Collins
School
Dictionary

Published by Collins
An imprint of HarperCollins Publishers
Westerhill Road
Bishopbriggs
Glasgow
G64 2QT

HarperCollins Publishers
1st Floor Watermarque Building
Ringsend Road
Dublin 4
Ireland

Sixth edition 2018

10 9 8 7 6 5

© HarperCollins Publishers 2018

UK hardback
ISBN 978-0-00-825793-4

Australian edition
ISBN 978-0-00-830118-7

Collins ® is a registered trademark of
HarperCollins Publishers Limited

www.collins.co.uk

Typeset by Davidson Publishing Solutions

Printed and bound in Italy by
Grafica Veneta S.p.A.

Acknowledgements
We would like to thank those authors
and publishers who kindly gave permission
for copyright material to be used in the
Collins Corpus. We would also like to thank
Times Newspapers Ltd for providing
valuable data.

MIX
Paper from
responsible sources
FSC™ C007454

Contents

Editorial Staff

Introduction

The ability to read, understand and write good English is vital for both success in exams and, ultimately, success in the world beyond school. Underpinning this ability is a thorough knowledge of spelling, grammar and punctuation, and *Collins School Dictionary* is an essential tool in achieving that knowledge.

Collins School Dictionary has been researched with teachers and students to ensure that it includes the information on language that students need to allow them to improve their performance and achieve exam success, not just in English but in all school subjects. As well as essential information on what words mean, it provides:

- Hundreds of tips on correct spelling, grammar and punctuation to help students avoid common errors

- Over 50 panels with brief but clear explanations of grammar terms and punctuation marks to help students understand them better

- Comprehensive coverage of core vocabulary from a range of curriculum subjects, with clear labelling of essential words in each subject

- The *Essential Guide to Spelling*, a supplementary section that recognises the importance of spelling, containing strategies for learning spelling, the key spelling rules, and words that students have been found to confuse or misspell, to help students to master the trickiest spelling problems

Collins School Dictionary is exceptionally easy to use. It is relevant to curriculum teaching in all subjects, it is accessible and student-friendly, and it offers essential help on the route to success.

How to Use the Dictionary

Collins School Dictionary is easy to use and understand. Below are some entries showing the dictionary's main features, along with an explanation of what they are.

The headword is the word you are looking up.

Word history notes explain where words come from.

There can be other forms of the word after the headword. These might be the plural of a noun, tenses of a verb, or comparative and superlative forms of adjectives.

Similar words notes list other words with the same meaning.

Grammar boxes give more information on the way English works. See page viii for a full list of grammar and punctuation boxes in the dictionary.

facetious [Said fas-**see**-shuss]
ADJECTIVE witty or amusing but in a rather silly or inappropriate way • *He didn't appreciate my facetious suggestion.*
WORD HISTORY: from Latin *facetiae* meaning 'witty remarks'

famished ADJECTIVE (*informal*) very hungry.

fish, fish or fishes, fishing, fished
NOUN ① a cold-blooded creature living in water that has a spine, gills, fins and a scaly skin. ② Fish is the flesh of fish eaten as food. ▶ VERB ③ To fish is to try to catch fish for food or sport. ④ If you fish for information, you try to get it in an indirect way. **fishing** NOUN **fisherman** NOUN

GRAMMAR TIP
The plural of the noun *fish* can be either *fish* or *fishes*, but *fish* is more common.

folly, follies NOUN Folly is a foolish act or foolish behaviour.
SIMILAR WORDS: foolishness, stupidity

interjection, interjections NOUN a word or phrase spoken suddenly to express surprise, pain or anger.
▶ SEE GRAMMAR BOX ON NEXT PAGE

The definition tells you what the word means.

Sometimes definitions include a label, such as *formal*, *informal* or *slang*, to give the appropriate context for a word.

Tips give more information on how the word is used or spelt.

The word class tells you if the headword is, for example, a noun, verb, adjective, adverb or pronoun.

Headwords with small numbers beside them have different origins.

minute¹, minutes, minuting, minuted [Said min-nit] NOUN ① a unit of time equal to sixty seconds. ② The minutes of a meeting are the written records of what was said and decided. ▶VERB ③ To minute a meeting is to write the official notes of it.

minute² [Said my-nyoot] ADJECTIVE extremely small • *a minute amount of pesticide.* **minutely** ADVERB

Other words that come from the main entry word

compare, compares, comparing, compared VERB ① EXAM TERM When you compare things, you look at them together and see in what ways they are different or similar. ② If you compare one thing to another, you say it is like the other thing • *Her voice is often compared to Adele's.*

Words used in exam questions are highlighted.

An example of the word being used

Core vocabulary from all curriculum subjects is labelled. See page ix for a full list of curriculum subject labels in the dictionary.

comparison, comparisons NOUN ENGLISH When you make a comparison, you consider two things together and see in what ways they are different or similar.

DNA NOUN SCIENCE DNA is deoxyribonucleic acid, a substance found in the cells of all living things. It determines the structure of every cell and is responsible for characteristics being passed on from parents to their children.

Some words can have more than one spelling or form.

primeval [Said pry-*mee*-vl] also spelt **primaeval** ADJECTIVE belonging to a very early period in the history of the world.

How to say the word

Where to Find Grammar and Punctuation Boxes

Throughout the dictionary there are 'grammar boxes' and 'punctuation boxes' that contain rules and advice on English grammar and punctuation, as well as helpful examples.

Curriculum Subject Labels

Collins School Dictionary gives you clear explanations of many words you need to know, not just for English but for many other school curriculum subjects.

If a word is important in a particular subject, you will find an eye-catching label with the name of the subject in the dictionary entry for that word.

A dictionary entry may also have a label if the word is particularly relevant to exams or using the library.

Here is a list of the subject labels used in the dictionary.

ART	Art
CITIZENSHIP	Citizenship
D&T	Design and technology
DRAMA	Drama
ENGLISH	English
EXAM TERM	Word used in exam questions
GEOGRAPHY	Geography
HISTORY	History
ICT	Information and communication technology
LIBRARY	Library skills
MATHS	Maths
MFL	Modern foreign languages
MUSIC	Music
PE	Physical education
PSHE	Personal, social and health education
RE	Religious education
SCIENCE	Science

Aa

a
b
c
d
e
f
g
h
i
j
k
l
m
n
o
p
q
r
s
t
u
v
w
x
y
z

The Indefinite Article

The word *a* is known as the **indefinite article**. You use it before a singular noun to refer to any example of that noun, or to avoid being specific about which example you mean:

a school
a woman

The word *an* is used instead of *a* when a word begins with a vowel sound:

an elephant
an umpire

The word *an* is also used instead of *a*

when words sound as though they begin with a vowel:

an hour
an honour

The word *a* is used instead of *an* when words that begin with a vowel sound as though they begin with a consonant:

a union
a European

Also look at the grammar box at **the**

---

a or **an** ADJECTIVE The indefinite article 'a', or 'an' if the next sound is a vowel, is used when you are talking about one of something • *an apple* • *There was a car parked behind the hedge.*

a- or **an-** PREFIX ① When 'a-' comes before an adjective it adds the meaning 'without' or 'opposite to'. 'An-' is the form used before a vowel • *amoral.* ② When 'a-' comes at the beginning of certain words it adds the meaning 'towards' or 'in the state of' • *aback* • *asleep.*

aardvark, aardvarks NOUN an ant-eating African animal with a long snout.
WORD HISTORY: from obsolete Afrikaans meaning 'earth pig'

aback ADVERB If you are taken aback, you are very surprised.

abacus, abacuses NOUN a frame with beads that slide along rods, used for counting.

abalone, abalones [Said ab-a-*lone*-ee] NOUN a shellfish which can be eaten.

abandon, abandons, abandoning, abandoned VERB ① If you abandon someone or something, you leave them or give them up for good.
▶ NOUN ② If you do something with abandon, you do it in an uncontrolled way • *He began to laugh with abandon.*
abandoned ADJECTIVE
abandonment NOUN
SIMILAR WORDS: ① desert, forsake, leave

abate, abates, abating, abated VERB If something abates, it becomes less • *His anger abated.*

abattoir, abattoirs [Said ab-a-*twahr*] NOUN a place where animals are killed for meat.

abbey, abbeys NOUN a church with

A
B
C
D
E
F
G
H
I
J
K
L
M
N
O
P
Q
R
S
T
U
V
W
X
Y
Z

buildings attached to it in which monks or nuns live.

abbot, abbots NOUN the monk or priest in charge of all the monks in a monastery.

abbreviate, abbreviates, abbreviating, abbreviated VERB To abbreviate something is to make it shorter.

abbreviation, abbreviations NOUN a short form of a word or phrase. An example is 'W', which is short for 'West'.

abdicate, abdicates, abdicating, abdicated VERB If a king or queen abdicates, he or she gives up being a king or queen. **abdication** NOUN

abdomen, abdomens NOUN the front part of your body below your chest, containing your stomach and intestines. **abdominal** ADJECTIVE

abduct, abducts, abducting, abducted VERB To abduct someone is to take them away by force. **abduction** NOUN

aberration, aberrations NOUN something that is not normal or usual.

abet, abets, abetting, abetted VERB If you abet someone, you help them to do something • You've aided and abetted criminals to evade justice.

abhor, abhors, abhorring, abhorred VERB (formal) If you abhor something, you hate it. **abhorrence** NOUN **abhorrent** ADJECTIVE

abide, abides, abiding, abided VERB ① If you can't abide something, you dislike it very much. ② If you abide by a decision or law, you act in agreement with it.

abiding ADJECTIVE lasting for ever • an abiding interest in history.

ability, abilities NOUN the intelligence or skill needed to do something • the ability to get on with others.

SIMILAR WORDS: capability, proficiency, skill

abject ADJECTIVE very bad • abject failure. **abjectly** ADVERB

ablaze ADJECTIVE on fire.

able, abler, ablest ADJECTIVE ① If you are able to do something, you can do it. ② PSHE Someone who is able is very clever or talented.

-able SUFFIX ① forming adjectives which have the meaning 'capable of' an action • enjoyable • breakable. ② forming adjectives with the meaning 'able to' or 'causing' • comfortable • miserable.

SPELLING TIP

When you are writing, it is easy to confuse the -able suffix with its other form, -ible. It can be helpful to know that the -able spelling is much commoner than -ible, and that you cannot make new words using -ible. Occasionally, it is correct to use either ending.

---

ably [Said ay-blee] ADVERB skilfully and successfully • He is ably supported by the cast.

abnormal ADJECTIVE not normal or usual. **abnormally** ADVERB

abnormality, abnormalities NOUN something that is not normal or usual.
SIMILAR WORDS: irregularity, oddity, peculiarity

aboard PREPOSITION or ADVERB on a ship or plane.

abode, abodes NOUN (old-fashioned) Your abode is your home.

abolish, abolishes, abolishing, abolished VERB To abolish something is to do away with it • the campaign to abolish hunting. **abolition** NOUN
SIMILAR WORDS: do away with, eliminate, end

abominable ADJECTIVE very unpleasant or shocking.
abominably ADVERB

Aboriginal [Said ab-or-rij-in-al] ADJECTIVE from the people who lived in Australia before Europeans arrived.

abort, aborts, aborting, aborted VERB If a plan or activity is aborted, it is stopped before it is finished.

abortion, abortions NOUN If a woman has an abortion, the pregnancy is ended deliberately before the foetus can live independently.

abortive ADJECTIVE unsuccessful • an abortive bank raid.

abound, abounds, abounding, abounded VERB If things abound, there are very large numbers of them.

about PREPOSITION or ADVERB ① of or concerning. ② approximately and not exactly. ▸ ADVERB ③ in different directions • There were some bottles scattered about. ▸ ADJECTIVE ④ present or in a place • Is Jane about? ▸ PHRASE ⑤ If you are **about to** do something, you are just going to do it.

above PREPOSITION or ADVERB ① directly over or higher than something • above the clouds. ② greater than a level or amount • The temperature didn't rise above freezing point.

above board ADJECTIVE completely open and legal • They assured me it was above board and properly licensed.
WORD HISTORY: an allusion to the difficulty of cheating at cards with your hands above the table

abrasion, abrasions NOUN ① an area where your skin has been broken. ② GEOGRAPHY erosion caused by the small stones, etc. carried by a river or glacier scraping against a surface.

abrasive ADJECTIVE ① An abrasive substance is rough and can be used to clean hard surfaces. ② Someone who is abrasive is unpleasant and rude.

abreast ADJECTIVE ① side by side • youths riding their motorbikes four abreast. ② If you keep abreast of a subject, you know all the most recent facts about it.

abroad ADVERB in a foreign country.

abrupt ADJECTIVE ① sudden and quick • His career came to an abrupt end. ② not friendly or polite.
abruptly ADVERB **abruptness** NOUN

abscess, abscesses [Said ab-sess] NOUN a painful swelling filled with pus.

abseiling NOUN Abseiling is the sport of going down a cliff or a tall building by sliding down ropes.

absent ADJECTIVE [Said ab-sent] Something that is absent is not present in a place or situation.
absence NOUN

absentee, absentees NOUN someone who is not present when they should be.

absent-minded ADJECTIVE forgetful and not paying attention. **absent-mindedly** ADVERB **absent-mindedness** NOUN

absolute ADJECTIVE ① total and complete • absolute honesty. ② having total power • the absolute ruler.
absolutely ADVERB

absolve, absolves, absolving, absolved VERB To absolve someone of something is to state they are not to blame for it.

absorb, absorbs, absorbing, absorbed VERB SCIENCE If something

A
B
C
D
E
F
G
H
I
J
K
L
M
N
O
P
Q
R
S
T
U
V
W
X
Y
Z

absorbs liquid or gas, it soaks it up or takes it in.

SIMILAR WORDS: soak up, take in

absorbent ADJECTIVE Absorbent materials soak up liquid easily.

absorption NOUN ① the soaking up of a liquid or taking in of a gas. ② great interest in something • *the artists' total absorption in their work.*

abstain, abstains, abstaining, abstained VERB ① If you abstain from something, you do not do it or have it • *The patients had to abstain from fatty foods.* ② If you abstain in a vote, you do not vote. **abstainer** NOUN **abstention** NOUN

SIMILAR WORDS: ① forbear, keep from, refrain

abstinence NOUN Abstinence is deliberately not doing something you enjoy.

abstract ADJECTIVE [Said *ab-strakt*] ① An abstract idea is based on thoughts and ideas rather than physical objects or events, for example 'bravery'. ② ART Abstract art is a style of art which uses shapes rather than images of people or objects. ③ Abstract nouns refer to qualities or ideas rather than to physical objects, for example 'happiness' or 'a question'. **abstraction** NOUN

absurd ADJECTIVE ridiculous and stupid. **absurdly** ADVERB **absurdity** NOUN

SIMILAR WORDS: ludicrous, preposterous, ridiculous

abundance NOUN Something that exists in abundance exists in large numbers • *an abundance of wildlife.*

SIMILAR WORDS: plenty, profusion

abundant ADJECTIVE present in large quantities. **abundantly** ADVERB

abuse, abuses, abusing, abused VERB [Said *ab-yooze*] ① If you abuse

someone, you speak insultingly to them. ② PSHE To abuse someone also means to treat them cruelly. ③ If you abuse something, you use it wrongly or for a bad purpose.
▸ NOUN [Said *ab-yoose*] ④ PSHE prolonged cruel treatment of someone. ⑤ rude and unkind remarks directed towards someone. ⑥ the wrong use of something • *an abuse of power* • *alcohol abuse.* **abuser** NOUN

SIMILAR WORDS: ② ill-treat, maltreat ④ ill-treatment, injury, maltreatment

abusive ADJECTIVE rude and unkind. **abusively** ADVERB **abusiveness** NOUN

abysmal [Said *ab-biz-ml*] ADJECTIVE very bad indeed • *an abysmal performance.* **abysmally** ADVERB

abyss, abysses NOUN a very deep hole.

WORD HISTORY: from Greek *abussos* meaning 'bottomless'

acacia, acacias [Said *a-kay-sha*] NOUN a type of thorny shrub with small yellow or white flowers.

academic, academics ADJECTIVE ① Academic work is work done in a school, college or university. ▸ NOUN ② someone who teaches or does research in a college or university. **academically** ADVERB

academy, academies NOUN ① a school or college, especially one that specialises in one particular subject • *the Royal Academy of Dramatic Art.* ② in England, a school that is funded by the central government rather than by a local authority. ③ an organisation of scientists, artists, writers or musicians.

WORD HISTORY: from Greek *akadēmeia*, the name of the grove where Plato taught

a cappella ADJECTIVE or ADVERB MUSIC without musical

accompaniment • *an a cappella version of the song* • *We decided to sing it a cappella*.

WORD HISTORY: an Italian phrase meaning 'according to (the style of the) chapel'

accelerate, accelerates, accelerating, accelerated VERB SCIENCE To accelerate is to go faster.

acceleration NOUN the rate at which the speed of something is increasing.

accelerator, accelerators NOUN the pedal in a vehicle which you press to make it go faster.

accent, accents NOUN ① a way of pronouncing a language • *She had an Australian accent.* ② MFL a mark placed above or below a letter in some languages, which affects the way the letter is pronounced. ③ ENGLISH stress placed on a particular word, syllable or note • *In Icelandic the accent usually falls on the first syllable of a word.* ④ an emphasis on something • *The accent is on action and special effects.*

accentuate, accentuates, accentuating, accentuated VERB To accentuate a feature of something is to make it more noticeable.

accept, accepts, accepting, accepted VERB ① If you accept something, you say yes to it or take it from someone. ② If you accept a situation, you realise that it cannot be changed • *He accepts criticism as part of his job.* ③ If you accept a statement or story, you believe it is true • *The teacher accepted his explanation.* ④ If a group accepts you, they treat you as one of the group.

acceptance NOUN

WORD HISTORY: from Latin *ad* meaning 'to' and *capere* meaning 'to take'

SPELLING TIP
Do not confuse the spellings of *accept* and *except*: *Please accept my apologies; He works every day except Tuesday.*

acceptable ADJECTIVE good enough to be accepted. **acceptably** ADVERB

access, accesses, accessing, accessed NOUN ① the right or opportunity to enter a place or to use something. ▶ VERB ② If you access information from a computer, you get it.

accessible ADJECTIVE ① easily reached or seen • *The village was accessible by foot only.* ② easily understood or used • *guidebooks which present information in a clear and accessible style.* **accessibility** NOUN

accession NOUN A ruler's accession is the time when he or she becomes the ruler of a country.

accessory, accessories NOUN ① an extra part. ② someone who helps another person commit a crime.

accident, accidents NOUN ① an unexpected event in which people are injured or killed. ② Something that happens by accident happens by chance.

accidental ADJECTIVE happening by chance. **accidentally** ADVERB
SIMILAR WORDS: inadvertent, unintentional, unplanned

acclaimed ADJECTIVE If someone or something is acclaimed, they are praised enthusiastically.

accolade, accolades NOUN (*formal*) great praise or an award given to someone.

accommodate, accommodates, accommodating, accommodated VERB ① If you accommodate someone, you provide them with a place to sleep, live or work. ② If a place can accommodate a number of things or people, it has enough room for them.

SPELLING TIP
Accommodate has two cs and two ms.

---

accommodating ADJECTIVE willing to help and to adjust to new situations.

accommodation NOUN a place provided for someone to sleep, live or work in.

accompaniment, accompaniments NOUN ① The accompaniment to a song is the music played to go with it. ② An accompaniment to something is another thing that comes with it • *Melon is a good accompaniment to cold meats.*

accompany, accompanies, accompanying, accompanied VERB ① If you accompany someone, you go with them. ② If one thing accompanies another, the two things exist at the same time • *severe pain accompanied by fever.* ③ If you accompany a singer or musician, you play an instrument while they sing or play the main tune.

accomplice, accomplices NOUN a person who helps someone else to commit a crime.

accomplish, accomplishes, accomplishing, accomplished VERB If you accomplish something, you succeed in doing it.

USAGE NOTE
The *com* part of *accomplish* can sound like *kum* or *kom*.

---

accomplished ADJECTIVE very talented at something • *an accomplished cook.*

accomplishment, accomplishments NOUN Someone's accomplishments are the skills they have gained.

accord, accords, according, accorded VERB ① If you accord someone or something a particular treatment, you treat them in that way • *She was accorded proper respect for her status.* ▶ NOUN ② agreement. ▶ PHRASE ③ If you do something **of your own accord**, you do it willingly and not because you have been forced to do it.

accordance PHRASE If you act **in accordance with** a rule or belief, you act in the way the rule or belief says you should.

accordingly ADVERB in a way that is appropriate for the circumstances • *The street had changed its character, and the shops had changed accordingly.*

according to PREPOSITION ① If something is true according to a particular person, that person says that it is true. ② If something is done according to a principle or plan, that principle or plan is used as the basis for it.

accordion, accordions NOUN a musical instrument like an expanding box. It is played by squeezing the two sides together while pressing the keys on it.

accost, accosts, accosting, accosted VERB If someone accosts you, especially someone you do not know, they come up and speak to you • *She says she is accosted when she goes shopping.*

account, accounts, accounting, accounted NOUN ① a written or spoken report of something. ② If you have a bank account, you can leave money in the bank and take it out when you need it. ③ (*in plural*) Accounts are records of money spent and received by a person or business. ▶ PHRASE ④ If you **take something into account**, you include it in your planning. ⑤**On account of** means because of. ▶**VERB** ⑥To account for something is to explain it • *This might account for her strange behaviour.* ⑦If something accounts for a particular amount of something, it is that amount • *The brain accounts for three per cent of body weight.*

accountable ADJECTIVE If you are accountable for something, you are responsible for it and have to explain your actions • *The committee is accountable to Parliament.*
accountability NOUN

accountancy NOUN the job of keeping or inspecting financial accounts.

accountant, accountants NOUN a person whose job is to keep or inspect financial accounts.

accounting NOUN the keeping and checking of financial accounts.

accrue, accrues, accruing, accrued VERB If money or interest accrues, it increases gradually.

accumulate, accumulates, accumulating, accumulated VERB If you accumulate things or they accumulate, they collect over a period of time.

accurate ADJECTIVE completely correct or precise. **accurately** ADVERB **accuracy** NOUN
SIMILAR WORDS: correct, exact, precise

accuse, accuses, accusing, accused VERB If you accuse someone of doing something wrong, you say they have done it. **accusation** NOUN **accuser** NOUN

accustom, accustoms, accustoming, accustomed VERB If you accustom yourself to something new or different, you get used to it.

accustomed ADJECTIVE used to something.

ace, aces NOUN ① In a pack of cards, an ace is a card with a single symbol on it. ▶**ADJECTIVE** ②(*informal*) good or skilful • *an ace squash player.*

acerbic [*Said as-ser-bik*] ADJECTIVE (*formal*) Acerbic remarks are harsh and bitter.

ache, aches, aching, ached VERB ① If you ache, you feel a continuous dull pain in a part of your body. ② If you are aching for something, you want it very much. ▶**NOUN** ③ a continuous dull pain.

achieve, achieves, achieving, achieved VERB PSHE If you achieve something, you successfully do it or cause it to happen.
SIMILAR WORDS: accomplish, attain, fulfil

SPELLING TIP
The *i* comes before the *e* in *achieve*.

achievement, achievements NOUN PSHE something which you succeed in doing, especially after a lot of effort.

acid, acids NOUN ① SCIENCE An acid is a substance with a pH value of less than 7. There are many different acids; some are used in chemical processes and others in household substances. ▶**ADJECTIVE** ②Acid tastes are sharp or sour. ③Acid comments are unkind and critical. ▶**PHRASE** ④Something that is an **acid test** is used as a way of testing whether something is true or not, or whether it is of good quality or not. **acidly** ADVERB **acidic** ADJECTIVE **acidity** NOUN
WORD HISTORY: from Latin *acidus* meaning 'sour'

acid rain NOUN GEOGRAPHY rain polluted by acid in the atmosphere which has come from factories.

a
b
c
d
e
f
g
h
i
j
k
l
m
n
o
p
q
r
s
t
u
v
w
x
y
z

A
B
C
D
E
F
G
H
I
J
K
L
M
N
O
P
Q
R
S
T
U
V
W
X
Y
Z

acknowledge, acknowledges, acknowledging, acknowledged VERB ① If you acknowledge a fact or situation, you agree or admit it is true. ② If you acknowledge someone, you show that you have seen and recognised them. ③ If you acknowledge a message, you tell the person who sent it that you have received it. **acknowledgment**; also spelt **acknowledgement** NOUN SIMILAR WORDS: ① accept, admit, grant

SPELLING TIP
Acknowledgment and *acknowledgement* are both correct spellings.

acne [*Said ak-nee*] NOUN lumpy spots that cover someone's face.

acorn, acorns NOUN the fruit of the oak tree, consisting of a pale oval nut in a cup-shaped base.

acoustic [*Said a-koo-stik*] ADJECTIVE ① relating to sound or hearing. ② An acoustic guitar is not made louder with an electric amplifier.

acoustics PLURAL NOUN The acoustics of a room are its structural features which are responsible for how clearly you can hear sounds made in it.

acquaintance, acquaintances NOUN someone you know slightly but not well.

acquainted ADJECTIVE If you are acquainted with someone, you know them slightly but not well.

GRAMMAR TIP
You say that you are *acquainted with* someone.

acquire, acquires, acquiring, acquired VERB If you acquire something, you obtain it.

acquisition, acquisitions NOUN something you have obtained.

acquit, acquits, acquitting, acquitted VERB ① If someone is acquitted of a crime, they have been tried in a court and found not guilty. ② If you acquit yourself well on a particular occasion, you behave or perform well. **acquittal** NOUN

acre, acres NOUN a unit for measuring areas of land. One acre is equal to 4840 square yards or about 4047 square metres.
WORD HISTORY: from Old English *æcer* meaning 'field'

acrid ADJECTIVE sharp and bitter • *the acrid smell of burning plastic.*

acrimony [*Said ak-rim-on-ee*] NOUN (*formal*) bitterness and anger.
acrimonious ADJECTIVE

acrobat, acrobats NOUN an entertainer who performs gymnastic tricks. **acrobatic** ADJECTIVE **acrobatics** PLURAL NOUN
WORD HISTORY: from Greek *akrobates* meaning 'someone who walks on tiptoe'

acronym, acronyms NOUN a word made up of the initial letters of a phrase. An example of an acronym is 'BAFTA', which stands for 'British Academy of Film and Television Arts'.

across PREPOSITION or ADVERB ① going from one side of something to the other. ② on the other side of a road or river.

acrylic, acrylics [*Said a-kril-lik*] NOUN ① Acrylic is a type of synthetic cloth. ② ART Acrylics, or acrylic paints, are thick artists' paints which can be used like oil paints or thinned down with water.

act, acts, acting, acted VERB ① If you act, you do something • *It would be irresponsible not to act swiftly.* ② If you act in a particular way, you behave in that way. ③ If a person or thing acts as something else, it has the function or does the job of that thing • *She was able to act as an interpreter.* ④ If you act in a play or film, you play a part. ▶ **NOUN** ⑤ a single thing someone does • *It was an act of disloyalty to the King.* ⑥ An Act of Parliament is a law passed by the government. ⑦ In a play, ballet or opera, an act is one of the main parts it is divided into.

SIMILAR WORDS: ④ perform, play ⑤ action, deed ⑥ bill, decree, law

acting NOUN the profession of performing in plays or films.

action, actions NOUN ① the process of doing something. ② something that is done. ③ a physical movement. ④ In law, an action is a legal proceeding • *a libel action.*

action plan, action plans NOUN a detailed account of things that need to be done in order to achieve a goal.

activate, activates, activating, activated VERB To activate something is to make it start working.

SIMILAR WORDS: set in motion, start

active ADJECTIVE ① PE full of energy. ② busy and hardworking. ③ ENGLISH In grammar, a verb in the active voice is one where the subject does the action, rather than having it done to them. **actively** ADVERB

activist, activists NOUN a person who tries to bring about political and social change.

activity, activities NOUN ① Activity is a situation in which a lot of things are happening at the same time. ② PE something you do for pleasure • *sport and leisure activities.*

actor, actors NOUN a man or woman whose profession is acting.

actress, actresses NOUN a woman whose profession is acting.

actual ADJECTIVE real, rather than imaginary or guessed at • *That is the official figure: the actual figure is much higher.* **actually** ADVERB

USAGE NOTE
Don't use *actual* or *actually* when they don't add anything to the meaning of a sentence. Say *it's a fact* rather than *it's an actual fact.*

acumen NOUN the ability to make good decisions quickly • *business acumen.*

acupuncture NOUN the treatment of illness or pain by sticking small needles into specific places on a person's body.
WORD HISTORY: from Latin *acus* meaning 'needle' added to 'puncture'

acute ADJECTIVE ① severe or intense • *an acute shortage of accommodation.* ② very intelligent • *an acute mind.* ③ MATHS An acute angle is less than 90°. ④ MFL In French and some other languages, an acute accent is a line sloping upwards from left to right placed over a vowel to indicate

The Active Voice

The **active** voice and the **passive** voice are two different ways of presenting information in a sentence. When a sentence is written in the **active** voice, the subject of the verb is doing the action. This is the most

natural way of presenting information:

Anna is feeding the cat.
The cat chased a mouse.

Also look at the grammar box at **passive**

a b c d e f g h i j k l m n o p q r s t u v w x y z

a change in pronunciation, as in the word *café*.

ad, ads NOUN (*informal*) an advertisement.

AD You use 'AD' in dates to indicate the number of years after the birth of Jesus Christ.

adage, adages [*Said ad-dij*] NOUN a saying that expresses some general truth about life.

adagio [*Said ad-ah-jee-oh*] ADVERB MUSIC In music, adagio is an instruction to play or sing something slowly.

adamant ADJECTIVE If you are adamant, you are determined not to change your mind. **adamantly** ADVERB

Adam's apple, Adam's apples NOUN the larynx, a lump at the front of the neck which is more obvious in men than in women and young boys.
WORD HISTORY: from the story that a piece of the forbidden apple got stuck in Adam's throat

adapt, adapts, adapting, adapted VERB ① If you adapt to a new situation, you change so you can deal with it successfully. ② If you adapt something, you change it so it is suitable for a new purpose or situation. ③ SCIENCE If a plant or animal adapts, it gradually changes over generations to become better suited to its environment.
adaptable ADJECTIVE **adaptation** NOUN

adaptor, adaptors; also spelt **adapter** NOUN a type of electric plug which can be used to connect two or more plugs to one socket.

add, adds, adding, added VERB ① If you add something to a number of things, you put it with the things. ② If you add numbers together or add them up, you work out the total.

adder, adders NOUN a small poisonous snake.

addict, addicts NOUN PSHE someone who cannot stop doing something, especially something harmful. **addicted** ADJECTIVE **addiction** NOUN

addictive ADJECTIVE If something is addictive, people cannot stop once they have started to do it.

addition, additions NOUN ① something that has been added to something else. ② MATHS the process of adding numbers together.
SIMILAR WORDS: ① extra, supplement

additional ADJECTIVE extra or more • *They made the decision to take on additional staff.* **additionally** ADVERB

additive, additives NOUN something added to something else, usually in order to improve it.

address, addresses, addressing, addressed NOUN ① the number of the house where you live, together with the name of the street and the town or village. ② a group of words or letters that identifies a location on the internet • *my email address*. ③ a speech given to a group of people. ▶VERB ④ If a letter is addressed to you, it has your name and address written on it. ⑤ If you address a problem or task, you start to deal with it.

adept ADJECTIVE very skilful at doing something • *She is adept at motivating others*.

adequate ADJECTIVE enough in amount or good enough for a purpose • *an adequate diet*.
adequately ADVERB **adequacy** NOUN
SIMILAR WORDS: enough, satisfactory, sufficient

adhere, adheres, adhering, adhered VERB ① If one thing adheres to another, it sticks firmly to it. ② If you adhere to a rule or agreement, you do what it says. ③ If you adhere to an opinion or belief, you firmly hold that opinion or belief. **adherence** NOUN

adherent, adherents NOUN An adherent of a belief is someone who holds that belief.

adhesive, adhesives NOUN ① any substance used to stick two things together, for example glue. ▸ ADJECTIVE ② Adhesive substances are sticky and able to stick to things.

adjacent [Said ad-*jay*-sent] ADJECTIVE (formal) ① If two things are adjacent, they are next to each other • a hotel adjacent to the beach. ② MATHS Adjacent angles share one side and have the same point opposite to their bases.

adjective, adjectives NOUN ENGLISH MFL a word that adds to the description given by a noun. For example, in 'They live in a large white Georgian house', 'large', 'white' and 'Georgian' are all adjectives. **adjectival** ADJECTIVE

adjoining ADJECTIVE If two rooms are next to each other and are connected, they are adjoining.

adjourn, adjourns, adjourning, adjourned VERB ① If a meeting or trial is adjourned, it stops for a time • The case was adjourned until September. ② If people adjourn to another place, they go there together after a meeting • We adjourned to the lounge. **adjournment** NOUN

adjust, adjusts, adjusting, adjusted VERB ① If you adjust something, you change its position or alter it in some other way. ② If you adjust to a new situation, you get used to it. **adjustment** NOUN **adjustable** ADJECTIVE

ad-lib, ad-libs, ad-libbing, ad-libbed VERB ① If you ad-lib, you say something that has not been prepared beforehand • I ad-lib on radio but use a script on TV. ▸ NOUN ② a comment that has not been prepared beforehand. **WORD HISTORY:** short for Latin ad libitum meaning 'according to desire'

What is an Adjective?

An adjective is a word that tells you something about a noun. Adjectives are sometimes called 'describing words'.

Adjectives may indicate how many of a person or thing there are:

three men
some fish

Adjectives may describe feelings or qualities:

a **happy** child
a **strange** girl

Adjectives may describe size, age, temperature or measurement:

a **large** envelope
an **old** jacket

Adjectives may indicate colour:

red socks
dark hair

Adjectives may indicate nationality or origin:

my **Indian** cousin
a **northern** accent

Adjectives may indicate the material from which something is made:

a **wooden** box
denim trousers

a b c d e f g h i j k l m n o p q r s t u v w x y z

A
B
C
D
E
F
G
H
I
J
K
L
M
N
O
P
Q
R
S
T
U
V
W
X
Y
Z

administer, administers, administering, administered VERB
①To administer an organisation is to be responsible for managing it. ②To administer the law or administer justice is to put it into practice and apply it. ③If medicine is administered to someone, it is given to them.

administration, administrations NOUN ①Administration is the work of organising and supervising an organisation. ②Administration is also the process of administering something • *the administration of criminal justice*. ③The administration is the group of people that manages an organisation or a country.
administrative ADJECTIVE
administrator NOUN

admirable ADJECTIVE very good and deserving to be admired. **admirably** ADVERB

admiral, admirals NOUN the commander of a navy.
WORD HISTORY: from Arabic *amir* meaning 'commander'

admiration NOUN a feeling of great liking and respect.

admire, admires, admiring, admired VERB If you admire someone or something, you respect and approve of them. **admirer** NOUN **admiring** ADJECTIVE **admiringly** ADVERB

admission, admissions NOUN ①If you are allowed admission to a place, you are allowed to go in. ②If you make an admission of something, you agree, often reluctantly, it is true • *It was an admission of guilt*.

admit, admits, admitting, admitted VERB ①If you admit something, you agree, often reluctantly, it is true. ②To admit someone or something to a place or organisation is to allow them to enter it. ③If you are admitted to hospital, you are taken there to stay until you are better.

admittedly ADVERB People use 'admittedly' to show that what they are saying contrasts with something they have already said or are about to say, and weakens their argument • *My studies, admittedly only from books, taught me much.*

adolescent, adolescents NOUN
SCIENCE a young person who is no longer a child but who is not yet an adult. **adolescence** NOUN
WORD HISTORY: from Latin *adolescere* meaning 'to grow up'

adopt, adopts, adopting, adopted VERB ①If you adopt a child that is not your own, you take him or her into your family as your son or daughter. ②(*formal*) If you adopt a particular attitude, you start to have it. **adoption** NOUN

adorable ADJECTIVE sweet and attractive.

adore, adores, adoring, adored VERB If you adore someone, you feel deep love and admiration for them. **adoration** NOUN

adorn, adorns, adorning, adorned VERB To adorn something is to decorate it • *The cathedral is adorned with statues.* **adornment** NOUN

adrenalin [*Said a-dren-al-in*]; also spelt **adrenaline** NOUN Adrenalin is a hormone which is produced by your body when you are angry, nervous or excited. Adrenalin makes your heart beat faster, and gives you more energy.

adrift ADJECTIVE OR ADVERB If a boat is adrift or goes adrift, it floats on the water without being controlled.

adulation [*Said ad-yoo-lay-shn*] NOUN great admiration and praise for someone. **adulatory** ADJECTIVE

adult, adults NOUN a mature and fully developed person or animal.

adultery NOUN a sexual relationship between a married person and someone he or she is not married to. **adulterous** ADJECTIVE

adulthood NOUN the time during someone's life when they are an adult.

advance, advances, advancing, advanced VERB ①To advance is to move forward. ②To advance a cause or interest is to help it to be successful. ③If you advance someone a sum of money, you lend it to them. ▶ NOUN ④Advance in something is progress in it • *scientific advance*. ⑤ a sum of money lent to someone. ▶ ADJECTIVE ⑥happening before an event • *The event received little advance publicity*. ▶ PHRASE ⑦If you do something **in advance**, you do it before something else happens • *We booked the room well in advance*. SIMILAR WORDS: ④development, progress

advantage, advantages NOUN ①a benefit or something that puts you in a better position. ▶ PHRASE ②If you **take advantage of** someone, you

treat them unfairly for your own benefit. ③If you **take advantage of** something, you make use of it.

advantageous ADJECTIVE likely to benefit you in some way • *an advantageous marriage*.

advent NOUN ①The advent of something is its start or its coming into existence • *The advent of the submarine changed naval warfare*. ②Advent is the season just before Christmas in the Christian calendar.

adventure, adventures NOUN a series of events that are unusual and exciting.

adventurer, adventurers NOUN someone who enjoys doing dangerous and exciting things.

adventurous ADJECTIVE willing to take risks and do new and exciting things. **adventurously** ADVERB

adverb, adverbs NOUN ENGLISH MFL a word that adds information about a verb or a following adjective or other adverb, for example, 'slowly', 'now' and 'here', which say how, when or where something is done. **adverbial** ADJECTIVE

What is an Adverb?

An adverb is a word that gives information about a verb. Many adverbs end with the letters *-ly*.

Adverbs of manner answer the question 'how?':

*She runs **quickly**.*
*She sings **badly**.*

Adverbs of place answer the question 'where?':

*We travelled **northwards**.*
*I live **here**.*

Adverbs of time answer the question 'when?':

*You must stop **immediately**.*

*I arrived **yesterday**.*

Adverbs of degree answer the question 'to what extent?':

*I **really** hope you will stay.*
*I play golf **fairly** often.*

Adverbs of frequency answer the question 'how often?':

*We **sometimes** meet for lunch.*
*You **never** answer my questions.*

Sometimes adverbs can refer to the whole sentence rather than just the verb:

***Fortunately**, she was not badly hurt.*

adversary, adversaries [Said ad-ver-sar-ee] NOUN someone who is your enemy or who opposes what you are doing.

adverse ADJECTIVE not helpful to you, or opposite to what you want or need • *adverse weather conditions*. **adversely** ADVERB

adversity, adversities NOUN a time of danger or difficulty.

advert, adverts NOUN (*informal*) an advertisement.

advertise, advertises, advertising, advertised VERB ① If you advertise something, you tell people about it in a newspaper or poster, or on TV or the internet. ② To advertise is to make an announcement in a newspaper or poster, or on TV or the internet. **advertiser** NOUN **advertising** NOUN

advertisement, advertisements [Said ad-**ver**-tiss-ment] NOUN an announcement about something in a newspaper or poster, or on TV or the internet.
SIMILAR WORDS: ad, advert, commercial

advice NOUN a suggestion from someone about what you should do.
SIMILAR WORDS: counsel, guidance, suggestion

SPELLING TIP
The noun *advice* is spelt with a c and the verb *advise* is spelt with an s.

advisable ADJECTIVE sensible and likely to achieve the result you want • *It is advisable to buy the visa before travelling*. **advisably** ADVERB **advisability** NOUN

advise, advises, advising, advised VERB ① If you advise someone to do something, you tell them you think they should do it. ② (*formal*) If you advise someone of something, you inform them of it. **advisory** ADJECTIVE

SIMILAR WORDS: ① counsel, recommend, suggest

SPELLING TIP
The verb *advise* is spelt with an s and the noun *advice* is spelt with a c.

adviser, advisers NOUN a person whose job is to give advice.

advocate, advocates, advocating, advocated VERB ① If you advocate a course of action or plan, you support it publicly. ▶ NOUN ② An advocate of something is someone who supports it publicly. ③ (*formal*) a lawyer who represents clients in court. **advocacy** NOUN

aerial, aerials [Said air-ee-al] ADJECTIVE ① Aerial means happening in the air • *aerial combat*. ▶ NOUN ② a piece of wire for receiving television or radio signals.

aerial top dressing NOUN In Australia and New Zealand, aerial top dressing is the spreading of fertiliser from an aeroplane onto land in remote country areas.

aero- PREFIX 'Aero-' means involving the air, the atmosphere, or aircraft • *aerobatics*.

aerobic ADJECTIVE SCIENCE Aerobic respiration is a type of breathing that uses oxygen.

aerobics NOUN a type of fast physical exercise, which increases the oxygen in your blood and strengthens your heart and lungs.

aerodynamic ADJECTIVE having a streamlined shape that moves easily through the air.

aeroplane, aeroplanes NOUN a vehicle with wings and engines that enable it to fly.

aerosol, aerosols NOUN SCIENCE a small metal container in which liquid is kept under pressure so that it can be forced out as a spray.

aerospace ADJECTIVE involved in making and designing aeroplanes and spacecraft.

aesthetic [*Said eess-thet-ik*]; also spelt **esthetic** ADJECTIVE DGT (*formal*) relating to the appreciation of beauty or art. **aesthetically** or **esthetically** ADVERB **aesthetics** or **esthetics** NOUN

afar NOUN (*literary*) From afar means from a long way away.

affable ADJECTIVE pleasant and easy to talk to. **affably** ADVERB **affability** NOUN

affair, affairs NOUN ① an event or series of events • *The funeral was a sad affair.* ② To have an affair is to have a secret romantic relationship, especially when one of the people involved is married. ③ (*in plural*) Your affairs are your private and personal life • *Why had he meddled in her affairs?*

affect, affects, affecting, affected VERB ① If something affects you, it influences you in some way. ② (*formal*) If you affect a particular way of behaving, you behave in that way • *He affected an Italian accent.*

affectation, affectations NOUN An affectation is behaviour that is not genuine but is put on to impress people.

affection, affections NOUN ① a feeling of love and fondness for someone. ② (*in plural*) Your affections are feelings of love you have for someone.

affectionate ADJECTIVE full of fondness for someone • *an affectionate embrace.* **affectionately** ADVERB

affiliate, affiliates, affiliating, affiliated VERB If a group affiliates itself to another, larger group, it forms a close association with it • *organisations affiliated to the ANC.* **affiliation** NOUN

affinity, affinities NOUN a close similarity or understanding between two things or people • *There are affinities between the two poets.*

affirm, affirms, affirming, affirmed VERB If you affirm an idea or belief, you clearly indicate your support for it • *We affirm our commitment to broadcast quality programmes.* **affirmation** NOUN

affirmative ADJECTIVE An affirmative word or gesture is one that means yes.

afflict, afflicts, afflicting, afflicted VERB If illness or pain afflicts someone, they suffer from it • *She was afflicted by depression.* **affliction** NOUN

affluent ADJECTIVE having a lot of money and possessions. **affluence** NOUN

afford, affords, affording, afforded VERB ① If you can afford to do something, you have enough money or time to do it. ② If you cannot afford something to happen, it would be harmful or embarrassing for you if it happened • *We cannot afford to be complacent.*

affordable ADJECTIVE If something is affordable, most people have enough money to buy it • *the availability of affordable housing.*

affray, affrays NOUN (*formal*) a noisy and violent fight.

a
b
c
d
e
f
g
h
i
j
k
l
m
n
o
p
q
r
s
t
u
v
w
x
y
z

affront, affronts, affronting, affronted VERB ① If you are affronted by something, you are insulted and angered by it. ▶ NOUN ② something that is an insult • *He took my question as a personal affront.*

GRAMMAR TIP
Notice that *affront*, the noun, is followed by *to*.

---

afield ADVERB Far afield means a long way away • *competitors from as far afield as Russia and China.*

afloat ADVERB or ADJECTIVE ① floating on water. ② successful and making enough money • *Companies are struggling hard to stay afloat.*

afoot ADJECTIVE or ADVERB happening or being planned, especially secretly • *Plans are afoot to build a new museum.*

afraid ADJECTIVE ① If you are afraid, you think that something bad is going to happen. ② If you are afraid something might happen, you are worried it might happen.
SIMILAR WORDS: ① fearful, frightened, scared

afresh ADVERB again and in a new way • *The couple moved abroad to start life afresh.*

Africa NOUN Africa is the second largest continent. It is almost surrounded by sea, with the Atlantic on its west side, the Mediterranean to the north, and the Indian Ocean and the Red Sea to the east.

African, Africans ADJECTIVE ① belonging or relating to Africa. ▶ NOUN ② someone, especially a Black person, who comes from Africa.

African-American, African-Americans NOUN an American whose ancestors came from Africa.

Afrikaans [*Said af-rik-ahns*] NOUN a language spoken in South Africa, similar to Dutch.

Afrikaner, Afrikaners NOUN a white South African with Dutch ancestors.

aft ADVERB or ADJECTIVE towards the back of a ship or boat.

after PREPOSITION or ADVERB ① later than a particular time, date or event. ② behind and following someone or something • *They ran after her.*
SIMILAR WORDS: ① afterwards, following, later

afterlife NOUN The afterlife is a life some people believe begins when you die.

aftermath, aftermaths NOUN The aftermath of a disaster is the situation that comes after it.

afternoon, afternoons NOUN the part of the day between noon and about six o'clock.

aftershave NOUN a pleasant-smelling liquid men put on their faces after shaving.

aftershock, aftershocks NOUN one of a series of minor tremors occurring after the main shock of an earthquake.

afterthought, afterthoughts NOUN something you do or say as an addition to something else you have already done or said.

afterwards ADVERB after an event or time.

again ADVERB ① happening one more time • *He looked forward to becoming a father again.* ② returning to the same state or place as before • *there and back again.*
SIMILAR WORDS: ① anew, once more

against PREPOSITION ① touching and leaning on • *He leaned against the wall.* ② in opposition to • *the Test match against England.* ③ in preparation for or in case of something • *precautions against fire.* ④in comparison with • *The pound is now at its lowest rate against the dollar.*

age, ages, ageing or aging, aged NOUN ①The age of something or someone is the number of years they have lived or existed. ②Age is the quality of being old • *The fabric was showing signs of age.* ③a particular period in history • *the Iron Age.* ④(in plural, informal) Ages means a very long time • *He's been talking for ages.* ▶VERB ⑤To age is to grow old or to appear older.

SPELLING TIP
Ageing and *aging* are both correct spellings.

aged ADJECTIVE ① [Rhymes with *raged*] having a particular age • *people aged 16 to 24.* ② [Said **ay**-jid] very old • *an aged horse.*
SIMILAR WORDS: ②elderly, old

ageism NOUN PSHE Ageism is the belief that older people are not as useful or important as younger people. **ageist** ADJECTIVE or NOUN

age limit, age limits NOUN CITIZENSHIP a minimum age at which people are legally allowed to do something, such as vote or drive.

agency, agencies NOUN an organisation or business which provides certain services • *a detective agency.*

agenda, agendas NOUN a list of items to be discussed at a meeting.

agent, agents NOUN ①someone who arranges work or business for other people, especially actors or singers. ②someone who works for their country's secret service.

aggravate, aggravates, aggravating, aggravated VERB ①To aggravate a bad situation is to make it worse. ②(*informal*) If someone or something aggravates you, they make you annoyed.
aggravating ADJECTIVE
aggravation NOUN

USAGE NOTE
Some people think that using *aggravate* to mean 'annoy' is wrong.

aggregate, aggregates NOUN a total that is made up of several smaller amounts.

aggression NOUN violent and hostile behaviour.

aggressive ADJECTIVE full of hostility and violence. **aggressively** ADVERB
aggressiveness NOUN
SIMILAR WORDS: belligerent, hostile

aggressor, aggressors NOUN a person or country that starts a fight or a war.

aggrieved ADJECTIVE upset and angry about the way you have been treated.

aghast [Said a-*gast*] ADJECTIVE shocked and horrified.

agile ADJECTIVE PE able to move quickly and easily • *He is as agile as a cat.* **agilely** ADVERB **agility** NOUN

agitate, agitates, agitating, agitated VERB ①If you agitate for something, you campaign energetically to get it. ②If something agitates you, it worries you. **agitation** NOUN **agitator** NOUN

agnostic, agnostics NOUN RE someone who believes we cannot know definitely whether God exists or not. **agnosticism** NOUN
WORD HISTORY: from Greek *agnōstos* meaning 'unknown'

ago ADVERB in the past • *He came to Britain six years ago.*

agog ADJECTIVE excited and eager to know more about an event or situation • *She was agog to hear his news.*

agonising; also spelt **agonizing**
ADJECTIVE extremely painful, either physically or mentally • *an agonising decision.*

agony NOUN very great physical or mental pain.
SIMILAR WORDS: pain, suffering, torment

agoraphobia [*Said a-gor-a-foe-bee-a*] NOUN the fear of open spaces.
agoraphobic ADJECTIVE
WORD HISTORY: from Greek *agora* meaning 'market place' + *phobia*

agrarian [*Said ag-rare-ee-an*] ADJECTIVE (*formal*) relating to farming and agriculture • *agrarian economies.*

agree, agrees, agreeing, agreed VERB ① If you agree with someone, you have the same opinion as them. ② If you agree to do something, you say you will do it. ③ If two stories or totals agree, they are the same. ④ Food that doesn't agree with you makes you ill.
SIMILAR WORDS: ① be of the same opinion, concur ② comply, consent

agreeable ADJECTIVE ① pleasant or enjoyable. ② If you are agreeable to something, you are willing to allow it or to do it • *She was agreeable to the project.* **agreeably** ADVERB

agreement, agreements NOUN ① a decision that has been reached by two or more people. ② Two people who are in agreement have the same opinion about something.

agriculture NOUN Agriculture is farming. **agricultural** ADJECTIVE

aground ADVERB If a boat runs aground, it becomes stuck in a shallow stretch of water.

ahead ADVERB ① in front • *He looked ahead.* ② more advanced than someone or something else • *We are*

five years ahead of the competition. ③ in the future • *I haven't had time to think far ahead.*

aid, aids, aiding, aided NOUN ① Aid is money, equipment or services provided for people in need • *food and medical aid.* ② something that makes a task easier • *teaching aids.* ▶ VERB ③ (*formal*) If you aid a person or an organisation, you help or support them.

aide, aides NOUN an assistant to an important person, especially in the government or the army • *the Prime Minister's closest aides.*

AIDS NOUN a disease which destroys the body's natural system of immunity to diseases. AIDS is an abbreviation for 'acquired immune deficiency syndrome'.

ailing ADJECTIVE ① sick or ill, and not getting better. ② getting into difficulties, especially with money • *an ailing company.*

ailment, ailments NOUN a minor illness.

aim, aims, aiming, aimed VERB ① If you aim an object or weapon at someone or something, you point it at them. ② If you aim to do something, you are planning or hoping to do it. ▶ NOUN ③ Your aim is what you intend to achieve. ④ If you take aim, you point an object or weapon at someone or something.
SIMILAR WORDS: ① point ② intend, mean, plan ③ goal, intention, objective

aimless ADJECTIVE having no clear purpose or plan. **aimlessly** ADVERB **aimlessness** NOUN

air, airs, airing, aired NOUN ① Air is the mixture of oxygen and other gases which we breathe and which forms the earth's atmosphere. ② 'Air' is used to refer to travel in aircraft • *I have to travel by air a great deal.* ③ An air someone or something has is the impression they give • *an air of defiance.* ④ (*in plural*) If you give yourself airs, you behave as if you were more important than you really are. ⑤ An air is a simple tune. ▶ **VERB** ⑥ If you air your opinions, you talk about them to other people.

airborne ADJECTIVE in the air and flying.

air-conditioning NOUN a system of providing cool, clean air in buildings. **air-conditioned** ADJECTIVE

aircraft NOUN any vehicle which can fly.

airfield, airfields NOUN an open area of ground with runways where small aircraft take off and land.

air force, air forces NOUN the part of a country's armed services that fights using aircraft.

air gun, air guns NOUN a gun which uses air pressure to fire pellets.

airless ADJECTIVE having no wind or fresh air.

airlift, airlifts NOUN an operation to move people or goods by air, especially in an emergency.

airline, airlines NOUN a company which provides air travel.

airliner, airliners NOUN a large passenger plane.

airmail NOUN the system of sending letters and parcels by air.

airman, airmen NOUN a man who serves in his country's air force.

airplane, airplanes NOUN In American English, an airplane is an aeroplane.

airport, airports NOUN a place where people go to catch planes.

air quality NOUN GEOGRAPHY a measurement of how much pollution there is in the air.

air raid, air raids NOUN an attack by enemy aircraft, in which bombs are dropped.

air resistance NOUN SCIENCE the friction which slows down something moving through the air. SIMILAR WORDS: drag

airship, airships NOUN a large, light aircraft, consisting of a rigid balloon filled with gas and powered by an engine, with a passenger compartment underneath.

airstrip, airstrips NOUN a stretch of land that has been cleared for aircraft to take off and land.

airtight ADJECTIVE not letting air in or out.

airy, airier, airiest ADJECTIVE full of fresh air and light. **airily** ADVERB

aisle, aisles [*Rhymes with* mile] NOUN a long narrow gap that people can walk along between rows of seats or shelves.

ajar ADJECTIVE A door or window that is ajar is slightly open.

akin ADJECTIVE (*formal*) similar • *The taste is akin to peach.*

alabaster NOUN a type of smooth stone used for making ornaments.

alacrity NOUN (*formal*) eager willingness • *He seized this offer with alacrity.*

alarm, alarms, alarming, alarmed NOUN ① a feeling of fear and worry • *The cat sprang back in alarm.* ② an automatic device used to warn people of something • *a car alarm.* ▶ **VERB** ③ If something alarms you, it makes you worried and anxious. **alarming** ADJECTIVE

alas ADVERB unfortunately or regrettably • *But, alas, it would not be true.*

Albanian, Albanians ADJECTIVE ① belonging or relating to Albania.

a
b
c
d
e
f
g
h
i
j
k
l
m
n
o
p
q
r
s
t
u
v
w
x
y
z

A
B
C
D
E
F
G
H
I
J
K
L
M
N
O
P
Q
R
S
T
U
V
W
X
Y
Z

▶ NOUN ② someone who comes from Albania. ③ Albanian is the main language spoken in Albania.

albatross, albatrosses NOUN a large white sea bird.

albeit [Said awl-**bee**-it] CONJUNCTION (formal) although • He was making progress, albeit slowly.

albino, albinos NOUN a person or animal with very white skin, white hair, and pink eyes.

album, albums NOUN ① a recording with a number of songs on it. ② a book in which you keep a collection of things such as photographs or stamps.

alchemy [Said al-kem-ee] NOUN a medieval science that attempted to change ordinary metals into gold. **alchemist** NOUN

alcheringa [Said al-cher-ring-ga] NOUN In the mythology of some Aboriginal Australians, Alcheringa is the time when the world was being made and the first people were created.

alcohol NOUN Alcohol is any drink that can make people drunk; also the colourless flammable liquid found in these drinks, produced by fermenting sugar.

alcoholic, alcoholics ADJECTIVE ① An alcoholic drink contains alcohol. ▶ NOUN ② someone who is addicted to alcohol. **alcoholism** NOUN

alcove, alcoves NOUN an area of a room which is set back slightly from the main part. WORD HISTORY: from Arabic al-qubbah meaning 'arch'

ale NOUN a type of beer.

alert, alerts, alerting, alerted ADJECTIVE ① paying full attention to what is happening • The criminal was spotted by an alert member of the public. ▶ NOUN ② a situation in which

people prepare themselves for danger • The troops were on a war alert. ▶ VERB ③ If you alert someone to a problem or danger, you warn them of it. **alertness** NOUN SIMILAR WORDS: ① attentive, vigilant, watchful

algae [Said al-jee] PLURAL NOUN plants that grow in water or on damp surfaces.

algebra NOUN [MATHS] a branch of mathematics in which symbols and letters are used instead of numbers to express relationships between quantities. **algebraic** ADJECTIVE WORD HISTORY: from Arabic al-jabr meaning 'reunion'

Algerian, Algerians ADJECTIVE ① belonging or relating to Algeria. ▶ NOUN ② someone who comes from Algeria.

algorithm, algorithms NOUN [ICT] a mathematical procedure for solving a particular problem. WORD HISTORY: from al-Khuwarizmi, the name of a 9th-century Arab mathematician

alias, aliases [Said ay-lee-ass] NOUN a false name • Zachary Quinto, alias Mr Spock.

alibi, alibis [Said al-li-bye] NOUN An alibi is evidence proving you were somewhere else when a crime was committed.

alien, aliens [Said ay-lee-an] ADJECTIVE ① not normal to you • a totally alien culture. ▶ NOUN ② someone who is not a citizen of the country in which he or she lives. ③ In science fiction, an alien is a creature from outer space.

alienate, alienates, alienating, alienated VERB If you alienate someone, you do something that makes them stop being sympathetic to you • The Council's approach

alienated many local residents.
alienation NOUN

alight, alights, alighting, alighted
ADJECTIVE ① Something that is alight
is burning. ▶ VERB ② If a bird or insect
alights somewhere, it lands there.
③ (*formal*) When passengers alight
from a vehicle, they get out of it at
the end of a journey.

align, aligns, aligning, aligned [*Said*
a-line] VERB ① If you align yourself
with a particular group, you support
them. ② If you align things, you place
them in a straight line. **alignment**
NOUN

alike ADJECTIVE ① Things that are
alike are similar in some way.
▶ ADVERB ② If people or things are
treated alike, they are treated in a
similar way.

alimony [*Said al-li-mon-ee*] NOUN
money someone has to pay regularly
to their wife or husband after they
are divorced.

alive ADJECTIVE ① living. ② lively and
active.
SIMILAR WORDS: ① animate, living

alkali, alkalis [*Said al-kal-eye*] NOUN
SCIENCE a chemical substance that
turns litmus paper blue. **alkaline**
ADJECTIVE **alkalinity** NOUN

alkali metal NOUN SCIENCE a
metal such as sodium or potassium
that forms an alkaline solution in
water and belongs to group 1A of the
periodic table.

all ADJECTIVE or PRONOUN or ADVERB
① used when referring to the whole
of something • *Why did he have to say*
all that? • *She managed to finish it all.*
▶ ADVERB ② 'All' is also used when
saying the two sides in a game or
contest have the same score • *The*
final score was six points all.

Allah PROPER NOUN RE the Arabic
word for God.

allay, allays, allaying, allayed VERB
To allay someone's fears or doubts is
to stop them feeling afraid or
doubtful.

SPELLING TIP

Do not confuse the spellings of *allay*
and *alley*: *I hope her explanation will*
allay my fears; the alley behind the
school.

---

allege, alleges, alleging, alleged
[*Said a-lej*] VERB If you allege that
something is true, you say it is true
but do not provide any proof • *It is*
alleged that she died as a result of
neglect. **allegation** NOUN **alleged**
ADJECTIVE

allegiance, allegiances [*Said*
al-lee-jenss] NOUN loyal support for a
person or organisation.

allegory, allegories [*Said al-li-gor-ee*]
NOUN a piece of writing or art in
which the characters and events are
symbols for something else.
Allegories usually make some moral,
religious or political point. For
example, George Orwell's novel
Animal Farm is an allegory in that the
animals who revolt in the farmyard
are symbols of the political leaders in
the Russian Revolution. **allegorical**
ADJECTIVE

allegro ADVERB MUSIC In music,
allegro is an instruction to play or
sing something quickly.

allele, alleles NOUN SCIENCE Alleles
are variations of genes that are
responsible for individuals having
alternative characteristics, such as
smooth or wrinkled seeds in peas.

allergy, allergies [*Said al-er-jee*]
NOUN a sensitivity someone has to
something, so that they become ill
when they eat it or touch it • *an*
allergy to cows' milk. **allergic**
ADJECTIVE

a
b
c
d
e
f
g
h
i
j
k
l
m
n
o
p
q
r
s
t
u
v
w
x
y
z

A
B
C
D
E
F
G
H
I
J
K
L
M
N
O
P
Q
R
S
T
U
V
W
X
Y
Z

alleviate, alleviates, alleviating, alleviated VERB To alleviate pain or a problem is to make it less severe • *measures to alleviate poverty*.
alleviation NOUN

alley, alleys NOUN a narrow passage between buildings.

SPELLING TIP
Do not confuse the spellings of *alley* and *allay*: *the alley behind the school; I hope her explanation will allay my fears*.

alliance, alliances NOUN a group of people, organisations or countries working together for similar aims.
SIMILAR WORDS: association, league, union

alligator, alligators NOUN a large animal, similar to a crocodile.
WORD HISTORY: from Spanish *el lagarto* meaning 'lizard'

alliteration NOUN ENGLISH
(*literary*) the use of several words together which all begin with the same sound, for example 'around the rugged rock the ragged rascal ran'.
alliterative ADJECTIVE

allocate, allocates, allocating, allocated VERB If you allocate something, you decide it should be given to a person or place, or used for a particular purpose • *funds allocated for nursery education*. **allocation** NOUN

allot, allots, allotting, allotted VERB If something is allotted to you, it is given to you as your share • *Space was allotted for visitors' cars*.

allotment, allotments NOUN ① a piece of land which people can rent to grow vegetables on. ② a share of something.

allow, allows, allowing, allowed VERB ① If you allow something, you say it is all right or let it happen. ② If you allow a period of time or an amount of something, you set it aside for a particular purpose • *Allow four hours for the paint to dry*.
allowable ADJECTIVE

SPELLING TIP
Do not confuse the spellings of the past tense form *allowed* and the adverb *aloud*, which sound the same.

allowance, allowances NOUN ① money given regularly to someone for a particular purpose • *a petrol allowance*. ▶ PHRASE ② If you **make allowances** for something, you take it into account • *The school made allowances for different cultural customs*.

alloy, alloys NOUN SCIENCE a mixture of two or more metals.

all right; also spelt **alright** ADJECTIVE ① If something is all right, it is acceptable. ② If someone is all right, they are safe and not harmed. ③ You say 'all right' to agree to something.

allude, alludes, alluding, alluded VERB If you allude to something, you refer to it in an indirect way.

GRAMMAR TIP
You *allude to* something.

SPELLING TIP
Do not confuse *allude* with *elude*: *She alluded to the report in the newspaper; I knew his face but his name eluded me*.

allure NOUN The allure of something is an exciting quality that makes it attractive • *the allure of foreign travel*.
alluring ADJECTIVE

allusion, allusions NOUN ENGLISH an indirect reference to or comment about something • *English literature is full of classical allusions*.

alluvium NOUN GEOGRAPHY Alluvium is a fine, fertile soil consisting of mud and silt that has been deposited by flowing water along the sides or at the mouth of a river. **alluvial** ADJECTIVE

ally, **allies**, **allying**, **allied** NOUN ① a person or country that helps and supports another. ▸ VERB ② If you ally yourself with someone, you agree to help and support each other.
SIMILAR WORDS: ① friend, helper, partner ② associate, join, unite

almanac, **almanacs** NOUN a book published every year giving information about a particular subject.

almighty ADJECTIVE ① very great or serious • *I've just had an almighty row with my dad.* ▸ PROPER NOUN ② The Almighty is another name for God.

almond, **almonds** NOUN a pale brown oval nut.

almost ADVERB very nearly • *Prices have almost doubled.*
SIMILAR WORDS: just about, nearly, practically

aloft ADVERB up in the air or in a high position • *He held aloft the trophy.*

alone ADJECTIVE OR ADVERB not with other people or things • *He just wanted to be alone.*
SIMILAR WORDS: by oneself, solitary, unaccompanied

along PREPOSITION ① moving, happening or existing continuously from one end to the other of something, or at various points beside it • *Put rivets along the top edge.* ▸ ADVERB ② moving forward • *We marched along, singing as we went.* ③ with someone • *Why could she not take her along?* ▸ PHRASE ④ **All along** means from the beginning of a period of time right up to now • *You've known that all along.*

alongside PREPOSITION OR ADVERB ① next to something • *They had a house in the park alongside the river.*

▸ PREPOSITION ② If you work alongside other people, you are working in the same place and cooperating with them • *He was thrilled to work alongside Robert De Niro.*

GRAMMAR TIP
Do not use *of* after *alongside*.

aloof ADJECTIVE emotionally distant from someone or something.

aloud ADVERB When you read or speak aloud, you speak loudly enough for other people to hear you.

SPELLING TIP
Do not confuse the spellings of *aloud* and *allowed*, the past tense form of *allow*.

alpha NOUN Alpha is the first letter in the Greek alphabet.

alphabet, **alphabets** NOUN ⟨LIBRARY⟩ a set of letters in a fixed order that is used in writing a language.
alphabetical ADJECTIVE
alphabetically ADVERB

alpine ADJECTIVE existing in or relating to high mountains • *alpine flowers.*

already ADVERB having happened before the present time or earlier than expected • *She has already gone to bed.*

alright another spelling of **all right**.

SPELLING TIP
Some people think that *all right* is the only correct spelling and that *alright* is wrong.

Alsatian, **Alsatians** [Said al-**say**-shn] NOUN a large wolflike dog.

also ADVERB in addition to something that has just been mentioned.

altar, **altars** NOUN a holy table in a church or temple.

a b c d e f g h i j k l m n o p q r s t u v w x y z

A
B
C
D
E
F
G
H
I
J
K
L
M
N
O
P
Q
R
S
T
U
V
W
X
Y
Z

SPELLING TIP
Do not confuse the spellings of *altar* and *alter*: *The priest stood at the altar; His tone altered suddenly.*

alter, alters, altering, altered VERB If something alters or if you alter it, it changes. **alteration** NOUN

SPELLING TIP
Do not confuse the spellings of *alter* and *altar*: *His tone altered suddenly; The priest stood at the altar.*

altercation, altercations NOUN (*formal*) a noisy disagreement.

alternate, alternates, alternating, alternated VERB [Said ol-tern-ate] ① If one thing alternates with another, the two things regularly occur one after the other. ▶ADJECTIVE [Said ol-**tern**-at] ② If something happens on alternate days, it happens on the first day but not the second, and happens again on the third day but not the fourth, and so on. ③ MATHS Alternate angles are two angles on opposite sides of a line that crosses two other lines. **alternately** ADVERB **alternation** NOUN

alternating current NOUN an electric current that regularly changes its direction, so that the electrons flow first one way and then the other.

alternative, alternatives NOUN ① something you can do or have instead of something else • *alternatives to prison such as community service.* ▶ADJECTIVE ② Alternative plans or actions can happen or be done instead of what is already happening or being done. **alternatively** ADVERB

USAGE NOTE
If there are more than two choices in a situation you should say *there are*

three choices rather than *there are three alternatives* because the strict meaning of *alternative* is a choice between two things.

although CONJUNCTION in spite of the fact that • *He wasn't well-known in America, although he did make a film there.*

altitude, altitudes NOUN
GEOGRAPHY The altitude of something is its height above sea level • *The mountain range reaches an altitude of 1330 metres.*

alto, altos MUSIC NOUN ① An alto is a person who sings the second highest part in four-part harmony. ▶ADJECTIVE ② An alto musical instrument has a range of notes that are of medium pitch.

altogether ADVERB ① entirely • *She wasn't altogether sorry to be leaving.* ② in total; used of amounts • *I get paid £1000 a month altogether.*

aluminium NOUN SCIENCE
Aluminium is a light silvery-white metallic element. It is used to make aircraft and other equipment, usually in the form of aluminium alloys.

alveoli PLURAL NOUN SCIENCE
Alveoli are tiny sacs of air in the lungs, through which oxygen is taken into the blood.

always ADVERB all the time or for ever • *She's always moaning.*

am the first person singular, present tense of **be**.

a.m. used to specify times between 12 midnight and 12 noon, eg *I get up at 6 a.m.* It is an abbreviation for the Latin phrase 'ante meridiem', which means 'before noon'.

amakhosi the plural of **inkhosi**.

amalgamate, amalgamates, amalgamating, amalgamated VERB If two organisations

amalgamate, they join together to form one new organisation.
amalgamation NOUN

amandla NOUN In South Africa, amandla is a political slogan which calls for power for Black people.

amass, **amasses**, **amassing**, **amassed** VERB If you amass something such as money or information, you collect large quantities of it • *He amassed a huge fortune.*

amateur, **amateurs** NOUN someone who does something as a hobby rather than as a job.

amateurish ADJECTIVE not skilfully made or done. **amateurishly** ADVERB

amaze, **amazes**, **amazing**, **amazed** VERB If something amazes you, it surprises you very much.
SIMILAR WORDS: astonish, astound, stun, surprise

amazement NOUN complete surprise.

amazing ADJECTIVE very surprising or remarkable. **amazingly** ADVERB

ambassador, **ambassadors** NOUN a person sent to a foreign country as the representative of his or her own government.

amber NOUN ① a hard, yellowish-brown substance used for making jewellery. ▸ NOUN or ADJECTIVE ② orange-brown.

ambi- PREFIX 'Ambi-' means 'both'. For example, something which is *ambiguous* can have either of two meanings.
WORD HISTORY: from Latin *ambo* meaning 'both'

ambidextrous ADJECTIVE Someone who is ambidextrous is able to use both hands equally skilfully.

ambience NOUN (*formal*) The ambience of a place is its atmosphere.

ambient ADJECTIVE ① surrounding • *low ambient temperatures.* ② creating a relaxing atmosphere • *ambient music.*

ambiguous ADJECTIVE A word or phrase that is ambiguous has more than one meaning. **ambiguously** ADVERB **ambiguity** NOUN

ambition, **ambitions** NOUN ① If you have an ambition to achieve something, you want very much to achieve it • *His ambition is to be an actor.* ② a great desire for success, power and wealth • *He's talented and full of ambition.*

ambitious ADJECTIVE ① Someone who is ambitious has a strong desire for success, power and wealth. ② An ambitious plan is a large one and requires a lot of work • *an ambitious rebuilding schedule.*

ambivalent ADJECTIVE having or showing two conflicting attitudes or emotions. **ambivalence** NOUN

amble, **ambles**, **ambling**, **ambled** VERB If you amble, you walk slowly and in a relaxed manner.

ambulance, **ambulances** NOUN a vehicle for taking sick and injured people to hospital.

ambush, **ambushes**, **ambushing**, **ambushed** VERB ① To ambush someone is to attack them after hiding and lying in wait for them. ▸ NOUN ② an attack on someone after hiding and lying in wait for them.

amen INTERJECTION 'Amen' is said at the end of a Christian prayer. It means 'so be it'.

amenable [*Said am-mee-na-bl*] ADJECTIVE willing to listen to suggestions, or to cooperate with someone • *Both brothers were amenable to the arrangement.*
amenably ADVERB **amenability** NOUN

a
b
c
d
e
f
g
h
i
j
k
l
m
n
o
p
q
r
s
t
u
v
w
x
y
z

amend, amends, amending, amended VERB To amend something that has been written or said is to alter it slightly • *Our constitution had to be amended.*
amendment NOUN

amends PLURAL NOUN If you make amends for something bad you have done, you say you are sorry and try to make up for it.

amenity, amenities [Said am-*mee-nit-ee*] NOUN GEOGRAPHY Amenities are things that are available for the public to use, such as sports facilities or shopping centres.

America NOUN America refers to the United States, or to the whole of North, South and Central America.

American, Americans ADJECTIVE ① belonging or relating to the United States, or to the whole of North, South and Central America. ▸ NOUN ② someone who comes from the United States.

amethyst, amethysts NOUN a type of purple semiprecious stone.
WORD HISTORY: from Greek *amethustos* meaning 'not drunk'. It was thought to prevent intoxication

amiable ADJECTIVE pleasant and friendly • *The hotel staff were very amiable.* **amiably** ADVERB **amiability** NOUN

amicable ADJECTIVE fairly friendly • *an amicable agreement.* **amicably** ADVERB

amid or **amidst** PREPOSITION (formal) ① If something happens amid events of some kind, it happens at the same time as those events • *The trial began amid scenes of chaos.* ② surrounded by • *The house is set amid trees and bushes.*

USAGE NOTE
The form *amidst* is a bit old-fashioned and *amid* is more often used.

amino acid, amino acids NOUN SCIENCE An amino acid is a compound containing an amino group, which forms a part of protein molecules.

amiss ADJECTIVE If something is amiss, there is something wrong.

ammeter, ammeters NOUN SCIENCE An ammeter is an instrument for measuring the strength of an electric current.

ammonia NOUN Ammonia is a colourless, strong-smelling gas or alkaline liquid. It is used in household cleaning materials, explosives and fertilisers. It has the chemical formula NH_3.

ammunition NOUN anything that can be fired from a gun or other weapon, for example bullets and shells.

amnesia NOUN loss of memory.

amnesty, amnesties NOUN an official pardon for political or other prisoners.

amniotic ADJECTIVE SCIENCE The amniotic sac is the protective membrane surrounding a baby in its mother's womb. It is filled with amniotic fluid, which protects the baby.

amoeba, amoebas or amoebae [Said am-*mee-ba*]; also spelt **ameba** NOUN the smallest kind of living creature, consisting of one cell. Amoebas reproduce by dividing into two.

amok [Said am-*muk*] PHRASE If a person or animal **runs amok**, they behave in a violent and uncontrolled way.
WORD HISTORY: a Malay word

among or **amongst** PREPOSITION ① surrounded by • *The bike lay among piles of chains and pedals.* ② in the company of • *He was among friends.* ③ between more than two • *The* *money will be divided among seven charities.*

USAGE NOTE

If there are more than two things, you should use *among*. If there are only two things you should use *between*. The form *amongst* is a bit old-fashioned and *among* is more often used.

amoral ADJECTIVE Someone who is amoral has no moral standards by which to live.

SPELLING TIP

Do not confuse *amoral* and *immoral*. You use *amoral* to talk about people with no moral standards, but *immoral* for people who are aware of moral standards but go against them.

amorous ADJECTIVE passionately affectionate • *an amorous relationship*. **amorously** ADVERB **amorousness** NOUN

amount, amounts, amounting, amounted NOUN ①An amount of something is how much there is of it. ▶ VERB ②If something amounts to a particular total, all the parts of it add up to that total • *Her vocabulary amounted to only 50 words*. **SIMILAR WORDS:** ① extent, number, quantity

amp, amps NOUN ①An amp is the same as an amplifier. ②An amp is also the same as an ampere.

ampere, amperes [*Said am-pair*] NOUN SCIENCE The ampere is the SI unit of electrical current. One ampere of current is produced by one volt of electrical force when the resistance is one ohm. The ampere is named after the French physicist A.M. Ampère (1775–1836).

ampersand, ampersands NOUN the character &, meaning 'and'.

amphetamine, amphetamines NOUN a drug that increases people's energy and makes them excited. It can have dangerous and unpleasant side effects.

amphibian, amphibians NOUN SCIENCE a creature that lives partly on land and partly in water, for example a frog or a newt.

amphibious ADJECTIVE An amphibious animal, such as a frog, lives partly on land and partly in water.

WORD HISTORY: from Greek *amphibios* meaning 'having a double life'

amphitheatre, amphitheatres NOUN HISTORY An amphitheatre is a large, circular open area with sloping sides covered with rows of seats. Amphitheatres were built originally by the Greeks and Romans as venues for sport and entertainment.

ample ADJECTIVE If there is an ample amount of something, there is more than enough of it. **amply** ADVERB

amplifier, amplifiers NOUN a piece of equipment which causes sounds or electrical signals to become louder.

amplify, amplifies, amplifying, amplified VERB If you amplify a sound, you make it louder. **amplification** NOUN

amplitude NOUN SCIENCE In physics, the amplitude of a wave is how far its curve moves away from its normal position.

amputate, amputates, amputating, amputated VERB To amputate an arm or a leg is to cut it off as a surgical operation. **amputation** NOUN

Amrit NOUN ① In the Sikh religion, Amrit is a special mixture of sugar and water used in rituals. ② The Amrit or Amrit ceremony takes place

a b c d e f g h i j k l m n o p q r s t u v w x y z

when someone is accepted as a full member of the Sikh community, and drinks Amrit as part of the ceremony.

amuse, amuses, amusing, amused VERB ① If something amuses you, you think it is funny. ② If you amuse yourself, you find things to do which stop you from being bored. **amused** ADJECTIVE **amusing** ADJECTIVE

amusement, amusements NOUN ① Amusement is the state of thinking something is funny. ② Amusement is also the pleasure you get from being entertained or from doing something interesting. ③ Amusements are ways of passing the time pleasantly.

an ADJECTIVE 'An' is used instead of 'a' in front of words that begin with a vowel sound.

GRAMMAR TIP
You use an in front of abbreviations that start with a vowel sound when they are read out loud: an MA; an OBE.

-an SUFFIX '-an' comes at the end of nouns and adjectives which show where or what someone or something comes from or belongs to • American • Victorian • Christian.

anachronism, anachronisms [Said an-**ak**-kron-izm] NOUN something that belongs or seems to belong to another time. **anachronistic** ADJECTIVE
WORD HISTORY: from Greek anakhronismos meaning 'mistake in time'

anaemia [Said a-**nee**-mee-a] NOUN a medical condition resulting from too few red cells in a person's blood. People with anaemia look pale and feel very tired. **anaemic** ADJECTIVE

anaerobic ADJECTIVE [SCIENCE] Anaerobic respiration is a type of breathing that does not use oxygen.

anaesthetic, anaesthetics [Said an-niss-**thet**-ik] NOUN a substance that stops you feeling pain. A general anaesthetic stops you from feeling pain in the whole of your body by putting you to sleep, and a local anaesthetic makes just one part of your body go numb.

anaesthetise, anaesthetises, anaesthetising, anaesthetised; also spelt **anesthetize** or **anaethetize** VERB To anaesthetise someone is to give them an anaesthetic to make them unconscious.

anaesthetist, anaesthetists; also spelt **anesthetist** NOUN a doctor who is specially trained to give anaesthetics.

anagram, anagrams NOUN a word or phrase formed by changing the order of the letters of another word or phrase. For example, 'triangle' is an anagram of 'integral'.

anal [Said ay-nl] ADJECTIVE relating to the anus.

analgesic, analgesics [Said an-al-**jee**-sik] NOUN a substance that relieves pain.

analogue; also spelt **analog** ADJECTIVE An analogue clock or instrument displays information using a dial rather than a digital display.

analogy, analogies [Said an-**al**-o-jee] NOUN a comparison showing that two things are similar in some ways. **analogous** ADJECTIVE

analyse, analyses, analysing, analysed VERB [EXAM TERM] To analyse something is to break it down into parts, or investigate it carefully, so that you can describe its main aspects, or find out what it consists of.

analysis, analyses NOUN the process of investigating something in order to understand it or find out what it consists of • *a full analysis of the problem*.

analyst, analysts NOUN a person whose job is to analyse things to find out about them.

analytic or **analytical** ADJECTIVE using logical reasoning • *Planning in detail requires an acute analytical mind.* **analytically** ADVERB

anarchy [Said an-nar-kee] NOUN a situation where nobody obeys laws or rules.
WORD HISTORY: from Greek *anarkhos* meaning 'without a ruler'

anatomy, anatomies NOUN ① the study of the structure of the human body or of the bodies of animals. ② An animal's anatomy is the structure of its body. **anatomical** ADJECTIVE **anatomically** ADVERB

ANC NOUN one of the main political parties in South Africa. ANC is an abbreviation for 'African National Congress'.

ancestor, ancestors NOUN Your ancestors are the members of your family who lived many years ago and from whom you are descended. **ancestral** ADJECTIVE
SIMILAR WORDS: forebear, forefather

ancestry, ancestries NOUN Your ancestry consists of the people from whom you are descended • *a French citizen of Greek ancestry*.

anchor, anchors, anchoring, anchored NOUN ① a heavy, hooked object at the end of a chain, dropped from a boat into the water to keep the boat in one place. ▶ VERB ② To anchor a boat or another object is to stop it from moving by dropping an anchor or attaching it to something solid.

anchorage, anchorages NOUN a place where a boat can safely be anchored.

anchovy, anchovies NOUN a type of small edible fish with a very strong salty taste.

ancient [Said ayn-shent] ADJECTIVE ① existing or happening in the distant past • *ancient Greece*. ② very old or having a very long history • *an ancient monastery*.

ancillary [Said an-sil-lar-ee] ADJECTIVE The ancillary workers in an institution are the people such as cooks and cleaners, whose work supports the main work of the institution.
WORD HISTORY: from Latin *ancilla* meaning 'maidservant'

and CONJUNCTION You use 'and' to link two or more words or phrases together.

andante, andantes [MUSIC] ADVERB ① In music, andante is an instruction to play or sing something at a moderately slow tempo. ▶ NOUN ② a piece of music that should be performed at a moderately slow tempo.
WORD HISTORY: an Italian word

androgynous [Said an-droj-in-uss] ADJECTIVE (*formal*) having both male and female characteristics.

android, androids NOUN In science fiction, an android is a robot that looks like a human being.

anecdote, anecdotes NOUN a short, entertaining story about a person or event. **anecdotal** ADJECTIVE

anemone, anemones [Said an-em-on-ee] NOUN a plant with red, purple or white flowers.

anew ADVERB If you do something anew, you do it again • *They left their life in Britain to start anew in France*.

angel, angels NOUN Angels are spiritual beings some people believe live in heaven and act as messengers for God. **angelic** ADJECTIVE

SPELLING TIP
Remember this mnemonic: *an ELegant angEL.*

anger, angers, angering, angered NOUN ① the strong feeling you get when you feel someone has behaved in an unfair or cruel way. ▶ VERB ② If something angers you, it makes you feel angry.
SIMILAR WORDS: ① fury, rage, wrath ② enrage, infuriate, madden

angina [*Said an-jy-na*] NOUN a brief but very severe heart pain, caused by lack of blood supply to the heart. It is also known as 'angina pectoris'.

angle, angles NOUN ① MATHS the difference in direction between two lines or surfaces. Angles are measured in degrees. ② the direction from which you look at something • *He had painted the vase from all angles.* ③ An angle on something is a particular way of considering it • *the same story from a German angle.*

SPELLING TIP
Remember this mnemonic: *LEt's measure the angLE.*

angler, anglers NOUN someone who fishes with a fishing rod as a hobby. **angling** NOUN

Anglican, Anglicans NOUN or ADJECTIVE RE (a member of one of the churches) belonging to the Anglican Communion, a group of Protestant churches which includes the Church of England.

Anglo-Saxon, Anglo-Saxons NOUN ① HISTORY The Anglo-Saxons were a race of people who settled in England from the fifth century AD and were the dominant people until the Norman invasion in 1066. They

were composed of three West Germanic tribes, the Angles, Saxons and Jutes. ② Anglo-Saxon is another name for **Old English**.

Angolan, Angolans [*Said ang-goh-ln*] ADJECTIVE ① belonging or relating to Angola. ▶ NOUN ② someone who comes from Angola.

angora ADJECTIVE ① An angora goat or rabbit is a breed with long, silky hair. ▶ NOUN ② Angora is this hair, usually mixed with other fibres to make clothing.
WORD HISTORY: from *Angora*, the former name of Ankara in Turkey

angry, angrier, angriest ADJECTIVE very cross or annoyed. **angrily** ADVERB
SIMILAR WORDS: enraged, furious, infuriated, mad

angst NOUN a feeling of anxiety and worry.

anguish NOUN extreme suffering. **anguished** ADJECTIVE

angular ADJECTIVE Angular things have straight lines and sharp points • *He has an angular face and pointed chin.*

animal, animals NOUN any living being except a plant, or any mammal except a human being.
WORD HISTORY: from Latin *anima* meaning 'life' or 'soul'

animate, animates, animating, animated VERB To animate something is to make it lively and interesting.

animated ADJECTIVE lively and interesting • *an animated conversation.* **animatedly** ADVERB

animation NOUN ① a method of film-making in which a series of drawings are photographed. When the film is projected, the characters in the drawings appear to move. ② Someone who has animation shows liveliness in the way they speak and act • *The crowd showed no sign of animation.* **animator** NOUN

animosity, animosities NOUN a feeling of strong dislike and anger towards someone.

aniseed NOUN a substance made from the seeds of a Mediterranean plant and used as a flavouring in sweets, drinks and medicine.

ankle, ankles NOUN the joint which connects your foot to your leg.

annex, annexes, annexing, annexed; also spelt **annexe** NOUN ① an extra building which is joined to a larger main building. ② an extra part added to a document. ▸ VERB ③ If one country annexes another, it seizes the other country and takes control of it. **annexation** NOUN

annihilate, annihilates, annihilating, annihilated *[Said an-nye-ill-ate]* VERB If something is annihilated, it is completely destroyed. **annihilation** NOUN

anniversary, anniversaries NOUN a date which is remembered because something special happened on that date in a previous year.

announce, announces, announcing, announced VERB If you announce something, you tell people about it publicly or officially • *The team was announced on Friday morning.*
SIMILAR WORDS: broadcast, make known, proclaim

announcement, announcements NOUN a statement giving information about something.

announcer, announcers NOUN someone who introduces programmes on radio or television.

annoy, annoys, annoying, annoyed VERB If someone or something annoys you, they irritate you and make you fairly angry. **annoyed** ADJECTIVE
SIMILAR WORDS: bother, exasperate, irritate, vex

annoyance NOUN ① a feeling of irritation. ② something that causes irritation.

annual, annuals ADJECTIVE ① happening or done once a year • *their annual conference.* ② happening or calculated over a period of one year • *the United States' annual budget for national defence.* ▸ NOUN ③ a book or magazine published once a year. ④ a plant that grows, flowers and dies within one year. **annually** ADVERB

annuity, annuities NOUN a fixed sum of money paid to someone every year from an investment or insurance policy.

annul, annuls, annulling, annulled VERB If a marriage or contract is annulled, it is declared invalid, so that legally it is considered never to have existed. **annulment** NOUN

anoint, anoints, anointing, anointed VERB To anoint someone is to put oil on them as part of a ceremony. **anointment** NOUN

anomaly, anomalies *[Said an-nom-al-ee]* NOUN Something is an anomaly if it is unusual or different from normal. **anomalous** ADJECTIVE

anon. an abbreviation for **anonymous**.

anonymous ADJECTIVE If something is anonymous, nobody knows who is responsible for it • *The police received an anonymous phone call.* **anonymously** ADVERB **anonymity** NOUN

anorak, anoraks NOUN a warm waterproof jacket, usually with a hood.
WORD HISTORY: an Inuit word

anorexia NOUN a psychological condition in which a person may eat too little in order to keep their weight as low as possible. **anorexic** ADJECTIVE

WORD HISTORY: from Greek *an-* + *orexis* meaning 'no appetite'

another ADJECTIVE or PRONOUN Another thing or person is an additional thing or person.

answer, answers, answering, answered VERB ① If you answer someone, you reply to them using words or actions or in writing. ▸ NOUN ② the reply you give when you answer someone. ③ a solution to a problem.

SIMILAR WORDS: ① reply, respond, retort ② reply, response, retort

answerable ADJECTIVE If you are answerable to someone for something, you are responsible for it • *He must be made answerable for these terrible crimes.*

ant, ants NOUN Ants are small insects that live in large groups.

-ant SUFFIX '-ant' is used to form adjectives • *important.*

antacid, antacids NOUN [SCIENCE] a substance that reduces the level of acid in the stomach.

antagonise, antagonises, antagonising, antagonised; also spelt **antagonize** VERB If someone is antagonised, they are made to feel anger and hostility.

antagonism NOUN hatred or hostility.

antagonist, antagonists NOUN an enemy or opponent.

antagonistic ADJECTIVE Someone who is antagonistic towards you shows hate or hostility. **antagonistically** ADVERB

Antarctic NOUN The Antarctic is the region south of the Antarctic Circle.

Antarctic Circle NOUN The Antarctic Circle is an imaginary circle around the southern part of the world.

ante- PREFIX 'Ante-' means 'before'. For example, *antenatal* means 'before birth'.

WORD HISTORY: from Latin *ante*, a preposition or adverb meaning 'before'

antecedent, antecedents [*Said an-tis-see-dent*] NOUN ① An antecedent of a thing or event is something which happened or existed before it and is related to it in some way • *the prehistoric antecedents of the horse.* ② Your antecedents are your ancestors, the relatives from whom you are descended.

antelope, antelopes NOUN an animal which looks like a deer.

antenatal ADJECTIVE concerned with the care of pregnant women and their unborn children • *an antenatal clinic.*

antenna, antennae or antennas NOUN ① The antennae of insects and certain other animals are the two long, thin parts attached to their heads which they use to feel with. ② In Australian, New Zealand and American English, an antenna is a radio or television aerial.

GRAMMAR TIP
The plural of the part of an insect is *antennae*. The plural of the aerial is *antennas*.

---

anthem, anthems NOUN a hymn written for a special occasion.

anther, anthers NOUN [SCIENCE] in a flower, the part of the stamen that makes pollen grains.

anthology, anthologies NOUN [LIBRARY] a collection of writings by various authors published in one book.

anthropology NOUN the study of human beings and their society and culture. **anthropological** ADJECTIVE **anthropologist** NOUN

anti- PREFIX 'Anti-' means opposed to or opposite to something • *antiwar marches*.
WORD HISTORY: from Greek *anti-* meaning 'opposite' or 'against'

antibiotic, antibiotics NOUN a drug or chemical used in medicine to kill bacteria and cure infections.

antibody, antibodies NOUN a substance produced in the blood which can kill the harmful bacteria that cause disease.

anticipate, anticipates, anticipating, anticipated VERB If you anticipate an event, you are expecting it and are prepared for it • *She had anticipated his visit*.
anticipation NOUN

anticlimax, anticlimaxes NOUN something that disappoints you because it is not as exciting as expected, or because it occurs after something that was very exciting.

anticlockwise ADJECTIVE OR ADVERB moving in the opposite direction to the hands of a clock.

antics PLURAL NOUN funny or silly ways of behaving.

anticyclone, anticyclones NOUN
GEOGRAPHY An anticyclone is an area of high air pressure which causes settled weather.

antidote, antidotes NOUN a chemical substance that acts against the effect of a poison.

antihistamine, antihistamines NOUN a drug used to treat an allergy.

antipathy NOUN a strong feeling of dislike or hostility towards something or someone.

antiperspirant, antiperspirants NOUN a substance which stops you sweating when you put it on your skin.

antipodes [Said an-**tip**-pod-eez] PLURAL NOUN any two points on the earth's surface that are situated directly opposite each other. In Britain, Australia and New Zealand are sometimes called the Antipodes as they are opposite Britain on the globe. **antipodean** ADJECTIVE
WORD HISTORY: from Greek *antipous* meaning 'with the feet opposite'

antiquarian ADJECTIVE relating to or involving old and rare objects • *antiquarian books*.

antiquated ADJECTIVE very old-fashioned • *an antiquated method of teaching*.

antique, antiques [Said an-**teek**] NOUN ① an object from the past that is collected because of its value or beauty. ▸ADJECTIVE ② from or concerning the past • *antique furniture*.

antiquity, antiquities NOUN ① Antiquity is the distant past, especially the time of the ancient Egyptians, Greeks and Romans. ② Antiquities are interesting works of art and buildings from the distant past.

anti-Semitism NOUN hatred of Jewish people. **anti-Semitic** ADJECTIVE **anti-Semite** NOUN

antiseptic ADJECTIVE Something that is antiseptic kills germs.

antisocial ADJECTIVE ① An antisocial person is unwilling to meet and be friendly with other people. ② Antisocial behaviour is annoying or upsetting to other people • *Smoking in public is antisocial*.

antithesis, antitheses [Said an-**tith**-iss-iss] NOUN (formal) The antithesis of something is its exact opposite • *Work is the antithesis of leisure.*

antivenene, antivenenes NOUN a substance which reduces the effect of a venom, especially a snake venom.

antler, antlers NOUN A male deer's antlers are the branched horns on its head.

antonym, antonyms NOUN ENGLISH a word which means the opposite of another word. For example, 'hot' is the antonym of 'cold'.

anus, anuses NOUN the hole between the buttocks.

anvil, anvils NOUN a heavy iron block on which hot metal is beaten into shape.

anxiety, anxieties NOUN nervousness or worry.

anxious ADJECTIVE ① If you are anxious, you are nervous or worried. ② If you are anxious to do something or anxious that something should happen, you very much want to do it or want it to happen • *He was anxious to get back to playing football.*

anxiously ADVERB

any ADJECTIVE or PRONOUN ① one, some or several • *Do you have any paperclips I could borrow?* ② even the smallest amount or even one • *He was unable to tolerate any dairy products.* ③ whatever or whichever, no matter what or which • *Any type of cooking oil will do.*

anybody PRONOUN any person.

USAGE NOTE
Anybody and *anyone* mean the same.

anyhow ADVERB ① in any case. ② in a careless way • *They were all shoved in anyhow.*

anyone PRONOUN any person.

USAGE NOTE
Anyone and *anybody* mean the same.

anything PRONOUN any object, event, situation or action.

anyway ADVERB in any case.

anywhere ADVERB in, at or to any place.

Anzac, Anzacs NOUN ① HISTORY In World War I, an Anzac was a soldier with the Australia and New Zealand Army Corps. ② an Australian or New Zealand soldier.

aorta [Said ay-or-ta] NOUN SCIENCE the main artery in the body, which carries blood away from the heart.

apart ADVERB or ADJECTIVE ① When something is apart from something else, there is a space or a distance between them • *The couple separated and lived apart for four years* • *The gliders landed about seventy metres apart.*
▶ ADVERB ② If you take something apart, you separate it into pieces.

apartheid [Said ap-par-tide] NOUN HISTORY In South Africa, apartheid was the government policy and laws which kept people of different races apart. It was abolished in 1994.

apartment, apartments NOUN a set of rooms for living in, usually on one floor of a building.

apathetic ADJECTIVE not interested in anything.
SIMILAR WORDS: indifferent, uninterested

apathy [Said ap-path-ee] NOUN a state of mind in which you do not care about anything.

ape, apes, aping, aped NOUN ① Apes are animals with a very short tail or no tail. They are closely related to humans. Apes include chimpanzees, gorillas and gibbons. ▶ VERB ② If you ape someone's speech or behaviour, you imitate it.

aphid, aphids NOUN a small insect that feeds by sucking the juices from plants.

aphorism, aphorisms NOUN An aphorism is a short, clever sentence that expresses a general truth.

apiece ADVERB If people have a particular number of things apiece, they have that number each.

aplomb [Said uh-**plom**] NOUN If you do something with aplomb, you do it with great confidence.

apocalypse [Said uh-**pok**-ka-lips] NOUN The Apocalypse is the end of the world. **apocalyptic** ADJECTIVE WORD HISTORY: from Greek apokaluptein meaning 'to reveal'; the way the world will end is considered to be revealed in the last book of the Bible, called 'Apocalypse' or 'Revelation'

apocryphal ADJECTIVE A story that is apocryphal is generally believed not to have really happened.

apolitical [Said ay-poll-**it**-i-kl] ADJECTIVE not interested in politics.

apologetic ADJECTIVE showing or saying you are sorry. **apologetically** ADVERB

apologise, apologises, apologising, apologised; also spelt **apologize** VERB When you apologise to someone, you say you are sorry for something you have said or done.

apology, apologies NOUN something you say or write to tell someone you are sorry.

apostle, apostles NOUN RE The apostles are the twelve followers who were chosen by Christ.

apostrophe, apostrophes [Said ap-**poss**-troff-ee] NOUN ENGLISH a punctuation mark that is used to show that one or more letters have been missed out of a word. Apostrophes are also used with -s at the end of a noun to show that what follows belongs to or relates to the noun.

PUNCTUATION TIP
You do not use an apostrophe to make the plural of a word: pizzas and pastas (not pizza's and pasta's).

app, apps NOUN ICT a computer program designed to do a particular task, especially one that you can download to a mobile electronic device.

What does the Apostrophe do?

The **apostrophe** (') is used to show possession. It is usually added to the end of a word and followed by an s:

Jana's book
children's programmes

If a plural word already ends in -s, the apostrophe follows that letter:

my parents' generation
seven years' bad luck

You should not use an apostrophe to form plurals or possessive pronouns:

a pound of tomatoes [not tomato's]

I happen to be a fan of hers [not her's]

You can, however, add an apostrophe to form the plural of a number, letter or symbol:

P's and Q's
7's
£'s

The apostrophe is also used to show that a letter or letters have been omitted:

rock 'n' roll
Who's next?

a b c d e f g h i j k l m n o p q r s t u v w x y z

appal, appals, appalling, appalled
VERB If something appals you, it shocks you because it is very bad.

appalling ADJECTIVE so bad as to be shocking • *She escaped with appalling injuries.*

apparatus NOUN The apparatus for a particular task is the equipment used for it.

apparent ADJECTIVE ① seeming real rather than actually being real • *an apparent hit and run accident.*
② obvious • *It was apparent that he had lost interest.* **apparently** ADVERB
SIMILAR WORDS: ① ostensible, seeming

apparition, apparitions NOUN something you think you see but that is not really there • *a ghostly apparition on the windscreen.*

appeal, appeals, appealing, appealed VERB ① If you appeal for something, you make an urgent request for it • *The police appealed for witnesses to come forward.* ② If you appeal to someone in authority against a decision, you formally ask them to change it. ③ If something appeals to you, you find it attractive or interesting. ▸ NOUN ④ a formal or serious request • *an appeal for peace.* ⑤ The appeal of something is the quality it has which people find attractive or interesting • *the rugged appeal of the Rockies.* **appealing** ADJECTIVE

appear, appears, appearing, appeared VERB ① When something which you could not see appears, it moves (or you move) so that you can see it. ② When something new appears, it begins to exist. ③ When an actor or actress appears in a film or show, they take part in it. ④ If something appears to be a certain way, it seems or looks that way • *He appeared to be searching for something.*

SIMILAR WORDS: ① come into view, emerge, show up

appearance, appearances NOUN ① The appearance of someone in a place is their arrival there, especially when it is unexpected. ② The appearance of something new is the time when it begins to exist • *the appearance of computer technology.* ③ Someone's or something's appearance is the way they look to other people • *We were taken aback by his tired appearance.*

appease, appeases, appeasing, appeased VERB If you try to appease someone, you try to calm them down when they are angry, for example by giving them what they want. **appeasement** NOUN

appendage, appendages NOUN a less important part attached to a main part.

appendicitis [Said app-end-i-*site*-uss] NOUN a painful illness in which a person's appendix becomes infected.

appendix, appendices or appendixes NOUN ① a small closed tube forming part of your digestive system. ② An appendix to a book is extra information placed after the end of the main text.

GRAMMAR TIP
The plural of the part of the body is *appendixes*. The plural of the extra section in a book is *appendices*.

---

appetising; also spelt **appetizing** ADJECTIVE Food that is appetising looks and smells good, and makes you want to eat it.

appetite, appetites NOUN ① Your appetite is your desire to eat. ② If you have an appetite for something, you have a strong desire for it and enjoyment of it • *She had lost her appetite for air travel.*

applaud, applauds, applauding, applauded VERB ①When a group of people applaud, they clap their hands in approval or praise. ②When an action or attitude is applauded, people praise it.

applause NOUN Applause is clapping by a group of people.

apple, apples NOUN a round fruit with smooth skin and firm white flesh.

appliance, appliances NOUN any machine in your home you use to do a job like cleaning or cooking • *kitchen appliances.*

applicable ADJECTIVE Something that is applicable to a situation is relevant to it • *The rules are applicable to everyone.*

applicant, applicants NOUN someone who is applying for something • *We had problems recruiting applicants for the post.*

application, applications NOUN ①a formal request for something, usually in writing. ②The application of a rule, system or skill is the use of it in a particular situation. ③ ICT Application is short for 'application program'.

application program, application programs NOUN ICT An application program is an app.

apply, applies, applying, applied VERB ①If you apply for something, you formally ask for it, usually by sending an email or writing a letter. ②If you apply a rule or skill, you use it in a situation • *He applied his mind to the problem.* ③If something applies to a person or a situation, it is relevant to that person or situation • *The legislation applies only to people living in England and Wales.* ④If you apply something to a surface, you put it on • *She applied lipstick to her mouth.*

appoint, appoints, appointing, appointed VERB ①If you appoint someone to a job or position, you formally choose them for it. ②If you appoint a time or place for something to happen, you decide when or where it will happen. **appointed** ADJECTIVE

appointment, appointments NOUN ①an arrangement you have with someone to meet them. ②The appointment of a person to do a particular job is the choosing of that person to do it. ③a job or a position of responsibility • *He applied for an appointment in Russia.*
SIMILAR WORDS: ①date, engagement, meeting

apposite [Said app-o-zit] ADJECTIVE well suited for a particular purpose • *He went before Cameron could think of anything apposite to say.*

appraise, appraises, appraising, appraised VERB If you appraise something, you think about it carefully and form an opinion about it. **appraisal** NOUN

appreciable [Said a-**pree**-shuh-bl] ADJECTIVE large enough to be noticed • *an appreciable difference.*
appreciably ADVERB

appreciate, appreciates, appreciating, appreciated VERB ①If you appreciate something, you like it because you recognise its good qualities • *He appreciates fine art.* ②If you appreciate a situation or problem, you understand it and know what it involves. ③If you appreciate something someone has done for you, you are grateful to them for it • *I really appreciate you coming to visit me.* ④If something appreciates over a period of time, its value increases • *The property appreciated by 50% in two years.*
SIMILAR WORDS: ①prize, rate highly, value

appreciation NOUN ①Appreciation is gratitude for something. ②Appreciation is awareness and understanding of a problem. ③Appreciation is also the recognition of a person's abilities, qualities or efforts. ④Appreciation means an increase in the value of something.

appreciative ADJECTIVE ①understanding and enthusiastic • *They were a very appreciative audience.* ②thankful and grateful • *I am particularly appreciative of the help my family and friends have given me.*

appreciatively ADVERB

apprehend, apprehends, apprehending, apprehended VERB (*formal*) ①When the police apprehend someone, they arrest them and take them into custody. ②If you apprehend something, you understand it fully • *They were unable to apprehend his hidden meaning.*

apprehensive ADJECTIVE afraid something bad may happen • *I was a little apprehensive about meeting him.*

apprehensively ADVERB

apprehension NOUN

apprentice, apprentices NOUN a person who works with someone for a period of time in order to learn their skill or trade. **apprenticeship** NOUN **WORD HISTORY:** from Old French *aprendre* meaning 'to learn'

approach, approaches, approaching, approached VERB ①To approach something is to come near or nearer to it. ②When a future event approaches, it gradually gets nearer • *As winter approached, tents were set up to accommodate refugees.* ③If you approach someone about something, you ask them about it. ④If you approach a situation or problem in a particular way, you think about it or deal with it in that way. ▶ NOUN ⑤The approach of something is the process of it coming closer • *the approach of spring.* ⑥An approach to a situation or problem is a way of thinking about it or dealing with it. ⑦a road or path that leads to a place. **approaching** ADJECTIVE

appropriate, appropriates, appropriating, appropriated ADJECTIVE [*Said a-proh-pri-it*] ①suitable or acceptable for a particular situation • *He didn't think jeans were appropriate for a vice-president.* ▶ VERB [*Said a-proh-pri-ate*] ②(*formal*) If you appropriate something which does not belong to you, you take it without permission.

appropriately ADVERB

appropriation NOUN

approval NOUN ①Approval is agreement given to a plan or request • *The plan will require approval from the local authority.* ② PSHE Approval is also admiration • *She looked at James with approval.*

SIMILAR WORDS: ①agreement, consent, permission

approve, approves, approving, approved VERB ① PSHE If you approve of something or someone, you think that thing or person is acceptable or good. ②If someone in a position of authority approves a plan or idea, they formally agree to it. **approved** ADJECTIVE **approving** ADJECTIVE

SIMILAR WORDS: ①commend, favour, like ②agree to, authorise, pass, permit

approximate ADJECTIVE MATHS almost exact • *What was the approximate distance between the cars?*

approximately ADVERB

SIMILAR WORDS: close, near

apricot, apricots NOUN a small, soft, yellowish-orange fruit. **WORD HISTORY:** from Latin *praecox* meaning 'early ripening'

April NOUN the fourth month of the year. April has 30 days.

apron, aprons NOUN a piece of clothing worn over the front of normal clothing to protect it.

apse, apses NOUN a domed recess in the east wall of a church.

apt ADJECTIVE ① suitable or relevant • *a very apt description.* ② having a particular tendency • *They are apt to jump to the wrong conclusions.*

aptitude NOUN Someone's aptitude for something is their ability to learn it quickly and to do it well • *I have a natural aptitude for painting.*

aquarium, aquaria or aquariums NOUN a glass tank filled with water in which fish are kept.

Aquarius NOUN Aquarius is the eleventh sign of the zodiac, represented by a person carrying water. People born between January 20th and February 18th are born under this sign.

aquatic ADJECTIVE ① An aquatic animal or plant lives or grows in water. ② involving water • *aquatic sports.*

aqueduct, aqueducts NOUN a long bridge with many arches carrying a water supply over a valley.

Arab, Arabs NOUN a member of a group of people who used to live in Arabia but who now live throughout the Middle East and North Africa.

Arabic NOUN a language spoken by many people in the Middle East and North Africa.

arable ADJECTIVE Arable land is used for growing crops.

arbiter, arbiters NOUN the person who decides about something.
SIMILAR WORDS: judge, referee, adjudicator

arbitrary ADJECTIVE An arbitrary decision or action is one that is not based on a plan or system.
arbitrarily ADVERB

arbitrate, arbitrates, arbitrating, arbitrated VERB When someone arbitrates between two people or groups who are in disagreement, they consider the facts and decide who is right. **arbitration** NOUN **arbitrator** NOUN

arc, arcs NOUN ① a smoothly curving line. ② MATHS in geometry, a section of the circumference of a circle.

SPELLING TIP
Do not confuse the spellings of *arc* and *ark*.

arcade, arcades NOUN a covered passage with shops or market stalls along one or both sides.

arcane ADJECTIVE mysterious and difficult to understand.

arch, arches, arching, arched NOUN ① a structure that has a curved top supported on either side by a pillar or wall. ② the curved part of bone at the top of the foot. ▶ VERB ③ When something arches, it forms a curved line or shape. ▶ ADJECTIVE ④ most important • *my arch enemy.*

arch- PREFIX 'Arch-' means 'most important' or 'chief' • *archangel.*

archaeology [Said ar-kee-ol-loj-ee]; also spelt **archeology** NOUN the study of the past by digging up and examining the remains of buildings, tools and other things.
archaeological; also spelt **archeological** ADJECTIVE **archaeologist**; also spelt **archeologist** NOUN
WORD HISTORY: from Greek *arkhaios* meaning 'ancient'

archaic [Said ar-kay-ik] ADJECTIVE very old or old-fashioned.

archbishop, archbishops NOUN [RE] a bishop of the highest rank in a Christian Church.

archeology another spelling of **archaeology**.

archer, archers NOUN someone who shoots with a bow and arrow.

archery NOUN a sport in which people shoot at a target with a bow and arrow.

archetype, archetypes [Said ark-i-type] NOUN An archetype is anything that is a perfect example of its kind • He is the archetype of a first-class athlete. **archetypal** ADJECTIVE

archipelago, archipelagos [Said ar-kip-**pel**-lag-oh] NOUN a group of small islands.
WORD HISTORY: from Italian arcipelago meaning 'chief sea'; originally referring to the Aegean Sea

architect, architects [Said ar-kit-tekt] NOUN [ART] a person who designs buildings.

architecture NOUN [ART] the art or practice of designing buildings. **architectural** ADJECTIVE

archive, archives [Said ar-kive] NOUN Archives are collections of documents and records about the history of a family or some other group of people.

arctic NOUN ①The Arctic is the region north of the Arctic Circle. ▸ADJECTIVE ②Arctic means very cold indeed • arctic conditions.
WORD HISTORY: from Greek arktos meaning 'bear'; originally it referred to the northern constellation of the Great Bear

Arctic Circle NOUN The Arctic Circle is an imaginary circle around the northern part of the world.

ardent ADJECTIVE full of enthusiasm and passion. **ardently** ADVERB

ardour NOUN a strong and passionate feeling of love or enthusiasm.

arduous [Said ard-yoo-uss] ADJECTIVE tiring and needing a lot of effort • the arduous task of rebuilding the country.

are the plural form of the present tense of **be**.

area, areas NOUN ①a particular part of a place, country or the world • a built-up area of the city. ②The area of a piece of ground or a surface is the amount of space it covers, measured in square metres or square feet. ③ [MATHS] The area of a geometric object is the amount of space enclosed within its lines.
SIMILAR WORDS: ①district, region, zone

arena, arenas NOUN ①a place where sports and other public events take place. ②A particular arena is the centre of attention or activity in a particular situation • the political arena.
WORD HISTORY: from Latin harena meaning 'sand', hence the sandy centre of an amphitheatre where gladiators fought

Argentinian, Argentinians [Said ar-jen-**tin**-ee-an] ADJECTIVE ①belonging or relating to Argentina. ▸NOUN ②someone who comes from Argentina.

arguable ADJECTIVE An arguable idea or point is not necessarily true or correct and should be questioned. **arguably** ADVERB

argue, argues, arguing, argued VERB ①If you argue with someone about something, you disagree with them about it, sometimes in an angry way. ②If you argue that something is the case, you give reasons why you think it is so • She argued that her client had been wrongly accused.

argument, arguments NOUN ① a disagreement between two people which causes a quarrel. ② a point or a set of reasons you use to try to convince people about something.

argumentative ADJECTIVE An argumentative person is always disagreeing with other people.

aria, arias [Said ah-ree-a] NOUN a song sung by one of the leading singers in an opera.

arid ADJECTIVE Arid land is very dry because it has very little rain.

Aries [Said air-reez] NOUN Aries is the first sign of the zodiac, represented by a ram. People born between March 21st and April 19th are born under this sign.

arise, arises, arising, arose, arisen VERB ① When something such as an opportunity or problem arises, it begins to exist. ② (formal) To arise also means to stand up from a sitting, kneeling or lying position.

aristocracy, aristocracies NOUN a class of people who have a high social rank and special titles.

aristocrat, aristocrats NOUN someone whose family has a high social rank, and who has a title. **aristocratic** ADJECTIVE

arithmetic NOUN the part of mathematics which is to do with the addition, subtraction, multiplication and division of numbers. **arithmetical** ADJECTIVE **arithmetically** ADVERB WORD HISTORY: from Greek *arithmos* meaning 'number'

SPELLING TIP
Remember this mnemonic: *A Rude Idiot Thought He Might Eat Toffee In Church.*

arithmetic sequence, arithmetic sequences NOUN [MATHS] a sequence of numbers in which each differs from the next by a constant amount, such as 3, 6, 9, 12, ...

ark NOUN ① [RE] In the Bible, the ark was the boat built by Noah for his family and the animals during the Flood. ② [RE] In Judaism, the ark is the cupboard at the front of a synagogue in which the Torah scrolls are kept.

SPELLING TIP
Do not confuse the spellings of *arc* and *ark*.

arm, arms, arming, armed NOUN ① Your arms are the part of your body between your shoulder and your wrist. ② The arms of a chair are the parts on which you rest your arms. ③ An arm of an organisation is a section of it • *the political arm of the armed forces*. ④ (in plural) Arms are weapons used in a war. ▶ VERB ⑤ To arm someone is to provide them with weapons.

armada, armadas [Said ar-**mah**-da] NOUN An armada is a large fleet of warships. In 1588, the Spanish Armada was sent against England by Philip II of Spain, but was defeated in the Channel by the English and destroyed. WORD HISTORY: a Spanish word

armadillo, armadillos NOUN a mammal from South America which is covered with strong bony plates like armour. WORD HISTORY: a Spanish word meaning 'little armed man'

Armageddon NOUN In Christianity, Armageddon is the final battle between good and evil at the end of the world. WORD HISTORY: from Hebrew *har megiddon*, the mountain district of Megiddo, the site of many battles

armament, armaments NOUN
Armaments are the weapons and military equipment that belong to a country.

armchair, armchairs NOUN a comfortable chair with a support on each side for your arms.

armed ADJECTIVE A person who is armed is carrying a weapon or weapons.

armistice, armistices [Said ar-miss-tiss] NOUN HISTORY an agreement in a war to stop fighting in order to discuss peace.

armour NOUN HISTORY In the past, armour was metal clothing worn for protection in battle.

armoured ADJECTIVE covered with thick steel for protection from gunfire and other missiles • an armoured car.

armoury, armouries NOUN a place where weapons are stored.

armpit, armpits NOUN the area under your arm where your arm joins your shoulder.

army, armies NOUN a large group of soldiers organised into divisions for fighting on land.

aroma, aromas NOUN a strong, pleasant smell. **aromatic** ADJECTIVE

aromatherapy NOUN a type of therapy that involves massaging the body with special fragrant oils.

arose the past tense of **arise**.

around PREPOSITION ① placed at various points in a place or area • There are many seats around the building. ② from place to place inside an area • We walked around the showroom. ③ at approximately the time or place mentioned • The attacks began around noon. ▶ ADVERB ④ here and there • His papers were scattered around.

arouse, arouses, arousing, aroused VERB If something arouses a feeling in you, it causes you to begin to have this feeling • The song arouses sad memories. **arousal** NOUN

arpeggio, arpeggios [Said ar-pej-ee-oh] NOUN MUSIC In music, an arpeggio is a chord in which the notes are played very quickly one after the other.

WORD HISTORY: from Italian arpeggiare meaning 'to play the harp'

arrange, arranges, arranging, arranged VERB ① If you arrange to do something, you make plans for it. ② If you arrange something for someone, you make it possible for them to have it or do it • The bank has arranged a loan for her. ③ If you arrange objects, you set them out in a particular position • He started to arrange the books in piles.

arrangement NOUN

arranged marriage, arranged marriages NOUN a marriage that has been agreed between the families of the bride and groom, rather than the bride and groom themselves.

array, arrays NOUN ① An array of different things is a large number of them displayed together. ② ICT In computing, an array is a sequence of items of data that each have a fixed length and is each referred to by its position.

arrears PLURAL NOUN ① Arrears are amounts of money you owe • mortgage arrears. ▶ PHRASE ② If you are paid in arrears, you are paid at the end of the period for which the payment is due.

arrest, arrests, arresting, arrested VERB ① If the police arrest someone, they take them into custody to decide whether to charge them with an offence. ▶ NOUN ② An arrest is the act of taking a person into custody. **arresting** ADJECTIVE

arrival, arrivals NOUN ① the act or time of arriving • *The arrival of the train was delayed.* ② something or someone that has arrived • *The tourist authority reported record arrivals over Christmas.*

arrive, arrives, arriving, arrived VERB ① When you arrive at a place, you reach it at the end of your journey. ② When a letter or a piece of news arrives, it is brought to you • *A letter arrived at her lawyer's office.* ③ When you arrive at an idea or decision you reach it. ④ When a moment, event or new thing arrives, it begins to happen • *The Easter holidays arrived.*

arrogant ADJECTIVE Someone who is arrogant behaves as if they are better than other people. **arrogantly** ADVERB **arrogance** NOUN

arrow, arrows NOUN a long, thin weapon with a sharp point at one end, shot from a bow.

arsenal, arsenals NOUN a place where weapons and ammunition are stored or produced. WORD HISTORY: from Italian *arsenale* meaning 'dockyard', originally in Venice

arsenic NOUN SCIENCE Arsenic is a strongly poisonous element used in insecticides and weedkillers. Arsenic's atomic number is 33 and its symbol is As.

arson NOUN the crime of deliberately setting fire to something, especially a building.

art, arts NOUN ① Art is the creation of objects such as paintings and sculptures, which are thought to be beautiful or which express a particular idea; also used to refer to the objects themselves. ② An activity is called an art when it requires special skill or ability • *the art of diplomacy.* ③ (*in plural*) The arts are literature, music, painting and sculpture, considered together.

artefact, artefacts [*Said ar-tif-fact*] NOUN any object made by people.

artery, arteries NOUN ① Your arteries are the tubes that carry blood from your heart to the rest of your body. ② a main road or major section of any system of communication or transport.

artesian well, artesian wells NOUN GEOGRAPHY An artesian well is a well in which water is continually forced upwards under pressure.

artful ADJECTIVE clever and skilful, often in a cunning way. **artfully** ADVERB

arthritis NOUN SCIENCE a condition in which the joints in someone's body become swollen and painful. **arthritic** ADJECTIVE

artichoke, artichokes NOUN ① the round, green, partly edible flower head of a thistle-like plant; the flower head is made up of clusters of leaves that have a soft fleshy part that is eaten as a vegetable. ② A Jerusalem artichoke is a small yellowish-white vegetable that grows underground and looks like a potato.

article, articles NOUN ① LIBRARY a piece of writing in a newspaper or magazine. ② a particular item • *an article of clothing.* ③ In English grammar, 'a' and 'the' are sometimes called articles: 'a' (or 'an') is the indefinite article; 'the' is the definite article.

articulate, articulates, articulating, articulated ADJECTIVE ① If you are articulate, you are able to express yourself well in words. ▸ VERB ② When you articulate your ideas or feelings, you express in words what you think or feel • *She could not articulate her grief.* ③ When you articulate a sound or word, you speak it clearly. **articulation** NOUN

artificial ADJECTIVE ① created by people rather than occurring naturally • *artificial colouring.* ② pretending to have attitudes and feelings which other people realise are not real • *an artificial smile.* **artificially** ADVERB

artillery NOUN ① Artillery consists of large, powerful guns such as cannons. ② The artillery is the branch of an army which uses large, powerful guns.

artist, artists NOUN ① a person who draws or paints or produces other works of art. ② a person who is very skilled at a particular activity.

artiste, artistes [*Said ar-teest*] NOUN a professional entertainer, for example a singer or a dancer.

artistic ADJECTIVE ① able to create good paintings, sculpture or other works of art. ② concerning or involving art or artists. **artistically** ADVERB

artistry NOUN Artistry is the creative skill of an artist, writer, actor or musician • *a supreme demonstration of his artistry as a cellist.*

arty, artier, artiest ADJECTIVE (*informal*) interested in painting, sculpture and other works of art.

as CONJUNCTION ① at the same time that • *She waved at fans as she arrived for the concert.* ② in the way that • *They had talked as only the best of friends can.* ③ because • *As I won't be back tonight, don't bother to cook a meal.* ④ You use the structure **as … as** when you are comparing things that are similar • *It was as big as four football pitches.* ▶ PREPOSITION ⑤ You use 'as' when you are saying what role someone or something has • *She worked as a waitress.* ▶ PHRASE ⑥ You use **as if** or **as though** when you are giving a possible explanation for something • *He looked at me as if I were mad.*

asbestos NOUN a grey heat-resistant material used in the past to make fireproof articles.

ASBO, ASBOs NOUN An ASBO is an order from a judge preventing people who have been persistently annoying or upsetting other people from continuing to do so. ASBO is an abbreviation for 'antisocial behaviour order'.

ascend, ascends, ascending, ascended [*Said ass-end*] VERB (*formal*) To ascend is to move or lead upwards • *We finally ascended to the brow of a steep hill.*

ascendancy NOUN (*formal*) If one group has ascendancy over another, it has more power or influence than the other.

ascendant ADJECTIVE ① rising or moving upwards. ▶ PHRASE ② Someone or something **in the ascendant** is increasing in power or popularity.

ascent, ascents NOUN an upward journey, for example up a mountain.

SPELLING TIP
Do not confuse the spellings of *ascent* and *assent*: *the first successful ascent of Everest; We can go on the trip if our parents give their assent.*

ascertain, ascertains, ascertaining, ascertained [*Said ass-er-tain*] VERB (*formal*) If you ascertain that something is the case, you find out it is the case • *The police were still trying to ascertain the facts about the incident.*

ascribe, ascribes, ascribing, ascribed VERB ① If you ascribe an event or state of affairs to a particular cause, you think that it is the cause of it • *Global warming is often ascribed to human activity.* ② If you ascribe a quality to someone, you think they have it.

ash, ashes NOUN ① the grey or black powdery remains of anything that has been burnt. ② a tree with grey bark and hard tough wood used for timber.

ashamed ADJECTIVE ① feeling embarrassed or guilty. ② If you are ashamed of someone, you feel embarrassed to be connected with them.

ashen ADJECTIVE grey or pale • *Her face was ashen with fatigue.*

ashore ADVERB on land or onto the land.

ashtray, ashtrays NOUN a small dish for ash from cigarettes and cigars.

Asia NOUN Asia is the largest continent. It has Europe on its western side, with the Arctic to the north, the Pacific to the east, and the Indian Ocean to the south. Asia includes several island groups, including Japan, Indonesia and the Philippines.

Asian, Asians ADJECTIVE ① belonging or relating to Asia. ▶NOUN ② someone who comes from Asia.

aside, asides ADVERB ① If you move something aside, you move it to one side. ▶NOUN ② a comment made away from the main conversation or dialogue that all those talking are not meant to hear.

ask, asks, asking, asked VERB ① If you ask someone a question, you put a question to them for them to answer. ② If you ask someone to do something or give you something, you tell them you want them to do it

or to give it to you. ③ If you ask someone's permission or forgiveness, you try to obtain it. ④ If you ask someone somewhere, you invite them there • *Not everybody had been asked to the wedding.*

askew ADJECTIVE not straight.

asleep ADJECTIVE sleeping.

AS level, AS levels NOUN an exam taken by students in many British schools and colleges, more advanced than GCSE but less advanced than A level.

asparagus NOUN a vegetable that has long shoots which are cooked and eaten.

aspect, aspects NOUN ① An aspect of something is one of its features • *Exam results illustrate only one aspect of a school's success.* ② An aspect of a person is one part of his or her character or nature. ③ The aspect of a building is the direction it faces • *The southern aspect of the cottage faces over fields.*

asphalt NOUN a black substance used to make road surfaces and playgrounds.

aspiration, aspirations NOUN Someone's aspirations are their desires and ambitions.

aspire, aspires, aspiring, aspired VERB If you aspire to something, you have an ambition to achieve it • *He aspired to work in music journalism.* **aspiring** ADJECTIVE

aspirin, aspirins NOUN ① a white drug used to relieve pain, fever and colds. ② a tablet of this drug.

ass, asses NOUN a donkey.

assailant, assailants NOUN someone who attacks another person.

assassin, assassins NOUN someone who has murdered a political or religious leader.

a b c d e f g h i j k l m n o p q r s t u v w x y z

WORD HISTORY: from Arabic *hashshashin* meaning 'people who eat hashish'; the name comes from a medieval Muslim sect who ate hashish and went about murdering Crusaders

assassinate, assassinates, assassinating, assassinated VERB To assassinate a political or religious leader is to murder him or her. **assassination** NOUN

assault, assaults, assaulting, assaulted NOUN ① a violent attack on someone. ▶ VERB ② To assault someone is to attack them violently.

assegai, assegais [Said ass-i-guy]; also spelt **assagai** NOUN In South African English, a sharp, light spear.

assemble, assembles, assembling, assembled VERB ① To assemble is to gather together. ② If you assemble something, you fit the parts of it together.

assembly, assemblies NOUN ① a group of people who have gathered together for a meeting. ② The assembly of an object is the fitting together of its parts • *DIY assembly of units*.

assent, assents, assenting, assented [Said as-*sent*] NOUN ① If you give your assent to something, you agree to it. ▶ VERB ② If you assent to something, you agree to it.

SPELLING TIP
Do not confuse the spellings of *assent* and *ascent*: *We can go on the trip if our parents give their assent; the first successful ascent of Everest.*

assert, asserts, asserting, asserted VERB ① If you assert a fact or belief, you state it firmly and forcefully. ② If you assert yourself, you speak and behave in a confident and direct way, so that people pay attention to you.

assertion, assertions NOUN a statement or claim.

assertive ADJECTIVE If you are assertive, you speak and behave in a confident and direct way, so that people pay attention to you. **assertively** ADVERB **assertiveness** NOUN

assess, assesses, assessing, assessed VERB ① EXAM TERM If you assess something, you consider it carefully and make a judgment about it. ② If a student is assessed, his or her learning and achievements are measured through course work or examinations. **assessment** NOUN
SIMILAR WORDS: ① appraise, judge, size up

assessor, assessors NOUN someone whose job is to assess the value of something.

asset, assets NOUN ① a person or thing considered useful • *He will be a great asset to the club.* ② (in plural) The assets of a person or company are all the things they own that could be sold to raise money.

assign, assigns, assigning, assigned VERB ① To assign something to someone is to give it to them officially or to make them responsible for it. ② If someone is assigned to do something, they are officially told to do it.
SIMILAR WORDS: ① allocate, allot, give ② appoint, choose, select

assignation, assignations [Said ass-ig-*nay*-shn] NOUN (literary) a secret or forbidden meeting with someone.

assignment, assignments NOUN a job someone is given to do.

assimilate, assimilates, assimilating, assimilated VERB ① If you assimilate ideas or experiences, you learn and understand them.

②When people are assimilated into a group, they become part of it. **assimilation** NOUN

assist, assists, assisting, assisted VERB To assist someone is to help them do something. **assistance** NOUN

assistant, assistants NOUN someone whose job is to help another person in their work.

associate, associates, associating, associated VERB ①If you associate one thing with another, you connect the two things in your mind. ②If you associate with a group of people, you spend a lot of time with them.
▶ NOUN ③Your associates are the people you work with or spend a lot of time with.
SIMILAR WORDS: ①connect, link, relate ②consort, mix, socialise

association, associations NOUN ①an organisation for people who have similar interests, jobs or aims. ②Your association with a person or group is the connection or involvement you have with them. ③An association between two things is a link you make in your mind between them • The place contained associations for her.

assonance NOUN ENGLISH the use of similar vowel or consonant sounds in words near to each other or in the same word, for example 'a nice white bike'.

assorted ADJECTIVE Assorted things are different in size and colour • assorted swimsuits.

assortment, assortments NOUN a group of similar things that are different sizes and colours • an amazing assortment of old toys.

assume, assumes, assuming, assumed VERB ①If you assume that something is true, you accept it is

true even though you have not thought about it • I assumed that he would turn up. ②To assume responsibility for something is to put yourself in charge of it.
SIMILAR WORDS: ①believe, presume, suppose, take for granted ②accept, shoulder, take on

assumption, assumptions NOUN ①a belief that something is true, without thinking about it. ②Assumption of power or responsibility is the taking of it.

assurance, assurances NOUN ①something said which is intended to make people less worried • She was emphatic in her assurances that she wanted to stay. ②Assurance is a feeling of confidence • He handled the car with ease and assurance. ③Life assurance is a type of insurance that pays money to your dependants when you die.

assure, assures, assuring, assured VERB If you assure someone that something is true, you tell them it is true.

asterisk, asterisks NOUN the symbol (*) used in printing and writing.
WORD HISTORY: from Greek asteriskos meaning 'small star'

astern ADVERB or ADJECTIVE (Nautical) backwards or at the back.

asteroid, asteroids NOUN one of the large number of very small planets that move around the sun between the orbits of Jupiter and Mars.

asthma [Said ass-ma] NOUN SCIENCE a disease of the chest which causes wheezing and difficulty in breathing. **asthmatic** ADJECTIVE

astonish, astonishes, astonishing, astonished VERB If something astonishes you, it surprises you very much. **astonished** ADJECTIVE **astonishing** ADJECTIVE

a
b
c
d
e
f
g
h
i
j
k
l
m
n
o
p
q
r
s
t
u
v
w
x
y
z

astonishingly ADVERB
astonishment NOUN

astound, astounds, astounding, astounded VERB If something astounds you, it shocks and amazes you. **astounded** ADJECTIVE **astounding** ADJECTIVE

astray PHRASE ① To **lead someone astray** is to influence them to do something wrong. ② If something **goes astray**, it gets lost • *The money had gone astray.*

astride PREPOSITION with one leg on either side of something • *He is pictured astride his new motorbike.*

astringent, astringents [*Said ass-trin-jent*] NOUN a liquid that makes skin less greasy and stops bleeding.

astrology NOUN the study of the sun, moon and stars in order to predict the future. **astrological** ADJECTIVE **astrologer** NOUN

astronaut, astronauts NOUN a person who operates a spacecraft. **WORD HISTORY:** from Greek *astron* meaning 'star' and *nautēs* meaning 'sailor'

astronomical ADJECTIVE ① involved with or relating to astronomy. ② extremely large in amount • *astronomical legal costs.*
astronomically ADVERB

astronomy NOUN the scientific study of stars and planets.
astronomer NOUN

astute ADJECTIVE clever and quick at understanding situations and behaviour • *an astute diplomat.*

asunder ADVERB (*literary*) If something is torn asunder, it is violently torn apart.

asylum, asylums [*Said ass-eye-lum*] NOUN ① (*old-fashioned*) a hospital for psychiatric patients. ② Political asylum is protection given by a government to someone who has fled from their own country for political reasons.

asymmetrical [*Said ay-sim-met-ri-kl*] or **asymmetric** ADJECTIVE unbalanced or with one half not exactly the same as the other half. **asymmetry** NOUN

at PREPOSITION ① used to say where someone or something is • *Bert met us at the airport.* ② used to mention the direction something is going in • *He threw his plate at the wall.* ③ used to say when something happens • *The game starts at 3 o'clock.* ④ used to mention the rate or price of something • *The shares were priced at fifty pence.*

ate the past tense of **eat**.

atheist, atheists [*Said ayth-ee-ist*] NOUN RE someone who believes there is no God. **atheistic** ADJECTIVE **atheism** NOUN

athlete, athletes NOUN PE someone who is good at sport and takes part in sporting events.

athletic ADJECTIVE ① PE strong, healthy and good at sports. ② involving athletes or athletics • *I lost two years of my athletic career because of injury.*

athletics PLURAL NOUN Sporting events such as running, jumping and throwing are called athletics.

Atlantic NOUN The Atlantic is the ocean separating North and South America from Europe and Africa.

atlas, atlases NOUN GEOGRAPHY a book of maps.
WORD HISTORY: from the giant *Atlas* in Greek mythology, who supported the sky on his shoulders

atmosphere, atmospheres NOUN ① SCIENCE GEOGRAPHY the air and other gases that surround a planet; also the air in a particular place • *a*

musty atmosphere. ② the general mood of a place • *a relaxed atmosphere.* ③ ENGLISH the mood created by the writer of a novel or play.
atmospheric ADJECTIVE

atom, atoms NOUN SCIENCE the smallest part of an element that can take part in a chemical reaction.

atomic ADJECTIVE relating to atoms or to the power released by splitting atoms • *atomic energy.*

atomic bomb, atomic bombs NOUN an extremely powerful bomb which explodes because of the energy that comes from splitting atoms.

atomic number, atomic numbers NOUN SCIENCE The atomic number of a chemical element is a number used to classify it, which is equal to the number of protons in the nucleus of the atom of the element.

atone, atones, atoning, atoned VERB (*formal*) If you atone for something wrong you have done, you say you are sorry and try to make up for it. **atonement** NOUN

atrium, atriums NOUN SCIENCE a chamber of the heart that receives blood from the veins.

atrocious ADJECTIVE extremely bad. **atrociously** ADVERB

atrocity, atrocities NOUN an extremely cruel and shocking act.

attach, attaches, attaching, attached VERB If you attach something to something else, you join or fasten the two things together.

attaché, attachés [*Said at-tash-ay*] NOUN a member of staff in an embassy • *the Russian cultural attaché.*

attached ADJECTIVE If you are attached to someone, you are very fond of them.

attachment, attachments NOUN ① Attachment to someone is a feeling of love and affection for them. ② Attachment to a cause or ideal is a strong belief in it and support for it. ③ a piece of equipment attached to a tool or machine to do a particular job. ④ an extra document attached to or included with another document. ⑤ a file that is attached to an electronic message.

attack, attacks, attacking, attacked VERB ① To attack someone is to use violence against them so as to hurt or kill them. ② If you attack someone or their ideas, you criticise them strongly • *He attacked the government's economic policies.* ③ If a disease or chemical attacks something, it damages or destroys it • *fungal diseases that attack crops.* ④ In a game such as football or hockey, to attack is to get the ball into a position from which a goal can be scored. ▸ NOUN ⑤ An attack is violent physical action against someone. ⑥ An attack on someone or on their ideas is strong criticism of them. ⑦ An attack of an illness is a short time in which you suffer badly with it. **attacker** NOUN
SIMILAR WORDS: ① assault, set upon ② censure, criticise ⑤ assault, onslaught

attain, attains, attaining, attained VERB (*formal*) If you attain something, you manage to achieve it • *He eventually attained the rank of major.* **attainable** ADJECTIVE **attainment** NOUN

attempt, attempts, attempting, attempted VERB ① If you attempt to do something, you try to do it or achieve it, but may not succeed • *They attempted to escape.* ▸ NOUN ② an act of trying to do something • *He made no attempt to go for the ball.*

attend, attends, attending, attended VERB ① If you attend an event, you are present at it. ② To

a b c d e f g h i j k l m n o p q r s t u v w x y z

attend school, church or hospital is to go there regularly. ③ If you attend to something, you deal with it • *We have business to attend to first*.
attendance NOUN

attendant, attendants NOUN someone whose job is to look after people in a place such as a cloakroom or swimming pool.

attention NOUN Attention is the thought or care you give to something • *The woman needed medical attention*.

attentive ADJECTIVE paying close attention to something • *an attentive audience*. **attentively** ADVERB **attentiveness** NOUN

attest, attests, attesting, attested VERB *(formal)* To attest something is to show or declare it is true.
attestation NOUN

attic, attics NOUN a room at the top of a house immediately below the roof.

attire NOUN *(formal)* Attire is clothing • *We will be wearing traditional wedding attire*.

attitude, attitudes NOUN Your attitude to someone or something is the way you think about them and behave towards them.

attorney, attorneys *[Said at-**turn**-ee]* NOUN In America, an attorney is the same as a lawyer.

attract, attracts, attracting, attracted VERB ① If something attracts people, it interests them and makes them want to go to it • *The trials have attracted many leading riders*. ② If someone attracts you, you like and admire them • *He was attracted to her outgoing personality*. ③ If something attracts support or publicity, it gets it. ④ SCIENCE If something attracts objects to it, it has a force that pulls them towards it.

attraction, attractions NOUN ① Attraction is a feeling of liking someone or something very much. ② something people visit for interest or pleasure • *The temple is a major tourist attraction*. ③ a quality that attracts someone or something • *the attraction of moving to seaside resorts*.

attractive ADJECTIVE ① interesting and possibly advantageous • *an attractive proposition*. ② pleasant to look at or be with • *an attractive woman* • *an attractive personality*.
attractively ADVERB **attractiveness** NOUN
SIMILAR WORDS: ① appealing, tempting ② charming, lovely, pleasant

attribute, attributes, attributing, attributed VERB *[Said a-**trib**-yoot]* ① If you attribute something to a person or thing, you believe it was caused or created by that person or thing • *a painting attributed to Raphael* • *Water pollution was attributed to the use of fertilisers*. ▶ NOUN *[Said **at**-rib-yoot]* ② a quality or feature someone or something has. **attribution** NOUN **attributable** ADJECTIVE

attrition NOUN ① Attrition is the constant wearing down of an enemy. ② GEOGRAPHY the process by which rocks gradually become smaller and smoother as they rub against one another in moving water.

attuned ADJECTIVE accustomed or well adjusted to something • *His eyes quickly became attuned to the dark*.

aubergine, aubergines *[Said oh-ber-jeen]* NOUN a dark purple, pear-shaped fruit that is eaten as a vegetable. It is also called an **eggplant**.

auburn ADJECTIVE Auburn hair is reddish brown.

auction, auctions, auctioning, auctioned NOUN ① a public sale in which goods are sold to the person who offers the highest price. ▶ VERB ② To auction something is to sell it in an auction.

auctioneer, auctioneers NOUN the person in charge of an auction.

audacious ADJECTIVE very daring
• *an audacious escape from jail*.
audaciously ADVERB **audacity** NOUN

audible ADJECTIVE loud enough to be heard • *She spoke in a barely audible whisper*. **audibly** ADVERB **audibility** NOUN

audience, audiences NOUN ① the group of people who are watching or listening to a performance. ② the group of people who are reached by a piece of writing, film or television programme. ③ a private or formal meeting with an important person
• *an audience with the Queen*.

audio ADJECTIVE used in recording and reproducing sound • *audio equipment*.

audit, audits, auditing, audited VERB ① To audit a set of financial accounts is to examine them officially to check they are correct. ▶ NOUN ② an official examination of an organisation's accounts. **auditor** NOUN

audition, auditions NOUN a short performance given by an actor or musician, so that a director can decide whether they are suitable for a part in a play or film or for a place in an orchestra.

auditorium, auditoriums or auditoria NOUN the part of a theatre where the audience sits.

auditory ADJECTIVE SCIENCE relating to hearing • *the auditory nerve*.

augment, augments, augmenting, augmented VERB (*formal*) To augment something is to add something to it.

August NOUN the eighth month of the year. August has 31 days.
WORD HISTORY: from the name of the Roman emperor *Augustus*

aunt, aunts NOUN Your aunt is the sister of your mother or father, or the wife of one of your parents' siblings.

au pair, au pairs [*Said oh* pair] NOUN a young foreign person who lives with a family to help with the children and housework and sometimes to learn the language.
WORD HISTORY: a French expression meaning 'on equal terms'

aura, auras NOUN an atmosphere that surrounds a person or thing
• *She has a great aura of calmness*.

aural [*Rhymes with* **floral**] ADJECTIVE relating to or done through the sense of hearing • *an aural comprehension test*.

SPELLING TIP
Do not confuse the spellings of *aural* and *oral*: *sounds that test aural function; I failed the oral examination*.

---

aurora borealis [*Said* aw-*roh*-ra bor-ee-*ay*-liss] NOUN SCIENCE The aurora borealis consists of bands of glowing coloured light sometimes seen in the sky in the Arctic. It is caused by charged particles discharged from the sun hitting the earth's atmosphere at an acute angle. A similar phenomenon in the Antarctic is called the **aurora australis**.
WORD HISTORY: from Latin meaning 'northern dawn'

auspices [*Said* aw-*spiss*-eez] PLURAL NOUN (*formal*) If you do something under the auspices of a person or organisation, you do it with their support • *military intervention under the auspices of the United Nations*.

auspicious ADJECTIVE (*formal*) favourable and seeming to promise success • *It was an auspicious start to the month*.

austere ADJECTIVE plain and simple, and without luxury • *an austere grey office block*. **austerity** NOUN

Australasia [*Said ost-ral-lay-sha*] NOUN Australasia consists of Australia, New Zealand and neighbouring islands in the Pacific. **Australasian** ADJECTIVE

Australia NOUN Australia is the smallest continent and the largest island in the world, situated between the Indian Ocean and the Pacific.

Australian, Australians ADJECTIVE ① belonging or relating to Australia. ▶ NOUN ② someone who comes from Australia.

Austrian, Austrians ADJECTIVE ① belonging or relating to Austria. ▶ NOUN ② someone who comes from Austria.

authentic ADJECTIVE real and genuine. **authentically** ADVERB **authenticity** NOUN

author, authors NOUN ENGLISH The author of a book is the person who wrote it.

USAGE NOTE
Use *author* to talk about both men and women writers, as *authoress* is now felt to be insulting.

---

authorise, authorises, authorising, authorised; also spelt **authorize** VERB To authorise something is to give official permission for it to happen. **authorisation** NOUN

authoritarian ADJECTIVE believing in strict obedience • *thirty years of authoritarian government*. **authoritarianism** NOUN

authoritative ADJECTIVE ① having authority • *a deep, authoritative voice*. ② accepted as being reliable and accurate • *an authoritative biography of the President*. **authoritatively** ADVERB

authority, authorities NOUN ① Authority is the power to control people • *the authority of the state*. ② In Britain, an authority is a local government department • *local health authorities*. ③ Someone who is an authority on something knows a lot about it • *the world's leading authority on fashion*. ④ (*in plural*) The authorities are the people who have the power to make decisions.

autism NOUN a developmental condition that can cause someone to have difficulty in communicating with and responding to other people. **autistic** ADJECTIVE

auto- PREFIX 'Auto-' means 'self'. For example, an *automatic* machine works by itself without needing to be operated by hand.

autobiography, autobiographies NOUN Someone's autobiography is an account of their life which they have written themselves. **autobiographical** ADJECTIVE

autograph, autographs NOUN the signature of a famous person.

automated ADJECTIVE If a factory or way of making things is automated, it works using machinery rather than people. **automation** NOUN

automatic ADJECTIVE ① An automatic machine is programmed to perform tasks without needing a person to operate it • *The plane was flying on automatic pilot*. ② Automatic actions or reactions take place without involving conscious thought. ③ A process or punishment that is automatic always happens as a direct result of something • *Certain crimes carry an automatic prison sentence.* **automatically** ADVERB

automobile, automobiles NOUN In American English, an automobile is a car.

autonomous [*Said aw-ton-nom-uss*] ADJECTIVE An autonomous country governs itself rather than being controlled by anyone else. **autonomy** NOUN

autopsy, autopsies NOUN a medical examination of a dead body to discover the cause of death.

autumn, autumns NOUN the season between summer and winter. **autumnal** ADJECTIVE

auxiliary, auxiliaries NOUN ① a person employed to help other members of staff • *nursing auxiliaries.* ▶ ADJECTIVE ② Auxiliary equipment is used when necessary in addition to the main equipment • *Auxiliary fuel tanks were stored in the bomb bay.*

auxiliary verb, auxiliary verbs NOUN ENGLISH MFL In grammar, an auxiliary verb is a verb which forms tenses of other verbs or questions. For example, in 'He has gone', 'has' is the auxiliary verb and in 'Do you understand?', 'do' is the auxiliary verb.

avail PHRASE If something you do is **of no avail** or **to no avail**, it is not successful or helpful.

available ADJECTIVE ① Something that is available can be obtained • *Artichokes are available in supermarkets.* ② Someone who is available is ready for work or free for people to talk to • *She will no longer be available at weekends.* **availability** NOUN

SIMILAR WORDS: ② accessible

avalanche, avalanches [*Said av-a-lahnsh*] NOUN a huge mass of snow and ice that falls down a mountain side.

avant-garde [*Said av-vong-gard*] ADJECTIVE extremely modern or experimental, especially in art, literature or music.

avarice NOUN (*formal*) greed for money and possessions. **avaricious** ADJECTIVE

avatar, avatars NOUN ICT an image that represents a person on a computer screen, for example in a computer game.

avenge, avenges, avenging, avenged VERB If you avenge something harmful someone has done to you or your family, you punish or harm the other person in return • *He was prepared to avenge the death of his friend.* **avenger** NOUN

avenue, avenues NOUN a street, especially one with trees along it.

average, averages, averaging, averaged NOUN ① MATHS a measure which represents the typical central or normal value in a set of data • *Six pupils were examined in a total of 39 subjects, an average of 6.5 subjects per pupil.* ▶ ADJECTIVE ② Average means standard or normal • *the average American teenager.* ▶ VERB ③ To average a number is to produce that number as an average over a period of time • *Monthly sales averaged more than 110,000.* ▶ PHRASE ④ You say **on average** when mentioning what usually happens in a situation • *Men are, on average, taller than women.*

SIMILAR WORDS: ② normal, ordinary, typical, usual

averse ADJECTIVE unwilling to do something • *He was averse to eating vegetables.*

aversion, aversions NOUN If you have an aversion to someone or

a
b
c
d
e
f
g
h
i
j
k
l
m
n
o
p
q
r
s
t
u
v
w
x
y
z

something, you dislike them very much.

avert, averts, averting, averted
VERB ① If you avert an unpleasant event, you prevent it from happening. ② If you avert your eyes from something, you turn your eyes away from it.

aviary, aviaries NOUN a large cage or group of cages in which birds are kept.

aviation NOUN the science of flying aircraft.

aviator, aviators NOUN (old-fashioned) a pilot of an aircraft.

avid ADJECTIVE eager and enthusiastic for something. **avidly** ADVERB

avocado, avocados NOUN a pear-shaped fruit, with dark green skin, soft greenish yellow flesh, and a large stone.

avoid, avoids, avoiding, avoided
VERB ① If you avoid doing something, you make a deliberate effort not to do it. ② If you avoid someone, you keep away from them. **avoidable** ADJECTIVE **avoidance** NOUN
SIMILAR WORDS: ① dodge, refrain from, shirk ② dodge, evade, keep away from

avowed ADJECTIVE (formal) ① If you are an avowed supporter or opponent of something, you have declared that you support it or oppose it. ② An avowed belief or aim is one you hold very strongly.

avuncular ADJECTIVE friendly and helpful in manner towards younger people, rather like an uncle.

await, awaits, awaiting, awaited
VERB ① If you await something, you expect it. ② If something awaits you, it will happen to you in the future.

awake, awakes, awaking, awoke, awoken ADJECTIVE ① Someone who is awake is not sleeping. ▶ VERB ② When you awake, you wake up. ③ If you are awoken by something, it wakes you up.

awaken, awakens, awakening, awakened VERB If something awakens an emotion or interest in you, you start to feel this emotion or interest.

award, awards, awarding, awarded
NOUN ① a prize or certificate for doing something well. ② a sum of money an organisation gives to students for training or study. ▶ VERB ③ If you award someone something, you give it to them formally or officially.

aware ADJECTIVE ① If you are aware of something, you realise it is there. ② If you are aware of something, you know about it. **awareness** NOUN
SIMILAR WORDS: ① conscious of, knowing about, mindful of ② conscious of, knowing about, mindful of

awash ADJECTIVE or ADVERB covered with water • After the downpour the road was awash.

away ADVERB ① moving from a place • I saw them walk away. ② at a distance from a place • Our nearest vet is 12 kilometres away. ③ in its proper place • He put his wallet away. ④ not at home, school or work • She had been away from home for years.

awe NOUN (formal) a feeling of great respect mixed with amazement and sometimes slight fear.

awesome ADJECTIVE ① Something that is awesome is very impressive and frightening. ② (informal) Awesome also means excellent or outstanding.

awful ADJECTIVE ① very unpleasant or very bad. ② (informal) very great • It took an awful lot of courage. **awfully** ADVERB

SIMILAR WORDS: ① appalling, dreadful, terrible

awkward ADJECTIVE ① clumsy and uncomfortable • *an awkward gesture*. ② embarrassed or nervous • *He was a shy, awkward young man*. ③ difficult to deal with • *I found myself in an awkward situation*.

WORD HISTORY: from Old Norse *ofugr* meaning 'turned the wrong way'

awning, awnings NOUN a large roof of canvas or plastic attached to a building or vehicle.

awoke the past tense of **awake**.

awoken the past participle of **awake**.

awry [*Said a-rye*] ADJECTIVE wrong or not as planned • *Why had their plans*

gone so badly awry?

axe, axes, axing, axed NOUN ① a tool with a handle and a sharp blade, used for chopping wood. ▶ VERB ② To axe something is to end it.

axiom, axioms NOUN a statement or saying that is generally accepted to be true. **axiomatic** ADJECTIVE

axis, axes [*Said ak-siss*] NOUN ① MATHS an imaginary line through the centre of something, around which it moves. ② MATHS one of the two sides of a graph.

axle, axles NOUN the long bar that connects a pair of wheels on a vehicle.

azure [*Said az-yoor*] ADJECTIVE (*literary*) bright blue.

a
b
c
d
e
f
g
h
i
j
k
l
m
n
o
p
q
r
s
t
u
v
w
x
y
z

Bb

babble, babbles, babbling, babbled
VERB When someone babbles, they
talk in a confused or excited way.

baboon, baboons NOUN an African
monkey with a pointed face, large
teeth, and a long tail.
WORD HISTORY: from Old French
baboue meaning 'grimace'

baby, babies NOUN a child in the first
year or two of its life. **babyhood**
NOUN **babyish** ADJECTIVE
SIMILAR WORDS: babe, infant

baby-sit, baby-sits, baby-sitting,
baby-sat VERB To baby-sit for
someone means to look after their
children while that person is out.
baby-sitter NOUN **baby-sitting**
NOUN

baccalaureate, baccalaureates
[Said back-uh-law-ree-it] NOUN an
internationally recognised course of
study made up of several different
subjects, offered by some schools as
an alternative to A levels.

bach, baches, baching, bached [Said
batch] NOUN ① In New Zealand, a
bach is a small holiday cottage.
▶ VERB ② (informal) In Australian and
New Zealand English, to bach is to
live and keep a house on your own,
especially when you are not used to it.

bachelor, bachelors NOUN a man
who has never been married.

back, backs, backing, backed
ADVERB ① When people or things
move back, they move in the
opposite direction from the one they
are facing. ② When people or things

go back to a place or situation, they
return to it • *She went back to sleep.*
③ If you get something back, it is
returned to you. ④ If you do
something back to someone, you do
to them what they have done to you
• *I smiled back at them.* ⑤ Back also
means in the past • *It happened back in
the early eighties.* ▶ NOUN ⑥ the rear
part of your body. ⑦ the part of
something that is behind the front.
▶ ADJECTIVE ⑧ The back parts of
something are the ones near the rear
• *an animal's back legs.* ▶ VERB ⑨ If a
building backs onto something, its
back faces in that direction. ⑩ When
a car backs, it moves backwards.
⑪ To back a person or organisation
means to support or finance that
person or organisation. **back down**
VERB If you back down on a demand
or claim, you withdraw and give up.
back out VERB If you back out of a
promise or commitment, you decide
not to do what you had promised to
do. **back up** VERB ① If you back up a
claim or story, you produce evidence
to show that it is true. ② If you back
someone up, you help and support
them.

backbencher, backbenchers NOUN
A backbencher is a Member of
Parliament who is not a government
minister and who does not have an
official position as a spokesperson for
an opposition party.

backbone, backbones NOUN ① the
column of linked bones along the
middle of a person's or animal's back.

② strength of character.

backdate, backdates, backdating, backdated **VERB** If an arrangement is backdated, it is valid from a date earlier than the one on which it is completed or signed.

backdrop, backdrops **NOUN** the background to a situation or event • *The visit occurred against the backdrop of the political crisis*.

backer, backers **NOUN** The backers of a project are the people who give it financial help.

backfire, backfires, backfiring, backfired **VERB** ① If a plan backfires, it fails. ② When a car backfires, there is a small but noisy explosion in its exhaust pipe.

background, backgrounds **NOUN** ① the circumstances which help to explain an event or caused it to happen. ② the kind of home you come from and your education and experience • *a rich background*. ③ If sounds are in the background, they are there but no one really pays any attention to them • *She could hear voices in the background*.

backhand, backhands **NOUN** or **ADJECTIVE** PE (a stroke in tennis, squash or badminton) made in front of your body with the back of your hand facing in the direction that you hit the ball.

backing **NOUN** support or help • *The project got government backing*.

backlash, backlashes **NOUN** a hostile reaction to a new development or a new policy.

backlog, backlogs **NOUN** a number of things which have not yet been done, but which need to be done.

backpack, backpacks **NOUN** a large bag that hikers or campers carry on their backs.

backside, backsides **NOUN** (*informal*)

the part of your body that you sit on.

backstroke **NOUN** PE Backstroke is a swimming stroke in which you lie on your back, kick your legs, and move your arms back over your head.

backward **ADJECTIVE** ① Backward means directed behind you • *without a backward glance*. ② A backward country or society is one that does not have modern industries or technology. **backwardness** **NOUN**

backwards **ADVERB** ① Backwards means behind you • *Lucille looked backwards*. ② If you do something backwards, you do it the opposite of the usual way • *He instructed them to count backwards*.

bacon **NOUN** meat from the back or sides of a pig, which has been salted or smoked.

bacteria **PLURAL NOUN** SCIENCE Bacteria are very tiny organisms which live in air, water, soil, plants and the bodies of animals. Some bacteria provide food for plants, others cause diseases such as typhoid. **bacterial** **ADJECTIVE** **WORD HISTORY:** from Greek *baktērion* meaning 'little rod'; some bacteria are rod-shaped

GRAMMAR TIP
The word *bacteria* is plural. The singular form is *bacterium*.

bad, worse, worst **ADJECTIVE** ① Anything harmful or upsetting can be described as bad • *Is the pain bad?* • *I have some bad news*. ② insufficient or of poor quality • *bad roads*. ③ evil or immoral in character or behaviour • *a bad person*. ④ lacking skill in something • *I was bad at sports*. ⑤ Bad language consists of swearwords. ⑥ If you have a bad temper, you become angry easily. **badness** **NOUN** **SIMILAR WORDS:** ③ evil, sinful, wicked, wrong

a
b
c
d
e
f
g
h
i
j
k
l
m
n
o
p
q
r
s
t
u
v
w
x
y
z

bade a form of the past tense of **bid**.

badge, badges NOUN a piece of plastic or metal with a design or message on it that you can pin to your clothes.

badger, badgers, badgering, badgered NOUN ① a wild animal that has a white head with two black stripes on it. ▶ VERB ② If you badger someone, you keep asking them questions or pestering them to do something.

badly ADVERB in an inferior or unimpressive way.

badminton NOUN PE Badminton is a game in which two or four players use rackets to hit a shuttlecock over a high net. It was first played at Badminton House in Gloucestershire.

Bafana bafana PLURAL NOUN In South Africa, Bafana bafana is a name for the South African national soccer team.

baffle, baffles, baffling, baffled VERB If something baffles you, you cannot understand or explain it • *The symptoms baffled the doctors.* **baffled** ADJECTIVE **baffling** ADJECTIVE

bag, bags NOUN ① a container for carrying things in. ② (*in plural, informal*) Bags of something is a lot of it • *bags of fun.*

baggage NOUN the suitcases and bags that you take on a journey.

baggy, baggier, baggiest ADJECTIVE Baggy clothing hangs loosely.

bagpipes PLURAL NOUN MUSIC a musical instrument played by squeezing air out of a leather bag through pipes, on which a tune is played.

bail, bails, bailing, bailed NOUN ① Bail is a sum of money paid to a court to allow an accused person to go free until the time of the trial • *He was released on bail.* ▶ VERB ② If you bail water from a boat, you scoop it out. **bail out**; also spelt **bale out** VERB ① To bail out of an aircraft means to jump out of it with a parachute. ② If you bail someone out, you help them out of a difficult situation.

bailiff, bailiffs NOUN ① a law officer who makes sure that the decisions of a court are obeyed. ② a person employed to look after land or property for the owner.

Baisakhi [Said buy-sah-kee] NOUN RE a Sikh festival celebrated every April.

bait, baits, baiting, baited NOUN ① a small amount of food placed on a hook or in a trap, to attract a fish or wild animal so that it gets caught. ② something used to tempt a person to do something. ▶ VERB ③ If you bait a hook or trap, you put some food on it to catch a fish or wild animal.

baize NOUN a smooth woollen material, usually green, used for covering snooker tables.

bake, bakes, baking, baked VERB ① To bake food means to cook it in an oven without using liquid or fat. ② To bake earth or clay means to heat it until it becomes hard.

baker, bakers NOUN a person who makes and sells bread and cakes.

bakery, bakeries NOUN a building where bread and cakes are baked and sold.

bakkie, bakkies [Said buck-ee] NOUN In South African English, a bakkie is a small truck.

balaclava, balaclavas NOUN A balaclava is a close-fitting woollen hood that covers every part of your head except your face. Balaclava is the name of a place in Crimea; at a battle there in 1854, British soldiers wore these hoods to protect themselves from the cold.

balance, balances, balancing, balanced VERB ①When someone or something balances, they remain steady and do not fall over. ▶NOUN ②Balance is the state of being upright and steady. ③Balance is also a situation in which all the parts involved have a stable relationship with each other • the chemical balance of the brain • a good work-life balance. ④The balance in someone's bank account is the amount of money in it.

balanced ADJECTIVE ①A balanced account or report presents information in a fair and objective way. ② PSHE If you lead a balanced life, you are able to spend time with your family and pursue hobbies as well as doing your work.

balcony, balconies NOUN ①a platform on the outside of a building with a wall or railing round it. ②an area of upstairs seats in a theatre or cinema.

bald, balder, baldest ADJECTIVE ①A bald person has little or no hair on their head. ②A bald statement or question is made in the simplest way without any attempt to be polite.
baldly ADVERB **baldness** NOUN
WORD HISTORY: from Middle English ballede meaning 'having a white patch'

bale, bales, baling, baled NOUN ①a large bundle of something, such as paper or hay, tied tightly. ▶VERB ②If you bale water from a boat, you remove it using a container; also spelt **bail**. **bale out**; also spelt **bail out** VERB To bale out of an aircraft means to jump out of it with a parachute.

balk, balks, balking, balked; also spelt **baulk** VERB If you balk at something, you object to it and may

refuse to do it • He balked at the cost.

ball, balls NOUN ①a round object, especially one used in games such as cricket and soccer. ②The ball of your foot or thumb is the rounded part where your toes join your foot or your thumb joins your hand. ③a large formal social event at which people dance.
SIMILAR WORDS: ①globe, orb, sphere

ballad, ballads NOUN ① ENGLISH a long song or poem which tells a story. ②a slow, romantic pop song.
WORD HISTORY: from Old French ballade meaning 'song for dancing to'

ballast NOUN any heavy material placed in a ship to make it more stable.

ballerina, ballerinas NOUN a female ballet dancer.

ballet [Said bal-lay] NOUN Ballet is a type of artistic dancing based on precise steps.

balloon, balloons NOUN ①a small bag made of thin rubber that you blow into until it becomes larger and rounder. ②a large, strong bag filled with gas or hot air, which travels through the air carrying passengers in a compartment underneath.
WORD HISTORY: from Italian ballone meaning 'large round object'

ballot, ballots, balloting, balloted NOUN ①a secret vote in which people select a candidate in an election, or express their opinion about something. ▶VERB ②When a group of people are balloted, they are asked questions to find out what they think about a particular problem or question.
WORD HISTORY: from Italian ballotta meaning 'little round object'; in medieval Venice votes were cast by dropping black or white pebbles or balls into a box

ballpoint, ballpoints NOUN a pen with a small metal ball at the end which transfers the ink onto the paper.

ballroom, ballrooms NOUN a very large room used for dancing or formal balls.

balm [Said bahm] or **balsam** NOUN (old-fashioned) Balm is a soothing ointment made from a fragrant oily resin produced by certain kinds of tropical trees.

balmy, balmier, balmiest ADJECTIVE mild and pleasant • balmy summer evenings.

balsa NOUN Balsa is very lightweight wood.

balustrade, balustrades NOUN a railing or wall on a balcony or staircase.

bamboo NOUN Bamboo is a tall tropical plant with hard, hollow stems used for making furniture. It is a species of giant grass. The young shoots can be eaten.

ban, bans, banning, banned VERB ① If something is banned, or if you are banned from doing it or using it, you are not allowed to do it or use it. ▶ NOUN ② If there is a ban on something, it is not allowed.
SIMILAR WORDS: ① forbid, outlaw, prohibit ② disqualification, embargo, prohibition

banal [Said ba-nahl] ADJECTIVE very ordinary and not at all interesting • He made some banal remark.
banality NOUN
WORD HISTORY: Old French banal referred to military service which all tenants had to do; hence the word came to mean 'common to everyone' or 'ordinary'

banana, bananas NOUN a long curved fruit with a yellow skin.
WORD HISTORY: from a West African language, via Portuguese

band, bands NOUN ① a group of musicians who play jazz or pop music together, or a group who play brass instruments together. ② a group of people who share a common purpose • a band of rebels. ③ a narrow strip of something used to hold things together or worn as a decoration • an elastic band • a headband. **band together** VERB When people band together, they join together for a particular purpose.

bandage, bandages, bandaging, bandaged NOUN ① a strip of cloth wrapped round a wound to protect it. ▶ VERB ② If you bandage a wound, you tie a bandage round it.

bandanna, bandannas; also spelt **bandana** NOUN a large brightly coloured handkerchief or cloth for tying round the head or neck.

bandicoot, bandicoots NOUN a small Australian marsupial with a long pointed muzzle and a long tail.

bandit, bandits NOUN (old-fashioned) a member of an armed gang who rob travellers.
WORD HISTORY: from Italian bandito meaning 'man who has been banished or outlawed'

bandstand, bandstands NOUN a platform, usually with a roof, where a band can play outdoors.

bandwagon PHRASE To **jump on the bandwagon** means to become involved in something because it is fashionable or likely to be successful.

bandwidth, bandwidths NOUN The bandwidth of a telecommunications signal is the range of frequencies used to transmit it.

bandy, bandies, bandying, bandied VERB If a name is bandied about, many people mention it.

WORD HISTORY: from Old French *bander* meaning 'to hit a tennis ball back and forth'

bane NOUN (*literary*) Someone or something that is the bane of a person or organisation causes a lot of trouble for them • *the bane of my life.*

WORD HISTORY: from Old English *bana* meaning 'murderer'

bang, bangs, banging, banged VERB ① If you bang something, you hit it or put it somewhere violently, so that it makes a loud noise • *He banged down the receiver.* ② If you bang a part of your body against something, you accidentally bump it. ▶ NOUN ③ a sudden, short, loud noise. ④ a hard or painful bump against something.

Bangladeshi, Bangladeshis [*Said bang-glad-desh-ee*] ADJECTIVE ① belonging or relating to Bangladesh. ▶ NOUN ② someone who comes from Bangladesh.

bangle, bangles NOUN an ornamental band worn round someone's wrist or ankle.

banish, banishes, banishing, banished VERB ① To banish someone means to send them into exile. ② To banish something means to get rid of it • *It will be a long time before poverty is banished.* **banishment** NOUN

SIMILAR WORDS: ① exile, expel, outlaw

banister, banisters; also spelt **bannister** NOUN a rail supported by posts along the side of a staircase.

banjo, banjos or **banjoes** NOUN a musical instrument, like a small guitar with a round body.

bank, banks, banking, banked NOUN ① a business that looks after people's money. ② A bank of something is a store of it kept ready for use • *a blood bank.* ③ the raised ground along the edge of a river or lake. ④ the sloping side of an area of raised ground. ▶ VERB ⑤ When you bank money, you pay it into a bank. ⑥ If you bank on something happening, you expect it and rely on it.

banker, bankers NOUN a senior worker in a bank.

bank holiday, bank holidays NOUN a public holiday, when banks are officially closed.

banking NOUN the business of looking after people's money.

banknote, banknotes NOUN a piece of paper money.

bankrupt, bankrupts, bankrupting, bankrupted ADJECTIVE ① People or organisations that go bankrupt do not have enough money to pay their debts. ▶ NOUN ② someone who has been declared bankrupt. ▶ VERB ③ To bankrupt someone means to make them bankrupt • *Restoring the house nearly bankrupted them.* **bankruptcy** NOUN

banksia, banksias NOUN an evergreen Australian tree or shrub with yellow flowers.

banner, banners NOUN a long strip of cloth with a message or slogan on it.

bannister another spelling of **banister**.

banquet, banquets NOUN a grand formal dinner, often followed by speeches.

banter NOUN Banter is friendly joking and teasing.

baobab, baobabs [*Said bay-oh-bab*] NOUN a small fruit tree with a very thick trunk which grows in Africa and northern Australia.

baptise, baptises, baptising, baptised; also spelt **baptize** VERB When someone is baptised, water is sprinkled on them, or they are immersed in water, as a sign that they have become a Christian.

a
b
c
d
e
f
g
h
i
j
k
l
m
n
o
p
q
r
s
t
u
v
w
x
y
z

baptism, baptisms NOUN RE
a ceremony in which someone is
baptised.

Baptist, Baptists NOUN RE a
member of a Protestant church who
believe that people should be
baptised when they are adults rather
than when they are babies.

bar, bars, barring, barred NOUN
① a long, straight piece of metal.
② a piece of something made in a
rectangular shape • *a bar of soap*.
③ a counter or room where alcoholic
drinks are served. ④ The bars in a
piece of music are the many short
parts of equal length that the piece is
divided into. ⑤ GEOGRAPHY In
meteorology, a bar is a unit of
pressure, equivalent to 100,000
newtons per square metre. ▸ VERB
⑥ If you bar a door, you place
something across it to stop it being
opened. ⑦ If you bar someone's way,
you stop them going somewhere by
standing in front of them.

barb, barbs NOUN a sharp curved
point on the end of an arrow or
fish-hook.

barbarian, barbarians NOUN a
member of a wild or uncivilised
people.
WORD HISTORY: from Greek *barbaros*
meaning 'foreigner', originally
'person saying *bar-bar*'

barbaric ADJECTIVE cruel or brutal
• *The judge described the crime as
barbaric.* **barbarity** NOUN

barbecue, barbecues, barbecuing,
barbecued NOUN ① a grill with a
charcoal fire on which you cook food,
usually outdoors; also an outdoor
party where you eat food cooked on
a barbecue. ▸ VERB ② When food is
barbecued, it is cooked over a
charcoal grill.
WORD HISTORY: from a Caribbean
word meaning 'framework'

barbed ADJECTIVE A barbed remark is
one that seems straightforward but
is really unkind or spiteful.

barbed wire NOUN Barbed wire is
strong wire with sharp points
sticking out of it, used to make
fences.

barber, barbers NOUN a person who
cuts men's hair.

barbiturate, barbiturates NOUN a
drug that people take to make them
calm or to help them sleep.

bar code, bar codes NOUN a small
pattern of numbers and lines on
something you buy in a shop, which
can be electronically scanned at a
checkout to give the price.

bard, bards NOUN (*literary*) A bard is a
poet. Some people call Shakespeare
the Bard.

bare, barer, barest; bares, baring,
bared ADJECTIVE ① If a part of your
body is bare, it is not covered by any
clothing. ② If something is bare, it
has nothing on top of it or inside it
• *bare floorboards* • *a small bare office*.
③ When trees are bare, they have no
leaves on them. ④ The bare
minimum or bare essentials means
the very least that is needed • *They
were fed the bare minimum.* ▸ VERB ⑤ If
you bare something, you uncover or
show it.
SIMILAR WORDS: ① naked, nude,
uncovered ② plain, stark

barefoot ADJECTIVE or ADVERB not
wearing anything on your feet.

barely ADVERB only just • *The girl was
barely sixteen.*

GRAMMAR TIP
Do not use *barely* with negative
words like *not*: *she was barely sixteen*
rather than *she was not barely sixteen*.

bargain, bargains, bargaining,
bargained NOUN ① an agreement in

which two people or groups discuss and agree what each will do, pay or receive in a matter which involves them both. ② something which is sold at a low price and which is good value. ▶ VERB ③ When people bargain with each other, they discuss and agree terms about what each will do, pay or receive in a matter which involves both. **bargain for** VERB If you had not bargained for or on something, you were not prepared for it.

barge, barges, barging, barged NOUN ① a boat with a flat bottom used for carrying heavy loads, especially on canals. ▶ VERB ②(*informal*) If you barge into a place, you push into it in a rough or rude way.

bar graph, bar graphs or **bar chart**, bar charts NOUN MATHS a graph with vertical and horizontal bars whose lengths are proportional to the numbers or quantities they represent.

baritone, baritones NOUN MUSIC A baritone is a man with a fairly deep singing voice, between that of a tenor and a bass.

bark, barks, barking, barked VERB ① When a dog barks, it makes a short, loud noise, once or several times. ▶ NOUN ② the short, loud noise that a dog makes. ③ the tough material that covers the outside of a tree.

barley NOUN a cereal that is grown for food and is also used for making beer and whisky.

bar mitzvah, bar mitzvahs NOUN A Jewish boy's bar mitzvah is a ceremony that takes place on his 13th birthday, after which he is regarded as an adult.
WORD HISTORY: a Hebrew phrase meaning 'son of the law'

barmy, barmier, barmiest ADJECTIVE (*slang*) eccentric or very foolish.

barn, barns NOUN a large farm building used for storing crops or animal food.

barnacle, barnacles NOUN a small shellfish that fixes itself to rocks and to the bottom of boats.

barometer, barometers NOUN GEOGRAPHY an instrument that measures air pressure and shows when the weather is changing.

baron, barons NOUN a member of the lowest rank of the nobility. **baronial** ADJECTIVE

baroness, baronesses NOUN a woman who has the rank of baron, or who is the wife of a baron.

baronet, baronets NOUN A baronet is a man who is given the title 'baronet' by the King or Queen, and who can pass this title on to his son. Baronets are addressed as 'Sir'. **baronetcy** NOUN

baroque [Said ba-**rok**] ADJECTIVE HISTORY Baroque describes an elaborate, highly ornamental style of architecture and art popular in Europe in the 17th and 18th centuries.

barracks PLURAL NOUN a building where soldiers live.

barracuda, barracudas NOUN a large, fierce tropical fish with sharp teeth.

barrage, barrages NOUN ① A barrage of questions or complaints is a lot of them all coming at the same time. ② A barrage is continuous artillery fire over a wide area, to prevent the enemy from moving.
SIMILAR WORDS: ① deluge, stream, torrent ② bombardment, fusillade, volley

barrel, barrels NOUN ① a wooden container with rounded sides and flat ends. ② The barrel of a gun is the long

a
b
c
d
e
f
g
h
i
j
k
l
m
n
o
p
q
r
s
t
u
v
w
x
y
z

tube through which the bullet is fired.

barren ADJECTIVE ① Barren land has soil of such poor quality that plants cannot grow on it. ② A barren female animal is not able to have young. **barrenness** NOUN
SIMILAR WORDS: ① desert, empty, unproductive ② infertile, sterile

barricade, barricades, barricading, barricaded NOUN ① a temporary barrier put up to stop people getting past. ▶ VERB ② If you barricade yourself inside a room or building, you put something heavy against the door to stop people getting in.

barrier, barriers NOUN ① a fence or wall that prevents people or animals getting from one area to another. ② If something is a barrier, it prevents two people or groups from agreeing or communicating, or prevents something from being achieved • *Cost is a major barrier to using the law*. SIMILAR WORDS: ① barricade, fence, wall

barrister, barristers NOUN a lawyer who is qualified to represent people in the higher courts.

barrow, barrows NOUN ① the same as a **wheelbarrow**. ② a large cart from which fruit or other goods are sold in the street.

barter, barters, bartering, bartered VERB ① If you barter goods, you exchange them for other goods, rather than selling them for money. ▶ NOUN ② Barter is the activity of exchanging goods.

base, bases, basing, based NOUN ① the lowest part of something, which often supports the rest. ② a place which part of an army, navy or air force works from. ③ SCIENCE In chemistry, a base is any compound that reacts with an acid to form a salt. ④ MATHS In mathematics, a base is a system of counting and expressing numbers. The decimal system uses base 10, and the binary system uses base 2. ⑤ MATHS The base of a shape is the side or face that is at the bottom. ▶ VERB ⑥ To base something on something else means to use the second thing as a foundation or starting point of the first • *The film is based on a traditional folk tale*. ⑦ If you are based somewhere, you live there or work from there.
SIMILAR WORDS: ① bottom, foot, stand, support

baseball NOUN Baseball is a team game played with a bat and a ball, similar to rounders.

basement, basements NOUN a floor of a building built completely or partly below the ground.

bases PLURAL NOUN ① [*Said* bay-seez] the plural of **basis**. ② [*Said* bay-siz] the plural of **base**.

bash, bashes, bashing, bashed (*informal*) VERB ① If you bash someone or bash into them, you hit them hard. ▶ NOUN ② A bash is a hard blow. ▶ PHRASE ③ If you **have a bash** at something, you try to do it.

bashful ADJECTIVE shy and easily embarrassed.

basic ADJECTIVE ① The basic aspects of something are the most necessary ones • *the basic necessities of life*. ② Something that is basic has only the necessary features without any extras or luxuries • *The accommodation is pretty basic*. **basically** ADVERB
SIMILAR WORDS: ① essential, necessary, vital

basics PLURAL NOUN The basics of something are the things you need to know or understand • *the basics of map-reading*.

basil NOUN Basil is a herb used for flavouring in cooking.

basin, **basins** NOUN ① a round wide container which is open at the top. ② The basin of a river is a bowl of land from which water runs into the river.

basis, **bases** NOUN ① The basis of something is the essential main principle from which it can be developed • *The same colour theme is used as the basis for several patterns*. ② The basis for a belief is the facts that support it • *There is no basis for this assumption*.

SIMILAR WORDS: ① base, foundation ② foundation, ground, support

bask, **basks**, **basking**, **basked** VERB If you bask in the sun, you sit or lie in it, enjoying its warmth.

basket, **baskets** NOUN a container made of thin strips of cane woven together.

basketball NOUN Basketball is a game in which two teams try to score goals by throwing a large ball through one of two circular nets suspended high up at each end of the court.

bass¹, **basses** [*Rhymes with lace*] NOUN ① MUSIC a man with a very deep singing voice. ② MUSIC A bass is also a musical instrument that provides the rhythm and lowest part in the harmonies. A bass may be either a large guitar or a very large member of the violin family.

bass², **basses** [*Rhymes with gas*] NOUN a type of edible sea fish.

basset hound, **basset hounds** NOUN a smooth-haired dog with a long body and ears, and short legs.

bassoon, **bassoons** NOUN a large woodwind instrument.

bastard, **bastards** NOUN ① (*offensive*) People sometimes call someone a bastard when they dislike them or are very angry with them. ② (*old-fashioned*) A bastard is someone whose parents were not married when he or she was born.

baste, **bastes**, **basting**, **basted** VERB When you baste meat that is roasting, you pour hot fat over it so that it does not become dry while cooking.

bastion, **bastions** NOUN (*literary*) something that protects a system or way of life • *The country is the last bastion of communism*.

bat, **bats**, **batting**, **batted** NOUN ① a specially shaped piece of wood with a handle, used for hitting the ball in a game such as cricket or table tennis. ② a small flying animal, active at night, that looks like a mouse with wings. ▶ VERB ③ In certain sports, when someone is batting, it is their turn to try to hit the ball and score runs.

batch, **batches** NOUN a group of things of the same kind produced or dealt with together.

bated PHRASE With bated breath means very anxiously.

bath, **baths** NOUN a long container which you fill with water and sit in to wash yourself.

bathe, **bathes**, **bathing**, **bathed** VERB ① When you bathe, you swim or play in open water. ② When you bathe a wound, you wash it gently. ③ In American English, to bathe means to wash in a bath. ④ (*literary*) If a place is bathed in light, a lot of light reaches it • *The room was bathed in spring sunshine*. **bather** NOUN **bathing** NOUN

bathroom, **bathrooms** NOUN a room with a bath or shower, a washbasin, and often a toilet in it.

baths PLURAL NOUN The baths is a public swimming pool.

bat mitzvah, bat mitzvahs NOUN
RE A Jewish girl's bat mitzvah is a ceremony that takes place when she is 12 or 13, after which she is regarded as a responsible person.
WORD HISTORY: a Hebrew phrase meaning 'daughter of the law'

baton, batons NOUN ① a light, thin stick that a conductor uses to direct an orchestra or choir. ② In athletics, the baton is a short stick passed from one runner to another in a relay race. ③ A baton is also a short stick used as a weapon by police officers in some countries.

batsman, batsmen NOUN In cricket, the batsman is the person who is batting.

battalion, battalions NOUN an army unit consisting of three or more companies.

batten, battens, battening, battened NOUN a strip of wood that is fixed to something to strengthen it or hold it firm. **batten down** VERB If you batten something down, you make it secure by fixing battens across it.

batter, batters, battering, battered VERB ① To batter someone or something means to hit them many times • *The waves kept battering the life raft.* ▶ NOUN ② Batter is a mixture of flour, eggs and milk, used to make pancakes, or to coat food before frying it. **battering** NOUN

battery, batteries NOUN ① a device, containing two or more cells, for storing and producing electricity, for example in a torch or a car. ② a large group of things or people.
▶ ADJECTIVE ③ A battery hen is one of a large number of hens kept in small cages for the mass production of eggs.

battle, battles NOUN ① HISTORY a fight between armed forces or a struggle between two people or groups with conflicting aims • *the battle between town and country.* ② A battle for something difficult is a determined attempt to obtain or achieve it • *the battle for equality in the workplace.*

battlefield, battlefields NOUN a place where a battle is or has been fought.

battlements PLURAL NOUN HISTORY The battlements of a castle consist of a wall built round the top, with gaps through which guns or arrows could be fired.

battleship, battleships NOUN a large, heavily armoured warship.

batty, battier, battiest ADJECTIVE (*informal*) foolish or eccentric.

bauble, baubles NOUN a pretty but cheap ornament or piece of jewellery.

baulk another spelling of **balk**.

bawl, bawls, bawling, bawled VERB ① (*informal*) To bawl at someone means to shout at them loudly and harshly. ② When a child is bawling, it is crying very loudly and angrily.

bay, bays, baying, bayed NOUN ① GEOGRAPHY a part of a coastline where the land curves inwards. ② a space or area used for a particular purpose • *a loading bay.* ③ Bay is a kind of tree similar to the laurel, with leaves used for flavouring in cooking.
▶ PHRASE ④ If you **keep something at bay**, you prevent it from reaching you • *Eating oranges keeps colds at bay.*
▶ VERB ⑤ When a hound or wolf bays, it makes a deep howling noise.
SIMILAR WORDS: ① cove, gulf, inlet

bayonet, bayonets NOUN a sharp blade that can be fixed to the end of a rifle and used for stabbing.
WORD HISTORY: named after *Bayonne* in France, where it originated

bazaar, bazaars NOUN ① an area with many small shops and stalls, especially in Asia or North Africa. ② a sale to raise money for charity.

BC BC means 'before Christ'. You use 'BC' in dates to indicate the number of years before the traditional date of the birth of Jesus Christ • *in 49 BC*.

BCE BCE means 'before the Common Era'. Non-Christians use 'BCE' in dates as an alternative to 'BC' • *399 BCE*.

be, **am**, **is**, **are**; **being**; **was**, **were**; **been** AUXILIARY VERB ① 'Be' is used with a present participle to form the continuous tense • *Crimes of violence are increasing*. ② 'Be' is also used to say that something will happen • *We are going to America next month*. ③ 'Be' is used to form the passive voice • *The walls were being repaired*. ▶ VERB ④ 'Be' is used to give more information about the subject of a sentence • *Her name is Melanie*.

be- PREFIX ① 'Be-' is used to form verbs from nouns and adds the meaning 'treat as'. For example, to *befriend* someone is to make friends with them. ② 'Be-' is also sometimes used to form verbs from verbs when it is used for emphasis or to mean 'covering completely'. For example, to *besmear* means to smear all over.

beach, beaches NOUN an area of sand or pebbles beside the sea.
SIMILAR WORDS: seashore, seaside, shore

SPELLING TIP

Do not confuse the spellings of *beach* and *beech*: *a day at the beach; a forest of oak, ash and beech.*

---

beach nourishment NOUN
GEOGRAPHY a process in which sand lost by coastal erosion is replaced by material moved from another area.

beacon, beacons NOUN In the past, a beacon was a light or fire on a hill, which acted as a signal or warning.

bead, beads NOUN ① Beads are small

The Verb Be

The verb **to be** has a lot of unusual forms, and does not follow the usual rules.

The main form is *be*. This is used with an auxiliary verb to make compound tenses, and after the preposition *to*:

*She will **be** five years old in April.*

The verb forms *am*, *are* and *is* are used to talk about the present time. *Am* is used for the first person singular; *are* is used for the second person and for all plural forms; *is* is used for the third person singular:

*I **am** exhausted.*
*You **are** very welcome.*
*Robbie **is** always cheerful.*
*They **are** a pair of rascals.*

The present participle is *being*.

This form is used with an auxiliary verb to make compound tenses:

*Ali **was being** very helpful.*

The verb forms *was* and *were* talk about past time. *Was* is used for the first and third person singular; *were* is used for the second person and for all plural forms:

*I **was** exhausted.*
*You **were** very welcome.*
*Robbie **was** always cheerful.*
*They **were** a pair of rascals.*

The past participle is *been*. This form is used with an auxiliary verb to make compound tenses:

*I **shall have been** here five years in April.*
*Ali **has been** polite at all times.*

a b c d e f g h i j k l m n o p q r s t u v w x y z

pieces of coloured glass or wood with a hole through the middle, strung together to make necklaces. ② Beads of liquid are drops of it.

beady, beadier, beadiest ADJECTIVE Beady eyes are small and bright like beads.

beagle, beagles NOUN a short-haired dog with long ears and short legs.

beak, beaks NOUN A bird's beak is the hard part of its mouth that sticks out.

beaker, beakers NOUN ① a cup for drinking out of, usually made of plastic and without a handle. ② a glass container with a lip which is used in laboratories.

beam, beams, beaming, beamed NOUN ① a broad smile. ② A beam of light is a band of light that shines from something such as a torch. ③ a long, thick bar of wood or metal, especially one that supports a roof. ▶VERB ④ If you beam, you smile because you are happy.

bean, beans NOUN Beans are the seeds or pods of a climbing plant, which are eaten as a vegetable; also used of some other seeds, for example the seeds from which coffee is made.

bear, bears, bearing, bore, borne NOUN ① a large, strong wild animal with thick fur and sharp claws. ▶VERB ② (formal) To bear something means to carry it or support its weight • The ice wasn't thick enough to bear their weight. ③ If something bears a mark or typical feature, it has it • The room bore all the signs of a violent struggle. ④ If you bear something difficult, you accept it and are able to deal with it • He bore his last illness with courage. ⑤ If you can't bear someone or something, you dislike them very much. ⑥ (formal)

When a plant or tree bears flowers, fruit or leaves, it produces them. **bearable** ADJECTIVE **bear out** VERB To bear someone out or to bear out their story or report means to support what they are saying • These claims are not borne out by the evidence.

beard, beards NOUN the hair that grows on the lower part of a man's face. **bearded** ADJECTIVE

bearer, bearers NOUN The bearer of something is the person who carries or presents it • the bearer of bad news.

bearing NOUN ① If something has a bearing on a situation, it is relevant to it. ② the way in which a person moves or stands.

beast, beasts NOUN ① (old-fashioned) a large wild animal. ② (informal) If you call someone a beast, you mean that they are cruel or spiteful.

beastly, beastlier, beastliest ADJECTIVE (old-fashioned, informal) cruel or spiteful.

beat, beats, beating, beat, beaten VERB ① To beat someone or something means to hit them hard and repeatedly. ② If you beat someone in a race or game, you defeat them or do better than them. ③ When a bird or insect beats its wings, it moves them up and down. ④ When your heart is beating, it is pumping blood with a regular rhythm. ⑤ If you beat eggs or butter, you mix them vigorously using a fork or a whisk. ▶NOUN ⑥ The beat of your heart is its regular pumping action. ⑦ MUSIC The beat of a piece of music is its main rhythm. ⑧ A police officer's beat is the area which he or she patrols. **beater** NOUN **beating** NOUN **beat up** VERB To beat someone up means to hit or kick them repeatedly.
SIMILAR WORDS: ① batter, hit, strike ② conquer, defeat, vanquish

Beaufort scale [Said boh-fort] NOUN
GEOGRAPHY The Beaufort scale is a
scale for measuring the speed of
wind, ranging from 0 (calm) to 12
(hurricane force). It was devised by
Sir Francis Beaufort (1774–1857), an
English admiral.

beaut, beauts (informal) NOUN ① In
Australian and New Zealand English,
a beaut is an outstanding person or
thing. ▶ ADJECTIVE ② In Australian
and New Zealand English, beaut
means good or excellent • a beaut
house.

beautiful ADJECTIVE very attractive
or pleasing • a beautiful girl • beautiful
music. **beautifully** ADVERB
SIMILAR WORDS: attractive,
gorgeous, lovely

SPELLING TIP
Remember this mnemonic: Beautiful
Elephants Are Usually Tiny.

---

beauty, beauties NOUN ① Beauty is
the quality of being beautiful.
②(old-fashioned) a very attractive
woman. ③ The beauty of an idea or
plan is what makes it attractive or
worthwhile • The beauty of the idea is
its simplicity.

beaver, beavers NOUN an animal
with a big, flat tail and webbed hind
feet. Beavers build dams.

became the past tense of **become**.

because CONJUNCTION ① 'Because' is
used with a clause that gives the
reason for something • I went home
because I was tired. ▶ PHRASE
② **Because of** is used with a noun
that gives the reason for something
• He quit playing because of a knee
injury.

SPELLING TIP
Remember this mnemonic: Betty Eats
Cakes And Uses Seven Eggs.

---

beck PHRASE If you are at someone's
beck and call, you are always
available to do what they ask.

beckon, beckons, beckoning,
beckoned VERB ① If you beckon to
someone, you signal with your hand
that you want them to come to you.
② If you say that something beckons,
you mean that you find it very
attractive • A career in journalism
beckons.

become, becomes, becoming,
became, become VERB To become
something means to start feeling or
being that thing • I became very angry
• He became an actor.

bed, beds NOUN ① a piece of furniture
that you lie on when you sleep. ② A
bed in a garden is an area of ground in
which plants are grown. ③ The bed
of a sea or river is the ground at the
bottom of it.

bedclothes PLURAL NOUN the sheets
and covers that you put over you
when you get into bed.

bedding NOUN Bedding is sheets,
blankets and other covers that are
used on beds.

bedlam NOUN You can refer to a noisy
and disorderly place or situation as
bedlam • The delay caused bedlam at
the station.
WORD HISTORY: from Bedlam, a
shortened form of the Hospital of St
Mary of Bethlehem in London, which
was an institution for people with
mental illness

bedpan, bedpans NOUN a container
used as a toilet by people who are too
ill to get out of bed.

bedraggled ADJECTIVE A bedraggled
person or animal is in a messy or
untidy state.

bedridden ADJECTIVE Someone
who is bedridden is too ill to get
out of bed.

a
b
c
d
e
f
g
h
i
j
k
l
m
n
o
p
q
r
s
t
u
v
w
x
y
z

bedrock NOUN ① Bedrock is the solid rock under the soil. ② The bedrock of something is the foundation and principles on which it is based • *His life was built on the bedrock of integrity.*

bedroom, bedrooms NOUN a room used for sleeping in.

bedspread, bedspreads NOUN a cover put over a bed, on top of the sheets and blankets.

bedstead, bedsteads NOUN the metal or wooden frame of an old-fashioned bed.

bee, bees NOUN a winged insect that makes honey and lives in large groups.

beech, beeches NOUN a tree with a smooth grey trunk and shiny leaves.

SPELLING TIP
Do not confuse the spellings of *beech* and *beach*: *a forest of oak, ash and beech; a day at the beach.*

beef NOUN Beef is the meat of a cow, bull or ox.

beefy, beefier, beefiest ADJECTIVE (*informal*) A beefy person is strong and muscular.

beehive, beehives NOUN a container in which bees live and make their honey.

beeline PHRASE (*informal*) If you **make a beeline** for a place, you go there as quickly and directly as possible.

been the past participle of **be**.

beer, beers NOUN an alcoholic drink made from malt and flavoured with hops.

beet, beets NOUN Beet is a plant with an edible root and leaves. Sugar is made from the root of one type of beet, and another type is used as food for farm animals.

beetle, beetles NOUN a flying insect with hard wings which cover its body when it is not flying.

beetroot, beetroots NOUN A beetroot is the round, dark red root of a type of beet. It is cooked and eaten, especially cold as a salad vegetable or preserved in vinegar.

befall, befalls, befalling, befell, befallen VERB (*old-fashioned*) If something befalls you, it happens to you • *A similar fate befell my cousin.*

before ADVERB or PREPOSITION or CONJUNCTION ① 'Before' is used to refer to a previous time • *Apply the ointment before going to bed.* ▶ ADVERB ② If you have done something before, you have done it on a previous occasion • *Never before had he seen such poverty.* ▶ PREPOSITION ③ (*formal*) Before also means in front of • *They stopped before a large white villa.*
SIMILAR WORDS: ① earlier than, prior to ② previously

beforehand ADVERB before • *It had been agreed beforehand that they would spend the night there.*

befriend, befriends, befriending, befriended VERB If you befriend someone, you act in a kind and helpful way and so become friends with them.

beg, begs, begging, begged VERB ① When people beg, they ask for food or money, because they are very poor. ② If you beg someone to do something, you ask them very anxiously to do it.
SIMILAR WORDS: ② beseech, implore, plead

began the past tense of **begin**.

beggar, beggars NOUN someone who lives by asking people for money or food.

begin, begins, beginning, began, begun VERB If you begin to do something, you start doing it. When something begins, it starts.

SIMILAR WORDS: commence, start

beginner, beginners NOUN someone who has just started learning to do something and cannot do it very well yet.

SIMILAR WORDS: learner, novice

beginning, beginnings NOUN The beginning of something is the first part of it or the time when it starts • *They had now reached the beginning of the city.*

SPELLING TIP
Remember that *beginning* has one *g* and two *n*s.

begonia, begonias [Said be-*go*-nya] NOUN A begonia is a garden plant or house plant with brightly coloured flowers. Begonia is named after Michel Bégon (1638–1710), a French patron of botany.

begrudge, begrudges, begrudging, begrudged VERB If you begrudge someone something, you are angry or envious because they have it • *No one could begrudge him the glory.*

beguiling [Rhymes with *smiling*] ADJECTIVE charming, but often in a deceptive way.

begun the past participle of **begin**.

behalf PHRASE To do something **on behalf of** someone or something means to do it for their benefit or as their representative.

behave, behaves, behaving, behaved VERB ① If you behave in a particular way, you act in that way • *They were behaving like animals.* ② To behave yourself means to act correctly or properly.

behaviour NOUN Your behaviour is the way in which you behave.

behead, beheads, beheading, beheaded VERB To behead someone means to cut their head off.

beheld the past tense of **behold**.

behind PREPOSITION ① at the back of • *He was seated behind the desk.* ② responsible for or causing • *He was the driving force behind the move.* ③ supporting someone • *The whole country was behind him.* ▶ ADVERB ④ If you stay behind, you remain after other people have gone. ⑤ If you leave something behind, you do not take it with you.

behold, beholds, beholding, beheld (*literary*) VERB ① To behold something means to notice it or look at it. ▶ INTERJECTION ② You say 'behold' when you want someone to look at something. **beholder** NOUN

beige, beiges [Said *bayj*] NOUN or ADJECTIVE pale creamy-brown.

being, beings ① Being is the present participle of **be**. ▶ NOUN ② Being is the state or fact of existing • *The party came into being in 1923.* ③ a living creature, either real or imaginary • *alien beings from a distant galaxy.*

belated ADJECTIVE (*formal*) A belated action happens later than it should have done • *a belated birthday present.* **belatedly** ADVERB

belch, belches, belching, belched VERB ① If you belch, you make a sudden noise in your throat because air has risen up from your stomach. ② If something belches smoke or fire, it sends it out in large amounts • *Smoke belched from the steelworks.* ▶ NOUN ③ the noise you make when you belch.

beleaguered ADJECTIVE ① struggling against difficulties or criticism • *the beleaguered aviation industry.* ② besieged by an enemy • *the beleaguered garrison.*

belfry, belfries NOUN the part of a church tower where the bells are.

A
B
C
D
E
F
G
H
I
J
K
L
M
N
O
P
Q
R
S
T
U
V
W
X
Y
Z

Belgian, Belgians ADJECTIVE
① belonging or relating to Belgium.
▶ NOUN ② someone who comes from
Belgium.

belief, beliefs NOUN ① a feeling of
certainty that something exists or is
true. ② one of the principles of a
religion or moral system.
SIMILAR WORDS: ② creed, doctrine,
faith

believable ADJECTIVE possible or
likely to be the case.

believe, believes, believing,
believed VERB ① If you believe that
something is true, you accept that it
is true. ② If you believe someone, you
accept that they are telling the truth.
③ If you believe in things such as God
and miracles, you accept that they
exist or happen. ④ If you believe in
something such as a plan or system,
you are in favour of it • *They really
believe in education*. **believer** NOUN

belittle, belittles, belittling,
belittled VERB If you belittle
someone or something, you make
them seem unimportant • *He belittled
my opinions*.
SIMILAR WORDS: deprecate,
disparage, scoff at

bell, bells NOUN ① a cup-shaped
metal object with a piece inside that
swings and hits the sides, producing
a ringing sound. ② an electrical
device that rings or buzzes in order to
attract attention.

bellbird, bellbirds NOUN an
Australian or New Zealand bird that
makes a sound like a bell.

belligerent ADJECTIVE aggressive
and keen to start a fight or an
argument. **belligerently** ADVERB
belligerence NOUN

bellow, bellows, bellowing,
bellowed VERB ① When an animal
such as a bull bellows, it makes a
loud, deep roaring noise. ② If
someone bellows, they shout in a
loud, deep voice.

bellows PLURAL NOUN Bellows are a
piece of equipment used for blowing
air into a fire to make it burn more
fiercely.

belly, bellies NOUN ① Your belly is
your stomach or the front of your
body below your chest. ② An
animal's belly is the underneath part
of its body.

belong, belongs, belonging,
belonged VERB ① If something
belongs to you, it is yours and you
own it. ② To belong to a group
means to be a member of it. ③ If
something belongs in a particular
place, that is where it should be • *It
did not belong in the music room*.

belongings PLURAL NOUN Your
belongings are the things that you
own.

beloved [Said bil-*luv*-id] ADJECTIVE A
beloved person or thing is one that
you feel great affection for.
SIMILAR WORDS: adored, dear, loved,
precious

below PREPOSITION or ADVERB ① If
something is below a line or the
surface of something else, it is lower
down • *six inches below soil level*.
② Below also means at or to a lower
point, level or rate • *The temperature
fell below zero degrees*.

belt, belts, belting, belted NOUN ① a
strip of leather or cloth that you
fasten round your waist to hold your
trousers or skirt up. ② In a machine,
a belt is a circular strip of rubber that
drives moving parts or carries objects
along. ③ a specific area of a country
• *Poland's industrial belt*. ▶ VERB
④ (*informal*) To belt someone means
to hit them very hard.

bemused ADJECTIVE If you are

bemused, you are puzzled or confused.

bench, benches NOUN ① a long seat that two or more people can sit on. ② a long, narrow table for working at, for example in a laboratory.
SIMILAR WORDS: ① form, pew, seat

benchmark, benchmarks NOUN a standard used when measuring or comparing something • *This exercise is a good benchmark to show how much students have learnt.*

bend, bends, bending, bent VERB ① When you bend something, you use force to make it curved or angular. ② When you bend, you move your head and shoulders forwards and downwards. ▸ NOUN ③ a curved part of something.
SIMILAR WORDS: ① arch, bow, curve ③ arch, bow, curve

beneath PREPOSITION or ADJECTIVE or ADVERB ① an old-fashioned word for **underneath**. ▸ PREPOSITION ② If someone thinks something is beneath them, they think that it is too unimportant for them to bother with it.

benefactor, benefactors NOUN a person who helps to support a person or institution by giving money.
SIMILAR WORDS: patron, sponsor, supporter

beneficial ADJECTIVE Something that is beneficial is good for people • *the beneficial effects of exercise.*
beneficially ADVERB
SIMILAR WORDS: advantageous, favourable, helpful

beneficiary, beneficiaries NOUN A beneficiary of something is someone who receives money or other benefits from it.

benefit, benefits, benefiting, benefited NOUN ① The benefits of

something are the advantages that it brings to people • *the benefits of relaxation.* ② Benefit is money given by the government to people who are unemployed or ill. ▸ VERB ③ If you benefit from something or something benefits you, it helps you.
SIMILAR WORDS: ① advantage, good, help ③ gain, profit

SPELLING TIP
Benefit is spelt with two *e*s, not two *i*s.

benevolent ADJECTIVE kind and helpful. **benevolence** NOUN **benevolently** ADVERB

benign [Said be-*nine*] ADJECTIVE ① Someone who is benign is kind and gentle. ② A benign tumour is one that will not cause death or serious illness. **benignly** ADVERB

bent ① Bent is the past tense and past participle of **bend**. ▸ PHRASE ② If you are **bent on** doing something, you are determined to do it.

berate, berates, berating, berated VERB (formal) If you berate someone, you scold them angrily • *He berated them for getting caught.*

bereaved ADJECTIVE (formal) You say that someone is bereaved when a close relative or friend of theirs has recently died. **bereavement** NOUN

bereft ADJECTIVE (literary) If you are bereft of something, you no longer have it • *The government seems bereft of ideas.*

beret, berets [Said ber-*ray*] NOUN a circular flat hat with no brim.

berm, berms NOUN ① a narrow path at the edge of a slope, road or canal. ② In New Zealand English, a strip of grass between the road and the footpath in areas where people live.

berry, berries NOUN Berries are small, round fruits that grow on bushes or trees.

berserk PHRASE If someone **goes berserk**, they lose control of themselves and become very violent. WORD HISTORY: from Icelandic *berserkr*, a kind of Viking who wore a shirt (*serkr*) made from the skin of a bear (*björn*). They worked themselves into a frenzy before battle

berth, berths NOUN ① a space in a harbour where a ship stays when it is being loaded or unloaded. ② In a boat or caravan, a berth is a bed.

SPELLING TIP
Do not confuse the spellings of *berth* and *birth*: *The yacht has six berths; the birth of their daughter.*

---

beseech, beseeches, beseeching, beseeched or besought VERB (*literary*) If you beseech someone to do something, you ask them very earnestly to do it • *Her eyes beseeched him to show mercy.* **beseeching** ADJECTIVE

beset ADJECTIVE (*formal*) If you are beset by difficulties or doubts, you have a lot of them.

beside PREPOSITION If one thing is beside something else, they are next to each other.
SIMILAR WORDS: adjacent to, alongside, next to

besiege, besieges, besieging, besieged VERB ① When soldiers besiege a place, they surround it and wait for the people inside to surrender. ② If you are besieged by people, many people want something from you and continually bother you.

besought a past tense and past participle of **beseech**.

best ADJECTIVE or ADVERB ① the superlative of **good** and **well**. ▸ ADVERB ② The thing that you like best is the thing that you prefer to everything else. ▸ NOUN ③ the thing most preferred.
SIMILAR WORDS: ① finest, supreme, top

best man NOUN The best man at a wedding is the man who acts as the bridegroom's attendant.

bestow, bestows, bestowing, bestowed VERB (*formal*) If you bestow something on someone, you give it to them.

bet, bets, betting, bet VERB ① If you bet on the result of an event, you will win money if something happens and lose money if it does not. ▸ NOUN ② the act of betting on something, or the amount of money that you agree to risk. ▸ PHRASE ③ (*informal*) You say **I bet** to indicate that you are sure that something is or will be so • *I bet the answer is no.* **betting** NOUN

beta NOUN Beta is the second letter in the Greek alphabet.

betray, betrays, betraying, betrayed VERB ① If you betray someone who trusts you, you do something which harms them, such as helping their enemies. ② If you betray your feelings or thoughts, you show them without intending to. **betrayal** NOUN **betrayer** NOUN
SIMILAR WORDS: ① be disloyal to, double-cross ② give away, reveal

betrothal, betrothals NOUN (*old-fashioned*) an engagement to be married. **betrothed** ADJECTIVE or NOUN

better ADJECTIVE or ADVERB ① the comparative of **good** and **well**. ▸ ADVERB ② If you like one thing better than another, you like it more than the other thing. ▸ ADJECTIVE ③ If you are better after an illness, you are no longer ill.
SIMILAR WORDS: ① finer, greater, superior

between PREPOSITION or ADVERB
① If something is between two other things, it is situated or happens in the space or time that separates them • *flights between Europe and Asia*. ② A relationship or difference between two people or things involves only those two.

USAGE NOTE
If there are two things you should use *between*. If there are more than two things you should use *among*.

beverage, beverages NOUN (*formal*) a drink.

bevy, bevies NOUN a group of people • *a bevy of lawyers*.

beware VERB If you tell someone to beware of something, you are warning them that it might be dangerous or harmful.

bewilder, bewilders, bewildering, bewildered VERB If something bewilders you, it is too confusing or difficult for you to understand. **bewildered** ADJECTIVE **bewildering** ADJECTIVE **bewilderment** NOUN

bewitch, bewitches, bewitching, bewitched VERB ① To bewitch someone means to cast a spell on them. ② If something bewitches you, you are so attracted to it that you cannot pay attention to anything else. **bewitched** ADJECTIVE **bewitching** ADJECTIVE

beyond PREPOSITION ① If something is beyond a certain place, it is on the other side of it • *Beyond the hills was the Sahara*. ② If something continues beyond a particular point, it continues further than that point • *an education beyond the age of 16*. ③ If someone or something is beyond understanding or help, they cannot be understood or helped.

bi- PREFIX 'Bi-' means 'two' or 'twice' • *bicycle* • *biannual*.

biannual ADJECTIVE occurring twice a year. **biannually** ADVERB

bias NOUN Someone who shows bias favours one person or thing unfairly.
SIMILAR WORDS: favouritism, partiality, prejudice

biased; also spelt **biassed** ADJECTIVE favouring one person or thing unfairly • *biased attitudes*.
SIMILAR WORDS: one-sided, prejudiced

bib, bibs NOUN a piece of cloth or plastic which is worn under the chin of very young children when they are eating, to keep their clothes clean.

Bible, Bibles NOUN RE The Bible is the sacred book of the Christian and Jewish religions. **biblical** ADJECTIVE
WORD HISTORY: from Greek *biblia* meaning 'the books'

bicentenary, bicentenaries NOUN The bicentenary of an event is its two-hundredth anniversary.

biceps, biceps NOUN PE the large muscle on your upper arms.
WORD HISTORY: from Latin *bi-* + *caput* meaning 'two-headed' (because the muscle has two points of origin)

bicker, bickers, bickering, bickered VERB When people bicker, they argue or quarrel about unimportant things.

bicycle, bicycles NOUN a two-wheeled vehicle which you ride by pushing two pedals with your feet.

bid, bids, bidding, bade or bid, bidden or bid NOUN ① an attempt to obtain or do something • *He made a bid for freedom*. ② an offer to buy something for a certain sum of money. ▶ VERB ③ If you bid for something, you offer to pay a certain sum of money for it. ④ (*old-fashioned*) If you bid someone a greeting or a farewell, you say it to them.

A
B
C
D
E
F
G
H
I
J
K
L
M
N
O
P
Q
R
S
T
U
V
W
X
Y
Z

GRAMMAR TIP
When *bid* means 'offer to pay a certain sum of money' (sense 3), the past tense and past participle is *bid*. When *bid* means 'say a greeting or farewell' (sense 4), the past tense is *bade* and the past participle is *bidden*.

biddy-biddy, biddy-biddies **NOUN** a prickly low-growing plant found in New Zealand.

bide, bides, biding, bided **PHRASE** If you **bide your time**, you wait for a good opportunity before doing something.

bidet, bidets [Said *bee-day*] **NOUN** a low basin in a bathroom which is used for washing your bottom in.
WORD HISTORY: a French word meaning 'small horse'

bifocals **PLURAL NOUN** Bifocals are glasses with lenses made in two halves, the upper halves for looking at distant objects and the lower ones for reading.

big, bigger, biggest **ADJECTIVE** ① of a large size. ② of great importance.
biggish **ADJECTIVE** **bigness** **NOUN**
SIMILAR WORDS: ① enormous, huge, large ② enormous, huge, large

bigamy **NOUN** Bigamy is the crime of marrying someone when you are already married to someone else.
bigamist **NOUN**

bigot, bigots **NOUN** someone who has strong and unreasonable opinions which they refuse to change. **bigoted** **ADJECTIVE** **bigotry** **NOUN**

bike, bikes **NOUN** (*informal*) a bicycle or motorcycle.

bikini, bikinis **NOUN** a small two-piece swimming costume worn by women.
WORD HISTORY: after *Bikini* atoll, from a comparison between the effect of an atom-bomb test there

and the effect caused by women wearing bikinis

bilateral **ADJECTIVE** A bilateral agreement is one made between two groups or countries.

bile **NOUN** Bile is a bitter yellow liquid produced by the liver which helps the digestion of fat. In the Middle Ages, it was believed to cause anger.

bilge **NOUN** the lowest part of a ship, where dirty water collects.

bilingual **ADJECTIVE** involving or using two languages • *bilingual street signs*.

bill, bills, billing, billed **NOUN** ① a written statement of how much is owed for goods or services. ② a formal statement of a proposed new law that is discussed and then voted on in Parliament. ③ a notice or a poster. ④ A bird's bill is its beak.
▶ **VERB** ⑤ If you bill someone, you give or send them a bill for goods or services you have supplied.
SIMILAR WORDS: ① charges, invoice

billabong, billabongs **NOUN** In Australia, a billabong is a lagoon or pool formed from part of a river.

billboard, billboards **NOUN** a large board on which advertisements are displayed.

billet, billets, billeting, billeted **VERB** When soldiers are billeted in a building, arrangements are made for them to stay there.

billiards **NOUN** Billiards is a game played on a large table, in which a long stick called a cue is used to strike one of three balls. The aim is to hit a second ball with the first so that either the third ball is also hit or one of the balls goes into one of the six pockets at the edges of the table.

billion, billions **NOUN** a thousand million. Formerly, a billion was a million million. **billionth** **ADJECTIVE**

USAGE NOTE
As the meaning of *billion* has changed from one million million to one thousand million, a writer may mean either of these things when using it, depending on when the book or article was written.

billionaire, billionaires NOUN a very rich person who has money or property worth billions of pounds or dollars.

billow, billows, billowing, billowed VERB ① When things made of cloth billow, they swell out and flap slowly in the wind. ② When smoke or cloud billows, it spreads upwards and outwards. ▸ NOUN ③ a large wave.

billy, billies or **billycan**, billycans NOUN In Australian and New Zealand English, a metal pot for boiling water over a camp fire.

biltong NOUN Biltong is a South African dish of strips of meat that have been dried and cured in the sun.

bin, bins NOUN a container, especially one that you put rubbish in.

binary [Said by-nar-ee] ADJECTIVE ICT The binary system expresses numbers using only two digits, 0 and 1.

bind, binds, binding, bound VERB ① If you bind something, you tie rope or string round it so that it is held firmly. ② If something binds you to a course of action, it makes you act in that way • *He was bound by that decision.*

bindi-eye, bindi-eyes NOUN a small Australian plant with prickly fruits.

binding, bindings ADJECTIVE ① If a promise or agreement is binding, it must be obeyed. ▸ NOUN ② The binding of a book is its cover.

binge, binges NOUN (*informal*) a wild bout of drinking or eating too much.

bingo NOUN Bingo is a game in which players aim to match the numbers that someone calls out with the numbers on the card that they have been given.

binoculars PLURAL NOUN Binoculars are an instrument with lenses for both eyes, which you look through in order to see objects far away.

bio- PREFIX 'Bio-' means 'life' or 'living things'. For example, a *biography* is the story of someone's life and *biology* is the study of living things.

bioaccumulation NOUN SCIENCE Bioaccumulation is the process by which chemicals and poisons gradually build up in the tissues of living things.

biochemistry NOUN Biochemistry is the study of the chemistry of living things. **biochemical** ADJECTIVE **biochemist** NOUN

biodegradable ADJECTIVE If something is biodegradable, it can be broken down into its natural elements by the action of bacteria • *biodegradable cleaning products*.

biodiversity NOUN SCIENCE the existence of a wide variety of plant and animal species in a particular area.

biography, biographies NOUN A biography is an account of someone's life, written by someone else. Compare **autobiography**. **biographer** NOUN **biographical** ADJECTIVE
WORD HISTORY: from Greek *bios* meaning 'life' and *graphein* meaning 'to write'

biological weapon, biological weapons NOUN a weapon that uses living organisms or their toxic products to cause death or injury to people.

a
b
c
d
e
f
g
h
i
j
k
l
m
n
o
p
q
r
s
t
u
v
w
x
y
z

biology NOUN Biology is the study of living things. **biological** ADJECTIVE **biologically** ADVERB **biologist** NOUN

biometric ADJECTIVE relating to biometrics • *a biometric passport*.

biometrics NOUN the use of mathematical measurements to analyse physical characteristics, especially to identify people.

bionic ADJECTIVE having a part of the body that works electronically.

biopsy, biopsies NOUN an examination under a microscope of tissue from a living body to find out the cause of a disease.

biosphere NOUN SCIENCE The biosphere is the part of the earth's surface and atmosphere where life exists.

biotechnology NOUN Biotechnology is the use of living things such as cells or bacteria in industry and technology.

birch, birches NOUN a tall deciduous tree with thin branches and thin bark.

bird, birds NOUN an animal with two legs, two wings, and feathers.

birth, births NOUN ① The birth of a baby is when it comes out of its mother's womb at the beginning of its life. ② The birth of something is its beginning • *the birth of modern art*.

SPELLING TIP
Do not confuse the spellings of *birth* and *berth*: *the birth of their daughter*; *The yacht has six berths*.

---

birthday, birthdays NOUN Your birthday is the anniversary of the date on which you were born.

birthmark, birthmarks NOUN a mark on someone's skin that has been there since they were born.

biscuit, biscuits NOUN a small flat cake made of baked dough.
WORD HISTORY: from Old French *bes* + *cuit* meaning 'twice-cooked'

bisect, bisects, bisecting, bisected VERB To bisect a line or area means to divide it in half.

bisexual ADJECTIVE attracted to both males and females.

bishop, bishops NOUN ① RE a high-ranking member of the clergy in some Christian Churches. ② In chess, a bishop is a piece that is moved diagonally across the board.

bison NOUN A bison is a large hairy animal, related to cattle, with a large head and shoulders. Bison used to be very common on the prairies in North America, but they are now almost extinct.

bistro, bistros [*Said* **bee**-*stroh*] NOUN a small informal restaurant.

bit, bits ① Bit is the past tense of **bite**.
▶ NOUN ② A bit of something is a small amount of it • *a bit of coal*.
▶ PHRASE ③ **A bit** means slightly or to a small extent • *That's a bit tricky*.
SIMILAR WORDS: ②fragment, part, piece

bitch, bitches NOUN ① a female dog. ② (*offensive*) If someone refers to a woman as a bitch, it means that they think she behaves in a spiteful way.
bitchy ADJECTIVE

bite, bites, biting, bit, bitten VERB ① To bite something or someone is to cut it or cut through it with the teeth.
▶ NOUN ② a small amount that you bite off something with your teeth. ③ the injury you get when an animal or insect bites you.

bitmap, bitmaps NOUN ICT a computer graphics file that breaks down an image into a grid of squares, each representing a particular colour.

bitter, bitterer, bitterest ADJECTIVE
① If someone is bitter, they feel angry and resentful. ② A bitter disappointment or experience makes people feel angry or unhappy for a long time afterwards. ③ In a bitter argument or war, people argue or fight fiercely and angrily • *a bitter power struggle*. ④ A bitter wind is an extremely cold wind. ⑤ Something that tastes bitter has a sharp, unpleasant taste. **bitterly** ADVERB **bitterness** NOUN
SIMILAR WORDS: ① acrimonious, resentful, sour ⑤ acid, sharp, sour

bivouac, bivouacs [*Said biv-oo-ak*] NOUN a temporary camp in the open air.

bizarre [*Said biz-zahr*] ADJECTIVE very strange or eccentric.

blab, blabs, blabbing, blabbed VERB (*informal*) When someone blabs, they give away secrets by talking carelessly.

black, blacker, blackest; blacks NOUN or ADJECTIVE ① Black is the darkest possible colour, like tar or soot. ② Someone who is Black is a member of a dark-skinned race. ③ Black coffee or tea has no milk or cream added to it. ④ Black humour involves jokes about death or suffering. **blackness** NOUN
black out VERB If you black out, you lose consciousness.
SIMILAR WORDS: ① dark, jet, pitch-black

SPELLING TIP
When you are writing about a person or people, *Black* should start with a capital letter.

blackberry, blackberries NOUN
Blackberries are small black fruits that grow on prickly bushes called brambles.

blackbird, blackbirds NOUN a common European bird, the male of which has black feathers and a yellow beak.

blackboard, blackboards NOUN a dark-coloured board on which people can write or draw using chalk.

black box, black boxes NOUN A black box is an electronic device in an aircraft which collects and stores information during flights. This information can be used to provide evidence if an accident occurs.

blackcurrant, blackcurrants NOUN
Blackcurrants are very small dark purple fruits that grow in bunches on bushes.

blacken, blackens, blackening, blackened VERB To blacken something means to make it black • *The smoke from the chimney blackened the roof*.

blackhead, blackheads NOUN a very small black spot on the skin caused by a pore being blocked with dirt.

blacklist, blacklists, blacklisting, blacklisted NOUN ① a list of people or organisations who are thought to be untrustworthy or disloyal. ▸ VERB ② When someone is blacklisted, they are put on a blacklist.

blackmail, blackmails, blackmailing, blackmailed VERB ① If someone blackmails another person, they threaten to reveal an unpleasant secret about them unless that person gives them money or does something for them. ▸ NOUN ② Blackmail is the action of blackmailing people. **blackmailer** NOUN

black market NOUN If something is bought or sold on the black market, it is bought or sold illegally.

blackout, blackouts NOUN If you have a blackout, you lose consciousness for a short time.

blacksmith, blacksmiths NOUN
a person whose job is making things out of iron, such as horseshoes.

bladder, bladders NOUN the part of your body where urine is held until it leaves your body.

blade, blades NOUN ①The blade of a weapon or cutting tool is the sharp part of it. ②The blades of a propeller are the thin, flat parts that turn round. ③A blade of grass is a single piece of it.

blame, blames, blaming, blamed VERB ① If someone blames you for something bad that has happened, they believe you caused it. ▶ NOUN ②The blame for something bad that happens is the responsibility for letting it happen.
SIMILAR WORDS: ① accuse, hold responsible

blameless ADJECTIVE Someone who is blameless has not done anything wrong.

blanch, blanches, blanching, blanched VERB If you blanch, you suddenly become very pale.

bland, blander, blandest ADJECTIVE tasteless, dull or boring • a bland diet • bland pop music. **blandly** ADVERB

blank, blanker, blankest; blanks ADJECTIVE ① Something that is blank has nothing on it • a blank sheet of paper. ② If you look blank, your face shows no feeling or interest. ▶ NOUN ③ If your mind is a blank, you cannot think of anything or remember anything.

blanket, blankets NOUN ① a large rectangle of thick cloth that is put on a bed to keep people warm. ②A blanket of something such as snow is a thick covering of it.

blare, blares, blaring, blared VERB To blare means to make a loud, unpleasant noise • The radio blared pop music.

blaspheme, blasphemes, blaspheming, blasphemed VERB When people blaspheme, they are disrespectful about God or religion.
WORD HISTORY: from Greek *blapsis* meaning 'evil' and *phēmein* meaning 'to speak'

blasphemy, blasphemies NOUN Blasphemy is speech or behaviour that shows disrespect for God or religion. **blasphemous** ADJECTIVE

blast, blasts, blasting, blasted VERB ①When people blast a hole in something they make a hole with an explosion. ▶ NOUN ②a big explosion, especially one caused by a bomb. ③a sudden strong rush of wind or air.

blatant ADJECTIVE If you describe something you think is bad as blatant, you mean that rather than hide it, those responsible actually seem to be making it obvious • a blatant disregard for the law.

blaze, blazes, blazing, blazed NOUN ① a large, hot fire. ②A blaze of light or colour is a great or strong amount of it • a blaze of red. ③A blaze of publicity or attention is a lot of it. ▶ VERB ④ If something blazes, it burns or shines brightly.

blazer, blazers NOUN a kind of jacket, often in the colours of a school or sports team.

bleach, bleaches, bleaching, bleached VERB ①To bleach material or hair means to make it white, usually by using a chemical. ▶ NOUN ②Bleach is a chemical that is used to make material white or to clean thoroughly and kill germs.

bleak, bleaker, bleakest ADJECTIVE ① If a situation is bleak, it is bad and seems unlikely to improve. ②If a place is bleak, it is cold, bare and exposed to the wind.

bleary, blearier, bleariest ADJECTIVE
If your eyes are bleary, they are red
and watery, usually because you are
tired.

bleat, bleats, bleating, bleated VERB
①When sheep or goats bleat, they
make a high-pitched cry. ▸NOUN
②the high-pitched cry that a sheep
or goat makes.

bleed, bleeds, bleeding, bled VERB
When you bleed, you lose blood as a
result of an injury.

bleep, bleeps NOUN a short
high-pitched sound made by an
electrical device such as an alarm.

blemish, blemishes NOUN a mark
that spoils the appearance of
something.

blend, blends, blending, blended
VERB ①When you blend substances,
you mix them together to form a
single substance. ②When colours or
sounds blend, they combine in a
pleasing way. ▸NOUN ③A blend of
things is a mixture of them,
especially one that is pleasing. ④a
word formed by joining together the
beginning and the end of two other
words; for example, 'brunch' is a
blend of 'breakfast' and 'lunch'.

blended family, blended families
NOUN a family unit consisting of two
parents who have been married
before and the children of their
previous marriages.

blender, blenders NOUN a machine
used for mixing liquids and foods at
high speed.

bless, blesses, blessing, blessed or
blest VERB When a priest blesses
people or things, he or she asks for
God's protection for them.
WORD HISTORY: from Old English
blædsian meaning 'to sprinkle with
sacrificial blood'

blessed [Said _blest_] ADJECTIVE If

someone is blessed with a particular
quality or skill, they have it • _He was
blessed with a sense of humour._

blessing, blessings NOUN
①something good that you are
thankful for • _Good health is the
greatest blessing._ ▸PHRASE ②If
something is done **with someone's
blessing**, they approve of it and
support it.

blew the past tense of **blow**.

blight, blights, blighting, blighted
NOUN ①something that damages or
spoils other things • _the blight of the
recession._ ▸VERB ②When something
is blighted, it is seriously harmed
• _His life had been blighted by sickness._

blind, blinder, blindest; blinds,
blinding, blinded ADJECTIVE
①Someone who is blind cannot see.
②If someone is blind to a particular
fact, they are not aware of it. ▸VERB
③If something blinds you, you
become unable to see, either for a
short time or permanently. ▸NOUN
④a roll of cloth or paper that you pull
down over a window to keep out the
light. **blindly** ADVERB **blindness**
NOUN

blindfold, blindfolds, blindfolding,
blindfolded NOUN ①a strip of cloth
tied over someone's eyes so that they
cannot see. ▸VERB ②To blindfold
someone means to cover their eyes
with a strip of cloth.

blinding ADJECTIVE A blinding light is
so bright that it hurts your eyes
• _There was a blinding flash._

blindingly ADVERB (informal) If
something is blindingly obvious, it is
very obvious indeed.

bling, blinger, blingest (informal)
NOUN ①jewellery that looks
expensive in a vulgar way.
▸ADJECTIVE ②flashy; expensive-
looking in a vulgar way.

a b c d e f g h i j k l m n o p q r s t u v w x y z

blink, blinks, blinking, blinked VERB
When you blink, you close your eyes
rapidly for a moment. Blinking is an
involuntary action that keeps the
eyes moist.

blinkers PLURAL NOUN Blinkers are
two pieces of leather placed at the
side of a horse's eyes so that it can
only see straight ahead.

bliss NOUN Bliss is a state of complete
happiness. **blissful** ADJECTIVE
blissfully ADVERB

blister, blisters, blistering, blistered
NOUN ① a small bubble on your skin
containing watery liquid, caused by a
burn or rubbing. ▶ VERB ② If
someone's skin blisters, blisters
appear on it as result of burning or
rubbing.

blistering ADJECTIVE ① Blistering
heat is very hot. ② A blistering
remark expresses great anger or
criticism.

blithe, blither, blithest ADJECTIVE
casual and done without serious
thought • *a blithe disregard for their
safety*. **blithely** ADVERB

blitz, blitzes, blitzing, blitzed NOUN
① HISTORY a bombing attack by
enemy aircraft on a city. ② a sudden
intensive attack or concerted effort.
▶ VERB ③ HISTORY When a city is
blitzed, it is bombed by aircraft and is
damaged or destroyed.

blizzard, blizzards NOUN a heavy
snowstorm with strong winds.

bloated ADJECTIVE Something that is
bloated is much larger than normal,
often because there is a lot of liquid
or gas inside it.

blob, blobs NOUN a small amount of a
thick or sticky substance.

bloc, blocs NOUN A group of countries
or political parties with similar aims
acting together is often called a bloc
• *the world's largest trading bloc*.

block, blocks, blocking, blocked
NOUN ① A block of flats or offices is a
large building containing flats or
offices. ② In a town, a block is an
area of land with streets on all its
sides • *He lives a few blocks down*. ③ A
block of something is a large
rectangular piece of it. ▶ VERB ④ To
block a road or channel means to put
something across it so that nothing
can get through. ⑤ If something
blocks your view, it is in the way and
prevents you from seeing what you
want to see. ⑥ If someone blocks
something, they prevent it from
happening • *The council blocked his
plans*.
SIMILAR WORDS: ③ bar, chunk, piece
④ obstruct ⑤ obstruct ⑥ obstruct

blockade, blockades, blockading,
blockaded NOUN ① an action that
prevents goods from reaching a
place. ▶ VERB ② When a place is
blockaded, supplies are prevented
from reaching it.

blockage, blockages NOUN When
there is a blockage in a pipe or tunnel,
something is clogging it.
SIMILAR WORDS: impediment,
obstruction, stoppage

blockbuster, blockbusters NOUN
(*informal*) a film or book that is very
popular and successful.

blog, blogs, blogging, blogged NOUN
① a person's online diary that he or
she puts on the internet so that other
people can read it. ▶ VERB ② If you
blog, you write a blog. **blogging**
NOUN

blogger, bloggers NOUN a person
who keeps a blog.

bloke, blokes NOUN (*informal*) a man.

blonde, blondes; also spelt **blond**,
blonds; blonder, blondest
ADJECTIVE ① Blonde hair is pale
yellow in colour. The spelling 'blond' is

used when referring to men. ▶ NOUN ②A blonde, or blond, is a person with light-coloured hair.

blood NOUN ① Blood is the red liquid that is pumped by the heart round the bodies of human beings and other mammals. ▶ PHRASE ②If something cruel is done **in cold blood**, it is done deliberately and without showing any emotion.

bloodhound, bloodhounds NOUN A bloodhound is a large dog with an excellent sense of smell. Bloodhounds were used to follow fugitives or to find people when they were lost.

bloodless ADJECTIVE ①If someone's face or skin is bloodless, it is very pale. ②In a bloodless coup or revolution, nobody is killed.

blood pressure NOUN Your blood pressure is a measure of the force with which your blood is being pumped round your body.

bloodshed NOUN When there is bloodshed, people are killed or wounded.

bloodshot ADJECTIVE If a person's eyes are bloodshot, the white parts have become red.

blood sport, blood sports NOUN any sport that involves deliberately killing or injuring animals.

bloodstained ADJECTIVE covered with blood.

bloodstream NOUN the flow of blood through your body.

bloodthirsty ADJECTIVE Someone who is bloodthirsty enjoys using or watching violence.

blood transfusion, blood transfusions NOUN a process in which blood is injected into the body of someone who has lost a lot of blood.

blood vessel, blood vessels NOUN Blood vessels are the narrow tubes in your body through which your blood flows.

bloody, bloodier, bloodiest ADJECTIVE or ADVERB ①'Bloody' is a common swearword, used to express anger or annoyance. ▶ ADJECTIVE ②A bloody event is one in which a lot of people are killed • *a bloody revolution*. ③Bloody also means covered with blood • *a bloody gash on his head*.

bloom, blooms, blooming, bloomed NOUN ①a flower on a plant. ▶ VERB ②When a plant blooms, it produces flowers. ③When something like a feeling blooms, it grows • *Romance can bloom where you least expect it*.

blossom, blossoms, blossoming, blossomed NOUN ①Blossom is the growth of flowers that appears on a tree before the fruit. ▶ VERB ②When a tree blossoms, it produces blossom.

blot, blots, blotting, blotted NOUN ①a drop of ink that has been spilled on a surface. ②A blot on someone's reputation is a mistake or piece of bad behaviour that spoils their reputation. **blot out** VERB To blot something out means to be in front of it and prevent it from being seen • *The smoke blotted out the sky*.

blotch, blotches NOUN a stain or a patch of a different colour. **blotchy** ADJECTIVE

blouse, blouses NOUN a light shirt, worn by a girl or a woman.

blow, blows, blowing, blew, blown VERB ①When the wind blows, the air moves. ②If something blows or is blown somewhere, the wind moves it there. ③If you blow a whistle or horn, you make a sound by blowing into it. ▶ NOUN ④If you receive a blow, someone or something hits you. ⑤something that makes you very disappointed or unhappy • *Marc's death was a terrible blow*.

a
b
c
d
e
f
g
h
i
j
k
l
m
n
o
p
q
r
s
t
u
v
w
x
y
z

blow up VERB ① To blow something up means to destroy it with an explosion. ② To blow up a balloon or a tyre means to fill it with air.

blubber NOUN The blubber of animals such as whales and seals is the layer of fat that protects them from the cold.

bludge, bludges, bludging, bludged VERB (*informal*) ① In Australian and New Zealand English, to bludge is to scrounge or cadge. ② In Australian and New Zealand English, to bludge is also to avoid work or responsibilities.

bludgeon, bludgeons, bludgeoning, bludgeoned VERB To bludgeon someone means to hit them several times with a heavy object.

blue, bluer, bluest; blues ADJECTIVE or NOUN ① Blue is the colour of the sky on a clear, sunny day. ▶ PHRASE ② If something happens **out of the blue**, it happens suddenly and unexpectedly. **bluish**; also spelt **blueish** ADJECTIVE

bluebell, bluebells NOUN a woodland plant with blue, bell-shaped flowers.

bluebottle, bluebottles NOUN ① a large fly with a shiny dark-blue body. ② In Australia and New Zealand, a bluebottle is also a small stinging jellyfish.

blue-collar ADJECTIVE Blue-collar workers do physical work as opposed to office work.

blueprint, blueprints NOUN a plan of how something is expected to work • *the blueprint for a successful school career.*

blues NOUN The blues is a type of music which is similar to jazz, but is always slow and sad.

Bluetooth NOUN Bluetooth is a technology that allows computers, mobile phones and other devices to communicate with each other without being connected by wires.

bluff, bluffs, bluffing, bluffed NOUN ① an attempt to make someone wrongly believe that you are in a strong position. ▶ VERB ② If you are bluffing, you are trying to make someone believe that you are in a position of strength.

blunder, blunders, blundering, blundered VERB ① If you blunder, you make a silly mistake. ▶ NOUN ② a silly mistake.

blunt, blunter, bluntest ADJECTIVE ① A blunt object has a rounded point or edge, rather than a sharp one. ② If you are blunt, you say exactly what you think, without trying to be polite.
SIMILAR WORDS: ② forthright, outspoken, straightforward

blur, blurs, blurring, blurred NOUN ① a shape or area which you cannot see clearly because it has no distinct outline or because it is moving very fast. ▶ VERB ② To blur the differences between things means to make them no longer clear • *The dreams blurred confusingly with her memories.* **blurred** ADJECTIVE

Blu-Ray, Blu-Rays NOUN (*trademark*) a type of disk that is used for storing digital information such as high-definition video.

blurt out, blurts out, blurting out, blurted out VERB If you blurt something out, you say it suddenly, after trying to keep it a secret.

blush, blushes, blushing, blushed VERB ① If you blush, your face becomes red, because you are embarrassed or ashamed. ▶ NOUN ② the red colour on someone's face when they are embarrassed or ashamed.

bluster, blusters, blustering, blustered VERB ①When someone blusters, they behave aggressively because they are angry or frightened. ▶ NOUN ②Bluster is aggressive behaviour by someone who is angry or frightened.

blustery ADJECTIVE Blustery weather is rough and windy.

BMI NOUN an index used to define whether a person is overweight or underweight, calculated by height and weight. BMI is an abbreviation for 'body mass index'.

boa, boas NOUN ①A boa, or a boa constrictor, is a large snake that kills its prey by coiling round it and crushing it. ②a long thin scarf of feathers or fur.

boar, boars NOUN a male wild pig, or a male domestic pig used for breeding.

board, boards, boarding, boarded NOUN ①a long, flat piece of wood. ②the group of people who control a company or organisation. ③Board is the meals provided when you stay somewhere • *The price includes full board.* ▶ VERB ④If you board a ship or aircraft, you get on it or in it. ▶ PHRASE ⑤If you are **on board** a ship or aircraft, you are on it or in it.

SPELLING TIP
Do not confuse the spellings of *board* and *bored*: *The coin slipped between the boards in the kitchen floor; Lucy was bored without anyone to play with.*

---

boarder, boarders NOUN a pupil who lives at school during the term.

boarding school, boarding schools NOUN a school where the pupils live during the term.

boardroom, boardrooms NOUN a room where the board of a company meets.

boast, boasts, boasting, boasted VERB ①If you boast about your possessions or achievements, you talk about them proudly. ▶ NOUN ②something that you say which shows that you are proud of what you own or have done.
SIMILAR WORDS: ①blow your own trumpet, brag, crow

boastful ADJECTIVE tending to brag about things.

boat, boats NOUN a small vehicle for travelling across water.

bob, bobs, bobbing, bobbed VERB ①When something bobs, it moves up and down. ▶ NOUN ②a woman's hair style in which her hair is cut level with her chin.

bobbin, bobbins NOUN a small round object on which thread or wool is wound.

bobby, bobbies NOUN (*old-fashioned*, *informal*) A bobby is a police officer. Bobbies were named after Robert Peel, who founded the Metropolitan Police Force in 1828.

bobotie [*Said ba-boot-ee*] NOUN Bobotie is a South African dish of curried minced meat with a topping of beaten egg baked to a crust.

bode, bodes, boding, boded PHRASE (*literary*) If something **bodes ill**, or **bodes well**, it makes you think that something bad, or good, will happen.

bodice, bodices NOUN the upper part of a dress.

bodily ADJECTIVE ①relating to the body • *bodily contact.* ▶ ADVERB ②involving the whole of someone's body • *He was carried bodily up the steps.*

body, bodies NOUN ①Your body is either all your physical parts, or just the main part not including your head, arms and legs. ②a person's dead body. ③the main part of a car

a
b
c
d
e
f
g
h
i
j
k
l
m
n
o
p
q
r
s
t
u
v
w
x
y
z

or aircraft, not including the engine.
④A body of people is also an
organised group.
SIMILAR WORDS: ① build, figure,
form, physique

bodyguard, bodyguards NOUN a
person employed to protect
someone.

body image NOUN PSHE Your body
image is the idea that you have about
how your own body looks.

bodywork NOUN the outer part of a
motor vehicle.

boer, boers [Said boh-er] NOUN In
South Africa, a boer is a white farmer,
especially one who is descended
from the Dutch people who went to
live in South Africa.

boerewors [Said boo-rih-vorse] NOUN
In South Africa, boerewors is a type of
meat sausage.

bog, bogs NOUN an area of land which
is always wet and spongy.

boggle, boggles, boggling, boggled
VERB If your mind boggles at
something, you find it difficult to
imagine or understand.

bogus ADJECTIVE not genuine • a
bogus doctor.

bohemian [Said boh-hee-mee-an]
ADJECTIVE Someone who is
bohemian does not behave in the
same way as most other people in
society, and is usually involved in the
arts.

boil, boils, boiling, boiled VERB
①When a hot liquid boils, bubbles
appear in it and it starts to give off
steam. ②When you boil a kettle, you
heat it until the water in it boils.
③When you boil food, you cook it in
boiling water. ▶NOUN ④a red
swelling on your skin.

boiler, boilers NOUN a piece of
equipment which burns fuel to
provide hot water.

boiling ADJECTIVE (informal) very hot.

boiling point, boiling points
NOUN SCIENCE the temperature at
which a liquid starts to boil and turn
to vapour.

boisterous ADJECTIVE Someone who
is boisterous is noisy and lively.
SIMILAR WORDS: loud, noisy, rowdy,
unruly

bold, bolder, boldest ADJECTIVE
①confident and not shy or
embarrassed • He was not bold enough
to ask them. ② not afraid of risk or
danger. ③ clear and noticeable • bold
colours. **boldly** ADVERB **boldness**
NOUN

bollard, bollards NOUN a short, thick
post used to keep vehicles out of a
road.

bolster, bolsters, bolstering,
bolstered VERB To bolster
something means to support it or
make it stronger • She relied on others
to bolster her self-esteem.

bolt, bolts, bolting, bolted NOUN ①a
metal bar that you slide across a door
or window in order to fasten it. ②a
metal object which screws into a nut
and is used to fasten things together.
▶VERB ③If you bolt a door or
window, you fasten it using a bolt. If
you bolt things together, you fasten
them together using a bolt. ④To bolt
means to escape or run away. ⑤To
bolt food means to eat it very quickly.

bomb, bombs, bombing, bombed
NOUN ①a container filled with
material that explodes when it hits
something or is set off by a timer.
▶VERB ②When a place is bombed, it
is attacked with bombs.

bombard, bombards, bombarding,
bombarded VERB ①To bombard a
place means to attack it with heavy
gunfire or bombs. ②If you are
bombarded with something you are

made to face a great deal of it • *I was bombarded with criticism*.

bombardment NOUN

bomber, bombers NOUN an aircraft that drops bombs.

bombshell, bombshells NOUN a sudden piece of shocking or upsetting news.

bona fide [*Said boh-na fie-dee*] ADJECTIVE genuine • *We are happy to donate to bona fide charities*.
WORD HISTORY: a Latin expression meaning 'in good faith'

bonanza, bonanzas NOUN An event or thing from which people suddenly become rich is called a bonanza.
WORD HISTORY: a Spanish word literally meaning 'calm sea' and therefore 'good luck'

bond, bonds, bonding, bonded NOUN ① a close relationship between people. ② (*literary*) Bonds are chains or ropes used to tie a prisoner up. ③ a certificate which records that you have lent money to a business and that it will repay you the loan with interest. ④ SCIENCE In chemistry, a bond is the means by which atoms or groups of atoms are combined in molecules. ⑤ Bonds are also feelings or obligations that force you to behave in a particular way • *the social bonds of community*. ▶VERB ⑥ When two things bond or are bonded, they become closely linked or attached.
SIMILAR WORDS: ① connection, link, tie

bondage NOUN Bondage is the condition of being someone's slave.

bone, bones NOUN Bones are the hard parts that form the framework of a person's or animal's body.
boneless ADJECTIVE

bonfire, bonfires NOUN a large fire made outdoors, often to burn rubbish.

WORD HISTORY: from 'bone' + 'fire'; bones were used as fuel in the Middle Ages

bonnet, bonnets NOUN ① the metal cover over a car's engine. ② a baby's or woman's hat tied under the chin.

bonny, bonnier, bonniest ADJECTIVE In Scotland and Northern England, a term meaning nice to look at.

bonus, bonuses NOUN ① an amount of money added to your usual pay. ② Something that is a bonus is a good thing that you get in addition to something else • *The view from the hotel was an added bonus*.

bony, bonier, boniest ADJECTIVE Bony people or animals are thin, with very little flesh covering their bones.

boo, boos, booing, booed NOUN ① a shout of disapproval. ▶VERB ② When people boo, they shout 'boo' to show their disapproval.

boobook, boobooks NOUN a small brown Australian owl with a spotted back and wings.

book, books, booking, booked NOUN ① a number of pages held together inside a cover. ▶VERB ② When you book something such as a room, you arrange to have it or use it at a particular time.

bookcase, bookcases NOUN a piece of furniture with shelves for books.

bookie, bookies NOUN (*informal*) a bookmaker.

booking, bookings NOUN an arrangement to book something such as a hotel room.

book-keeping NOUN Book-keeping is the keeping of a record of the money spent and received by a business.

booklet, booklets NOUN a small book with a paper cover.

a b c d e f g h i j k l m n o p q r s t u v w x y z

A
B
C
D
E
F
G
H
I
J
K
L
M
N
O
P
Q
R
S
T
U
V
W
X
Y
Z

bookmaker, bookmakers NOUN a person who makes a living by taking people's bets and paying them when they win.

bookmark, bookmarks, bookmarking, bookmarked NOUN ① a piece of card which you put between the pages of a book to mark your place. ② In computing, a bookmark is the address of a website that you put into a list on your computer so that you can return to it easily. ▶ VERB ③ If you bookmark a website, you put its address into a list on your computer so that you can return to it easily.

Boolean ADJECTIVE ICT A Boolean system is one which allows only two possible positions, such as 'Yes' or 'No'.

boom, booms, booming, boomed NOUN ① a rapid increase in something • the baby boom. ② a loud deep echoing sound. ▶ VERB ③ When something booms, it increases rapidly • Sales are booming. ④ To boom means to make a loud deep echoing sound.

boomerang, boomerangs NOUN a curved wooden missile that can be thrown so that it returns to the thrower, originally used as a weapon by Aboriginal Australians.

boon, boons NOUN Something that is a boon makes life better or easier • Subtitles are a boon for deaf people.

boost, boosts, boosting, boosted VERB ① To boost something means to cause it to improve or increase • The campaign had boosted sales. ▶ NOUN ② an improvement or increase • a boost to the economy. **booster** NOUN

boot, boots, booting, booted NOUN ① Boots are strong shoes that come up over your ankle and sometimes your calf. ② the covered space in a

car, usually at the back, for carrying things in. ▶ VERB ③ (informal) If you boot something, you kick it.
▶ PHRASE ④ To boot means also or in addition • The story was compelling and well written to boot.

booth, booths NOUN ① a small partly enclosed area • a photo booth. ② a stall where you can buy goods.

booty NOUN Booty is valuable things taken from a place, especially by soldiers after a battle.

booze, boozes, boozing, boozed (informal) NOUN ① Booze is alcoholic drink. ▶ VERB ② When people booze, they drink alcohol. **boozer** NOUN **boozy** ADJECTIVE

border, borders, bordering, bordered NOUN ① the dividing line between two places or things. ② a strip or band round the edge of something • plain tiles with a bright border. ③ a long flower bed in a garden. ▶ VERB ④ To border something means to form a boundary along the side of it • Tall poplar trees bordered the fields.

borderline ADJECTIVE only just acceptable as a member of a class or group • a borderline case.

bore, bores, boring, bored VERB ① If something bores you, you find it dull and not at all interesting. ② If you bore a hole in something, you make it using a tool such as a drill. ③ Bore is also the past tense of **bear**. ▶ NOUN ④ someone or something that bores you.

bored ADJECTIVE If you are bored, you are impatient because you do not find something interesting or because you have nothing to do.

GRAMMAR TIP
You can say that you are bored with or bored by someone or something, but you should not say bored of.

SPELLING TIP
Do not confuse the spellings of *bored* and *board*: *Lucy was bored without anyone to play with*; *The coin slipped between the boards in the kitchen floor.*

boredom NOUN a lack of interest.

boring ADJECTIVE dull and lacking interest.
SIMILAR WORDS: dull, tedious, uninteresting

born VERB ① When a baby is born, it comes out of its mother's womb at the beginning of its life. ▸ ADJECTIVE ② You use 'born' to mean that someone has a particular quality from birth • *He was a born pessimist.*

borne the past participle of **bear**.

borough, boroughs [*Said bur-uh*] NOUN a town, or a district within a large town, that has its own council.

borrow, borrows, borrowing, borrowed VERB If you borrow something that belongs to someone else, they let you have it for a period of time. **borrower** NOUN

GRAMMAR TIP
You *borrow* something *from* a person, not *off* them.

USAGE NOTE
Do not confuse *borrow* and *lend*. If you *borrow* something, you get it from another person for a while; if you *lend* something, someone gets it from you for a while.

Bosnian, Bosnians ADJECTIVE ① belonging or relating to Bosnia. ▸ NOUN ② someone who comes from Bosnia.

bosom, bosoms NOUN ① A woman's bosom is her chest. ▸ ADJECTIVE ② A bosom friend is a very close friend.

boss, bosses, bossing, bossed NOUN ① Someone's boss is the person in charge of the place where they work.
▸ VERB ② If someone bosses you around, they keep telling you what to do.

bossy, bossier, bossiest ADJECTIVE A bossy person enjoys telling other people what to do. **bossiness** NOUN
SIMILAR WORDS: dictatorial, domineering, overbearing

bot, bots NOUN a computer program that carries out tasks for other programs or users.

botany NOUN Botany is the scientific study of plants. **botanic** or **botanical** ADJECTIVE **botanist** NOUN

botch, botches, botching, botched VERB (*informal*) If you botch something, you do it badly or clumsily.
SIMILAR WORDS: bungle, mess up

both ADJECTIVE or PRONOUN 'Both' is used when saying something about two things or people.

GRAMMAR TIP
You can use *of* after *both*, but it is not essential. *Both the boys* means the same as *both of the boys*.

bother, bothers, bothering, bothered VERB ① If you do not bother to do something, you do not do it because it takes too much effort or it seems unnecessary. ② If something bothers you, you are worried or concerned about it. If you do not bother about it, you are not concerned about it • *She is not bothered about money.* ③ If you bother someone, you interrupt them when they are busy. ▸ NOUN ④ Bother is trouble, fuss or difficulty.
bothersome ADJECTIVE

bottle, bottles, bottling, bottled NOUN ① a glass or plastic container for keeping liquids in. ▸ VERB ② To bottle something means to store it in

A
B
C
D
E
F
G
H
I
J
K
L
M
N
O
P
Q
R
S
T
U
V
W
X
Y
Z

bottles. **bottle up** VERB If you bottle up strong feelings, you do not let yourself think about them.

bottleneck, bottlenecks NOUN a narrow section of road where traffic has to slow down or stop.

bottle store, bottle stores NOUN In Australian, New Zealand and South African English, a bottle store is a shop that sells sealed alcoholic drinks which can be drunk elsewhere.

bottom, bottoms NOUN ① The bottom of something is its lowest part. ② Your bottom is your buttocks. ▶ ADJECTIVE ③ The bottom thing in a series of things is the lowest one. **bottomless** ADJECTIVE

bough, boughs [Rhymes with now] NOUN a large branch of a tree.

bought the past tense and past participle of **buy**.

SPELLING TIP
Do not confuse *bought* and *brought*. *Bought* comes from *buy* and *brought* comes from *bring*.

boulder, boulders NOUN a large rounded rock.

boulevard, boulevards [Said boo-le-vard] NOUN a wide street in a city, usually with trees along each side.

bounce, bounces, bouncing, bounced VERB ① When an object bounces, it springs back from something after hitting it. ② To bounce also means to move up and down • *Her long black hair bounced as she walked*.

SIMILAR WORDS: ① rebound, recoil, ricochet

bouncy, bouncier, bounciest ADJECTIVE ① Someone who is bouncy is lively and enthusiastic. ② Something that is bouncy is capable of bouncing or being

bounced on • *a bouncy ball* • *a bouncy castle*.

bound, bounds, bounding, bounded ADJECTIVE ① If you say that something is bound to happen, you mean that it is certain to happen. ② If a person or a vehicle is bound for a place, they are going there. ③ If someone is bound by an agreement or regulation, they must obey it. ▶ NOUN ④ a large leap. ⑤ (*in plural*) Bounds are limits which restrict or control something • *Their enthusiasm knew no bounds*. ▶ PHRASE ⑥ If a place is **out of bounds**, you are forbidden to go there. ▶ VERB ⑦ When animals or people bound, they move quickly with large leaps • *He bounded up the stairway*. ⑧ Bound is also the past tense and past participle of **bind**.

boundary, boundaries NOUN ① something that indicates the farthest limit of anything • *the city boundary*. ② PSHE The boundaries of an activity are the limits that people think that it should have • *You have every right to set boundaries on what you are comfortable with*.

boundless ADJECTIVE without end or limit • *her boundless energy*.

bountiful ADJECTIVE (*literary*) freely available in large amounts • *a bountiful harvest*.

bounty NOUN ① (*literary*) Bounty is a generous supply • *autumn's bounty of fruits*. ② Someone's bounty is their generosity in giving a lot of something.

bouquet, bouquets [Said boo-kay] NOUN an attractively arranged bunch of flowers.

bout, bouts NOUN ① If you have a bout of something such as an illness, you have it for a short time • *a bout of flu*. ② If you have a bout of doing something, you do it enthusiastically for a short time. ③ a boxing or wrestling match.

boutique, boutiques [Said boo-**teek**] NOUN a small shop that sells fashionable clothes.

bovine ADJECTIVE (technical) relating to cattle.

bow¹, bows, bowing, bowed [Rhymes with **now**] VERB ① When you bow, you bend your body or lower your head as a sign of respect or greeting. ② If you bow to something, you give in to it • He bowed to pressure from his friends. ▸ NOUN ③ the movement you make when you bow. ④ the front part of a ship.

bow², bows [Rhymes with **low**] NOUN ① a knot with two loops and two loose ends. ② a long thin piece of wood with horsehair stretched along it, which you use to play a violin. ③ a long flexible piece of wood used for shooting arrows.

bowel, bowels [Rhymes with **towel**] NOUN Your bowels are the tubes leading from your stomach, through which waste passes before it leaves your body.

bowerbird, bowerbirds NOUN a bird found in Australia, the male of which builds a shelter during courtship.

bowl, bowls, bowling, bowled [Rhymes with **mole**] NOUN ① A bowl is a round container with a wide uncovered top, used for holding liquid or for serving food. ② A bowl is also the hollow, rounded part of something • a toilet bowl • the bowl of his pipe. ③ PE A bowl is a large heavy ball used in the game of bowls or in bowling. ▸ VERB ④ PE In cricket, to bowl means to throw the ball towards the batsman; if a batsman is bowled, or bowled out, their wicket is knocked over by the ball and they are out. **bowler** NOUN

bowling NOUN Bowling is a game in which you roll a heavy ball down a narrow track towards a group of wooden objects called pins and try to knock them down.

bowls NOUN Bowls is a game in which the players try to roll large wooden balls as near as possible to a small ball.

bow tie, bow ties [Rhymes with **low**] NOUN a man's tie in the form of a bow, often worn at formal occasions.

box, boxes, boxing, boxed NOUN ① a container with a firm base and sides and usually a lid. ② On a form, a box is a rectangular space which you have to fill in. ③ In a theatre, a box is a small separate area where a few people can watch the performance together. ▸ VERB ④ To box means to fight someone according to the rules of boxing.

boxer, boxers NOUN ① a person who boxes. ② a type of medium-sized, smooth-haired dog with a flat face.

boxing NOUN Boxing is a sport in which two people fight using their fists, wearing padded gloves.

box office, box offices NOUN the place where tickets are sold in a theatre or cinema.

boy, boys NOUN a male child. **boyhood** NOUN **boyish** ADJECTIVE SIMILAR WORDS: lad, youngster, youth

boycott, boycotts, boycotting, boycotted VERB ① If you boycott an organisation or event, you refuse to have anything to do with it. ▸ NOUN ② the boycotting of an organisation or event • a boycott of the elections. SIMILAR WORDS: ① ban, blacklist, embargo WORD HISTORY: from the name of Captain C.C. Boycott (1832–1897), an Irish land agent, who offended the

A
B
C
D
E
F
G
H
I
J
K
L
M
N
O
P
Q
R
S
T
U
V
W
X
Y
Z

What do Brackets do?

Brackets ( ) enclose material that has been added to the text, but could be omitted and still leave a meaningful sentence. In formal writing this sort of material is usually marked off with commas or dashes, and brackets are used for giving references or translations of foreign phrases:

Buddhism is discussed in Chapter 7

(see pages 152–197).
The boat was called 'La Ardilla Roja' (The Red Squirrel).

Square brackets [ ] are used to enclose remarks and explanations which are inserted by a writer to make a quotation clearer:

The minister said, 'I think that five million [pounds] should do it.'

---

tenants, so that they refused to pay their rents

boyfriend, boyfriends NOUN Someone's boyfriend is the man or boy with whom they are having a romantic relationship.

bra, bras NOUN a piece of underwear worn by a woman to support her breasts.

braaivleis, braaivleises [Said *bry-flayss*] or **braai**, braais NOUN In South African English, a braaivleis is a picnic where meat is cooked on an open fire.

brace, braces, bracing, braced VERB ①When you brace yourself, you stiffen your body to steady yourself • *The ship lurched and he braced himself.* ②If you brace yourself for something unpleasant, you prepare yourself to deal with it • *The country braced itself for an invasion.* ▸ NOUN ③an object fastened to something to straighten or support it • *a neck brace.* ④(in plural) Braces are a pair of straps worn over the shoulders and fastened to the trousers to hold them up.

bracelet, bracelets NOUN a chain or band worn around someone's wrist as an ornament.

bracing ADJECTIVE Something that is bracing makes you feel fit and full of energy • *the bracing sea air.*

bracken NOUN Bracken is a plant like a large fern that grows on hills and in woods.

bracket, brackets NOUN ① ENGLISH Brackets are a pair of written marks, ( ) or [ ], placed round a word or sentence that is not part of the main text, or to show that the items inside the brackets belong together. ②a range between two limits, for example of ages or prices • *the four-figure price bracket.* ③a piece of metal or wood fastened to a wall to support something such as a shelf.

PUNCTUATION TIP
Keep punctuation outside brackets unless it applies to the bracketed section only: *You will need t-shirts (at least three), shorts and sandals; Ali and Anum (have you met her?) will both be at the party.*

---

brag, brags, bragging, bragged VERB When someone brags, they boast about their achievements • *Both leaders bragged they could win by a landslide.*

braggart, braggarts NOUN someone who brags.

Brahma [Said *brah-ma*] PROPER NOUN RE Brahma is a Hindu god and is one of the Trimurti.

Brahman [Said *brah-men*] NOUN RE

In the Hindu religion Brahman is the ultimate and impersonal divine reality of the universe.

brahmin, brahmins [Said brah-min] NOUN RE a member of the highest or priestly caste in Hindu society.

braid, braids, braiding, braided NOUN ① Braid is a strip of decorated cloth used to decorate clothes or curtains. ② a length of hair which has been plaited and tied. ▶ VERB ③ To braid hair or thread means to plait it.

Braille NOUN Braille is a system of printing for blind people in which letters are represented by raised dots that can be felt with the fingers. It was invented by the French inventor Louis Braille in the 19th century.

brain, brains NOUN ① Your brain is the mass of nerve tissue inside your head that controls your body and enables you to think and feel; also used to refer to your mind and the way that you think • *I admired his legal brain.* ② (*in plural*) If you say that someone has brains, you mean that they are very intelligent.

brainchild NOUN (*informal*) Someone's brainchild is something that they have invented or created.

brainwash, brainwashes, brainwashing, brainwashed VERB If people are brainwashed into believing something, they accept it without question because they are told it repeatedly. **brainwashing** NOUN

brainwave, brainwaves NOUN (*informal*) a clever idea you think of suddenly.

brainy, brainier, brainiest ADJECTIVE (*informal*) clever.

braise, braises, braising, braised VERB To braise food means to fry it for a short time, then cook it slowly in a little liquid.

brake, brakes, braking, braked NOUN ① a device for making a vehicle stop or slow down. ▶ VERB ② When a driver brakes, he or she makes a vehicle stop or slow down by using its brakes.

SPELLING TIP
Do not confuse the spellings of *brake* and *break*, or *braking* and *breaking*.

SPELLING TIP
Remember this mnemonic: *there's a rAKE in the brAKEs.*

---

bramble, brambles NOUN a wild, thorny bush that produces blackberries.

bran NOUN Bran is the ground husks that are left over after flour has been made from wheat grains.

branch, branches, branching, branched NOUN ① The branches of a tree are the parts that grow out from its trunk. ② A branch of an organisation is one of a number of its offices or shops. ③ A branch of a subject is one of its areas of study or activity • *specialists in certain branches of medicine.* ▶ VERB ④ A road that branches off from another road splits off from it to lead in a different direction. **branch out** VERB To branch out means to take up an additional pursuit.

brand, brands, branding, branded NOUN ① A brand of something is a particular kind or make of it • *a popular brand of chocolate.* ▶ VERB ② When an animal is branded, a mark is burned on its skin to show who owns it.

brandish, brandishes, brandishing, brandished VERB (*literary*) If you brandish something, you wave it vigorously • *He brandished his sword over his head.*

a
b
c
d
e
f
g
h
i
j
k
l
m
n
o
p
q
r
s
t
u
v
w
x
y
z

brand-new ADJECTIVE completely new.

brandy, brandies NOUN a strong alcoholic drink, usually made from wine.

WORD HISTORY: from Dutch *brandewijn* meaning 'burnt wine'

brash, brasher, brashest ADJECTIVE If someone is brash, they are overconfident or rather rude.

brass NOUN ① Brass is a yellow-coloured metal made from copper and zinc. ② In an orchestra, the brass or brass section consists of instruments made of brass such as trumpets and trombones.

brassière, brassières NOUN (formal) a bra.

brat, brats NOUN (informal) A badly behaved child may be referred to as a brat.

bravado [Said bra-*vah*-doh] NOUN Bravado is a display of courage intended to impress other people.

brave, braver, bravest; braves, braving, braved ADJECTIVE ① A brave person is willing to do dangerous things and does not show any fear. ▶ VERB ② If you brave an unpleasant or dangerous situation, you face up to it in order to do something • *His fans braved the rain to hear him sing.* **bravely** ADVERB
SIMILAR WORDS: ① courageous, daring, fearless, plucky

bravery NOUN the quality of being courageous.

bravo INTERJECTION People shout 'Bravo!' to express appreciation when something has been done well.

brawl, brawls, brawling, brawled NOUN ① a rough fight. ▶ VERB ② When people brawl, they take part in a rough fight.

brawn NOUN Brawn is physical strength. **brawny** ADJECTIVE

bray, brays, braying, brayed VERB ① When a donkey brays, it makes a loud, harsh sound. ▶ NOUN ② the sound a donkey makes.

brazen ADJECTIVE When someone's behaviour is brazen, they do not care if other people think they are behaving wrongly. **brazenly** ADVERB

brazier, braziers NOUN a metal container in which coal or charcoal is burned to keep people warm out of doors.

Brazilian, Brazilians ADJECTIVE ① belonging or relating to Brazil. ▶ NOUN ② someone who comes from Brazil.

breach, breaches, breaching, breached VERB ① (formal) If you breach an agreement or law, you break it. ② To breach a barrier means to make a gap in it • *The river breached its banks.* ▶ NOUN ③ A breach of an agreement or law is an action that breaks it • *a breach of contract.* ④ a gap or break.
SIMILAR WORDS: ③ contravention, infringement, violation

bread NOUN a food made from flour and water, usually raised with yeast, and baked.

breadth NOUN The breadth of something is the distance between its two sides.

breadwinner, breadwinners NOUN the person who earns the money in a family.

break, breaks, breaking, broke, broken VERB ① When an object breaks, it is damaged and separates into pieces. ② If you break a rule or promise, you fail to keep it. ③ When a boy's voice breaks, it becomes permanently deeper. ④ When a wave breaks, it falls and becomes foam. ▶ NOUN ⑤ a short period during which you rest or do something different. **breakable** ADJECTIVE

break down VERB ①When a machine or a vehicle breaks down, it stops working. ②When a discussion or relationship breaks down, it ends because of problems or disagreements. **break up** VERB If something breaks up, it ends • *The marriage broke up after a year.*
SIMILAR WORDS: ①crack, fracture, separate, snap ②breach, contravene, disobey, violate

---

SPELLING TIP
Do not confuse the spellings of *break* and *brake*, or *breaking* and *braking*.

SPELLING TIP
Remember this mnemonic: *you'll brEAK that Electrical Aerial, Kitty.*

---

breakage, breakages NOUN the act of breaking something or a thing that has been broken.

breakaway ADJECTIVE A breakaway group is one that has separated from a larger group.

breakdown, breakdowns NOUN ①The breakdown of something such as a system is its failure • *a breakdown in communications.* ②the same as a nervous breakdown. ③If a driver has a breakdown, their car stops working. ④A breakdown of something complex is a summary of its important points • *He demanded a breakdown of the costs.*

breaker, breakers NOUN Breakers are big sea waves.

breakfast, breakfasts NOUN the first meal of the day.

break-in, break-ins NOUN the illegal entering of a building, especially by a burglar.

breakneck ADJECTIVE (*informal*) Someone or something that is travelling at breakneck speed is travelling dangerously fast.

breakthrough, breakthroughs NOUN a sudden important development • *a medical breakthrough.*

breakwater, breakwaters NOUN a wall extending into the sea which protects a coast from the force of the waves.

bream, breams NOUN an edible fish.

breast, breasts NOUN ①A woman's breasts are the two soft, fleshy parts on her chest, which secrete milk after she has had a baby. ②(*literary or old-fashioned*) The human breast is the upper front part of the body, sometimes regarded as the place where emotions are felt • *His breast was red with blood* • *I felt hope rise in my breast.*

breaststroke NOUN PE
Breaststroke is a swimming stroke in which you lie on your front, moving your arms horizontally through the water and kicking both legs at the same time.

breath, breaths NOUN ①Your breath is the air you take into your lungs and let out again when you breathe.
▶ PHRASE ②If you are **out of breath**, you are breathing with difficulty after doing something energetic. ③If you say something **under your breath**, you say it in a very quiet voice.

SPELLING TIP
Do not confuse the spellings of the noun *breath* and the verb *breathe*: *I took a breath and then started to explain; Breathe deeply and count to ten.*

---

breathe, breathes, breathing, breathed VERB When you breathe, you take air into your lungs and let it out again.

SPELLING TIP
Do not confuse the spellings of the verb *breathe* and the noun *breath*:

Breathe deeply and count to ten; I took a breath and then started to explain.

breathless ADJECTIVE If you are breathless, you are breathing fast or with difficulty. **breathlessly** ADVERB **breathlessness** NOUN

breathtaking ADJECTIVE If you say that something is breathtaking, you mean that it is very beautiful or exciting.

bred the past tense and past participle of **breed**.

breeches [Said *brit-chiz*] PLURAL NOUN Breeches are trousers reaching to just below the knee, worn especially for riding.

breed, breeds, breeding, bred NOUN ① A breed of a species of domestic animal is a particular type of it. ▸ VERB ② Someone who breeds animals or plants keeps them in order to produce more animals or plants with particular qualities. ③ When animals breed, they mate and produce offspring.
SIMILAR WORDS: ③ multiply, procreate, reproduce

breeze, breezes NOUN a gentle wind.

brevity NOUN (*formal*) Brevity means shortness • *the brevity of his report*.

brew, brews, brewing, brewed VERB ① If you brew tea or coffee, you make it in a pot by pouring hot water over it. ② To brew beer means to make it, by boiling and fermenting malt. ③ If an unpleasant situation is brewing, it is about to happen • *Another scandal is brewing*. **brewer** NOUN

brewery, breweries NOUN a place where beer is made.

briar, briars NOUN a wild rose that grows on a dense prickly bush.

Brexit NOUN 'Brexit' is used to refer to the United Kingdom leaving the European Union.

bribe, bribes, bribing, bribed NOUN ① a gift or money given to an official to persuade them to make a favourable decision. ▸ VERB ② To bribe someone means to give them a bribe. **bribery** NOUN

bric-a-brac NOUN Bric-a-brac consists of small ornaments or pieces of furniture of no great value.
WORD HISTORY: from an obsolete French phrase *à bric et à brac* meaning 'at random'

brick, bricks NOUN Bricks are rectangular blocks of baked clay used in building.

bricklayer, bricklayers NOUN a person whose job is to build with bricks.

bride, brides NOUN a woman who is getting married or who has just got married. **bridal** ADJECTIVE

bridegroom, bridegrooms NOUN a man who is getting married or who has just got married.

bridesmaid, bridesmaids NOUN a woman who helps and accompanies a bride on her wedding day.

bridge, bridges NOUN ① a structure built over a river, road or railway so that vehicles and people can cross. ② the platform from which a ship is steered and controlled. ③ the hard ridge at the top of your nose. ④ Bridge is a card game for four players based on whist.

bridle, bridles NOUN a set of straps round a horse's head and mouth, which the rider uses to control the horse.

brief, briefer, briefest; briefs, briefing, briefed ADJECTIVE ① Something that is brief lasts only a short time. ▸ VERB ② DGT When you brief someone on a task, you give them all the necessary instructions and information about it. **briefly** ADVERB

SIMILAR WORDS: ①fleeting, momentary, quick, short

briefcase, briefcases NOUN a small flat case for carrying papers.

briefing, briefings NOUN a meeting at which information and instructions are given.

brier another spelling of **briar**.

brigade, brigades NOUN an army unit consisting of three battalions.

brigadier, brigadiers [Said brig-ad-*ear*] NOUN an army officer of the rank immediately above colonel.

brigalow, brigalows NOUN a type of Australian acacia tree that grows in the bush.

bright, brighter, brightest ADJECTIVE ①strong and startling • *a bright light*. ②clever • *my brightest student*. ③cheerful • *a bright smile*. **brightly** ADVERB **brightness** NOUN SIMILAR WORDS: ①brilliant, dazzling, shining, vivid

brighten, brightens, brightening, brightened VERB ①If something brightens, it becomes brighter • *The weather had brightened*. ②If someone brightens, they suddenly look happier. **brighten up** VERB To brighten something up means to make it more attractive and cheerful.

brilliant ADJECTIVE ①A brilliant light or colour is extremely bright. ②A brilliant person is extremely clever. ③A brilliant career is extremely successful. **brilliantly** ADVERB **brilliance** NOUN

brim, brims NOUN ①the wide part of a hat that sticks outwards at the bottom. ▶ PHRASE ②If a container is filled **to the brim**, it is filled right to the top.

brine NOUN Brine is salt water.

bring, brings, bringing, brought VERB ①If you bring something or someone with you when you go to a place, you take them with you • *You can bring a friend to the party*. ②To bring something to a particular state means to cause it to be like that • *Bring the vegetables to the boil*.

bring about VERB To bring something about means to cause it to happen • *We must try to bring about a better world*. **bring off** VERB If you bring off something difficult, you succeed in doing it. **bring out** VERB ①To bring out a new product means to produce it and offer it for sale. ②If something brings out a particular kind of behaviour, it causes it to occur • *Sunny days seem to bring out the best in us*. **bring up** VERB ①To bring up children means to look after them while they grow up. ②If you bring up a subject, you introduce it into the conversation • *She brought up the subject at dinner*.

brinjal, brinjals NOUN In Indian and South African English, an aubergine.

brink NOUN If you are on the brink of something, you are just about to do it or experience it.

brisk, brisker, briskest ADJECTIVE ①A brisk action is done quickly and energetically • *A brisk walk restores your energy*. ②If someone's manner is brisk, it shows that they want to get things done quickly and efficiently. **briskly** ADVERB **briskness** NOUN

bristle, bristles, bristling, bristled NOUN ①Bristles are strong animal hairs used to make brushes. ▶ VERB ②If the hairs on an animal's body bristle, they rise up, because it is frightened. **bristly** ADJECTIVE

British ADJECTIVE belonging or relating to the United Kingdom of Great Britain and Northern Ireland.

Briton, Britons NOUN someone who comes from the United Kingdom of Great Britain and Northern Ireland.

a
b
c
d
e
f
g
h
i
j
k
l
m
n
o
p
q
r
s
t
u
v
w
x
y
z

brittle ADJECTIVE An object that is brittle is hard but breaks easily.

broach, broaches, broaching, broached VERB When you broach a subject, you introduce it into a discussion.

SPELLING TIP

Do not confuse the spellings of *broach* and *brooch*: *I'm scared to broach the subject of a pay rise; a gold brooch with diamonds and rubies.*

---

broad, broader, broadest ADJECTIVE ① wide • *a broad smile*. ② having many different aspects or concerning many different people • *A broad range of issues was discussed*. ③ general rather than detailed • *the broad concerns of the movement*. ④ If someone has a broad accent, the way that they speak makes it very clear where they come from • *She spoke in a broad Irish accent*.

broadband NOUN Broadband is a digital system used on the internet and in other forms of telecommunication which can process and transfer information input from various sources, such as from telephones, computers or televisions.

broad bean, broad beans NOUN Broad beans are light-green beans with thick flat edible seeds.

broadcast, broadcasts, broadcasting, broadcast NOUN ① a programme or announcement on radio or television. ▶ VERB ② To broadcast something means to send it out by radio waves, so that it can be seen on television or heard on radio. **broadcaster** NOUN **broadcasting** NOUN

broaden, broadens, broadening, broadened VERB ① When something broadens, it becomes wider • *His smile broadened*. ② To broaden something means to cause it to involve more things or concern more people • *We must broaden the scope of this job*.

broadly ADVERB true to a large extent or in most cases • *There are broadly two schools of thought on this*.

broad-minded ADJECTIVE Someone who is broad-minded does not disapprove of behaviour or attitudes that many other people disapprove of.
SIMILAR WORDS: liberal, open-minded, tolerant

broadsheet, broadsheets NOUN ENGLISH a newspaper with large pages and detailed news stories.

brocade NOUN Brocade is a heavy, expensive material, often made of silk, with a raised pattern.

broccoli NOUN Broccoli is a green vegetable, similar to cauliflower.

brochure, brochures [Said broh-sher] NOUN a booklet which gives information about a product or service.

brogue, brogues [Said broag] NOUN ① a strong accent, especially an Irish one. ② Brogues are thick leather shoes.
WORD HISTORY: from Irish Gaelic bróg meaning 'boot' or 'shoe'

broil, broils, broiling, broiled NOUN In American English, to broil food is to cook it on or under a grill.

broke ① the past tense of **break**. ▶ ADJECTIVE ② (informal) If you are broke, you have no money.

broken ① the past participle of **break**. ▶ ADJECTIVE ② in pieces. ③ not kept.

broker, brokers NOUN a person whose job is to buy and sell shares for other people.

brolga, brolgas NOUN a large grey

Australian crane with a red-and-green head.

brolly, brollies NOUN (*informal*) an umbrella.

bromine NOUN SCIENCE Bromine is a heavy, corrosive liquid element used in fumigants and dyes. Its atomic number is 35 and its symbol is Br.

bronchial tube, bronchial tubes NOUN SCIENCE Your bronchial tubes are the two tubes which connect your windpipe to your lungs.
WORD HISTORY: from Greek *bronkhus* meaning 'windpipe'

bronchiole, bronchioles NOUN SCIENCE The bronchioles are the smallest branches of the bronchial tubes, which usually end in alveoli.

bronchitis NOUN Bronchitis is an illness in which the two tubes which connect your windpipe to your lungs become infected, making you cough.

bronchus, bronchi NOUN SCIENCE one of the two tubes that carry air from your windpipe into your lungs.

bronze NOUN Bronze is a yellowish-brown metal which is a mixture of copper and tin; also the yellowish-brown colour of this metal.

brooch, brooches [Rhymes with *coach*] NOUN a piece of jewellery with a pin at the back for attaching to clothes.

SPELLING TIP
Do not confuse the spellings of *brooch* and *broach*: *a gold brooch with diamonds and rubies; I'm scared to broach the subject of a pay rise.*

brood, broods, brooding, brooded NOUN ① a family of baby birds. ▸ VERB ② If you brood about something, you keep thinking about it in a serious or unhappy way.

brook, brooks NOUN a stream.

broom, brooms NOUN ① a long-handled brush. ② Broom is a shrub with yellow flowers.

broth NOUN Broth is soup, usually with vegetables in it.

brother, brothers NOUN Your brother is a boy or man who has the same parents as you. **brotherly** ADJECTIVE

brotherhood, brotherhoods NOUN ① Brotherhood is the affection and loyalty that brothers or close male friends feel for each other. ② a group of men with common interests or beliefs.

brother-in-law, brothers-in-law NOUN Someone's brother-in-law is the brother of their husband or wife, or their sibling's husband.

brought the past tense and past participle of **bring**.

SPELLING TIP
Do not confuse *brought* and *bought*. *Brought* comes from *bring* and *bought* comes from *buy*.

brow, brows NOUN ① Your brow is your forehead. ② Your brows are your eyebrows. ③ The brow of a hill is the top of it.

brown, browner, brownest; browns ADJECTIVE or NOUN Brown is the colour of earth or wood.

browned off ADJECTIVE (*informal*) Someone who is browned off is feeling fed up.

brownie, brownies NOUN a junior member of the Guides.

browse, browses, browsing, browsed VERB ① If you browse through a book or magazine, you look through it in a casual way. ② If you browse in a shop, you look at the things in it for interest rather than because you want to buy something. ③ If you browse on a computer, you search for information on the World Wide Web.

browser, browsers NOUN a piece of computer software that lets you look at websites on the World Wide Web.

bruise, bruises, bruising, bruised NOUN ① a purple mark that appears on your skin after something has hit it. ▶ VERB ② If something bruises you, it hits you so that a bruise appears on your skin.

brumby, brumbies NOUN In Australia and New Zealand, a brumby is a wild horse.

brunette, brunettes NOUN a girl or woman with dark brown hair.

brunt PHRASE If you bear the brunt of something unpleasant, you are the person who suffers most • *Young people bear the brunt of unemployment*.

brush, brushes, brushing, brushed NOUN ① an object with bristles which you use for cleaning things, painting, or tidying your hair. ▶ VERB ② If you brush something, you clean it or tidy it with a brush. ③ To brush against something means to touch it while passing it • *Her lips brushed his cheek*. **brush up** VERB If you brush up on a subject, you improve your knowledge of it • *They need to brush up their French*.

brusque, brusquer, brusquest [Said *broosk*] ADJECTIVE Someone who is brusque deals with people quickly and without considering their feelings. **brusquely** ADVERB **brusqueness** NOUN

brussels sprout, brussels sprouts NOUN Brussels sprouts are vegetables that look like tiny cabbages.

brutal ADJECTIVE Brutal behaviour is cruel and violent • *a brutal murder*. **brutally** ADVERB **brutality** NOUN

brute, brutes NOUN ① a rough and insensitive man. ▶ ADJECTIVE ② Brute force is strength alone, without any skill • *You have to use brute force to open the gates*. **brutish** ADJECTIVE

bubble, bubbles, bubbling, bubbled NOUN ① a ball of air in a liquid. ② a hollow, delicate ball of soapy liquid. ▶ VERB ③ When a liquid bubbles, bubbles form in it. ④ If you are bubbling with something like excitement, you are full of it. **bubbly** ADJECTIVE

bubonic plague [Said *byoo-bon-ik*] NOUN HISTORY Bubonic plague is a disease transmitted by fleas on rats. Until a cure was discovered in the 19th century, it was a widespread cause of epidemics and death. Swellings, called buboes, appeared in the armpits and groin of people who caught it.

buck, bucks, bucking, bucked NOUN ① the male of various animals, including the deer and the rabbit. ② (informal) a dollar. ▶ VERB ③ If a horse bucks, it jumps into the air with its feet off the ground.

bucket, buckets NOUN a deep round container with an open top and a handle.

buckle, buckles, buckling, buckled NOUN ① a fastening on the end of a belt or strap. ▶ VERB ② If you buckle a belt or strap, you fasten it. ③ If something buckles, it becomes bent because of severe heat or pressure.

bud, buds, budding, budded NOUN ① a small, tight swelling on a tree or plant, which develops into a flower or a cluster of leaves. ▶ VERB ② When a tree or plant buds, new buds appear on it.

Buddhism NOUN RE an Eastern religion which teaches that the way to end suffering is by overcoming your desires. It was founded in the 6th century BC by the Buddha (a title meaning 'the enlightened one'),

Gautama Siddhartha, a nobleman and religious teacher of northern India. **Buddhist** NOUN or ADJECTIVE

budding ADJECTIVE just beginning to develop • *a budding artist*.

buddy, buddies NOUN (*informal*) a friend.

budge, budges, budging, budged VERB If something will not budge, you cannot move it.

budgerigar, budgerigars NOUN A budgerigar is a small brightly coloured pet bird. Budgerigars originated in Australia.

WORD HISTORY: from an Aboriginal language, from *budgeri* + *gar* meaning 'good cockatoo'

budget, budgets, budgeting, budgeted NOUN ① CITIZENSHIP a plan showing how much money will be available and how it will be spent. ▸ VERB ② CITIZENSHIP If you budget for something, you plan your money carefully, so that you are able to afford it. **budgetary** ADJECTIVE

budgie, budgies NOUN (*informal*) a budgerigar.

buff, buffs ADJECTIVE ① a pale brown colour. ▸ NOUN ② (*informal*) someone who knows a lot about a subject • *a film buff*.

buffalo, buffaloes NOUN a wild animal like a large cow with long curved horns.

buffer, buffers NOUN ① Buffers on a train or at the end of a railway line are metal discs on springs that reduce shock when they are hit. ② something that prevents something else from being harmed • *Keep savings as a buffer against unexpected cash needs*.

buffet¹, buffets [*Said boof-ay or buf-ay*] NOUN ① a café at a station. ② a meal at which people serve themselves.

buffet², buffets, buffeting, buffeted

[*Said buff-it*] VERB If the wind or sea buffets a place or person, it strikes them violently and repeatedly.

bug, bugs, bugging, bugged NOUN ① an insect, especially one that causes damage. ② a small error in a computer program which means that the program will not work properly. ③ (*informal*) a virus or minor infection • *a stomach bug*. ▸ VERB ④ If a place is bugged, tiny microphones are hidden there to pick up what people are saying.

buggy, buggies NOUN a small lightweight vehicle or carriage.

bugle, bugles NOUN MUSIC a brass musical instrument that looks like a small trumpet. **bugler** NOUN

build, builds, building, built VERB ① To build something such as a house means to make it from its parts. ② To build something such as an organisation means to develop it gradually. ▸ NOUN ③ Your build is the shape and size of your body. **builder** NOUN

SIMILAR WORDS: ① assemble, construct, erect

building, buildings NOUN a structure with walls and a roof.

building society, building societies NOUN a business in which some people invest their money, while others borrow from it to buy a house.

bulb, bulbs NOUN ① the glass part of an electric lamp. ② an onion-shaped root that grows into a flower or plant.

Bulgarian, Bulgarians ADJECTIVE ① belonging or relating to Bulgaria. ▸ NOUN ② someone who comes from Bulgaria. ③ the main language spoken in Bulgaria.

bulge, bulges, bulging, bulged VERB ① If something bulges, it swells out from a surface. ▸ NOUN ② a lump on a normally flat surface.

a
b
c
d
e
f
g
h
i
j
k
l
m
n
o
p
q
r
s
t
u
v
w
x
y
z

bulimia NOUN a psychological condition in which a person may make themselves vomit after eating in order to keep their weight as low as possible.

bulk, bulks NOUN ① a large mass of something • *The book is more impressive for its bulk than its content.* ② The bulk of something is most of it • *the bulk of the world's great poetry.* ▶ PHRASE ③ To buy something **in bulk** means to buy it in large quantities.

bulky, bulkier, bulkiest ADJECTIVE large and heavy • *a bulky package.*
SIMILAR WORDS: cumbersome, large, unwieldy

bull, bulls NOUN the male of some species of animals, including the cow family, elephants and whales.

bulldog, bulldogs NOUN a squat dog with a broad head and muscular body.

bulldozer, bulldozers NOUN a powerful tractor with a broad blade in front, which is used for moving earth or knocking things down.

bullet, bullets NOUN a small piece of metal fired from a gun.

bulletin, bulletins NOUN ① a short news report on radio or television. ② a leaflet or small newspaper regularly produced by a group or organisation.
WORD HISTORY: from Italian *bulletino* meaning 'small Papal edict'

bulletin board, bulletin boards NOUN ① In American English, a bulletin board is a notice board. ② In computing, a bulletin board is a system that allows people to send and receive messages of general interest.

bullet point, bullet points NOUN one of a series of items that are listed in a document, each marked by a square or round symbol.

bullion NOUN Bullion is gold or silver in the form of bars.

bullock, bullocks NOUN a young castrated bull.

bullroarer, bullroarers NOUN a wooden slat attached to a string that is whirled round to make a roaring noise. Bullroarers are used especially by Aboriginal Australians in religious ceremonies.

bully, bullies, bullying, bullied NOUN ① someone who repeatedly tries to hurt or frighten other people. ▶ VERB ② If you bully someone, you frighten or hurt them deliberately. ③ If someone bullies you into doing something, they make you do it by using force or threats.

bump, bumps, bumping, bumped VERB ① If you bump or bump into something, you knock it with a jolt. ▶ NOUN ② a soft or dull noise made by something knocking into something else. ③ a raised, uneven part of a surface. **bumpy** ADJECTIVE **bump off** VERB (*informal*) To bump someone off means to kill them.
SIMILAR WORDS: ③ bulge, lump, protuberance

bumper, bumpers NOUN ① Bumpers are bars on the front and back of a vehicle which protect it if there is a collision. ▶ ADJECTIVE ② A bumper crop or harvest is larger than usual.

bun, buns NOUN a small, round cake.

bunch, bunches, bunching, bunched NOUN ① a group of people. ② a number of flowers held or tied together. ③ a group of things. ④ a group of bananas or grapes growing on the same stem. ▶ VERB ⑤ When people bunch together or bunch up, they stay very close to each other.

bundle, bundles, bundling, bundled NOUN ① a number of things tied together or wrapped up in a cloth.

▶ **VERB** ② If you bundle someone or something somewhere, you push them there quickly and roughly.

bung, bungs, bunging, bunged **NOUN** ① a stopper used to close a hole in something such as a barrel. ▶ **VERB** ② (informal) If you bung something somewhere, you put it there quickly and carelessly.

bungalow, bungalows **NOUN** a one-storey house. **WORD HISTORY:** from Hindi bangla meaning 'of Bengal'

bungle, bungles, bungling, bungled **VERB** To bungle something means to fail to do it properly.

bunion, bunions **NOUN** a painful lump on the first joint of a person's big toe.

bunk, bunks **NOUN** a bed fixed to a wall in a ship or caravan.

bunker, bunkers **NOUN** ① On a golf course, a bunker is a large hole filled with sand. ② an underground shelter with strong walls to protect it from bombing.

bunny, bunnies **NOUN** (informal) a rabbit.

bunting **NOUN** Bunting is strips of small coloured flags displayed on streets and buildings on special occasions.

bunyip, bunyips **NOUN** a legendary monster said to live in swamps and lakes in Australia.

buoy, buoys [Said boy] **NOUN** a floating object anchored to the bottom of the sea, marking a channel or warning of danger.

buoyant **ADJECTIVE** ① able to float. ② lively and cheerful • She was in a buoyant mood. **buoyancy** **NOUN**

burble, burbles, burbling, burbled **VERB** To burble means to make a soft bubbling sound • The water burbled over the gravel.

burden, burdens **NOUN** ① a heavy load. ② If something is a burden to you, it causes you a lot of worry or hard work. **burdensome** **ADJECTIVE** **SIMILAR WORDS:** ① load, weight ② millstone, trouble, worry

bureau, bureaux [Said byoo-roh] **NOUN** ① an office that provides a service • an employment bureau. ② a writing desk with shelves and drawers. ③ In American English, a bureau is a chest of drawers.

bureaucracy **NOUN** Bureaucracy is the complex system of rules and procedures which operates in government departments. **bureaucratic** **ADJECTIVE**

bureaucrat, bureaucrats **NOUN** a person who works in a government department, especially one who follows rules and procedures strictly.

burgeoning **ADJECTIVE** growing or developing rapidly • a burgeoning political crisis.

burger, burgers **NOUN** a flat round mass of minced meat or vegetables which is fried and often eaten in a bread roll.

burglar, burglars **NOUN** a thief who breaks into a building.

burglary, burglaries **NOUN** Burglary is the act of breaking into a building in order to steal things.

burgle, burgles, burgling, burgled **VERB** If your house is burgled, someone breaks into it and steals things.

burial, burials **NOUN** a ceremony held when a dead person is buried.

burly, burlier, burliest **ADJECTIVE** If you are burly, you have a broad body and strong muscles. **SIMILAR WORDS:** brawny, well-built

burn, burns, burning, burned or **burnt** **VERB** ① If something is burning, it is on fire. ② To burn

A

B

C

D

E

F

G

H

I

J

K

L

M

N

O

P

Q

R

S

T

U

V

W

X

Y

Z

something means to destroy it with fire. ③ If you burn yourself or are burned, you are injured by fire or by something hot. ▸ **NOUN** ④ an injury caused by fire or by something hot.
SIMILAR WORDS: ① be on fire, blaze ② incinerate, set on fire

SPELLING TIP
You can write either *burned* or *burnt* as the past form of *burn*.

burp, burps, burping, burped **VERB**
① If you burp, you make a noise because air from your stomach has been forced up through your throat.
▸ **NOUN** ② the noise that you make when you burp.

burqa, burqas; also spelt **burka** [*Said bur-kuh*] **NOUN** RE a long garment that covers the head and body and is traditionally worn by some women in Islamic countries.

burrow, burrows, burrowing, burrowed **NOUN** ① a tunnel or hole in the ground dug by a small animal.
▸ **VERB** ② When an animal burrows, it digs a burrow.

bursary, bursaries **NOUN** a sum of money given to someone to help fund their education.

burst, bursts, bursting, burst **VERB**
① When something bursts, it splits open because of pressure from inside it. ② If you burst into a room, you enter it suddenly. ③ To burst means to happen or come suddenly and with force • *The aircraft burst into flames*. ④ (*informal*) If you are bursting with something, you find it difficult to keep it to yourself • *We were bursting with joy*. ▸ **NOUN** ⑤ A burst of something is a short period of it • *He had a sudden burst of energy*.
SIMILAR WORDS: ⑤ outbreak, rush, spate

bury, buries, burying, buried **VERB**
① When a dead person is buried, their

body is put into a grave and covered with earth. ② To bury something means to put it in a hole in the ground and cover it up. ③ If something is buried under something, it is covered by it • *My bag was buried under a pile of old newspapers*.

bus, buses **NOUN** a large motor vehicle that carries passengers.
WORD HISTORY: from Latin *omnibus* meaning 'for all'; buses were originally called omnibuses

bush, bushes **NOUN** ① a thick plant with many stems branching out from ground level. ② In Australia and South Africa, the bush is an area of land in its natural state outside of city areas. ③ In New Zealand, the bush is land covered with rainforest.

bushman, bushmen **NOUN** ① In Australia and New Zealand, a bushman is someone who lives or travels in the bush. ② In New Zealand, a bushman is also someone whose job it is to clear the bush for farming.

Bushman, Bushmen **NOUN** A Bushman is a member of a group of people in southern Africa who live by hunting and gathering food.

bushranger, bushrangers **NOUN** In Australia and New Zealand in the past, a bushranger was an outlaw living in the bush.

bushveld [*Said bush-felt*] **NOUN** In South Africa, bushveld is countryside where a lot of shrubs grow.

bushy, bushier, bushiest **ADJECTIVE** Bushy hair or fur grows very thickly • *bushy eyebrows*.

business, businesses **NOUN** ① Business is work relating to the buying and selling of goods and services. ② an organisation which produces or sells goods or provides a service. ③ You can refer to any event, situation or activity as a business • *This whole business has upset me.*

businessman NOUN
businesswoman NOUN
SIMILAR WORDS: ② company, establishment, firm, organisation

businesslike ADJECTIVE dealing with things in an efficient way.

busker, buskers NOUN someone who plays music or sings for money in public places.

bust, busts, busting, bust or busted NOUN ① a statue of someone's head and shoulders • *a bust of Beethoven.* ② A woman's bust is her chest and her breasts. ▶ VERB ③ (*informal*) If you bust something, you break it. ▶ ADJECTIVE ④ (*informal*) If a business goes bust, it becomes bankrupt and closes down.

bustle, bustles, bustling, bustled VERB ① When people bustle, they move in a busy, hurried way. ▶ NOUN ② Bustle is busy, noisy activity.

busy, busier, busiest; busies, busying, busied ADJECTIVE ① If you are busy, you are in the middle of doing something. ② A busy place is full of people doing things or moving about • *a busy seaside resort.* ▶ VERB ③ If you busy yourself with something, you occupy yourself by doing it. **busily** ADVERB
SIMILAR WORDS: ① employed, engaged, occupied

but CONJUNCTION ① used to introduce an idea that is opposite to what has gone before • *I don't like apples, but I do like oranges.* ② used when apologising • *I'm sorry, but I can't come tonight.* ③ except • *We can't do anything but wait.*

butcher, butchers NOUN a shopkeeper who sells meat.

butler, butlers NOUN the chief male servant in a rich household.
WORD HISTORY: from Old French *bouteillier* meaning 'a dealer in bottles'

butt, butts, butting, butted NOUN ① The butt of a weapon is the thick end of its handle. ② If you are the butt of teasing, you are the target of it. ▶ VERB ③ If you butt something, you ram it with your head. **butt in** VERB If you butt in, you join in a private conversation or activity without being asked to.

butter, butters, buttering, buttered NOUN ① Butter is a soft fatty food made from cream, which is spread on bread and used in cooking. ▶ VERB ② To butter bread means to spread butter on it.

buttercup, buttercups NOUN a wild plant with bright yellow flowers.

butterfly, butterflies NOUN a type of insect with large colourful wings.

buttocks PLURAL NOUN Your buttocks are the part of your body that you sit on.

button, buttons, buttoning, buttoned NOUN ① Buttons are small, hard objects sewn on to clothing, and used to fasten two surfaces together. ② a small object on a piece of equipment that you press to make it work. ▶ VERB ③ If you button a piece of clothing, you fasten it using its buttons.

buttonhole, buttonholes NOUN ① a hole that you push a button through to fasten a piece of clothing. ② a flower worn in your lapel.

buxom ADJECTIVE A buxom woman is large, healthy and attractive.

buy, buys, buying, bought VERB If you buy something, you obtain it by paying money for it. **buyer** NOUN

buzz, buzzes, buzzing, buzzed VERB ① If something buzzes, it makes a

humming sound, like a bee. ▸ **NOUN**
② the sound something makes when
it buzzes.

buzzard, buzzards **NOUN** a large
brown and white bird of prey.

buzzer, buzzers **NOUN** a device that
makes a buzzing sound, to attract
attention.

by **PREPOSITION** ① used to indicate
who or what has done something
• *The class was taken by a new teacher.*
② used to indicate how something is
done • *He frightened her by hiding
behind the door.* ③ located next to • *I
sat by her bed.* ④ before a particular
time • *It should be ready by next spring.*
▸ **PREPOSITION** or **ADVERB** ⑤ going
past • *We drove by his house.*

by-election, by-elections **NOUN**
an election held to choose a new
member of parliament after the
previous member has resigned or
died.

bygone **ADJECTIVE** (*literary*)
happening or existing a long time
ago • *the ceremonies of a bygone era*.

bypass, bypasses **NOUN** a main road
which takes traffic round a town
rather than through it.

bystander, bystanders **NOUN**
someone who is not included or
involved in something but is there to
see it happen.

byte, bytes **NOUN** ICT a unit of
computer memory size.

Cc

cab, **cabs** NOUN ① a taxi. ② In a lorry, bus or train, the cab is where the driver sits.
WORD HISTORY: from French *cabriolet* meaning 'light two-wheeled carriage'. Cabs were originally horse-drawn

cabaret, **cabarets** [Said *kab-bar-ray*] NOUN a show consisting of dancing, singing or comedy acts.
WORD HISTORY: from French *cabaret* meaning 'tavern'

cabbage, **cabbages** NOUN a large green or reddish-purple leafy vegetable.
WORD HISTORY: from Norman French *cabache* meaning 'head'

cabbage tree, **cabbage trees** NOUN a palm-like tree found in New Zealand with a tall bare trunk and big bunches of spiky leaves; also a similar tree found in eastern Australia.

cabin, **cabins** NOUN ① a room in a ship where a passenger sleeps. ② a small house, usually in the country and often made of wood. ③ the area where the passengers or the crew sit in a plane.

cabinet, **cabinets** NOUN ① a small cupboard. ② The cabinet in a government is a group of ministers who advise the leader and decide policies.

cable, **cables** NOUN ① a strong, thick rope or chain. ② a bundle of wires with a rubber covering, which carries electricity. ③ a message sent abroad by using electrical signals sent along a wire.

cable car, **cable cars** NOUN a vehicle pulled by a moving cable, for taking people up and down mountains.

cable television NOUN a television service people can receive from underground wires which carry the signals.

cacao, **cacaos** [Said *ka-kah-oh*] NOUN A cacao is a type of small tropical evergreen tree, whose berries are used to produce chocolate and cocoa.

cache, **caches** [Said *kash*] NOUN a store of things hidden away • *a cache of guns*.

cachet [Said *kash-shay*] NOUN (formal) Cachet is the status and respect something has • *the cachet of shopping at Harrods*.

cackle, **cackles**, **cackling**, **cackled** VERB ① If you cackle, you laugh harshly. ▶ NOUN ② a harsh laugh.

cacophony [Said *kak-koff-fon-nee*] NOUN (formal) a loud, unpleasant noise • *a cacophony of barking dogs*.
WORD HISTORY: from Greek *kakos* + *phōnē* meaning 'bad sound'

cactus, **cacti** or **cactuses** NOUN a thick, fleshy plant that grows in deserts and is usually covered in spikes.

caddie, **caddies**; also spelt **caddy** NOUN ① a person who carries golf clubs for a golf player. ② A tea caddy is a box for keeping tea in.

cadence, **cadences** [Said *kay-denss*] NOUN The cadence of someone's voice is the way it goes up and down as they speak.

cadet, cadets NOUN a young person being trained in the armed forces or police.

cadge, cadges, cadging, cadged VERB If you cadge something off someone, you get it from them and don't give them anything in return • *I cadged a lift ashore.*

caesarean, caesareans [Said *siz-air-ee-an*]; also spelt **caesarian** or **cesarean** NOUN A caesarean or caesarean section is an operation in which a baby is lifted out of a woman's womb through a cut in her abdomen.

café, cafés [Said *kaf-fay*] NOUN ① a place where you can buy light meals and drinks. ② In South African English, a café is a corner shop or grocer's shop.

cafeteria, cafeterias [Said *kaf-fit-ee-ree-ya*] NOUN a restaurant where you serve yourself.

caffeine [Said *kaf-feen*] NOUN Caffeine is a chemical in coffee and tea which makes you more active.

cage, cages NOUN a box made of wire or bars in which birds or animals are kept. **caged** ADJECTIVE

cagey, cagier, cagiest [Said *kay-jee*] ADJECTIVE (informal) cautious and not open • *They're very cagey when they talk to me.*

cagoule, cagoules [Said *ka-gool*] NOUN a lightweight waterproof jacket with a hood.

cahoots PHRASE (informal) If you are **in cahoots** with someone, you are working closely with them on a secret plan.

cairn, cairns NOUN a pile of stones built as a memorial or a landmark. WORD HISTORY: from Gaelic *carn* meaning 'heap of stones' or 'hill'

cajole, cajoles, cajoling, cajoled VERB If you cajole someone into doing something, you persuade them to do it by saying nice things to them.

cake, cakes, caking, caked NOUN ① a sweet food made by baking flour, eggs, fat and sugar. ② a block of a hard substance such as soap. ▶ VERB ③ If something cakes or is caked, it forms or becomes covered with a solid layer • *caked with mud.* WORD HISTORY: from Old Norse *kaka* meaning 'oatcake'

calamity, calamities NOUN an event that causes disaster or distress. **calamitous** ADJECTIVE

calcium [Said *kal-see-um*] NOUN SCIENCE Calcium is a soft white element found in bones and teeth. Its atomic number is 20 and its symbol is Ca.

calculate, calculates, calculating, calculated VERB MATHS If you calculate something, you work it out, usually by doing some arithmetic. **calculation** NOUN WORD HISTORY: from Latin *calculus* meaning 'stone' or 'pebble'. The Romans used pebbles to count with

calculated ADJECTIVE deliberately planned to have a particular effect.

calculating ADJECTIVE carefully planning situations to get what you want • *Toby was always a calculating type.*

calculator, calculators NOUN a small electronic machine used for doing mathematical calculations.

calculus NOUN Calculus is a branch of mathematics concerned with amounts that can change and rates of change.

calendar, calendars NOUN ① a chart showing the date of each day in a particular year. ② a system of dividing time into fixed periods of days, months and years • *the Jewish calendar*.

WORD HISTORY: from Latin *kalendae*, the day of the month on which interest on debts was due

calf, **calves** NOUN ① a young cow, bull, elephant, whale or seal. ② the thick part at the back of your leg below your knee.

calibre, **calibres** [*Said kal-lib-ber*] NOUN ① the ability or intelligence someone has • *a player of her calibre*. ② The calibre of a gun is the width of the inside of the barrel of the gun.

call, **calls**, **calling**, **called** VERB ① If someone or something is called a particular name, that is their name • *a man called Jeffrey*. ② If you call people or situations something, you use words to describe your opinion of them • *They called me unfriendly*. ③ If you call someone, you telephone them. ④ If you call or call out something, you say it loudly • *He called out his daughter's name*. ⑤ If you call on someone, you pay them a short visit • *Don't hesitate to call on me*. ▶ NOUN ⑥ If you get a call from someone, they telephone you or pay you a visit. ⑦ a cry or shout • *a call for help*. ⑧ a demand for something • *The call for art teachers was small*. **call off** VERB If you call something off, you cancel it. **call up** VERB If someone is called up, they are ordered to join the army, navy or air force.

SIMILAR WORDS: ① christen, label, name

call centre, **call centres** NOUN an office in which most staff are employed to answer telephone calls on behalf of a particular company or organisation.

calling NOUN ① a profession or career. ② If you have a calling to a particular job, you have a strong feeling that you should do it.

callous ADJECTIVE cruel and not concerned with other people's feelings. **callously** ADVERB **callousness** NOUN

SIMILAR WORDS: hard-hearted, heartless, unfeeling

calm, **calmer**, **calmest**; **calms**, **calming**, **calmed** ADJECTIVE ① Someone who is calm is quiet and does not show any worry or excitement. ② If the weather or the sea is calm, it is still because there is no strong wind. ▶ NOUN ③ Calm is a state of quietness and peacefulness • *He liked the calm of the evening*. ▶ VERB ④ To calm someone means to make them less upset or excited.

calmly ADVERB **calmness** NOUN

SIMILAR WORDS: ① composed, cool, self-possessed ③ peacefulness, quiet ④ quieten, soothe

calorie, **calories** NOUN a unit of measurement for the energy food and drink gives you • *Chocolate cake is high in calories*. **calorific** ADJECTIVE

calves the plural of **calf**.

calypso, **calypsos** [*Said kal-lip-soh*] NOUN a type of song originally from Trinidad, accompanied by a rhythmic beat, about something happening at the time.

calyx, **calyxes** or **calyces** [*Said kay-lix*] NOUN (*technical*) In a flower, a calyx is the ring of petal-like sepals that protects the developing bud.

camaraderie [*Said kam-mer-rah-der-ree*] NOUN Camaraderie is a feeling of trust and friendship between a group of people.

camber, **cambers** NOUN a slight downward slope from the centre of a road to each side of it.

came the past tense of **come**.

camel, **camels** NOUN a large mammal with either one or two humps on its back. Camels live in hot desert areas and are sometimes used for carrying things.

WORD HISTORY: from Hebrew *gamal*

cameo, **cameos** NOUN ① a small but important part in a play or film played by a well-known actor or actress. ② a brooch with a raised stone design on a flat stone of another colour.

camera, **cameras** NOUN a piece of equipment used for taking photographs or for filming.

WORD HISTORY: from Latin *camera* meaning 'vault'

camomile NOUN Camomile is a plant with a strong smell and daisy-like flowers which are used to make herbal tea.

WORD HISTORY: from Greek *khamaimēlon* meaning 'apple on the ground'

camouflage, **camouflages**, **camouflaging**, **camouflaged** [Said *kam-mof-flahj*] NOUN ① Camouflage is a way of avoiding being seen by having the same colour or appearance as the surroundings. ▸ VERB ② To camouflage something is to hide it by giving it the same colour or appearance as its surroundings.

camp, **camps**, **camping**, **camped** NOUN ① a place where people live in tents or stay in tents on holiday. ② a collection of buildings for a particular group of people such as soldiers or prisoners. ③ a group of people who support a particular idea or belief • *the pro-government camp.* ▸ VERB ④ If you camp, you stay in a tent. **camper** NOUN **camping** NOUN

campaign, **campaigns**, **campaigning**, **campaigned** [Said *kam-pane*] NOUN ① a set of actions aiming to achieve a particular result • *a campaign to educate people.* ▸ VERB ② To campaign means to carry out a campaign • *He has campaigned against smoking.* **campaigner** NOUN

camp-drafting NOUN In Australia, camp-drafting is a competition in which men on horseback select cattle or sheep from a herd or flock.

campus, **campuses** NOUN the area of land and the buildings that make up a university or college.

can¹, **could** VERB ① If you can do something, it is possible for you to do it or you are allowed to do it • *You can go to the cinema.* ② If you can do something, you have the ability to do it • *I can speak Italian.*

can², **cans**, **canning**, **canned** NOUN ① a metal container, often a sealed one with food or drink inside. ▸ VERB ② To can food or drink is to seal it in cans.

Canadian, **Canadians** ADJECTIVE ① belonging or relating to Canada. ▸ NOUN ② someone who comes from Canada.

canal, **canals** NOUN a long, narrow man-made stretch of water.

canary, **canaries** NOUN a small yellow bird.

can-can, **can-cans** NOUN a lively dance in which women kick their legs high in the air to fast music.

cancel, **cancels**, **cancelling**, **cancelled** VERB ① If you cancel something that has been arranged, you stop it from happening. ② If you cancel a cheque or an agreement, you make sure that it is no longer valid. **cancellation** NOUN

cancer, **cancers** NOUN ① a serious disease in which abnormal cells in a part of the body increase rapidly, causing growths. ② Cancer is also the fourth sign of the zodiac, represented by a crab. People born between June 21st and July 22nd are

born under this sign. **cancerous**
ADJECTIVE
WORD HISTORY: from Latin *cancer* meaning 'crab'

candelabra, candelabras or **candelabrum** NOUN an ornamental holder for a number of candles.

candid ADJECTIVE honest and frank. **candidly** ADVERB **candour** NOUN

candidate, candidates NOUN ① a person who is being considered for a job. ② a person standing for election. ③ a person taking an examination. **candidacy** NOUN
WORD HISTORY: from Latin *candidatus* meaning 'white-robed'. In Rome, a candidate wore a white toga

candied ADJECTIVE covered or cooked in sugar • *candied fruit*.

candle, candles NOUN a stick of hard wax with a wick through the middle. The lighted wick gives a flame that provides light.

candlestick, candlesticks NOUN a holder for a candle.

candy, candies NOUN In America, candy is sweets.
WORD HISTORY: from Arabic *qand* meaning 'cane sugar'

cane, canes, caning, caned NOUN ① Cane is the long, hollow stems of a plant such as bamboo. ② Cane is also strips of cane used for weaving things such as baskets. ③ a long narrow stick, often one used to beat people as a punishment. ▶ VERB ④ To cane someone means to beat them with a cane as a punishment.

cane toad, cane toads NOUN In Australia, a cane toad is a large toad that is used to control insects that eat crops.

canine [*Said kay-nine*] ADJECTIVE ① relating to dogs. ▶ NOUN ② SCIENCE A canine, or a canine

tooth, is one of the pointed teeth near the front of the mouth in humans and some animals.

canister, canisters NOUN a container with a lid, used for storing foods such as sugar or tea.

cannabis NOUN Cannabis is an illegal drug made from the hemp plant, which some people smoke.

canned ADJECTIVE ① Canned food is kept in cans. ② Canned music or laughter on a television or radio show is recorded beforehand.

cannibal, cannibals NOUN a person who eats other human beings; also used of animals that eat animals of their own type. **cannibalism** NOUN

cannon, cannons, cannoning, cannoned NOUN ① A cannon is a large gun, usually on wheels, used in battles to fire heavy metal balls. ▶ VERB ② To cannon into people or things means to collide into them with force.
WORD HISTORY: from Italian *canna* meaning 'tube'

SPELLING TIP
Do not confuse the spellings of *cannon* and *canon*: *the onslaught from the French cannon; the canons of Canterbury Cathedral.*

cannot VERB Cannot is the same as can not • *She cannot come home yet*.

canny, cannier, canniest ADJECTIVE clever and cautious • *canny business people*. **cannily** ADVERB

canoe, canoes [*Said ka-noo*] NOUN a small, narrow boat that you row using a paddle. **canoeing** NOUN **canoeist** NOUN

canon, canons NOUN ① a member of the clergy in a cathedral. ② a basic rule or principle • *the canons of political economy*. ③ In literature, a canon is all the writings by a particular author which are known to be genuine.

SPELLING TIP
Do not confuse the spellings of *canon* and *cannon*: *the canons of Canterbury Cathedral; the onslaught from the French cannon.*

canopy, canopies NOUN a cover for something, used for shelter or decoration • *a frilly canopy over the bed.* WORD HISTORY: from Greek *kōnōpeion* meaning 'bed with a mosquito net'

cantankerous ADJECTIVE Cantankerous people are quarrelsome and bad-tempered.

canteen, canteens NOUN ① In a place such as a school or office, the canteen is a place where people can go to eat. ② A canteen of cutlery is a set of cutlery in a box.

canter, canters, cantering, cantered VERB When a horse canters, it moves at a speed between a gallop and a trot.

cantilever, cantilevers NOUN a long beam or bar fixed at only one end and supporting a bridge or other structure at the other end.

canton, cantons NOUN a political and administrative region of a country, especially in Switzerland.

canvas, canvases NOUN ① Canvas is strong, heavy cloth used for making things such as sails and tents. ② a piece of canvas on which an artist does a painting.

SPELLING TIP
Do not confuse the spellings of *canvas* and *canvass*: *a hammock made from heavy canvas; Campaigners have been sent to canvass opinion before the election.*

canvass, canvasses, canvassing, canvassed VERB ① If you canvass people or a place, you go round trying to persuade people to vote for a particular candidate or party in an election. ② If you canvass opinion, you find out what people think about a particular subject by asking them.

SPELLING TIP
Do not confuse the spellings of *canvass* and *canvas*: *Campaigners have been sent to canvass opinion before the election; a hammock made from heavy canvas.*

canyon, canyons NOUN GEOGRAPHY a narrow river valley with steep sides.

cap, caps, capping, capped NOUN ① a soft, flat hat, often with a peak at the front. ② the top of a bottle. ③ Caps are small explosives used in toy guns. ▶ VERB ④ To cap something is to cover it with something. ⑤ If you cap a story or a joke that someone has just told, you tell a better one.

capable ADJECTIVE ① able to do something • *a man capable of writing great books.* ② skilful or talented • *She was a very capable woman.* **capably** ADVERB **capability** NOUN

capacity, capacities [Said *kap-pas-sit-tee*] NOUN ① the maximum amount that something can hold or produce • *a seating capacity of eleven thousand.* ② a person's power or ability to do something • *his capacity for consuming hamburgers.* ③ someone's position or role • *in his capacity as councillor.*

cape, capes NOUN ① a short cloak with no sleeves. ② a large piece of land sticking out into the sea • *the Cape of Good Hope.*

caper, capers NOUN ① Capers are the flower buds of a spiky Mediterranean shrub, which are pickled and used to flavour food. ② a light-hearted practical joke • *Jack would have nothing to do with such capers.*

capillary, capillaries [Said kap-**pill**-lar-ree] NOUN SCIENCE Capillaries are very thin blood vessels.

capital, capitals NOUN ① The capital of a country is the city where the government meets. ② Capital is the amount of money or property owned or used by a business. ③ Capital is also a sum of money that you save or invest in order to gain interest. ④ A capital or capital letter is a larger letter used at the beginning of a sentence or a name.

PUNCTUATION TIP
Capitals, or capital letters, are used at the start of proper nouns and the first word in a sentence: *Lionel Messi*; *Eve likes dogs*. Avoid using capitals for other nouns: *My teacher is ill* (not *My Teacher is ill*).

---

capitalise, capitalises, capitalising, capitalised; also spelt **capitalize** VERB If you capitalise on a situation, you use it to get an advantage.

capitalism NOUN Capitalism is an economic and political system where businesses and industries are not owned and run by the government, but by individuals who can make a profit from them. **capitalist** ADJECTIVE or NOUN

capital punishment NOUN Capital punishment is legally killing someone as a punishment for a crime they have committed.

capitulate, capitulates, capitulating, capitulated VERB To capitulate is to give in and stop fighting or resisting • *The Finns capitulated in March 1940.* **capitulation** NOUN

cappuccino, cappuccinos [Said kap-poot-**sheen**-oh] NOUN coffee made with frothy milk.

capricious [Said kap-**prish**-uss] ADJECTIVE often changing unexpectedly • *the capricious English weather*.

Capricorn NOUN Capricorn is the tenth sign of the zodiac, represented by a goat. People born between December 22nd and January 19th are born under this sign.
WORD HISTORY: from Latin *caper* meaning 'goat' and *cornu* meaning 'horn'

capsize, capsizes, capsizing, capsized VERB If a boat capsizes, it turns upside down.

capsule, capsules NOUN ① a small container with medicine inside which you swallow. ② the part of a spacecraft in which astronauts travel.

captain, captains, captaining, captained NOUN ① the officer in charge of a ship or aeroplane. ② an army officer of the rank immediately above lieutenant. ③ a navy officer of the rank immediately above commander. ④ the leader of a sports team • *captain of the cricket team*.
▶ VERB ⑤ If you captain a group of people, you are their leader.

caption, captions NOUN a title printed underneath a picture or photograph.

captivate, captivates, captivating, captivated VERB To captivate someone is to fascinate or attract them so that they cannot take their attention away • *I was captivated by her*. **captivating** ADJECTIVE

captive, captives NOUN ① a person who has been captured and kept prisoner. ▶ ADJECTIVE ② imprisoned or enclosed • *a captive bird*. **captivity** NOUN

captor, captors NOUN someone who has captured a person or animal.

a b c d e f g h i j k l m n o p q r s t u v w x y z

capture, captures, capturing, captured VERB ①To capture someone is to take them prisoner. ②To capture a quality or mood means to succeed in representing or describing it • *capturing the mood of the riots.* ▶NOUN ③The capture of someone or something is the action of taking them prisoner • *the fifth anniversary of his capture.*

car, cars NOUN ①a four-wheeled road vehicle with room for a small number of people. ②a railway carriage used for a particular purpose • *the buffet car.*

carafe, carafes [*Said kar-raf*] NOUN a glass bottle for serving water or wine.
WORD HISTORY: from Arabic *gharrafah* meaning 'vessel for liquid'

caramel, caramels NOUN ①a chewy sweet made from sugar, butter and milk. ②Caramel is burnt sugar used for colouring or flavouring food.

carat, carats NOUN ①A carat is a unit for measuring the weight of diamonds and other precious stones, equal to 0.2 grams. ②A carat is also a unit for measuring the purity of gold. The purest gold is 24 carats.

SPELLING TIP
Do not confuse the spellings of *carat* and *carrot*: *a huge 55 carat diamond*; *Rabbits love lettuce and carrots.*

caravan, caravans NOUN ①a vehicle pulled by a car in which people live or spend their holidays. ②a group of people and animals travelling together, usually across a desert.
WORD HISTORY: from Persian *karwan*

carbohydrate, carbohydrates NOUN DG-T SCIENCE Carbohydrate is a substance that gives you energy. It is found in foods like sugar and bread.

carbon NOUN SCIENCE Carbon is a chemical element that is pure in diamonds and also found in coal. All living things contain carbon. Its atomic number is 6 and its symbol is C.
WORD HISTORY: from Latin *carbo* meaning 'charcoal'

carbonated ADJECTIVE Carbonated drinks contain bubbles of carbon dioxide that make them fizzy.

carbon cycle, carbon cycles NOUN SCIENCE The carbon cycle is the circulation of carbon between living organisms and their surroundings.

carbon dioxide NOUN SCIENCE Carbon dioxide is a colourless, odourless gas that humans and animals breathe out. It is used in industry, for example in making fizzy drinks and in fire extinguishers.

carbon monoxide NOUN SCIENCE Carbon monoxide is a colourless, poisonous gas formed when carbon burns in a very small amount of air.

carburettor, carburettors [*Said kahr-bur-ret-ter*] NOUN the part of the engine in a vehicle in which air and petrol are mixed together.

carcass, carcasses; also spelt **carcase** NOUN the body of a dead animal.

carcinogen, carcinogens [*Said kahr-sin-ne-jen*] NOUN SCIENCE A carcinogen is a substance that causes cancer. **carcinogenic** ADJECTIVE

card, cards NOUN ①a piece of stiff paper or plastic with information or a message on it • *a birthday card.* ②Cards can mean playing cards • *a poor set of cards with which to play.* ③When you play cards, you play any game using playing cards. ④Card is thick, stiff paper.
WORD HISTORY: from Greek *khartēs* meaning 'papyrus leaf'

cardboard NOUN Cardboard is thick, stiff paper.

cardiac ADJECTIVE relating to the heart • *cardiac disease.*

cardigan, cardigans NOUN a knitted jacket that fastens up the front.

cardinal, cardinals NOUN ① a high-ranking member of the Roman Catholic clergy who chooses and advises the Pope. ▶ ADJECTIVE ② extremely important • *a cardinal principle of law.*

WORD HISTORY: from Latin *cardo* meaning 'hinge'. When something is important, other things hinge on it

cardiovascular ADJECTIVE of or relating to the heart and the blood vessels • *Exercise is important for maintaining cardiovascular fitness.*

care, cares, caring, cared VERB ① If you care about something, you are concerned about it and interested in it. ② If you care about someone, you feel affection towards them. ③ If you care for someone, you look after them. ▶ NOUN ④ Care is concern or worry. ⑤ Care of someone or something is treatment for them or looking after them • *the care of young children.* ⑥ If you do something with care, you do it with close attention.

career, careers, careering, careered NOUN ① PSHE the series of jobs that someone has in life, usually in the same occupation • *a career in insurance.* ▶ VERB ② To career somewhere is to move very quickly, often out of control • *His car careered off the road.*

carefree ADJECTIVE having no worries or responsibilities.

careful ADJECTIVE ① acting sensibly and with care • *Be careful what you say to him.* ② complete and well done • *It needs very careful planning.* **carefully** ADVERB

SIMILAR WORDS: ① cautious, prudent

careless ADJECTIVE ① done badly without enough attention • *careless driving.* ② relaxed and unconcerned • *careless laughter.* **carelessly** ADVERB **carelessness** NOUN

SIMILAR WORDS: ① slapdash, sloppy

carer, carers NOUN a person who looks after someone who is ill or elderly, often a relative.

caress, caresses, caressing, caressed VERB ① If you caress someone, you stroke them gently and affectionately. ▶ NOUN ② a gentle, affectionate stroke.

SIMILAR WORDS: ① fondle, stroke

caretaker, caretakers NOUN ① a person who looks after a large building such as a school. ▶ ADJECTIVE ② having an important position for a short time until a new person is appointed • *O'Leary was named caretaker manager.*

cargo, cargoes NOUN the goods carried on a ship or plane.

Caribbean NOUN The Caribbean consists of the Caribbean Sea east of Central America and the islands in it.

caricature, caricatures, caricaturing, caricatured NOUN ① a drawing or description of someone that exaggerates striking parts of their appearance or personality. ▶ VERB ② To caricature someone is to give a caricature of them.

carjack, carjacks, carjacking, carjacked VERB If a car is carjacked, its driver is attacked and robbed, or the car is stolen.

carnage [Said *kahr-nij*] NOUN Carnage is the violent killing of large numbers of people.

carnal ADJECTIVE (formal) relating to the body rather than the spirit • *carnal pleasure.*

carnation, carnations NOUN a plant

with a long stem and white, pink or red flowers.

carnival, carnivals NOUN a public festival with music, processions and dancing.

carnivore, carnivores NOUN an animal that eats meat. **carnivorous** ADJECTIVE

carol, carols NOUN a religious song sung at Christmas time.

carousel, carousels [Said kar-ros-**sel**] NOUN a merry-go-round.

carp, carps, carping, carped NOUN ① a large edible freshwater fish. ▶ VERB ② To carp means to complain about unimportant things.

carpel, carpels NOUN SCIENCE the seed-bearing female part of a flower.

carpenter, carpenters NOUN a person who makes and repairs wooden structures. **carpentry** NOUN

carpet, carpets, carpeting, carpeted NOUN ① a thick covering for a floor, usually made of a material like wool. ▶ VERB ② To carpet a floor means to cover it with a carpet.

carpet snake, carpet snakes NOUN a large harmless Australian snake with a carpet-like pattern on its back.

carriage, carriages NOUN ① one of the separate sections of a passenger train. ② an old-fashioned vehicle for carrying passengers, usually pulled by horses.

carriageway, carriageways NOUN one of the sides of a road which traffic travels along in one direction only.

carrier, carriers NOUN ① a vehicle that is used for carrying things • *a troop carrier*. ② A carrier of a germ or disease is a person or animal that can pass it on to others.

carrier bag, carrier bags NOUN a bag made of plastic or paper, which is used for carrying shopping.

carrion NOUN Carrion is the decaying flesh of dead animals.

carrot, carrots NOUN a long, thin orange root vegetable.

SPELLING TIP

Do not confuse the spellings of *carrot* and *carat*: *Rabbits love lettuce and carrots; a huge 55 carat diamond*.

carry, carries, carrying, carried VERB ① To carry something is to hold it and take it somewhere. ② When a vehicle carries people, they travel in it. ③ A person or animal that carries a germ can pass it on to other people or animals • *I still carry the disease*. ④ If a sound carries, it can be heard far away • *Jake's voice carried over the cheering*. ⑤ In a meeting, if a proposal is carried, it is accepted by a majority of the people there. **carry away** VERB If you are carried away, you are so excited by something that you do not behave sensibly. **carry on** VERB To carry on doing something means to continue doing it. **carry out** VERB To carry something out means to do it and complete it • *The conversion was carried out by a local builder*.

SIMILAR WORDS: ② bear, convey, take

carrying capacity, carrying capacities NOUN GEOGRAPHY the number of people or the amount of livestock that an area can support in terms of available resources.

cart, carts NOUN a vehicle with wheels, used to carry goods and often pulled by horses or cattle.

cartilage NOUN SCIENCE Cartilage is a strong, flexible substance found around the joints and in the nose and ears.

carton, cartons NOUN a cardboard or plastic container.

cartoon, cartoons NOUN ① a drawing or a series of drawings which are funny or make a point. ② a film in which the characters and scenes are drawn. **cartoonist** NOUN
WORD HISTORY: from Italian *cartone* meaning 'sketch on stiff paper'

cartridge, cartridges NOUN ① a tube containing a bullet and an explosive substance, used in guns. ② a plastic container full of ink that you put in a printer or pen.

cartwheel, cartwheels NOUN an acrobatic movement in which you throw yourself sideways onto one hand and move round in a circle with arms and legs stretched until you land on your feet again.

carve, carves, carving, carved VERB ① To carve an object means to cut it out of a substance such as stone or wood. ② To carve meat means to cut slices from it.

carving, carvings NOUN a carved object.

cascade, cascades, cascading, cascaded NOUN ① a waterfall or group of waterfalls. ▶VERB ② To cascade means to flow downwards quickly • *Gallons of water cascaded from the attic.*

case, cases NOUN ① a particular situation, event or example • *a clear case of mistaken identity.* ② a container for something, or a suitcase • *a camera case.* ③ Doctors sometimes refer to a patient as a case. ④ Police detectives refer to a crime they are investigating as a case. ⑤ In an argument, the case for an idea is the reasons used to support it. ⑥ In law, a case is a trial or other inquiry. ⑦ In grammar, the case of a noun or pronoun is the form

of it which shows its relationship with other words in a sentence • *the accusative case.* ▶PHRASE ⑧ You say **in case** to explain something that you do because a particular thing might happen • *I didn't want to shout in case I startled you.* ⑨ You say **in that case** to show that you are assuming something said before is true • *In that case we won't do it.*
SIMILAR WORDS: ① instance, circumstance, circumstances, situation

casement, casements NOUN a window that opens on hinges at one side.

cash NOUN Cash is money in notes and coins.
WORD HISTORY: from Italian *cassa* meaning 'money-box'

cashew, cashews [Said kash-oo] NOUN a curved, edible nut.

cash flow NOUN Cash flow is the money that a business makes and spends.

cashier, cashiers NOUN the person that customers pay in a shop or get money from in a bank.

cashmere NOUN Cashmere is very soft, fine wool from goats.

cash register, cash registers NOUN a machine in a shop which records sales, and where the money is kept.

casing, casings NOUN a protective covering for something.

casino, casinos [Said kass-ee-noh] NOUN a place where people go to play gambling games.

cask, casks NOUN a wooden barrel.

casket, caskets NOUN ① a small box for jewellery or other valuables. ② In American English, a casket is a coffin.
WORD HISTORY: from Old French *cassette* meaning 'little box'

casserole, casseroles NOUN a dish made by cooking a mixture of meat

a b c d e f g h i j k l m n o p q r s t u v w x y z

and vegetables slowly in an oven; also used to refer to the pot a casserole is cooked in.

cassock, **cassocks** NOUN a long robe that is worn by some members of the clergy.

cassowary, **cassowaries** NOUN a large bird found in Australia with black feathers and a brightly coloured neck. Cassowaries cannot fly.

cast, **casts**, **casting**, **cast** NOUN ① all the people who act in a play or film. ② an object made by pouring liquid into a mould and leaving it to harden • *the casts of classical sculptures*. ③ a stiff plaster covering put on broken bones to keep them still so that they heal properly. ▶ VERB ④ To cast actors is to choose them for roles in a play or film. ⑤ When people cast their votes in an election, they vote. ⑥ To cast something is to throw it. ⑦ If you cast your eyes somewhere, you look there • *I cast my eyes down briefly*. ⑧ To cast an object is to make it by pouring liquid into a mould and leaving it to harden • *An image of him has been cast in bronze*. **cast off** VERB If you cast off, you untie the rope fastening a boat to a harbour or shore.

castanets PLURAL NOUN Castanets are a Spanish musical instrument consisting of two small round pieces of wood that are clicked together with the fingers.

WORD HISTORY: from Spanish *castañetas* meaning 'little chestnuts'

castaway, **castaways** NOUN a person who has been shipwrecked.

caste, **castes** NOUN ① RE one of the four classes into which Hindu society is divided. ② Caste is a system of social classes decided according to family, wealth and position.

caster sugar; also spelt **castor sugar** NOUN Caster sugar is very fine white sugar used in cooking.

castigate, **castigates**, **castigating**, **castigated** VERB (*formal*) To castigate someone is to criticise them severely.

cast iron NOUN ① Cast iron is iron which is made into objects by casting. ▶ ADJECTIVE ② A cast-iron excuse or guarantee is absolutely certain and firm.

castle, **castles** NOUN ① HISTORY a large building with walls or ditches round it to protect it from attack. ② In chess, a castle is the same as a rook.

cast-off, **cast-offs** NOUN a piece of outgrown or discarded clothing that has been passed on to someone else.

castor, **castors**; also spelt **caster** NOUN a small wheel fitted to furniture so that it can be moved easily.

castrate, **castrates**, **castrating**, **castrated** VERB To castrate a male animal is to remove its testicles so that it can no longer produce sperm. **castration** NOUN

casual ADJECTIVE ① happening by chance without planning • *a casual remark*. ② careless or without interest • *a casual glance over his shoulder*. ③ Casual clothes are suitable for informal occasions. ④ Casual work is not regular or permanent. **casually** ADVERB **casualness** NOUN
SIMILAR WORDS: ② careless, nonchalant, offhand

casualty, **casualties** NOUN a person killed or injured in an accident or war • *Many of the casualties were office workers*.

casuarina, **casuarinas** [Said *kass-you-a-rine-a*] NOUN an

Australian tree with jointed green branches.

cat, cats NOUN ① a small furry animal with whiskers, a tail, and sharp claws, often kept as a pet. ② any of the family of mammals that includes lions and tigers.

catacomb, catacombs [Said *kat-a-koom*] NOUN Catacombs are underground passages where dead bodies are buried.

catalogue, catalogues, cataloguing, catalogued NOUN ① a book containing pictures and descriptions of goods that you can buy in a shop or through the post. ② LIBRARY a list of things such as the objects in a museum or the books in a library. ▶ VERB ③ To catalogue a collection of things means to list them in a catalogue.

catalyst, catalysts [Said *kat-a-list*] NOUN ① something that causes a change to happen • *the catalyst which provoked civil war*. ② SCIENCE a substance that speeds up a chemical reaction without changing itself.

catalytic converter, catalytic converters NOUN SCIENCE a device that is fitted to a car's exhaust to reduce the pollution coming from it.

catamaran, catamarans NOUN a sailing boat with two hulls connected to each other.

WORD HISTORY: from Tamil *kattumaram* meaning 'tied logs'

catapult, catapults, catapulting, catapulted NOUN ① a Y-shaped object with a piece of elastic tied between the two top ends, used for shooting small stones. ▶ VERB ② To catapult something is to throw it violently through the air. ③ If someone is catapulted into a situation, they find themselves unexpectedly in that situation • *Tony*

has been catapulted into the limelight.

cataract, cataracts NOUN an area of the lens of someone's eye that has become white instead of clear, so that they cannot see properly.

catarrh [Said *kat-tahr*] NOUN Catarrh is a condition in which you get a lot of mucus in your nose and throat.

catastrophe, catastrophes [Said *kat-tass-trif-fee*] NOUN a terrible disaster. **catastrophic** ADJECTIVE

catch, catches, catching, caught VERB ① If you catch a ball moving in the air, you grasp hold of it when it comes near you. ② To catch an animal means to trap it • *I caught ten fish*. ③ When the police catch criminals, they find them and arrest them. ④ If you catch someone doing something they should not be doing, you discover them doing it • *He caught me playing the church organ*. ⑤ If you catch a bus or train, you get on it and travel somewhere. ⑥ If you catch a cold or a disease, you become infected with it. ⑦ If something catches on an object, it sticks to it or gets trapped • *The white fibres caught on the mesh*. ▶ NOUN ⑧ a device that fastens something. ⑨ a problem or hidden complication in something.
catch on VERB ① If you catch on to something, you understand it. ② If something catches on, it becomes popular • *The show has never really caught on with TV viewers*. **catch out** VERB To catch someone out is to trick them or trap them. **catch up** VERB ① To catch up with someone in front of you is to reach the place where they are by moving slightly faster than them. ② To catch up with someone is also to reach the same level or standard as them.
SIMILAR WORDS: ② capture, snare, trap ③ apprehend, arrest, capture ⑥ contract, develop, go down with

catching ADJECTIVE tending to spread very quickly • *Measles is catching.*

catchment area, catchment areas NOUN A catchment area is the area that a school, hospital or other institution serves.

catchy, catchier, catchiest ADJECTIVE attractive and easily remembered • *a catchy little tune.*

catechism, catechisms [*Said* kat-ik-kizm*]* NOUN a set of questions and answers about the main beliefs of a religion.

categorical ADJECTIVE absolutely certain and direct • *a categorical denial.* **categorically** ADVERB

categorise, categorises, categorising, categorised; also spelt **categorize** VERB To categorise things is to arrange them in different categories.

category, categories NOUN a set of things with a particular characteristic in common • *Occupations can be divided into four categories.*

cater, caters, catering, catered VERB To cater for people is to provide them with what they need, especially food.

caterer, caterers NOUN a person or business that provides food for parties and groups.

caterpillar, caterpillars NOUN the larva of a butterfly or moth. It looks like a small coloured worm and feeds on plants.
WORD HISTORY: from Old French *catepelose* meaning 'hairy cat'

catharsis, catharses [*Said* kath-ar-siss*]* NOUN (*formal*) Catharsis is the release of strong emotions and feelings by expressing them through drama or literature.

cathedral, cathedrals NOUN
HISTORY an important church with a bishop in charge of it.

Catholic, Catholics NOUN or ADJECTIVE ① (a) Roman Catholic.
▶ ADJECTIVE ② If a person has catholic interests, they have a wide range of interests. **Catholicism** NOUN
WORD HISTORY: from Greek *katholikos* meaning 'universal'

SPELLING TIP
When *Catholic* begins with a capital letter, it refers to the religion. When it begins with a small letter, it means 'covering a wide range'.

cattle PLURAL NOUN Cattle are cows and bulls kept by farmers.

catty, cattier, cattiest ADJECTIVE unpleasant and spiteful. **cattiness** NOUN

catwalk, catwalks NOUN a narrow pathway that people walk along, for example over a stage.

Caucasian, Caucasians [*Said* kaw-kayz-yn*]* NOUN a person belonging to a race of people with fair or light-brown skin.
WORD HISTORY: from *Caucasia*, a region in SW Russia, Georgia, Armenia and Azerbaijan

caught the past tense and past participle of **catch**.

cauldron, cauldrons NOUN a large, round, metal cooking pot, especially one that sits over a fire.

cauliflower, cauliflowers NOUN a large, round, white vegetable surrounded by green leaves.

cause, causes, causing, caused NOUN ① The cause of something is the thing that makes it happen • *the most common cause of back pain.* ② an aim or principle which a group of people are working for • *dedication to the cause of peace.* ③ If you have cause for something, you have a reason for it • *They gave us no cause to believe that.*

▶ **VERB** ④ To cause something is to make it happen • *This can cause delays*.

causal ADJECTIVE

WORD HISTORY: from Latin *causa* meaning 'cause' or 'reason'

causeway, causeways NOUN a raised path or road across water or marshland.

WORD HISTORY: from Latin *calciatus* meaning 'paved with limestone'

caustic ADJECTIVE ① A caustic chemical can destroy substances • *caustic liquids such as acids*. ② bitter or sarcastic • *your caustic sense of humour*.

caution, cautions, cautioning, cautioned NOUN ① Caution is great care which you take to avoid danger • *You will need to proceed with caution*. ② a warning • *Sutton was let off with a caution*. ▶ VERB ③ If someone cautions you, they warn you, usually not to do something again • *A man has been cautioned by police*.

cautionary ADJECTIVE

cautious ADJECTIVE acting very carefully to avoid danger • *a cautious approach*. **cautiously** ADVERB

cavalcade, cavalcades NOUN a procession of people on horses or in cars or carriages.

cavalier [Said kav-val-**eer**] ADJECTIVE Someone who is cavalier behaves without sensitivity, or does not take something seriously enough • *a cavalier attitude to friendships*.

cavalry NOUN The cavalry is the part of an army that uses armoured vehicles or horses.

cave, caves, caving, caved NOUN ① a large hole in rock, that is underground or in the side of a cliff. ▶ VERB ② If a roof caves in, it collapses inwards.

caveman, cavemen NOUN Cavemen were people who lived in caves in prehistoric times.

cavern, caverns NOUN a large cave.

cavernous ADJECTIVE large, deep and hollow • *a cavernous warehouse*.

caviar [Said kav-vee-ar] NOUN Caviar is the tiny salted eggs of a fish called the sturgeon.

cavity, cavities NOUN a small hole in something solid • *There were dark cavities in his back teeth*.

cavort, cavorts, cavorting, cavorted VERB When people cavort, they jump around excitedly.

cc an abbreviation for 'cubic centimetres'.

CD an abbreviation for 'compact disc'.

CE CE means 'Common Era'. Non-Christians use 'CE' in dates as an alternative to 'AD' • *410 CE*.

cease, ceases, ceasing, ceased VERB ① If something ceases, it stops happening. ② If you cease to do something, or cease doing it, you stop doing it.

ceasefire, ceasefires NOUN an agreement between groups that are fighting each other to stop for a period and discuss peace.

ceaseless ADJECTIVE going on without stopping • *ceaseless chatter*. **ceaselessly** ADVERB

cedar, cedars NOUN a large evergreen tree with wide branches and needle-shaped leaves.

cede, cedes, ceding, ceded [Said seed] VERB To cede something is to give it up to someone else • *Haiti was ceded to France in 1697*.

ceiling, ceilings NOUN the top inside surface of a room.

celebrate, celebrates, celebrating, celebrated VERB ① If you celebrate or celebrate something, you do something special and enjoyable because of it • *a party to celebrate the* end of the exams. ② When a priest celebrates Mass, he performs the ceremonies of the Mass.

celebrated ADJECTIVE famous • *the celebrated Italian mountaineer.*

celebration, celebrations NOUN an event in honour of a special occasion. **celebratory** ADJECTIVE

celebrity, celebrities NOUN a famous person.

celery NOUN Celery is a vegetable with long, pale green stalks.

celestial [*Said* sil-**lest**-yal] ADJECTIVE (*formal*) concerning the sky or heaven • *The telescope is pointed at a celestial object.*

celibate [*Said* sel-**lib**-bit] ADJECTIVE Someone who is celibate does not marry. **celibacy** NOUN

cell, cells NOUN ① SCIENCE In biology, a cell is the smallest part of an animal or plant that can exist by itself. Each cell contains a nucleus. ② a small room where a prisoner is kept in a prison or police station. ③ a small group of people set up to work together as part of a larger organisation. ④ DGT a device that converts chemical energy to electricity.

cellar, cellars NOUN a room underneath a building, often used to store wine.

cello, cellos [*Said* **chel**-loh] NOUN MUSIC a large musical stringed instrument which you play sitting down, holding the instrument upright with your knees. **cellist** NOUN

Cellophane NOUN DGT (*trademark*) Cellophane is thin, transparent plastic material used as a protective covering.

cellphone, cellphones NOUN a small portable telephone.

cellular ADJECTIVE Cellular means relating to the cells of animals or plants.

Celsius [*Said* **sel**-see-yuss] NOUN SCIENCE Celsius is a scale for measuring temperature in which water freezes at 0 degrees (0°C) and boils at 100 degrees (100°C). It is named after Anders Celsius (1701–1744), who invented it. Celsius is the same as 'Centigrade'.

Celtic [*Said* **kel**-tik] ADJECTIVE A Celtic language is one of a group of languages that includes Gaelic and Welsh.

cement, cements, cementing, cemented NOUN ① Cement is a fine powder made from limestone and clay, which is mixed with sand and water to make concrete. ▶ VERB ② To cement things is to stick them together with cement or cover them with cement. ③ Something that cements a relationship makes it stronger • *to cement relations between them.*

cemetery, cemeteries NOUN an area of land where dead people are buried.

cenotaph, cenotaphs [*Said* **sen**-not-ahf] NOUN a monument built in memory of dead people, especially soldiers buried elsewhere.
WORD HISTORY: from Greek *kenos* + *taphos* meaning 'empty tomb'

censor, censors, censoring, censored NOUN ① a person officially appointed to examine books or films and to ban parts that are considered unsuitable. ▶ VERB ② If someone censors a book or film, they cut or ban parts of it that are considered unsuitable for the public.
censorship NOUN

censure, censures, censuring, censured [*Said* **sen**-sher] NOUN ① Censure is strong disapproval of something. ▶ VERB ②To censure someone is to criticise them severely.

census, censuses NOUN an official survey of the population of a country.

cent, cents NOUN a unit of currency. In the USA and the Caribbean, a cent is worth one hundredth of a dollar; in Europe, it is worth one hundredth of a euro.

centaur, centaurs [Said sen-tawr] NOUN a creature in Greek mythology with the top half of a man and the lower body and legs of a horse.

centenary, centenaries [Said sen-teen-er-ee] NOUN the hundredth anniversary of something.

centi- PREFIX 'Centi-' is used to form words that have 'hundred' as part of their meaning • centimetre.

Centigrade Centigrade is another name for **Celsius**.

USAGE NOTE

Scientists say and write Celsius rather than Centigrade.

---

centimetre, centimetres NOUN a unit of length equal to ten millimetres or one hundredth of a metre.

centipede, centipedes NOUN a long, thin, insect-like creature with many pairs of legs.

central ADJECTIVE ①in or near the centre of an object or area • central ceiling lights. ②main or most important • the central idea of this work. **centrally** ADVERB **centrality** NOUN

Central America NOUN Central America is the area of land joining North America to South America.

central bank, central banks NOUN a national bank that acts as the government's banker, controls credit, and issues currency.

central heating NOUN Central heating is a system of heating a building in which water or air is heated in a tank and travels through pipes and radiators round the building.

centralise, centralises, centralising, centralised; also spelt **centralize** VERB To centralise a system is to bring the organisation of it under the control of one central group. **centralisation** NOUN

centre, centres, centring, centred NOUN ①the middle of an object or area. ②a building where people go for activities, meetings or help • a health centre. ③Someone or something that is the centre of attention attracts a lot of attention. ▶ VERB ④To centre something is to move it so that it is balanced or at the centre of something else. ⑤If something centres on or around a particular thing, that thing is the main subject of attention • The discussion centred on his request.

SIMILAR WORDS: ①heart, middle

centurion, centurions NOUN HISTORY an ancient Roman officer in charge of a hundred soldiers.

century, centuries NOUN ①a period of one hundred years. ②In cricket, a century is one hundred runs scored by a batsman.

ceramic, ceramics [Said si-ram-mik] NOUN ① SCIENCE Ceramic is a hard material made by baking clay to a very high temperature. ②Ceramics is the art of making objects out of clay.

cereal, cereals NOUN ①a food made from grain, often eaten with milk for breakfast. ②a plant that produces edible grain, such as wheat or oats.

SPELLING TIP

Do not confuse the spellings of cereal

and *serial*: *my favourite breakfast cereal; a new drama serial.*

cerebral [Said **ser**-reb-ral] ADJECTIVE (formal) relating to the brain • *a cerebral haemorrhage.*

cerebral palsy NOUN Cerebral palsy is an illness caused by damage to a baby's brain, which makes its muscles and limbs very weak.

ceremonial ADJECTIVE ① relating to a ceremony • *ceremonial dress.* ② If a job is ceremonial, it does not have any influence or authority attached to it. **ceremonially** ADVERB

ceremony, ceremonies NOUN ① a set of formal actions performed at a special occasion or important public event • *his recent coronation ceremony.* ② Ceremony is very formal and polite behaviour • *He hung up without ceremony.*

certain ADJECTIVE ① definite or reliable • *He is certain to be in Italy.* ② having no doubt in your mind. ③ You use 'certain' to refer to a specific person or thing • *certain aspects of the job.* ④ You use 'certain' to suggest that a quality is noticeable but not obvious • *There's a certain resemblance to Joe.*

certainly ADVERB ① without doubt • *My boss was certainly interested.* ② of course • *'Will you be there?' — 'Certainly.'*

certainty, certainties NOUN ① Certainty is the state of being certain. ② something that is known without doubt • *There are no certainties and no guarantees.*

certificate, certificates NOUN a document stating particular facts, for example of someone's birth or death • *a marriage certificate.*

certify, certifies, certifying, certified VERB ① To certify something means to declare formally that it is true • *certifying the cause of*

death. ② To certify someone means to declare officially that they are insane.

cervical [Said **ser**-vik-kl] ADJECTIVE (technical) relating to the cervix.

cervix, cervixes or cervices NOUN (technical) The cervix is the entrance to the womb.
WORD HISTORY: from Latin *cervix* meaning 'neck'

cessation NOUN (formal) The cessation of something is the stopping of it • *a swift cessation of hostilities.*

cf. cf. means 'compare'. It is written after something in a text to mention something else which the reader should compare with what has just been written.

CFC, CFCs NOUN CFCs are manufactured chemicals that were formerly used in aerosol sprays and refrigerators. They damage the ozone layer. CFC is an abbreviation for 'chlorofluorocarbon'.

CGI NOUN CGI is computer technology that is used to make special effects in cinema and on television. CGI is an abbreviation for 'computer-generated imagery'.

chaff NOUN Chaff is the outer parts of grain separated from the seeds by beating.

chaffinch, chaffinches NOUN a small European bird with black and white wings.

chagrin [Said **shag**-rin] NOUN (formal) Chagrin is a feeling of annoyance or disappointment.

chain, chains, chaining, chained NOUN ① a number of metal rings connected together in a line • *a bicycle chain.* ② a number of things in a series or connected to each other • *a chain of shops.* ▶VERB ③ If you chain one thing to another, you fasten them together with a chain • *They had chained themselves to railings*.

chain saw, chain saws NOUN a large saw with teeth fixed in a chain that is driven round by a motor.

chair, chairs, chairing, chaired NOUN ① a seat with a back and four legs for one person. ② the person in charge of a meeting who decides when each person may speak. ▶ VERB ③ The person who chairs a meeting is in charge of it.

chair lift, chair lifts NOUN a line of chairs that hang from a moving cable and carry people up and down a mountain.

chairperson, chairpersons NOUN ① the person in charge of a meeting who decides when each person may speak. ② the head of a company or committee. **chairman** NOUN **chairwoman** NOUN

chalet, chalets [*Said shall-lay*] NOUN a wooden house with a sloping roof, especially in a mountain area or a holiday camp.

chalice, chalices [*Said chal-liss*] NOUN RE a gold or silver cup used in churches to hold the Communion wine.

chalk, chalks, chalking, chalked NOUN ① ART Chalk is a soft white rock. Small sticks of chalk are used for writing or drawing on a blackboard. ▶ VERB ② To chalk up a result is to achieve it • *He chalked up his first win*. **chalky** ADJECTIVE

challenge, challenges, challenging, challenged NOUN ① something that is new and exciting but requires a lot of effort • *It's a new challenge at the right time in my career*. ② a suggestion from someone to compete with them. ③ A challenge to something is a questioning of whether it is correct

or true • *a challenge to authority*. ▶ VERB ④ If someone challenges you, they suggest that you compete with them in some way. ⑤ If you challenge something, you question whether it is correct or true. **challenger** NOUN **challenging** ADJECTIVE

SIMILAR WORDS: ⑤ dispute, question

chamber, chambers NOUN ① a large room, especially one used for formal meetings • *the Council Chamber*. ② a group of people chosen to decide laws or administrative matters. ③ a hollow place or compartment inside something, especially inside an animal's body or inside a gun • *the chambers of the heart*. ④ (in plural) Chambers are a room where judges hear cases that are not being heard in an open court.

chambermaid, chambermaids NOUN a woman who cleans and tidies rooms in a hotel.

chameleon, chameleons [*Said kam-mee-lee-on*] NOUN a lizard which is able to change the colour of its skin to match the colour of its surroundings.

WORD HISTORY: from Greek *khamai* + *leōn* meaning 'ground lion'

chamois leather, chamois leathers [*Said sham-mee*] NOUN a soft leather cloth used for polishing.

chamomile another spelling of **camomile**.

champagne, champagnes [*Said sham-pain*] NOUN Champagne is a sparkling white wine made in France.

champion, champions, championing, championed NOUN ① a person who wins a competition. ② someone who supports or defends a cause or principle • *a champion of women's causes*. ▶ VERB ③ Someone who champions a cause or principle supports or defends it.

a b c d e f g h i j k l m n o p q r s t u v w x y z

championship, championships
NOUN a competition to find the
champion of a sport.

chance, chances, chancing,
chanced NOUN ① The chance of
something happening is how
possible or likely it is • *There's a chance
of rain later*. ② an opportunity to do
something • *Your chance to be a TV
star!* ③ a possibility that something
dangerous or unpleasant may
happen • *Don't take chances, he's
armed*. ④ Chance is also the way
things happen unexpectedly without
being planned • *I only found out by
chance*. ▶ VERB ⑤ If you chance
something, you try it although you
are taking a risk.
SIMILAR WORDS: ④ accident,
coincidence, luck

chancellor, chancellors NOUN
① the head of government in some
European countries. ② In Britain, the
Chancellor is the Chancellor of the
Exchequer. ③ the honorary head of a
university.

Chancellor of the Exchequer
NOUN In Britain, the Chancellor of
the Exchequer is the minister
responsible for finance and taxes.

chandelier, chandeliers [Said
shan-del-leer] NOUN an ornamental
light fitting which hangs from the
ceiling.

change, changes, changing,
changed NOUN ① a difference or
alteration in something • *Steven soon
noticed a change in Penny's attitude*.
② a replacement of something by
something else • *a change of clothes*.
③ Change is money you get back
when you have paid more than the
actual price of something. ▶ VERB
④ When something changes or when
you change it, it becomes different
• *It changed my life*. ⑤ If you change
something, you exchange it for

something else. ⑥ When you
change, you put on different clothes.
⑦ To change money means to
exchange it for smaller coins of the
same total value, or to exchange it
for foreign currency.

changeable ADJECTIVE likely to
change all the time.
SIMILAR WORDS: erratic, inconstant,
variable

changeover, changeovers NOUN a
change from one system or activity
to another • *the changeover between
day and night*.

channel, channels, channelling,
channelled NOUN ① a wavelength
used to receive programmes
broadcast by a television or radio
station; also the station itself • *I was
watching another channel*. ② a passage
along which water flows or along
which something is carried. ③ The
Channel or the English Channel is the
stretch of sea between England and
France. ④ a method of achieving
something • *We have tried to do things
through the right channels*. ▶ VERB
⑤ To channel something such as
money or energy means to direct it in
a particular way • *Their efforts are
being channelled into worthy causes*.

chant, chants, chanting, chanted
NOUN ① a group of words repeated
over and over again • *a rousing chant*.
② a religious song sung on only a few
notes. ▶ VERB ③ If people chant a
group of words, they repeat them
over and over again • *Crowds chanted
his name*.

Chanukah another spelling of
Hanukkah.

chaos [Said *kay-oss*] NOUN Chaos is a
state of complete disorder and
confusion. **chaotic** ADJECTIVE

chap, chaps, chapping, chapped
NOUN ① (*informal*) a man. ▶ VERB ② If

your skin chaps, it becomes dry and cracked, usually as a result of cold or wind.

chapel, chapels NOUN ① a section of a church or cathedral with its own altar. ② a type of small church. **WORD HISTORY:** from Latin *capella* meaning 'small cloak'; originally used of the place where St Martin's cloak was kept as a relic

chaperone, chaperones *[Said shap-per-rone]*; also spelt **chaperon** NOUN an older woman who accompanies a young unmarried woman on social occasions, or any person who accompanies a group of younger people.

chaplain, chaplains NOUN a member of the Christian clergy who regularly works in a hospital, school or prison. **chaplaincy** NOUN

chapter, chapters NOUN ① one of the parts into which a book is divided. ② a particular period in someone's life or in history.

char, chars, charring, charred VERB If something chars, it gets partly burned and goes black. **charred** ADJECTIVE

character, characters NOUN ① all the qualities which combine to form the personality of a person or the atmosphere of a place. ② A person or place that has character has an interesting, attractive or admirable quality • *an inn of great character and simplicity.* ③ ENGLISH The characters in a film, play or book are the people in it. ④ a person • *an odd character.* ⑤ a letter, number or other written symbol. **SIMILAR WORDS:** ① nature, personality, quality

characterise, characterises, characterising, characterised; also spelt **characterize** VERB A quality that characterises something is typical of it • *a condition characterised by muscle stiffness.*

characteristic, characteristics NOUN ① a quality that is typical of a particular person or thing • *Silence is the characteristic of the place.* ② SCIENCE a feature that is typical of a particular living thing. ▶ ADJECTIVE ③ Characteristic means typical of a particular person or thing • *Two things are very characteristic of his driving.* **characteristically** ADVERB

characterless ADJECTIVE dull and uninteresting • *a tiny characterless flat.*

charade, charades *[Said shar-rahd]* NOUN a ridiculous and unnecessary activity or pretence. **WORD HISTORY:** from Provençal *charrado* meaning 'chat'

charcoal NOUN Charcoal is a black form of carbon made by burning wood without air, used as a fuel and also for drawing.

charge, charges, charging, charged VERB ① If someone charges you money, they ask you to pay it for something you have bought or received • *The company charged £150 on each loan.* ② To charge someone means to accuse them formally of having committed a crime. ③ To charge the battery of an electrical device means to pass an electrical current through it to make it store electricity. ④ To charge somewhere means to rush forward, often to attack someone • *The rhino charged at her.* ▶ NOUN ⑤ the price that you have to pay for something. ⑥ a formal accusation that a person is guilty of a crime and has to go to court. ⑦ To have charge or be in charge of someone or something means to be responsible for them and be in control of them. ⑧ an explosive put in a gun or other weapon. ⑨ SCIENCE An electrical charge is the amount of electricity that something carries.

charger, chargers NOUN a device for charging or recharging batteries.

chariot, chariots NOUN a two-wheeled open vehicle pulled by horses.

charisma [Said kar-riz-ma] NOUN Charisma is a special ability to attract or influence people by your personality. **charismatic** ADJECTIVE

charity, charities NOUN ① an organisation that raises money to help people or animals in need. ② Charity is money or other help given to people or animals in need • to help raise money for charity. ③ Charity is also a kind, sympathetic attitude towards people. **charitable** ADJECTIVE

charlatan, charlatans [Said shar-lat-tn] NOUN someone who pretends to have skill or knowledge that they do not really have.

charm, charms, charming, charmed NOUN ① Charm is an attractive and pleasing quality that some people and things have • a man of great personal charm. ② a small ornament worn on a bracelet. ③ a magical spell or an object that is supposed to bring good luck. ▸ VERB ④ If you charm someone, you use your charm to please them.

charmer, charmers NOUN someone who uses their charm to influence people.

charming ADJECTIVE very pleasant and attractive • a rather charming man. **charmingly** ADVERB

chart, charts, charting, charted NOUN ① a diagram or table showing information • He noted the score on his chart. ② a map of the sea or stars.

▸ VERB ③ If you chart something, you observe and record it carefully.

charter, charters, chartering, chartered NOUN ① a document stating the rights or aims of a group or organisation, often written by the government • the new charter for commuters. ▸ VERB ② To charter transport such as a plane or boat is to hire it for private use. **chartered** ADJECTIVE

chase, chases, chasing, chased VERB ① If you chase someone or something, you run after them in order to catch them. ② If you chase someone, you force them to go somewhere else. ▸ NOUN ③ the activity of chasing or hunting someone or something • a high-speed car chase.

SIMILAR WORDS: ① hunt, pursue

chasm, chasms [Said kazm] NOUN ① a deep crack in the earth's surface. ② a very large difference between two ideas or groups of people • the chasm between rich and poor in America.

chassis, chassis [Said shas-ee] NOUN the frame on which a vehicle is built.

GRAMMAR TIP
The plural of chassis is also chassis.

chaste [Said chayst] ADJECTIVE (old-fashioned) pure and well-behaved. **chastity** NOUN

chastise, chastises, chastising, chastised VERB (formal) If someone chastises you, they criticise you or punish you for something that you have done.

chat, chats, chatting, chatted NOUN ① a friendly talk with someone, usually about things that are not very important. ② the exchange of messages on a computer network.
▸ VERB ③ When people chat, they talk to each other in a friendly way.

chat up VERB (*informal*) If you chat up someone, you talk to them in a friendly way, because you are attracted to them.
SIMILAR WORDS: ① gossip, natter, talk ③ gossip, natter, talk

chateau, chateaux [*Said shat-toe*] NOUN a large country house or castle in France.

chatroom, chatrooms NOUN an internet site where people read and post messages.

chatter, chatters, chattering, chattered VERB ① When people chatter, they talk very fast. ② If your teeth are chattering, they are knocking together and making a clicking noise because you are cold. ▶ NOUN ③ Chatter is a lot of fast unimportant talk.

chatty, chattier, chattiest ADJECTIVE talkative and friendly.

chauffeur, chauffeurs [*Said show-fur*] NOUN a person whose job is to drive another person's car.

chauvinist, chauvinists NOUN ① a person who thinks their country is always right. ② A male chauvinist is a man who believes that men are superior to women. **chauvinistic** ADJECTIVE **chauvinism** NOUN

chav, chavs NOUN (*offensive*) In Britain, a chav is a young working-class person who is considered to have vulgar tastes.

cheap, cheaper, cheapest ADJECTIVE ① costing very little money. ② inexpensive but of poor quality. ③ A cheap joke or cheap remark is unfair and unkind. **cheaply** ADVERB
SIMILAR WORDS: ① inexpensive, reasonable

cheat, cheats, cheating, cheated VERB ① If someone cheats, they do wrong or unfair things to win or get something that they want. ② If you are cheated of or out of something, you do not get what you are entitled to. ▶ NOUN ③ a person who cheats.
SIMILAR WORDS: ① con, deceive, swindle

check, checks, checking, checked VERB ① To check something is to examine it in order to make sure that everything is all right. ② To check the growth or spread of something is to make it stop • *a policy to check fast population growth*. ▶ NOUN ③ an inspection to make sure that everything is all right. ④ In American English, a check is a bill in a restaurant. ⑤ (*in plural*) Checks are different coloured squares which form a pattern. ▶ PHRASE ⑥ If you keep something **in check**, you keep it under control • *She kept her emotions in check*. ▶ ADJECTIVE ⑦ Check or checked means marked with a pattern of squares • *check design*.

check in VERB When you check in at a hotel or airport, you arrive and sign your name or show your ticket.

check out VERB ① If you check something out, you inspect it and find out whether everything about it is right. ② When you check out of a hotel, you pay the bill and leave.

checkers PLURAL NOUN Checkers is the American name for the game of draughts.

checkmate NOUN In chess, checkmate is a situation where one player cannot stop their king being captured and so loses the game.
WORD HISTORY: from Arabic *shah mat* meaning 'the King is dead'

checkout, checkouts NOUN a counter in a supermarket where the customers pay for their goods.

checkpoint, checkpoints NOUN a place where traffic has to stop in order to be checked.

a b c d e f g h i j k l m n o p q r s t u v w x y z

checkup, checkups NOUN an examination by a doctor or dentist to see if you are healthy.

cheek, cheeks NOUN ① Your cheeks are the sides of your face below your eyes. ② Cheek is speech or behaviour that is rude or disrespectful • *an expression of sheer cheek*.

SIMILAR WORDS: ② impertinence, impudence, insolence

cheeky, cheekier, cheekiest ADJECTIVE rather rude and disrespectful.

cheer, cheers, cheering, cheered VERB ① When people cheer, they shout with approval or in order to show support for a person or team. ▶ NOUN ② a shout of approval or support. **cheer up** VERB When you cheer up, you feel more cheerful.

cheerful ADJECTIVE ① happy and in good spirits • *I had never seen her so cheerful*. ② bright and pleasant-looking • *a cheerful and charming place*. **cheerfully** ADVERB **cheerfulness** NOUN

cheerio INTERJECTION Cheerio is a friendly way of saying goodbye.

cheery, cheerier, cheeriest ADJECTIVE happy and cheerful • *He gave me a cheery nod*.

cheese, cheeses NOUN a hard or creamy food made from milk.

cheesecake, cheesecakes NOUN a dessert made of biscuit covered with smooth soft cheese.

cheetah, cheetahs NOUN a wild animal like a large cat with black spots.

WORD HISTORY: from Sanskrit *citra* + *kaya* meaning 'speckled body'

chef, chefs NOUN a head cook in a restaurant or hotel.

chemical, chemicals NOUN SCIENCE ① Chemicals are substances manufactured by chemistry.

▶ ADJECTIVE ② involved in chemistry or using chemicals • *chemical weapons*. **chemically** ADVERB

chemist, chemists NOUN ① a person who is qualified to make up drugs and medicines prescribed by a doctor. ② a shop where medicines and cosmetics are sold. ③ a scientist who does research in chemistry.

chemistry NOUN Chemistry is the scientific study of substances and the ways in which they change when they are combined with other substances.

chemotherapy [Said keem-oh-*ther-a*-pee] NOUN Chemotherapy is a way of treating diseases such as cancer by using chemicals.

cheque, cheques NOUN a printed form on which you write an amount of money that you have to pay. You sign the cheque and your bank pays the money from your account.

chequered [Said chek-kerd] ADJECTIVE ① covered with a pattern of squares. ② A chequered career is a varied career that has both good and bad parts.

cherish, cherishes, cherishing, cherished VERB ① If you cherish something, you care deeply about it and want to keep it or look after it lovingly. ② If you cherish a memory or hope, you have it in your mind and care deeply about it • *I cherish the good memories I have of him*.

cherry, cherries NOUN ① a small, juicy fruit with a red or black skin and a hard stone in the centre. ② a tree that produces cherries.

cherub, cherubs or cherubim NOUN an angel, shown in pictures as a plump, naked child with wings. **cherubic** ADJECTIVE

chess NOUN Chess is a board game for two people in which each player has

16 pieces and tries to move his or her pieces so that the other player's king cannot escape.

chessboard, chessboards NOUN A chessboard is a board divided into 64 squares of two alternating colours on which chess is played.

chest, chests NOUN ① the front part of your body between your shoulders and your waist. ② a large wooden box with a hinged lid.

chestnut, chestnuts NOUN ① Chestnuts are reddish-brown nuts that grow inside a prickly green outer covering. ② a tree that produces these nuts. ▶ADJECTIVE ③ Something that is chestnut is reddish-brown.

chest of drawers, chests of drawers NOUN a piece of furniture with drawers in it, used for storing clothes.

chew, chews, chewing, chewed VERB When you chew something, you use your teeth to break it up in your mouth before swallowing it. **chewy** ADJECTIVE

chewing gum NOUN Chewing gum is a kind of sweet that you chew for a long time, but which you do not swallow.

chic, chicer, chicest [Said sheek] ADJECTIVE elegant and fashionable • a chic restaurant.

chick, chicks NOUN a young bird.

chicken, chickens, chickening, chickened NOUN a bird kept on a farm for its eggs and meat; also the meat of this bird • roast chicken. **chicken out** VERB (informal) If you chicken out of something, you do not do it because you are afraid.

chickenpox NOUN Chickenpox is an illness which produces a fever and blister-like spots on the skin.

chicory NOUN Chicory is a plant with bitter leaves that are used in salads.

chide, chides, chiding, chided VERB (old-fashioned) To chide someone is to tell them off.

chief, chiefs NOUN ① the leader of a group or organisation. ▶ADJECTIVE ② most important • the chief source of oil. **chiefly** ADVERB

chieftain, chieftains NOUN the leader of a tribe or clan.

chiffon [Said shif-fon] NOUN Chiffon is a very thin lightweight cloth made of silk or nylon.

chihuahua, chihuahuas [Said chi-wah-wah] NOUN a breed of very small dog with short hair and pointed ears.

child, children NOUN ① a young person who is not yet an adult. ② Someone's child is their son or daughter.
SIMILAR WORDS: ① baby, kid, youngster

childbirth NOUN Childbirth is the act of giving birth to a child.

childhood, childhoods NOUN Someone's childhood is the time when they are a child.

childish ADJECTIVE immature and foolish • I don't have time for childish arguments. **childishly** ADVERB **childishness** NOUN
SIMILAR WORDS: immature, infantile, juvenile

USAGE NOTE
If you call someone childish, you think they are immature or foolish. If you call them childlike, you think they are innocent like a young child.

---

childless ADJECTIVE having no children.

childlike ADJECTIVE like a child in appearance or behaviour • childlike enthusiasm.

a
b
c
d
e
f
g
h
i
j
k
l
m
n
o
p
q
r
s
t
u
v
w
x
y
z

childminder, childminders NOUN a person who is qualified and paid to look after other people's children while they are at work.

Chilean, Chileans ADJECTIVE ① belonging or relating to Chile. ▸ NOUN ② someone who comes from Chile.

chill, chills, chilling, chilled VERB ① To chill something is to make it cold • *Chill the cheesecake*. ② If something chills you, it makes you feel worried or frightened • *The thought chilled her*. ▸ NOUN ③ a feverish cold. ④ a feeling of cold • *the chill of the night air*.

chilli, chillies NOUN the red or green seed pod of a type of pepper which has a very hot, spicy taste.

chilly, chillier, chilliest ADJECTIVE ① rather cold • *the chilly November breeze*. ② unfriendly and without enthusiasm • *a chilly reception*.

chilly-bin, chilly-bins NOUN (*informal*) In New Zealand English, a container for keeping food and drink cool that can be carried.

chime, chimes, chiming, chimed VERB When a bell chimes, it makes a clear ringing sound.

chimney, chimneys NOUN a vertical pipe or other hollow structure above a fireplace or furnace through which smoke from a fire escapes.

chimpanzee, chimpanzees NOUN a small ape with dark fur that lives in forests in Africa.

chin, chins NOUN the part of your face below your mouth.

china, chinas NOUN ① China is items like cups, saucers and plates made from very fine clay. ② (*informal*) In British and South African English, a china is a friend.

Chinese ADJECTIVE ① belonging or relating to China. ▸ NOUN ② someone who comes from China. ③ Chinese refers to any of a group of related languages and dialects spoken by Chinese people.

chink, chinks NOUN ① a small, narrow opening • *a chink in the roof*. ② a short, light, ringing sound, like one made by glasses touching each other.

chintz NOUN Chintz is a type of brightly patterned cotton fabric. WORD HISTORY: from Hindi *chint* meaning 'brightly coloured'

chip, chips, chipping, chipped NOUN ① Chips are thin strips of fried potato. ② In American English, chips are thin slices of potato fried until they are hard and crunchy. ③ In electronics, a chip is a tiny piece of silicon inside a computer which is used to form electronic circuits. ④ a small piece broken off an object, or the mark made when a piece breaks off. ▸ VERB ⑤ If you chip an object, you break a small piece off it.

chipboard NOUN Chipboard is a material made from wood scraps pressed together into hard sheets.

chipmunk, chipmunks NOUN a small rodent with a striped back.

chiropodist, chiropodists [*Said kir-rop-pod-dist*] NOUN a person whose job is treating people's feet. **chiropody** NOUN

chirp, chirps, chirping, chirped VERB When a bird chirps, it makes a short, high-pitched sound.

chisel, chisels, chiselling, chiselled NOUN ① a tool with a long metal blade and a sharp edge at the end which is used for cutting and shaping wood, stone or metal. ▸ VERB ② To chisel wood, stone or metal is to cut or shape it using a chisel.

chivalry [*Said shiv-val-ree*] NOUN Chivalry is polite and helpful behaviour, especially by men towards women. **chivalrous** ADJECTIVE

WORD HISTORY: from Latin *caballarius* meaning 'horseman'

chive, chives NOUN Chives are grasslike hollow leaves that have a mild onion flavour.

chlorine [Said klaw-reen] NOUN SCIENCE Chlorine is a chemical element which is a poisonous greenish-yellow gas with a strong, unpleasant smell. It is used to disinfect water and to make bleach. Its atomic number is 17 and its symbol is Cl.

chloroform [Said klor-rof-form] NOUN Chloroform is a colourless liquid with a strong, sweet smell used in cleaning products.

chlorophyll [Said klor-rof-fil] NOUN SCIENCE Chlorophyll is a green substance in plants which enables them to use the energy from sunlight in order to grow.

chloroplast NOUN SCIENCE Chloroplast is a substance containing chlorophyll and other pigments, which occurs in plants that carry out photosynthesis.

chock-a-block or **chock-full** ADJECTIVE completely full.

chocolate, chocolates NOUN ① Chocolate is a sweet food made from cacao seeds. ② a sweet made of chocolate. ▶ ADJECTIVE ③ dark brown.

WORD HISTORY: from Aztec *xococ* + *atl* meaning 'bitter water'

choice, choices NOUN ① a range of different things that are available to choose from • *a wider choice of treatments*. ② something that you choose • *You've made a good choice*. ③ Choice is the power or right to choose • *I had no choice*.

SIMILAR WORDS: ① range, selection, variety

choir, choirs [Said kwire] NOUN MUSIC a group of singers, for example in a church.

choke, chokes, choking, choked VERB ① If you choke, you stop being able to breathe properly, usually because something is blocking your windpipe • *the diner who choked on a fish bone*. ② If things choke a place, they fill it so much that it is blocked or clogged up • *The canal was choked with old tyres*.

choko, chokos NOUN a fruit that is shaped like a pear and used as a vegetable in Australia, New Zealand and the Caribbean.

cholera [Said kol-ler-ra] NOUN Cholera is a serious disease causing severe diarrhoea and vomiting. It is caused by infected food or water.

cholesterol [Said kol-less-ter-rol] NOUN Cholesterol is a substance found in all animal fats, tissues and blood.

chook, chooks NOUN (informal) In Australian and New Zealand English, a chook is a chicken.

choose, chooses, choosing, chose, chosen VERB To choose something is to decide to have it or do it • *He chose to live in Kenya*.

SIMILAR WORDS: opt for, pick, select

choosy, choosier, choosiest ADJECTIVE fussy and difficult to satisfy • *You can't be too choosy about jobs*.

chop, chops, chopping, chopped VERB ① To chop something is to cut it with quick, heavy strokes using an axe or a knife. ▶ NOUN ② a small piece of lamb or pork containing a bone, usually cut from the ribs.

chopper, choppers NOUN (informal) a helicopter.

choppy, choppier, choppiest
ADJECTIVE Choppy water has a lot of waves because it is windy.

chopstick, chopsticks NOUN Chopsticks are a pair of thin sticks used, especially in East Asian countries, for eating food.

choral ADJECTIVE relating to singing by a choir • *choral music*.

chord, chords NOUN ① MUSIC a group of three or more musical notes played together. ② MATHS In geometry, a chord is a straight line connecting two points on a curve.

SPELLING TIP

Do not confuse the spellings of *chord* and *cord*: *I only know how to play one chord on the guitar; a package tied with cord.*

---

chore, chores NOUN an uninteresting job that has to be done • *the chore of cleaning*.

choreograph, choreographs, choreographing, choreographed VERB If a person choreographs a dance, he or she decides which steps and movements should be in it.

choreography [Said kor-ree-og-raf-fee] NOUN Choreography is the art of composing dance steps and movements. **choreographer** NOUN

chortle, chortles, chortling, chortled VERB To chortle is to laugh with amusement.

chorus, choruses, chorusing, chorused MUSIC NOUN ① a large group of singers; also a piece of music for a large group of singers. ② a part of a song which is repeated after each verse. ▶VERB ③ If people chorus something, they all say or sing it at the same time.
WORD HISTORY: from Greek *khoros*, the group of actors who gave the commentary in Classical plays

chose the past tense of **choose**.

chosen the past participle of **choose**.

Christ PROPER NOUN RE Christ is the name for Jesus. Christians believe that Jesus is the son of God.

christen, christens, christening, christened VERB RE When a baby is christened, it is named by a member of the clergy in a religious ceremony.

Christian, Christians NOUN RE ① a person who believes in Jesus Christ and his teachings. ▶ADJECTIVE ② relating to Christ and his teachings • *the Christian faith*. ③ good, kind and considerate. **Christianity** NOUN

Christian name, Christian names NOUN the name given to someone when they were born or christened.

Christmas, Christmases NOUN RE the Christian festival celebrating the birth of Christ, falling on December 25th.

chromatic [Said kro-ma-tik] ADJECTIVE MUSIC A chromatic scale is one which is based on an octave of 12 semitones.

chromatography NOUN SCIENCE a technique used to discover the components of mixtures of gases or liquids. It involves passing the mixture through a material that absorbs the components at different rates.

chrome [Said krome] NOUN Chrome is metal plated with chromium, a hard grey metal.

chromosome, chromosomes NOUN SCIENCE In biology, a chromosome is one of a number of rod-shaped parts in the nucleus of a cell which contains genes that determine the characteristics of an animal or plant.
WORD HISTORY: from Greek *khrōma* meaning 'colour' and *sōma* meaning 'body'

chronic *[Said kron-nik]* ADJECTIVE lasting a very long time or never stopping • *a chronic illness.* **chronically** ADVERB

chronicle, chronicles, chronicling, chronicled NOUN ① a record of a series of events described in the order in which they happened. ▶ VERB ② To chronicle a series of events is to record or describe them in the order in which they happened.

chronological *[Said kron-nol-loj-i-kl]* ADJECTIVE HISTORY arranged in the order in which things happened • *Tell me the whole story in chronological order.* **chronologically** ADVERB

chronology *[Said kron-nol-loj-jee]* NOUN HISTORY The chronology of events is the order in which they happened. WORD HISTORY: from Greek *khronos* meaning 'time' and *legein* meaning 'to say'

chrysalis, chrysalises *[Said kriss-sal-liss]* NOUN a butterfly or moth when it is developing from being a caterpillar to being a fully grown adult.

chrysanthemum, chrysanthemums *[Said kriss-an-thim-mum]* NOUN a plant with large, brightly coloured flowers.

chubby, chubbier, chubbiest ADJECTIVE plump and round • *his chubby cheeks.*

chuck, chucks, chucking, chucked VERB *(informal)* To chuck something is to throw it casually.

chuckle, chuckles, chuckling, chuckled VERB When you chuckle, you laugh quietly.

chug, chugs, chugging, chugged VERB When a machine or engine chugs, it makes a continuous dull thudding sound.

chum, chums NOUN *(informal)* a friend.

chunk, chunks NOUN a thick piece of something. SIMILAR WORDS: hunk, lump, piece

chunky, chunkier, chunkiest ADJECTIVE Someone who is chunky is broad and heavy but usually short.

church, churches NOUN ① a building where Christians go for religious services and worship. ② In the Christian religion, a church is one of the groups with their own particular beliefs, customs and clergy • *the Catholic Church.* WORD HISTORY: from Greek *kuriakon* meaning 'master's house'

Church of England NOUN RE The Church of England is the Anglican church in England, where it is the state church, with the King or Queen as its head.

churchyard, churchyards NOUN an area of land around a church, often used as a graveyard.

churn, churns NOUN a container used for making milk or cream into butter.

chute, chutes *[Said shoot]* NOUN a steep slope or channel used to slide things down • *a rubbish chute.*

chutney, chutneys NOUN Chutney is a strong-tasting thick sauce made from fruit, vinegar and spices.

cider, ciders NOUN Cider is an alcoholic drink made from apples.

cigar, cigars NOUN a roll of dried tobacco leaves which people smoke. WORD HISTORY: from Mayan *sicar* meaning 'to smoke'

cigarette, cigarettes NOUN a thin roll of tobacco covered in thin paper which people smoke.

cinder, cinders NOUN Cinders are small pieces of burnt material left

a b **c** d e f g h i j k l m n o p q r s t u v w x y z

after something such as wood or coal has burned.

cinema, cinemas NOUN ① a place where people go to watch films. ② Cinema is the business of making films.

cinnamon NOUN Cinnamon is a sweet spice which comes from the bark of an Asian tree.

cipher, ciphers [Said *sy-fer*]; also spelt **cypher** NOUN a secret code or system of writing used to send secret messages.

circa [Said *sur-ka*] PREPOSITION (formal) about or approximately; used especially before dates • *portrait of a lady, circa 1840.*

circle, circles, circling, circled NOUN ① MATHS a completely regular round shape. Every point on its edge is the same distance from the centre. ② a group of people with the same interest or profession • *a character well known in yachting circles.* ③ an area of seats on an upper floor of a theatre. ▶ VERB ④ To circle is to move round and round as though going round the edge of a circle • *A police helicopter circled above.*

circuit, circuits [Said *sur-kit*] NOUN ① any closed line or path, often circular, for example a racing track; also the distance round this path • *three circuits of the 26-lap race remaining.* ② SCIENCE An electrical circuit is a complete route around which an electric current can flow. A **closed circuit** is a complete electrical circuit around which current can flow; a **parallel circuit** is a closed circuit in which the current divides into two or more paths before coming back together to complete the circuit; a **series circuit** is an electrical circuit in which the elements are connected one after the other so that the same current flows through them all.

circuit breaker, circuit breakers NOUN SCIENCE a device which can stop the flow of electricity around a circuit by switching itself off if anything goes wrong.

circular, circulars ADJECTIVE ① in the shape of a circle. ② A circular argument or theory is not valid because it uses a statement to prove a conclusion and the conclusion to prove the statement. ▶ NOUN ③ a letter or advert sent to a lot of people at the same time. **circularity** NOUN

circulate, circulates, circulating, circulated VERB ① When something circulates or when you circulate it, it moves easily around an area • *an open position where the air can circulate freely.* ② When you circulate something among people, you pass it round or tell it to all the people • *We circulate a regular newsletter.*

circulation, circulations NOUN ① The circulation of something is the act of circulating it or the action of it circulating • *traffic circulation.* ② The circulation of a newspaper or magazine is the number of copies that are sold of each issue. ③ SCIENCE Your circulation is the movement of blood through your body. **circulatory** ADJECTIVE

circumcise, circumcises, circumcising, circumcised VERB RE If a boy or man is circumcised, the foreskin at the end of his penis is removed. This is carried out mainly as part of a Muslim or Jewish religious ceremony. **circumcision** NOUN

circumference, circumferences NOUN MATHS The circumference of a circle is its outer line or edge; also the length of this line.

circumstance, circumstances NOUN ① The circumstances of a situation or event are the conditions that affect what happens • *He did well* *in the circumstances*. ② Someone's circumstances are their position and conditions in life • *Her circumstances had changed*.

circus, circuses NOUN a show given by a travelling group of entertainers such as clowns, acrobats and specially trained animals.

cirrus NOUN GEOGRAPHY Cirrus is a type of thin cloud high up in the sky.

cistern, cisterns NOUN a tank in which water is stored, for example one in the roof of a house or above a toilet.

citadel, citadels NOUN a fortress in or near a city.

cite, cites, citing, cited VERB ① (*formal*) If you cite something, you quote it or refer to it • *He cited a letter written by Newall*. ② If someone is cited in a legal action, they are officially called to appear in court.

citizen, citizens NOUN CITIZENSHIP The citizens of a country or city are the people who live in it or belong to it • *American citizens*.

citizenship NOUN CITIZENSHIP the status of being a citizen, with all the rights and duties that go with it • *I'm applying for Australian citizenship*.

citrus fruit, citrus fruits NOUN Citrus fruits are juicy, sharp-tasting fruits such as oranges, lemons and grapefruit.

city, cities NOUN a large town where many people live and work.

civic ADJECTIVE relating to a city or citizens • *the Civic Centre*.

civil ADJECTIVE ① relating to the citizens of a country • *civil rights*. ② relating to people or things that are not connected with the armed forces • *the history of civil aviation*. ③ polite. **civilly** ADVERB **civility** NOUN

civil engineering NOUN Civil engineering is the design and construction of roads, bridges and public buildings.

civilian, civilians NOUN a person who is not in the armed forces.

civilisation, civilisations; also spelt **civilization** NOUN ① HISTORY a society which has a highly developed organisation and culture • *the tale of a lost civilisation*. ② Civilisation is an advanced state of social organisation and culture.

civilised; also spelt **civilized** ADJECTIVE ① A civilised society is one with a developed social organisation and way of life. ② A civilised person is polite and reasonable.

civil partnership, civil partnerships NOUN a legal relationship between two people of the same sex that is similar to marriage.

civil servant, civil servants NOUN a person who works in the civil service.

civil service NOUN The civil service is the government departments responsible for the administration of a country.

civil war, civil wars NOUN a war between groups of people who live in the same country.

clad ADJECTIVE (*literary*) Someone who is clad in particular clothes is wearing them.

claim, claims, claiming, claimed VERB ① If you claim that something is the case, you say that it is the case • *He claims to have lived in the same house all his life*. ② If you claim something, you ask for it because it belongs to you or you have a right to it • *Cartier claimed the land for the King of France*. ▶ NOUN ③ a statement that something is the case, or that you have a right to something • *She will make a claim for damages*.

a
b
c
d
e
f
g
h
i
j
k
l
m
n
o
p
q
r
s
t
u
v
w
x
y
z

SIMILAR WORDS: ① allege, assert, maintain

claimant, claimants NOUN someone who is making a claim, especially for money.

clairvoyant, clairvoyants ADJECTIVE ① able to know about things that will happen in the future. ▶ NOUN ② a person who is, or claims to be, clairvoyant. WORD HISTORY: from French *clair* + *voyant* meaning 'clear-seeing'

clam, clams NOUN a kind of shellfish.

clamber, clambers, clambering, clambered VERB If you clamber somewhere, you climb there with difficulty.

clammy, clammier, clammiest ADJECTIVE unpleasantly damp and sticky • *clammy hands.*

clamour, clamours, clamouring, clamoured VERB ① If people clamour for something, they demand it noisily or angrily • *We clamoured for an explanation.* ▶ NOUN ② Clamour is noisy or angry shouts or demands by a lot of people.

clamp, clamps, clamping, clamped NOUN ① an object with movable parts that are used to hold two things firmly together. ▶ VERB ② To clamp things together is to fasten them or hold them firmly with a clamp. **clamp down on** VERB To clamp down on something is to become stricter in controlling it • *The Queen has clamped down on all expenditure.*

clan, clans NOUN a group of families related to each other by being descended from the same ancestor.

clandestine ADJECTIVE secret and hidden • *a clandestine meeting with friends.*

clang, clangs, clanging, clanged VERB When something metal clangs or when you clang it, it makes a loud, deep sound.

clank, clanks, clanking, clanked VERB If something metal clanks, it makes a loud noise.

clap, claps, clapping, clapped VERB ① When you clap, you hit your hands together loudly to show your appreciation. ② If you clap someone on the back or shoulder, you hit them in a friendly way. ③ If you clap something somewhere, you put it there quickly and firmly • *I clapped a hand over her mouth.* ▶ NOUN ④ a sound made by clapping your hands. ⑤ A clap of thunder is a sudden loud noise of thunder.

clapper, clappers NOUN A clapper is a small piece of metal that hangs inside a bell and strikes the side to make the bell sound.

claret, clarets NOUN a type of red wine, especially one from the Bordeaux region of France.

clarify, clarifies, clarifying, clarified VERB EXAM TERM To clarify something is to make it clear and easier to understand • *Discussion will clarify your thoughts.* **clarification** NOUN

clarinet, clarinets NOUN MUSIC a woodwind instrument with a straight tube and a single reed in its mouthpiece.

clarity NOUN The clarity of something is its clearness.

clash, clashes, clashing, clashed VERB ① If people clash with each other, they fight or argue. ② Ideas or styles that clash are so different that they do not go together. ③ If two events clash, they happen at the same time so you cannot go to both. ④ When metal objects clash, they hit each other with a loud noise. ▶ NOUN ⑤ a fight or argument. ⑥ A clash of ideas, styles or events is a situation in which they do not go together. ⑦ a loud noise made by metal objects when they hit each other.

clasp, clasps, clasping, clasped VERB ①To clasp something means to hold it tightly or fasten it • *He clasped his hands.* ▸NOUN ② a fastening such as a hook or catch.

class, classes, classing, classed NOUN ①A class of people or things is a group of them of a particular type or quality • *the old class of politicians.* ② a group of pupils or students taught together, or a lesson that they have together. ③ Someone who has class is elegant in appearance or behaviour. ▸VERB ④To class something means to arrange it in a particular group or to consider it as belonging to a particular group • *They are officially classed as visitors.*

SIMILAR WORDS: ①category, group, kind, type

classic, classics ADJECTIVE ①typical and therefore a good model or example of something • *a classic case of misuse.* ②of very high quality • *one of the classic films of all time.* ③simple in style and form • *the classic dinner suit.* ▸NOUN ④something of the highest quality • *one of the great classics of rock music.* ⑤Classics is the study of Latin and Greek, and the literature of ancient Greece and Rome.

classical ADJECTIVE ①traditional in style, form and content • *classical ballet.* ②Classical music is serious music considered to be of lasting value. ③characteristic of the style of ancient Greece and Rome • *Classical friezes decorate the walls.* **classically** ADVERB

classified ADJECTIVE officially declared secret by the government • *access to classified information.*

classify, classifies, classifying, classified VERB LIBRARY To classify things is to arrange them into groups with similar characteristics • *We can classify the differences into three groups.* **classification** NOUN

classroom, classrooms NOUN a room in a school where pupils have lessons.

classy, classier, classiest ADJECTIVE (*informal*) stylish and elegant.

clatter, clatters, clattering, clattered VERB ①When things clatter, they hit each other with a loud rattling noise. ▸NOUN ② a loud rattling noise made by hard things hitting each other.

clause, clauses NOUN ① a section of a legal document. ② ENGLISH In grammar, a clause is a group of words with a subject and a verb, which may be a complete sentence or one of the parts of a sentence.

▸SEE GRAMMAR BOX ON NEXT PAGE

claustrophobia [*Said klos-trof-foe-bee-ya*] NOUN Claustrophobia is a fear of being in enclosed spaces. **claustrophobic** ADJECTIVE

claw, claws, clawing, clawed NOUN ①An animal's claws are hard, curved nails at the end of its feet. ②The claws of a crab or lobster are the two jointed parts, used for grasping things. ▸VERB ③If an animal claws something, it digs its claws into it.

clay NOUN Clay is a type of earth that is soft and sticky when wet and hard when baked dry. It is used to make pottery and bricks.

clean, cleaner, cleanest; cleans, cleaning, cleaned ADJECTIVE ①free from dirt or marks. ②free from germs or infection. ③If humour is clean, it is not rude and does not involve bad language. ④A clean movement is skilful and accurate. ⑤Clean also means free from fault or error • *a clean driving licence.* ▸VERB ⑥To clean something is to

A B **C** D E F G H I J K L M N O P Q R S T U V W X Y Z

What is a Clause?

A **clause** is a group of words which form part of a sentence and express an idea or describe a situation. A clause often gives information about the main idea or situation:

*Matthew ate a cake **which was covered in chocolate**.*
*Jana crossed the street **after looking carefully in both directions**.*

Main Clauses and Subordinate Clauses

Clauses can be either **main clauses** or **subordinate clauses**.

A **main clause** is the core of a sentence. It would make sense if it stood on its own. Every sentence contains a main clause:

***Matthew ate a cake** which was covered in chocolate.*
*After looking carefully in both directions, **Jana crossed the road**.*

A **subordinate clause** is a less important part of a sentence. It would not make sense on its own, but gives information about the main clause:

***After looking carefully**, Jana crossed the road.*
*Jana had to cross the road, **which was often very busy**.*

Relative clauses

Relative clauses give additional information about a person or thing mentioned in the main clause.

Relative clauses are introduced by a relative pronoun – *who, whom, whose, which* or *that*:

*Jamal has a cat **who likes fish**.*
*Jana has one sister, **whose name is Rosa**.*

---

remove dirt from it. **cleanly** ADVERB **cleaner** NOUN

cleanliness [*Said* klen-lin-ness] NOUN Cleanliness is the practice of keeping yourself and your surroundings clean.

cleanse, **cleanses**, **cleansing**, **cleansed** [*Said* klenz] VERB To cleanse something is to make it completely free from dirt.

clear, **clearer**, **clearest**; **clears**, **clearing**, **cleared** ADJECTIVE ① easy to understand, see or hear • *He made it clear he did not want to talk.* ② easy to see through • *a clear liquid.* ③ free from obstructions or unwanted things • *clear of snow.* ▶ VERB ④ To clear an area is to remove unwanted things from it. ⑤ If you clear a fence or other obstacle, you jump over it without touching it. ⑥ When fog or mist clears, it disappears. ⑦ If

someone is cleared of a crime, they are proved to be not guilty. **clearly** ADVERB **clear out** VERB ① If you clear out a room or cupboard, you tidy it and throw away unwanted things. ② (*informal*) To clear out means to leave • *You can clear out right now!* **clear up** VERB ① If you clear up, you tidy a place and put things away. ② If a problem or misunderstanding is cleared up, it is solved or settled. SIMILAR WORDS: ① evident, obvious, plain

clearance NOUN ① Clearance is the removal of old buildings in an area. ② If someone is given clearance to do something, they get official permission to do it.

clearing, **clearings** NOUN an area of bare ground in a forest.

cleavage, **cleavages** NOUN the space between a woman's breasts.

cleaver, cleavers NOUN a knife with a large square blade, used especially by butchers.

clef, clefs NOUN In written music, a clef is a symbol at the beginning of each line which indicates the pitch of the notes.

WORD HISTORY: from Latin *clavis* meaning 'key'

cleft, clefts NOUN a narrow opening in a rock.

clench, clenches, clenching, clenched VERB ①When you clench your fist, you curl your fingers up tightly. ②When you clench your teeth, you squeeze them together tightly.

clergy PLURAL NOUN RE The clergy are the ministers of the Christian Church.

clergyman, clergymen NOUN a male member of the clergy.

clerical ADJECTIVE ①relating to work done in an office • *clerical jobs with the City Council*. ②relating to the clergy.

clerihew, clerihews NOUN ENGLISH a kind of humorous poem that has two rhyming couplets and an irregular metre.

clerk, clerks [Said klahrk] NOUN a person who keeps records or accounts in an office, bank or law court.

clever, cleverer, cleverest ADJECTIVE ①intelligent and quick to understand things. ②very effective or skilful • *a clever plan*. **cleverly** ADVERB **cleverness** NOUN
SIMILAR WORDS: ①bright, intelligent, smart

clianthus [Said klee-an-thuss] NOUN A clianthus is a plant found in Australia and New Zealand which has clusters of scarlet flowers.

cliché, clichés [Said klee-shay] NOUN ENGLISH an idea or phrase which is no longer effective because it has been used so much.

click, clicks, clicking, clicked VERB ①When something clicks or when you click it, it makes a short snapping sound. ②When you click on an area of a computer screen, you point the cursor at it and press one of the buttons on the mouse in order to make something happen. ▸ NOUN ③a sound of something clicking • *I heard the click of a bolt*.

client, clients NOUN someone who pays a professional person or company for a service.

clientele [Said klee-on-tell] PLURAL NOUN The clientele of a place are its customers.

cliff, cliffs NOUN a steep, high rock face by the sea.

climactic ADJECTIVE (formal) bringing a climax • *Her death is the climactic point of the film*.

climate, climates NOUN ① GEOGRAPHY The climate of a place is the average weather conditions there • *The climate was dry in the summer*. ②the general attitude and opinion of people at a particular time • *the American political climate*. **climatic** ADJECTIVE

climax, climaxes NOUN ENGLISH The climax of a process, story or piece of music is the most exciting moment in it, usually near the end.

WORD HISTORY: from Greek *klimax* meaning 'ladder'

climb, climbs, climbing, climbed VERB ①To climb is to move upwards. ②If you climb somewhere, you move there with difficulty • *She climbed out of the driving seat*. ▸ NOUN ③a movement upwards • *this long climb up the slope* • *the rapid climb in murders*. **climber** NOUN

a
b
c
d
e
f
g
h
i
j
k
l
m
n
o
p
q
r
s
t
u
v
w
x
y
z

clinch, clinches, clinching, clinched VERB If you clinch an agreement or an argument, you settle it in a definite way • *Peter clinched a deal*.

cling, clings, clinging, clung VERB To cling to something is to hold onto it or stay closely attached to it • *still clinging to old-fashioned values*.

Clingfilm NOUN (*trademark*) a clear thin plastic used for wrapping food.

clinic, clinics NOUN a building where people go for medical treatment.

clinical ADJECTIVE ① relating to the medical treatment of patients • *clinical tests*. ② Clinical behaviour or thought is logical and unemotional • *the cold, clinical attitudes of his colleagues*. **clinically** ADVERB

clip, clips, clipping, clipped NOUN ① a small metal or plastic object used for holding things together. ② a short piece of a film shown by itself. ▶ VERB ③ If you clip things together, you fasten them with clips. ④ If you clip something, you cut bits from it to shape it • *clipped hedges*.

clippers PLURAL NOUN Clippers are tools used for cutting.

clipping, clippings NOUN an article cut from a newspaper or magazine.

clique, cliques [*Rhymes with* **seek**] NOUN a small group of people who stick together and do not mix with other people.

clitoris, clitorises [*Said* **klit-tor-riss**] NOUN a small highly sensitive piece of flesh near the opening of a woman's vagina.

cloak, cloaks, cloaking, cloaked NOUN ① a wide, loose coat without sleeves. ▶ VERB ② To cloak something is to cover or hide it • *a land permanently cloaked in mist*.

cloakroom, cloakrooms NOUN a room for coats or a room with toilets and washbasins in a public building.

clock, clocks NOUN ① a device that measures and shows the time. ▶ PHRASE ② If you work **round the clock**, you work all day and night.

clockwise ADJECTIVE OR ADVERB in the same direction as the hands on a clock.

clockwork NOUN ① Toys that work by clockwork move when they are wound up with a key. ▶ PHRASE ② If something happens **like clockwork**, it happens with no problems or delays.

clog, clogs, clogging, clogged VERB ① To clog something is to block it • *pavements clogged up with people*. ▶ NOUN ② Clogs are heavy wooden shoes.

cloister, cloisters NOUN a covered area in a monastery or a cathedral for walking around a square.

clone, clones, cloning, cloned | SCIENCE | NOUN ① In biology, a clone is an animal or plant that has been produced artificially from the cells of another animal or plant and is therefore identical to it. ▶ VERB ② To clone an animal or plant is to produce it as a clone.

close, closes, closing, closed; closer, closest VERB [*Said* **kloze**] ① To close something is to shut it. ② To close a road or entrance is to block it so that no-one can go in or out. ③ If a shop closes at a certain time, then it does not do business after that time. ▶ ADJECTIVE OR ADVERB [*Said* **kloass**] ④ near to something • *a restaurant close to their home*. ▶ ADJECTIVE [*Said* **kloass**] ⑤ People who are close to each other are very friendly and know each other well. ⑥ You say the weather is close when it is uncomfortably warm and there is not enough air. **closely** ADVERB **closeness** NOUN **closed** ADJECTIVE **close down** VERB If a business closes down, all work stops there permanently.

SIMILAR WORDS: ④ near, nearby

closet, closets, closeting, closeted NOUN ① a cupboard. ▸ VERB ② If you are closeted somewhere, you shut yourself away alone or in private with another person. ▸ ADJECTIVE ③ Closet beliefs or habits are kept private and secret • *a closet romantic*.

close-up, close-ups NOUN a detailed close view of something, especially a photograph taken close to the subject.

closure, closures [Said *klohz-yur*] NOUN ① The closure of a business is the permanent shutting of it. ② The closure of a road is the blocking of it so it cannot be used.

clot, clots, clotting, clotted NOUN ① a lump, especially one that forms when blood thickens. ▸ VERB ② When a substance such as blood clots, it thickens and forms a lump.

cloth, cloths NOUN ① Cloth is fabric made by a process such as weaving. ② a piece of material used for wiping or protecting things.

clothe, clothes, clothing, clothed VERB To clothe someone is to give them clothes to wear.

clothes PLURAL NOUN the things people wear on their bodies.

clothing NOUN the clothes people wear.

cloud, clouds, clouding, clouded NOUN ① a mass of water vapour, smoke or dust that forms in the air and is seen floating in the sky. ② ICT **The cloud** is a name for a network of servers on the internet used to store data and services. ▸ VERB ③ If something clouds or is clouded, it becomes cloudy or difficult to see through • *The sky clouded over*. ④ Something that clouds an issue

makes it more confusing.

cloud computing NOUN ICT Cloud computing is a system where a person's files and programs are stored on the internet so that the person can use them at any time from any place.

cloudy, cloudier, cloudiest ADJECTIVE ① full of clouds • *the cloudy sky*. ② difficult to see through • *a glass of cloudy liquid*.

SIMILAR WORDS: ① dull, overcast

clout, clouts, clouting, clouted (*informal*) NOUN ① Someone who has clout has influence. ② A clout is a hit • *a clout on the head*. ▸ VERB ③ If you clout someone, you hit them.

clove, cloves NOUN ① Cloves are small, strong-smelling dried flower buds from a tropical tree, used as a spice in cooking. ② A clove of garlic is one of the separate sections of the bulb.

clover NOUN Clover is a small plant with leaves made up of three similar parts.

clown, clowns, clowning, clowned NOUN ① a circus performer who wears funny clothes and make-up and does silly things to make people laugh. ▸ VERB ② If you clown around, you do silly things to make people laugh.

cloying ADJECTIVE unpleasantly sickly, sweet or sentimental • *something less cloying than whipped cream*.

club, clubs, clubbing, clubbed NOUN ① an organisation of people with a particular interest, who meet regularly; also the place where they meet. ② a thick, heavy stick used as a weapon. ③ a stick with a shaped head that a golf player uses to hit the ball. ④ Clubs is one of the four suits in a pack of playing cards. It is marked

a
b
c
d
e
f
g
h
i
j
k
l
m
n
o
p
q
r
s
t
u
v
w
x
y
z

by a black symbol in the shape of a clover leaf. ▶ VERB ⑤ To club someone is to hit them hard with a heavy object. **club together** VERB If people club together, they all join together to give money to buy something.

SIMILAR WORDS: ① association, group, society

cluck, clucks, clucking, clucked VERB When a hen clucks, it makes a short, repeated, high-pitched sound.

clue, clues NOUN something that helps to solve a problem or mystery.

clump, clumps, clumping, clumped NOUN ① a small group of things close together. ▶ VERB ② If you clump about, you walk with heavy footsteps.

clumsiness NOUN awkwardness in the way someone or something moves.

clumsy, clumsier, clumsiest ADJECTIVE ① moving awkwardly and carelessly. ② said or done without thought or tact • *his clumsy attempts to catch her out.* **clumsily** ADVERB SIMILAR WORDS: ① awkward, gauche, ungainly

clung the past tense and past participle of **cling**.

cluster, clusters, clustering, clustered NOUN ① A cluster of things is a group of them together • *a cluster of huts at the foot of the mountains.* ▶ VERB ② If people cluster together, they stay together in a close group.

clutch, clutches, clutching, clutched VERB If you clutch something, you hold it tightly or seize it.

clutter, clutters, cluttering, cluttered NOUN ① Clutter is an untidy mess. ▶ VERB ② Things that clutter a place fill it and make it untidy.

cm an abbreviation for 'centimetres'.

CO- PREFIX 'Co-' means 'together' • *Paula is now co-writing a book with Pierre.*

coach, coaches, coaching, coached NOUN ① a long motor vehicle used for taking passengers on long journeys. ② a section of a train that carries passengers. ③ a four-wheeled vehicle with a roof pulled by horses, which people used to travel in. ④ a person who coaches a sport or a subject. ▶ VERB ⑤ If someone coaches you, they teach you and help you to get better at a sport or a subject.

SIMILAR WORDS: ④ instructor, trainer ⑤ instruct, train

coal, coals NOUN ① Coal is a hard black rock obtained from under the earth and burned as a fuel. ② Coals are burning pieces of coal.

coalition, coalitions NOUN a temporary alliance, especially between different political parties forming a government.

coarse, coarser, coarsest ADJECTIVE ① Something that is coarse is rough in texture, often consisting of large particles • *a coarse blanket.* ② Someone who is coarse talks or behaves in a rude or rather offensive way. **coarsely** ADVERB **coarseness** NOUN

SPELLING TIP
Do not confuse the spellings of *coarse* and *course*: *a coarse cloth; a course in conversational Italian.*

coast, coasts, coasting, coasted NOUN ① the edge of the land where it meets the sea. ▶ VERB ② A vehicle that is coasting is moving without engine power. **coastal** ADJECTIVE

coastguard, coastguards NOUN an official who watches the sea near a

A
B
C
D
E
F
G
H
I
J
K
L
M
N
O
P
Q
R
S
T
U
V
W
X
Y
Z

coast to get help for sailors when they need it, and to prevent smuggling.

coastline, coastlines NOUN the outline of a coast, especially its appearance as seen from the sea or air.

coat, coats, coating, coated NOUN ① a piece of clothing with sleeves which you wear over your other clothes. ② An animal's coat is the fur or hair on its body. ③ A coat of paint or varnish is a layer of it. ▶ VERB ④ To coat something means to cover it with a thin layer of something • *walnuts coated with chocolate*.

coat hanger, coat hangers NOUN a curved piece of wood, metal or plastic that you hang clothes on.

coating, coatings NOUN a layer of something.

coax, coaxes, coaxing, coaxed VERB If you coax someone to do something, you gently persuade them to do it.

SIMILAR WORDS: cajole, persuade, talk into, wheedle

cobalt NOUN SCIENCE Cobalt is a hard silvery-white metallic element which is used in alloys and for producing a blue dye. Its atomic number is 27 and its symbol is Co.

cobble, cobbles NOUN Cobbles or cobblestones are stones with a rounded surface that were used in the past for making roads.

cobbler, cobblers NOUN a person who makes or mends shoes.

cobra, cobras [Said koh-bra] NOUN a type of large poisonous snake from Africa and Asia.

cobweb, cobwebs NOUN the very thin net that a spider spins for catching insects.

cocaine NOUN Cocaine is an illegal addictive drug.

cock, cocks NOUN an adult male chicken; also used of any male bird.

cockatoo, cockatoos NOUN a type of parrot with a crest, found in Australia and New Guinea.

cockerel, cockerels NOUN a young cock.

Cockney, Cockneys NOUN a person born in the East End of London.

cockpit, cockpits NOUN The place in a small plane where the pilot sits.

cockroach, cockroaches NOUN a large dark-coloured insect often found in dirty rooms.

cocktail, cocktails NOUN an alcoholic drink made from several ingredients.

cocky, cockier, cockiest; cockies (*informal*) ADJECTIVE ① cheeky or too self-confident. ▶ NOUN ② in Australian English, a cockatoo. ③ in Australian and New Zealand English, a farmer, especially one whose farm is small. **cockiness** NOUN

cocoa NOUN Cocoa is a brown powder made from the seeds of a tropical tree and used for making chocolate; also a hot drink made from this powder.

coconut, coconuts NOUN a very large nut with white flesh, milky juice, and a hard hairy shell.

cocoon, cocoons NOUN a silky covering over the larvae of moths and some other insects.

WORD HISTORY: from Provençal *coucoun* meaning 'eggshell'

cod, cod NOUN a large edible fish.

GRAMMAR TIP
The plural of *cod* is also *cod*.

coda, codas NOUN MUSIC a passage of music at the end of a section, for example at the end of a movement in a concerto.

a b c d e f g h i j k l m n o p q r s t u v w x y z

WORD HISTORY: an Italian word meaning 'tail'

code, codes, coding, coded NOUN
① a system of replacing the letters or words in a message with other letters or words, so that nobody can understand the message unless they know the system. ② a group of numbers and letters which is used to identify something • *the telephone code for Melbourne*. ③ ICT Code is the instructions used to create a computer program. ▶ VERB ④ If you code a message, you put it into code. ⑤ To code is also to write computer programs. **coded** ADJECTIVE

coefficient, coefficients NOUN
MATHS a number that expresses a measurement of a particular quality of a substance or object under specified conditions.

coerce, coerces, coercing, coerced
[*Said koh-erss*] VERB If you coerce someone into doing something, you make them do it against their will. **coercion** NOUN
WORD HISTORY: from Latin *coercere* meaning 'to restrain'

coexist, coexists, coexisting, coexisted VERB When two or more things coexist, they exist together in the same place or at the same time. **coexistence** NOUN **coexistent** ADJECTIVE

coffee NOUN Coffee is a substance made by roasting and grinding the beans of a tropical shrub; also a hot drink made from this substance.
WORD HISTORY: from Arabic *qahwah* meaning 'wine' or 'coffee'

coffin, coffins NOUN a box in which a dead body is buried or cremated.

cog, cogs NOUN a wheel with teeth which turns another wheel or part of a machine.

cognac, cognacs [*Said kon-yak*] NOUN Cognac is a kind of brandy.

coherent ADJECTIVE ① If something such as a theory is coherent, its parts fit together well and do not contradict each other. ② If someone is coherent, what they are saying makes sense and is not jumbled or confused. **coherence** NOUN

cohesive ADJECTIVE If something is cohesive, its parts fit together well • *The team must work as a cohesive unit.* **cohesion** NOUN

coil, coils, coiling, coiled NOUN ① a length of rope or wire wound into a series of loops; also one of the loops. ▶ VERB ② If something coils, it turns into a series of loops.

coin, coins, coining, coined NOUN ① a small metal disc which is used as money. ▶ VERB ② If you coin a word or a phrase, you invent it.

coinage NOUN The coinage of a country is the coins that are used there.

coincide, coincides, coinciding, coincided VERB ① If two events coincide, they happen at about the same time. ② When two people's ideas or opinions coincide, they agree • *What she said coincided exactly with his own thinking.*

coincidence, coincidences NOUN ① what happens when two similar things occur at the same time by chance • *I had moved to London, and by coincidence, Helen had too.* ② the fact that two things are surprisingly the same. **coincidental** ADJECTIVE **coincidentally** ADVERB

coke NOUN Coke is a grey solid fuel produced from coal.

colander, colanders [*Said kol-an-der*] NOUN a bowl-shaped container with holes in it, used for washing or draining food.

cold, colder, coldest; colds ADJECTIVE
① having a low temperature.
② Someone who is cold does not show much affection. ▸ NOUN ③ You can refer to cold weather as the cold • *She was complaining about the cold.* ④ a minor illness in which you sneeze and may have a sore throat. **coldly** ADVERB **coldness** NOUN

cold-blooded ADJECTIVE
① Someone who is cold-blooded does not show any pity • *two cold-blooded killers*. ② A cold-blooded animal has a body temperature that changes according to the surrounding temperature.

cold war NOUN Cold war is a state of extreme unfriendliness between countries not actually at war.

coleslaw NOUN Coleslaw is a salad of chopped cabbage and other vegetables in mayonnaise.
WORD HISTORY: from Dutch *koolsla* meaning 'cabbage salad'

colic NOUN Colic is pain in a baby's stomach.

collaborate, collaborates, collaborating, collaborated VERB
When people collaborate, they work together to produce something • *The two bands have collaborated in the past*. **collaboration** NOUN **collaborator** NOUN

collage, collages [Said *kol-lahj*] NOUN
ART a picture made by sticking pieces of paper or cloth onto a surface.

collapse, collapses, collapsing, collapsed VERB ① If something such as a building collapses, it falls down suddenly. If a person collapses, they fall down suddenly because they are ill. ② If something such as a system or a business collapses, it suddenly stops working • *50,000 small firms collapsed last year*. ▸ NOUN ③ The collapse of something is what

happens when it stops working • *the collapse of the country's economy*.

collapsible ADJECTIVE A collapsible object can be folded flat when it is not in use • *a collapsible ironing board*.

collar, collars NOUN ① The collar of a shirt or coat is the part round the neck which is usually folded over. ② a leather band round the neck of a dog or cat.

collarbone, collarbones NOUN Your collarbones are the two long bones which run from the base of your neck to your shoulders.

collateral NOUN Collateral is money or property which is used as a guarantee that someone will repay a loan, and which the lender can take if the loan is not repaid.

colleague, colleagues NOUN A person's colleagues are the people he or she works with.

collect, collects, collecting, collected VERB ① To collect things is to gather them together for a special purpose or as a hobby • *collecting money for charity*. ② If you collect someone or something from a place, you call there and take them away • *We had to collect her from school*. ③ When things collect in a place, they gather there over a period of time • *Food collects in holes in the teeth*. **collector** NOUN

collected ADJECTIVE calm and self-controlled.

collection, collections NOUN
① ART a group of things acquired over a period of time • *a collection of paintings*. ② Collection is the collecting of something • *tax collection*. ③ the organised collecting of money, for example for charity, or the sum of money collected.
SIMILAR WORDS: ① accumulation, compilation, set

a
b
c
d
e
f
g
h
i
j
k
l
m
n
o
p
q
r
s
t
u
v
w
x
y
z

collective, collectives ADJECTIVE
① involving every member of a group
of people • *The school's teachers took a
collective decision.* ▶ NOUN ② a group
of people who share the
responsibility both for running
something and for doing the work.
collectively ADVERB

collective noun, collective nouns
NOUN ENGLISH a noun that refers to
a single unit made up of a number of
things, for example 'flock' and 'swarm'.

college, colleges NOUN ① a place
where students study after they have
left school. ② a name given to some
secondary schools. ③ one of the
institutions into which some
universities are divided. ④ In New
Zealand English, a college can also
refer to a teacher training college.

collide, collides, colliding, collided
VERB If a moving object collides with
something, it hits it.

collie, collies NOUN a dog that is used
for rounding up sheep.

colliery, collieries NOUN a coal mine.

collision, collisions NOUN A collision
occurs when a moving object hits
something.
SIMILAR WORDS: crash, impact, smash

colloquial [*Said kol-loh-kwee-al*]
ADJECTIVE ENGLISH Colloquial
words and phrases are informal and
used especially in conversation.

colloquially ADVERB **colloquialism**
NOUN

cologne [*Said kol-lone*] NOUN Cologne
is a kind of weak perfume.

colon, colons NOUN ① ENGLISH the
punctuation mark (:). ② part of your
intestine.

PUNCTUATION TIP
Use a colon to introduce lists or
reasons: *He has two brothers: Jim and
Robert; I can't come to the wedding: I will
be on holiday.*

---

colonel, colonels [*Said kur-nl*] NOUN
an army officer with a fairly high rank.

colonial ADJECTIVE ① relating to a
colony. ② In Australia, 'colonial' is
used to relate to the period of
Australian history before the
Federation in 1901.

colonise, colonises, colonising,
colonised; also spelt **colonize** VERB
① HISTORY When people colonise a
place, they go to live there and take
control of it • *the Europeans who
colonised North America.* ② When a lot
of animals colonise a place, they go
there and make it their home • *Toads
are colonising the whole place.*
colonisation NOUN **colonist** NOUN

colony, colonies NOUN ① HISTORY
a country controlled by a more
powerful country. ② a group of

What does the Colon do?

The **colon** (:) and the **semicolon** (;) are
often confused and used incorrectly.

The **colon** is used to introduce a list:

*I bought fruit: pears, apples, grapes and
plums.*

The colon can also be used to
introduce a quotation:

He received a message which read: 'You

can't fool all of the people all of the time.'

Another use of the colon is to
introduce an explanation of a
statement:

*They did not enjoy the meal: the food
was cold.*

Also look at the punctuation box
at **semicolon**

people who settle in a country controlled by their homeland.

colossal ADJECTIVE very large indeed.

colour, colours, colouring, coloured NOUN ① ART the appearance something has as a result of reflecting light. ② a substance used to give colour. ③ Someone's colour is the normal colour of their skin. ④ Colour is also a quality that makes something interesting or exciting • *bringing more culture and colour to the city*. ▶ VERB ⑤ If you colour something, you give it a colour. ⑥ If something colours your opinion, it affects the way you think about something. **coloured** ADJECTIVE **colourless** ADJECTIVE **colouring** NOUN

SIMILAR WORDS: ① hue, shade, tint

colour blind ADJECTIVE Someone who is colour blind cannot distinguish between colours.

Coloured, Coloureds ADJECTIVE ① In South Africa, a Coloured person has mixed White and non-White parentage. ▶ NOUN ② In South Africa, a Coloured is a person of racially mixed parentage or descent.

colourful ADJECTIVE ① full of colour. ② interesting or exciting. **colourfully** ADVERB

colt, colts NOUN a young male horse.

column, columns NOUN ① a tall solid upright cylinder, especially one supporting a part of a building. ② a group of people moving in a long line. ③ a vertical section of writing. ④ a regular article in a newspaper or magazine.

columnist, columnists NOUN a journalist who writes a regular article in a newspaper or magazine.

coma, comas NOUN Someone who is in a coma is in a state of deep unconsciousness.

comb, combs, combing, combed NOUN ① a flat object with pointed teeth used for tidying your hair. ▶ VERB ② When you comb your hair, you tidy it with a comb. ③ If you comb a place, you search it thoroughly to try to find someone or something.

combat, combats, combating, combated NOUN ① Combat is fighting • *his first experience of combat*. ▶ VERB ② To combat something means to try to stop it happening or developing • *a way to combat crime*.

combination, combinations NOUN ① a mixture of things • *a combination of charm and skill*. ② a series of letters or numbers used to open a special lock.

combine, combines, combining, combined VERB ① To combine things is to cause them to exist together • *to combine a career with being a mother*. ② To combine things also means to join them together to make a single thing • *Combine all the ingredients*. ③ If something combines two qualities or features, it has them both • *a film that combines great charm and scintillating performances*.

combustion NOUN SCIENCE Combustion is the act of burning something or the process of burning.

come, comes, coming, came, come VERB ① To come to a place is to move there or arrive there. ② To come to a place also means to reach as far as that place • *The sea water came up to his waist*. ③ 'Come' is used to say that someone or something reaches a particular state • *They came to power in 2016* • *We had come to a decision*. ④ When a particular time or event comes, it happens • *The peak of his career came early in 2000*. ⑤ If you come from a place, you were born there or it is your home. ▶ PHRASE ⑥ A time or event **to come** is a future time or event • *The public will thank*

a
b
c
d
e
f
g
h
i
j
k
l
m
n
o
p
q
r
s
t
u
v
w
x
y
z

A
B
C
D
E
F
G
H
I
J
K
L
M
N
O
P
Q
R
S
T
U
V
W
X
Y
Z

What does the Comma do?

The **comma** (,) indicates a short pause between different elements within a sentence. This happens, for example, when a sentence consists of two main clauses joined by a conjunction:

Anna likes swimming, but Matthew prefers fishing.

A comma may also separate an introductory phrase or a subordinate clause from the main clause in a sentence:

After a month of sunshine, it rained on Thursday.

However, a short introductory phrase does not need to be followed by a comma:

After lunch the classes continued.

When words such as *therefore*, *however* and *moreover* are put into a sentence to show how a train of thought is progressing, they should be marked off by commas:

We are confident, however, that the operation will be successful.

The comma also separates items in a list or series:

I made this soup with carrots, beans, leeks and potatoes.

Commas separate the name of a person or people being addressed from the rest of the sentence:

Thank you, ladies and gentlemen, for your attention.

The comma also separates words in quotation marks from the rest of the sentence, if there is no question or exclamation mark at the end of the quotation:

'This is a terrific picture,' she said.

them in years to come. **come about** VERB The way something comes about is the way it happens • *The discussion came about because of the proposed changes.* **come across** VERB If you come across something, you find it by chance. **come off** VERB If something comes off, it succeeds • *His rescue plan had come off.* **come on** VERB If something is coming on, it is making progress • *How is your essay coming on?* **come round** VERB ①To come round means to recover consciousness. ②To come round to an idea or situation means to eventually accept it. ③When a regular event comes round, it happens • *Beginning of term came round too quickly.* **come to** VERB To come to means to recover consciousness. **come up** VERB If

something comes up in a conversation or meeting, it is mentioned or discussed. **come up with** VERB If you come up with a plan or idea, you suggest it.

comeback, comebacks NOUN To make a comeback means to be popular or successful again.

comedian, comedians NOUN an entertainer whose job is to make people laugh.

comedienne, comediennes *[Said kom-mee-dee-en]* NOUN a female comedian.

comedy, comedies NOUN a light-hearted play or film with a happy ending.
WORD HISTORY: from Greek *kōmos* meaning 'village festival' and *aeidein* meaning 'to sing'

comet, comets NOUN an object that travels around the sun leaving a bright trail behind it.

comfort, comforts, comforting, comforted NOUN ①Comfort is the state of being physically relaxed • *He settled back in comfort.* ②Comfort is also a feeling of relief from worries or unhappiness • *The thought is a great comfort to me.* ③(in plural) Comforts are things which make your life easier and more pleasant • *all the comforts of home.* ▶VERB ④To comfort someone is to make them less worried or unhappy.

comfortable ADJECTIVE ①If you are comfortable, you are physically relaxed. ②Something that is comfortable makes you feel relaxed • *a comfortable bed.* ③If you feel comfortable in a particular situation, you are not afraid or embarrassed.
comfortably ADVERB

comic, comics ADJECTIVE ①funny • *a comic monologue.* ▶NOUN ②someone who tells jokes. ③a magazine that contains stories told in pictures.

comical ADJECTIVE funny • *a comical sight.*

comma, commas NOUN ENGLISH the punctuation mark (,).

PUNCTUATION TIP
Commas are used when there are three or more items in a list or series, but there is no need to use a comma between the last two items in the list: *We had fish, peas and rice for lunch.* There is no need to use a comma at all when there are only two items: *We had fish and rice for lunch.*

command, commands, commanding, commanded VERB ①To command someone to do something is to order them to do it. ②If you command something such as respect, you receive it because of your personal qualities. ③An officer who commands part of an army or navy is in charge of it. ▶NOUN ④an order to do something. ⑤Your command of something is your knowledge of it and your ability to use this knowledge • *a good command of English.*
SIMILAR WORDS: ①direct, order

commandant, commandants [*Said* kom-man-dant] NOUN an army officer in charge of a place or group of people.

commander, commanders NOUN an officer in charge of a military operation or organisation.

a
b
c
d
e
f
g
h
i
j
k
l
m
n
o
p
q
r
s
t
u
v
w
x
y
z

What is a Command?

Commands are used to give orders, instructions or warnings.

Commands are made by putting the verb at the start of the sentence. The verb is used in its **imperative form**, which is the basic form without any endings added:

Come over here.

Commands do not need a subject, as people who are being told to do something already know who they

are. So commands may consist of a single verb:

Stop!

The negative form of a command is introduced by *do not* or *don't*:

Don't *put that on the table.*

Commands often end with an exclamation mark rather than a full stop, especially if they express urgency:

Run for your life!

commandment, commandments
NOUN RE The ten commandments
are ten important rules of behaviour
that, according to the Old
Testament, people should obey.

commando, commandos NOUN
Commandos are soldiers who have
been specially trained to carry out
raids.

commemorate, commemorates,
commemorating, commemorated
VERB ① An object that
commemorates a person or an event
is intended to remind people of that
person or event. ② If you
commemorate an event, you do
something special to show that you
remember it. **commemorative**
ADJECTIVE **commemoration** NOUN

commence, commences,
commencing, commenced VERB
(formal) To commence is to begin.
commencement NOUN

commend, commends,
commending, commended VERB To
commend someone or something is
to praise them • He has been
commended for his work.
commendation NOUN
commendable ADJECTIVE

comment, comments,
commenting, commented VERB
① If you comment on something, you
make a remark about it. ▶ NOUN ② a
remark about something • She
received many comments about her
performance.
SIMILAR WORDS: ① observe, remark

commentary, commentaries
NOUN a description of an event which
is broadcast on radio or television
while the event is happening.

commentator, commentators
NOUN someone who gives a radio or
television commentary.

commerce NOUN Commerce is the
buying and selling of goods.

commercial, commercials
ADJECTIVE ① relating to commerce.
② Commercial activities involve
producing goods on a large scale in
order to make money • the commercial
fishing world. ▶ NOUN ③ an
advertisement on television or radio.
commercially ADVERB

commission, commissions,
commissioning, commissioned
VERB ① If someone commissions a
piece of work, they formally ask
someone to do it • a study
commissioned by the government.
▶ NOUN ② a piece of work that has
been commissioned. ③ Commission
is money paid to a salesperson each
time a sale is made. ④ an official
body appointed to investigate or
control something.

commit, commits, committing,
committed VERB ① To commit a
crime or sin is to do it. ② If you
commit yourself, you state an
opinion or state that you will do
something. ③ If someone is
committed to hospital or prison,
they are officially sent there.
committal NOUN
SIMILAR WORDS: ① do, perform,
perpetrate

commitment, commitments NOUN
① Commitment is a strong belief in
an idea or system. ② something that
regularly takes up some of your time
• business commitments.

committed ADJECTIVE A committed
person has strong beliefs • a
committed feminist.

committee, committees NOUN a
group of people who make decisions
on behalf of a larger group.

commodity, commodities NOUN
(formal) Commodities are things that
are sold.

common, commoner, **commonest**;
commons ADJECTIVE ① Something
that is common exists in large
numbers or happens often • *a
common complaint*. ② If something is
common to two or more people, they
all have it or use it • *I realised we had a
common interest*. ③ 'Common' is used
to indicate that something is of the
ordinary kind and not special. ④ If
you describe someone as common,
you mean they do not have good
taste or good manners. ▶ NOUN ⑤ an
area of grassy land where everyone
can go. ▶ PHRASE ⑥ If two things or
people have something **in common**,
they both have it. **commonly** ADVERB
SIMILAR WORDS: ① customary,
frequent ④ coarse, vulgar

commoner, commoners NOUN
someone who is not a member of the
nobility.

commonplace ADJECTIVE
Something that is commonplace
happens often • *Foreign holidays have
become commonplace*.

common sense NOUN Your common
sense is your natural ability to behave
sensibly and make good judgments.

Commonwealth NOUN ① The
Commonwealth is an association of
countries around the world that are
or used to be ruled by Britain. ② a
country made up of a number of
states • *the Commonwealth of Australia*.

commotion, commotions NOUN A
commotion is a lot of noise and
excitement.

communal ADJECTIVE shared by a
group of people • *a communal canteen*.

commune, communes [*Said kom-yoon*]
NOUN a group of people who live
together and share everything.

communicate, communicates,
communicating, communicated
VERB ① If you communicate with
someone, you keep in touch with
them. ② If you communicate
information or a feeling to someone,
you make them aware of it.
SIMILAR WORDS: ② convey, make
known

communication, communications
NOUN ① PSHE Communication is
the process by which people or
animals exchange information.
② (*in plural*) Communications are
the systems by which people
communicate or broadcast
information, especially using
electricity or radio waves. ③ (*formal*)
a letter or telephone call.

communicative ADJECTIVE
Someone who is communicative is
willing to talk to people.

communion NOUN ① Communion
is the sharing of thoughts and
feelings. ② RE In Christianity,
Communion is a religious service in
which people share bread and wine
in remembrance of the death and
resurrection of Jesus Christ.

communism NOUN Communism is
the doctrine that the state should
own the means of production and
that there should be no private
property. **communist** ADJECTIVE or
NOUN

community, communities
NOUN CITIZENSHIP all the people
living in a particular area; also used
to refer to particular groups within a
society • *the heart of the local
community* • *the Asian community*.

commute, commutes, commuting,
commuted VERB People who
commute travel a long distance to
work every day. **commuter** NOUN

compact ADJECTIVE taking up very
little space • *a compact microwave*.

compact disc, compact discs NOUN
a music or video recording in the

form of a plastic disc which is played using a laser on a special machine, and gives good quality sound or pictures.

companion, companions NOUN someone you travel or spend time with. **companionship** NOUN WORD HISTORY: from Latin *com-* meaning 'together' and *panis* meaning 'bread'. A companion was originally someone you shared a meal with

company, companies NOUN ① a business that sells goods or provides a service • *the record company*. ② a group of actors, opera singers or dancers • *the Royal Shakespeare Company*. ③ If you have company, you have a friend or visitor with you • *I enjoyed her company*.

comparable [Said **kom-pra-bl**] ADJECTIVE If two things are comparable, they are similar in size or quality • *The skill is comparable to playing the violin*. **comparably** ADVERB
SIMILAR WORDS: equal, equivalent, on a par

comparative, comparatives ADJECTIVE ① You add comparative to indicate that something is true only when compared with what is normal • *eight years of comparative calm*.
▶ NOUN ② ENGLISH In grammar, the comparative is the form of an adjective which indicates that the person or thing described has more of a particular quality than someone or something else. For example, 'quicker', 'better' and 'easier' are all comparatives. **comparatively** ADVERB

What is a Comparative?

Many adjectives have three different forms. These are known as the **positive**, the **comparative** and the **superlative**. The comparative and superlative are used when you make comparisons.

The **positive** form of an adjective is given as the entry in the dictionary. It is used when there is no comparison between different objects:

*Matthew is **tall**.*

The **comparative** form is usually made by adding the ending *-er* to the positive form of the adjective. It shows that something possesses a quality to a greater extent than the thing it is being compared with:

*Matthew is **taller** than Jana.*

You can also make comparisons by using the words *more* or *less* with the positive (not the comparative) form

of the adjective:

*Matthew is **more energetic** than Robbie.*

Irregular Comparative Forms
When the comparative and superlative of an adjective are not formed in the regular way, the irregular forms of the adjective are shown in the dictionary after the main entry.

Many adjectives – especially ones that have more than one syllable and do not end in -*y* – do not have separate spelling forms for the comparative and superlative. For these adjectives comparisons must be made using *more*, *less*, *most* and *least*:

beautiful → *more beautiful* → *most beautiful*
boring → *less boring* → *least boring*

Also look at the grammar box at **the**

compare, compares, comparing, compared VERB ① EXAM TERM When you compare things, you look at them together and see in what ways they are different or similar. ② If you compare one thing to another, you say it is like the other thing • *Her voice is often compared to Adele's.*

comparison, comparisons NOUN ENGLISH When you make a comparison, you consider two things together and see in what ways they are different or similar.

compartment, compartments NOUN ① a section of a railway carriage. ② one of the separate parts of an object • *a special compartment inside your vehicle.*

compass, compasses NOUN ① SCIENCE an instrument with a magnetic needle for finding directions. ② (*in plural*) Compasses are a hinged instrument for drawing circles.

GRAMMAR TIP
The proper name for the drawing instrument is *a pair of compasses.*

compassion NOUN pity and sympathy for someone who is suffering.
WORD HISTORY: from Latin *compati* meaning 'to suffer with'

compassionate ADJECTIVE feeling or showing sympathy and pity for others. **compassionately** ADVERB

compatible ADJECTIVE If people or things are compatible, they can live or work together successfully. **compatibility** NOUN

compatriot, compatriots NOUN Your compatriots are people from your own country.

compel, compels, compelling, compelled VERB To compel someone to do something is to force them to do it.

compelling ADJECTIVE ① If a story or event is compelling, it is extremely interesting • *a compelling novel.* ② A compelling argument or reason makes you believe that something is true or should be done • *compelling new evidence.*

compensate, compensates, compensating, compensated VERB ① To compensate someone is to give them money to replace something lost or damaged. ② If one thing compensates for another, it cancels out its bad effects • *The trip more than compensated for the hardship.*
compensatory ADJECTIVE
SIMILAR WORDS: ① recompense, refund ② make up for

compensation, compensations NOUN something that makes up for loss or damage.

compere, comperes, compering, compered [*Said kom-pare*] NOUN ① the person who introduces the guests or performers in a show.
▶ VERB ② To compere a show is to introduce the guests or performers.

compete, competes, competing, competed VERB ① When people or firms compete, each tries to prove that they or their products are the best. ② If you compete in a contest or game, you take part in it.

competent ADJECTIVE Someone who is competent at something can do it satisfactorily • *a very competent engineer.* **competently** ADVERB **competence** NOUN

competition, competitions NOUN ① When there is competition between people or groups, they are all trying to get something that not everyone can have • *There's a lot of competition for places.* ② an event in which people take part to find who is best at something. ③When there is competition between firms, each firm is trying to get people to buy its own goods.

competitive ADJECTIVE ①A competitive situation is one in which people or firms are competing with each other • *a crowded and competitive market*. ②A competitive person is eager to be more successful than others. ③Goods sold at competitive prices are cheaper than other goods of the same kind. **competitively** ADVERB

competitor, competitors NOUN a person or firm that is competing to become the most successful.

compilation, compilations NOUN A compilation is a book, recording or programme consisting of several items that were originally produced separately • *this compilation of his solo work*.

compile, compiles, compiling, compiled VERB When someone compiles a book or report, they make it by putting together several items.

complacent ADJECTIVE If someone is complacent, they are unconcerned about a serious situation and do nothing about it. **complacently** ADVERB **complacency** NOUN

complain, complains, complaining, complained VERB ①If you complain, you say that you are not satisfied with something. ②If you complain of pain or illness, you say that you have it.
SIMILAR WORDS: ①find fault, grumble, moan

complaint, complaints NOUN If you make a complaint, you complain about something.

complement, complements, complementing, complemented

VERB ①If one thing complements another, the two things go well together • *The tiled floor complements the pine furniture*. ▶NOUN ②If one thing is a complement to another, it goes well with it. ③In grammar, a complement is a word or phrase that gives information about the subject or object of a sentence. For example, in the sentence 'Rover is a dog', 'a dog' is a complement. **complementary** ADJECTIVE

SPELLING TIP
Do not confuse the spellings of *complement* and *compliment*: *The rice should complement the curry nicely; I must compliment you on your garden*.

complementary angle, complementary angles NOUN
MATHS A complementary angle is either of the two angles that together make up 90°.

complete, completes, completing, completed ADJECTIVE ①to the greatest degree possible • *a complete mess*. ②If something is complete, none of it is missing • *a complete set of tools*. ③When a task is complete, it is finished • *The planning stage is now complete*. ▶VERB ④If you complete something, you finish it. ⑤If you complete a form, you fill it in.
completely ADVERB **completion** NOUN

SIMILAR WORDS: ①absolute, thorough, total ②entire, full, whole

complex, complexes ADJECTIVE ①Something that is complex has many different parts • *a very complex problem*. ②In grammar, a complex sentence consists of a main clause with one or more subordinate clauses joined to it. ▶NOUN ③A complex is a group of buildings, roads or other things connected with each other in some way • *a hotel and* *restaurant complex.* ④If someone has a complex, they have an emotional problem because of a past experience • *an inferiority complex.* **complexity** NOUN

SIMILAR WORDS: ① complicated, intricate, involved

complexion, complexions NOUN the quality of the skin on your face • *a healthy glowing complexion.*

complicate, complicates, complicating, complicated VERB To complicate something is to make it more difficult to understand or deal with.

complicated ADJECTIVE Something that is complicated has so many parts or aspects that it is difficult to understand or deal with.

complication, complications NOUN something that makes a situation more difficult to deal with • *One possible complication was that it was late in the year.*

compliment, compliments, complimenting, complimented NOUN ① If you pay someone a compliment, you tell them you admire something about them. ② (*in plural, formal*) When someone sends their compliments, they formally express their good wishes • *Inspector Paget sends his compliments.* ▶ VERB ③ If you compliment someone, you pay them a compliment.

SPELLING TIP
Do not confuse the spellings of *compliment* and *complement*: *I must compliment you on your garden; The rice should complement the curry nicely.*

complimentary ADJECTIVE ① If you are complimentary about something, you express admiration for it. ② A complimentary seat, ticket or magazine is given to you free.

comply, complies, complying, complied VERB If you comply with an order or rule, you obey it. **compliance** NOUN

component, components NOUN
DGT SCIENCE The components of something are the parts it is made of.

compose, composes, composing, composed VERB ① If something is composed of particular things or people, it is made up of them. ② To compose a piece of music, letter or speech means to write it. ③ If you compose yourself, you become calm after being excited or upset.

composed ADJECTIVE calm and in control of your feelings.

composer, composers NOUN someone who writes music.

composition, compositions NOUN ① The composition of something is the things it consists of • *the composition of the ozone layer.* ② MUSIC The composition of a poem or piece of music is the writing of it. ③ MUSIC a piece of music or writing.

compost NOUN Compost is a mixture of decaying plants and manure added to soil to help plants grow.

composure NOUN Someone's composure is their ability to stay calm • *Jarvis was able to recover his composure.*

compound, compounds, compounding, compounded NOUN ① an enclosed area of land with buildings used for a particular purpose • *the prison compound.* ② a word formed from two existing words, for example, *keyboard.* ③ SCIENCE In chemistry, a compound is a substance consisting of two or more different substances or chemical elements. ▶ VERB ④ To compound something is to put

a
b
c
d
e
f
g
h
i
j
k
l
m
n
o
p
q
r
s
t
u
v
w
x
y
z

together different parts to make a whole. ⑤ To compound a problem is to make it worse by adding to it • *Water shortages were compounded by taps left running*.

comprehend, comprehends, comprehending, comprehended VERB (*formal*) To comprehend something is to understand or appreciate it • *He did not fully comprehend what was puzzling me*.
comprehension NOUN

comprehensible ADJECTIVE able to be understood.

comprehensive, comprehensives ADJECTIVE ① Something that is comprehensive includes everything necessary or relevant • *a comprehensive guide*. ▶ NOUN ② a school where children of all abilities are taught together.
comprehensively ADVERB

compress, compresses, compressing, compressed VERB To compress something is to squeeze it or shorten it so that it takes up less space • *compressed air*. **compression** NOUN

comprise, comprises, comprising, comprised VERB (*formal*) What something comprises is what it consists of • *The district then comprised 66 villages*.

GRAMMAR TIP
You do not need *of* after *comprise*. For example, you say *the library comprises 500,000 books*.

---

compromise, compromises, compromising, compromised NOUN ① an agreement in which people accept less than they originally wanted • *In the end they reached a compromise*. ▶ VERB ② When people compromise, they agree to accept less than they originally wanted.

compulsion, compulsions NOUN a very strong desire to do something.

compulsive ADJECTIVE ① You use 'compulsive' to describe someone who cannot stop doing something • *a compulsive letter writer*. ② If you find something such as a book or television programme compulsive, you cannot stop reading or watching it.

compulsory ADJECTIVE If something is compulsory, you have to do it • *School attendance is compulsory*.
SIMILAR WORDS: mandatory, obligatory

computer, computers NOUN an electronic machine that can quickly make calculations or store and find information.

computer-aided design NOUN Computer-aided design is the use of computers and computer graphics to help design things.

computerise, computerises, computerising, computerised; also spelt **computerize** VERB When a system or process is computerised, the work is done by computers.

computing NOUN Computing is the use of computers and the writing of programs for them.

comrade, comrades NOUN A soldier's comrades are his or her fellow soldiers, especially in battle.
comradeship NOUN

con, cons, conning, conned (*informal*) VERB ① If someone cons you, they trick you into doing or believing something. ▶ NOUN ② a trick in which someone deceives you into doing or believing something.

concave ADJECTIVE MATHS A concave surface curves inwards, rather than being level or bulging outwards.

conceal, conceals, concealing, concealed VERB To conceal something is to hide it • *He had concealed his gun.* **concealment** NOUN

concede, concedes, conceding, conceded [*Said* kon-**seed**] VERB ① If you concede something, you admit that it is true • *I conceded that he was entitled to his views.* ② When someone concedes defeat, they accept that they have lost something such as a contest or an election.

conceit NOUN Conceit is someone's excessive pride in their appearance or abilities.
SIMILAR WORDS: pride, self-importance

conceited ADJECTIVE Someone who is conceited is too proud of their appearance or abilities.
SIMILAR WORDS: bigheaded, full of oneself, self-important

conceivable ADJECTIVE If something is conceivable, you can believe that it could exist or be true • *It's conceivable that you also met her.* **conceivably** ADVERB

conceive, conceives, conceiving, conceived VERB ① If you can conceive of something, you can imagine it or believe it • *Could you conceive of doing such a thing yourself?* ② If you conceive something such as a plan, you think of it and work out how it could be done. ③ When a woman conceives, she becomes pregnant.

concentrate, concentrates, concentrating, concentrated VERB ① If you concentrate on something, you give it all your attention. ② When something is concentrated in one place, it is all there rather than in several places • *They are mostly concentrated in the urban areas.* **concentration** NOUN

concentrated ADJECTIVE A concentrated liquid has been made stronger by having water removed from it • *concentrated apple juice.*

concentration camp, concentration camps NOUN
HISTORY a prison camp, especially one set up by the Nazis during World War Two.

concept, concepts NOUN an abstract or general idea • *the concept of tolerance.* **conceptual** ADJECTIVE **conceptually** ADVERB

conception, conceptions NOUN ① Your conception of something is the idea you have of it. ② Conception is the process by which a woman becomes pregnant.

concern, concerns, concerning, concerned NOUN ① Concern is a feeling of worry about something or someone • *public concern about violence.* ② If something is your concern, it is your responsibility. ③ a business • *a large manufacturing concern.* ▶ VERB ④ If something concerns you or if you are concerned about it, it worries you. ⑤ You say that something concerns you if it affects or involves you • *My business does not concern you.* ▶ PHRASE ⑥ If something is **of concern** to you, it is important to you. **concerned** ADJECTIVE
SIMILAR WORDS: ⑤ be relevant to, involve, regard

concerning PREPOSITION You use 'concerning' to show what something is about • *studies concerning the environment.*

concert, concerts NOUN a public performance by musicians.

concerted ADJECTIVE A concerted action is done by several people together • *concerted action to cut interest rates.*

concerto, concertos or concerti [Said kon-**cher**-toe] NOUN MUSIC a piece of music for a solo instrument and an orchestra.

concession, concessions NOUN If you make a concession, you agree to let someone have or do something • Her one concession was to let me come into the building.

conch, conches NOUN a shellfish with a large, brightly coloured shell; also the shell itself.

concise ADJECTIVE giving all the necessary information using as few words as necessary • a concise guide. **concisely** ADVERB
SIMILAR WORDS: brief, short, succinct

conclude, concludes, concluding, concluded VERB ① If you conclude something, you decide that it is so because of the other things that you know • An inquiry concluded that this was untrue. ② When you conclude something, you finish it • At that point I intend to conclude the interview. **concluding** ADJECTIVE

conclusion, conclusions NOUN ① a decision made after thinking carefully about something. ② the finish or ending of something.

conclusive ADJECTIVE Facts that are conclusive show that something is certainly true. **conclusively** ADVERB

concoct, concocts, concocting, concocted VERB ① If you concoct an excuse or explanation, you invent one. ② If you concoct something, you make it by mixing several things together. **concoction** NOUN

concourse, concourses NOUN a wide hall in a building where people walk about or gather together.

concrete NOUN ① Concrete is a solid building material made by mixing cement, sand and water. ▶ ADJECTIVE ② definite, rather than general or

vague • I don't really have any concrete plans. ③ real and physical, rather than abstract • concrete evidence.

concur, concurs, concurring, concurred VERB (formal) To concur is to agree • She concurred with me.

concurrent ADJECTIVE If things are concurrent, they happen at the same time. **concurrently** ADVERB

concussed ADJECTIVE confused or unconscious because of a blow to the head. **concussion** NOUN

condemn, condemns, condemning, condemned VERB ① If you condemn something, you say it is bad and unacceptable • Teachers condemned the new plans. ② If someone is condemned to a punishment, they are given it • She was condemned to death. ③ If you are condemned to something unpleasant, you must suffer it • Many people are condemned to poverty. ④ When a building is condemned, it is going to be pulled down because it is unsafe.
condemnation NOUN
SIMILAR WORDS: ① censure, criticise, disapprove of ② sentence ③ doom

condensation NOUN SCIENCE Condensation is a coating of tiny drops formed on a surface by steam or vapour.

condense, condenses, condensing, condensed VERB ① If you condense a piece of writing or a speech, you shorten it. ② SCIENCE When a gas or vapour condenses, it changes into a liquid.

condescending ADJECTIVE If you are condescending, you behave in a way that shows you think you are superior to other people.
SIMILAR WORDS: patronising, superior

condition, conditions, conditioning, conditioned NOUN

① the state someone or something is in. ② (*in plural*) The conditions in which something is done are the location and other factors likely to affect it • *The very difficult conditions continued to affect our performance*. ③ a requirement that must be met for something else to be possible • *He had to report to the police each week as a condition of bail*. ④ You can refer to an illness or other medical problem as a condition • *a heart condition*.
▶ PHRASE ⑤ If you are **out of condition**, you are unfit. ▶ VERB ⑥ If someone is conditioned to behave or think in a certain way, they do it as a result of their upbringing or training.
SIMILAR WORDS: ③ prerequisite, requirement, stipulation

conditional ADJECTIVE If one thing is conditional on another, it can only happen if the other thing happens • *Admission to the course is conditional on you getting good grades*.

condolence, condolences NOUN Condolence is sympathy expressed for a bereaved person.

condom, condoms NOUN a rubber sheath worn by a man on his penis or by a woman inside her vagina as a contraceptive.

condominium, condominiums NOUN In Canadian, Australian and New Zealand English, a condominium is an apartment block in which each apartment is owned by the person who lives in it.

condone, condones, condoning, condoned VERB If you condone someone's bad behaviour, you accept it and do not try to stop it • *We cannot condone violence*.

conducive [Said kon-*joo*-siv] ADJECTIVE If something is conducive to something else, it makes it likely to happen • *a situation that is conducive to relaxation*.

conduct, conducts, conducting, conducted VERB ① To conduct an activity or task is to carry it out • *He seemed to be conducting a conversation*. ② (*formal*) The way you conduct yourself is the way you behave. ③ MUSIC When someone conducts an orchestra or choir, they stand in front of it and direct it. ④ SCIENCE If something conducts heat or electricity, heat or electricity can pass through it. ▶ NOUN ⑤ If you take part in the conduct of an activity or task, you help to carry it out. ⑥ Your conduct is your behaviour.

conductor, conductors NOUN ① MUSIC someone who conducts an orchestra or choir. ② someone who moves round a train, bus or tram selling tickets. ③ In American English, a railway official in charge of a train. ④ SCIENCE a substance that conducts heat or electricity.

cone, cones NOUN ① a regular three-dimensional shape with a circular base and a point at the top. ② A fir cone or pine cone is the fruit of a fir or pine tree.

confectionery NOUN Confectionery is sweets.

confederation, confederations NOUN an organisation formed for business or political purposes.

confer, confers, conferring, conferred VERB When people confer, they discuss something in order to make a decision.

conference, conferences NOUN a meeting at which formal discussions take place.

confess, confesses, confessing, confessed VERB If you confess to something, you admit it • *Your son has confessed to his crimes*.
SIMILAR WORDS: admit, own up

a
b
c
d
e
f
g
h
i
j
k
l
m
n
o
p
q
r
s
t
u
v
w
x
y
z

confession, confessions NOUN ① If you make a confession, you admit you have done something wrong. ② Confession is the act of confessing something, especially a religious act in which people confess their sins to a priest.

SIMILAR WORDS:
① acknowledgment, admission

confessional, confessionals NOUN RE a small room in some churches where people confess their sins to a priest.

confetti NOUN Confetti is small pieces of coloured paper thrown over the newly married couple after a wedding.
WORD HISTORY: from Italian *confetto* meaning 'a sweet'

confidant, confidants [Said kon-fid-dant] NOUN (formal) a person you discuss your private problems with.

SPELLING TIP
Do not confuse the spellings of *confidant* and *confident*: *My brother is my only confidant; She was confident she could remember the way home*. When the person you discuss your private problems with is a girl or a woman, the word is spelt *confidante*.

---

confide, confides, confiding, confided VERB If you confide in or to someone, you tell them a secret • *Marian confided in me that she was very worried*.

confidence, confidences NOUN ① If you have confidence in someone, you feel you can trust them. ② Someone who has confidence is sure of their own abilities or qualities. ③ a secret you tell someone.

confidence trick, confidence tricks NOUN A confidence trick is the same as a con. **confidence trickster** NOUN

confident ADJECTIVE ① If you are confident about something, you are sure it will happen the way you want it to. ② People who are confident are sure of their own abilities or qualities. **confidently** ADVERB
SIMILAR WORDS: ① certain, positive, sure ② assured, self-assured

---

SPELLING TIP
Do not confuse the spellings of *confident* and *confidant*: *She was confident she could remember the way home; My brother is my only confidant*.

---

confidential ADJECTIVE Confidential information is meant to be kept secret. **confidentially** ADVERB **confidentiality** NOUN

confine, confines, confining, confined VERB ① If something is confined to one place, person or thing, it exists only in that place or affects only that person or thing. ② If you confine yourself to doing or saying something, it is the only thing you do or say • *They confined themselves to discussing the weather*. ③ If you are confined to a place, you cannot leave it • *She was confined to bed for two days*. ▶ PLURAL NOUN ④ The confines of a place are its boundaries • *outside the confines of the prison*. **confinement** NOUN

confined ADJECTIVE A confined space is small and enclosed by walls.

confirm, confirms, confirming, confirmed VERB ① To confirm something is to say or show that it is true • *Police confirmed that they had received a call*. ② If you confirm an arrangement or appointment, you say it is definite. ③ RE When someone is confirmed, they are formally accepted as a member of a Christian Church. **confirmation** NOUN
SIMILAR WORDS: ① prove, verify

confirmed ADJECTIVE You use 'confirmed' to describe someone who has a belief or way of life that is unlikely to change • *a confirmed bachelor*.

confiscate, confiscates, confiscating, confiscated VERB To confiscate something is to take it away from someone as a punishment.

conflict, conflicts, conflicting, conflicted NOUN [Said *kon-flikt*] ① Conflict is disagreement and argument • *conflict between teenagers and their parents*. ② HISTORY a war or battle. ③ When there is a conflict of ideas or interests, people have different ideas or interests which cannot all be satisfied. ▶ VERB [Said *kon-flikt*] ④ When ideas or interests conflict, they are different and cannot all be satisfied.
SIMILAR WORDS: ① disagreement, dissension ② battle, clash ④ be incompatible, clash, disagree

confluence, confluences NOUN GEOGRAPHY the place where two rivers join.

conform, conforms, conforming, conformed VERB ① If you conform, you behave the way people expect you to. ② If something conforms to a law or to someone's wishes, it is what is required or wanted.
conformist NOUN or ADJECTIVE

confound, confounds, confounding, confounded VERB If someone or something confounds you, they make you feel surprised or confused.

confront, confronts, confronting, confronted VERB ① If you are confronted with a problem or task, you have to deal with it. ② If you confront someone, you meet them face to face like an enemy. ③ If you confront someone with evidence or a fact, you present it to them in order to accuse them of something.

confrontation, confrontations NOUN a serious dispute or fight • *a confrontation between police and protesters*.

confuse, confuses, confusing, confused VERB ① If you confuse two things, you mix them up and think one of them is the other • *You are confusing facts with opinion*. ② To confuse someone means to make them uncertain about what is happening or what to do. ③ To confuse a situation means to make it more complicated.
SIMILAR WORDS: ② baffle, bewilder

confused ADJECTIVE ① uncertain about what is happening or what to do. ② in an untidy mess.

confusing ADJECTIVE puzzling or bewildering.

confusion NOUN ① a bewildering state. ② an untidy mess.

congeal, congeals, congealing, congealed [Said *kon-jeel*] VERB When a liquid congeals, it becomes very thick and sticky.

congenial [Said *kon-jeen-yal*] ADJECTIVE If something is congenial, it is pleasant and suits you • *We wanted to talk in congenial surroundings*.

congenital ADJECTIVE If someone has a congenital disease or disability, they have had it from birth but did not inherit it.

congested ADJECTIVE ① When a road is congested, it is so full of traffic that normal movement is impossible. ② If your nose is congested, it is blocked and you cannot breathe properly.
congestion NOUN

conglomerate, conglomerates NOUN a large business organisation consisting of several companies.

a b **c** d e f g h i j k l m n o p q r s t u v w x y z

A
B
C
D
E
F
G
H
I
J
K
L
M
N
O
P
Q
R
S
T
U
V
W
X
Y
Z

What is a Conjunction?

A conjunction is a word that joins two words or two parts of a sentence together. Conjunctions are sometimes called 'joining words'.

Coordinating conjunctions join items of equal importance:

I ordered fish and chips.

Contrasting conjunctions are a type of coordinating conjunction which are used to join opposites or contrasting items:

He was not walking but running.

Correlative conjunctions are pairs of conjunctions, such as *either ... or*, or *both ... and*, each of which introduces a separate item in the sentence:

She speaks both French and German.
You can drink either tea or coffee.

Subordinating conjunctions join additional items to the main part of the sentence:

He was happy because he had finished his work.
I will come if I have time.

congratulate, congratulates, congratulating, **congratulated** VERB If you congratulate someone, you express pleasure at something good that has happened to them, or praise them for something they have achieved. **congratulation** NOUN **congratulatory** ADJECTIVE

congregate, congregates, congregating, congregated VERB When people congregate, they gather together somewhere.

congregation, congregations NOUN the congregation are the people attending a service in a church.

congress, congresses NOUN a large meeting held to discuss ideas or policies • *a medical congress*.

congruent ADJECTIVE Two triangles are congruent if they are exactly the same shape and size.

conical ADJECTIVE shaped like a cone.

conifer, conifers NOUN any type of evergreen tree that produces cones. **coniferous** ADJECTIVE

conjecture NOUN Conjecture is guesswork about something • *There was no evidence, only conjecture.*

conjugate, conjugates, conjugating, conjugated [*Said kon-joo-gate*] VERB ENGLISH MFL When you conjugate a verb, you list the different forms of it you use with the pronouns 'I', 'you' (singular), 'he', 'she', 'it', 'you' (plural) and 'they'.

conjunction, conjunctions NOUN ① ENGLISH MFL In grammar, a conjunction is a word that links two other words or two clauses, for example 'and', 'but', 'while' and 'that'. ▶ PHRASE ② If two or more things are done **in conjunction**, they are done together.

conjurer, conjurers NOUN someone who entertains people by doing magic tricks.

conker, conkers NOUN Conkers are hard brown nuts from a horse chestnut tree.

connect, connects, connecting, **connected** VERB ①To connect two things is to join them together. ② If you connect something with something else, you think of them as being linked • *High blood pressure is closely connected to heart disease.*

connection, connections; also spelt **connexion** NOUN ① a link or relationship between things. ② the point where two wires or pipes are joined together • *a loose connection*. ③ (*in plural*) Someone's connections are the people they know • *He had powerful connections in the army.*

connective, connectives NOUN ENGLISH MFL a word or short phrase that connects clauses, phrases or words.

connectivity NOUN ① Connectivity is the state of being connected. ② ICT The connectivity of an application program or piece of equipment is its ability to connect to another application or piece of equipment.

connoisseur, connoisseurs [*Said kon-nis-sur*] NOUN someone who knows a lot about the arts, or about food or drink • *a great connoisseur of coffee.*

WORD HISTORY: from Old French *connoistre* meaning 'to know'

connotation, connotations NOUN ENGLISH The connotations of a word or name are what it makes you think of • *the word grey has connotations of dullness.*

conquer, conquers, conquering, conquered VERB ① To conquer people is to take control of their country by force. ② If you conquer something difficult or dangerous, you succeed in controlling it • *Conquer your fear!* **conqueror** NOUN

conquest, conquests NOUN ① Conquest is the conquering of a country or group of people. ② Conquests are lands captured by conquest.

conscience, consciences NOUN the part of your mind that tells you what is right and wrong.

SPELLING TIP
Do not confuse the spellings of *conscience* and *conscious: a guilty conscience; I made a conscious effort to smile at her.*

conscientious [*Said kon-shee-en-shus*] ADJECTIVE Someone who is conscientious is very careful to do their work properly.
conscientiously ADVERB
SIMILAR WORDS: careful, meticulous, thorough

conscious ADJECTIVE ① If you are conscious of something, you are aware of it • *She was not conscious of the time.* ② A conscious action or effort is done deliberately • *I made a conscious decision not to hide.* ③ Someone who is conscious is awake, rather than asleep or unconscious • *Still conscious, she was taken to hospital.* **consciously** ADVERB **consciousness** NOUN

SPELLING TIP
Do not confuse the spellings of *conscious* and *conscience: I made a conscious effort to smile at her; a guilty conscience.*

consecrated ADJECTIVE A consecrated building or place is one that has been officially declared to be holy.

consecutive ADJECTIVE Consecutive events or periods of time happen one after the other • *eight consecutive games.*

consensus NOUN Consensus is general agreement among a group of people • *The consensus was that it could be done.*

SPELLING TIP
There are three ss in *consensus*; do not confuse the spelling with *census*.

USAGE NOTE
You should not say *consensus of opinion*, as *consensus* already has *of opinion* in its meaning.

consent, consents, consenting, consented NOUN ① PSHE Consent is permission to do something • *Thomas reluctantly gave his consent to my writing this book.* ② Consent is also agreement between two or more people • *By common consent it was the best game of these championships.*
▶ VERB ③ PSHE If you consent to something, you agree to it or allow it.

consequence, consequences NOUN ① The consequences of something are its results or effects • *the dire consequences of major war.* ② (*formal*) If something is of consequence, it is important.

consequent ADJECTIVE Consequent describes something as being the result of something else • *an earthquake in 1980 and its consequent damage.* **consequently** ADVERB

conservation NOUN Conservation is the preservation of the environment. **conservationist** NOUN or ADJECTIVE

conservative, conservatives NOUN ① In Britain, a Conservative is a member or supporter of the Conservative Party, a political party that believes that the government should interfere as little as possible in the running of the economy.
▶ ADJECTIVE ② In Britain, Conservative views and policies are those of the Conservative Party. ③ Someone who is conservative is opposed to radical change and values tradition and stability. ④ A conservative estimate or guess is a cautious or moderate one. **conservatively** ADVERB **conservatism** NOUN

conservatory, conservatories NOUN a room with glass walls and a glass roof attached to a house.

conserve, conserves, conserving, conserved VERB If you conserve a supply of something, you make it last • *the only way to conserve energy.*

consider, considers, considering, considered VERB ① If you consider something to be the case, you think or judge it to be so • *The manager does not consider him an ideal team member.* ② EXAM TERM To consider something is to think about it carefully • *If an offer were made, we would consider it.* ③ If you consider someone's needs or feelings, you take account of them.
SIMILAR WORDS: ② contemplate, think about

considerable ADJECTIVE A considerable amount of something is a lot of it • *a considerable sum of money.* **considerably** ADVERB

considerate ADJECTIVE Someone who is considerate pays attention to other people's needs and feelings.

consideration, considerations NOUN ① Consideration is careful thought about something • *a decision demanding careful consideration.* ② If you show consideration for someone, you take account of their needs and feelings. ③ something that has to be taken into account • *Money was also a consideration.*
SIMILAR WORDS: ① deliberation, thought

considered ADJECTIVE A considered opinion or judgment is arrived at by careful thought.

considering CONJUNCTION or PREPOSITION You say 'considering' to indicate that you are taking something into account • *It's a great game considering that it's free.*

consign, consigns, consigning, consigned VERB (*formal*) To consign something to a particular place is to send or put it there.

consignment, consignments NOUN A consignment of goods is a load of them being delivered somewhere.

consist, consists, consisting, consisted VERB What something consists of is its different parts or members • *The brain consists of millions of nerve cells.*

consistency, consistencies NOUN ① Consistency is the quality of being consistent. ② The consistency of a substance is how thick or smooth it is • *the consistency of single cream.*

consistent ADJECTIVE ① If you are consistent, you keep doing something the same way • *one of our most consistent performers.* ② If something such as a statement or argument is consistent, there are no contradictions in it. **consistently** ADVERB

console, consoles, consoling, consoled VERB [Said con-**sole**] ① To console someone who is unhappy is to make them more cheerful. ▶ NOUN [Said **con**-sole] ② a panel with switches or knobs for operating a machine. **consolation** NOUN

consolidate, consolidates, consolidating, consolidated VERB To consolidate something you have gained or achieved is to make it more secure. **consolidation** NOUN

consonant, consonants NOUN ENGLISH a sound such as 'p' or 'm' which you make by stopping the air flowing freely through your mouth. WORD HISTORY: from Latin *consonare* meaning 'to sound at the same time'

consort, consorts, consorting, consorted VERB [Said con-**sort**] ① (formal) If you consort with someone, you spend a lot of time with them. ▶ NOUN [Said **con**-sort] ② the wife or husband of the king or queen.

consortium, consortia or consortiums NOUN a group of businesses working together.

conspicuous ADJECTIVE If something is conspicuous, people can see or notice it very easily. **conspicuously** ADVERB

conspiracy, conspiracies NOUN When there is a conspiracy, a group of people plan something illegal, often for a political purpose.

conspirator, conspirators NOUN someone involved in a conspiracy.

conspire, conspires, conspiring, conspired VERB ① When people conspire, they plan together to do something illegal, often for a political purpose. ② (literary) When events conspire towards a particular result, they seem to work together to cause it • *Circumstances conspired to doom the business.*

constable, constables NOUN a police officer of the lowest rank. WORD HISTORY: from Latin *comes stabuli* meaning 'officer of the stable'

constabulary, constabularies NOUN a police force.

constant ADJECTIVE ① Something that is constant happens all the time or is always there • *a city under constant attack.* ② If an amount or level is constant, it stays the same. ③ People who are constant stay loyal to a person or idea. **constantly** ADVERB **constancy** NOUN SIMILAR WORDS: ② fixed, steady, unchanging

constellation, constellations NOUN a group of stars.

consternation NOUN Consternation is anxiety or dismay • *There was some consternation when it began raining.*

constipated ADJECTIVE Someone who is constipated is unable to pass solid waste from their bowels. **constipation** NOUN

a b c d e f g h i j k l m n o p q r s t u v w x y z

constituency, constituencies
NOUN a town or area represented by
an MP.

constituent, constituents NOUN
①An MP's constituents are the
voters who live in his or her
constituency. ②The constituents of
something are its parts • *the major
constituents of bone.*

constitute, constitutes,
constituting, constituted VERB If a
group of things constitute something,
they are what it consists of • *Jewellery
constitutes 80 per cent of the stock.*

constitution, constitutions NOUN
① HISTORY The constitution of a
country is a system of laws and
principles by which the country
should be governed. ②Your
constitution is your health • *a very
strong constitution.* **constitutional**
ADJECTIVE **constitutionally** ADVERB

constrained ADJECTIVE If a person
feels constrained to do something,
they feel that they should do that.

constraint, constraints NOUN
something that limits someone's
freedom of action • *the financial
constraints on schools.*

constrict, constricts, constricting,
constricted VERB To constrict
something is to squeeze it tightly.
constriction NOUN

construct, constructs,
constructing, constructed VERB To
construct something is to build or
make it.

construction, constructions NOUN
①The construction of something is
the building or making of it • *the
construction of the harbour.*
②something built or made • *a shoddy
modern construction built of concrete.*

constructive ADJECTIVE
Constructive criticisms and
comments are helpful.

constructively ADVERB

consul, consuls NOUN an official who
lives in a foreign city and who looks
after people there who are citizens of
his or her own country. **consular**
ADJECTIVE

consulate, consulates NOUN the
place where a consul works.

consult, consults, consulting,
consulted VERB ①If you consult
someone, you ask for their opinion or
advice. ②When people consult each
other, they exchange ideas and
opinions. ③If you consult a book or
map, you look at it for information.

consultancy, consultancies NOUN
an organisation whose members
give expert advice on a subject.

consultant, consultants NOUN
①an experienced doctor who
specialises in one type of medicine.
②someone who gives expert advice
• *a management consultant.*

consultation, consultations NOUN
①a meeting held to discuss
something. ②Consultation is
discussion or the seeking of advice
• *There has to be much better
consultation with the public.*
consultative ADJECTIVE

consume, consumes, consuming,
consumed VERB ①(*formal*) If you
consume something, you eat or drink
it. ②To consume fuel or energy is to
use it up.

consumer, consumers NOUN
someone who buys things or uses
services • *two new magazines for
teenage consumers.*

consumerism NOUN Consumerism
is the belief that a country will have a
strong economy if its people buy a lot
of goods and spend a lot of money.

consuming ADJECTIVE A consuming
passion or interest is more important
to you than anything else.

consummate, consummates, consummating, consummated
VERB [Said **kons**-yum-mate] ①To consummate something is to make it complete. ▸ADJECTIVE [Said **kon**-sum-mit] ②You use 'consummate' to describe someone who is very good at something • a consummate politician.
consummation NOUN

consumption NOUN The consumption of fuel or food is the using of it, or the amount used.

contact, contacts, contacting, contacted NOUN ①If you are in contact with someone, you regularly talk to them or write to them. ②When things are in contact, they are touching each other. ③someone you know in a place or organisation from whom you can get help or information. ▸VERB ④If you contact someone, you telephone them or write to them.
SIMILAR WORDS: ④ get in touch with, reach

contact lens, contact lenses NOUN Contact lenses are small plastic lenses that you put in your eyes instead of wearing glasses, to help you see better.

contagious ADJECTIVE A contagious disease can be caught by touching people or things infected with it.

contain, contains, containing, contained VERB ①If a substance contains something, that thing is a part of it • Alcohol contains sugar. ②The things a box or room contains are the things inside it. ③(formal) To contain something also means to stop it increasing or spreading • efforts to contain the disease.
containment NOUN

container, containers NOUN ①something such as a box or a bottle that you keep things in. ②a large

sealed metal box for transporting things.
SIMILAR WORDS: ① holder, receptacle

contaminate, contaminates, contaminating, contaminated VERB If something is contaminated by dirt, chemicals or radiation, it is made impure and harmful • foods contaminated with lead.
contamination NOUN

contemplate, contemplates, contemplating, contemplated VERB ①To contemplate is to think carefully about something for a long time. ②If you contemplate doing something, you consider doing it • I never contemplated going to university. ③If you contemplate something, you look at it for a long time • He contemplated his drawings.
contemplation NOUN
contemplative ADJECTIVE

contemporary, contemporaries ADJECTIVE ①produced or happening now • contemporary literature. ②produced or happening at the time you are talking about • contemporary descriptions of Lizzie Borden. ▸NOUN ③Someone's contemporaries are other people living or active at the same time as them • Shakespeare and his contemporaries.

contempt NOUN If you treat someone or something with contempt, you show no respect for them at all.

contemptible ADJECTIVE not worthy of any respect • this contemptible piece of nonsense.

contemptuous ADJECTIVE showing contempt. **contemptuously** ADVERB

contend, contends, contending, contended VERB ①To contend with a difficulty is to deal with it • They had to contend with injuries. ②(formal) If you contend that something is true, you say firmly that it is true. ③ When people contend for something, they compete for it. **contender** NOUN

content, contents, contenting, contented NOUN *[Said con-***tent***]* ① (*in plural*) The contents of something are the things inside it. ▶ ADJECTIVE *[Said con-***tent***]* ② happy and satisfied with your life. ③ willing to do or have something • *He would be content to phone her.* ▶ VERB *[Said con-***tent***]* ④ If you content yourself with doing something, you do it and do not try to do anything else • *He contented himself with an early morning lecture.*

contented ADJECTIVE happy and satisfied with your life. **contentedly** ADVERB **contentment** NOUN

contention, contentions NOUN (*formal*) ① Someone's contention is the idea or opinion they are expressing • *Is your contention that government employees should not be jailed for breaking the law?* ② Contention is disagreement and argument about something • *What had brought about all this contention?*

contentious ADJECTIVE causing disagreement and argument • *His contentious view is that the Prime Minister should resign.*

contest, contests, contesting, contested NOUN *[Said con-*test*]* ① a competition or game • *a boxing contest.* ② a struggle for power • *a presidential contest.* ▶ VERB *[Said con-*test*]* ③ If you contest a statement or decision, you object to it formally. SIMILAR WORDS: ① competition, game, match

contestant, contestants NOUN someone taking part in a competition.
SIMILAR WORDS: competitor, player

context, contexts NOUN ① The context of something consists of

matters related to it which help to explain it • *English history is treated in a European context.* ② ENGLISH The context of a word or sentence consists of the words or sentences before and after it.

continent, continents NOUN ① a very large area of land, such as Africa or Asia. ② The Continent is the mainland of Europe. **continental** ADJECTIVE

contingency, contingencies *[Said kon-***tin***-jen-see]* NOUN something that might happen in the future • *I need to examine all possible contingencies.*

contingent, contingents NOUN ① a group of people representing a country or organisation • *a strong South African contingent.* ② a group of police or soldiers.

continual ADJECTIVE ① happening all the time without stopping • *continual headaches.* ② happening again and again • *the continual snide remarks.* **continually** ADVERB
SIMILAR WORDS: ① constant, incessant ② constant, incessant

continuation, continuations NOUN ① The continuation of something is the continuing of it • *the continuation of the human race.* ② Something that is a continuation of an event follows it and seems like a part of it • *a meeting which was a continuation of a conference.*

continue, continues, continuing, continued VERB ① If you continue to do something, you keep doing it. ② If something continues, it does not stop. ③ You also say something continues when it starts again after stopping • *She continued after a pause.*
SIMILAR WORDS: ② carry on, go on, proceed ③ carry on, go on, proceed

continuous ADJECTIVE ① Continuous means happening or

existing without stopping. ② MATHS A continuous line or surface has no gaps or holes in it. A continuous set of data has an unlimited amount of numbers or items in it.

continuously ADVERB **continuity** NOUN

contorted ADJECTIVE twisted into an unnatural, unattractive shape.

contour, contours NOUN ①The contours of something are its general shape. ② GEOGRAPHY On a map, a contour is a line joining points of equal height.

contra- PREFIX 'Contra-' means 'against' or 'opposite to' • *contraflow* • *contraindication*.

contraception NOUN Contraception is methods of preventing pregnancy.

contraceptive, contraceptives NOUN a device or pill for preventing pregnancy.

contract, contracts, contracting, contracted NOUN [Said con-**trakt**] ①a written legal agreement about the sale of something or work done for money. ▶ VERB [Said con-**trakt**] ②When something contracts, it gets smaller or shorter. ③ (formal) If you contract an illness, you get it • *Her husband contracted a virus.*

contractual ADJECTIVE

contraction, contractions NOUN ①A contraction is an act of becoming smaller. ② ENGLISH a shortened form of a word or words, for example *I'm* for *I am.*

contractor, contractors NOUN a person or company who does work for other people or companies • *a building contractor.*

contradict, contradicts, contradicting, contradicted VERB If you contradict someone, you say that what they have just said is not true, and that something else is.

contradiction NOUN
contradictory ADJECTIVE

contraption, contraptions NOUN a strange-looking machine or piece of equipment.

contrary ADJECTIVE ①Contrary ideas or opinions are opposed to each other and cannot be held by the same person. ▶ PHRASE ②You say **on the contrary** when you are contradicting what someone has just said.

contrast, contrasts, contrasting, contrasted NOUN [Said con-trast] ①a great difference between things • *the real contrast between the two poems.* ②If one thing is a contrast to another, it is very different from it • *I couldn't imagine a greater contrast to Maxwell.* ▶ VERB [Said con-**trast**] ③ EXAM TERM If you contrast things, you describe or emphasise the differences between them • *The painter contrasted her image of rural America with striking representations of New York.* ④If one thing contrasts with another, it is very different from it • *The interview completely contrasted with the one she gave after Tokyo.*

contravene, contravenes, contravening, contravened VERB (formal) If you contravene a law or rule, you do something that it forbids.

contribute, contributes, contributing, contributed VERB ①If you contribute to something, you do things to help it succeed • *Young people have much to contribute to the community.* ②If you contribute money, you give it to help to pay for something. ③If something contributes to an event or situation, it is one of its causes • *The dry summer has contributed to perfect conditions.*

contribution NOUN **contributor**

A
B
C
D
E
F
G
H
I
J
K
L
M
N
O
P
Q
R
S
T
U
V
W
X
Y
Z

NOUN **contributory** ADJECTIVE
SIMILAR WORDS: ② donate, give

contrive, contrives, contriving, contrived VERB (formal) If you contrive to do something difficult, you succeed in doing it • Anthony contrived to escape with a few companions.

contrived ADJECTIVE Something that is contrived is unnatural • a contrived compliment.

control, controls, controlling, controlled NOUN ① Control of a country or organisation is the power to make the important decisions about how it is run. ② Your control over something is your ability to make it work the way you want it to. ③ The controls on a machine are knobs or other devices used to work it. ▶ VERB ④ To control a country or organisation means to have the power to make decisions about how it is run. ⑤ To control something such as a machine or system means to make it work the way you want it to. ⑥ If you control yourself, you make yourself behave calmly when you are angry or upset. ▶ PHRASE ⑦ If something is **out of control**, nobody has any power over it. **controller** NOUN
SIMILAR WORDS: ⑥ hold back, restrain

controversial ADJECTIVE Something that is controversial causes a lot of discussion and argument, because many people disapprove of it.

controversy, controversies [Said kon-triv-ver-see or kon-trov-ver-see] NOUN discussion and argument because many people disapprove of something.
WORD HISTORY: from Latin controversus meaning 'turned in an opposite direction'

USAGE NOTE
Notice that there are two ways to say controversy. The first way is older, and the second is becoming more common.

conundrum, conundrums NOUN (formal) a puzzling problem.

conurbation, conurbations NOUN
GEOGRAPHY A conurbation is a very large urban area formed by towns or cities spreading towards each other.

convalesce, convalesces, convalescing, convalesced VERB When people convalesce, they rest and regain their health after an illness or operation.

convection NOUN SCIENCE Convection is the process by which heat travels through gases and liquids.

convene, convenes, convening, convened VERB ① (formal) To convene a meeting is to arrange for it to take place. ② When people convene, they come together for a meeting.

convenience, conveniences NOUN ① The convenience of something is the fact that it is easy to use or that it makes something easy to do. ② something useful.

convenient ADJECTIVE If something is convenient, it is easy to use or it makes something easy to do. **conveniently** ADVERB
SIMILAR WORDS: handy, useful

convent, convents NOUN a building where nuns live, or a school run by nuns.

convention, conventions NOUN ① an accepted way of behaving or doing something. ② a large meeting of an organisation or political group • the Democratic Convention. ③ a formal agreement between nations.

conventional ADJECTIVE ① You say that people are conventional when there is nothing unusual about their way of life. ②Conventional methods are the ones that are usually used. **conventionally** ADVERB

converge, converges, converging, converged VERB To converge is to meet or join at a particular place.

conversation, conversations NOUN If you have a conversation with someone, you spend time talking to them. **conversational** ADJECTIVE **conversationalist** NOUN

converse, converses, conversing, conversed VERB [Said con-**verse**] ① (formal) When people converse, they talk to each other. ▶ NOUN [Said con-verse] ②The converse of something is its opposite • Don't you think that the converse might also be possible? **conversely** ADVERB

convert, converts, converting, converted VERB [Said con-**vert**] ①To convert one thing into another is to change it so that it becomes the other thing. ② MATHS If you convert a unit or measurement, you express it in terms of another unit or scale of measurement. For example, you can convert inches to centimetres by multiplying by 2.54. ③If someone converts you, they persuade you to change your religious or political beliefs. ▶ NOUN [Said con-vert] ④someone who has changed their religious or political beliefs. **conversion** NOUN **convertible** ADJECTIVE

convex ADJECTIVE MATHS A convex surface bulges outwards, rather than being level or curving inwards.

convey, conveys, conveying, conveyed VERB ①To convey information or ideas is to cause them to be known or understood. ② (formal) To convey someone or something to a place is to transport them there.

conveyor belt, conveyor belts NOUN a moving strip used in factories for moving objects along.

convict, convicts, convicting, convicted VERB [Said kon-**vikt**] ①To convict someone of a crime is to find them guilty. ▶ NOUN [Said **kon**-vikt] ②someone serving a prison sentence.

conviction, convictions NOUN ①a strong belief or opinion. ②The conviction of someone is what happens when they are found guilty in a court of law.

convince, convinces, convincing, convinced VERB To convince someone of something is to persuade them that it is true. SIMILAR WORDS: persuade, sway

convincing ADJECTIVE 'Convincing' is used to describe things or people that can make you believe something is true • a convincing argument. **convincingly** ADVERB SIMILAR WORDS: credible, persuasive, plausible

convoluted [Said kon-vol-**oo**-tid] ADJECTIVE Something that is convoluted has many twists and bends • the convoluted patterns of these designs.

convoy, convoys NOUN a group of vehicles or ships travelling together.

convulsion, convulsions NOUN If someone has convulsions, their muscles move violently and uncontrollably.

coo, coos, cooing, cooed VERB When pigeons and doves coo, they make a soft flutelike sound.

cook, cooks, cooking, cooked VERB ①To cook food is to prepare it for eating by heating it. ▶ NOUN ②someone who prepares and cooks food, often as their job.

cooker, cookers NOUN a device for cooking food.

A B C D E F G H I J K L M N O P Q R S T U V W X Y Z

cookery NOUN Cookery is the activity of preparing and cooking food.

cookie, cookies NOUN ① a sweet biscuit. ② a small file placed on a user's computer by a website, containing information about the user's preferences that will be used on any future visits he or she may make to the site.

cool, cooler, coolest; cools, cooling, cooled ADJECTIVE ① Something cool has a low temperature but is not cold. ② If you are cool in a difficult situation, you stay calm and unemotional. ▶ VERB ③ When something cools or when you cool it, it becomes less warm. **coolly** ADVERB **coolness** NOUN

coolabah, coolabahs; also spelt **coolibah** NOUN an Australian eucalypt that grows along rivers.

coop, coops NOUN a cage for chickens or rabbits.

cooperate, cooperates, cooperating, cooperated [Said koh-op-er-rate] VERB ① When people cooperate, they work or act together. ② To cooperate also means to do what someone asks. **cooperation** NOUN

cooperative, cooperatives [Said koh-op-er-ut-tiv] NOUN ① a business or organisation run by the people who work for it, and who share its benefits or profits. ▶ ADJECTIVE ② A cooperative activity is done by people working together. ③ Someone who is cooperative does what you ask them to.

coordinate, coordinates, coordinating, coordinated [Said koh-or-din-ate] VERB ① To coordinate an activity is to organise the people or things involved in it • to coordinate the campaign. ▶ NOUN ② MATHS (in plural) Coordinates are a pair of numbers or letters which tell you how far along and up or down a point is on a grid. **coordination** NOUN **coordinator** NOUN

cop, cops NOUN (slang) a police officer.

cope, copes, coping, coped VERB If you cope with a problem or task, you deal with it successfully.

copious ADJECTIVE (formal) existing or produced in large quantities • He wrote copious notes in every class.

copper, coppers NOUN ① SCIENCE Copper is a reddish-brown metallic element. Its atomic number is 29 and its symbol is Cu. ② Coppers are brown metal coins of low value. ③ (informal) A copper is also a police officer.

copse, copses NOUN a small group of trees growing close together.

copy, copies, copying, copied NOUN ① something made to look like something else. ② A copy of something such as a book, magazine or DVD is one of many identical ones produced at the same time. ▶ VERB ③ If you copy what someone does, you do the same thing. ④ If you copy something, you make a copy of it. **copier** NOUN
SIMILAR WORDS: ① duplicate, replica, reproduction ④ duplicate, reproduce

copyright, copyrights NOUN LIBRARY If someone has the copyright on a piece of writing or music, it cannot be copied or performed without their permission.

coral, corals NOUN Coral is a hard substance that forms in the sea from the skeletons of tiny animals called corals.

cor anglais, cors anglais [Said kohr ong-glay] NOUN MUSIC A cor anglais is a woodwind instrument with a double reed. It has a slightly lower pitch than an oboe.

cord, cords NOUN ① Cord is strong, thick string. ② Electrical wire covered in rubber or plastic is also called cord.

SPELLING TIP

Do not confuse the spellings of *cord* and *chord*: *a package tied with cord; I only know how to play one chord on the guitar.*

---

cordial, cordials ADJECTIVE ① warm and friendly. ▶ NOUN ② a sweet drink made from fruit juice.

cordon, cordons, cordoning, cordoned NOUN ① a line or ring of police or soldiers preventing people entering or leaving a place. ▶ VERB ② If police or soldiers cordon off an area, they stop people entering or leaving by forming themselves into a line or ring.

corduroy NOUN Corduroy is a thick cloth with parallel raised lines on the outside.

core, cores NOUN ① the hard central part of a fruit such as an apple. ② the most important part of something • *the core of Asia's problems*. ③ GEOGRAPHY the central part of the earth that lies beneath the mantle.

coriander [*Said kor-ree-an-der*] NOUN a plant with seeds that are used as a spice and leaves that are used as a herb for flavouring in cooking.

cork, corks NOUN ① Cork is the spongelike bark of a Mediterranean tree. ② a piece of cork pushed into the end of a bottle to close it.

corkscrew, corkscrews NOUN a device for pulling corks out of bottles.

cormorant, cormorants NOUN a dark-coloured bird with a long neck.

corn, corns NOUN ① Corn refers to crops such as wheat and barley and to their seeds. ② In American English, corn is the same as maize. ③ a small painful area of hard skin on your foot.

cornea, corneas [*Said kor-nee-a*] NOUN the transparent skin that covers the outside of your eyeball.

corner, corners, cornering, cornered NOUN ① a place where two sides or edges of something meet • *a small corner of one shelf* • *a street corner*. ▶ VERB ② To corner a person or animal is to get them into a place they cannot escape from.

cornerstone, cornerstones NOUN The cornerstone of something is the basic part of it on which its existence or success depends • *Food is one of the cornerstones of good health*.

cornet, cornets NOUN MUSIC a small brass instrument used in brass and military bands.

cornflour NOUN Cornflour is a fine white flour made from maize and used in cooking to thicken sauces.

cornflower, cornflowers NOUN a small plant with bright flowers, usually blue.

cornice, cornices NOUN a decorative strip of plaster, wood or stone along the top edge of a wall.

corny, cornier, corniest ADJECTIVE very obvious or sentimental and not at all original • *corny old love songs*.

coronary, coronaries NOUN If someone has a coronary, blood cannot reach their heart because of a blood clot.

coronation, coronations NOUN the ceremony at which a king or queen is crowned.

coronavirus, coronaviruses NOUN a type of virus that causes colds and diseases such as COVID-19.

coroner, coroners NOUN an official who investigates the deaths of people who have died in a violent or unusual way.

coronet, coronets NOUN a small crown.

corporal, corporals NOUN an officer of low rank in the army or air force.

corporal punishment NOUN Corporal punishment is the punishing of people by beating them.

corporate ADJECTIVE (*formal*) belonging to or done by all members of a group together • *a corporate decision*.

corporation, corporations NOUN ① a large business. ② a group of people responsible for running a city.

corps, corps [*Rhymes with* **more**] NOUN ① a part of an army with special duties • *the Engineering Corps*. ② a small group of people who do a special job • *the world press corps*.

GRAMMAR TIP
The plural of *corps* is also *corps*.

---

corpse, corpses NOUN a dead body.

correa, correas NOUN an Australian shrub with large green and white flowers.

correct, corrects, correcting, corrected ADJECTIVE ① If something is correct, there are no mistakes in it. ② The correct thing in a particular situation is the right one • *Each has the correct number of coins*. ③ Correct behaviour is considered to be socially acceptable. ▶ VERB ④ If you correct something which is wrong, you make it right. **correctly** ADVERB **corrective** ADJECTIVE or NOUN SIMILAR WORDS: ④ amend, rectify

correction, corrections NOUN the act of making something right.

correlate, correlates, correlating, correlated VERB If two things correlate or are correlated, they are closely connected or strongly

influence each other • *Obesity correlates with health problems*.
correlation NOUN

correspond, corresponds, corresponding, corresponded VERB ① If one thing corresponds to another, it has a similar purpose, function or status. ② MATHS If numbers or amounts correspond, they are the same. ③ When people correspond, they write to each other.

correspondence, correspondences NOUN ① Correspondence is the writing of letters; also the letters written. ② If there is a correspondence between two things, they are closely related or very similar.

correspondent, correspondents NOUN a newspaper, television or radio reporter.

corresponding ADJECTIVE ① You use 'corresponding' to describe a change that results from a change in something else • *the rise in inflation and corresponding rise in prices*. ② You also use 'corresponding' to describe something which has a similar purpose or status to something else • *Alfard is the corresponding Western name for the star*. **correspondingly** ADVERB

corresponding angle, corresponding angles NOUN MATHS Corresponding angles occur where a line crosses two or more parallel lines. They are the equivalent angles on the same side of the intersection.

corridor, corridors NOUN a passage that connects different parts of a building.

corroboree, corroborees NOUN an Aboriginal gathering or dance that is festive or warlike.

corrode, corrodes, corroding, corroded VERB SCIENCE When metal corrodes, it is gradually destroyed by a chemical or rust.

corrosion NOUN **corrosive** ADJECTIVE

corrugated ADJECTIVE Corrugated metal or cardboard is made in parallel folds to make it stronger.
WORD HISTORY: from Latin *corrugare* meaning 'to wrinkle up'

corrupt, corrupts, corrupting, corrupted ADJECTIVE ①Corrupt people act dishonestly or illegally in return for money or power • *corrupt ministers*. ▶VERB ②To corrupt someone means to make them dishonest. ③To corrupt someone also means to make them immoral.
corruptible ADJECTIVE
SIMILAR WORDS: ①crooked, dishonest③deprave

corruption NOUN Corruption is dishonesty and illegal behaviour by people in positions of power.
SIMILAR WORDS: depravity, immorality, vice

corset, corsets NOUN Corsets are stiff underwear worn round the hips and waist to make them look slimmer.

cortex, cortices NOUN The cortex of the brain or other organ is its outer layer.

cosine, cosines NOUN MATHS In mathematics, a cosine is a function of an angle. If B is the right angle in a right-angled triangle ABC, the cosine of the angle at A is AB divided by AC.

cosmetic, cosmetics NOUN ①Cosmetics are substances such as lipstick and face powder which are intended to make someone more attractive. ▶ADJECTIVE ②Cosmetic changes improve the appearance of something without changing its basic nature.

cosmic ADJECTIVE belonging or relating to the universe.

cosmopolitan ADJECTIVE A cosmopolitan place is full of people from many countries.
WORD HISTORY: from Greek *kosmos* meaning 'universe' and *politēs* meaning 'citizen'

cosmos NOUN The cosmos is the universe.

cosset, cossets, cosseting, cosseted VERB If you cosset someone, you spoil them and protect them too much.

cost, costs, costing, cost NOUN ①The cost of something is the amount of money needed to buy it, do it, or make it. ②The cost of achieving something is the loss or injury in achieving it • *the total cost in human misery*. ▶VERB ③You use 'cost' to talk about the amount of money you have to pay for things • *The air fares were going to cost a lot.* ④If a mistake costs you something, you lose that thing because of the mistake • *a reckless gamble that could cost him his job.*

costly, costlier, costliest ADJECTIVE expensive • *a costly piece of furniture.*

costume, costumes NOUN ① DRAMA a set of clothes worn by an actor. ②Costume is the clothing worn in a particular place or during a particular period • *eighteenth-century costume.*

cosy, cosier, cosiest ADJECTIVE ①warm and comfortable • *her cosy new flat.* ②Cosy activities are pleasant and friendly • *a cosy chat.*
cosily ADVERB **cosiness** NOUN

cot, cots NOUN a small bed for a baby, with bars or panels round it to stop the baby falling out.

cottage, cottages NOUN a small house in the country.

cottage cheese NOUN Cottage

a
b
c
d
e
f
g
h
i
j
k
l
m
n
o
p
q
r
s
t
u
v
w
x
y
z

cheese is a type of soft white lumpy cheese.

cotton, cottons NOUN ① Cotton is cloth made from the soft fibres of the cotton plant. ② Cotton is also thread used for sewing.

cotton wool NOUN Cotton wool is soft fluffy cotton, often used for dressing wounds.

couch, couches, couching, couched NOUN ① a long, soft piece of furniture which more than one person can sit on. ▸VERB ② If a statement is couched in a particular type of language, it is expressed in that language • *a comment couched in impertinent terms*.

cough, coughs, coughing, coughed [Said *koff*] VERB ① When you cough, you force air out of your throat with a sudden harsh noise. ▸NOUN ② an illness that makes you cough a lot; also the noise you make when you cough.

could VERB ① You use 'could' to say that you were able or allowed to do something • *He could hear voices* • *She could come and go as she wanted*. ② You also use 'could' to say that something might happen or might be the case • *It could rain*. ③ You use 'could' when you are asking for something politely • *Could you tell me the name of that film?*

council, councils NOUN ① CITIZENSHIP a group of people elected to look after the affairs of a town, district or county. ② Some other groups have Council as part of their name • *the World Gold Council*.

SPELLING TIP
Do not confuse the spellings of *council* and *counsel*: *Her husband works for the local council; She offers counsel at difficult times; I counsel you to stop this before it is too late.*

councillor, councillors NOUN CITIZENSHIP an elected member of a local council.

counsel, counsels, counselling, counselled NOUN ① (formal) To give someone counsel is to give them advice. ▸VERB ② To counsel people is to give them advice about their problems. **counselling** NOUN **counsellor** NOUN

SPELLING TIP
Do not confuse the spellings of *counsel* and *council*: *She offers counsel at difficult times; I counsel you to stop this before it is too late; Her husband works for the local council.*

count, counts, counting, counted VERB ① To count is to say all the numbers in order up to a particular number. ② If you count all the things in a group, you add them up to see how many there are. ③ What counts in a situation is whatever is most important. ④ To count as something means to be regarded as that thing • *I'm not sure whether this counts as harassment*. ⑤ If you can count on someone or something, you can rely on them. ▸NOUN ⑥ a number reached by counting. ⑦ (formal) If something is wrong on a particular count, it is wrong in that respect. ⑧ a European nobleman.
SIMILAR WORDS: ② add up, calculate, reckon

countdown, countdowns NOUN the counting aloud of numbers in reverse order before something happens, especially before a spacecraft is launched.

countenance, countenances, countenancing, countenanced (formal) NOUN ① Someone's countenance is their face. ▸VERB ② To countenance something means to allow or accept it • *I will not* *countenance behaviour of this sort.*

counter, counters, countering, countered NOUN ① a long, flat surface over which goods are sold in a shop. ② a small, flat, round object used in board games. ▸ VERB ③ If you counter something that is being done, you take action to make it less effective • *I countered that argument with a reference to our sales report.*

counteract, counteracts, counteracting, counteracted VERB To counteract something is to reduce its effect by producing an opposite effect.

counterclockwise ADJECTIVE or ADVERB In American English, counterclockwise means anticlockwise.

counterfeit, counterfeits, counterfeiting, counterfeited [Said **kown-ter-fit**] ADJECTIVE ① Something counterfeit is not genuine but has been made to look genuine to deceive people • *counterfeit money.* ▸ VERB ② To counterfeit something is to make a counterfeit version of it.

counterpart, counterparts NOUN The counterpart of a person or thing is another person or thing with a similar function in a different place • *The Irish prime minister called his French counterpart to discuss the issue.*

counterterrorism NOUN Counterterrorism is action to prevent terrorist attacks or destroy terrorist groups.

countess, countesses NOUN the wife of a count or earl, or a woman with the same rank as a count or earl.

counting PREPOSITION You say 'counting' when including something in a calculation • *six students, not counting me.*

countless ADJECTIVE too many to

count • *There had been countless demonstrations.*
SIMILAR WORDS: incalculable, innumerable

country, countries NOUN ① GEOGRAPHY one of the political areas the world is divided into. ② The country is land away from towns and cities. ③ 'Country' is used to refer to an area with particular features or associations • *the heart of coal country.*
SIMILAR WORDS: ① nation, state

countryman, countrymen NOUN Your countrymen are people from your own country.

countryside NOUN The countryside is land away from towns and cities.

county, counties NOUN GEOGRAPHY a region with its own local government.
WORD HISTORY: from Old French *conté* meaning 'land belonging to a count'

coup, coups [Said **koo**] or **coup d'état**, coups d'état [Said **koo day-tah**] NOUN HISTORY When there is a coup, a group of people seize power in a country.
WORD HISTORY: from French *coup* meaning 'a blow'

couple, couples, coupling, coupled NOUN ① two people who are married or are involved in a romantic relationship. ② A couple of things or people means two of them • *a couple of weeks ago.* ▸ VERB ③ If one thing is coupled with another, the two things are done or dealt with together • *Its stores offer high quality coupled with low prices.*

couplet, couplets NOUN ENGLISH two lines of poetry together, especially two that rhyme.

coupon, coupons NOUN ① a piece of printed paper which, when you hand it in, entitles you to pay less than

a b **c** d e f g h i j k l m n o p q r s t u v w x y z

usual for something. ② a form you fill in to ask for information or to enter a competition.

courage NOUN Courage is the quality shown by people who do things knowing they are dangerous or difficult. **courageous** ADJECTIVE **courageously** ADVERB

courgette, courgettes [Said koor-**jet**] NOUN a type of small marrow with dark green skin. Courgettes are also called **zucchini**.

courier, couriers [Said koo-ree-er] NOUN someone employed to collect and deliver letters and packages.

course, courses NOUN ① a series of lessons or lectures. ② a series of medical treatments • a course of injections. ③ one of the parts of a meal. ④ A course or a course of action is one of the things you can do in a situation. ⑤ a piece of land where a sport such as golf is played. ⑥ the route a ship or aircraft takes. ⑦ If something happens in the course of a period of time, it happens during that period • One hundred people joined in the course of the day. ▶ PHRASE ⑧ If you say **of course**, you are showing that something is totally expected or that you are sure about something • Of course she wouldn't do that.

SPELLING TIP

Do not confuse the spellings of course and coarse: a course in conversational Italian; a coarse cloth.

---

court, courts, courting, courted NOUN ① CITIZENSHIP a place where legal matters are decided by a judge and jury or a magistrate. The judge and jury or magistrate can also be referred to as the court. ② a place where a game such as tennis or badminton is played. ③ the place where a king or queen lives and carries out ceremonial duties.

▶ VERB ④ (old-fashioned) If two people are courting, they are spending a lot of time together because they intend to get married.

courteous [Said kur-tee-yuss] ADJECTIVE Courteous behaviour is polite and considerate.

courtesy NOUN Courtesy is polite, considerate behaviour.

courtier, courtiers NOUN Courtiers were noblemen and noblewomen at the court of a king or queen.

court-martial, court-martials, court-martialling, court-martialled NOUN ① a military trial. ▶ VERB ② If a member of the armed forces is court-martialled, he or she is tried by a court-martial.

courtship NOUN (formal) Courtship is the activity of courting or the period of time during which two people are courting.

courtyard, courtyards NOUN a flat area of ground surrounded by buildings or walls.

cousin, cousins NOUN Your cousin is the child of your uncle or aunt.

cove, coves NOUN a small bay.

covenant, covenants [Said kuv-vi-nant] NOUN a formal written agreement or promise.

cover, covers, covering, covered VERB ① If you cover something, you put something else over it to protect it or hide it. ② If something covers something else, it forms a layer over it • Tears covered his face. ③ If you cover a particular distance, you travel that distance • He covered 52 kilometres in 210 laps. ▶ NOUN ④ something put over an object to protect it or keep it warm. ⑤ The cover of a book or magazine is its outside. ⑥ Insurance cover is a guarantee that money will be paid if something is lost or harmed. ⑦ In the open, cover consists of trees, rocks or other places where you can shelter or hide. **cover up** VERB If you cover up something you do not want people to know about, you hide it from them • *He lied to cover up his crime.* **cover-up** NOUN

coverage NOUN The coverage of something in the news is the reporting of it.

covering, coverings NOUN a layer of something which protects or conceals something else • *A morning blizzard left a covering of snow.*

covert [Said koh-vert] ADJECTIVE (formal) Covert activities are secret, rather than open. **covertly** ADVERB

SPELLING TIP
Do not confuse the spellings of *covert* and *covet*: *a covert military operation*; *It's hard not to covet the life she has.*

covet, covets, coveting, coveted [Said kuv-vit] VERB (formal) If you covet something, you want it very much.

COVID-19; also spelt **Covid-19** NOUN a serious infectious disease that affects the lungs.

cow, cows NOUN a large animal kept on farms for its milk.

coward, cowards NOUN someone who is easily frightened and who avoids dangerous or difficult situations. **cowardice** NOUN

cowardly ADJECTIVE easily scared.

cowboy, cowboys NOUN a man employed to look after cattle in America.

cower, cowers, cowering, cowered VERB When someone cowers, they crouch or move backwards because they are afraid.
SIMILAR WORDS: cringe, shrink

COX, coxes NOUN A cox is a coxswain.

coxswain, coxswains [Said kok-sn] NOUN The coxswain of a boat is the person who steers it.

coy, coyer, coyest ADJECTIVE If someone is coy, they pretend to be shy and modest. **coyly** ADVERB

coyote, coyotes [Said koy-ote-ee] NOUN a North American animal like a small wolf.

CPU, CPUs NOUN [ICT] the part of a computer that controls all the other parts. CPU is an abbreviation for 'central processing unit'.

crab, crabs NOUN a sea creature with four pairs of legs, two pincers, and a flat, round body covered by a shell.

crack, cracks, cracking, cracked VERB ① If something cracks, it becomes damaged, with lines appearing on its surface. ② If you crack a joke, you tell it. ③ If you crack a problem or code, you solve it. ▶ NOUN ④ one of the lines appearing on something when it cracks. ⑤ a narrow gap. ▶ ADJECTIVE ⑥ A crack soldier, sportsman or sportswoman is highly trained and skilful.
SIMILAR WORDS: ④ break, fracture ⑤ gap

cracker, crackers NOUN ① a thin, crisp biscuit that is often eaten with cheese. ② a paper-covered tube that pulls apart with a bang and usually has a toy and paper hat inside.

crackle, crackles, crackling, crackled VERB ① If something crackles, it makes a rapid series of short, harsh noises. ▶ NOUN ② a short, harsh noise.

cradle, cradles, cradling, cradled NOUN ① a box-shaped bed for a baby. ▶ VERB ② If you cradle something in your arms or hands, you hold it there carefully.

craft, crafts NOUN ① an activity such as weaving, carving or pottery.

② a skilful occupation • *the writer's craft*. ③ a boat, plane or spacecraft.

GRAMMAR TIP
When *craft* means 'a boat, plane or spacecraft' (sense 3), the plural is *craft*.

---

craftsman, craftsmen NOUN a man who makes things skilfully with his hands. **craftsmanship** NOUN

craftswoman, craftswomen NOUN a woman who makes things skilfully with her hands.

craftwork, craftworks NOUN Craftwork is the act of making things skilfully by hand.

crafty, craftier, craftiest ADJECTIVE Someone who is crafty gets what they want by tricking people in a clever way.

crag, crags NOUN a steep rugged rock or peak.

craggy, craggier, craggiest ADJECTIVE A craggy mountain or cliff is steep and rocky.

cram, crams, cramming, crammed VERB If you cram people or things into a place, you put more in than there is room for.
SIMILAR WORDS: pack, squeeze, stuff

cramp, cramps NOUN Cramp or cramps is a pain caused by a muscle contracting.

cramped ADJECTIVE If a room or building is cramped, it is not big enough for the people or things in it.

cranberry, cranberries NOUN Cranberries are sour-tasting red berries, often made into a sauce.

crane, cranes, craning, craned NOUN ① a machine that moves heavy things by lifting them in the air. ② a large bird with a long neck and long legs. ▶ VERB ③ If you crane your neck, you extend your head in a particular direction to see or hear something better.

crank, cranks, cranking, cranked NOUN ① (*informal*) someone with strange ideas who behaves in an odd way. ② a device you turn to make something move • *The adjustment is made by turning the crank.* ▶ VERB ③ If you crank something, you make it move by turning a handle.

cranny, crannies NOUN a very narrow opening in a wall or rock • *nooks and crannies*.

crash, crashes, crashing, crashed NOUN ① an accident in which a moving vehicle hits something violently. ② a sudden loud noise • *the crash of the waves on the rocks*. ③ the sudden failure of a business or financial institution. ▶ VERB ④ When a vehicle crashes, it hits something and is badly damaged. ⑤ If a computer or a computer program crashes, it fails suddenly.

crash helmet, crash helmets NOUN a helmet worn by motorcyclists for protection when they are riding.

crate, crates NOUN a large box used for transporting or storing things.

crater, craters NOUN GEOGRAPHY a wide hole in the ground caused by something hitting it or by an explosion.

cravat, cravats NOUN a piece of cloth a man can wear round his neck tucked into his shirt collar.
WORD HISTORY: from Serbo-Croat *Hrvat* meaning 'Croat'. Croat soldiers wore cravats during the Thirty Years' War

crave, craves, craving, craved VERB If you crave something, you want it very much • *He craves attention.*
craving NOUN

crawl, crawls, crawling, crawled VERB ① When you crawl, you move forward on your hands and knees. ②When a vehicle crawls, it moves very slowly. ③ (*informal*) If a place is crawling with people or things, it is full of them • *The place is crawling with tourists.* **crawler** NOUN

crayfish, crayfishes or crayfish NOUN a small shellfish like a lobster.

crayon, crayons NOUN a coloured pencil or a stick of coloured wax.

craze, crazes NOUN something that is very popular for a short time.

crazy, crazier, craziest ADJECTIVE (*informal*) ① very strange or foolish • *The guy is crazy* • *a crazy idea.* ② If you are crazy about something, you are very keen on it • *I was crazy about dancing.* **crazily** ADVERB **craziness** NOUN

creak, creaks, creaking, creaked VERB ① If something creaks, it makes a harsh sound when it moves or when you stand on it. ▶ NOUN ② a harsh squeaking noise. **creaky** ADJECTIVE

SPELLING TIP

Do not confuse the spellings of *creak* and *creek*: *The door opened with a creak; The yacht was anchored in the creek below the house.*

---

cream, creams NOUN ① Cream is a thick, yellowish-white liquid taken from the top of milk. ② Cream is also a substance people can rub on their skin. ▶ ADJECTIVE ③ yellowish-white. **creamy** ADJECTIVE

crease, creases, creasing, creased NOUN ① an irregular line that appears on cloth or paper when it is crumpled. ② a straight line on something that has been pressed or folded neatly. ▶ VERB ③ To crease something is to make lines appear on it. **creased** ADJECTIVE

create, creates, creating, created

VERB ① To create something is to cause it to happen or exist • *This is absolutely vital but creates a problem.* ② When someone creates a new product or process, they invent it. **creator** NOUN **creation** NOUN

creative ADJECTIVE ① Creative people are able to invent and develop original ideas. ② Creative activities involve the inventing and developing of original ideas • *creative writing.* **creatively** ADVERB **creativity** NOUN

creature, creatures NOUN any living thing that moves about.

crèche, crèches [*Said* **kresh**] NOUN a place where small children are looked after while their parents are working.

credence NOUN (*formal*) If something gives credence to a theory or story, it makes it easier to believe.

credentials PLURAL NOUN Your credentials are your past achievements or other things in your background that make you qualified for something.

credible ADJECTIVE If someone or something is credible, you can believe or trust them. **credibility** NOUN

credit, credits, crediting, credited NOUN ① If you are allowed credit, you can take something and pay for it later • *to buy goods on credit.* ② If you get the credit for something, people praise you for it. ③ If you say someone is a credit to their family or school, you mean that their family or school should be proud of them. ④ (*in plural*) The list of people who helped make a film, recording or television programme is called the credits. ▶ PHRASE ⑤ If someone or their bank account is **in credit**, their account has money in it. ▶ VERB ⑥ If you are credited with an achievement, people believe that you were responsible for it.

creditable ADJECTIVE satisfactory or fairly good • *a creditable performance*.

credit card, credit cards NOUN a plastic card that allows someone to buy goods on credit.

creditor, creditors NOUN Your creditors are the people you owe money to.

creed, creeds NOUN ① a religion. ② any set of beliefs • *her political creed*.

creek, creeks NOUN a narrow inlet where the sea comes a long way into the land.

WORD HISTORY: from Old Norse *kriki* meaning 'nook'

SPELLING TIP
Do not confuse the spellings of *creek* and *creak*: *The yacht was anchored in the creek below the house; The door opened with a creak.*

creep, creeps, creeping, crept VERB To creep is to move quietly and slowly.

creepy, creepier, creepiest ADJECTIVE (*informal*) strange and frightening • *a creepy feeling*.

cremate, cremates, cremating, cremated VERB When someone is cremated, their dead body is burned during a funeral service. **cremation** NOUN

crematorium, crematoriums or crematoria NOUN a building in which the bodies of dead people are burned.

creole, creoles [*Said* kree-ohl] NOUN A creole is a language that has developed from a mixture of different languages and has become the main language in a particular place.

crepe [*Said* krayp] NOUN ① Crepe is a thin ridged material made from cotton, silk or wool. ② Crepe is also a type of rubber with a rough surface.

crept the past tense and past participle of **creep**.

crescendo, crescendos [*Said* krish-en-doe*] NOUN MUSIC When there is a crescendo in a piece of music, the music gets louder.

crescent, crescents NOUN a curved shape that is wider in its middle than at the ends, which are pointed.

cress NOUN Cress is a plant with small, strong-tasting leaves. It is used in salads.

crest, crests NOUN ① The crest of a hill or wave is its highest part. ② a tuft of feathers on top of a bird's head. ③ a small picture or design that is the emblem of a noble family, a town, or an organisation. **crested** ADJECTIVE

crevice, crevices NOUN a narrow crack or gap in rock.

crew, crews NOUN ① The crew of a ship, aeroplane or spacecraft are the people who operate it. ② people with special technical skills who work together • *the camera crew*.

crib, cribs, cribbing, cribbed VERB ① (*informal*) If you crib, you copy what someone else has written and pretend it is your own work. ▶ NOUN ② (*old-fashioned*) a baby's cot.

crib-wall, crib-walls NOUN in New Zealand English, a wooden wall built against a bank of earth to support it.

crick, cricks NOUN a pain in your neck or back caused by muscles becoming stiff.

cricket, crickets NOUN ① Cricket is an outdoor game played by two teams who take turns at scoring runs by hitting a ball with a bat. ② a small jumping insect that produces sounds by rubbing its wings together. **cricketer** NOUN

crime, crimes NOUN an action for

which you can be punished by law • *a serious crime*.
SIMILAR WORDS: misdemeanour, offence

criminal, criminals NOUN ① someone who has committed a crime. ▸ ADJECTIVE ② involving or related to crime • *criminal activities*.
criminally ADVERB
SIMILAR WORDS: ① crook, lawbreaker, offender

criminology NOUN the scientific study of crime and criminals.
criminologist NOUN

crimson NOUN or ADJECTIVE dark purplish-red.

cringe, cringes, cringing, cringed VERB If you cringe, you back away from someone or something because you are afraid or embarrassed.

crinkle, crinkles, crinkling, crinkled VERB ① If something crinkles, it becomes slightly creased or folded. ▸ NOUN ② Crinkles are small creases or folds.

cripple, cripples, crippling, crippled VERB ① To cripple someone is to injure them severely. ② To cripple a company or country is to prevent it from working. **crippled** ADJECTIVE **crippling** ADJECTIVE

crisis, crises [*Said* **kry**-*seez in the plural*] NOUN a serious or dangerous situation.

crisp, crisper, crispest; crisps ADJECTIVE ① Something that is crisp is pleasantly fresh and firm • *crisp lettuce leaves*. ② If the air or the weather is crisp, it is pleasantly fresh, cold and dry • *crisp wintry days*. ▸ NOUN ③ Crisps are thin slices of potato fried until they are hard and crunchy.

crispy, crispier, crispiest ADJECTIVE Crispy food is pleasantly hard and crunchy • *a crispy salad*.

criterion, criteria [*Said* kry-**teer**-ee-on] NOUN a standard by which you judge or decide something.

GRAMMAR TIP
Criteria is the plural of *criterion*, and needs to be used with a plural verb.

critic, critics NOUN ① someone who writes reviews of books, films, plays or musical performances. ② A critic of a person or system is someone who criticises them publicly • *the government's critics*.

critical ADJECTIVE ① A critical time is one which is very important in determining what happens in the future • *critical months in the history of the world*. ② A critical situation is a very serious one • *Rock music is in a critical state*. ③ If an ill or injured person is critical, they are in danger of dying. ④ If you are critical of something or someone, you express severe judgments or opinions about them. ⑤ If you are critical, you examine and judge something carefully • *Learning facts is not so important as critical thinking*.
critically ADVERB

criticise, criticises, criticising, criticised; also spelt **criticize** VERB If you criticise someone or something, you say what you think is wrong with them.
SIMILAR WORDS: disparage, find fault with

criticism, criticisms NOUN ① When there is criticism of someone or something, people express disapproval of them. ② If you make a criticism, you point out a fault you think someone or something has.

croak, croaks, croaking, croaked VERB ① When animals and birds croak, they make harsh, low sounds. ▸ NOUN ② a harsh, low sound.

Croatian, Croatians ADJECTIVE
① belonging or relating to Croatia.
▶ NOUN ② someone who comes from Croatia. ③ Croatian is the form of Serbo-Croat spoken in Croatia.

crochet, crochets, crocheting, crocheted [Said kroh-shay] NOUN ① Crochet is a way of making clothes and other things out of thread using a needle with a small hook at the end. ▶ VERB ② If someone crochets clothes, they make them out of thread using a needle with a small hook at the end.

crockery NOUN Crockery is plates, cups and saucers.

crocodile, crocodiles NOUN a large, scaly, meat-eating reptile which lives in tropical rivers.

crocus, crocuses NOUN Crocuses are yellow, purple or white flowers that grow in early spring.

croft, crofts NOUN a small piece of land, especially in Scotland, which is farmed by one family. **crofter** NOUN

croissant, croissants [Said krwah-son] NOUN a light, crescent-shaped roll eaten at breakfast.
WORD HISTORY: from French croissant meaning 'crescent'

crony, cronies NOUN (old-fashioned) Your cronies are the friends you spend a lot of time with.

crook, crooks NOUN ① (informal) a criminal. ② The crook of your arm or leg is the soft inside part where you bend your elbow or knee. ▶ ADJECTIVE ③ In Australian English, crook means ill.

crooked [Said kroo-kid] ADJECTIVE ① bent or twisted. ② (informal) Someone who is crooked is dishonest.

croon, croons, crooning, crooned VERB To croon is to sing or hum quietly and gently • He crooned a love song.

WORD HISTORY: from Old Dutch kronen meaning 'to groan'

crop, crops, cropping, cropped NOUN ① Crops are plants such as wheat and potatoes that are grown for food. ② the plants collected at harvest time • You should have two crops in the year. ▶ VERB ③ To crop someone's hair is to cut it very short.
crop up VERB (informal) If something crops up, it happens unexpectedly.

croquet [Said kroh-kay] NOUN Croquet is a game in which the players use long-handled mallets to hit balls through metal arches pushed into a lawn.

cross, crosses, crossing, crossed; crosser, crossest VERB ① If you cross something such as a room or a road, you go to the other side of it. ② Lines or roads that cross meet and go across each other. ③ If a thought crosses your mind, you think of it. ④ If you cross your arms, legs or fingers, you put one on top of the other. ▶ NOUN ⑤ a vertical bar or line crossed by a shorter horizontal bar or line; also used to describe any object shaped like this. ⑥ [RE] The Cross is the cross-shaped structure on which Jesus Christ was crucified. A cross is also any symbol representing Christ's Cross. ⑦ a written mark shaped like an X • Mark the wrong answers with a cross. ⑧ Something that is a cross between two things is neither one thing nor the other, but a mixture of both. ▶ ADJECTIVE ⑨ Someone who is cross is rather angry. **crossly** ADVERB **cross out** VERB If you cross out words on a page, you draw a line through them because they are wrong or because you do not want people to read them.

crossbow, crossbows NOUN [HISTORY] a weapon consisting of a small bow fixed at the end of a piece of wood.

cross-country NOUN ① Cross-country is the sport of running across open countryside, rather than on roads or on a track. ▸ADVERB or ADJECTIVE ② across open countryside.

cross-eyed ADJECTIVE A cross-eyed person has eyes that seem to look towards each other.

crossfire NOUN Crossfire is gunfire crossing the same place from opposite directions.

crosshatching NOUN ART Crosshatching is drawing an area of shade in a picture using two or more sets of parallel lines.

crossing, crossings NOUN ① a place where you can cross a road safely. ② a journey by ship to a place on the other side of the sea.

cross-legged ADJECTIVE If you are sitting cross-legged, you are sitting on the floor with your knees pointing outwards and your feet tucked under them.

crossroads, crossroads NOUN a place where two roads meet and cross each other.

cross section, cross sections NOUN A cross section of a group of people is a representative sample of them.

crossword, crosswords NOUN a puzzle in which you work out the answers to clues and write them in the white squares of a pattern of black and white squares.

crotch, crotches NOUN the part of your body between the tops of your legs.

crotchet, crotchets NOUN MUSIC A crotchet is a musical note equal to two quavers or half a minim.

crouch, crouches, crouching, crouched VERB If you are crouching, you are leaning forward with your legs bent under you.

crow, crows, crowing, crowed NOUN ① a large black bird which makes a loud, harsh noise. ▸VERB ② When a cock crows, it utters a loud squawking sound.

crowbar, crowbars NOUN a heavy iron bar used as a lever or for forcing things open.

crowd, crowds, crowding, crowded NOUN ① a large group of people gathered together. ▸VERB ② When people crowd somewhere, they gather there close together or in large numbers.
SIMILAR WORDS: ① mass, mob, multitude, throng

crowded ADJECTIVE A crowded place is full of people.

crowdfunding NOUN Crowdfunding is when a large number of people each give an amount of money to pay for something.

crown, crowns, crowning, crowned NOUN ① a circular ornament worn on a royal person's head. ② The crown of something such as your head is the top part of it. ▸VERB ③ When a king or queen is crowned, a crown is put on their head during their coronation ceremony. ④ When something crowns an event, it is the final part of it • *The news crowned a dreadful week.*

crucial [Said kroo-shl] ADJECTIVE If something is crucial, it is very important in determining how something else will be in the future.
SIMILAR WORDS: critical, decisive, vital
WORD HISTORY: from Latin *crux* meaning 'a cross'

crucifix, crucifixes NOUN RE a cross with a figure representing Jesus Christ being crucified on it.

crucify, crucifies, crucifying, crucified VERB RE To crucify someone is to tie or nail them to a

a
b
c
d
e
f
g
h
i
j
k
l
m
n
o
p
q
r
s
t
u
v
w
x
y
z

large wooden cross and leave them there to die. **crucifixion** NOUN

crude, cruder, crudest ADJECTIVE ① rough and simple • *a crude weapon* • *a crude method of entry.* ② A crude person speaks or behaves in a rude and offensive way • *You can be quite crude at times.* **crudely** ADVERB **crudity** NOUN
SIMILAR WORDS: ① makeshift, primitive ② coarse, vulgar

cruel, crueller, cruellest ADJECTIVE Cruel people deliberately cause pain or distress to other people or to animals. **cruelly** ADVERB
SIMILAR WORDS: brutal, callous, unkind

cruelty NOUN cruel behaviour.

cruise, cruises, cruising, cruised NOUN ① a holiday in which you travel on a ship and visit places. ▸ VERB ② When a vehicle cruises, it moves at a constant moderate speed.

cruiser, cruisers NOUN ① a motor boat with a cabin you can sleep in. ② a large, fast warship.

crumb, crumbs NOUN Crumbs are very small pieces of bread or cake.

crumble, crumbles, crumbling, crumbled VERB When something crumbles, it breaks into small pieces.

crumbly, crumblier, crumbliest ADJECTIVE Something crumbly easily breaks into small pieces.

crumpet, crumpets NOUN a round, flat, breadlike cake which you eat toasted.

crumple, crumples, crumpling, crumpled VERB To crumple paper or cloth is to squash it so that it is full of creases and folds.

crunch, crunches, crunching, crunched VERB If you crunch something, you crush it noisily, for example between your teeth or under your feet.

crunchy, crunchier, crunchiest ADJECTIVE Crunchy food is hard or crisp and makes a noise when you eat it.

crusade, crusades NOUN a long and determined attempt to achieve something • *the crusade for human rights.* **crusader** NOUN

crush, crushes, crushing, crushed VERB ① To crush something is to destroy its shape by squeezing it. ② To crush a substance is to turn it into liquid or powder by squeezing or grinding it. ③ To crush an army or political organisation is to defeat it completely. ▸ NOUN ④ a dense crowd of people.

crust, crusts NOUN ① the hard outside part of a loaf. ② a hard layer on top of something • *The snow had a fine crust on it.* ③ GEOGRAPHY the outer layer of the earth.

crustacean, crustaceans [Said kruss-tay-shn] NOUN SCIENCE A crustacean is a creature with a shell and several pairs of legs. Crabs, lobsters and shrimps are crustaceans.

crusty, crustier, crustiest ADJECTIVE ① Something that is crusty has a hard outside layer. ② Crusty people are impatient and irritable.

crutch, crutches NOUN a support like a long stick which you lean on to help you walk when you have an injured foot or leg.

crux, cruxes NOUN the most important or difficult part of a problem or argument.

cry, cries, crying, cried VERB ① When you cry, tears appear in your eyes. ② To cry something is to shout it or say it loudly • *'See you soon!' they cried.* ▸ NOUN ③ If you have a cry, you cry for a period of time. ④ a shout or other loud sound made with your voice. ⑤ a loud sound made by some birds • *the cry of a seagull*. **cry off** VERB (*informal*) If you cry off, you change your mind and decide not to do something. **cry out for** VERB (*informal*) If something is crying out for something else, it needs it very much.

SIMILAR WORDS: ① sob, weep

crypt, **crypts** NOUN an underground room beneath a church, usually used as a burial place.

WORD HISTORY: from Greek *kruptein* meaning 'to hide'

cryptic ADJECTIVE A cryptic remark or message has a hidden meaning.

crystal, **crystals** NOUN ① a piece of a mineral that has formed naturally into a regular shape. ② Crystal is a type of transparent rock, used in jewellery. ③ Crystal is also a kind of very high quality glass. **crystalline** ADJECTIVE

crystallise, **crystallises**, **crystallising**, **crystallised**; also spelt **crystallize** VERB ① If a substance crystallises, it turns into crystals. ② If an idea crystallises, it becomes clear in your mind.

cub, **cubs** NOUN ① Some young wild animals are called cubs • *a lion cub*. ② The Cubs is an organisation for young boys before they join the Scouts.

Cuban, **Cubans** [*Said* kyoo-*ban*] ADJECTIVE ① belonging or relating to Cuba. ▶ NOUN ② someone who comes from Cuba.

cube, **cubes**, **cubing**, **cubed** MATHS NOUN ① a three-dimensional shape with six equally-sized square surfaces. ② The cube of a number is the number multiplied by itself twice. For example, the cube of 4, written 4^3, is 4 x 4 x 4. ▶ VERB ③ To cube a number is to multiply it by itself twice.

cube root, cube roots NOUN MATHS The cube root of a number is another number that makes the first number when it is multiplied by itself twice. For example, the cube root of 27 is 3.

cubic ADJECTIVE MATHS used in measurements of volume • *cubic centimetres*.

cubicle, **cubicles** NOUN a small enclosed area in a place such as a sports centre, where you can dress and undress.

cuboid, **cuboids** NOUN ① MATHS a three-dimensional shape with six rectangular faces. ▶ ADJECTIVE ② shaped like a cube • *a cuboid structure*.

cuckoo, **cuckoos** NOUN a grey bird with a two-note call that lays its eggs in other birds' nests.

cucumber, **cucumbers** NOUN a long, thin, green-skinned fruit eaten raw in salads.

cuddle, **cuddles**, **cuddling**, **cuddled** VERB ① If you cuddle someone, you hold them affectionately in your arms. ▶ NOUN ② If you give someone a cuddle, you hold them affectionately in your arms.

cuddly, **cuddlier**, **cuddliest** ADJECTIVE Cuddly people, animals or toys are soft or pleasing in some way so that you want to cuddle them.

cue, **cues** NOUN ① something said or done by a performer that is a signal for another performer to begin • *Chris never misses a cue*. ② a long stick used to hit the balls in snooker and billiards.

SPELLING TIP
Do not confuse the spellings of *cue* and *queue*: *That's the lead singer's cue; a long queue at the bank.*

cuff, **cuffs** NOUN the end part of a sleeve.

a
b
c
d
e
f
g
h
i
j
k
l
m
n
o
p
q
r
s
t
u
v
w
x
y
z

cufflink, cufflinks NOUN Cufflinks are small objects for holding shirt cuffs together.

cuisine, cuisines [Said kwiz-*een*] NOUN The cuisine of a region is the style of cooking that is typical of it. WORD HISTORY: from French *cuisine* meaning 'kitchen'

cul-de-sac, cul-de-sacs [Said *kul-des-sak*] NOUN a road that does not lead to any other roads because one end is blocked off.

culinary ADJECTIVE (*formal*) connected with the kitchen or cooking. WORD HISTORY: from Latin *culina* meaning 'kitchen'

cull, culls, culling, culled VERB ① If you cull things, you gather them from different places or sources • *information culled from movies.* ② If you cull animals, you kill them in order to reduce their numbers • *culling infected chickens.* ▶ NOUN ③ When there is a cull, weaker animals are killed to reduce the numbers in a group.

culminate, culminates, culminating, culminated VERB To culminate in something is to finally develop into it • *a campaign that culminated in a stunning success.* **culmination** NOUN

culprit, culprits NOUN someone who has done something harmful or wrong.

cult, cults NOUN ① A cult is a religious group with special rituals, usually connected with the worship of a particular person. ② 'Cult' is used to refer to any situation in which someone or something is very popular with a large group of people • *the American sports car cult.*

cultivate, cultivates, cultivating, cultivated VERB ① To cultivate land is to grow crops on it. ② If you cultivate a feeling or attitude, you try to develop it in yourself or other people. **cultivation** NOUN

cultural ADJECTIVE ① of or relating to artistic activities • *a cultural festival.* ② of or relating to a culture or civilisation • *cultural diversity.*

culture, cultures NOUN ① Culture refers to the arts and to people's appreciation of them • *He was a man of culture.* ② The culture of a particular society is its ideas, customs and art • *Japanese culture.* ③ In science, a culture is a group of bacteria or cells grown in a laboratory. **cultured** ADJECTIVE

cumulative ADJECTIVE Something that is cumulative keeps being added to.

cunjevoi, cunjevois [Said *kun-jiv-voi*] NOUN a very small Australian sea creature that lives on rocks.

cunning ADJECTIVE ① Someone who is cunning uses clever and deceitful methods to get what they want. ▶ NOUN ② Cunning is the ability to get what you want using clever and deceitful methods. **cunningly** ADVERB SIMILAR WORDS: ① crafty, sly, wily

cup, cups, cupping, cupped NOUN ① a small, round container with a handle, which you drink out of. ② a large metal container with two handles, given as a prize. ▶ VERB ③ If you cup your hands, you put them together to make a shape like a cup.

cupboard, cupboards NOUN a piece of furniture with doors and shelves.

curable ADJECTIVE If a disease or illness is curable, it can be cured.

curate, curates NOUN a member of the clergy who helps a vicar or a priest.

curator, curators NOUN the person in a museum or art gallery in charge of its contents.

curb, curbs, curbing, curbed VERB
① To curb something is to keep it within limits • *policies designed to curb inflation.* ▶ NOUN ② If a curb is placed on something, it is kept within limits • *the curb on spending.*

SPELLING TIP

Do not confuse the spellings of *curb* and *kerb*: *There is a curb on public spending; A taxi drew up at the kerb.*

---

curdle, curdles, curdling, curdled
VERB When milk curdles, it turns sour.

curds PLURAL NOUN Curds are the thick white substance formed when milk turns sour.

cure, cures, curing, cured VERB
① To cure an illness is to end it. ② To cure a sick or injured person is to make them well. ③ If something cures you of a habit or attitude, it stops you having it. ④ To cure food, tobacco or animal skin is to treat it in order to preserve it. ▶ NOUN ⑤ A cure for an illness is something that cures it.
SIMILAR WORDS: ② heal, make better

curfew, curfews NOUN If there is a curfew, people must stay indoors between particular times at night.

curiosity, curiosities NOUN
① Curiosity is the desire to know about something or about many things. ② something unusual and interesting.

curious ADJECTIVE ① Someone who is curious wants to know more about something. ② Something that is curious is unusual and hard to explain. **curiously** ADVERB
SIMILAR WORDS: ① inquiring, inquisitive, nosy

curl, curls, curling, curled NOUN
① Curls are lengths of hair shaped in tight curves and circles. ② a curved or spiral shape • *the curls of morning fog.* ▶ VERB ③ If something curls, it moves in a curve or spiral. **curly** ADJECTIVE

curler, curlers NOUN Curlers are plastic or metal tubes that you can roll your hair round to make it curly.

curlew, curlews [*Said* kur-lyoo] NOUN a large brown bird with a long curved beak and a loud cry.

currant, currants NOUN ① Currants are small dried grapes often put in cakes and puddings. ② Currants are also blackcurrants or redcurrants.
WORD HISTORY: sense 1 is from Middle English *rayson of Corannte* meaning 'Corinth raisin'

SPELLING TIP

Do not confuse the spellings of *currant* and *current*: *a cake with cherries and currants; At this point in the river the current is very strong.*

---

currawong, currawongs NOUN an Australian bird like a crow.

currency, currencies NOUN ① A country's currency is its coins and banknotes or its monetary system generally • *foreign currency* • *a strong economy and a weak currency.* ② If something such as an idea has currency, it is used a lot at a particular time.

current, currents NOUN
① GEOGRAPHY a strong continuous movement of the water in a river or in the sea. ② GEOGRAPHY An air current is a flowing movement in the air. ③ SCIENCE An electric current is a flow of electricity through a wire or circuit. ▶ ADJECTIVE ④ Something that is current is happening, being done, or being used now. **currently** ADVERB

a b c d e f g h i j k l m n o p q r s t u v w x y z

SPELLING TIP
Do not confuse the spellings of *current* and *currant*: *At this point in the river the current is very strong; a cake with cherries and currants.*

current affairs PLURAL NOUN
Current affairs are political and social events discussed in newspapers and on television and radio.

curriculum, curriculums or **curricula** [Said *kur-rik-yoo-lum*] NOUN the different courses taught at a school or university.

curriculum vitae, curricula vitae [Said *vee-tie*] NOUN Someone's curriculum vitae is a written account of their personal details, education and work experience which they send when they apply for a job.

curried ADJECTIVE Curried food has been flavoured with hot spices • *curried vegetables.*

curry, curries, currying, curried NOUN ① Curry is an Indian dish made with hot spices. ▸ PHRASE ② To **curry favour** with someone means to try to please them by flattering them or doing things to help them.
WORD HISTORY: sense 1 is from Tamil *kari* meaning 'sauce'; sense 2 is from Old French *correer* meaning 'to make ready'

curse, curses, cursing, cursed VERB ① To curse is to swear because you are angry. ② If you curse someone or something, you say angry things about them using rude words. ▸ NOUN ③ what you say when you curse. ④ something supernatural that is supposed to cause unpleasant things to happen to someone. ⑤ a thing or person that causes a lot of trouble or distress • *the curse of summer colds.* **cursed** ADJECTIVE

cursor, cursors NOUN [ICT] an arrow or box on a computer screen which indicates where the next letter or symbol will be inserted.

cursory ADJECTIVE When you give something a cursory glance or examination, you look at it briefly without paying attention to detail.

curt, curter, curtest ADJECTIVE If someone is curt, they speak in a brief and rather rude way. **curtly** ADVERB

curtail, curtails, curtailing, curtailed VERB (formal) To curtail something is to reduce or restrict it • *Injury curtailed his career.*

curtain, curtains NOUN ① a hanging piece of material which can be pulled across a window for privacy or to keep out the light. ② [DRAMA] a large piece of material which hangs in front of the stage in a theatre until a performance begins.

curtsy, curtsies, curtsying, curtsied; also spelt **curtsey** VERB ① When a woman curtsies, she lowers her body briefly, bending her knees, to show respect. ▸ NOUN ② the movement a woman makes when she curtsies • *She gave a mock curtsy.*

curve, curves, curving, curved NOUN ① a smooth, gradually bending line. ▸ VERB ② When something curves, it moves in a curve or has the shape of a curve • *The track curved away below him* • *His mouth curved slightly.* **curved** ADJECTIVE **curvy** ADJECTIVE

cushion, cushions, cushioning, cushioned NOUN ① a soft object put on a seat to make it more comfortable. ▸ VERB ② To cushion something is to reduce its effect • *We might have helped to cushion the shock for her.*

custard NOUN Custard is a sweet yellow sauce made from milk and eggs or milk and a powder.

custodian, custodians NOUN the person in charge of a collection in an art gallery or a museum.

custody NOUN ① To have custody of a child means to have the legal right to keep it and look after it • *She won custody of her younger son.* ▶ PHRASE ② Someone who is **in custody** is being kept in prison until they can be tried in a court. **custodial** ADJECTIVE

custom, customs NOUN ① a traditional activity • *an ancient Chinese custom.* ② something usually done at a particular time or in particular circumstances by a person or by the people in a society • *It was also my custom to do Christmas shows.* ③ Customs is the place at a border, airport or harbour where you have to declare any goods you are bringing into a country. ④ (*formal*) If a shop or business has your custom, you buy things or go there regularly • *Banks are desperate to get your custom.* SIMILAR WORDS: ① convention, tradition ② habit, practice

customary ADJECTIVE usual • *his customary modesty* • *her customary greeting.* **customarily** ADVERB

custom-built or **custom-made** ADJECTIVE Something that is custom-built or custom-made is made to someone's special requirements.

customer, customers NOUN ① A shop's or firm's customers are the people who buy its goods. ② (*informal*) You can use 'customer' to refer to someone when describing what they are like to deal with • *a tough customer.* SIMILAR WORDS: ① buyer, client, consumer

customise, customises, customising, customised; also spelt **customize** VERB To customise a car means to alter its appearance to

make it look unusual.

cut, cuts, cutting, cut VERB ① If you cut something, you use a knife, scissors or some other sharp tool to mark it or remove parts of it. ② If you cut yourself, you injure yourself on a sharp object. ③ If you cut the amount of something, you reduce it • *Some costs could be cut.* ④ When writing is cut, parts of it are not printed or broadcast. ⑤ To cut from one scene or shot to another in a film is to go instantly to the other scene or shot. ▶ NOUN ⑥ a mark or injury made with a knife or other sharp tool. ⑦ a reduction • *another cut in interest rates.* ⑧ a part in something written that is not printed or broadcast. ⑨ a large piece of meat ready for cooking. ▶ ADJECTIVE ⑩ Well cut clothes have been well designed and made • *this beautifully cut coat.* **cut back** VERB To cut back or cut back on spending means to reduce it. **cutback** NOUN **cut down** VERB If you cut down on an activity, you do it less often • *cutting down on smoking.* **cut off** VERB ① To cut someone or something off means to separate them from things they are normally connected with • *The President had cut himself off from the people.* ② If a supply of something is cut off, you no longer get it • *The water had been cut off.* ③ If your telephone or telephone call is cut off, it is disconnected. **cut out** VERB ① If you cut out something you are doing, you stop doing it • *Cut out eating fatty foods.* ② If an engine cuts out, it suddenly stops working.

cute, cuter, cutest ADJECTIVE pretty or attractive.

cuticle, cuticles NOUN SCIENCE Cuticles are the pieces of skin that cover the base of your fingernails and toenails.

a b c d e f g h i j k l m n o p q r s t u v w x y z

cutlass, **cutlasses** NOUN a curved sword that was used by sailors.

cutlery NOUN Cutlery is knives, forks and spoons.

cutlet, **cutlets** NOUN a small piece of meat which you fry or grill.

cutting, **cuttings** NOUN ① something cut from a newspaper or magazine. ② a part cut from a plant and used to grow a new plant. ▸ ADJECTIVE ③ A cutting remark is unkind and likely to hurt someone.

CV an abbreviation for **curriculum vitae**.

cyanide [Said sigh-an-nide] NOUN Cyanide is an extremely poisonous chemical.

cyber- PREFIX Words that begin with 'cyber-' have something to do with computers in their meaning. For example *cybercrime* is crime that involves the use of computers. WORD HISTORY: from Greek *kybernētēs* meaning 'a steersman'

cyberattack, **cyberattacks** NOUN an attempt to damage or disrupt a computer system.

cyberbullying NOUN Cyberbullying is the act of threatening or intimidating a person using electronic communication such as email or social media.

cybersecurity NOUN Cybersecurity means the precautions that people take to protect themselves against criminals who use the internet.

cyberspace NOUN all of the data stored in a large computer or network, seen as a place.

cycle, **cycles**, **cycling**, **cycled** VERB ① When you cycle, you ride a bicycle. ▸ NOUN ② a bicycle or a motorcycle. ③ a series of events which is repeated again and again in the same order • *the cycle of births and deaths*. ④ a series of songs or poems intended to be performed or read together. WORD HISTORY: from Greek *kuklos* meaning 'ring' or 'wheel'

cyclical or **cyclic** ADJECTIVE happening over and over again in cycles • *a clear cyclical pattern*.

cyclist, **cyclists** NOUN someone who rides a bicycle.

cyclone, **cyclones** NOUN a violent tropical storm.

cygnet, **cygnets** [Said sig-net] NOUN a young swan.

cylinder, **cylinders** NOUN ① MATHS a three-dimensional shape with two equally-sized flat circular ends joined by a curved surface. ② the part in a motor engine in which the piston moves backwards and forwards. **cylindrical** ADJECTIVE

cymbal, **cymbals** NOUN a circular brass plate used as a percussion instrument. Cymbals are clashed together or hit with a stick.

SPELLING TIP
Do not confuse the spellings of *cymbal* and *symbol*: *a sudden crash of cymbals; The dove is the symbol of peace*.

cynic, **cynics** [Said sin-nik] NOUN a cynical person. WORD HISTORY: from Greek *kunikos* meaning 'dog-like'

cynical ADJECTIVE believing that people always behave selfishly or dishonestly. **cynically** ADVERB **cynicism** NOUN

cypher another spelling of **cipher**.

cypress, **cypresses** NOUN a type of evergreen tree with small dark green leaves and round cones.

cyst, **cysts** [Said sist] NOUN a growth containing liquid that can form under your skin or inside your body.

cytoplasm [Said **sigh**-toh-plazm]
 NOUN SCIENCE all the substances
 and structures inside a cell except the
 nucleus.

czar another spelling of **tsar**.

czarina another spelling of **tsarina**.

Czech, Czechs [Said **chek**] ADJECTIVE
 ① belonging or relating to the Czech
 Republic. ▶ NOUN ② someone who
 comes from the Czech Republic.
 ③ Czech is the language spoken in
 the Czech Republic.

a
b
c
d
e
f
g
h
i
j
k
l
m
n
o
p
q
r
s
t
u
v
w
x
y
z

Dd

dab, dabs, dabbing, dabbed VERB
① If you dab something, you touch it with quick light strokes • *He dabbed some disinfectant onto the gash.*
▶ NOUN ② a small amount of something that is put on a surface • *a dab of perfume.*

dabble, dabbles, dabbling, dabbled VERB If you dabble in something, you work or play at it without being seriously involved in it • *All his life he dabbled in poetry.*

dace NOUN A dace is a type of small freshwater fish.

dachshund, dachshunds [*Said daks-hoond*] NOUN a small dog with a long body and very short legs.
WORD HISTORY: a German word meaning 'badger-dog'

dad, dads or **daddy**, daddies NOUN (*informal*) Your dad or your daddy is your father.

daddy-long-legs NOUN a harmless flying insect with very long legs.

daffodil, daffodils NOUN A daffodil is an early spring flowering plant, with a yellow trumpet-shaped flower grown from a bulb.

daft, dafter, daftest ADJECTIVE (*informal*) stupid and not sensible.
WORD HISTORY: from Old English *gedæfte* meaning 'gentle'

dagger, daggers NOUN a weapon like a short knife.

dahlia, dahlias [*Said dale-ya*] NOUN A dahlia is a type of brightly coloured garden flower growing from a tuberous root. It is named after Anders Dahl, a Swedish botanist.

daily ADJECTIVE ① happening or appearing every day • *our daily visit to the gym.* ▶ ADVERB ② every day • *New messages arrived daily.*

dainty, daintier, daintiest ADJECTIVE very delicate and pretty. **daintily** ADVERB

dairy, dairies NOUN ① a shop or company that supplies milk and milk products. ② in New Zealand, a small shop selling groceries, often outside usual opening hours. ▶ ADJECTIVE ③ Dairy products are foods made from milk, such as butter, cheese, cream and yogurt. ④ A dairy farm is one which keeps cattle to produce milk.

SPELLING TIP
Do not confuse the order of the vowels in *dairy* and *diary*.

---

dais, daises [*Said day-is*] NOUN a raised platform, normally at one end of a hall and used by a speaker.

daisy, daisies NOUN a small wild flower with a yellow centre and small white petals.
WORD HISTORY: from Old English *dæges eage* meaning 'day's eye', because the daisy opens in the daytime and closes at night

dale, dales NOUN a valley.

dalmatian, dalmatians NOUN A dalmatian is a large dog with short smooth white hair and black or brown spots. Dalmatians are named after Dalmatia, a region of Croatia.

dam, dams NOUN a barrier built across a river to hold back water.

damage, damages, damaging, damaged VERB ①To damage something means to harm or spoil it. ▸ NOUN ②Damage to something is injury or harm done to it. ③Damages is the money awarded by a court to compensate someone for loss or harm. **damaging** ADJECTIVE

dame, dames NOUN the title given to a woman who has been awarded the OBE or one of the other British orders of chivalry.

damn, damns, damning, damned [Said **dam**] VERB ①To damn something or someone means to curse or condemn them. ▸ INTERJECTION ②'Damn' is a swearword. **damned** ADJECTIVE

damnation [Said dam-nay-shun] NOUN Damnation is eternal punishment in Hell after death.

damp, damper, dampest ADJECTIVE ①slightly wet. ▸ NOUN ②Damp is slight wetness, especially in the air or in the walls of a building. **dampness** NOUN

dampen, dampens, dampening, dampened VERB ①If you dampen something, you make it slightly wet. ②To dampen something also means to reduce its liveliness or strength • The whole episode has rather dampened my enthusiasm.

damper PHRASE (informal) To **put a damper on** something means to stop it being enjoyable.

damson, damsons NOUN a small blue-black plum; also the tree that the fruit grows on. WORD HISTORY: from Latin prunum Damascenum meaning 'Damascus plum'

dance, dances, dancing, danced

VERB ①To dance means to move your feet and body rhythmically in time to music. ▸ NOUN ②a series of rhythmic movements or steps in time to music. ③a social event where people dance with each other. **dancer** NOUN **dancing** NOUN

dandelion, dandelions NOUN a wild plant with yellow flowers which form a ball of fluffy seeds.

dandruff NOUN Dandruff is small, loose scales of dead skin in someone's hair.

D and T an abbreviation for 'Design and Technology'.

Dane, Danes NOUN someone who comes from Denmark.

danger, dangers NOUN ①Danger is the possibility that someone may be harmed or killed. ②something or someone that can hurt or harm you. SIMILAR WORDS: ① hazard, peril, risk

dangerous ADJECTIVE able to or likely to cause hurt or harm. **dangerously** ADVERB SIMILAR WORDS: hazardous, perilous, unsafe

dangle, dangles, dangling, dangled VERB When something dangles or when you dangle it, it swings or hangs loosely.

Danish ADJECTIVE ①belonging or relating to Denmark. ▸ NOUN ②Danish is the main language spoken in Denmark.

dank, danker, dankest ADJECTIVE A dank place is unpleasantly damp and chilly.

dapper ADJECTIVE slim and neatly dressed. WORD HISTORY: from Old Dutch dapper meaning 'active' or 'nimble'

dappled ADJECTIVE marked with patches of a different or darker shade.

dare, dares, daring, dared VERB ①To

a b c d e f g h i j k l m n o p q r s t u v w x y z

dare someone means to challenge them to do something in order to prove their courage. ② To dare to do something means to have the courage to do it. ▶ NOUN ③ a challenge to do something dangerous.

GRAMMAR TIP
When *dare* is used in a question or with a negative, it does not add an *s*: *Dare she come?*; *He dare not come*.

daredevil, daredevils NOUN a person who enjoys doing dangerous things.

daring ADJECTIVE ① bold and willing to take risks. ▶ NOUN ② the courage required to do things which are dangerous.

dark, darker, darkest ADJECTIVE ① If it is dark, there is not enough light to see properly. ② Dark colours or surfaces reflect little light and so look deep-coloured or dull. ③ 'Dark' is also used to describe thoughts or ideas which are sinister or unpleasant. ▶ NOUN ④ The dark is the lack of light in a place. **darkly** ADVERB **darkness** NOUN
SIMILAR WORDS: ① dim, murky

Dark Ages PLURAL NOUN HISTORY
In European history, the Dark Ages were the period between about 500 AD and 1000 AD.

darken, darkens, darkening, darkened VERB If something darkens, or if you darken it, it becomes darker than it was.

darling, darlings NOUN ① Someone who is lovable or a favourite may be called a darling. ▶ ADJECTIVE ② much admired or loved • *his darling daughter*.

darn, darns, darning, darned VERB ① To darn a hole in a garment means to mend it with crossing stitches. ▶ NOUN ② a part of a garment that has been darned.

dart, darts, darting, darted NOUN ① a small pointed arrow. ② Darts is a game in which the players throw darts at a round board divided into numbered sections. ▶ VERB ③ To dart about means to move quickly and suddenly from one place to another.

dash, dashes, dashing, dashed VERB ① To dash somewhere means to rush there. ② If something is dashed against something else, it strikes it or is thrown violently against it. ③ If hopes or ambitions are dashed, they are ruined or frustrated. ▶ NOUN ④ a sudden movement or rush. ⑤ a small quantity of something. ⑥ ENGLISH the punctuation mark (—) which shows a change of subject, or which may be used instead of brackets.

PUNCTUATION TIP
Do not confuse a dash with a hyphen when you are writing. A dash is longer than a hyphen: *I picked up my phone — Sarah had returned it to me earlier — and threw it across the room.*

What does the Dash do?

The **dash** (–) marks an abrupt change in the flow of a sentence, either showing a sudden change of subject, or marking off extra information. The dash can also show that a speech has been cut off suddenly:

I'm not sure – what was the question again?
'Go ahead and – ' He broke off as Luca seized his arm.

dashboard, dashboards NOUN the instrument panel in a motor vehicle.

dashing ADJECTIVE A dashing man is stylish and confident • *He was a dashing figure in forties cinema*.

dasyure, dasyures [Said *dass-ee-your*] NOUN a small marsupial that lives in Australia and eats meat.

data NOUN ① information, usually in the form of facts or statistics. ② ICT any information put into a computer and which the computer works on or processes.

WORD HISTORY: from Latin *data* meaning 'things given'

GRAMMAR TIP
Data is really a plural word, but it is usually used as a singular.

---

database, databases NOUN ICT a collection of information stored in a computer.

date, dates, dating, dated NOUN ① a particular day or year that can be named. ② If you have a date, you have an appointment to meet someone; also used to refer to the person you are meeting. ③ a small dark-brown sticky fruit with a stone inside, which grows on palm trees. ▶ VERB ④ If you are dating someone, you have a romantic relationship with them. ⑤ If you date something, you find out the time when it began or was made. ⑥ If something dates from a particular time, that is when it happened or was made. ▶ PHRASE ⑦ If something is **out of date**, it is old-fashioned or no longer valid.

dated ADJECTIVE no longer fashionable.

datum the singular form of **data**.

daub, daubs, daubing, daubed VERB If you daub something such as mud or paint on a surface, you smear it there.

daughter, daughters NOUN Someone's daughter is their female child.

daughter-in-law, daughters-in-law NOUN Someone's daughter-in-law is the wife of their grown-up child.

daunt, daunts, daunting, daunted VERB If something daunts you, you feel worried about whether you can succeed in doing it • *He was not the type of man to be daunted by adversity*.
daunting ADJECTIVE

dauphin, dauphins [Said *doe-fan*] NOUN HISTORY The dauphin was the name given to the eldest son of the King of France from the 14th to the 19th century.

dawn, dawns, dawning, dawned NOUN ① the time in the morning when light first appears in the sky. ② the beginning of something • *the dawn of the radio age*. ▶ VERB ③ If day is dawning, morning light is beginning to appear. ④ If an idea or fact dawns on you, you realise it.

day, days NOUN ① one of the seven 24-hour periods of time in a week, measured from one midnight to the next. ② Day is the period of light between sunrise and sunset. ③ You can refer to a particular day or days meaning a particular period in history • *in Gladstone's day*.

daybreak NOUN Daybreak is the time in the morning when light first appears in the sky.

daydream, daydreams, daydreaming, daydreamed NOUN ① a series of pleasant thoughts about things that you would like to happen. ▶ VERB ② When you daydream, you drift off into a daydream.

daylight NOUN ① Daylight is the period during the day when it is light.

② Daylight is also the light from the sun.

daytime NOUN Daytime is the part of a day between the time when it gets light and the time when it gets dark.

day-to-day ADJECTIVE happening every day as part of ordinary routine life.

day trip, day trips NOUN a journey for pleasure to a place and back again on the same day.

daze PHRASE If you are **in a daze**, you are confused and bewildered.

dazed ADJECTIVE If you are dazed, you are stunned and unable to think clearly.

dazzle, dazzles, dazzling, dazzled VERB ① If someone or something dazzles you, you are very impressed by their brilliance. ② If a bright light dazzles you, it blinds you for a moment. **dazzling** ADJECTIVE

de- PREFIX When 'de-' is added to a noun or verb, it changes the meaning to its opposite • *de-ice*.

deacon, deacons NOUN ① In the Church of England or Roman Catholic Church, a deacon is a member of the clergy below the rank of priest. ② In some other churches, a deacon is a church official appointed to help the minister. **deaconess** NOUN

dead ADJECTIVE ① no longer living or supporting life. ② no longer used or no longer functioning • *a dead language*. ③ If part of your body goes dead, it loses sensation and feels numb. ▶ PHRASE ④ **The dead of night** is the middle part of the night, when it is most quiet and dark.

dead end, dead ends NOUN a street that is closed off at one end.

deadline, deadlines NOUN a time or date before which something must be completed.

deadlock, deadlocks NOUN a situation in which neither side in a dispute is willing to give in.
SIMILAR WORDS: impasse, stalemate

deadly, deadlier, deadliest ADJECTIVE ① likely or able to cause death. ▶ ADVERB or ADJECTIVE ② 'Deadly' is used to emphasise how serious or unpleasant a situation is • *He is deadly serious about his comeback.*

deadpan ADJECTIVE or ADVERB showing no emotion or expression.

deaf, deafer, deafest ADJECTIVE ① partially or totally unable to hear. ② refusing to listen or pay attention to something • *He was deaf to all pleas for financial help.* **deafness** NOUN

deafen, deafens, deafening, deafened VERB If you are deafened by a noise, it is so loud that you cannot hear anything else.

deafening ADJECTIVE If a noise is deafening, it is so loud that you cannot hear anything else.

deal, deals, dealing, dealt NOUN ① an agreement or arrangement, especially in business. ▶ VERB ② If you deal with something, you do what is necessary to sort it out • *He must learn to deal with stress.* ③ If you deal in a particular type of goods, you buy and sell those goods. ④ If you deal someone or something a blow, you hurt or harm them • *Competition from abroad dealt a heavy blow to the industry.*

dealer, dealers NOUN a person or firm whose business involves buying or selling things.

dealings PLURAL NOUN Your dealings with people are the relations you have with them or the business you do with them.

dean, deans NOUN ① In a university or college, a dean is a person responsible for administration or for

the welfare of students. ② In the Church of England, a dean is a member of the clergy who is responsible for administration.
WORD HISTORY: from Latin *decanus* meaning 'someone in charge of ten people'

dear, dears; dearer, dearest NOUN ① 'Dear' is used as a sign of affection • *What's the matter, dear?* ▶ ADJECTIVE ② much loved • *my dear son*. ③ Something that is dear is expensive. ④ You use 'dear' at the beginning of a letter before the name of the person you are writing to.
dearly ADVERB
SIMILAR WORDS: ② beloved, cherished ③ costly, expensive

dearth [*Said* **derth**] NOUN a shortage of something.

death, deaths NOUN Death is the end of the life of a person or animal.

debacle, debacles [*Said* **day-bah-kl**] NOUN (*formal*) a sudden disastrous failure.

debase, debases, debasing, debased VERB To debase something means to reduce its value or quality.

debatable ADJECTIVE not absolutely certain • *The justness of these wars is debatable.*
SIMILAR WORDS: doubtful, questionable

debate, debates, debating, debated NOUN ① Debate is argument or discussion • *There is some debate as to what causes global warming.* ② CITIZENSHIP a formal discussion in which opposing views are expressed. ▶ VERB ③ When people debate something, they discuss it in a fairly formal manner. ④ If you are debating whether or not to do something, you are considering it • *He was debating whether or not he should tell her.*

debilitating ADJECTIVE (*formal*) If something is debilitating, it makes you very weak • *a debilitating illness*.

debit, debits, debiting, debited VERB ① to take money from a person's bank account. ▶ NOUN ② a record of the money that has been taken out of a person's bank account.

debrief, debriefs, debriefing, debriefed VERB When someone is debriefed, they are asked to give a report on a task they have just completed. **debriefing** NOUN

debris [*Said* **day-bree**] NOUN Debris is fragments or rubble left after something has been destroyed.
WORD HISTORY: from Old French *débriser* meaning 'to shatter'

debt, debts [*Said* **det**] NOUN ① a sum of money that is owed to one person by another. ② Debt is the state of owing money.

debtor, debtors NOUN a person who owes money.

debut, debuts [*Said* **day-byoo**] NOUN a performer's first public appearance.

debutante, debutantes [*Said* **deb-yoo-tant**] NOUN (*old-fashioned*) a girl from the upper classes who has started going to social events.

dec- or **deca-** PREFIX Words beginning with 'dec-' or 'deca-' have 'ten' in their meaning • *decathlon*.

decade, decades NOUN a period of ten years.

decadence NOUN Decadence is a decline in standards of morality and behaviour. **decadent** ADJECTIVE

decaffeinated [*Said* **dee-kaf-in-ate-ed**] ADJECTIVE Decaffeinated coffee or tea has had most of the caffeine removed.

decagon, decagons NOUN MATHS a shape with ten straight sides.

decanter, decanters NOUN a glass

a
b
c
d
e
f
g
h
i
j
k
l
m
n
o
p
q
r
s
t
u
v
w
x
y
z

bottle with a stopper, from which wine and other drinks are served.

decapitate, **decapitates**, **decapitating**, **decapitated** VERB To decapitate someone means to cut off their head.

decathlon, **decathlons** [Said de-*cath*-lon] NOUN a sports contest in which athletes compete in ten different events.
WORD HISTORY: from Greek *deka* meaning 'ten' and *athlon* meaning 'contest'

decay, **decays**, **decaying**, **decayed** VERB ① When things decay, they rot or go bad. ▶ NOUN ② Decay is the process of decaying.

deceased (*formal*) ADJECTIVE ① A deceased person is someone who has recently died. ▶ NOUN ② The deceased is someone who has recently died.

deceit NOUN Deceit is behaviour that is intended to make people believe something that is not true. **deceitful** ADJECTIVE

deceive, **deceives**, **deceiving**, **deceived** VERB If you deceive someone, you make them believe something that is not true.

decelerate, **decelerates**, **decelerating**, **decelerated** VERB If something decelerates, it slows down. **deceleration** NOUN

December NOUN December is the twelfth and last month of the year. It has 31 days.
WORD HISTORY: from Latin *December* meaning 'the tenth month'

decency NOUN ① Decency is behaviour that is respectable and follows accepted moral standards. ② Decency is also behaviour which shows kindness and respect towards people • *No one had the decency to tell me to my face.*

decent ADJECTIVE ① of an acceptable standard or quality • *She went to a decent school.* ② Decent people are honest and respectable • *a decent man.* **decently** ADVERB
SIMILAR WORDS: ② respectable

decentralise, **decentralises**, **decentralising**, **decentralised**; also spelt **decentralize** VERB To decentralise an organisation means to reorganise it so that power is transferred from one main administrative centre to smaller local units. **decentralisation** NOUN

deception, **deceptions** NOUN ① something that is intended to trick or deceive someone. ② Deception is the act of deceiving someone.

deceptive ADJECTIVE likely to make people believe something that is not true. **deceptively** ADVERB
SIMILAR WORDS: false, misleading

decibel, **decibels** NOUN SCIENCE a unit of the intensity of sound.

decide, **decides**, **deciding**, **decided** VERB If you decide to do something, you choose to do it.
SIMILAR WORDS: make up one's mind, reach a decision, come to a decision

deciduous ADJECTIVE Deciduous trees lose their leaves in the autumn every year.

decimal, **decimals** MATHS ADJECTIVE ① The decimal system expresses numbers using all the digits from 0 to 9. ▶ NOUN ② a fraction in which a dot called a decimal point is followed by numbers representing tenths, hundredths and thousandths. For example, 0.5 represents $5/10$ (or $1/2$); 0.05 represents $5/100$ (or $1/20$).

decimate, **decimates**, **decimating**, **decimated** VERB To decimate a group of people or animals means to kill or destroy a large number of them.

WORD HISTORY: from Latin *decimare*, from *decem* meaning 'ten'. In the Roman Army, mutiny was punished by the killing of every tenth man

decipher, deciphers, deciphering, deciphered VERB If you decipher a piece of writing or a message, you work out its meaning.

decision, decisions NOUN a choice or judgment that is made about something • *The editor's decision is final*.
SIMILAR WORDS: judgment, resolution

decisive *[Said dis-sigh-siv]* ADJECTIVE ① having great influence on the result of something • *It was the decisive moment of the race*. ② A decisive person is able to make decisions firmly and quickly.
decisively ADVERB **decisiveness** NOUN

deck, decks NOUN ① a floor or platform built into a ship, or one of the two floors on a bus. ② a pack of cards.

deck chair, deck chairs NOUN a light folding chair, usually made from canvas and wood, used outdoors.

declaration, declarations NOUN a firm, forceful statement, often an official announcement • *a declaration of war*.
SIMILAR WORDS: assertion, statement

declare, declares, declaring, declared VERB ① If you declare something, you state it forcefully or officially. ② If you declare goods or earnings, you state what you have bought or earned, in order to pay tax or duty.
SIMILAR WORDS: ① announce, proclaim, state

decline, declines, declining, declined VERB ① If something

declines, it becomes smaller or weaker. ② If you decline something, you politely refuse to accept it or do it. ▶ NOUN ③ a gradual weakening or decrease • *a decline in the birth rate*.

decode, decodes, decoding, decoded VERB If you decode a coded message, you convert it into ordinary language. **decoder** NOUN

decommission, decommissions, decommissioning, decommissioned VERB When something such as a nuclear reactor or large machine is decommissioned, it is taken to pieces or removed from service because it is no longer going to be used.

decompose, decomposes, decomposing, decomposed VERB
[SCIENCE] If something decomposes, it decays through chemical or bacterial action. **decomposition** NOUN

decor *[Said day-kor]* NOUN The decor of a room or house is the style in which it is decorated and furnished.

decorate, decorates, decorating, decorated VERB ① If you decorate something, you make it more attractive by adding some ornament or colour to it. ② If you decorate a room or building, you paint or wallpaper it.
SIMILAR WORDS: ① adorn, ornament

decoration, decorations NOUN ① Decorations are features added to something to make it more attractive. ② The decoration in a building or room is the style of the furniture and wallpaper.

decorative ADJECTIVE intended to look attractive.

decorator, decorators NOUN a person whose job is painting and putting up wallpaper in rooms and buildings.

a b c d e f g h i j k l m n o p q r s t u v w x y z

decorum [Said dik-*ore*-um] NOUN
(*formal*) Decorum is polite and correct
behaviour.

decoy, decoys NOUN a person or
object that is used to lead someone
or something into danger.

decrease, decreases, decreasing,
decreased VERB ① If something
decreases or if you decrease it, it
becomes less in quantity or size.
▶ NOUN ② a lessening in the amount
of something; also the amount by
which something becomes less.
decreasing ADJECTIVE

decree, decrees, decreeing, decreed
VERB ① If someone decrees
something, they state formally that
it will happen. ▶ NOUN ② an official
decision or order, usually by
governments or rulers.

decrepit ADJECTIVE broken or worn
out by use or old age. **decrepitude**
NOUN

decrescendo, decrescendos [Said
day-krish-*en*-doe] NOUN MUSIC
When there is a decrescendo in a
piece of music, the music gets
quieter.

decriminalise, decriminalises,
decriminalising, decriminalised;
also spelt **decriminalize** VERB To
decriminalise something illegal is to
change the law so that it is no longer
illegal.

dedicate, dedicates, dedicating,
dedicated VERB If you dedicate
yourself to something, you devote
your time and energy to it.
dedication NOUN
SIMILAR WORDS: commit,
devote

deduce, deduces, deducing,
deduced VERB If you deduce
something, you work it out from
other facts that you know are true.
SIMILAR WORDS: conclude, reason

deduct, deducts, deducting,
deducted VERB To deduct an
amount from a total amount means
to subtract it from the total.

deduction, deductions NOUN ① an
amount which is taken away from a
total. ② a conclusion that you have
reached because of other things that
you know are true.

deed, deeds NOUN ① something that
is done. ② a legal document,
especially concerning the ownership
of land or buildings.

deem, deems, deeming, deemed
VERB (*formal*) If you deem something
to be true, you judge or consider it to
be true • *His ideas were deemed
unacceptable.*

deep, deeper, deepest ADJECTIVE
① situated or extending a long way
down from the top surface of
something, or a long way inwards • *a
deep hole.* ② great or intense • *deep
suspicion.* ③ low in pitch • *a deep voice.*
④ strong and fairly dark in colour
• *The juice was deep orange in colour.*
deeply ADVERB

deepen, deepens, deepening,
deepened VERB If something
deepens or is deepened, it becomes
deeper or more intense.

deer, deer NOUN a large, hoofed
mammal that lives wild in parts of
Britain.

deface, defaces, defacing, defaced
VERB If you deface a wall or notice,
you spoil it by writing or drawing on
it • *She spitefully defaced her sister's
poster.*

default, defaults, defaulting,
defaulted VERB ① If someone
defaults on something they have
legally agreed to do, they fail to do it
• *He defaulted on repayment of the loan.*
▶ PHRASE ② If something happens
by default, it happens because

something else which might have prevented it has failed to happen.

defeat, defeats, defeating, defeated VERB ① If you defeat someone or something, you win a victory over them, or cause them to fail. ▶ NOUN ② the state of being beaten or of failing or an occasion on which someone is beaten or fails to achieve something • *He was gracious in defeat*.

defecate, defecates, defecating, defecated VERB To defecate means to get rid of waste matter from the bowels through the anus.

defect, defects, defecting, defected NOUN ① a fault or flaw in something. ▶ VERB ② If someone defects, they leave their own country or organisation and join an opposing one. **defection** NOUN

defective ADJECTIVE imperfect or faulty • *defective eyesight*.

defence, defences NOUN ① Defence is action that is taken to protect someone or something from attack. ② any arguments used in support of something that has been criticised or questioned. ③ the case presented, in a court of law, by a lawyer for the person on trial; also the person on trial and his or her lawyers. ④ HISTORY A country's defences are its military resources, such as its armed forces and weapons.

defend, defends, defending, defended VERB ① To defend someone or something means to protect them from harm or danger. ② If you defend a person or their ideas and beliefs, you argue in support of them. ③ To defend someone in court means to represent them and argue their case for them. ④ In a game such as football or hockey, to defend means to try to prevent goals being scored by your opponents.

defendant, defendants NOUN a person who has been accused of a crime in a court of law.

defender, defenders NOUN ① a person who protects someone or something from harm or danger. ② a person who argues in support of something. ③ a person who tries to stop goals being scored in certain sports.

defensible ADJECTIVE able to be defended against criticism or attack.

defensive ADJECTIVE ① intended or designed for protection • *defensive weapons*. ② Someone who is defensive feels unsure and threatened by other people's opinions and attitudes • *Don't get defensive, I was only joking about your cooking*. **defensively** ADVERB **defensiveness** NOUN

defer, defers, deferring, deferred VERB ① If you defer something, you delay or postpone it until a future time. ② If you defer to someone, you agree with them or do what they want because you respect them.

deference [Said *def-er-enss*] NOUN Deference is polite and respectful behaviour. **deferential** ADJECTIVE **deferentially** ADVERB

defiance NOUN Defiance is behaviour which shows that you are not willing to obey or behave in the expected way • *a gesture of defiance*. **defiant** ADJECTIVE **defiantly** ADVERB

deficiency, deficiencies NOUN a lack of something • *vitamin deficiency*.

deficient ADJECTIVE lacking in something.

deficit, deficits [Said *def-iss-it*] NOUN the amount by which money received by an organisation is less than money spent.

define, defines, defining, defined VERB EXAM TERM If you define something, you say clearly what it is or what it means • *Culture can be defined in hundreds of ways.*

definite ADJECTIVE ① firm and unlikely to be changed • *The answer is a definite 'yes'.* ② certain or true rather than guessed or imagined • *definite proof.* **definitely** ADVERB

SPELLING TIP

There is no *a* in *definite* or *definitely*. Remember this mnemonic: *inFINITy is deFINITe*.

---

definite article, definite articles NOUN the grammatical term for 'the'.

definition, definitions NOUN a statement explaining the meaning of a word or idea.

definitive ADJECTIVE ① final and unable to be questioned or altered • *a definitive answer.* ② most complete, or the best of its kind • *a definitive history of science fiction.* **definitively** ADVERB

deflate, deflates, deflating, deflated VERB ① If you deflate something such as a tyre or balloon, you let out all the air or gas in it. ② If you deflate someone, you make them seem less important.

deflation NOUN Deflation is a reduction in economic activity that leads to lower levels of industrial output, trade, investment and prices.

deflect, deflects, deflecting, deflected VERB To deflect something means to turn it aside or make it change direction. **deflection** NOUN

deforestation NOUN GEOGRAPHY Deforestation is the cutting down of all the trees in an area.

deform, deforms, deforming, deformed VERB To deform something means to put it out of shape or spoil its appearance

• *Badly fitting shoes can deform the feet.* **deformity** NOUN

deformed ADJECTIVE disfigured or abnormally shaped.

defraud, defrauds, defrauding, defrauded VERB If someone defrauds you, they cheat you out of something that should be yours.

defrost, defrosts, defrosting, defrosted VERB ① If you defrost a freezer or refrigerator, you remove the ice from it. ② If you defrost frozen food, you let it thaw out.

deft, defter, deftest ADJECTIVE Someone who is deft is quick and skilful in their movements. **deftly** ADVERB

defunct ADJECTIVE no longer existing or functioning.

defuse, defuses, defusing, defused VERB ① To defuse a dangerous or tense situation means to make it less dangerous or tense. ② To defuse a bomb means to remove its fuse or detonator so that it cannot explode.

SPELLING TIP

Do not confuse the spellings of *defuse* and *diffuse*: *The soldiers learn how to defuse bombs; The wind made the gas diffuse over many miles.*

---

defy, defies, defying, defied VERB ① If you defy a person or a law, you openly refuse to obey. ② (*formal*) If you defy someone to do something that you think is impossible, you challenge them to do it.

SIMILAR WORDS: ① disregard, flout, resist

degenerate, degenerates, degenerating, degenerated VERB [Said de-**jen**-er-ate] ① If something degenerates, it becomes worse • *The election campaign degenerated into farce.* ▸ ADJECTIVE [Said de-**jen**-e-rit] ② having low standards of morality.

▶ NOUN [Said de-jen-e-rit] ③ someone whose standards of morality are so low that people find their behaviour shocking or disgusting.
degeneration NOUN

degradation NOUN Degradation is a state of poverty and misery.

degrade, degrades, degrading, degraded VERB If something degrades people, it humiliates them and makes them feel that they are not respected. **degrading** ADJECTIVE
SIMILAR WORDS: debase, demean

degree, degrees NOUN ① an amount of a feeling or quality • *a degree of pain*. ② SCIENCE a unit of measurement of temperature; often written as ° after a number • 20°C. ③ MATHS a unit of measurement of angles in mathematics, and of latitude and longitude • *The yacht was 20° off course*. ④ a course of study at a university or college; also the qualification awarded after passing the course.

dehydrate, dehydrates, dehydrating, dehydrated VERB ① If something is dehydrated, water is removed or lost from it. ② If someone is dehydrated, they are weak or ill because they have lost too much water from their body. **dehydrated** ADJECTIVE **dehydration** NOUN

deign, deigns, deigning, deigned [Said dane] VERB (formal) If you deign to do something, you do it even though you think you are too important to do such a thing.

deity, deities NOUN a god or goddess.

deja vu [Said day-ja voo] NOUN Deja vu is the feeling that you have already experienced in the past exactly the same sequence of events as is happening now.
WORD HISTORY: from French déjà vu meaning 'already seen'

dejected ADJECTIVE miserable and unhappy. **dejectedly** ADVERB **dejection** NOUN

delay, delays, delaying, delayed VERB ① If you delay doing something, you put it off until a later time. ② If something delays you, it hinders you or slows you down: ▶ NOUN ③ Delay is time during which something is delayed.
SIMILAR WORDS: ① postpone, put off

delectable ADJECTIVE very pleasing or delightful.

delegate, delegates, delegating, delegated NOUN ① a person appointed to vote or to make decisions on behalf of a group of people. ▶ VERB ② If you delegate duties, you give them to someone who can then act on your behalf.

delegation, delegations NOUN ① a group of people chosen to represent a larger group of people. ② Delegation is the giving of duties, responsibilities or power to someone who can then act on your behalf.

delete, deletes, deleting, deleted VERB ICT To delete something means to cross it out or remove it • *He had deleted the computer file by mistake*. **deletion** NOUN

deliberate, deliberates, deliberating, deliberated ADJECTIVE [Said di-lib-er-it] ① done on purpose or planned in advance • *It was a deliberate insult*. ② careful and not hurried in speech and action • *She was very deliberate in her movements*. ▶ VERB [Said di-lib-er-ayt] ③ If you deliberate about something, you think about it seriously and carefully. **deliberately** ADVERB
SIMILAR WORDS: ① intentional, planned

deliberation, deliberations NOUN Deliberation is careful consideration of a subject.

a b c d e f g h i j k l m n o p q r s t u v w x y z

delicacy, delicacies NOUN
① Delicacy is grace and attractiveness. ② Something said or done with delicacy is said or done tactfully so that nobody is offended. ③ Delicacies are rare or expensive foods that are considered especially nice to eat.

delicate ADJECTIVE ① fine, graceful or subtle in character • *a delicate fragrance*. ② fragile and needing to be handled carefully • *delicate antique lace*. ③ precise or sensitive, and able to notice very small changes • *a delicate instrument*. **delicately** ADVERB

delicatessen, delicatessens NOUN a shop selling unusual or imported foods.

WORD HISTORY: from German *Delikatessen* meaning 'delicacies'

delicious ADJECTIVE very pleasing, especially to taste. **deliciously** ADVERB

SIMILAR WORDS: delectable, scrumptious

delight, delights, delighting, delighted NOUN ① Delight is great pleasure or joy. ▶ VERB ② If something delights you or if you are delighted by it, it gives you a lot of pleasure. **delighted** ADJECTIVE

delightful ADJECTIVE very pleasant and attractive. **delightfully** ADVERB

delinquent, delinquents NOUN a young person who commits minor crimes. **delinquency** NOUN

delirious ADJECTIVE ① unable to speak or act in a rational way because of illness or fever. ② wildly excited and happy. **deliriously** ADVERB

deliver, delivers, delivering, delivered VERB ① If you deliver something to someone, you take it to them and give them it. ② To deliver a lecture or speech means to give it.

delivery, deliveries NOUN ① Delivery or a delivery is the bringing of letters or goods to a person or firm. ② Someone's delivery is the way in which they give a speech.

dell, dells NOUN (*literary*) a small wooded valley.

delta, deltas NOUN GEOGRAPHY a low, flat area at the mouth of a river where the river has split into several branches to enter the sea.

delude, deludes, deluding, deluded VERB To delude people means to deceive them into believing something that is not true.

deluge, deluges, deluging, deluged NOUN ① a sudden, heavy downpour of rain. ▶ VERB ② To be deluged with things means to be overwhelmed by a great number of them.

delusion, delusions NOUN a mistaken or misleading belief or idea.

de luxe [*Said de luks*] ADJECTIVE rich, luxurious or of superior quality.

delve, delves, delving, delved VERB If you delve into something, you seek out more information about it.

demand, demands, demanding, demanded VERB ① If you demand something, you ask for it forcefully and urgently. ② If a job or situation demands a particular quality, it needs it • *This situation demands hard work*. ▶ NOUN ③ a forceful request for something. ④ If there is a demand for something, a lot of people want to buy it or have it.

GRAMMAR TIP
The verb *demand* is either followed by *of* or *from*: *At least one important decision was demanded of me; He had demanded an explanation from Daphne.*

demean, demeans, demeaning,

demeaned VERB If you demean yourself, you do something which makes people have less respect for you. **demeaning** ADJECTIVE

demeanour NOUN Your demeanour is the way you behave and the impression that this creates.

demented ADJECTIVE Someone who is demented behaves in a wild or violent way.

dementia [Said dee-**men**-sha] NOUN Dementia is a serious illness of the brain that affects people's ability to think clearly and remember things.

demerara sugar NOUN a type of brown cane sugar originally from Guyana.

demi- PREFIX 'Demi-' means 'half'.

demise [Said dee-**myz**] NOUN (formal) Someone's demise is their death.

demo, demos NOUN (informal) a demonstration.

democracy, democracies NOUN CITIZENSHIP Democracy is a system of government in which the people choose their leaders by voting for them in elections.

democrat, democrats NOUN a person who believes in democracy, personal freedom and equality.

democratic ADJECTIVE having representatives elected by the people. **democratically** ADVERB WORD HISTORY: from Greek dēmos meaning 'the people' and kratos meaning 'power'

demography NOUN Demography is the study of the changes in the size and structure of populations. **demographic** ADJECTIVE

demolish, demolishes, demolishing, demolished VERB To demolish a building means to pull it down or break it up. **demolition** NOUN

demon, demons NOUN ① an evil spirit or devil. ▸ ADJECTIVE ② skilful, keen and energetic • a demon squash player. **demonic** ADJECTIVE

demonstrate, demonstrates, demonstrating, demonstrated VERB ① EXAM TERM To demonstrate a fact or theory means to prove or show it to be true. ② If you demonstrate something to somebody, you show and explain it by using or doing the thing itself • She demonstrated how to apply the make-up. ③ If people demonstrate, they take part in a march or rally to show their opposition or support for something.

demonstration, demonstrations NOUN ① a talk or explanation to show how to do or use something. ② Demonstration is proof that something exists or is true. ③ a public march or rally in support of or opposition to something. **demonstrator** NOUN

demoralise, demoralises, demoralising, demoralised; also spelt **demoralize** VERB If something demoralises someone, it makes them feel depressed and lose their confidence.

demote, demotes, demoting, demoted VERB A person who is demoted is put in a lower rank or position, often as a punishment. **demotion** NOUN

demure ADJECTIVE Someone who is demure is quiet and shy and behaves very modestly. **demurely** ADVERB

den, dens NOUN ① the home of some wild animals such as lions or foxes. ② a secret place where people meet.

denial, denials NOUN ① A denial of something is a statement that it is untrue • He published a firm denial of the report. ② The denial of a request

a
b
c
d
e
f
g
h
i
j
k
l
m
n
o
p
q
r
s
t
u
v
w
x
y
z

or something to which you have a right is the refusal of it • *the denial of human rights*.

denigrate, denigrates, denigrating, denigrated VERB *(formal)* To denigrate someone or something means to criticise them in order to damage their reputation.

denim, denims NOUN ① Denim is strong cotton cloth, used for making clothes. ② *(in plural)* Denims are jeans made from denim.
WORD HISTORY: from French *serge de Nîmes*, meaning 'serge (a type of cloth) from Nîmes'

denomination, denominations NOUN ① a particular group which has slightly different religious beliefs from other groups within the same faith. ② a unit in a system of weights, values or measures • *bank notes of different denominations*.

denominator, denominators NOUN MATHS In maths, the denominator is the bottom part of a fraction.

denote, denotes, denoting, denoted VERB If one thing denotes another, it is a sign of it or it represents it • *Red eyes denote tiredness*.

denouement, denouements *[Said day-noo-mon]* NOUN ENGLISH The denouement of a story is the explanation at the end of it of something that has previously been unclear or kept secret.

denounce, denounces, denouncing, denounced VERB ① If you denounce someone or something, you express very strong disapproval of them • *He publicly denounced government nuclear policy*. ② If you denounce someone, you give information against them • *He was denounced as a dangerous agitator*.

dense, denser, densest ADJECTIVE ① thickly crowded or packed together • *the dense crowd*. ② difficult to see through • *dense black smoke*.
densely ADVERB

density, densities NOUN ① the degree to which something is filled or occupied • *a very high population density*. ② SCIENCE The density of a substance is its compactness, measured by the relation of its mass to its volume.

dent, dents, denting, dented VERB ① To dent something means to damage it by hitting it and making a hollow in its surface. ▶ NOUN ② a hollow in the surface of something.

dental ADJECTIVE relating to the teeth.

dentist, dentists NOUN a person who is qualified to treat people's teeth.

dentistry NOUN Dentistry is the branch of medicine concerned with disorders of the teeth.

dentures PLURAL NOUN Dentures are false teeth.

denunciation, denunciations NOUN A denunciation of someone or something is severe public criticism of them.

deny, denies, denying, denied VERB ① If you deny something that has been said, you state that it is untrue. ② If you deny that something is the case, you refuse to believe it • *He denied the existence of God*. ③ If you deny someone something, you refuse to give it to them • *They were denied permission to attend*.
SIMILAR WORDS: ① contradict, gainsay

deodorant, deodorants NOUN a substance or spray used to hide the smell of sweat.

depart, departs, departing, departed VERB When you depart, you leave. **departure** NOUN

department, departments NOUN
one of the sections into which an
organisation is divided • *the art
department*. **departmental**
ADJECTIVE

depend, depends, depending,
depended VERB ① If you depend on
someone or something, you trust
them and rely on them. ② If one
thing depends on another, it is
influenced by it • *Success depends on
how hard you work*.
SIMILAR WORDS: ① count on, rely on,
trust

dependable ADJECTIVE reliable and
trustworthy.

dependant, dependants NOUN
PSHE someone who relies on
another person for financial support.

SPELLING TIP
Do not confuse the spellings of the
noun *dependant* and the adjective
dependent: *Do you have children or other
dependants?*; *The flood victims are
dependent on aid*.

---

dependence NOUN Dependence is a
constant need that someone has for
something or someone in order to
survive or operate properly • *She was
frustrated by her dependence on her
sister*.

dependency, dependencies NOUN
① PSHE Dependency is relying on
someone or something to give you
what you need • *drug dependency*. ② a
country or area controlled by another
country.

dependent ADJECTIVE reliant on
someone or something.

SPELLING TIP
Do not confuse the spellings of the
adjective *dependent* and the noun
dependant: *The flood victims are
dependent on aid; Do you have children
or other dependants?*

---

dependent variable, dependent
variables NOUN SCIENCE a variable
in a mathematical equation whose
value depends on the value taken on
by another variable. For example, in
the equation $x = y+1$, x is the
dependent variable as it depends on
the value of y.

depict, depicts, depicting, depicted
VERB To depict someone or
something means to represent them
in painting or sculpture. **depiction**
NOUN

deplete, depletes, depleting,
depleted VERB To deplete something
means to reduce greatly the amount
of it available. **depletion** NOUN

deplorable ADJECTIVE shocking or
regrettable • *deplorable conditions*.

deplore, deplores, deploring,
deplored VERB If you deplore
something, you condemn it because
you feel it is wrong.

deploy, deploys, deploying,
deployed VERB To deploy troops or
resources means to organise or
position them so that they can be
used effectively. **deployment** NOUN

depopulation NOUN GEOGRAPHY
Depopulation is when the
population of an area or town is
reduced • *the depopulation of rural
areas*.

deport, deports, deporting,
deported VERB If a government
deports someone, it sends them out
of the country because they have
committed a crime or because they
do not have the right to be there.
deportation NOUN

depose, deposes, deposing,
deposed VERB If someone is
deposed, they are removed from a
position of power.

deposit, deposits, depositing,
deposited VERB ① If you deposit

a
b
c
d
e
f
g
h
i
j
k
l
m
n
o
p
q
r
s
t
u
v
w
x
y
z

something, you put it down or leave it somewhere. ②If you deposit money or valuables, you put them somewhere for safekeeping. ③ GEOGRAPHY If something is deposited on a surface, a layer of it is left there as a result of chemical or geological action. ▸NOUN ④a sum of money given in part payment for goods or services. ⑤ GEOGRAPHY an underground accumulation of ores, coal, etc • *massive gold deposits*.

deposition, depositions NOUN ① GEOGRAPHY Deposition is the geological process which causes layers of minerals to be formed in the ground by the action of wind, waves, rivers or ice. ②A deposition is a formal written statement of evidence, given under oath.

depot, depots [*Said dep-oh*] NOUN a place where large supplies of materials or equipment may be stored.

depraved ADJECTIVE morally bad.

depress, depresses, depressing, depressed VERB ①If something depresses you, it makes you feel sad and gloomy. ②If wages or prices are depressed, their value falls.

depressive ADJECTIVE

depressant, depressants NOUN a drug which reduces nervous activity and so has a calming effect.

depressed ADJECTIVE ①unhappy and gloomy. ②A place that is depressed has little economic activity and therefore low incomes and high unemployment • *depressed industrial areas*.

SIMILAR WORDS: ①dejected, despondent, low-spirited

depression, depressions NOUN ①a state of mind in which someone feels unhappy and has no energy or enthusiasm. ②a time of industrial and economic decline. ③ GEOGRAPHY In meteorology, a depression is a mass of air that has low pressure and brings cloud, wind and rain. ④ GEOGRAPHY A depression in the surface of something is a part which is lower than the rest.

deprive, deprives, depriving, deprived VERB If you deprive someone of something, you take it away or prevent them from having it.

deprived ADJECTIVE **deprivation** NOUN

depth, depths NOUN ①The depth of something is the measurement or distance between its top and bottom, or between its front and back. ②The depth of something such as emotion is its intensity • *the depth of her hostility*.

deputation, deputations NOUN a small group of people sent to speak or act on behalf of others.

deputy, deputies NOUN Someone's deputy is a person appointed to act in their place.

deranged ADJECTIVE behaving in a wild and uncontrolled way.

derby, derbies [*Said dar-bee*] NOUN A local derby is a sporting event between two teams from the same area.

derelict ADJECTIVE abandoned and falling into ruins.

deride, derides, deriding, derided VERB To deride someone or something means to mock or jeer at them with contempt.

derision NOUN Derision is an attitude of contempt or scorn towards something or someone.

derivation, derivations NOUN The derivation of something is its origin or source.

derivative, derivatives NOUN
① something which has developed from an earlier source. ▶ ADJECTIVE ② not original, but based on or copied from something else • *The record was not deliberately derivative.*

derive, derives, deriving, derived VERB ① (*formal*) If you derive something from someone or something, you get it from them • *He derived so much joy from music.* ② If something derives from something else, it develops from it.

derogatory ADJECTIVE critical and scornful • *He made derogatory remarks about them.*

descant, descants NOUN MUSIC The descant to a tune is another tune played at the same time and at a higher pitch.

descend, descends, descending, descended VERB ① To descend means to move downwards. ② If you descend on people or on a place, you arrive unexpectedly.

descendant, descendants NOUN A person's descendants are the people in later generations who are related to them.

descended ADJECTIVE If you are descended from someone who lived in the past, your family originally derived from them.

descent, descents NOUN ① a movement or slope from a higher to a lower position or level. ② Your descent is your family's origins.

describe, describes, describing, described VERB To describe someone or something means to give an account or a picture of them in words.

description, descriptions NOUN an account or picture of something in words. **descriptive** ADJECTIVE

desert¹, deserts [*Said dez-ert*] NOUN GEOGRAPHY a region of land with very little plant life, usually because of low rainfall.

desert², deserts, deserting, deserted [*Said dez-zert*] VERB To desert a person means to leave or abandon them • *His friends had deserted him.* **desertion** NOUN

SPELLING TIP

Do not confuse the spellings of *desert* and *dessert*: *The residents are ready to desert the city; What would you like for dessert?*

---

deserter, deserters NOUN someone who leaves the armed forces without permission.

deserve, deserves, deserving, deserved VERB If you deserve something, you are entitled to it or earn it because of your qualities, achievements or actions • *He deserved a rest.*
SIMILAR WORDS: be worthy of, justify, merit

deserving ADJECTIVE worthy of being helped, rewarded or praised • *a deserving charity.*

design, designs, designing, designed DGT VERB ① To design something means to plan it, especially by preparing a detailed sketch or drawings from which it can be built or made. ▶ NOUN ② a drawing or plan from which something can be built or made. ③ The design of something is its shape and style. **designer** NOUN

designate, designates, designating, designated [*Said dez-ig-nate*] VERB ① To designate someone or something means to formally label or name them • *The cathedral was designated a World Heritage site.* ② If you designate someone to do something, you appoint them to do it • *He designated his son as his successor.*

designation, designations NOUN a name or title.

designing ADJECTIVE crafty and cunning.

desirable ADJECTIVE worth having or doing • *a desirable job*. **desirability** NOUN

desire, desires, desiring, desired VERB ① If you desire something, you want it very much. ▸ NOUN ② a strong feeling of wanting something.
SIMILAR WORDS: ① long for, want, wish for ② longing, want, wish

desist, desists, desisting, desisted VERB (*formal*) To desist from doing something means to stop doing it.

desk, desks NOUN ① a piece of furniture designed for working at or writing on. ② a counter or table in a public building behind which a receptionist sits.

desktop ADJECTIVE of a convenient size to be used on a desk or table • *a desktop computer*.

desolate ADJECTIVE ① deserted and bleak • *a desolate mountainous region*. ② lonely, very sad, and without hope • *He was desolate without her*. **desolation** NOUN

despair, despairs, despairing, despaired NOUN ① Despair is a total loss of hope. ▸ VERB ② If you despair, you lose hope • *He despaired of finishing it*. **despairing** ADJECTIVE
SIMILAR WORDS: ① desperation, hopelessness

despatch another spelling of **dispatch**.

desperate ADJECTIVE ① If you are desperate, you are so worried or frightened that you will try anything to improve your situation • *a desperate attempt to win*. ② A desperate person is violent and dangerous. ③ A desperate situation is extremely dangerous or serious.

desperately ADVERB **desperation** NOUN

despicable ADJECTIVE deserving contempt.

despise, despises, despising, despised VERB If you despise someone or something, you dislike them very much.

despite PREPOSITION in spite of • *He fell asleep despite all the coffee he'd drunk*.
SIMILAR WORDS: in spite of, regardless of

despondent ADJECTIVE dejected and unhappy. **despondency** NOUN

despot, despots NOUN A despot is a ruler with total power, who uses it cruelly.

dessert, desserts [*Said diz-ert*] NOUN a sweet food served after the main course of a meal.
WORD HISTORY: from French *desservir* meaning 'to clear the table after a meal'

SPELLING TIP
Do not confuse the spellings of *dessert* and *desert*: *What would you like for dessert?*; *The residents are ready to desert the city*.

---

destination, destinations NOUN a place to which someone or something is going or is being sent.

destined ADJECTIVE meant or intended to happen • *I was destined for fame and fortune*.

destiny, destinies NOUN ① Your destiny is all the things that happen to you in your life, especially when they are considered to be outside human control. ② Destiny is the force which some people believe controls everyone's life.

destitute ADJECTIVE without money or possessions, and therefore in great need. **destitution** NOUN

destroy, destroys, destroying, destroyed VERB ①To destroy something means to damage it so much that it is completely ruined. ②To destroy something means to put an end to it • *The holiday destroyed their friendship.*
SIMILAR WORDS: ① demolish, ruin, wreck

destruction NOUN Destruction is the act of destroying something or the state of being destroyed.
SIMILAR WORDS: devastation, ruin

destructive ADJECTIVE causing or able to cause great harm, damage or injury. **destructiveness** NOUN

desultory [*Said dez-ul-tree*] ADJECTIVE passing from one thing to another in a fitful or random way • *A desultory, embarrassed chatter began again.*
desultorily ADVERB

detach, detaches, detaching, detached VERB To detach something means to remove it • *The hood can be detached.* **detachable** ADJECTIVE

detached ADJECTIVE ① separate or standing apart • *a detached house.* ② having no real interest or emotional involvement in something • *He observed me with a detached curiosity.*

detachment, detachments NOUN ① Detachment is the feeling of not being personally involved with something • *A stranger can view your problems with detachment.* ② a small group of soldiers sent to do a special job.

detail, details NOUN ① an individual fact or feature of something • *We discussed every detail of the performance.* ② Detail is all the small features that make up the whole of something • *Look at the detail.*
detailed ADJECTIVE

detain, detains, detaining, detained VERB ①To detain someone means to force them to stay • *She was being detained for interrogation.* ② If you detain someone, you delay them • *I mustn't detain you.*

detect, detects, detecting, detected VERB ① If you detect something, you notice it • *I detected a glimmer of interest in his eyes.* ②To detect something means to find it • *Bone injuries can be detected by X-rays.*
detectable ADJECTIVE

detection NOUN ① Detection is the act of noticing, discovering or sensing something. ② Detection is also the work of investigating crime.

detective, detectives NOUN a person, usually a police officer, whose job is to investigate crimes.

detector, detectors NOUN an instrument which is used to detect the presence of something • *a metal detector.*

detention NOUN The detention of someone is their arrest or imprisonment.

deter, deters, deterring, deterred VERB To deter someone means to discourage or prevent them from doing something by creating a feeling of fear or doubt • *Many burglars are deterred by the sight of an alarm box.*

detergent, detergents NOUN a chemical substance used for washing or cleaning things.

deteriorate, deteriorates, deteriorating, deteriorated VERB If something deteriorates, it gets worse • *My father's health has deteriorated lately.* **deterioration** NOUN

determination NOUN Determination is great firmness, after you have made up your mind to do something • *They shared a determination to win the war.*

a
b
c
d
e
f
g
h
i
j
k
l
m
n
o
p
q
r
s
t
u
v
w
x
y
z

determine, determines, determining, **determined** VERB ① If something determines a situation or result, it causes it or controls it • *The track surface determines his tactics in a race.* ② To determine something means to decide or settle it firmly • *The date has still to be determined.* ③ To determine something means to find out or calculate the facts about it • *He bit the coin to determine whether it was genuine.*
SIMILAR WORDS: ② decide, settle ③ ascertain, find out, verify

determined ADJECTIVE firmly decided • *She was determined not to repeat her error.* **determinedly** ADVERB
SIMILAR WORDS: intent on, resolute

determiner, determiners NOUN
ENGLISH | MFL a word that can go before a noun or noun group to show, for instance, which thing you are referring to or whether you are referring to one thing or several. For example, in 'my house', 'the windows', 'this red book' and 'each time', 'my', 'the', 'this' and 'each' can be called determiners.

deterrent, deterrents NOUN something that prevents you from doing something by making you afraid of what will happen if you do it • *The cameras act as a deterrent to would-be thieves.* **deterrence** NOUN

detest, detests, detesting, detested VERB If you detest someone or something, you strongly dislike them.

detonate, detonates, detonating, detonated VERB To detonate a bomb or mine means to cause it to explode. **detonator** NOUN

detour, detours NOUN an alternative, less direct route.

detract, detracts, detracting,

detracted VERB To detract from something means to make it seem less good or valuable.

detriment NOUN Detriment is disadvantage or harm • *a detriment to their health.* **detrimental** ADJECTIVE

deuce, deuces [Said *joos*] NOUN In tennis, deuce is the score of forty all.

devalue, devalues, devaluing, devalued VERB To devalue something means to lower its status, importance or worth. **devaluation** NOUN

devastate, devastates, devastating, devastated VERB To devastate an area or place means to damage it severely or destroy it. **devastation** NOUN

devastated ADJECTIVE very shocked or upset • *The family are devastated by the news.*

develop, develops, developing, developed VERB ① When something develops or is developed, it grows or becomes more advanced • *The sneezing developed into a full-blown cold.* ② To develop an area of land means to build on it. ③ To develop an illness or a fault means to become affected by it.

developer, developers NOUN a person or company that builds on land.

development, developments NOUN ① Development is gradual growth or progress. ② The development of land or water is the process of making it more useful or profitable by the expansion of industry or housing • *the development of the old docks.* ③ a new stage in a series of events • *developments in technology.* **developmental** ADJECTIVE

deviant, deviants ADJECTIVE ① Deviant behaviour is unacceptable or different from what people consider as normal. ▸ NOUN ② someone whose behaviour or beliefs are different from what people consider to be acceptable. **deviance** NOUN

deviate, deviates, deviating, deviated VERB To deviate means to differ or depart from what is usual or acceptable. **deviation** NOUN

device, devices NOUN ① a machine or tool that is used for a particular purpose • *a device to warn you when the batteries need changing.* ② a plan or scheme • *a device to pressurise him into selling.*

SPELLING TIP

Do not confuse the spellings of the noun *device* and the verb *devise: a device for picking up litter; They need to devise a new plan to deal with unemployment.*

---

devil, devils NOUN ① RE In Christianity and Judaism, the Devil is the spirit of evil and enemy of God. ② an evil spirit.

devious ADJECTIVE insincere and dishonest. **deviousness** NOUN

devise, devises, devising, devised VERB To devise something means to work it out • *Besides diets, he devised punishing exercise routines.*

SPELLING TIP

The verb *devise* is spelt with an s and the noun *device* is spelt with a c.

---

devoid ADJECTIVE lacking in a particular thing or quality • *His glance was devoid of expression.*

devolution NOUN Devolution is the transfer of power from a central government or organisation to local government departments or smaller organisations.

devote, devotes, devoting, devoted VERB If you devote yourself to something, you give all your time, energy or money to it • *She has devoted herself to women's causes.*

devoted ADJECTIVE very loving and loyal.

devotee, devotees NOUN a fanatical or enthusiastic follower of something.

devotion NOUN Devotion to someone or something is great love or affection for them. **devotional** ADJECTIVE

devour, devours, devouring, devoured VERB If you devour something, you eat it hungrily or greedily.

devout ADJECTIVE deeply and sincerely religious • *a devout Buddhist.* **devoutly** ADVERB

dew NOUN Dew is drops of moisture that form on the ground and other cool surfaces at night.

dexterity NOUN Dexterity is skill or agility in using your hands or mind • *He had learned to use the crutches with dexterity.* **dexterous** ADJECTIVE

dharma [Said *dar-ma*] NOUN ① RE In the Buddhist religion, dharma is ideal truth as set out in the teaching of the Buddha. ② RE In the Hindu religion, dharma is the moral law that Hindus should follow.

WORD HISTORY: a Sanskrit word

diabetes [Said *dy-a-bee-tiss*] NOUN Diabetes is a disease in which someone has too much sugar in their blood, because they do not produce enough insulin to absorb it. **diabetic** ADJECTIVE

diabolic ADJECTIVE extremely wicked or cruel.

diabolical ADJECTIVE ① (informal) dreadful and very annoying • *The pain was diabolical.* ② extremely wicked and cruel.

a b c d e f g h i j k l m n o p q r s t u v w x y z

A
B
C
D
E
F
G
H
I
J
K
L
M
N
O
P
Q
R
S
T
U
V
W
X
Y
Z

diadem, diadems NOUN A diadem is a small jewelled crown or headband, usually worn by royalty.

diagnose, diagnoses, diagnosing, diagnosed VERB To diagnose an illness or problem means to identify exactly what is wrong.

diagnosis, diagnoses NOUN the identification of what is wrong with someone who is ill. **diagnostic** ADJECTIVE

diagonal ADJECTIVE in a slanting direction. **diagonally** ADVERB

diagram, diagrams NOUN a drawing that shows or explains something.

dial, dials, dialling, dialled NOUN ① the face of a clock or meter, with divisions marked on it so that a time or measurement can be recorded and read. ② a part of a device, such as a radio, used to control or tune it. ▶ VERB ③ To dial a telephone number means to press the number keys to select the required number.

dialect, dialects NOUN a form of a language spoken in a particular geographical area.

dialogue, dialogues NOUN ① ENGLISH In a novel, play or film, dialogue is conversation. ② Dialogue is communication or discussion between people or groups of people • The union sought dialogue with the council.

dialysis NOUN Dialysis is a treatment used for some kidney diseases, in which blood is filtered by a special machine to remove waste products. WORD HISTORY: from Greek dialuein meaning 'to rip apart'

diameter, diameters NOUN MATHS The diameter of a circle is the length of a straight line drawn across it through its centre.

diamond, diamonds NOUN ① A diamond is a precious stone made of pure carbon. Diamonds are the hardest known substance in the world and are used for cutting substances and for making jewellery. ② A diamond is also a shape with four straight sides of equal length forming two opposite angles less than 90° and two opposite angles greater than 90°. ③ Diamonds is one of the four suits in a pack of playing cards. It is marked by a red diamond-shaped symbol.
▶ ADJECTIVE ④ A diamond anniversary is the 60th anniversary of an event • a diamond wedding.

diaper, diapers NOUN In American English, a diaper is a nappy.

diaphragm, diaphragms [Said dy-a-fram] NOUN SCIENCE In mammals, the diaphragm is the muscular wall that separates the lungs from the stomach.

diarrhoea [Said dy-a-ree-a] NOUN Diarrhoea is a condition in which the faeces are more liquid and frequent than usual.

diary, diaries NOUN a book which has a separate space or page for each day of the year on which to keep a record of appointments. **diarist** NOUN

SPELLING TIP
Do not confuse the order of the vowels in diary and dairy.

dice, dices, dicing, diced NOUN ① a small cube which has each side marked with dots representing the numbers one to six. ▶ VERB ② To dice food means to cut it into small cubes. **diced** ADJECTIVE

dictate, dictates, dictating, dictated VERB ① If you dictate something, you say or read it aloud for someone else to write down. ② To dictate something means to command or state what must happen • What we wear is largely *dictated by our daily routine.* **dictation** NOUN

dictator, dictators NOUN HISTORY
A dictator is a ruler who has complete power in a country, especially one who has taken power by force. **dictatorial** ADJECTIVE

diction NOUN Someone's diction is the clarity with which they speak or sing.

dictionary, dictionaries NOUN LIBRARY a book in which words are listed alphabetically and explained, or equivalent words are given in another language.
WORD HISTORY: from Latin *dictio* meaning 'phrase' or 'word'

did the past tense of **do**.

didgeridoo, didgeridoos NOUN an Australian musical wind instrument made in the shape of a long wooden tube.

die, dies, dying, died VERB ①When people, animals or plants die, they stop living. ②When something dies, dies away or dies down, it gradually fades away • *The footsteps died away.* ▶NOUN ③a dice. **die out** VERB When something dies out, it ceases to exist.
SIMILAR WORDS: ①expire, pass away, perish

diesel [Said *dee-zel*] NOUN ①a heavy fuel used in trains, buses, lorries and some cars. ②a vehicle with a diesel engine.

diesel engine, diesel engines NOUN A diesel engine is an internal-combustion engine in which the fuel is ignited by hot air produced by compression in the cylinders. It is named after Rudolf Diesel, who invented it in 1892.

diet, diets NOUN ①Someone's diet is the usual food that they eat • *a vegetarian diet.* ②PSHE a special restricted selection of foods that someone eats to improve their health or regulate their weight.

dietary ADJECTIVE **dieter** NOUN
WORD HISTORY: from Greek *diaita* meaning 'mode of living'

dietician, dieticians; also spelt **dietitian** NOUN a person trained to advise people about healthy eating.

differ, differs, differing, differed VERB ①If two or more things differ, they are unlike each other. ②If people differ, they have opposing views or disagree about something.

difference, differences NOUN ①The difference between things is the way in which they are unlike each other. ②The difference between two numbers is the amount by which one is less than another. ③A difference in someone or something is a significant change in them • *You wouldn't believe the difference in her.*
SIMILAR WORDS: ①disparity, dissimilarity, distinction

different ADJECTIVE ①unlike something else. ②unusual and out of the ordinary. ③distinct and separate, although of the same kind • *The school supports a different charity each year.* **differently** ADVERB
SIMILAR WORDS: ①dissimilar, unlike

GRAMMAR TIP
You should say that one thing is *different from* another thing. Some people think that *different to* is incorrect. *Different than* is American.

differentiate, differentiates, differentiating, differentiated VERB ①To differentiate between things means to recognise or show how one is unlike the other. ②Something that differentiates one thing from another makes it distinct and unlike the other. **differentiation** NOUN

difficult ADJECTIVE ①not easy to do, understand or solve • *a very difficult*

a
b
c
d
e
f
g
h
i
j
k
l
m
n
o
p
q
r
s
t
u
v
w
x
y
z

decision to make. ② hard to deal with, especially because of being unreasonable or unpredictable • *a difficult child.*

SIMILAR WORDS: ① demanding, hard, laborious

difficulty, difficulties NOUN ① a problem • *The main difficulty is memorising the shortcut keys.* ② Difficulty is the fact or quality of being difficult.

diffident ADJECTIVE timid and lacking in self-confidence. **diffidently** ADVERB **diffidence** NOUN

diffract, diffracts, diffracting, diffracted VERB SCIENCE When rays of light or sound waves diffract, they break up after hitting an obstacle. **diffraction** NOUN

diffuse, diffuses, diffusing, diffused VERB *[Said dif-yooz]* ① If something diffuses, it spreads out or scatters in all directions. ② SCIENCE If particles of a gas, liquid or solid diffuse, they mix together, especially by moving from an area where they are very concentrated to one where there are fewer of them. ▶ ADJECTIVE *[Said dif-yoos]* ③ spread out over a wide area. **diffusion** NOUN

SPELLING TIP

Do not confuse the spellings of *diffuse* and *defuse*: *The wind made the gas diffuse over many miles; The soldiers learn how to defuse bombs.*

dig, digs, digging, dug VERB ① If you dig, you break up soil or sand, especially with a spade or garden fork. ② To dig something into an object means to push, thrust or poke it in. ▶ NOUN ③ a prod or jab, especially in the ribs. ④ (*informal*) A dig at someone is a spiteful or unpleasant remark intended to hurt or embarrass them.

digest, digests, digesting, digested

VERB ① To digest food means to break it down in the gut so that it can be easily absorbed and used by the body. ② If you digest information or a fact, you understand it and take it in. **digestible** ADJECTIVE

digestion, digestions NOUN ① SCIENCE Digestion is the process of digesting food. ② Your digestion is your ability to digest food • *Camomile tea aids poor digestion.* **digestive** ADJECTIVE

digger, diggers NOUN In Australian English, digger is a friendly name to call a man.

digit, digits *[Said dij-it]* NOUN ① (*formal*) Your digits are your fingers or toes. ② MATHS a written symbol for any of the numbers from 0 to 9.

digital ADJECTIVE ① Digital technology involves recording or transmitting information in the form of thousands of very small electronic signals • *a digital camera* • *digital shopping.* ② Digital displays show information, especially time, by numbers, rather than by a pointer moving round a dial • *a digital watch.* **digitally** ADVERB

digital immigrant, digital immigrants NOUN a person who was born before it was common to use things such as personal computers and mobile phones.

digital native, digital natives NOUN someone who has used the internet and mobile phones since they were a child.

dignified ADJECTIVE full of dignity.

dignitary, dignitaries NOUN a person who holds a high official position.

dignity NOUN Dignity is behaviour which is serious, calm and controlled • *She conducted herself with dignity.*

digression, digressions NOUN A digression in speech or writing is leaving the main subject for a while.

dilapidated ADJECTIVE falling to pieces and generally in a bad condition • *a dilapidated castle*.

dilate, dilates, dilating, dilated VERB To dilate means to become wider and larger • *The pupil of the eye dilates in the dark*. **dilated** ADJECTIVE **dilation** NOUN

dilemma, dilemmas NOUN PSHE a situation in which a choice has to be made between alternatives that are equally difficult or unpleasant. **WORD HISTORY:** from Greek *di-* meaning 'two' and *lemma* meaning 'assumption'

USAGE NOTE
A *dilemma* involves a difficult choice between two things. If there are more than two choices you should say *problem* or *difficulty*.

diligent ADJECTIVE hard-working, and showing care and perseverance. **diligently** ADVERB **diligence** NOUN SIMILAR WORDS: conscientious, hard-working, industrious

dill NOUN Dill is a herb with yellow flowers and a strong sweet smell.

dilly bag, dilly bags NOUN In Australian English, a dilly bag is a small bag used to carry food.

dilute, dilutes, diluting, diluted VERB To dilute a liquid means to add water or another liquid to it to make it less concentrated. **dilution** NOUN

dim, dimmer, dimmest; dims, dimming, dimmed ADJECTIVE ① badly lit and lacking in brightness. ② very vague and unclear in your mind • *dim recollections*. ③ (informal) stupid or mentally dull • *He is rather dim*. ▸ VERB ④ If lights dim or are dimmed, they become less bright. **dimly** ADVERB **dimness** NOUN

dime, dimes NOUN A dime is an American or Canadian coin worth ten cents.

dimension, dimensions NOUN ① A dimension of a situation is an aspect or factor that influences the way you understand it • *This process had a domestic and a foreign dimension*. ② You can talk about the size or extent of something as its dimensions • *It was an explosion of major dimensions*. ③ ART The dimensions of something are also its measurements, for example its length, breadth, height or diameter.

diminish, diminishes, diminishing, diminished VERB If something diminishes or if you diminish it, it becomes reduced in size or importance.

diminuendo, diminuendos NOUN MUSIC ① a gradual decrease in loudness. ▸ ADVERB ② gradually decreasing in loudness. **WORD HISTORY:** an Italian word meaning 'getting smaller'

diminutive ADJECTIVE very small.

dimmer switch, dimmer switches NOUN a switch that allows you to adjust the brightness of an electric light.

dimple, dimples NOUN a small hollow in someone's cheek or chin.

din, dins NOUN a loud and unpleasant noise.

dinar, dinars [Said dee-nar] NOUN a unit of currency in several countries in southern Europe, North Africa and the Middle East.

dine, dines, dining, dined VERB (formal) To dine means to eat dinner in the evening • *We dined together in the hotel*.

diner, diners NOUN ① a person who is having dinner in a restaurant. ② a small restaurant.

a b c d e f g h i j k l m n o p q r s t u v w x y z

dinghy, dinghies [Said *ding-ee*] NOUN a small boat which is rowed, sailed or powered by outboard motor.

dingo, dingoes NOUN an Australian wild dog.

dingy, dingier, dingiest [Said *din-jee*] ADJECTIVE dusty, dark and rather depressing • *a dingy room*.

dinkum ADJECTIVE (*informal*) In Australian and New Zealand English, dinkum means genuine or right • *a fair dinkum offer*.

dinner, dinners NOUN ① the main meal of the day, eaten either in the evening or at lunchtime. ② a formal social occasion in the evening, at which a meal is served.

dinosaur, dinosaurs [Said *dy-no-sor*] NOUN a large reptile which lived in prehistoric times.
WORD HISTORY: from Greek *deinos* + *sauros* meaning 'fearful lizard'

dint PHRASE By dint of means by means of • *He succeeds by dint of hard work*.

diocese, dioceses NOUN a district controlled by a bishop. **diocesan** ADJECTIVE

dip, dips, dipping, dipped VERB ① If you dip something into a liquid, you lower it or plunge it quickly into the liquid. ② If something dips, it slopes downwards or goes below a certain level • *The sun dipped below the horizon*. ③ To dip also means to make a quick, slight downward movement • *She dipped her fingers into the cool water*. ▸ NOUN ④ a rich creamy mixture which you scoop up with biscuits or raw vegetables and eat • *an avocado dip*. ⑤ (*informal*) a swim.

diphthong, diphthongs NOUN ⌐ENGLISH¬ A diphthong is a vowel in which the speaker's tongue changes position while it is being pronounced, so that the vowel sounds like a combination of two other vowels.

diploma, diplomas NOUN a certificate awarded to a student who has successfully completed a course of study.
WORD HISTORY: from Greek *diploma* meaning 'folded paper' or 'letter of recommendation'

diplomacy NOUN ① Diplomacy is the managing of relationships between countries. ② Diplomacy is also skill in dealing with people without offending or upsetting them. **diplomatic** ADJECTIVE **diplomatically** ADVERB

diplomat, diplomats NOUN an official who negotiates and deals with another country on behalf of his or her own country.

dire, direr, direst ADJECTIVE disastrous, urgent or terrible • *people in dire need*.

direct, directs, directing, directed ADJECTIVE ① moving or aimed in a straight line or by the shortest route • *the direct route*. ② straightforward, and without delay or evasion • *his direct manner*. ③ without anyone or anything intervening • *Schools can take direct control of their own funding*. ④ exact • *the direct opposite*. ▸ VERB ⑤ To direct something means to guide and control it. ⑥ To direct people or things means to send them, tell them, or show them the way. ⑦ To direct a film, a play, or a television programme means to organise the way it is made and performed.
SIMILAR WORDS: ② frank, open, straightforward

direct current NOUN an electric current that always flows in the same direction.

direction, directions NOUN ① the general line that someone or something is moving or pointing in. ② Direction is the controlling and guiding of something • *He was chopping vegetables under the chef's direction.* ③ (*in plural*) Directions are instructions that tell you how to do something or how to get somewhere.

directive, directives NOUN an instruction that must be obeyed • *a directive banning cigarette advertising.*

directly ADVERB in a straight line or immediately • *He looked directly at Rose.*

direct message, direct messages NOUN On a computer network, a direct message is a message that can be read only by the person you send it to.

director, directors NOUN ① a member of the board of a company or institution. ② DRAMA the person responsible for the making and performance of a programme, play or film. **directorial** ADJECTIVE

directorate, directorates NOUN a board of directors of a company or organisation.

directory, directories NOUN ① a book which gives lists of facts, such as names and addresses, and is usually arranged in alphabetical order. ② ICT another name for **folder**.

direct speech NOUN ENGLISH the reporting of what someone has said by quoting the exact words.

dirge, dirges NOUN a slow, sad piece of music, sometimes played or sung at funerals.

dirt NOUN ① Dirt is any unclean substance, such as dust, mud or stains. ② Dirt is also earth or soil.
SIMILAR WORDS: ① filth, grime, muck

dirty, dirtier, dirtiest ADJECTIVE ① marked or covered with dirt.

② unfair, unscrupulous or dishonest • *She accused her opponents of running a dirty campaign.*
SIMILAR WORDS: ① filthy, grubby, mucky, unclean

dis- PREFIX 'Dis-' is added to the beginning of a word to form a word that means the opposite • *discontented.*

disability, disabilities NOUN a physical or mental condition or illness that restricts someone's ability to move or use his or her senses.

disable, disables, disabling, disabled VERB ① If something disables someone, it restricts his or her ability to move or use his or her senses. ② If someone or something disables a system or mechanism, they stop it working, usually temporarily. **disablement** NOUN

disabled ADJECTIVE having a physical or mental condition that restricts your ability to move or use your senses.

disadvantage, disadvantages NOUN an unfavourable or harmful circumstance. **disadvantaged** ADJECTIVE
SIMILAR WORDS: drawback, handicap

disaffected ADJECTIVE If someone is disaffected with an idea or organisation, they no longer believe in it or support it • *disaffected voters.*

disagree, disagrees, disagreeing, disagreed VERB ① If you disagree with someone, you have a different view or opinion from theirs. ② If you disagree with an action or proposal, you disapprove of it and believe it is wrong • *He detested her and disagreed with her policies.* ③ If food or drink disagrees with you, it makes you feel unwell.
SIMILAR WORDS: ① differ, dispute, dissent

a
b
c
d
e
f
g
h
i
j
k
l
m
n
o
p
q
r
s
t
u
v
w
x
y
z

disagreeable ADJECTIVE unpleasant or unhelpful and unfriendly • *a disagreeable odour.*

disagreement, disagreements NOUN ① a dispute about something. ② an objection to something.

disappear, disappears, disappearing, disappeared VERB ① If something or someone disappears, they go out of sight or become lost. ② To disappear also means to stop existing or happening • *The pain has disappeared.*
disappearance NOUN
SIMILAR WORDS: ① fade away, vanish ② fade away, vanish

disappoint, disappoints, disappointing, disappointed VERB If someone or something disappoints you, it fails to live up to what you expected of it.

disappointed ADJECTIVE sad because something has not happened.

disappointment, disappointments NOUN ① a feeling of being disappointed. ② something that disappoints you.

disapproval NOUN the belief that something is wrong or inappropriate.

disapprove, disapproves, disapproving, disapproved VERB To disapprove of something or someone means to believe they are wrong or bad • *Everyone disapproved of their marrying so young.* **disapproving** ADJECTIVE

disarm, disarms, disarming, disarmed VERB ① To disarm means to get rid of weapons. ② If someone disarms you, they overcome your anger or doubt by charming or soothing you • *Mahoney was almost disarmed by his frankness.* **disarming** ADJECTIVE

disarmament NOUN Disarmament is the reducing or getting rid of military forces and weapons.

disarray NOUN Disarray is a state of disorder and confusion • *Our army was in disarray and practically weaponless.*

disassemble, disassembles, disassembling, disassembled VERB
DGT To disassemble a structure or object which has been made up or built from several smaller parts is to separate its parts from one another.

disaster, disasters NOUN ① an event or accident that causes great distress or destruction. ② a complete failure.
disastrous ADJECTIVE **disastrously** ADVERB
SIMILAR WORDS: ① calamity, catastrophe

disband, disbands, disbanding, disbanded VERB When a group of people disbands, it officially ceases to exist.

disc, discs; also spelt **disk** NOUN ① a flat round object • *a metal disc.* ② one of the thin circular pieces of cartilage that separate the bones in your spine. ③ ICT in computing, another spelling of **disk**.

discard, discards, discarding, discarded VERB To discard something means to get rid of it, because you no longer want it or find it useful.
SIMILAR WORDS: dump, get rid of, throw away

discern, discerns, discerning, discerned [*Said dis-**ern***] VERB (formal) To discern something means to notice or understand it clearly • *The film had no plot that I could discern.*

discernible ADJECTIVE able to be seen or recognised • *no discernible talent.*

discerning ADJECTIVE having good

taste and judgment. **discernment** NOUN

discharge, discharges, discharging, discharged VERB ① If something discharges or is discharged, it is given or sent out • *Oil discharged into the world's oceans.* ② To discharge someone from hospital means to allow them to leave. ③ If someone is discharged from a job, they are dismissed from it. ▶ NOUN ④ a substance that is released from the inside of something • *a thick nasal discharge.* ⑤ a dismissal or release from a job or an institution.

disciple, disciples [*Said dis-sigh-pl*] NOUN RE a follower of someone or something, especially one of the twelve men who were followers and helpers of Christ.

discipline, disciplines, disciplining, disciplined NOUN ① Discipline is making people obey rules and punishing them when they break them. ② Discipline is the ability to behave and work in a controlled way. ▶ VERB ③ If you discipline yourself, you train yourself to behave and work in an ordered way. ④ To discipline someone means to punish them. **disciplinary** ADJECTIVE **disciplined** ADJECTIVE

disc jockey, disc jockeys NOUN someone who introduces and plays music on the radio or at a night club.

disclose, discloses, disclosing, disclosed VERB To disclose something means to make it known or allow it to be seen. **disclosure** NOUN

disco, discos NOUN a party or a club where people dance to recorded music.

discomfort, discomforts NOUN ① Discomfort is distress or slight pain. ② Discomfort is also a feeling of worry or embarrassment.

③ Discomforts are things that make you uncomfortable.

disconcert, disconcerts, disconcerting, disconcerted VERB If something disconcerts you, it makes you feel uneasy or embarrassed. **disconcerting** ADJECTIVE

disconnect, disconnects, disconnecting, disconnected VERB ① To disconnect something means to detach it from something else. ② If someone disconnects your fuel supply or telephone, they cut you off.

discontent NOUN Discontent is a feeling of dissatisfaction with conditions or with life in general • *He was aware of the discontent this policy had caused.* **discontented** ADJECTIVE

discontinue, discontinues, discontinuing, discontinued VERB To discontinue something means to stop doing it.

discord NOUN Discord is unpleasantness or quarrelling between people.

discount, discounts, discounting, discounted NOUN ① a reduction in the price of something. ▶ VERB ② If you discount something, you reject it or ignore it • *We shouldn't discount the possibility that things could get a lot worse.*

discourage, discourages, discouraging, discouraged VERB To discourage someone means to take away their enthusiasm to do something. **discouraging** ADJECTIVE **discouragement** NOUN SIMILAR WORDS: demoralise, dishearten, put off

discourse, discourses (*formal*) NOUN ① a formal talk or piece of writing intended to teach or explain something. ② Discourse is serious conversation between people on a particular subject.

a b c d e f g h i j k l m n o p q r s t u v w x y z

discover, discovers, discovering, discovered VERB When you discover something, you find it or find out about it. **discovery** NOUN **discoverer** NOUN

discredit, discredits, discrediting, discredited VERB ① To discredit someone means to damage their reputation. ② To discredit an idea means to cause it to be doubted or not believed.

discreet ADJECTIVE If you are discreet, you avoid causing embarrassment when dealing with secret or private matters. **discreetly** ADVERB

SPELLING TIP
Do not confuse the spellings of *discreet* and *discrete*: *I don't want anyone to know about this so please be discreet; Anna has two discrete sets of friends.*

discrepancy, discrepancies NOUN a difference between two things which ought to be the same • *discrepancies in his police interviews.*

discrete ADJECTIVE ① (formal) separate and distinct • *two discrete sets of nerves.* ② MATHS A discrete line or set of data is made up of a limited number of separate points or items.

SPELLING TIP
Do not confuse the spellings of *discrete* and *discreet*: *Anna has two discrete sets of friends; I don't want anyone to know about this so please be discreet.*

discretion NOUN ① Discretion is the quality of behaving with care and tact so as to avoid embarrassment or distress to other people • *You can count on my discretion.* ② Discretion is also freedom and authority to make decisions and take action according to your own judgment • *Class teachers* have some discretion in decision-making. **discretionary** ADJECTIVE

discriminate, discriminates, discriminating, discriminated VERB ① To discriminate between things means to recognise and understand the differences between them. ② PSHE To discriminate against a person or group means to treat them unfairly, for example because of their gender, race or colour. ③ To discriminate in favour of a person or group means to treat them more favourably than others. **discrimination** NOUN **discriminatory** ADJECTIVE

discursive ADJECTIVE ENGLISH A discursive essay presents different arguments about a topic.

discus, discuses NOUN a disc-shaped object with a heavy middle, thrown by athletes.

discuss, discusses, discussing, discussed VERB ① When people discuss something, they talk about it in detail. ② EXAM TERM To discuss a question is to look at the points or arguments of both sides and try to reach your own opinion.

discussion, discussions NOUN PSHE a conversation or piece of writing in which a subject is considered in detail.
SIMILAR WORDS: conversation, discourse, talk

disdain NOUN Disdain is a feeling of superiority over or contempt for someone or something • *The candidates showed disdain for the press.* **disdainful** ADJECTIVE

disease, diseases NOUN SCIENCE an unhealthy condition in people, animals or plants. **diseased** ADJECTIVE

disembark, disembarks, disembarking, disembarked VERB

To disembark means to land or unload from a ship, aircraft or bus.

disembodied ADJECTIVE ① separate from or existing without a body • *a disembodied skull*. ② seeming not to be attached or to come from anyone • *disembodied voices*.

disenchanted ADJECTIVE disappointed with something, and no longer believing that it is good or worthwhile • *Students can become disenchanted with learning*.

disenchantment NOUN

disfigure, disfigures, disfiguring, disfigured VERB To disfigure something means to spoil its appearance • *Graffiti or posters disfigured every wall*.

disgrace, disgraces, disgracing, disgraced NOUN ① Disgrace is a state in which people disapprove of someone. ② If something is a disgrace, it is unacceptable • *The overcrowded prisons were a disgrace*. ③ If someone is a disgrace to a group of people, their behaviour makes the group feel ashamed • *You're a disgrace to the school*. ▶ VERB ④ If you disgrace yourself or disgrace someone else, you cause yourself or them to be strongly disapproved of by other people.

SIMILAR WORDS: ① dishonour, shame ④ discredit, dishonour, shame

disgraceful ADJECTIVE If something is disgraceful, people disapprove of it strongly and think that those who are responsible for it should be ashamed. **disgracefully** ADVERB

SIMILAR WORDS: scandalous, shameful, shocking

disgruntled ADJECTIVE discontented or in a bad mood.

disguise, disguises, disguising, disguised VERB ① To disguise something means to change its appearance so that people do not recognise it. ② To disguise a feeling means to hide it • *I tried to disguise my relief*. ▶ NOUN ③ something you wear or something you do to alter your appearance so that you cannot be recognised by other people.

disgust, disgusts, disgusting, disgusted NOUN ① Disgust is a strong feeling of dislike or disapproval. ▶ VERB ② To disgust someone means to make them feel a strong sense of dislike or disapproval. **disgusted** ADJECTIVE

SIMILAR WORDS: ① loathing, repugnance, revulsion ② revolt, sicken

disgusting ADJECTIVE very unpleasant and offensive.

dish, dishes NOUN ① a shallow container for cooking or serving food. ② food of a particular kind or food cooked in a particular way • *two fish dishes to choose from*.

dishearten, disheartens, disheartening, disheartened VERB If you dishearten someone, you take away their hope and confidence in something.

disheartened ADJECTIVE If you are disheartened, you feel disappointed.

dishevelled [Said dish-ev-ld] ADJECTIVE If someone looks dishevelled, their clothes or hair look untidy.

dishonest ADJECTIVE not truthful or able to be trusted. **dishonestly** ADVERB

dishonesty NOUN Dishonesty is behaviour which is meant to deceive people, either by not telling the truth or by cheating.

dishwasher, dishwashers NOUN an electrically operated machine that washes plates, saucepans and cutlery.

a b c **d** e f g h i j k l m n o p q r s t u v w x y z

disillusion, disillusions, disillusioning, disillusioned VERB If something or someone disillusions you, you discover that you were mistaken about something you valued, and so you feel disappointed with it. **disillusionment** NOUN

disillusioned ADJECTIVE If you are disillusioned with something, you are disappointed because it is not as good as you had expected.

disinfectant, disinfectants NOUN a chemical substance that kills germs.

disintegrate, disintegrates, disintegrating, disintegrated VERB ① If something disintegrates, it becomes weakened and is not effective • *My confidence disintegrated.* ② If an object disintegrates, it breaks into many pieces and so is destroyed. **disintegration** NOUN

disinterest NOUN ① Disinterest is a lack of interest. ② Disinterest is also a lack of personal involvement in a situation.

disinterested ADJECTIVE If someone is disinterested, they are not going to gain or lose from the situation they are involved in, and so can act in a way that is fair to both sides • *a disinterested judge.*

USAGE NOTE
Some people use *disinterested* to mean 'not interested', but the word they should use is *uninterested*.

disjointed ADJECTIVE If thought or speech is disjointed, it jumps from subject to subject and so is difficult to follow.

disk, disks NOUN ① ICT In a computer, the disk is the part where information is stored • *The program takes up 2.5 megabytes of disk space.* ② another spelling of **disc**.

dislike, dislikes, disliking, disliked VERB ① If you dislike something or someone, you think they are unpleasant and do not like them. ▶ NOUN ② Dislike is a feeling that you have when you do not like someone or something.
SIMILAR WORDS: ② aversion, distaste

dislocate, dislocates, dislocating, dislocated VERB To dislocate your bone or joint means to put it out of place.

dislodge, dislodges, dislodging, dislodged VERB To dislodge something means to move it or force it out of place.

dismal [*Said diz-mal*] ADJECTIVE rather gloomy and depressing • *dismal weather.* **dismally** ADVERB
WORD HISTORY: from Latin *dies mali* meaning 'evil days'

dismantle, dismantles, dismantling, dismantled VERB To dismantle something means to take it apart.

dismay, dismays, dismaying, dismayed NOUN ① Dismay is a feeling of fear and worry. ▶ VERB ② If someone or something dismays you, it fills you with alarm and worry.

dismember, dismembers, dismembering, dismembered VERB (*formal*) To dismember a person or animal means to cut or tear their body into pieces.

dismiss, dismisses, dismissing, dismissed VERB ① If you dismiss something, you decide to ignore it because it is not important enough for you to think about. ② To dismiss an employee means to ask that person to leave their job. ③ If someone in authority dismisses you, they tell you to leave. **dismissal** NOUN

dismissive ADJECTIVE If you are dismissive of something or someone, you show that you think they are of little importance or value • *a dismissive gesture*.

disobey, disobeys, disobeying, disobeyed VERB To disobey a person or an order means to deliberately refuse to do what you are told.

disorder, disorders NOUN ① Disorder is a state of untidiness. ② Disorder is also a lack of organisation • *The men fled in disorder*. ③ a disease • *a stomach disorder*. SIMILAR WORDS: ② chaos, confusion

disorganised; also spelt **disorganized** ADJECTIVE If something is disorganised, it is confused and badly prepared or badly arranged. **disorganisation** NOUN

disown, disowns, disowning, disowned VERB To disown someone or something means to refuse to admit any connection with them.

disparaging ADJECTIVE critical and scornful • *disparaging remarks*.

disparate ADJECTIVE (*formal*) Things that are disparate are utterly different from one another. **disparity** NOUN

dispatch, dispatches, dispatching, dispatched; also spelt **despatch** VERB ① To dispatch someone or something to a particular place means to send them there for a special reason • *The president dispatched him on a fact-finding visit*. ▶ NOUN ② an official written message, often sent to an army or government headquarters.

dispel, dispels, dispelling, dispelled VERB To dispel fears or beliefs means to drive them away or to destroy them • *The myths are being dispelled*.

dispensary, dispensaries NOUN a place where medicines are prepared and given out.

dispense, dispenses, dispensing, dispensed VERB ① (*formal*) To dispense something means to give it out • *They dispense advice*. ② To dispense medicines means to prepare them and give them out. ③ To dispense with something means to do without it or do away with it • *When she stood up to speak she dispensed with her notes*.

dispenser, dispensers NOUN a machine or container from which you can get things • *a cash dispenser*.

disperse, disperses, dispersing, dispersed VERB ① When something disperses, it scatters over a wide area. ② When people disperse or when someone disperses them, they move apart and go in different directions. **dispersal** NOUN **dispersion** NOUN

dispirited ADJECTIVE depressed and having no enthusiasm for anything.

dispiriting ADJECTIVE Something dispiriting makes you depressed • *a dispiriting defeat*.

displace, displaces, displacing, displaced VERB ① If one thing displaces another, it forces the thing out of its usual place and occupies that place itself. ② If people are displaced, they are forced to leave their home or country.

displacement NOUN ① Displacement is the removal of something from its usual or correct place or position. ② SCIENCE In physics, displacement is the weight or volume of liquid displaced by an object submerged or floating in it.

display, displays, displaying, displayed VERB ① If you display something, you show it or make it visible to people. ② If you display something such as an emotion, you behave in a way that shows you feel it.

a
b
c
d
e
f
g
h
i
j
k
l
m
n
o
p
q
r
s
t
u
v
w
x
y
z

▸ NOUN ③ ART an arrangement of things designed to attract people's attention.

displease, displeases, displeasing, displeased VERB If someone or something displeases you, they make you annoyed, dissatisfied or offended. **displeasure** NOUN

disposable ADJECTIVE designed to be thrown away after use • *disposable nappies*.

disposal NOUN Disposal is the act of getting rid of something that is no longer wanted or needed.

dispose, disposes, disposing, disposed VERB ① To dispose of something means to get rid of it. ② If you are not disposed to do something, you are not willing to do it.

disprove, disproves, disproving, disproved VERB If someone disproves an idea, belief or theory, they show that it is not true.

dispute, disputes, disputing, disputed NOUN ① an argument. ▸ VERB ② To dispute a fact or theory means to question the truth of it.

disqualify, disqualifies, disqualifying, disqualified VERB If someone is disqualified from a competition or activity, they are officially stopped from taking part in it • *He was disqualified from driving for 18 months.* **disqualification** NOUN

disquiet NOUN Disquiet is worry or anxiety. **disquieting** ADJECTIVE

disregard, disregards, disregarding, disregarded VERB ① To disregard something means to pay little or no attention to it. ▸ NOUN ② Disregard is a lack of attention or respect for something • *He exhibited a flagrant disregard of the law.*

disrepair PHRASE If something is **in disrepair** or **in a state of disrepair**, it is broken or in poor condition.

disrespect NOUN Disrespect is contempt or lack of respect • *his disrespect for authority.* **disrespectful** ADJECTIVE

disrupt, disrupts, disrupting, disrupted VERB To disrupt something such as an event or system means to break it up or throw it into confusion • *Ash from the volcano disrupted air traffic.* **disruption** NOUN **disruptive** ADJECTIVE

dissatisfied ADJECTIVE not pleased or not contented. **dissatisfaction** NOUN

dissect, dissects, dissecting, dissected VERB To dissect a plant or a dead body means to cut it up so that it can be scientifically examined. **dissection** NOUN

dissent, dissents, dissenting, dissented NOUN ① Dissent is strong difference of opinion • *political dissent.* ▸ VERB ② When people dissent, they express a difference of opinion about something. **dissenting** ADJECTIVE

dissertation, dissertations NOUN a long essay, especially for a university degree.

disservice NOUN To do someone a disservice means to do something that harms them.

dissident, dissidents NOUN someone who disagrees with and criticises the government of their country.

dissimilar ADJECTIVE If things are dissimilar, they are unlike each other.

dissipate, dissipates, dissipating, dissipated VERB ① (*formal*) When something dissipates or is dissipated, it completely disappears • *The cloud seemed to dissipate there.* ② If someone dissipates time, money or effort, they waste it.

dissipated ADJECTIVE Someone who is dissipated shows signs of indulging too much in things such as food and drink.

dissolve, dissolves, dissolving, dissolved VERB ① SCIENCE If you dissolve something or if it dissolves in a liquid, it becomes mixed with and absorbed in the liquid. ② To dissolve an organisation or institution means to officially end it.

dissuade, dissuades, dissuading, dissuaded [Said dis-**wade**] VERB To dissuade someone from doing something or from believing something means to persuade them not to do it or not to believe it.

distance, distances, distancing, distanced NOUN ① The distance between two points is how far it is between them. ② Distance is the fact of being far away in space or time. ▶ VERB ③ If you distance yourself from someone or something or are distanced from them, you become less involved with them.

distant ADJECTIVE ① far away in space or time. ② A distant relative is one who is not closely related to you. ③ Someone who is distant is cold and unfriendly. **distantly** ADVERB
SIMILAR WORDS: ③ aloof, reserved, standoffish

distaste NOUN Distaste is a dislike of something which you find offensive.

distasteful ADJECTIVE If you find something distasteful, you think it is unpleasant or offensive.

distil, distils, distilling, distilled VERB SCIENCE When a liquid is distilled, it is heated until it evaporates and then cooled to enable purified liquid to be collected. **distillation** NOUN

distillery, distilleries NOUN a place where whisky or other strong

alcoholic drink is made, using a process of distillation.

distinct ADJECTIVE ① If one thing is distinct from another, it is recognisably different from it • A word may have two quite distinct meanings. ② If something is distinct, you can hear, smell or see it clearly and plainly • There was a distinct buzzing noise. ③ If something such as a fact, idea or intention is distinct, it is clear and definite • She had a distinct feeling that someone was watching them. **distinctly** ADVERB

distinction, distinctions NOUN ① a difference between two things • a distinction between the body and the soul. ② Distinction is a quality of excellence and superiority • a man of distinction. ③ a special honour or claim • It had the distinction of being the largest square in Europe. ④ A distinction is the highest level of achievement in an examination.

distinctive ADJECTIVE Something that is distinctive has a special quality which makes it recognisable • a distinctive voice. **distinctively** ADVERB

distinguish, distinguishes, distinguishing, distinguished VERB ① To distinguish between things means to recognise the difference between them • I've learned to distinguish business and friendship. ② To distinguish something means to make it out by seeing, hearing or tasting it • I heard shouting but was unable to distinguish the words. ③ If you distinguish yourself, you do something that makes people think highly of you. **distinguishable** ADJECTIVE **distinguishing** ADJECTIVE

distinguished ADJECTIVE ① dignified in appearance or behaviour. ② having a very high reputation • He was a distinguished professor.

a b c d e f g h i j k l m n o p q r s t u v w x y z

distort, distorts, distorting, distorted VERB ① If you distort a statement or an argument, you represent it in an untrue or misleading way. ② If something is distorted, it is changed so that it seems strange or unclear • *His voice was distorted.* ③ If an object is distorted, it is twisted or pulled out of shape. **distorted** ADJECTIVE **distortion** NOUN

distract, distracts, distracting, distracted VERB If something distracts you, your attention is taken away from what you are doing. **distracted** ADJECTIVE **distractedly** ADVERB **distracting** ADJECTIVE
SIMILAR WORDS: divert, sidetrack

distraction, distractions NOUN ① something that takes people's attention away from something. ② an activity that is intended to amuse or relax someone.

distraught ADJECTIVE so upset and worried that you cannot think clearly • *He was distraught over the accident.*

distress, distresses, distressing, distressed NOUN ① Distress is great suffering caused by pain or sorrow. ② Distress is also the state of needing help because of difficulties or danger. ▶ VERB ③ To distress someone means to make them feel alarmed or unhappy • *Her letter had profoundly distressed me.*
SIMILAR WORDS: ③ trouble, upset

distressing ADJECTIVE very worrying or upsetting.

distribute, distributes, distributing, distributed VERB ① To distribute something such as leaflets means to hand them out or deliver them • *They publish and distribute brochures.* ② If things are distributed, they are spread throughout an area or space • *Distribute the cheese evenly on top of the pizza.* ③ To distribute something

means to divide it and share it out among a number of people.
SIMILAR WORDS: ③ dispense, share out

distribution, distributions NOUN ① Distribution is the delivering of something to various people or organisations • *the distribution of political leaflets.* ② Distribution is the sharing out of something to various people • *distribution of power.*

distributor, distributors NOUN a company that supplies goods to other businesses who then sell them to the public.

district, districts NOUN an area of a town or country • *a residential district.*

district nurse, district nurses NOUN a nurse who visits and treats people in their own homes.

distrust, distrusts, distrusting, distrusted VERB ① If you distrust someone, you are suspicious of them because you are not sure whether they are honest. ▶ NOUN ② Distrust is suspicion. **distrustful** ADJECTIVE

disturb, disturbs, disturbing, disturbed VERB ① If you disturb someone, you break their peace or privacy. ② If something disturbs you, it makes you feel upset or worried. ③ If something is disturbed, it is moved out of position or meddled with. **disturbing** ADJECTIVE
SIMILAR WORDS: ② trouble, upset, worry

disturbance, disturbances NOUN ① Disturbance is the state of being disturbed. ② a violent or unruly incident in public.

disuse NOUN Something that has fallen into disuse is neglected or no longer used. **disused** ADJECTIVE

ditch, ditches NOUN a channel at the side of a road or field, to drain away excess water.

dither, dithers, dithering, dithered VERB To dither means to be unsure and hesitant.

ditto 'Ditto' means 'the same'. In written lists, 'ditto' is represented by a mark (") to avoid repetition. WORD HISTORY: from Italian *detto* meaning 'said'

ditty, ditties NOUN (*old-fashioned*) a short simple song or poem.

diva, divas NOUN a great or leading female singer, especially in opera. WORD HISTORY: from Latin *diva* meaning 'a goddess'

dive, dives, diving, dived VERB ①To dive means to jump into water with your arms held straight above your head, usually head first. ②If you go diving, you go down under the surface of the sea or a lake using special breathing equipment. ③If an aircraft or bird dives, it flies in a steep downward path, or drops sharply. **diver** NOUN **diving** NOUN

diverge, diverges, diverging, diverged VERB ①If opinions or facts diverge, they differ • *Theory and practice sometimes diverged*. ②If two things such as roads or paths which have been going in the same direction diverge, they separate and go off in different directions. **divergence** NOUN **divergent** ADJECTIVE

diverse ADJECTIVE ① CITIZENSHIP If a group of people or things is diverse, it is made up of several different kinds • *a racially diverse community*. ②People, ideas or objects that are diverse are very different from each other. **diversity** NOUN

diversify, diversifies, diversifying, diversified VERB To diversify means to increase the variety of something • *Has the company diversified into new areas?* **diversification** NOUN

diversion, diversions NOUN ①a special route arranged for traffic when the usual route is closed. ②something that takes your attention away from what you should be concentrating on • *A break for tea created a welcome diversion*. ③a pleasant or amusing activity.

divert, diverts, diverting, diverted VERB To divert something means to change the course or direction it is following.

divide, divides, dividing, divided VERB ①When something divides or is divided, it is split up and separated into two or more parts. ②If something divides two areas, it forms a barrier between them. ③If people divide over something or if something divides them, it causes strong disagreement between them. ④ MATHS When you divide one number by another, you calculate how many times the first number contains the other. ▶ NOUN ⑤a separation • *the class divide*.

dividend, dividends NOUN ① MATHS a number that is divided by another number. ②a portion of a company's profits that is paid to shareholders.

divination NOUN Divination is the foretelling of the future as though by supernatural power.

divine, divines, divining, divined ADJECTIVE ①having the qualities of a god or goddess. ▶ VERB ②To divine something means to discover it by guessing. **divinely** ADVERB

divinity, divinities NOUN ①Divinity is the study of religion. ②Divinity is the state of being a god. ③a god or goddess.

division, divisions NOUN ①Division is the separation of something into two or more distinct parts. ② MATHS Division is also the process of dividing

a b c **d** e f g h i j k l m n o p q r s t u v w x y z

A B C **D** E F G H I J K L M N O P Q R S T U V W X Y Z

one number by another. ③ a difference of opinion that causes separation between ideas or groups of people • *There were divisions in the Party on economic policy.* ④ any one of the parts or groups into which something is split • *the Research Division.* **divisional** ADJECTIVE

divisive ADJECTIVE causing hostility between people so that they split into different groups • *He was seen as a divisive and meddling figure.*

divisor, divisors NOUN MATHS a number by which another number is divided.

divorce, divorces, divorcing, divorced NOUN ① Divorce is the formal and legal ending of a marriage. ▸ VERB ② When a married couple divorce, their marriage is legally ended. **divorced** ADJECTIVE **divorcee** NOUN

divulge, divulges, divulging, divulged VERB To divulge information means to reveal it.

Diwali [Said dih-*wah*-lee] NOUN RE a Hindu religious festival in honour of the goddess of wealth. It is celebrated by feasting, exchanging gifts and lighting lamps.

DIY NOUN DIY is the activity of making or repairing things yourself. DIY is an abbreviation for 'do-it-yourself'.

dizzy, dizzier, dizziest ADJECTIVE having or causing a whirling sensation. **dizziness** NOUN

DJ, DJs NOUN A DJ is a disc jockey.

DM, DMs NOUN an abbreviation for 'direct message'.

DNA NOUN SCIENCE DNA is deoxyribonucleic acid, a substance found in the cells of all living things. It determines the structure of every cell and is responsible for characteristics being passed on from parents to their children.

do, does, doing, did, done; dos VERB ① 'Do' is an auxiliary verb, which is used to form questions and negatives and to give emphasis to the main verb of a sentence. ② If someone does a task or activity, they perform it and finish it • *He just didn't want to do any work.* ③ If you ask what people do, you want to know what their job is • *What will you do when you leave school?* ④ If you do well at something, you are successful. If you do badly, you are unsuccessful. ⑤ If something will do, it is adequate but not the most suitable option • *If you don't have a tennis ball, a rolled-up sock will do.* ▸ NOUN ⑥ (*informal*) a party or other social event. **do away with** VERB To do away with something means to get rid of it. **do up** VERB ① To do something up means to fasten it. ② To do up something old means to repair and decorate it.

SIMILAR WORDS: ② carry out, execute, perform

docile ADJECTIVE quiet, calm and easily controlled.

dock, docks, docking, docked NOUN ① an enclosed area in a harbour where ships go to be loaded, unloaded or repaired. ② In a court of law, the dock is the place where the accused person stands or sits. ③ a stand in which a portable electronic device can be placed to charge its battery or to connect it to other devices. ▸ VERB ④ When a ship docks, it is brought into dock at the end of its voyage. ⑤ To dock someone's wages means to deduct an amount from the sum they would normally receive. ⑥ To dock an animal's tail means to cut part of it off. **docker** NOUN

doctor, doctors, doctoring, doctored NOUN ① a person who is qualified in medicine and treats people who are ill. ②A doctor of an academic subject is someone who has been awarded the highest academic degree • *She is a doctor of philosophy.* ▸VERB ③To doctor something means to alter it in order to deceive people • *Stamps can be doctored.*

doctorate, doctorates NOUN the highest university degree. **doctoral** ADJECTIVE

doctrine, doctrines NOUN a set of beliefs or principles held by a group. **doctrinal** ADJECTIVE

document, documents, documenting, documented NOUN ① HISTORY a piece of paper which provides an official record of something. ② ICT a piece of text or graphics stored in a computer as a file that can be amended or altered by document processing software. ▸VERB ③ HISTORY If you document something, you make a detailed record of it. **documentation** NOUN

documentary, documentaries NOUN ①a radio or television programme, or a film, which gives information on real events. ▸ADJECTIVE ②Documentary evidence is made up of written or official records.

dodge, dodges, dodging, dodged VERB ①If you dodge or dodge something, you move suddenly to avoid being seen, hit or caught. ②If you dodge something such as an issue or accusation, you avoid dealing with it.

dodgy, dodgier, dodgiest ADJECTIVE (*informal*) dangerous, risky or unreliable • *He has a dodgy knee.*

dodo, dodos NOUN A dodo was a large, flightless bird that lived in Mauritius and became extinct in the late 17th century.

doe, does NOUN a female deer, rabbit or hare.

does the third person singular of the present tense of **do**.

dog, dogs, dogging, dogged NOUN ①a four-legged, meat-eating animal, kept as a pet, or to guard property or go hunting. ▸VERB ②If you dog someone, you follow them very closely and never leave them.

dog collar, dog collars NOUN (*informal*) a white collar with no front opening worn by Christian clergy.

dog-eared ADJECTIVE A book that is dog-eared has been used so much that the corners of the pages are turned down or worn.

dogged [*Said dog-ged*] ADJECTIVE showing determination to continue with something, even if it is very difficult • *dogged persistence.* **doggedly** ADVERB

doggerel NOUN ENGLISH Doggerel is funny or silly verse, often written quickly and not intended to be serious.

dogma, dogmas NOUN a belief or system of beliefs held by a religious or political group.

dogmatic ADJECTIVE Someone who is dogmatic about something is convinced that they are right about it. **dogmatism** NOUN

dolce [*Said dol-chay*] ADVERB MUSIC In music, dolce is an instruction to play or sing something gently and sweetly.
WORD HISTORY: an Italian word meaning 'sweet'

doldrums PHRASE (*informal*) If you are **in the doldrums**, you are depressed or bored.

dole, doles, doling, doled VERB If you dole something out, you give a certain amount of it to each individual in a group.

doll, dolls NOUN a child's toy which looks like a baby or person.

dollar, dollars NOUN the main unit of currency in Australia, New Zealand, the USA, Canada and some other countries. A dollar is worth 100 cents.

dollop, dollops NOUN an amount of food, served casually in a lump.

dolphin, dolphins NOUN a mammal which lives in the sea and looks like a large fish with a long snout.

domain, domains NOUN ① a particular area of activity or interest • *the domain of science*. ② an area over which someone has control or influence • *This reservation was the largest of the Apache domains*.

dome, domes NOUN a round roof. **domed** ADJECTIVE

domestic ADJECTIVE ① happening or existing within one particular country • *domestic and foreign politics*. ② involving or concerned with the home and family • *routine domestic tasks*.

domesticated ADJECTIVE If a wild animal or plant has been domesticated, it has been controlled or cultivated.

domesticity NOUN (formal) Domesticity is life at home with your family.

dominance NOUN ① Dominance is power or control. ② If something has dominance over other similar things, it is more powerful or important than they are • *the dominance of the United States in the film business*. ③ SCIENCE In genetics, dominance is ability of a gene to produce a particular characteristic in the next generation even if only one parent passes on the gene. **dominant** ADJECTIVE

dominate, dominates, dominating, dominated VERB ① If something or someone dominates a situation or event, they are the most powerful or important thing in it and have control over it • *The artist dominated the music charts this year*. ② If a person or country dominates other people or places, they have power or control over them. ③ If something dominates an area, it towers over it • *The valley was dominated by high surrounding cliffs*. **dominating** ADJECTIVE **domination** NOUN

dominee, dominees [Said *doom-in-nee*] NOUN In South Africa, a dominee is a minister of the Dutch Reformed Church.

domineering ADJECTIVE Someone who is domineering tries to control other people.

dominion NOUN Dominion is control or authority that a person or a country has over other people.

domino, dominoes NOUN Dominoes are small rectangular blocks marked with two groups of spots on one side, used for playing the game called dominoes.

don, dons, donning, donned VERB (literary) If you don clothing, you put it on.

donate, donates, donating, donated VERB To donate something to a charity or organisation means to give it as a gift. **donation** NOUN

done the past participle of **do**.

donkey, donkeys NOUN an animal like a horse, but smaller and with longer ears.

donor, donors NOUN ① someone who gives some of their blood or an organ to be used to help someone who is ill • *a kidney donor*. ② someone who gives something such as money to a charity or other organisation.

doodle, doodles, doodling, doodled NOUN ① a drawing done when you are thinking about something else or when you are bored. ▶ **VERB** ② To doodle means to draw doodles.

doom NOUN Doom is a terrible fate or event in the future which you can do nothing to prevent.

doomed ADJECTIVE If someone or something is doomed to an unpleasant or unhappy experience, they are certain to suffer it • *doomed to failure.*

doomsday NOUN Doomsday is the end of the world.

door, doors NOUN a swinging or sliding panel for opening or closing the entrance to something; also the entrance itself.

doorstep, doorsteps NOUN a step in front of a door on the outside of a building.

doorway, doorways NOUN an opening in a wall for a door.

dope, dopes, doping, doped NOUN ① (informal) Dope is an illegal drug. ▶ **VERB** ② If someone dopes you, they put a drug into your food or drink. **WORD HISTORY:** from Dutch *doop* meaning 'sauce'

dormant ADJECTIVE Something that is dormant is not active, growing or being used • *The buds will remain dormant until spring.*

dormitory, dormitories NOUN a large bedroom where several people sleep.

dormouse, dormice NOUN an animal, like a large mouse, with a furry tail.

dorp, dorps NOUN In South African English, a dorp is a small town or village.

dosage, dosages NOUN the amount of a medicine or a drug that should be taken.

dose, doses NOUN a measured amount of a medicine or drug.

dossier, dossiers [*Said doss-ee-ay*] NOUN a collection of papers with information on a particular subject or person.

dot, dots, dotting, dotted NOUN ① a very small, round mark. ▶ **VERB** ② If things dot an area, they are scattered all over it • *Fishing villages dot the coastline.* ▶ **PHRASE** ③ If you arrive somewhere **on the dot**, you arrive there at exactly the right time.

dotcom, dotcoms NOUN a company that does most of its business on the internet.

dote, dotes, doting, doted VERB If you dote on someone, you love them very much. **doting** ADJECTIVE

double, doubles, doubling, doubled ADJECTIVE ① twice the usual size • *a double portion of cheesecake.* ② consisting of two parts • *a double album.* ▶ **VERB** ③ If something doubles, it becomes twice as large. ④ To double as something means to have a second job or use as well as the main one • *Their home doubles as an office.* ▶ **NOUN** ⑤ Your double is someone who looks exactly like you. ⑥ Doubles is a game of tennis or badminton which two people play against two other people. **doubly** ADVERB

double bass, double basses NOUN a musical instrument like a large violin, which you play standing up.

double-cross, double-crosses, double-crossing, double-crossed VERB If someone double-crosses you, they cheat you by pretending to do what you both planned, when in fact they do the opposite.

double-decker, double-deckers ADJECTIVE ① having two tiers or layers. ▶ **NOUN** ② a bus with two floors.

double glazing NOUN Double glazing is a second layer of glass

a b c d e f g h i j k l m n o p q r s t u v w x y z

fitted to windows to keep the building quieter or warmer.

double helix, **double helixes** or **double helices** NOUN SCIENCE a shape consisting of two helixes coiled around the same axis, which is the form of the molecular structure of DNA.

doubt, **doubts**, **doubting**, **doubted** NOUN ① Doubt is a feeling of uncertainty about whether something is true or possible. ▶ VERB ② If you doubt something, you think that it is probably not true or possible.
SIMILAR WORDS: ① misgiving, qualm, uncertainty

doubtful ADJECTIVE unlikely or uncertain.

dough [Rhymes with go] NOUN ① Dough is a mixture of flour and water and sometimes other ingredients, used to make bread, pastry or biscuits. ② (slang) Dough is money.

doughnut, **doughnuts** NOUN a ring or ball of sweet dough cooked in hot fat.

dour, **dourer**, **dourest** [Rhymes with poor] ADJECTIVE severe and unfriendly • a dour portrait of his personality.

douse, **douses**, **dousing**, **doused**; also spelt **dowse** VERB If you douse a fire, you stop it burning by throwing water over it.

dove, **doves** NOUN a bird like a small pigeon.

dovetail, **dovetails**, **dovetailing**, **dovetailed** VERB If two things dovetail together, they fit together closely or neatly.

dowager, **dowagers** NOUN a woman who has inherited a title from her dead husband • the Empress Dowager.

dowdy, **dowdier**, **dowdiest** ADJECTIVE wearing dull and unfashionable clothes.

dowel, **dowels** NOUN DGT A dowel is a short, thin piece of wood or metal which is fitted into holes in larger pieces of wood or metal to join them together.

down, **downs**, **downing**, **downed** PREPOSITION or ADVERB ① Down means towards the ground, towards a lower level, or in a lower place. ② If you go down a road or river, you go along it. ▶ ADVERB ③ If you put something down, you place it on a surface. ④ If an amount of something goes down, it decreases. ▶ ADJECTIVE ⑤ If you feel down, you feel unhappy. ▶ VERB ⑥ If you down a drink, you drink it quickly. ▶ NOUN ⑦ Down is the small, soft feathers on young birds.

downbeat ADJECTIVE If you are downbeat, you are depressed or gloomy about a situation.

down beat, **down beats** NOUN MUSIC the first beat of a bar of music.

downcast ADJECTIVE ① feeling sad and dejected. ② If your eyes are downcast, they are looking towards the ground.

downfall NOUN ① The downfall of a successful or powerful person or institution is their failure. ② Something that is someone's downfall is the thing that causes their failure • His pride may be his downfall.

downgrade, **downgrades**, **downgrading**, **downgraded** VERB If you downgrade something, you give it less importance or make it less valuable.

downhill ADVERB ① moving down a slope. ② becoming worse • The press has gone downhill in the last 10 years.

download, downloads, downloading, downloaded ICT VERB ① If you download data, you transfer it from the memory of a large computer system to a smaller computer. ▶ NOUN ② a piece of data transferred in this way.

downpour, downpours NOUN a heavy fall of rain.

downright ADJECTIVE or ADVERB You use 'downright' to emphasise that something is extremely unpleasant or bad • *Staff are often discourteous and sometimes downright rude.*

downs PLURAL NOUN an area of low grassy hills, especially in the south of England.

downside, downsides NOUN The downside of a situation is the aspect of it which is less positive, pleasant or useful than its other aspects.

downsize, downsizes, downsizing, downsized VERB To downsize something such as a business means to make it smaller.

Down's syndrome NOUN Down's syndrome is a genetic condition that results in physical differences and learning disability.

downstairs ADVERB ① If you go downstairs in a building, you go down to a lower floor. ▶ ADJECTIVE or ADVERB ② on a lower floor or on the ground floor. ▶ NOUN ③ The downstairs of a building is its lower floor or floors.

downstream ADVERB towards the mouth of a river • *The raft drifted downstream.*

down-to-earth ADJECTIVE sensible and practical • *a down-to-earth approach.*

downtrodden ADJECTIVE People who are downtrodden are treated badly by those with power and do not have the ability to fight back.

downturn, downturns NOUN a decline in the economy or in the success of a company or industry.

down under (*informal*) NOUN ① Australia or New Zealand. ▶ ADVERB ② in or to Australia or New Zealand.

downwards ADVERB ① If you move or look downwards, you move or look towards the ground or towards a lower level • *His eyes travelled downwards.* ② If an amount or rate moves downwards, it decreases. **downward** ADJECTIVE

downwind ADVERB If something moves downwind, it moves in the same direction as the wind • *Sparks drifted downwind.*

dowry, dowries NOUN In some societies, a woman's dowry is money or property which her father gives to the man she marries.

doze, dozes, dozing, dozed VERB ① When you doze, you sleep lightly for a short period. ▶ NOUN ② a short, light sleep.

dozen, dozens NOUN A dozen things are twelve of them.

Dr ① [*Said* **dock**-*ter*] 'Dr' is short for 'Doctor' and is used before the name of someone with the highest form of academic degree or who practises medicine. ② 'Dr' is short for 'drive' in addresses.

drab, drabber, drabbest ADJECTIVE dull and unattractive. **drabness** NOUN

SIMILAR WORDS: dreary, dull

draft, drafts, drafting, drafted NOUN ① an early rough version of a document or speech. ▶ VERB ② When you draft a document or speech, you write the first rough version of it. ③ To draft people somewhere means to move them there so that they can do a specific job • *Various different presenters were drafted in.* ④ In Australian and New Zealand English, to draft cattle or sheep is to select some from a herd or flock.

SPELLING TIP
Do not confuse the spellings of *draft* and *draught: I would like to see a draft of that report by tomorrow; There's a draught coming under that door.*

---

drag, drags, dragging, dragged
VERB ① If you drag a heavy object somewhere, you pull it slowly and with difficulty. ② If you drag someone somewhere, you make them go although they may be unwilling. ③ If things drag behind you, they trail along the ground as you move along. ④ If an event or a period of time drags, it is boring and seems to last a long time. ▸ **NOUN** ⑤ SCIENCE Drag is the resistance to the motion of a body passing through air or a fluid.
SIMILAR WORDS: ① draw, haul, pull

dragon, dragons **NOUN** In stories and legends, a dragon is a fierce animal like a large lizard with wings and claws that breathes fire.

dragonfly, dragonflies **NOUN** a colourful insect which is often found near water.

dragoon, dragoons, dragooning, dragooned **NOUN** ① Dragoons are soldiers. Originally, they were mounted infantry soldiers. ▸ **VERB** ② If you dragoon someone into something, you force them to do it.

drain, drains, draining, drained
VERB ① If you drain something, you cause liquid to flow out of it. ② If you drain a glass, you drink all its contents. ③ If liquid drains somewhere, it flows there. ④ If something drains strength or resources, it gradually uses them up

• *The job seems to have drained him of energy.* ▸ **NOUN** ⑤ a pipe or channel that carries water or sewage away from a place. ⑥ a metal grid in a road, through which rainwater flows.

drainage **NOUN** ① Drainage is the system of pipes, drains or ditches used to drain water or other liquid away from a place. ② Drainage is also the process of draining water away, or the way in which a place drains • *To grow these plants well, all you need is good drainage.*

drainage basin, drainage basins
NOUN GEOGRAPHY the area of land from which rainwater drains into a particular river or reservoir.

drake, drakes **NOUN** a male duck.

drama, dramas **NOUN** ① a serious play for the theatre, television or radio. ② Drama is plays and the theatre in general • *Japanese drama.* ③ You can refer to the exciting events or aspects of a situation as drama • *the drama of real life.*

dramatic **ADJECTIVE** A dramatic change or event happens suddenly and is very noticeable • *a dramatic departure from tradition.*
dramatically **ADVERB**

dramatist, dramatists **NOUN** DRAMA a person who writes plays.

drank the past tense of **drink**.

drape, drapes, draping, draped
VERB ① If you drape a piece of cloth, you arrange it so that it hangs down or covers something in loose folds.
▸ **NOUN** ② Drapes are curtains, especially in American English.

drastic **ADJECTIVE** A drastic course of action is very severe and is usually taken urgently • *It's time for drastic measures to stop people littering.*
drastically **ADVERB**
SIMILAR WORDS: extreme, radical

draught, draughts [*Said draft*] **NOUN**

① a current of cold air. ② an amount of liquid that you swallow. ③ Draughts is a game for two people played on a chessboard with round pieces. ▶ ADJECTIVE ④ Draught beer is served straight from barrels rather than in bottles.

SPELLING TIP
Do not confuse the spellings of *draught* and *draft*: *There's a draught coming under that door; I would like to see a draft of that report by tomorrow.*

draughtsman, draughtsmen NOUN a person who prepares detailed drawings or plans.

draughty, draughtier, draughtiest ADJECTIVE A place that is draughty has currents of cold air blowing through it.

draw, draws, drawing, drew, drawn VERB ① When you draw, you use a pen or crayon to make a picture or diagram. ② To draw near means to move closer. To draw away or draw back means to move away. ③ If you draw something in a particular direction, you pull it there smoothly and gently • *He drew his feet under the chair.* ④ If you draw a deep breath, you breathe in deeply. ⑤ If you draw the curtains, you pull them so that they cover or uncover the window. ⑥ If something such as water or energy is drawn from a source, it is taken from it. ⑦ If you draw a conclusion, you arrive at it from the facts you know. ⑧ If you draw a distinction or a comparison between two things, you point out that it exists. ▶ NOUN ⑨ the result of a game or competition in which nobody wins. **draw up** VERB To draw up a plan, document or list means to prepare it and write it out.

drawback, drawbacks NOUN a problem that makes something less

acceptable or desirable • *Shortcuts usually have a drawback.*

drawbridge, drawbridges NOUN a bridge that can be pulled up or lowered.

drawer, drawers NOUN a sliding box-shaped part of a piece of furniture used for storing things.

drawing, drawings NOUN ① a picture made with a pencil, pen or crayon. ② Drawing is the skill or work of making drawings.

drawing pin, drawing pins NOUN [DGT] A drawing pin is a short nail with a broad, flat top.

drawing room, drawing rooms NOUN (*old-fashioned*) a room in a house where people relax or entertain guests.

drawl, drawls, drawling, drawled VERB If someone drawls, they speak slowly with long vowel sounds.

drawn Drawn is the past participle of **draw**.

dread, dreads, dreading, dreaded VERB ① If you dread something, you feel very worried and frightened about it • *He was dreading the journey.* ▶ NOUN ② Dread is a feeling of great fear or anxiety. **dreaded** ADJECTIVE

dreadful ADJECTIVE very bad or unpleasant. **dreadfully** ADVERB SIMILAR WORDS: atrocious, awful, terrible

dreadlocks PLURAL NOUN hair worn in the Rastafarian style of tightly curled strands.

dream, dreams, dreaming, dreamed or **dreamt** NOUN ① a series of events that you experience in your mind while asleep. ② a situation or event which you often think about because you would very much like it to happen • *his dream of winning the lottery.* ▶ VERB ③ When you dream, you see events in your mind while

you are asleep. ④When you dream about something happening, you often think about it because you would very much like it to happen. ⑤If someone dreams up a plan or idea, they invent it. ⑥If you say you would not dream of doing something, you are emphasising that you would not do it • *I wouldn't dream of giving the plot away*.
▶ ADJECTIVE ⑦too good to be true • *a dream holiday*. **dreamer** NOUN

Dreamtime NOUN Dreamtime is the same as Alcheringa.

dreamy, dreamier, dreamiest ADJECTIVE Someone with a dreamy expression looks as if they are thinking about something very pleasant.

dreary, drearier, dreariest ADJECTIVE dull or boring.

dregs PLURAL NOUN The dregs of a liquid are the last drops left at the bottom of a container, and any sediment left with it.

drenched ADJECTIVE soaking wet.

dress, dresses, dressing, dressed NOUN ①a piece of clothing made up of a skirt and top attached. ②Dress is any clothing.
▶ VERB ③When you dress, you put clothes on. ④If you dress for a special occasion, you put on formal clothes. ⑤To dress a wound means to clean it up and treat it.

dresser, dressers NOUN a piece of kitchen or dining room furniture with cupboards or drawers in the lower part and open shelves in the top part.

dressage [*Said dres-ahj*] NOUN the method of training horses to perform controlled movements.

dressing gown, dressing gowns NOUN an item of clothing shaped like a coat and put on over nightwear.

dressing room, dressing rooms NOUN a room used for getting changed and putting on make-up, especially a backstage room at a theatre.

dress rehearsal, dress rehearsals NOUN the last rehearsal of a show or play, using costumes, scenery and lighting.

drew the past tense of **draw**.

dribble, dribbles, dribbling, dribbled VERB ①When liquid dribbles down a surface, it trickles down it in drops or a thin stream. ②If a person or animal dribbles, saliva trickles from their mouth. ③In sport, to dribble a ball means to move it along by repeatedly tapping it with your foot or a stick.
▶ NOUN ④a small quantity of liquid flowing in a thin stream or drops.

drift, drifts, drifting, drifted VERB ①When something drifts, it is carried along by the wind or by water. ②When people drift somewhere, they wander or move there gradually. ③When people drift in life, they move without any aims from place to place or from one activity to another. ④If you drift off to sleep, you gradually fall asleep. ▶ NOUN ⑤A snow drift is a pile of snow heaped up by the wind. ⑥The drift of an argument or speech is its main point.
drifter NOUN
WORD HISTORY: from Old Norse *drift* meaning 'snow drift'

drill, drills, drilling, drilled NOUN ① DGT a tool for making holes • *an electric drill*. ②Drill is a routine exercise or routine training • *lifeboat drill*. ▶ VERB ③ DGT To drill into something means to make a hole in it using a drill. ④If you drill people, you teach them to do something by repetition.

drink, drinks, drinking, drank, drunk VERB ①When you drink, you take

liquid into your mouth and swallow it. ②To drink also means to drink alcohol • *He drinks little and eats carefully.* ▶ NOUN ③an amount of liquid suitable for drinking. ④an alcoholic drink. **drinker NOUN**
SIMILAR WORDS: ①imbibe, sip, swallow ②booze, tipple

drip, drips, dripping, dripped VERB
①When liquid drips, it falls in small drops. ②When an object drips, drops of liquid fall from it. ▶ NOUN ③a drop of liquid falling from something. ④a device for allowing liquid food or medicine to enter the bloodstream of a person who is ill.

drive, drives, driving, drove, driven
VERB ①To drive a vehicle means to operate it and control its movements. ②If something or someone drives you to do something, they force you to do it • *His lack of progress drove him to start again.* ③If you drive a post or nail into something, you force it in by hitting it with a hammer. ④If something drives a machine, it supplies the power that makes it work. ▶ NOUN ⑤a journey in a vehicle. ⑥a private road that leads from a public road to a person's house. ⑦Drive is energy and determination. **driver NOUN**
driving NOUN

drive-in, drive-ins NOUN a restaurant, cinema or other commercial place that is specially designed for customers to use while staying in their cars.

drivel NOUN Drivel is nonsense • *He is still writing mindless drivel.*

drizzle NOUN Drizzle is light rain.

dromedary, dromedaries NOUN a camel which has one hump.

drone, drones, droning, droned
VERB ①If something drones, it makes a low, continuous humming noise. ②If someone drones on, they keep talking or reading aloud in a boring way. ▶ NOUN ③a low, continuous humming sound. ④a type of aircraft that does not have a pilot and is controlled by someone on the ground.

drool, drools, drooling, drooled
VERB If someone drools, saliva dribbles from their mouth without them being able to stop it.

droop, droops, drooping, drooped
VERB If something droops, it hangs or sags downwards with no strength or firmness.

drop, drops, dropping, dropped
VERB ①If you drop something, you let it fall. ②If something drops, it falls straight down. ③If a level or amount drops, it becomes less. ④If your voice drops, or if you drop your voice, you speak more quietly. ⑤If you drop something that you are doing or dealing with, you stop doing it or dealing with it • *She dropped the subject and never mentioned it again.* ⑥If you drop a hint, you give someone a hint in a casual way. ⑦If you drop something or someone somewhere, you deposit or leave them there.
▶ NOUN ⑧A drop of liquid is a very small quantity of it that forms or falls in a round shape. ⑨a decrease • *a huge drop in income.* ⑩the distance between the top and bottom of something tall, such as a cliff or building • *It is a sheer drop to the foot of the cliff.*

droplet, droplets NOUN a small drop.

droppings PLURAL NOUN Droppings are the faeces of birds and small animals.

drought, droughts [*Rhymes with shout*] NOUN GEOGRAPHY a long period during which there is no rain.

drove, droves, droving, droved
①Drove is the past tense of **drive**.

▶ **VERB** ② To drove cattle or sheep is to drive them over a long distance.

drown, drowns, drowning, drowned **VERB** ① When someone drowns or is drowned, they die because they have gone under water and cannot breathe. ② If a noise drowns a sound, it is louder than the sound and makes it impossible to hear it.

drowsy, drowsier, drowsiest **ADJECTIVE** sleepy.

drudgery **NOUN** Drudgery is hard boring work.

drug, drugs, drugging, drugged **NOUN** ① a chemical given to people to treat disease. ② PSHE Drugs are chemical substances that some people smoke, swallow, inhale or inject because of their stimulating effects. ▶ **VERB** ③ To drug a person or animal means to give them a drug to make them unconscious. ④ To drug food or drink means to add a drug to it in order to make someone unconscious. **drugged** **ADJECTIVE**

druid, druids [Said droo-id] **NOUN** a priest of an ancient religion in Northern Europe.

drum, drums, drumming, drummed **NOUN** ① a musical instrument consisting of a skin stretched tightly over a round frame. ② an object or container shaped like a drum • an oil drum. ③ (informal) In Australian English, the drum is information or advice • The manager gave me the drum. ▶ **VERB** ④ If something is drumming on a surface, it is hitting it regularly, making a continuous beating sound. ⑤ If you drum something into someone, you keep saying it to them until they understand it or remember it. **drummer** **NOUN**

drumstick, drumsticks **NOUN** ① a stick used for beating a drum. ② A chicken drumstick is the lower part of the leg of a chicken, which is cooked and eaten.

drunk, drunks ① Drunk is the past participle of **drink**. ▶ **ADJECTIVE** ② If someone is drunk, they have drunk so much alcohol that they cannot speak clearly or behave sensibly. ▶ **NOUN** ③ a person who is drunk, or who often gets drunk. **drunken** **ADJECTIVE** **drunkenly** **ADVERB** **drunkenness** **NOUN**
SIMILAR WORDS: ② inebriated, intoxicated

dry, drier or dryer, driest or dryest; dries, drying, dried **ADJECTIVE** ① Something that is dry contains or uses no water or liquid. ② Dry bread or toast is eaten without a topping. ③ Dry sherry or wine does not taste sweet. ④ Dry also means plain and sometimes boring • the dry facts. ⑤ Dry humour is subtle and sarcastic. ▶ **VERB** ⑥ When you dry something, or when it dries, liquid is removed from it. **dryness** **NOUN** **drily** **ADVERB** **dry up** **VERB** ① If something dries up, it becomes completely dry. ② (informal) If you dry up, you forget what you were going to say, or find that you have nothing left to say.
SIMILAR WORDS: ① arid, dehydrated, parched

dry-clean, dry-cleans, dry-cleaning, dry-cleaned **VERB** When clothes are dry-cleaned, they are cleaned with a liquid chemical rather than with water.

dryer, dryers; also spelt **drier** **NOUN** a device for removing moisture from something by heating or by hot air • a hair dryer.

dual **ADJECTIVE** having two parts, functions or aspects • a dual-purpose trimmer.

SPELLING TIP
Do not confuse the spellings of *dual* and *duel*: *I have dual citizenship of Britain and the US; He was killed in a duel during the Civil War.*

dual-heritage ADJECTIVE A dual-heritage family has parents with different ethnic or religious backgrounds.

dub, dubs, dubbing, dubbed VERB ① If something is dubbed a particular name, it is given that name • *Smiling has been dubbed 'nature's secret weapon'.* ② If a film is dubbed, the voices on the soundtrack are not those of the actors, but those of other actors speaking in a different language.

dubious [Said **dyoo-bee-uss**] ADJECTIVE ① not entirely honest, safe or reliable • *dubious sales techniques.* ② doubtful • *I felt dubious about the entire proposition.* **dubiously** ADVERB SIMILAR WORDS: ① questionable, suspect

duchess, duchesses NOUN a woman who has the same rank as a duke, or who is a duke's wife or widow.

duchy, duchies [Said **dut-shee**] NOUN the land owned and ruled by a duke or duchess.

duck, ducks, ducking, ducked NOUN ① a bird that lives in water and has webbed feet and a large flat bill. ▸ VERB ② If you duck, you move your head quickly downwards in order to avoid being hit by something. ③ If you duck a duty or responsibility, you avoid it. ④ To duck someone means to push them briefly under water.

duckling, ducklings NOUN a young duck.

duct, ducts NOUN ① a pipe or channel through which liquid or gas is sent. ② a bodily passage through which liquid such as tears can pass.

ductile ADJECTIVE DGT Material that is ductile is soft enough be shaped, moulded or drawn out into threads • *Copper is a ductile metal.*

dud, duds NOUN something which does not function properly.

due, dues ADJECTIVE ① expected to happen or arrive • *The baby is due at Christmas.* ② If you give something due consideration, you give it the consideration it needs. ▸ PHRASE ③ **Due to** means caused by • *Headaches can be due to stress.* ▸ ADVERB ④ Due means exactly in a particular direction • *About a mile due west lay the ocean.* ▸ NOUN ⑤ (in plural) Dues are sums of money that you pay regularly to an organisation you belong to.

duel, duels NOUN ① a fight arranged between two people using deadly weapons, to settle a quarrel. ② Any contest or conflict between two people can be referred to as a duel.

SPELLING TIP
Do not confuse the spellings of *duel* and *dual*: *He was killed in a duel during the Civil War; I have dual citizenship of Britain and the US.*

duet, duets NOUN MUSIC a piece of music sung or played by two people.

dug Dug is the past tense and past participle of **dig**.

dugout, dugouts NOUN ① a canoe made by hollowing out a log. ② (Military) a shelter dug in the ground for protection.

duiker, duikers [Said **dike-er**] NOUN a small African antelope. **WORD HISTORY**: a Dutch word meaning 'diver'

duke, dukes NOUN a nobleman with a rank just below that of a prince. **WORD HISTORY**: from Latin *dux* meaning 'leader'

dull, duller, dullest; dulls, dulling, dulled ADJECTIVE ① not at all interesting in any way. ② not bright, sharp or clear. ③ A dull day or dull sky is very cloudy. ④ Dull feelings are weak and not intense • *He should have been angry but felt only dull resentment.* ▶ VERB ⑤ If something dulls or is dulled, it becomes less bright, sharp or clear. **dully** ADVERB **dullness** NOUN

SIMILAR WORDS: ③ cloudy, overcast

duly ADVERB ① (*formal*) If something is duly done, it is done in the correct way • *I wish to record my support for the duly elected council.* ② If something duly happens, it is something that you expected to happen • *Two chicks duly emerged from their eggs.*

dumb, dumber, dumbest ADJECTIVE ① unable to speak • *She was dumb with rage.* ② (*informal*) slow to understand or stupid.

dumbfounded ADJECTIVE speechless with amazement • *She was too dumbfounded to answer.*

dummy, dummies NOUN ① a rubber teat which a baby sucks or bites on. ② an imitation or model of something which is used for display. ▶ ADJECTIVE ③ imitation or substitute.

dump, dumps, dumping, dumped VERB ① When unwanted waste is dumped, it is left somewhere. ② If you dump something, you throw it down or put it down somewhere in a careless way. ▶ NOUN ③ a place where rubbish is left. ④ a storage place, especially used by the military for storing supplies. ⑤ (*informal*) You refer to a place as a dump when it is unattractive and unpleasant to live in.

dumpling, dumplings NOUN a small lump of dough that is cooked and eaten with meat and vegetables.

dunce, dunces NOUN a person who cannot learn what someone is trying to teach them.

dune, dunes NOUN A dune or sand dune is a hill of sand near the sea or in the desert.

dung NOUN Dung is the faeces from large animals, sometimes called manure.

dungarees PLURAL NOUN Dungarees are trousers which have a bib covering the chest and straps over the shoulders. They are named after Dungri in India, where dungaree material was first made.

dungeon, dungeons [*Said dun-jen*] NOUN an underground prison.

dunk, dunks, dunking, dunked VERB To dunk something means to dip it briefly into a liquid • *He dunked a single tea bag into two cups.*

duo, duos NOUN ① a pair of musical performers; also a piece of music written for two players. ② Any two people doing something together can be referred to as a duo.

dupe, dupes, duping, duped VERB ① If someone dupes you, they trick you. ▶ NOUN ② someone who has been tricked.

WORD HISTORY: from Old French *de huppe* meaning 'of the hoopoe', a bird thought to be stupid

duplicate, duplicates, duplicating, duplicated VERB [*Said dyoop-lik-ayt*] ① To duplicate something means to make an exact copy of it. ▶ NOUN [*Said dyoop-lik-it*] ② something that is identical to something else. ▶ ADJECTIVE [*Said dyoop-lik-it*] ③ identical to or an exact copy of • *a duplicate key.* **duplication** NOUN

durable ADJECTIVE strong and lasting for a long time. **durability** NOUN

duration NOUN The duration of something is the length of time during which it happens or exists.

duress [Said dyoo-**ress**] NOUN If you do something under duress, you are forced to do it, and you do it very unwillingly.

during PREPOSITION happening throughout a particular time or at a particular point in time • *The mussels will open naturally during cooking.*

dusk NOUN Dusk is the time just before nightfall when it is not completely dark.

WORD HISTORY: from Old English *dox* meaning 'dark' or 'swarthy'

dust, dusts, dusting, dusted NOUN ① Dust is dry fine powdery material such as particles of earth, dirt or pollen. ▶ VERB ② When you dust furniture or other objects, you remove dust from them using a duster. ③ If you dust a surface with powder, you cover it lightly with the powder.

dustbin, dustbins NOUN a large container for rubbish.

duster, dusters NOUN a cloth used for removing dust from furniture and other objects.

dustman, dustmen NOUN someone whose job is to collect the rubbish from people's houses.

dusty, dustier, dustiest ADJECTIVE covered with dust.

Dutch ADJECTIVE ① belonging or relating to Holland. ▶ NOUN ② Dutch is the main language spoken in Holland.

dutiful ADJECTIVE doing everything you are expected to do. **dutifully** ADVERB

duty, duties NOUN ① something you ought to do or feel you should do, because it is your responsibility • *Adults have a duty to listen to children.* ② a task which you do as part of your job. ③ Duty is tax paid to the government on some goods, especially imports.

SIMILAR WORDS: ① obligation, responsibility

duty-free ADJECTIVE Duty-free goods are sold at airports or on planes or ships at a cheaper price than usual because they are not taxed.

duvet, duvets [Said doo-**vay**] NOUN a cotton quilt filled with feathers or other material, which you put over yourself in bed.

DVD, DVDs NOUN A DVD is a disc that can store large amounts of video and sound information. DVD is an abbreviation for 'digital video disc' or 'digital versatile disc'.

dwarf, dwarfs, dwarfing, dwarfed VERB ① If one thing dwarfs another, it is so much bigger that it makes it look very small. ▶ ADJECTIVE ② smaller than average. ▶ NOUN ③ a person who is much smaller than average size.

dwell, dwells, dwelling, dwelled or dwelt VERB ① (*literary*) To dwell somewhere means to live there. ② If you dwell on something or dwell upon it, you think or write about it a lot.

dwelling, dwellings NOUN (*formal*) Someone's dwelling is the house or other place where they live.

dwindle, dwindles, dwindling, dwindled VERB If something dwindles, it becomes smaller or weaker.

dye, dyes, dyeing, dyed VERB ① To dye something means to change its colour by applying coloured liquid to it. ▶ NOUN ② a colouring substance which is used to change the colour of something such as cloth or hair.

dying ADJECTIVE ① likely to die soon. ② (*informal*) If you are **dying for something**, you want it very much.

a
b
c
d
e
f
g
h
i
j
k
l
m
n
o
p
q
r
s
t
u
v
w
x
y
z

SPELLING TIP
Do not confuse the spellings of *dying* and *dyeing*: *Children are dying of hunger every day; I warned her against dyeing her hair that colour.*

dyke, dykes; also spelt **dike** NOUN a thick wall that prevents water flooding onto land from a river or from the sea.

dynamic, dynamics ADJECTIVE ① A dynamic person is full of energy, ambition and new ideas. ② relating to energy or forces which produce motion.

dynamics PLURAL NOUN ① The dynamics of a society or a situation are the forces that cause it to change. ② MUSIC Dynamics is the various degrees of loudness needed in the performance of a piece of music, or the symbols used to indicate this in written music.

dynamite NOUN Dynamite is an explosive made of nitroglycerine.

dynamo, dynamos NOUN SCIENCE a device that converts mechanical energy into electricity.

dynasty, dynasties NOUN HISTORY a series of rulers of a country all belonging to the same family.

dysentery [Said *diss-en-tree*] NOUN an infection of the bowel which causes fever, stomach pain and severe diarrhoea.

dyslexia [Said *dis-lek-see-a*] NOUN Dyslexia is difficulty with reading and spelling caused by a slight disorder of the brain. **dyslexic** ADJECTIVE

Ee

e- PREFIX Words beginning with 'e-' have something to do with the internet • *e-reader*.
WORD HISTORY: from *electronic*

each ADJECTIVE or PRONOUN ① every one taken separately • *Each time she went out, she would buy a plant.*
▶ PHRASE ② If people do something to **each other**, each person does it to the other or others • *She and Chris smiled at each other.*

USAGE NOTE
Wherever you use *each other*, you could also use *one another*.

---

eager ADJECTIVE wanting very much to do or have something. **eagerly** ADVERB **eagerness** NOUN

eagle, eagles NOUN a large bird of prey.

ear, ears NOUN ① the parts of your body on either side of your head with which you hear sounds. ② An ear of corn or wheat is the top part of the stalk which contains seeds.

eardrum, eardrums NOUN Your eardrums are thin pieces of tightly stretched skin inside your ears which vibrate so that you can hear sounds.

earl, earls NOUN a British nobleman.
WORD HISTORY: from Old English *eorl* meaning 'chieftain'

early, earlier, earliest ADJECTIVE ① before the arranged or expected time • *He wasn't late for our meeting, I was early.* ② near the beginning of a day, evening or other period of time • *the early 2000s.* ▶ ADVERB ③ before the arranged or expected time • *I arrived early.*
SIMILAR WORDS: ① premature, untimely

earmark, earmarks, earmarking, earmarked VERB If you earmark something for a special purpose, you keep it for that purpose.
WORD HISTORY: from identification marks on the ears of domestic or farm animals

earn, earns, earning, earned VERB ① If you earn money, you get it in return for work that you do. ② If you earn something such as praise, you receive it because you deserve it.
earner NOUN

earnest ADJECTIVE ① sincere in what you say or do • *I answered with an earnest smile.* ▶ PHRASE ② If something begins **in earnest**, it happens to a greater or more serious extent than before • *The battle began in earnest.* **earnestly** ADVERB

earnings PLURAL NOUN Your earnings are money that you earn.

earphones PLURAL NOUN small speakers which you wear on your ears to listen to sounds from an electronic device.

earring, earrings NOUN Earrings are pieces of jewellery that you wear on your ear lobes.

earshot PHRASE If you are **within earshot** of something, you can hear it.

earth, earths NOUN ① The earth is the planet on which we live. ② Earth is the dry land on the surface of the earth, especially the soil in which things grow. ③ a hole in the ground where a fox lives. ④ The earth in a piece of electrical equipment is the wire through which electricity can pass into the ground and so make the equipment safe for use.

earthenware NOUN pottery made of baked clay.

earthly, **earthlier**, **earthliest** ADJECTIVE concerned with life on earth rather than heaven or life after death.

earthquake, **earthquakes** NOUN SCIENCE GEOGRAPHY a shaking of the ground caused by movement of the earth.

earthworm, **earthworms** NOUN a worm that lives under the ground.

earthy, **earthier**, **earthiest** ADJECTIVE ① looking or smelling like earth. ② Someone who is earthy is open and direct, often in a crude way • *earthy language*.

earwig, **earwigs** NOUN a small, thin, brown insect which has a pair of pincers at the end of its body.
WORD HISTORY: from Old English *earwicga* meaning 'ear insect'; it was believed to creep into people's ears

ease, **eases**, **easing**, **eased** NOUN ① lack of difficulty, worry or hardship • *He had sailed through life with relative ease.* ▶ VERB ② When something eases, or when you ease it, it becomes less severe or less intense • *to ease the pain.* ③ If you ease something somewhere, you move it there slowly and carefully • *He eased himself into his chair.*
SIMILAR WORDS: ① easiness, effortlessness ② alleviate, relieve

easel, **easels** NOUN ART an upright frame which supports a picture that someone is painting.

WORD HISTORY: from Dutch *ezel* meaning 'ass' or 'donkey'

easily ADVERB ① without difficulty. ② without a doubt • *The song is easily one of their finest.*

east NOUN ① East is the direction in which you look to see the sun rise. ② The east of a place is the part which is towards the east when you are in the centre • *the east of Africa.* ③ The East is the countries in the south and east of Asia. ▶ ADJECTIVE or ADVERB ④ East means in or towards the east • *The entrance faces east.* ▶ ADJECTIVE ⑤ An east wind blows from the east.

Easter NOUN RE a Christian religious festival celebrating Jesus Christ's coming back to life after he had been killed.
WORD HISTORY: from Old English *Eostre*, a pre-Christian Germanic goddess whose festival was at the spring equinox

easterly ADJECTIVE ① Easterly means to or towards the east. ② An easterly wind blows from the east.

eastern ADJECTIVE in or from the east • *a remote eastern corner of the country.*

eastward or **eastwards** ADVERB ① Eastward or eastwards means towards the east • *The city expanded eastward.* ▶ ADJECTIVE ② The eastward part of something is the east part.

easy, **easier**, **easiest** ADJECTIVE ① able to be done without difficulty • *It's easy to fall.* ② comfortable and without any worries • *an easy life.*

GRAMMAR TIP
Although *easy* is an adjective, it can be used as an adverb in fixed phrases like *take it easy*.

eat, **eats**, **eating**, **ate**, **eaten** VERB ① To eat means to chew and swallow food. ② When you eat, you have a

meal • *We like to eat early.* **eat away**
VERB If something is eaten away, it is
slowly destroyed • *The sea had eaten
away at the headland.*

eaves **PLURAL NOUN** The eaves of a
roof are the lower edges which jut
out over the walls.

eavesdrop, eavesdrops,
eavesdropping, eavesdropped
VERB If you eavesdrop, you listen
secretly to what other people are
saying.
WORD HISTORY: from Old English
yfesdrype meaning 'water dripping
down from the eaves'; people were
supposed to stand outside in the rain
to hear what was being said inside
the house

ebb, ebbs, ebbing, ebbed **VERB**
①When the sea or the tide ebbs, it
flows back. ②If a person's feeling or
strength ebbs, it gets weaker • *The
strength ebbed from his body.*

Ebola virus **NOUN** a virus that causes
a severe infectious disease.

ebony **NOUN** ①a hard, dark-coloured
wood, used for making furniture.
▶ **NOUN** or **ADJECTIVE** ②very deep
black.

e-book, e-books **NOUN** a book that is
produced in a format that can be read
using a portable electronic device.

ebullient **ADJECTIVE** (*formal*) lively
and full of enthusiasm. **ebullience**
NOUN

e-card, e-cards **NOUN** ICT a
greetings card that is sent by
computer.

eccentric, eccentrics *[Said ik-sen-trik]*
ADJECTIVE ①having habits or
opinions which other people think
are odd or peculiar. ▶ **NOUN**
②someone who is eccentric.
eccentricity **NOUN** **eccentrically**
ADVERB
SIMILAR WORDS: ①odd, peculiar,

strange ②crank, oddball, weirdo

ecclesiastical *[Said ik-leez-ee-ass-ti-kl]*
ADJECTIVE of or relating to the
Christian Church.
WORD HISTORY: from Greek *ekklēsia*
meaning 'assembly' or 'church'

echelon, echelons *[Said esh-el-on]*
NOUN ①An echelon is a level of
power or responsibility in an
organisation; also used of the group
of people at that level. ②An echelon
is also a military formation in the
shape of an arrowhead.
WORD HISTORY: from French *échelon*
meaning 'rung of a ladder'

echidna, echidnas or echidnae *[Said
ik-kid-na]* **NOUN** a small, spiny
mammal that lays eggs and has a
long snout and claws, found in
Australia.

echo, echoes, echoing, echoed
NOUN ① SCIENCE a sound which is
caused by sound waves reflecting off
a surface. ②a repetition, imitation
or reminder of something • *Echoes of
the past are everywhere.* ▶ **VERB** ③If a
sound echoes, it is reflected off a
surface so that you can hear it again
after the original sound has stopped.

eclipse, eclipses **NOUN** An eclipse
occurs when one planet passes in
front of another and hides it from
view for a short time.

eco- **PREFIX** Words beginning with
'eco-' have something to do with
ecology or the environment.
WORD HISTORY: from Greek *oikos*
meaning 'environment'

eco-friendly, eco-friendlier,
eco-friendliest **ADJECTIVE** If a
product is eco-friendly, it does not
cause any damage to the
environment • *eco-friendly washing
powder.*

ecology **NOUN** SCIENCE the
relationship between living things

a
b
c
d
e
f
g
h
i
j
k
l
m
n
o
p
q
r
s
t
u
v
w
x
y
z

and their environment; also used of the study of this relationship.

ecological ADJECTIVE **ecologically** ADVERB **ecologist** NOUN

economic ADJECTIVE ① concerning the management of the money, industry and trade of a country. ② concerning making a profit • *economic ways to produce dairy foods.*

economical ADJECTIVE ① another word for **economic**. ② Something that is economical is cheap to use or operate. ③ Someone who is economical spends money carefully and sensibly. **economically** ADVERB

economics NOUN Economics is the study of the production and distribution of goods, services and wealth in a society and the organisation of its money, industry and trade.

economist, economists NOUN a person who studies or writes about economics.

economy, economies NOUN ① HISTORY The economy of a country is the system it uses to organise and manage its money, industry and trade; also used of the wealth that a country gets from business and industry. ② Economy is the careful use of things to save money, time or energy • *There is a wonderful economy of effort about this recipe.*
WORD HISTORY: from Greek *oikonomia* meaning 'domestic management'

ecosystem, ecosystems NOUN SCIENCE the relationship between plants and animals and their environment.

ecstasy, ecstasies NOUN ① Ecstasy is a feeling of extreme happiness. ② (*informal*) a strong illegal drug that can cause hallucinations. **ecstatic** ADJECTIVE **ecstatically** ADVERB

eczema [*Said* **ek**-*sim-ma or* ek-**see**-*ma*] NOUN a skin disease that causes the surface of the skin to become rough and itchy.
WORD HISTORY: from Greek *ekzein* meaning 'to boil over'

-ed SUFFIX '-ed' is used to form the past tense of most English verbs • *jumped* • *tried.*

eddy, eddies NOUN a circular movement in water or air.

edge, edges, edging, edged NOUN ① The edge of something is a border or line where it ends or meets something else. ② The edge of a blade is its thin, sharp side. ③ If you have the edge over someone, you have an advantage over them.
▸ VERB ④ If you edge something, you make a border for it • *The veil was edged with matching lace.* ⑤ If you edge somewhere, you move there very gradually • *The ferry edged its way out into the river.*
SIMILAR WORDS: ① border, brink, margin

edgy, edgier, edgiest ADJECTIVE anxious and irritable.

edible ADJECTIVE safe and pleasant to eat.

edifice, edifices [*Said* ed-*if-iss*] NOUN (*formal*) a large and impressive building.

edit, edits, editing, edited VERB ① If you edit a piece of writing, you correct it so that it is fit for publishing. ② To edit a film or television programme means to select different parts of it and arrange them in a particular order. ③ Someone who edits a newspaper or magazine is in charge of it.

edition, editions NOUN ① ENGLISH An edition of a book, magazine or newspaper is a particular version of it printed at one time; also the total

number of copies printed at one time. ②An edition of a television or radio programme is a single programme that is one of a series • *tonight's edition of the news*.
WORD HISTORY: from Latin *edere* meaning 'to give out'

editor, editors NOUN ①a person who is responsible for the content of a newspaper or magazine. ② LIBRARY a person who checks books and makes corrections to them before they are published. ③a person who selects different parts of a television programme or a film and arranges them in a particular order.
editorship NOUN

editorial, editorials ADJECTIVE ①involved in preparing a newspaper, book or magazine for publication. ②involving the contents and the opinions of a newspaper or magazine • *an editorial comment*. ▶ NOUN ③an article in a newspaper or magazine which gives the opinions of the editor or publisher on a particular topic.
editorially ADVERB

educate, educates, educating, educated VERB To educate someone means to teach them so that they gain knowledge about something.

educated ADJECTIVE having a high standard of learning and culture.

education NOUN the process of gaining knowledge and understanding through learning or the system of teaching people.
educational ADJECTIVE
educationally ADVERB

eel, eels NOUN a long, thin, snakelike fish.

eerie, eerier, eeriest ADJECTIVE strange and frightening • *an eerie silence*. **eerily** ADVERB

effect, effects NOUN ①a direct result of someone or something on another

person or thing • *the effects of bullying on children*. ②An effect that someone or something has is the overall impression or result that they have • *The effect of the decor was cosy and antique*. ▶ PHRASE ③If something **takes effect** at a particular time, it starts to happen or starts to produce results at that time • *The law will take effect next year*.

SPELLING TIP
Do not confuse the spelling of the noun *effect* with the verb *affect*. Something that *affects* you has an *effect* on you.

---

effective ADJECTIVE ①working well and producing the intended results. ②coming into operation or beginning officially • *The agreement has become effective immediately*.
effectively ADVERB

effeminate ADJECTIVE A man who is effeminate behaves, looks or sounds like a woman.

effervescent ADJECTIVE ①An effervescent liquid is fizzy and gives off bubbles of gas. ②Someone who is effervescent is lively and enthusiastic. **effervescence** NOUN

efficient ADJECTIVE capable of doing something well without wasting time or energy. **efficiently** ADVERB
efficiency NOUN
SIMILAR WORDS: capable, competent, proficient

effigy, effigies [Said ef-fij-ee] NOUN a statue or model of a person.

effluent [Said ef-loo-ent] NOUN Effluent is liquid waste that comes out of factories or sewage works.

effort, efforts NOUN ① PSHE Effort is the physical or mental energy needed to do something. ②an attempt or struggle to do something • *The town has banned cars*

A
B
C
D
E
F
G
H
I
J
K
L
M
N
O
P
Q
R
S
T
U
V
W
X
Y
Z

in an effort to cut pollution.
SIMILAR WORDS: ① exertion, trouble, work

effortless ADJECTIVE done easily.
effortlessly ADVERB

eg or **e.g.** Eg means 'for example', and is abbreviated from the Latin expression 'exempli gratia'.

egalitarian ADJECTIVE favouring equality for all people • *an egalitarian country.*

egg, eggs, egging, egged NOUN ① an oval or rounded object laid by female birds, reptiles, fishes and insects. A baby creature develops inside the egg until it is ready to be born. ② a hen's egg used as food. ③ In a female animal, an egg is a cell produced in its body which can develop into a baby if it is fertilised.
egg on VERB If you egg someone on, you encourage them to do something foolish or daring.

eggplant, eggplants NOUN a dark purple pear-shaped fruit eaten as a vegetable. It is also called **aubergine**.

ego, egos [Said *ee-goh*] NOUN Your ego is your opinion of what you are worth • *It'll do her good and boost her ego.*
WORD HISTORY: from Latin *ego* meaning 'I'

egocentric ADJECTIVE only thinking of yourself.

egoism or **egotism** NOUN Egoism is behaviour and attitudes which show that you believe that you are more important than other people. **egoist** or **egotist** NOUN **egoistic** or **egotistic** or **egotistical** ADJECTIVE

Egyptian, Egyptians [Said *ij-jip-shn*] ADJECTIVE ① belonging or relating to Egypt. ▶ NOUN ② An Egyptian is someone who comes from Egypt.

eiderdown, eiderdowns NOUN An eiderdown is a thick bed covering that is filled with feathers.

Eid-ul-Adha [Said *eed-dool-ah-duh*] NOUN RE an annual Muslim festival marking the end of the pilgrimage to Mecca known as the hajj. Animals are sacrificed and their meat is shared among the poor.
WORD HISTORY: from Arabic *id ul adha* meaning 'festival of sacrifice'

Eid ul-Fitr [Said *eed-dool-fee-tuh*] NOUN RE an annual Muslim festival marking the end of Ramadan.
WORD HISTORY: from Arabic *id ul fitr* meaning 'festival of fast-breaking'

eight, eights ① the number 8. ▶ NOUN ② In rowing, an eight is the crew of a narrow racing boat, consisting of eight rowers. **eighth** ADJECTIVE

eighteen the number 18.
eighteenth ADJECTIVE

eighty, eighties the number 80.
eightieth ADJECTIVE

either ADJECTIVE or PRONOUN or CONJUNCTION ① one or the other of two possible alternatives • *You can spell it either way* • *Either of these schemes would cost billions of pounds* • *Either take it or leave it.* ▶ ADJECTIVE ② both one and the other • *on either side of the head.*

GRAMMAR TIP
When *either* is followed by a plural noun, the following verb can be plural too: *either of these books are useful.*

ejaculate, ejaculates, ejaculating, ejaculated VERB If you ejaculate, you suddenly say something.
ejaculation NOUN
WORD HISTORY: from Latin *jacere* meaning 'to throw'

eject, ejects, ejecting, ejected VERB If you eject something or someone, you forcefully push or send them out • *He was ejected from the club.*
ejection NOUN
SIMILAR WORDS: expel, throw out

elaborate, elaborates, elaborating, elaborated ADJECTIVE [Said e-la-bor-it] ① having many different parts • *an elaborate system of drains.* ② carefully planned, detailed and exact • *elaborate plans.* ③ highly decorated and complicated • *elaborate designs.* ▶ VERB [Said e-la-bor-ate] ④ If you elaborate on something, you add more information or detail about it. **elaborately** ADVERB **elaboration** NOUN

SIMILAR WORDS: ③ complicated, fancy, ornate

eland, elands NOUN a large African antelope with twisted horns.

elapse, elapses, elapsing, elapsed VERB When time elapses, it passes by • *Eleven years elapsed before you got this job.*

elastic ADJECTIVE ① able to stretch easily. ▶ NOUN ② Elastic is rubber material which stretches and returns to its original shape. **elasticity** NOUN

elation NOUN Elation is a feeling of great happiness. **elated** ADJECTIVE

elbow, elbows, elbowing, elbowed NOUN ① Your elbow is the joint between the upper part of your arm and your forearm. ▶ VERB ② If you elbow someone aside, you push them away with your elbow.

elder, eldest; elders ADJECTIVE ① Your elder brother or sister is older than you. ▶ NOUN ② a senior member of a group who has influence or authority. ③ a bush or small tree with dark purple berries.

USAGE NOTE
The adjectives *elder* and *eldest* can only be used when talking about the age of people within families. You can use *older* and *oldest* to talk about the age of other people or things.

elderly ADJECTIVE Elderly is a polite way to describe an old person • *our elderly relatives.*

elect, elects, electing, elected VERB ① CITIZENSHIP If you elect someone, you choose them to fill a position, by voting • *He's just been elected president.* ② (formal) If you elect to do something, you choose to do it • *I have elected to stay.* ▶ ADJECTIVE ③ (formal) voted into a position, but not yet carrying out the duties of the position • *the vice-president elect.*

election, elections NOUN CITIZENSHIP the selection of one or more people for an official position by voting. **electoral** ADJECTIVE

electorate, electorates NOUN all the people who have the right to vote in an election.

electric ADJECTIVE ① powered or produced by electricity. ② very tense or exciting • *The atmosphere is electric.*

GRAMMAR TIP
The word *electric* is an adjective and should not be used as a noun.

electrical ADJECTIVE using or producing electricity • *electrical goods.* **electrically** ADVERB

electrician, electricians NOUN a person whose job is to install and repair electrical equipment.

electricity NOUN Electricity is a form of energy used for heating and lighting, and to provide power for machines.

WORD HISTORY: from Greek *ēlektron* meaning 'amber'; in early experiments, scientists rubbed amber in order to get an electrical charge

electrified ADJECTIVE connected to a supply of electricity.

electrifying ADJECTIVE Something

that is electrifying makes you feel very excited.

electro- PREFIX 'Electro-' means 'electric' or involving electricity.

electrocute, electrocutes, electrocuting, electrocuted VERB If someone is electrocuted, they are killed by touching something that is connected to electricity. **electrocution** NOUN

electrode, electrodes NOUN a small piece of metal which allows an electric current to pass between a source of power and a piece of equipment.

electrolysis [Said il-ek-**trol**-iss-iss] NOUN SCIENCE Electrolysis is the process of passing an electric current through a substance in order to produce chemical changes in it.

electromagnet, electromagnets NOUN SCIENCE a magnet made up of an iron or steel core with a coil of wire round it, through which an electric current is passed. **electromagnetic** ADJECTIVE

electron, electrons NOUN ① SCIENCE In physics, an electron is a tiny particle of matter, smaller than an atom. ② SCIENCE An **electron shell** is the orbit of an electron around the nucleus of an atom.

electronic ADJECTIVE ICT having transistors or silicon chips which control an electric current. **electronically** ADVERB

electronics NOUN Electronics is the technology of electronic devices such as televisions and computers; also the study of how these devices work.

electrostatic ADJECTIVE SCIENCE An electrostatic effect is an effect that relates to an electric field, or is created by an electric charge.

elegant ADJECTIVE attractive and graceful or stylish • an elegant and

beautiful city. **elegantly** ADVERB **elegance** NOUN

elegiac [Said el-lij-**eye**-ak] ADJECTIVE ENGLISH (literary) (literary) expressing or showing sadness.

elegy, elegies [Said el-lij-ee] NOUN a sad poem or song about someone who has died.

element, elements NOUN ① a part of something which combines with others to make a whole. ② SCIENCE In chemistry, an element is a substance that is made up of only one type of atom. ③ A particular element within a large group of people is a section of it which is similar • criminal elements. ④ An element of a quality is a certain amount of it • Their attack has largely lost the element of surprise. ⑤ The elements of a subject are the basic and most important points. ⑥ The elements are the weather conditions • Our open boat is exposed to the elements.

elemental ADJECTIVE (formal) simple and basic, but powerful • elemental emotions.

elementary ADJECTIVE simple, basic and straightforward • an elementary course in woodwork.

elephant, elephants NOUN a very large four-legged mammal with a long trunk, large ears, and ivory tusks.

elevate, elevates, elevating, elevated VERB ① To elevate someone to a higher status or position means to give them greater status or importance • He was elevated to the rank of major in the army. ② To elevate something means to raise it up.

elevation, elevations NOUN ① The elevation of someone or something is the raising of them to a higher level or position. ② The elevation of a place is its height above sea level or above the ground.

elevator, elevators NOUN In American English, an elevator is a lift for carrying people.

eleven, elevens ① the number 11. ▸NOUN ② a team of cricket or soccer players. **eleventh** ADJECTIVE

elf, elves NOUN In folklore, an elf is a small mischievous fairy.

elicit, elicits, eliciting, elicited [Said il-*iss*-it] VERB ① (formal) If you elicit information, you find it out by asking careful questions. ② If you elicit a response or reaction, you make it happen • *He elicited sympathy from the audience.*

SPELLING TIP

Do not confuse the spellings of *elicit* and *illicit*: *It is the police's job to elicit the truth from the suspect; an illicit business deal.*

---

eligible [Said el-*lij*-i-bl] ADJECTIVE suitable or having the right qualifications for something • *You will be eligible for a grant in the future.* **eligibility** NOUN

SPELLING TIP

Do not confuse the spellings of *eligible* and *illegible*: *George is not eligible to vote; Your handwriting is illegible.*

---

eliminate, eliminates, eliminating, eliminated VERB ① If you eliminate something or someone, you get rid of them • *They eliminated him from their inquiries.* ② If a team or a person is eliminated from a competition, they can no longer take part. **elimination** NOUN

elite, elites [Said ill-*eet*] NOUN a group of the most powerful, rich or talented people in a society.

Elizabethan HISTORY ADJECTIVE Someone or something that is

Elizabethan lived or was made during the reign of Elizabeth I.

elk, elks NOUN a large kind of deer.

ellipse, ellipses NOUN a regular oval shape, like a circle seen from an angle.

ellipsis, ellipses NOUN ENGLISH Ellipsis is the omission of parts of a sentence when the sentence can be understood without these parts. An example is 'You coming too?', where 'Are' has been omitted from the beginning of the question.

elm, elms NOUN a tall tree with broad leaves.

elocution NOUN the art or study of speaking clearly or well in public.

elongated ADJECTIVE long and thin.

elope, elopes, eloping, eloped VERB If someone elopes, they run away secretly with their lover to get married.

eloquent ADJECTIVE able to speak or write skilfully and with ease • *an eloquent politician.* **eloquently** ADVERB **eloquence** NOUN

else ADVERB ① other than this or more than this • *Can you think of anything else?* ▸PHRASE ② You say **or else** to introduce a possibility or an alternative • *You have to go with the flow or else be left behind in the rush.*

elsewhere ADVERB in or to another place • *He would rather be elsewhere.*

elude, eludes, eluding, eluded [Said ill-*ood*] VERB ① If a fact or idea eludes you, you cannot understand it or remember it. ② If you elude someone or something, you avoid them or escape from them • *He eluded the authorities.*

SPELLING TIP

Do not confuse *elude* with *allude*: *I knew his face but his name eluded me; She alluded to the report in the newspaper.*

---

elusive ADJECTIVE difficult to find, achieve, describe or remember • *the elusive million dollar prize.*

elves the plural of **elf**.

em- PREFIX 'Em-' is another form of the prefix **en-**.

SPELLING TIP
em- is the form which is used before the letters *b*, *m* and *p*.

---

emaciated [*Said im-**may**-see-ate-ed*] ADJECTIVE extremely thin and weak, because of illness or lack of food.

email; also spelt **e-mail** NOUN ① the sending of messages from one computer to another. ② a message sent in this way. ▶ VERB ③ If you email someone, you send an email to them. ④ If you email something to someone, you send it to them by email.

emancipate, emancipates, emancipating, emancipated VERB To emancipate someone means to free them from situations or restrictions which are unpleasant or harmful. **emancipation** NOUN
WORD HISTORY: from Latin *emancipare* meaning 'to give independence to a son'

emancipation NOUN The emancipation of a person means the act of freeing them from harmful or unpleasant restrictions.

embargo, embargoes NOUN an order made by a government to stop trade with another country.

embark, embarks, embarking, embarked VERB ① If you embark, you go onto a ship at the start of a journey. ② If you embark on something, you start it • *He embarked on a huge spending spree.*

embarrass, embarrasses, embarrassing, embarrassed VERB If you embarrass someone, you make them feel ashamed or awkward • *I won't embarrass you by asking for details.* **embarrassing** ADJECTIVE

embarrassed ADJECTIVE ashamed or awkward.

embarrassment, embarrassments NOUN shame and awkwardness.

embassy, embassies NOUN the building in which an ambassador and his or her staff work; also used of the ambassador and his or her staff.

embedded ADJECTIVE Something that is embedded is fixed firmly and deeply • *glass decorated with embedded threads.*

ember, embers NOUN Embers are glowing pieces of coal or wood from a dying fire.

embittered ADJECTIVE If you are embittered, you are angry and resentful about things that have happened to you.

emblazoned [*Said im-**blaze**-nd*] ADJECTIVE If something is emblazoned with designs, it is decorated with them • *vases emblazoned with bold and colourful images.*
WORD HISTORY: originally a heraldic term from Old French *blason* meaning 'shield'

emblem, emblems NOUN an object or a design representing an organisation or an idea • *a flower emblem of Japan.*

embody, embodies, embodying, embodied VERB ① To embody a quality or idea means to contain it or express it • *A young dancer embodies the spirit of fun.* ② If a number of things are embodied in one thing, they are contained in it • *the principles embodied in his report.* **embodiment** NOUN

embossed ADJECTIVE decorated with designs that stand up slightly from the surface • *embossed wallpaper*.

embrace, **embraces**, **embracing**, **embraced** VERB ① If you embrace someone, you hug them to show affection or as a greeting. ② If you embrace a belief or cause, you accept it and believe in it. ▸ NOUN ③ a hug.

embroider, **embroiders**, **embroidering**, **embroidered** VERB If you embroider fabric, you sew a decorative design onto it.

embroidery NOUN Embroidery is decorative designs sewn onto fabric; also the art or skill of embroidering.

embroiled ADJECTIVE If someone is embroiled in an argument or conflict, they are deeply involved in it and cannot get out of it • *The two companies are now embroiled in the courts*.

embryo, **embryos** [*Said* em-bree-oh] NOUN SCIENCE an animal or human being in the very early stages of development in the womb.
embryonic ADJECTIVE
WORD HISTORY: from Greek *embruon* meaning 'new-born animal'

emerald, **emeralds** NOUN ① a bright green precious stone. ▸ NOUN or ADJECTIVE ② bright green.

emerge, **emerges**, **emerging**, **emerged** VERB ① If someone emerges from a place, they come out of it so that they can be seen. ② If something emerges, it becomes known or begins to be recognised as existing • *It later emerged that he had left the band*. **emergence** NOUN **emergent** ADJECTIVE

emergency, **emergencies** NOUN an unexpected and serious event which needs immediate action to deal with it.
SIMILAR WORDS: crisis, extremity

emigrant, **emigrants** NOUN HISTORY someone who leaves their native country and goes to live permanently in another one.

emigrate VERB **emigration** NOUN

SPELLING TIP
Do not confuse the spellings of *emigrate* and *immigrate*. Try this mnemonic: *if you Emigrate, you Exit your country*.

eminence NOUN ① Eminence is the quality of being well-known and respected for what you do • *lawyers of eminence*. ② 'Your Eminence' is a title of respect used to address a Roman Catholic cardinal.

eminent ADJECTIVE well-known and respected for what you do • *an eminent scientist*.

SPELLING TIP
Do not confuse the spellings of *eminent* and *imminent*: *an eminent professor of archaeology; The wedding is imminent*.

eminently ADVERB (formal) very • *eminently reasonable*.

emir, **emirs** [*Said* em-**eer**] NOUN a Muslim ruler or nobleman.

emission, **emissions** NOUN (formal) The emission of something such as gas or radiation is the release of it into the atmosphere.

SPELLING TIP
Do not confuse the spellings of *emission* and *omission*: *the plan to cut carbon emissions; Her omission from the team is a big surprise*.

emit, **emits**, **emitting**, **emitted** VERB To emit something means to give it out or release it • *She emitted a long, low whistle*.
SIMILAR WORDS: exude, give off, give out

emoji, **emojis** [*Said* im-**moh**-jee] NOUN an image used in electronic communication to represent an emotion.

emoticon, emoticons NOUN a symbol used in electronic communication which represents a particular emotion and is made up of normal keyboard characters that are viewed sideways. For example, the symbol (:+(means 'frightened' or 'scared'.

emotion, emotions NOUN PSHE a strong feeling, such as love or fear.

emotional ADJECTIVE ① causing strong feelings • an emotional appeal for help. ② PSHE to do with feelings rather than your physical condition • emotional support. ③ showing your feelings openly • The child is in a very emotional state. **emotionally** ADVERB

emotive ADJECTIVE concerning emotions, or stirring up strong emotions • emotive language.

empathise, empathises, empathising, empathised; also spelt **empathize** VERB PSHE If you empathise with someone, you understand how they are feeling. **empathy** NOUN

emperor, emperors NOUN a male ruler of an empire.

emphasis, emphases NOUN Emphasis is special importance or extra stress given to something.

emphasise, emphasises, emphasising, emphasised; also spelt **emphasize** VERB If you emphasise something, you make it known that it is very important • It was emphasised that the matter was of international concern.

emphatic ADJECTIVE expressed strongly and with force to show how important something is • I answered both questions with an emphatic 'Yes'. **emphatically** ADVERB

empire, empires NOUN ① a group of countries controlled by one country. ② a powerful group of companies controlled by one person.

employ, employs, employing, employed VERB ① If you employ someone, you pay them to work for you. ② If you employ something for a particular purpose, you make use of it • the techniques employed in turning milk into cheese.
SIMILAR WORDS: ① engage, hire, take on

employable ADJECTIVE PSHE Someone who is employable has skills or abilities that will make someone want to give them a job. **employability** NOUN

employee, employees NOUN a person who is paid to work for another person or for an organisation.

employer, employers NOUN Someone's employer is the person or organisation that they work for.

employment NOUN GEOGRAPHY Employment is the state of having a paid job, or the activity of recruiting people for a job.

empower, empowers, empowering, empowered VERB If you are empowered to do something, you have the authority or power to do it. **empowerment** NOUN

empress, empresses NOUN a woman who rules an empire, or the wife of an emperor.

empty, emptier, emptiest; empties, emptying, emptied ADJECTIVE ① having nothing or nobody inside. ② without purpose, value or meaning • empty promises. ▶ VERB ③ If you empty something, or empty its contents, you remove the contents. **emptiness** NOUN
SIMILAR WORDS: ① bare, blank,

vacant ③ clear, evacuate

empty set, empty sets NOUN
MATHS a set that has no members.

emu, emus *[Said ee-myoo]* NOUN a
large Australian bird which can run
fast but cannot fly.

emulate, emulates, emulating,
emulated VERB If you emulate
someone or something, you imitate
them because you admire them.
emulation NOUN

emulsion, emulsions NOUN a
water-based paint.

en- PREFIX ① 'En-' means to surround
or cover • *enclose* • *encrusted*. ② 'En-'
means to cause to be in a certain
state or condition • *enamoured*
• *endanger*.
WORD HISTORY: from Latin prefix *in-*

enable, enables, enabling, enabled
VERB To enable something to happen
means to make it possible.

enact, enacts, enacting, enacted
VERB ① If a government enacts a law
or bill, it officially passes it so that it
becomes law. ② If you enact a story
or play, you act it out. **enactment**
NOUN

enamel, enamels, enamelling,
enamelled NOUN ① a substance like
glass, used to decorate or protect
metal or china. ② The enamel on
your teeth is the hard, white
substance that forms the outer part.
▶ VERB ③ If you enamel something,
you decorate or cover it with enamel.
enamelled ADJECTIVE

enamoured *[Said in-am-erd]*
ADJECTIVE If you are enamoured of
someone or something, you like
them very much.

encapsulate, encapsulates,
encapsulating, encapsulated VERB
If something encapsulates facts or
ideas, it contains or represents them
in a small space.

encased ADJECTIVE Something that
is encased is surrounded or covered
with a substance • *encased in plaster*.

-ence SUFFIX '-ence' is used to form
nouns which mean a state, condition
or quality • *residence* • *patience*.

enchanted ADJECTIVE If you are
enchanted by something or
someone, you are fascinated or
charmed by them.

enchanting ADJECTIVE attractive,
delightful or charming • *an enchanting
baby*.

encircle, encircles, encircling,
encircled VERB To encircle
something or someone means to
completely surround them.

enclave, enclaves NOUN a place that
is surrounded by areas that are
different from it in some important
way, for example because the people
there are from a different culture • *an
Armenian enclave in Azerbaijan*.

enclose, encloses, enclosing,
enclosed VERB To enclose an object
or area means to surround it with
something solid. **enclosed**
ADJECTIVE

enclosure, enclosures NOUN an area
of land surrounded by a wall or fence
and used for a particular purpose.

encompass, encompasses,
encompassing, encompassed VERB
To encompass a number of things
means to include all of those things
• *The book encompassed all aspects of
maths*.

encore, encores *[Said ong-kor]* NOUN
a short extra performance given by
an entertainer because the audience
asks for it.
WORD HISTORY: from French *encore*
meaning 'again'

encounter, encounters,
encountering, encountered VERB
① If you encounter someone or

something, you meet them or are faced with them • *She was the most gifted child he ever encountered.* ▶ NOUN ② a meeting, especially when it is difficult or unexpected.

encourage, **encourages**, **encouraging**, **encouraged** VERB ① PSHE If you encourage someone, you give them courage and confidence to do something. ② If someone or something encourages a particular activity, they support it • *The government will encourage the creation of nursery places.* **encouraging** ADJECTIVE **encouragement** NOUN
SIMILAR WORDS: ① hearten, inspire

encroach, **encroaches**, **encroaching**, **encroached** VERB If something encroaches on a place or on your time or rights, it gradually takes up or takes away more and more of it. **encroachment** NOUN

encrusted ADJECTIVE covered with a crust or layer of something • *a necklace encrusted with gold.*

encrypt, **encrypts**, **encrypting**, **encrypted** VERB If a document is encrypted, it is written in a code, so that only certain people can read it. **encryption** NOUN

encyclopedia, **encyclopedias** [Said en-sigh-klo-**pee**-dee-a]; also spelt **encyclopaedia** NOUN LIBRARY a book or set of books giving information about many different subjects.
WORD HISTORY: from Greek *enkuklios paideia* meaning 'general education'

encyclopedic; also spelt **encyclopaedic** ADJECTIVE knowing or giving information about many different things.

end, **ends**, **ending**, **ended** NOUN ① The end of a period of time or an event is the last part. ② The end of

something is the farthest point of it • *the room at the end of the passage.* ③ the purpose for which something is done • *He made friends with me for his own ends.* ▶ VERB ④ If something ends or if you end it, it comes to a finish.

endanger, **endangers**, **endangering**, **endangered** VERB To endanger something means to cause it to be in a dangerous and harmful situation • *a driver who endangers the safety of others.*
SIMILAR WORDS: jeopardise, put at risk

endangered species NOUN SCIENCE a plant or animal that is in danger of becoming extinct • *Grey wolves are now an endangered species.*

endear, **endears**, **endearing**, **endeared** VERB If someone's behaviour endears them to you, it makes you fond of them. **endearing** ADJECTIVE **endearingly** ADVERB

endeavour, **endeavours**, **endeavouring**, **endeavoured** [Said in-**dev**-er] VERB ① (formal) If you endeavour to do something, you try very hard to do it. ▶ NOUN ② an effort to do or achieve something.

endless ADJECTIVE having or seeming to have no end. **endlessly** ADVERB

endorse, **endorses**, **endorsing**, **endorsed** VERB ① If you endorse someone or something, you give approval and support to them. ② If you endorse a document, you write your signature or a comment on it, to show that you approve of it. **endorsement** NOUN

endothermic ADJECTIVE SCIENCE If a chemical reaction is endothermic, then heat is absorbed.

endowed ADJECTIVE If someone is endowed with a quality or ability, they have it or are given it • *She was* *endowed with great willpower.*

endurance NOUN Endurance is the ability to put up with a difficult situation for a period of time.

endure, endures, enduring, endured VERB ① If you endure a difficult situation, you put up with it calmly and patiently. ② If something endures, it lasts or continues to exist • *The old alliance still endures.* **enduring** ADJECTIVE

enemy, enemies NOUN a person or group that is hostile or opposed to another person or group.
SIMILAR WORDS: adversary, foe

energetic ADJECTIVE having or showing energy or enthusiasm. **energetically** ADVERB
SIMILAR WORDS: active, lively, vigorous

energy, energies NOUN ① the physical strength to do active things. ② the power which drives machinery. ③ SCIENCE In physics, energy is the capacity of a body or system to do work. It is measured in joules.
SIMILAR WORDS: ① drive, stamina, vigour

enforce, enforces, enforcing, enforced VERB If you enforce a law or a rule, you make sure that it is obeyed. **enforceable** ADJECTIVE **enforcement** NOUN

engage, engages, engaging, engaged VERB ① If you engage in an activity, you take part in it • *Officials have declined to engage in a debate.* ② To engage someone or their attention means to make or keep someone interested in something • *He engaged the driver in conversation.*

engaged ADJECTIVE ① When two people are engaged, they have agreed to marry each other. ② If someone or something is engaged, they are occupied or busy • *Mr*

Anderson was otherwise engaged • *The emergency number was always engaged.*

engagement, engagements NOUN ① an appointment that you have with someone. ② an agreement that two people have made with each other to get married.

engine, engines NOUN ① a machine designed to convert heat or other kinds of energy into mechanical movement. ② a railway locomotive.
WORD HISTORY: from Latin *ingenium* meaning 'ingenious device'

engineer, engineers, engineering, engineered NOUN ① a person trained in designing and building machinery and electrical devices, or roads and bridges. ② a person who repairs mechanical or electrical devices. ▶ VERB ③ If you engineer an event or situation, you arrange it cleverly, usually for your own advantage.

engineering NOUN Engineering is the profession of designing and constructing machinery and electrical devices, or roads and bridges.

English ADJECTIVE ① belonging or relating to England. ▶ NOUN ② English is the main language spoken in the United Kingdom, the USA, Canada, Australia, New Zealand and many other countries.

Englishman, Englishmen NOUN a man who comes from England.

Englishwoman, Englishwomen NOUN a woman who comes from England.

engrave, engraves, engraving, engraved VERB To engrave means to cut letters or designs into a hard surface with a tool.

engraving, engravings NOUN a picture or design that has been cut into a hard surface. **engraver** NOUN

a b c d e f g h i j k l m n o p q r s t u v w x y z

engrossed ADJECTIVE If you are engrossed in something, it holds all your attention • *He was engrossed in a video game.*

engulf, engulfs, engulfing, engulfed VERB To engulf something means to completely cover or surround it • *Black smoke engulfed him.*

enhance, enhances, enhancing, enhanced VERB To enhance something means to make it more valuable or attractive • *an outfit that really enhances your colouring.*
enhancement NOUN

enigma, enigmas NOUN anything which is puzzling or difficult to understand.

enigmatic ADJECTIVE mysterious, puzzling or difficult to understand • *an enigmatic stranger.*
enigmatically ADVERB

enjambment [Said in-jam-ment]; also spelt **enjambement** NOUN ENGLISH In poetry, enjambment is when a sentence or phrase runs from one line of verse over to the next without a pause between lines.

enjoy, enjoys, enjoying, enjoyed VERB ① If you enjoy something, you find pleasure and satisfaction in it. ② If you enjoy something, you are lucky to have it or experience it • *She has enjoyed a long life.*

enjoyable ADJECTIVE giving pleasure or satisfaction.

enjoyment NOUN Enjoyment is the feeling of pleasure or satisfaction you get from something nice.

enlarge, enlarges, enlarging, enlarged VERB ① When you enlarge something, it gets bigger. ② If you enlarge on a subject, you give more details about it.

enlargement, enlargements NOUN ① An enlargement of something is the action of making it bigger.

② something, especially a photograph, which has been made bigger.

enlighten, enlightens, enlightening, enlightened VERB To enlighten someone means to give them more knowledge or understanding of something.
enlightening ADJECTIVE
enlightenment NOUN

enlightened ADJECTIVE well-informed and willing to consider different opinions • *an enlightened government.*

enlist, enlists, enlisting, enlisted VERB ① If someone enlists, they join the army, navy or air force. ② If you enlist someone's help, you persuade them to help you in something you are doing.

enliven, enlivens, enlivening, enlivened VERB To enliven something means to make it more lively or more cheerful.

en masse [Said on mass] ADVERB If a group of people do something en masse, they do it together and at the same time.

enormity, enormities NOUN ① The enormity of a problem or difficulty is its great size and seriousness. ② something that is thought to be a terrible crime or offence.

enormous ADJECTIVE very large in size or amount. **enormously** ADVERB

enough ADJECTIVE or ADVERB ① as much or as many as required • *He did not have enough money for sweets.* ▶ NOUN ② Enough is the quantity necessary for something • *There's not enough to go round.* ▶ ADVERB ③ very or fairly • *She could manage well enough without me.*

enquire, enquires, enquiring, enquired; also spelt **inquire** VERB

If you enquire about something or someone, you ask about them.

enquiry, **enquiries**; also spelt **inquiry** NOUN ① a question that you ask in order to find something out. ② an investigation into something that has happened and that needs explaining.

enrage, **enrages**, **enraging**, **enraged** VERB If something enrages you, it makes you very angry. **enraged** ADJECTIVE

enrich, **enriches**, **enriching**, **enriched** VERB To enrich something means to improve the quality or value of it • *new woods to enrich our countryside.* **enriched** ADJECTIVE **enrichment** NOUN

enrol, **enrols**, **enrolling**, **enrolled** VERB If you enrol for something such as a course or a college, you register to join or become a member of it. **enrolment** NOUN

en route [*Said on root*] ADVERB If something happens en route to a place, it happens on the way there.

ensconced ADJECTIVE If you are ensconced in a particular place, you are settled there firmly and comfortably.

ensemble, **ensembles** [*Said on-som-bl*] NOUN ① a group of things or people considered as a whole rather than separately. ② a small group of musicians who play or sing together.

enshrine, **enshrines**, **enshrining**, **enshrined** VERB If something such as an idea or a right is enshrined in a society, constitution or a law, it is protected by it • *Freedom of speech is enshrined in the American Constitution.*

ensign, **ensigns** NOUN a flag flown by a ship to show what country that ship belongs to.

ensue, **ensues**, **ensuing**, **ensued** [*Said en-syoo*] VERB If something ensues, it happens after another event, usually as a result of it • *He entered the house and an argument ensued.* **ensuing** ADJECTIVE

ensure, **ensures**, **ensuring**, **ensured** VERB To ensure that something happens means to make certain that it happens • *We make every effort to ensure the information given is correct.*

SPELLING TIP
Do not confuse the spellings of *ensure* and *insure*: *Please ensure that the door is locked; Callum forgot to insure the car.*

entangled ADJECTIVE If you are entangled in problems or difficulties, you are involved in them.

enter, **enters**, **entering**, **entered** VERB ① To enter a place means to go into it. ② If you enter an organisation or institution, you join and become a member of it • *He entered Parliament in 2015.* ③ If you enter a competition or examination, you take part in it. ④ If you enter data into a form or database, you record it by writing or typing it in an empty space.

enterprise, **enterprises** NOUN ① a business or company. ② a project or task, especially one that involves risk or difficulty.

enterprising ADJECTIVE ready to start new projects and tasks and full of boldness and initiative • *an enterprising company.*

entertain, **entertains**, **entertaining**, **entertained** VERB ① If you entertain people, you keep them amused or interested. ② If you entertain guests, you receive them into your house and give them food and hospitality.

entertainer, **entertainers** NOUN someone whose job is to amuse and please audiences, for example a comedian or singer.

a
b
c
d
e
f
g
h
i
j
k
l
m
n
o
p
q
r
s
t
u
v
w
x
y
z

A
B
C
D
E
F
G
H
I
J
K
L
M
N
O
P
Q
R
S
T
U
V
W
X
Y
Z

entertaining ADJECTIVE ① amusing and full of interest. ▶ NOUN ② Entertaining is the hospitality that you give to guests • *He enjoys entertaining at home.*

entertainment, entertainments NOUN anything people watch or do for pleasure.

enthral, enthrals, enthralling, enthralled [Said in-**thrawl**] VERB If you enthral someone, you hold their attention and interest completely.
enthralling ADJECTIVE

enthuse, enthuses, enthusing, enthused [Said inth-**yooz**] VERB If you enthuse about something, you talk about it with enthusiasm and excitement.

enthusiasm, enthusiasms NOUN Enthusiasm is interest, eagerness or delight in something.
SIMILAR WORDS: keenness, passion, zeal
WORD HISTORY: from Greek *enthousiasmos* meaning 'possessed or inspired by the gods'

enthusiastic ADJECTIVE showing great excitement, eagerness or approval for something • *She was enthusiastic about poetry.*
enthusiastically ADVERB

entice, entices, enticing, enticed VERB If you entice someone to do something, you tempt them to do it • *We tried to entice the mouse out of the hole.*

enticing ADJECTIVE extremely attractive and tempting.

entire ADJECTIVE including all of something • *the entire month of July.*

entirely ADVERB wholly and completely • *He and I were entirely different.*

entirety [Said en-**tire**-it-tee] PHRASE If something happens to something **in its entirety**, it happens to all of it • *This message will now be repeated in its entirety.*

entitle, entitles, entitling, entitled VERB If something entitles you to have or do something, it gives you the right to have or do it.
entitlement NOUN

entity, entities [Said en-**tit**-ee] NOUN any complete thing that is not divided and not part of anything else.

entourage, entourages [Said on-too-**rahj**] NOUN a group of people who follow or travel with a famous or important person.

entrails PLURAL NOUN Entrails are the inner parts, especially the intestines, of people or animals.

entrance¹, entrances [Said en-**trunss**] NOUN ① The entrance of a building or area is its doorway or gate. ② A person's entrance is their arrival in a place, or the way in which they arrive • *She likes to make a dramatic entrance.* ③ DRAMA In the theatre, an actor makes his or her entrance when he or she comes onto the stage. ④ Entrance is the right to enter a place • *He had gained entrance by pretending to be a heating engineer.*

entrance², entrances, entrancing, entranced [Said en-**trahnss**] VERB If something entrances you, it gives you a feeling of wonder and delight.
entrancing ADJECTIVE

entrant, entrants NOUN a person who officially enters a competition or an organisation.

entrenched ADJECTIVE If a belief, custom or power is entrenched, it is firmly established.

entrepreneur, entrepreneurs [Said on-tre-pren-**ur**] NOUN a person who sets up business deals, especially ones in which risks are involved, in order to make a profit.
entrepreneurial ADJECTIVE

entrust, entrusts, entrusting, entrusted VERB If you entrust something to someone, you give them the care and protection of it • *Miss Fry was entrusted with the children's education.*

entry, entries NOUN ① Entry is the act of entering a place. ② a place through which you enter somewhere. ③ anything which is entered or recorded • *Send your entry to the address below.*

SIMILAR WORDS: ② entrance, way in

envelop, envelops, enveloping, enveloped VERB To envelop something means to cover or surround it completely • *A dense fog enveloped the area.*

SPELLING TIP

Do not confuse the spellings of the verb *envelop* and the noun *envelope*: *The mist seemed to envelop the town; I have included a cheque in the envelope.*

---

envelope, envelopes NOUN a flat covering of paper with a flap that can be folded over to seal it, which is used to hold a letter.

enviable ADJECTIVE If you describe something as enviable, you mean that you wish you had it yourself.

envious ADJECTIVE full of envy. **enviously** ADVERB

environment, environments NOUN ① Your environment is the circumstances and conditions in which you live or work • *a good environment to grow up in.* ② SCIENCE The environment is the natural world around us • *the waste which is dumped in the environment.* **environmental** ADJECTIVE **environmentally** ADVERB

SPELLING TIP

There is an *n* before the *m* in *environment*.

---

environmentalist, environmentalists NOUN a person who is concerned with the problems of the natural environment, such as pollution.

envisage, envisages, envisaging, envisaged VERB If you envisage a situation or state of affairs, you can picture it in your mind as being true or likely to happen.

envoy, envoys NOUN a messenger, sent especially from one government to another.

envy, envies, envying, envied NOUN ① Envy is a feeling of resentment you have when you wish you could have what someone else has. ▸ VERB ② If you envy someone, you wish that you had what they have.

enzyme, enzymes NOUN SCIENCE a chemical substance, usually a protein, produced by cells in the body.

ephemeral [Said if-**em**-er-al] ADJECTIVE lasting only a short time.

epic, epics NOUN ① a long story of heroic events and actions. ▸ ADJECTIVE ② very impressive or ambitious • *epic adventures.*

epicentre, epicentres NOUN GEOGRAPHY The epicentre of an earthquake is the place on the surface of the earth immediately above where the earthquake started.

epidemic, epidemics NOUN ① an occurrence of a disease in one area, spreading quickly and affecting many people. ② a rapid development or spread of something • *the country's crime epidemic.*

epidermis [Said ep-pid-**der**-miss] NOUN SCIENCE The epidermis is the top layer of skin.

epigram, epigrams NOUN a short saying which expresses an idea in a clever and amusing way.

a b c d e f g h i j k l m n o p q r s t u v w x y z

epigraph NOUN ① a quotation at the beginning of a book. ② an inscription on a monument or building.

epilepsy NOUN Epilepsy is a condition of the brain which causes fits and periods of unconsciousness. **epileptic** ADJECTIVE

epilogue, epilogues [Said ep-ill-og] NOUN ENGLISH An epilogue is a passage added to the end of a book or play as a conclusion.

episode, episodes NOUN ① an event or period • *After this episode, she found it impossible to trust him.* ② ENGLISH one of several parts of a novel or drama appearing for example on television • *I never miss an episode of the show.*

epistle, epistles [Said ip-**piss**-sl] NOUN (formal) a letter.

epitaph, epitaphs [Said **ep**-it-ahf] NOUN some words on a tomb about the person who has died.

epithet, epithets NOUN a word or short phrase used to describe some characteristic of a person.

epitome [Said ip-**pit**-om-ee] NOUN (formal) The epitome of something is the most typical example of its sort • *She was the epitome of the successful woman.*

USAGE NOTE
Do not use *epitome* to mean 'the peak of something'. It means 'the most typical example of something'.

epoch, epochs [Said **ee**-pok] NOUN a long period of time.

eponymous [Said ip-**on**-im-uss] ADJECTIVE (formal) The eponymous hero or heroine of a play or book is the person whose name forms its title • *the eponymous hero of 'Eric the Viking'.*

equal, equals, equalling, equalled ADJECTIVE ① having the same size, amount, value or standard. ② If you are equal to a task, you have the necessary ability to deal with it. ▶ NOUN ③ Your equals are people who have the same ability, status or rights as you. ▶ VERB ④ If one thing equals another, it is as good or remarkable as the other • *He equalled the course record of 63.* **equally** ADVERB **equality** NOUN

equal set, equal sets NOUN MATHS Equal sets are sets with the same members.

equate, equates, equating, equated VERB If you equate a particular thing with something else, you believe that it is similar or equal • *You can't equate lives with money.*

equation, equations NOUN MATHS a mathematical statement showing that two expressions are equal.

equator [Said ik-**way**-tor] NOUN GEOGRAPHY an imaginary line drawn round the middle of the earth, lying halfway between the North and South poles. **equatorial** ADJECTIVE

equestrian [Said ik-**west**-ree-an] ADJECTIVE relating to or involving horses.

equidistant ADJECTIVE Things that are equidistant are at an equal distance from each other or from a central point • *The three houses are equidistant.*

equilateral ADJECTIVE MATHS An equilateral triangle has sides that are all the same length.

equilibrium, equilibria NOUN a state of balance or stability in a situation.

equine ADJECTIVE relating to horses. WORD HISTORY: from Latin *equus* meaning 'horse'

equinox, equinoxes NOUN one of the two days in the year when the day and night are of equal length,

occurring in September and March.
WORD HISTORY: from Latin
aequinoctium meaning 'equal night'

equip, **equips**, **equipping**, **equipped**
VERB If a person or thing is equipped
with something, they have it or are
provided with it • *The test boat was
equipped with a folding propeller*.
SIMILAR WORDS: provide, supply

equipment **NOUN** Equipment is all
the things that are needed or used for
a particular job or activity.
SIMILAR WORDS: apparatus, gear,
tools

equitable **ADJECTIVE** fair and
reasonable.

equity **NOUN** Equity is the quality of
being fair and reasonable • *It is
important to distribute income with
some sense of equity*.

equivalent, **equivalents** **ADJECTIVE**
① equal in use, size, value or effect.
▶ **NOUN** ② something that has the
same use, value or effect as
something else • *911 is the American
equivalent of the British 999 service*.
equivalence **NOUN**
SIMILAR WORDS: ② equal, match

equivalent fraction, **equivalent
fractions** **NOUN** MATHS a fraction
that can be reduced to the same
proper fraction as another. $^2/_4$ and $^3/_6$
are equivalent fractions that can be
reduced to $^1/_2$.

equivalent ratio, **equivalent ratios**
NOUN MATHS a ratio that has the
same comparison as another ratio.
For example, 12:8 and 3:2 are
equivalent ratios.

equivalent set, **equivalent sets**
NOUN MATHS Equivalent sets are
sets with the same number of
members.

equivocal **ADJECTIVE** deliberately
vague and capable of many different
interpretations.

-er **SUFFIX** ① When '-er' is used to form
some nouns it means 'for' or
'belonging to' • *fastener* • *Highlander*.
② '-er' is also used to form nouns
which mean someone or something
that does something • *climber*
• *teacher* • *baker*. ③ '-er' is used to
make adjectives and adverbs that
have the meaning 'more' • *lighter*
• *funnier*.

era, **eras** [*Said **ear**-a*] **NOUN** a period of
time distinguished by a particular
feature • *a new era of prosperity*.

eradicate, **eradicates**, **eradicating**,
eradicated **VERB** To eradicate
something means to get rid of it or
destroy it completely. **eradication**
NOUN

erase, **erases**, **erasing**, **erased** **VERB**
To erase something means to
remove it.

eraser, **erasers** **NOUN** anything
which erases, especially a rubber
used for rubbing out writing.

e-reader, **e-readers** **NOUN** a portable
electronic gadget for reading books.

erect, **erects**, **erecting**, **erected** **VERB**
① To erect something means to put it
up or construct it • *The building was
erected in 1900*. ▶ **ADJECTIVE** ② in a
straight and upright position • *She
held herself erect and looked directly at
him*.
SIMILAR WORDS: ② straight, upright,
vertical

erection, **erections** **NOUN** ① the
process of erecting something.
② anything which has been erected.

ermine, **ermines** **NOUN** ① An ermine
is a weasel whose brown fur turns
white in winter. ② Ermine is the
white fur from the ermine.

erode, **erodes**, **eroding**, **eroded** **VERB**
If something erodes or is eroded, it is
gradually worn or eaten away and
destroyed.

a
b
c
d
e
f
g
h
i
j
k
l
m
n
o
p
q
r
s
t
u
v
w
x
y
z

A
B
C
D
E
F
G
H
I
J
K
L
M
N
O
P
Q
R
S
T
U
V
W
X
Y
Z

erosion NOUN GEOGRAPHY the gradual wearing away and destruction of something • *soil erosion*.

err, errs, erring, erred VERB If you err, you make a mistake.

errand, errands NOUN a short trip you make in order to do a job for someone.

erratic ADJECTIVE not following a regular pattern or a fixed course • *Police officers noticed his erratic driving*. **erratically** ADVERB

erroneous [*Said ir-rone-ee-uss*] ADJECTIVE Ideas or methods that are erroneous are incorrect or only partly correct. **erroneously** ADVERB

error, errors NOUN a mistake or something which you have done wrong.

erudite [*Said eh-roo-dite*] ADJECTIVE having great academic knowledge.

erupt, erupts, erupting, erupted VERB ① When a volcano erupts, it violently throws out a lot of hot lava and ash. ② When a situation erupts, it starts up suddenly and violently • *A family row erupted*. **eruption** NOUN

e-safety NOUN the state of being safe from harm or danger when using the internet, for example by not giving away any personal details.

escalate, escalates, escalating, escalated VERB If a situation escalates, it becomes greater in size, seriousness or intensity.

escalator, escalators NOUN a mechanical moving staircase.

escapade, escapades NOUN an adventurous or daring incident that causes trouble.

escape, escapes, escaping, escaped VERB ① To escape means to get free from someone or something. ② If you escape something unpleasant or difficult, you manage to avoid it • *He escaped the death penalty*. ③ If something escapes you, you cannot remember it • *It was an actor whose name escapes me for the moment*. ▶ NOUN ④ an act of escaping from a particular place or situation • *his escape from North Korea*. ⑤ a situation or activity which distracts you from something unpleasant • *Television provides an escape*.

escapee, escapees [*Said is-kay-pee*] NOUN someone who has escaped, especially an escaped prisoner.

escapism NOUN avoiding the real and unpleasant things in life by thinking about pleasant or exciting things • *Most horror movies are simple escapism*. **escapist** ADJECTIVE

eschew, eschews, eschewing, eschewed [*Said is-chew*] VERB (formal) If you eschew something, you deliberately avoid or keep away from it.

escort, escorts, escorting, escorted NOUN ① a person or vehicle that travels with another in order to protect or guide them. ② a person who accompanies another person to a social event. ▶ VERB ③ If you escort someone, you go with them somewhere, especially in order to protect or guide them.

-ese [*Said -eez*] SUFFIX '-ese' forms adjectives and nouns which show where a person or thing comes from • *Japanese*.

Eskimo, Eskimos NOUN (offensive) a name that was formerly used for the Inuit and their language.

especially ADVERB You say especially to show that something applies more to one thing, person or situation than to any other • *Regular eye tests are important, especially for older people*.

espionage [Said ess-pee-on-ahj]
NOUN Espionage is the act of spying to get secret information, especially to find out military or political secrets.
WORD HISTORY: from French *espionner* meaning 'to spy'

espouse, espouses, espousing, espoused VERB (formal) If you espouse a particular policy, cause or plan, you give your support to it • *They espoused the values of freedom and human rights.*

espresso NOUN Espresso is strong coffee made by forcing steam through ground coffee.
WORD HISTORY: from Italian *caffè espresso* meaning 'pressed coffee'

SPELLING TIP
The second letter of *espresso* is s and not x.

-ess SUFFIX '-ess' added at the end of a noun indicates a female • *lioness*.

USAGE NOTE
Special words for a woman who does a particular job or activity, such as *actress*, *poetess* and *authoress*, are now used less often because many women prefer to be referred to simply as an *actor*, *poet* or *author*.

essay, essays NOUN a short piece of writing on a particular subject, for example one done as an exercise by a student.

essence, essences NOUN ① The essence of something is its most basic and most important part, which gives it its identity • *the very essence of life.* ② a concentrated liquid used for flavouring food • *vanilla essence.*

essential ADJECTIVE ① vitally important and absolutely necessary • *Good ventilation is essential in the greenhouse.* ② very basic, important and typical • *the essential aspects of international banking.* **essentially** ADVERB

essentials PLURAL NOUN Essentials are things that are very important or necessary • *the bare essentials of furnishing.*

-est SUFFIX '-est' is used to form adjectives and adverbs that have the meaning 'most' • *greatest* • *furthest*.

establish, establishes, establishing, established VERB ① To establish something means to set it up in a permanent way. ② If you establish yourself or become established as something, you achieve a strong reputation for a particular activity • *He had just established himself as a film star.* ③ If you establish a fact or establish the truth of something, you discover it and can prove it • *Our first priority is to establish the cause of the accident.* **established** ADJECTIVE
SIMILAR WORDS: ① create, found, set up

establishment, establishments NOUN ① The establishment of an organisation or system is the act of setting it up. ② a shop, business or some other sort of organisation or institution. ③ The Establishment is the group of people in a country who have power and influence • *lawyers and other pillars of the Establishment.*

estate, estates NOUN ① a large area of privately owned land in the country, together with all the property on it. ② an area of land, usually in or near a city, which has been developed for housing or industry. ③ (Law) A person's estate consists of all the possessions they leave behind when they die.

estate agent, estate agents NOUN a person who works for a company that sells houses and land.

esteem NOUN admiration and respect that you feel for another person. **esteemed** ADJECTIVE

estimate, estimates, estimating, estimated VERB ① MATHS If you estimate an amount or quantity, you calculate it approximately. ② If you estimate something, you make a guess about it based on the evidence you have available • *Often it's possible to estimate a person's age just by knowing their name.* ▶ NOUN ③ a guess at an amount, quantity or outcome, based on the evidence you have available. ④ a formal statement from a company who may do some work for you, telling you how much it is likely to cost.

estimation, estimations NOUN ① an approximate calculation of something that can be measured. ② the opinion or impression you form about a person or situation.

estranged ADJECTIVE ① If someone is estranged from their husband or wife, they no longer live with them. ② If someone is estranged from their family or friends, they have quarrelled with them and no longer keep in touch with them.

estrogen NOUN SCIENCE a female hormone which regulates the reproductive cycle.

estuary, estuaries [Said *est*-yoo-ree] NOUN GEOGRAPHY the wide part of a river near where it joins the sea and where fresh water mixes with salt water.

etc. a written abbreviation for **et cetera**.

et cetera [Said it *set*-ra] 'Et cetera' is used at the end of a list to indicate that other items of the same type you have mentioned could have been mentioned if there had been time or space.

USAGE NOTE
As *etc.* means 'and the rest', you should not write *and etc.*

etch, etches, etching, etched VERB ① If you etch a design or pattern on a surface, you cut it into the surface by using acid or a sharp tool. ② If something is etched on your mind or memory, it has made such a strong impression on you that you feel you will never forget it. **etched** ADJECTIVE

etching, etchings NOUN a picture printed from a metal plate that has had a design cut into it.

eternal ADJECTIVE lasting forever, or seeming to last forever • *eternal life.* **eternally** ADVERB
SIMILAR WORDS: endless, everlasting, perpetual

eternity, eternities NOUN ① Eternity is time without end, or a state of existing outside time, especially the state some people believe they will pass into when they die. ② a period of time which seems to go on forever • *We arrived there after an eternity.*

ether [Said *eeth*-er] NOUN a colourless liquid that burns easily, used in industry as a solvent and in medicine as an anaesthetic.

ethereal [Said *ith*-ee-ree-al] ADJECTIVE light and delicate • *misty ethereal landscapes.* **ethereally** ADVERB

ethical ADJECTIVE in agreement with accepted principles of behaviour that are thought to be right • *teenagers who become vegetarian for ethical reasons.* **ethically** ADVERB

ethics PLURAL NOUN Ethics are moral beliefs about right and wrong • *The medical profession has a code of ethics.*

Ethiopian, Ethiopians [Said *eeth*-ee-oh-pee-an] ADJECTIVE ① belonging or relating to Ethiopia.

▶ NOUN ② someone who comes from Ethiopia.

ethnic ADJECTIVE ① involving different racial groups of people • *ethnic minorities*. ② relating to a particular racial or cultural group, especially when very different from modern western culture • *ethnic food*. **ethnically** ADVERB **ethnicity** NOUN

ethos [Said *eeth-oss*] NOUN a set of ideas and attitudes that is associated with a particular group of people • *the ethos of journalism*.

etiquette [Said *et-ik-ket*] NOUN a set of rules for behaviour in a particular social situation.

-ette SUFFIX '-ette' is used to form nouns which have 'small' as part of their meaning • *kitchenette* • *pipette*.

etymology [Said *et-tim-ol-loj-ee*] NOUN ENGLISH Etymology is the study of the origin and changes of form in words.

EU an abbreviation for **European Union**.

eucalyptus, eucalyptuses or **eucalypt**, eucalypts NOUN an evergreen tree, grown mostly in Australia; also the wood and oil from this tree.

Eucharist, Eucharists [Said *yoo-kar-rist*] NOUN RE a religious ceremony in which Christians remember and celebrate Christ's last meal with his disciples. **WORD HISTORY:** from Greek *eucharistia* meaning 'thanksgiving'

eukaryote, eukaryotes NOUN SCIENCE a living organism whose cells have a nucleus containing the genetic material. Eukaryotes include fungi, plants and animals.

eunuch, eunuchs [Said *yoo-nuk*] NOUN a man who has been castrated.

euphemism, euphemisms NOUN a polite word or expression that you can use instead of one that might offend or upset people • *'Passing on' is a euphemism for death*. **euphemistic** ADJECTIVE **euphemistically** ADVERB

euphoria NOUN a feeling of great happiness. **euphoric** ADJECTIVE

euro, euros NOUN the official unit of currency in some countries of the European Union, replacing their old currencies at the beginning of January 2002.

Europe NOUN Europe is the second smallest continent. It has Asia on its eastern side, with the Arctic to the north, the Atlantic to the west, and the Mediterranean and Africa to the south.

European, Europeans ADJECTIVE ① belonging or relating to Europe. ▶ NOUN ② someone who comes from Europe.

European Union NOUN The group of countries who have joined together under the Treaty of Rome for economic and trade purposes are officially known as the European Union.

euthanasia [Said *yooth-a-nay-zee-a*] NOUN Euthanasia is the act of painlessly killing a dying person in order to stop their suffering. **WORD HISTORY:** from Greek *eu-* meaning 'easy' and *thanatos* meaning 'death'

evacuate, evacuates, evacuating, evacuated VERB If someone is evacuated, they are removed from a place of danger to a place of safety • *A crowd of shoppers had to be evacuated from a store after a bomb scare*. **evacuation** NOUN **evacuee** NOUN

evade, evades, evading, evaded VERB ① If you evade something or someone, you keep moving in order to keep out of their way • *For two months he evaded police*. ② If you evade a problem or question, you avoid dealing with it.

evaluate, evaluates, evaluating, evaluated VERB EXAM TERM If you evaluate something, you assess its strengths and weaknesses.

evaluation, evaluations NOUN ① Evaluation is assessing the strengths and weaknesses of something. ② DGT To carry out an evaluation of a design, product or system is to do an assessment to find out how well it works or will work.

evangelical [Said ee-van-**jel**-ik-kl] ADJECTIVE Evangelical beliefs are Christian beliefs that stress the importance of the gospels and a personal belief in Christ.

evangelist, evangelists [Said iv-**van**-jel-ist] NOUN RE a person who travels from place to place preaching Christianity. **evangelise** VERB **evangelism** NOUN WORD HISTORY: from Greek *evangelion* meaning 'good news'

evaporate, evaporates, evaporating, evaporated VERB ① SCIENCE When a liquid evaporates, it gradually changes into a gas. ② SCIENCE If a substance has been evaporated, all the liquid has been taken out so that it is dry or concentrated. **evaporation** NOUN

evasion, evasions NOUN deliberately avoiding doing something • *evasion of arrest*.

evasive ADJECTIVE deliberately trying to avoid talking about or doing something • *He was evasive about his past*.

eve, eves NOUN the evening or day before an event or occasion • *on the eve of the battle*.

even, evens, evening, evened ADJECTIVE ① flat and level • *an even layer of chocolate*. ② regular and

without variation • *an even temperature*. ③ In maths, numbers that are even can be divided exactly by two • *4 is an even number*. ④ Scores that are even are exactly the same. ▸ ADVERB ⑤ 'Even' is used to suggest that something is unexpected or surprising • *I haven't even got a bank account*. ⑥ 'Even' is also used to say that something is greater in degree than something else • *This was an opportunity to obtain even more money*. ▸ PHRASE ⑦ **Even if** or **even though** is used to introduce something that is surprising in relation to the main part of the sentence • *She was too kind to say anything, even though she was jealous*. **evenly** ADVERB SIMILAR WORDS: ① flat, level, straight ④ equal, level

evening, evenings NOUN the part of the day between late afternoon and night.

event, events NOUN ① something that happens, especially when it is unusual or important. ② one of the competitions that are part of an organised occasion, especially in sports. ▸ PHRASE ③ If you say **in any event**, you mean whatever happens • *In any event we must get on with our own lives*. SIMILAR WORDS: ① happening, incident, occurrence

eventful ADJECTIVE full of interesting and important events.

eventual ADJECTIVE happening or being achieved in the end • *He remained confident of eventual victory*.

eventuality, eventualities NOUN a possible future event or result • *equipment to cope with most eventualities*.

eventually ADVERB in the end • *Eventually I got to Berlin*.

ever ADVERB ① at any time • *Have you*

ever seen anything like it? ② more all the time • *They grew ever further apart.* ③ 'Ever' is used to give emphasis to what you are saying • *I'm as happy here as ever I was in England.* ▶ PHRASE ④ (*informal*) **Ever so** means very • *Thank you ever so much.*

evergreen, evergreens NOUN a tree or bush which has green leaves all the year round.

everlasting ADJECTIVE never coming to an end.

every ADJECTIVE ① 'Every' is used to refer to all the members of a particular group, separately and one by one • *We eat out every night.* ② 'Every' is used to mean the greatest or the best possible degree of something • *He has every reason to avoid the subject.* ③ 'Every' is also used to indicate that something happens at regular intervals • *renewable every five years.* ▶ PHRASE ④ **Every other** means each alternate • *I see Lisa at least every other week.*

everybody PRONOUN ① all the people in a group • *He obviously thinks everybody in the place knows him.* ② all the people in the world • *Everybody has a hobby.*

USAGE NOTE
Everybody and *everyone* mean the same.

everyday ADJECTIVE usual or ordinary • *the everyday drudgery of work.*

everyone PRONOUN ① all the people in a group. ② all the people in the world.

USAGE NOTE
Everyone and *everybody* mean the same.

everything PRONOUN ① all or the whole of something. ② the most

important thing • *Friends were everything to me.*

everywhere ADVERB in or to all places.

evict, evicts, evicting, evicted VERB To evict someone means to officially force them to leave a place they are occupying. **eviction** NOUN

evidence NOUN ① Evidence is anything you see, read or are told which gives you reason to believe something. ② Evidence is the information used in court to attempt to prove or disprove something.

evident ADJECTIVE easily noticed or understood • *His love of nature is evident in his paintings.* **evidently** ADVERB

evil, evils NOUN ① Evil is a force or power that is believed to cause wicked or bad things to happen. ② a very unpleasant or harmful situation or activity • *the evils of war.* ▶ ADJECTIVE ③ Someone or something that is evil is morally wrong or bad • *evil influences.*

evoke, evokes, evoking, evoked VERB To evoke an emotion, memory or reaction means to cause it • *Enthusiasm was evoked by the appearance of the Prince.*

evolution [*Said ee-vol-oo-shn*] NOUN ① SCIENCE Evolution is a process of gradual change taking place over many generations during which living things slowly change as they adapt to different environments. ② Evolution is also any process of gradual change and development over a period of time • *the evolution of the European Union.* **evolutionary** ADJECTIVE

evolve, evolves, evolving, evolved VERB ① If something evolves or if you evolve it, it develops gradually over a period of time • *I was given a brief to*

a
b
c
d
e
f
g
h
i
j
k
l
m
n
o
p
q
r
s
t
u
v
w
x
y
z

A
B
C
D
E
F
G
H
I
J
K
L
M
N
O
P
Q
R
S
T
U
V
W
X
Y
Z

evolve a system of training. ② When living things evolve, they gradually change and develop into different forms over a period of time.

ewe, ewes *[Said yoo]* NOUN a female sheep.

ex- PREFIX 'Ex-' means 'former' • *her ex-husband.*

exacerbate, exacerbates, exacerbating, exacerbated *[Said ig-zass-er-bate]* VERB To exacerbate something means to make it worse.

exact, exacts, exacting, exacted ADJECTIVE ① correct and complete in every detail • *an exact replica of the Santa Maria.* ② accurate and precise, as opposed to approximate • *Mystery surrounds the exact circumstances of his death.* ▶ VERB ③ *(formal)* If somebody or something exacts something from you, they demand or obtain it from you, especially through force • *The navy was on its way to exact a terrible revenge.*

exactly ADVERB ① with complete accuracy and precision • *That's exactly what happened.* ② You can use 'exactly' to emphasise the truth of a statement, or a similarity or close relationship between one thing and another • *It's exactly the same colour.* ▶ INTERJECTION ③ an expression implying total agreement.

exaggerate, exaggerates, exaggerating, exaggerated VERB ① If you exaggerate, you make the thing you are describing seem better, worse, bigger or more important than it really is. ② To exaggerate something means to make it more noticeable than usual • *He exaggerated his Irish accent for the benefit of the joke he was telling.* **exaggeration** NOUN

exalted ADJECTIVE *(formal)* Someone who is exalted is very important.

exam, exams NOUN an official test set to find out your knowledge or skill in a subject.

examination, examinations NOUN ① an exam. ② If you make an examination of something, you inspect it very carefully • *I carried out a careful examination of the hull.* ③ A medical examination is a check by a doctor to find out the state of your health.

examine, examines, examining, examined VERB ① If you examine something, you inspect it very carefully. ② EXAM TERM To examine a subject is to look closely at the issues involved and form your own opinion. ③ To examine someone means to find out their knowledge or skill in a particular subject by testing them. ④ If a doctor examines you, he or she checks your body to find out the state of your health.

examiner, examiners NOUN a person who sets or marks an exam.

example, examples NOUN ① something which represents or is typical of a group or set • *some examples of early Spanish music.* ② If you say someone or something is an example to people, you mean that people can imitate and learn from them. ▶ PHRASE ③ You use **for example** to give an example of something you are talking about. SIMILAR WORDS: ① sample, specimen

exasperate, exasperates, exasperating, exasperated VERB If someone or something exasperates you, they irritate you and make you angry. **exasperating** ADJECTIVE **exasperation** NOUN

excavate, excavates, excavating, excavated VERB To excavate means to remove earth from the ground by digging. **excavation** NOUN

exceed, exceeds, exceeding, exceeded VERB To exceed something such as a limit means to go beyond it or to become greater than it • *the first aircraft to exceed the speed of sound.*

exceedingly ADVERB extremely or very much.

excel, excels, excelling, excelled VERB If someone excels in something, they are very good at doing it.

Excellency, Excellencies NOUN a title used to address an official of very high rank, such as an ambassador or a governor.

excellent ADJECTIVE very good indeed. **excellence** NOUN
SIMILAR WORDS: first-rate, outstanding, superb

except PREPOSITION Except or except for means other than or apart from • *All my family were musicians except my father.*

SPELLING TIP
Do not confuse the spellings of *except* and *accept: He works every day except Tuesday; Please accept my apologies.*

---

exception, exceptions NOUN somebody or something that is not included in a general statement or rule • *English, like every language, has exceptions to its rules.*

exceptional ADJECTIVE ① unusually talented or clever. ② unusual and likely to happen very rarely. **exceptionally** ADVERB

excerpt, excerpts NOUN a short piece of writing or music which is taken from a larger piece.

excess, excesses NOUN ① Excess is behaviour which goes beyond normally acceptable limits • *a life of excess.* ② a larger amount of something than is needed, usual or healthy • *an excess of energy.*

▶ADJECTIVE ③ more than is needed, allowed or healthy • *excess weight.*
▶PHRASE ④ **In excess of** a particular amount means more than that amount • *a fortune in excess of 150 million pounds.* ⑤ If you do something **to excess**, you do it too much • *She exercised to excess.*

excessive ADJECTIVE too great in amount or degree • *using excessive force.* **excessively** ADVERB

exchange, exchanges, exchanging, exchanged VERB ① To exchange things means to give or receive one thing in return for another • *They exchange small presents on Christmas Eve.* ▶NOUN ② the act of giving or receiving something in return for something else • *an exchange of letters* • *exchanges of gunfire.* ③ a place where people trade and do business • *the stock exchange.*

exchequer [Said iks-**chek**-er] NOUN The exchequer is the department in the government in Britain and other countries which is responsible for money belonging to the state.

excise NOUN Excise is a tax put on goods produced for sale in the country that produces them.

excitable ADJECTIVE easily excited.

excite, excites, exciting, excited VERB ① If somebody or something excites you, they make you feel very happy and nervous or very interested and enthusiastic. ② If something excites a particular feeling, it causes somebody to have that feeling • *This excited my suspicion.*
SIMILAR WORDS: ① arouse, thrill

excited ADJECTIVE happy and unable to relax. **excitedly** ADVERB

excitement NOUN happiness and enthusiasm.

exciting ADJECTIVE making you feel happy and enthusiastic.

a
b
c
e
f
g
h
i
j
k
l
m
n
o
p
q
r
s
t
u
v
w
x
y
z

A
B
C
D
E
F
G
H
I
J
K
L
M
N
O
P
Q
R
S
T
U
V
W
X
Y
Z

What does the Exclamation Mark do?

The **exclamation mark (!)** is used after emphatic expressions and exclamations:

I can't believe it!

The exclamation mark can lose its effect if used too much. After a sentence expressing mild excitement or humour, it is better to use a full stop:

It is a beautiful day.

exclaim, exclaims, exclaiming, exclaimed VERB When you exclaim, you cry out suddenly or loudly because you are excited or shocked.

exclamation, exclamations NOUN ENGLISH a word or phrase spoken suddenly to express a strong feeling.

exclamation mark, exclamation marks NOUN a punctuation mark (!) used in writing to express a strong feeling.

PUNCTUATION TIP
If a piece of direct speech ends in an exclamation, you put the exclamation mark inside the quotation marks: *When the door opened we all shouted, 'Surprise!'*.

exclude, excludes, excluding, excluded VERB ① If you exclude something, you deliberately do not include it or do not consider it. ② If you exclude somebody from a place or an activity, you prevent them from entering the place or taking part in the activity.
exclusion NOUN

exclusive, exclusives ADJECTIVE ① available to or for the use of a small group of rich or privileged people • *an exclusive club*. ② belonging to a particular person or group only • *exclusive rights to coverage of the concerts*. ▶ NOUN ③ a story or interview which appears in only one newspaper or on only one television programme. **exclusively** ADVERB

excrement [Said **eks-krim-ment**] NOUN Excrement is the solid waste matter that is passed out of a person's or animal's body through their bowels.

excrete, excretes, excreting, excreted VERB SCIENCE When you excrete waste matter from your body, you get rid of it, for example by going to the lavatory or by sweating. **excretion** NOUN **excretory** ADJECTIVE

excruciating [Said **iks-kroo-shee-ate-ing**] ADJECTIVE unbearably painful. **excruciatingly** ADVERB
WORD HISTORY: from Latin *excruciare* meaning 'to torture'

excursion, excursions NOUN a short journey or outing.

excuse, excuses, excusing, excused NOUN [Said **iks-kyoos**] ① a reason which you give to explain why something has been done, has not been done, or will not be done. ▶ VERB [Said **iks-kyooz**] ② If you excuse yourself or something that you have done, you give reasons defending your actions. ③ If you excuse somebody for something wrong they have done, you forgive them for it. ④ If you excuse somebody from a duty or responsibility, you free them from it • *He was excused from standing trial because of ill health.* ▶ PHRASE ⑤ You say **excuse me** to try to catch somebody's attention or to apologise for an interruption or for rude behaviour.

execute, executes, executing, executed VERB ①To execute somebody means to kill them as a punishment for a crime. ②If you execute something such as a plan or an action, you carry it out or perform it • *The crime had been planned and executed in Montreal.* **execution** NOUN

executioner, executioners NOUN a person whose job is to execute criminals.

executive, executives NOUN ①a person who is employed by a company at a senior level. ②The executive of an organisation is a committee which has the authority to make decisions and ensure that they are carried out. ▶ADJECTIVE ③concerned with making important decisions and ensuring that they are carried out • *the commission's executive director.*

executor, executors [*Said ig-zek-yoo-tor*] NOUN a person you appoint to carry out the instructions in your will.

exemplary ADJECTIVE ①being a good example and worthy of imitation • *an exemplary performance.* ②serving as a warning • *an exemplary tale.*

exemplify, exemplifies, exemplifying, exemplified VERB ①To exemplify something means to be a typical example of it • *This aircraft exemplifies the advantages of European technological cooperation.* ②If you exemplify something, you give an example of it.

exempt, exempts, exempting, exempted ADJECTIVE ①excused from a rule or duty • *people exempt from prescription charges.* ▶VERB ②To exempt someone from a rule, duty or obligation means to excuse them from it. **exemption** NOUN

exercise, exercises, exercising, exercised NOUN ① PE Exercise is any activity which you do to get fit or remain healthy. ②Exercises are also activities which you do to practise and train for a particular skill • *piano exercises* • *a mathematical exercise.* ▶VERB ③When you exercise, you do activities which help you to get fit and remain healthy. ④If you exercise your rights or responsibilities, you use them.

exert, exerts, exerting, exerted VERB ①To exert pressure means to apply it. ②If you exert yourself, you make a physical or mental effort to do something.

exertion, exertions NOUN Exertion is vigorous physical effort or exercise.

exhale, exhales, exhaling, exhaled VERB SCIENCE When you exhale, you breathe out. **exhalation** NOUN

exhaust, exhausts, exhausting, exhausted VERB ①To exhaust somebody means to make them very tired • *Several lengths of the pool left her exhausted.* ②If you exhaust a supply of something such as money or food, you use it up completely. ③If you exhaust a subject, you talk about it so much that there is nothing else to say about it. ▶NOUN ④a pipe which carries the gas or steam out of the engine of a vehicle. ⑤Exhaust is the gas or steam produced by the engine of a vehicle. **exhaustion** NOUN
SIMILAR WORDS: ①fatigue, tire out, wear out

exhaustive ADJECTIVE thorough and complete • *an exhaustive series of tests.* **exhaustively** ADVERB

exhibit, exhibits, exhibiting, exhibited VERB ①To exhibit things means to show them in a public place for people to see. ②If you exhibit your feelings or abilities, you display them so that other people can see

a
b
c
e
f
g
h
i
j
k
l
m
n
o
p
q
r
s
t
u
v
w
x
y
z

them. ▶ NOUN ③ anything which is put on show for the public to see.

exhibition, exhibitions NOUN ART a public display of works of art, products or skills.

exhibitor, exhibitors NOUN a person whose work is being shown in an exhibition.

exhilarating ADJECTIVE Something that is exhilarating makes you feel very happy and excited.

exile, exiles, exiling, exiled NOUN ① If somebody lives in exile, they live in a foreign country because they cannot live in their own country, usually for political reasons. ② a person who lives in exile. ▶ VERB ③ If somebody is exiled, they are sent away from their own country and not allowed to return.

exist, exists, existing, existed VERB If something exists, it is present in the world as a real or living thing.

existence NOUN ① Existence is the state of being or existing. ② a way of living or being • an idyllic existence.

exit, exits, exiting, exited NOUN ① a way out of a place. ② If you make an exit, you leave a place. ▶ VERB ③ To exit means to go out. ④ DRAMA An actor exits when he or she leaves the stage.

exodus NOUN An exodus is the departure of a large number of people from a place.

exothermic ADJECTIVE SCIENCE If a chemical reaction is exothermic, heat is produced.

exotic ADJECTIVE ① attractive or interesting through being unusual • exotic fabrics. ② coming from a foreign country • exotic plants.
WORD HISTORY: from Greek exōtikos meaning 'foreign'

expand, expands, expanding, expanded VERB ① If something

expands or you expand it, it becomes larger in number or size. ② If you expand on something, you give more details about it • Use the following paragraphs to expand on the points you made in the first. **expansion** NOUN

expanse, expanses NOUN a very large or widespread area • a vast expanse of pine forests.

expansive ADJECTIVE ① Something that is expansive is very wide or extends over a very large area • the expansive countryside. ② Someone who is expansive is friendly, open or talkative.

expatriate, expatriates [Said eks-pat-ree-it] NOUN someone who is living in a country which is not their own.

expect, expects, expecting, expected VERB ① If you expect something to happen, you believe that it will happen • The group is expected to arrive today. ② If you are expecting somebody or something, you believe that they are going to arrive or to happen • Mr Jenkins was expecting you this morning. ③ If you expect something, you believe that it is your right to get it or have it • He seemed to expect a reply.
SIMILAR WORDS: ① anticipate, look forward to

expectancy NOUN Expectancy is the feeling that something is about to happen, especially something exciting.

expectant ADJECTIVE ① If you are expectant, you believe that something is about to happen, especially something exciting. ② An expectant mother or father is someone whose baby is going to be born soon. **expectantly** ADVERB

expectation, expectations NOUN Expectation or an expectation is a

A B C D E F G H I J K L M N O P Q R S T U V W X Y Z

strong belief or hope that something will happen.

expedient, expedients [Said *iks-pee-dee-ent*] NOUN ① an action or plan that achieves a particular purpose but that may not be morally acceptable • *Many firms have improved their profitability by the simple expedient of cutting staff.* ▶ ADJECTIVE ② Something that is expedient is useful or convenient in a particular situation. **expediency** NOUN

expedition, expeditions NOUN ① an organised journey made for a special purpose, such as to explore; also the party of people who make such a journey. ② a short journey or outing • *shopping expeditions.*
expeditionary ADJECTIVE

expel, expels, expelling, expelled VERB ① If someone is expelled from a school or club, they are officially told to leave because they have behaved badly. ② If a gas or liquid is expelled from a place, it is forced out of it.

expend, expends, expending, expended VERB To expend energy, time or money means to use it up or spend it.

expendable ADJECTIVE no longer useful or necessary, and therefore able to be got rid of.

expenditure NOUN Expenditure is the total amount of money spent on something.

expense, expenses NOUN ① Expense is the money that something costs • *the expense of installing a burglar alarm.* ② (in plural) Expenses are the money somebody spends while doing something connected with their work, which is paid back to them by their employer • *travelling expenses.*
SIMILAR WORDS: ① cost, expenditure, outlay

expensive ADJECTIVE costing a lot of money. **expensively** ADVERB

experience, experiences, experiencing, experienced NOUN ① Experience consists of all the things that you have done or that have happened to you. ② the knowledge or skill you have in a particular activity. ③ something that you do or something that happens to you, especially something new or unusual. ▶ VERB ④ If you experience a situation or feeling, it happens to you or you are affected by it.
SIMILAR WORDS: ④ go through, undergo

experienced ADJECTIVE skilled or knowledgeable through doing something for a long time.

experiment, experiments, experimenting, experimented NOUN ① the testing of something, either to find out its effect or to prove something. ▶ VERB ② If you experiment with something, you do a scientific test on it to prove or discover something.
experimentation NOUN
experimental ADJECTIVE
experimentally ADVERB

expert, experts NOUN ① a person who is very skilled at doing something or very knowledgeable about a particular subject. ▶ ADJECTIVE ② having or requiring special skill or knowledge • *expert advice.* **expertly** ADVERB
SIMILAR WORDS: ① authority, master, specialist

expertise [Said *eks-per-teez*] NOUN Expertise is special skill or knowledge.

expire, expires, expiring, expired VERB When something expires, it reaches the end of the period of time for which it is valid • *My contract expires in the summer.* **expiry** NOUN

A
B
C
D
E
F
G
H
I
J
K
L
M
N
O
P
Q
R
S
T
U
V
W
X
Y
Z

explain, explains, explaining, explained VERB If you explain something, you give details about it or reasons for it so that it can be understood.
SIMILAR WORDS: clarify, elucidate, make clear

explanation, explanations NOUN a helpful or clear description. **explanatory** ADJECTIVE

explicit ADJECTIVE shown or expressed clearly and openly • *an explicit warning.* **explicitly** ADVERB

explode, explodes, exploding, exploded VERB ① If something such as a bomb explodes, it bursts loudly and with great force, often causing damage. ② If somebody explodes, they express strong feelings suddenly or violently • *I half expected him to explode in anger.* ③ When something increases suddenly and rapidly, it can be said to explode • *Sales of men's toiletries have exploded.*
WORD HISTORY: from Latin *explodere* meaning 'to clap someone offstage', from *ex* meaning 'out of' + *plaudere* meaning 'to clap'

exploit, exploits, exploiting, exploited VERB [Said iks-**ploit**] ① If somebody exploits a person or a situation, they take advantage of them for their own ends • *Critics claim the record label exploited young musicians.* ② If you exploit something, you make the best use of it, often for profit • *The company wants to exploit the power of social media.* ▸ NOUN [Said **eks**-ploit] ③ something daring or interesting that somebody has done • *The diver's courage and exploits were legendary.* **exploitation** NOUN

explore, explores, exploring, explored VERB ① If you explore a place, you travel in it to find out what it is like. ② If you explore an idea, you think about it carefully. **exploration** NOUN **exploratory** ADJECTIVE **explorer** NOUN

explosion, explosions NOUN a sudden violent burst of energy, for example one caused by a bomb.

explosive, explosives ADJECTIVE ① capable of exploding or likely to explode. ② happening suddenly and making a loud noise. ③ An explosive situation is one which is likely to have serious or dangerous effects. ▸ NOUN ④ a substance or device that can explode.

exponent, exponents NOUN ① An exponent of an idea or plan is someone who puts it forward. ② (formal) An exponent of a skill or activity is someone who is good at it. ③ MATHS a number or symbol placed above and to the right of a number, indicating how many times the number is to be multiplied by itself • 2^3 equals $2 \times 2 \times 2$.

export, exports, exporting, exported VERB [Said ik-**sport**] ① If you export goods, you send them to another country and sell them there. ② ICT If you export data, you save it in a format that can be used by another software program. ▸ NOUN [Said **ek**-sport] ③ Exports are goods which are sent to another country and sold there. **exporter** NOUN

expose, exposes, exposing, exposed VERB ① To expose something means to uncover it and make it visible. ② To expose a person to something dangerous means to put them in a situation in which it might harm them • *exposed to tobacco smoke.* ③ To expose a person or situation means to reveal the truth about them.

exposition, expositions NOUN ENGLISH a detailed explanation of a particular subject.

exposure, exposures NOUN
① Exposure is the exposing of something. ② Exposure is the harmful effect on the body caused by very cold weather.

express, expresses, expressing, expressed VERB ① When you express an idea or feeling, you show what you think or feel by saying or doing something. ② If you express a quantity in a particular form, you write it down in that form • *The result of the equation is usually expressed as a percentage.* ▶ ADJECTIVE ③ very fast • *express delivery service.* ▶ NOUN ④ a fast train or coach which stops at only a few places.

expression, expressions NOUN
① Your expression is the look on your face which shows what you are thinking or feeling. ② ENGLISH The expression of ideas or feelings is the showing of them through words, actions or art. ③ a word or phrase used in communicating • *the expression 'nosey parker'.* ④ MATHS a symbol or equation that represents a quantity or problem.

expressive ADJECTIVE ① showing feelings clearly. ② full of expression.

expressway, expressways NOUN a road designed for fast-moving traffic.

expulsion, expulsions NOUN The expulsion of someone from a place or institution is the act of officially banning them from that place or institution • *the high number of school expulsions.*

exquisite ADJECTIVE extremely beautiful and pleasing.

extend, extends, extending, extended VERB ① If something extends for a distance, it continues and stretches into the distance. ② If something extends from a surface or an object, it sticks out from it. ③ If you extend something, you make it larger or longer • *The table had been extended to seat fifty.*

extension, extensions NOUN ① a room or building which is added to an existing building. ② an extra period of time for which something continues to exist or be valid • *an extension to his visa.* ③ an additional telephone connected to the same line as another telephone.

extensive ADJECTIVE ① covering a large area. ② very great in effect • *extensive repairs.* **extensively** ADVERB

extent, extents NOUN The extent of something is its length, area or size.

exterior, exteriors NOUN ① The exterior of something is its outside. ② Your exterior is your outward appearance.

exterior angle, exterior angles NOUN MATHS the angle formed between a line extending from one side of a polygon and the side next to it.

exterminate, exterminates, exterminating, exterminated VERB When animals or people are exterminated, they are deliberately killed. **extermination** NOUN

external ADJECTIVE existing or happening on the outside or outer part of something. **externally** ADVERB

extinct ADJECTIVE ① SCIENCE An extinct species of animal or plant is no longer in existence. ② SCIENCE An extinct volcano is no longer likely to erupt. **extinction** NOUN

extinguish, extinguishes, extinguishing, extinguished VERB To extinguish a light or fire means to put it out.

extortionate ADJECTIVE more expensive than you consider to be fair.

a b c d e f g h i j k l m n o p q r s t u v w x y z

extra, **extras** ADJECTIVE ① more than is usual, necessary or expected.
▸ NOUN ② anything which is additional. ③ a person who is hired to play a very small and unimportant part in a film.
SIMILAR WORDS: ① added, additional, further

extra- PREFIX 'Extra-' means 'outside' or 'beyond' • *extraordinary*.

extract, **extracts**, **extracting**, **extracted** VERB [*Said iks-**tract***] ① To extract something from a place means to take it out or get it out, often by force. ② If you extract information from someone, you get it from them with difficulty. ▸ NOUN [*Said **eks**-tract*] LIBRARY ③ a small section taken from a book or piece of music.

extraction NOUN ① Your extraction is the country or people that your family originally comes from • *a Malaysian citizen of Australian extraction*. ② Extraction is the process of taking or getting something out of a place.

extraordinary ADJECTIVE unusual or surprising. **extraordinarily** ADVERB
SIMILAR WORDS: exceptional, remarkable, unusual

extraterrestrial ADJECTIVE happening or existing beyond the earth's atmosphere.

extravagant ADJECTIVE ① spending or costing more money than is reasonable or affordable. ② going beyond reasonable limits.
extravagantly ADVERB
extravagance NOUN

extravaganza, **extravaganzas** NOUN a spectacular and expensive public show.

extreme, **extremes** ADJECTIVE ① very great in degree or intensity • *extreme caution*. ② going beyond what is usual or reasonable • *extreme weather conditions*. ③ at the furthest point or edge of something • *the extreme northern corner of Spain*.
▸ NOUN ④ the highest or furthest degree of something. **extremely** ADVERB

extremist, **extremists** NOUN a person who uses unreasonable or violent methods to bring about political change. **extremism** NOUN

extremity, **extremities** NOUN The extremities of something are its furthest ends or edges.

extricate, **extricates**, **extricating**, **extricated** VERB To extricate someone from a place or a situation means to free them from it.

extrovert, **extroverts** NOUN a person who is more interested in other people and the world around them than their own thoughts and feelings.
WORD HISTORY: from Latin *extra* meaning 'outwards' + *vertere* meaning 'to turn'

exuberant ADJECTIVE full of energy and cheerfulness. **exuberantly** ADVERB **exuberance** NOUN

exude, **exudes**, **exuding**, **exuded** VERB If someone exudes a quality or feeling, they seem to have it to a great degree.

eye, **eyes**, **eyeing** or **eying**, **eyed** NOUN ① the organ of sight. ② the small hole at the end of a needle through which you pass the thread.
▸ VERB ③ To eye something means to look at it carefully or suspiciously.

eyeball, **eyeballs** NOUN the whole of the ball-shaped part of the eye.

eyebrow, **eyebrows** NOUN Your eyebrows are the lines of hair which grow on the ridges of bone above your eyes.

eyelash, **eyelashes** NOUN Your

eyelashes are hairs that grow on the edges of your eyelids.

eyelid, eyelids NOUN Your eyelids are the folds of skin which cover your eyes when they are closed.

eyesight NOUN Your eyesight is your ability to see.

eyesore, eyesores NOUN Something that is an eyesore is extremely ugly.

eyewitness, eyewitnesses NOUN a person who has seen an event and can describe what happened.

eyrie, eyries [Said ear-ee] NOUN the nest of an eagle or other bird of prey.

Ff

fable, fables NOUN a story intended to teach a moral lesson.

fabled ADJECTIVE well-known because many stories have been told about it • *the fabled city of Troy*.

fabric, fabrics NOUN ① DGT cloth • *tough fabric for tents*. ②The fabric of a building is its walls, roof and other parts. ③The fabric of a society or system is its structure, laws and customs • *the democratic fabric of American society*.

fabricate, fabricates, fabricating, fabricated VERB ① If you fabricate a story or an explanation, you invent it in order to deceive people. ②To fabricate something is to make or manufacture it. **fabrication** NOUN

fabulous ADJECTIVE ①wonderful or very impressive • *a fabulous picnic*. ②not real, but happening in stories and legends • *fabulous creatures*.

facade, facades [Said fas-**sahd**] NOUN ①the front outside wall of a building. ②a false outward appearance • *the facade of honesty*.

face, faces, facing, faced NOUN ①the front part of your head from your chin to your forehead. ②the expression someone has or is making • *a grim face*. ③a surface or side of something, especially the most important side • *the north face of Everest*. ④the main aspect or general appearance of something • *We have changed the face of language study*. ▶VERB ⑤To face something or someone is to be opposite them or to look at them or towards them • *a room that faces onto the street*. ⑥If you face something difficult or unpleasant, you have to deal with it • *She faced a terrible dilemma*. ▶PHRASE ⑦**On the face of it** means judging by the appearance of something or your initial reaction to it • *On the face of it the palace looks gigantic*.

SIMILAR WORDS: ①countenance, visage

faceless ADJECTIVE without character or individuality • *anonymous shops and faceless coffee-bars*.

facelift, facelifts NOUN ①an operation to tighten the skin on someone's face to make them look younger. ②If you give something a face-lift, you clean it or improve its appearance.

facet, facets [Said fas-it] NOUN ①a single part or aspect of something • *the many facets of his talent*. ②one of the flat, cut surfaces of a precious stone.

WORD HISTORY: from French *facette* meaning 'little face'

FaceTime, FaceTimes, FaceTiming, FaceTimed NOUN (*trademark*) ①a computer program for making video calls on the internet. ▶VERB ②If you FaceTime someone, you use a computer program to speak to them while you look at each other on a video display.

facetious [Said fas-**see**-shuss] ADJECTIVE witty or amusing but in a rather silly or inappropriate way • *He didn't appreciate my facetious suggestion.*

WORD HISTORY: from Latin *facetiae* meaning 'witty remarks'

facial [Said **fay-shal**] **ADJECTIVE** appearing on or being part of the face • *facial expressions.*

facilitate, **facilitates**, **facilitating**, **facilitated** **VERB** To facilitate something is to make it easier for it to happen • *a process that will facilitate individual development.*

facility, **facilities** **NOUN** ①a service or piece of equipment which makes it possible to do something • *excellent shopping facilities.* ②A facility for something is an ability to do it easily or well • *a facility for novel-writing.*

fact, **facts** **NOUN** ①a piece of knowledge or information that is true or something that has actually happened. ▶ **PHRASE** ②**In fact**, **as a matter of fact** and **in point of fact** mean 'actually' or 'really' and are used for emphasis or when making an additional comment • *Very few people, in fact, have this type of skin.* **factual** **ADJECTIVE** **factually** **ADVERB**

faction, **factions** **NOUN** a small group of people belonging to a larger group, but differing from the larger group in some aims or ideas • *a conservative faction in the Church.*

SPELLING TIP

Do not confuse the spellings of *faction* and *fraction*: *a disagreement between factions of the Anglican Church; Write 50 per cent as a fraction.*

---

fact of life, **facts of life** **NOUN** ①The facts of life are details about how babies are conceived and born. ②If you say that something is a fact of life, you mean that it is something that people expect to happen, even though they might find it shocking or unpleasant • *War is a fact of life.*

factor, **factors** **NOUN** ①something that helps to cause a result • *House dust mites are a major factor in asthma.* ②The factors of a number are the whole numbers that will divide exactly into it. For example, 2 and 5 are factors of 10. ③If something increases by a particular factor, it is multiplied that number of times • *The amount of energy used has increased by a factor of eight.*

SIMILAR WORDS: ①cause, element, part

factory, **factories** **NOUN** a building or group of buildings where goods are made in large quantities.

faculty, **faculties** **NOUN** ①Your faculties are your physical and mental abilities • *My mental faculties are as sharp as ever.* ②In some universities, a Faculty is a group of related departments • *the Science Faculty.*

fad, **fads** **NOUN** a temporary fashion or craze • *the latest exercise fad.*

fade, **fades**, **fading**, **faded** **VERB** If something fades, the intensity of its colour, brightness or sound is gradually reduced.

faeces [Said **fee-seez**]; also spelt **feces** **PLURAL NOUN** the solid waste substances discharged from a person's or animal's body.

fag, **fags** **NOUN** (*informal*) a cigarette.

Fahrenheit [Said **far-ren-hite**] **NOUN** a scale of temperature in which the freezing point of water is 32° and the boiling point is 212°.

fail, **fails**, **failing**, **failed** **VERB** ①If someone fails to achieve something, they are not successful. ②If you fail an exam, your marks are too low and you do not pass. ③If you fail to do something that you should have done, you do not do it • *They failed to*

a
b
c
d
e
f
g
h
i
j
k
l
m
n
o
p
q
r
s
t
u
v
w
x
y
z

phone her. ④ If something fails, it becomes less effective or stops working properly • *The power failed* • *His grandmother's eyesight began to fail.* ▶ NOUN ⑤ In an exam, a fail is a piece of work that is not good enough to pass. ▶ PHRASE ⑥ **Without fail** means definitely or regularly • *Every Sunday her mum would ring without fail.*

SIMILAR WORDS: ① be unsuccessful, flop

failing, failings NOUN ① a fault in something or someone.
▶ PREPOSITION ② used to introduce an alternative • *Failing that, get a market stall.*

failure, failures NOUN ① lack of success • *Not all conservation programmes ended in failure.* ② an unsuccessful person, thing or action • *The venture was a complete failure.* ③ Your failure to do something is not doing something that you were expected to do • *a statement explaining his failure to turn up as a speaker.* ④ a weakness in something.

SIMILAR WORDS: ② flop, loser, washout

faint, fainter, faintest; faints, fainting, fainted ADJECTIVE ① A sound, colour or feeling that is faint is not very strong or intense. ② If you feel faint, you feel weak, dizzy and unsteady. ▶ VERB ③ If you faint, you lose consciousness for a short time. **faintly** ADVERB

SIMILAR WORDS: ③ black out, pass out, swoon

fair, fairer, fairest; fairs ADJECTIVE ① reasonable and just • *fair and prompt trials for political prisoners.* ② quite large • *a fair size.* ③ moderately good or likely to be correct • *He had a fair idea of what to expect.* ④ having light-coloured hair or pale skin. ⑤ with pleasant and dry

weather • *Ireland's fair weather months.* ▶ NOUN ⑥ a form of entertainment that takes place outside, with stalls, sideshows and machines to ride on. ⑦ an exhibition of goods produced by a particular industry • *International Food Fair.*

fairly ADVERB **fairness** NOUN
SIMILAR WORDS: ① impartial, just, unbiased

fairground, fairgrounds NOUN an outdoor area where a fair is set up.

fairway, fairways NOUN the area of trimmed grass between a tee and a green on a golf course.

fairy, fairies NOUN In stories, fairies are small, supernatural creatures with magical powers.

fairy tale, fairy tales NOUN a story of magical events.

faith, faiths NOUN ① Faith is a feeling of confidence, trust or optimism about something. ② RE Someone's faith is their religion.

faithful ADJECTIVE ① loyal to someone or something and remaining firm in support of them. ② accurate and truthful • *a faithful copy of an original.* **faithfully** ADVERB **faithfulness** NOUN
SIMILAR WORDS: ① loyal, steadfast, trusty

faith school, faith schools NOUN a school where the staff and pupils follow a particular religion.

fake, fakes, faking, faked NOUN ① an imitation of something made to trick people into thinking that it is genuine. ▶ ADJECTIVE ② imitation and not genuine • *fake fur.* ▶ VERB ③ If you fake a feeling, you pretend that you are experiencing it.

SIMILAR WORDS: ① copy, imitation, sham ② artificial, false, phoney ③ feign, pretend, simulate

falcon, falcons NOUN a bird of prey

that can be trained to hunt other birds or small animals.

fall, falls, falling, fell, fallen VERB ① If someone or something falls or falls over, they drop towards the ground. ② If something falls somewhere, it lands there • *The spotlight fell on her.* ③ If something falls in amount or strength, it becomes less • *Steel production fell about 25 per cent.* ④ If a person or group in a position of power falls, they lose their position and someone else takes control. ⑤ Someone who falls in battle is killed. ⑥ If, for example, you fall asleep, fall ill, or fall in love, you change quite quickly to that new state. ⑦ If you fall for someone, you become strongly attracted to them and fall in love. ⑧ If you fall for a trick or lie, you are deceived by it. ⑨ Something that falls on a particular date occurs on that date. ▶ NOUN ⑩ If you have a fall, you accidentally fall over. ⑪ A fall of snow, soot or other substance is a quantity of it that has fallen to the ground. ⑫ A fall in something is a reduction in its amount or strength. ⑬ In America, autumn is called fall.

fall down VERB An argument or idea that falls down on a particular point is weak on that point and as a result will be unsuccessful. **fall out** VERB If people fall out, they disagree and quarrel. **fall through** VERB If an arrangement or plan falls through, it fails or is abandoned.

fallacy, fallacies [Said *fal-lass-ee*] NOUN something false that is generally believed to be true.

fallopian tube, fallopian tubes [Said *fal-loh-pee-an*] NOUN one of two tubes in a woman's body along which the eggs pass from the ovaries to the uterus.

fallout NOUN radioactive particles that fall to the earth after a nuclear explosion.

fallow ADJECTIVE Land that is fallow is not being used for crop growing so that it has the chance to rest and improve.

false, falser, falsest ADJECTIVE ① untrue or incorrect • *I think that's a false argument.* ② not real or genuine but intended to seem real • *false teeth.* ③ unfaithful or deceitful. **falsely** ADVERB **falseness** NOUN **falsity** NOUN

falsehood, falsehoods NOUN ① the quality or fact of being untrue • *the difference between truth and falsehood.* ② a lie.

falsetto, falsettos NOUN MUSIC A falsetto is a man's very high-pitched speaking or singing voice.

falsify, falsifies, falsifying, falsified VERB If you falsify something, you change it in order to deceive people. **falsification** NOUN

falter, falters, faltering, faltered VERB If someone or something falters, they hesitate or become unsure or unsteady • *Her voice faltered.*

fame NOUN the state of being very well-known.
SIMILAR WORDS: prominence, renown, repute

famed ADJECTIVE very well-known • *an area famed for its beauty.*

familiar ADJECTIVE ① well-known or easy to recognise • *familiar faces.* ② knowing or understanding something well • *Most children are familiar with stories.* **familiarity** NOUN **familiarise** VERB
SIMILAR WORDS: ① recognisable, well-known

family, families NOUN ① a group consisting of parents and their children; also all the people who are

a
b
c
d
e
f
g
h
i
j
k
l
m
n
o
p
q
r
s
t
u
v
w
x
y
z

A
B
C
D
E
F
G
H
I
J
K
L
M
N
O
P
Q
R
S
T
U
V
W
X
Y
Z

related to each other, including aunts and uncles, cousins and grandparents. ② a group of related species of animals or plants. It is smaller than an order and larger than a genus. **familial** ADJECTIVE

family planning NOUN PSHE
Family planning is the practice of controlling the number of children you have, usually by using contraception.

family tree, family trees NOUN A family tree is a chart showing all the people in a family and their relationship to others over many generations.

famine, famines NOUN a serious shortage of food which may cause many deaths.

famished ADJECTIVE (informal) very hungry.

famous ADJECTIVE very well-known.
SIMILAR WORDS: prominent, renowned, well-known

famously ADVERB (old-fashioned) If people get on famously, they enjoy each other's company very much.

fan, fans, fanning, fanned NOUN ① If you are a fan of someone or something, you like them very much and are very enthusiastic about them. ② a hand-held or mechanical object which creates a draught of cool air when it moves. ▶ VERB ③ To fan someone or something is to create a draught in their direction • The gentle wind fanned her from all sides. **fan out** VERB If things or people fan out, they move outwards in different directions.
SIMILAR WORDS: ① admirer, enthusiast, supporter

fanatic, fanatics NOUN a person who is very extreme in their support for a cause or in their enthusiasm for a particular activity. **fanaticism** NOUN

WORD HISTORY: from Latin *fanaticus* meaning 'possessed by a god'

fanatical ADJECTIVE If you are fanatical about something, you are very extreme in your enthusiasm or support for it. **fanatically** ADVERB
SIMILAR WORDS: obsessive, overenthusiastic

fancy, fancies, fancying, fancied; fancier, fanciest VERB ① If you fancy something, you want to have it or do it • She fancied living in Canada.
▶ ADJECTIVE ② special and elaborate • dressed up in some fancy clothes.
fanciful ADJECTIVE
SIMILAR WORDS: ② elaborate, ornate

fancy dress NOUN clothing worn for a party at which people dress up to look like a particular character or animal.

fanfare, fanfares NOUN a short, loud musical introduction to a special event, usually played on trumpets.

fang, fangs NOUN Fangs are long, pointed teeth.

fantail, fantails NOUN ① a pigeon with a large tail that can be opened out like a fan. ② In Australia and New Zealand, a fantail is also a small, insect-eating bird with a fan-shaped tail.

fantasise, fantasises, fantasising, fantasised; also spelt **fantasize** VERB If you fantasise, you imagine pleasant but unlikely events or situations.

fantastic ADJECTIVE ① wonderful and very pleasing • a fantastic view of the sea. ② extremely large in degree or amount • fantastic debts.
③ strange and difficult to believe • fantastic animals found nowhere else on earth. **fantastically** ADVERB
SIMILAR WORDS: ① marvellous, wonderful

fantasy, fantasies NOUN ① an imagined story or situation.

②Fantasy is the activity of imagining things or the things that you imagine • *She can't distinguish between fantasy and reality.* ③In books and films, fantasy is the people or situations which are created in the writer's imagination and do not reflect reality.
WORD HISTORY: from Greek *phantasia* meaning 'imagination'

far, farther, farthest; further, furthest **ADVERB** ①If something is far away from other things, it is a long distance away. ②Far also means very much or to a great extent or degree • *far more important.* ▸**ADJECTIVE** ③Far means very distant • *in the far south of Africa.* ④Far also describes the more distant of two things rather than the nearer one • *the far corner of the goal.* ▸**PHRASE** ⑤**By far** and **far and away** are used to say that something is so to a great degree • *Walking is by far the best way to get around.* ⑥**So far** means up to the present moment • *So far, it's been good news.* ⑦**As far as**, **so far as** and **in so far as** mean to the degree or extent that something is true • *As far as I know he is progressing well.*
SIMILAR WORDS: ②considerably, much ③distant, remote

USAGE NOTE
When you are talking about a physical distance you can use *farther* and *farthest* or *further* and *furthest*. If you are talking about extra effort or time, use *further* and *furthest*: *A further delay is likely.*

farce, farces **NOUN** ①a humorous play in which ridiculous and unlikely situations occur. ②a disorganised and ridiculous situation. **farcical ADJECTIVE**

fare, fares, faring, fared **NOUN** ①the amount charged for a journey on a

bus, train or plane. ▸**VERB** ②How someone fares in a particular situation is how they get on • *The team have not fared well in this tournament.*

Far East NOUN The Far East consists of the countries of East Asia, including China, Japan and Malaysia. **Far Eastern ADJECTIVE**

farewell INTERJECTION ①Farewell means goodbye. ▸**ADJECTIVE** ②A farewell act is performed by or for someone who is leaving a particular job or career • *a farewell speech.*

far-fetched ADJECTIVE unlikely to be true.

farm, farms, farming, farmed **NOUN** ①an area of land together with buildings, used for growing crops and raising animals. ▸**VERB** ②Someone who farms uses land to grow crops and raise animals. **farmer NOUN farming NOUN**
WORD HISTORY: from Old French *ferme* meaning 'rented land'

farmhouse, farmhouses **NOUN** the main house on a farm.

farmyard, farmyards **NOUN** an area surrounded by farm buildings.

fascinate, fascinates, fascinating, fascinated **VERB** If something fascinates you, it interests you very much. **fascinating ADJECTIVE**
SIMILAR WORDS: absorb, enthral, intrigue

fascism [*Said fash-izm*] **NOUN** ⌐HISTORY⌐ an extreme political ideology or system of government with a powerful dictator and state control of most activities. Nationalism is encouraged and political opposition is not allowed. **fascist NOUN** or **ADJECTIVE**

fashion, fashions, fashioning, fashioned **NOUN** ①a style of dress or way of behaving that is popular at a particular time. ②The fashion in which someone does something is the way in which they do it. ▶ VERB ③If you fashion something, you make or shape it.

SIMILAR WORDS: ① style, trend, vogue

fashionable ADJECTIVE Something that is fashionable is very popular with a lot of people at the same time. **fashionably** ADVERB

SIMILAR WORDS: in, in vogue, popular, trendy

fast, faster, fastest; fasts, fasting, fasted ADJECTIVE ①moving or done at great speed. ②If a clock is fast, it shows a time that is later than the real time. ▶ ADVERB ③quickly and without delay. ④Something that is held fast is firmly fixed. ▶ PHRASE ⑤If you are **fast asleep**, you are in a deep sleep. ▶ VERB ⑥If you fast, you eat no food at all for a period of time, usually for religious reasons. ▶ NOUN ⑦a period of time during which someone does not eat food.

SIMILAR WORDS: ① quick, rapid, speedy, swift

fasten, fastens, fastening, fastened VERB ①To fasten something is to close it or attach it firmly to something else. ②If you fasten your hands or teeth around or onto something, you hold it tightly with them. **fastener** NOUN **fastening** NOUN

SIMILAR WORDS: ①fix, secure

fast food NOUN hot food that is prepared and served quickly after you have ordered it.

fastidious ADJECTIVE extremely choosy and concerned about neatness and cleanliness.

fast-track, fast-tracks, fast-tracking, fast-tracked VERB To fast-track something is to make it happen or put it into effect as quickly

as possible, usually giving it priority over other things.

fat, fatter, fattest; fats ADJECTIVE ①Someone who is fat has too much weight on their body. ②large or great • *a fat pile of letters.* ▶ NOUN ③Fat is the greasy, cream-coloured substance that animals and humans have under their skin, which is used to store energy and to help keep them warm. ④Fat is also the greasy solid or liquid substance obtained from animals and plants and used in cooking. **fatness** NOUN **fatty** ADJECTIVE

SIMILAR WORDS: ①overweight, plump, podgy, tubby

fatal ADJECTIVE ①causing death • *fatal injuries.* ②very important or significant and likely to have an undesirable effect • *The mistake was fatal to my plans.* **fatally** ADVERB

SIMILAR WORDS: ①deadly, lethal, mortal

fatality, fatalities NOUN a death caused by accident or violence.

fate, fates NOUN ①Fate is a power that is believed to control events. ②Someone's fate is what happens to them • *She was resigned to her fate.*

SIMILAR WORDS: ①destiny, providence

fateful ADJECTIVE having an important, often disastrous, effect • *fateful political decisions.*

father, fathers NOUN ①A person's father is their male parent. ②The father of something is the man who invented or started it • *the father of Italian painting.* ③'Father' is used to address a priest in some Christian churches. ④Father is another name for God. **fatherly** ADJECTIVE **fatherhood** NOUN

father-in-law, fathers-in-law NOUN A person's father-in-law is the father of their husband or wife.

fathom, fathoms, fathoming, fathomed NOUN ① a unit for measuring the depth of water. It is equal to 6 feet or about 1.83 metres. ▸ VERB ② If you fathom something, you understand it after careful thought • *Daisy tries to fathom what it means*.

fatigue, fatigues, fatiguing, fatigued [*Said* fat-*eeg*] NOUN ① Fatigue is extreme tiredness. ▸ VERB ② If you are fatigued by something, it makes you extremely tired.

fatten, fattens, fattening, fattened VERB If you fatten animals, you feed them so that they put on weight.

faucet, faucets [*Said* faw-*sit*] NOUN Mainly in American English, a faucet is a tap.

fault, faults, faulting, faulted NOUN ① If something bad is your fault, you are to blame for it. ② a weakness or imperfection in someone or something. ③ GEOGRAPHY a large crack in rock caused by movement of the earth's crust. ▸ PHRASE ④ If you are **at fault**, you are mistaken or are to blame for something • *If you were at fault, you accept it*. ▸ VERB ⑤ If you fault someone, you criticise them for what they are doing because they are not doing it well. **faultless** ADJECTIVE

SIMILAR WORDS: ② defect, failing, flaw

faulty, faultier, faultiest ADJECTIVE containing flaws or errors.

fauna [*Said* faw-*na*] NOUN GEOGRAPHY The fauna of a particular area is all the animals found in that area • *the flora and fauna of Africa*.

favour, favours, favouring, favoured NOUN ① If you regard someone or something with favour, you like or support them. ② If you do someone a favour, you do something helpful for them. ▸ PHRASE ③ Something that is **in someone's favour** is a help or advantage to them • *The arguments seemed to be in our favour*. ④ If you are **in favour of** something, you agree with it and think it should happen. ▸ VERB ⑤ If you favour something or someone, you prefer that person or thing.

favourable ADJECTIVE ① of advantage or benefit to someone. ② positive and expressing approval. **favourably** ADVERB

favourite, favourites ADJECTIVE ① Your favourite person or thing is the one you like best. ▸ NOUN ② Someone's favourite is the person or thing they like best. ③ the animal or person expected to win in a race or contest.

favouritism NOUN Favouritism is behaviour in which you are unfairly more helpful or more generous to one person than to other people.

fawn, fawns, fawning, fawned NOUN or ADJECTIVE ① pale yellowish-brown. ▸ NOUN ② a very young deer. ▸ VERB ③ To fawn on someone is to seek their approval by flattering them.

fear, fears, fearing, feared NOUN ① Fear is an unpleasant feeling of danger. ② a thought that something undesirable or unpleasant might happen • *You have a fear of failure*. ▸ VERB ③ If you fear someone or something, you are frightened of them. ④ If you fear something unpleasant, you are worried that it is likely to happen • *Artists feared that their pictures would be forgotten*. **fearless** ADJECTIVE **fearlessly** ADVERB

SIMILAR WORDS: ① dread, fright, terror

fearful ADJECTIVE ① afraid and full of fear. ② extremely unpleasant or

A
B
C
D
E
F
G
H
I
J
K
L
M
N
O
P
Q
R
S
T
U
V
W
X
Y
Z

worrying • *The world's in such a fearful mess.* **fearfully ADVERB**

fearsome ADJECTIVE terrible or frightening • *a powerful, fearsome weapon*.

feasible ADJECTIVE possible and likely to happen • *The proposal is just not feasible.* **feasibility NOUN**

feast, feasts NOUN a large and special meal for many people.

feat, feats NOUN an impressive and difficult achievement • *It was an astonishing feat for Leeds to score six away from home.*

feather, feathers NOUN one of the light fluffy things covering a bird's body. **feathery ADJECTIVE**

feature, features, featuring, featured NOUN ① an interesting or important part or characteristic of something. ② Someone's features are the various parts of their face. ③ a special article or programme dealing with a particular subject. ④ the main film in a cinema programme. ▶ VERB ⑤ To feature something is to include it or emphasise it as an important part or subject. **featureless ADJECTIVE**

February NOUN February is the second month of the year. It has 28 days, except in a leap year, when it has 29 days.
WORD HISTORY: from *Februa*, a Roman festival of purification

fed the past tense and past participle of **feed**.

federal ADJECTIVE relating to a system of government in which a group of states is controlled by a central government, but each state has its own local powers • *The United States of America is a federal country.*

federation, federations NOUN a group of organisations or states that have joined together for a common purpose.

fed up ADJECTIVE (*informal*) unhappy or bored.

fee, fees NOUN a charge or payment for a job, service or activity.

feeble, feebler, feeblest ADJECTIVE weak or lacking in power or influence • *feeble and stupid arguments*.

feed, feeds, feeding, fed VERB ① To feed a person or animal is to give them food. ② When an animal or baby feeds, it eats. ③ To feed something is to supply what is needed for it to operate or exist • *The information was fed into a computer database.* ▶ NOUN ④ Feed is food for animals. ⑤ In computer networks, a feed is a system that tells a user when something is available for them to read.

feedback NOUN ① Feedback is comments and information about the quality or success of something. ② Feedback is also a condition in which some of the power, sound or information produced by electronic equipment goes back into it.

feel, feels, feeling, felt VERB ① If you feel an emotion or sensation, you experience it • *I felt a bit ashamed.* ② If you feel that something is the case, you believe it to be so • *She feels that she is in control of her life.* ③ If you feel something, you touch it. ④ If something feels warm or cold, for example, you experience its warmth or coldness through the sense of touch • *Real marble feels cold to the touch.* ⑤ To feel the effect of something is to be affected by it • *The shock waves of this fire will be felt by people from all over the world.* ▶ NOUN ⑥ The feel of something is how it feels to you when you touch it • *skin with a velvety smooth feel.* ▶ PHRASE ⑦ If you **feel like** doing something, you want to do it.
SIMILAR WORDS: ① be aware of, experience ② believe, consider, think

feeler, feelers NOUN An insect's feelers are the two thin antennae on its head with which it senses things around it.

feeling, feelings NOUN ① an emotion or reaction • *feelings of envy*. ② a physical sensation • *a feeling of pain*. ③ Feeling is the ability to experience the sense of touch in your body • *He had no feeling in his hands*. ④ (*in plural*) Your feelings about something are your general attitudes or thoughts about it • *He has strong feelings about our national sport*.

feet the plural of **foot**.

feign, feigns, feigning, feigned [*Rhymes with rain*] VERB If you feign an emotion or state, you pretend to experience it • *I feigned a headache*.

feisty, feistier, feistiest [*Said fie-stee*] ADJECTIVE tough, independent and spirited • *a feisty woman with a great sense of humour*.

feline [*Said fee-line*] ADJECTIVE belonging or relating to the cat family.

fell, fells, felling, felled ① the past tense of **fall**. ▶ VERB ② To fell a tree is to cut it down.

fellow, fellows NOUN ① (*old-fashioned, informal*) a man • *I knew a fellow by that name*. ② a senior member of a learned society or a university college. ③ Your fellows are the people who share work or an activity

with you. ▶ ADJECTIVE ④ You use 'fellow' to describe people who have something in common with you • *his fellow editors*.

fellowship, fellowships NOUN ① a feeling of friendliness that a group of people have when they are doing things together. ② a group of people that join together because they have interests in common • *the Dickens Fellowship*. ③ an academic post at a university which involves research work.

felt ① the past tense and past participle of **feel**. ▶ NOUN ② [D-G-T] Felt is a thick cloth made by pressing short threads together.

female, females NOUN ① a person or animal belonging to the sex that can have babies or lay eggs. ▶ ADJECTIVE ② concerning or relating to females.

feminine ADJECTIVE ① relating to women or considered to be typical of women. ② belonging to a particular class of nouns in some languages, such as French, German and Latin. **femininity** NOUN

feminism NOUN Feminism is the belief that women should have the same rights and opportunities as men. **feminist** NOUN OR ADJECTIVE

fen, fens NOUN The fens are an area of low, flat, very wet land in the east of England.

What is a Feminine Noun?

Feminine nouns refer to female people and animals:

The girl put on her coat. → *girl is **feminine***

It is customary to refer to countries and vehicles as if they were feminine:

The ship came into view, her sails swelling in the breeze.

Common nouns may be either masculine or feminine. Other words in the sentence may tell us if they are male or female:

The doctor parked his car.
The doctor parked her car.

Also look at the grammar boxes at **gender**; **masculine**; **neuter**

fence, fences, fencing, fenced NOUN
① a wooden or wire barrier between two areas of land. ② a barrier or hedge for the horses to jump over in horse racing or show jumping.
▶ VERB ③ To fence an area of land is to surround it with a fence. ④ When two people fence, they use special swords to fight each other as a sport.

fend, fends, fending, fended PHRASE
If you have to **fend for yourself**, you have to look after yourself. **fend off** VERB If you fend off an attack or unwelcome questions or attention, you defend and protect yourself.

ferment, ferments, fermenting, fermented VERB When wine, beer or fruit ferments, a chemical change takes place in it, often producing alcohol. **fermentation** NOUN

fern, ferns NOUN a plant with long feathery leaves and no flowers.

ferocious ADJECTIVE violent and fierce • *ferocious dogs* • *ferocious storms*. **ferociously** ADVERB **ferocity** NOUN
WORD HISTORY: from Latin *ferox* meaning 'like a wild animal'

ferret, ferrets NOUN a small, fierce animal related to the weasel and kept for hunting rats and rabbits.
WORD HISTORY: from Old French *furet* meaning 'little thief'

ferry, ferries, ferrying, ferried NOUN
① a boat that carries people and vehicles across short stretches of water. ▶ VERB ② To ferry people or goods somewhere is to transport them there, usually on a short, regular journey.

fertile ADJECTIVE ① capable of producing offspring or plants. ② creative • *fertile minds*. **fertility** NOUN

fertilise, fertilises, fertilising, fertilised; also spelt **fertilize** VERB
① SCIENCE When an egg, plant or female is fertilised, the process of reproduction begins by sperm joining with the egg, or by pollen coming into contact with the reproductive part of a plant. ② To fertilise land is to put manure or chemicals onto it to feed the plants.

fertiliser, fertilisers; also spelt **fertilizer** NOUN GEOGRAPHY a substance put onto soil to improve plant growth.

fervent ADJECTIVE showing strong, sincere and enthusiastic feeling • *a fervent nationalist*. **fervently** ADVERB

fervour NOUN a very strong feeling for or belief in something • *a wave of revolutionary fervour*.
WORD HISTORY: from Latin *fervor* meaning 'heat'

fester, festers, festering, festered VERB If a wound festers, it becomes infected and produces pus.
WORD HISTORY: from Latin *fistula* meaning 'ulcer'

festival, festivals NOUN ① an organised series of events and performances • *the Cannes Film Festival*. ② RE a day or period of religious celebration.

festive ADJECTIVE full of happiness and celebration • *a festive time of singing and dancing*.

festivity, festivities NOUN celebration and happiness • *the wedding festivities*.

festooned ADJECTIVE If something is festooned with objects, the objects are hanging across it in large numbers.

fetch, fetches, fetching, fetched VERB ① If you fetch something, you go to where it is and bring it back. ② If something fetches a particular sum of money, it is sold for that amount • *Portraits fetch the highest prices*.

fetching ADJECTIVE attractive in appearance • *a fetching purple frock*.

fete, fetes, feting, feted *[Rhymes with date]* NOUN ① an outdoor event with competitions, displays and goods for sale. ▶ VERB ② Someone who is feted receives a public welcome or entertainment as an honour.

feud, feuds, feuding, feuded *[Said fyood]* NOUN ① a long-term and very bitter quarrel, especially between families. ▶ VERB ② When people feud, they take part in a feud.

feudalism NOUN HISTORY Feudalism is a social and political system that was common in the Middle Ages in Europe. Under this system, ordinary people were given land and protection by a lord, and in return they worked and fought for him. **feudal** ADJECTIVE

fever, fevers NOUN ① Fever is a condition occurring during illness, in which the patient has a very high body temperature. ② A fever is extreme excitement or agitation • *a fever of impatience*.

feverish ADJECTIVE ① in a state of extreme excitement or agitation • *increasingly feverish activity*. ② suffering from a high body temperature. **feverishly** ADVERB

few, fewer, fewest ADJECTIVE or NOUN ① used to refer to a small number of things • *I saw him a few moments ago* • *one of only a few*. ▶ PHRASE ② **Quite a few** or **a good few** means quite a large number of things.

GRAMMAR TIP
You use *fewer* to talk about things that can be counted: *fewer than five visits*. When you are talking about amounts that can't be counted you should use *less*.

---

fiancé, fiancés *[Said fee-on-say]* NOUN A person's fiancé is the man to whom they are engaged.

fiancée, fiancées *[Said fee-on-say]* NOUN A person's fiancée is the woman to whom they are engaged.

fiasco, fiascos *[Said fee-ass-koh]* NOUN an event or attempt that fails completely, especially in a ridiculous or disorganised way • *The game ended in a complete fiasco*.

fib, fibs, fibbing, fibbed NOUN ① a small, unimportant lie. ▶ VERB ② If you fib, you tell a small lie.

fibre, fibres NOUN ① DGT a thin thread of a substance used to make cloth. ② SCIENCE Fibre is also a part of plants that can be eaten but not digested; it helps food pass quickly through the body. **fibrous** ADJECTIVE

fibreglass NOUN DGT Fibreglass is a material made from thin threads of glass. It can be mixed with plastic to make boats, cars and furniture, and is often used as an insulating material.

fibre optics NOUN Fibre optics is the use of long, thin threads of glass to carry information in the form of light.

fickle ADJECTIVE A fickle person keeps changing their mind about who or what they like or want.

fiction, fictions NOUN ① Fiction is stories about people and events that have been invented by the author. ② something that is not true. **fictional** ADJECTIVE **fictitious** ADJECTIVE

fiddle, fiddles, fiddling, fiddled VERB ① If you fiddle with something, you keep moving it or touching it restlessly. ② (*informal*) If someone fiddles something such as an account, they alter it dishonestly to get money for themselves. ▶ NOUN (*informal*) ③ a dishonest action or

a
b
c
d
e
f
g
h
i
j
k
l
m
n
o
p
q
r
s
t
u
v
w
x
y
z

scheme to get money. ④ a violin.
fiddler NOUN

fiddly, fiddlier, fiddliest ADJECTIVE
small and difficult to do or use • *fiddly
nuts and bolts.*

fidelity NOUN Fidelity is remaining
firm in your beliefs, friendships or
loyalty to another person.

fidget, fidgets, fidgeting, fidgeted
VERB ① If you fidget, you keep
changing your position because of
nervousness or boredom. ▸ NOUN
② someone who fidgets. **fidgety**
ADJECTIVE

field, fields, fielding, fielded NOUN
① an area of land where crops are
grown or animals are kept. ② PE an
area of land where sports are played
• *a hockey field.* ③ A coal field, oil field
or gold field is an area where coal, oil
or gold is found. ④ a particular
subject or area of interest • *He was
doing well in the field of chemistry.*
⑤ SCIENCE A magnetic field or
gravitational field is the area in which
magnetism or gravity has an effect.
▸ ADJECTIVE ⑥ A field trip or a field
study involves research or activity in
the natural environment rather than
theoretical or laboratory work. ⑦ In
an athletics competition, the field
events are the events such as the
high jump and the javelin which do
not take place on a running track.
▸ VERB ⑧ In cricket, when you field
the ball, you stop it after the
batsman has hit it. ⑨ To field
questions is to answer or deal with
them skilfully.

fielder, fielders NOUN In cricket, the
fielders are the team members who
stand at various parts of the pitch
and try to get the batsmen out or to
prevent runs from being scored.

field marshal, field marshals NOUN
an army officer of the highest rank.

fieldwork NOUN Fieldwork is the
study of something in the
environment where it naturally lives
or occurs, rather than in a class or
laboratory.

fiend, fiends [Said *feend*] NOUN ① a
devil or evil spirit. ② a very wicked or
cruel person. ③ (informal) someone
who is very keen on a particular thing
• *a fitness fiend.*

fierce, fiercer, fiercest ADJECTIVE
① very aggressive or angry.
② extremely strong or intense • *a
sudden fierce pain* • *a fierce storm.*
fiercely ADVERB
SIMILAR WORDS: ① ferocious, savage,
wild

fiery, fierier, fieriest ADJECTIVE
① involving fire or seeming like fire • *a
huge fiery sun.* ② showing great
anger, energy or passion • *a fiery
debate.*

fifteen the number 15. **fifteenth**
ADJECTIVE

fifth, fifths ADJECTIVE ① The fifth item
in a series is the one counted as
number five. ▸ NOUN ② one of five
equal parts.

fifty, fifties the number 50. **fiftieth**
ADJECTIVE

fifty-fifty ADVERB ① divided equally
into two portions. ▸ ADJECTIVE
② just as likely not to happen as to
happen • *You've got a fifty-fifty chance
of being right.*

fig, figs NOUN a soft, sweet fruit full of
tiny seeds. It grows in hot countries
and is often eaten dried.

fight, fights, fighting, fought VERB
① When people fight, they take part
in a battle, a war, a boxing match, or
in some other attempt to hurt or kill
someone. ② To fight for something is
to try in a very determined way to
achieve it • *I must fight for respect.*
▸ NOUN ③ a situation in which

people hit or try to hurt each other. ④ a determined attempt to prevent or achieve something • *the fight for independence.* ⑤ an angry disagreement.

SIMILAR WORDS: ① battle, come to blows, struggle ③ battle, conflict, struggle

fighter, fighters NOUN someone who physically fights another person.

figurative ADJECTIVE ENGLISH If you use a word or expression in a figurative sense, you use it with a more abstract or imaginative meaning than its ordinary one.
figuratively ADVERB

figure, figures, figuring, figured NOUN ① a written number or the amount a number stands for. ② a geometrical shape. ③ a diagram or table in a written text. ④ the shape of a human body, sometimes one that you cannot see properly • *his slim and supple figure* • *A human figure leaped at him.* ⑤ a person • *He was a major figure in the trial.* ▸ VERB ⑥ To figure in something is to appear or be included in it • *the many people who have figured in his life.* ⑦ (*informal*) If you figure that something is the case, you guess or conclude this • *We figure the fire broke out around four in the morning.*

figurehead, figureheads NOUN the leader of a movement or organisation who has no real power.

figure of speech, figures of speech NOUN ENGLISH A figure of speech is an expression such as a simile or idiom in which the words are not used in their literal sense.

filament, filaments NOUN ① SCIENCE A filament is a very fine wire or thread, especially the wire that produces light in a light bulb. ② SCIENCE In a flower, the filament is the stalk of a stamen.

file, files, filing, filed NOUN ① a box or folder in which a group of papers or records is kept; also used of the information kept in the file. ② In computing, a file is a stored set of related data with its own name. ③ a line of people one behind the other. ④ DGT a long steel tool with a rough surface, used for smoothing and shaping hard materials. ▸ VERB ⑤ When someone files a document, they put it in its correct place with similar documents. ⑥ When a group of people file somewhere, they walk one behind the other in a line. ⑦ If you file something, you smooth or shape it with a file.

file extension, file extensions NOUN ICT a group of letters that appears after the dot in the name of a computer file and indicates the application program that created the file.

fill, fills, filling, filled VERB ① If you fill something or if it fills up, it becomes full. ② If something fills a need, it satisfies the need • *Ella had in some small way filled the gap left by Molly's absence.* ③ To fill a job vacancy is to appoint someone to do that job. ▸ NOUN ④ If you have had your fill of something, you do not want any more. **fill in** VERB ① If you fill in a form, you write information in the appropriate spaces. ② If you fill someone in, you give them information to bring them up to date.

fillet, fillets, filleting, filleted NOUN ① a strip of tender, boneless beef, veal or pork. ② a piece of fish with the bones removed. ▸ VERB ③ To fillet meat or fish is to prepare it by cutting out the bones.

filling, fillings NOUN ① the soft food mixture inside a sandwich, cake or pie. ② a small amount of metal or plastic put into a hole in a tooth by a dentist.

filly, **fillies** NOUN a female horse or pony under the age of four.

film, **films**, **filming**, **filmed** NOUN ① a series of moving pictures projected onto a screen and shown at the cinema or on television. ② a thin flexible strip of plastic used in some cameras to record images when exposed to light. ③ a very thin layer of powder or liquid on a surface. ④ Plastic film is a very thin sheet of plastic used for wrapping things. ▶ VERB ⑤ If you film someone, you use a video camera to record their movements.

filter, **filters**, **filtering**, **filtered** NOUN ① a device that allows some things to pass through it, but not others • *a filter against the harmful rays of the sun* • *a filter to block unwanted email.* ▶ VERB ② To filter something is to pass it through a filter. ③ If something filters somewhere, it gets there slowly or faintly • *Traffic filtered into the city.* **filtration** NOUN

filth NOUN ① Filth is disgusting dirt and muck. ② People often use the word filth to refer to very bad language or to things that are thought to be crude and offensive. **filthy** ADJECTIVE **filthiness** NOUN SIMILAR WORDS: ① dirt, muck, squalor

fin, **fins** NOUN a thin, flat structure on the body of a fish, used to help guide it through the water.

final, **finals** ADJECTIVE ① last in a series or happening at the end of something. ② A decision that is final cannot be changed or questioned. ▶ NOUN ③ the last game or contest in a series which decides the overall winner. ④ (*in plural*) Finals are the last and most important examinations of a university or college course.

SIMILAR WORDS: ① concluding, last

SPELLING TIP
Do not confuse the spellings of *final* and *finale*: *Nathan will miss the cup final; All the dancers were on stage for the show's finale.*

finale, **finales** [*Said fin-nah-lee*] NOUN the last section of a piece of music or show.

finalise, **finalises**, **finalising**, **finalised**; also spelt **finalize** VERB If you finalise something, you complete all the arrangements for it.

finalist, **finalists** NOUN a person taking part in the final of a competition.

finally ADVERB ① If something finally happens, it happens after a long delay. ② You use 'finally' to introduce a final point, question or topic that you are talking or writing about. SIMILAR WORDS: ① at last, eventually

finance, **finances**, **financing**, **financed** VERB ① To finance a project or a large purchase is to provide the money for it. ▶ NOUN ② Finance for something is the money or loans used to pay for it. ③ Finance is also the management of money, loans and investments.

financial ADJECTIVE relating to or involving money. **financially** ADVERB

financier, **financiers** NOUN a person who deals with the finance for large businesses.

finch, **finches** NOUN a small bird with a short, strong beak.

find, **finds**, **finding**, **found** VERB ① If you find someone or something, you discover them, either as a result of searching or by coming across them unexpectedly. ② If you find that something is the case, you become aware of it or realise it • *I found my fists* *were clenched.* ③ Something that is found in a particular place typically lives or exists there. ④ When a court or jury finds a person guilty or not guilty, they decide that the person is guilty or innocent • *He was found guilty and sentenced to life imprisonment.* ▶ NOUN ⑤ If you describe something or someone as a find, you mean that you have recently discovered them and they are valuable or useful. **finder** NOUN

find out VERB ① If you find out something, you learn or discover something that you did not know. ② If you find someone out, you discover that they have been doing something they should not have been doing.

SIMILAR WORDS: ① come across, discover

findings PLURAL NOUN Someone's findings are the conclusions they reach as a result of investigation.

fine, finer, finest; fines, fining, fined ADJECTIVE ① very good or very beautiful • *a fine school* • *fine clothes.* ② satisfactory or suitable • *If you're on a diet, pasta dishes are fine if not served with a rich sauce.* ③ very narrow or thin. ④ A fine detail, adjustment or distinction is very delicate, exact or subtle. ⑤ When the weather is fine, it is not raining and is bright or sunny. ▶ NOUN ⑥ a sum of money paid as a punishment. ▶ VERB ⑦ Someone who is fined has to pay a sum of money as a punishment.

finery NOUN Finery is very beautiful clothing and jewellery.

finesse [*Said* fin-**ness**] NOUN If you do something with finesse, you do it with skill and subtlety.

finger, fingers, fingering, fingered NOUN ① Your fingers are the four long jointed parts of your hands, sometimes including the thumbs.

▶ VERB ② If you finger something, you feel it with your fingers.

fingernail, fingernails NOUN Your fingernails are the hard coverings at the ends of your fingers.

fingerprint, fingerprints NOUN a mark made showing the pattern on the skin at the tip of a person's finger.

finish, finishes, finishing, finished VERB ① When you finish something, you reach the end of it and complete it. ② When something finishes, it ends or stops. ▶ NOUN ③ The finish of something is the end or last part of it. ④ DGT The finish that something has is the texture or appearance of its surface • *a healthy, glossy finish.*
SIMILAR WORDS: ① complete, conclude, end ③ close, conclusion, end

finite [*Said* fie-**nite**] ADJECTIVE having a particular size or limit which cannot be increased • *There's only finite money to spend.*

Finn, Finns NOUN someone who comes from Finland.

Finnish ADJECTIVE ① belonging or relating to Finland. ▶ NOUN ② Finnish is the main language spoken in Finland.

fir, firs NOUN a tall, pointed evergreen tree that has thin, needle-like leaves and produces cones.

fire, fires, firing, fired NOUN ① Fire is the flames produced when something burns. ② a pile or mass of burning material. ③ a piece of equipment that is used as a heater • *a gas fire.* ▶ VERB ④ If you fire a weapon or fire a bullet, you operate the weapon so that the bullet or missile is released. ⑤ If you fire questions at someone, you ask them a lot of questions very quickly. ⑥ (*informal*) If an employer fires someone, he or she dismisses that person from their job.

▶ PHRASE ⑦ If someone **opens fire**, they start shooting.

firearm, firearms NOUN a gun.

fire brigade, fire brigades NOUN the organisation which has the job of putting out fires.

fire engine, fire engines NOUN a large vehicle that carries equipment for putting out fires.

fire escape, fire escapes NOUN an emergency exit or staircase for use if there is a fire.

fire extinguisher, fire extinguishers NOUN a metal cylinder containing water or foam for spraying onto a fire.

firefighter, firefighters NOUN a person whose job is to put out fires and rescue trapped people.

firefly, fireflies NOUN an insect that glows in the dark.

fireplace, fireplaces NOUN the opening beneath a chimney where a fire can be lit.

fireproof ADJECTIVE resistant to fire.

fire station, fire stations NOUN a building where fire engines are kept and where firefighters wait to be called out.

firewall, firewalls NOUN a computer system or program that automatically prevents an unauthorised person from gaining access to a computer when it is connected to the internet.

firework, fireworks NOUN a small container of gunpowder and other chemicals which explodes and produces coloured sparks or smoke when lit.

firing squad, firing squads NOUN a group of soldiers ordered to shoot a person condemned to death.

firm, firmer, firmest; firms ADJECTIVE ① Something that is firm does not move easily when pressed or pushed, or when weight is put on it. ② A firm grasp or push is one with controlled force or pressure. ③ A firm decision is definite. ④ Someone who is firm behaves with authority that shows they will not change their mind. ▶ NOUN ⑤ a business selling or producing something. **firmly** ADVERB **firmness** NOUN

first ADJECTIVE ① done or in existence before anything else. ② more important than anything else • *Her story won first prize.* ▶ ADVERB ③ done or occurring before anything else. ▶ NOUN ④ something that has never happened or been done before. **firstly** ADVERB

SIMILAR WORDS: ② chief, foremost, principal

first aid NOUN First aid is medical treatment given to an injured person.

first-class ADJECTIVE ① Something that is first-class is of the highest quality or standard • *This machine produces first-class results.* ② First-class services are more expensive and therefore faster or more comfortable than second-class ones.

first-hand ADJECTIVE First-hand knowledge or experience is gained directly rather than from books or other people.

First Lady, First Ladies NOUN The First Lady of a country is the wife of its president.

first-past-the-post ADJECTIVE In politics, a first-past-the-post system is a voting system in which the candidate with the most votes wins outright.

first person NOUN ENGLISH MFL In grammar, the first person is the person who is speaking (*I* or *we*).

first-person narrator NOUN ENGLISH A first-person narrator is the principal character in a story and uses the pronoun 'I'.

first-rate ADJECTIVE excellent.

fiscal ADJECTIVE involving government or public money, especially taxes.

WORD HISTORY: from Latin *fiscus* meaning 'money-bag' or 'treasury'

fish, fish or fishes, fishing, fished NOUN ① a cold-blooded creature living in water that has a spine, gills, fins and a scaly skin. ② Fish is the flesh of fish eaten as food. ▶ VERB ③ To fish is to try to catch fish for food or sport. ④ If you fish for information, you try to get it in an indirect way. **fishing** NOUN **fisherman** NOUN

GRAMMAR TIP

The plural of the noun *fish* can be either *fish* or *fishes*, but *fish* is more common.

---

fisherman, fishermen NOUN a person who catches fish as a job or for sport.

fishery, fisheries NOUN an area of the sea where fish are caught commercially.

fishmonger, fishmongers NOUN a shopkeeper who sells fish; also the shop itself.

fishy, fishier, fishiest ADJECTIVE ① smelling of fish. ② (*informal*) suspicious or doubtful • *He spotted something fishy going on*.

fissure, fissures NOUN a deep crack in rock.

fist, fists NOUN a hand with the fingers curled tightly towards the palm.

fit, fits, fitting, fitted; fitter, fittest VERB ① Something that fits is the right shape or size for a particular person or position. ② If you fit something somewhere, you put it there carefully or securely • *Very carefully he fitted the files inside the compartment*. ③ If something fits a particular situation, person or thing, it is suitable or appropriate • *a sentence that fitted the crime*. ▶ NOUN ④ The fit of something is how it fits • *This bolt must be a good fit*. ⑤ If someone has a fit, their muscles suddenly start contracting violently and they may lose consciousness. ⑥ A fit of laughter, coughing, anger or panic is a sudden uncontrolled outburst. ▶ ADJECTIVE ⑦ good enough or suitable • *Housing fit for young families*. ⑧ Someone who is fit is healthy and has strong muscles as a result of regular exercise. **fitness** NOUN **fit out** VERB To fit someone or something out means to provide them with the necessary equipment. SIMILAR WORDS: ③ match, suit ⑤ convulsion, seizure, spasm

fitful ADJECTIVE happening at irregular intervals and not continuous • *a fitful breeze*. **fitfully** ADVERB

fitter, fitters NOUN a person who assembles or installs machinery.

fitting, fittings ADJECTIVE ① right or suitable • *a fitting reward for his efforts*. ▶ NOUN ② a small part that is fixed to a piece of equipment or furniture. ③ If you have a fitting, you try on a garment that is being made to see if it fits properly.

five, fives ① the number 5. ▶ NOUN ② Fives is a ball game similar to squash, in which you hit the ball with your hand.

fix, fixes, fixing, fixed VERB ① If you fix something somewhere, you attach it or put it there securely. ② If you fix something broken, you mend it. ③ If you fix your attention on something, you concentrate on it. ④ If you fix something, you make

a b c d e f g h i j k l m n o p q r s t u v w x y z

arrangements for it • *The opening party is fixed for the 24th September.* ⑤ (*informal*) To fix something is to arrange the outcome unfairly or dishonestly. ▶ **NOUN** ⑥ (*informal*) something that has been unfairly or dishonestly arranged. ⑦ (*informal*) If you are in a fix, you are in a difficult situation. **fixed** ADJECTIVE **fixedly** ADVERB

SIMILAR WORDS: ② mend, repair

fixation, fixations NOUN an extreme and obsessive interest in something.

fixture, fixtures NOUN ① a piece of furniture or equipment that is fixed into position in a house. ② a sports event due to take place on a particular date • *a series of difficult away fixtures*.

fizz, fizzes, fizzing, fizzed VERB Something that fizzes makes a hissing sound.

fizzle, fizzles, fizzling, fizzled VERB Something that fizzles makes a weak hissing or spitting sound.

fizzy, fizzier, fizziest ADJECTIVE Fizzy drinks have carbon dioxide in them to make them bubbly.

fjord, fjords [*Said fee-ord*]; also spelt **fiord** NOUN a long, narrow inlet of the sea between very high cliffs, especially in Norway.
WORD HISTORY: a Norwegian word

flab NOUN Flab is large amounts of surplus fat on someone's body.

flabbergasted ADJECTIVE extremely surprised.

flabby, flabbier, flabbiest ADJECTIVE Someone who is flabby is rather fat and unfit, with loose flesh on their body.

flag, flags, flagging, flagged NOUN ① a rectangular or square cloth which has a particular colour and design, and is used as the symbol of a nation or as a signal. ▶ **VERB** ② If you or your spirits flag, you start to lose energy or enthusiasm. **flag down** VERB If you flag down a vehicle, you signal to the driver to stop.

flagrant [*Said flay-grant*] ADJECTIVE very shocking and bad in an obvious way • *a flagrant defiance of the rules.* **flagrantly** ADVERB

SPELLING TIP
Do not confuse the spellings of *flagrant* and *fragrant*: *a flagrant attack on democracy; a bunch of fragrant flowers.*

flagship, flagships NOUN ① a ship carrying the commander of the fleet. ② the most modern or impressive product or asset of an organisation.

flail, flails, flailing, flailed VERB If someone's arms or legs flail about, they move in a wild, uncontrolled way.

flair NOUN Flair is a natural ability to do something well or stylishly.

SPELLING TIP
Do not confuse the spellings of *flair* and *flare*: *I think she has a flair for mathematics; The sailor used a flare to attract attention.*

flak NOUN ① Flak is anti-aircraft fire. ② If you get flak for doing something, you get a lot of severe criticism.
WORD HISTORY: from the first letters of the parts of German *Fliegerabwehrkanone* meaning 'anti-aircraft gun'

flake, flakes, flaking, flaked NOUN ① a small, thin piece of something. ▶ **VERB** ② When something such as paint flakes, small thin pieces of it come off. **flaky** ADJECTIVE **flaked** ADJECTIVE **flake out** VERB (*informal*) If you flake out, you collapse, go to sleep, or lose consciousness.

flamboyant ADJECTIVE behaving in a very showy and confident way.
flamboyance NOUN

flame, **flames** NOUN ① a hot bright stream of burning gas. ② A flame of passion, desire or anger is a sudden strong feeling.

flamenco NOUN Flamenco is a type of very lively, fast Spanish dancing, accompanied by guitar music.

flamingo, **flamingos** or **flamingoes** NOUN a long-legged wading bird with pink feathers and a long neck.

flammable ADJECTIVE likely to catch fire and burn easily.

USAGE NOTE
Although *flammable* and *inflammable* both mean 'likely to catch fire', *flammable* is used more often as people sometimes think that *inflammable* means 'not likely to catch fire'.

flan, **flans** NOUN an open sweet or savoury tart with a pastry or cake base.

flank, **flanks**, **flanking**, **flanked** NOUN ① the side of an animal between the ribs and the hip. ▶ VERB ② Someone or something that is flanked by a particular thing or person has them at their side • *He was flanked by four bodyguards.*

flannel, **flannels** NOUN ① Flannel is a lightweight woollen fabric. ② a small square of towelling, used for washing yourself. In Australian English it is called a **washer**.

flap, **flaps**, **flapping**, **flapped** VERB ① Something that flaps moves up and down or from side to side with a snapping sound. ▶ NOUN ② a loose piece of something such as paper or skin that is attached at one edge.

flare, **flares**, **flaring**, **flared** NOUN ① a device that produces a brightly coloured flame, used especially as an emergency signal. ▶ VERB ② If a fire flares, it suddenly burns much more vigorously. ③ If violence or a conflict flares or flares up, it suddenly starts or becomes more serious.

SPELLING TIP
Do not confuse the spellings of *flare* and *flair*: *The sailor used a flare to attract attention; I think she has a flair for mathematics.*

flash, **flashes**, **flashing**, **flashed** NOUN ① a sudden, short burst of light. ▶ VERB ② If a light flashes, it shines for a very short period, often repeatedly. ③ Something that flashes past moves or happens so fast that you almost miss it. ④ If you flash something, you show it briefly • *Rihanna flashed her face at the crowd.* ▶ PHRASE ⑤ Something that happens **in a flash** happens suddenly and lasts a very short time.

flashback, **flashbacks** NOUN a scene in a film, play or book that returns to events in the past.

flash drive, **flash drives** NOUN ICT a small, portable device that can be used to transfer data between computers and other electronic devices.

flashlight, **flashlights** NOUN a large, powerful torch.

flashy, **flashier**, **flashiest** ADJECTIVE expensive and fashionable in appearance, in a vulgar way • *flashy clothes.*

flask, **flasks** NOUN a bottle used for carrying alcoholic or hot drinks around with you.

flat, **flats**, **flatting**, **flatted**; **flatter**, **flattest** NOUN ① a self-contained set of rooms, usually on one level, for living in. ② In music, a flat is a note or key a semitone lower than that

described by the same letter. It is represented by the symbol (♭). ▶ **VERB** ③ In Australian and New Zealand English, to flat is to live in a flat • *flatting in London.* ▶ **ADJECTIVE** ④ Something that is flat is level and smooth. ⑤ A flat object is not very tall or deep • *a low, flat building.* ⑥ A flat tyre or ball has not got enough air in it. ⑦ A flat battery has lost its electrical charge. ⑧ A flat refusal or denial is complete and firm. ⑨ Something that is flat is without emotion or interest. ⑩ A flat rate or price is fixed and the same for everyone • *The company charges a flat fee for its advice.* ⑪ A musical instrument or note that is flat is slightly too low in pitch. ▶ **ADVERB** ⑫ Something that is done in a particular time flat, takes exactly that time • *They would find them in two minutes flat.* **flatly ADVERB flatness NOUN**
SIMILAR WORDS: ④ even, level

flat character NOUN ENGLISH A flat character is a character in a story who plays a minor role, does not seem complicated or realistic, and does not undergo any kind of change during the story.

flatfish NOUN a sea fish with a wide flat body, such as a plaice or sole.

flathead, flatheads NOUN a common Australian edible fish.

flatten, flattens, flattening, flattened VERB If you flatten something or if it flattens, it becomes flat or flatter.

flatter, flatters, flattering, flattered VERB ① If you flatter someone, you praise them in an exaggerated way, either to please them or to persuade them to do something. ② If you are flattered by something, it makes you feel pleased and important • *He was very flattered because she liked him.* ③ If

you flatter yourself that something is the case, you believe, perhaps mistakenly, something good about yourself or your abilities. ④ Something that flatters you makes you appear more attractive. **flattering ADJECTIVE**
SIMILAR WORDS: ① butter up, praise

flattery NOUN Flattery is flattering words or behaviour.

flatting PHRASE In New Zealand English, to **go flatting** is to leave home and live with others in a shared house or flat.

flatulence NOUN Flatulence is the uncomfortable state of having too much gas in your stomach or intestine.

flaunt, flaunts, flaunting, flaunted VERB If you flaunt your possessions or talents, you display them too obviously or proudly.

SPELLING TIP
Be careful not to confuse *flaunt* with *flout*, which means 'disobey'.

---

flautist, flautists NOUN someone who plays the flute.

flavour, flavours, flavouring, flavoured NOUN ① DGT The flavour of food is its taste. ② The flavour of something is its distinctive characteristic or quality. ▶ **VERB** ③ DGT If you flavour food with a spice or herb, you add it to the food to give it a particular taste. **flavouring NOUN**

flaw, flaws NOUN ① a fault or mark in a piece of fabric or glass, or in a decorative pattern. ② a weak point or undesirable quality in a theory, plan or person's character. **flawed ADJECTIVE flawless ADJECTIVE**
SIMILAR WORDS: ① blemish, spot ② fault, weakness

flax NOUN Flax is a plant used for making rope and cloth.

flay, flays, flaying, flayed VERB ①To flay a dead animal is to cut off its skin. ②To flay someone is to criticise them severely.

flea, fleas NOUN a small wingless jumping insect which feeds on blood.

fleck, flecks NOUN a small coloured mark or particle. **flecked** ADJECTIVE

fled the past tense and past participle of **flee**.

fledgling, fledglings NOUN ①a young bird that is learning to fly. ▶ADJECTIVE ② Fledgling means new, or young and inexperienced • *the fledgling American President*.

flee, flees, fleeing, fled VERB To flee from someone or something is to run away from them.

fleece, fleeces, fleecing, fleeced NOUN ①A sheep's fleece is its coat of wool. ▶VERB ② (*informal*) To fleece someone is to swindle them or charge them too much money.

fleet, fleets NOUN a group of ships or vehicles owned by the same organisation or travelling together.

fleeting ADJECTIVE lasting for a very short time.

Flemish NOUN Flemish is a language spoken in many parts of Belgium.

flesh NOUN ① Flesh is the soft part of the body. ②The flesh of a fruit or vegetable is the soft inner part that you eat. **fleshy** ADJECTIVE

flew the past tense of **fly**.

SPELLING TIP

Do not confuse the spellings of *flew* and *flue*: *I flew home last week; The flue needs to be cleaned.*

---

flex, flexes, flexing, flexed NOUN ①a length of wire covered in plastic, which carries electricity to an appliance. ▶VERB ②If you flex your muscles, you bend and stretch them.

flexible ADJECTIVE ① able to be bent easily without breaking. ② able to adapt to changing circumstances. **flexibility** NOUN

flick, flicks, flicking, flicked VERB ① If you flick something, you move it sharply with your finger. ② If something flicks somewhere, it moves with a short sudden movement • *His foot flicked forward.* ▶ NOUN ③ a short sudden movement or sharp touch with the finger • *a sideways flick of the head.*

flicker, flickers, flickering, flickered VERB ①If a light or a flame flickers, it shines and moves unsteadily. ▶ NOUN ②a short unsteady light or movement of light • *the flicker of candlelight.* ③A flicker of a feeling is a very brief experience of it • *a flicker of interest.*

flight, flights NOUN ①a journey made by aeroplane. ②Flight is the action of flying or the ability to fly. ③Flight is also the act of running away. ④A flight of stairs or steps is a set running in a single direction.

flight attendant, flight attendants NOUN a person who looks after passengers on an aircraft.

flightless ADJECTIVE Flightless birds, such as penguins and ostriches, are birds that cannot fly.

flimsy, flimsier, flimsiest ADJECTIVE ①made of something very thin or weak and not providing much protection. ②not very convincing • *flimsy evidence.*

flinch, flinches, flinching, flinched VERB If you flinch, you make a sudden small movement in fear or pain. SIMILAR WORDS: cringe, recoil, wince

fling, flings, flinging, flung VERB ①If you fling something, you throw it with a lot of force. ▶ NOUN ②a short period devoted to pleasure and free from any restrictions or rules.

a b c d e f g h i j k l m n o p q r s t u v w x y z

flint, flints NOUN Flint is a hard greyish-black form of quartz. It produces a spark when struck with steel.

flip, flips, flipping, flipped VERB If you flip something, you turn or move it quickly and sharply • *He flipped over the first page.*

flippant ADJECTIVE showing an inappropriate lack of seriousness • *a flippant attitude to money.* **flippantly** ADVERB **flippancy** NOUN

flipper, flippers NOUN ① one of the broad, flat limbs of sea animals, for example seals or penguins, used for swimming. ② Flippers are broad, flat pieces of rubber that you can attach to your feet to help you swim.

flirt, flirts, flirting, flirted VERB ① If you flirt with someone, you behave as if you are attracted to them but without serious intentions. ② If you flirt with an idea, you consider it without seriously intending to do anything about it. ▶ NOUN ③ someone who often flirts with people. **flirtation** NOUN **flirtatious** ADJECTIVE

flit, flits, flitting, flitted VERB To flit somewhere is to fly or move there with quick, light movements.

float, floats, floating, floated VERB ① Something that floats is supported by water. ② Something that floats through the air moves along gently, supported by the air. ③ If a company is floated, shares are sold to the public for the first time and the company gains a listing on the stock exchange. ▶ NOUN ④ a light object that floats and either supports something or someone or regulates the level of liquid in a tank or cistern. ⑤ In Australian English, a float is also a vehicle for transporting horses.

flock, flocks, flocking, flocked NOUN ① a group of birds, sheep or goats.
▶ VERB ② If people flock somewhere, they go there in large numbers.

flog, flogs, flogging, flogged VERB ① (*informal*) If you flog something, you sell it. ② To flog someone is to beat them with a whip or stick. **flogging** NOUN

flood, floods, flooding, flooded NOUN ① a large amount of water covering an area that is usually dry. ② A flood of something is a large amount of it suddenly occurring • *a flood of angry language.* ▶ VERB ③ If liquid floods an area, or if a river floods, the water or liquid overflows, covering the surrounding area. ④ If people or things flood into a place, they come there in large numbers • *Tourists have flooded into the city in recent years.*
SIMILAR WORDS: ① deluge, spate, torrent ② stream, torrent

floodgates PHRASE To **open the floodgates** is suddenly to give a lot of people the opportunity to do something they could not do before.

floodlight, floodlights NOUN a very powerful outdoor lamp used to light up public buildings and sports grounds. **floodlit** ADJECTIVE

floor, floors, flooring, floored NOUN ① the part of a room you walk on. ② one of the levels in a building • *the top floor of a factory.* ③ the ground at the bottom of a valley, forest or the sea. ▶ VERB ④ If a remark or question floors you, you are completely unable to deal with it or answer it.

floorboard, floorboards NOUN one of the long planks of wood from which a floor is made.

flop, flops, flopping, flopped VERB ① If someone or something flops, they fall loosely and rather heavily. ② (*informal*) Something that flops fails. ▶ NOUN ③ (*informal*) something that is completely unsuccessful.

floppy, floppier, floppiest ADJECTIVE tending to hang downwards in a rather loose way • *a floppy, outsize jacket*.

SIMILAR WORDS: droopy, limp

floral ADJECTIVE patterned with flowers or made from flowers • *floral cotton dresses*.

florid [*Rhymes with* **horrid**] ADJECTIVE ① highly elaborate and extravagant • *florid language*. ② having a red face.

florist, florists NOUN a person or shop selling flowers.

floss NOUN Dental floss is soft silky threads or fibre which you use to clean between your teeth.

flotation, flotations NOUN ① The flotation of a business is the issuing of shares in order to launch it or to raise money. ② Flotation is the act of floating.

flotilla, flotillas [*Said* flot-**til**-la] NOUN a small fleet or group of small ships. WORD HISTORY: from Spanish *flotilla* meaning 'little fleet'

flotsam NOUN Flotsam is rubbish or wreckage floating at sea or washed up on the shore.

flounce, flounces, flouncing, flounced VERB ① If you flounce somewhere, you walk there with exaggerated movements suggesting that you are feeling angry or impatient about something • *She flounced out of the office*. ▶ NOUN ② a big frill around the bottom of a dress or skirt.

flounder, flounders, floundering, floundered VERB ① To flounder is to struggle to move or stay upright, for example in water or mud. ② If you flounder in a conversation or situation, you find it difficult to decide what to say or do. ▶ NOUN ③ a type of edible flatfish.

flour NOUN DGT Flour is a powder made from finely ground grain, usually wheat, and used for baking and cooking. **floured** ADJECTIVE **floury** ADJECTIVE

SPELLING TIP
Do not confuse the spellings of *flour* and *flower*: *I need to buy flour for the birthday cake; Fiona is picking flowers in the garden.*

flourish, flourishes, flourishing, flourished VERB ① Something that flourishes develops or functions successfully or healthily. ② If you flourish something, you wave or display it so that people notice it. ▶ NOUN ③ a bold sweeping or waving movement.

flout, flouts, flouting, flouted VERB If you flout a convention or law, you deliberately disobey it.

SPELLING TIP
Be careful not to confuse *flout* with *flaunt*, which means 'display obviously'.

flow, flows, flowing, flowed VERB ① If something flows, it moves or happens in a steady continuous stream. ▶ NOUN ② A flow of something is a steady continuous movement of it; also the rate at which it flows • *a steady flow of complaints*.

flow chart, flow charts NOUN DGT a diagram showing the sequence of steps that lead to various results.

flower, flowers, flowering, flowered NOUN ① SCIENCE the part of a plant containing the reproductive organs from which the fruit or seeds develop. A **complete flower** is a flower that has all the flower parts, particularly the stamens and pistils; an **incomplete flower** is a flower without one or more of the main flower parts; a **perfect flower** is a flower that has both stamens and pistils. ▶ **VERB** ② When a plant flowers, it produces flowers.

SPELLING TIP
Do not confuse the spellings of *flower* and *flour*: *Fiona is picking flowers in the garden; I need to buy flour for the birthday cake.*

flowery ADJECTIVE Flowery language is full of elaborate expressions.

flown the past participle of **fly**.

flu NOUN Flu is an illness similar to a very bad cold, which causes headaches, sore throat, weakness and aching muscles. Flu is short for 'influenza'.

fluctuate, fluctuates, fluctuating, fluctuated VERB Something that fluctuates is irregular and changeable • *fluctuating between feeling well and not so well.* **fluctuation** NOUN

flue, flues NOUN a pipe which takes fumes and smoke away from a stove or boiler.

SPELLING TIP
Do not confuse the spellings of *flue* and *flew*, the past tense of fly: *The flue needs to be cleaned; I flew home last week.*

fluent ADJECTIVE ① able to speak a foreign language correctly and without hesitation. ② able to express yourself clearly and without hesitation. **fluently** ADVERB

fluff, fluffs, fluffing, fluffed NOUN ① Fluff is soft, light, woolly threads or fibres bunched together. ▶ **VERB** ② If you fluff something up or out, you brush or shake it to make it seem larger and lighter • *Fluff the rice up with a fork before serving.* **fluffy** ADJECTIVE

fluid, fluids NOUN ① a liquid. ▶ **ADJECTIVE** ② Fluid movement is smooth and flowing. ③ A fluid arrangement or plan is flexible and without a fixed structure. **fluidity** NOUN

fluke, flukes NOUN an accidental success or piece of good luck.

flung the past tense and past participle of **fling**.

fluorescent [Said floo-er-ess-nt] ADJECTIVE ① having a very bright appearance when light is shone on it, as if it is shining itself • *fluorescent yellow dye.* ② A fluorescent light is in the form of a tube and shines with a hard bright light.

fluoride NOUN Fluoride is a mixture of chemicals that is meant to prevent tooth decay.

fluorine NOUN SCIENCE Fluorine is a chemical element which is a toxic, pungent, pale yellow gas. Its atomic number is 9 and its symbol is F.

flurry, flurries NOUN a short rush of activity or movement.

flush, flushes, flushing, flushed; flusher, flushest NOUN ① A flush is a rosy red colour • *The flowers are cream with a pink flush.* ② In cards, a flush is a hand all of one suit. ▶ **VERB** ③ If you flush, your face goes red. ④ If you flush a toilet or something such as a pipe, you force water through it to clean it. ▶ **ADJECTIVE** ⑤ (*informal*) Someone who is flush has plenty of money. ⑥ Something that is flush with a surface is level with it or flat against it.

flustered ADJECTIVE If you are flustered, you feel confused, nervous and rushed.

flute, flutes NOUN a musical wind instrument consisting of a long metal tube with holes and keys. It is held sideways to the mouth and played by blowing across a hole in its side.

fluted ADJECTIVE decorated with long grooves.

flutter, flutters, fluttering, fluttered VERB ① If something flutters, it flaps or waves with small, quick movements. ▶ NOUN ② If you are in a flutter, you are excited and nervous. ③ (informal) If you have a flutter, you have a small bet.

flux NOUN Flux is a state of constant change • *stability in a world of flux*.

fly, flies, flying, flew, flown NOUN ① an insect with two pairs of wings. ② The front opening on a pair of trousers is the fly or the flies. ③ The fly or fly sheet of a tent is either a flap at the entrance or an outer layer providing protection from rain. ▶ VERB ④ When a bird, insect or aircraft flies, it moves through the air. ⑤ If someone or something flies, they move or go very quickly. ⑥ If you fly at someone or let fly at them, you attack or criticise them suddenly and aggressively. **flying** ADJECTIVE or NOUN **flyer** NOUN

fly-fishing NOUN Fly-fishing is a method of fishing using imitation flies as bait.

flying fox, flying foxes NOUN ① a large bat that eats fruit, found in Australia and Africa. ② In Australia and New Zealand, a flying fox is a cable car used to carry people over rivers and gorges.

flying saucer, flying saucers NOUN a large disc-shaped spacecraft, which some people claim to have seen.

flyover, flyovers NOUN a structure carrying one road over another at a junction or intersection.

foal, foals, foaling, foaled NOUN ① a young horse. ▶ VERB ② When a female horse foals, she gives birth.

foam, foams, foaming, foamed NOUN ① Foam is a mass of tiny bubbles. ② DGT Foam is light spongy material used, for example, in furniture or packaging. ▶ VERB ③ When something foams, it forms a mass of small bubbles.
SIMILAR WORDS: ① bubbles, froth

fob off, fobs off, fobbing off, fobbed off VERB (informal) If you fob someone off, you provide them with something that is not very good or not adequate.

focus, focuses or focusses, focusing or focussing, focused or focussed; focuses or foci VERB ① If you focus your eyes or an instrument on an object, you adjust them so that the image is clear. ▶ NOUN ② The focus of something is its centre of attention • *The focus of the conversation had moved around during the meal*. **focal** ADJECTIVE

SPELLING TIP
When you add the verb endings to *focus*, you can either add them straight to *focus* (*focuses, focusing, focused*), or you can put another s at the end of *focus* before adding the endings (*focusses, focussing, focussed*). Either way is correct, but the first way is much more common. The plural of the noun is either *focuses* or *foci*, but *focuses* is the commoner.

fodder NOUN Fodder is food for farm animals or horses.

foe, foes NOUN an enemy.

foetus, foetuses [Said *fee-tus*]; also spelt **fetus** NOUN SCIENCE an unborn child or animal in the womb. **foetal** ADJECTIVE

fog, fogs, fogging, fogged NOUN ① Fog is a thick mist of water droplets suspended in the air. ▶ VERB ② If glass fogs up, it becomes clouded

a
b
c
d
e
f
g
h
i
j
k
l
m
n
o
p
q
r
s
t
u
v
w
x
y
z

with steam or condensation.
foggy ADJECTIVE

foil, foils, foiling, foiled VERB ① If you foil someone's attempt at something, you prevent them from succeeding. ▶ NOUN ② Foil is thin, paper-like sheets of metal used to wrap food. ③ Something that is a good foil for something else contrasts with it and makes its good qualities more noticeable. ④ a thin, light sword with a button on the tip, used in fencing.

foist, foists, foisting, foisted VERB If you foist something on someone, you force or impose it on them.

fold, folds, folding, folded VERB ① If you fold something, you bend it so that one part lies over another. ② (informal) If a business folds, it fails and closes down. ③ In cooking, if you fold one ingredient into another, you mix it in gently. ▶ NOUN ④ a crease or bend in paper or cloth. ⑤ a small enclosed area for sheep.
SIMILAR WORDS: ① bend, crease, double over

-fold SUFFIX '-fold' is used with a number to indicate that something has a certain number of parts or is multiplied by that number • *The problems were two-fold*.

folder, folders NOUN ① a thin piece of folded cardboard for keeping loose papers together. ② In computing, a folder is a named area of a computer disk where you can group together files and subdirectories.

foliage NOUN Foliage is leaves and plants.

folk, folks PLURAL NOUN ① Folk or folks are people. ▶ ADJECTIVE ② Folk music, dance or art is traditional or representative of the ordinary people of an area.

folklore NOUN Folklore is the traditional stories and beliefs of a community.

folk tale, folk tales NOUN A folk tale is a traditional story in a community.

follicle, follicles NOUN a small sac or cavity in the body • *hair follicles*.

follow, follows, following, followed VERB ① If you follow someone, you move along behind them. If you follow a path or a sign, you move along in that direction. ② Something that follows a particular thing happens after it. ③ Something that follows is true or logical as a result of something else being the case • *Just because she is pretty, it doesn't follow that she can sing*. ④ If you follow instructions or advice, you do what you are told. ⑤ If you follow an explanation or the plot of a story, you understand each stage of it. ⑥ If you follow a person on a social networking site, you regularly read the messages he or she writes.
follow up VERB If you follow up a suggestion or discovery, you find out more about it or act upon it.

follower, followers NOUN ① The followers of a person or belief are the people who support them. ② On a social networking site, the followers of a person are the people who regularly read their messages.
SIMILAR WORDS: ① adherent, supporter

folly, follies NOUN Folly is a foolish act or foolish behaviour.
SIMILAR WORDS: foolishness, stupidity

fond, fonder, fondest ADJECTIVE ① If you are fond of someone or something, you like them. ② A fond hope or belief is thought of with happiness but is unlikely to happen.
fondly ADVERB **fondness** NOUN
SIMILAR WORDS: ① affectionate, loving

fondle, fondles, fondling, fondled **VERB** To fondle something is to stroke it affectionately.

font, fonts **NOUN** ① In printing, a font is a set of characters of the same style and size. ② a large stone bowl in a church that holds the water for baptisms.

food, foods **NOUN** Food is any substance consumed by an animal or plant to provide energy.
SIMILAR WORDS: fare, nourishment

food chain, food chains **NOUN** SCIENCE a series of living things which are linked because each one feeds on the next one in the series. For example, a plant may be eaten by a rabbit which may be eaten by a fox.

foodstuff, foodstuffs **NOUN** anything used for food.

food technology **NOUN** Food technology is the study of foods and what they consist of, and their effect on the body.

fool, fools, fooling, fooled **NOUN** ① someone who behaves in a silly or stupid way. ② a dessert made from fruit, cream and sugar whipped together. ▶ **VERB** ③ If you fool someone, you deceive or trick them.

foolhardy **ADJECTIVE** foolish and involving too great a risk.

foolish **ADJECTIVE** very silly or unwise. **foolishly** **ADVERB** **foolishness** **NOUN**

foolproof **ADJECTIVE** Something that is foolproof is so well designed or simple to use that it cannot fail.

foot, feet **NOUN** ① the part of your body at the end of your leg. ② the bottom, base or lower end of something • *the foot of the mountain*. ③ a unit of length equal to 12 inches or about 30.5 centimetres. ④ ENGLISH In poetry, a foot is the basic unit of rhythm containing two or three syllables. ▶ **ADJECTIVE** ⑤ A

foot brake, pedal or pump is operated by your foot.

footage **NOUN** Footage is a length of film • *exclusive footage of the summer festivals*.

foot-and-mouth disease **NOUN** Foot-and-mouth disease is a serious infectious disease affecting cattle, sheep, pigs and goats which causes swellings around the animal's hooves and mouth.

football, footballs **NOUN** ① Football is any game in which the ball can be kicked, such as soccer, Australian Rules, rugby union and American football. ② a ball used in any of these games. **footballer** **NOUN**

foothills **PLURAL NOUN** GEOGRAPHY Foothills are hills at the base of mountains.

foothold, footholds **NOUN** ① a place where you can put your foot when climbing. ② a position from which further progress can be made.

footing **NOUN** ① Footing is a secure grip by or for your feet • *He missed his footing and fell flat*. ② a footing is the basis or nature of a relationship or situation • *Steps to put the nation on a war footing*.

footman, footmen **NOUN** a male servant in a large house who wears uniform.

footnote, footnotes **NOUN** a note at the bottom of a page or an additional comment giving extra information.

footpath, footpaths **NOUN** a path for people to walk on.

footprint, footprints **NOUN** ① a mark left by a foot or shoe. ② The footprint of something is the permanent effect that it leaves behind • *a scheme to reduce our environmental footprint*.

footstep, footsteps **NOUN** the sound or mark made by someone walking.

a
b
c
d
e
f
g
h
i
j
k
l
m
n
o
p
q
r
s
t
u
v
w
x
y
z

for PREPOSITION ① meant to be given to or used by a particular person, or done in order to help or benefit them • *private beaches for their exclusive use.* ② 'For' is used when explaining the reason, cause or purpose of something • *This is my excuse for going to Italy.* ③ You use 'for' to express a quantity, time or distance • *I'll play for ages* • *the only house for miles around.* ④ If you are for something, you support it or approve of it • *votes for or against independence.*

forage, forages, foraging, foraged VERB When a person or animal forages, they search for food.

foray, forays NOUN ① a brief attempt to do or get something • *her first foray into acting.* ② an attack or raid by soldiers.

forbid, forbids, forbidding, forbade, forbidden VERB If you forbid someone to do something, you order them not to do it. **forbidden** ADJECTIVE

force, forces, forcing, forced VERB ① To force someone to do something is to make them do it. ② To force something is to use violence or great strength to move or open it. ▶ NOUN ③ a pressure to do something, sometimes with the use of violence or great strength. ④ The force of something is its strength or power • *The force of the explosion shook buildings.* ⑤ a person or thing that has a lot of influence or effect • *She became the dominant force in tennis.* ⑥ an organised group of soldiers or police. ⑦ SCIENCE In physics, force is a pushing or pulling influence that changes a body from a state of rest to one of motion, or changes its rate of motion. ▶ PHRASE ⑧ A law or rule that is **in force** is currently valid and must be obeyed.

SIMILAR WORDS: ① compel, drive, make

forceful ADJECTIVE powerful and convincing • *a forceful, highly respected lawyer.* **forcefully** ADVERB

forceps PLURAL NOUN Forceps are a pair of long tongs or pincers used by a doctor or surgeon.

forcible ADJECTIVE ① involving physical force or violence. ② convincing and making a strong impression • *a forcible reminder.* **forcibly** ADVERB

ford, fords, fording, forded NOUN ① a shallow place in a river where it is possible to cross on foot or in a vehicle. ▶ VERB ② To ford a river is to cross it on foot or in a vehicle.

fore PHRASE Someone or something that comes **to the fore** becomes important or popular.

forearm, forearms NOUN the part of your arm between your elbow and your wrist.

forebear, forebears NOUN Your forebears are your ancestors.

foreboding, forebodings NOUN a strong feeling of approaching disaster.

forecast, forecasts, forecasting, forecast or forecasted NOUN ① a prediction of what will happen, especially a statement about what the weather will be like. ▶ VERB ② To forecast an event is to predict what will happen.

forecourt, forecourts NOUN an open area at the front of a petrol station or large building.

forefather, forefathers NOUN Your forefathers are your ancestors.

forefinger, forefingers NOUN the finger next to your thumb.

forefront NOUN The forefront of something is the most important and progressive part of it.

forego, foregoes, foregoing, forewent, foregone; also spelt **forgo** VERB If you forego something pleasant, you give it up or do not insist on having it.

foregoing PHRASE (formal) You can say **the foregoing** when talking about something that has just been said • *The foregoing discussion has highlighted the difficulties*.

foregone conclusion, foregone conclusions NOUN A foregone conclusion is a result or conclusion that is bound to happen.

foreground NOUN ART In a picture, the foreground is the part that seems nearest to you.

forehand, forehands NOUN or ADJECTIVE PE (a stroke in tennis, squash or badminton) made with the palm of your hand facing in the direction that you hit the ball.

forehead, foreheads NOUN the area at the front of your head, above your eyebrows and below your hairline.

foreign ADJECTIVE ① belonging to or involving countries other than your own • *foreign coins* • *foreign travel*. ② unfamiliar or uncharacteristic • *Such daft enthusiasm was foreign to him*. ③ A foreign object has got into something, usually by accident, and should not be there • *a foreign object in my eye*. **foreigner** NOUN
SIMILAR WORDS: ② alien, unfamiliar

foreman, foremen NOUN ① a person in charge of a group of workers, for example on a building site. ② The foreman of a jury is its spokesperson.

foremost ADJECTIVE The foremost of a group of things is the most important or the best.

forensic ADJECTIVE ① relating to or involving the scientific examination of objects involved in a crime. ② relating to or involving the legal profession.

forerunner, forerunners NOUN The forerunner of something is the person who first introduced or achieved it, or the first example of it.

foresee, foresees, foreseeing, foresaw, foreseen VERB If you foresee something, you predict or expect that it will happen. **foreseeable** ADJECTIVE

foresight NOUN Foresight is the ability to know what is going to happen in the future.

foreskin, foreskins NOUN A man's foreskin is the fold of skin covering the end of his penis.

forest, forests NOUN a large area of trees growing close together.

forestry NOUN Forestry is the study and work of growing and maintaining forests.

foretaste, foretastes NOUN a slight taste or experience of something in advance.

foretell, foretells, foretelling, foretold VERB If you foretell something, you predict that it will happen.

forever ADVERB permanently or continually.

forewarn, forewarns, forewarning, forewarned VERB If you forewarn someone, you warn them in advance about something.

forewent the past tense of **forego**.

foreword, forewords NOUN an introduction in a book.

forfeit, forfeits, forfeiting, forfeited VERB ① If you forfeit something, you have to give it up as a penalty. ▶ NOUN ② something that you have to give up or do as a penalty.

forgave the past tense of **forgive**.

forge, forges, forging, forged NOUN ① a place where a blacksmith works making metal goods by hand. ▶ VERB

②To forge metal is to hammer and bend it into shape while hot. ③To forge a relationship is to create a strong and lasting relationship. ④To forge money, documents or paintings is to make illegal copies of them. ⑤To forge ahead is to progress quickly.

forgery, forgeries NOUN Forgery is the crime of forging money, documents or paintings; also something that has been forged. **forger** NOUN

forget, forgets, forgetting, forgot, forgotten VERB ①If you forget something, you fail to remember or think about it. ②If you forget yourself, you behave in an unacceptable, uncontrolled way. **forgetful** ADJECTIVE

forget-me-not, forget-me-nots NOUN a small plant with tiny blue flowers.

forgive, forgives, forgiving, forgave, forgiven VERB If you forgive someone for doing something bad, you stop feeling angry and resentful towards them. **forgiving** ADJECTIVE SIMILAR WORDS: absolve, excuse, pardon

forgiveness NOUN the act of forgiving.

forgo another spelling of **forego**.

forgot the past tense of **forget**.

forgotten the past participle of **forget**.

fork, forks, forking, forked NOUN ①a pronged instrument used for eating food. ②a large garden tool with three or four prongs. ③a Y-shaped junction or division in a road, river or branch. ▶VERB ④To fork something is to move or turn it with a fork. **fork out** VERB (informal) If you fork out for something, you pay for it, often unwillingly.

forlorn ADJECTIVE ①lonely, unhappy and pitiful. ②desperate and without any expectation of success • a forlorn fight for a draw. **forlornly** ADVERB

form, forms, forming, formed NOUN ①A particular form of something is a type or kind of it • a new form of weapon. ②The form of something is the shape or pattern of something • a brooch in the form of a bright green lizard. ③a sheet of paper with questions and spaces for you to fill in the answers. ④a class in a school. ▶VERB ⑤The things that form something are the things it consists of • events that were to form the basis of her novel. ⑥When someone forms something or when it forms, it is created, organised or started.

formal ADJECTIVE ①correct, serious and conforming to accepted conventions • a very formal letter of apology. ②official and publicly recognised • the first formal agreement of its kind. **formally** ADVERB

formaldehyde [Said for-mal-di-hide] NOUN Formaldehyde is a poisonous, strong-smelling gas, used in the manufacture of plastics and for preserving biological specimens. Its formula is HCHO.

formality, formalities NOUN an action or process that is carried out as part of an official procedure.

format, formats NOUN ①the way in which something is arranged or presented. ② ICT The format of a computer file is the way in which the data is stored in it.

formation, formations NOUN ①The formation of something is the process of developing and creating it. ②the pattern or shape of something.

formative ADJECTIVE having an important and lasting influence on character and development • the formative days of his young manhood.

former ADJECTIVE ① happening or existing before now or in the past • *a former tennis champion.* ▶ NOUN ② You use 'the former' to refer to the first of two things just mentioned • *If I had to choose between happiness and money, I would have the former.* **formerly** ADVERB

formidable ADJECTIVE very difficult to deal with or overcome, and therefore rather frightening or impressive • *formidable enemies.*
SIMILAR WORDS: daunting, intimidating

formula, **formulae** or **formulas** NOUN ① MATHS a group of letters, numbers and symbols which stand for a mathematical or scientific rule. ② SCIENCE a list of quantities of substances that when mixed make another substance, for example in chemistry. ③ a plan or set of rules for dealing with a particular problem • *my secret formula for keeping myself fit.*

formulate, **formulates**, **formulating**, **formulated** VERB If you formulate a plan or thought, you create it and express it in a clear and precise way.

forsake, **forsakes**, **forsaking**, **forsook**, **forsaken** VERB To forsake someone or something is to give them up or abandon them.

fort, **forts** NOUN ① a strong building built for defence. ▶ PHRASE ② If you **hold the fort** for someone, you manage their affairs while they are away.

forte, **fortes** [*Said for-tay*] ADVERB ① MUSIC In music, forte is an instruction to play or sing something loudly. ▶ NOUN ② If something is your forte, you are particularly good at doing it.
SIMILAR WORDS: ② speciality, strong point

forth ADVERB ① out and forward from a starting place • *Christopher Columbus set forth on his epic voyage of discovery.* ② into view • *He brought forth a slim volume of his newly published verse.*

SPELLING TIP
Do not confuse the spellings of *forth* and *fourth*: *They set forth at the beginning of June; This is the fourth time you have been late.*

---

forthcoming ADJECTIVE ① planned to happen soon • *their forthcoming holiday.* ② given or made available • *Medical aid might be forthcoming.* ③ willing to give information • *He was not too forthcoming about this.*

forthright ADJECTIVE Someone who is forthright is direct and honest about their opinions and feelings.

fortification, **fortifications** NOUN Fortifications are buildings, walls and ditches used to protect a place.

fortify, **fortifies**, **fortifying**, **fortified** VERB To fortify a place is to strengthen it against attack.

fortissimo ADVERB MUSIC In music, fortissimo is an instruction to play or sing something very loudly.

fortitude NOUN Fortitude is calm and patient courage.

fortnight, **fortnights** NOUN a period of two weeks. **fortnightly** ADVERB or ADJECTIVE

fortress, **fortresses** NOUN a castle or well-protected town built for defence.

fortuitous [*Said for-tyoo-it-uss*] ADJECTIVE happening by chance or good luck • *a fortuitous winning goal.*

fortunate ADJECTIVE ① Someone who is fortunate is lucky. ② Something that is fortunate brings success or advantage. **fortunately** ADVERB

a
b
c
d
e
f
g
h
i
j
k
l
m
n
o
p
q
r
s
t
u
v
w
x
y
z

fortune, fortunes NOUN ① Fortune or good fortune is good luck. ② A fortune is a large amount of money. ▶ PHRASE ③ If someone **tells your fortune**, they predict your future.

forty, forties the number 40. **fortieth** ADJECTIVE

forum, forums NOUN ① a place or meeting in which people can exchange ideas and discuss public issues. ② a website where people discuss a particular topic. ③ a square in Roman towns where people met to discuss business and politics.

forward, forwards, forwarding, forwarded ADVERB or ADJECTIVE ① Forward or forwards means in the front or towards the front • *A photographer moved forward to capture the moment.* ② Forward means in or towards a future time • *a positive atmosphere of looking forward and making fresh starts.* ③ Forward or forwards also means developing or progressing • *The new committee would push forward government plans.* ▶ ADVERB ④ If someone or something is put forward, they are suggested as being suitable for something. ▶ VERB ⑤ If you forward a message or document that you have received, you send it on to another person. ▶ NOUN ⑥ In a game such as football or hockey, a forward is a player in an attacking position.
SIMILAR WORDS: ③ ahead, on

fossick, fossicks, fossicking, fossicked VERB ① In Australian and New Zealand English, to fossick for gold nuggets or precious stones is to look for them in rivers or old mines. ② In Australian and New Zealand English, to fossick for something is to search for it.

fossil, fossils NOUN SCIENCE the remains or impression of an animal or plant from a previous age,
preserved in rock. **fossilise** VERB

fossil fuel, fossil fuels NOUN
GEOGRAPHY SCIENCE Fossil fuels are fuels such as coal, oil and natural gas, which have been formed by rotting animals and plants from millions of years ago.

foster, fosters, fostering, fostered VERB ① If someone fosters a child, they are paid to look after the child for a period, but do not become its legal parent. ② If you foster something such as an activity or an idea, you help its development and growth by encouraging people to do or think it • *to foster and maintain this goodwill.* **foster child** NOUN **foster home** NOUN **foster parent** NOUN

fought the past tense and past participle of **fight**.

foul, fouler, foulest; fouls, fouling, fouled ADJECTIVE ① Something that is foul is very unpleasant, especially because it is dirty, wicked or obscene. ▶ VERB ② To foul something is to make it dirty, especially with faeces • *Dogs must not be allowed to foul the pavement.* ▶ NOUN ③ In sport, a foul is an act of breaking the rules.

found, founds, founding, founded ① Found is the past tense and past participle of **find**. ▶ VERB ② If someone founds an organisation or institution, they start it and set it up.

foundation, foundations NOUN ① The foundation of a belief or way of life is the basic ideas or attitudes on which it is built. ② a solid layer of concrete or bricks in the ground, on which a building is built to give it a firm base. ③ an organisation set up by money donated to or left in someone's will for research or charity.

founder, founders, foundering, foundered NOUN ① The founder of an institution or organisation is the person who sets it up. ▶ **VERB** ② If something founders, it fails.

foundry, foundries NOUN a factory where metal is melted and cast.

fountain, fountains NOUN an ornamental structure consisting of a jet of water forced into the air by a pump.

fountain pen, fountain pens NOUN a pen which is supplied with ink from a container inside the pen.

four, fours ① the number 4.
▶ **PHRASE** ② If you are on **all fours**, you are on your hands and knees.

four-poster, four-posters NOUN a bed with a tall post at each corner supporting a canopy and curtains.

fourteen the number 14.
fourteenth ADJECTIVE

fourth ADJECTIVE The fourth item in a series is the one counted as number four.

SPELLING TIP
Do not confuse the spellings of *fourth* and *forth*: *This is the fourth time you have been late; They set forth at the beginning of June.*

fowl, fowls NOUN a bird such as chicken or duck that is kept or hunted for its meat or eggs.

fox, foxes, foxing, foxed NOUN ① a dog-like wild animal with reddish-brown fur, a pointed face and ears, and a thick tail. ▶ **VERB** ② If something foxes you, it is too confusing or puzzling for you to understand.

foxglove, foxgloves NOUN a plant with a tall spike of purple or white trumpet-shaped flowers.

foyer, foyers [Said foy-ay] NOUN a large area just inside the main doors of a cinema, hotel or public building.

fracas [Said frak-ah] NOUN a rough noisy quarrel or fight.

fracking NOUN Fracking is the extraction of oil or gas by forcing liquid into rock at high pressure.

fraction, fractions NOUN ① [MATHS] In arithmetic, a fraction is a part of a whole number. A **proper fraction** is a fraction in which the number above the line is lower than the number below it; an **improper fraction** has the greater number above the line • $3/4$ *is a proper fraction.* ② a tiny proportion or amount of something • *an area a fraction of the size of London.* **fractional** ADJECTIVE **fractionally** ADVERB

SPELLING TIP
Do not confuse the spellings of *fraction* and *faction*: *Write 50 per cent as a fraction; a disagreement between factions of the Anglican Church.*

fractious ADJECTIVE When small children are fractious, they become upset or angry very easily, often because they are tired.

fracture, fractures, fracturing, fractured NOUN ① a crack or break in something, especially a bone.
▶ **VERB** ② If something fractures, it breaks.

fragile ADJECTIVE easily broken or damaged • *fragile glass* • *a fragile relationship.* **fragility** NOUN
SIMILAR WORDS: breakable, delicate, frail

fragment, fragments, fragmenting, fragmented NOUN ① a small piece or part of something. ▶ **VERB** ② If something fragments, it breaks into small pieces or different parts.
fragmentation NOUN **fragmented** ADJECTIVE

fragmentary ADJECTIVE made up of small pieces, or parts that are not

a b c d e f g h i j k l m n o p q r s t u v w x y z

connected • *fragmentary notes in a journal*.

fragrance, fragrances NOUN a sweet or pleasant smell.
SIMILAR WORDS: aroma, perfume, scent

fragrant ADJECTIVE Something that is fragrant smells sweet or pleasant.

SPELLING TIP
Do not confuse the spellings of *fragrant* and *flagrant*: *a bunch of fragrant flowers; a flagrant attack on democracy*.

frail, frailer, frailest ADJECTIVE ① Someone who is frail is not strong or healthy. ② Something that is frail is easily broken or damaged. **frailty** NOUN

frame, frames, framing, framed NOUN ① the structure surrounding a door, window or picture. ② an arrangement of connected bars over which something is built. ③ The frames of a pair of glasses are the wire or plastic parts that hold the lenses. ④ Your frame is your body • *his large frame*. ⑤ one of the many separate photographs of which a cinema film is made up. ▶ VERB ⑥ To frame a picture is to put it into a frame • *I've framed pictures I've pulled out of magazines*. ⑦ The language something is framed in is the language used to express it.

framework, frameworks NOUN ① [DGT] a structure acting as a support or frame. ② a set of rules, beliefs or ideas which you use to decide what to do.

franc, francs NOUN the main unit of currency in Switzerland, and formerly in France and Belgium. A franc is worth 100 centimes.

franchise, franchises NOUN ① The franchise is the right to vote in an election • *a franchise that gave the vote to less than 2% of the population*. ② the right given by a company to someone to allow them to sell its goods or services.

frank, franker, frankest ADJECTIVE If you are frank, you say things in an open and honest way. **frankly** ADVERB **frankness** NOUN
SIMILAR WORDS: candid, honest, open

frantic ADJECTIVE If you are frantic, you behave in a wild, desperate way because you are anxious or frightened. **frantically** ADVERB

fraternal ADJECTIVE 'Fraternal' is used to describe friendly actions and feelings between groups of people • *an affectionate fraternal greeting*.

fraternity, fraternities NOUN ① Fraternity is friendship between groups of people. ② a group of people with something in common • *the golfing fraternity*.

fraud, frauds NOUN ① Fraud is the crime of getting money by deceit or trickery. ② something that deceives people in an illegal or immoral way. ③ Someone who is not what they pretend to be.

fraudulent ADJECTIVE dishonest or deceitful • *fraudulent use of credit cards*.

fraught ADJECTIVE If something is fraught with problems or difficulties, it is full of them • *Modern life was fraught with hazards*.

fray, frays, fraying, frayed VERB ① If cloth or rope frays, its threads or strands become worn and it is likely to tear or break. ▶ NOUN ② a fight or argument.

freak, freaks NOUN ① someone whose appearance or behaviour is very unusual. ▶ ADJECTIVE ② A freak event is very unusual and unlikely to happen • *a freak snowstorm in summer.*

freckle, freckles NOUN Freckles are small, light brown spots on someone's skin, especially their face. **freckled** ADJECTIVE

free, freer, freest; frees, freeing, freed ADJECTIVE ① not controlled or limited • *the free flow of aid* • *free trade.* ② Someone who is free is no longer a prisoner. ③ To be free of something unpleasant is not to have it • *She wanted her aunt's life to be free of worry.* ④ If someone is free, they are not busy or occupied. If a place, seat or machine is free, it is not occupied or not being used • *Are you free for dinner?* ⑤ If something is free, you can have it without paying for it. ▶ VERB ⑥ If you free someone or something that is imprisoned, fastened or trapped, you release them.

SIMILAR WORDS: ② at liberty, liberated ⑤ complimentary, gratis ⑥ liberate, release

freedom NOUN ① If you have the freedom to do something, you have the scope or are allowed to do it • *We have the freedom to decide our own futures.* ② When prisoners gain their freedom, they escape or are released. ③ When there is freedom from something unpleasant, people are not affected by it • *freedom from guilt.*

SIMILAR WORDS: ② liberty, release

freedom fighter, freedom fighters NOUN a person who is involved in a revolution to overthrow a government or system.

freehold, freeholds NOUN the right to own a house or piece of land for life without conditions.

freelance ADJECTIVE or ADVERB A freelance journalist or photographer is not employed by one organisation, but is paid for each job he or she does.

freely ADVERB Freely means without restriction • *the pleasure of being able to walk about freely.*

free-range ADJECTIVE Free-range eggs are laid by hens that can move and feed freely on an area of open ground.

freestyle NOUN Freestyle refers to sports competitions, especially swimming, in which competitors can use any style or method.

freeway, freeways NOUN In Australia, South Africa and the United States, a freeway is a road designed for fast-moving traffic.

free will PHRASE If you do something **of your own free will**, you do it by choice and not because you are forced to.

freeze, freezes, freezing, froze, frozen VERB ① SCIENCE When a liquid freezes, it becomes solid because it is very cold. ② If you freeze, you suddenly become very still and quiet. ③ DRAMA To freeze the action in a film is to stop the film at a particular frame. ④ If you freeze food, you put it in a freezer to preserve it. ⑤ When wages or prices are frozen, they are officially prevented from rising. ▶ NOUN ⑥ an official action taken to prevent wages or prices from rising. ⑦ a period of freezing weather.

SPELLING TIP

Do not confuse the spellings of *freeze* and *frieze*: *Freeze raw meat on the day you buy it; an intricate plaster frieze.*

freezer, freezers NOUN a large refrigerator which freezes and stores food for a long time.

freeze-thaw cycle, freeze-thaw cycles NOUN GEOGRAPHY the continuous process, for example in rocks on high mountains, of the freezing and thawing of water which results in the rocks cracking and eroding.

freezing ADJECTIVE extremely cold.

freight NOUN Freight is goods moved by lorries, ships or other transport; also the moving of these goods.

SPELLING TIP

Do not confuse the spellings of *freight* and *fright*: *Our lorries carry freight all over Europe; The door banged and we all jumped in fright.*

French ADJECTIVE ① belonging or relating to France. ▶ NOUN ② French is the main language spoken in France, and is also spoken by many people in Belgium, Switzerland and Canada.

French bean, French beans NOUN French beans are green pods eaten as a vegetable, which grow on a climbing plant with white or mauve flowers.

French horn, French horns NOUN a brass musical wind instrument consisting of a tube wound in a circle.

Frenchman, Frenchmen NOUN a man who comes from France.

french window, french windows NOUN French windows are glass doors that lead into a garden or onto a balcony.

Frenchwoman, Frenchwomen NOUN a woman who comes from France.

frenetic ADJECTIVE Frenetic behaviour is wild and excited. **frenetically** ADVERB

frenzy, frenzies NOUN If someone is in a frenzy, their behaviour is wild and uncontrolled. **frenzied** ADJECTIVE

frequency, frequencies NOUN ① The frequency of an event is how often it happens • *He did not call anyone with great frequency.* ② SCIENCE The frequency of a sound

or radio wave is the rate at which it vibrates. ③ MATHS In statistics, the frequency of a particular class is the number of individuals in it.

frequent, frequents, frequenting, frequented ADJECTIVE [Said *free-kwuhnt*] ① often happening • *His visits were frequent* • *They move at frequent intervals.* ▶ VERB [Said *free-kwent*] ② If you frequent a place, you go there often. **frequently** ADVERB

fresco, frescoes NOUN a picture painted on a plastered wall while the plaster is still wet.

fresh, fresher, freshest ADJECTIVE ① A fresh thing replaces a previous one, or is added to it • *footprints filled in by fresh snow* • *fresh evidence.* ② Fresh food is newly made or obtained, and not tinned or frozen. ③ Fresh water is not salty, for example the water in a stream. ④ If the weather is fresh, it is fairly cold and windy. ⑤ If you are fresh from something, you have experienced it recently • *a teacher fresh from college.* **freshly** ADVERB **freshness** NOUN

freshwater ADJECTIVE ① A freshwater lake or pool contains water that is not salty. ② A freshwater creature lives in a river, lake or pool that is not salty.

fret, frets, fretting, fretted VERB ① If you fret about something, you worry about it. ▶ NOUN ② The frets on a stringed instrument, such as a guitar, are the metal ridges across its neck. **fretful** ADJECTIVE

Freudian slip, Freudian slips NOUN something that you say or do that is said to reveal your unconscious thoughts.

friar, friars NOUN a member of a men's Catholic religious order.

friction NOUN ① SCIENCE the force

that stops things from moving freely when they rub against each other. ② Friction between people is disagreement and quarrels.

Friday, Fridays NOUN the day between Thursday and Saturday. **WORD HISTORY:** from Old English *Frigedæg* meaning 'Freya's day'. Freya was the Norse goddess of love

fridge, fridges NOUN the same as a **refrigerator**.

friend, friends, friending, friended NOUN ① Your friends are people you know well and like to spend time with. ② someone with whom you can exchange posts and messages on a social networking site. ▶ VERB ③ If you friend someone on a social networking site, you allow them to exchange posts and messages with you.
SIMILAR WORDS: ① chum, companion, mate, pal

SPELLING TIP
Remember this mnemonic: *I always visit my FRIend on a FRIday.*

---

friendly, friendlier, friendliest ADJECTIVE ① If you are friendly to someone, you behave in a kind and pleasant way to them. ② People who are friendly with each other like each other and enjoy spending time together. **friendliness** NOUN
SIMILAR WORDS: ① amicable, cordial, genial

friendship, friendships NOUN ① Your friendships are the special relationships that you have with your friends. ② Friendship is the state of being friends with someone.
SIMILAR WORDS: ② friendliness, goodwill

fries PLURAL NOUN Fries are thin strips of fried potato.

frieze, friezes NOUN ① a strip of decoration or carving along the top of a wall or column. ② ART a picture on a long strip of paper which is hung along a wall.

SPELLING TIP
Do not confuse the spellings of *frieze* and *freeze*: *an intricate plaster frieze; Freeze raw meat on the day you buy it.*

---

frigate, frigates [*Said* frig-it] NOUN a small, fast warship.

fright NOUN Fright is a sudden feeling of fear.

SPELLING TIP
Do not confuse the spellings of *fright* and *freight*: *The door banged and we all jumped in fright; Our lorries carry freight all over Europe.*

---

frighten, frightens, frightening, frightened VERB If something frightens you, it makes you afraid.

frightened ADJECTIVE having feelings of fear about something.

frightening ADJECTIVE causing someone to feel fear.

frightful ADJECTIVE very bad or unpleasant • *a frightful bully*. **frightfully** ADVERB

frigid ADJECTIVE Frigid behaviour is cold and unfriendly • *frigid stares*.

frill, frills NOUN a strip of cloth with many folds, attached to something as a decoration. **frilly** ADJECTIVE

fringe, fringes NOUN ① the hair that hangs over a person's forehead. ② a decoration on clothes and other objects, consisting of a row of hanging strips or threads. ③ The fringes of a place are the parts farthest from its centre • *the western fringe of the Amazon basin.* **fringed** ADJECTIVE

frisk, frisks, frisking, frisked VERB (*informal*) If someone frisks you, they search you quickly with their hands to see if you are hiding illegal items in your clothes.

frisky, friskier, friskiest ADJECTIVE A frisky animal or child is energetic and wants to have fun.

fritter, fritters, frittering, frittered NOUN ① Fritters consist of food dipped in batter and fried • *apple fritters*. ▶ VERB ② If you fritter away your time or money, you waste it on unimportant things.

frivolous ADJECTIVE Someone who is frivolous behaves in a silly or light-hearted way, especially when they should be serious or sensible. **frivolity** NOUN
SIMILAR WORDS: flippant, silly

frizzy, frizzier, frizziest ADJECTIVE Frizzy hair has stiff, wiry curls.

frock, frocks NOUN (*old-fashioned*) a dress.

frog, frogs NOUN a small amphibious creature with smooth skin, prominent eyes, and long back legs which it uses for jumping.

frolic, frolics, frolicking, frolicked VERB When animals or children frolic, they run around and play in a lively way.
SIMILAR WORDS: frisk, play, romp
WORD HISTORY: from Dutch *vrolijk* meaning 'joyful'

from PREPOSITION ① You use 'from' to say what the source, origin or starting point of something is • *a call from a mobile phone* • *people from a city 100 miles away*. ② If you take something from an amount, you reduce the amount by that much • *A sum of money was wrongly taken from his account*. ③ You also use 'from' when stating the range of something • *a score from one to five*.

frond, fronds NOUN Fronds are long feathery leaves.

front, fronts, fronting, fronted NOUN ① The front of something is the part that faces forward. ② In a war, the front is the place where two armies are fighting. ③ In meteorology, a front is the line where a mass of cold air meets a mass of warm air. ④ A front is an outward appearance, often one that is false • *I put up a brave front* • *He's no more than a respectable front for some very dubious happenings*. ▶ PHRASE ⑤ **In front** means ahead or further forward. ⑥ If you do something **in front of** someone, you do it when they are present. **frontal** ADJECTIVE

frontage, frontages NOUN The frontage of a building is the wall that faces a street.

frontier, frontiers NOUN a border between two countries.

frontispiece, frontispieces NOUN a picture opposite the title page of a book.

frost, frosts NOUN When there is a frost, the temperature outside falls below freezing.

frostbite NOUN Frostbite is damage to your fingers, toes or ears caused by extreme cold.

frosting NOUN In American English, frosting is icing.

frosty, frostier, frostiest ADJECTIVE ① If it is frosty, the temperature outside is below freezing point. ② If someone is frosty, they are unfriendly or disapproving. **frostily** ADVERB

froth, froths, frothing, frothed NOUN ① Froth is a mass of small bubbles on the surface of a liquid. ▶ VERB ② If a liquid froths, small bubbles appear on its surface. **frothy** ADJECTIVE

frown, frowns, frowning, frowned VERB ① If you frown, you move your eyebrows closer together, because you are annoyed, worried or concentrating. ▶ NOUN ② a cross expression on someone's face.

froze the past tense of **freeze**.

frozen ① Frozen is the past participle of **freeze**. ▶ ADJECTIVE ② If you say you are frozen, you mean you are extremely cold.
SIMILAR WORDS: ② chilled, ice-cold, icy

fructose [Said frook-toes] NOUN Fructose is a type of sugar found in many fruits and in honey.

frugal ADJECTIVE ① Someone who is frugal spends very little money. ② A frugal meal is small and cheap. **frugally** ADVERB **frugality** NOUN
SIMILAR WORDS: ① economical, thrifty

fruit, fruits NOUN ① the part of a plant that develops after the flower and contains the seeds. Many fruits are edible. ② (in plural) The fruits of something are its good results • the fruits of his labours.

fruitful ADJECTIVE Something that is fruitful has good and useful results • a fruitful experience.

fruitless ADJECTIVE Something that is fruitless does not achieve anything • a fruitless effort.

fruit machine, fruit machines NOUN a coin-operated gambling machine which pays out money when a particular series of symbols, usually fruit, appears on a screen.

fruit salad, fruit salads NOUN a mixture of pieces of different fruits served in a juice as a dessert.

fruity, fruitier, fruitiest ADJECTIVE Something that is fruity smells or tastes of fruit.

frustrate, frustrates, frustrating, frustrated VERB ① If something frustrates you, it prevents you doing what you want and makes you upset and angry • Everyone gets frustrated with their work. ② To frustrate something such as a plan is to prevent it • She hopes to frustrate the building of the new road. **frustrated** ADJECTIVE **frustrating** ADJECTIVE **frustration** NOUN
SIMILAR WORDS: ② foil, thwart

fry, fries, frying, fried VERB When you fry food, you cook it in a pan containing hot fat or oil.

fuchsia, fuchsias [Said fyoo-sha] NOUN a plant or small bush with pink, purple or white flowers that hang downwards.

fudge, fudges, fudging, fudged NOUN ① Fudge is a soft brown sweet made from butter, milk and sugar. ▶ VERB ② If you fudge something, you avoid making clear or definite decisions or statements about it • He was carefully fudging his message.

fuel, fuels, fuelling, fuelled NOUN ① Fuel is a substance such as coal or petrol that is burned to provide heat or power. ▶ VERB ② A machine or vehicle that is fuelled by a substance works by burning the substance as a fuel • power stations fuelled by wood.

fug NOUN A fug is an airless, smoky atmosphere.

fugitive, fugitives [Said fyoo-jit-tiv] NOUN someone who is running away or hiding, especially from the police.

-ful SUFFIX ① '-ful' is used to form adjectives with the meaning 'full of' • careful. ② '-ful' is used to form nouns which mean 'the amount needed to fill' • spoonful.

fulcrum, fulcrums or fulcra NOUN
DGT the point at which something is balancing or pivoting.

fulfil, fulfils, fulfilling, fulfilled VERB ① If you fulfil a promise, hope or duty, you carry it out or achieve it. ② If something fulfils you, it gives you satisfaction. **fulfilling** ADJECTIVE **fulfilment** NOUN

A
B
C
D
E
F
G
H
I
J
K
L
M
N
O
P
Q
R
S
T
U
V
W
X
Y
Z

What does the Full Stop do?

The **full stop** (.) marks the end of any sentence which is not a question or an exclamation:

The train is leaving.

A full stop is also used after an abbreviation or initial:

etc.
J.R. Hartley

A full stop is also used after an expression that stands by itself but is not a complete sentence:

Good morning.

full, fuller, fullest ADJECTIVE
① containing or having as much as it is possible to hold • *His room is full of posters.* ② complete or whole • *They had taken a full meal* • *a full 20 years later.* ③ loose and made from a lot of fabric • *full sleeves.* ④ rich and strong • *a full, pungent cheese.*
▶ ADVERB ⑤ completely and directly • *Turn the taps full on.* ▶ PHRASE ⑥ Something that has been done or described **in full** has been dealt with completely. **fullness** NOUN
fully ADVERB
SIMILAR WORDS: ① filled, loaded, packed

full-blooded ADJECTIVE having great commitment and enthusiasm • *a full-blooded sprint for third place.*

full-blown ADJECTIVE complete and fully developed • *a full-blown crisis.*

full moon, full moons NOUN the moon when it appears as a complete circle.

full stop, full stops NOUN ENGLISH the punctuation mark (.) used at the end of a sentence and after an abbreviation or initial.

PUNCTUATION TIP
You put a full stop at the end of every sentence or greeting unless it already ends with a question mark or exclamation mark: *I'm sorry.*

---

full-time ADJECTIVE ① involving work for the whole of each normal working week. ▶ NOUN ② In games such as football, full time is the end of the match.

fully-fledged ADJECTIVE completely developed • *I was a fully-fledged and mature human being.*

fulsome ADJECTIVE exaggerated and elaborate, and often sounding insincere • *His most fulsome praise was reserved for his mother.*

fumble, fumbles, fumbling, fumbled VERB If you fumble, you feel or handle something clumsily.

fume, fumes, fuming, fumed NOUN ① Fumes are unpleasant-smelling gases and smoke, often toxic, that are produced by burning and by some chemicals. ▶ VERB ② If you are fuming, you are very angry.

fun NOUN ① Fun is pleasant, enjoyable and light-hearted activity. ▶ PHRASE ② If you **make fun** of someone, you tease them or make jokes about them.

function, functions, functioning, functioned NOUN ① The function of something or someone is their purpose or the job they have to do. ② a large formal dinner, reception or party. ③ MATHS A function is a variable whose value depends on the value of other independent variables. 'y is a function of x' is written $y = f(x)$.
▶ VERB ④ When something functions, it operates or works.

functional ADJECTIVE ① relating to the way something works.

②designed for practical use rather than for decoration or attractiveness • *The buildings are functional but not nice to look at.* ③working properly • *fully functional smoke alarms.*

fund, funds, funding, funded NOUN ①an amount of available money, usually for a particular purpose • *a pension fund.* ②A fund of something is a lot of it • *He had a fund of hilarious tales on the subject.* ▶VERB ③Someone who funds something provides money for it • *research funded by pharmaceutical companies.*
SIMILAR WORDS: ③finance, subsidise

fundamental, fundamentals ADJECTIVE ①basic and central • *the fundamental right of freedom of choice* • *fundamental changes.* ▶NOUN ②The fundamentals of something are its most basic and important parts • *teaching small children the fundamentals of road safety.*

fundi, fundis NOUN In South Africa, a fundi is an expert.

funeral, funerals [*Said* fyoo-ner-al] NOUN a ceremony or religious service for the burial or cremation of a dead person.

funereal [*Said* few-*nee*-ree-al] ADJECTIVE depressing and gloomy.

funfair, funfairs NOUN a place of entertainment with things like amusement arcades and rides.

fungicide, fungicides NOUN a chemical used to kill or prevent fungus.

fungus, fungi or funguses NOUN SCIENCE a plant such as a mushroom or mould that does not have leaves and grows on other living things. **fungal** ADJECTIVE

funky, funkier, funkiest ADJECTIVE (*informal*) If you describe something or someone as funky, you like them because they are unconventional or unusual • *a funky little café.*

funnel, funnels, funnelling, funnelled NOUN ①an open cone narrowing to a tube, used to pour substances into containers. ②a metal chimney on a ship or steam engine. ▶VERB ③If something is funnelled somewhere, it is directed through a narrow space into that place.

funnel-web, funnel-webs NOUN a large black poisonous Australian spider that builds funnel-shaped webs.

funny, funnier, funniest ADJECTIVE ①strange or puzzling • *Young children get some very funny ideas sometimes!* ②causing amusement or laughter • *a funny old film.* **funnily** ADVERB
SIMILAR WORDS: ①odd, peculiar, strange ②amusing, comical, humorous

fur, furs NOUN ①Fur is the soft thick body hair of many animals. ②a coat made from an animal's fur. **furry** ADJECTIVE

furious ADJECTIVE ①extremely angry. ②involving great energy, effort or speed • *the furious speed of technological development.* **furiously** ADVERB

furlong, furlongs NOUN a unit of length equal to 220 yards or about 201.2 metres. Furlong originally referred to the length of the average furrow.

furnace, furnaces NOUN a container for a very large, hot fire used, for example, in the steel industry for melting ore.

furnish, furnishes, furnishing, furnished VERB ①If you furnish a room, you put furniture into it. ②(*formal*) If you furnish someone with something, you supply or provide it for them.

a
b
c
d
e
f
g
h
i
j
k
l
m
n
o
p
q
r
s
t
u
v
w
x
y
z

furnishings PLURAL NOUN The furnishings of a room or house are the furniture and fittings in it.

furniture NOUN Furniture is movable objects such as tables, chairs and wardrobes.

furore [Said fyoo-**roh**-ree] NOUN an angry and excited reaction or protest.
WORD HISTORY: from Italian furore meaning 'rage'

furrow, furrows, furrowing, furrowed NOUN ① a long, shallow trench made by a plough. ▶ VERB ② When someone furrows their brow, they frown.

further, furthers, furthering, furthered ① a comparative form of far. ▶ ADJECTIVE ② additional or more • There was no further rain. ▶ VERB ③ If you further something, you help it to progress • He wants to further his acting career.
SIMILAR WORDS: ③ advance, promote

further education NOUN Further education is education at a college after leaving school, but not at a university.

furthermore ADVERB (formal) used to introduce additional information • There is no record of such a letter. Furthermore, it is company policy never to send such letters.

furthest a superlative form of **far**.

furtive ADJECTIVE secretive, sly and cautious • a furtive smile. **furtively** ADVERB

fury NOUN Fury is violent or extreme anger.

fuse, fuses, fusing, fused NOUN ① a safety device in a plug or electrical appliance consisting of a piece of wire which melts to stop the electric current if a fault occurs. ② a long cord attached to some types of simple bomb which is lit to detonate. ▶ VERB ③ When an electrical appliance fuses, it stops working because the fuse has melted to protect it. ④ If two things fuse, they join or become combined • Christianity slowly fused with existing beliefs.

fuselage, fuselages [Said **fyoo**-zil-ahj] NOUN the main part of an aeroplane or rocket.

fusion NOUN ① Fusion is what happens when two substances join by melting together. ② Fusion is also nuclear fusion. ▶ ADJECTIVE ③ Fusion is used to refer to food or a style of cooking that brings together ingredients or cooking techniques from several different countries.

fuss, fusses, fussing, fussed NOUN ① Fuss is unnecessarily anxious or excited behaviour. ▶ VERB ② If someone fusses, they behave with unnecessary anxiety and concern for unimportant things.
SIMILAR WORDS: ① bother, commotion, palaver

fussy, fussier, fussiest ADJECTIVE ① likely to fuss a lot • He was unusually fussy about keeping things perfect. ② with too much elaborate detail or decoration • fussy chiffon evening wear.
SIMILAR WORDS: ① finicky, particular

futile ADJECTIVE having no chance of success • a futile attempt to calm the storm. **futility** NOUN
SIMILAR WORDS: useless, vain

future, futures NOUN ① The future is the period of time after the present. ② Something that has a future is likely to succeed • She sees no future in a modelling career. ▶ ADJECTIVE ③ relating to or occurring at a time after the present • to predict future events. ④ ENGLISH MFL The future tense of a verb is the form used to express something that will happen in the future.

Talking about the Future

There is no simple future tense in English. To talk about an event that will happen in the future, we usually use **compound tenses**.

The auxiliary verbs *will* and *shall* are used before the basic form of the verb to show that an action will happen:

His father **will cook** *the dinner.*
I **shall cook** *the dinner.*

You can also talk about the future by putting the verbs *will have* or *shall have* before the verb, and adding the ending *-ed*. This form shows that an action will be completed in the future:

His father **will have cooked** *the dinner.*
I **shall have cooked** *the dinner.*

You can also talk about the future by using the phrase *be about to* or *be going to* in front of the dictionary form of the verb. This shows that the action will take place very soon:

He **is about to cook** *the dinner.*
I **am going to cook** *the dinner.*

You can sometimes use a form of the present tense to talk about future events, but only if the sentence contains a clear reference to the future:

His father **is cooking** *the dinner tonight.*
The plane **leaves** *at three o'clock.*

Also look at the grammar box at **the**

futuristic ADJECTIVE very modern and strange, as if belonging to a time in the future • *futuristic cars*.

fuzz NOUN short fluffy hair. **fuzzy** ADJECTIVE

fynbos [*Said* **fain**-*bos*] NOUN Fynbos is a type of vegetation of southern and southwestern South Africa. It consists of evergreen hard-leaved shrubs and almost no trees.
WORD HISTORY: an Afrikaans word meaning 'fine bush'

a
b
c
d
e
f
g
h
i
j
k
l
m
n
o
p
q
r
s
t
u
v
w
x
y
z

Gg

g an abbreviation for 'gram' or 'grams'.

gabble, gabbles, gabbling, gabbled **VERB** If you gabble, you talk so fast that it is difficult for people to understand you.

gable, gables **NOUN** Gables are the triangular parts at the top of the outside walls at each end of a house.

gadget, gadgets **NOUN** a small machine or tool. **gadgetry NOUN** SIMILAR WORDS: contraption, device

Gaelic [Said gay-lik] **NOUN** a language spoken in some parts of Scotland and Ireland.

gaffe, gaffes [Said gaf] **NOUN** a social blunder or mistake.

gaffer, gaffers **NOUN** (informal) a boss.

gag, gags, gagging, gagged **NOUN** ① a strip of cloth that is tied round someone's mouth to stop them speaking. ② (informal) a joke told by a comedian. ▶ **VERB** ③ To gag someone means to put a gag round their mouth. ④ If you gag, you choke and nearly vomit.

gaggle, gaggles **NOUN** ① a group of geese. ② (informal) a noisy group • a gaggle of schoolboys.

gaiety [Said gay-yet-tee] **NOUN** liveliness and fun.

gaily **ADVERB** in a happy and cheerful way.

gain, gains, gaining, gained **VERB** ① If you gain something, you get it gradually • I spent years at night school trying to gain qualifications. ② If you gain from a situation, you get some advantage from it. ③ If you gain on someone, you gradually catch them up. ▶ **NOUN** ④ an increase • a gain in speed. ⑤ an advantage that you get for yourself • People use whatever influence they have for personal gain.

gait, gaits **NOUN** Someone's gait is their way of walking • an awkward gait.

gala, galas **NOUN** a special public celebration or performance • the opening gala of the London Film Festival.

galah, galahs **NOUN** ① an Australian cockatoo with a pink breast and a grey back and wings. ② (informal) In Australian English, a galah is also a stupid person.

galaxy, galaxies **NOUN** SCIENCE A galaxy is an enormous group of stars that extends over many millions of miles. The galaxy to which the earth's solar system belongs is called the Milky Way. **galactic ADJECTIVE**

gale, gales **NOUN** an extremely strong wind.

gall, galls, galling, galled [Rhymes with ball] **NOUN** ① If someone has the gall to do something, they have enough courage or impudence to do it • He even has the gall to visit her. ▶ **VERB** ② If something galls you, it makes you extremely annoyed.

gallant **ADJECTIVE** ① brave and honourable • They have put up a gallant fight for pensioners' rights. ② polite and considerate towards women. **gallantly ADVERB** **gallantry NOUN**

gall bladder, gall bladders NOUN an organ in your body which stores bile and which is next to your liver.

galleon, galleons NOUN [HISTORY] a large sailing ship used in the sixteenth and seventeenth centuries.

SPELLING TIP
Do not confuse the spellings of *galleon* and *gallon*: *a fleet of Spanish galleons; a gallon of water*.

---

gallery, galleries NOUN ① [ART] a building or room where works of art are shown. ② In a theatre or large hall, the gallery is a raised area at the back or sides • *the public gallery in Parliament*.

galley, galleys NOUN ① a kitchen in a ship or aircraft. ② a ship, driven by oars, used in ancient and medieval times.

Gallic [Said *gal*-lik] ADJECTIVE (*formal or literary*) French.

gallon, gallons NOUN a unit of liquid volume equal to eight pints or about 4.55 litres.

gallop, gallops, galloping, galloped VERB ① When a horse gallops, it runs very fast, so that during each stride all four feet are off the ground at the same time. ▸ NOUN ② a very fast run.

gallows NOUN A gallows is a framework on which criminals used to be hanged.

gallstone, gallstones NOUN a small painful lump that can develop in your gall bladder.

galore ADJECTIVE in very large numbers • *chocolates galore*.
WORD HISTORY: from Irish Gaelic *go leór* meaning 'to sufficiency'

galoshes PLURAL NOUN Galoshes are waterproof rubber shoes which you wear over your ordinary shoes to stop them getting wet.

galvanised; also spelt **galvanized**

ADJECTIVE Galvanised metal has been coated with zinc by an electrical process to protect it from rust.

gambit, gambits NOUN something which someone does to gain an advantage in a situation
• *Commentators are calling the plan a clever political gambit*.
WORD HISTORY: from Italian *gambetto* meaning 'a tripping up'

gamble, gambles, gambling, gambled VERB ① When people gamble, they bet money on the result of a game or race. ② If you gamble something, you risk losing it in the hope of gaining an advantage • *The company gambled everything on the new factory*. ▸ NOUN ③ If you take a gamble, you take a risk in the hope of gaining an advantage. **gambler** NOUN **gambling** NOUN
SIMILAR WORDS: ① bet, wager

game, games, gaming, gamed; gamer, gamest NOUN ① an enjoyable activity with a set of rules which is played by individuals or teams against each other. ② an enjoyable imaginative activity played by small children • *childhood games of cowboys and Indians*. ③ You might describe something as a game when it is designed to gain advantage • *the political game*. ④ Game is wild animals or birds that are hunted for sport or for food. ⑤ (*in plural*) Games are sports played at school or in a competition. ▸ VERB ⑥ To game means to play games, especially computer games. ▸ ADJECTIVE ⑦ (*informal*) Someone who is game is willing to try something unusual or difficult. **gamer** NOUN **gamely** ADVERB
SIMILAR WORDS: ① amusement, pastime

gamekeeper, gamekeepers NOUN a person employed to look after game animals and birds on a country estate.

gamete, gametes [Said *gam-meet*] NOUN SCIENCE In biology, a gamete is a cell that can unite with another during reproduction to form a new organism.

gammon NOUN Gammon is cured meat from a pig, similar to bacon.

gamut [Said *gam-mut*] NOUN (formal) The gamut of something is the whole range of things that can be included in it • *the whole gamut of human emotions*.

gander, ganders NOUN a male goose.

gang, gangs, ganging, ganged NOUN a group of people who join together for some purpose, for example to commit a crime.
gang up VERB (informal) If people gang up on you, they join together to oppose you.

gangplank, gangplanks NOUN a plank used for boarding and leaving a ship or boat.

gangrene [Said *gang-green*] NOUN Gangrene is decay in the tissues of part of the body, caused by inadequate blood supply.
gangrenous ADJECTIVE

gangster, gangsters NOUN a violent criminal who is a member of a gang.

gannet, gannets NOUN a large sea bird which dives to catch fish.

gaol another spelling of **jail**.

gap, gaps NOUN ① a space between two things or a hole in something solid. ② a period of time. ③ A gap between things, people or ideas is a great difference between them • *the gap between fantasy and reality*.
SIMILAR WORDS: ① hole, opening, space

gape, gapes, gaping, gaped VERB ① If you gape at someone or

something, you stare at them with your mouth open in surprise. ② Something that gapes is wide open • *gaping holes in the wall*.

garage, garages NOUN ① a building where a car can be kept. ② a place where cars are repaired and where petrol is sold.

garb NOUN (formal) Someone's garb is their clothes • *his usual garb of a dark suit*.

garbage NOUN ① Garbage is rubbish, especially household rubbish. ② (informal) If you say something is garbage, you mean it is nonsense.
WORD HISTORY: from Anglo-French *garbelage* meaning 'removal of discarded matter'

garbled ADJECTIVE Garbled messages are jumbled and the details may be wrong.

garden, gardens NOUN ① an area of land next to a house, where flowers, fruit or vegetables are grown. ② (in plural) Gardens are a type of park in a town or around a large house. ▶ VERB ③ If you garden, you do work in your garden such as weeding or planting.
gardening NOUN

gardener, gardeners NOUN a person who looks after a garden as a job or as a hobby.

gargle, gargles, gargling, gargled VERB When you gargle, you rinse the back of your throat by putting some liquid in your mouth and making a bubbling sound without swallowing.

gargoyle, gargoyles NOUN a stone carving below the roof of an old building, in the shape of an ugly person or animal and often having a water spout at the mouth.

garish [Said *gair-rish*] ADJECTIVE bright and harsh to look at • *garish bright red boots*.

garland, garlands NOUN a circle of

flowers and leaves which is worn around the neck or head.

garlic NOUN Garlic is the small white bulb of an onion-like plant which has a strong taste and smell and is used in cooking.

garment, garments NOUN a piece of clothing.

garnet, garnets NOUN a type of gemstone, usually red in colour.

garnish, garnishes, garnishing, garnished NOUN ① something such as a sprig of parsley, that is used in cooking for decoration. ▶ VERB ② To garnish food means to decorate it with a garnish.

garret, garrets NOUN an attic.

garrison, garrisons NOUN a group of soldiers stationed in a town in order to guard it; also used of the buildings in which these soldiers live.

garter, garters NOUN a piece of elastic worn round the top of a stocking to hold it up.

gas, gases; gasses, gassing, gassed NOUN ① SCIENCE any airlike substance that is not liquid or solid, such as oxygen or the gas used as a fuel in heating. ② In American English, gas is petrol. ▶ VERB ③ To gas people or animals means to kill them with poisonous gas.

SPELLING TIP
The plural of the noun *gas* is *gases*. The verb forms of *gas* are spelt with a double s.

gas chamber, gas chambers NOUN a room in which people or animals are killed with poisonous gas.

gaseous [Said *gas-see-uss*] ADJECTIVE consisting of gas or like gas.

gash, gashes, gashing, gashed NOUN ① a long, deep cut. ▶ VERB ② If you gash something, you make a long, deep cut in it.

gas mask, gas masks NOUN a large mask with special filters attached which people wear over their face to protect them from poisonous gas.

gasoline NOUN In American English, gasoline is petrol.

gasp, gasps, gasping, gasped VERB ① If you gasp, you quickly draw in your breath through your mouth because you are surprised or in pain. ▶ NOUN ② a sharp intake of breath through the mouth.

gastric ADJECTIVE occurring in the stomach or involving the stomach • *gastric pain*.

gate, gates NOUN ① a barrier which can open and shut and is used to close the entrance to a garden or field. ② The gate at a sports event is the number of people who have attended it.

gateau, gateaux [Said *gat-toe*] NOUN a rich layered cake with cream in it.

gatecrash, gatecrashes, gatecrashing, gatecrashed VERB If you gatecrash a party, you go to it when you have not been invited.

gateway, gateways NOUN ① an entrance through a wall or fence where there is a gate. ② Something that is considered to be the entrance to a larger or more important thing can be described as the gateway to the larger thing • *New York is the great gateway to America*.

gather, gathers, gathering, gathered VERB ① When people gather, they come together in a group. ② If you gather a number of things, you bring them together in one place. ③ If something gathers speed or strength, it gets faster or stronger. ④ If you gather something, you learn it, often from what someone says.
SIMILAR WORDS: ① assemble, congregate ② amass, assemble, collect

gathering, gatherings NOUN a meeting of people who have come together for a particular purpose.

gauche [Said gohsh] ADJECTIVE (formal) socially awkward.
WORD HISTORY: from French gauche meaning 'left'

gaudy, gaudier, gaudiest [Said gaw-dee] ADJECTIVE very colourful in a vulgar way.
SIMILAR WORDS: bright, flashy, garish

gauge, gauges, gauging, gauged [Said gayj] VERB ① If you gauge something, you estimate it or calculate it • He gauged the wind at over 30 knots. ▶ NOUN ② a piece of equipment that measures the amount of something • a rain gauge. ③ something that is used as a standard by which you judge a situation • They see profit as a gauge of efficiency. ④ On railways, the gauge is the distance between the two rails on a railway line.

gaunt ADJECTIVE A person who looks gaunt is thin and bony.

gauntlet, gauntlets NOUN ① Gauntlets are long thick gloves worn for protection, for example by motorcyclists. ▶ PHRASE ② If you **throw down the gauntlet**, you challenge someone. ③ If you **run the gauntlet**, you have an unpleasant experience in which you are attacked or criticised by people.

gave the past tense of **give**.

gay, gayer, gayest; gays ADJECTIVE ① Someone who is gay is homosexual. ② (old-fashioned) Gay people or places are lively and full of fun. ▶ NOUN ③ a homosexual person.

GRAMMAR TIP
The most common meaning of gay now is 'homosexual'. In some older books it may have its old-fashioned meaning of 'lively and full of fun'. The

noun gaiety is related to this older meaning of gay. The noun that means 'the state of being homosexual' is gayness.

gaze, gazes, gazing, gazed VERB If you gaze at something, you look steadily at it for a long time.

gazelle, gazelles NOUN a small antelope found in Africa and Asia.

gazette, gazettes NOUN a newspaper or journal.

GB an abbreviation for **Great Britain**.

GCSE, GCSEs NOUN In Britain, the GCSE is an examination taken by school students aged 15 and 16. GCSE is an abbreviation for 'General Certificate of Secondary Education'.

gear, gears, gearing, geared NOUN ① DGT a piece of machinery which controls the rate at which energy is converted into movement. Gears in vehicles control the speed and power of the vehicle. ② PE The gear for an activity is the clothes and equipment that you need for it. ▶ VERB ③ If someone or something is geared to a particular event or purpose, they are prepared for it.

geek, geeks NOUN (informal) a person who is obsessive about an interest or hobby, especially computers.

geese the plural of **goose**.

geisha, geishas [Said gay-sha] NOUN A geisha is a Japanese woman whose job is to entertain men, for example by dancing and making conversation.

gel, gels, gelling, gelled [Said jel] NOUN ① a smooth, soft, jelly-like substance • shower gel. ▶ VERB ② If a liquid gels, it turns into a gel. ③ If a vague thought or plan gels, it becomes more definite.

gelatine or **gelatin** [Said jel-lat-tin] NOUN a clear tasteless substance, obtained from meat and bones, used to make liquids firm and jelly-like.

gelding, geldings [Said **gel**-ding] NOUN a horse which has been castrated.

gem, gems NOUN ① a jewel or precious stone. ② You can describe something or someone that is extremely good or beautiful as a gem • *a gem of a novel*.

Gemini [Said **jem**-in-nye] NOUN Gemini is the third sign of the zodiac, represented by a pair of twins. People born between May 21st and June 20th are born under this sign.

gemsbok, gemsbok or gemsboks; also spelt **gemsbuck** NOUN In South African English, a gemsbok is an oryx, a type of large antelope with straight horns.

gen NOUN (*informal*) The gen on something is information about it.

gender, genders NOUN ① PSHE The gender of a person or animal is whether they are male or female • *the female gender*. ② MFL the classification of nouns as masculine, feminine and neuter in certain languages.

gene, genes [Said jeen] NOUN
SCIENCE one of the parts of a living cell which controls the physical characteristics of an organism and which are passed on from one generation to the next.

genealogy, genealogies [Said jeen-nee-al-loj-ee] NOUN Genealogy is the study of the history of families, or the history of a particular family.

genera the plural of **genus**.

general, generals ADJECTIVE ① relating to the whole of something or to most things in a group • *your general health*. ② true, suitable or relevant in most situations • *the general truth of science*. ③ including or involving a wide range of different things • *a general hospital*. ④ having complete responsibility over a wide area of work or a large number of people • *the general secretary*. ▶ NOUN ⑤ an army officer of very high rank. ▶ PHRASE ⑥ **In general** means usually. **generally** ADVERB
SIMILAR WORDS: ① overall ② common, universal, widespread

a
b
c
d
e
f
g
h
i
j
k
l
m
n
o
p
q
r
s
t
u
v
w
x
y
z

What is Gender?

When we talk about the gender of a noun, we mean whether it is referred to as *he*, *she* or *it*. There are three genders: **masculine** (things referred to as *he*), **feminine** (things referred to as *she*) and **neuter** (things referred to as *it*).

Masculine nouns refer to male people and animals:

The boy put on his coat. → *boy is* **masculine**

Feminine nouns denote female people and animals:

The girl put on her coat. → *girl is* **feminine**

It is customary to refer to countries and vehicles as if they were feminine:

The ship came into view, her sails swelling in the breeze.

Neuter nouns refer to inanimate objects and abstract ideas:

The kettle will switch itself off. → *kettle is* **neuter**

Common nouns may be either masculine or feminine. Other words in the sentence may tell us if they are male or female:

The doctor parked <u>his</u> car.
The doctor parked <u>her</u> car.

general election, general elections NOUN an election for a new government, which all the people of a country may vote in.

generalise, generalises, generalising, generalised; also spelt **generalize** VERB To generalise means to say that something is true in most cases, ignoring minor details. **generalisation** NOUN

general practitioner, general practitioners NOUN a doctor who works in the community rather than in a hospital.

generate, generates, generating, generated VERB To generate something means to create or produce it • *using wind power to generate electricity*.

generation, generations NOUN all the people of about the same age; also the period of time between one generation and the next, usually considered to be about 25–30 years.

generator, generators NOUN a machine which produces electricity from another form of energy such as wind or water power.

generic ADJECTIVE A generic term is a name that applies to all the members of a group of similar things.

generosity NOUN PSHE the willingness to give money, time or help.

generous ADJECTIVE ① PSHE A generous person is very willing to give money or time. ② Something that is generous is very large • *a generous waist*. **generously** ADVERB SIMILAR WORDS: ① lavish, liberal ② abundant, ample, lavish

genesis, geneses NOUN (formal) The genesis of something is its beginning.

genetically modified ADJECTIVE SCIENCE Genetically modified plants and animals have had one or more genes changed, for example so that they grow larger or resist diseases better.

genetics NOUN SCIENCE Genetics is the science of the way that characteristics are passed on from generation to generation by means of genes. **genetic** ADJECTIVE **genetically** ADVERB

genial ADJECTIVE cheerful, friendly and kind. **genially** ADVERB

genie, genies [Said jee-nee] NOUN a magical being that obeys the wishes of the person who controls it. WORD HISTORY: from Arabic *jinni* meaning 'demon'

genitals PLURAL NOUN The genitals are the reproductive organs. The technical name is **genitalia**. **genital** ADJECTIVE

genius, geniuses NOUN ① a highly intelligent, creative or talented person. ② Genius is great intelligence, creativity or talent • *a poet of genius*.

genocide [Said jen-nos-side] NOUN (formal) Genocide is the systematic murder of all members of a particular race or group.

genome, genomes [Said jee-nome] NOUN SCIENCE all of the genes contained in a single cell of an organism.

genre, genres [Said jahn-ra] NOUN ENGLISH LIBRARY (formal) a particular style in literature or art.

genteel ADJECTIVE very polite and refined.

Gentile, Gentiles [Said jen-tile] NOUN RE a person who is not Jewish.

gentility NOUN Gentility is excessive politeness and refinement.

gentle, gentler, gentlest ADJECTIVE mild and calm; not violent or rough • *a gentle man*. **gently** ADVERB **gentleness** NOUN

gentleman, gentlemen NOUN a man who is polite and well-educated; also a polite way of referring to any man. **gentlemanly** ADJECTIVE

gentry PLURAL NOUN The gentry are wealthy landowners who are not members of the nobility.

genuine [Said jen-yoo-in] ADJECTIVE ① real and not false or pretend • *a genuine smile* • *genuine silver*. ② A genuine person is sincere and honest. **genuinely** ADVERB **genuineness** NOUN

genus, genera [Said jee-nuss] NOUN SCIENCE In biology, a genus is a class of animals or closely related plants. It is smaller than a family and larger than a species.

geo- PREFIX 'Geo-' means 'earth' • *geography* • *geologist*. WORD HISTORY: from Greek *gē* meaning 'earth'

geography NOUN the study of the physical features of the earth, together with the climate, natural resources and population in different parts of the world. **geographic** or **geographical** ADJECTIVE **geographically** ADVERB WORD HISTORY: from Greek *gē* meaning 'earth' and *-graphia* meaning 'writing'

geology NOUN the study of the earth's structure, especially the layers of rock and soil that make up the surface of the earth. **geological** ADJECTIVE **geologist** NOUN

geometric or **geometrical** ADJECTIVE ① consisting of regular lines and shapes, such as squares, triangles and circles • *bold geometric designs*. ② involving geometry.

geometric sequence, geometric sequences NOUN MATHS a sequence of numbers in which each differs from the next by a constant ratio, such as 1, 2, 4, 8, ...

geometry NOUN Geometry is the branch of mathematics that deals with lines, angles, curves and spaces.

Georgian ADJECTIVE HISTORY belonging to or typical of the time from 1714 to 1830, when George I to George IV reigned in Britain.

geranium, geraniums NOUN a garden plant with red, pink or white flowers.

gerbil, gerbils [Said jer-bil] NOUN a small rodent with long back legs, often kept as a pet.

geriatrics [Said jer-ree-at-riks] NOUN Geriatrics is the medical care of elderly people. **geriatric** ADJECTIVE WORD HISTORY: from Greek *gēras* meaning 'old age' and *iatrikos* meaning 'of healing'

germ, germs NOUN ① a very small organism that causes disease. ② (formal) The germ of an idea or plan is the beginning of it.

German, Germans ADJECTIVE ① belonging or relating to Germany. ▶ NOUN ② someone who comes from Germany. ③ German is the main language spoken in Germany and Austria and is also spoken by many people in Switzerland.

Germanic ADJECTIVE ① typical of Germany or the German people. ② The Germanic group of languages includes English, Dutch, German, Danish, Swedish and Norwegian.

German measles NOUN German measles is a contagious disease that gives you a cough, a sore throat and red spots. It is dangerous to unborn babies if their mothers catch it.

germinate, germinates, germinating, germinated VERB ① SCIENCE When a seed germinates, it starts to grow.

② When an idea or plan germinates, it starts to develop. **germination** NOUN

gerrymander, gerrymanders, gerrymandering, gerrymandered VERB To gerrymander is to change political boundaries in an area so that a particular party or politician gets a bigger share of votes in an election.

gestation [Said jes-**tay**-shn] NOUN SCIENCE Gestation is the time during which a foetus is growing inside its mother's womb.

gesticulate, gesticulates, gesticulating, gesticulated [Said jes-**stik**-yoo-late] VERB If you gesticulate, you move your hands and arms around while you are talking. **gesticulation** NOUN

gesture, gestures, gesturing, gestured NOUN ① a movement of your hands or head that conveys a message or feeling. ② an action symbolising something • a gesture of support. ▶ VERB ③ If you gesture, you move your hands or head in order to communicate a message or feeling.

get, gets, getting, got VERB ① Get often means the same as become • People draw the curtains once it gets dark. ② If you get into a particular situation, you put yourself in that situation • We are going to get into a hopeless muddle. ③ If you get something done, you do it or someone does it for you • You can get your homework done in time. ④ If you get somewhere, you go there • I must get home. ⑤ If you get something, you fetch it or are given it • I'll get us all a cup of coffee • I got your message. ⑥ If you get a joke or get the point of something, you understand it. ⑦ If you get a train, bus or plane, you travel on it • You can get a bus. **get across** VERB If you get an idea across, you make people understand it. **get at** VERB ① If someone is getting at you, they are criticising you in an unkind way. ② If you ask someone what they are getting at, you are asking them to explain what they mean. **get away with** VERB If you get away with something dishonest, you are not found out or punished for doing it. **get by** VERB If you get by, you have just enough money to live on. **get on** VERB ① If two people get on well together, they like each other's company. ② If you get on with a task, you do it. **get over with** VERB If you want to get something unpleasant over with, you want it to be finished quickly. **get through** VERB ① If you get through to someone, you make them understand what you are saying. ② If you get through to someone on the telephone, you succeed in talking to them.

SIMILAR WORDS: ① become, grow ⑤ acquire, obtain, procure

getaway, getaways NOUN an escape made by criminals.

Gethsemane [Said geth-**sem**-an-i] NOUN RE the garden in Jerusalem where Christ was betrayed by Judas Iscariot on the night before his Crucifixion.

get-together, get-togethers NOUN (informal) an informal meeting or party.

geyser, geysers [Said gee-zer] NOUN GEOGRAPHY a spring through which hot water and steam gush up in spurts. WORD HISTORY: from Old Norse geysa meaning 'to gush'

Ghanaian, Ghanaians [Said gah-**nay**-an] ADJECTIVE ① belonging or relating to Ghana. ▶ NOUN ② someone who comes from Ghana.

ghastly, ghastlier, ghastliest ADJECTIVE extremely horrible and unpleasant • *a ghastly crime* • *ghastly food*.

gherkin, gherkins NOUN a small pickled cucumber.

ghetto, ghettoes or ghettos NOUN a part of a city where many poor people of a particular ethnic group live. WORD HISTORY: from Italian *borghetto* meaning 'settlement outside the city walls'

ghost, ghosts NOUN the spirit of a dead person, believed to haunt people or places. SIMILAR WORDS: phantom, spectre, spirit

ghoulish [Said *gool-ish*] ADJECTIVE very interested in unpleasant things such as death and murder.

giant, giants NOUN ① a huge person in a myth or legend. ▶ ADJECTIVE ② much larger than other similar things • *giant prawns* • *a giant wave*.

gibberish [Said *jib-ir-ish*] NOUN Gibberish is speech that makes no sense at all.

gibbon, gibbons NOUN an ape with very long arms.

gibe, gibes; also spelt **jibe** NOUN an insulting remark.

gidday INTERJECTION In Australia and New Zealand, 'gidday' is a term for 'hello'.

giddy, giddier, giddiest ADJECTIVE If you feel giddy, you feel unsteady on your feet usually because you are ill. **giddily** ADVERB

gift, gifts NOUN ① a present. ② a natural skill or ability • *a gift for comedy*.

gifted ADJECTIVE having a special ability • *gifted tennis players*.

gig, gigs NOUN a rock or jazz concert.

gigabyte, gigabytes NOUN ICT a unit of computer memory size, equal to 1024 megabytes.

gigantic ADJECTIVE extremely large.

giggle, giggles, giggling, giggled VERB ① To giggle means to laugh in a silly or nervous way. ▶ NOUN ② a silly or nervous laugh. **giggly** ADJECTIVE

gilded ADJECTIVE Something which is gilded is covered with a thin layer of gold.

gill, gills NOUN ① [Said *gil*] The gills of a fish are the organs on its sides which it uses for breathing. ② [Said *jil*] a unit of liquid volume equal to one quarter of a pint or about 0.142 litres.

gilt, gilts NOUN ① a thin layer of gold. ▶ ADJECTIVE ② covered with a thin layer of gold • *a gilt writing-table*.

SPELLING TIP
Do not confuse the spellings of *gilt* and *guilt*: *The lid of the jewellery box is gilt; I still feel guilt for the way I behaved towards him.*

gimmick, gimmicks NOUN a device that is not really necessary but is used to attract interest • *All pop stars need a good gimmick*. **gimmicky** ADJECTIVE

gin NOUN Gin is a strong, colourless alcoholic drink made from grain and juniper berries.

ginger NOUN ① Ginger is a plant root with a hot, spicy flavour, used in cooking. ▶ ADJECTIVE ② bright orange or red • *ginger hair*.

gingerbread NOUN Gingerbread is a sweet, ginger-flavoured cake.

gingerly ADVERB If you move gingerly, you move cautiously • *They walked gingerly down the stairs*.

gingham NOUN Gingham is checked cotton cloth. WORD HISTORY: from Malay *ginggang* meaning 'striped cloth'

Gipsy another spelling of **Gypsy**.

a
b
c
d
e
f
g
h
i
j
k
l
m
n
o
p
q
r
s
t
u
v
w
x
y
z

giraffe, giraffes NOUN a tall, four-legged African mammal with a very long neck.

girder, girders NOUN a large metal beam used in the construction of a bridge or a building.

girdle, girdles NOUN a woman's corset.

girl, girls NOUN a female child. **girlhood** NOUN **girlish** ADJECTIVE

girlfriend, girlfriends NOUN Someone's girlfriend is the woman or girl with whom they are having a romantic relationship.

girth NOUN The girth of something is the measurement round it.

gist [Said **jist**] NOUN the general meaning or most important points in a piece of writing or speech.

give, gives, giving, gave, given VERB ① If you give someone something, you hand it to them or provide it for them • I gave her a card • George gave me my job. ② 'Give' is also used to express physical actions and speech • He gave a fierce smile • Rosa gave a lovely performance. ③ If you give a party or a meal, you are the host at it. ④ If something gives, it collapses under pressure. ▶ NOUN ⑤ If material has give, it will bend or stretch when pulled or put under pressure. ▶ PHRASE ⑥ You use **give or take** to indicate that an amount you are mentioning is not exact • About two years, give or take a month or so. ⑦ If something **gives way** to something else, it is replaced by it. ⑧ If something **gives way**, it collapses. **give in** VERB If you give in, you admit that you are defeated. **give out** VERB If something gives out, it stops working • the electricity gave out. **give up** VERB ① If you give something up, you stop doing it • I can't give up my job. ② If you give up,

you admit that you cannot do something. ③ If you give someone up, you let the police know where they are hiding.
SIMILAR WORDS: ① grant, present, provide

given ① the past participle of **give**. ▶ ADJECTIVE ② fixed or specified • My style can change at any given moment.

glacé [Said **glass**-say] ADJECTIVE Glacé fruits are fruits soaked and coated with sugar • glacé cherries.

glaciation [Said glay-see-ay-shn] NOUN GEOGRAPHY the condition of being covered with sheet ice.

glacier, glaciers [Said **glass**-yer] NOUN GEOGRAPHY a huge frozen river of slow-moving ice.

glad, gladder, gladdest ADJECTIVE happy and pleased • They'll be glad to get away from it all. **gladly** ADVERB **gladness** NOUN

glade, glades NOUN a grassy space in a forest.

gladiator, gladiators NOUN HISTORY In ancient Rome, gladiators were slaves trained to fight in arenas to provide entertainment.
WORD HISTORY: from Latin gladius meaning 'sword'

gladiolus, gladioli NOUN a garden plant with spikes of brightly coloured flowers on a long stem.

glamour NOUN The glamour of a fashionable or attractive person or place is the charm and excitement that they have • the glamour of Paris. **glamorous** ADJECTIVE

glance, glances, glancing, glanced VERB ① If you glance at something, you look at it quickly. ② If one object glances off another, it hits it at an angle and bounces away in another direction. ▶ NOUN ③ a quick look.

gland, glands NOUN an organ in your body, such as the thyroid gland and the sweat glands, which either produce chemical substances for your body to use, or which help to get rid of waste products from your body. **glandular** ADJECTIVE

glare, glares, glaring, glared VERB ① If you glare at someone, you look at them angrily. ▶ NOUN ② a hard, angry look. ③ Glare is extremely bright light.

glass, glasses NOUN ① Glass is a hard, transparent substance that is easily broken, used to make windows and bottles. ② a container for drinking out of, made from glass.

glasses PLURAL NOUN Glasses are two lenses in a frame, which some people wear over their eyes to improve their eyesight.

glassy, glassier, glassiest ADJECTIVE ① smooth and shiny like glass • *glassy water*. ② A glassy look shows no feeling or expression.

glaze, glazes, glazing, glazed NOUN ① A glaze on pottery or on food is a smooth shiny surface. ▶ VERB ② To glaze pottery or food means to cover it with a glaze. ③ To glaze a window means to fit a sheet of glass into a window frame. **glaze over** VERB If your eyes glaze over, they lose all expression, usually because you are bored.

glazed ADJECTIVE Someone who has a glazed expression looks bored.

gleam, gleams, gleaming, gleamed VERB ① If something gleams, it shines and reflects light. ▶ NOUN ② a pale shining light.

glean, gleans, gleaning, gleaned VERB To glean information means to collect it from various sources.

glee NOUN (*old-fashioned*) Glee is joy and delight. **gleeful** ADJECTIVE **gleefully** ADVERB

glen, glens NOUN a deep, narrow valley, especially in Scotland or Ireland.

glide, glides, gliding, glided VERB ① To glide means to move smoothly • *cygnets gliding up the stream*. ② When birds or aeroplanes glide, they float on air currents.

glider, gliders NOUN an aeroplane without an engine, which flies by floating on air currents.

glimmer, glimmers, glimmering, glimmered NOUN ① a faint, unsteady light. ② A glimmer of a feeling or quality is a faint sign of it • *a glimmer of intelligence*.

glimpse, glimpses, glimpsing, glimpsed NOUN ① a brief sight of something • *They caught a glimpse of their hero*. ▶ VERB ② If you glimpse something, you see it very briefly.

glint, glints, glinting, glinted VERB ① If something glints, it reflects quick flashes of light. ▶ NOUN ② a quick flash of light. ③ A glint in someone's eye is a brightness expressing some emotion • *A glint of mischief in her blue-grey eyes*.

glisten, glistens, glistening, glistened [*Said gliss-sn*] VERB If something glistens, it shines or sparkles.

glitch, glitches NOUN (*informal*) a problem which stops something from working properly.

glitter, glitters, glittering, glittered VERB ① If something glitters, it shines in a sparkling way • *a glittering crown*. ▶ NOUN ② Glitter is sparkling light.

gloat, gloats, gloating, gloated VERB If you gloat, you cruelly show your pleasure about your own success or someone else's failure • *Their rivals were gloating over their triumph*.

global ADJECTIVE concerning the whole world • *a global tour*.

a
b
c
d
e
f
g
h
i
j
k
l
m
n
o
p
q
r
s
t
u
v
w
x
y
z

globalisation; also spelt **globalization** NOUN ①the process by which a company expands so that it can do business internationally. ②the process by which cultures throughout the world become more and more similar for a variety of reasons including increased global business and better international communications.

global warming NOUN GEOGRAPHY SCIENCE an increase in the world's overall temperature believed to be caused by the greenhouse effect.

globe, globes NOUN ①a ball-shaped object, especially one with a map of the earth on it. ② GEOGRAPHY You can refer to the world as the globe. ③In South African, Australian and New Zealand English, a globe is an electric light bulb.

gloom NOUN ①Gloom is darkness or dimness. ②Gloom is also a feeling of unhappiness or despair.

gloomy, gloomier, gloomiest ADJECTIVE ①dark and depressing. ②feeling very sad. **gloomily** ADVERB

glorify, glorifies, glorifying, glorified VERB If you glorify someone or something, you make them seem better than they really are • *songs glorifying war*. **glorification** NOUN

glorious ADJECTIVE ①beautiful and impressive to look at • *glorious beaches*. ②very pleasant and giving a feeling of happiness • *glorious sunshine*. ③involving great fame and success • *a glorious career*. **gloriously** ADVERB

glory, glories, glorying, gloried NOUN ①Glory is fame and admiration for an achievement. ②something considered splendid or admirable • *the true glories of the Alps*. ▶VERB ③If you glory in something, you take great delight in it.

glory box, glory boxes NOUN (*old-fashioned*) In Australian and New Zealand English, a chest in which a young woman stores household goods and linen for her marriage.

gloss, glosses, glossing, glossed NOUN ①Gloss is a bright shine on a surface. ②Gloss is also an attractive appearance which may hide less attractive qualities • *to put a positive gloss on the events*.

glossary, glossaries NOUN LIBRARY a list of explanations of specialist words, usually found at the back of a book.

glossy, glossier, glossiest ADJECTIVE smooth and shiny • *glossy lipstick* • *glossy paper*.
SIMILAR WORDS: lustrous, shiny

glove, gloves NOUN Gloves are coverings which you wear over your hands for warmth or protection.

glow, glows, glowing, glowed NOUN ①a dull, steady light. ②a strong feeling of pleasure or happiness. ▶VERB ③If something glows, it shines with a dull, steady light • *A light glowed behind the curtains*. ④If you are glowing, you look very happy or healthy.

glower, glowers, glowering, glowered [*Rhymes with shower*] VERB If you glower, you stare angrily.
SIMILAR WORDS: glare, scowl

glowing ADJECTIVE A glowing description praises someone or something very highly • *a glowing character reference*.

glucose NOUN SCIENCE Glucose is a type of sugar found in plants and that animals and people make in their bodies from food to provide energy.

glue, glues, gluing or glueing, glued NOUN ①a substance used for sticking things together. ▶VERB ②If you glue one object to another, you stick them together using glue.

glum, glummer, glummest
ADJECTIVE miserable and depressed.
glumly ADVERB

glut, gluts NOUN a greater quantity of
things than is needed.

gluten [Said gloo-ten] NOUN a sticky
protein found in cereal grains, such
as wheat.

glutton, gluttons NOUN ① a person
who eats too much. ② If you are a
glutton for something, such as
punishment or hard work, you seem
very eager for it. **gluttony** NOUN

glycogen [Said gly-koh-jen] NOUN
SCIENCE Glycogen is a type of
carbohydrate found in the cells of
humans and animals, which can
easily be converted to glucose.

GM an abbreviation for 'genetically
modified'.

gnarled [Said narld] ADJECTIVE old,
twisted and rough • gnarled fingers.

gnat, gnats [Said nat] NOUN a tiny
flying insect that bites.

gnaw, gnaws, gnawing, gnawed
[Said naw] VERB ① To gnaw
something means to bite at it
repeatedly. ② If a feeling gnaws at
you, it keeps worrying you • a
question gnawed at him.

gnome, gnomes [Said nome] NOUN a
tiny old man in fairy stories.

gnu, gnus [Said noo] NOUN a large
African antelope.

go, goes, going, went, gone VERB
① If you go somewhere, you move or
travel there. ② You can use 'go' to
mean become • She felt she was going
mad. ③ You can use 'go' to describe
the state that someone or something
is in • Our arrival went unnoticed. ④ If
something goes well, it is successful.
If it goes badly, it is unsuccessful. ⑤ If
you are going to do something, you
will do it. ⑥ If a machine or clock
goes, it works and is not broken.

⑦ You use 'go' before giving the sound
something makes or before quoting
a song or saying • The bell goes
ding-dong. ⑧ If something goes on
something or to someone, it is
allotted to them. ⑨ If one thing goes
with another, they are appropriate
together. ⑩ If one number goes into
another, it can be divided into it.
▶ NOUN ⑪ an attempt at doing
something. ▶ PHRASE ⑫ If someone
is always **on the go**, they are always
busy and active. ⑬ **To go** means
remaining • I've got one more year of my
course to go. **go back on** VERB If you
go back on a promise or agreement,
you do not do what you promised or
agreed. **go down** VERB ① If
something goes down well, people
like it. If it goes down badly, they do
not like it. ② If you go down with an
illness, you catch it. **go for** VERB If
someone goes for you, they attack
you. **go in** VERB If you go in for
something, you decide to do it as
your job. **go off** VERB ① If you go off
someone or something, you stop
liking them. ② If a bomb goes off, it
explodes. **go on** VERB ① If you go on
doing something, you continue to do
it. ② If you go on about something,
you keep talking about it in a rather
boring way. ③ Something that is
going on is happening. **go out** VERB
If you go out with someone, you have
a romantic relationship with them.
go over VERB If you go over
something, you think about it or
discuss it carefully. **go through**
VERB ① If you go through an
unpleasant event, you experience it.
② If a law or agreement goes
through, it is approved and becomes
official. ③ If you go through with
something, you do it even though it
is unpleasant.

goad, goads, goading, goaded VERB
If you goad someone, you encourage

them to do something by making them angry or excited • *He had goaded the man into losing his temper.*

go-ahead NOUN If someone gives you the go-ahead for something, they give you permission to do it.

goal, goals NOUN ① the space, in games like football or hockey, into which the players try to get the ball in order to score a point. ② an instance of this. ③ Your goal is something that you hope to achieve.

goalkeeper, goalkeepers NOUN the player, in games like soccer or hockey, who stands in the goal and tries to stop the other team from scoring.

goanna, goannas NOUN a large Australian lizard.

goat, goats NOUN an animal, like a sheep, with coarse hair, a beard and horns.

go-away bird, go-away birds NOUN In South Africa, a go-away bird is a grey lourie, a type of bird which lives in open grassland.

gob, gobs NOUN (*informal*) Your gob is your mouth.

gobble, gobbles, gobbling, gobbled VERB ① If you gobble food, you eat it very quickly. ② When a turkey gobbles, it makes a loud gurgling sound.

SIMILAR WORDS: ① devour, guzzle, wolf

gobbledygook; also spelt **gobbledegook** NOUN Gobbledygook is language that is impossible to understand because it is so formal or complicated.

goblet, goblets NOUN a glass with a long stem.

goblin, goblins NOUN an ugly, mischievous creature in fairy stories.

god, gods PROPER NOUN ① RE The name God is given to the being who is worshipped by Christians, Jews and Muslims as the creator and ruler of the world. ▶ NOUN ② any of the beings that are believed in many religions to have power over an aspect of life or a part of the world • *Mars, the Roman god of war.* ③ If someone is your god, you admire them very much. ④ (*in plural*) In a theatre, the gods are the highest seats farthest from the stage.

godchild, godchildren NOUN If you are someone's godchild, they agreed to be responsible for your religious upbringing when you were baptised in a Christian Church. **goddaughter** NOUN **godson** NOUN

goddess, goddesses NOUN a female god.

godparent, godparents NOUN A person's godparent is someone who agrees to be responsible for their religious upbringing when they are baptised in a Christian Church. **godfather** NOUN **godmother** NOUN

godsend, godsends NOUN something that comes unexpectedly and helps you very much.

goggles PLURAL NOUN Goggles are special glasses that fit closely round your eyes to protect them.

going NOUN The going is the conditions that affect your ability to do something • *He found the going very slow indeed.*

gold NOUN ① SCIENCE Gold is a valuable, yellow-coloured metallic element. It is used for making jewellery and as an international currency. Its atomic number is 79 and its symbol is Au. ② 'Gold' is also used to mean things that are made of gold. ▶ ADJECTIVE ③ bright yellow.

golden ADJECTIVE ① gold in colour • *golden syrup.* ② made of gold

• *a golden chain*. ③ excellent or ideal
• *a golden hero*.

golden rule, golden rules NOUN a very important rule to remember in order to be able to do something successfully.

golden wedding, golden weddings NOUN A married couple's golden wedding is their 50th wedding anniversary.

goldfish, goldfish NOUN a small orange-coloured fish, often kept in ponds or bowls.

goldsmith, goldsmiths NOUN a person whose job is making jewellery out of gold.

golf NOUN Golf is a game in which players use special clubs to hit a small ball into holes that are spread out over a large area of grassy land. **golfer** NOUN

golf course, golf courses NOUN an area of grassy land where people play golf.

gondola, gondolas [Said gon-dol-la] NOUN a long narrow boat used in Venice, which is propelled with a long pole.

gone the past participle of **go**.

gong, gongs NOUN a flat, circular piece of metal that is hit with a hammer to make a loud sound, often as a signal for something.

good, better, best; goods ADJECTIVE ① pleasant, acceptable or satisfactory • *good news* • *a good film*. ② skilful or successful • *good at art*. ③ kind, thoughtful and loving • *She was grateful to her parents for being so good to her*. ④ well-behaved • *Have the children been good?* ⑤ used to emphasise something • *a good few million pounds*. ▶ NOUN ⑥ Good is moral and spiritual justice and virtue • *the forces of good and evil*. ⑦ Good also refers to anything that is

desirable or beneficial as opposed to harmful • *The break has done me good*. ⑧ (*in plural*) Goods are objects that people own or that are sold in shops • *leather goods*. ▶ PHRASE ⑨ **For good** means for ever. ⑩ **As good as** means almost • *The election is as good as decided*.

GRAMMAR TIP
Good is an adjective, and should not be used as an adverb. You should say that *a person did well* not *did good*.

---

goodbye INTERJECTION You say goodbye when you are leaving someone or ending a telephone conversation.

Good Friday NOUN RE Good Friday is the Friday before Easter, when Christians remember the crucifixion of Christ.

good-natured ADJECTIVE friendly, pleasant and even-tempered.

goodness NOUN ① Goodness is the quality of being kind. ▶ INTERJECTION ② People say 'Goodness!' or 'My goodness!' when they are surprised.

goodwill NOUN Goodwill is kindness and helpfulness • *Messages of goodwill were exchanged*.

goody, goodies NOUN (*informal*) ① Goodies are enjoyable things, often food. ② You can call a hero in a film or book a goody.

google, googles, googling, googled VERB ICT If you google a person or thing, you search the internet for information about them.

goose, geese NOUN a fairly large bird with webbed feet and a long neck.

gooseberry, gooseberries NOUN a round, green berry that grows on a bush and has a sharp taste.

gore, gores, goring, gored VERB ① If an animal gores someone, it wounds them badly with its horns or tusks.

▶ **NOUN** ② Gore is clotted blood from a wound.

gorge, gorges, gorging, gorged **NOUN** ① GEOGRAPHY a deep, narrow valley. ▶ **VERB** ② If you gorge yourself, you eat a lot of food greedily.

gorgeous **ADJECTIVE** extremely pleasant or attractive • *a gorgeous view.*

gorilla, gorillas **NOUN** a very large, strong ape with very dark fur.
WORD HISTORY: from *Gorillai*, the Greek name for an African tribe with hairy bodies

gorse **NOUN** Gorse is a dark green wild shrub that has sharp prickles and small yellow flowers.

gory, gorier, goriest **ADJECTIVE** Gory situations involve people being injured in horrible ways.

gosling, goslings [*Said goz-ling*] **NOUN** a young goose.

gospel, gospels **NOUN** ① RE The Gospels are the four books in the New Testament which describe the life and teachings of Jesus Christ. ② a set of ideas that someone strongly believes in • *The chef wants to spread the gospel of good food.* ▶ **ADJECTIVE** ③ Gospel music is a style of religious music popular among Black Christians in the United States.

gossip, gossips, gossiping, gossiped **NOUN** ① Gossip is informal conversation, often concerning people's private affairs. ② Someone who is a gossip enjoys talking about other people's private affairs. ▶ **VERB** ③ If you gossip, you talk informally with someone, especially about other people.

got ① Got is the past tense and past participle of **get**. ② You can use 'have got' instead of the more formal 'have' when talking about possessing

things • *The director has got a map.* ③ You can use 'have got to' instead of the more formal 'have to' when talking about something that must be done • *He has got to win.*

Gothic **ADJECTIVE** ① ART Gothic buildings have tall pillars, high vaulted ceilings, and pointed arches. ② ART Gothic printing or writing has letters that are very ornate.

gouge, gouges, gouging, gouged [*Said gowj*] **VERB** ① If you gouge a hole in something, you make a hole in it with a pointed object. ② If you gouge something out, you force it out of position with your fingers or a sharp tool.

goulash [*Said goo-lash*] **NOUN** Goulash is a type of rich meat stew, originally from Hungary.

gourd, gourds [*Said goord*] **NOUN** a large fruit with a hard outside.

gourmet, gourmets [*Said goor-may*] **NOUN** a person who enjoys good food and drink and knows a lot about it.

gout **NOUN** Gout is a disease which causes someone's joints to swell painfully, especially in their toes.

govern, governs, governing, governed **VERB** ① To govern a country means to control it. ② Something that governs a situation influences it • *Our thinking is as much governed by habit as by behaviour.*

governance **NOUN** ① Governance is the same as government or authority. ② Governance of an area or organisation is also the way in which it is governed • *The new minister promised good governance.*

governess, governesses **NOUN** a woman who is employed to teach the children in a family and who lives with the family.

government, governments **NOUN**

① CITIZENSHIP The government is the group of people who govern a country. ② CITIZENSHIP Government is the control and organisation of a country. **governmental** ADJECTIVE

governor, governors NOUN ① a person who controls and organises a state or an institution. ② In Australia, the Governor is the representative of the King or Queen in a State.

governor-general, governors-general NOUN the chief representative of the King or Queen in Australia, New Zealand and other Commonwealth countries.

gown, gowns NOUN ① a long, formal dress. ② a long, dark cloak worn by people such as judges and lawyers.

GP an abbreviation for **general practitioner**.

grab, grabs, grabbing, grabbed VERB ① If you grab something, you take it or pick it up roughly. ② If you grab an opportunity, you take advantage of it eagerly. ③ (informal) If an idea grabs you, it excites you. ▶ NOUN ④ A grab at an object is an attempt to grab it.
SIMILAR WORDS: ① grasp, seize, snatch ② grasp, seize, snatch

grace, graces, gracing, graced NOUN ① Grace is an elegant way of moving. ② Grace is also a pleasant, kind way of behaving. ③ Grace is also a short prayer of thanks said before a meal. ④ Dukes and archbishops are addressed as 'Your Grace' and referred to as 'His Grace'. ▶ VERB ⑤ Something that graces a place makes it more attractive. ⑥ If someone important graces an event, they kindly agree to be present at it.
graceful ADJECTIVE **gracefully** ADVERB
SIMILAR WORDS: ① elegance, poise

gracious ADJECTIVE ① kind, polite and pleasant. ▶ INTERJECTION ② 'Good gracious' is an exclamation of surprise. **graciously** ADVERB

grade, grades, grading, graded VERB ① To grade things means to arrange them according to quality. ▶ NOUN ② The grade of something is its quality. ③ the mark that you get for an exam or piece of written work. ④ Your grade in a company or organisation is your level of importance or your rank.

gradient, gradients NOUN a slope or the steepness of a slope.

gradual ADJECTIVE happening or changing slowly over a long period of time. **gradually** ADVERB

graduate, graduates, graduating, graduated NOUN [Said **grad**-yoo-it] ① a person who has completed a first degree at a university or college. ▶ VERB [Said **grad**-yoo-ate] ② When students graduate, they complete a first degree at a university or college. ③ To graduate from one thing to another means to progress gradually towards the second thing.
graduation NOUN

graffiti [Said graf-**fee**-tee] NOUN Graffiti is slogans or drawings scribbled on walls.
WORD HISTORY: from Italian graffiare meaning 'to scratch a surface'

GRAMMAR TIP
Although graffiti is a plural in Italian, the language it comes from, in English it can be used as a singular noun or a plural noun.

graft, grafts, grafting, grafted NOUN ① a piece of living tissue which is used to replace by surgery a damaged or unhealthy part of a person's body. ② (informal) Graft is hard work. ▶ VERB ③ To graft one thing to another means to attach it.

grain, grains NOUN ① a cereal plant, such as wheat, that is grown as a crop and used for food. ② Grains are seeds of a cereal plant. ③ A grain of sand or salt is a tiny particle of it. ④ The grain of a piece of wood is the pattern of lines made by the fibres in it. ▶ PHRASE ⑤ If something **goes against the grain**, you find it difficult to accept because it is against your principles.

SIMILAR WORDS: ③ bit, granule, particle

gram, grams; also spelt **gramme** NOUN a unit of weight equal to one thousandth of a kilogram.

grammar NOUN ENGLISH MFL Grammar is the rules of a language relating to the ways you can combine words to form sentences.

grammar school, grammar schools NOUN ① a secondary school for pupils of high academic ability. ② In Australia, a grammar school is a private school, usually one controlled by a church.

grammatical ADJECTIVE ① relating to grammar • *grammatical knowledge*. ② following the rules of grammar correctly • *grammatical sentences*. **grammatically** ADVERB

gran, grans NOUN (*informal*) Your gran is your grandmother.

granary, granaries NOUN ① a building for storing grain. ▶ ADJECTIVE ② (*trademark*) Granary bread contains whole grains of wheat.

grand, grander, grandest ADJECTIVE ① magnificent in appearance and size • *a grand house*. ② very important • *the grand scheme of your life*. ③ (*informal*) very pleasant or enjoyable • *It was a grand day*. ④ A grand total is the final complete

amount. ▶ NOUN ⑤ (*informal*) a thousand pounds or dollars. **grandly** ADVERB

SIMILAR WORDS: ① impressive, magnificent, splendid

grandad, grandads NOUN (*informal*) Your grandad is your grandfather.

grandchild, grandchildren NOUN Someone's grandchildren are the children of their son or daughter.

granddaughter, granddaughters NOUN Someone's granddaughter is the daughter of their son or daughter.

grandeur [*Said* grand-yer] NOUN Grandeur is great beauty and magnificence.

grandfather, grandfathers NOUN Your grandfather is your father's father or your mother's father.

grandfather clock, grandfather clocks NOUN a clock in a tall wooden case that stands on the floor.

grandiose [*Said* gran-dee-ose] ADJECTIVE intended to be very impressive, but seeming ridiculous • *a grandiose gesture of love*.

grandma, grandmas NOUN (*informal*) Your grandma is your grandmother.

grandmother, grandmothers NOUN Your grandmother is your father's mother or your mother's mother.

grandparent, grandparents NOUN Your grandparents are your parents' parents.

grand piano, grand pianos NOUN a large flat piano with horizontal strings.

grandson, grandsons NOUN Someone's grandson is the son of their son or daughter.

grandstand, grandstands NOUN a structure with a roof and seats for spectators at a sports ground.

granite [Said gran-nit] NOUN Granite is a very hard rock used in building.

granny, grannies NOUN (informal) Your granny is your grandmother.

grant, grants, granting, granted NOUN ① an amount of money that an official body gives to someone for a particular purpose • *a grant to carry out repairs.* ▸ VERB ② If you grant something to someone, you allow them to have it. ③ If you grant that something is true, you admit that it is true. ▸ PHRASE ④ If you **take something for granted**, you believe it without thinking about it. If you **take someone for granted**, you benefit from them without showing that you are grateful.

granule, granules NOUN a very small piece of something • *granules of salt.*

grape, grapes NOUN a small green or purple fruit, eaten raw or used to make wine.

grapefruit, grapefruit or grapefruits NOUN a large, round, yellow citrus fruit.

grapevine, grapevines NOUN ① a climbing plant which grapes grow on. ▸ PHRASE ② If you hear some news **on the grapevine**, it has been passed on from person to person, usually unofficially or secretly.

graph, graphs NOUN MATHS a diagram which shows how sets of numbers or measurements are related.

-graph SUFFIX '-graph' means a writer or recorder of some sort or something made by writing, drawing or recording • *telegraph* • *autograph.*

graphic ADJECTIVE ① A graphic description is very detailed and lifelike. ② relating to drawing or painting. **graphically** ADVERB

graphics PLURAL NOUN ICT Graphics are drawings and pictures composed of simple lines and strong colours • *computerised graphics.*

graphite NOUN a black form of carbon that is used in pencil leads. WORD HISTORY: from Greek *graphein* meaning 'to write'

grapple, grapples, grappling, grappled VERB ① If you grapple with someone, you struggle with them while fighting. ② If you grapple with a problem, you try hard to solve it.

grasp, grasps, grasping, grasped VERB ① If you grasp something, you hold it firmly. ② If you grasp an idea, you understand it. ▸ NOUN ③ a firm hold. ④ Your grasp of something is your understanding of it.

grass, grasses NOUN Grass is the common green plant that grows on lawns and in parks. **grassy** ADJECTIVE

grasshopper, grasshoppers NOUN an insect with long back legs which it uses for jumping and making a high-pitched sound.

grate, grates, grating, grated NOUN ① a framework of metal bars in a fireplace. ▸ VERB ② To grate food means to shred it into small pieces by rubbing it against a metal tool. ③ When something grates on something else, it rubs against it making a harsh sound. ④ If something grates on you, it irritates you.

SPELLING TIP
Do not confuse the spellings of *grate* and *great*: *Grate 250g of cheddar; the great Amazon River.*

grateful ADJECTIVE If you are grateful for something, you are glad you have it and want to thank the person who gave it to you. **gratefully** ADVERB SIMILAR WORDS: appreciative, thankful

a
b
c
d
e
f
g
h
i
j
k
l
m
n
o
p
q
r
s
t
u
v
w
x
y
z

grater, graters NOUN a small metal tool used for grating food.

gratify, gratifies, gratifying, gratified VERB ① If you are gratified by something, you are pleased by it. ② If you gratify a wish or feeling, you satisfy it.

grating, gratings NOUN ① a metal frame with bars across it fastened over a hole in a wall or in the ground. ▶ ADJECTIVE ② A grating sound is harsh and unpleasant • *grating melodies*.

gratis [Said grah-tis] ADVERB or ADJECTIVE free • *food and drink supplied gratis*.

gratitude NOUN Gratitude is the feeling of being grateful.
SIMILAR WORDS: appreciation, thankfulness

gratuitous [Said grat-*yoo*-it-tuss] ADJECTIVE unnecessary • *a gratuitous attack*. **gratuitously** ADVERB

grave¹, graves; graver, gravest [Rhymes with **save**] NOUN ① a place where a corpse is buried. ▶ ADJECTIVE ② (formal) very serious • *grave danger*.

grave² [Said grahv] ADJECTIVE MFL In French and some other languages, a grave accent is a line sloping downwards from left to right placed over a vowel to indicate a change in pronunciation, as in the word *lièvre* (a hare).

gravel NOUN Gravel is small stones used for making roads and paths.

gravestone, gravestones NOUN a large stone placed over someone's grave, with their name on it.

graveyard, graveyards NOUN an area of land where corpses are buried.

gravitate, gravitates, gravitating, gravitated VERB When people gravitate towards something, they go towards it because they are attracted by it.

gravitation NOUN SCIENCE Gravitation is the force which causes objects to be attracted to each other. **gravitational** ADJECTIVE

gravity NOUN ① SCIENCE Gravity is the force that makes things fall when you drop them. ② (formal) The gravity of a situation is its seriousness.

gravy NOUN Gravy is a brown sauce made from meat juices.

graze, grazes, grazing, grazed VERB ① When animals graze, they eat grass. ② If something grazes a part of your body, it scrapes against it, injuring you slightly. ▶ NOUN ③ a slight injury caused by something scraping against your skin.

grease, greases, greasing, greased NOUN ① Grease is an oily substance used for lubricating machines. ② Grease is also melted animal fat, used in cooking. ③ Grease is also an oily substance produced by your skin and found in your hair. ▶ VERB ④ If you grease something, you lubricate it with grease. **greasy** ADJECTIVE

great, greater, greatest ADJECTIVE ① very large • *a great sea* • *great efforts*. ② very important • *a great artist*. ③ (informal) very good • *Paul had a great time*. **greatly** ADVERB **greatness** NOUN

SPELLING TIP
Do not confuse the spellings of *great* and *grate*: *the great Amazon River; Grate 250g of cheddar.*

Great Britain NOUN Great Britain is the largest of the British Isles, consisting of England, Scotland and Wales.

Great Dane, Great Danes NOUN a very large dog with short hair.

great-grandfather, great-grandfathers NOUN Your great-grandfather is your father's or mother's grandfather.

great-grandmother, great-grandmothers NOUN Your great-grandmother is your father's or mother's grandmother.

greed NOUN Greed is a desire for more of something than you really need.

greedy, greedier, greediest ADJECTIVE wanting more of something than you really need. **greedily** ADVERB **greediness** NOUN

SIMILAR WORDS: grasping, insatiable, voracious

Greek, Greeks ADJECTIVE ① belonging or relating to Greece. ▶NOUN ② someone who comes from Greece. ③ Greek is the main language spoken in Greece.

green, greener, greenest; greens ADJECTIVE or NOUN ① Green is a colour between yellow and blue on the spectrum. ▶NOUN ② an area of grass in the middle of a village. ③ A putting green or bowling green is a grassy area on which putting or bowls is played. ④ an area of smooth short grass around each hole on a golf course. ⑤ (in plural) Greens are green vegetables. ▶ADJECTIVE ⑥ 'Green' is used to describe political movements which are concerned with environmental issues. ⑦ (informal) Someone who is green is young and inexperienced.

green belt, green belts NOUN GEOGRAPHY The green belt is the area of countryside round a city where people are not allowed to build houses and factories.

greenery NOUN Greenery is a lot of trees, bushes or other green plants together in one place.

greenfly, greenfly NOUN Greenfly are small green insects that damage plants.

greengrocer, greengrocers NOUN a shopkeeper who sells vegetables and fruit.

greenhouse, greenhouses NOUN a glass building in which people grow plants that need to be kept warm.

greenhouse effect NOUN GEOGRAPHY SCIENCE the gradual rise in temperature in the earth's atmosphere due to heat being absorbed from the sun and being trapped by gases such as carbon dioxide in the air around the earth.

green paper, green papers NOUN In Britain, Australia and New Zealand, a green paper is a report published by the government containing proposals to be discussed before decisions are made about them.

greenstone NOUN a type of jade found in New Zealand and used for making ornaments, weapons and tools.

greet, greets, greeting, greeted VERB ① If you greet someone, you say something friendly like 'hello' to them when you meet them. ② If you greet something in a particular way, you react to it in that way • *He was greeted with deep suspicion*.

SIMILAR WORDS: ① hail, salute

greeting, greetings NOUN something friendly that you say to someone when you meet them • *Her greeting was warm*.

gregarious [Said grig-*air*-ee-uss] ADJECTIVE (formal) Someone who is gregarious enjoys being with other people.

grenade, grenades NOUN a small bomb, containing explosive or tear gas, which can be thrown.

WORD HISTORY: from Spanish *granada* meaning 'pomegranate'

a b c d e f g h i j k l m n o p q r s t u v w x y z

grevillea, grevilleas NOUN an evergreen Australian tree or shrub.

grew the past tense of **grow**.

grey, greyer, greyest; greys, greying, greyed ADJECTIVE or NOUN ① Grey is a colour between black and white. ▶ ADJECTIVE ② dull and boring • *He's a bit of a grey man.* ▶ VERB ③ If someone is greying, their hair is going grey. **greyness** NOUN

greyhound, greyhounds NOUN a thin dog with long legs that can run very fast.

grid, grids NOUN ① a pattern of lines crossing each other to form squares. ② The grid is the network of wires and cables by which electricity is distributed throughout a country.

grid reference, grid references NOUN GEOGRAPHY a number that identifies a place on a map by referring to the numbered lines of a grid drawn on the map.

grief NOUN ① Grief is extreme sadness. ▶ PHRASE ② If someone or something **comes to grief**, they fail or are injured.
SIMILAR WORDS: ① heartache, sadness, sorrow

grievance, grievances NOUN a reason for complaining.

grieve, grieves, grieving, grieved VERB ① If you grieve, you are extremely sad, especially because someone has died. ② If something grieves you, it makes you feel very sad.
SIMILAR WORDS: ① lament, mourn

grievous ADJECTIVE (*formal*) extremely serious • *grievous damage.* **grievously** ADVERB

grill, grills, grilling, grilled NOUN ① a part on a cooker where food is cooked by strong heat from above. ② a metal frame on which you cook food over a fire. ▶ VERB ③ If you grill food, you cook it on or under a grill. ④ (*informal*) If you grill someone, you ask them a lot of questions in a very intense way.

grille, grilles [*Rhymes with* **pill**]; also spelt **grill** NOUN a metal framework over a window or piece of machinery, used for protection.

grim, grimmer, grimmest ADJECTIVE ① If a situation or piece of news is grim, it is very unpleasant and worrying • *There are grim times ahead.* ② Grim places are unattractive and depressing. ③ If someone is grim, they are very serious or stern. **grimly** ADVERB

grimace, grimaces, grimacing, grimaced [*Said* **grim**-*iss or* grim-**mace**] NOUN ① a twisted facial expression indicating disgust or pain. ▶ VERB ② When someone grimaces, they make a grimace.

grime NOUN Grime is thick dirt which gathers on the surface of something. **grimy** ADJECTIVE

grin, grins, grinning, grinned VERB ① If you grin, you smile broadly. ▶ NOUN ② a broad smile. ▶ PHRASE ③ If you **grin and bear it**, you accept a difficult situation without complaining.

grind, grinds, grinding, ground VERB ① If you grind something such as pepper, you crush it into a fine powder. ② If you grind your teeth, you rub your upper and lower teeth together. ▶ PHRASE ③ If something **grinds to a halt**, it stops • *Progress ground to a halt.*
SIMILAR WORDS: ① crush, powder, pulverise

grip, grips, gripping, gripped NOUN ① a firm hold. ② a handle on a bat or a racket. ③ Your grip on a situation is your control over it. ▶ VERB ④ If you grip something, you hold it firmly.

▶ PHRASE ⑤ If you **get to grips with** a situation or problem, you start to deal with it effectively.

grisly, grislier, grisliest ADJECTIVE very nasty and horrible • *a grisly murder scene*.

grit, grits, gritting, gritted NOUN ① Grit consists of very small stones. It is put on icy roads to make them less slippery. ▶ VERB ② When workmen grit an icy road, they put grit on it. ▶ PHRASE ③ To **grit your teeth** means to decide to carry on in a difficult situation. **gritty** ADJECTIVE

grizzled ADJECTIVE Grizzled hair is grey. A grizzled person has grey hair.

grizzly bear, grizzly bears NOUN a large, greyish-brown bear from North America.

groan, groans, groaning, groaned VERB ① If you groan, you make a long, low sound of pain, unhappiness or disapproval. ▶ NOUN ② the sound you make when you groan.

grocer, grocers NOUN a shopkeeper who sells many kinds of food and other household goods.

grocery, groceries NOUN ① a grocer's shop. ② (*in plural*) Groceries are the goods that you buy in a grocer's shop.

grog NOUN (*informal*) In Australian and New Zealand English, grog is any alcoholic drink.

groin, groins NOUN the area where your legs join the main part of your body at the front.

groom, grooms, grooming, groomed NOUN ① someone who looks after horses in a stable. ② At a wedding, the groom is the bridegroom. ▶ VERB ③ To groom an animal means to clean its fur. ④ If you groom someone for a job, you prepare them for it by teaching them the skills they will need.

groove, grooves NOUN a deep line cut into a surface. **grooved** ADJECTIVE

grope, gropes, groping, groped VERB ① If you grope for something you cannot see, you search for it with your hands. ② If you grope for something such as the solution to a problem, you try to think of it.

gross, grosser, grossest; grosses, grossing, grossed ADJECTIVE ① extremely bad • *a gross betrayal*. ② Gross speech or behaviour is very rude. ③ Gross things are ugly • *gross holiday outfits*. ④ Someone's gross income is their total income before any deductions are made. ⑤ The gross weight of something is its total weight including the weight of its container. ▶ VERB ⑥ If you gross an amount of money, you earn that amount in total. **grossly** ADVERB

grotesque [*Said groh-tesk*] ADJECTIVE ① exaggerated and absurd • *It was the most grotesque thing she had ever heard*. ② very strange and ugly • *grotesque animal puppets*. **grotesquely** ADVERB WORD HISTORY: from Old Italian *pittura grottesca* meaning 'cave paintings'

grotto, grottoes or grottos NOUN a small cave that people visit because it is attractive.

ground, grounds, grounding, grounded NOUN ① The ground is the surface of the earth. ② a piece of land that is used for a particular purpose • *the training ground*. ③ The ground covered by a book or course is the range of subjects it deals with. ④ (*in plural*) The grounds of a large building are the land belonging to it and surrounding it. ⑤ (*in plural, formal*) The grounds for something are the reasons for it • *genuine grounds for caution*. ▶ VERB ⑥ (*formal*) If something is grounded in something

a
b
c
d
e
f
g
h
i
j
k
l
m
n
o
p
q
r
s
t
u
v
w
x
y
z

else, it is based on it. ⑦ If an aircraft is grounded, it has to remain on the ground. ⑧ Ground is the past tense and past participle of **grind**.

ground floor, ground floors NOUN The ground floor of a building is the floor that is approximately level with the ground.

grounding NOUN If you have a grounding in a skill or subject, you have had basic instruction in it.

groundless ADJECTIVE not based on reason or evidence • *groundless accusations*.

group, groups, grouping, grouped NOUN ① A group of things or people is a number of them that are linked together in some way. ② a number of musicians who perform pop music together. ▶ VERB ③ When things or people are grouped together, they are linked together in some way. SIMILAR WORDS: ① band, bunch, crowd, set

grouping, groupings NOUN a number of things or people that are linked together in some way.

grouse, grouse NOUN a fat brown or grey bird, often shot for sport.

grove, groves NOUN (*literary*) a group of trees growing close together.

grovel, grovels, grovelling, grovelled VERB If you grovel, you behave in an unpleasantly humble way towards someone you regard as important.

grow, grows, growing, grew, grown VERB ① To grow means to increase in size or amount. ② If a tree or plant grows somewhere, it is alive there. ③ When people grow plants, they plant them and look after them. ④ If a man grows a beard or moustache, he lets it develop by not shaving. ⑤ To grow also means to pass gradually into a particular state. ⑥ If

one thing grows from another, it develops from it. ⑦ (*informal*) If something grows on you, you gradually get to like it. **grow up** VERB When a child grows up, he or she becomes an adult. SIMILAR WORDS: ① expand, get bigger, increase

growl, growls, growling, growled VERB ① When an animal growls, it makes a low rumbling sound, usually because it is angry. ② If you growl something, you say it in a low, rough, rather angry voice. ▶ NOUN ③ the sound an animal makes when it growls.

grown-up, grown-ups NOUN ① (*informal*) an adult. ▶ ADJECTIVE ② Someone who is grown-up is adult, or behaves like an adult.

growth, growths NOUN ① When there is a growth in something, it gets bigger • *the growth of the fishing industry*. ② Growth is the process by which something develops to its full size. ③ an abnormal lump that grows inside or on a person, animal or plant. SIMILAR WORDS: ① expansion, increase

grub, grubs NOUN ① a wormlike insect that has just hatched from its egg. ② (*informal*) Grub is food.

grubby, grubbier, grubbiest ADJECTIVE rather dirty.

grudge, grudges, grudging, grudged NOUN ① If you have a grudge against someone, you resent them because they have harmed you in the past. ▶ VERB ② If you grudge someone something, you give it to them unwillingly, or are displeased that they have it.

grudging ADJECTIVE done or felt unwillingly • *grudging admiration*. **grudgingly** ADVERB

gruel NOUN Gruel is oatmeal boiled in water or milk.

gruelling ADJECTIVE difficult and tiring • *a gruelling race*.

gruesome ADJECTIVE shocking and horrible • *gruesome pictures*.

gruff, gruffer, gruffest ADJECTIVE If someone's voice is gruff, it sounds rough and unfriendly.

grumble, grumbles, grumbling, grumbled VERB ① If you grumble, you complain in a bad-tempered way. ▶ NOUN ② a bad-tempered complaint.

grumpy, grumpier, grumpiest ADJECTIVE bad-tempered and fed-up. SIMILAR WORDS: ill-tempered, irritable

grunt, grunts, grunting, grunted VERB ① If a person or a pig grunts, they make a short, low, gruff sound. ▶ NOUN ② the sound a person or a pig makes when they grunt.

guarantee, guarantees, guaranteeing, guaranteed NOUN ① If something is a guarantee of something else, it makes it certain that it will happen. ② a written promise that if a product develops a fault it will be replaced or repaired free. ▶ VERB ③ If something or someone guarantees something, they make certain that it will happen • *Money may not guarantee success*. **guarantor** NOUN SIMILAR WORDS: ① assurance, pledge, promise ③ ensure, promise

guard, guards, guarding, guarded VERB ① If you guard a person or object, you stay near to them to protect them. ② If you guard a person, you stop them making trouble or escaping. ③ If you guard against something, you are careful to avoid it happening. ▶ NOUN ④ a person or group of people who guard a person, object or place. ⑤ a railway official in charge of a train. ⑥ Any object which covers something to prevent it causing harm can be called a guard • *a fire guard*. SIMILAR WORDS: ① defend, protect, watch over ④ protector, sentry, watchman

guardian, guardians NOUN ① someone who has been legally appointed to look after a child. ② A guardian of something is someone who protects it • *a guardian of the law*. **guardianship** NOUN

guernsey, guernseys NOUN ① In Australian and New Zealand English, a jersey. ② a sleeveless top worn by an Australian Rules football player.

guerrilla, guerrillas [Said ger-ril-la]; also spelt **guerilla** NOUN a member of a small unofficial army fighting an official army. WORD HISTORY: from Spanish *guerrilla* meaning 'little war'

guess, guesses, guessing, guessed VERB ① If you guess something, you form or express an opinion that it is the case, without having much information. ▶ NOUN ② an attempt to give the correct answer to something without having much information, or without working it out properly. SIMILAR WORDS: ① conjecture, suppose ② conjecture, speculation, supposition

guest, guests NOUN ① someone who stays at your home or who attends an occasion because they have been invited. ② The guests in a hotel are the people staying there.

guffaw NOUN a loud, coarse laugh.

guidance NOUN Guidance is help and advice.

guide, guides, guiding, guided NOUN ① someone who shows you round places, or leads the way through difficult country. ② a book which gives you information or instructions • *a Sydney street guide*. ③ A Guide is a girl who is a member of an organisation that encourages discipline and practical skills. ▸ **VERB** ④ If you guide someone in a particular direction, you lead them in that direction. ⑤ If you are guided by something, it influences your actions or decisions.

guidebook, guidebooks NOUN a book which gives information about a place.

guide dog, guide dogs NOUN a dog that has been trained to lead a blind person.

guideline, guidelines NOUN a piece of advice about how something should be done.

guild, guilds NOUN a society of people • *the Screen Writers' Guild*.

guile [Rhymes with **mile**] NOUN Guile is cunning and deceit. **guileless** ADJECTIVE

guillotine, guillotines [Said *gil-lot-teen*] NOUN ① HISTORY In the past, the guillotine was a machine used for beheading people, especially in France. It was named after Joseph-Ignace Guillotin, who first recommended its use. ② A guillotine is also a piece of equipment with a long sharp blade, used for cutting paper.

guilt NOUN ① Guilt is an unhappy feeling of having done something wrong. ② Someone's guilt is the fact that they have done something wrong • *The law will decide their guilt*.

SPELLING TIP

Do not confuse the spellings of *guilt* and *gilt*: *I still feel guilt for the way I behaved towards him; The lid of the jewellery box is gilt*.

guilty, guiltier, guiltiest ADJECTIVE ① If you are guilty of doing something wrong, you did it • *He was guilty of theft*. ② If you feel guilty, you are unhappy because you have done something wrong. **guiltily** ADVERB

guinea, guineas [Said *gin-ee*] NOUN an old British unit of money, worth 21 shillings.

guinea pig, guinea pigs NOUN ① a small furry animal without a tail, often kept as a pet. ② a person used to try something out on • *a guinea pig for a new drug*.

guise, guises [Rhymes with **prize**] NOUN a misleading appearance • *political statements in the guise of religious talk*.

guitar, guitars NOUN a musical instrument with six strings which are strummed or plucked. **guitarist** NOUN

gulf, gulfs NOUN ① GEOGRAPHY a very large bay. ② a wide gap or difference between two things or people.

gull, gulls NOUN a sea bird with long wings, white and grey or black feathers, and webbed feet. WORD HISTORY: from Welsh *gwylan*

gullet, gullets NOUN the tube that goes from your mouth to your stomach.

gullible ADJECTIVE easily tricked. **gullibility** NOUN SIMILAR WORDS: credulous, naive

gully, gullies NOUN a long, narrow valley.

gulp, gulps, gulping, gulped VERB ① If you gulp food or drink, you swallow large quantities of it. ② If you gulp, you swallow air, because you are nervous. ▸ NOUN ③ A gulp of food or drink is a large quantity of it swallowed at one time.

gum, gums NOUN ① Gum is a soft flavoured substance that people chew but do not swallow. ②Gum is also glue for sticking paper. ③Your gums are the firm flesh in which your teeth are set.

gumboot, gumboots NOUN Gumboots are long waterproof boots.

gumtree, gumtrees NOUN a eucalyptus, or other tree which produces gum.

gun, guns NOUN a weapon which fires bullets or shells.

gunfire NOUN Gunfire is the repeated firing of guns.

gunpowder NOUN Gunpowder is an explosive powder made from a mixture of potassium nitrate and other substances.

gunshot, gunshots NOUN the sound of a gun being fired.

gunyah, gunyahs NOUN In Australia, a gunyah is a hut or shelter in the bush.

guppy, guppies NOUN a small, brightly coloured tropical fish.

gurdwara NOUN RE a Sikh place of worship.
WORD HISTORY: from Sanskrit *guru* meaning 'teacher' + *dvārā* meaning 'door'

gurgle, gurgles, gurgling, gurgled VERB ①To gurgle means to make a bubbling sound. ▶NOUN ②a bubbling sound.

guru, gurus [*Said* goo-rooh] NOUN RE a spiritual leader and teacher, especially in India.
WORD HISTORY: from Sanskrit *guruh* meaning 'weighty' or 'of importance'

gush, gushes, gushing, gushed VERB ①When liquid gushes from something, it flows out of it in large quantities. ②When people gush, they express admiration or pleasure in an exaggerated way. **gushing** ADJECTIVE

SIMILAR WORDS: ①flow, pour, spurt, stream

gust, gusts NOUN a sudden rush of wind. **gusty** ADJECTIVE

gusto NOUN Gusto is energy and enthusiasm • *Her gusto for life was amazing.*

gut, guts, gutting, gutted NOUN (*in plural*) ①Your guts are your internal organs, especially your intestines. ②(*informal*) Guts is courage. ▶VERB ③To gut a dead fish means to remove its internal organs. ④If a building is gutted, the inside of it is destroyed, especially by fire.
SIMILAR WORDS: ①entrails, innards, intestines

gutsy, gutsier, gutsiest ADJECTIVE (*informal*) If you describe someone as gutsy, you mean they show courage or determination.

gutter, gutters NOUN ①the edge of a road next to the pavement, where rain collects and flows away. ②a channel fixed to the edge of a roof, where rain collects and flows away. **guttering** NOUN

guttural [*Said* gut-ter-al] ADJECTIVE Guttural sounds are produced at the back of a person's throat and are often considered to be unpleasant.

guy, guys NOUN ①(*informal*) a man or boy. ②a crude model of Guy Fawkes, that is burnt on top of a bonfire on Guy Fawkes Day (November 5).
WORD HISTORY: short for *Guy Fawkes*, who plotted to blow up the British Houses of Parliament

guzzle, guzzles, guzzling, guzzled VERB To guzzle something means to drink or eat it quickly and greedily.

gym, gyms NOUN ①a gymnasium. ②PE Gym is gymnastics.

gymkhana, gymkhanas [*Said* jim-kah-na] NOUN an event in which people take part in horse-riding contests.

a b c d e f g h i j k l m n o p q r s t u v w x y z

WORD HISTORY: from Hindi *gend-khana* literally meaning 'ball house', where sports were held

gymnasium, **gymnasiums** NOUN a room with special equipment for physical exercises.

gymnast, **gymnasts** NOUN someone who is trained in gymnastics.
gymnastic ADJECTIVE

gymnastics NOUN PE Gymnastics is physical exercises, especially ones using equipment such as bars and ropes.

gynaecology [Said gie-nak-**kol**-loj-ee]; also spelt **gynecology** NOUN Gynaecology is the branch of medical science concerned with the female reproductive system.
gynaecologist NOUN
gynaecological ADJECTIVE

Gypsy, **Gypsies**; also spelt **Gipsy** NOUN a member of a race of people who travel from place to place, usually in caravans, rather than living in one place. Some Gypsies object to this name, and prefer to be called Romany.
WORD HISTORY: from 'Egyptian', because people used to think Gypsies came from Egypt

gyrate, **gyrates**, **gyrating**, **gyrated** [Said jy-**rate**] VERB To gyrate means to move round in a circle.

Hh

habit, habits NOUN ① something that you do often • *He got into the habit of eating out.* ② something that you keep doing and find it difficult to stop doing • *a habit of picking at her spots.* ③ A monk's or nun's habit is a garment like a loose dress.
habitual ADJECTIVE **habitually** ADVERB

habitat, habitats NOUN GEOGRAPHY the natural home of a plant or animal.

hack, hacks, hacking, hacked VERB ① If you hack at something, you cut it using rough strokes. ② If you hack into a computer system, you gain access to it without permission.
▶ NOUN ③ a writer or journalist who produces work fast without worrying about quality.

hacker, hackers NOUN someone who uses a computer to break into the computer system of a company or government.

hackles PLURAL NOUN ① A dog's hackles are the hairs on the back of its neck which rise when it is angry.
▶ PHRASE ② Something that **makes your hackles rise** makes you angry.

hackneyed ADJECTIVE A hackneyed phrase is meaningless because it has been used too often.
SIMILAR WORDS: clichéd, unoriginal

hacksaw, hacksaws NOUN a small saw with a narrow blade set in a frame.

had the past tense and past participle of **have**.

haddock, haddocks NOUN an edible sea fish.

haemoglobin [Said hee-moh-**gloh**-bin] NOUN SCIENCE Haemoglobin is a substance in red blood cells which carries oxygen round the body.

haemophilia [Said hee-moh-**fil**-lee-a]; also spelt **hemophilia** NOUN Haemophilia is a disease in which a person's blood does not clot so they bleed for too long when they are injured. **haemophiliac** or **hemophiliac** NOUN

haemorrhage [Said hem-er-rij] NOUN A haemorrhage is serious bleeding especially inside a person's body.

haemorrhoids [Said hem-er-roydz] PLURAL NOUN Haemorrhoids are painful lumps around the anus that are caused by swollen veins.

hag, hags NOUN (*offensive*) an ugly old woman.

haggard ADJECTIVE A person who is haggard looks very tired and ill.

haggis NOUN Haggis is a Scottish dish made of the internal organs of a sheep, boiled together with oatmeal and spices in a skin.

haggle, haggles, haggling, haggled VERB If you haggle with someone, you argue with them, usually about the cost of something.

haiku, haiku [Said high-koo] NOUN ENGLISH a type of very short Japanese poem which has 17 syllables.

GRAMMAR TIP
The plural of *haiku* is *haiku*.

hail, hails, hailing, hailed NOUN ① Hail is frozen rain. ②A hail of things is a lot of them falling together • *a hail of bullets* • *a hail of protest.* ▸VERB ③When it is hailing, frozen rain is falling. ④If someone hails you, they call you to attract your attention or greet you • *He hailed a taxi.*

hair, hairs NOUN Hair consists of the long, threadlike strands that grow from the skin of animals and humans.

haircut, haircuts NOUN the cutting of someone's hair; also the style in which it is cut.

hairdo, hairdos NOUN a hairstyle.

hairdresser, hairdressers NOUN someone who is trained to cut and style people's hair; also a shop where this is done. **hairdressing** NOUN or ADJECTIVE

hairline, hairlines NOUN ① the edge of the area on your forehead where your hair grows. ▸ADJECTIVE ②A hairline crack is so fine that you can hardly see it.

hairpin, hairpins NOUN ① a U-shaped wire used to hold hair in position. ▸ADJECTIVE ②A hairpin bend is a U-shaped bend in the road.

hair-raising ADJECTIVE very frightening or exciting.

hairstyle, hairstyles NOUN Someone's hairstyle is the way in which their hair is arranged or cut.

hairy, hairier, hairiest ADJECTIVE ① covered in a lot of hair. ② (*informal*) difficult, exciting and rather frightening • *He had lived through many hairy adventures.*

hajj, hajjes [*Rhymes with* **badge**] NOUN RE The hajj is the pilgrimage to Mecca that every Muslim must make at least once in their life if they are healthy and wealthy enough to do so.

haka, haka or hakas NOUN ① In New Zealand, a haka is a ceremonial Māori dance made up of various postures and accompanied by a chant. ② an imitation of this dance performed by New Zealand sports teams before matches as a challenge.

hake, hakes NOUN an edible sea fish related to the cod.

hakea, hakeas NOUN a large Australian shrub with bright flowers and hard, woody fruit.

halal ADJECTIVE RE Halal meat is from animals that have been killed in the correct way according to Islamic law.

halcyon [*Said* **hal-see-on**] ADJECTIVE ① (*literary*) peaceful, gentle and calm • *halcyon colours of yellow and turquoise.* ▸PHRASE ②Halcyon days are a happy and carefree time in the past • *halcyon days in the sun.*

half, halves NOUN or ADJECTIVE or ADVERB ① Half refers to one of two equal parts that make up a whole • *the two halves of the brain* • *They chatted for another half hour* • *The bottle was only half full.* ▸ADVERB ②You can use 'half' to say that something is only partly true • *I half expected him to explode in anger.*

half-baked ADJECTIVE (*informal*) Half-baked ideas or plans have not been properly thought out.

half board NOUN Half board at a hotel includes breakfast and dinner but not lunch.

half-brother, half-brothers NOUN Your half-brother is the son of either your mother or your father but not of your other parent.

half-hearted ADJECTIVE showing no real effort or enthusiasm.

half-pie ADJECTIVE (*informal*) In New Zealand English, half-pie means incomplete or not properly done • *finished in a half-pie way.*

half-sister, **half-sisters** NOUN Your half-sister is the daughter of either your mother or your father but not of your other parent.

half-timbered ADJECTIVE A half-timbered building has a framework of wooden beams showing in the walls.

half-time NOUN Half-time is a short break between two parts of a game when the players have a rest.

halfway ADVERB at the middle of the distance between two points in place or time • *He stopped halfway down the ladder* • *halfway through the term*.

halibut, **halibuts** NOUN a large edible flat fish.

hall, **halls** NOUN ① the room just inside the front entrance of a house which leads into other rooms. ② a large room or building used for public events • *a concert hall*.

hallmark, **hallmarks** NOUN ① The hallmark of a person or group is their most typical quality • *A warm, hospitable welcome is the hallmark of island people*. ② an official mark on gold or silver indicating the quality of the metal.

hallowed [Said hal-lode] ADJECTIVE respected as being holy • *hallowed ground*.

Halloween NOUN Halloween is October 31st, and is celebrated by children dressing up, often as ghosts and witches.
WORD HISTORY: from Old English *halig* + *æfen* meaning 'holy evening', the evening before All Saints' Day

hallucinate, **hallucinates**, **hallucinating**, **hallucinated** [Said hal-**loo**-sin-ate] VERB If you hallucinate, you see strange things in your mind because of illness or drugs.
hallucination NOUN **hallucinatory** ADJECTIVE

WORD HISTORY: from Latin *alucinari* meaning 'to wander in thought'

halo, **haloes** or **halos** NOUN a circle of light around the head of a holy figure.
WORD HISTORY: from Greek *halos* meaning 'disc shape of the sun or moon'

halogen [Said hal-o-jen] NOUN SCIENCE A halogen is any of the chemical elements fluorine, chlorine, bromine, iodine and astatine. They form group VIII in the periodic table.

halt, **halts**, **halting**, **halted** VERB ① To halt when moving means to stop. ② To halt development or action means to stop it. ▶ NOUN ③ a short standstill.

halter, **halters** NOUN a strap fastened round a horse's head so that it can be led easily.

halve, **halves**, **halving**, **halved** [Said hahv] VERB ① If you halve something, you divide it into two equal parts. ② To halve something also means to reduce its size or amount by half.

ham, **hams** NOUN ① Ham is meat from the hind leg of a pig, salted and cured. ② (*informal*) a bad actor who exaggerates emotions and gestures. ③ someone who is interested in amateur radio.

hamburger, **hamburgers** NOUN a flat disc of minced meat, seasoned and fried; often eaten in a bread roll.
WORD HISTORY: named after its city of origin *Hamburg* in Germany

hammer, **hammers**, **hammering**, **hammered** NOUN ① a tool consisting of a heavy piece of metal at the end of a handle, used for hitting nails into things. ▶ VERB ② If you hammer something, you hit it repeatedly, with a hammer or with your fist. ③ If you hammer an idea into someone, you keep repeating it

and telling them about it.
④ (*informal*) If you hammer someone, you criticise or attack them severely.

hammock, hammocks NOUN a piece of net or canvas hung between two supports and used as a bed.

hamper, hampers, hampering, hampered NOUN ① a rectangular wicker basket with a lid, used for carrying food. ▸ VERB ② If you hamper someone, you make it difficult for them to move or progress.

SIMILAR WORDS: ② handicap, hinder, impede

hamster, hamsters NOUN a small furry rodent which is often kept as a pet.

SPELLING TIP
There is no *p* in *hamster*.

---

hamstring, hamstrings NOUN PE
Your hamstring is a tendon behind your knee joining your thigh muscles to the bones of your lower leg.

hand, hands, handing, handed NOUN ① Your hand is the part of your body beyond the wrist, with four fingers and a thumb. ② Your hand is also your writing style. ③ The hand of someone in a situation is their influence or the part they play in it • *He had a hand in its design.* ④ If you give someone a hand, you help them to do something. ⑤ When an audience gives someone a big hand, they applaud. ⑥ The hands of a clock or watch are the pointers that point to the numbers. ⑦ In cards, your hand is the cards you are holding. ▸ VERB ⑧ If you hand something to someone, you give it to them. ▸ PHRASE ⑨ Something that is at hand, to hand or on hand is available, close by, and ready for use. ⑩ You use on the one hand to introduce the first part of an

argument or discussion with two different points of view. ⑪ You use on the other hand to introduce the second part of an argument or discussion with two different points of view. ⑫ If you do something by hand, you do it using your hands rather than a machine. hand down VERB Something that is handed down is passed from one generation to another.

handbag, handbags NOUN a small bag used mainly by women to carry money and personal items.

handbook, handbooks NOUN a book giving information and instructions about something.

handcuff, handcuffs NOUN Handcuffs are two metal rings linked by a chain which are locked around a prisoner's wrists.

handful, handfuls NOUN ① A handful of something is the amount of it you can hold in your hand • *He picked up a handful of seeds.* ② a small quantity • *Only a handful of people knew.* ③ Someone who is a handful is difficult to control • *He is a bit of a handful.*

handicap, handicaps, handicapping, handicapped NOUN ① (*old-fashioned, offensive*) a physical or mental disability. ② something that makes it difficult for you to achieve something. ③ In sport, a handicap is a disadvantage or advantage given to competitors according to their skill, in order to give them an equal chance of winning. ▸ VERB ④ If something handicaps someone, it makes it difficult for them to achieve something.

handicraft, handicrafts NOUN Handicrafts are activities such as embroidery or pottery which involve making things with your hands;

also the items produced.

handiwork NOUN Your handiwork is something that you have done or made yourself.

handkerchief, handkerchiefs NOUN a small square of fabric used for blowing your nose.

handle, handles, handling, handled NOUN ① The handle of an object is the part by which it is held or controlled. ② a small lever used to open and close a door or window. ▶ VERB ③ If you handle an object, you hold it in your hands to examine it. ④ If you handle something, you deal with it or control it • *I have learned how to handle pressure.*

handlebar, handlebars NOUN Handlebars are the bar and handles at the front of a bicycle, used for steering.

handout, handouts NOUN ① a gift of food, clothing or money given to a person in need. ② a piece of paper giving information about something.

hand-picked ADJECTIVE carefully chosen • *a hand-picked team of bodyguards.*

handset, handsets NOUN The handset of a telephone is the part that you speak into and listen with.

handshake, handshakes NOUN the grasping and shaking of a person's hand by another person.

handsome ADJECTIVE ① very attractive in appearance. ② large and generous • *a handsome profit.* **handsomely** ADVERB
SIMILAR WORDS: ① attractive, good-looking

SPELLING TIP
There is a *d* in *handsome*.

---

handwriting NOUN Someone's handwriting is their style of writing as it looks on the page.

handy, handier, handiest ADJECTIVE ① conveniently near. ② easy to handle or use. ③ skilful.

hang, hangs, hanging, hung VERB ① If you hang something somewhere, you attach it to a high point • *She hung heavy red velvet curtains in the sitting room.* ② If something is hanging on something, it is attached by its top to it • *His jacket hung from a hook behind the door.* ③ If a future event or possibility is hanging over you, it worries or frightens you • *She has an eviction notice hanging over her.* ④ When you hang wallpaper, you stick it onto a wall. ⑤ To hang someone means to kill them by suspending them by a rope around the neck. ▶ PHRASE ⑥ When you **get the hang of something**, you understand it and are able to do it. **hang about** or **hang around** VERB ① (*informal*) To hang about or hang around means to wait somewhere. ② To hang about or hang around with someone means to spend a lot of time with them. **hang back** VERB To hang back means to wait or hesitate. **hang on** VERB ① If you hang on to something, you hold it tightly or keep it. ② (*informal*) To hang on means to wait. **hang out** VERB (*informal*) If you hang out somewhere or with someone, you spend a lot of time there or with them. **hang up** VERB When you hang up, you end a telephone call.

GRAMMAR TIP
When *hang* means 'kill someone by suspending them by a rope' (sense 5), the past tense and past participle are *hanged*: *He was hanged for murder in 1959.*

---

hangar, hangars NOUN a large building where aircraft are kept.

hanger, hangers NOUN a coat hanger.

hanger-on, hangers-on NOUN an unwelcome follower of an important person.

hang-glider, hang-gliders NOUN an aircraft without an engine and consisting of a large frame covered in fabric, from which the pilot hangs in a harness.

hangi, hangi or hangis [Said *hung-ee*] NOUN In New Zealand, a Māori oven made from a hole in the ground lined with hot stones.

hangover, hangovers NOUN a feeling of sickness and headache after drinking too much alcohol.

hang-up, hang-ups NOUN A hang-up about something is a continual feeling of embarrassment or fear about it.

hanker, hankers, hankering, hankered VERB If you hanker after something, you continually want it. **hankering** NOUN

hanky, hankies NOUN a handkerchief.

Hanukkah [Said *hah-na-ka*]; also spelt **Chanukah** NOUN RE Hanukkah is an eight-day Jewish festival of lights.
WORD HISTORY: a Hebrew word meaning 'a dedication'

haphazard [Said *hap-haz-ard*] ADJECTIVE not organised or planned. **haphazardly** ADVERB
WORD HISTORY: from Old Norse *hap* meaning 'chance' and Arabic *az-zahr* meaning 'gaming dice'

hapless ADJECTIVE (literary) unlucky.

happen, happens, happening, happened VERB ① When something happens, it occurs or takes place. ② If you happen to do something, you do it by chance. **happening** NOUN
SIMILAR WORDS: ① come about, occur, take place

happiness NOUN a feeling of great contentment or pleasure.

happy, happier, happiest ADJECTIVE ① feeling, showing or producing contentment or pleasure • *a happy smile* • *a happy atmosphere*. ② satisfied that something is right • *I wasn't very happy about the layout*. ③ willing • *I would be happy to help*. ④ fortunate or lucky • *a happy coincidence*. **happily** ADVERB
SIMILAR WORDS: ① blissful, content, glad, joyful

happy-go-lucky ADJECTIVE carefree and unconcerned.

harangue, harangues, haranguing, harangued [Said *har-rang*] NOUN ① a long, forceful, passionate speech. ▶ VERB ② To harangue someone means to talk to them at length passionately and forcefully about something.
WORD HISTORY: from Old Italian *aringa* meaning 'public speech'

harass, harasses, harassing, harassed [Said *har-rass*] VERB If someone harasses you, they trouble or annoy you continually. **harassed** ADJECTIVE **harassment** NOUN

harbinger, harbingers [Said *har-bin-jer*] NOUN a person or thing that announces or indicates the approach of a future event • *The cold wind was a harbinger of winter*.

harbour, harbours, harbouring, harboured NOUN ① a protected area of deep water where boats can be moored. ▶ VERB ② To harbour someone means to hide them secretly in your house. ③ If you harbour a feeling, you have it for a long time • *She's still harbouring great bitterness*.
WORD HISTORY: from Old English *here* + *beorg* meaning 'army shelter'

hard, harder, hardest ADJECTIVE
① Something that is hard is firm, solid or stiff • *a hard piece of cheese.*
② requiring a lot of effort • *hard work.*
③ difficult • *That is a hard question.*
④ Someone who is hard has no kindness or pity • *Don't be hard on him.*
⑤ A hard colour or voice is harsh and unpleasant. ⑥ Hard evidence or facts can be proved to be true. ⑦ Hard water contains a lot of lime and does not easily produce a lather. ⑧ Hard drink is strong alcohol. ▶ ADVERB
⑨ earnestly or intently • *They tried hard to attract tourists.* ⑩ An event that follows hard upon something takes place immediately afterwards.
hardness NOUN
SIMILAR WORDS: ① firm, rigid, solid, stiff

hard and fast ADJECTIVE fixed and not able to be changed • *hard and fast rules.*

hardback, hardbacks NOUN a book with a stiff cover.

hard-bitten ADJECTIVE tough and determined.

hard core NOUN The hard core in an organisation is the group of people who most resist change.

harden, hardens, hardening, hardened VERB To harden means to become hard or get harder.
hardening NOUN **hardened** ADJECTIVE

hard labour NOUN physical work which is difficult and tiring, used in some countries as a punishment for a crime.

hardly ADVERB ① almost not or not quite • *I could hardly believe it.*
② certainly not • *It's hardly a secret.*

GRAMMAR TIP
You should not use *hardly* with a negative word like *not* or *no*: *He could hardly hear her*, not *He could not hardly hear her.*

hard-nosed ADJECTIVE tough, practical and realistic.

hard of hearing ADJECTIVE not able to hear properly.

hardship, hardships NOUN Hardship is a time or situation of suffering and difficulty.

hard shoulder, hard shoulders NOUN the area at the edge of a motorway where a driver can stop in the event of a breakdown.

hard up ADJECTIVE (*informal*) having hardly any money.

hardware NOUN ① Hardware is tools and equipment for use in the home and garden. ② ICT Hardware is also computer machinery rather than computer programs.

hard-wearing ADJECTIVE strong, well-made and long-lasting.

hardwood, hardwoods NOUN strong, hard wood from a tree such as an oak; also the tree itself.

hardy, hardier, hardiest ADJECTIVE tough and able to endure very difficult or cold conditions • *The environment produced hardy and independent people.* **hardiness** NOUN

hare, hares, haring, hared NOUN ① an animal like a large rabbit, but with longer ears and legs. ▶ VERB ② To hare means to run very fast • *He hared off down the corridor.*

harem, harems [*Said har-reem*] NOUN in the past, the place in a Muslim house or palace where the women lived.

hark, harks, harking, harked VERB ① (*old-fashioned*) To hark means to listen. ② To hark back to something in the past means to refer back to it or recall it.

harlequin [*Said har-lik-win*] ADJECTIVE having many different colours.

harm, harms, harming, harmed VERB ① To harm someone or

something means to injure or damage them. ▸ **NOUN** ② Harm is injury or damage.

SIMILAR WORDS: ① damage, hurt, injure

harmful ADJECTIVE having a bad effect on something • *Whilst most stress is harmful, some is beneficial.*

harmless ADJECTIVE ① safe to use or be near. ② unlikely to cause problems or annoyance • *He's harmless really.* **harmlessly** ADVERB

harmonic ADJECTIVE using musical harmony.

harmonica, harmonicas NOUN a small musical instrument which you play by blowing and sucking while moving it across your lips.

harmonious [*Said har-moh-nee-uss*] ADJECTIVE ① showing agreement, peacefulness and friendship • *a harmonious relationship.* ② consisting of parts which blend well together making an attractive whole • *harmonious interior decor.* **harmoniously** ADVERB

harmonise, harmonises, harmonising, harmonised; also spelt **harmonize** VERB If things harmonise, they fit in with each other or interact in an agreeable way.

harmony, harmonies NOUN ① Harmony is a state of peaceful agreement and cooperation • *the promotion of racial harmony.* ② MUSIC Harmony is the structure and relationship of chords in a piece of music. ③ Harmony is the pleasant combination of two or more notes played at the same time.

harness, harnesses, harnessing, harnessed NOUN ① a set of straps and fittings fastened round a horse so that it can pull a vehicle, or fastened round someone's body to attach something • *a safety harness.*

▸ **VERB** ② If you harness something, you bring it under control to use it • *harnessing your natural energy.*

harp, harps, harping, harped NOUN ① a musical instrument consisting of a triangular frame with vertical strings which you pluck with your fingers. ▸ **VERB** ② (*informal*) If someone harps on about something, they keep talking about it, especially in a boring way. **harpist** NOUN

harpoon, harpoons NOUN a barbed spear attached to a rope, thrown or fired from a gun and used for catching whales or large fish.

harpsichord, harpsichords NOUN a musical instrument like a small piano, with strings which are plucked when the keys are pressed.

harrowing ADJECTIVE very upsetting or disturbing • *a harrowing experience.*

harsh, harsher, harshest ADJECTIVE severe, difficult and unpleasant • *harsh weather conditions* • *harsh criticism.* **harshly** ADVERB **harshness** NOUN

SIMILAR WORDS: hard, severe, tough

harvest, harvests, harvesting, harvested NOUN ① the cutting and gathering of a crop; also the ripe crop when it is gathered and the time of gathering. ▸ **VERB** ② To harvest food means to gather it when it is ripe. **harvester** NOUN

WORD HISTORY: from Old German *herbist* meaning 'autumn'

has-been, has-beens NOUN (*informal*) a person who is no longer important or successful.

hash, hashes PHRASE ① If you **make a hash of** a job, you do it badly. ▸ **NOUN** ② the name for the symbol #. ③ Hash is a dish made of small pieces of meat and vegetables cooked together.

hashish [Said *hash-eesh*] NOUN Hashish is a drug made from the hemp plant. It is usually smoked, and is illegal in many countries.

hashtag, hashtags NOUN ICT a word or phrase that is used to indicate the topic of a post on a social networking website.

hassle, hassles, hassling, hassled (*informal*) NOUN ① Something that is a hassle is difficult or causes trouble. ▶ VERB ② If you hassle someone, you annoy them by repeatedly asking them to do something.

haste NOUN Haste is doing something quickly, especially too quickly.

hasten, hastens, hastening, hastened [Said *hay-sn*] VERB To hasten means to move quickly or do something quickly.

hasty, hastier, hastiest ADJECTIVE done or happening suddenly and quickly, often without enough care or thought. **hastily** ADVERB

hat, hats NOUN a covering for the head.

hatch, hatches, hatching, hatched VERB ① When an egg hatches, or when a bird or reptile hatches, the egg breaks open and the young bird or reptile emerges. ② To hatch a plot means to plan it. ▶ NOUN ③ a covered opening in a floor or wall.

hatchback, hatchbacks NOUN a car with a door at the back which opens upwards.

hatchet, hatchets NOUN ① a small axe. ▶ PHRASE ② To **bury the hatchet** means to resolve a disagreement and become friends again.

hate, hates, hating, hated VERB ① If you hate someone or something, you have a strong dislike for them. ▶ NOUN ② Hate is a strong dislike.

SIMILAR WORDS: ① detest, loathe

hateful ADJECTIVE extremely unpleasant.

hatred [Said *hay-trid*] NOUN Hatred is an extremely strong feeling of dislike.

hat trick, hat tricks NOUN In sport, a hat trick is three achievements, for example when a footballer scores three goals in a match • *Crawford completed his hat trick in the 60th minute.*

haughty, haughtier, haughtiest [*Rhymes with* **naughty**] ADJECTIVE showing excessive pride • *He behaved in a haughty manner.* **haughtily** ADVERB

SIMILAR WORDS: disdainful, proud, supercilious

haul, hauls, hauling, hauled VERB ① To haul something somewhere means to pull it with great effort. ▶ NOUN ② a quantity of something obtained • *a good haul of fish.* ▶ PHRASE ③ Something that you describe as **a long haul** takes a lot of time and effort to achieve • *So women began the long haul to equality.*

haulage [Said *hawl-lij*] NOUN Haulage is the business or cost of transporting goods by road.

haunches PLURAL NOUN Your haunches are your buttocks and the tops of your legs • *He squatted on his haunches.*

haunt, haunts, haunting, haunted VERB ① If a ghost haunts a place, it is seen or heard there regularly. ② If a memory or a fear haunts you, it continually worries you. ▶ NOUN ③ A person's favourite haunt is a place they like to visit often.

haunted ADJECTIVE ① regularly visited by a ghost • *a haunted house.* ② very worried or troubled • *a haunted expression.*

haunting ADJECTIVE extremely beautiful or sad so that it makes a lasting impression on you • *haunting landscapes*.

have, **has**, **having**, **had** VERB ① Have is an auxiliary verb, used to form the past tense or to express completed actions • *They have never met* • *I have lost it.* ② If you have something, you own or possess it • *We have two tickets for the concert.* ③ If you have something, you experience it, it happens to you, or you are affected by it • *I have an idea!* • *He had a marvellous time.* ④ To have a child or baby animal means to give birth to it • *When is she having the baby?* ▶ PHRASE ⑤ If you **have to** do something, you must do it. If you **had better** do something, you ought to do it.

haven, **havens** [*Said* **hay-ven**] NOUN a safe place.

havoc NOUN ① Havoc is disorder and confusion. ▶ PHRASE ② To **play havoc** with something means to cause great disorder and confusion • *Food allergies often play havoc with the immune system.*

hawk, **hawks**, **hawking**, **hawked** NOUN ① a bird of prey with short rounded wings and a long tail. ▶ VERB ② To hawk goods means to sell them by taking them around from place to place.

hawthorn, **hawthorns** NOUN a small, thorny tree producing white blossom and red berries.

hay NOUN Hay is grass which has been cut and dried and is used as animal feed.

hay fever NOUN Hay fever is an allergy to pollen, causing sneezing and watering eyes.

haystack, **haystacks** NOUN a large, firmly built pile of hay, usually covered and left out in the open.

hazard, **hazards**, **hazarding**, **hazarded** NOUN ① SCIENCE a substance, object or action which could be dangerous to you. ▶ VERB ② If you hazard something, you put it at risk • *hazarding the health of his crew.* ▶ PHRASE ③ If you **hazard a guess**, you make a guess. **hazardous** ADJECTIVE

WORD HISTORY: from Arabic *az-zahr* meaning 'gaming dice'

haze NOUN If there is a haze, you cannot see clearly because there is moisture or smoke in the air.

hazel, **hazels** NOUN ① a small tree producing edible nuts. ▶ ADJECTIVE ② greenish brown in colour.

hazy, **hazier**, **haziest** ADJECTIVE dim or vague • *hazy sunshine* • *a hazy memory.*

he PRONOUN 'He' is used to refer to a man, boy or male animal.

head, **heads**, **heading**, **headed** NOUN ① Your head is the part of your body which has your eyes, brain and mouth in it. ② Your head is also your mind and mental abilities • *He has a head for figures.* ③ The head of something is the top, start or most important end • *at the head of the table.* ④ The head of a group or organisation is the person in charge. ⑤ The head on beer is the layer of froth on the top. ⑥ The head on a computer or tape recorder is the part that can read or write information. ⑦ When you toss a coin, the side called heads is the one with the head on it. ▶ VERB ⑧ To head a group or organisation means to be in charge • *Bryce heads the aid organisation.* ⑨ To head in a particular direction means to move in that direction • *She is heading for the city centre.* ⑩ To head a ball means to hit it with your head. ▶ PHRASE ⑪ If you **lose your head**, you panic. ⑫ If you say that someone is **off their head**, you mean that they are mad. ⑬ If something is **over someone's head**, it is too difficult for them to understand. ⑭ If you **can't make head nor tail of something**, you cannot understand it. **head off** VERB If you head off someone or something, you make them change direction or prevent something from happening • *He hopes to head off a public squabble.*

headache, headaches NOUN ① a pain in your head. ② Something that is a headache is causing a lot of difficulty or worry • *Homework can be a headache for school students.*

header, headers NOUN A header in soccer is hitting the ball with your head.

heading, headings NOUN a piece of writing that is written or printed at the top of a page or section.

headland, headlands NOUN
GEOGRAPHY a narrow piece of land jutting out into the sea.

headlight, headlights NOUN The headlights on a motor vehicle are the large powerful lights at the front.

headline, headlines NOUN ① A newspaper headline is the title of a newspaper article printed in large, bold type. ② The headlines are the main points of the radio or television news.

headmaster, headmasters NOUN a man who is the head teacher of a school.

headmistress, headmistresses NOUN a woman who is the head teacher of a school.

head of state, heads of state NOUN the highest-ranking person in a country, such as the president or monarch.

headphones PLURAL NOUN Headphones are a pair of small speakers which you wear in or over your ears to listen to music without other people hearing.

headquarters NOUN The headquarters of an organisation is the main place or the place from which it is run.

headroom NOUN Headroom is the amount of space below a roof or surface under which an object must pass or fit.

headstone, headstones NOUN a large stone standing at one end of a grave and showing the name of the person buried there.

headstrong ADJECTIVE determined to do something in your own way and ignoring other people's advice.

head teacher, head teachers NOUN the teacher who is in charge of a school.

headway PHRASE If you are **making headway**, you are making progress.

headwind, headwinds NOUN a wind blowing in the opposite direction to the way you are travelling.

heady, headier, headiest ADJECTIVE extremely exciting • *the heady days of the civil rights era.*

heal, heals, healing, healed VERB If something heals or if you heal it, it becomes healthy or normal again • *He had a nasty wound which had not healed properly.*

healer, healers NOUN a person who heals people.

health NOUN ① PSHE Your health is the condition of your body • *His health is not good.* ② Health is also the state of being free from disease and feeling well.
SIMILAR WORDS: ② fitness, wellbeing
WORD HISTORY: from Old English *hælth* a toast drunk to a person's wellbeing

health care NOUN Health care is the provision of medical services.

health food, health foods NOUN food which is free from added chemicals and is considered to be good for your health.

healthy, healthier, healthiest ADJECTIVE ① PSHE Someone who is healthy is fit and strong and does not have any diseases. ② Something that is healthy is good for you • *a healthy diet*. ③ An organisation or system that is healthy is successful • *a healthy economy*. **healthily** ADVERB
SIMILAR WORDS: ① fit, well

heap, heaps, heaping, heaped NOUN ① a pile of things. ② (*in plural, informal*) Heaps of something means plenty of it • *His performance earned him heaps of praise*. ▶ VERB ③ If you heap things, you pile them up. ④ To heap something such as praise on someone means to give them a lot of it.
SIMILAR WORDS: ① mass, mound, pile

hear, hears, hearing, heard VERB ① When you hear sounds, you are aware of them because they reach your ears. ② When you hear from someone, they write to you or phone you. ③ When you hear about something, you are informed about it. ④ When a judge hears a case, he or she listens to it in court in order to make a decision on it. ▶ PHRASE ⑤ If you say that you **won't hear of** something, you mean you refuse to allow it. **hear out** VERB If you hear someone out, you listen to all they have to say without interrupting.

SPELLING TIP
Do not confuse the spellings of *hear* and *here*: *I hear a dog barking; Come over here*.

SPELLING TIP
Do not confuse the spellings of *heard* and *herd*: *I thought I heard the doorbell; a herd of buffalo*.

hearing, hearings NOUN ① Hearing is the sense which makes it possible for you to be aware of sounds • *My hearing is poor*. ② a court trial or official meeting to hear facts about an incident. ③ If someone gives you a hearing, they let you give your point of view and listen to you.

hearsay NOUN Hearsay is information that you have heard from other people rather than something that you know personally to be true.

hearse, hearses [*Rhymes with verse*] NOUN a large car that carries the coffin at a funeral.

heart, hearts NOUN ① the organ in your chest that pumps the blood around your body. ② Your heart is also thought of as the centre of your emotions. ③ Heart is courage, determination or enthusiasm • *They were losing heart*. ④ The heart of something is the most central and important part of it. ⑤ a shape similar to a heart, used especially as a symbol of love. ⑥ Hearts is one of the four suits in a pack of playing cards. It is marked by a red heart-shaped symbol.

heartache, heartaches NOUN Heartache is very great sadness and emotional suffering.

heart attack, heart attacks NOUN a serious medical condition in which the heart suddenly beats irregularly or stops completely.

heartbreak, heartbreaks NOUN Heartbreak is great sadness and emotional suffering. **heartbreaking** ADJECTIVE

heartbroken ADJECTIVE very sad and

emotionally upset • *She was heartbroken when her cat was lost.*

heartburn NOUN Heartburn is a painful burning sensation in your chest, caused by indigestion.

heartening ADJECTIVE encouraging or uplifting • *heartening news.*

heart failure NOUN Heart failure is a serious condition in which someone's heart does not work as well as it should, sometimes stopping completely.

heartfelt ADJECTIVE sincerely and deeply felt • *Our heartfelt sympathy goes out to you.*

hearth, hearths [*Said* harth] NOUN the floor of a fireplace.

heartless ADJECTIVE cruel and unkind.

heart-rending ADJECTIVE causing great sadness and pity • *a heart-rending story.*

heart-throb, heart-throbs NOUN someone who is attractive to a lot of people.

heart-to-heart, heart-to-hearts NOUN a discussion in which two people talk about their deepest feelings.

hearty, heartier, heartiest ADJECTIVE ①cheerful and enthusiastic • *hearty congratulations.* ②strongly felt • *a hearty dislike for her teacher.* ③A hearty meal is large and satisfying. **heartily** ADVERB

heat, heats, heating, heated NOUN ①Heat is warmth or the quality of being hot; also the temperature of something that is warm or hot. ②Heat is strength of feeling, especially of anger or excitement. ③a contest or race in a competition held to decide who will play in the final. ▶VERB ④To heat something means to raise its temperature. ▶PHRASE ⑤When a female animal is

on heat, she is ready for mating.

heater, heaters NOUN a piece of equipment or a machine which is used to raise the temperature of something.

heath, heaths NOUN an area of open land covered with rough grass or heather.

heathen, heathens NOUN (*old-fashioned*) someone who does not believe in one of the established religions.

heather NOUN a plant with small purple or white flowers that grows wild on hills and moorland.

heating NOUN Heating is the equipment used to heat a building; also the process and cost of running the equipment to provide heat.

heatwave, heatwaves NOUN a period of time during which the weather is much hotter than usual.

heave, heaves, heaving, heaved VERB ①To heave something means to move or throw it with a lot of effort. ②If your stomach heaves, you vomit or suddenly feel sick. ③If you heave a sigh, you sigh loudly. ▶NOUN ④If you give something a heave, you move or throw it with a lot of effort.

heaven, heavens NOUN ① RE a place of happiness where God is believed to live and where good people are believed to go when they die. ②(*informal*) If you describe something as heaven, you mean that it is wonderful • *The cake was pure heaven.* ▶PHRASE ③You say **Good heavens** to express surprise.

heavenly ADJECTIVE ①relating to heaven • *a heavenly choir.* ②(*informal*) wonderful • *heavenly chocolate ice cream.*

heavy, heavier, heaviest; heavies ADJECTIVE ①great in weight or force • *How heavy are you?* • *a heavy blow.*

② great in degree or amount • *heavy casualties*. ③ solid and thick in appearance • *heavy shoes*. ④ using a lot of something quickly • *The van is heavy on petrol*. ⑤ serious and difficult to deal with or understand • *It all got a bit heavy when the police arrived* • *a heavy speech*. ⑥ Food that is heavy is solid and difficult to digest • *a heavy meal*. ⑦ When it is heavy, the weather is hot, humid and still. ⑧ Someone with a heavy heart is very sad. ▸ NOUN ⑨ (*informal*) a large, strong man employed to protect someone or something. **heavily** ADVERB **heaviness** NOUN

heavy-duty ADJECTIVE Heavy-duty equipment is strong and hard-wearing.

heavy-handed ADJECTIVE showing a lack of care or thought and using too much authority • *The demonstration was broken up in a heavy-handed way*.

heavyweight, heavyweights NOUN ① a boxer in the heaviest weight group. ② an important person with a lot of influence.

Hebrew, Hebrews [*Said* hee-broo] NOUN ① Hebrew is an ancient language now spoken in Israel, where it is the official language. ② In the past, the Hebrews were Hebrew-speaking Jews who lived in Israel. ▸ ADJECTIVE ③ relating to the Hebrews and their customs.

heckle, heckles, heckling, heckled VERB If members of an audience heckle a speaker, they interrupt and shout rude remarks. **heckler** NOUN

hectare, hectares NOUN a unit for measuring areas of land, equal to 10,000 square metres or about 2.471 acres.

hectic ADJECTIVE involving a lot of rushed activity • *a hectic schedule*.

hedge, hedges, hedging, hedged NOUN ① a row of bushes forming a barrier or boundary. ▸ VERB ② If you hedge against something unpleasant happening, you protect yourself. ③ If you hedge, you avoid answering a question or dealing with a problem. ▸ PHRASE ④ If you **hedge your bets**, you support two or more people or courses of action to avoid the risk of losing a lot.

hedgehog, hedgehogs NOUN a small, brown animal with sharp spikes covering its back.

hedonism [*Said* hee-dn-izm] NOUN Hedonism is the belief that gaining pleasure is the most important thing in life. **hedonistic** ADJECTIVE

heed, heeds, heeding, heeded VERB ① If you heed someone's advice, you pay attention to it. ▸ NOUN ② If you take or pay heed to something, you give it careful attention.
SIMILAR WORDS: ① listen to, mind, pay attention to

heel, heels, heeling, heeled NOUN ① the back part of your foot. ② The heel of a shoe or sock is the part that fits over your heel. ▸ VERB ③ To heel a pair of shoes means to put a new piece on the heel. ▸ PHRASE ④ A person or place that looks **down at heel** looks untidy and in poor condition.

heeler, heelers NOUN In Australia and New Zealand, a heeler is a dog that herds cattle by biting at their heels.

hefty, heftier, heftiest ADJECTIVE of great size, force or weight • *a hefty fine* • *hefty volumes*.

height, heights NOUN ① The height of an object is its measurement from the bottom to the top. ② a high position or place • *Their nesting rarely takes place at any great height*. ③ The height of something is its peak, or the time when it is most successful or intense • *the height of the tourist season* • *at the height of his career.* ④ MATHS In maths, the height of a triangle is the point where two sides meet at a peak opposite the base.

heighten, heightens, heightening, heightened VERB If something heightens a feeling or experience, it increases its intensity.

heinous [Said *hay-nuss* or *hee-nuss*] ADJECTIVE evil and terrible • *heinous crimes.*

heir, heirs [Said *air*] NOUN A person's heir is the person who is entitled to inherit their property or title.

heiress, heiresses [Said *air-iss*] NOUN a female with the right to inherit property or a title.

heirloom, heirlooms [Said *air-loom*] NOUN something belonging to a family that has been passed from one generation to another.

held the past tense and past participle of **hold**.

helicopter, helicopters NOUN an aircraft with rotating blades above it which enable it to take off vertically, hover and fly.
WORD HISTORY: from Greek *heliko* + *pteron* meaning 'spiral wing'

helium [Said *hee-lee-um*] NOUN SCIENCE Helium is an element which is a colourless inert gas. It occurs in some natural gases, and is used in air balloons. Its atomic number is 2 and its symbol is He.
WORD HISTORY: from Greek *hēlios* meaning 'sun', because helium was first discovered in the solar spectrum

hell NOUN ① RE Hell is the place where souls of evil people are believed to go to be punished after death. ② (*informal*) If you say that something is hell, you mean it is very

unpleasant. ▸ INTERJECTION ③ 'Hell' is also a swearword.

hell-bent ADJECTIVE determined to do something whatever the consequences.

hellish ADJECTIVE (*informal*) very unpleasant.

hello INTERJECTION You say 'Hello' as a greeting or when you answer the phone.

helm, helms NOUN ① The helm on a boat is the position from which it is steered and the wheel or tiller.
▸ PHRASE ② **At the helm** means in a position of leadership or control.

helmet, helmets NOUN a hard hat worn to protect the head.

help, helps, helping, helped VERB ① To help someone means to make something easier or better for them. ▸ NOUN ② If you need or give help, you need or give assistance. ③ someone or something that helps you • *He really is a good help.* ▸ PHRASE ④ If you **help yourself** to something, you take it. ⑤ If you **can't help** something, you cannot control it or change it • *I can't help feeling sorry for him.*

helper, helpers NOUN a person who gives assistance.

helpful ADJECTIVE ① If someone is helpful, they help you by doing something for you. ② Something that is helpful makes a situation more pleasant or easier to tolerate.
helpfully ADVERB
SIMILAR WORDS: ① cooperative, supportive ② beneficial, useful

helping, helpings NOUN an amount of food that you get in a single serving.

helpless ADJECTIVE ① unable to cope on your own • *a helpless child.* ② weak or powerless • *helpless despair.*
helplessly ADVERB **helplessness** NOUN

a b c d e f g **h** i j k l m n o p q r s t u v w x y z

hem, hems, hemming, hemmed
NOUN ①The hem of a garment is an edge which has been turned over and sewn in place. ▶VERB ②To hem something means to make a hem on it. **hem in** VERB If someone is hemmed in, they are surrounded and prevented from moving.

hemisphere, hemispheres [Said hem-iss-feer] NOUN one half of the earth, the brain or a sphere. **hemispherical** ADJECTIVE

hemp NOUN Hemp is a tall plant, some varieties of which are used to make rope, and others to produce the drug cannabis.

hen, hens NOUN a female chicken; also any female bird.

hence ADVERB ①(formal) for this reason • I was tired when I sat the test, hence I made mistakes. ②from now or from the time mentioned • The convention is due to start two weeks hence.

henceforth ADVERB (formal) from this time onwards • His life henceforth was to revolve around her.

henchman, henchmen NOUN The henchmen of a powerful person are the people employed to do violent or dishonest work for that person.

hepatitis NOUN Hepatitis is a serious infectious disease causing inflammation of the liver.

heptagon, heptagons NOUN MATHS a shape with seven straight sides. **heptagonal** ADJECTIVE

her PRONOUN or ADJECTIVE 'Her' is used to refer to a woman, girl or female animal that has already been mentioned, or to show that something belongs to a particular female.

herald, heralds, heralding, heralded NOUN ①In the past, a herald was a messenger. ▶VERB ②Something that heralds a future event is a sign of that event.

herb, herbs NOUN a plant whose leaves are used in medicine or to flavour food. **herbal** ADJECTIVE **herbalist** NOUN

herbicide, herbicides NOUN SCIENCE a chemical used to kill plants, especially weeds.

herbivore, herbivores NOUN an animal that eats only plants. **herbivorous** ADJECTIVE

herd, herds, herding, herded NOUN ①a large group of animals. ▶VERB ②To herd animals or people means to make them move together as a group.

SPELLING TIP
Do not confuse the spellings of herd and heard, the past tense of hear: a herd of buffalo; I thought I heard the doorbell.

---

here ADVERB ①at, to or in the place where you are, or the place mentioned or indicated. ▶PHRASE ②**Here and there** means in various unspecified places • dense forests broken here and there by small towns.

SPELLING TIP
Do not confuse the spellings of here and hear: Come over here; I hear a dog barking.

---

hereafter ADVERB (formal) after this time or point • the South China Morning Post (referred to hereafter as SCMP).

hereby ADVERB (formal) used in documents and statements to indicate that a declaration is official • All leave is hereby cancelled.

hereditary ADJECTIVE passed on to a child from a parent • a hereditary disease.

A
B
C
D
E
F
G
H
I
J
K
L
M
N
O
P
Q
R
S
T
U
V
W
X
Y
Z

SPELLING TIP
Do not confuse the spellings of *hereditary* and *heredity*: *Her curly hair is hereditary; Eye colour is determined by heredity.*

heredity NOUN Heredity is the process by which characteristics are passed from parents to their children through the genes.

SPELLING TIP
Do not confuse the spellings of *heredity* and *hereditary*: *Eye colour is determined by heredity; Her curly hair is hereditary.*

herein ADVERB (*formal*) in this place or document.

heresy, heresies [*Said* **herr**-*ess-ee*] NOUN Heresy is belief or behaviour considered to be wrong because it disagrees with what is generally accepted, especially with regard to religion. **heretic** NOUN **heretical** ADJECTIVE

heritage NOUN the possessions or traditions that have been passed from one generation to another.

hermit, hermits NOUN a person who lives alone with a simple way of life, especially for religious reasons.
WORD HISTORY: from Greek *erēmitēs* meaning 'living in the desert'

hernia, hernias [*Said* **her**-*nee-a*] NOUN a medical condition in which part of the intestine sticks through a weak point in the surrounding tissue.

hero, heroes NOUN ① the main male character in a book, film or play. ② a person who has done something brave or good.

heroic ADJECTIVE brave, courageous and determined. **heroically** ADVERB

heroin [*Said* **herr**-*oh-in*] NOUN Heroin is a powerful drug formerly used as an anaesthetic and now taken illegally by some people for pleasure.

SPELLING TIP
Do not confuse the spellings of *heroin* and *heroine*: *addicted to heroin; The heroine of the book is Elizabeth Bennet.*

heroine, heroines [*Said* **herr**-*oh-in*] NOUN ① the main female character in a book, film or play. ② a woman who has done something brave or good.

SPELLING TIP
Do not confuse the spellings of *heroine* and *heroin*: *The heroine of the book is Elizabeth Bennet; addicted to heroin.*

heroism [*Said* **herr**-*oh-izm*] NOUN Heroism is great courage and bravery.

heron, herons NOUN a wading bird with very long legs and a long beak and neck.

herpes [*Said* **her**-*peez*] NOUN Herpes is a virus which causes painful red spots on the skin.

herring, herrings NOUN a silvery fish that lives in large shoals in northern seas.

hers PRONOUN 'Hers' refers to something that belongs or relates to a woman, girl or female animal.

herself PRONOUN ① 'Herself' is used when the same woman, girl or female animal does an action and is affected by it • *She pulled herself out of the water.* ② 'Herself' is used to emphasise 'she' • *She herself was not a keen gardener.*

hertz NOUN A hertz is a unit of frequency equal to one cycle per second. It is named after the German physicist H.R. Hertz (1857–1894).

hesitant ADJECTIVE If you are hesitant, you do not do something immediately because you are uncertain or worried. **hesitantly** ADVERB

a
b
c
d
e
f
g
h
i
j
k
l
m
n
o
p
q
r
s
t
u
v
w
x
y
z

SIMILAR WORDS: irresolute, uncertain, unsure

hesitate, hesitates, hesitating, hesitated VERB To hesitate means to pause or show uncertainty. **hesitation** NOUN

hessian NOUN Hessian is a thick, rough fabric used for making sacks.

heterosexual, heterosexuals [Said het-roh-*seks*-yool] NOUN ① a person who is attracted to people of the opposite sex. ▸ ADJECTIVE ② attracted to people of the opposite sex.

hewn ADJECTIVE carved from a substance • *a cave, hewn out of the hillside*.

hexagon, hexagons NOUN MATHS a shape with six straight sides; a **regular hexagon** has six straight sides of the same length. **hexagonal** ADJECTIVE

hexameter, hexameters NOUN ENGLISH a line of verse that has six metrical feet.

heyday [Said *hay*-day] NOUN The heyday of a person or thing is the period when they are most successful or popular • *Hollywood in its heyday*.

hi INTERJECTION 'Hi!' is an informal greeting.

hiatus, hiatuses [Said high-*ay*-tuss] NOUN (formal) a pause or gap.

hibernate, hibernates, hibernating, hibernated VERB Animals that hibernate spend the winter in a state like deep sleep. **hibernation** NOUN WORD HISTORY: from Latin *hibernare* meaning 'to spend the winter'

hibiscus, hibiscuses [Said hie-*bis*-kuss] NOUN a type of tropical shrub with brightly coloured flowers.

hiccup, hiccups, hiccupping, hiccupped [Said *hik*-kup] NOUN ① Hiccups are short, uncontrolled choking sounds in your throat that you sometimes get if you have been eating or drinking too quickly. ② (informal) a minor problem. ▸ VERB ③ When you hiccup, you make little choking sounds.

hide, hides, hiding, hid, hidden VERB ① To hide something means to put it where it cannot be seen, or to prevent it from being discovered • *He was unable to hide his disappointment*. ▸ NOUN ② the skin of a large animal. SIMILAR WORDS: ① conceal, disguise

hideous [Said *hid*-ee-uss] ADJECTIVE extremely ugly or unpleasant. **hideously** ADVERB

hideout, hideouts NOUN a hiding place.

hiding, hidings NOUN (informal) To give someone a hiding means to beat them severely.

hierarchy, hierarchies [Said high-er-ar-kee] NOUN a system in which people or things are ranked according to how important they are. **hierarchical** ADJECTIVE

high, higher, highest; highs ADJECTIVE ① tall or a long way above the ground. ② great in degree, quantity or intensity • *high interest rates* • *There is a high risk of failure*. ③ towards the top of a scale of importance or quality • *high fashion*. ④ close to the top of a range of sound or notes • *the human voice reaches a very high pitch*. ⑤ (informal) Someone who is high on a drug is affected by having taken it. ▸ ADVERB ⑥ at or to a height. ▸ NOUN ⑦ a high point or level • *Morale reached a new high*. ▸ PHRASE ⑧ (informal) Someone who is **on a high** is in a very excited and optimistic mood. SIMILAR WORDS: ① lofty, tall, towering

highbrow ADJECTIVE concerned with serious, intellectual subjects.

higher education NOUN Higher education is education at universities and colleges.

highest common factor, highest common factors NOUN MATHS In a group of numbers, the highest common factor is the largest number that divides equally into each number in the group. For example, the highest common factor of 8, 12 and 16 is 4.

high jump NOUN The high jump is an athletics event involving jumping over a high bar.

highlands PLURAL NOUN Highlands are mountainous or hilly areas of land.

highlight, highlights, highlighting, highlighted VERB ① If you highlight a point or problem, you emphasise and draw attention to it. ▶ NOUN ② The highlight of something is the most interesting part of it • *His show was the highlight of the Festival.* ③ ART a lighter area of a painting, showing where light shines on things. ④ Highlights are also light-coloured streaks in someone's hair.

highly ADVERB ① extremely • *It is highly unlikely I'll be able to replace it.* ② towards the top of a scale of importance, admiration or respect • *She thought highly of him* • *highly qualified personnel.*

high-minded ADJECTIVE Someone who is high-minded has strong moral principles.

Highness NOUN 'Highness' is used in titles and forms of address for members of the royal family other than a king or queen • *Her Royal Highness, Princess Alexandra.*

high-pitched ADJECTIVE A high-pitched sound is high and often rather shrill.

high-rise ADJECTIVE High-rise buildings are very tall.

high school, high schools NOUN a secondary school.

high technology NOUN High technology is the development and use of advanced electronics and computers.

high tide NOUN On a coast, high tide is the time, usually twice a day, when the sea is at its highest level.

highveld [Said hai-felt] NOUN The highveld is a grassy region of eastern South Africa that is high above sea level.

high-water mark NOUN GEOGRAPHY The high-water mark is the highest level reached by the sea at high tide or a river in a flood.

highway, highways NOUN a road along which vehicles have the right to pass.

highwayman, highwaymen NOUN In the past, highwaymen were robbers on horseback who used to rob travellers.

hijab, hijabs NOUN a head-covering worn by some Muslim women.

hijack, hijacks, hijacking, hijacked VERB If someone hijacks a plane or vehicle, they illegally take control of it during a journey. **hijacker** NOUN **hijacking** NOUN

hike, hikes, hiking, hiked NOUN ① a long country walk. ▶ VERB ② To hike means to walk long distances in the country. **hiker** NOUN

hilarious ADJECTIVE very funny. **hilariously** ADVERB SIMILAR WORDS: funny, humorous, uproarious

hilarity NOUN Hilarity is great amusement and laughter.

hill, hills NOUN a rounded area of land higher than the land surrounding it. **hilly** ADJECTIVE

hillbilly, hillbillies NOUN someone

who lives in the country away from other people, especially in remote areas in the southern United States.

hilt, hilts NOUN The hilt of a sword or knife is its handle.

him PRONOUN You use 'him' to refer to a man, boy or male animal that has already been mentioned.

himself PRONOUN ① 'Himself' is used when the same man, boy or male animal does an action and is affected by it • *He discharged himself from hospital*. ② 'Himself' is used to emphasise 'he' • *He himself was not keen to join the others*.

hind, hinds [*Rhymes with blind*] ADJECTIVE ① used to refer to the back part of an animal • *the hind legs*. ▶ NOUN ② a female deer.

hinder, hinders, hindering, hindered VERB ① [*Said hin-der*] If you hinder someone or something, you get in their way and make something difficult for them. ▶ ADJECTIVE ② [*Said hine-der*] The hinder parts of an animal are the parts at the back.

Hindi [*Said hin-dee*] NOUN Hindi is a language spoken in northern India.

hindrance, hindrances NOUN ① Someone or something that is a hindrance causes difficulties or is an obstruction. ② Hindrance is the act of hindering someone or something.

hindsight NOUN Hindsight is the ability to understand an event after it has actually taken place • *With hindsight, I realised how odd he is*.

Hindu, Hindus [*Said hin-doo*] NOUN RE a person who believes in Hinduism, an Indian religion which has many gods and believes that people have another life on earth after death. **Hinduism** NOUN

hinge, hinges, hinging, hinged NOUN ① the movable joint which attaches a door or window to its frame. ▶ VERB ② Something that hinges on a situation or event depends entirely on that situation or event • *Victory or defeat hinged on her final putt*.

hint, hints, hinting, hinted NOUN ① an indirect suggestion. ② a helpful piece of advice. ▶ VERB ③ If you hint at something, you suggest it indirectly.
SIMILAR WORDS: ① clue, indication, suggestion ③ imply, insinuate, suggest

hinterland, hinterlands NOUN The hinterland of a coastline or a port is the area of land behind it or around it.

hip, hips NOUN Your hips are the two parts at the sides of your body between your waist and your upper legs.

hip-hop NOUN Hip-hop is a form of popular culture which started in the United States in the 1980s. It includes rap music and graffiti art.

hippo, hippos NOUN (*informal*) a hippopotamus.

hippopotamus, hippopotamuses or **hippopotami** NOUN a large African animal with thick wrinkled skin and short legs, that lives near rivers.
WORD HISTORY: from Greek *hippo* + *potamos* meaning 'river horse'

hippy, hippies; also spelt **hippie** NOUN In the 1960s and 1970s hippies were people who rejected conventional society and tried to live a life based on peace and love.

hire, hires, hiring, hired VERB ① If you hire something, you pay money to be able to use it for a period of time. ② If you hire someone, you pay them to do a job for you. ▶ PHRASE ③ Something that is **for hire** is available for people to hire.

hire-purchase NOUN Hire-purchase is a way of buying something by making regular payments over a period of time.

hirsute [Said hir-syoot] ADJECTIVE (formal) hairy.

his ADJECTIVE OR PRONOUN 'His' refers to something that belongs or relates to a man, boy or male animal that has already been mentioned, and sometimes also to any person whose gender is not known.

hiss, hisses, hissing, hissed VERB ① To hiss means to make a long 's' sound, especially to show disapproval or aggression. ▶ NOUN ② a long 's' sound.

histogram, histograms NOUN MATHS a graph consisting of rectangles of varying sizes, that shows the frequency of values of a quantity.

historian, historians NOUN a person who studies and writes about history.

historic ADJECTIVE important in the past or likely to be seen as important in the future.

historical ADJECTIVE ① occurring in the past, or relating to the study of the past • historical events. ② describing or representing the past • historical novels. **historically** ADVERB

history, histories NOUN History is the study of the past. A history is a record of the past • The village is steeped in history • my family history.

histrionic, histrionics [Said hiss-tree-on-ik] ADJECTIVE ① Histrionic behaviour is very dramatic and full of exaggerated emotion. ② (formal) relating to drama and acting • a young man of marked histrionic ability.

histrionics PLURAL NOUN Histrionics are dramatic behaviour full of exaggerated emotion.

hit, hits, hitting, hit VERB ① If you hit someone, you strike them forcefully, usually causing hurt or damage. ② If you hit an object, you collide with it. ③ To hit a ball or other object means to make it move by hitting it with something. ④ If something hits you, it affects you badly and suddenly • The recession has hit the tourist industry hard. ⑤ If something hits a particular point or place, it reaches it • The book hit Britain just at the right time. ⑥ If you hit on an idea or solution, you suddenly think of it. ▶ NOUN ⑦ a person or thing that is popular and successful. ⑧ the action of hitting something • Give it a good hard hit with the hammer. ▶ PHRASE ⑨ (informal) If you **hit it off** with someone, you become friendly with them the first time you meet them.

hit and miss ADJECTIVE happening in an unpredictable way or without being properly organised.

hit-and-run ADJECTIVE A hit-and-run car accident is one in which the person who has caused the damage drives away without stopping.

hitch, hitches, hitching, hitched NOUN ① A hitch is a slight problem or difficulty • The whole process was completed without a hitch • an administrative hitch. ▶ VERB ② (informal) If you hitch, you hitchhike • Which country is the safest to hitch round? ③ To hitch something somewhere means to hook it or fasten it there • Each wagon was hitched onto the one in front. ▶ PHRASE ④ (informal) If you **get hitched**, you get married.

hitchhike, hitchhikes, hitchhiking, hitchhiked VERB To hitchhike means to travel by getting lifts from passing vehicles. **hitchhiker** NOUN

hitchhiking NOUN Hitchhiking is travelling by getting free lifts from passing vehicles.

hi tech ADJECTIVE designed using the most modern methods and equipment, especially electronic equipment.

hither (*old-fashioned*) ADVERB ① used to refer to movement towards the place where you are. ▶ PHRASE ② Something that moves **hither and thither** moves in all directions.

hitherto ADVERB (*formal*) until now • *What he was aiming at had not hitherto been attempted*.

HIV NOUN HIV is a virus that reduces people's resistance to illness and can cause AIDS. HIV is an abbreviation for 'human immunodeficiency virus'.

hive, hives, hiving, hived NOUN ① a beehive. ② A place that is a hive of activity is very busy with a lot of people working hard. ▶ VERB ③ If part of something such as a business is hived off, it is transferred to new ownership • *The company is poised to hive off its music interests*.

hoard, hoards, hoarding, hoarded VERB ① To hoard things means to save them even though they may no longer be useful. ▶ NOUN ② a store of things that has been saved or hidden. SIMILAR WORDS: ① save, stockpile, store ② cache, stash, store

---

SPELLING TIP
Do not confuse the spellings of *hoard* and *horde*: *a hoard of Viking treasure*; *hordes of Christmas shoppers*.

---

hoarding, hoardings NOUN a large advertising board by the side of the road.

hoarse, hoarser, hoarsest ADJECTIVE A hoarse voice sounds rough and unclear. **hoarsely** ADVERB

hoax, hoaxes, hoaxing, hoaxed NOUN ① a trick or an attempt to deceive someone. ▶ VERB ② To hoax someone means to trick or deceive them. **hoaxer** NOUN

hob, hobs NOUN a surface on top of a cooker which can be heated in order to cook things.

hobble, hobbles, hobbling, hobbled VERB ① If you hobble, you walk awkwardly because of pain or injury. ② If you hobble an animal, you tie its legs together to restrict its movement.

hobby, hobbies NOUN something that you do for enjoyment in your spare time.

hock, hocks NOUN The hock of a horse or other animal is the angled joint in its back leg.

hockey NOUN Hockey is a game in which two teams use long sticks with curved ends to try to hit a small ball into the other team's goal.

hoe, hoes, hoeing, hoed NOUN ① a long-handled gardening tool with a small square blade, used to remove weeds and break up the soil. ▶ VERB ② To hoe the ground means to use a hoe on it.

hog, hogs, hogging, hogged NOUN ① a castrated male pig. ▶ VERB ② (*informal*) If you hog something, you take more than your share of it, or keep it for too long. ▶ PHRASE ③ (*informal*) If you **go the whole hog**, you do something completely or thoroughly in a bold or extravagant way.

hoist, hoists, hoisting, hoisted VERB ① To hoist something means to lift it, especially using a crane or other machinery. ▶ NOUN ② a machine for lifting heavy things.

hokey-pokey NOUN In New Zealand, hokey-pokey is a kind of brittle toffee.

hold, holds, holding, held VERB
① To hold something means to carry or keep it in place, usually with your hand or arms. ② Someone who holds power, office or an opinion has it or possesses it. ③ If you hold something such as a meeting or an election, you arrange it and cause it to happen. ④ If something holds, it is still available or valid • *The offer still holds*. ⑤ If you hold someone responsible for something, you consider them responsible for it. ⑥ If something holds a certain number or amount, it can contain that number or amount • *The theatre holds 150 people*. ⑦ If you hold something such as theatre tickets, a telephone call, or the price of something, you keep or reserve it for a period of time • *The line is engaged – will you hold?* ⑧ To hold something down means to keep it or to keep it under control • *I managed to hold down a job for years*. ⑨ If you hold on to something, you continue it or keep it even though it might be difficult • *They are keen to hold on to their culture*. ⑩ To hold something back means to prevent it, keep it under control, or not reveal it • *She failed to hold back the tears*. ▸ NOUN ⑪ If someone or something has a hold over you, they have power, control or influence over you • *The party has a considerable hold over its own leader*. ⑫ a way of holding something or the act of holding it • *He grabbed the rope and got a hold on it*. ⑬ the place where cargo or luggage is stored in a ship or a plane. **holder** NOUN **hold out** VERB If you hold out, you stand firm and manage to resist opposition in difficult circumstances • *The rebels could hold out for ten years*. **hold up** VERB If something holds you up, it delays you.

holdall, holdalls NOUN a large, soft bag for carrying clothing.

hole, holes, holing, holed NOUN ① an opening or hollow in something. ② (*informal*) If you are in a hole, you are in a difficult situation. ③ (*informal*) A hole in a theory or argument is a weakness or error in it. ④ In golf, a hole is one of the small holes into which you have to hit the ball. ▸ VERB ⑤ When you hole the ball in golf, you hit the ball into one of the holes.
SIMILAR WORDS: ① aperture, gap, opening

SPELLING TIP
Do not confuse the spellings of *hole* and *whole*: *You have a hole in your sock; Emily was away for the whole of July*.

Holi NOUN RE Holi is a Hindu festival celebrated in spring.

holiday, holidays, holidaying, holidayed NOUN ① a period of time spent away from home for enjoyment. ② a time when you are not working or not at school. ▸ VERB ③ When you holiday somewhere, you take a holiday there • *She is currently holidaying in Italy*.
WORD HISTORY: from Old English *haligdæg* meaning 'holy day'

holidaymaker, holidaymakers NOUN a person who is away from home on holiday.

holiness NOUN ① Holiness is the state or quality of being holy. ② 'Your Holiness' and 'His Holiness' are titles used to address or refer to the Pope or to leaders of some other religions.

hollow, hollows, hollowing, hollowed ADJECTIVE ① Something that is hollow has space inside it rather than being solid. ② An opinion or situation that is hollow has no real value or worth • *a hollow gesture*.

a b c d e f g h i j k l m n o p q r s t u v w x y z

③A hollow sound is dull and has a slight echo • *the hollow sound of his footsteps on the stairs.* ▶ NOUN ④a hole in something or a part of a surface that is lower than the rest • *It is a pleasant village in a lush hollow.* ▶ VERB ⑤To hollow means to make a hollow • *They hollowed out crude dwellings from the soft rock.*

holly NOUN Holly is an evergreen tree or shrub with spiky leaves. It often has red berries in winter.

holocaust, holocausts [*Said hol-o-kawst*] NOUN ①a large-scale destruction or loss of life, especially the result of war or fire. ② HISTORY The Holocaust was the mass murder of the Jews in Europe by the Nazis during World War II.
WORD HISTORY: from Greek *holos* + *kaustos* meaning 'completely burnt'

holster, holsters NOUN a holder for a hand gun, worn at the side of the body or under the arm.

holy, holier, holiest ADJECTIVE ① RE relating to God or to a particular religion • *the holy city.* ② Someone who is holy is religious and leads a pure and good life.
SIMILAR WORDS: ① hallowed, sacred ② devout, pious

homage [*Said hom-ij*] NOUN Homage is an act of respect and admiration • *The thronging crowds paid homage to their assassinated president.*

home, homes, homing, homed NOUN ①Your home is the building or place in which you live or feel you belong. ②a building in which elderly or ill people live and are looked after • *He has been living in a nursing home since his stroke.* ▶ ADJECTIVE ③connected with or involving your home or country • *He gave them his home phone number* • *coverage of both home and overseas news.* **home in** VERB If something homes in on a

target, it moves directly and quickly towards it.
SIMILAR WORDS: ① abode, dwelling, residence

SPELLING TIP
Do not confuse the spellings of *home* and *hone*: *The police are homing in on a suspect; He spent hours honing his basketball skills.*

homeland, homelands NOUN Your homeland is your native country.

homeless ADJECTIVE ①having no home. ▶ PLURAL NOUN ②The homeless are people who have no home. **homelessness** NOUN

homely, homelier, homeliest ADJECTIVE simple, ordinary and comfortable • *The room was small and homely.*

homeopathy [*Said home-ee-op-path-ee*] NOUN Homeopathy is a way of treating illness by giving the patient tiny amounts of a substance that would normally cause illness in a healthy person. **homeopathic** ADJECTIVE **homeopath** NOUN

homeowner, homeowners NOUN a person who owns the home in which he or she lives.

homesick ADJECTIVE unhappy because of being away from home and missing family and friends. **homesickness** NOUN

homespun ADJECTIVE not sophisticated or complicated • *The book contains simple homespun philosophy.*

homestead, homesteads NOUN a house and its land and other buildings, especially a farm.

home truth, home truths NOUN Home truths are unpleasant facts about yourself that you are told by someone else.

homeward or **homewards**
ADJECTIVE or ADVERB towards home
• *the homeward journey*.

homework NOUN ① Homework is
school work given to pupils to be
done in the evening at home.
② Homework is also research and
preparation • *You certainly need to do
your homework before buying a horse*.

homicide, homicides NOUN
Homicide is the crime of murder.
homicidal ADJECTIVE

homing ADJECTIVE A homing device is
able to guide itself to a target. An
animal with a homing instinct is able
to guide itself home.

homonym, homonyms NOUN
[ENGLISH] Homonyms are words
which are pronounced or spelt in the
same way but which have different
meanings. For example, *swift* is an
adjective meaning 'fast', and the
name for a type of bird; *meat* is the
flesh of animals, and *meet* is a verb
meaning 'encounter'.

homophobia NOUN Homophobia is
a strong and unreasonable dislike of
homosexual people.

homophone, homophones NOUN
[ENGLISH] Homophones are words
with different meanings which are
pronounced in the same way but are
spelt differently. For example, 'write'
and 'right' are homophones.

homo sapiens [*Said hoh-moh
sap-ee-enz*] NOUN (*formal*) Homo
sapiens is the scientific name for
human beings.
WORD HISTORY: from Latin *homo*
meaning 'man' and *sapiens* meaning
'wise'

homosexual, homosexuals NOUN
① a person who is attracted to
people of the same sex. ▶ ADJECTIVE
② attracted to people of the same
sex. **homosexuality** NOUN

hone, hones, honing, honed VERB
① If you hone a tool, you sharpen it.
② If you hone a quality or ability, you
develop and improve it • *He had a
sharply honed sense of justice*.

SPELLING TIP
Do not confuse the spellings of *hone*
and *home*: *He spent hours honing his
basketball skills; The police are homing in
on a suspect*.

honest ADJECTIVE truthful and
trustworthy. **honestly** ADVERB
SIMILAR WORDS: honourable,
trustworthy, truthful

honesty NOUN Honesty is the quality
of being truthful and trustworthy.
SIMILAR WORDS: honour, integrity,
truthfulness

honey NOUN ① Honey is a sweet,
edible, sticky substance produced by
bees. ② 'Honey' means 'sweetheart'
or 'darling' • *What is it, honey?*

honeycomb, honeycombs NOUN a
wax structure consisting of rows of
six-sided cells made by bees for
storage of honey and eggs.

honeyeater, honeyeaters NOUN a
small Australian bird that feeds on
nectar from flowers.

honeymoon, honeymoons NOUN a
holiday taken by a couple who have
just got married.

honeysuckle NOUN Honeysuckle is
a climbing plant with fragrant pink or
cream flowers.

hongi [*Said hong-ee*] NOUN In New
Zealand, hongi is a Māori greeting in
which people touch noses.

honk, honks, honking, honked
NOUN ① a short, loud sound like that
made by a car horn or a goose.
▶ VERB ② When something honks, it
makes a short, loud sound.

honorary ADJECTIVE An honorary
title or job is given as a mark of

a
b
c
d
e
f
g
h
i
j
k
l
m
n
o
p
q
r
s
t
u
v
w
x
y
z

respect, and does not involve the usual qualifications or work • *She was awarded an honorary degree.*

honour, honours, honouring, honoured NOUN ① Your honour is your good reputation and the respect that other people have for you • *This is a war fought by men totally without honour.* ② an award or privilege given as a mark of respect. ③ Honours is a class of university degree which is higher than a pass or ordinary degree. ▶ PHRASE ④ If something is done **in honour of** someone, it is done out of respect for them • *Egypt celebrated frequent minor festivals in honour of the dead.* ▶ VERB ⑤ If you honour someone, you give them special praise or attention, or an award. ⑥ If you honour an agreement or promise, you do what was agreed or promised • *There is enough cash to honour the existing pledges.*

honourable ADJECTIVE worthy of respect or admiration • *He should do the honourable thing and resign.*

hood, hoods NOUN ① a loose covering for the head, usually part of a coat or jacket. ② a cover on a piece of equipment or vehicle, usually curved and movable • *The mechanic had the hood up to work on the engine.* **hooded** ADJECTIVE

-hood SUFFIX '-hood' is added at the end of words to form nouns that indicate a state or condition • *childhood* • *priesthood.*

hoodie, hoodies NOUN a type of casual jacket with a hood.

hoof, hooves or hoofs NOUN the hard bony part of certain animals' feet.

hook, hooks, hooking, hooked NOUN ① a curved piece of metal or plastic that is used for catching, holding or hanging things • *picture hooks.* ② a curving movement, for example

of the fist in boxing, or of a golf ball. ▶ VERB ③ If you hook one thing onto another, you attach it there using a hook. ▶ PHRASE ④ If you are **let off the hook**, something happens so that you avoid punishment or a difficult situation.

hooked ADJECTIVE addicted to something; also obsessed by something • *hooked on soap operas* • *I'm hooked on exercise.*

hooligan, hooligans NOUN a destructive and violent young person. **hooliganism** NOUN
SIMILAR WORDS: delinquent, ruffian, yob

hoop, hoops NOUN a large ring, often used as a toy.

hooray INTERJECTION another spelling of **hurray**.

hoot, hoots, hooting, hooted VERB ① To hoot means to make a long 'oo' sound like an owl • *hooting with laughter.* ② If a car horn hoots, it makes a loud honking noise. ▶ NOUN ③ a sound like that made by an owl or a car horn.

hoover, hoovers, hoovering, hoovered NOUN (*trademark*) ① a vacuum cleaner. ▶ VERB ② When you hoover, you use a vacuum cleaner to clean the floor.

hooves a plural of **hoof**.

hop, hops, hopping, hopped VERB ① If you hop, you jump on one foot. ② When animals or birds hop, they jump with two feet together. ③ (*informal*) If you hop into or out of something, you move there quickly and easily • *You only have to hop on the ferry to get there.* ▶ NOUN ④ a jump on one leg. ⑤ Hops are flowers of the hop plant, which are dried and used for making beer.

hope, hopes, hoping, hoped VERB ① If you hope that something will happen or hope that it is true, you want it to happen or be true. ▶ NOUN ② Hope is a wish or feeling of desire and expectation • *There was little hope of recovery.* **hopeful** ADJECTIVE **hopefully** ADVERB

USAGE NOTE
Some people do not like the use of *hopeful* to mean 'it is hoped', for example *Hopefully, we can get a good result on Saturday.* Although it is very common in speech, it should be avoided in written work.

hopeless ADJECTIVE ① having no hope • *She shook her head in hopeless bewilderment.* ② certain to fail or be unsuccessful. ③ bad or inadequate • *I'm hopeless at remembering birthdays* • *hopeless athletes.* **hopelessly** ADVERB **hopelessness** NOUN

hopper, hoppers NOUN a large, funnel-shaped container for storing things such as grain or sand.

horde, hordes *[Rhymes with bored]* NOUN a large group or number of people or animals • *hordes of tourists.*

SPELLING TIP
Do not confuse the spellings of *horde* and *hoard*: *hordes of Christmas shoppers; a hoard of Viking treasure.*

horizon, horizons *[Said hor-eye-zn]* NOUN ① the distant line where the sky seems to touch the land or sea. ② Your horizons are the limits of what you want to do or are interested in • *Travel broadens your horizons.* ▶ PHRASE ③ If something is **on the horizon**, it is almost certainly going to happen or be done in the future • *Political change was on the horizon.*

horizontal *[Said hor-riz-zon-tl]* ADJECTIVE MATHS flat and parallel with the horizon or with a line considered as a base • *a patchwork of* vertical and horizontal black lines. **horizontally** ADVERB

hormone, hormones NOUN a chemical made by one part of your body that stimulates or has a specific effect on another part of your body. **hormonal** ADJECTIVE

horn, horns NOUN ① one of the hard, pointed growths on the heads of animals such as goats. ② a musical instrument made of brass, consisting of a tube that is narrow at one end and wide at the other. ③ On vehicles, a horn is a warning device which makes a loud noise.

hornet, hornets NOUN a type of very large wasp.

horoscope, horoscopes *[Said hor-ros-kope]* NOUN a prediction about what is going to happen to someone, based on the position of the stars when they were born. WORD HISTORY: from Greek *hōra* + *skopos* meaning 'hour observer'

horrendous ADJECTIVE very unpleasant and shocking • *horrendous injuries.*

horrible ADJECTIVE ① disagreeable and unpleasant • *A horrible nausea rose within him.* ② causing shock, fear or disgust • *horrible crimes.* **horribly** ADVERB
SIMILAR WORDS: ① disagreeable, nasty, unpleasant ② dreadful, ghastly, shocking

horrid ADJECTIVE (*old-fashioned*) very unpleasant indeed • *We were all so horrid to him.*

horrific ADJECTIVE so bad or unpleasant that people are horrified • *a horrific attack.*

horrify, horrifies, horrifying, horrified VERB If something horrifies you, it makes you feel dismay or disgust • *a crime trend that will horrify parents.* **horrifying** ADJECTIVE

a b c d e f g h i j k l m n o p q r s t u v w x y z

horror, horrors NOUN ① a strong feeling of alarm, dismay and disgust • *He gazed in horror at the knife.* ② If you have a horror of something, you fear it very much • *He had a horror of fire.*

horse, horses NOUN ① a large animal with a mane and long tail, on which people can ride. ② a piece of gymnastics equipment with four legs, used for jumping over.

horseback NOUN or ADJECTIVE You refer to someone who is riding a horse as someone 'on horseback', or a horseback rider.

horsepower NOUN Horsepower is a unit used for measuring how powerful an engine is, equal to about 746 watts.

horseradish NOUN Horseradish is the white root of a plant made into a hot-tasting sauce, often served cold with beef.

horseshoe, horseshoes NOUN a U-shaped piece of metal, nailed to the hard surface of a horse's hoof to protect it; also anything of this shape, often regarded as a good luck symbol.

horsey; also spelt **horsy**, **horsier**, **horsiest** ADJECTIVE ① very keen on horses and riding. ② having a face similar to that of a horse.

horticulture NOUN Horticulture is the study and practice of growing flowers, fruit and vegetables. **horticultural** ADJECTIVE

hose, hoses, hosing, hosed NOUN ① a long flexible tube through which liquid or gas can be passed • *He left the garden hose on.* ▶ VERB ② If you hose something, you wash or water it using a hose • *The street cleaners need to hose the square down.*

hosiery [Said *hoze-ee-yer-ee*] NOUN Hosiery consists of tights, socks and similar items, especially in shops.

hospice, hospices [Said *hoss-piss*] NOUN a hospital which provides care for people who are dying.

hospitable ADJECTIVE friendly, generous and welcoming to guests or strangers. **hospitality** NOUN

hospital, hospitals NOUN a place where sick and injured people are treated and cared for.

host, hosts, hosting, hosted NOUN ① The host of an event is the person that welcomes guests and provides food or accommodation for them • *He is a most generous host who takes his guests to the best restaurants in town.* ② The host of a radio or television show is the person who introduces it and talks to other people who take part in it • *the host of a comedy quiz show.* ③ a plant or animal with smaller plants or animals living on or in it. ④ A host of things is a large number of them • *a host of close friends.* ⑤ In the Christian Church, the Host is the consecrated bread used in Mass or Holy Communion. ▶ VERB ⑥ To host an event or programme means to act as its host.

hostage, hostages NOUN a person who is illegally held prisoner and threatened with injury or death unless certain demands are met by other people.

hostel, hostels NOUN a large building in which people can stay or live • *a hostel for homeless people.*

hostess, hostesses NOUN a woman who welcomes guests or visitors and provides food or accommodation for them.

hostile ADJECTIVE ① unfriendly, aggressive and unpleasant • *a hostile audience.* ② relating to or involving the enemies of a country • *hostile territory.*

hostility, hostilities NOUN
aggression or unfriendly behaviour
towards a person or thing.

hot, hotter, hottest ADJECTIVE
① having a high temperature • *a hot climate*. ② very spicy and causing a burning sensation in your mouth • *a hot curry*. ③ new, recent and exciting • *hot news from Tinseltown*. ④ dangerous or difficult to deal with • *Animal testing is a hot issue*. **hotly** ADVERB

hotbed, hotbeds NOUN A hotbed of some type of activity is a place that seems to encourage it • *The city was a hotbed of rumour*.

hot dog, hot dogs NOUN a sausage served in a roll split lengthways.

hotel, hotels NOUN a building where people stay, paying for their room and sometimes also meals.

hothouse, hothouses NOUN ① a large heated greenhouse. ② a place or situation of intense intellectual or emotional activity • *a hothouse of radical ideas*.

hot seat NOUN (informal) Someone who is in the hot seat has to make difficult decisions for which they will be held responsible.

hotspot, hotspots NOUN ① an exciting place where there is a lot of activity or entertainment. ② a place where computer users can gain access to the internet through a wireless network.

hound, hounds, hounding, hounded NOUN ① a dog, especially one used for hunting or racing. ▶ VERB ② If someone hounds you, they constantly pursue or trouble you.

hour, hours NOUN ① a unit of time equal to 60 minutes, of which there are 24 in a day. ② The hour for something is the time when it happens • *The hour for launching*

approached. ③ The hour is also the time of day • *What are you doing up at this hour?* ④ an important or difficult time • *The hour has come* • *He is the hero of the hour*. ⑤ (in plural) The hours that you keep are the times that you usually go to bed and get up. **hourly** ADJECTIVE or ADVERB

house, houses, housing, housed NOUN [Said **hows**] ① a building where a person or family lives. ② a building used for a particular purpose • *an auction house* • *the opera house*. ③ In a theatre or cinema, the house is the part where the audience sits; also the audience itself • *The show had a packed house calling for more*. ▶ VERB [Said **howz**] ④ To house something means to keep it or contain it • *The west wing housed a store of valuable antiques*.

houseboat, houseboats NOUN a small boat which people live on that is tied up at a particular place on a river or canal.

household, households NOUN ① all the people who live as a group in a house or flat. ▶ PHRASE ② Someone who is **a household name** is very well-known. **householder** NOUN

housekeeper, housekeepers NOUN a person who is employed to do the cooking and cleaning in a house.

House of Commons NOUN The House of Commons is the more powerful of the two parts of the British Parliament. Its members are elected by the public.

House of Lords NOUN The House of Lords is the less powerful of the two parts of the British Parliament. Its members are unelected and come from noble families or are appointed by the monarch as an honour for a life of public service.

House of Representatives NOUN ① In Australia, the House of

Representatives is the larger of the two parts of the Federal Parliament. ②In New Zealand, the House of Representatives is the Parliament.

housewife, **housewives** NOUN a married woman who does the chores in her home, and does not have a paid job.

housing NOUN Housing is the buildings in which people live • *the serious housing shortage*.

hovel, **hovels** NOUN a small hut or house that is dirty or badly in need of repair.

hover, **hovers**, **hovering**, **hovered** VERB ①When a bird, insect or aircraft hovers, it stays in the same position in the air. ②If someone is hovering, they are hesitating because they cannot decide what to do • *He was hovering nervously around the sick animal*.

hovercraft, **hovercraft** or **hovercrafts** NOUN a vehicle which can travel over water or land supported by a cushion of air.

how ADVERB ①'How' is used to ask about, explain or refer to the way in which something is done, known or experienced • *How did this happen?* • *He knew how quickly rumours could spread*. ②'How' is used to ask about or refer to a measurement or quantity • *How much is it for the weekend?* • *I wonder how old he is*. ③'How' is used to emphasise the following word or statement • *How odd!*

however ADVERB ①You use 'however' when you are adding a comment that seems to contradict or contrast with what has just been said • *For all his compassion, he is, however, surprisingly restrained*. ②You use 'however' to say that something makes no difference to a situation • *However hard she tried, nothing seemed to work*.

howl, **howls**, **howling**, **howled** VERB ①To howl means to make a long, loud wailing noise such as that made by a dog when it is upset • *A distant coyote howled at the moon* • *The wind howled through the trees*. ▶ NOUN ②a long, loud wailing noise.

HQ an abbreviation for **headquarters**.

HTML NOUN ⟨ICT⟩ HTML is a computer programming language that is used to design the layout of web pages. HTML is an abbreviation for 'hypertext markup language'.

hub, **hubs** NOUN ①the centre part of a wheel. ②the most important or active part of a place or organisation • *The kitchen is the hub of most households*.

hubbub NOUN Hubbub is great noise or confusion • *the general hubbub of conversation*.

huddle, **huddles**, **huddling**, **huddled** VERB ①If you huddle up or are huddled, you are curled up with your arms and legs close to your body. ②When people or animals huddle together, they sit or stand close to each other, often for warmth. ▶ NOUN ③A huddle of people or things is a small group of them.

hue, **hues** NOUN ①(*literary*) a colour or a particular shade of a colour. ▶ PHRASE ②If people raise a **hue and cry**, they are very angry about something and protest.

huff PHRASE (*informal*) If you are **in a huff**, you are sulking or offended about something. **huffy** ADJECTIVE **huffily** ADVERB

hug, **hugs**, **hugging**, **hugged** VERB ①If you hug someone, you put your arms round them and hold them close to you. ②To hug the ground or a stretch of water or land means to keep very close to it • *The road hugs the coast for hundreds of miles.* ▶ NOUN ③ If you give someone a hug, you hold them close to you.

WORD HISTORY: from Old Norse *hugga* meaning 'to comfort' or 'to console'

huge, **huger**, **hugest** ADJECTIVE extremely large in amount, size or degree • *a huge success* • *a huge crowd*.
hugely ADVERB
SIMILAR WORDS: enormous, gigantic, vast

hui, **hui** or **huis** [*Said hoo-ee*] NOUN ① In New Zealand, a hui is a meeting of Māori people. ② (*informal*) In New Zealand English, a hui is a party.

hulk, **hulks** NOUN ① a large, heavy person or thing. ② the body of a ship that has been wrecked or abandoned. **hulking** ADJECTIVE

hull, **hulls** NOUN The hull of a ship is the main part of its body that sits in the water.

hum, **hums**, **humming**, **hummed** VERB ① To hum means to make a continuous low noise • *The generator hummed faintly.* ② If you hum, you sing with your lips closed. ▶ NOUN ③ a continuous low noise • *the hum of the fridge.*

human, **humans** ADJECTIVE ① relating to, concerning or typical of people • *Intolerance appears deeply ingrained in human nature.* ▶ NOUN ② a person. **humanly** ADVERB

human being, **human beings** NOUN a person.

Human Development Index NOUN GEOGRAPHY a way of measuring how much a country has developed by gathering data about things such as life expectancy, adult literacy and standard of living, and comparing them with data about the same things in other countries.

humane ADJECTIVE showing kindness and sympathy towards others • *Medicine is regarded as the most humane of professions.*
humanely ADVERB

humanism NOUN RE Humanism is the belief in mankind's ability to achieve happiness and fulfilment without depending on religion or superstition.

humanitarian, **humanitarians** NOUN ① a person who works for the welfare of mankind. ▶ ADJECTIVE ② concerned with the welfare of mankind • *humanitarian aid*.
humanitarianism NOUN

humanity NOUN ① Humanity is people in general • *I have faith in humanity.* ② Humanity is also the condition of being human • *He is so full of hatred he has lost his humanity.* ③ Someone who has humanity is kind and sympathetic.

human rights PLURAL NOUN CITIZENSHIP Human rights are the rights of individuals to freedom and justice.

humble, **humbler**, **humblest**; **humbles**, **humbling**, **humbled** ADJECTIVE ① A humble person is modest and thinks that he or she has very little value. ② Something that is humble is small, or not very important or special • *Just a splash of this sauce will transform a humble casserole.* ▶ VERB ③ To humble someone means to make them feel humiliated. **humbly** ADVERB **humbled** ADJECTIVE
SIMILAR WORDS: ① modest, unassuming

humbug, **humbugs** NOUN ① a hard black and white striped sweet that tastes of peppermint. ② Humbug is speech or writing that is obviously dishonest or untrue • *hypocritical humbug.*

a
b
c
d
e
f
g
h
i
j
k
l
m
n
o
p
q
r
s
t
u
v
w
x
y
z

humdrum ADJECTIVE ordinary, dull and boring • *humdrum domestic tasks*.

humid ADJECTIVE If it is humid, the air feels damp, heavy and warm.

humidity NOUN Humidity is the amount of moisture in the air, or the state of being humid.

humiliate, humiliates, humiliating, humiliated VERB To humiliate someone means to make them feel ashamed or appear stupid to other people. **humiliation** NOUN
SIMILAR WORDS: embarrass, mortify, shame

humility NOUN Humility is the quality of being modest and humble.

hummingbird, hummingbirds NOUN a small bird with powerful wings that make a humming noise as they beat.

humour, humours, humouring, humoured NOUN ① Humour is the quality of being funny • *They discussed it with tact and humour*. ② Humour is also the ability to be amused by certain things • *Helen's got a peculiar sense of humour*. ③ Someone's humour is the mood they are in • *He hasn't been in a good humour lately*. ▶ VERB ④ If you humour someone, you are especially kind to them and do whatever they want. **humorous** ADJECTIVE
SIMILAR WORDS: ① comedy, funniness, wit

hump, humps, humping, humped NOUN ① a small, rounded lump or mound • *a camel's hump*. ▶ VERB ② (informal) If you hump something heavy, you carry or move it with difficulty.

hunch, hunches, hunching, hunched NOUN ① a feeling or suspicion about something, not based on facts or evidence. ▶ VERB ② If you hunch your shoulders, you raise your shoulders and lean forwards.

hunchback, hunchbacks NOUN (old-fashioned) someone who has a large hump on their back.

hundred, hundreds the number 100. **hundredth** ADJECTIVE

hung a past tense and past participle of **hang**.

Hungarian, Hungarians [Said *hung-gair-ee-an*] ADJECTIVE ① belonging or relating to Hungary. ▶ NOUN ② someone who comes from Hungary. ③ Hungarian is the main language spoken in Hungary.

hunger, hungers, hungering, hungered NOUN ① Hunger is the need to eat or the desire to eat. ② A hunger for something is a strong need or desire for it • *a hunger for winning*. ▶ VERB ③ If you hunger for something, you want it very much.

hunger strike, hunger strikes NOUN a refusal to eat anything at all, especially by prisoners, as a form of protest.

hungry, hungrier, hungriest ADJECTIVE needing or wanting to eat • *People are going hungry*. **hungrily** ADVERB

hunk, hunks NOUN A hunk of something is a large piece of it.

hunt, hunts, hunting, hunted VERB ① To hunt means to chase wild animals to kill them for food or for sport. ② If you hunt for something, you search for it. ▶ NOUN ③ the act of hunting • *Police launched a hunt for an abandoned car*. **hunter** NOUN **hunting** ADJECTIVE or NOUN

huntaway, huntaways NOUN In Australia and New Zealand, a huntaway is a dog trained to drive sheep forward.

hurdle, hurdles NOUN ① one of the frames or barriers that you jump over in an athletics race called hurdles • *She won the 400-metre hurdles*.

②a problem or difficulty • *Several hurdles exist for anyone seeking to do postgraduate study.*

hurl, hurls, hurling, hurled VERB ①To hurl something means to throw it with great force. ②If you hurl insults at someone, you insult them aggressively and repeatedly.

hurray or **hurrah** or **hooray** INTERJECTION an exclamation of excitement or approval.

hurricane, hurricanes NOUN GEOGRAPHY A hurricane is a violent wind or storm, usually force 12 or above on the Beaufort scale.

hurry, hurries, hurrying, hurried VERB ①To hurry means to move or do something as quickly as possible • *She hurried through the empty streets.* ②To hurry something means to make it happen more quickly • *You can't hurry nature.* ▶NOUN ③Hurry is the speed with which you do something quickly • *He was in a hurry to leave.* **hurried** ADJECTIVE **hurriedly** ADVERB
SIMILAR WORDS: ①dash, fly, rush ③haste, rush

hurt, hurts, hurting, hurt VERB ①To hurt someone means to cause them physical pain. ②If a part of your body hurts, you feel pain there. ③If you hurt yourself, you injure yourself. ④To hurt someone also means to make them unhappy by being unkind or thoughtless towards them • *I didn't want to hurt his feelings.* ▶ADJECTIVE ⑤If someone feels hurt, they feel unhappy because of someone's unkindness towards them • *He felt hurt by all the lies.* **hurtful** ADJECTIVE

hurtle, hurtles, hurtling, hurtled VERB To hurtle means to move or travel very fast indeed, especially in an uncontrolled way.

husband, husbands NOUN A person's husband is the man they are married to.

husbandry NOUN ①Husbandry is the art or skill of farming. ②Husbandry is also the art or skill of managing something carefully and economically.

hush, hushes, hushing, hushed VERB ①If you tell someone to hush, you are telling them to be quiet. ②To hush something up means to keep it secret, especially something dishonest involving important people • *The government has hushed up a series of scandals.* ▶NOUN ③If there is a hush, it is quiet and still • *A graveyard hush fell over the group.* **hushed** ADJECTIVE

husk, husks NOUN Husks are the dry outer coverings of grain or seed.

husky, huskier, huskiest; huskies ADJECTIVE ①A husky voice is rough or hoarse. ▶NOUN ②a large, strong dog with a thick coat, often used to pull sledges across snow. **huskily** ADVERB

hustle, hustles, hustling, hustled VERB To hustle someone means to make them move by pushing and jostling them • *The guards hustled him out of the car.*

hut, huts NOUN a small, simple building, with one or two rooms.

hutch, hutches NOUN a wooden box with wire mesh at one side, in which small pets can be kept.

hyacinth, hyacinths [Said *high-as-sinth*] NOUN a spring flower with many small, bell-shaped flowers.

hybrid, hybrids NOUN ①a plant or animal that has been bred from two different types of plant or animal. ②anything that is a mixture of two other things.

hydra, hydras or hydrae NOUN a microscopic freshwater creature that has a slender tubular body and tentacles round the mouth.

a
b
c
d
e
f
g
h
i
j
k
l
m
n
o
p
q
r
s
t
u
v
w
x
y
z

hydrangea, hydrangeas *[Said high-**drain**-ja]* NOUN a garden shrub with large clusters of pink or blue flowers.

hydraulic *[Said high-**drol**-lik]* ADJECTIVE operated by water or other fluid which is under pressure.

hydraulics NOUN Hydraulics is the study and use of systems that work using hydraulic pressure.

hydro- PREFIX 'Hydro-' means 'water'. For example, *hydroelectricity* is electricity made using water power. WORD HISTORY: from Greek *hudōr* meaning 'water'

hydrocarbon, hydrocarbons NOUN ⟦SCIENCE⟧ A hydrocarbon is a chemical compound that is a mixture of hydrogen and carbon.

hydrogen NOUN ⟦SCIENCE⟧ Hydrogen is the lightest gas and the simplest chemical element. It is colourless and odourless. Its atomic number is 1 and its symbol is H.

hydrology NOUN ⟦GEOGRAPHY⟧ the study of the distribution and use of water on the earth and in its atmosphere.

hyena, hyenas *[Said high-**ee**-na]*; also spelt **hyaena** NOUN a wild doglike animal of Africa and Asia that hunts in packs.

hygiene *[Said high-jeen]* NOUN ⟦DGT⟧ Hygiene is the practice of keeping yourself and your surroundings clean, especially to stop the spread of disease. **hygienic** ADJECTIVE

hygienically ADVERB

hymn, hymns NOUN ⟦RE⟧ a Christian song in praise of God.

hype, hypes, hyping, hyped NOUN ① Hype is the use of a lot of publicity and advertising to make people interested in something. ▶ VERB ② To hype or hype up a product means to advertise or praise it a lot.

hyper- PREFIX 'Hyper-' means 'very much' or 'excessively' • *hyperactive*. WORD HISTORY: from Greek *huper* meaning 'over'

hyperactive ADJECTIVE A hyperactive person is unable to relax and is always in a state of restless activity.

hyperbole *[Said high-**per**-bol-lee]* NOUN Hyperbole is a style of speech or writing which uses exaggeration.

hyperlink, hyperlinks NOUN a word, phrase or picture in a computer document which a user may click to move to another part of the document, or to another document.

hypertension NOUN Hypertension is a medical condition in which a person has high blood pressure.

hypertext, hypertexts NOUN computer software that allows users to create, store and view text and move between related items easily.

hyphen, hyphens NOUN ⟦ENGLISH⟧ a punctuation mark used to join together words or parts of words, as for example in the word 'left-handed'. **hyphenate** VERB **hyphenation** NOUN

What does the Hyphen do?

The **hyphen** (-) separates the different parts of certain words. A hyphen is often used when there would otherwise be an awkward combination of letters, or confusion with another word:

Anna was re-elected president.
She adopted a no-nonsense approach.

In printed texts, the hyphen also divides a word that will not fit at the end of a line and has to be continued on the next line.

PUNCTUATION TIP
You do not put a hyphen between the parts of a phrasal verb but you do when you are writing a noun that comes from it: *The match will kick off at 6 o'clock; Kick-off has been delayed by an hour.*

hypnosis [*Said* hip-*noh*-siss] NOUN Hypnosis is an artificially produced state of relaxation in which the mind is very receptive to suggestion.
WORD HISTORY: from Greek *hupnos* meaning 'sleep'

hypnotise, hypnotises, hypnotising, **hypnotised**; also spelt **hypnotize** VERB To hypnotise someone means to put them into a state in which they seem to be asleep but can respond to questions and suggestions. **hypnotic** ADJECTIVE **hypnotism** NOUN **hypnotist** NOUN

hypochondriac, hypochondriacs [*Said* high-pok-*kon*-dree-ak] NOUN a person who continually worries about their health, being convinced that they are ill when there is actually nothing wrong with them. **hypochondria** NOUN

hypocrisy, hypocrisies NOUN Hypocrisy is pretending to have beliefs or qualities that you do not really have, so that you seem a better person than you are. **hypocritical** ADJECTIVE **hypocritically** ADVERB **hypocrite** NOUN

hypodermic, hypodermics NOUN a medical instrument with a hollow needle, used for giving people injections, or taking blood samples.

hypotenuse, hypotenuses [*Said* high-*pot*-tin-yooz] NOUN MATHS In a triangle that has a right angle, the hypotenuse is the longest side and is opposite the right angle.

hypothermia NOUN SCIENCE Hypothermia is a condition in which a person is very ill because their body temperature has been unusually low for a long time.

hypothesis, hypotheses NOUN SCIENCE an explanation or theory which has not yet been proved to be correct.

hypothetical ADJECTIVE based on assumption rather than on fact or reality. **hypothetically** ADVERB

hysterectomy, hysterectomies [*Said* his-ter-*rek*-tom-ee] NOUN an operation to remove a woman's womb.

hysteria [*Said* hiss-*teer*-ee-a] NOUN Hysteria is a state of uncontrolled excitement or panic.

hysterical ADJECTIVE ① Someone who is hysterical is in a state of uncontrolled excitement or panic. ② (*informal*) Something that is hysterical is extremely funny. **hysterically** ADVERB **hysterics** NOUN SIMILAR WORDS: ① frantic, frenzied

a
b
c
d
e
f
g
h
i
j
k
l
m
n
o
p
q
r
s
t
u
v
w
x
y
z

Ii

I PRONOUN A speaker or writer uses 'I' to refer to himself or herself • *I like the colour*.

iambic ADJECTIVE ENGLISH If a line of verse is iambic, it is made up of rhythmic units called *iambs*, which have one unstressed syllable followed by a stressed one.

ibis, ibises [*Said eye-biss*] NOUN a large wading bird with a long, thin, curved bill that lives in warm countries.

-ible SUFFIX another form of the suffix **-able**.

-ic or **-ical** SUFFIX '-ic' and '-ical' form adjectives from nouns. For example, *ironic* or *ironical* can be formed from *irony*.

ice, ices, icing, iced NOUN ① water that has frozen solid. ② an ice cream. ▶ VERB ③ If you ice cakes, you cover them with icing. ④ If something ices over or ices up, it becomes covered with a layer of ice. ▶ PHRASE ⑤ If you do something to **break the ice**, you make people feel relaxed and comfortable.

Ice Age, Ice Ages NOUN a period of time lasting thousands of years when a lot of the earth's surface was covered with ice.

iceberg, icebergs NOUN a large mass of ice floating in the sea.
WORD HISTORY: from Dutch *ijsberg* meaning 'ice mountain'

icebreaker, icebreakers NOUN ① An icebreaker is a ship that breaks a channel through ice. ② An icebreaker is also something, such as a question, that starts people talking in a relaxed way at a social or business gathering.

icecap, icecaps NOUN a layer of ice and snow that permanently covers the North or South Pole.

ice cream, ice creams NOUN a very cold sweet food made from frozen cream.

ice cube, ice cubes NOUN Ice cubes are small cubes of ice put in drinks to make them cold.

ice hockey NOUN a type of hockey played on ice, with two teams of six players.

Icelandic ADJECTIVE ① belonging or relating to Iceland. ▶ NOUN ② the main language spoken in Iceland.

ice-skate, ice-skates, ice-skating, ice-skated NOUN ① a boot with a metal blade on the bottom, which you wear when skating on ice. ▶ VERB ② If you ice-skate, you move about on ice wearing ice-skates.

icicle, icicles [*Said eye-sik-kl*] NOUN a piece of ice shaped like a pointed stick that hangs down from a surface.

icing NOUN a mixture of powdered sugar and water or egg whites, used to decorate cakes.

icon, icons [*Said eye-kon*] NOUN ① ICT a picture on a computer screen representing a program that can be activated by moving the cursor over it. ② in the Orthodox Churches, a holy picture of Christ, the Virgin Mary or a saint.

WORD HISTORY: from Greek *eikōn* meaning 'likeness' or 'image'

ICT an abbreviation for 'Information and Communication Technology'.

icy, icier, iciest ADJECTIVE
① Something which is icy is very cold • *an icy wind*. ② An icy road has ice on it. **icily** ADVERB

id NOUN In psychology, your id is your basic instincts and unconscious thoughts.

ID NOUN (*informal*) ID is something which proves who you are, such as a passport. ID is an abbreviation for 'identification document'.

idea, ideas NOUN ① a plan, suggestion or thought that you have after thinking about a problem. ② an opinion or belief • *old-fashioned ideas about women*. ③ An idea of something is what you know about it • *They had no idea of their position*.
SIMILAR WORDS: ① impression, thought ② belief, notion, opinion

ideal, ideals NOUN ① a principle or idea that you try to achieve because it seems perfect to you. ② Your ideal of something is the person or thing that seems the best example of it.
▶ ADJECTIVE ③ The ideal person or thing is the best possible person or thing for the situation.

idealise, idealises, idealising, idealised; also spelt **idealize** VERB If you idealise someone or something, you regard them as being perfect.
idealisation NOUN

idealism [*Said eye-dee-il-izm*] NOUN behaviour that is based on a person's ideals. **idealist** NOUN **idealistic** ADJECTIVE

ideally ADVERB ① If you say that ideally something should happen, you mean that you would like it to happen but you know that it is not likely. ② Ideally means perfectly

• *The hotel is ideally placed for business travellers*.

identical ADJECTIVE exactly the same • *identical twins*. **identically** ADVERB

identification NOUN ① The identification of someone or something is the act of identifying them. ② Identification is a document, such as a driving licence or passport, which proves who you are.

identify, identifies, identifying, identified VERB ① To identify someone or something is to recognise them or name them. ② If you identify with someone, you understand their feelings and ideas.
identifiable ADJECTIVE

identity, identities NOUN ① the characteristics that make you who you are. ② MATHS an equation that is valid for all values of its variables.

identity theft NOUN Identity theft is the crime of pretending to be another person and using that person's private information to get money illegally.

ideology, ideologies NOUN a set of political beliefs. **ideological** ADJECTIVE **ideologically** ADVERB

idiom, idioms NOUN ENGLISH a group of words whose meaning together is different from all the words taken individually. For example, 'It's raining cats and dogs' is an idiom.
WORD HISTORY: from Greek *idiōma* meaning 'special phraseology'

idiosyncrasy, idiosyncrasies [*Said id-ee-oh-sing-krass-ee*] NOUN Someone's idiosyncrasies are their own habits and likes or dislikes.
idiosyncratic ADJECTIVE

idiot, idiots NOUN someone who is stupid or foolish.
SIMILAR WORDS: fool, halfwit, moron

a
b
c
d
e
f
g
h
i
j
k
l
m
n
o
p
q
r
s
t
u
v
w
x
y
z

WORD HISTORY: from Greek *idiōtēs* meaning 'ignorant person'

idiotic ADJECTIVE extremely foolish or silly. **idiotically** ADVERB

SIMILAR WORDS: foolish, senseless, stupid

idle, idler, idlest; idles, idling, idled ADJECTIVE If you are idle, you are doing nothing. **idleness** NOUN **idly** ADVERB

WORD HISTORY: from Saxon *idal* meaning 'worthless' or 'empty'

SPELLING TIP

Do not confuse the spellings of *idle* and *idol*: *You can't be idle while I do all the work; Murray is my tennis idol.*

---

idol, idols [Said *eye-doll*] NOUN ① a famous person who is loved and admired by fans. ② RE a picture or statue which is worshipped as if it were a god.

SPELLING TIP

Do not confuse the spellings of *idol* and *idle*: *Murray is my tennis idol; You can't be idle while I do all the work.*

---

idyll, idylls [Said *id-ill*] NOUN a situation which is peaceful and beautiful. **idyllic** ADJECTIVE

i.e. i.e. means 'that is', and is used before giving more information. It is an abbreviation for the Latin expression 'id est'.

if CONJUNCTION ① on the condition that • *I shall stay if I can.* ② whether • *I asked her if she wanted to go.*

igloo, igloos NOUN a dome-shaped house built out of blocks of snow by Inuit.

igneous [Said *ig-nee-uss*] ADJECTIVE GEOGRAPHY Igneous rocks are formed by hot liquid rock cooling and going hard.

WORD HISTORY: from Latin *igneus* meaning 'fiery'

ignite, ignites, igniting, ignited VERB If you ignite something or if it ignites, it starts burning.

WORD HISTORY: from Latin *ignis* meaning 'fire'

ignition, ignitions NOUN In a car, the ignition is the part of the engine where the fuel is ignited.

ignominious ADJECTIVE shameful or considered wrong • *It was an ignominious end to a brilliant career.* **ignominiously** ADVERB **ignominy** NOUN

ignoramus, ignoramuses [Said *ig-nor-ray-muss*] NOUN an ignorant person.

WORD HISTORY: from the character *Ignoramus*, an uneducated lawyer in a 17th-century play by Ruggle. In Latin *ignoramus* means 'we do not know'

ignorant ADJECTIVE ① If you are ignorant of something, you do not know about it • *He was completely ignorant of the rules.* ② Someone who is ignorant does not know about things in general • *I thought of asking, but didn't want to seem ignorant.* **ignorantly** ADVERB **ignorance** NOUN

SIMILAR WORDS: ① unaware, unconscious, uninformed

ignore, ignores, ignoring, ignored VERB If you ignore someone or something, you deliberately do not take any notice of them.

iguana, iguanas [Said *ig-wah-na*] NOUN a large, tropical lizard.

il- PREFIX 'il-' means 'not' or 'the opposite of', and is the form of 'in-' that is used before the letter *l* • *illegible.*

ill, ills ADJECTIVE ① unhealthy or sick. ② harmful or unpleasant • *ill effects.* ▸ PLURAL NOUN ③ Ills are difficulties or problems. ▸ PHRASE ④ If you feel

ill at ease, you feel unable to relax.
SIMILAR WORDS: ① sick, unhealthy, unwell
WORD HISTORY: from Norse *illr* meaning 'bad'

illegal ADJECTIVE forbidden by the law. **illegally** ADVERB **illegality** NOUN
SIMILAR WORDS: criminal, illicit, unlawful

illegible [Said il-**lej**-i-bl] ADJECTIVE Writing which is illegible is unclear and very difficult to read.

SPELLING TIP
Do not confuse the spellings of *illegible* and *eligible*: *Your handwriting is illegible; George is not eligible to vote.*

---

illegitimate [Said il-lij-**it**-tim-it] ADJECTIVE A person who is illegitimate was born to parents who were not married at the time. **illegitimacy** NOUN

ill-fated ADJECTIVE doomed to end unhappily • *his ill-fated attempt on the world record.*

illicit [Said il-**liss**-it] ADJECTIVE not allowed by law or not approved of by society • *illicit drugs.*

SPELLING TIP
Do not confuse the spellings of *illicit* and *elicit*: *an illicit business deal; It is the police's job to elicit the truth from the suspect.*

---

illiterate ADJECTIVE unable to read or write. **illiteracy** NOUN

illness, illnesses NOUN ① Illness is the experience of being ill. ② a particular disease • *the treatment of common illnesses.*
SIMILAR WORDS: ② ailment, disease, malady, sickness

illogical ADJECTIVE An illogical feeling or action is not reasonable or sensible. **illogically** ADVERB

ill-treat, ill-treats, ill-treating, ill-treated VERB If you ill-treat someone or something you hurt or damage them or treat them cruelly. **ill-treatment** NOUN

illuminate, illuminates, illuminating, illuminated VERB To illuminate something is to shine light on it to make it easier to see.

illumination, illuminations NOUN ① Illumination is lighting. ② Illuminations are the coloured lights put up to decorate a town, especially at Christmas.

illusion, illusions NOUN ① a false belief which you think is true • *Their hopes proved to be an illusion.* ② ART a false appearance of reality which deceives the eye • *Painters create the illusion of space.*

illusory [Said ill-**yoo**-ser-ee] ADJECTIVE seeming to be true, but actually false • *an illusory truce.*

illustrate, illustrates, illustrating, illustrated VERB ① EXAM TERM If you illustrate a point, you explain it or make it clearer, often by using examples. ② If you illustrate a book, you put pictures in it. **illustrator** NOUN **illustrative** ADJECTIVE

illustration, illustrations NOUN ① an example or a story which is used to make a point clear. ② a picture in a book.

illustrious ADJECTIVE An illustrious person is famous and respected.

ill will NOUN Ill will is a feeling of hostility.

IM, IMs NOUN an abbreviation for 'instant message'.

im- PREFIX 'Im-' means 'not' or 'the opposite of', and is the form of 'in-' which is used before the letters *b*, *m* and *p* • *imbalance* • *immature* • *impatient*.

image, images NOUN ① a mental

a b c d e f g h i j k l m n o p q r s t u v w x y z

picture of someone or something.
② the appearance which a person,
group or organisation presents to the
public.

imagery NOUN ENGLISH The
imagery of a poem or book is the
descriptive language used in it.

imaginary ADJECTIVE Something
that is imaginary exists only in your
mind, not in real life.

imagination, imaginations NOUN
the ability to form new and exciting
ideas.

imaginative ADJECTIVE Someone
who is imaginative can easily form
new or exciting ideas in their mind.
imaginatively ADVERB

imagine, imagines, imagining,
imagined VERB ① If you imagine
something, you form an idea of it in
your mind, or you think you have
seen or heard it but you have not
really. ② If you imagine that
something is the case, you believe it
is the case • *I imagine that's what you
aim to do.* **imaginable** ADJECTIVE
SIMILAR WORDS: ① conceive,
envisage, picture, visualise ② believe,
suppose, think

imam [Said ih-**mam**] NOUN RE a
person who leads a group in prayer in
a mosque.

imbalance, imbalances NOUN If
there is an imbalance between
things, they are unequal • *the
imbalance between rich and poor.*

imbecile, imbeciles [Said im-bis-seel]
NOUN a stupid person.

imitate, imitates, imitating,
imitated VERB To imitate someone
or something is to copy them.
imitator NOUN **imitative**
ADJECTIVE
SIMILAR WORDS: copy, mimic

imitation, imitations NOUN a copy
of something else.

immaculate [Said im-mak-yoo-lit]
ADJECTIVE ① completely clean and
tidy • *The flat was immaculate.*
② without any mistakes at all
• *his usual immaculate guitar
accompaniment.* **immaculately**
ADVERB

immaterial ADJECTIVE Something
that is immaterial is not important.

immature ADJECTIVE ① Something
that is immature has not finished
growing or developing. ② A person
who is immature does not behave in
a sensible adult way. **immaturity**
NOUN

immediate ADJECTIVE ① Something
that is immediate happens or is done
without delay. ② Your immediate
relatives and friends are the ones
most closely connected or related to
you. **immediacy** NOUN

immediately ADVERB ① If
something happens immediately, it
happens right away. ② Immediately
means very near in time or position
• *immediately behind the house.*

immemorial ADJECTIVE If something
has been happening from time
immemorial, it has been happening
longer than anyone can remember.

immense ADJECTIVE very large or
huge. **immensely** ADVERB
immensity NOUN

immerse, immerses, immersing,
immersed VERB ① If you are
immersed in an activity, you are
completely involved in it. ② If you
immerse something in a liquid, you
put it into the liquid so that it is
completely covered. **immersion**
NOUN

immigrant, immigrants NOUN
HISTORY someone who has come to
live permanently in a new country.
immigrate VERB **immigration**
NOUN

SPELLING TIP
Do not confuse the spellings of *immigrate* and *emigrate*. Try this mnemonic: *if someone Immigrates, they come Into a country.*

imminent ADJECTIVE If something is imminent, it is going to happen very soon. **imminently** ADVERB **imminence** NOUN
SIMILAR WORDS: coming, impending, near

SPELLING TIP
Do not confuse the spellings of *imminent* and *eminent*: *The wedding is imminent; an eminent professor of archaeology.*

immobile ADJECTIVE not moving. **immobility** NOUN

immoral ADJECTIVE RE If you describe someone or their behaviour as immoral, you mean that they do not fit in with most people's idea of what is right and proper. **immorality** NOUN

SPELLING TIP
Do not confuse *immoral* and *amoral*. You use *immoral* to talk about people who are aware of moral standards, but go against them. *Amoral* applies to people with no moral standards.

immortal ADJECTIVE ① Something that is immortal is famous and will be remembered for a long time • *Emily Brontë's immortal love story.* ② In stories, someone who is immortal will never die.

immortality NOUN RE Immortality is never dying. In many religions, people believe that the soul or some other essential part of a person lives forever or continues to exist in some form.

immovable; also spelt **immoveable** ADJECTIVE Something that is immovable is fixed and cannot be moved. **immovably** ADVERB

immune [Said im-**yoon**] ADJECTIVE ① If you are immune to a particular disease, you cannot catch it. ② If someone or something is immune to something, they are able to avoid it or are not affected by it • *The captain was immune to prosecution.* **immunity** NOUN

immune system NOUN SCIENCE Your body's immune system consists of your white blood cells, which fight disease by producing antibodies or germs to kill germs which come into your body.

immunise, **immunises**, **immunising**, **immunised**; also spelt **immunize** VERB SCIENCE To immunise a person or animal means to make them immune to a particular disease, usually by giving them an injection. **immunisation** NOUN

imp, **imps** NOUN a small mischievous creature in fairy stories. **impish** ADJECTIVE

impact, **impacts** NOUN ① The impact that someone or something has is the impression that they make or the effect that they have. ② Impact is the action of one object hitting another, usually with a lot of force • *The aircraft crashed into a ditch, exploding on impact.*

impair, **impairs**, **impairing**, **impaired** VERB To impair something is to damage it so that it stops working properly • *Travel had made him weary and impaired his judgement.*

impale, **impales**, **impaling**, **impaled** VERB If you impale something, you pierce it with a sharp object.

impart, **imparts**, **imparting**, **imparted** VERB (formal) To impart information to someone is to pass it on to them.

impartial ADJECTIVE Someone who is impartial has a view of something which is fair or not biased.
impartially ADVERB **impartiality** NOUN
SIMILAR WORDS: fair, neutral, objective

impasse [Said am-pass] NOUN a difficult situation in which it is impossible to find a solution.
WORD HISTORY: from French impasse meaning 'dead end'

impassioned ADJECTIVE full of emotion • an impassioned plea.

impassive ADJECTIVE showing no emotion. **impassively** ADVERB

impasto NOUN ART a technique of painting with thick paint so that brush strokes or palette knife marks can be seen.
WORD HISTORY: an Italian word, from pasta meaning 'paste'

impatient ADJECTIVE ① Someone who is impatient becomes annoyed easily or is quick to lose their temper when things go wrong. ② If you are impatient to do something, you are eager and do not want to wait • He was impatient to get back.
impatiently ADVERB **impatience** NOUN

impeccable [Said im-pek-i-bl] ADJECTIVE excellent, without any faults. **impeccably** ADVERB

impede, impedes, impeding, impeded VERB If you impede someone, you make their progress difficult.

impediment, impediments NOUN something that makes it difficult to move, develop or do something properly • a speech impediment.

impelled ADJECTIVE If you feel impelled to do something, you feel strongly that you must do it.

impending ADJECTIVE (formal) You use 'impending' to describe something that is going to happen very soon • a sense of impending doom.

impenetrable ADJECTIVE impossible to get through.

imperative ADJECTIVE ① Something that is imperative is extremely urgent or important. ▶ NOUN ② ENGLISH In grammar, an imperative is the form of a verb that is used for giving orders.

imperfect ADJECTIVE ① Something that is imperfect has faults or problems. ▶ NOUN ② ENGLISH MFL In grammar, the imperfect is a tense used to describe continuous or repeated actions which happened in the past. **imperfectly** ADVERB **imperfection** NOUN
SIMILAR WORDS: ① faulty, flawed

imperial ADJECTIVE ① HISTORY Imperial means relating to an empire or an emperor or empress • the Imperial Palace. ② The imperial system of measurement is the measuring system which uses inches, feet and yards, ounces and pounds, and pints and gallons.

imperialism NOUN HISTORY a system of rule in which a rich and powerful nation controls other nations. **imperialist** ADJECTIVE or NOUN

imperious ADJECTIVE proud and domineering • an imperious manner. **imperiously** ADVERB

impersonal ADJECTIVE Something that is impersonal makes you feel that individuals and their feelings do not matter • impersonal cold rooms. **impersonally** ADVERB
SIMILAR WORDS: detached, dispassionate, inhuman

impersonate, impersonates, impersonating, impersonated VERB If you impersonate someone, you pretend to be that person.

impersonation NOUN
impersonator NOUN

impertinent ADJECTIVE disrespectful and rude • *impertinent questions*.
impertinently ADVERB
impertinence NOUN

impetuous ADJECTIVE If you are impetuous, you act quickly without thinking • *an impetuous gamble*.
impetuously ADVERB **impetuosity** NOUN

impetus NOUN ① An impetus is the stimulating effect that something has on a situation, which causes it to develop more quickly. ② In physics, impetus is the force that starts an object moving and resists changes in speed or direction.

impinge, impinges, impinging, impinged VERB If something impinges on your life, it has an effect on you and influences you • *My private life doesn't impinge on my professional life*.

implacable [Said im-**plak**-a-bl] ADJECTIVE Someone who is implacable is being harsh and refuses to change their mind. **implacably** ADVERB **implacability** NOUN

implant, implants, implanting, implanted VERB [Said im-**plant**] ① To implant something into a person's body is to put it there, usually by means of an operation. ▶ NOUN [Said im-**plant**] ② something that has been implanted into someone's body.

implausible ADJECTIVE very unlikely • *implausible stories*. **implausibly** ADVERB

implement, implements, implementing, implemented VERB ① If you implement something such as a plan, you carry it out • *The government has failed to implement promised reforms*. ▶ NOUN ② An implement is a tool.

implementation NOUN

implicate, implicates, implicating, implicated VERB If you are implicated in a crime, you are shown to be involved in it.

implication, implications NOUN something that is suggested or implied but not stated directly.

implicit [Said im-**pliss**-it] ADJECTIVE ① expressed in an indirect way • *implicit criticism*. ② If you have an implicit belief in something, you have no doubts about it • *He had implicit faith in the noble intentions of the Emperor*. **implicitly** ADVERB

implore, implores, imploring, implored VERB If you implore someone to do something, you beg them to do it.

imply, implies, implying, implied VERB If you imply that something is the case, you suggest it in an indirect way.

import, imports, importing, imported VERB [Said im-**port**] ① If you import something from another country, you bring it into your country or have it sent there. ② ICT If you import data, you open it using a different software program. ▶ NOUN [Said im-**port**] ③ Imports are goods that are made in another country and sent to your own country to be sold there.
importation NOUN **importer** NOUN

important ADJECTIVE ① Something that is important is very valuable, necessary or significant. ② An important person has great influence or power. **importantly** ADVERB **importance** NOUN
SIMILAR WORDS: ① momentous, significant

impose, imposes, imposing, imposed VERB ① If you impose

a
b
c
d
e
f
g
h
i
j
k
l
m
n
o
p
q
r
s
t
u
v
w
x
y
z

something on people, you force it on them • *Many companies imposed a pay freeze on their employees.* ② If someone imposes on you, they unreasonably expect you to do something for them. **imposition** NOUN

imposing ADJECTIVE having an impressive appearance or manner • *an imposing building.*

impossible ADJECTIVE Something that is impossible cannot happen, be done, or be believed. **impossibly** ADVERB **impossibility** NOUN

imposter, imposters; also spelt **impostor** NOUN a person who pretends to be someone else in order to get things they want.

impotent ADJECTIVE Someone who is impotent has no power to influence people or events. **impotently** ADVERB **impotence** NOUN

impound, impounds, impounding, impounded VERB If something you own is impounded, the police or other officials take it.

impoverished ADJECTIVE Someone who is impoverished is very poor.

impractical ADJECTIVE not practical, sensible or realistic.

impregnable ADJECTIVE A building or other structure that is impregnable is so strong that it cannot be broken into or captured.

impregnated ADJECTIVE If something is impregnated with a substance, it has absorbed the substance so that it spreads right through it • *sponges impregnated with detergent and water.*

impresario, impresarios [Said im-pris-**sar**-ee-oh] NOUN a person who manages theatrical or musical events or companies.

impress, impresses, impressing, impressed VERB ① If you impress

someone, you make them admire or respect you. ② If you impress something on someone, you make them understand the importance of it.

impression, impressions NOUN An impression of someone or something is the way they look or seem to you.

impressionable ADJECTIVE easy to influence • *impressionable young children.*

impressionism NOUN Impressionism is a style of painting which is concerned with the impressions created by light and shapes, rather than with neat realistic details. Impressionism was particularly popular in France between 1870 and 1900, especially with artists such as Monet and Renoir. **impressionist** NOUN

impressive ADJECTIVE If something is impressive, it impresses you • *an impressive display of old-fashioned American cars.*

imprint, imprints, imprinting, imprinted NOUN [Said im-**print**] ① If something leaves an imprint on your mind, it has a strong and lasting effect. ② the mark left by the pressure of one object on another. ▶ VERB [Said im-**print**] ③ If something is imprinted on your memory, it is firmly fixed there.

imprison, imprisons, imprisoning, imprisoned VERB If you are imprisoned, you are locked up, usually in a prison. **imprisonment** NOUN

improbable ADJECTIVE not probable or likely to happen. **improbably** ADVERB **improbability** NOUN SIMILAR WORDS: doubtful, unlikely

impromptu [Said im-**prompt**-yoo] ADJECTIVE An impromptu action is one done without planning or organisation.

SIMILAR WORDS: improvised, off the cuff, unprepared
WORD HISTORY: from Latin *in promptu* meaning 'in readiness'

improper ADJECTIVE ① rude or shocking • *improper behaviour.* ② illegal or dishonest • *improper dealings.* ③ not suitable or correct • *an improper diet.* **improperly** ADVERB

improper fraction, improper fractions NOUN MATHS a fraction in which the numerator has a higher value than the denominator, for example, $5/3$.

impropriety NOUN (*formal*) Impropriety is improper behaviour.

improve, improves, improving, improved VERB If something improves or if you improve it, it gets better or becomes more valuable.
SIMILAR WORDS: better, enhance

improvement, improvements NOUN ① the fact or process of getting better. ② An improvement in something is a change in something that makes it better.

improvise, improvises, improvising, improvised VERB ① If you improvise something, you make or do something without planning in advance, and with whatever materials are available. ② DRAMA MUSIC When musicians or actors improvise, they make up the music or words as they go along. **improvised** ADJECTIVE **improvisation** NOUN

impudence NOUN disrespectful talk or behaviour towards someone.

impudent ADJECTIVE If someone is impudent, something they say or do is cheeky and lacking in respect. **impudently** ADVERB

impulse, impulses NOUN a strong urge to do something • *She felt a sudden impulse to confide in her.*

impulsive ADJECTIVE If you are impulsive, you do things suddenly, without thinking about them carefully. **impulsively** ADVERB

impure ADJECTIVE Something which is impure contains small amounts of other things, such as dirt.

impurity, impurities NOUN ① Impurity is the quality of being impure • *the impurity of the water.* ② If something contains impurities, it contains small amounts of dirt or other substances that should not be there.

in PREPOSITION or ADVERB 'In' is used to indicate position, direction, time and manner • *boarding schools in England* • *in the past few years.*

in- PREFIX ① 'In-' is added to the beginning of some words to form a word with the opposite meaning • *insincere.* ② 'In-' also means in, into or in the course of • *infiltrate.*

inability NOUN a lack of ability to do something.

inaccessible ADJECTIVE impossible or very difficult to reach.

inaccurate ADJECTIVE not accurate or correct.

inadequate ADJECTIVE ① If something is inadequate, there is not enough of it. ② not good enough in quality for a particular purpose. ③ If someone feels inadequate, they feel they do not possess the skills necessary to do a particular job or to cope with life in general.
inadequately ADVERB **inadequacy** NOUN
SIMILAR WORDS: ① insufficient, meagre

inadvertent ADJECTIVE not intentional • *The insult had been inadvertent.* **inadvertently** ADVERB

inane ADJECTIVE silly or stupid. **inanely** ADVERB **inanity** NOUN

a
b
c
d
e
f
g
h
i
j
k
l
m
n
o
p
q
r
s
t
u
v
w
x
y
z

inanimate ADJECTIVE An inanimate object is not alive.

inappropriate ADJECTIVE not suitable for a particular purpose or occasion • *It was quite inappropriate to ask such questions.* **inappropriately** ADVERB

SIMILAR WORDS: out of place, unfitting, unsuitable

inarticulate ADJECTIVE If you are inarticulate, you are unable to express yourself well or easily in speech.

inasmuch CONJUNCTION 'Inasmuch as' means 'to the extent that' • *She's giving herself a hard time inasmuch as she feels guilty.*

inaudible ADJECTIVE not loud enough to be heard. **inaudibly** ADVERB

inaugurate, inaugurates, inaugurating, inaugurated [*Said in-awg-yoo-rate*] VERB ① To inaugurate a new scheme is to start it. ② To inaugurate a new leader is to officially establish them in their new position in a special ceremony • *Albania's Orthodox Church inaugurated its first archbishop in 25 years.* **inauguration** NOUN **inaugural** ADJECTIVE

inborn ADJECTIVE An inborn quality is one that you were born with.

inbox, inboxes NOUN a folder on a computer or phone where emails are received.

incandescent ADJECTIVE Something which is incandescent gives out light when it is heated. **incandescence** NOUN

WORD HISTORY: from Latin *candescere* meaning 'to glow white'

incapable ADJECTIVE ① Someone who is incapable of doing something is not able to do it • *He is incapable of changing a fuse.* ② An incapable person is weak and helpless.

incarcerate, incarcerates, incarcerating, incarcerated [*Said in-kar-ser-rate*] VERB To incarcerate someone is to lock them up. **incarceration** NOUN

Incarnation NOUN The Incarnation is the Christian belief that God took human form in Jesus Christ.

incendiary [*Said in-send-yer-ee*] ADJECTIVE An incendiary weapon is one which sets fire to things • *incendiary bombs.*

incense NOUN Incense is a spicy substance which is burned to create a sweet smell, especially during religious services.

incensed ADJECTIVE If you are incensed by something, it makes you extremely angry.

incentive, incentives NOUN something that encourages you to do something.

inception NOUN (*formal*) The inception of a project is the start of it. WORD HISTORY: from Latin *incipere* meaning 'to take up' or 'to begin'

incessant ADJECTIVE continuing without stopping • *her incessant talking.* **incessantly** ADVERB

inch, inches, inching, inched NOUN ① a unit of length equal to about 2.54 centimetres. ▶VERB ② To inch forward is to move forward slowly. WORD HISTORY: from Latin *uncia* meaning 'twelfth part'; there are twelve inches to the foot

incident, incidents NOUN an event • *a shooting incident.*

incidental ADJECTIVE occurring as a minor part of something • *full of vivid incidental detail.* **incidentally** ADVERB

incinerate, incinerates, incinerating, incinerated VERB If you incinerate something, you burn it. **incineration** NOUN

incinerator, incinerators NOUN a furnace for burning rubbish.

incipient ADJECTIVE beginning to happen or appear • *incipient panic*.

incision, incisions NOUN a sharp cut, usually made by a surgeon operating on a patient.

incisive ADJECTIVE Incisive language is clear and forceful.

incisor, incisors NOUN SCIENCE An incisor is a flat tooth with a sharp cutting edge at the front of your mouth.

incite, incites, inciting, incited VERB If you incite someone to do something, you encourage them to do it by making them angry or excited. **incitement** NOUN
SIMILAR WORDS: encourage, provoke, spur

inclination, inclinations NOUN If you have an inclination to do something, you want to do it.

incline, inclines, inclining, inclined VERB ① If you are inclined to behave in a certain way, you often behave that way or you want to behave that way. ▶ NOUN ② a slope.

include, includes, including, included VERB If one thing includes another, it has the second thing as one of its parts. **including** PREPOSITION
SIMILAR WORDS: contain, incorporate

inclusion NOUN The inclusion of one thing in another is the act of making it part of the other thing.

inclusive ADJECTIVE A price that is inclusive includes all the goods and services that are being offered, with no extra charge for any of them.

incognito [Said in-kog-**nee**-toe] ADVERB If you are travelling incognito, you are travelling in disguise.

WORD HISTORY: from Latin in- + *cognitus* meaning 'not known'

incoherent ADJECTIVE If someone is incoherent, they are talking in an unclear or rambling way. **incoherently** ADVERB **incoherence** NOUN

income, incomes NOUN the money a person earns.

income tax NOUN Income tax is a part of someone's salary which they have to pay regularly to the government.

incoming ADJECTIVE coming in • *incoming trains* • *an incoming phone call*.

incomparable ADJECTIVE Something that is incomparable is so good that it cannot be compared with anything else. **incomparably** ADVERB
SIMILAR WORDS: matchless, unequalled, unparalleled

incompatible ADJECTIVE Two things or people are incompatible if they are unable to live or exist together because they are completely different. **incompatibility** NOUN

incompetent ADJECTIVE Someone who is incompetent does not have the ability to do something properly. **incompetently** ADVERB **incompetence** NOUN

incomplete ADJECTIVE not complete or finished. **incompletely** ADVERB

incomprehensible ADJECTIVE not able to be understood.

inconceivable ADJECTIVE impossible to believe.

inconclusive ADJECTIVE not leading to a decision or to a definite result.

incongruous ADJECTIVE Something that is incongruous seems strange because it does not fit in to a place or situation. **incongruously** ADVERB

inconsequential ADJECTIVE
Something that is inconsequential is not very important.

inconsistent ADJECTIVE Someone or something that is inconsistent is unpredictable and behaves differently in similar situations. **inconsistently** ADVERB **inconsistency** NOUN

inconspicuous ADJECTIVE not easily seen or obvious. **inconspicuously** ADVERB

incontinent ADJECTIVE Someone who is incontinent is unable to control their bladder or bowels.

inconvenience, inconveniences, inconveniencing, inconvenienced NOUN ① If something causes inconvenience, it causes difficulty or problems. ▸ VERB ② To inconvenience someone is to cause them trouble, difficulty or problems. **inconvenient** ADJECTIVE **inconveniently** ADVERB

incorporate, incorporates, incorporating, incorporated VERB If something is incorporated into another thing, it becomes part of that thing. **incorporation** NOUN

incorrect ADJECTIVE wrong or untrue. **incorrectly** ADVERB

increase, increases, increasing, increased VERB ① If something increases, it becomes larger in amount. ▸ NOUN ② a rise in the number, level or amount of something. **increasingly** ADVERB

incredible ADJECTIVE ① totally amazing. ② impossible to believe. **incredibly** ADVERB
SIMILAR WORDS: ① amazing, unbelievable

incredulous ADJECTIVE If you are incredulous, you are unable to believe something because it is very surprising or shocking.

incredulously ADVERB **incredulity** NOUN

increment, increments NOUN the amount by which something increases, or a regular increase in someone's salary. **incremental** ADJECTIVE

incriminate, incriminates, incriminating, incriminated VERB If something incriminates you, it suggests that you are involved in a crime.

incubate, incubates, incubating, incubated [Said in-kyoo-bate] VERB When eggs incubate, they are kept warm until they are ready to hatch. **incubation** NOUN

incubator, incubators NOUN a piece of hospital equipment in which sick or weak newborn babies are kept warm.

incumbent, incumbents (formal) ADJECTIVE ① If it is incumbent on you to do something, it is your duty to do it. ▸ NOUN ② the person in a particular official position.

incur, incurs, incurring, incurred VERB If you incur something unpleasant, you cause it to happen.

incurable ADJECTIVE ① An incurable disease is one which cannot be cured. ② An incurable habit is one which cannot be changed • an incurable romantic. **incurably** ADVERB

indaba, indabas [Said in-dah-ba] NOUN ① In southern Africa, an indaba is a meeting to discuss a serious topic. ② (informal) In South African English, an indaba is a matter of concern.

indebted ADJECTIVE If you are indebted to someone, you are grateful to them. **indebtedness** NOUN

indecent ADJECTIVE Something that is indecent is shocking or rude.

indecently ADVERB **indecency** NOUN

indeed ADVERB You use 'indeed' to strengthen a point that you are making • *The desserts are very good indeed.*

indefatigable [Said in-dif-**fat**-ig-a-bl] ADJECTIVE People who never get tired of doing something are indefatigable.

indefinite ADJECTIVE ① If something is indefinite, no time to finish has been decided • *an indefinite strike.* ② Indefinite also means vague or not exact • *indefinite words and pictures.* **indefinitely** ADVERB

indefinite article, indefinite articles NOUN the grammatical term for 'a' and 'an'.

indelible ADJECTIVE unable to be removed • *indelible ink.* **indelibly** ADVERB

indemnity NOUN (*formal*) Indemnity is protection against damage or loss.

indentation, indentations NOUN a dent or a groove in a surface or on the edge of something.

independence NOUN ① Independence is not relying on anyone else. ② HISTORY A nation or state gains its independence when it stops being ruled or governed by another country and has its own government and laws.

independent ADJECTIVE ① Something that is independent happens or exists separately from other people or things • *Results are assessed by an independent panel.* ② Someone who is independent does not need other people's help • *a fiercely independent teenager.* ③ An independent nation is one that is not ruled or governed by another country. ④ An independent candidate in an election does not represent any political party.

independently ADVERB SIMILAR WORDS: ③ autonomous, self-governing

independent variable, independent variables NOUN SCIENCE a variable in a mathematical equation whose value does not depend on the value taken on by another variable. For example, in the equation x = y+1, y is the independent variable as it does not depends on the value of x.

indeterminate ADJECTIVE not certain or definite • *some indeterminate point in the future.*

index, indexes or **indices**; indexing, indexed NOUN ① ENGLISH An index is an alphabetical list at the back of a book, referring to items in the book. ② LIBRARY An index is also an alphabetical list of all the books in a library, arranged by title, author or subject. ③ MATHS a number or symbol placed above and to the right of a number, indicating the number of times the number is to be multiplied by itself. ▶ VERB ④ To index a book or collection of information means to provide an index for it.

GRAMMAR TIP
The usual plural of the alphabetical list is *indexes*. The plural of the mathematical term is *indices*.

index finger, index fingers NOUN your first finger, next to your thumb.

Indian, Indians ADJECTIVE ① belonging or relating to India. ▶ NOUN ② someone who comes from India. ③ someone descended from the people who lived in North, South or Central America before Europeans arrived.

indicate, indicates, indicating, indicated VERB ① If something indicates something, it shows that it

is true • *a gesture which clearly indicates his relief.* ② If you indicate something to someone, you point to it. ③ If you indicate a fact, you mention it. ④ If the driver of a vehicle indicates, they give a signal to show which way they are going to turn.
SIMILAR WORDS: ① denote, show, signify

indication, indications NOUN a sign of what someone feels or what is likely to happen.

indicative ADJECTIVE ① If something is indicative of something else, it is a sign of that thing • *Clean, pink tongues are indicative of a good, healthy digestion.* ▶ NOUN ② ENGLISH If a verb is used in the indicative, it is in the form used for making statements.

indicator, indicators NOUN ① something which tells you what something is like or what is happening. ② A car's indicators are the lights at the front and back which are used to show when it is turning left or right. ③ SCIENCE a substance used in chemistry that shows if another substance is an acid or alkali by changing colour when it comes into contact with it.

indict, indicts, indicting, indicted [*Said in-***dite***] VERB (formal) To indict someone is to charge them officially with a crime. **indictment** NOUN **indictable** ADJECTIVE

indie ADJECTIVE Indie music refers to rock or pop music produced by bands working with small, independent record companies.

indifferent ADJECTIVE ① If you are indifferent to something, you have no interest in it. ② If something is indifferent, it is of a poor quality or low standard • *a pair of rather indifferent paintings.* **indifferently** ADVERB **indifference** NOUN

indigenous [*Said in-***dij**-*in-uss*] ADJECTIVE If something is indigenous to a country, it comes from that country • *a plant indigenous to Asia.*

indigestible ADJECTIVE Food that is indigestible cannot be digested easily, and may give you indigestion.

indigestion NOUN Indigestion is a pain you get when you find it difficult to digest food.

indignant ADJECTIVE If you are indignant, you feel angry about something that you think is unfair. **indignantly** ADVERB

indignation NOUN Indignation is anger about something that you think is unfair.

indignity, indignities NOUN something that makes you feel embarrassed or humiliated • *the indignity of having to flee angry protesters.*

indigo, indigos or indigoes NOUN or ADJECTIVE dark violet-blue.

indirect ADJECTIVE ① not moving in a straight line or by the shortest route . ② not done or caused directly by a particular person or thing, but by someone or something else. **indirectly** ADVERB
SIMILAR WORDS: ① circuitous, roundabout

indiscriminate ADJECTIVE not involving careful thought or choice • *an indiscriminate bombing campaign.* **indiscriminately** ADVERB

indispensable ADJECTIVE If something is indispensable, you cannot do without it • *A good pair of walking shoes is indispensable.*

indistinct ADJECTIVE not clear • *indistinct voices.* **indistinctly** ADVERB

individual, individuals ADJECTIVE ① relating to one particular person or thing • *Each family needs individual* attention. ② Someone who is individual behaves quite differently from the way other people behave. ▶ NOUN ③ a person, different from any other person • *wealthy individuals*. **individually** ADVERB

individualist, individualists NOUN someone who likes to do things in their own way. **individualistic** ADJECTIVE

individuality NOUN If something has individuality, it is different from all other things, and therefore is very interesting and noticeable.

indomitable ADJECTIVE (*formal*) impossible to overcome • *an indomitable spirit*.

Indonesian, Indonesians [*Said in-don-nee-zee-an*] ADJECTIVE ① belonging or relating to Indonesia. ▶ NOUN ② someone who comes from Indonesia. ③ Indonesian is the official language of Indonesia.

indoor ADJECTIVE situated or happening inside a building.

indoors ADVERB If something happens indoors, it takes place inside a building.

induce, induces, inducing, induced VERB ① To induce a state is to cause it • *His manner was rough and suspicious but he did not induce fear*. ② If you induce someone to do something, you persuade them to do it.

inducement, inducements NOUN something offered to encourage someone to do something.

indulge, indulges, indulging, indulged VERB ① If you indulge in something, you allow yourself to do something that you enjoy. ② If you indulge someone, you let them have or do what they want, often in a way that is not good for them.

indulgence, indulgences NOUN ① something you allow yourself to

have because it gives you pleasure. ② Indulgence is the act of indulging yourself or another person.

indulgent ADJECTIVE If you are indulgent, you treat someone with special kindness • *a rich, indulgent father*. **indulgently** ADVERB

industrial ADJECTIVE relating to industry.

industrial action NOUN Industrial action is action such as striking taken by workers in protest over pay or working conditions.

industrialist, industrialists NOUN a person who owns or controls a lot of factories.

Industrial Revolution NOUN HISTORY The Industrial Revolution was a period when machines began to be used more in factories and more goods were produced as a result. It started in Britain in the late eighteenth and early nineteenth century.

industrious ADJECTIVE An industrious person works very hard.

industry, industries NOUN ① Industry is the work and processes involved in manufacturing things in factories. ② all the people and processes involved in manufacturing a particular thing.

inedible ADJECTIVE too nasty or poisonous to eat.

inefficient ADJECTIVE badly organised, wasteful and slow • *a corrupt and inefficient administration*. **inefficiently** ADVERB **inefficiency** NOUN

inept ADJECTIVE without skill • *an inept lawyer*. **ineptitude** NOUN

inequality, inequalities NOUN a difference in size, status, wealth or position, between different things, groups or people.

inert ADJECTIVE ① Something that is

a b c d e f g h i j k l m n o p q r s t u v w x y z

inert does not move and appears lifeless • *an inert body lying on the floor.* ② In chemistry, an inert gas does not react with other substances. The inert gases are also called **noble gases**.

inertia *[Said in-ner-sha]* NOUN If you have a feeling of inertia, you feel very lazy and unwilling to do anything.

inevitable ADJECTIVE certain to happen. **inevitably** ADVERB **inevitability** NOUN

inexhaustible ADJECTIVE Something that is inexhaustible will never be used up • *an inexhaustible supply of ideas.*

inexorable ADJECTIVE (*formal*) Something that is inexorable cannot be prevented from continuing • *the inexorable increase in the number of cars.* **inexorably** ADVERB

inexpensive ADJECTIVE not costing much.

inexperienced ADJECTIVE lacking experience of a situation or activity • *inexperienced drivers.* **inexperience** NOUN
SIMILAR WORDS: new, raw, unpractised

inexplicable ADJECTIVE If something is inexplicable, you cannot explain it • *For some inexplicable reason I still felt uneasy.* **inexplicably** ADVERB

inextricably ADVERB If two or more things are inextricably linked, they cannot be separated.

infallible ADJECTIVE never wrong • *No machine is infallible.* **infallibility** NOUN

infamous *[Said in-fe-muss]* ADJECTIVE well-known because of something bad or evil • *a book about the country's most infamous murder cases.*

infant, infants NOUN ① a baby or very young child. ▸ ADJECTIVE ② designed for young children • *an infant school.* **infancy** NOUN

infantile ADJECTIVE
WORD HISTORY: from Latin *infans* meaning 'unable to speak'

infantry NOUN In an army, the infantry are soldiers who fight on foot rather than in tanks or on horses.

infatuated ADJECTIVE If you are infatuated with someone, you have such strong feelings of love or passion that you cannot think sensibly about them. **infatuation** NOUN

infect, infects, infecting, infected VERB To infect someone or something is to cause disease in them.

infection, infections NOUN ① a disease caused by germs • *a chest infection.* ② Infection is the state of being infected • *a very small risk of infection.*

infectious ADJECTIVE spreading from one person to another • *an infectious disease.*
SIMILAR WORDS: catching, contagious

infer, infers, inferring, inferred VERB If you infer something, you work out that it is true on the basis of information that you already have. **inference** NOUN

USAGE NOTE
Do not use *infer* to mean the same as *imply.*

inferior, inferiors ADJECTIVE ① having a lower position than something or someone else. ② of low quality • *inferior quality DVDs.* ▸ NOUN ③ Your inferiors are people in a lower position than you. **inferiority** NOUN

infernal ADJECTIVE (*old-fashioned*) very unpleasant • *an infernal bore.*
WORD HISTORY: from Latin *infernus* meaning 'hell'

inferno, infernos NOUN a very large dangerous fire.

infertile ADJECTIVE ① Infertile soil is of poor quality and plants cannot grow well in it. ② Someone who is infertile cannot have children.
infertility NOUN

infested ADJECTIVE Something that is infested has a large number of animals or insects living on or in it and causing damage • *The flats are damp and infested with rats.*
infestation NOUN

infighting NOUN Infighting is quarrelling or rivalry between members of the same organisation.

infiltrate, infiltrates, infiltrating, infiltrated VERB If people infiltrate an organisation, they gradually enter it in secret to spy on its activities.
infiltration NOUN **infiltrator** NOUN

infinite ADJECTIVE without any limit or end • *an infinite number of possibilities.* **infinitely** ADVERB
SIMILAR WORDS: limitless, never-ending

infinitive, infinitives NOUN In grammar, the infinitive is the base form of the verb. It often has 'to' in front of it, for example 'to go' or 'to see'.

infinity NOUN ① Infinity is a number that is larger than any other number and can never be given an exact value. ② Infinity is also a point that can never be reached, further away than any other point • *skies stretching on into infinity.*

infirm ADJECTIVE weak or ill.
infirmity NOUN

infirmary, infirmaries NOUN a hospital.

inflamed ADJECTIVE If part of your body is inflamed, it is red and swollen, usually because of infection.

inflammable ADJECTIVE An inflammable material burns easily.

USAGE NOTE
Although *inflammable* and *flammable* both mean 'likely to catch fire', *flammable* is used more often as people sometimes think that *inflammable* means 'not likely to catch fire'.

---

inflammation NOUN Inflammation is painful redness or swelling of part of the body.

inflammatory ADJECTIVE Inflammatory actions are likely to make people very angry.

inflate, inflates, inflating, inflated VERB When you inflate something, you fill it with air or gas to make it swell. **inflatable** ADJECTIVE

inflation NOUN Inflation is an increase in the price of goods and services in a country. **inflationary** ADJECTIVE

inflection, inflections; also spelt **inflexion** NOUN MFL a change in the form of a word that shows its grammatical function, for example a change that makes a noun plural.

inflexible ADJECTIVE fixed and unable to be altered • *an inflexible routine.*

inflict, inflicts, inflicting, inflicted VERB If you inflict something unpleasant on someone, you make them suffer it.

influence, influences, influencing, influenced NOUN ① Influence is power that a person has over other people. ② An influence is also the effect that someone or something has • *under the influence of alcohol.*
▶ VERB ③ To influence someone or something means to have an effect on them.
SIMILAR WORDS: ① hold, power, pull
WORD HISTORY: from Latin *influentia* meaning 'power flowing from the stars'

a
b
c
d
e
f
g
h
i
j
k
l
m
n
o
p
q
r
s
t
u
v
w
x
y
z

influential ADJECTIVE Someone who is influential has a lot of influence over people.

influenza NOUN (*formal*) Influenza is flu.

influx NOUN a steady arrival of people or things • *a large influx of tourists.*

inform, informs, informing, **informed** VERB ① If you inform someone of something, you tell them about it. ② If you inform on a person, you tell the police about a crime they have committed.
informant NOUN
SIMILAR WORDS: ① notify, tell ② betray, grass, shop

informal ADJECTIVE relaxed and casual • *an informal meeting.*
informally ADVERB **informality** NOUN

information NOUN If you have information on or about something, you know something about it.
SIMILAR WORDS: data, facts

informative ADJECTIVE Something that is informative gives you useful information.

informed ADJECTIVE ① having a lot of knowledge about something. ② PSHE based on definite knowledge or information • *an informed decision.*

informer, informers NOUN someone who tells the police that another person has committed a crime.

infrastructure, infrastructures NOUN GEOGRAPHY The infrastructure of a country consists of things like factories, schools and roads, which show how much money the country has and how strong its economy is.

infringe, infringes, infringing, **infringed** VERB ① If you infringe a law, you break it. ② To infringe people's rights is to not allow them the rights to which they are entitled.
infringement NOUN

infuriate, infuriates, infuriating, **infuriated** VERB If someone infuriates you, they make you very angry. **infuriating** ADJECTIVE

infuse, infuses, infusing, infused VERB ① If you infuse someone with a feeling such as enthusiasm or joy, you fill them with it. ② If you infuse a substance such as a herb or medicine, you pour hot water onto it and leave it for the water to absorb the flavour. **infusion** NOUN

ingenious [*Said in-jeen-yuss*] ADJECTIVE very clever and using new ideas • *his ingenious invention.*
ingeniously ADVERB

ingenuity [*Said in-jen-yoo-it-ee*] NOUN Ingenuity is cleverness and skill at inventing things or working out plans.

ingot, ingots NOUN a brick-shaped lump of metal, especially gold.

ingrained ADJECTIVE If habits and beliefs are ingrained, they are difficult to change or destroy.

ingredient, ingredients NOUN DGT Ingredients are the things that something is made from, especially in cookery.

inhabit, inhabits, inhabiting, **inhabited** VERB If you inhabit a place, you live there.

inhabitant, inhabitants NOUN The inhabitants of a place are the people who live there.
SIMILAR WORDS: citizen, dweller, resident

inhale, inhales, inhaling, inhaled VERB SCIENCE When you inhale, you breathe in. **inhalation** NOUN

inherent ADJECTIVE Inherent qualities or characteristics in something are a natural part of it • *her inherent common sense.*

inherently ADVERB

inherit, inherits, inheriting, inherited VERB ① If you inherit money or property, you receive it from someone who has died. ② SCIENCE If you inherit a quality or characteristic from a parent or ancestor, it is passed on to you at birth. **inheritor** NOUN

inheritance, inheritances NOUN something that is passed on from another person.

inhibit, inhibits, inhibiting, inhibited VERB If you inhibit someone from doing something, you prevent them from doing it.

inhibited ADJECTIVE People who are inhibited find it difficult to relax and to show their emotions.

inhibition, inhibitions NOUN Inhibitions are feelings of fear or embarrassment that make it difficult for someone to relax and to show their emotions.

inhospitable ADJECTIVE ① An inhospitable place is unpleasant or difficult to live in. ② If someone is inhospitable, they do not make people who visit them feel welcome.

inhuman ADJECTIVE not human or not behaving like a human • *the inhuman killing of their enemies.*

inhumane ADJECTIVE extremely cruel. **inhumanity** NOUN

inimitable ADJECTIVE If you have an inimitable characteristic, no one else can imitate it • *her inimitable sense of style.*

initial, initials [Said in-nish-l] ADJECTIVE ① first, or at the beginning • *Shock and dismay were my initial reactions.* ▶ NOUN ② the first letter of a name. **initially** ADVERB

initiate, initiates, initiating, initiated [Said in-nish-ee-ate] VERB ① If you initiate something, you make it start or happen. ② If you initiate someone into a group or club, you allow them to become a member of it, usually by means of a special ceremony. **initiation** NOUN

initiative, initiatives [Said in-nish-at-ive] NOUN ① an attempt to get something done. ② If you have initiative, you decide what to do and then do it, without needing the advice of other people.

inject, injects, injecting, injected VERB ① If a doctor or nurse injects you with a substance, they use a needle and syringe to put the substance into your body. ② If you inject something new into a situation, you add it. **injection** NOUN

injunction, injunctions NOUN an order issued by a court of law to stop someone doing something.

injure, injures, injuring, injured VERB To injure someone is to damage part of their body.

injury, injuries NOUN PE hurt or damage, especially to part of a person's body or to their feelings • *The knee injury forced him to retire from the professional game* • *He suffered acute injury to his pride.*

injustice, injustices NOUN ① Injustice is lack of justice and fairness. ② If you do someone an injustice, you judge them too harshly.

ink NOUN Ink is the coloured liquid used for writing or printing.

inkhosi, amakhosi [Said in-koh-see] NOUN a Zulu tribal chief.

inkling, inklings NOUN a vague idea about something.

inlaid ADJECTIVE decorated with small pieces of wood, metal or stone • *decorative plates inlaid with brass.*
inlay NOUN

inland ADJECTIVE ① near the middle of a country, away from the sea.
▶ADVERB ② towards the middle of a country, away from the sea.

in-law, in-laws NOUN Your in-laws are members of your husband's or wife's family.

inlet, inlets NOUN a narrow bay.

inmate, inmates NOUN someone who lives in a prison or psychiatric hospital.

inn, inns NOUN a small old country pub or hotel.

innards PLURAL NOUN The innards of something are its inside parts.

innate ADJECTIVE An innate quality is one that you were born with • *an innate sense of fairness*. **innately** ADVERB

inner ADJECTIVE contained inside a place or object • *an inner room*.

innermost ADJECTIVE deepest and most secret • *our innermost feelings*.

innings NOUN In cricket, an innings is a period when a particular team is batting.

innocence NOUN inexperience of evil or unpleasant things.

innocent ADJECTIVE ① not guilty of a crime. ② without experience of evil or unpleasant things • *an innocent child*. **innocently** ADVERB

innocuous [Said in-**nok**-yoo-uss] ADJECTIVE not harmful.

innovation, innovations NOUN DGT a completely new idea, product or system of doing things.

innuendo, innuendos or innuendoes [Said in-yoo-**en**-doe] NOUN an indirect reference to something rude or unpleasant. **WORD HISTORY:** from Latin *innuendo* meaning 'by hinting', from *innuere* meaning 'to convey by a nod'

innumerable ADJECTIVE too many to be counted • *innumerable cups of tea*.

inoculate, inoculates, inoculating, inoculated VERB To inoculate someone means to inject them with a weak form of a disease in order to protect them from that disease. **inoculation** NOUN

input, inputs NOUN ① Input consists of all the money, information and other resources that are put into a job, project or company to make it work. ② ICT In computing, input is information which is fed into a computer.

inquest, inquests NOUN an official inquiry to find out what caused a person's death.

inquire, inquires, inquiring, inquired; also spelt **enquire** VERB If you inquire about something, you ask for information about it. **inquiring** ADJECTIVE **inquiry** NOUN

inquisition, inquisitions NOUN an official investigation, especially one which is very thorough and uses harsh methods of questioning.

inquisitive ADJECTIVE Someone who is inquisitive is keen to find out about things. **inquisitively** ADVERB

inroads PLURAL NOUN If something makes inroads on or into something, it starts affecting it.

insane ADJECTIVE Someone who is insane has a serious mental illness that causes their mind not to work normally. **insanely** ADVERB **insanity** NOUN

insatiable [Said in-**saysh**-a-bl] ADJECTIVE A desire or urge that is insatiable is very great • *an insatiable curiosity*. **insatiably** ADVERB

inscribe, inscribes, inscribing, inscribed VERB If you inscribe words on an object, you write or carve them on it.

inscription, inscriptions NOUN the words that are written or carved on something.

inscrutable [Said in-**skroot**-a-bl] ADJECTIVE Someone who is inscrutable does not show what they are really thinking.

insect, insects NOUN SCIENCE a small creature with six legs, and usually wings.

insecticide, insecticides NOUN SCIENCE a poisonous chemical used to kill insects.

insecure ADJECTIVE ① If you are insecure, you feel unsure of yourself and doubt whether other people like you. ② Something that is insecure is not safe or well protected • *People still feel their jobs are insecure.* **insecurity** NOUN

insensitive ADJECTIVE If you are insensitive, you do not notice when you are upsetting people. **insensitivity** NOUN

insert, inserts, inserting, inserted VERB If you insert an object into something, you put it inside. **insertion** NOUN

inshore ADJECTIVE at sea but close to the shore • *inshore boats.*

inside, insides NOUN ① the part of something that is surrounded by the main part and often hidden • *The inside of the house was painted white.* ② (in plural) Your insides are the parts inside your body. ▶ ADJECTIVE ③ surrounded by the main part and often hidden • *an inside pocket.* ▶ PREPOSITION ④ in or to the interior of • *inside the house.* ▶ PHRASE ⑤ **Inside out** means with the inside part facing outwards.

GRAMMAR TIP
Do not use *of* after *inside*. You should write *she was waiting inside the school* and not *inside of the school.*

insider, insiders NOUN a person who is involved in a situation and so knows more about it than other people.

insidious ADJECTIVE Something that is insidious is unpleasant and develops slowly without being noticed • *the insidious progress of the disease.* **insidiously** ADVERB

insight, insights NOUN If you gain insight into a problem, you gradually get a deep and accurate understanding of it.

insignia [Said in-**sig**-nee-a] NOUN the badge or a sign of a particular organisation.

insignificant ADJECTIVE small and unimportant. **insignificance** NOUN

insincere ADJECTIVE Someone who is insincere pretends to have feelings which they do not really have. **insincerely** ADVERB **insincerity** NOUN

insinuate, insinuates, insinuating, insinuated VERB If you insinuate something unpleasant, you hint about it. **insinuation** NOUN

insipid ADJECTIVE ① An insipid person or activity is dull and boring. ② Food that is insipid has very little taste. SIMILAR WORDS: ① bland, colourless, uninteresting

insist, insists, insisting, insisted VERB If you insist on something, you demand it forcefully. **insistent** ADJECTIVE **insistence** NOUN

insolent ADJECTIVE very rude and disrespectful. **insolently** ADVERB **insolence** NOUN

insoluble [Said in-**soll**-yoo-bl] ADJECTIVE ① impossible to solve • *an insoluble problem.* ② SCIENCE unable to dissolve • *substances which are insoluble in water.*

insolvent ADJECTIVE unable to pay your debts. **insolvency** NOUN

insomnia NOUN Insomnia is difficulty in sleeping. **insomniac** NOUN

a
b
c
d
e
f
g
h
i
j
k
l
m
n
o
p
q
r
s
t
u
v
w
x
y
z

inspect, inspects, inspecting, inspected VERB To inspect something is to examine it carefully to check that everything is all right. **inspection** NOUN

inspector, inspectors NOUN ① someone who inspects things. ② a police officer just above a sergeant in rank.

inspire, inspires, inspiring, inspired VERB ① If something inspires you, it gives you new ideas and enthusiasm to do something. ② To inspire an emotion in someone is to make them feel this emotion. **inspired** ADJECTIVE **inspiring** ADJECTIVE **inspiration** NOUN

instability NOUN Instability is a lack of stability in a place • *political instability*.

install, installs, installing, installed VERB ① If you install a piece of equipment in a place, you put it there so it is ready to be used. ② If you install software on a computer, you transfer it there and make it ready to be used. ③ To install someone in an important job is to officially give them that position. ④ If you install yourself in a place, you settle there and make yourself comfortable. **installation** NOUN

instalment, instalments NOUN ① If you pay for something in instalments, you pay small amounts of money regularly over a period of time. ② one of the parts of a story or television series.

instance, instances NOUN ① a particular example or occurrence of an event, situation or person • *a serious instance of corruption*.
▶ PHRASE ② You use **for instance** to give an example of something you are talking about.

instant, instants NOUN ① a moment or short period of time • *In an instant they were gone.* ▶ ADJECTIVE ② immediate and without delay • *The record was an instant success.* **instantly** ADVERB

instantaneous ADJECTIVE happening immediately and without delay • *The applause was instantaneous.* **instantaneously** ADVERB

instant message, instant messages NOUN a message that appears immediately on the screen of the computer you send it to.

instead ADVERB in place of something • *Take the stairs instead of the lift.*

instigate, instigates, instigating, instigated VERB Someone who instigates a situation makes it happen. **instigation** NOUN **instigator** NOUN

instil, instils, instilling, instilled VERB If you instil an idea or feeling into someone, you make them feel or think it.

instinct, instincts NOUN a natural tendency to do something • *My first instinct was to protect myself.* **instinctive** ADJECTIVE **instinctively** ADVERB

institute, institutes, instituting, instituted NOUN ① an organisation for teaching or research. ▶ VERB ② (*formal*) If you institute a rule or system, you introduce it.

institution, institutions NOUN ① a custom or system regarded as an important tradition within a society • *the institution of marriage.* ② a large, important organisation, for example a university or bank. **institutional** ADJECTIVE

instruct, instructs, instructing, instructed VERB ① If you instruct someone to do something, you tell them to do it. ② If someone instructs you in a subject or skill, they teach you about it. **instructor** NOUN **instructive** ADJECTIVE **instruction** NOUN

instrument, instruments NOUN ① a tool or device used for a particular job • *a special instrument which cut through the metal.* ② MUSIC A musical instrument is an object, such as a piano or flute, played to make music.

instrumental ADJECTIVE ① If you are instrumental in doing something, you help to make it happen. ② MUSIC Instrumental music is performed using only musical instruments, and not voices.

insufficient ADJECTIVE not enough for a particular purpose. **insufficiently** ADVERB

insular [*Said* inss-yoo-lar] ADJECTIVE Someone who is insular is unwilling to meet new people or to consider new ideas. **insularity** NOUN

insulate, insulates, insulating, insulated VERB ① If you insulate a person from harmful things, you protect them from those things. ② If materials such as feathers, fur or foam insulate something, they keep it warm by covering it in a thick layer. ③ SCIENCE You insulate an electrical or metal object by covering it with rubber or plastic. This is to stop electricity passing through it and giving you an electric shock. **insulation** NOUN **insulator** NOUN

insulin [*Said* inss-yoo-lin] NOUN Insulin is a substance which controls the level of sugar in the blood. People who have diabetes do not produce insulin naturally and have to take regular doses of it.

insult, insults, insulting, insulted VERB ① If you insult someone, you

offend them by being rude to them. ▶ NOUN ② a rude remark which offends you. **insulting** ADJECTIVE SIMILAR WORDS: ① abuse, affront, offend ② abuse, affront, offence

insure, insures, insuring, insured VERB ① If you insure something or yourself, you pay money regularly to a company so that if there is an accident or damage, the company will pay for medical treatment or repairs. ② If you do something to insure against something unpleasant happening, you do it to prevent the unpleasant thing from happening or to protect yourself if it does happen. **insurance** NOUN

SPELLING TIP
Do not confuse the spellings of *insure* and *ensure*: *Callum forgot to insure the car; Please ensure that the door is locked.*

insurgent, insurgents NOUN Insurgents are people who are fighting against the government or army of their own country. **insurgency** NOUN
WORD HISTORY: from Latin *insurgere* meaning 'to rise up'

insurrection, insurrections NOUN a violent action taken against the rulers of a country.

intact ADJECTIVE complete, and not changed or damaged in any way • *The rear of the aircraft remained intact when it crashed.*

intake, intakes NOUN A person's intake of food, drink or air is the amount they take in.

integer, integers [*Said* in-ti-jer] NOUN MATHS In mathematics, an integer is any whole number.

integral ADJECTIVE If something is an integral part of a whole thing, it is an essential part.

integrate, integrates, integrating, integrated VERB ①If a person integrates into a group, they become part of it. ②To integrate things is to combine them so that they become closely linked or form one thing • *his plan to integrate the coal and steel industries.* **integration** NOUN

integrity NOUN ①Integrity is the quality of being honest and following your principles. ②The integrity of a group of people is their being united as one whole.

intellect, intellects NOUN Intellect is the ability to understand ideas and information.

intellectual, intellectuals ADJECTIVE ①involving thought, ideas and understanding • *an intellectual exercise.* ▶ NOUN ②someone who enjoys thinking about complicated ideas. **intellectually** ADVERB

intelligence NOUN A person's intelligence is their ability to understand and learn things quickly and well.

SIMILAR WORDS: brains, intellect, understanding

intelligent ADJECTIVE able to understand and learn things quickly and well. **intelligently** ADVERB

intelligentsia [Said in-tell-lee-jent-sya] NOUN The intelligentsia are intellectual people, considered as a group.

intelligible ADJECTIVE able to be understood • *very few intelligible remarks.*

intend, intends, intending, intended VERB ①If you intend to do something, you have decided or planned to do it • *She intended to move back to Cape Town.* ②If something is intended for a particular use, you have planned that it should have this use • *The booklet is intended to be kept handy.*

intense ADJECTIVE ①very great in strength or amount • *intense heat.* ②If a person is intense, they take things very seriously and have very strong feelings. **intensely** ADVERB **intensity** NOUN

intensify, intensifies, intensifying, intensified VERB To intensify something is to make it greater or stronger.

intensive ADJECTIVE involving a lot of energy or effort over a very short time • *an intensive training course.*

intent, intents NOUN ①(formal) A person's intent is their purpose or intention. ▶ ADJECTIVE ②If you are intent on doing something, you are determined to do it. **intently** ADVERB

intention, intentions NOUN If you have an intention to do something, you have a plan of what you are going to do.

intentional ADJECTIVE If something is intentional, it is done on purpose. **intentionally** ADVERB

inter- PREFIX 'Inter-' means 'between' • *inter-school competitions.*

interact, interacts, interacting, interacted VERB The way two people or things interact is the way they work together, communicate or react with each other. **interaction** NOUN

interactive ADJECTIVE ICT Interactive television, computers and games react to decisions taken by the viewer, user or player.

intercept, intercepts, intercepting, intercepted [Said in-ter-sept] VERB If you intercept someone or something that is going from one place to another, you stop them.

interchange, interchanges NOUN An interchange is the act or process of exchanging things or ideas.

interchangeable ADJECTIVE

intercom, intercoms NOUN a device consisting of a microphone and a loudspeaker, which you use to speak to people in another room.

intercourse NOUN Intercourse or sexual intercourse is the act of having sex.

interest, interests, interesting, interested NOUN ① If you have an interest in something or if something is of interest, you want to learn or hear more about it. ② Your interests are your hobbies. ③ If you have an interest in something being done, you want it to be done because it will benefit you. ④ Interest is an extra payment made to the lender by someone who has borrowed a sum of money, or by a bank or company to someone who has invested money in them. Interest is worked out as a percentage of the sum of money borrowed or invested. ▶ VERB ⑤ Something that interests you attracts your attention so that you want to learn or hear more about it. **interested** ADJECTIVE

interesting ADJECTIVE making you want to know, learn or hear more. **interestingly** ADVERB

interface, interfaces NOUN ① The interface between two subjects or systems is the area in which they affect each other or are linked. ② [ICT] The user interface of a computer program is how it is presented on the computer screen and how easy it is to operate.

interfere, interferes, interfering, interfered VERB ① If you interfere in a situation, you try to influence it, although it does not really concern you. ② Something that interferes with a situation has a damaging effect on it. **interference** NOUN **interfering** ADJECTIVE

SIMILAR WORDS: ① butt in, intrude, meddle

WORD HISTORY: from Old French *s'entreferir* meaning 'to collide'

interim ADJECTIVE intended for use only until something permanent is arranged • *an interim government*.

interior, interiors NOUN ① the inside part of something. ▶ ADJECTIVE ② Interior means inside • *They painted the interior walls white.*

interior angle NOUN MATHS An interior angle is the angle between any two adjacent sides of a polygon.

interjection, interjections NOUN a word or phrase spoken suddenly to express surprise, pain or anger.
▶ SEE GRAMMAR BOX ON NEXT PAGE

interlude, interludes [Rhymes with rude] NOUN a short break from an activity.

intermediary, intermediaries [Said in-ter-meed-yer-ee] NOUN someone who tries to get two groups of people to come to an agreement.

intermediate ADJECTIVE An intermediate level occurs in the middle, between two other stages • *intermediate students*.

interminable ADJECTIVE If something is interminable, it goes on for a very long time • *an interminable wait for the bus*. **interminably** ADVERB

intermission, intermissions NOUN an interval between two parts of a film or play.

intermittent ADJECTIVE happening only occasionally. **intermittently** ADVERB

internal ADJECTIVE happening inside a person, place or object. **internally** ADVERB

international, internationals ADJECTIVE GEOGRAPHY ① involving different countries. ▶ NOUN ② a

A
B
C
D
E
F
G
H
I
J
K
L
M
N
O
P
Q
R
S
T
U
V
W
X
Y
Z

What is an Interjection?

An interjection is a word that expresses a strong emotion, such as anger, surprise or excitement. Interjections often stand alone rather than as part of a sentence.

Some interjections express greetings:

Hello.
Congratulations!

Some interjections express agreement or disagreement:

Indeed.
No.

Some interjections express pain, anger or annoyance:

Ouch!
Blast!

Some interjections express approval, pleasure or excitement:

Bravo!
Hooray!

Some interjections express surprise or relief:

Wow!
Phew!

Sometimes an interjection is more like a noise than a word:

Sh!
Psst!

A group of words can be used together as an interjection:

Happy birthday!
Hey presto!

When an interjection does occur within a sentence, it is usually separated by commas or dashes:

I turned the key and, **bingo,** *the engine started.*

sports match between two countries. **internationally** ADVERB

internet or **Internet** NOUN ICT The internet is a global communication system of interconnected computer networks which supports the world wide web, email and instant messaging.

interplay NOUN The interplay between two things is the way they react with one another.

interpret, interprets, interpreting, interpreted VERB ① If you interpret what someone writes, says or does, you decide what it means. ② If you interpret a foreign language that someone is speaking, you translate it. **interpretation** NOUN **interpreter** NOUN

interrogate, interrogates, interrogating, interrogated VERB If you interrogate someone, you question them thoroughly to get information from them. **interrogation** NOUN **interrogator** NOUN

SIMILAR WORDS: cross-examine, question

interrogative, interrogatives ADJECTIVE ① ENGLISH An interrogative sentence is one that is in the form of a question. ▶ NOUN ② An interrogative is a word such as 'who' or 'why' that is used to ask a question.

interrupt, interrupts, interrupting, interrupted VERB ① If you interrupt someone, you start talking while they are talking. ② If you interrupt a process or activity, you stop it continuing for a time. **interruption** NOUN

intersect, intersects, intersecting, intersected VERB When two roads or lines intersect, they cross each other.

intersection, intersections NOUN ① An intersection is where two roads meet. ② MATHS In maths, an intersection is the point where two straight lines meet.

interspersed ADJECTIVE If something is interspersed with things, these things occur at various points in it.

interval, intervals NOUN ① the period of time between two moments or dates. ② a short break during a play or concert. ③ MUSIC In music, an interval is the difference in pitch between two musical notes.
SIMILAR WORDS: ② break, interlude, intermission

intervene, intervenes, intervening, intervened VERB If you intervene in a situation, you step in to prevent conflict between people.
intervention NOUN
SIMILAR WORDS: mediate, step in

intervening ADJECTIVE An intervening period of time is one which separates two events.

interview, interviews, interviewing, interviewed NOUN ① a meeting at which someone asks you questions about yourself to see if you are suitable for a particular job. ② a conversation in which a journalist asks a famous person questions. ▸ VERB ③ If you interview someone, you ask them questions about themselves. **interviewer** NOUN **interviewee** NOUN

intestine, intestines NOUN Your intestines are a long tube which carries food from your stomach through to your bowels, and in which the food is digested. **intestinal** ADJECTIVE

intimate, intimates, intimating, intimated ADJECTIVE [Said in-ti-mit]
① If two people are intimate, there is a close relationship between them. ② An intimate matter is very private and personal. ③ An intimate knowledge of something is very deep and detailed. ▸ VERB [Said in-ti-mate] ④ If you intimate something, you hint at it • He did intimate that he might give up.
intimately ADVERB **intimacy** NOUN **intimation** NOUN

intimidate, intimidates, intimidating, intimidated VERB If you intimidate someone, you frighten them in a threatening way.
intimidated ADJECTIVE
intimidating ADJECTIVE
intimidation NOUN

into PREPOSITION ① If something goes into something else, it goes inside it. ② If you bump or crash into something, you hit it. ③ (informal) If you are into something, you like it very much • Nowadays I'm really into healthy food.

intolerable ADJECTIVE If something is intolerable, it is so bad that it is difficult to put up with it.
intolerably ADVERB

intonation NOUN Your intonation is the way that your voice rises and falls as you speak.

intoxicated ADJECTIVE If someone is intoxicated, they are drunk.
intoxicating ADJECTIVE
intoxication NOUN

intra- PREFIX 'Intra-' means 'within' or 'inside' • intra-European conflicts.

intractable ADJECTIVE (formal) stubborn and difficult to deal with or control.

intransitive ADJECTIVE An intransitive verb is one that does not have a direct object. For example, 'sings' is intransitive in 'She sings', but not in 'She sings a song'.

intravenous [Said in-trav-**vee**-nuss] ADJECTIVE Intravenous foods or drugs are given to sick people through their veins. **intravenously** ADVERB

intrepid ADJECTIVE not worried by danger • *an intrepid explorer.* **intrepidly** ADVERB

intricate ADJECTIVE Something that is intricate has many fine details • *walls and ceilings covered with intricate patterns.* **intricately** ADVERB **intricacy** NOUN

intrigue, intrigues, intriguing, intrigued NOUN ① Intrigue is the making of secret plans, often with the intention of harming other people • *political intrigue.* ▶ VERB ② If something intrigues you, you are fascinated by it and curious about it. **intriguing** ADJECTIVE

intrinsic ADJECTIVE (*formal*) The intrinsic qualities of something are its basic qualities. **intrinsically** ADVERB

introduce, introduces, introducing, introduced VERB ① If you introduce one person to another, you tell them each other's name so that they can get to know each other. ② When someone introduces a radio or television show, they say a few words at the beginning to tell you about it. ③ If you introduce someone to something, they learn about it for the first time. **introductory** ADJECTIVE

introduction, introductions NOUN ① The introduction of someone or something is the act of presenting them for the first time. ② ENGLISH a piece of writing at the beginning of a book, which usually tells you what the book is about.
SIMILAR WORDS: ② foreword, opening, preface

introvert, introverts NOUN someone who spends more time thinking about their private feelings than about the world around them, and who often finds it difficult to talk to others. **introverted** ADJECTIVE

intrude, intrudes, intruding, intruded VERB To intrude on someone or something is to disturb them • *I don't want to intrude on your parents.* **intruder** NOUN **intrusion** NOUN **intrusive** ADJECTIVE
SIMILAR WORDS: butt in, trespass

intuition, intuitions [Said int-yoo-**ish**-n] NOUN Your intuition is a feeling you have about something that you cannot explain • *My intuition is right about him.* **intuitive** ADJECTIVE **intuitively** ADVERB

Inuit, Inuits; also spelt **Innuit** NOUN one of a group of peoples who live in Northern Canada, Greenland, Alaska and Eastern Siberia.

inundated ADJECTIVE If you are inundated by messages or requests, you receive so many that you cannot deal with them all.

invade, invades, invading, invaded VERB ① If an army invades a country, it enters it by force. ② If someone invades your privacy, they disturb you when you want to be alone. **invader** NOUN

invalid[1], invalids [Said **in**-va-lid] NOUN someone who is so ill that they need to be looked after by someone else.
WORD HISTORY: from Latin *invalidus* meaning 'infirm'

invalid[2] [Said in-**val**-id] ADJECTIVE ① If an argument or result is invalid, it is not acceptable because it is based on a mistake. ② If a law, marriage or election is invalid, it is illegal because it has not been carried out properly. **invalidate** VERB
WORD HISTORY: from Latin *invalidus* meaning 'without legal force'

invalidity [Said in-va-**lid**-dit-ee] NOUN Invalidity is the condition of being very ill for a very long time.

invaluable ADJECTIVE extremely useful • *This book contains invaluable tips.*

invariably ADVERB If something invariably happens, it almost always happens.

invasion, invasions NOUN
① HISTORY The invasion of a country or territory is the act of entering it by force. ② an unwanted disturbance or intrusion • *an invasion of her privacy.*

invective NOUN (*formal*) Invective is abusive language used by someone who is angry.

invent, invents, inventing, invented VERB ① If you invent a device or process, you are the first person to think of it or to use it. ② If you invent a story or an excuse, you make it up.
inventor NOUN **invention** NOUN **inventive** ADJECTIVE **inventiveness** NOUN
SIMILAR WORDS: ① conceive, create, devise

inventory, inventories [Said in-**vin**-to-ri] NOUN a written list of all the objects in a place.

inverse ADJECTIVE (*formal*) If there is an inverse relationship between two things, one decreases as the other increases.

invertebrate, invertebrates NOUN
SCIENCE An invertebrate is a creature which does not have a spine. Some invertebrates, for example crabs, have an external skeleton.

inverted ADJECTIVE upside down or back to front.

inverted comma, inverted commas NOUN Inverted commas are the punctuation marks " " or ' ', used to show where speech begins and ends.

invest, invests, investing, invested VERB ① If you invest money, you pay it into a bank or buy shares so that you will receive a profit. ② If you invest in something useful, you buy it because it will help you do something better. ③ If you invest money, time or energy in something, you try to make it a success. **investor** NOUN **investment** NOUN

investigate, investigates, investigating, investigated VERB To investigate something is to try to find out all the facts about it.

What do Inverted Commas do?

Inverted commas or **quotation marks** (" " or ' ') mark the beginning and end of a speaker's exact words or thoughts:

"I would like some more," said Matthew.

Inverted commas are not used when a speaker's words are reported indirectly rather than in their exact form:

Matthew said that he would like some more.

Inverted commas can also be used to indicate the title of a book, piece of music, etc:

The class had been reading 'The Little Prince'.

Inverted commas are also used to draw attention to the fact that a word or phrase is being used in an unusual way, or that a word itself is the subject of discussion:

Braille allows a blind person to "see" with the fingers.
What rhymes with "orange"?

a b c d e f g h i j k l m n o p q r s t u v w x y z

investigator NOUN **investigation** NOUN

SIMILAR WORDS: examine, look into, study

inveterate ADJECTIVE having lasted for a long time and not likely to stop • *an inveterate gambler.*

invincible ADJECTIVE unable to be defeated. **invincibility** NOUN

invisible ADJECTIVE If something is invisible, you cannot see it, because it is hidden, very small or imaginary. **invisibly** ADVERB **invisibility** NOUN

invite, invites, inviting, invited VERB ① If you invite someone to an event, you ask them to come to it. ② If you invite someone to do something, you ask them to do it • *Andrew has been invited to speak at the conference.* **inviting** ADJECTIVE **invitation** NOUN

invoice, invoices NOUN a bill for services or goods.

invoke, invokes, invoking, invoked VERB ① (formal) If you invoke a law, you use it to justify what you are doing. ② If you invoke certain feelings, you cause someone to have these feelings.
WORD HISTORY: from Latin *invocare* meaning 'to call upon'

involuntary ADJECTIVE sudden and uncontrollable. **involuntarily** ADVERB

involve, involves, involving, involved VERB PSHE If a situation involves someone or something, it includes them as a necessary part. **involvement** NOUN

inward ADJECTIVE or ADVERB ① Inward means towards the inside or centre of something • *inward motion.* ▸ ADJECTIVE ② Your inward thoughts and feelings are private • *She gave an inward sigh of relief.* **inwardly** ADVERB

inwards ADVERB towards the centre or inside • *Let your fingers curl inwards.*

iodine [Said *eye-oh-deen*] NOUN SCIENCE Iodine is a bluish-black element whose compounds are used in medicine and photography. Its atomic number is 53 and its symbol is I.

ion, ions [Said *eye-on*] NOUN Ions are electrically charged atoms.

iota NOUN an extremely small amount • *He did not have an iota of proof.*

IQ, IQs NOUN Your IQ is your level of intelligence shown by the results of a special test. IQ is an abbreviation for 'intelligence quotient'.

ir- PREFIX 'Ir-' means 'not' or 'the opposite of', and is the form of 'in-' which is used before the letter r • *irrational.*

Iranian, Iranians [Said *ir-rain-ee-an*] ADJECTIVE ① belonging or relating to Iran. ▸ NOUN ② someone who comes from Iran. ③ Iranian is the main language spoken in Iran. It is also known as Farsi.

Iraqi, Iraqis [Said *ir-ah-kee*] ADJECTIVE ① belonging or relating to Iraq. ▸ NOUN ② someone who comes from Iraq.

irate [Said *eye-rate*] ADJECTIVE very angry.

iris, irises [Said *eye-riss*] NOUN ① the round, coloured part of your eye. ② a tall plant with long leaves and large blue, yellow or white flowers.
WORD HISTORY: from Greek *iris* meaning 'rainbow' or 'coloured circle'

Irish ADJECTIVE ① belonging or relating to the Irish Republic, or to the whole of Ireland. ▸ NOUN ② Irish or Irish Gaelic is a language spoken in some parts of Ireland.

Irishman, Irishmen NOUN a man who comes from Ireland.

Irishwoman, Irishwomen NOUN a woman who comes from Ireland.

irk, irks, irking, irked VERB If something irks you, it annoys you. **irksome** ADJECTIVE

iron, irons, ironing, ironed NOUN ① SCIENCE Iron is a strong hard metallic element found in rocks. It is used in making tools and machines, and is also an important component of blood. Its atomic number is 26 and its symbol is Fe. ② An iron is a device which heats up and which you rub over clothes to remove creases.
▸ VERB ③ If you iron clothes, you use a hot iron to remove creases from them. **ironing** NOUN **iron out** VERB If you iron out difficulties, you solve them.

Iron Age NOUN HISTORY The Iron Age was a time about 3000 years ago when people first started to make tools out of iron.

ironbark, ironbarks NOUN an Australian eucalypt with a hard, rough bark.

irony, ironies [Said eye-ron-ee] NOUN ① ENGLISH Irony is a form of humour in which you say the opposite of what you really mean • This group could be described, without irony, as the fortunate ones. ② There is irony in a situation when there is an unexpected or unusual connection between things or events • It's a sad irony of life: once you are lost, a map is useless. **ironic** or **ironical** ADJECTIVE **ironically** ADVERB

irrational ADJECTIVE ① Irrational feelings are not based on logical reasons • irrational fears. ② MATHS An irrational number is a number that cannot be expressed as the ratio of two whole numbers. **irrationally** ADVERB **irrationality** NOUN

irregular ADJECTIVE ① not smooth or even • irregular walls. ② not forming a regular pattern. ③ MATHS Irregular things are uneven or unequal, or are not symmetrical. **irregularly** ADVERB **irregularity** NOUN SIMILAR WORDS: ② haphazard, random, variable

irrelevant ADJECTIVE not directly connected with a subject • He either ignored questions or gave irrelevant answers. **irrelevance** NOUN

irrepressible ADJECTIVE Someone who is irrepressible is lively and cheerful.

irresistible ADJECTIVE ① unable to be controlled • an irresistible urge to yawn. ② extremely attractive • irresistible freshly baked bread. **irresistibly** ADVERB

irrespective ADJECTIVE If you say something will be done irrespective of certain things, you mean it will be done without taking those things into account.

irresponsible ADJECTIVE An irresponsible person does things without considering the consequences • an irresponsible driver. **irresponsibly** ADVERB **irresponsibility** NOUN SIMILAR WORDS: careless, reckless, thoughtless

irrigate, irrigates, irrigating, irrigated VERB To irrigate land is to supply it with water brought through pipes or ditches. **irrigated** ADJECTIVE **irrigation** NOUN

irritable ADJECTIVE easily annoyed.

irritate, irritates, irritating, irritated VERB ① If something irritates you, it annoys you. ② If something irritates part of your body, it makes it tender, sore or itchy. **irritant** NOUN **irritation** NOUN SIMILAR WORDS: ① annoy, get on one's nerves

a b c d e f g h i j k l m n o p q r s t u v w x y z

is the third person singular, present tense of **be**.

-ise or **-ize** SUFFIX '-ise' and '-ize' form verbs. Most verbs can be spelt with either ending, though there are some that can only be spelt with '-ise', for example *advertise*, *improvise* and *revise*.

-ish SUFFIX '-ish' forms adjectives that mean 'fairly' or 'rather' • *smallish* • *greenish*.

isiXhosa NOUN IsiXhosa is another name for the Xhosa language.

isiZulu NOUN IsiZulu is another name for the Zulu language.

Islam [Said iz-lahm] NOUN RE Islam is the Muslim religion, which teaches that there is only one God, Allah, and Mohammed is his prophet. The holy book of Islam is the Qur'an. **Islamic** ADJECTIVE

WORD HISTORY: from Arabic *islam* meaning 'surrender to God'

Islamophobia NOUN Islamophobia is a strong and unreasonable dislike of Muslim people.

island, islands [Said *eye-land*] NOUN a piece of land surrounded on all sides by water. **islander** NOUN

isle, isles [Rhymes with **mile**] NOUN (*literary*) an island.

-ism SUFFIX ① '-ism' forms nouns that refer to an action or condition • *criticism* • *heroism*. ② '-ism' forms nouns that refer to a political or economic system or a system of beliefs • *Marxism* • *Sikhism*. ③ '-ism' forms nouns that refer to a type of prejudice • *racism* • *sexism*.

isobar, isobars [Said *eye-so-bar*] NOUN GEOGRAPHY An isobar is a line on a map which joins places of equal air pressure.

isolate, isolates, isolating, isolated VERB ① If something isolates you or if you isolate yourself, you are set apart

from other people. ② If you isolate something, you separate it from everything else. **isolated** ADJECTIVE **isolation** NOUN

isometric ADJECTIVE MATHS If two or more things are isometric they have equal dimensions.

isosceles [Said eye-soss-il-eez] ADJECTIVE MATHS An isosceles triangle has two sides of the same length.

WORD HISTORY: from Greek *iso-* meaning 'equal' and *skelos* meaning 'leg'

isotherm, isotherms NOUN GEOGRAPHY An isotherm is a line on a map which joins places of equal temperature.

ISP an abbreviation for 'internet service provider'.

Israeli, Israelis [Said iz-rail-ee] ADJECTIVE ① belonging or relating to Israel. ▶ NOUN ② someone who comes from Israel.

issue, issues, issuing, issued [Said ish-yoo] NOUN ① an important subject that people are talking about. ② a particular edition of a newspaper or magazine. ▶ VERB ③ If you issue a statement or a warning, you say it formally and publicly. ④ If someone issues something, they officially give it • *Staff were issued with plastic cards*.

SIMILAR WORDS: ④ distribute, give out

-ist SUFFIX ① '-ist' forms nouns and adjectives which refer to someone who is involved in a certain activity, or who believes in a certain system or religion • *chemist* • *motorist* • *Buddhist*. ② '-ist' forms nouns and adjectives which refer to someone who has a certain prejudice • *racist*.

isthmus, isthmuses NOUN a narrow strip of land connecting two larger areas.

it PRONOUN ① 'It' is used to refer to something that has already been mentioned, or to a situation or fact • *It was a difficult decision.* ② 'It' is used to refer to people or animals whose gender is not known • *If a baby is thirsty, it feeds more often.* ③ You use 'it' to make statements about the weather, time or date • *It's noon.*

IT NOUN IT is the use of computers to store and analyse information. IT is an abbreviation for 'information technology'.

Italian, Italians ADJECTIVE ① belonging or relating to Italy. ▶ NOUN ② someone who comes from Italy. ③ Italian is the main language spoken in Italy.

italics PLURAL NOUN Italics are letters printed in a special sloping way, and are often used to emphasise something. All the example sentences in this dictionary are in italics. **italic** ADJECTIVE

itch, itches, itching, itched VERB ① When your skin itches, it has an unpleasant feeling and you want to scratch it. ② If you are itching to do something, you are impatient to do it. ▶ NOUN ③ an unpleasant feeling on your skin that you want to scratch. **itchy** ADJECTIVE

item, items NOUN ① one of a collection or list of objects. ② a newspaper or magazine article.
SIMILAR WORDS: ② article, feature, piece

itinerary, itineraries NOUN a plan of a journey, showing a route to follow and places to visit.

-itis SUFFIX '-itis' is added to the name of a part of the body to refer to disease or inflammation in that part • *appendicitis* • *tonsillitis.*

its ADJECTIVE or PRONOUN 'Its' refers to something belonging to or relating to things, children or animals that have already been mentioned • *The lion lifted its head.*

GRAMMAR TIP
Many people are confused about the difference between *its* and *it's*. *Its*, without the apostrophe, is the possessive form of it: *The cat has hurt its paw*. *It's*, with the apostrophe, is a short form of *it is* or *it has*: *It's green; it's been snowing again*.

itself PRONOUN ① 'Itself' is used when the same thing, child or animal does an action and is affected by it • *The cat was washing itself.* ② 'Itself' is used to emphasise 'it'.

-ity SUFFIX '-ity' forms nouns that refer to a state or condition • *continuity* • *technicality*.

-ive SUFFIX '-ive' forms adjectives and some nouns • *massive* • *detective*.

IVF NOUN IVF is a method of helping a woman to have a baby by removing an egg from one of her ovaries, fertilising it outside her body, and then replacing it in her womb. It is an abbreviation for 'in-vitro fertilisation'.

ivory NOUN ① the valuable creamy-white bone which forms the tusk of an elephant. It is used to make ornaments. ▶ NOUN or ADJECTIVE ② creamy-white.

ivy NOUN an evergreen plant which creeps along the ground and up walls.

iwi, iwi or iwis NOUN In New Zealand, an iwi is a Māori tribe.

a b c d e f g h i j k l m n o p q r s t u v w x y z

Jj

jab, jabs, jabbing, jabbed VERB ① To jab something means to poke at it roughly. ▶ NOUN ② a sharp or sudden poke. ③ (*informal*) an injection.

jabiru, jabirus NOUN a white-and-green Australian stork with red legs.

jack, jacks, jacking, jacked NOUN ① a piece of equipment for lifting heavy objects, especially for lifting a car when changing a wheel. ② In a pack of cards, a jack is a card with a picture of a young prince on it. ▶ VERB ③ To jack up an object means to raise it, especially by using a jack. ④ (*informal*) In New Zealand English, to jack something up is to organise or prepare something.

jackal, jackals NOUN a wild animal related to the dog.

jackaroo, jackaroos; also spelt **jackeroo** NOUN In Australia, a jackaroo is a young person learning the work of a sheep or cattle station.

jackdaw, jackdaws NOUN a bird like a small crow with black and grey feathers.

jacket, jackets NOUN ① a short coat reaching to the waist or hips. ② an outer covering for something • *a book jacket*. ③ The jacket of a baked potato is its skin.

jackpot, jackpots NOUN In a gambling game, the jackpot is the top prize.

jade NOUN Jade is a hard green stone used for making jewellery and ornaments.

jagged ADJECTIVE sharp and spiky.
SIMILAR WORDS: serrated, spiked, uneven

jaguar, jaguars NOUN A jaguar is a large member of the cat family with spots on its back. Jaguars live in South and Central America.
WORD HISTORY: from *jaguara*, a South American Indian word

jail, jails, jailing, jailed; also spelt **gaol** NOUN ① a building where people convicted of a crime are locked up. ▶ VERB ② To jail someone means to lock them up in a jail.
SIMILAR WORDS: ① nick, penitentiary, prison

jailer, jailers; also spelt **gaoler** NOUN a person who is in charge of the prisoners in a jail.

jam, jams, jamming, jammed NOUN ① a food, made by boiling fruit and sugar together until it sets. ② a situation in which it is impossible to move • *a traffic jam*. ③ (*informal*) If someone is in a jam, they are in a difficult situation. ▶ VERB ④ If people or things are jammed into a place, they are squeezed together so closely that they can hardly move. ⑤ To jam something somewhere means to push it there roughly • *He jammed his foot on the brake*. ⑥ If something is jammed, it is stuck or unable to work properly. ⑦ To jam a radio signal means to interfere with it and prevent it from being received clearly.
SIMILAR WORDS: ③ fix, predicament, tight spot

Jamaican, Jamaicans [Said *jam-may-kn*] ADJECTIVE ① belonging or relating to Jamaica. ▶ NOUN ② someone who comes from Jamaica.

jamboree, jamborees NOUN a gathering of large numbers of people enjoying themselves.

Jandal, Jandals NOUN (*trademark*) In New Zealand, a Jandal is a sandal with a strap between the big toe and other toes and over the foot.

jangle, jangles, jangling, jangled VERB ① If something jangles, it makes a harsh metallic ringing noise. ▶ NOUN ② the sound made by metal objects striking against each other.

janitor, janitors NOUN the caretaker of a building.

January NOUN January is the first month of the year. It has 31 days.
WORD HISTORY: from Latin *Januarius* meaning 'the month of Janus', named after a Roman god

Japanese ADJECTIVE ① belonging or relating to Japan. ▶ NOUN ② someone who comes from Japan. ③ Japanese is the main language spoken in Japan.

jar, jars, jarring, jarred NOUN ① a glass container with a wide top used for storing food. ▶ VERB ② If something jars on you, you find it unpleasant or annoying.

jargon NOUN Jargon consists of words that are used in special or technical ways by particular groups of people, often making the language difficult to understand.

jarrah, jarrahs NOUN an Australian eucalypt tree that produces wood used for timber.

jasmine NOUN Jasmine is a climbing plant with small sweet-scented white flowers.

jaundice NOUN Jaundice is an illness affecting the liver, in which the skin and the whites of the eyes become yellow.

jaundiced ADJECTIVE pessimistic and lacking enthusiasm • *He takes a rather jaundiced view of politicians*.

jaunt, jaunts NOUN a journey or trip you go on for pleasure.

jaunty, jauntier, jauntiest ADJECTIVE expressing cheerfulness and self-confidence • *a jaunty tune*.
jauntily ADVERB

javelin, javelins NOUN a long spear that is thrown in sports competitions.

jaw, jaws NOUN ① A person's or animal's jaw is the bone in which the teeth are set. ② A person's or animal's jaws are their mouth and teeth.

jay, jays NOUN a kind of noisy chattering bird.

jazz, jazzes, jazzing, jazzed NOUN ① Jazz is a style of popular music with a forceful rhythm. ▶ VERB ② (*informal*) To jazz something up means to make it more colourful or exciting.

jazzy, jazzier, jazziest ADJECTIVE (*informal*) bright and showy.

jealous ADJECTIVE ① If you are jealous, you feel bitterness towards someone who has something that you would like to have. ② If you are jealous of something you have, you feel you must try to keep it from other people. **jealously** ADVERB **jealousy** NOUN
SIMILAR WORDS: ① covetous, envious ② possessive

jeans PLURAL NOUN Jeans are casual denim trousers.

Jeep, Jeeps NOUN (*trademark*) a small road vehicle with four-wheel drive.

jeer, jeers, jeering, jeered VERB ① If you jeer at someone, you insult them in a loud, unpleasant way. ▶ NOUN

a
b
c
d
e
f
g
h
i
j
k
l
m
n
o
p
q
r
s
t
u
v
w
x
y
z

② Jeers are rude and insulting remarks. **jeering** ADJECTIVE

Jehovah [Said ji-**hove**-ah] PROPER NOUN RE Jehovah is a name of God in the Old Testament. **WORD HISTORY:** from adding vowels to the Hebrew *JHVH*, the sacred name of God

jelly, jellies NOUN ① a clear, sweet food eaten as a dessert. ② a type of clear, set jam.

jellyfish, jellyfishes NOUN a sea animal with a clear soft body and tentacles which may sting.

jeopardise, jeopardises, jeopardising, jeopardised [Said *jep-par-dyz*]; also spelt **jeopardize** VERB To jeopardise something means to do something which puts it at risk • *Elaine jeopardised her health.*

jeopardy NOUN If someone or something is in jeopardy, they are at risk of failing or of being destroyed.

jerk, jerks, jerking, jerked VERB ① To jerk something means to give it a sudden, sharp pull. ② If something jerks, it moves suddenly and sharply. ▶ NOUN ③ a sudden sharp movement. ④ (*informal*) If you call someone a jerk, you mean they are stupid. **jerky** ADJECTIVE **jerkily** ADVERB

jerkin, jerkins NOUN a short sleeveless jacket.

jersey, jerseys NOUN ① a knitted garment for the upper half of the body. ② Jersey is a type of knitted woollen or cotton fabric used to make clothing.

jest, jests, jesting, jested NOUN ① a joke. ▶ VERB ② To jest means to speak jokingly.

jester, jesters NOUN In the past, a jester was a man who was kept to amuse the king or queen.

jet, jets, jetting, jetted NOUN ① a plane which is able to fly very fast. ② a stream of liquid, gas or flame forced out under pressure. ③ Jet is a hard black stone, usually highly polished and used in jewellery and ornaments. ▶ VERB ④ To jet somewhere means to fly there in a plane, especially a jet.

jet boat, jet boats NOUN In New Zealand, a jet boat is a motor boat that is powered by a jet of water at the rear.

jet lag NOUN Jet lag is a feeling of tiredness or confusion that people have after a long flight across different time zones.

jetsam NOUN Jetsam is rubbish thrown from a boat and left floating on the sea or washed up on the seashore.

jettison, jettisons, jettisoning, jettisoned VERB If you jettison something, you throw it away because you no longer want it.

jetty, jetties NOUN a wide stone wall or wooden platform at the edge of the sea or a river, where boats can be moored.

Jew, Jews [Said *joo*] NOUN RE a person who practises the religion of Judaism, or who is of Hebrew descent. **Jewish** ADJECTIVE **WORD HISTORY:** from *Judah*, the name of a Jewish patriarch

jewel, jewels NOUN a precious stone used to decorate valuable ornaments or jewellery. **jewelled** ADJECTIVE

jeweller, jewellers NOUN a person who makes jewellery or who sells and repairs jewellery and watches.

jewellery NOUN Jewellery consists of ornaments that people wear, such as rings or necklaces, made of valuable metals and sometimes decorated with precious stones.

jib, jibs NOUN a small sail towards the front of a sailing boat.

jibe another spelling of **gibe**.

jig, jigs, jigging, jigged NOUN ① A jig is a type of lively folk dance; also the music that accompanies it. ▶ VERB ② If you jig, you dance or jump around in a lively bouncy manner.

jiggle, jiggles, jiggling, jiggled VERB If you jiggle something, you move it around with quick jerky movements.

jigsaw, jigsaws NOUN a puzzle consisting of a picture on cardboard that has been cut up into small pieces which have to be put together again.

jihad, jihads [Said jee-had] NOUN ① RE a holy war waged to defend or further the ideals of Islam. ② RE Jihad also means the personal struggle of a Muslim against sin.

jihadi, jihadis [Said jee-had-ee] NOUN a person who takes part in a holy war to defend or further the ideals of Islam.

jilt, jilts, jilting, jilted VERB If you jilt someone, you suddenly break off your relationship with them. **jilted** ADJECTIVE

jingle, jingles, jingling, jingled NOUN ① a short, catchy phrase or rhyme set to music and used to advertise something on radio or television. ② the sound of something jingling. ▶ VERB ③ When something jingles, it makes a tinkling sound like small bells.

jinks PLURAL NOUN High jinks is boisterous and mischievous behaviour.

jinx, jinxes NOUN someone or something that is thought to bring bad luck • He was beginning to think he was a jinx.

jinxed ADJECTIVE If something is jinxed it is considered to be unlucky • I think this house is jinxed.

jitters PLURAL NOUN (informal) If you have got the jitters, you are feeling very nervous. **jittery** ADJECTIVE

job, jobs NOUN ① the work that someone does to earn money. ② a duty or responsibility • It is a captain's job to lead from the front. ▶ PHRASE ③ If something is **just the job**, it is exactly right or exactly what you wanted. SIMILAR WORDS: ① employment, occupation, work

job centre, job centres NOUN a government office where people can find out about job vacancies.

jobless ADJECTIVE without any work.

jockey, jockeys, jockeying, jockeyed NOUN ① someone who rides a horse in a race. ▶ VERB ② To jockey for position means to manoeuvre in order to gain an advantage over other people.

jocular ADJECTIVE A jocular comment is intended to make people laugh. **jocularly** ADVERB

jodhpurs [Said jod-purz] PLURAL NOUN Jodhpurs are close-fitting trousers worn when riding a horse. WORD HISTORY: from Jodhpur, the name of a town in northern India

joey, joeys NOUN In Australian English, a joey is a young kangaroo or other young animal.

jog, jogs, jogging, jogged VERB ① To jog means to run slowly and rhythmically, often as a form of exercise. ② If you jog something, you knock it slightly so that it shakes or moves. ③ If someone or something jogs your memory, they remind you of something. ▶ NOUN ④ a slow run. **jogger** NOUN **jogging** NOUN

join, joins, joining, joined VERB ① When two things join, or when one thing joins another, they come together. ② If you join a club or organisation, you become a member of it or start taking part in it.

A
B
C
D
E
F
G
H
I
J
K
L
M
N
O
P
Q
R
S
T
U
V
W
X
Y
Z

③To join two things means to fasten them. ▶ NOUN ④ a place where two things are fastened together. **join up** VERB If someone joins up, they become a member of the armed forces.

SIMILAR WORDS: ① connect, link, unite ② enlist, enrol, sign up ③ connect, link, unite

joiner, joiners NOUN a person who makes wooden window frames, doors and furniture.

joinery NOUN Joinery is the work done by a joiner.

joint, joints, jointing, jointed ADJECTIVE ① shared by or belonging to two or more people • *a joint building society account.* ▶ NOUN ② SCIENCE a part of the body where two bones meet and are joined together so that they can move, for example a knee or hip. ③ DGT a place where two things are fixed together. ④ a large piece of meat suitable for roasting. ⑤ (*informal*) any place of entertainment, such as a nightclub or pub. ▶ VERB ⑥ To joint meat means to cut it into large pieces according to where the bones are. **jointly** ADVERB **jointed** ADJECTIVE

joist, joists NOUN a large beam used to support floors or ceilings.

joke, jokes, joking, joked NOUN ① something that you say or do to make people laugh, such as a funny story. ② anything that you think is ridiculous and not worthy of respect • *The decision was a joke.* ▶ VERB ③ If you are joking, you are teasing someone. **jokingly** ADVERB

SIMILAR WORDS: ① gag, jest ③ jest, kid

joker, jokers NOUN In a pack of cards, a joker is an extra card that does not belong to any of the four suits, but is used in some games.

jolly, jollier, jolliest; jollies, jollying, jollied ADJECTIVE ① happy, cheerful and pleasant. ▶ ADVERB ② (*informal*) Jolly also means very • *It all sounds like jolly good fun.* ▶ VERB ③ If you jolly someone along, you encourage them in a cheerful and friendly way. **jolliness** NOUN

jolt, jolts, jolting, jolted VERB ① To jolt means to move or shake roughly and violently. ② If you are jolted by something, it gives you an unpleasant surprise. ▶ NOUN ③ a sudden jerky movement. ④ an unpleasant shock or surprise.

jostle, jostles, jostling, jostled VERB To jostle means to push roughly against people in a crowd.

jot, jots, jotting, jotted VERB ① If you jot something down, you write it quickly in the form of a short informal note. ▶ NOUN ② a very small amount. **jotting** NOUN

jotter, jotters NOUN a pad or notebook.

joule, joules [Rhymes with **school**] NOUN SCIENCE A joule is a unit of energy or work. A watt is equal to one joule per second. The joule is named after the English physicist J.P. Joule (1818–1889).

journal, journals NOUN ① a magazine that deals with a particular subject, trade or profession. ② a diary which someone keeps regularly.

journalism NOUN Journalism is the work of collecting, writing and publishing news in newspapers and magazines, and on television and radio. **journalist** NOUN **journalistic** ADJECTIVE

journey, journeys, journeying, journeyed NOUN ① the act of travelling from one place to another. ▶ VERB ② (*formal*) To journey somewhere means to travel there

• *He intended to journey up the Amazon.*

joust, jousts [HISTORY] NOUN In medieval times, a joust was a competition between knights fighting on horseback, using lances.

jovial ADJECTIVE cheerful and friendly. **jovially** ADVERB **joviality** NOUN

joy, joys NOUN ① Joy is a feeling of great happiness. ② (*informal*) Joy also means success or luck • *Any joy with getting cup final tickets?* ③ something that makes you happy or gives you pleasure.

joyful ADJECTIVE ① causing pleasure and happiness. ② Someone who is joyful is extremely happy. **joyfully** ADVERB

joyous ADJECTIVE (*formal*) joyful. **joyously** ADVERB

joyride, joyrides NOUN a drive in a stolen car for pleasure. **joyriding** NOUN **joyrider** NOUN

joystick, joysticks NOUN ① a lever in an aircraft which the pilot uses to control height and direction. ② In some computer games, the joystick is the lever used to control the movement of objects on the screen.

jube, jubes NOUN (*informal*) In Australian and New Zealand English, a jube is a fruit-flavoured jelly sweet.

jubilant ADJECTIVE feeling or expressing great happiness or triumph. **jubilantly** ADVERB

jubilation NOUN Jubilation is a feeling of great happiness and triumph.

jubilee, jubilees NOUN a special anniversary of an event such as a coronation • *Queen Elizabeth's Diamond Jubilee in 2012.*
WORD HISTORY: from Hebrew *yobhel* meaning 'ram's horn'; rams' horns were blown during festivals and celebrations

Judaism [*Said joo-day-i-zm*] NOUN [RE] Judaism is the religion of the Jewish people. It is based on a belief in one God, and draws its laws and authority from the Old Testament. **Judaic** ADJECTIVE

judder, judders, juddering, juddered VERB To judder means to shake and vibrate noisily and violently.

judder bar, judder bars NOUN In New Zealand English, a judder bar is a bump built across a road to stop drivers from going too fast. In Britain it is called a **speed bump**.

judge, judges, judging, judged NOUN ① the person in a law court who decides how the law should be applied to people who appear in the court. ② someone who decides the winner in a contest or competition. ▶ VERB ③ If you judge someone or something, you form an opinion about them based on the evidence that you have. ④ To judge a contest or competition means to decide on the winner.
SIMILAR WORDS: ② adjudicator, referee, umpire ④ adjudicate, referee, umpire

judgment, judgments; also spelt **judgement** NOUN an opinion or decision based on evidence.

SPELLING TIP
Judgment and *judgement* are both correct spellings.

---

judicial ADJECTIVE relating to judgment or to justice • *a judicial review.*

judiciary NOUN The judiciary is the branch of government concerned with justice and the legal system.

judicious ADJECTIVE sensible and showing good judgment. **judiciously** ADVERB

a b c d e f g h i j k l m n o p q r s t u v w x y z

judo NOUN Judo is a sport in which two people try to force each other to the ground using special throwing techniques. It originated in Japan as a form of self-defence.

WORD HISTORY: from Japanese *ju do* meaning 'gentleness art'

jug, jugs NOUN a container with a lip or spout used for holding or serving liquids.

juggernaut, juggernauts NOUN a large heavy lorry.

WORD HISTORY: from Hindi *Jagannath*, the name of a huge idol of the god Krishna, which every year is wheeled through the streets of Puri in India

juggle, juggles, juggling, juggled VERB ①To juggle means to throw objects into the air, catching them in sequence, and tossing them up again so there are several in the air at one time. ②If you juggle several different activities, you spend some time doing each of them rather than concentrating on just one • *He has to juggle work and family life.* **juggler** NOUN

jugular, jugulars NOUN The jugular or jugular vein is one of the veins in the neck which carry blood from the head back to the heart.

juice, juices NOUN ① Juice is the liquid that can be squeezed or extracted from fruit or other food. ② Juices in the body are fluids • *gastric juices*.

juicy, juicier, juiciest ADJECTIVE ① Juicy food has a lot of juice in it. ② Something that is juicy is interesting, exciting or scandalous • *a juicy bit of gossip.* **juiciness** NOUN

jukebox, jukeboxes NOUN a machine which automatically plays a selected piece of music when coins are inserted.

July NOUN July is the seventh month of the year. It has 31 days.

WORD HISTORY: from Latin *Julius*, the month of July, named after Julius Caesar by the Romans

jumble, jumbles, jumbling, jumbled NOUN ① an untidy muddle of things. ② Jumble consists of cheap articles that are given away to a charity so that they can be sold to raise money. ▶ VERB ③To jumble things means to mix them up untidily.

jumble sale, jumble sales NOUN an event at which cheap second-hand clothes and other articles are sold to raise money, usually for a charity.

jumbo, jumbos NOUN ①A jumbo or jumbo jet is a large jet aeroplane that can carry several hundred passengers. ▶ ADJECTIVE ②very large • *jumbo packs of elastic bands*.

WORD HISTORY: from *Jumbo*, the name of a famous 19th-century elephant

jumbuck, jumbucks NOUN (old-fashioned) In Australian English, a jumbuck is a sheep.

jump, jumps, jumping, jumped VERB ①To jump means to spring off the ground using your leg muscles. ②To jump something means to spring off the ground and move over or across it. ③If you jump at something, such as an opportunity, you accept it eagerly. ④If you jump on someone, you criticise them suddenly and forcefully. ⑤If someone jumps, they make a sudden sharp movement of surprise. ⑥If an amount or level jumps, it suddenly increases. ▶ NOUN ⑦a spring into the air, sometimes over an object.

SIMILAR WORDS: ①bound, leap, spring ⑦bound, leap, spring

jumper, jumpers NOUN a knitted garment for the top half of the body.

jumpy, jumpier, jumpiest ADJECTIVE nervous and worried.

junction, junctions NOUN a place where roads or railway lines meet or cross.

June NOUN June is the sixth month of the year. It has 30 days.
WORD HISTORY: from Latin *Junius*, the month of June, probably from the name of an important Roman family

jungle, jungles NOUN ① a dense tropical forest. ② a tangled mass of plants or other objects.

junior, juniors ADJECTIVE ① Someone who is junior to other people has a lower position in an organisation. ② Junior also means younger. ③ relating to childhood • *a junior school*. ▶ NOUN ④ someone who holds an unimportant position in an organisation.

juniper, junipers NOUN an evergreen shrub with purple berries used in cooking and medicine.

junk, junks NOUN ① Junk is old or second-hand articles which are sold cheaply or thrown away. ② If you think something is junk, you think it is worthless rubbish. ③ a Chinese sailing boat with a flat bottom and square sails.

junk food NOUN Junk food is food low in nutritional value which is eaten as well as or instead of proper meals.

junkie, junkies NOUN (*slang*) a drug addict.

Jupiter NOUN Jupiter is the largest planet in the solar system and the fifth from the sun.

jurisdiction NOUN ① (*formal*) Jurisdiction is the power or right of the courts to apply laws and make legal judgments • *The Court held that it did not have the jurisdiction to examine*

the merits of the case. ② Jurisdiction is power or authority • *The airport was under French jurisdiction*.

juror, jurors NOUN a member of a jury.

jury, juries NOUN a group of people in a court of law who have been selected to listen to the facts of a case on trial, and to decide whether the accused person is guilty or not.

just ADJECTIVE ① fair and impartial • *She arrived at a just decision*. ② morally right or proper • *a just reward*. ▶ ADVERB ③ If something has just happened, it happened a very short time ago. ④ If you just do something, you do it by a very small amount • *They only just won*. ⑤ simply or only • *It was just an excuse not to do any work*. ⑥ exactly • *It's just what she wanted*. ▶ PHRASE ⑦ In South African English, **just now** means in a little while. **justly** ADVERB

justice, justices NOUN ① Justice is fairness and reasonableness. ② CITIZENSHIP The system of justice in a country is the way in which laws are maintained by the courts. ③ a judge or magistrate.

justify, justifies, justifying, justified VERB ① If you justify an action or idea, you prove or explain why it is reasonable or necessary. ② ICT To justify text that you have typed or keyed into a computer is to adjust the spaces between the words so each full line in a paragraph fills the space between the left and right hand margins of the page. **justification** NOUN **justifiable** ADJECTIVE

jut, juts, jutting, jutted VERB If something juts out, it sticks out beyond or above a surface or edge.
SIMILAR WORDS: project, protrude, stick out

a b c d e f g h i j k l m n o p q r s t u v w x y z

jute NOUN Jute is a strong fibre made from the bark of an Asian plant, used to make rope and sacking.

juvenile, juveniles ADJECTIVE
① suitable for young people.
② childish and rather silly • *a juvenile game*. ▶ NOUN ③ a young person not old enough to be considered an adult.

juxtapose, juxtaposes, juxtaposing, juxtaposed VERB If you juxtapose things or ideas, you put them close together, often to emphasise the difference between them. **juxtaposition** NOUN

Kk

Kaaba NOUN RE a cube-shaped building inside the mosque at Mecca, which contains the Black Stone which Muslims believe God gave to Abraham. It is the most holy site in Islam and Muslims turn towards it when they pray.

kai NOUN (*informal*) In New Zealand, kai is another name for food.

kaleidoscope, kaleidoscopes [*Said kal-eye-dos-skope*] NOUN a toy consisting of a tube with a hole at one end. When you look through the hole and twist the other end of the tube, you can see a changing pattern of colours.
WORD HISTORY: from Greek *kalos* meaning 'beautiful', *eidos* meaning 'shape', and *skopein* meaning 'to look at'

kamikaze NOUN HISTORY In the Second World War, a kamikaze was a Japanese pilot who flew an aircraft loaded with explosives directly into an enemy target knowing he would be killed doing so.
WORD HISTORY: from Japanese *kami* meaning 'divine' + *kaze* meaning 'wind'

kangaroo, kangaroos NOUN a large Australian animal with very strong back legs which it uses for jumping.

karate [*Said kar-rat-ee*] NOUN Karate is a sport in which people fight each other using only their hands, elbows, feet and legs.
WORD HISTORY: from Japanese *kara* + *te* meaning 'empty hand'

karma NOUN RE In Buddhism, Hinduism and Sikhism, karma refers to the forces that influence people's fortune and rebirth.

Karoo, Karoos; also spelt **Karroo** NOUN In South Africa, the Karoos are areas of very dry land.

karri, karris NOUN an Australian eucalypt that produces a dark red wood used for building.

karyotype, karyotypes NOUN SCIENCE A karyotype of a person is a description of the number, size and shape of the chromosomes in their body cells.

katipo, katipo or katipos NOUN a small, poisonous spider with a red or orange stripe on its back, found in New Zealand.

kauri, kauri or kauris NOUN a large tree found in New Zealand which produces wood used for building and making furniture.

kayak, kayaks [*Said ky-ak*] NOUN a covered canoe with a small opening for the person sitting in it, originally used by the Inuit.

kea, kea or keas [*Said kay-ah*] NOUN ① a large, greenish parrot found in New Zealand. ② In New Zealand, Keas are the youngest members of the Scouts.

kebab, kebabs NOUN pieces of meat or vegetable stuck on a stick and grilled.

keel, keels, keeling, keeled NOUN ① the specially shaped bottom of a ship which supports the sides and sits in the water. ▶ **VERB** ② If someone or something keels over, they fall down sideways.

keen, keener, keenest **ADJECTIVE** ① Someone who is keen shows great eagerness and enthusiasm. ② If you are keen on someone or something, you are attracted to or fond of them. ③ quick to notice or understand things. ④ Keen senses let you see, hear, smell and taste things very clearly or strongly. **keenly ADVERB keenness NOUN**
SIMILAR WORDS: ① avid, eager, enthusiastic

keep, keeps, keeping, kept **VERB** ① To keep someone or something in a particular condition means to make them stay in that condition • *We'll walk to keep warm.* ② If you keep something, you have it and look after it. ③ To keep something also means to store it in the usual place. ④ If you keep doing something, you do it repeatedly or continuously • *I kept phoning the hospital.* ⑤ If you keep a promise, you do what you promised to do. ⑥ If you keep a secret, you do not tell anyone else. ⑦ If you keep a diary, you write something in it every day. ⑧ If you keep someone from going somewhere, you delay them so that they are late. ⑨ To keep someone means to provide them with money, food and clothing.
▶ **NOUN** ⑩ Your keep is the cost of the food you eat, your housing and your clothing • *He does not contribute towards his keep.* ⑪ **HISTORY** the main tower inside the walls of a castle. **keep up VERB** If you keep up with other people, you move or work at the same speed as they do.
SIMILAR WORDS: ② hold, maintain, preserve

keeper, keepers **NOUN** ① a person whose job is to look after the animals in a zoo. ② a goalkeeper in soccer or hockey.

keeping NOUN ① If something is in your keeping, it has been given to you to look after for a while.
▶ **PHRASE** ② If one thing is **in keeping with** another, the two things are suitable or appropriate together.

keepsake, keepsakes **NOUN** something that someone gives you to remind you of a particular person or event.
SIMILAR WORDS: memento, souvenir

keg, kegs **NOUN** a small barrel.

kelpie, kelpies; also spelt **kelpy NOUN** a smooth-haired Australian sheepdog with upright ears.

kennel, kennels **NOUN** ① a shelter for a dog. ② A kennels is a place where dogs can be kept for a time, or where they are bred.

Kenyan, Kenyans [*Said ken-yan or keen-yan*] **ADJECTIVE** ① belonging or relating to Kenya. ▶ **NOUN** ② someone who comes from Kenya.

kept the past tense and past participle of **keep**.

kerb, kerbs **NOUN** the raised edge at the point where a pavement joins onto a road.

SPELLING TIP
Do not confuse the spellings of *kerb* and *curb*: *A taxi drew up at the kerb; There is a curb on public spending.*

---

kernel, kernels **NOUN** the part of a nut that is inside the shell.

kerosene NOUN Kerosene is the same as paraffin.

kestrel, kestrels **NOUN** A kestrel is a type of small falcon that kills and eats other birds and small animals.

ketchup NOUN Ketchup is a cold sauce, usually made from tomatoes.

kettle, kettles NOUN a metal container with a spout, in which you boil water.

key, keys, keying, keyed NOUN ① a shaped piece of metal that fits into a hole so that you can unlock a door, wind something that is clockwork, or start a car. ② The keys on a computer keyboard, piano or cash register are the buttons that you press to use it. ③ an explanation of the symbols used in a map or diagram. ④ MUSIC In music, a key is a scale of notes. ⑤ The key to a situation or result is the way in which it can be achieved • *The key to success is to be ready from the start.* ▶ VERB ⑥ ICT If you key in information on a computer keyboard, you type it. ▶ ADJECTIVE ⑦ The key person or thing in a group is the most important one.

keyboard, keyboards NOUN ICT a row of buttons or levers on a computer, piano or cash register.

keynote, keynotes NOUN ① The keynote of a policy or idea is the main theme of it. ▶ ADJECTIVE ② A keynote presentation or speech is the most important one at a meeting.

Key Stage, Key Stages NOUN In England and Wales, one of the four age-group divisions to which each level of the National Curriculum applies (5–7; 7–11; 11–14; 14–16).

kg an abbreviation for 'kilogram' or 'kilograms'.

khaki [Said *kah-kee*] NOUN ① Khaki is a strong yellowish-brown material, used especially for military uniforms. ▶ NOUN or ADJECTIVE ② yellowish-brown.
WORD HISTORY: from Urdu *kaki* meaning 'dusty'

khanda, khandas [Said *kun-dah*] NOUN RE a sword used by Sikhs in the Amrit ceremony.

kia ora [Said *ki-or-ah*] INTERJECTION In New Zealand, 'kia ora' is a Māori greeting.

kibbutz, kibbutzim [Said kib-*boots*] NOUN a place of work in Israel, for example a farm or factory, where the workers live together and share all the duties and income.

kick, kicks, kicking, kicked VERB ① If you kick something, you hit it with your foot. ▶ NOUN ② If you give something a kick, you hit it with your foot. ③ (*informal*) If you get a kick out of doing something, you enjoy doing it very much. **kick off** VERB When players kick off, they start a soccer or rugby match. **kick-off** NOUN

kid, kids, kidding, kidded NOUN ① (*informal*) a child. ② a young goat. ▶ VERB ③ If you kid people, you tease them by deceiving them in fun.

kidnap, kidnaps, kidnapping, kidnapped VERB To kidnap someone is to take them away by force and demand a ransom in exchange for returning them. **kidnapper** NOUN **kidnapping** NOUN
SIMILAR WORDS: abduct, seize

kidney, kidneys NOUN ① Your kidneys are two organs in your body that remove waste products from your blood. ② Kidney is also the kidneys of some animals, which may be cooked and eaten.

kill, kills, killing, killed VERB ① To kill a person, animal or plant is to make them die. ② (*informal*) If something is killing you, it is causing you severe pain or discomfort • *My arms are killing me.* ▶ NOUN ③ The kill is the moment when a hunter kills an animal. **killer** NOUN
SIMILAR WORDS: ① murder, slay

kiln, kilns NOUN ART an oven for baking china or pottery until it becomes hard and dry.

a b c d e f g h i j k l m n o p q r s t u v w x y z

kilo, kilos NOUN a kilogram.

kilobyte, kilobytes NOUN ICT a unit of computer memory size, equal to 1024 bytes.

kilogram, kilograms NOUN a unit of weight equal to 1000 grams.

kilohertz NOUN A kilohertz is a unit of frequency equal to 1000 cycles per second.

kilojoule, kilojoules NOUN a unit of energy equal to 1000 joules.

kilometre, kilometres NOUN MATHS a unit of distance equal to 1000 metres.

kilowatt, kilowatts NOUN SCIENCE a unit of power equal to 1000 watts.

kilt, kilts NOUN a tartan skirt worn by men as part of Scottish Highland dress.

kimono, kimonos NOUN a long, loose garment with wide sleeves and a sash, worn in Japan.

kin PLURAL NOUN Your kin are your relatives.
SIMILAR WORDS: family, relatives

kind, kinds; kinder, kindest NOUN ① A particular kind of thing is something of the same type or sort as other things • *that kind of film*.
▶ ADJECTIVE ② Someone who is kind is considerate and generous towards other people. **kindly** ADVERB
SIMILAR WORDS: ① class, sort, type ② considerate, generous

GRAMMAR TIP
When you use *kind* in its singular form, the adjective before it should also be singular: *that kind of dog*. When you use the plural form *kinds*, the adjective before it should be plural: *those kinds of dog; those kinds of dogs*.

kindergarten, kindergartens NOUN a school for children who are too young to go to primary school.

WORD HISTORY: from German *Kinder* + *Garten* meaning 'children's garden'

kindle, kindles, kindling, kindled VERB ① If you kindle a fire, you light it. ② If something kindles a feeling in you, it causes you to have that feeling.

kindling NOUN Kindling is bits of dry wood or paper that you use to start a fire.

kindness NOUN the quality of being considerate towards other people.

kindred ADJECTIVE If you say that someone is a kindred spirit, you mean that they have the same interests or opinions as you.

kinetic, kinetics ADJECTIVE ① relating to movement. ▶ NOUN ② SCIENCE Kinetics is the scientific study of the way energy behaves when something moves.

kinetic energy NOUN SCIENCE Kinetic energy is the energy that is produced when something moves.

king, kings NOUN ① HISTORY The king of a country is a man who is the head of state in the country, and who inherited his position from his parents. ② In chess, the king is a piece which can only move one square at a time. When a king cannot move away from a position where it can be taken, the game is lost. ③ In a pack of cards, a king is a card with a picture of a king on it.
SIMILAR WORDS: ① monarch, ruler, sovereign

kingdom, kingdoms NOUN ① HISTORY a country that is governed by a king or queen. ② The largest divisions of the living organisms in the natural world are called kingdoms • *the animal kingdom*.

kingfisher, kingfishers NOUN a brightly coloured bird that lives near water and feeds on fish.

king-size or **king-sized** ADJECTIVE larger than the normal size • *a king-size bed*.

kink, kinks NOUN a dent or curve in something which is normally straight.

kinship NOUN Kinship is a family relationship to other people.

kiosk, kiosks [*Said* kee-osk] NOUN a covered stall on a street where you can buy newspapers, sweets or cigarettes.
WORD HISTORY: from Turkish *kösk* meaning 'pavilion'

kip, kips, kipping, kipped (*informal*) .NOUN ① a period of sleep. ▶VERB ② When you kip, you sleep.

kipper, kippers NOUN a smoked herring.

kirk, kirks NOUN In Scotland, a kirk is a church.

kiss, kisses, kissing, kissed VERB ① When you kiss someone, you touch them with your lips as a sign of love or affection. ▶NOUN ② When you give someone a kiss, you kiss them.

kiss of life NOUN The kiss of life is a method of reviving someone by blowing air into their lungs.

kit, kits NOUN ① a collection of things that you use for a sport or other activity. ② a set of parts that you put together to make something.

kitchen, kitchens NOUN a room used for cooking and preparing food.

kite, kites NOUN ① a frame covered with paper or cloth which is attached to a piece of string, and which you fly in the air. ② a shape with four sides, with two pairs of the same length, and none of the sides parallel to each other. ③ a large bird of prey with a long tail and long wings.

kitset, kitsets NOUN In New Zealand English, a kitset is a set of parts which you have to put together yourself to make an item such as a house or a piece of furniture.

kitten, kittens NOUN a young cat.

kitty, kitties NOUN a fund of money that has been given by a group of people who will use it to pay for or do things together.

kiwi, kiwi or kiwis [*Said* kee-wee] NOUN ① a type of bird found in New Zealand. Kiwis cannot fly. ② (*informal*) someone who comes from New Zealand. The plural of this sense is 'kiwis'.

kiwi fruit, kiwi fruits NOUN a fruit with a brown hairy skin and green flesh.

kloof, kloofs NOUN In South Africa, a kloof is a narrow valley.

km an abbreviation for 'kilometres'.

knack NOUN a skilful or clever way of doing something difficult • *the knack of making friends*.

knead, kneads, kneading, kneaded VERB If you knead dough, you press it and squeeze it with your hands before baking it.

knee, knees NOUN the joint in your leg between your ankle and your hip.

kneecap, kneecaps NOUN Your kneecaps are the bones at the front of your knees.

kneel, kneels, kneeling, knelt VERB When you kneel, you bend your legs and lower your body until your knees are touching the ground.

knell, knells NOUN (*literary*) the sound of a bell rung to announce a death or at a funeral.

knelt the past tense and past participle of **kneel**.

knew the past tense of **know**.

knickers PLURAL NOUN Knickers are underpants worn by women and girls.

a
b
c
d
e
f
g
h
i
j
k
l
m
n
o
p
q
r
s
t
u
v
w
x
y
z

knick-knacks PLURAL NOUN
Knick-knacks are small ornaments.

knife, knives; knifes, knifing, knifed
NOUN ① DGT a sharp metal tool
that you use to cut things. ▶ VERB
②To knife someone is to stab them
with a knife.

knight, knights, knighting,
knighted NOUN ① a man who has
been given the title 'Sir' by the King or
Queen. ② HISTORY In medieval
Europe, a knight was a man who
served a monarch or lord as a
mounted soldier. ③ a chess piece
that is usually in the shape of a
horse's head. ▶ VERB ④To knight a
man is to give him the title 'Sir'.
knighthood NOUN

knit, knits, knitting, knitted VERB
① If you knit a piece of clothing, you
make it by working lengths of wool
together, either using needles held in
the hand, or with a machine. ② If you
knit your brows, you frown. **knitting**
NOUN

knob, knobs NOUN ① a round handle.
② a round switch on a machine • *the
knobs of a radio*.

knobkerrie, knobkerries NOUN In
South Africa, a knobkerrie is a club or
stick with a rounded end.

knock, knocks, knocking, knocked
VERB ① If you knock on something,
you strike it with your hand or fist.
② If you knock a part of your body
against something, you bump into it
quite forcefully. ③ (*informal*) To knock
someone is to criticise them. ▶ NOUN
④ a firm blow on something solid
• *There was a knock at the door*.
knock out VERB To knock someone
out is to hit them so hard that they
become unconscious.

knocker, knockers NOUN a metal
lever attached to a door, which you
use to knock on the door.

knockout, knockouts NOUN
① a punch in boxing which knocks a
boxer unconscious. ② a competition
in which competitors are eliminated
in each round until only the winner
is left.

knoll, knolls [*Rhymes with* **roll**] NOUN
(*literary*) a gently sloping hill with a
rounded top.

knot, knots, knotting, knotted
NOUN ① a fastening made by looping
a piece of string around itself and
pulling the ends tight. ② a small
lump visible on the surface of a piece
of wood. ③ A knot of people is a small
group of them. ④ (*technical*) a unit of
speed used for ships and aircraft.
▶ VERB ⑤ If you knot a piece of string,
you tie a knot in it.

know, knows, knowing, knew,
known VERB ① If you know a fact,
you have it in your mind and you do
not need to learn it. ② People you
know are not strangers because you
have met them and spoken to them.
▶ PHRASE ③ (*informal*) If you are
in the know, you are one of a small
number of people who share a
secret.

SPELLING TIP
Do not confuse the spellings of *know*
and *now*: *I think I know that girl; Lunch
is ready now*.

know-how NOUN Know-how is the
ability to do something that is quite
difficult or technical.

knowing ADJECTIVE A knowing look
is one that shows that you know or
understand something that other
people do not. **knowingly** ADVERB

knowledge NOUN Knowledge is all
the information and facts that you
know.

knowledgeable ADJECTIVE
Someone who is knowledgeable

knows a lot about a subject • *She was very knowledgeable about Irish mythology.*

knuckle, knuckles NOUN Your knuckles are the joints at the end of your fingers where they join your hand.

koala, koalas NOUN an Australian animal with grey fur and small tufted ears. Koalas live in trees and eat eucalyptus leaves.

kohanga reo, kohanga reo or **kohanga** NOUN In New Zealand, a kohanga reo is an infant class where children are taught in Māori.
WORD HISTORY: a Māori term meaning 'language nest'

kookaburra, kookaburras NOUN a large Australian kingfisher.
WORD HISTORY: a native Australian word

koppie, koppies *[Said kop-i]*; also spelt **kopje** NOUN In South Africa, a koppie is a small hill with no other hills around it.

Koran *[Said kaw-rahn]*; also spelt **Qur'an** NOUN RE The Koran is the holy book of Islam.
WORD HISTORY: from Arabic *kara'a* meaning 'to read'

Korean, Koreans *[Said kor-ree-an]* ADJECTIVE ① relating or belonging to Korea. ▶ NOUN ② someone who comes from Korea. ③ Korean is the main language spoken in Korea.

kosher *[Said koh-sher]* ADJECTIVE RE Kosher food is acceptable for Jewish people to eat.
WORD HISTORY: from Hebrew *kasher* meaning 'right' or 'proper'

kowhai, kowhai or kowhais *[Said ko-wigh]* NOUN a small New Zealand tree with clusters of yellow flowers.

kraal, kraals NOUN In South Africa, a kraal is a village in which a tribe lives and which is often surrounded by a fence.

kudu, kudus; also spelt **koodoo** NOUN a large African antelope with curled horns.

kumara; also spelt **kumera**, kumara or **kumaras** *[Said koo-mih-rah]* NOUN In New Zealand English, a kumara is a sweet potato, a vegetable with yellow or orange flesh.

kumquat, kumquats *[Said koom-kwat]* NOUN a very small round or oval citrus fruit.

kung fu *[Said kung foo]* NOUN Kung fu is a Chinese style of fighting which involves using your hands and feet.

kura kaupapa Māori, kura kaupapa Māori *[Said koo-ra kow-puh-puh mow-ree]* NOUN In New Zealand, a kura kaupapa Māori is a primary school where teaching is based on Māori language and culture.

Kurd, Kurds NOUN The Kurds are a group of people who live mainly in eastern Turkey, northern Iraq and western Iran.

Kurdish ADJECTIVE ① belonging or relating to the Kurds • *Kurdish culture.* ▶ NOUN ② Kurdish is the language spoken by the Kurds.

kwaito *[Said kwai-toh]* NOUN Kwaito is a type of South African pop music with lyrics spoken over an instrumental backing.

a
b
c
d
e
f
g
h
i
j
k
l
m
n
o
p
q
r
s
t
u
v
w
x
y
z

Ll

l an abbreviation for 'litres'.

laager, laagers NOUN In South Africa, a laager is a camp defended by a circle of wagons.

lab, labs NOUN (*informal*) a laboratory.

label, labels, labelling, labelled NOUN ① a piece of paper or plastic attached to something as an identification. ▶VERB ② If you label something, you put a label on it.

laboratory, laboratories NOUN a place where scientific experiments are carried out.

laborious ADJECTIVE needing a lot of effort or time. **laboriously** ADVERB

Labor Party NOUN In Australia, the Labor Party is one of the major political parties.

labour, labours, labouring, laboured NOUN ① Labour is hard work. ② The workforce of a country or industry is sometimes called its labour • *unskilled labour*. ③ In Britain, the Labour Party is a political party that believes that wealth and power should be shared more equally among the population. ④ In New Zealand, the Labour Party is one of the main political parties. ⑤ Labour is also the last stage of pregnancy when a woman gives birth to a baby. ▶VERB ⑥ (*old-fashioned*) To labour means to work hard. **labourer** NOUN
SIMILAR WORDS: ① toil, work ⑥ slave, toil, work

labrador, labradors NOUN a large dog with short black, golden or brown hair.

labyrinth, labyrinths [*Said lab-er-inth*] NOUN a complicated series of paths or passages.

lace, laces, lacing, laced NOUN ① Lace is a very fine decorated cloth made with a lot of holes in it. ② Laces are cords with which you fasten your shoes. ▶VERB ③ When you lace up your shoes, you tie a bow in the laces. ④ To lace someone's food or drink means to put a small amount of alcohol, a drug, or poison in it. **lacy** ADJECTIVE

lack, lacks, lacking, lacked NOUN ① If there is a lack of something, it is not present when or where it is needed. ▶VERB ② If something is lacking, it is not present when or where it is needed. ③ If someone or something is lacking in something, they do not have it or do not have enough of it • *Francis was lacking in stamina*.
SIMILAR WORDS: ① absence, scarcity, shortage

lacklustre [*Said lak-luss-ter*] ADJECTIVE not interesting or exciting.

laconic [*Said lak-kon-ik*] ADJECTIVE using very few words.
WORD HISTORY: from Greek *Lakōnikos* meaning 'Spartan'. The Spartans were famous for using few words

lacquer, lacquers [*Said lak-er*] NOUN Lacquer is thin, clear paint that you put on wood to protect it and make it shiny.

lacrosse NOUN Lacrosse is an outdoor ball game in which two teams try to score goals using long sticks with nets on the end of them. **WORD HISTORY:** from Canadian French *la crosse* meaning 'the hooked stick'

lactic acid NOUN SCIENCE an acid that is in sour milk and is also produced in your muscles after you have done a lot of exercise.

lad, lads NOUN a boy or young man.

ladder, ladders, laddering, laddered NOUN ① a wooden or metal frame used for climbing which consists of horizontal steps fixed to two vertical poles. ② If your stockings or tights have a ladder in them, they have a vertical, ladder-like tear in them. ▸ VERB ③ If you ladder your stockings or tights, you get a ladder in them.

laden [*Said* lay-den] ADJECTIVE To be laden with something means to be carrying or holding a lot of it • *baskets laden with fruit.*

ladle, ladles, ladling, ladled NOUN ① a long-handled spoon with a deep, round bowl, which you use to serve soup. ▸ VERB ② If you ladle out food, you serve it with a ladle.

lady, ladies NOUN ① a woman, especially one who is considered to be well-mannered. ② Lady is a title used in front of the name of a woman from the nobility, such as a lord's wife.

ladybird, ladybirds NOUN a small flying beetle with a round red body patterned with black spots.

lady-in-waiting, ladies-in-waiting NOUN a woman who acts as companion to a queen or princess.

ladylike ADJECTIVE behaving in a polite and socially correct way.

Ladyship, Ladyships NOUN You address a woman who has the title 'Lady' as 'Your Ladyship'.

lag, lags, lagging, lagged VERB ① To lag behind is to make slower progress than other people. ② To lag pipes is to wrap cloth round them to stop the water inside freezing in cold weather.

lager, lagers NOUN Lager is light-coloured beer. **WORD HISTORY:** from German *Lagerbier* meaning 'beer for storing'

lagoon, lagoons NOUN an area of water separated from the sea by reefs or sand.

laid the past tense and past participle of **lay**.

lain the past participle of some meanings of **lie¹**.

lair, lairs NOUN a place where a wild animal lives.

laird, lairds [*Rhymes with* dared] NOUN a landowner in Scotland.

lake, lakes NOUN an area of fresh water surrounded by land.

lama, lamas NOUN a Buddhist priest or monk.

SPELLING TIP

Do not confuse the spellings of *lama* and *llama*: *a revered Tibetan lama; hats and gloves made from llama wool.*

lamb, lambs NOUN ① a young sheep. ② Lamb is the meat from a lamb.

lame, lamer, lamest ADJECTIVE ① unable to walk easily because of an injured leg. ② A lame excuse is not very convincing. **lamely** ADVERB **lameness** NOUN SIMILAR WORDS: ② feeble, flimsy, weak

lament, laments, lamenting, lamented VERB ① To lament something means to express sorrow or regret about it. ▸ NOUN ② an expression of sorrow or regret. ③ a song or poem expressing grief at someone's death.

a b c d e f g h i j k **l** m n o p q r s t u v w x y z

lamentable ADJECTIVE
disappointing and regrettable.

laminated ADJECTIVE consisting of several thin sheets or layers stuck together • *laminated glass*.

lamp, lamps NOUN a device that produces light.

lamppost, lampposts NOUN a tall column in a street, with a lamp at the top.

lampshade, lampshades NOUN a decorative covering over an electric light bulb which prevents the bulb giving out too harsh a light.

LAN, LANs NOUN ICT a group of computers and associated equipment that are linked by cables or wireless technology, for example in a school. LAN is an abbreviation for 'local area network'.

lance, lances, lancing, lanced VERB ①To lance a boil or abscess means to stick a sharp instrument into it in order to release the fluid. ▶ NOUN ②a long spear that used to be used by soldiers on horseback.

land, lands, landing, landed NOUN ①Land is an area of ground. ②Land is also the part of the earth that is not covered by water. ③a country • *our native land*. ▶ VERB ④When a plane lands, it arrives back on the ground after a flight. ⑤If you land something you have been trying to get, you succeed in getting it • *She eventually landed a job with a local radio station*. ⑥To land a fish means to catch it while fishing. ⑦If you land someone with something unpleasant, you cause them to have to deal with it.

landfill, landfills NOUN ①Landfill is the disposing of rubbish by covering it with earth. ②A landfill is an area where rubbish is disposed of in this way.

landing, landings NOUN ①a flat area in a building at the top of a flight of stairs. ②The landing of an aeroplane is its arrival back on the ground after a flight • *a smooth landing*.

landlady, landladies NOUN a woman who owns a house or small hotel and who lets rooms to people.

landlord, landlords NOUN a man who owns a house or small hotel and who lets rooms to people.

landmark, landmarks NOUN ①a noticeable feature in a landscape, which you can use to check your position. ②an important stage in the development of something • *The play is a landmark in Japanese theatre*.

landowner, landowners NOUN someone who owns land, especially a large area of the countryside.

landscape, landscapes NOUN ① GEOGRAPHY The landscape is the view over an area of open land. ② ART a painting of the countryside.

landslide, landslides NOUN ①a large amount of loose earth and rocks falling down a mountain side. ②a victory in an election won by a large number of votes.

lane, lanes NOUN ①a narrow road, especially in the country. ②one of the strips on a road marked with lines to guide drivers.

language, languages NOUN ①the system of words that the people of a country use to communicate with each other. ②Your language is the style in which you express yourself • *His language is often obscure*. ③Language is the study of the words and grammar of a particular language.

SIMILAR WORDS: ②expression, speech

languid [*Said lang-gwid*] ADJECTIVE slow and lacking energy. **languidly** ADVERB

languish, languishes, languishing, languished VERB If you languish, you endure an unpleasant situation for a long time • *Many languished in poverty*.

lanky, lankier, lankiest ADJECTIVE Someone who is lanky is tall and thin and moves rather awkwardly.

lantana, lantanas NOUN In Australia, a lantana is a shrub with yellow or orange flowers which is regarded as a pest in some areas.

lantern, lanterns NOUN a lamp in a metal frame with glass sides.

lap, laps, lapping, lapped NOUN ① Your lap is the flat area formed by your thighs when you are sitting down. ② one circuit of a running track or racecourse. ▸ VERB ③ When an animal laps up liquid, it drinks using its tongue to get the liquid into its mouth. ④ If you lap someone in a race, you overtake them when they are still on the previous lap. ⑤ When water laps against something, it gently moves against it in little waves.

lapel, lapels [*Said* lap-**el**] NOUN a flap which is joined on to the collar of a jacket or coat.

lapse, lapses, lapsing, lapsed NOUN ① a moment of bad behaviour by someone who usually behaves well. ② a slight mistake. ③ a period of time between two events. ▸ VERB ④ If you lapse into a different way of behaving, you start behaving that way • *The offenders lapsed into a sullen silence*. ⑤ If a legal document or contract lapses, it is not renewed on the date when it expires.

laptop, laptops NOUN ICT a type of small portable computer.

lard NOUN Lard is fat from a pig, used in cooking.

larder, larders NOUN a room in which you store food, often next to a kitchen.

large, larger, largest ADJECTIVE ① Someone or something that is large is much bigger than average. ▸ PHRASE ② If a prisoner is **at large**, he or she has escaped from prison.

largely ADVERB to a great extent • *The public are largely unaware of this*.

lark, larks NOUN ① a small brown bird with a distinctive song. ② If you do something for a lark, you do it in a high-spirited or mischievous way for fun.

larrikin, larrikins NOUN (*informal*) In Australian and New Zealand English, a larrikin is a young person who behaves in a wild or irresponsible way.

larva, larvae NOUN an insect, which looks like a short, fat worm, at the stage before it becomes an adult.

SPELLING TIP
Do not confuse the spellings of *larva* and *lava*: *a mosquito larva; Their home was destroyed by molten lava*.

laryngitis [*Said* lar-in-**jie**-tiss] NOUN Laryngitis is an infection of the throat which causes you to lose your voice.

larynx, larynxes or larynges NOUN the part of your throat containing the vocal cords, through which air passes between your nose and lungs.

lasagne [*Said* laz-**zan**-ya] NOUN Lasagne is an Italian dish made with wide flat sheets of pasta, meat and cheese sauce.
WORD HISTORY: from Latin *lasanum* meaning 'cooking pot'

laser, lasers NOUN a machine that produces a powerful concentrated beam of light which is used to cut very hard materials and in some kinds of surgery.
WORD HISTORY: from the first letters of 'Light Amplification by Stimulated Emission of Radiation'

a b c d e f g h i j k l m n o p q r s t u v w x y z

lash, lashes, lashing, lashed NOUN ① Your lashes are the hairs growing on the edge of your eyelids. ② a strip of leather at the end of a whip. ③ Lashes are blows struck with a whip. **lash out** VERB To lash out at someone means to criticise them severely.

lass, lasses NOUN a girl or young woman.

lasso, lassoes or lassos, lassoing, lassoed [Said las-**soo**] NOUN ① a length of rope with a noose at one end, used by cowboys to catch cattle and horses. ▸ VERB ② To lasso an animal means to catch it by throwing the noose of a lasso around its neck.

last, lasts, lasting, lasted ADJECTIVE ① The last thing or event is the most recent one • last year. ② The last thing that remains is the only one left after all the others have gone • The last family left in 1990. ▸ ADVERB ③ If you last did something on a particular occasion, you have not done it since then • They last met in Rome. ④ The thing that happens last in a sequence of events is the final one • He added the milk last. ▸ VERB ⑤ If something lasts, it continues to exist or happen • Her speech lasted fifty minutes. ⑥ To last also means to remain in good condition • The mixture will last for up to 2 weeks in the fridge. ▸ PHRASE ⑦ At last means after a long time. **lastly** ADVERB

last-ditch ADJECTIVE A last-ditch attempt to do something is a final attempt to succeed when everything else has failed.

latch, latches, latching, latched NOUN ① a simple door fastening consisting of a metal bar which falls into a hook. ② a type of door lock which locks automatically when you close the door and which has to be opened with a key. ▸ VERB

③ (informal) If you latch onto someone or something, you become attached to them.

late, later, latest ADJECTIVE or ADVERB ① Something that happens late happens towards the end of a period of time • the late evening • late in the morning. ② If you arrive late, or do something late, you arrive or do it after the time you were expected to. ▸ ADJECTIVE ③ A late event happens after the time when it usually takes place • a late breakfast. ④ (formal) Late means dead • my late grandmother.

lately ADVERB Events that happened lately happened recently.

latent ADJECTIVE A latent quality is hidden at the moment, but may emerge in the future • a latent talent for art.

lateral ADJECTIVE relating to the sides of something, or moving in a sideways direction.

lathe, lathes NOUN a machine which holds and turns a piece of wood or metal against a tool to cut and shape it.

lather, lathers NOUN Lather is the foam that you get when you rub soap in water.

Latin, Latins NOUN ① Latin is the language of ancient Rome. ② Latins are people who speak languages closely related to Latin, such as French, Italian, Spanish and Portuguese.

Latin America NOUN Latin America consists of the countries in North, South and Central America where Spanish or Portuguese is the main language. **Latin American** ADJECTIVE

latitude, latitudes NOUN
GEOGRAPHY The latitude of a place is its distance north or south of the equator measured in degrees.

latrine, latrines [Said lat-**reen**] NOUN a hole or trench in the ground used as a toilet at a camp.

latter ADJECTIVE or NOUN ①You use 'latter' to refer to the second of two things that are mentioned • *They were eating sandwiches and cakes (the latter bought from Mrs Paul's bakery).*
▶ ADJECTIVE ②'Latter' also describes the second or end part of something • *the latter part of his career.*

USAGE NOTE
You use *latter* to talk about the second of two items. To talk about the last of three or more items you should use *last-named*.

latterly ADVERB (*formal*) Latterly means recently • *It's only latterly that this has become an issue.*

lattice, lattices NOUN a structure made of strips which cross over each other diagonally leaving holes in between.

laudable ADJECTIVE (*formal*) deserving praise • *It is a laudable aim.*
laudably ADVERB

laugh, laughs, laughing, laughed VERB ①When you laugh, you make a noise which shows that you are amused or happy. ▶ NOUN ②the noise you make when you laugh.

laughable ADJECTIVE quite absurd.

laughing stock NOUN someone who has been made to seem ridiculous.

laughter NOUN Laughter is a noise which shows that you are amused or happy.

launch, launches, launching, launched VERB ①To launch a ship means to send it into the water for the first time. ②To launch a rocket means to send it into space. ③When a company launches a new product, they have an advertising campaign to promote it as they start to sell it.
▶ NOUN ④a motorboat.

launch pad, launch pads NOUN A launch pad, or a launching pad, is the place from which space rockets take off.

launder, launders, laundering, laundered VERB (*old-fashioned*) To launder clothes, sheets or towels means to wash and iron them.

laundry, laundries NOUN ①a business that washes and irons clothes and sheets. ②Laundry is also the dirty clothes and sheets that are being washed, or are about to be washed.

laurel, laurels NOUN an evergreen tree with shiny leaves.

lava NOUN GEOGRAPHY Lava is the very hot liquid rock that comes shooting out of an erupting volcano, and becomes solid as it cools.

SPELLING TIP
Do not confuse the spellings of *lava* and *larva*: *Their home was destroyed by molten lava; a mosquito larva.*

lavatory, lavatories NOUN a toilet.

lavender NOUN ①Lavender is a small bush with bluish-pink flowers that have a strong, pleasant scent.
▶ ADJECTIVE ②bluish-pink.

lavish, lavishes, lavishing, lavished ADJECTIVE ①If you are lavish, you are very generous with your time, money or gifts. ②A lavish amount is a large amount. ▶ VERB ③If you lavish money or affection on someone, you give them a lot of it. **lavishly** ADVERB

law, laws NOUN ① CITIZENSHIP The law is the system of rules developed by the government of a country, which regulate what people may and may not do and deals with people who break these rules. ②The law is also the profession of people such as

a
b
c
d
e
f
g
h
i
j
k
l
m
n
o
p
q
r
s
t
u
v
w
x
y
z

lawyers, whose job involves the application of the laws of a country. ③ CITIZENSHIP one of the rules established by a government or a religion, which tells people what they may or may not do. ④ a scientific fact which allows you to explain how things work in the physical world. **lawful** ADJECTIVE **lawfully** ADVERB

law-abiding ADJECTIVE obeying the law and not causing any trouble.

lawless ADJECTIVE having no regard for the law.

lawn, lawns NOUN an area of grass that is kept cut short.

lawnmower, lawnmowers NOUN a machine for cutting grass.

lawsuit, lawsuits NOUN a civil court case between two people, as opposed to the police prosecuting someone for a criminal offence.

lawyer, lawyers NOUN a person who is qualified in law, and whose job is to advise people about the law and represent them in court.

lax, laxer, laxest ADJECTIVE careless and not keeping up the usual standards • *a lax accounting system*.

laxative, laxatives NOUN something that you eat or drink to stop you being constipated.

lay, lays, laying, laid VERB ① When you lay something somewhere, you put it down so that it lies there. ② If you lay something, you arrange it or set it out. ③ If you lay the table, you put cutlery on the table ready for a meal. ④ When a bird lays an egg, it produces the egg out of its body. ⑤ If you lay a trap for someone, you create a situation in which you will be able to catch them out. ⑥ If you lay emphasis on something, you refer to it in a way that shows you think it

is very important. ⑦ If you lay odds on something, you bet that it will happen. ⑧ Lay is the past tense of **lie**[1]. ▶ ADJECTIVE ⑨ You use 'lay' to describe people who are involved with a Christian church but are not members of the clergy • *a lay preacher*.

lay off VERB ① When workers are laid off, their employers tell them not to come to work for a while because there is a shortage of work. ② (*informal*) If you tell someone to lay off, you want them to stop doing something annoying. **lay on** VERB If you lay on a meal or entertainment, you provide it.

GRAMMAR TIP

People often get confused about *lay* and *lie*. The verb *lay* takes an object: *Lay the table please; The Queen laid a wreath*. The verb *lie* does not take an object: *The book was lying on the table; I'm going to lie down*.

---

lay-by, lay-bys NOUN ① an area by the side of a main road where motorists can stop for a short while. ② In Australia and New Zealand, lay-by is a system where you pay a deposit on an item in a shop so that it will be kept for you until you pay the rest of the price.

layer, layers NOUN a single thickness of something • *layers of clothing*.

layman, laymen NOUN ① someone who does not have specialised knowledge of a subject • *a layman's guide to computers*. ② someone who belongs to the church but is not a member of the clergy.

layout, layouts NOUN The layout of something is the pattern in which it is arranged.

laze, lazes, lazing, lazed VERB If you laze, you relax and do no work • *We spent a few days lazing around by the pool*.

lazy, lazier, laziest ADJECTIVE idle and unwilling to work. **lazily** ADVERB **laziness** NOUN
SIMILAR WORDS: idle, indolent, slothful

lb an abbreviation for 'pounds' • 3lb of sugar.

lbw In cricket, lbw is a way of dismissing a batsman when his or her legs prevent the ball from hitting the wicket. lbw is an abbreviation for 'leg before wicket'.

leach, leaches, leaching, leached VERB When minerals are leached from rocks, they are dissolved by water which filters through the rock.

lead¹, leads, leading, led [Rhymes with feed] VERB ① If you lead someone somewhere, you go in front of them in order to show them the way. ② If one thing leads to another, it causes the second thing to happen. ③ a person who leads a group of people is in charge of them. ▶ NOUN ④ a length of leather or chain attached to a dog's collar, so that the dog can be kept under control. ⑤ If the police have a lead, they have a clue which might help them to solve a crime.
SIMILAR WORDS: ① conduct, escort, guide

lead² [Rhymes with fed] NOUN SCIENCE Lead is a soft metallic element. Its atomic number is 82 and its symbol is Pb.

leader, leaders NOUN ① someone who is in charge of a country, an organisation, or a group of people. ② the person who is winning in a competition or race. ③ a newspaper article that expresses the newspaper's opinions.

leadership NOUN ① the group of people in charge of an organisation. ② Leadership is the ability to be a good leader.

leading ADJECTIVE particularly important, respected or advanced.

leaf, leaves; leafs, leafing, leafed NOUN ① the flat green growth on the end of a twig or branch of a tree or other plant. ▶ VERB ② If you leaf through a book, magazine or newspaper, you turn the pages over quickly. **leafy** ADJECTIVE

leaflet, leaflets NOUN a piece of paper with information or advertising printed on it.

league, leagues [Said leeg] NOUN ① PE a group of countries, clubs or people who have joined together for a particular purpose or because they share a common interest • the League of Red Cross Societies • the Australian Football League. ② a unit of distance used in former times, equal to about 3 miles.

leak, leaks, leaking, leaked VERB ① If a pipe or container leaks, it has a hole which lets gas or liquid escape. ② If liquid or gas leaks, it escapes from a pipe or container. ③ If someone in an organisation leaks information, they give the information to someone who is not supposed to have it • The letter was leaked to the press. ▶ NOUN ④ If a pipe or container has a leak, it has a hole which lets gas or liquid escape. ⑤ If there is a leak in an organisation, someone inside the organisation is giving information to people who are not supposed to have it. **leaky** ADJECTIVE

leakage, leakages NOUN an escape of gas or liquid from a pipe or container.

lean, leans, leaning, leant or leaned; leaner, leanest VERB ① When you lean in a particular direction, you bend your body in that direction. ② When you lean on something, you rest your body against it for support. ③ If you lean on someone, you depend on them. ④ If you lean towards particular ideas, you approve of them and follow them • *parents who lean towards strictness.* ▶ **ADJECTIVE** ⑤ having little or no fat • *lean cuts of meat.* ⑥ A lean period is a time when food or money is in short supply.

SPELLING TIP
Do not confuse the spellings of *leant*, the past tense and past participle of lean, and *lent*, the past tense and past participle of lend: *I leant against the wall; She lent me her bike.*

leap, leaps, leaping, leapt or leaped **VERB** ① If you leap somewhere, you jump over a long distance or high in the air. ▶ **NOUN** ② a jump over a long distance or high in the air.

leap year, leap years **NOUN** a year, occurring every four years, in which there are 366 days.

learn, learns, learning, learnt or learned **VERB** ① When you learn something, you gain knowledge or a skill through studying or training. ② If you learn of something, you find out about it • *She had first learnt of the accident that morning.* **learner NOUN**
SIMILAR WORDS: ② discover, find out, hear

learned [Said ler-nid] **ADJECTIVE** A learned person has a lot of knowledge gained from years of study.

learning NOUN Learning is knowledge that has been acquired through serious study.

lease, leases, leasing, leased **NOUN** ① an agreement which allows someone to use a house or flat in return for rent. ▶ **VERB** ② To lease property to someone means to allow them to use it in return for rent.

leash, leashes **NOUN** a length of leather or chain attached to a dog's collar so that the dog can be controlled.

least NOUN ① The least is the smallest possible amount of something. ▶ **ADJECTIVE** ② as small or as few as possible. ▶ **ADVERB** ③ Least is a superlative form of **little**. ▶ **PHRASE** ④ You use **at least** to show that you are referring to the minimum amount of something, and that you think the true amount is greater • *At least 200 hundred people turned up at the rally.*

leather NOUN Leather is the tanned skin of some animals, used to make shoes and clothes. **leathery ADJECTIVE**

leave, leaves, leaving, left **VERB** ① When you leave a place, you go away from it. ② If you leave someone somewhere, they stay behind after you go away. ③ If you leave a job or organisation, you stop being part of it • *He left his job shortly after Christmas.* ④ If someone leaves money or possessions to someone, they arrange for them to be given to them after their death. ⑤ In subtraction, when you take one number from another, it leaves a third number. ▶ **NOUN** ⑥ a period of holiday or absence from a job.
SIMILAR WORDS: ① depart, exit, go

Lebanese ADJECTIVE ① belonging or relating to Lebanon. ▶ **NOUN** ② someone who comes from Lebanon.

lectern, lecterns **NOUN** a sloping desk which people use to rest books or notes on.

lecture, lectures, lecturing, lectured **NOUN** ① a formal talk intended to teach people about a particular subject. ② a talk intended to tell someone off. ▶ **VERB** ③ Someone who lectures teaches in a college or university.

lecturer, **lecturers** NOUN a teacher in a college or university.

led the past tense and past participle of **lead**[1].

SPELLING TIP

Do not confuse the spellings of *led*, the past tense and past participle of the verb lead, and *lead*, the metal: *I led her through to the garden; The pipes are made of lead.*

ledge, **ledges** NOUN a narrow shelf on the side of a cliff or rock face, or on the outside of a building, directly under a window.

ledger, **ledgers** NOUN a book in which accounts are kept.

lee NOUN ① the sheltered side of a place • *the lee of the mountain.* ▶ ADJECTIVE ② on the side of a ship away from the wind.

leech, **leeches** NOUN a small worm that lives in water and feeds by sucking the blood from other animals.

leek, **leeks** NOUN a long vegetable of the onion family, which is white at one end and has green leaves at the other.

leer, **leers**, **leering**, **leered** VERB ① To leer at someone means to smile at them in an unpleasant or suggestive way. ▶ NOUN ② an unpleasant or suggestive smile.

leeward GEOGRAPHY NOUN ① an area or direction that is sheltered from the wind. ▶ ADJECTIVE or ADVERB ② towards or in an area sheltered from the wind • *the leeward side of a boat.*

leeway NOUN If something gives you some leeway, it allows you more flexibility in your plans, for example by giving you time to finish an activity.

left NOUN ① The left is one of two sides of something. For example, on a page, English writing begins on the left. ② People and political groups who hold socialist or communist views are referred to as the Left. ③ Left is the past tense and past participle of **leave**. ▶ ADJECTIVE or ADVERB ④ Left means on or towards the left side of something • *He had a mark above his left eye* • *Turn left down Govan Road.*

left-handed ADJECTIVE or ADVERB Someone who is left-handed does things such as writing with their left hand.

leftist, **leftists** NOUN or ADJECTIVE (a person) holding left-wing political views.

leftovers PLURAL NOUN the bits of food which have not been eaten at the end of a meal.

left-wing ADJECTIVE believing more strongly in socialism, or less strongly in capitalism or conservatism, than other members of the same party or group. **left-winger** NOUN

leg, **legs** NOUN ① Your legs are the two limbs which stretch from your hips to your feet. ② The legs of a pair of trousers are the parts that cover your legs. ③ The legs of an object such as a table are the parts which rest on the floor and support the object's weight. ④ A leg of a journey is one part of it. ⑤ one of two matches played between two sports teams • *He will miss the second leg of their qualifying tie.*

legacy, **legacies** NOUN ① property or money that someone gets in the will of a person who has died. ② something that exists as a result of a previous event or time • *the legacy of a strict upbringing.*

SIMILAR WORDS: ① bequest, inheritance

legal ADJECTIVE ① relating to the law • *the Dutch legal system*. ② allowed by the law • *The strike was perfectly legal*. **legally** ADVERB

legal aid NOUN Legal aid is a system which provides the services of a lawyer free, or very cheaply, to people who cannot afford the full fees.

legalise, legalises, legalising, legalised; also spelt **legalize** VERB To legalise something that is illegal means to change the law so that it becomes legal. **legalisation** NOUN

legality NOUN The legality of an action means whether or not it is allowed by the law • *They challenged the legality of the scheme*.

legend, legends NOUN ① an old story which was once believed to be true, but which is probably untrue. ② If you refer to someone or something as a legend, you mean they are very famous • *His career has become a legend*. **legendary** ADJECTIVE

leggings PLURAL NOUN ① Leggings are very close-fitting trousers made of stretchy material. ② Leggings are also a waterproof covering worn over ordinary trousers to protect them.

legible ADJECTIVE Writing that is legible is clear enough to be read.

legion, legions NOUN ① HISTORY In ancient Rome, a legion was a military unit of between 3000 and 6000 soldiers. ② a large military force • *the French Foreign Legion*. ③ Legions of people are large numbers of them.

legislate, legislates, legislating, legislated VERB (*formal*) When a government legislates, it creates new laws.

legislation NOUN Legislation is a law or set of laws created by a government.

legislative ADJECTIVE relating to the making of new laws • *a legislative council*.

legislator, legislators NOUN (*formal*) a person involved in making or passing laws.

legislature NOUN (*formal*) the parliament in a country, which is responsible for making new laws.

legitimate [*Said lij-it-tim-it*] ADJECTIVE Something that is legitimate is reasonable or acceptable according to existing laws or standards • *a legitimate charge for parking the car*. **legitimacy** NOUN **legitimately** ADVERB

leisure [*Rhymes with measure*] NOUN ① Leisure is time during which you do not have to work, and can do what you enjoy doing. ▶ PHRASE ② If you do something **at leisure**, or **at your leisure**, you do it at a convenient time.

leisurely ADJECTIVE or ADVERB A leisurely action is done in an unhurried and calm way.

lekgotla, lekgotlas [*Said leh-hot-la*] NOUN ① In South Africa, a lekgotla is a meeting place for village assemblies, court cases and meetings of village leaders. ② In South African English, a lekgotla is also a conference or business meeting.

lekker ADJECTIVE (*slang*) ① In South African English, lekker means pleasant. ② In South African English, lekker can also mean tasty.

lemming, lemmings NOUN a small rodent which lives in cold, northern countries. Lemmings were believed in the past to jump off cliffs to their death in large numbers.

lemon, lemons NOUN ① a yellow citrus fruit with a sour taste. ▶ ADJECTIVE ② pale yellow.

lemonade NOUN a sweet, fizzy drink made from lemons, water and sugar.

lend, lends, lending, lent VERB ① If you lend someone something, you give it to them for a period of time and then they give it back to you. ② If a bank lends money, it gives the money to someone and the money has to be repaid in the future, usually with interest. ▶ PHRASE ③ If you **lend someone a hand**, you help them. **lender** NOUN

length, lengths NOUN ① The length of something is the horizontal distance from one end to the other. ② The length of an event or activity is the amount of time it lasts for. ③ The length of something is also the fact that it is long rather than short • Despite its length, the novel is a rewarding read. ④ a long piece of something.

lengthen, lengthens, lengthening, lengthened VERB To lengthen something means to make it longer. SIMILAR WORDS: elongate, extend, prolong

lengthways or **lengthwise** ADVERB If you measure something lengthways, you measure the horizontal distance from one end to the other.

lengthy, lengthier, lengthiest ADJECTIVE Something that is lengthy lasts for a long time.

lenient ADJECTIVE If someone in authority is lenient, they are less severe than expected. **leniently** ADVERB **leniency** NOUN

lens, lenses NOUN ① a curved piece of glass designed to focus light in a certain way, for example in a camera, telescope or pair of glasses. ② The lens in your eye is the part behind the iris, which focuses light.

lent ① the past tense and past participle of **lend**. ▶ NOUN ② RE Lent is the period of forty days leading up to Easter, during which Christians give up something they enjoy.

SPELLING TIP
Do not confuse the spellings of lent, the past tense and past participle of lend, and leant, the past tense and past participle of lean: She lent me her bike; I leant against the wall.

lentil, lentils NOUN Lentils are small dried red, green or brown seeds which are cooked and eaten in soups and curries.

Leo NOUN Leo is the fifth sign of the zodiac, represented by a lion. People born between July 23rd and August 22nd are born under this sign.

leopard, leopards NOUN a wild Asian or African big cat, with yellow fur and black or brown spots.

leotard, leotards [Said lee-eh-tard] NOUN A leotard is a tight-fitting costume covering the body, which is worn for dancing or exercise. It is named after a French acrobat called Jules Léotard.

leper, lepers NOUN (offensive) someone who has leprosy. WORD HISTORY: from Greek lepros meaning 'scaly'

leprosy NOUN Leprosy is an infectious disease which attacks the skin and nerves, and which can lead to fingers or toes dropping off.

lesbian, lesbians NOUN a homosexual woman. **lesbianism** NOUN

lesion, lesions [Said lee-zhen] NOUN a wound or injury.

less ADJECTIVE OR ADVERB ① Less means a smaller amount, or not as much in quality • They left less than three weeks ago • She had become less *frightened of the dark now.* ② Less is a comparative form of **little**.

▶ **PREPOSITION** ③ You use 'less' to show that you are subtracting one number from another • *Eight less two leaves six.*

GRAMMAR TIP
You use *less* to talk about things that can't be counted: *less time.* When you are talking about amounts that can be counted you should use *fewer*.

-less SUFFIX '-less' means without • *hopeless* • *fearless.*

lessen, **lessens**, **lessening**, **lessened** VERB If something lessens, it is reduced in amount, size or quality.
SIMILAR WORDS: decrease, diminish, reduce

lesser ADJECTIVE smaller in importance or amount than something else.

lesson, **lessons** NOUN ① a fixed period of time during which a class of pupils is taught by a teacher. ② an experience that makes you understand something important which you had not realised before.

lest CONJUNCTION (*old-fashioned*) as a precaution in case something unpleasant or unwanted happens • *I was afraid to open the door lest he should follow me.*

let, **lets**, **letting**, **let** VERB ① If you let someone do something, you allow them to do it. ② If someone lets a house or flat that they own, they rent it out. ③ You can say 'let's' or 'let us' when you want to suggest doing something with someone else • *Let's go.* ④ If you let yourself in for something, you agree to do it although you do not really want to.
let down VERB If you let someone down, you fail to do something you had agreed to do for them. **let off** VERB ① If someone in authority lets

you off, they do not punish you for something you have done wrong. ② If you let off a firework or explosive, you light it or detonate it.

lethal [*Said lee-thal*] ADJECTIVE able to kill someone • *a lethal weapon.*

lethargic [*Said lith-ar-jik*] ADJECTIVE If you feel lethargic, you have no energy or enthusiasm.

lethargy [*Said leth-ar-jee*] NOUN Lethargy is a lack of energy and enthusiasm.

letter, **letters** NOUN ① Letters are written symbols which go together to make words. ② a piece of writing addressed to someone, and usually sent through the post.

letter box, **letter boxes** NOUN ① an oblong gap in the front door of a house or flat, through which letters are delivered. ② a large metal container in the street, where you post letters.

lettering NOUN Lettering is writing, especially when you are describing the type of letters used • *bold lettering.*

lettuce, **lettuces** NOUN a vegetable with large green leaves eaten raw in salad.

leukaemia [*Said loo-kee-mee-a*]; also spelt **leukemia** NOUN Leukaemia is a serious illness which affects the blood.

level, **levels**, **levelling**, **levelled** ADJECTIVE ① A surface that is level is smooth, flat and parallel to the ground. ▶ VERB ② To level a piece of land means to make it flat. ③ If you level a criticism at someone, you say or write something critical about them. ▶ ADVERB ④ If you draw level with someone, you get closer to them so that you are moving next to them. ▶ NOUN ⑤ a point on a scale which measures the amount,

importance or difficulty of something. ⑥ The level of a liquid is the height it comes up to in a container. **level off** or **level out** VERB If something levels off or levels out, it stops increasing or decreasing • *Profits are beginning to level off.*
SIMILAR WORDS: ⑤ grade, position, stage

level crossing, level crossings NOUN a place where road traffic is allowed to drive across a railway track.

level-headed ADJECTIVE Someone who is level-headed is sensible and calm in emergencies.

lever, levers NOUN ① a handle on a machine that you pull in order to make the machine work. ② a long bar that you wedge underneath a heavy object and press down on to make the object move.

leverage NOUN Leverage is knowledge or influence that you can use to make someone do something.

levy, levies, levying, levied [*Said lev-ee*] (*formal*) NOUN ① an amount of money that you pay in tax. ▸ VERB ② When a government levies a tax, it makes people pay the tax and organises the collection of the money.

lewd, lewder, lewdest [*Rhymes with rude*] ADJECTIVE unpleasantly coarse and crude.

lexicography NOUN the profession of writing dictionaries.
lexicographer NOUN
WORD HISTORY: from Greek *lexis* meaning 'word' and *graphein* meaning 'to write'

liability, liabilities NOUN ① Someone's liability is their responsibility for something they have done wrong. ② In business, a company's liabilities are its debts.

③ (*informal*) If you describe someone as a liability, you mean that they cause a lot of problems or embarrassment.

liable ADJECTIVE ① If you say that something is liable to happen, you mean that you think it will probably happen. ② If you are liable for something you have done, you are legally responsible for it.

USAGE NOTE
It used to be wrong to use *liable* to mean 'probable or likely', but that use is now considered correct.

---

liaise, liaises, liaising, liaised [*Said lee-aze*] VERB To liaise with someone or an organisation means to cooperate with them and keep them informed.

liaison, liaisons [*Said lee-aze-on*] NOUN Liaison is communication between two organisations or two sections of an organisation.

liar, liars NOUN a person who tells lies.

libel, libels, libelling, libelled [*Said lie-bel*] NOUN ① Libel is something written about someone which is not true, and for which the writer can be made to pay damages in court. ▸ VERB ② To libel someone means to write or say something untrue about them. **libellous** ADJECTIVE
WORD HISTORY: from Latin *libellus* meaning 'little book'

liberal, liberals NOUN ① someone who believes in political progress, social welfare and individual freedom. ▸ ADJECTIVE ② Someone who is liberal is tolerant of a wide range of behaviour, standards or opinions. ③ To be liberal with something means to be generous with it. ④ A liberal quantity of something is a large amount of it.
liberally ADVERB **liberalism** NOUN

a
b
c
d
e
f
g
h
i
j
k
l
m
n
o
p
q
r
s
t
u
v
w
x
y
z

Liberal Party NOUN In Australia, the Liberal Party is one of the major political parties.

liberalise, liberalises, liberalising, liberalised; also spelt **liberalize** VERB If a country liberalises its laws, it makes them less severe.

liberate, liberates, liberating, liberated VERB To liberate people means to free them from prison or from an unpleasant situation. **liberation** NOUN **liberator** NOUN

liberty NOUN CITIZENSHIP ① Liberty is the freedom to choose how you want to live, without government restrictions. ▶ PHRASE ② If you are **not at liberty** to do something, you are not allowed to do it.

Libra NOUN Libra is the seventh sign of the zodiac, represented by a pair of scales. People born between September 23rd and October 22nd are born under this sign.

librarian, librarians NOUN LIBRARY a person who works in, or is in charge of, a library.

library, libraries NOUN ① a building in which books are kept for people to come and read or borrow. ② a collection of things such as books or music.

Libyan, Libyans ADJECTIVE ① belonging or relating to Libya. ▶ NOUN ② someone who comes from Libya.

lice the plural of **louse**.

licence, licences NOUN ① an official document which entitles you to carry out a particular activity, for example to drive a car. ② Licence is the freedom to do what you want, especially when other people consider that it is being used irresponsibly.

SPELLING TIP
Do not confuse the spellings of the noun *licence* and the verb *license*: *a driving licence; Are you licensed to fly a plane?*

SPELLING TIP
Remember this mnemonic: *I want to see (C) your licenCe.*

license, licenses, licensing, licensed VERB To license an activity means to give official permission for it to be carried out.

SPELLING TIP
Do not confuse the spellings of the verb *license* and the noun *licence*: *Are you licensed to fly a plane?; a driving licence.*

SPELLING TIP
Remember this mnemonic: *The government licenSes Spaniels.*

lichen, lichens [*Said* lie-ken] NOUN Lichen is a green, moss-like growth on rocks or tree trunks.

lick, licks, licking, licked VERB ① If you lick something, you move your tongue over it. ▶ NOUN ② the action of licking.

lid, lids NOUN the top of a container, which you open in order to reach what is inside.

lie¹, lies, lying, lay, lain VERB ① To lie somewhere means to rest there horizontally. ② If you say where something lies, you are describing where it is • *The farm lies between two valleys.*

SPELLING TIP
The past tense of this verb *lie* is *lay*. Do not confuse it with the verb *lay* meaning 'put'.

lie², lies, lying, lied VERB ① To lie means to say something that is not

true. ▸ NOUN ② something you say
that is not true.

lieu [Said **lyoo**] PHRASE If one thing
happens **in lieu** of another, it
happens instead of it.

lieutenant, lieutenants [Said
loo-**ten**-ant or lef-**ten**-ent] NOUN a
junior officer in the army or navy.
WORD HISTORY: from Old French
lieutenant meaning literally 'holding a
place'

life, lives NOUN ① Life is the quality of
being able to grow and develop,
which is present in people, plants
and animals. ② Your life is your
existence from the time you are born
until the time you die. ③ The life of a
machine is the period of time for
which it is likely to work. ④ If you
refer to the life in a place, you are
talking about the amount of activity
there • *The town was full of life.* ⑤ If
criminals are sentenced to life, they
are sent to prison for the rest of their
lives, or until they are granted parole.

life assurance NOUN Life assurance
is an insurance which provides a sum
of money in the event of the policy
holder's death.

lifeblood NOUN The lifeblood of
something is the most essential part
of it.

lifeboat, lifeboats NOUN ① a boat
kept on shore, which is sent out to
rescue people who are in danger at
sea. ② a small boat kept on a ship,
which is used if the ship starts to
sink.

life expectancy, life expectancies
NOUN GEOGRAPHY Your life
expectancy is the number of years
you can expect to live.

lifeguard, lifeguards NOUN a person
whose job is to rescue people who
are in difficulty in the sea or in a
swimming pool.

life jacket, life jackets NOUN a
sleeveless inflatable jacket that
keeps you afloat in water.

lifeless ADJECTIVE ① Someone who is
lifeless is dead. ② If you describe a
place or person as lifeless, you mean
that they are dull.

lifelike ADJECTIVE A picture or sculpture
that is lifelike looks very real or alive.

lifeline, lifelines NOUN ① something
which helps you to survive or helps
an activity to continue. ② a rope
thrown to someone who is in danger
of drowning.

lifelong ADJECTIVE existing
throughout someone's life • *He had a
lifelong interest in music.*

lifesaver, lifesavers NOUN In Australia
and New Zealand, a lifesaver is a
person whose job is to rescue people
who are in difficulty in the sea.

life span, life spans NOUN
① Someone's life span is the length of
time during which they are alive.
② The life span of a product or
organisation is the length of time it
exists or is useful.

lifestyle, lifestyles NOUN PSHE the
living conditions, behaviour and
habits that a person chooses to have.

lifetime, lifetimes NOUN Your
lifetime is the period of time during
which you are alive.

lift, lifts, lifting, lifted VERB ① To lift
something means to move it to a
higher position. ② When fog or mist
lifts, it clears away. ③ To lift a ban on
something means to remove it.
④ (informal) To lift things means to
steal them. ▸ NOUN ⑤ a machine like
a large box which carries passengers
from one floor to another in a
building. ⑥ If you give someone a lift,
you drive them somewhere in a car or
on a motorcycle.
SIMILAR WORDS: ① elevate, raise

a
b
c
d
e
f
g
h
i
j
k
l
m
n
o
p
q
r
s
t
u
v
w
x
y
z

ligament, ligaments NOUN SCIENCE a piece of tough tissue in your body which connects your bones.

light, lights, lighting, lighted or lit; lighter, lightest NOUN ① Light is brightness from the sun, fire or lamps, that enables you to see things. ② a lamp or other device that gives out brightness. ③ If you give someone a light, you give them a match or lighter to light their cigarette. ▶ ADJECTIVE ④ A place that is light is bright because of the sun or the use of lamps. ⑤ A light colour is pale. ⑥ A light object does not weigh much. ⑦ A light task is fairly easy. ⑧ Light books or music are entertaining and are not intended to be serious. ▶ VERB ⑨ To light a place means to cause it to be filled with light. ⑩ To light a fire means to make it start burning. ⑪ To light upon something means to find it by accident. **lightly** ADVERB **lightness** NOUN

lighten, lightens, lightening, lightened VERB ① When something lightens, it becomes less dark. ② To lighten a load means to make it less heavy.

lighter, lighters NOUN a device for lighting a cigarette or cigar.

light-headed ADJECTIVE If you feel light-headed, you feel slightly dizzy or drunk.

light-hearted ADJECTIVE Someone who is light-hearted is cheerful and has no worries.
SIMILAR WORDS: blithe, carefree, happy-go-lucky

lighthouse, lighthouses NOUN a tower by the sea, which sends out a powerful light to guide ships and warn them of danger.

lighting NOUN ① The lighting in a room or building is the way that it

is lit. ② DRAMA Lighting in the theatre or for a film is the special lights that are directed on the performers or scene.

lightning NOUN Lightning is the bright flashes of light in the sky which are produced by natural electricity during a thunderstorm.

lightweight, lightweights NOUN ① a boxer in one of the lighter weight groups. ▶ ADJECTIVE ② Something that is lightweight does not weigh very much • a lightweight jacket.

light year, light years NOUN SCIENCE a unit of distance equal to the distance that light travels in a year.

likable; also spelt **likeable** ADJECTIVE Someone who is likable is very pleasant and friendly.

like, likes, liking, liked PREPOSITION ① If one thing is like another, it is similar to it. ▶ NOUN ② 'The like' means other similar things of the sort just mentioned • nappies, prams, cots and the like. ▶ PHRASE ③ If you **feel like** something, you want to do it or have it • I feel like a walk. ▶ VERB ④ If you like something or someone, you find them pleasant.

-like SUFFIX '-like' means resembling or similar to • a balloonlike object.

likelihood NOUN If you say that there is a likelihood that something will happen, you mean that you think it will probably happen.

likely, likelier, likeliest ADJECTIVE Something that is likely will probably happen or is probably true.

liken, likens, likening, likened VERB If you liken one thing to another, you say that they are similar.

likeness, likenesses NOUN If two things have a likeness to each other, they are similar in appearance.

likewise ADVERB Likewise means

similarly • *She sat down and he did likewise.*

liking NOUN If you have a liking for someone or something, you like them.

lilac NOUN ① a shrub with large clusters of pink, white or mauve flowers. ▸ADJECTIVE ② pale mauve.

lilt, lilts NOUN A lilt in someone's voice is a pleasant rising and falling sound in it. **lilting** ADJECTIVE

lily, lilies NOUN a plant with trumpet-shaped flowers of various colours.

limb, limbs NOUN ① Your limbs are your arms and legs. ② The limbs of a tree are its branches. ▸PHRASE ③ If you have gone **out on a limb**, you have said or done something risky.

limber up, limbers up, limbering up, limbered up VERB If you limber up, you stretch your muscles before doing a sport.

limbo NOUN ① If you are in limbo, you are in an uncertain situation over which you feel you have no control. ② The limbo is a dance, originally from Trinidad, in which the dancer has to pass under a low bar while leaning backwards.
WORD HISTORY: sense 1 is from Latin *in limbo* meaning 'on the border (of Hell)'

lime, limes NOUN ① a small, green citrus fruit, rather like a lemon. ② A lime tree is a large tree with pale green leaves. ③ Lime is a chemical substance that is used in cement and as a fertiliser.

limelight NOUN If someone is in the limelight, they are getting a lot of attention.

limerick, limericks NOUN an amusing nonsense poem of five lines.

limestone NOUN Limestone is a white rock which is used for building and making cement.

limit, limits, limiting, limited NOUN ① a boundary or an extreme beyond which something cannot go • *the speed limit.* ▸VERB ② To limit something means to prevent it from becoming bigger, spreading or making progress • *He did all he could to limit the damage.*

limitation, limitations NOUN ① The limitation of something is the reducing or controlling of it. ② If you talk about the limitations of a person or thing, you are talking about the limits of their abilities.

limited ADJECTIVE Something that is limited is rather small in amount or extent • *a limited number of bedrooms.*

limousine, limousines [*Said lim-o-zeen*] NOUN a large, luxurious car, usually driven by a chauffeur.

limp, limps, limping, limped; limper, limpest VERB ① If you limp, you walk unevenly because you have hurt your leg or foot. ▸NOUN ② an uneven way of walking. ▸ADJECTIVE ③ Something that is limp is soft and floppy, and not stiff or firm • *a limp lettuce.*

limpet, limpets NOUN a shellfish with a pointed shell, that attaches itself very firmly to rocks.

line, lines, lining, lined NOUN ① a long, thin mark. ② a number of people or things positioned one behind the other. ③ a route along which someone or something moves • *a railway line.* ④ In a piece of writing, a line is a number of words together • *I often used to change my lines as an actor.* ⑤ MATHS In maths, a line is the straight, one-dimensional space between two points. ⑥ Someone's line of work is the kind of work they do. ⑦ The line someone takes is the attitude they have towards something • *He took a hard line with truancy.* ⑧ In a shop or business, a line is a type of product • *That line has* been discontinued. ▸ **VERB** ⑨ To line something means to cover its inside surface or edge with something • *Cottages lined the edge of the harbour.*

line up VERB ① When people line up, they stand in a line. ② When you line something up, you arrange it for a special occasion • *A tour is being lined up for July.*

lineage, lineages [*Said* lin-ee-ij] **NOUN** Someone's lineage is all the people from whom they are directly descended.

linear [*Said* lin-ee-ar] **ADJECTIVE** arranged in a line or in a strict sequence, or happening at a constant rate.

line dancing NOUN a type of dancing performed by rows of people to country music.

line graph, line graphs NOUN MATHS a graph where each value is plotted as a point, joined by a straight line to the points on either side of it.

linen NOUN ① DGT Linen is a type of cloth made from a plant called flax. ② Linen is also household goods made of cloth, such as sheets and tablecloths.

liner, liners NOUN a large passenger ship that makes long journeys.

linesman, linesmen NOUN an official at a sports match who watches the lines of the field or court and indicates when the ball goes outside them.

-ling SUFFIX '-ling' means 'small' • *duckling.*

linger, lingers, lingering, lingered VERB To linger means to remain for a long time • *The smell of the flowers lingered in the air.*

lingerie [*Said* lan-jer-ee] **NOUN** Lingerie is women's nightclothes and underclothes.

lingo, lingoes NOUN (*informal*) a foreign language.

linguist, linguists NOUN MFL someone who studies foreign languages or the way in which language works.

linguistic ADJECTIVE ENGLISH relating to language or to linguistics.

linguistics NOUN ENGLISH Linguistics is the study of language and of how it works.

lining, linings NOUN any material used to line the inside of something.

link, links, linking, linked NOUN ① a relationship or connection between two things • *the link between good diet and health.* ② a physical connection between two things or places • *a high-speed rail link between the cities.* ③ one of the rings in a chain. ④ In computing, a link is a connection between different documents, or between different parts of the same document. ▸ **VERB** ⑤ To link people, places or things means to join them together. **linkage** NOUN

lino NOUN Lino is the same as linoleum.

linoleum NOUN a floor covering with a shiny surface.

lint NOUN soft cloth made from linen, used to dress wounds.

lion, lions NOUN a large member of the cat family which comes from Africa. Lions have light brown fur, and the male has a long mane. A female lion is called a lioness.

lip, lips NOUN ① Your lips are the edges of your mouth. ② The lip of a jug is the slightly pointed part through which liquids are poured out.

lip-read, lip-reads, lip-reading, lip-read VERB To lip-read means to watch someone's lips when they are talking in order to understand what they are saying. Deaf people often lip-read. **lip-reading** NOUN

lipstick, lipsticks NOUN a coloured substance which is worn on the lips.

liqueur, liqueurs [Said lik-**yoor**] NOUN a strong sweet alcoholic drink, usually drunk after a meal.

liquid, liquids NOUN ① SCIENCE any substance which is not a solid or a gas, and which can be poured. ▶ADJECTIVE ② Something that is liquid is in the form of a liquid • liquid nitrogen. ③ In commerce and finance, a person's or company's liquid assets are the things that can be sold quickly to raise cash.

liquidate, liquidates, liquidating, liquidated VERB To liquidate a company means to close it down and use its assets to pay off its debts. **liquidation** NOUN **liquidator** NOUN

liquor NOUN Liquor is any strong alcoholic drink.

liquorice [Said lik-ker-iss] NOUN Liquorice is a root used to flavour sweets; also the sweets themselves.

lisp, lisps, lisping, lisped NOUN ① Someone who has a lisp pronounces the sounds 's' and 'z' like 'th'. ▶VERB ② To lisp means to speak with a lisp.

list, lists, listing, listed NOUN ① a set of words or items written one below the other. ▶VERB ② If you list a number of things, you make a list of them.

listen, listens, listening, listened VERB If you listen to something, you hear it and pay attention to it. **listener** NOUN

listless ADJECTIVE lacking energy and enthusiasm. **listlessly** ADVERB WORD HISTORY: from Old English list meaning 'desire'

lit a past tense and past participle of **light**.

litany, litanies NOUN ① a part of a church service in which the priest says or chants prayers and the people give responses. ② something, especially a list of things, that is repeated often or in a boring or insincere way • a tedious litany of complaints.

literacy NOUN Literacy is the ability to read and write. **literate** ADJECTIVE

literal ADJECTIVE ① ENGLISH The literal meaning of a word is its most basic meaning. ② A literal translation from a foreign language is one that has been translated exactly word for word. **literally** ADVERB

USAGE NOTE
Be careful where you use literally. It can emphasise something without changing the meaning: The house was literally only five minutes' walk away. However, it can make nonsense of some things: He literally swept me off my feet. This sentence is ridiculous unless he actually took a broom and swept the speaker over.

literary ADJECTIVE ENGLISH connected with literature • literary critics.

literature NOUN ① ENGLISH Literature consists of novels, plays and poetry. ② The literature on a subject is everything that has been written about it.

lithe, lither, lithest ADJECTIVE supple and graceful.

lithium NOUN SCIENCE Lithium is a chemical element. It is the lightest known solid. Its atomic number is 3 and its symbol is Li.

litmus NOUN SCIENCE In chemistry, litmus is a substance that turns red under acid and blue under alkali conditions.

a
b
c
d
e
f
g
h
i
j
k
l
m
n
o
p
q
r
s
t
u
v
w
x
y
z

litmus test, litmus tests NOUN something which is regarded as a simple and accurate test of a particular thing, such as a person's attitude to an issue • *The match will be a litmus test of the team's confidence.*

litre, litres NOUN MATHS a unit of liquid volume equal to about 1.76 pints.

litter, litters, littering, littered NOUN ① Litter is rubbish in the street and other public places. ② Cat litter is a gravelly substance you put in a container where you want your cat to urinate and defecate. ③ a number of baby animals born at the same time to the same mother. ▶ VERB ④ If things litter a place, they are scattered all over it.

little, less, lesser, least ADJECTIVE ① small in size or amount. ▶ NOUN ② A little is a small amount or degree • *Would you like a little of this?* ③ Little also means not much • *He has little to say.* ▶ ADVERB ④ to a small amount or degree • *a little afraid* • *She ate little.*

live, lives, living, lived [*Said* liv] VERB ① If you live in a place, that is where your home is. ② To live means to be alive. ③ If something lives up to your expectations, it is as good as you thought it would be. ▶ ADJECTIVE or ADVERB [*Rhymes with* hive] ④ Live television or radio is broadcast while the event is taking place • *a live football match* • *The concert will go out live.* ▶ ADJECTIVE ⑤ Live animals or plants are alive, rather than dead or artificial • *a live spider.* ⑥ Something is live if it is directly connected to an electricity supply • *Careful – those wires are live.* ⑦ Live bullets or ammunition have not yet been exploded. **live down** VERB If you cannot live down a mistake or failure, you cannot make people forget it.

livelihood, livelihoods NOUN Someone's livelihood is their job or the source of their income.

lively, livelier, liveliest ADJECTIVE full of life and enthusiasm • *lively conversation.* **liveliness** NOUN
SIMILAR WORDS: brisk, energetic, vigorous

liven, livens, livening, livened VERB To liven things up means to make them more lively or interesting.

liver, livers NOUN ① Your liver is a large organ in your body which cleans your blood and helps digestion. ② Liver is also the liver of some animals, which may be cooked and eaten.
WORD HISTORY: from Greek *liparos* meaning 'fat'

livestock NOUN Livestock is farm animals.

livid ADJECTIVE ① extremely angry. ② dark purple or bluish • *livid bruises.*

living ADJECTIVE ① If someone is living, they are alive • *her only living relative.* ▶ NOUN ② The work you do for a living is the work you do in order to earn money to live.

living room, living rooms NOUN the room where people relax and entertain in their homes.

lizard, lizards NOUN a long, thin, dry-skinned reptile found in hot, dry countries.

llama, llamas NOUN a South American animal related to the camel.

SPELLING TIP
Do not confuse the spellings of *llama* and *lama*: *hats and gloves made from llama wool; a revered Tibetan lama.*

load, loads, loading, loaded NOUN ① something being carried. ② (*informal*) Loads means a lot • *loads of work.* ▶ VERB ③ To load a vehicle or animal means to put a large number of things into it or onto it.

loaf, loaves; loafs, loafing, loafed NOUN ① a large piece of bread baked in a shape that can be cut into slices. ▸ VERB ② To loaf around means to be lazy and not do any work.

loan, loans, loaning, loaned NOUN ① a sum of money that you borrow. ② the act of borrowing or lending something • *I am grateful to Jane for the loan of her book.* ▸ VERB ③ If you loan something to someone, you lend it to them.

loath [*Rhymes with* both] ADJECTIVE If you are loath to do something, you are very unwilling to do it.

SPELLING TIP

Do not confuse the spellings of *loath* the adjective and *loathe* the verb: *I'm loath to ask him for money; I loathe that song.*

---

loathe, loathes, loathing, loathed VERB To loathe someone or something means to feel strong dislike for them. **loathing** NOUN **loathsome** ADJECTIVE

SPELLING TIP

Do not confuse the spellings of *loathe* the verb and *loath* the adjective: *I loathe that song; I'm loath to ask him for money.*

---

lob, lobs, lobbing, lobbed VERB ① If you lob something, you throw it high in the air. ▸ NOUN ② In tennis, a lob is a stroke in which the player hits the ball high in the air.

lobby, lobbies, lobbying, lobbied NOUN ① The lobby in a building is the main entrance area with corridors and doors leading off it. ② a group of people trying to persuade an organisation that something should be done • *the environmental lobby.*

▸ VERB ③ To lobby an MP or an organisation means to try to persuade them to do something, for example by writing them lots of letters.

lobe, lobes NOUN ① The lobe of your ear is the rounded soft part at the bottom. ② any rounded part of something • *the frontal lobe of the brain.*

lobola [*Said* law-baw-la] NOUN Lobola is a southern African custom by which a bridegroom's family makes a payment in cattle or cash to the bride's family shortly before the marriage.

lobster, lobsters NOUN an edible shellfish with two front claws and eight legs.

local, locals ADJECTIVE ① Local means in, near or belonging to the area in which you live • *the local newspaper.* ② A local anaesthetic numbs only one part of your body and does not send you to sleep. ▸ NOUN ③ The locals are the people who live in a particular area. ④ (*informal*) Someone's local is the pub nearest their home. **locally** ADVERB
SIMILAR WORDS: ① provincial, regional

localised; also spelt **localized** ADJECTIVE existing or happening in only one place • *localised pain.*

locality, localities NOUN an area of a country or city • *a large map of the locality.*

locate, locates, locating, located VERB ① To locate someone or something means to find out where they are. ② If something is located in a place, it is in that place.

location, locations NOUN ① GEOGRAPHY a place, or the position of something. ② In South Africa, a location was a small town where only Black people or Coloured people were allowed to live.

SIMILAR WORDS: ① place, position

loch, lochs NOUN In Scottish English, a loch is a lake.

lock, locks, locking, locked VERB ① If you lock something, you close it and fasten it with a key. ② If something locks into place, it moves into place and becomes firmly fixed there. ▶ NOUN ③ a device on something which fastens it and prevents it from being opened except with a key. ④ A lock on a canal is a place where the water level can be raised or lowered to allow boats to go between two parts of the canal which have different water levels. ⑤ A lock of hair is a small bunch of hair.

lockdown, lockdowns NOUN If there is a lockdown, or a place is in lockdown, people must stay indoors in order to keep themselves and other people safe.

locker, lockers NOUN a small cupboard for your personal belongings, for example in a changing room.

locket, lockets NOUN a piece of jewellery consisting of a small case which you can keep a photograph in, and which you wear on a chain round your neck.

locksmith, locksmiths NOUN a person who makes or mends locks.

locomotion NOUN Locomotion is movement or the power to move.

locomotive, locomotives NOUN a railway engine.

locomotor ADJECTIVE to do with locomotion • *locomotor skills such as running*.

locus, loci NOUN MATHS A locus is a set of points whose position satisfies a particular condition. For example, a circle is the locus of points in the plane at the same distance from a central point.

locust, locusts NOUN an insect like a large grasshopper, which travels in huge swarms and eats crops.

lodge, lodges, lodging, lodged NOUN ① a small house in the grounds of a large country house, or a small house used for holidays. ▶ VERB ② If you lodge in someone else's house, you live there and pay them rent. ③ If something lodges somewhere, it gets stuck there.

lodger, lodgers NOUN a person who lives in someone's house and pays rent.

loft, lofts NOUN the space immediately under the roof of a house, often used for storing things.

lofty, loftier, loftiest ADJECTIVE ① very high • *a lofty hall*. ② very noble and important • *lofty ideals*. ③ proud and superior • *her lofty manner*.

log, logs, logging, logged NOUN ① a thick branch or piece of tree trunk which has fallen or been cut down. ② the captain's official record of everything that happens on board a ship. ▶ VERB ③ If you log something, you officially make a record of it, for example in a ship's log. ④ To log into a computer system means to gain access to it, usually by giving your name and password. To log out means to finish using the system.

logarithm, logarithms NOUN MATHS In mathematics, every number has a logarithm to a particular base. Logarithms to the base 10 are arranged in tables to make calculations easier. For example, you can add or subtract the logarithms of two numbers instead of multiplying or dividing the numbers.

logic NOUN Logic is a way of reasoning involving a series of statements, each of which must be true if the statement before it is true.

logical ADJECTIVE ①A logical argument uses logic. ②A logical course of action or decision is sensible or reasonable in the circumstances. **logically** ADVERB

logistics NOUN (formal) The logistics of a complicated undertaking is the skilful organisation of it.

logo, logos [Said **loh-goh**] NOUN The logo of an organisation is a special design that is put on all its products.
WORD HISTORY: from Greek logos meaning 'word'

-logy SUFFIX '-logy' is used to form words that refer to the study of something • biology • geology • anthropology.

loin, loins NOUN ① (old-fashioned) Your loins are the front part of your body between your waist and your thighs. ② Loin is a piece of meat from the back or sides of an animal • loin of pork.

loiter, loiters, loitering, loitered VERB To loiter means to stand about idly with no real purpose.

loll, lolls, lolling, lolled VERB ① If you loll somewhere, you sit or lie there in an idle, relaxed way. ② If your head or tongue lolls, it hangs loosely.

lollipop, lollipops NOUN a hard sweet on the end of a stick.

lolly, lollies NOUN ① a lollipop. ② a piece of flavoured ice or ice cream on a stick. ③ In Australian and New Zealand English, a lolly is a sweet.

lolly scramble, lolly scrambles NOUN In New Zealand, a lolly scramble is a lot of sweets thrown on the ground for children to pick up.

lone ADJECTIVE A lone person or thing is the only one in a particular place • a lone climber.
SIMILAR WORDS: single, solitary

lonely, lonelier, loneliest ADJECTIVE ① If you are lonely, you are unhappy because you are alone. ② A lonely place is an isolated one which very few people visit • a lonely hillside.
loneliness NOUN

loner, loners NOUN a person who likes to be alone.

lonesome ADJECTIVE lonely and sad.

long, longer, longest; longs, longing, longed ADJECTIVE ① continuing for a great amount of time • There had been no rain for a long time. ▶ ADJECTIVE ② great in length or distance • a long dress • a long road. ▶ ADVERB ③ for a certain period of time • How long will it last? ④ for an extensive period of time • long into the following year. ▶ PHRASE ⑤ If something **no longer** happens, it does not happen any more. ⑥ **Before long** means soon. ⑦ If one thing is true **as long as** another thing is true, it is true only if the other thing is true. ▶ VERB ⑧ If you long for something, you want it very much.

longbow, longbows NOUN HISTORY a very tall bow used to fire long arrows in medieval times.

longevity [Said lon-**jev**-it-ee] NOUN (formal) Longevity is long life.

longhand NOUN If you write something in longhand, you do it in your own handwriting rather than using shorthand or a computer.

longing, longings NOUN a strong wish for something.

longitude, longitudes NOUN GEOGRAPHY The longitude of a place is its distance east or west of a meridian line passing through Greenwich, measured in degrees.

a
b
c
d
e
f
g
h
i
j
k
l
m
n
o
p
q
r
s
t
u
v
w
x
y
z

longitudinal ADJECTIVE SCIENCE
Longitudinal is used to describe something that goes in the same direction as something else rather than at right angles to it • *longitudinal waves*.

long jump NOUN The long jump is an athletics event in which you jump as far as possible after taking a long run.

long-range ADJECTIVE ① able to be used over a great distance • *long-range artillery*. ② extending a long way into the future • *a long-range weather forecast*.

longship, longships NOUN HISTORY a narrow open ship with oars and a square sail, used by the Vikings.

long-sighted ADJECTIVE If you are long-sighted, you have difficulty seeing things that are close.

long-standing ADJECTIVE having existed for a long time • *a long-standing tradition*.

long-suffering ADJECTIVE very patient • *her long-suffering father*.

long-term ADJECTIVE extending a long way into the future • *a long-term investment*.

long-winded ADJECTIVE long and boring • *a long-winded letter*.

loo, loos NOUN (*informal*) a toilet.

look, looks, looking, looked VERB ① If you look at something, you turn your eyes towards it so that you can see it. ② If you look at a subject or situation, you study it or judge it. ③ If you look down on someone, you think that they are inferior to you. ④ If you are looking forward to something, you want it to happen because you think you will enjoy it. ⑤ If you look up to someone, you admire and respect them. ⑥ If you describe the way that something or someone looks, you are describing the appearance of it or them. ▶ NOUN ⑦ If you have a look at something, you look at it. ⑧ the way someone or something appears, especially the expression on a person's face. ⑨ If you talk about someone's looks, you are talking about how attractive they are. ▶ INTERJECTION ⑩ You say 'look out' to warn someone of danger.

look after VERB If you look after someone or something, you take care of them. **look for** VERB If you look for someone or something, you try to find them. **look up** VERB ① To look up information means to find it out in a book. ② If you look someone up, you go to see them after not having seen them for a long time. ③ If a situation is looking up, it is improving.

SIMILAR WORDS: ① gaze, glance, see, watch ⑦ glance, glimpse, peek ⑧ appearance, expression

lookalike, lookalikes NOUN a person who looks very like someone else • *an Elvis lookalike*.

lookout, lookouts NOUN ① someone who is watching for danger, or a place where they watch for danger. ▶ PHRASE ② If you are **on the lookout** for something, you are watching for it or waiting expectantly for it.

loom, looms, looming, loomed NOUN ① a machine for weaving cloth. ▶ VERB ② If something looms in front of you, it suddenly appears as a tall, unclear and sometimes frightening shape. ③ If a situation or event is looming, it is likely to happen soon and is rather worrying.

loony, loonier, looniest; loonies (*slang*) ADJECTIVE ① Behaviour might be described as loony if it is very foolish or eccentric. ▶ NOUN ② a very foolish or eccentric person.

loop, loops, looping, looped NOUN ① a curved or circular shape in something long such as a piece of string. ▶ VERB ② If you loop rope or string around an object, you place it in a loop around the object.

loophole, loopholes NOUN a small mistake or omission in the law which allows you to do something that the law really intends that you should not do.

loose, looser, loosest ADJECTIVE ① If something is loose, it is not firmly held, fixed or attached. ② Loose clothes are rather large and do not fit closely. ▶ ADVERB ③ To set animals loose means to set them free after they have been tied up or kept in a cage. **loosely** ADVERB

SPELLING TIP
The adjective and adverb *loose* is spelt with two *o*s. Do not confuse it with the verb *lose*.

loosen, loosens, loosening, loosened VERB To loosen something means to make it looser.

loot, loots, looting, looted VERB ① To loot shops and houses means to steal goods from them during a battle or riot. ▶ NOUN ② Loot is stolen money or goods.
SIMILAR WORDS: ① pillage, plunder, ransack ② booty, plunder, spoils
WORD HISTORY: from Hindi *lut*

lop, lops, lopping, lopped VERB If you lop something off, you cut it off with one quick stroke.

lopsided ADJECTIVE Something that is lopsided is uneven because its two sides are different sizes or shapes.

lord, lords NOUN ① a nobleman. ② Lord is a title used in front of the names of some noblemen, and of bishops, archbishops, judges and some high-ranking officials • *the Lord Mayor of London*. ③ In Christianity, Lord is a name given to God and Jesus Christ.

Lordship, Lordships NOUN You address a lord, judge or bishop as Your Lordship.

lore NOUN The lore of a place, people or subject is all the traditional knowledge and stories about it.

lorikeet, lorikeets NOUN a type of small parrot found in Australia.

lorry, lorries NOUN a large vehicle for transporting goods by road.

lory, lories [Said *law-ree*] NOUN a small, brightly coloured parrot found in Australia.

lose, loses, losing, lost VERB ① If you lose something, you cannot find it, or you no longer have it because it has been taken away from you • *I lost my jacket*. ② If you lose a relative or friend, they die • *She lost her brother in the war*. ③ If you lose a fight or an argument, you are beaten. ④ If a business loses money, it is spending more money than it is earning.

SPELLING TIP
The verb *lose* is spelt with one *o*. Do not confuse it with the adjective and adverb *loose*.

loser NOUN ① a person who is defeated in a game, contest or struggle. ② (*informal*) If you refer to someone as a loser, you have a low opinion of them because you think they are always unsuccessful.

loss, losses NOUN ① The loss of something is the losing of it. ▶ PHRASE ② If you are **at a loss**, you do not know what to do.

lost ADJECTIVE ① If you are lost, you do not know where you are. ② If something is lost, you cannot find it. ③ Lost is the past tense and past participle of **lose**.

lot, lots PHRASE ① **A lot** of something, or lots of something, is a large amount of it. ② **A lot** means very

a
b
c
d
e
f
g
h
i
j
k
l
m
n
o
p
q
r
s
t
u
v
w
x
y
z

much or very often • *I love him a lot.*
▶ NOUN ③ an amount of something or a number of things • *I've answered the first lot of questions.* ④ In an auction, a lot is one of the things being sold.

SIMILAR WORDS: ① abundance, loads, plenty

SPELLING TIP
Remember that *a lot* is written as two separate words.

lotion, lotions NOUN a liquid that you put on your skin to protect or soften it • *suntan lotion.*

lottery, lotteries NOUN a method of raising money by selling tickets by which a winner is selected at random.

lotus, lotuses NOUN a large water lily, found in Africa and Asia.

loud, louder, loudest ADJECTIVE or ADVERB ① A loud noise has a high volume of sound • *a loud explosion.* ② If you describe clothing as loud, you mean that it is too bright • *a loud tie.* **loudly** ADVERB **loudness** NOUN

loudspeaker, loudspeakers NOUN a piece of equipment that makes your voice louder when you speak into a microphone connected to it.

lounge, lounges, lounging, lounged NOUN ① a room in a house or hotel with comfortable chairs where people can relax. ② The lounge or lounge bar in a pub or hotel is a more expensive and comfortably furnished bar. ▶ VERB ③ If you lounge around, you lean against something or sit or lie around in a lazy and comfortable way.

lourie, louries [*Rhymes with floury*] NOUN one of two types of bird found in South Africa. The grey lourie lives in open grassland and the other more brightly coloured species lives in forests and wooded areas.

louse, lice NOUN Lice are small insects that live on people's bodies • *head lice.*

lousy, lousier, lousiest ADJECTIVE (*informal*) ① of bad quality or very unpleasant • *The weather is lousy.* ② ill or unhappy.

lout, louts NOUN a young man who behaves in an aggressive and rude way.

lovable; also spelt **loveable** ADJECTIVE having very attractive qualities and therefore easy to love • *a lovable black mongrel.*

love, loves, loving, loved VERB ① If you love someone, you have strong emotional feelings of affection for them. ② If you love something, you like it very much • *We both love fishing.* ③ If you would love to do something, you want very much to do it • *I would love to live there.* ▶ NOUN ④ Love is a strong emotional feeling of affection for someone or something. ⑤ a strong liking for something. ⑥ In tennis, love is a score of zero.
▶ PHRASE ⑦ If you are **in love** with someone, you feel strongly attracted to them romantically.
SIMILAR WORDS: ① adore, dote on

love affair, love affairs NOUN a romantic relationship between two people.

love life, love lives NOUN a person's romantic relationships.

lovelorn ADJECTIVE miserable because of unreturned love or an unhappy love affair.

lovely, lovelier, loveliest ADJECTIVE very beautiful, attractive and pleasant. **loveliness** NOUN

lover, lovers NOUN ① Someone who is a lover of something, for example art or music, is very fond of it. ② A person's lover is someone that they have a romantic relationship with but are not married to.

loving ADJECTIVE feeling or showing love. **lovingly** ADVERB

low, lower, lowest ADJECTIVE
① Something that is low is close to the ground, or measures a short distance from the ground to the top • *a low stool*. ② Low means small in value or amount. ③ A low sound is deep and quiet. ④ 'Low' is used to describe people who are considered not respectable • *mixing with low company*. ▶ ADVERB ⑤ in a low position, level or degree. ▶ NOUN ⑥ a level or amount that is less than before • *Sales hit a new low*.

lowboy, lowboys NOUN In Australian and New Zealand English, a lowboy is a small wardrobe or chest of drawers.

lower, lowers, lowering, lowered VERB ① To lower something means to move it downwards. ② To lower something also means to make it less in value or amount.

lower case ADJECTIVE ENGLISH Lower case letters are the small letters used in printing.

lowest common multiple, lowest common multiples NOUN MATHS In a group of numbers, the lowest common multiple is the smallest number that can be divided by each number in the group and leave no remainder. For example, the lowest common multiple of 3, 5 and 6 is 30.

lowlands PLURAL NOUN Lowlands are an area of flat, low land. **lowland** ADJECTIVE

lowly, lowlier, lowliest ADJECTIVE low in importance, rank or status.

low tide, low tides NOUN On a coast, low tide is the time, usually twice a day, when the sea is at its lowest level.

lowveld [*Said loh-felt*] NOUN Lowveld is another name for bushveld.

loyal ADJECTIVE firm in your friendship or support for someone or something. **loyally** ADVERB **loyalty** NOUN

loyalist, loyalists NOUN a person who remains firm in their support for a government or ruler.

lozenge, lozenges NOUN ① a type of sweet with medicine in it, which you suck to relieve a sore throat or cough. ② a diamond shape.

Ltd an abbreviation for 'limited'; used after the names of some companies.

lubricate, lubricates, lubricating, lubricated VERB To lubricate something such as a machine means to put oil or an oily substance onto it, so that it moves smoothly and friction is reduced. **lubrication** NOUN **lubricant** NOUN

lucid ADJECTIVE ① Lucid writing or speech is clear and easy to understand. ② Someone who is lucid after having been ill or delirious is able to think clearly again.

luck NOUN Luck is anything that seems to happen by chance and not through your own efforts.
SIMILAR WORDS: chance, fortune

luckless ADJECTIVE unsuccessful or unfortunate • *We reduced our luckless opponents to shattered wrecks*.

lucky, luckier, luckiest ADJECTIVE ① Someone who is lucky has a lot of good luck. ② Something that is lucky happens by chance and has good effects or consequences. **luckily** ADVERB

lucrative ADJECTIVE Something that is lucrative earns you a lot of money • *a lucrative sponsorship deal*.

lucre NOUN another word for money, often used humorously.

Luddite, Luddites NOUN ① HISTORY The Luddites were a group of workers who destroyed machines in order to protest against industrialization in

a b c d e f g h i j k l m n o p q r s t u v w x y z

the early 19th century. ② someone who opposes the introduction of new machines and working methods.

ludicrous ADJECTIVE completely foolish, unsuitable or ridiculous.

lug, lugs, lugging, lugged VERB If you lug a heavy object around, you carry it with difficulty.

luggage NOUN Your luggage is the bags and suitcases that you take with you when you travel.

lukewarm ADJECTIVE ① slightly warm • *a mug of lukewarm tea.* ② not very enthusiastic or interested • *The report was given a polite but lukewarm response.*

lull, lulls, lulling, lulled NOUN ① a pause in something, or a short time when it is quiet and nothing much happens • *There was a temporary lull in the fighting.* ▶ VERB ② If you are lulled into feeling safe, someone or something causes you to feel safe at a time when you are not safe • *We had been lulled into a false sense of security.*

lullaby, lullabies NOUN a song used for sending a baby or child to sleep.

lumber, lumbers, lumbering, lumbered NOUN ① Lumber is wood that has been roughly cut up. ② Lumber is also old unwanted furniture and other items. ▶ VERB ③ If you lumber around, you move heavily and clumsily. ④ (*informal*) If you are lumbered with something, you are given it to deal with even though you do not want it • *I was lumbered with looking after my little brother.*

luminary, luminaries NOUN (*literary*) a person who is famous or an expert in a particular subject.

luminous ADJECTIVE Something that is luminous glows in the dark, usually

because it has been treated with a special substance • *The luminous dial on her clock.* **luminosity** NOUN

lump, lumps, lumping, lumped NOUN ① A lump of something is a solid piece of it, of any shape or size • *a big lump of dough.* ② a bump on the surface of something. ▶ VERB ③ If you lump people or things together, you combine them into one group or consider them as being similar in some way. **lumpy** ADJECTIVE

lump sum, lump sums NOUN a large sum of money given or received all at once.

lunacy NOUN ① Lunacy is extremely foolish or eccentric behaviour. ② (*old-fashioned*) insanity.

lunar ADJECTIVE relating to the moon. WORD HISTORY: from Latin *luna* meaning 'moon'

lunatic, lunatics NOUN ① If you call someone a lunatic, you mean that they are very foolish • *He drives like a lunatic!* ▶ ADJECTIVE ② Lunatic behaviour is very stupid, foolish or dangerous.

lunch, lunches, lunching, lunched NOUN ① a meal eaten in the middle of the day. ▶ VERB ② When you lunch, you eat lunch.

luncheon, luncheons [*Said* **lun**-shen] NOUN (*formal*) Luncheon is lunch.

lung, lungs NOUN Your lungs are the two organs inside your ribcage with which you breathe.

lunge, lunges, lunging, lunged NOUN ① a sudden forward movement • *He made a lunge for the door.* ▶ VERB ② To lunge means to make a sudden movement in a particular direction.

lurch, lurches, lurching, lurched VERB ① To lurch means to make a sudden, jerky movement. ▶ NOUN ② a sudden, jerky movement.

lure, lures, luring, lured VERB ① To lure someone means to attract them into going somewhere or doing something. ▶ NOUN ② something that you find very attractive.

lurid [Said loo-rid] ADJECTIVE ① involving a lot of sensational detail • *lurid stories in the press.* ② very brightly coloured or patterned.

lurk, lurks, lurking, lurked VERB To lurk somewhere means to remain there hidden from the person you are waiting for.

luscious ADJECTIVE very tasty • *luscious fruit.*

lush, lusher, lushest ADJECTIVE In a lush field or garden, the grass or plants are healthy and growing thickly.

lust, lusts, lusting, lusted NOUN ① A lust for something is a strong desire to have it • *a lust for money.* ▶ VERB ② If you lust for or after something, you have a very strong desire to possess it • *She lusted after fame.*

lustre [Said lus-ter] NOUN Lustre is soft shining light reflected from the surface of something • *the lustre of silk.*

lute, lutes NOUN an old-fashioned stringed musical instrument which is plucked like a guitar.

luxuriant ADJECTIVE Luxuriant plants, trees and gardens are large, healthy and growing strongly.

luxurious ADJECTIVE very expensive and full of luxury. **luxuriously** ADVERB

SIMILAR WORDS: opulent, splendid, sumptuous

luxury, luxuries NOUN ① Luxury is great comfort in expensive and beautiful surroundings • *a life of luxury.* ② something that you enjoy very much but do not have very often, usually because it is expensive.
SIMILAR WORDS: ① extravagance, indulgence, treat

-ly SUFFIX ① '-ly' forms adjectives that describe a quality • *friendly.* ② '-ly' forms adjectives that refer to how often something happens or is done • *yearly.* ③ '-ly' forms adverbs that refer to how or in what way something is done • *quickly* • *nicely.*

lying NOUN ① Lying is telling lies. ▶ ADJECTIVE ② A lying person is telling lies. ③ Lying is also the present participle of **lie²**.

lynch, lynches, lynching, lynched VERB If a crowd lynches someone, it kills them in a violent way without first holding a legal trial.

lynx, lynxes NOUN a wildcat with a short tail and tufted ears.

lyre, lyres NOUN a stringed instrument rather like a small harp, which was used in ancient Greece.

lyric, lyrics NOUN ① MUSIC The lyrics of a song are the words. ▶ ADJECTIVE ② Lyric poetry is written in a simple and direct style, and is usually about love.

lyrical ADJECTIVE poetic and romantic.

Essential Guide to Spelling

Tips for Learning Hard Words

You can improve your spelling a lot by learning the rules and getting to know the patterns that come up regularly. However, knowing the principles of spelling can only get you so far. There are times when you just have to learn how to spell a particular word. So here are some tips for getting the tricky words right and getting them to stay in your mind.

① Mnemonics

A **mnemonic**, which is pronounced nim-**on**-nik, is a saying or rhyme that helps you remember something. Mnemonics can help you remember anything, not just spelling. You may already know mnemonics for other things, for example *Richard Of York Gives Battle In Vain*, which is often used as a way to remember the colours of the rainbow (because the first letters of each word correspond to the first letters of the colours red, orange, yellow, green, blue, indigo and violet). Another well-known mnemonic is the verse beginning 'Thirty days has September', which helps you remember how many days are in each month.

Here are some types of mnemonics that can help with spelling.

Initial-letter mnemonics

In some mnemonics, the word you want to remember is spelt out by the initial letters of all the words in a sentence or phrase.

beautiful	=	*Bella escorts an uncle to Italy for unforgettable lunch*
buoy	=	*Big unsinkable ocean yacht*
chaos	=	*Citizens have abolished our system*
gauge	=	*Great Aunt Una grows eggplants*
heir	=	*Happy Edward is rich*
rhythm	=	*Roger hates your terrible heavy metal*

Partial initial-letter mnemonics

In some mnemonics, a phrase just acts as a reminder of how to spell the tricky bits of a word, but does not spell out the whole word.

accelerate	=	*If it can **accele**rate, **a c**ar can **e**asily **l**ead **e**very **r**ace*
attach	=	*Att**ach a c**oat **h**ook to the wall*
familiar	=	*Someone who is famil**iar is a** regular*
jodhpurs	=	*You wear jo**dh**purs when you ride a **d**appled **h**orse*
neurotic	=	*The government is **neu**rotic about the **E**uropean **U**nion*
surgeon	=	*Sur**geon**s **g**raft **e**ars **on***

Partial mnemonics

Another type of mnemonic uses words or syllables that are contained within the difficult word to help you remember it.

address	=	***Add** your **add**ress*
beggar	=	*There is a be**ggar** in the **gar**den*
cemetery	=	*A cemet**ery** is **very** scary*
friend	=	*My **fri**end likes **fri**es*
interrupt	=	*It is **terr**ibly rude to inte**rr**upt*
optimistic	=	***Tim** is op**tim**istic*

But the best mnemonics are often ones that you make up yourself. If you base these phrases around words and topics that mean something to you, you are more likely to remember them. For example, you might use the names of your friends, your pets, or your family members, or you might make up sentences that relate to your interests. Try to make up your own mnemonics for words you find hard to remember.

② Look, Say, Cover, Write, Check

Another way of learning how to spell a word is to go through five stages: look, say, cover, write, check.

- **Look** at the word carefully.
- **Say** the word aloud to yourself, listening to how it sounds.
- **Cover** the word and try to remember what it looks like.
- **Write** the word.
- **Check** what you have written to see if you got it right.

If you haven't got the word right, go through the five steps again until you can spell it correctly.

③ Breaking down the word into its parts

Another good way of learning a word is to break it down into its syllables, and sound them out, pronouncing even the silent letters.

business	=	*bus + i + ness*
dictionary	=	*dic + ti + on + ar + y*
ecstasy	=	*ec + sta + sy*
handkerchief	=	*hand + ker + chief*
laboratory	=	*lab + or + a + tor + y*
material	=	*ma + te + ri + al*
separate	=	*se + par + ate*
Wednesday	=	*Wed + nes + day*

Get into the habit of looking at words in this way and you will find it easier to remember how to spell them.

④ Word families

Look for patterns and relations between words. If you know that one word is related to another word, it can help you remember how the word is spelt.

The words below are all related to *act*.

act	**act**ion	**act**ivity
re**act**	re**act**ion	re**act**ive

Other useful related words include:

definite	+	definitive
disciple	+	discipline
excel	+	excellent
irritable	+	irritate
minute	+	minuscule
muscle	+	muscular
sign	+	signature
vehicle	+	vehicular

⑤ Words within words

Look for complete words within the word you are trying to remember, for example:

govern	in	government
iron	in	environment
reign	in	foreign and sovereign
finite	in	definite
get	in	vegetable
vile	in	privilege

Spelling Rules

① **ie** or **ei** The rule is: *i* before *e*, except after *c*:

ach**ie**ve	br**ie**f	ch**ie**f
f**ie**rce	gr**ie**ve	n**ie**ce
rel**ie**f	s**ie**ge	th**ie**f
c**ei**ling	conc**ei**t	dec**ei**t
dec**ei**ve	rec**ei**pt	rec**ei**ve

There are some exceptions:

s**ei**ze	prot**ei**n

② **-ise** or **-ize** In this dictionary, the endings *-ise* (and *-isation*) are used for verbs (and their nouns) such as *emphasise*, *organise* (*organisation*) and *patronise*. Many of these words can also be spelled with the endings *-ize* (and *-ization*), and that is the normal spelling in American English. Care should be taken, however, because some words can only be spelled with *-ize* and others only with *-ise*.

Verbs (and nouns) only spelled with *-ize*:

caps**ize**	pr**ize** [= *value highly*]

Verbs (and nouns) only spelled with *-ise*:

advert**ise**	adv**ise**	chast**ise**	compr**ise**	comprom**ise**	desp**ise**
dev**ise**	disgu**ise**	exc**ise**	exerc**ise**	franch**ise**	improv**ise**
pr**ise** [= *force open*]	rev**ise**	superv**ise**	surpr**ise**	telev**ise**	

③ **a**. A final silent *e* is dropped when an ending that begins with a vowel is added:

servile + ity	=	servil**ity**
response + ible	=	respons**ible**
tolerate + ing	=	tolerat**ing**
value + able	=	valu**able**
excuse + ed	=	excus**ed**

b. But the *e* is kept if an ending beginning with a vowel is added to a word that ends in *-ce* or *-ge*:

change + able	=	chang**e**able
notice + able	=	notic**e**able
outrage + ous	=	outrag**e**ous
peace + able	=	peac**e**able

④ When an ending beginning with a vowel is added to a word that ends in a single vowel + a consonant, the consonant is doubled if the stress is on the end of the word:

admit + ance	=	admi**tt**ance
begin + ing	=	begi**nn**ing
occur + ence	=	occu**rr**ence
equip + ed	=	equi**pp**ed

⑤ When an ending beginning with a vowel is added to a word that ends in a vowel + *l* or *p*, the *l* or *p* is usually doubled:

cancel + ation	=	cance**ll**ation
dial + ing	=	dia**ll**ing
fulfil + ed	=	fulfi**ll**ed
kidnap + er	=	kidna**pp**er
slip + ing	=	sli**pp**ing

⑥ When the adverb suffix -*ly* is added to an adjective that ends in a consonant followed by -*le*, the -*le* in the adjective is usually dropped:

gentle + ly	=	gent**ly**
idle + ly	=	id**ly**
subtle + ly	=	subt**ly**

⑦ When the adjective suffix -*ous* or -*ary* is added to a word that ends in -*our*, the *u* of the -*our* is dropped:

glamour + ous	=	glam**o**rous
honour + ary	=	hon**o**rary
humour + ous	=	hum**o**rous

⑧ When an ending beginning with *e*, *i* or *y* is added to a word that ends in *c*, a *k* is added to the *c* to keep its hard sound:

mimic + ed	=	mimic**k**ed
picnic + ing	=	picnic**k**ing

⑨ **a**. When an ending is added to a word that ends in a consonant + *y*, the *y* changes to *i*:

beauty + ful	=	beaut**i**ful
crazy + ly	=	craz**i**ly
woolly + er	=	wooll**i**er

b. But, with certain short adjectives that end in a consonant + *y*, the -*ly* ending to make an adverb is added after the *y*:

shy + ly	=	shy**ly**
wry + ly	=	wry**ly**

⑩ The plural of a word that ends in a consonant + *y* is made by changing the *y* to *i* and adding -*es*:

story + es	=	stor**ies**
quality + es	=	qualit**ies**
spy + es	=	sp**ies**

⑪ The plural of a word that ends in a vowel plus *y* is made by adding -*s*:

donkey + s	=	donkey**s**
holiday + s	=	holiday**s**
boy + s	=	boy**s**
buoy + s	=	buoy**s**

⑫ The plural of a word that ends in *s*, *x*, *z*, *sh* or *ch* is made by adding -*es*:

bus + es	=	bus**es**
mass + es	=	mass**es**
fox + es	=	fox**es**
buzz + es	=	buzz**es**
rash + es	=	rash**es**
match + es	=	match**es**

⑬ The plural of a word that ends in -*eau* is made by adding -*x*:

gateau + x	=	gateau**x**
bureau + x	=	bureau**x**
(bureau**s** is also allowable)		

⑭ **a**. The suffix -*ful* is always spelt with one *l*:

grateful	faithful	cupful

b. But -*fully* is always spelt with two:

gratefully	faithfully	beautifully

Commonly Confused Words and Spellings

accept – verb **except** – prep	*Please accept my apologies.* *He works every day except Tuesday.*
affect – verb **effect** – noun	*Tiredness affects concentration.* *the beneficial effects of the medicine*
aid – noun & verb **aide** – noun	*a plane carrying aid to famine victims • Rest will aid recovery from illness.* *a personal aide to the President*
air – noun & verb **heir** – noun	*The air was full of smoke. • She's always happy to air her views on climate change.* *the heir to his father's business*
allude – verb **elude** – verb	*She alluded to the recent reports in the newspapers.* *I recognised his face, but his name eluded me.*
altar – noun **alter** – verb	*The couple stood before the altar to take their marriage vows.* *His tone altered suddenly.*
ascent – noun **assent** – noun	*the ascent of Everest by Edmund Hillary and Tenzing Norgay* *The king gave his assent to the government's revised bill.*
aural – adjective **oral** – adjective	*high- and low-pitched sounds which test aural function* *He stumbled over his words in the oral examination.*
base – noun **bass** – noun	*the base of the mountain* *the bass player in the band*
born – verb **borne** – verb	*Murray was born in Glasgow.* *He has borne his illness bravely.*
bough – noun **bow** – verb & noun	*the bough of an apple tree* *The men bowed before the king. • a low bow of respect*

breath – noun **breathe** – verb	There wasn't a breath of wind. Breathe deeply a couple of times.
bridal – adjective **bridle** – noun	The bridal party arrived late. I removed the horse's bridle and reins.
broach – verb **brooch** – noun	She didn't dare broach the subject of a pay rise. a gold brooch set with emeralds and diamonds
canvas – noun **canvass** – verb	a hammock made from heavy canvas TV reporters canvassing opinion
chute – noun **shoot** – verb & noun	Put the rubbish bag down the chute. He likes to shoot pheasants. • a turkey shoot
coarse – adjective **course** – noun	a coarse cloth which scratched the skin The river widens along its course.
complement – noun **compliment** – noun	Rice is a good complement to curry. My compliments to the chef.
council – noun **counsel** – verb & noun	the local council • a council of war He counsels victims of crime. • give good counsel
cue – noun **queue** – noun	That's the leading lady's cue. a long queue at the post office
curb – verb **kerb** – noun	trying hard to curb her appetite for chocolate The taxi drew up at the kerb.
currant – noun **current** – noun & adjective	raisins, sultanas and currants ocean currents • current affairs
dependant – noun **dependent** – adjective	Do you have children or other dependants? The flood victims are dependent on international aid.
desert – noun & verb **dessert** – noun	the Gobi Desert • The sentry deserted his post. Would you like ice-cream or fresh fruit for dessert?

draft – noun & verb **draught** – noun	*a first draft of the report • He's drafting a letter to his MP.* *There's a draught coming under that door.*
dual – adjective **duel** – noun **jewel** – noun	*Their children have dual citizenship of Britain and France.* *The two men fought a duel with pistols at dawn.* *I only wear my jewels on special occasions.*
dyeing – verb **dying** – verb	*Have you been dyeing your hair again?* *The weakest are dying first, of hunger and cold.*
emit – verb **omit** – verb	*The child emitted a loud cry.* *The manager omitted him from the team.*
envelop – verb **envelope** – noun	*A greenish haze seemed to envelop the landscape.* *Send a stamped addressed envelope.*
flair – noun **flare** – noun & verb	*a flair for design* *The fishermen lit a flare to attract attention. • The horse's nostrils flared.*
forth – adverb **fourth** – adjective	*They rode forth from the black gates in a great mass.* *the fourth day of July*
foul – adjective, verb & noun **fowl** – noun	*a foul crime • Please do not allow your dog to foul the pavement. • The referee saw the foul but did nothing.* *ducks and other wild fowl*
gamble – verb **gambol** – verb	*gambling on the lottery* *puppies gambolling in the sunshine*
gilt – noun **guilt** – noun	*a clock decorated with silver gilt* *The evidence proves his guilt.*
gorilla – noun **guerrilla** – noun	*the habitat of the mountain gorilla* *The guerrillas have released their prisoners.*
grisly – adjective **grizzly** – adjective	*a series of grisly murders* *We were chased by a grizzly bear.*

hangar – noun **hanger** – noun	*an aircraft hangar* *Your coat is on a hanger in the wardrobe.*
hoard – noun & verb **horde** – noun	*a hoard of treasure • Many people hoard cooking ingredients years past their sell-by date.* *hordes of noisy football fans*
its – adjective **it's** – short form	*The dog broke free of its lead and ran off.* *It's rude to stare.*
lead – verb & noun **led** – verb	*You lead the way. • pipes made of lead* *He was led astray by the other children.*
leant – verb **lent** – verb	*He leant against the tree.* *She lent me her bike.*
licence – noun **license** – verb	*a driving licence* *licensed to drive heavy goods vehicles*
lightening – verb **lightning** – noun	*The sky is lightening now that dawn is approaching.* *The dogs are scared of thunder and lightning.*
loath – adjective **loathe** – verb	*I'm loath to ask him for money.* *We loathe each other.*
loose – adjective **lose** – verb	*His front tooth is loose.* *Be careful not to lose your pocket money.*
mat – noun **matt** – adjective	*Wipe your feet on the mat before you come in.* *I chose a matt paint for the sitting room.*
miner – noun **minor** – adjective & noun	*a coal miner* *a minor inconvenience • a 14-year-old minor*
palate – noun **palette** – noun	*An ulcer on your palate can be very painful.* *The museum has a number of Turner's palettes on display.*
practice – noun **practise** – verb	*a common practice • a dental practice* *He has a law degree but has never practised.*

precede – verb **proceed** – verb	*Summer precedes autumn.* *Let's proceed with the meeting.*
principal – adjective & noun **principle** – noun	*the principal reason • the school principal* *Telling fibs is against my principles.*
program – noun & verb **programme** – noun	*a computer program • The early computers were not easy to program.* *There's a programme I want to watch tonight on Channel 4.*
ring – verb & noun **wring** – verb	*Ring the bell before you open the door. • a ring of trees in the middle of the field* *Wring your towel out and hang it on the line.*
rye – noun **wry** – adjective	*a loaf of rye bread* *She gave me a wry smile as she left the room.*
stationary – adjective **stationery** – noun	*The bus skidded and hit a stationary vehicle.* *paper, envelopes, and other office stationery*
stile – noun **style** – noun & verb	*We climbed the stile and went into the field.* *I enjoy their style of play. • I get my hair styled every two weeks.*
their – adjective **they're** – short form **there** – adverb	*It's not their fault.* *They're not to blame.* *She is standing there.*
tide – noun **tied** – verb	*The tide can come in quickly so you must be careful.* *She tied the parcel with string.*
vain – adjective **vein** – noun	*He's vain and self-opinionated.* *Veins carry blood back to the heart.*
wander – verb **wonder** – verb & noun	*They wandered through the old town looking at the buildings.* *We wondered where the others had got to. • It's a wonder you ever get any work done.*

Commonly Misspelled Words

The English language is notorious for its difficult spelling rules. In the first place, we often have more than one way to spell one sound. *mete*, *meet* and *meat* are pronounced identically, and the same sound is found in *deceit*. While groups like the Spelling Society and even a university professor or two have advocated a simpler approach to English spelling, the rules are unlikely to change in the near future. So in the meantime, we had better learn to spell words in the traditional way. Here is a list of words that are particularly tricky to get right.

accompany	believe	controversy	euthanasia
according	besiege	convenience	exaggerate
achieve	biased	correspond	excellent
address	blatant	criticise	excerpt
advertise	broccoli	curiosity	exist
aggressive	bruise	curriculum	existence
amateur	budget	deceive	explanation
anaesthetic	business	definite	extraordinary
analysis	camouflage	despair	extrovert
ancient	cappuccino	desperate	facetious
anoint	Caribbean	detach	familiar
apartment	category	determined	fascinate
appal	cemetery	develop	February
appalling	cinnamon	dictionary	fluorescent
apparent	commemorate	disappear	foreign
appreciate	commitment	disappoint	forty
aqueduct	committee	disastrous	freight
archaeology	communicate	dissatisfied	frequently
argument	community	ecstasy	fulfil
artefact	comparative	eighth	gauge
attached	compatible	embarrass	glamorous
available	competition	enthral	gorgeous
average	connoisseur	environment	government
awkward	conscience	equip	guarantee
bargain	conscious	equipment	guard
beautiful	consensus	especially	guardian
beige	contemporary	espresso	haemorrhage

hamster	manoeuvre	possession	soldier
handkerchief	margarine	prejudice	sovereign
harass	marvellous	privilege	stomach
height	mathematician	profession	successful
hindrance	mayonnaise	professor	sufficient
honorary	medieval	programme	suggest
humorous	Mediterranean	pronunciation	supersede
hygiene	memento	psychology	suppress
hypocrisy	millennium	query	surprise
identity	millionaire	questionnaire	symbol
idiosyncrasy	miniature	queue	system
immediate	minuscule	receipt	temperature
immediately	mischievous	receive	thorough
independent	misspell	recognise	threshold
indict	mortgage	recommend	tomorrow
individual	muscle	reconnaissance	truly
innocuous	necessary	refrigerator	twelfth
inoculate	neighbour	relevant	unconscious
instalment	niece	restaurant	usual
integrate	nuisance	rhinoceros	until
intelligent	occasion	rhyme	unwieldy
interfere	occupy	rhythm	vacuum
interrupt	occur	sacrifice	vague
introvert	occurrence	sacrilege	variety
irritable	omit	satellite	vegetable
itinerary	opportunity	sausage	vehicle
jealousy	paradigm	schedule	veil
jeopardy	parliament	secretary	veterinary
jewellery	parallel	seize	weight
knight	peculiar	separate	weird
knowledge	perceive	sergeant	whinge
label	permanent	shoulder	wilful
laboratory	persuade	siege	withhold
language	pharaoh	sieve	xylophone
leisure	phlegm	signature	yacht
liaison	physical	silhouette	yield
lieutenant	piece	sincere	
lightning	pigeon	sincerely	
maintenance	playwright	skilful	

Mm

m an abbreviation for 'metres' or 'miles'.

macabre [Said mak-**kahb**-ra] ADJECTIVE A macabre event or story is strange and horrible • *a macabre horror story*.

macadamia, macadamias [Said ma-ka-**dame**-ee-a] NOUN an Australian tree, also grown in New Zealand, that produces edible nuts.

macaroni NOUN Macaroni is short hollow tubes of pasta.
WORD HISTORY: an Italian word; from Greek *makaria* meaning 'food made from barley'

macaroon, macaroons NOUN a sweet biscuit flavoured with almonds or coconut.

mace, maces NOUN an ornamental pole carried by an official during ceremonies as a symbol of authority.

machete, machetes [Said mash-**ett**-ee] NOUN a large, heavy knife with a big blade.

machine, machines, machining, machined NOUN ① DGT a piece of equipment which uses electricity or power from an engine to make it work. ▶VERB ② If you machine something, you make it or work on it using a machine.

machine-gun, machine-guns NOUN a gun that works automatically, firing bullets one after the other.

machinery NOUN Machinery is machines in general.

machismo [Said mak-**kiz**-moe] NOUN Machismo is exaggerated aggressive male behaviour.

macho [Said **mat**-shoh] ADJECTIVE A man who is described as macho behaves in an aggressively masculine way.
WORD HISTORY: from Spanish *macho* meaning 'male'

mackerel, mackerels NOUN a sea fish with blue and silver stripes.

mackintosh, mackintoshes NOUN a raincoat made from specially treated waterproof cloth.

mad, madder, maddest ADJECTIVE ① Someone who is mad does not think in a normal way and may behave in strange ways. ② (*informal*) If you describe someone as mad, you mean that they are very foolish • *He said we were mad to share a flat*. ③ (*informal*) Someone who is mad is angry. ④ (*informal*) If you are mad about someone or something, you like them very much • *Alan was mad about golf*. **madness** NOUN **madman** NOUN
SIMILAR WORDS: ① crazy, deranged, insane ② daft, foolish

madam NOUN 'Madam' is a very formal way of addressing a woman.

maddening ADJECTIVE irritating or frustrating • *She had many maddening habits*.

made the past tense and past participle of **make**.

madly ADVERB If you do something madly, you do it in a fast, excited way.

madrigal, madrigals NOUN a song sung by several people without instruments.

maestro, maestros [Said **mye-stroh**] NOUN a skilled and well-known musician.

Mafia NOUN The Mafia is a large crime organisation operating in Italy and the USA.

magazine, magazines NOUN ① LIBRARY a weekly or monthly publication with articles and photographs. ② a compartment in a gun for cartridges.
WORD HISTORY: from Arabic *makhzan* meaning 'storehouse'

magenta [Said **maj-jen-ta**] NOUN or ADJECTIVE dark reddish-purple.

maggot, maggots NOUN a creature that looks like a small worm and lives on decaying things. Maggots turn into flies.

magic NOUN ① In fairy stories, magic is a special power that can make impossible things happen. ② Magic is the art of performing tricks to entertain people.

magical ADJECTIVE wonderful and exciting. **magically** ADVERB

magician, magicians NOUN ① a person who performs tricks as entertainment. ② In fairy stories, a magician is a man with magical powers.

magistrate, magistrates NOUN an official who acts as a judge in a law court that deals with less serious crimes.

magma NOUN GEOGRAPHY Magma is a hot liquid beneath the earth's surface which forms igneous rock when it solidifies.

magnanimous ADJECTIVE generous and forgiving.

magnate, magnates NOUN someone who is very rich and powerful in business.

magnesium NOUN SCIENCE Magnesium is a metallic element which burns with a bright white flame. It is used in fireworks, flashbulbs and flares. Its atomic number is 12 and its symbol is Mg.

magnet, magnets NOUN SCIENCE a piece of iron which attracts iron or steel towards it, and which points towards north if allowed to swing freely. A **permanent magnet** is a magnet that is still magnetic when the magnetic field that produced it is taken away; a **temporary magnet** is a magnet that loses its magnetism when the magnetic field that produced it is taken away. **magnetic** ADJECTIVE **magnetism** NOUN

magnetic field, magnetic fields NOUN SCIENCE the area around a magnet inside which a magnetic force is felt.

magnificent ADJECTIVE extremely beautiful or impressive.
magnificently ADVERB
magnificence NOUN

magnify, magnifies, magnifying, magnified VERB SCIENCE When a microscope or lens magnifies something, it makes it appear bigger than it actually is. **magnification** NOUN

magnifying glass, magnifying glasses NOUN a lens which makes things appear bigger than they really are.

magnitude NOUN The magnitude of something is its great size or importance.

magnolia, magnolias NOUN a tree which has large white or pink flowers in spring.

magpie, magpies NOUN a large black and white bird with a long tail.

mahogany NOUN Mahogany is a hard, reddish-brown wood used for making furniture.

maid, maids NOUN a female servant.

maiden, maidens NOUN ① (*literary*) a young woman. ▸ ADJECTIVE ② first • *a maiden voyage*.

maiden name, maiden names NOUN the surname a woman had before she married.

mail, mails, mailing, mailed NOUN ① Your mail is the letters and parcels delivered to you by the post office. ▸ VERB ② If you mail a letter, you send it by post.

mailbox, mailboxes NOUN ① Mainly in American English, a mailbox is a postbox. ② On a computer, your mailbox is the file where your email is stored.

mail order NOUN Mail order is a system of buying goods by post.

maim, maims, maiming, maimed VERB To maim someone is to injure them very badly for life.

main, mains ADJECTIVE ① most important • *the main event*. ▸ NOUN ② The mains are large pipes or wires that carry gas, water or electricity. SIMILAR WORDS: ① chief, major, principal

mainframe, mainframes NOUN a large computer which can be used by many people at the same time.

mainland NOUN The mainland is the main part of a country in contrast to islands around its coast.

mainly ADVERB true in most cases.

mainstay NOUN The mainstay of something is the most important part of it.

mainstream NOUN The mainstream is the most ordinary and conventional group of people or ideas in a society.

maintain, maintains, maintaining, maintained VERB ① If you maintain something, you keep it going or keep it at a particular rate or level • *I wanted to maintain our friendship.* ② If you maintain someone, you provide them regularly with money for what they need. ③ To maintain a machine or a building is to keep it in good condition. ④ If you maintain that something is true, you believe it is true and say so.

maintenance NOUN ① Maintenance is the process of keeping something in good condition. ② Maintenance is also money that a person sends regularly to someone to provide for the things they need.

maize NOUN Maize is a tall plant which produces sweet corn.

majesty, majesties NOUN ① Majesty is great dignity and impressiveness. ② 'Majesty' is used in the title and form of address for kings and queens • *Her Majesty, Queen Victoria.* **majestic** ADJECTIVE **majestically** ADVERB

major, majors ADJECTIVE ① more important or more significant than other things • *the major political parties.* ② MUSIC A major key is one of the keys in which most European music is written. In a major key the third note is four semitones higher than the first. ▸ NOUN ③ an army officer of the rank immediately above captain.

majority, majorities NOUN ① The majority of people or things in a group is more than half of the group. ② In an election, the majority is the difference between the number of votes gained by the winner and the number gained by the runner-up.

a b c d e f g h i j k l **m** n o p q r s t u v w x y z

USAGE NOTE
You should use *majority* only to talk about things that can be counted: *the majority of car owners*. To talk about an amount that cannot be counted you should use *most*: *Most of the harvest was saved.*

make, makes, making, made VERB
① To make something is to produce or construct it, or to cause it to happen. ② To make something is to do it • *He was about to make a speech.* ③ To make something is to prepare it • *I'll make some salad dressing.* ④ If someone makes you do something, they force you to do it • *Mum made me clean the bathroom.* ▶ NOUN ⑤ The make of a product is the name of the company that manufactured it • *'What make of car do you drive?'* — *'A Toyota.'* **make up** VERB ① If a number of things make up something, they form that thing. ② If you make up a story, you invent it. ③ If you make yourself up, you put make-up on. ④ If two people make it up, they become friends again after a quarrel.
SIMILAR WORDS: ① create, fashion, form, produce ⑤ brand, kind, type

makeshift ADJECTIVE temporary and of poor quality • *The refugees were put into makeshift shelters.*

make-up NOUN ① Make-up is coloured creams and powders which people put on their faces to make themselves look more attractive. ② Someone's make-up is their character or personality.

making NOUN ① The making of something is the act or process of creating or producing it. ▶ PHRASE ② When you describe someone as something **in the making**, you mean that they are gradually becoming that thing • *a captain in the making.*

maladjusted ADJECTIVE A maladjusted person has psychological or behaviour problems.

malaise [*Said mal-laze*] NOUN (*formal*) Malaise is a feeling of dissatisfaction or unhappiness.

malaria [*Said mal-lay-ree-a*] NOUN Malaria is a tropical disease caught from mosquitoes which causes fever and shivering.

Malaysian, Malaysians ADJECTIVE ① belonging or relating to Malaysia. ▶ NOUN ② someone who comes from Malaysia.

male, males NOUN ① a person or animal belonging to the sex that cannot give birth or lay eggs. ▶ ADJECTIVE ② concerning or relating to males.

male chauvinist, male chauvinists NOUN a man who thinks that men are better than women.

malevolent [*Said mal-lev-oh-lent*] ADJECTIVE (*formal*) wanting or intending to cause harm. **malevolence** NOUN
SIMILAR WORDS: malicious, spiteful, vindictive

malfunction, malfunctions, malfunctioning, malfunctioned VERB ① If a machine or part of the body malfunctions, it fails to work properly. ▶ NOUN ② the failure of a machine or part of the body to work properly.

malice NOUN Malice is a desire to cause harm to people.

malicious ADJECTIVE Malicious talk or behaviour is intended to harm someone.

malign, maligns, maligning, maligned (*formal*) VERB ① To malign someone means to say unpleasant and untrue things about them. ▶ ADJECTIVE ② intended to harm someone.

WORD HISTORY: from Latin *malignus* meaning 'spiteful'

malignant ADJECTIVE ① harmful and cruel. ② A malignant disease or tumour could cause death if it is allowed to continue.

mall, **mall** NOUN a very large enclosed shopping area.

mallard, **mallards** NOUN a kind of wild duck. The male has a green head.

malleable ADJECTIVE (*formal*) ① easily influenced by other people. ② If a metal or other substance is malleable, it is soft enough to be made into different shapes • *Gold and silver are the most malleable of all metals.* **malleability** NOUN

mallee, **mallees** NOUN a eucalyptus that grows close to the ground in dry areas of Australia.

mallet, **mallets** NOUN a wooden hammer with a square head.

malnutrition NOUN SCIENCE Malnutrition is not eating enough food, or enough healthy food.

malodorous ADJECTIVE If you describe something as malodorous, you mean it smells bad.

malpractice NOUN If someone such as a doctor or lawyer breaks the rules of their profession, their behaviour is called malpractice.

malt NOUN Malt is roasted grain, usually barley, that is used in making beer and whisky.

malware NOUN Computer programs that are designed to damage or disrupt a system are known as malware.

mammal, **mammals** NOUN SCIENCE Animals that give birth to live babies and feed their young with milk from the mother's body are called mammals. Human beings, dogs and whales are all mammals.

mammoth, **mammoths** ADJECTIVE ① very large indeed • *a mammoth outdoor concert.* ▶ NOUN ② a huge animal that looked like a hairy elephant with long tusks. Mammoths became extinct a long time ago.

man, **men**; **mans**, **manning**, **manned** NOUN ① an adult male human being. ▶ PLURAL NOUN ② 'Man' is sometimes used to refer to human beings in general, including men and women • *Man's responsibility to look after the planet.* ▶ VERB ③ To man something is to be in charge of it or operate it • *Two officers were manning the radar screens.*
SIMILAR WORDS: ① bloke, chap, guy ② humanity, mankind

mana NOUN Mana is authority and influence such as that held by a New Zealand Māori chief.

manacle, **manacles** NOUN Manacles are metal rings or clamps attached to a prisoner's wrists or ankles.

manage, **manages**, **managing**, **managed** VERB ① If you manage to do something, you succeed in doing it • *We managed to find somewhere to sit.* ② If you manage an organisation or business, you are responsible for controlling it.
SIMILAR WORDS: ① accomplish, succeed

manageable ADJECTIVE able to be dealt with.

management NOUN ① The management of a business is the controlling and organising of it. ② The people who control an organisation are called the management.
SIMILAR WORDS: ① administration, control, running

manager, **managers** NOUN a person responsible for running a business or organisation • *a bank manager.*

a
b
c
d
e
f
g
h
i
j
k
l
m
n
o
p
q
r
s
t
u
v
w
x
y
z

USAGE NOTE
In business, the word *manager* can apply to either a man or a woman.

manageress, **manageresses** NOUN a woman responsible for running a business or organisation.

managing director, **managing directors** NOUN a company director who is responsible for the way the company is managed.

mandarin, **mandarins** NOUN a type of small orange which is easy to peel.

mandate, **mandates** NOUN (*formal*) A government's mandate is the authority it has to carry out particular policies as a result of winning an election.

mandatory ADJECTIVE If something is mandatory, there is a law or rule stating that it must be done • *Attendance at the meeting is mandatory.*

mandir, **mandirs** [*Said mun-dir*] NOUN a Hindu temple.
WORD HISTORY: a Hindi word

mandolin, **mandolins** NOUN a musical instrument like a small guitar with a deep, rounded body.

mane, **manes** NOUN the long hair growing from the neck of a lion or horse.

manger, **mangers** [*Said main-jir*] NOUN a feeding box in a barn or stable.

mangle, **mangles**, **mangling**, **mangled** VERB ① If something is mangled, it is crushed and twisted. ▸ NOUN ② an old-fashioned piece of equipment consisting of two large rollers which squeeze water out of wet clothes.

mango, **mangoes** or **mangos** NOUN a sweet yellowish fruit which grows in tropical countries.

manhole, **manholes** NOUN a covered hole in the ground leading to a drain or sewer.

manhood NOUN Manhood is the state of being a man rather than a boy.

mania, **manias** NOUN ① a strong liking for something • *a mania for plant collecting.* ② a mental condition characterised by periods of great excitement.
WORD HISTORY: from Greek *mania* meaning 'madness'

maniac, **maniacs** NOUN a person who is violent and dangerous.

manic ADJECTIVE energetic and excited • *a manic rush to the airport.*

manicure, **manicures**, **manicuring**, **manicured** VERB ① If you manicure your hands, you care for them by softening the skin and shaping and polishing the nails. ▸ NOUN ② A manicure is a special treatment for the hands and nails. **manicurist** NOUN

manifest, **manifests**, **manifesting**, **manifested** (*formal*) ADJECTIVE ① obvious or easily seen • *his manifest enthusiasm.* ▸ VERB ② To manifest something is to make people aware of it • *Fear can manifest itself in many ways.*

manifestation, **manifestations** NOUN (*formal*) A manifestation of something is a sign that it is happening or exists • *The illness may be a manifestation of stress.*

manifesto, **manifestoes** or **manifestos** NOUN a published statement of the aims and policies of a political party.

manipulate, **manipulates**, **manipulating**, **manipulated** VERB ① To manipulate people or events is to control or influence them to produce a particular result. ② If you manipulate a piece of equipment, you control it in a skilful way.

manipulation NOUN **manipulator** NOUN **manipulative** ADJECTIVE

mankind NOUN 'Mankind' is used to refer to all human beings • *a threat to mankind.*

manly, manlier, manliest ADJECTIVE having qualities that are typically masculine • *He laughed a deep, manly laugh.*

manner, manners NOUN ① The manner in which you do something is the way you do it. ② Your manner is the way in which you behave and talk • *his kind manner.* ③ (*in plural*) If you have good manners, you behave very politely.

mannerism, mannerisms NOUN a gesture or a way of speaking which is characteristic of a person.

manoeuvre, manoeuvres, manoeuvring, manoeuvred [*Said man-noo-ver*] VERB ① If you manoeuvre something into a place, you skilfully move it there • *It took expertise to manoeuvre the boat so close to the shore.* ▶ NOUN ② a clever move you make in order to change a situation to your advantage.

manor, manors NOUN a large country house with land.

manpower NOUN Workers can be referred to as manpower.

mansion, mansions NOUN a very large house.

manslaughter NOUN (*Law*) Manslaughter is the accidental killing of a person.

mantelpiece, mantelpieces NOUN a shelf over a fireplace.

mantle, mantles NOUN ① (*literary*) To take on the mantle of something is to accept the status or duties associated with it • *He has taken over the mantle of England's greatest living poet.* ② GEOGRAPHY the part of the earth between the crust and the core.

mantra, mantras NOUN RE a word or short piece of sacred text or prayer continually repeated to help concentration.

manual, manuals ADJECTIVE ① Manual work involves physical strength rather than mental skill. ② operated by hand rather than by electricity or by motor • *a manual typewriter.* ▶ NOUN ③ an instruction book which tells you how to use a machine. **manually** ADVERB

manufacture, manufactures, manufacturing, manufactured DGT VERB ① To manufacture goods is to make them in a factory. ▶ NOUN ② The manufacture of goods is the making of them in a factory • *the manufacture of computers.* **manufacturer** NOUN

manure NOUN Manure is animal faeces used to fertilise the soil.

manuscript, manuscripts NOUN a handwritten or typed document, especially a version of a book before it is printed.

Manx ADJECTIVE belonging or relating to the Isle of Man.

many ADJECTIVE ① If there are many people or things, there is a large number of them. ② You also use 'many' to ask how great a quantity is or to give information about it • *How many tickets do you require?* ▶ PRONOUN ③ a large number of people or things • *Many are too weak to walk.*

Māori, Māoris NOUN ① someone descended from the people who lived in New Zealand before Europeans arrived. ② Māori is a language spoken by Māoris. ▶ ADJECTIVE ③ belonging or relating to Māoris.

map, maps, mapping, mapped NOUN ① a detailed drawing of an area as it would appear if you saw it from above. ② MATHS the relationship between elements of a set and elements in the same or another set. **map out** VERB If you map out a plan, you work out in detail what you will do.

maple, maples NOUN a tree that has large leaves with five points.

mar, mars, marring, marred VERB To mar something is to spoil it • *The presentation was marred by technical problems*.

marae, marae or maraes [*Said* ma-**rye**] NOUN In New Zealand, a marae is a Māori meeting house; also the enclosed space in front of it.

marathon, marathons NOUN ① a race in which people run 26 miles along roads. ▶ ADJECTIVE ② A marathon task is a large one that takes a long time.

marble, marbles NOUN ① Marble is a very hard, cold stone which is often polished to show the coloured patterns in it. ② Marbles is a children's game played with small coloured glass balls. These balls are also called marbles.

march, marches, marching, marched NOUN ① March is the third month of the year. It has 31 days. ② an organised protest in which a large group of people walk somewhere together. ▶ VERB ③ When soldiers march, they walk with quick regular steps in time with each other. ④ To march somewhere is to walk quickly in a determined way • *He marched out of the room*. WORD HISTORY: sense 1 is from Latin *Martius* meaning (month) of Mars, the Roman god of war

SPELLING TIP
When *March* refers to the month it starts with a capital letter.

mare, mares NOUN an adult female horse.

margarine, margarines [*Said* mar-jar-reen] NOUN Margarine is a substance that is similar to butter but is made from vegetable oil and animal fats.

margin, margins NOUN ① If you win a contest by a large or small margin, you win it by a large or small amount. ② an extra amount that allows you more freedom in doing something • *a small margin of error*. ③ the blank space at each side on a written or printed page.

marginal ADJECTIVE ① small and not very important • *a marginal increase*. ② A marginal seat or constituency is a political constituency where the previous election was won by a very small majority. **marginally** ADVERB

marigold, marigolds NOUN a type of yellow or orange garden flower.

marijuana [*Said* mar-rih-**wan**-a] NOUN Marijuana is an illegal drug which people smoke.

marina, marinas NOUN a harbour for pleasure boats and yachts.

marinate, marinates, marinating, marinated VERB To marinate food is to soak it in a mixture of oil, vinegar, spices and herbs to flavour it before cooking.

marine, marines NOUN ① a soldier who serves with the navy. ▶ ADJECTIVE ② relating to or involving the sea • *marine life*.

marital ADJECTIVE relating to or involving marriage.

maritime ADJECTIVE relating to the sea and ships • *maritime trade*.

marjoram NOUN Marjoram is a herb with small rounded leaves and tiny pink flowers.

mark, marks, marking, marked NOUN ① a small stain or damaged area on a surface • *I can't get this mark off the curtain.* ② a written or printed symbol • *He made a few marks with his pen.* ③ a letter or number showing how well you have done in homework or in an exam. ▶ **VERB** ④ If something marks a surface, it damages it in some way. ⑤ If you mark something, you write a symbol on it or identify it in some other way. ⑥ When a teacher marks your work, he or she decides how good it is and gives it a mark. ⑦ To mark something is to be a sign of it • *The accident marked a tragic end to the day.* ⑧ In soccer or hockey, if you mark your opposing player, you stay close to them, trying to prevent them from getting the ball.

marked ADJECTIVE very obvious • *a marked improvement.* **markedly** ADVERB

market, markets, marketing, marketed NOUN ① a place where goods or animals are bought and sold. ② The market for a product is the number of people who want to buy it • *the market for cars.* ▶ **VERB** ③ To market a product is to organise its sale, by deciding its price, where it should be sold, and how it should be advertised.
SIMILAR WORDS: ① bazaar, fair, mart

marketing NOUN DGT Marketing is the part of a business concerned with the way a product is sold.

market research NOUN DGT Market research is research into what people want and buy.

marksman, marksmen NOUN someone who can shoot very accurately.

marlin, marlins NOUN a large fish found in tropical seas which has a very long upper jaw.

marmalade NOUN Marmalade is a jam made from citrus fruit, usually eaten at breakfast.
WORD HISTORY: from Latin *marmelo* meaning 'quince'

maroon NOUN or ADJECTIVE a dark reddish-purple colour.

marooned ADJECTIVE If you are marooned in a place, you are stranded there and cannot leave it.

marquee, marquees [Said mar-**kee**] NOUN a very large tent used at a fair or other outdoor entertainment.

marquis, marquises [Said mar-**kwiss**]; also spelt **marquess** NOUN a male member of the nobility of the rank between duke and earl.

marriage, marriages NOUN ① the legal relationship between a couple. ② Marriage is the act of marrying someone.
SIMILAR WORDS: ① matrimony, wedlock

marrow, marrows NOUN a long, thick, green-skinned fruit with cream-coloured flesh eaten as a vegetable.

marry, marries, marrying, married VERB ① When two people marry, they become each other's partner during a special ceremony. ② When a member of the clergy or a registrar marries a couple, he or she is in charge of their marriage ceremony. **married** ADJECTIVE

Mars NOUN Mars is the planet in the solar system which is fourth from the sun.

marsh, marshes NOUN an area of land which is permanently wet.

marshal, marshals, marshalling, marshalled VERB ① If you marshal things or people, you gather them together and organise them • *The students were marshalled into the assembly room.* ▶ **NOUN** ② an official who helps to organise a public event.

a
b
c
d
e
f
g
h
i
j
k
l
m
n
o
p
q
r
s
t
u
v
w
x
y
z

A B C D E F G H I J K L **M** N O P Q R S T U V W X Y Z

marshmallow, marshmallows
NOUN a soft, spongy, pink or white
sweet made using gelatine.

marsupial, marsupials [Said
mar-**syoo**-pee-al] NOUN an animal
that carries its young in a pouch.
Koalas and kangaroos are
marsupials.
WORD HISTORY: from Greek
marsupion meaning 'purse'

martial [Said mar-shal] ADJECTIVE
relating to or involving war or
soldiers • martial music.

martial arts PLURAL NOUN The
martial arts are the techniques of
self-defence that come from East
Asia, for example karate or judo.

Martian, Martians [Said mar-shan]
NOUN an imaginary creature from
the planet Mars.

martyr, martyrs, martyring,
martyred RE NOUN ① someone
who suffers or is killed rather than
change their beliefs. ▶VERB ② If
someone is martyred, they are killed
because of their beliefs. **martyrdom**
NOUN

marvel, marvels, marvelling,
marvelled VERB ① If you marvel at
something, it fills you with surprise
or admiration • Modern designers can
only marvel at his genius. ▶NOUN
② something that makes you feel
great surprise or admiration
• a marvel of high technology.

marvellous ADJECTIVE wonderful or

excellent. **marvellously** ADVERB

Marxism NOUN Marxism is a political
philosophy based on the writings of
Karl Marx. It states that society will
develop towards communism
through the struggle between
different social classes. **Marxist**
ADJECTIVE or NOUN

marzipan NOUN Marzipan is a paste
made of almonds, sugar and egg. It is
put on top of cakes or used to make
small sweets.

mascara NOUN Mascara is a
substance that can be used to colour
eyelashes and make them look
longer.

mascot, mascots NOUN a person,
animal or toy which is thought to
bring good luck.

masculine ADJECTIVE ① typical of
men, rather than women • masculine
characteristics like facial hair.
② belonging to a particular class of
nouns in some languages, such as
French, German and Latin.
masculinity NOUN

mash, mashes, mashing, mashed
VERB If you mash vegetables, you
crush them after they have been
cooked.

mask, masks, masking, masked
NOUN ① something you wear over
your face for protection or disguise
• a surgical mask. ▶VERB ② If you
mask something, you cover it so that
it is protected or cannot be seen.

What is a Masculine Noun?

Masculine nouns refer to male
people and animals:

The boy put on his coat. → boy is
masculine

Common nouns may be either
masculine or feminine. Other words

in the sentence may tell us if they
are male or female:

The doctor parked his car.
The doctor parked her car.

Also look at the grammar boxes at
gender; feminine; neuter

masochist, masochists [Said *mass-so-kist*] NOUN someone who gets pleasure from their own suffering. **masochism** NOUN

WORD HISTORY: named after the Austrian novelist Leopold von Sacher Masoch (1836–1895), who wrote about masochism

mason, masons NOUN a person who is skilled at making things with stone.

masonry NOUN Masonry is pieces of stone which form part of a wall or building.

masquerade, masquerades, masquerading, masqueraded [Said *mass-ker-raid*] VERB If you masquerade as something, you pretend to be it • *He masqueraded as a doctor*.

mass, masses, massing, massed NOUN ① a large amount of something. ② The masses are the ordinary people in society considered as a group • *opera for the masses*. ③ SCIENCE In physics, the mass of an object is the amount of physical matter that it has. ④ RE In the Roman Catholic Church, Mass is a religious service in which people share bread and wine in remembrance of the death and resurrection of Jesus Christ. ▶ ADJECTIVE ⑤ involving a large number of people • *mass unemployment*. ▶ VERB ⑥ When people mass, they gather together in a large group.

massacre, massacres, massacring, massacred [Said *mass-ik-ker*] NOUN ① the killing of a very large number of people in a violent and cruel way. ▶ VERB ② To massacre people is to kill large numbers of them in a violent and cruel way.

massage, massages, massaging, massaged VERB ① To massage someone is to rub their body in order to help them relax or to relieve pain. ▶ NOUN ② A massage is treatment which involves rubbing the body.

massive ADJECTIVE extremely large • *a massive iceberg*. **massively** ADVERB

mass-produce, mass-produces, mass-producing, mass-produced VERB To mass-produce something is to make it in large quantities • *They began mass-producing cameras after the war*.

mast, masts NOUN the tall upright pole that supports the sails of a boat.

master, masters, mastering, mastered NOUN ① a man who has authority over others, especially servants or slaves. ② the owner of an animal. ③ If you are master of a situation, you have control over it • *He was master of his own destiny*. ④ a male teacher at some schools. ▶ VERB ⑤ If you master a difficult situation, you succeed in controlling it. ⑥ If you master something, you learn how to do it properly • *She found it easy to master the game*.

masterful ADJECTIVE showing control and authority.

masterly ADJECTIVE extremely clever or well done • *a masterly exhibition of batting*.

mastermind, masterminds, masterminding, masterminded VERB ① If you mastermind a complicated activity, you plan and organise it. ▶ NOUN ② The mastermind behind something is the person responsible for planning it.

masterpiece, masterpieces NOUN an extremely good painting or other work of art.

mat, mats NOUN ① a small round or square piece of cloth, card or plastic that is placed on a table to protect it

a
b
c
d
e
f
g
h
i
j
k
l
m
n
o
p
q
r
s
t
u
v
w
x
y
z

from plates or glasses. ② a small piece of carpet or other thick material that is placed on the floor.

matador, matadors NOUN a man who fights and tries to kill bulls as part of a public entertainment, especially in Spain.
WORD HISTORY: from Spanish *matar* meaning 'to kill'

match, matches, matching, matched NOUN ① an organised game of football, cricket or some other sport. ② a small, thin stick of wood that produces a flame when you strike it against a rough surface. ▶ VERB ③ If one thing matches another, the two things look the same or have similar qualities.

mate, mates, mating, mated NOUN ① (*informal*) Your mates are your friends. ② The first mate on a ship is the officer who is next in importance to the captain. ③ An animal's mate is its partner for reproduction. ▶ VERB ④ When a male and female animal mate, they come together in order to breed.

material, materials NOUN ① DGT Material is cloth. ② DGT a substance from which something is made • *the materials to make red dye*. ③ DGT The equipment for a particular activity can be referred to as materials • *building materials*. ④ Material for a book, play or film is the information or ideas on which it is based. ▶ ADJECTIVE ⑤ involving possessions and money • *concerned with material comforts*. **materially** ADVERB

materialise, materialises, materialising, materialised; also spelt **materialize** VERB If something materialises, it actually happens or appears • *Fortunately, the attack did not materialise*.

materialism NOUN Materialism is thinking that money and possessions are the most important things in life. **materialistic** ADJECTIVE

maternal ADJECTIVE relating to or involving a mother • *her maternal instincts*.

maternity ADJECTIVE relating to or involving pregnant women and birth • *a maternity hospital*.

math NOUN In American English, math is mathematics.

mathematics NOUN Mathematics is the study of numbers, quantities and shapes. **mathematical** ADJECTIVE **mathematically** ADVERB **mathematician** NOUN

maths NOUN Maths is mathematics.

Matilda NOUN (*old-fashioned, informal*) In Australia, Matilda is the pack of belongings carried by a swagman in the bush. The word is now used only in the phrase 'waltzing Matilda', meaning travelling in the bush with few possessions.

matinee, matinees [*Said* mat-in-nay]; also spelt **matinée** NOUN an afternoon performance of a play or film.

matriarch, matriarchs [*Said* may-tree-ark*] NOUN a woman who is the head of a family in a society in which power passes from mother to daughter. **matriarchy** NOUN **matriarchal** ADJECTIVE

matrimony NOUN (*formal*) Matrimony is marriage. **matrimonial** ADJECTIVE

matrix, matrices [*Said* may-trix] NOUN ① (*formal*) the framework in which something grows and develops. ② In maths, a matrix is a set of numbers or elements set out in rows and columns.

matron, matrons NOUN In a hospital, a senior nurse in charge of all the nursing staff used to be known as matron.

matt ADJECTIVE A matt surface is dull rather than shiny • *matt black plastic*.

matted ADJECTIVE Hair that is matted is tangled with the strands sticking together.

matter, **matters**, **mattering**, **mattered** NOUN ① something that you have to deal with. ② Matter is any substance • *The atom is the smallest divisible particle of matter.* ③ Books and magazines are reading matter. ▶ VERB ④ If something matters to you, it is important. ▶ PHRASE ⑤ If you ask **What's the matter?**, you are asking what is wrong.
SIMILAR WORDS: ① affair, business, situation, subject

matter-of-fact ADJECTIVE showing no emotion.

matting NOUN Matting is thick woven material such as rope or straw, used as a floor covering.

mattress, **mattresses** NOUN a large thick pad filled with springs, foam or other material that is put on a bed to make it comfortable.

mature, **matures**, **maturing**, **matured** VERB ① When a child or young animal matures, it becomes an adult. ② When something matures, it reaches complete development. ▶ ADJECTIVE ③ Mature means fully developed and emotionally balanced. **maturely** ADVERB **maturity** NOUN

maudlin ADJECTIVE Someone who is maudlin is sad and sentimental, especially when they are drunk.

maul, **mauls**, **mauling**, **mauled** VERB If someone is mauled by an animal, they are savagely attacked and badly injured by it.

mausoleum, **mausoleums** [*Said maw-sal-lee-um*] NOUN a building which contains the grave of a famous person.

mauve [*Rhymes with grove*] NOUN or ADJECTIVE pale purple.

maxim, **maxims** NOUN a short saying which gives a rule for good or sensible behaviour • *Instant action: that's my maxim.*

maximise, **maximises**, **maximising**, **maximised**; also spelt **maximize** VERB To maximise something is to make it as great or effective as possible • *Their objective is to maximise profits.*

maximum ADJECTIVE ① The maximum amount is the most that is possible • *the maximum recommended intake.* ▶ NOUN ② The maximum is the most that is possible • *a maximum of 50 people.*

may VERB ① If something may happen, it is possible that it will happen • *It may rain today.* ② If someone may do something, they are allowed to do it • *Please may I be excused?* ③ You can use 'may' when saying that although something is true, something else is also true • *This may be true, but it is only part of the story.* ④ (formal) You also use 'may' to express a wish that something will happen • *May you live to be a hundred.* ▶ NOUN ⑤ May is the fifth month of the year. It has 31 days.

SPELLING TIP
When *May* refers to the month it starts with a capital letter.

USAGE NOTE
It used to be that you used *may* instead of *can* when asking for or giving someone permission to do something: *You may leave the table.* Nowadays *may* is usually only used in polite questions: *May I open the window?*

a
b
c
d
e
f
g
h
i
j
k
l
m
n
o
p
q
r
s
t
u
v
w
x
y
z

A
B
C
D
E
F
G
H
I
J
K
L
M
N
O
P
Q
R
S
T
U
V
W
X
Y
Z

maybe ADVERB You use 'maybe' when you are stating a possibility that you are not certain about • *Maybe I should lie about my age.*

mayhem NOUN You can refer to a confused and chaotic situation as mayhem • *There was complete mayhem in the classroom.*

mayonnaise [Said may-on-**nayz**] NOUN Mayonnaise is a thick salad dressing made with egg yolks and oil.

mayor, mayors NOUN a person who has been elected to lead and represent the people of a town.

maze, mazes NOUN a system of complicated passages which it is difficult to find your way through • *a maze of dark tunnels.*

MBE, MBEs NOUN a British honour granted by the King or Queen. MBE is an abbreviation for 'Member of the Order of the British Empire' • *Rory McIlroy, MBE.*

MD an abbreviation for 'Doctor of Medicine' or 'Managing Director'.

me PRONOUN A speaker or writer uses 'me' to refer to himself or herself.

meadow, meadows NOUN a field of grass.

meagre [Said *mee-ger*] ADJECTIVE very small and poor • *his meagre pension.*

meal, meals NOUN an occasion when people eat, or the food they eat at that time.

mealie, mealies; also spelt **mielie** NOUN In South African English, mealie is maize or an ear of maize.

mean, means, meaning, meant; meaner, meanest VERB ① If you ask what something means, you want to know what it refers to or what its message is. ② If you mean what you say, you are serious • *The head teacher means what she says.* ③ If something means a lot to you, it is important to you. ④ If one thing means another, it

shows that the second thing is true or will happen • *Major roadworks will mean long delays.* ⑤ If you mean to do something, you intend to do it • *I meant to phone you, but didn't have time.* ⑥ If something is meant to be true, it is supposed to be true • *I found a road that wasn't meant to be there.*
▶ ADJECTIVE ⑦ Someone who is mean is unwilling to spend much money. ⑧ Someone who is mean is unkind or cruel • *He apologised for being so mean to her.* ▶ NOUN ⑨ (in plural) A means of doing something is a method or object which makes it possible • *The tests were marked by means of a computer.* ⑩ (in plural) Someone's means are their money and income • *He's obviously a man of means.* ⑪ MATHS The mean of a set of numbers is the result obtained by adding all the numbers in the set and dividing the total by the number of members of the set. **meanness** NOUN **meanly** ADVERB
SIMILAR WORDS: ⑤ aim, intend, plan ⑦ miserly, parsimonious, stingy, tight-fisted

meander, meanders, meandering, meandered [Said *mee-an-der*] VERB If a road or river meanders, it has a lot of bends in it.

meaning, meanings NOUN ① The meaning of a word is what it refers to or expresses. ② The meaning of what someone says, or of a book or a film, is the thoughts or ideas that it is intended to express. ③ If something has meaning, it seems to be worthwhile and to have real purpose. **meaningful** ADJECTIVE **meaningfully** ADVERB **meaningless** ADJECTIVE
SIMILAR WORDS: ① gist, sense, significance

means test, means tests NOUN a check of a person's money and income to see whether they need money or benefits from the government or other organisation.

meantime PHRASE In the meantime means in the period of time between two events • *I'll call the nurse; in the meantime, you must rest.*

meanwhile ADVERB Meanwhile means while something else is happening.

measles NOUN Measles is an infectious illness in which you have red spots on your skin.

measly ADJECTIVE (*informal*) very small or inadequate • *a measly 4.3 per cent.*

measure, measures, measuring, measured VERB ① MATHS When you measure something, you find out how big it is. ② MATHS If something measures a particular distance, its length or depth is that distance • *slivers of glass measuring a few millimetres across.* ▶ NOUN ③ A measure of something is a certain amount of it • *There has been a measure of agreement.* ④ MATHS a unit in which size, speed or depth is expressed. ⑤ Measures are actions carried out to achieve a particular result • *Tough measures are needed to maintain order.* **measurement** NOUN

measured ADJECTIVE careful and deliberate • *walking at the same measured pace.*

measurement, measurements NOUN ① the result that you obtain when you measure something. ② Measurement is the activity of measuring something. ③ Your measurements are the sizes of your chest, waist and hips that you use to buy the correct size of clothes.

meat, meats NOUN Meat is the flesh of animals that is cooked and eaten. **meaty** ADJECTIVE

Mecca NOUN ① RE Mecca is the holiest city of Islam, to which many Muslims make pilgrimages. ② If a place is a mecca for people of a particular kind, many of them go there because it is of special interest to them • *The island is a mecca for bird lovers.*

USAGE NOTE
Most Muslims dislike this form and use the Arabic *Makkah*.

mechanic, mechanics NOUN ① a person who repairs and maintains engines and machines. ② (*in plural*) The mechanics of something are the way in which it works or is done • *the mechanics of accounting.* ③ (*in plural*) Mechanics is also the scientific study of movement and the forces that affect objects.

mechanical ADJECTIVE ① A mechanical device has moving parts and is used to do a physical task. ② A mechanical action is done automatically without thinking about it • *He gave a mechanical smile.* **mechanically** ADVERB

mechanism, mechanisms NOUN ① DGT a part of a machine that does a particular task • *a locking mechanism.* ② part of your behaviour that is automatic • *the body's defence mechanisms.*

medal, medals NOUN a small disc of metal given as an award for bravery or as a prize for sport.

medallion, medallions NOUN a round piece of metal worn as an ornament on a chain round the neck.

medallist, medallists NOUN a person who has won a medal in sport • *a gold medallist at the Olympics.*

meddle, meddles, meddling, meddled VERB To meddle is to interfere and try to change things without being asked.

media PLURAL NOUN You can refer to the television, radio and newspapers as the media.

mediaeval another spelling of **medieval**.

median, medians [Said *mee-dee-an*] ADJECTIVE MATHS The median value of a set is the middle value when the set is arranged in order.

mediate, mediates, mediating, mediated VERB If you mediate between two groups, you try to settle a dispute between them. **mediation** NOUN **mediator** NOUN

medical, medicals ADJECTIVE ① relating to the prevention and treatment of illness and injuries. ▸ NOUN ② a thorough examination of your body by a doctor. **medically** ADVERB

medication, medications NOUN Medication is a substance that is used to treat illness.

medicinal ADJECTIVE relating to the treatment of illness • *a valuable medicinal herb.*

medicine, medicines NOUN ① Medicine is the treatment of illness and injuries by doctors and nurses. ② a substance that you drink or swallow to help cure an illness.

medieval [Said *med-dee-ee-vul*]; also spelt **mediaeval** ADJECTIVE HISTORY relating to the period between about 1100 AD and 1500 AD, especially in Europe.

WORD HISTORY: from Latin *medium aevum* meaning 'the middle age'

mediocre [Said *meed-dee-oh-ker*] ADJECTIVE of rather poor quality

• *a mediocre string of performances.* **mediocrity** NOUN

meditate, meditates, meditating, meditated VERB ① If you meditate on something, you think about it very deeply. ② If you meditate, you remain in a calm, silent state for a period of time, often as part of a religious training. **meditation** NOUN

Mediterranean NOUN ① The Mediterranean is the large sea between southern Europe and northern Africa. ▸ ADJECTIVE ② relating to or typical of the Mediterranean or the European countries adjoining it.

medium, mediums or media ADJECTIVE ① If something is of medium size or degree, it is neither large nor small • *a medium-sized hotel.* ▸ NOUN ② a means that you use to communicate something • *the medium of television.* ③ a person who claims to be able to speak to the dead and to receive messages from them.

medley, medleys NOUN ① a mixture of different things creating an interesting effect. ② a number of different songs or tunes sung or played one after the other.

meek, meeker, meekest ADJECTIVE A meek person is timid and does what other people say. **meekly** ADVERB **meekness** NOUN
SIMILAR WORDS: submissive, timid

meet, meets, meeting, met VERB ① If you meet someone, you happen to be in the same place as them and start talking to them. ② If you meet a visitor you go to be with them when they arrive. ③ When a group of people meet, they gather together for a purpose. ④ If something meets a need, it can fulfil it • *services intended to meet the needs of people with disabilities.* ⑤ If something meets with a particular reaction, it gets that reaction from people • *I was met with silence.*

meeting, meetings NOUN ① an event in which people discuss proposals and make decisions together. ② what happens when you meet someone.

mega- PREFIX 'Mega-' means very great.

megabyte, megabytes NOUN ICT a unit of computer memory size, equal to 1024 kilobytes.

megalomaniac, megalomaniacs NOUN Someone who is a megalomaniac is always seeking power and enjoys feeling important.

megaphone, megaphones NOUN A megaphone is a cone-shaped device that makes your voice sound louder when you speak into it.

melaleuca, melaleucas [Said *mel-a-loo-ka*] NOUN an Australian tree or shrub that has black branches and a white trunk.

melancholy ADJECTIVE If you feel melancholy, you feel sad.

mêlée, mêlées [Said *mel-lay*] NOUN a situation where there are a lot of people rushing around.

mellow, mellower, mellowest; mellows, mellowing, mellowed ADJECTIVE ① Mellow light is soft and golden. ② A mellow sound is smooth and pleasant to listen to • *his mellow clarinet.* ▶ VERB ③ If someone mellows, they become more pleasant or relaxed • *He certainly hasn't mellowed with age.*

melodic ADJECTIVE relating to melody.

melodious ADJECTIVE pleasant to listen to • *soft melodious music.*

melodrama, melodramas NOUN a story or play in which people's emotions are exaggerated.

melodramatic ADJECTIVE behaving in an exaggerated, emotional way.
SIMILAR WORDS: histrionic, overdramatic, theatrical

melody, melodies NOUN MUSIC a tune.

melon, melons NOUN a large, juicy fruit with a green or yellow skin and many seeds inside.

melt, melts, melting, melted VERB ① When something melts or when you melt it, it changes from a solid to a liquid because it has been heated. ② If something melts, it disappears • *The crowd melted away* • *Her inhibitions melted.*

meltdown, meltdowns NOUN (informal) The meltdown of a company, organisation or system is its sudden and complete failure.

melting point, melting points NOUN SCIENCE the temperature at which a solid starts to turn to liquid.

member, members NOUN ① A member of a group is one of the people or things belonging to the group • *members of the family.* ② A member of an organisation is a person who has joined the organisation. ▶ ADJECTIVE ③ A country belonging to an international organisation is called a member country or a member state.

membership NOUN ① Membership of an organisation is the state of being a member of it. ② The people who belong to an organisation are its membership.

membrane, membranes NOUN SCIENCE a very thin piece of skin or tissue which connects or covers plant or animal organs or cells • *the nasal membrane.*

meme, memes NOUN something such as a video, picture or phrase that a lot of people send to each other on the internet.

a b c d e f g h i j k l m n o p q r s t u v w x y z

memento, mementos NOUN an object which you keep because it reminds you of a person or a special occasion • *a lasting memento of the holiday.*

memo, memos NOUN a note from one person to another within the same organisation. Memo is short for 'memorandum'.

memoirs [Said mem-*wahrz*] PLURAL NOUN ENGLISH If someone writes their memoirs, they write a book about their life and experiences.

memorable ADJECTIVE If something is memorable, it is likely to be remembered because it is special or unusual • *a memorable victory.* **memorably** ADVERB

memorandum, memorandums or memoranda NOUN a memo.

memorial, memorials NOUN ① a structure built to remind people of a famous person or event • *a war memorial.* ▶ ADJECTIVE ② A memorial event or prize is in honour of someone who has died, so that they will be remembered.

memorise, memorises, memorising, memorised; also spelt **memorize** VERB If you memorise something, you learn it thoroughly so you can remember it exactly.

memory, memories NOUN ① Your memory is your ability to remember things. ② something you remember about the past • *memories of their school days.* ③ ICT the part in which information is stored in a computer. SIMILAR WORDS: ① recall, recollection, remembrance

memory card, memory cards NOUN ICT a small device for storing information in a mobile phone or digital camera.

men the plural of **man**.

menace, menaces, menacing,

menaced NOUN ① someone or something that is likely to cause serious harm • *the menace of drugs in sport.* ② Menace is the quality of being threatening • *an atmosphere of menace.* ▶ VERB ③ If someone or something menaces you, they threaten to harm you. **menacingly** ADVERB

menagerie, menageries [Said men-*naj*-er-ree] NOUN a collection of different wild animals.
WORD HISTORY: from French *menagerie* meaning 'household management', which used to include the care of domestic animals

mend, mends, mending, mended VERB If you mend something that is broken, you repair it.

menial ADJECTIVE Menial work is boring and tiring and the people who do it have low status.

meningitis NOUN Meningitis is a serious infectious illness which affects your brain and spinal cord.

menopause NOUN The menopause is the time during which a woman gradually stops menstruating. This usually happens when she is about fifty.

menorah, menorahs [Said mi-*naw*-rah] NOUN RE a candelabra that usually has seven parts and is used in Jewish temples.

menstruate, menstruates, menstruating, menstruated VERB SCIENCE When a woman menstruates, blood comes from her womb. This normally happens about once a month. **menstruation** NOUN **menstrual** ADJECTIVE

-ment SUFFIX '-ment' forms nouns which refer to a state or a feeling • *contentment* • *resentment.*

mental ADJECTIVE ① relating to the process of thinking or intelligence

• *mental arithmetic.* ② relating to the health of the mind • *mental wellbeing.* **mentally** ADVERB

mentality, mentalities NOUN an attitude or way of thinking • *the traditional military mentality.*

mention, mentions, mentioning, mentioned VERB ① If you mention something, you talk about it briefly. ▶ NOUN ② a brief comment about someone or something • *He made no mention of his criminal past.* SIMILAR WORDS: ① bring up, refer to, touch upon

mentor, mentors NOUN Someone's mentor is a person who teaches them and gives them advice. **mentorship** NOUN

menu, menus NOUN ① a list of the foods you can eat in a restaurant. ② ICT a list of different options shown on a computer screen which the user must choose from.

MEP, MEPs NOUN a person who has been elected to represent people in the European Parliament. MEP is an abbreviation for 'Member of the European Parliament'.

mercenary, mercenaries NOUN ① a soldier who is paid to fight for a foreign country. ▶ ADJECTIVE ② Someone who is mercenary is mainly interested in getting money.

merchandise NOUN (*formal*) Merchandise is goods that are sold • *He had left me with more merchandise than I could sell.*

merchant, merchants NOUN a trader who imports and exports goods • *a coal merchant.*

merchant navy NOUN The merchant navy is the boats and sailors involved in carrying goods for trade.

merciful ADJECTIVE ① showing kindness. ② showing forgiveness. **mercifully** ADVERB

SIMILAR WORDS: ② compassionate, humane, kind

merciless ADJECTIVE showing no kindness or forgiveness. **mercilessly** ADVERB SIMILAR WORDS: cruel, heartless, ruthless

mercury NOUN ① SCIENCE Mercury is a silver-coloured metallic element that is liquid at room temperature. It is used in thermometers. Its atomic number is 80 and its symbol is Hg. ② Mercury is also the planet in the solar system which is nearest to the sun.

SPELLING TIP
When *Mercury* refers to the planet it starts with a capital letter.

mercy, mercies NOUN If you show mercy, you show forgiveness and do not punish someone as severely as you could. SIMILAR WORDS: compassion, kindness, pity

mere, merest ADJECTIVE used to emphasise how unimportant or small something is • *It's a mere seven-minute journey by boat.* **merely** ADVERB

merge, merges, merging, merged VERB When two things merge, they combine together to make one thing • *The firms merged in 2003.*

merger, mergers NOUN a joining together of two companies or organisations.

meringue, meringues [*Said mer-rang*] NOUN a type of crisp, sweet cake made with egg whites and sugar.

merino, merinos [*Said mer-ree-no*] NOUN a breed of sheep, common in Australia and New Zealand, with long, fine wool.

merit, merits, meriting, merited NOUN ① If something has merit, it is

a
b
c
d
e
f
g
h
i
j
k
l
m
n
o
p
q
r
s
t
u
v
w
x
y
z

good or worthwhile. ②The merits of something are its advantages or good qualities. ▸ VERB ③If something merits a particular treatment, it deserves that treatment • *He merits a place in the team.*

mermaid, mermaids NOUN In stories, a mermaid is a woman with a fish's tail instead of legs, who lives in the sea.

merry, merrier, merriest ADJECTIVE happy and cheerful • *He was, for all his shyness, a merry man.* **merrily** ADVERB

merry-go-round, merry-go-rounds NOUN a large rotating platform with models of animals or vehicles on it, on which children ride at a fair.

mesh NOUN Mesh is threads of wire or plastic twisted together like a net • *a fence made of wire mesh.*

mesolithic ADJECTIVE relating to the middle period of the Stone Age, roughly between 12,000 BC and 3000 BC.

mess, messes, messing, messed NOUN ①something untidy. ②a situation which is full of problems and trouble. ③a room or building in which members of the armed forces eat • *the officers' mess.* **messy** ADJECTIVE **mess about** or **mess around** VERB If you mess about or mess around, you do things without any particular purpose. **mess up** VERB If you mess something up, you spoil it or do it wrong.

message, messages NOUN ①a piece of information or a request that you send someone or leave for them. ②an idea that someone tries to communicate to people, for example in a play or a speech • *the story's anti-drugs message.* ▸ VERB ③If you

message someone, you send them a text message.

messaging NOUN Messaging or text messaging is the sending and receiving of short pieces of information between mobile phones, often using both letters and numbers to produce shortened forms of words.

messenger, messengers NOUN someone who takes a message to someone for someone else.
SIMILAR WORDS: courier, emissary, envoy

Messiah [Said miss-**eye**-ah] PROPER NOUN ① RE For Jews, the Messiah is the king of the Jews, who will be sent by God. ② RE For Christians, the Messiah is Jesus Christ.
WORD HISTORY: from Hebrew *mashiach* meaning 'anointed'

Messrs [Said **mes**-serz] Messrs is the plural of **Mr**. It is often used in the names of businesses • *Messrs Brown and Humberley, Solicitors.*

met the past tense and past participle of **meet**.

metabolism, metabolisms NOUN Your metabolism is the chemical processes in your body that use food for growth and energy. **metabolic** ADJECTIVE

metal, metals NOUN SCIENCE a chemical element such as iron, steel, copper or lead. Metals are good conductors of heat and electricity and form positive ions. **metallic** ADJECTIVE
WORD HISTORY: from Latin *metallum* meaning 'mine'

metamorphic ADJECTIVE GEOGRAPHY Metamorphic rock is rock that has been altered from its original state by heat or pressure.

metamorphosis, metamorphoses [Said met-am-**mor**-fiss-iss] NOUN (*formal*) When a metamorphosis occurs, a person or thing changes into something completely different • *the metamorphosis of a larva into an insect*.

metaphor, metaphors NOUN ENGLISH an imaginative way of describing something as another thing, and so suggesting that it has the typical qualities of that other thing. For example, if you wanted to say that someone is shy, you might say they are a mouse. **metaphorical** ADJECTIVE **metaphorically** ADVERB

meteor, meteors NOUN a piece of rock or metal that burns very brightly when it enters the earth's atmosphere from space.

meteoric ADJECTIVE A meteoric rise to power or success happens very quickly.

meteorite, meteorites NOUN a piece of rock from space that has landed on earth.

meteorological ADJECTIVE GEOGRAPHY relating to or involving the weather or weather forecasting. **meteorology** NOUN

meteorologist, meteorologists NOUN GEOGRAPHY someone who studies and forecasts the weather.

meter, meters NOUN a device that measures and records something • *a gas meter*.

SPELLING TIP
Do not confuse the spellings of *meter* and *metre*: *the electricity meter; The wall is a metre high*.

methane [*Said* mee-thane] NOUN Methane is a colourless gas with no smell that is found in coal gas and produced by decaying vegetable matter. It burns easily and can be used as a fuel.

method, methods NOUN a particular way of doing something • *the traditional method of making pasta*.

methodical ADJECTIVE Someone who is methodical does things carefully and in an organised way. **methodically** ADVERB

Methodist, Methodists NOUN RE someone who belongs to the Methodist Church, a Protestant church whose members worship God in a way begun by John Wesley and his followers.

meticulous ADJECTIVE A meticulous person does things very carefully and with great attention to detail. **meticulously** ADVERB

metre, metres NOUN ① a unit of length equal to 100 centimetres. ② ENGLISH In poetry, metre is the regular and rhythmic arrangement of words and syllables. **metrical** ADJECTIVE

SPELLING TIP
Do not confuse the spellings of *metre* and *meter*: *The wall is a metre high; the electricity meter*.

metric ADJECTIVE relating to the system of measurement that uses metres, grams and litres.

metropolis, metropolises NOUN a very large city.
WORD HISTORY: from Greek *mētēr* + *polis* meaning 'mother city'

metropolitan ADJECTIVE relating or belonging to a large, busy city • *metropolitan districts*.

mettle NOUN If you are on your mettle, you are ready to do something as well as you can because you know you are being tested or challenged.

mew, mews, mewing, mewed VERB ① When a cat mews, it makes a short high-pitched noise. ▶ NOUN ② the short high-pitched sound that a cat makes.

mews NOUN A mews is a quiet yard or street surrounded by houses.

Mexican, Mexicans ADJECTIVE ① belonging or relating to Mexico. ▸ NOUN ② someone who comes from Mexico.

mezzo forte [Said met-so for-tay] ADVERB MUSIC In music, mezzo forte is an instruction to play or sing something fairly loudly.
WORD HISTORY: an Italian term; 'mezzo' is Italian for 'half', and 'forte' means 'loud'

mezzo piano [Said met-so pee-an-oh] ADVERB MUSIC In music, mezzo piano is an instruction to play or sing something fairly quietly.
WORD HISTORY: an Italian term; 'mezzo' is Italian for 'half', and 'piano' means 'soft'

mg an abbreviation for 'milligram' or 'milligrams'.

miasma, miasmas or miasmata NOUN an unhealthy or unpleasant atmosphere, especially one caused by decaying things.

mice the plural of **mouse**.

micro- PREFIX 'Micro-' means very small.

microbe, microbes NOUN SCIENCE A microbe is a very small living thing which you can see only if you use a microscope.
WORD HISTORY: from Greek *mikros* meaning 'small' and *bios* meaning 'life'

microchip, microchips NOUN a very small piece of silicon inside a computer with electronic circuits on it, which can hold large quantities of information or perform mathematical or logical operations.

microphone, microphones NOUN a device that is used to make sounds louder or to record them.

microprocessor, microprocessors NOUN a microchip which can be programmed to do a large number of tasks or calculations.

microscope, microscopes NOUN SCIENCE a piece of equipment which magnifies very small objects so that you can study them.

microscopic ADJECTIVE very small indeed • *microscopic parasites*.

microwave, microwaves NOUN A microwave or microwave oven is a type of oven which cooks food very quickly by radiation.

mid- PREFIX 'Mid-' is used to form words that refer to the middle part of a place or period of time • *mid-Atlantic* • *the mid-70s*.

midday NOUN Midday is twelve o'clock in the middle of the day.

middle, middles NOUN ① The middle of something is the part furthest from the edges, ends or outside surface. ▸ ADJECTIVE ② The middle one in a series or a row is the one that has an equal number of people or things on each side of it • *the middle house*.

middle age NOUN Middle age is the period of your life when you are between about 40 and 60 years old. **middle-aged** ADJECTIVE

Middle Ages PLURAL NOUN HISTORY In European history, the Middle Ages were the period between about 1100 AD and 1500 AD.

middle class, middle classes NOUN The middle classes are the people in a society who are not working-class or upper-class, for example managers and lawyers.

Middle East NOUN The Middle East consists of Iran and the countries in Asia to the west and south-west of Iran.

Middle English NOUN Middle English

was the English language from about 1100 AD until about 1450 AD.

middle-of-the-road ADJECTIVE Middle-of-the-road opinions are moderate.

middle school, middle schools NOUN In England and Wales, a middle school is for children aged between about 8 and 12.

middling ADJECTIVE of average quality or ability.

midge, midges NOUN a small flying insect which can bite people.

midget, midgets NOUN ① a very small thing. ② (offensive) a very small person.

midnight NOUN Midnight is twelve o'clock at night.

midriff, midriffs NOUN the middle of your body between your waist and your chest.

midst NOUN If you are in the midst of a crowd or an event, you are in the middle of it.

midsummer ADJECTIVE relating to the period in the middle of summer • a lovely midsummer morning in July.

midway ADVERB in the middle of a distance or period of time • They scored midway through the second half.

midweek ADJECTIVE happening in the middle of the week • a midweek training session.

midwife, midwives NOUN a nurse who is trained to help women at the birth of a baby. **midwifery** NOUN

might VERB ① If you say something might happen, you mean that it is possible that it will happen • I might stay a while. ② If you say that someone might do something, you are suggesting that they do it • You might like to go and see it. ③ Might is also the past tense of **may**. ▶ NOUN ④ (literary) Might is strength or

power • the full might of the Navy.

mightily ADVERB (literary) to a great degree or extent • I was mightily relieved by the decision.

mighty, mightier, mightiest ADJECTIVE (literary) ① very powerful or strong • a mighty army on the march. ② very large and impressive • the world's mightiest mountain range.

migraine, migraines [Said mee-grane or my-grane] NOUN a severe headache that makes you feel very ill.
WORD HISTORY: from Latin hemicrania meaning 'pain in half the head'

migrant, migrants NOUN a person who moves from one place to another, especially to find work.

migrant worker, migrant workers NOUN GEOGRAPHY someone who travels to another country to work.

migrate, migrates, migrating, migrated VERB ① GEOGRAPHY If people migrate, they move from one place to another, especially to find work. ② SCIENCE When birds or animals migrate, they move at a particular season to a different place, usually to breed or to find new feeding grounds • the birds migrate each year to Mexico. **migration** NOUN **migratory** ADJECTIVE

mike, mikes NOUN (informal) a microphone.

mild, milder, mildest ADJECTIVE ① Something that is mild is not strong and does not have any powerful or damaging effects • a mild shampoo. ② Someone who is mild is gentle and kind. ③ Mild weather is warmer than usual • The region has mild winters and hot summers. ④ Mild

a
b
c
d
e
f
g
h
i
j
k
l
m
n
o
p
q
r
s
t
u
v
w
x
y
z

emotions or attitudes are not very great or extreme • *mild surprise*.

mildly ADVERB

mildew NOUN Mildew is a soft white fungus that grows on things when they are warm and damp.

mile, miles NOUN a unit of distance equal to 1760 yards or about 1.6 kilometres.

WORD HISTORY: from Latin *mille passuum* meaning 'a thousand paces'

mileage, mileages NOUN ① Your mileage is the distance that you have travelled, measured in miles. ② The amount of mileage that you get out of something is how useful it is to you.

milestone, milestones NOUN an important event in the history or development of something or someone • *a milestone in Zambian history*.

militant, militants ADJECTIVE ① A militant person is very active in trying to bring about extreme political or social change • *a militant party member*. ▶ NOUN ② a person who tries to bring about extreme political or social change. **militancy** NOUN

military ADJECTIVE ① related to or involving the armed forces of a country • *military bases*. ▶ NOUN ② The military are the armed forces of a country. **militarily** ADVERB

militia, militias [*Said* mil-**lish**-a] NOUN an organisation that operates like an army but whose members are not professional soldiers.

milk, milks, milking, milked NOUN ① Milk is the white liquid produced by female cows, goats and some other animals to feed their young. People drink milk and use it to make butter, cheese and yogurt. ② Milk is also the white liquid that a baby drinks from its mother's breasts.

▶ VERB ③ When someone milks a cow or a goat, they get milk from it by pulling its udders. ④ If you milk a situation, you get as much personal gain from it as possible • *They milked money from a hospital charity*.

milk tooth, milk teeth NOUN Your milk teeth are your first teeth, which fall out and are replaced by the permanent set.

milky, milkier, milkiest ADJECTIVE ① pale creamy white • *milky white skin*. ② containing a lot of milk • *a large mug of milky coffee*.

Milky Way NOUN The Milky Way is a strip of stars clustered closely together, appearing as a pale band in the sky.

mill, mills NOUN ① a building where grain is crushed to make flour. ② a factory for making materials such as steel, wool or cotton. ③ a small device for grinding coffee or spices into powder • *a pepper mill*.

millennium, millennia or millenniums NOUN (*formal*) a period of 1000 years.

miller, millers NOUN the person who operates a flour mill.

milli- PREFIX 'Milli-' is added to some measurement words to form words that refer to measurements a thousand times smaller.

WORD HISTORY: from Latin *mille* meaning 'thousand'

millibar, millibars NOUN GEOGRAPHY a unit of atmospheric pressure equal to one thousandth of a bar.

milligram, milligrams NOUN a unit of weight equal to one thousandth of a gram.

millilitre, millilitres NOUN a unit of liquid volume equal to one thousandth of a litre.

millimetre, millimetres NOUN a unit of length equal to one tenth of a centimetre or one thousandth of a metre.

million, millions the number 1,000,000. **millionth** ADJECTIVE

millionaire, millionaires NOUN a very rich person who has money or property worth millions of pounds or dollars.

millstone, millstones PHRASE If something is **a millstone round your neck**, it is an unpleasant problem or responsibility you cannot escape from.

mime, mimes, miming, mimed NOUN ① Mime is the use of movements and gestures to express something or to tell a story without using speech. ▶ VERB ② If you mime something, you describe or express it using mime.

mimic, mimics, mimicking, mimicked VERB ① If you mimic someone's actions or voice, you imitate them in an amusing way. ▶ NOUN ② a person who can imitate other people. **mimicry** NOUN

minaret, minarets NOUN RE a tall, thin tower on a mosque.

mince, minces, mincing, minced NOUN ① Mince is meat which has been chopped into very small pieces in a special machine. ▶ VERB ② If you mince meat, you chop it into very small pieces. ③ To mince about is to walk with small quick steps in an affected, effeminate way.

mind, minds, minding, minded NOUN ① Your mind is your ability to think, together with all the thoughts you have and your memory. ▶ PHRASE ② If you **change your mind**, you change a decision that you have made or an opinion that you have. ▶ VERB ③ If you do not mind something, you are not annoyed by it or bothered about it. ④ If you say

that you wouldn't mind something, you mean that you would quite like it • *I wouldn't mind something to eat.* ⑤ If you mind a child or mind something for someone, you look after it for a while • *My mother is minding the office.*

mindful ADJECTIVE (*formal*) If you are mindful of something, you think about it carefully before taking action • *mindful of their needs.*

mindless ADJECTIVE ① Mindless actions are regarded as stupid and destructive • *mindless violence.* ② A mindless job or activity is simple and repetitive.

mindset, mindsets NOUN PSHE the way that a person typically thinks about things.

mine, mines, mining, mined PRONOUN ① 'Mine' refers to something belonging or relating to the person who is speaking or writing • *a friend of mine.* ▶ NOUN ② a series of holes or tunnels in the ground from which diamonds, coal or other minerals are dug out • *a diamond mine.* ③ a bomb hidden in the ground or underwater, which explodes when people or things touch it. ▶ VERB ④ To mine diamonds, coal or other minerals is to obtain these substances from underneath the ground. **miner** NOUN **mining** NOUN

minefield, minefields NOUN an area of land or water where mines have been hidden.

mineral, minerals NOUN DGT SCIENCE a substance such as tin, salt or coal that is formed naturally in rocks and in the earth • *rich mineral deposits.*

mineral water NOUN Mineral water is water which comes from a natural spring.

a b c d e f g h i j k l m n o p q r s t u v w x y z

minestrone [Said min-nes-**strone**-ee]
NOUN Minestrone is soup containing small pieces of vegetable and pasta. WORD HISTORY: from Italian minestrare meaning 'to serve'

minesweeper, minesweepers
NOUN a ship for clearing away underwater mines.

mingle, mingles, mingling, mingled
VERB If things mingle, they become mixed together • His cries mingled with theirs.

mini- PREFIX 'Mini-' is used to form nouns referring to something smaller or less important than similar things • a TV mini-series.

miniature, miniatures [Said min-nit-cher] ADJECTIVE ① copying something on a much smaller scale. ▶ NOUN ② a very small detailed painting, often of a person.

minibus, minibuses NOUN a van with seats in the back which is used as a small bus.

minim, minims NOUN MUSIC a musical note (♩) that has a time value equal to half a semibreve. In the United States and Canada, a minim is called a half note.

minimal ADJECTIVE very small in quality, quantity or degree • He has minimal experience. **minimally** ADVERB

minimise, minimises, minimising, minimised; also spelt **minimize** VERB If you minimise something, you reduce it to the smallest amount possible • His route was changed to minimise jet lag.

minimum ADJECTIVE ① The minimum amount is the smallest amount that is possible • a minimum wage. ▶ NOUN ② The minimum is the smallest amount that is possible • a minimum of three weeks.

minister, ministers NOUN ① A minister is a person who is in charge of a particular government department • Portugal's deputy foreign minister. ② A minister in a Protestant church is a member of the clergy.

ministerial ADJECTIVE relating to a government minister or ministry • ministerial duties.

ministry, ministries NOUN ① a government department that deals with a particular area of work • the Ministry of Defence. ② Members of the clergy can be referred to as the ministry • Her son is in the ministry.

mink, minks NOUN Mink is an expensive fur used to make coats or hats.

minnow, minnows NOUN a very small freshwater fish.

minor, minors ADJECTIVE ① not as important or serious as other things • a minor injury. ② MUSIC A minor key is one of the keys in which most European music is written. In a minor key the third note is three semitones higher than the first. ▶ NOUN ③ (formal) a young person under the age of 18 • laws concerning the employment of minors.

SPELLING TIP
Do not confuse the spellings minor and miner: It is illegal to sell alcohol to minors; Three miners have been rescued from a diamond mine in South Africa.

minority, minorities NOUN ① The minority of people or things in a group is a number of them forming less than half of the whole • Only a minority of people want this. ② A minority is a group of people of a particular race or religion living in a place where most people are of a different race or religion • ethnic minorities.

minstrel, minstrels NOUN
a singer and entertainer in
medieval times.

mint, mints, minting, minted NOUN
① Mint is a herb used for flavouring in
cooking. ② a peppermint-flavoured
sweet. ③ The mint is the place where
the official coins of a country are
made. ▶ VERB ④ When coins or
medals are minted, they are made.
▶ ADJECTIVE ⑤ If something is in mint
condition, it is in very good
condition, like new.

minus ① You use 'minus' to show
that one number is being subtracted
from another • *Ten minus six equals
four.* ▶ ADJECTIVE ② 'Minus' is used
when talking about temperatures
below 0°C or 0°F.

minuscule [*Said* min-nus-kyool]
ADJECTIVE very small indeed.

minute¹, minutes, minuting,
minuted [*Said* min-nit] NOUN ① a
unit of time equal to sixty seconds.
② The minutes of a meeting are the
written records of what was said and
decided. ▶ VERB ③ To minute a
meeting is to write the official
notes of it.

minute² [*Said* my-nyoot] ADJECTIVE
extremely small • *a minute amount of
pesticide.* **minutely** ADVERB

minutiae [*Said* my-nyoo-shee-aye]
PLURAL NOUN (*formal*) Minutiae are
small, unimportant details.

miracle, miracles NOUN ① RE a
wonderful and surprising event,
believed to have been caused by God.
② any very surprising and fortunate
event • *My brother got a job. It was a
miracle.* **miraculous** ADJECTIVE
miraculously ADVERB

mirage, mirages [*Said* mir-ahj]
NOUN an image which you can see
in the distance in very hot weather,
but which does not actually exist.

mire NOUN (*literary*) Mire is swampy
ground or mud.

mirror, mirrors, mirroring, mirrored
NOUN ① a piece of glass which
reflects light and in which you can
see your reflection. ▶ VERB ② To
mirror something is to have similar
features to it • *His own shock was
mirrored on her face.*

mirth NOUN (*literary*) Mirth is great
amusement and laughter.

mis- PREFIX 'Mis-' means 'wrong' or
'false' • *misbehaviour* • *misconception*.

misbehave, misbehaves,
misbehaving, misbehaved VERB If a
child misbehaves, he or she is
naughty or behaves badly.
misbehaviour NOUN

miscarriage, miscarriages NOUN
① If a woman has a miscarriage, her
baby dies and she gives birth to it
before it is properly formed. ② A
miscarriage of justice is a wrong
decision made by a court, which
causes an innocent person to be
punished.

miscellaneous ADJECTIVE A
miscellaneous group is made up of
people or things that are different
from each other.

mischief NOUN Mischief is eagerness
to have fun by teasing people or
playing tricks. **mischievous**
ADJECTIVE

misconception, misconceptions
NOUN a wrong idea about something
• *the misconception that history is boring*.

misconduct NOUN Misconduct is
bad or unacceptable behaviour by a
professional person • *The Football
Association found him guilty of
misconduct.*

misdemeanour, misdemeanours
[*Said* miss-dem-**mee**-ner] NOUN
(*formal*) an act that is shocking or
unacceptable.

a
b
c
d
e
f
g
h
i
j
k
l
m
n
o
p
q
r
s
t
u
v
w
x
y
z

A
B
C
D
E
F
G
H
I
J
K
L
M
N
O
P
Q
R
S
T
U
V
W
X
Y
Z

miser, misers NOUN a person who enjoys saving money but hates spending it. **miserly** ADJECTIVE

miserable ADJECTIVE ① If you are miserable, you are very unhappy. ② If a place or a situation is miserable, it makes you feel depressed • *a miserable little flat*. **miserably** ADVERB
SIMILAR WORDS: ① dejected, unhappy, wretched ② gloomy, wretched

misery, miseries NOUN Misery is great unhappiness.

misfire, misfires, misfiring, misfired VERB If a plan misfires, it goes wrong.

misfit, misfits NOUN a person who is not accepted by other people because of being rather strange or eccentric.

misfortune, misfortunes NOUN an unpleasant occurrence that is regarded as bad luck • *I had the misfortune to fall off my bike.*

misgiving, misgivings NOUN If you have misgivings, you are worried or unhappy about something • *I had misgivings about his methods.*

misguided ADJECTIVE A misguided opinion or action is wrong because it is based on a misunderstanding or bad information.

misinform, misinforms, misinforming, misinformed VERB If you are misinformed, you are given wrong or inaccurate information. **misinformation** NOUN

misinterpret, misinterprets, misinterpreting, misinterpreted VERB To misinterpret something is to understand it wrongly • *You completely misinterpreted what I wrote.*

misjudge, misjudges, misjudging, misjudged VERB If you misjudge someone or something, you form an incorrect idea or opinion about them.

mislay, mislays, mislaying, mislaid VERB If you mislay something, you lose it because you have forgotten where you put it.

mislead, misleads, misleading, misled VERB To mislead someone is to make them believe something which is not true.

misplaced ADJECTIVE A misplaced feeling is inappropriate or directed at the wrong thing or person • *misplaced loyalty.*

misprint, misprints NOUN a mistake such as a spelling mistake in something that has been printed.

misrepresent, misrepresents, misrepresenting, misrepresented VERB To misrepresent someone is to give an inaccurate or misleading account of what they have said or done. **misrepresentation** NOUN

miss, misses, missing, missed VERB ① If you miss something, you do not notice it • *You can't miss it. It's on the second floor.* ② If you miss someone or something, you feel sad that they are no longer with you • *The boys miss their father.* ③ If you miss a chance or opportunity, you fail to take advantage of it. ④ If you miss a bus, plane or train, you arrive too late to catch it. ⑤ If you miss something, you fail to hit it when you aim at it • *His shot missed the target and went wide.* ▶ NOUN ⑥ an act of missing something that you were aiming at. ⑦ 'Miss' is used before the name of a woman or girl who is not married as a form of address • *Did you know Miss Smith?*

missile, missiles NOUN a weapon that moves long distances through the air and explodes when it reaches its target; also used of any object thrown as a weapon.

mission, missions NOUN ① an

important task that you have to do. ② a group of people who have been sent to a foreign country to carry out an official task. ③ a journey made by a military aeroplane or space rocket to carry out a task. ④ If you have a mission, there is something that you believe it is your duty to try to achieve. ⑤ the workplace of a group of Christians who are working for the Church.

missionary, missionaries NOUN RE a Christian who has been sent to a foreign country to work for the Church.

missive, missives NOUN (old-fashioned) a letter or message.

mist, mists, misting, misted NOUN ① Mist consists of a large number of tiny drops of water in the air, which make it hard to see clearly. ▶ VERB ② If your eyes mist, you cannot see very far because there are tears in your eyes. ③ If glass mists over or mists up, it becomes covered with condensation so that you cannot see through it.

mistake, mistakes, mistaking, mistook, mistaken NOUN ① an action or opinion that is wrong or is not what you intended. ▶ VERB ② If you mistake someone or something for another person or thing, you wrongly think that they are the other person or thing • *I mistook him for the owner of the house.*
SIMILAR WORDS: ① blunder, error, miscalculation, slip

mistaken ADJECTIVE ① If you are mistaken about something, you are wrong about it. ② If you have a mistaken belief or opinion, you believe something which is not true.
mistakenly ADVERB

mister NOUN A man is sometimes addressed in a very informal way as 'mister' • *Where do you live, mister?*

mistletoe [Said **mis-sel-toe**] NOUN Mistletoe is a plant which grows on trees and has white berries on it. It is used as a Christmas decoration.

mistook the past tense of **mistake**.

mistreat, mistreats, mistreating, mistreated VERB To mistreat a person or animal is to treat them badly and make them suffer.

mistress, mistresses NOUN ① A school mistress is a female teacher. ② A servant's mistress is the woman who is the servant's employer.

mistrust, mistrusts, mistrusting, mistrusted VERB ① If you mistrust someone, you do not feel that you can trust them. ▶ NOUN ② Mistrust is a feeling that you cannot trust someone.

misty, mistier, mistiest ADJECTIVE full of or covered with mist.

misunderstand, misunderstands, misunderstanding, misunderstood VERB If you misunderstand something, you do not properly understand what it means • *He misunderstood the problem.*

misunderstanding, misunderstandings NOUN If two people have a misunderstanding, they have a slight quarrel or disagreement.

misuse, misuses, misusing, misused NOUN [Said **mis-yoos**] ① The misuse of something is the incorrect or dishonest use of it • *the misuse of public money.* ▶ VERB [Said **mis-yooz**] ② To misuse something is to use it incorrectly or dishonestly.

mite, mites NOUN a very tiny creature that lives in the fur of animals.

mitigate, mitigates, mitigating, mitigated VERB (formal) To mitigate something means to make it less unpleasant, serious or painful.
mitigation NOUN

mitigating ADJECTIVE (*formal*)
Mitigating circumstances make a crime easier to understand, and perhaps justify it.

mitochondrion, mitochondria [*Said* mite-oh-**kon**-dree-on] NOUN SCIENCE part of a living cell that contains enzymes that produce energy.

mitten, mittens NOUN Mittens are gloves which have one section that covers your thumb and another section for the rest of your fingers together.

mix, mixes, mixing, mixed VERB If you mix things, you combine them or shake or stir them together. **mix up** VERB If you mix up two things or people, you confuse them • *People often mix us up and greet us by each other's names.*
SIMILAR WORDS: blend, combine, merge, mingle

mixed ADJECTIVE ① consisting of several things of the same general kind • *a mixed salad.* ② involving people from two or more different ethnic or religious groups • *mixed marriages.* ③ Mixed education or accommodation is for both males and females • *a mixed comprehensive.*

mixed number, mixed numbers NOUN MATHS a number that includes a whole number and a fraction, for example, $3\frac{1}{2}$.

mixed up ADJECTIVE ① If you are mixed up, you are confused • *I was all mixed up and forgot where I was.* ② If you are mixed up in a crime or a scandal, you are involved in it.

mixer, mixers NOUN a machine used for mixing things together • *a cement mixer.*

mixture, mixtures NOUN several different things mixed or shaken together.

SIMILAR WORDS: blend, medley, mix

mix-up, mix-ups NOUN a mistake in something that was planned • *a mix-up with the bookings.*

ml an abbreviation for 'millilitre' or 'millilitres'.

mm an abbreviation for 'millimetre' or 'millimetres'.

mnemonic, mnemonics [*Said* nim-**on**-nik] NOUN ENGLISH A mnemonic is a word or rhyme that helps you to remember things such as scientific facts or spelling rules. 'i before e, except after c' is an example of a mnemonic.

moa, moa or moas NOUN a large, flightless bird that lived in New Zealand and which became extinct in the late 18th century.

moan, moans, moaning, moaned VERB ① If you moan, you make a low, miserable sound because you are in pain or suffering. ② (*informal*) If you moan about something, you complain about it. ▶ NOUN ③ a low cry of pain or misery.

moat, moats NOUN a wide, water-filled ditch around a building such as a castle.

mob, mobs, mobbing, mobbed NOUN ① a large, disorganised crowd of people • *A mob attacked the team bus.* ▶ VERB ② If a lot of people mob someone, they crowd around the person in a disorderly way • *The band was mobbed by over a thousand fans.*
WORD HISTORY: from Latin *mobile vulgus* meaning 'the fickle public'

mobile, mobiles ADJECTIVE ① able to move or be moved freely and easily • *a mobile home.* ② PE If you are mobile, you are able to travel or move about from one place to another • *a mobile workforce.* ▶ NOUN ③ a decoration consisting of several small objects which hang from threads and move around when a breeze blows. ④ a mobile phone. **mobility** NOUN

mobile phone, mobile phones NOUN a small portable telephone.

mobilise, mobilises, mobilising, mobilised; also spelt **mobilize** VERB ① If you mobilise a group of people, you organise them to do something. ② If a country mobilises its armed forces, it prepares them to fight a war. **mobilisation** NOUN

moccasin, moccasins NOUN Moccasins are flat, soft leather shoes with a raised seam above the toe. WORD HISTORY: from *mocussin*, a North American Indian word meaning 'shoe'

mock, mocks, mocking, mocked VERB ① If you mock someone, you say something scornful or imitate their foolish behaviour. ▸ ADJECTIVE ② not genuine • *mock surprise* • *a mock Tudor house*. ③ A mock examination is one that you do as a practice before the real examination. SIMILAR WORDS: ① laugh at, make fun of, ridicule

mockery NOUN Mockery is the expression of scorn or ridicule of someone. SIMILAR WORDS: derision, ridicule

modal verb, modal verbs NOUN a verb that is used with another verb to express possibility, intention or permission. 'Can', 'might' and 'will' are examples of modal verbs in English, for example, 'I *might* come to your party'.

mode, modes NOUN ① A mode of life or behaviour is a particular way of living or behaving. ② MATHS In mathematics, the mode is the biggest in a set of groups.

model, models, modelling, modelled NOUN ① a copy of something that shows what it looks like or how it works • *a model of a ship*. ② Something that is described as, for example, a model of clarity or a model of perfection, is extremely clear or absolutely perfect. ③ a type or version of a machine • *Which model of washing machine did you choose?* ④ a person who poses for a painter or a photographer. ⑤ a person who wears the clothes that are being displayed at a fashion show or in a magazine. ▸ ADJECTIVE ⑥ Someone who is described as, for example, a model student is an excellent student. ▸ VERB ⑦ If you model yourself on someone, you copy their behaviour because you admire them. ⑧ To model clothes is to display them by wearing them. ⑨ To model shapes or figures is to make them out of clay or wood. SIMILAR WORDS: ② example, ideal, pattern

modem, modems [Said *moe-dem*] NOUN ICT a piece of equipment that links a computer to the telephone system so that data can be transferred from one machine to another via the telephone line.

moderate, moderates, moderating, moderated ADJECTIVE [Said *mod-i-rit*] ① Moderate views are not extreme, and usually favour gradual changes rather than major ones. ② A moderate amount of something is neither large nor small. ▸ NOUN [Said *mod-i-rit*] ③ a person whose political views are not extreme. ▸ VERB [Said *mod-i-rate*] ④ If you moderate something or if it moderates, it becomes less extreme or violent • *The weather moderated*. **moderately** ADVERB

moderation NOUN Moderation is control of your behaviour that stops you acting in an extreme way • *She*

a
b
c
d
e
f
g
h
i
j
k
l
m
n
o
p
q
r
s
t
u
v
w
x
y
z

showed fairness and moderation in her judgements.

modern ADJECTIVE ① relating to the present time • *modern society.* ② new and involving the latest ideas and equipment • *modern technology.* **modernity** NOUN

SIMILAR WORDS: ① contemporary, current, present-day

modernise, modernises, modernising, modernised; also spelt **modernize** VERB To modernise something is to introduce new methods or equipment to it.

modest ADJECTIVE ① quite small in size or amount. ② Someone who is modest does not boast about their abilities or possessions. ③ shy and easily embarrassed. **modestly** ADVERB **modesty** NOUN

modification, modifications NOUN a small change made to improve something • *Modifications to the undercarriage were made.*

modify, modifies, modifying, modified VERB If you modify something, you change it slightly in order to improve it.

module, modules NOUN ① one of the parts which when put together form a whole unit or object • *The course is divided into three modules.* ② ICT a part of a machine, system or program that does a particular task. ③ a part of a spacecraft which can do certain things away from the main body • *the lunar module.* **modular** ADJECTIVE

mogul, moguls NOUN an important, rich and powerful businessman or businesswoman.

mohair NOUN Mohair is very soft, fluffy wool obtained from angora goats.

moist, moister, moistest ADJECTIVE slightly wet.

moisten, moistens, moistening, moistened VERB If you moisten something, you make it slightly wet.

moisture NOUN Moisture is tiny drops of water in the air or on the ground.

molar, molars NOUN SCIENCE Your molars are the large teeth at the back of your mouth.

mole, moles NOUN ① a dark, slightly raised spot on your skin. ② a small animal with black fur. Moles live in tunnels underground. ③ (*informal*) a member of an organisation who is working as a spy for a rival organisation.

molecule, molecules NOUN SCIENCE the smallest amount of a substance that can exist. **molecular** ADJECTIVE

molest, molests, molesting, molested VERB ① If someone molests another person, they illegally touch or attack them. ② If someone molests you, they annoy or pester you. **molester** NOUN

mollify, mollifies, mollifying, mollified VERB To mollify someone is to do something to make them less upset or angry.

mollusc, molluscs NOUN an animal with a soft body and no backbone. Snails, slugs, clams and mussels are all molluscs.

molten ADJECTIVE Molten rock or metal has been heated to a very high temperature and has become a thick liquid.

mom, moms NOUN (*informal*) in American English, your mom is your mother.

moment, moments NOUN ① a very short period of time • *He paused for a moment.* ② The moment at which something happens is the point in time at which it happens • *At that moment, the doorbell rang.* ▶ PHRASE ③ If something is happening **at the**

moment, it is happening now.
SIMILAR WORDS: ① instant, second

momentary ADJECTIVE Something that is momentary lasts for only a few seconds • *a momentary lapse of concentration.* **momentarily** ADVERB

momentous ADJECTIVE (*formal*) very important, often because of its future effect • *a momentous occasion.*

momentum NOUN ① Momentum is the ability that something has to keep developing • *The campaign is gaining momentum.* ② Momentum is also the ability that an object has to continue moving as a result of the speed it already has.

monarch, monarchs [*Said* mon-nark] NOUN CITIZENSHIP a queen, king or other royal person who reigns over a country.

monarchy, monarchies NOUN a system in which a queen or king reigns in a country.

monastery, monasteries NOUN a building in which monks live. **monastic** ADJECTIVE

Monday, Mondays NOUN Monday is the day between Sunday and Tuesday.
WORD HISTORY: from Old English *monandæg* meaning 'moon's day'

monetary [*Said* mun-net-tree] ADJECTIVE (*formal*) relating to money, especially the total amount of money in a country.

money NOUN Money is the coins or banknotes that you use to buy something.

mongoose, mongooses NOUN A mongoose is a small animal with a long tail. Mongooses live in hot countries and kill snakes.

mongrel, mongrels NOUN a dog with parents of different breeds.

monitor, monitors, monitoring, monitored VERB ① If you monitor something, you regularly check its condition and progress • *Her health will be monitored daily.* ▶ NOUN ② a machine used to check or record things. ③ ICT the visual display unit of a computer. ④ a school pupil chosen to do special duties by the teacher.

monk, monks NOUN a member of a male religious community.

monkey, monkeys NOUN an animal which has a long tail and climbs trees. Monkeys live in hot countries.

mono- PREFIX 'Mono-' is used at the beginning of nouns and adjectives that have 'one' as part of their meaning • *monopoly* • *monogamy.*

monocle, monocles NOUN a glass lens worn in front of one eye only and held in place by the curve of the eye socket.

monogamy NOUN (*formal*) Monogamy is the custom of being married to only one person at a time. **monogamous** ADJECTIVE

monolith, monoliths NOUN A monolith is a very large upright piece of stone. **monolithic** ADJECTIVE

monologue, monologues [*Said* mon-nol-og] NOUN ENGLISH a long speech by one person during a play or a conversation.

monomer, monomers NOUN SCIENCE a compound whose molecules can join together to form a polymer.

monopoly, monopolies NOUN control of most of an industry by one or a few large firms.

monorail, monorails NOUN DGT A monorail is a railway running on a single rail usually raised above ground level.

monosyllable, monosyllables NOUN ENGLISH If someone speaks in monosyllables, they use only words containing one syllable, such

a
b
c
d
e
f
g
h
i
j
k
l
m
n
o
p
q
r
s
t
u
v
w
x
y
z

as 'yes' and 'no'. **monosyllabic**
ADJECTIVE

monotone, monotones NOUN a
tone which does not vary • *He droned
on in a boring monotone.*

monotonous ADJECTIVE having a
regular pattern which is very dull and
boring • *monotonous work.*
monotony NOUN

monotreme, monotremes NOUN a
mammal that lays eggs and excretes
waste matter through the same
opening in its body.

monounsaturated ADJECTIVE
Monounsaturated oils are made
mainly from vegetable fats and are
considered to be healthier than
saturated oils. **monounsaturate**
NOUN

monsoon, monsoons NOUN
GEOGRAPHY the season of very
heavy rain in South-east Asia.

monster, monsters NOUN ① a large,
imaginary creature that looks very
frightening. ② a cruel or frightening
person. ▶ ADJECTIVE ③ extremely
large • *a monster truck.*
WORD HISTORY: from Latin *monstrum*
meaning 'omen' or 'warning'

monstrosity, monstrosities NOUN
something that is large and
extremely ugly • *a concrete monstrosity
in the middle of the city.*

monstrous ADJECTIVE extremely
shocking or unfair • *a monstrous crime.*
monstrously ADVERB

montage, montages [Said mon-**tahj**]
NOUN a picture or film consisting of a
combination of several different
items arranged to produce an
unusual effect.

month, months NOUN one of the
twelve periods that a year is divided
into.

monthly ADJECTIVE ① happening or
appearing once a month • *monthly*

spelling tests. ▶ ADVERB ② once a
month • *I get paid monthly.*

monument, monuments NOUN a
large stone structure built to remind
people of a famous person or event
• *a monument to the dead.*

monumental ADJECTIVE ① A
monumental building or sculpture is
very large and important. ② very
large or extreme • *We face a
monumental task.*

moo, moos, mooing, mooed VERB
When a cow moos, it makes a long,
deep sound.

mood, moods NOUN the way you are
feeling at a particular time • *She was
in a really cheerful mood.*
SIMILAR WORDS: humour, state of
mind, temper

moody, moodier, moodiest
ADJECTIVE ① Someone who is moody
is depressed or unhappy • *Tony,
despite his charm, could sulk and be
moody.* ② Someone who is moody
often changes their mood for no
apparent reason.
SIMILAR WORDS: ① morose, sulky,
sullen ② mercurial, temperamental

moon, moons NOUN The moon is an
object moving round the earth which
you see as a shining circle or crescent
in the sky at night. Some other
planets have moons.

moonlight, moonlights,
moonlighting, moonlighted NOUN
① Moonlight is the light that comes
from the moon at night. ▶ VERB
② (informal) If someone is
moonlighting, they have a second
job that they have not informed the
tax office about. **moonlit** ADJECTIVE

moor, moors, mooring, moored
NOUN ① a high area of open land.
▶ VERB ② If a boat is moored, it is
attached to the land with a rope.

mooring, moorings NOUN a place
where a boat can be tied.

moose NOUN a large North American deer with flat antlers.

moot, moots, mooting, mooted VERB (*formal*) When something is mooted, it is suggested for discussion • *The project was first mooted in 2008.*

mop, mops, mopping, mopped NOUN ① a tool for washing floors, consisting of a sponge or string head attached to a long handle. ② a large amount of loose or untidy hair. ▶ VERB ③ To mop a floor is to clean it with a mop. ④ To mop a surface is to wipe it with a dry cloth to remove liquid.

mope, mopes, moping, moped VERB If you mope, you feel miserable and not interested in anything.

moped, mopeds [*Said moe-ped*] NOUN a type of small motorcycle.

mopoke, mopokes NOUN a small, spotted owl found in Australia and New Zealand. In New Zealand it is called a **morepork**.

moral, morals NOUN ① PSHE (*in plural*) Morals are values based on beliefs about the correct and acceptable way to behave. ▶ ADJECTIVE ② concerned with whether behaviour is right or acceptable • *moral values*. **morality** NOUN **morally** ADVERB

morale [*Said mor-rahl*] NOUN Morale is the amount of confidence and optimism that you have • *The morale of the team was high.*

morbid ADJECTIVE having a great interest in unpleasant things, especially death.

more ADJECTIVE ① More means a greater number or extent than something else • *He's got more chips than me.* ② used to refer to an additional thing or amount of something • *He found some more clues.*

▶ PRONOUN ③ a greater number or extent. ▶ ADVERB ④ to a greater degree or extent • *more amused than concerned.* ⑤ You can use 'more' in front of adjectives and adverbs to form comparatives • *You look more beautiful than ever.*

moreover ADVERB used to introduce a piece of information that supports or expands the previous statement • *They have accused the government of corruption. Moreover, they have named names.*

morepork, moreporks NOUN another name in New Zealand English for **mopoke**.

morgue, morgues [*Said morg*] NOUN a building where dead bodies are kept before being buried or cremated.

moribund ADJECTIVE no longer having a useful function and about to come to an end • *a moribund industry.*

morning, mornings NOUN the part of the day between midnight and noon • *He was born at three in the morning.*

SPELLING TIP
Do not confuse the spellings of *morning* and *mourning*: *a sunny morning; a week of national mourning.*

Moroccan, Moroccans [*Said mor-rok-an*] ADJECTIVE ① belonging or relating to Morocco. ▶ NOUN ② someone who comes from Morocco.

moron, morons NOUN (*informal*) a very stupid person. **moronic** ADJECTIVE

morose ADJECTIVE miserable and bad-tempered.

morphine NOUN Morphine is a drug which is used to relieve pain.

morphology NOUN ENGLISH In the study of language, morphology refers to the ways words are constructed with stems, prefixes and suffixes.

Morse or **Morse code** NOUN Morse or Morse code is a code used for sending messages in which each letter is represented by a series of dots and dashes. It is named after its American inventor, Samuel Morse.

morsel, morsels NOUN a small piece of food.

mortal, mortals ADJECTIVE ① unable to live forever • *Remember that you are mortal.* ② A mortal wound is one that causes death. ▶ NOUN ③ an ordinary person.

mortality NOUN ① Mortality is the fact that all people must die. ② Mortality also refers to the number of people who die at any particular time • *a low infant mortality rate.*

mortar, mortars NOUN ① a short cannon which fires missiles high into the air for a short distance. ② Mortar is a mixture of sand, water and cement used to hold bricks firmly together.

mortgage, mortgages, mortgaging, mortgaged [Said *mor-gij*] NOUN ① a loan which you get from a bank or a building society in order to buy a house. ▶ VERB ② If you mortgage your house, you use it as a guarantee to a company in order to borrow money from them. They can take the house from you if you do not pay back the money you have borrowed.

mortifying ADJECTIVE embarrassing or humiliating • *There were some mortifying setbacks.*

mortuary, mortuaries NOUN a special room in a hospital where dead bodies are kept before being buried or cremated.

mosaic, mosaics [Said *moe-zay-yik*] NOUN a design made of small coloured stones or pieces of coloured glass set into concrete or plaster.

Moslem an old-fashioned spelling of **Muslim**.

mosque, mosques [Said *mosk*] NOUN RE a building where Muslims go to worship.
WORD HISTORY: from Arabic *masjid* meaning 'temple'

mosquito, mosquitoes or mosquitos [Said *moss-kee-toe*] NOUN Mosquitoes are small insects which bite people in order to suck their blood.
WORD HISTORY: from Spanish *mosquito* meaning 'little fly'

moss, mosses NOUN Moss is a soft, low-growing, green plant which grows on damp soil or stone. **mossy** ADJECTIVE

most ADJECTIVE or PRONOUN ① Most of a group of things or people means nearly all of them • *Most people don't share your views* • *She is smarter than most.* ② The most means a larger amount than anyone or anything else • *She has the most talent.*
▶ ADVERB ③ You can use 'most' in front of adjectives or adverbs to form superlatives • *the most beautiful buildings in the world.*

mostly ADVERB 'Mostly' is used to show that a statement is generally true • *Her friends are mostly classmates.*

MOT, MOTs NOUN In Britain, the MOT test is an annual test for road vehicles to check that they are safe to drive.

motel, motels NOUN a hotel providing overnight accommodation for people in the middle of a car journey.

moth, moths NOUN an insect like a butterfly which usually flies at night.

mother, mothers, mothering, mothered NOUN ① A person's mother is their female parent.

▸**VERB** ② To mother someone is to look after them and bring them up.

motherhood NOUN Motherhood is the state of being a mother.

mother-in-law, mothers-in-law NOUN Someone's mother-in-law is the mother of their husband or wife.

motif, motifs [Said moe-**teef**] NOUN a design which is used as a decoration.

motion, motions, motioning, motioned NOUN ① Motion is the process of continually moving or changing position • the motion of the ship. ② an action or gesture • Apply with a brush using circular motions. ③ a proposal which people discuss and vote on at a meeting. ▸**VERB** ④ If you motion to someone, you make a movement with your hand in order to show them what they should do • I motioned him to proceed.

motionless ADJECTIVE not moving at all • He sat motionless.

motivate, motivates, motivating, motivated VERB ① If you are motivated by something, it makes you behave in a particular way • He is motivated by duty rather than ambition. ② If you motivate someone, you make them feel determined to do something. **motivated** ADJECTIVE **motivation** NOUN SIMILAR WORDS: ① drive, inspire, prompt

motive, motives NOUN a reason or purpose for doing something • There was no motive for the crime.

motley ADJECTIVE A motley collection is made up of people or things of very different types.

motor, motors NOUN DGT ① a part of a vehicle or a machine that uses electricity or fuel to produce movement so that the machine can work. ▸ADJECTIVE ② concerned with or relating to vehicles with a petrol or diesel engine • the motor industry.

motorbike, motorbikes NOUN (informal) a motorcycle.

motorboat, motorboats NOUN a boat with an engine.

motorcycle, motorcycles NOUN a two-wheeled vehicle with an engine which is ridden like a bicycle. **motorcyclist** NOUN

motoring ADJECTIVE relating to cars and driving • a motoring correspondent.

motorist, motorists NOUN a person who drives a car.

motorway, motorways NOUN a wide road built for fast travel over long distances.

mottled ADJECTIVE covered with patches of different colours • mottled leaves.

motto, mottoes or mottos NOUN a short sentence or phrase that is a rule for good or sensible behaviour.

mould, moulds, moulding, moulded VERB ① To mould someone or something is to influence and change them so they develop in a particular way • Early experiences mould our behaviour for life. ② DGT To mould a substance is to make it into a particular shape • Mould the mixture into flat round cakes. ▸NOUN ③ DGT a container used to make something into a particular shape • a jelly mould. ④ Mould is a soft grey or green substance that can form on old food or damp walls. **mouldy** ADJECTIVE

moult, moults, moulting, moulted VERB When an animal or bird moults, it loses its hair or feathers so new ones can grow.

mound, mounds NOUN ① a small man-made hill. ② a large, untidy pile • a mound of blankets.

mount, mounts, mounting, mounted VERB ① To mount a campaign or event is to organise it

a b c d e f g h i j k l m n o p q r s t u v w x y z

and carry it out. ② If something is mounting, it is increasing • *Economic problems are mounting*. ③ *(formal)* To mount something is to go to the top of it • *He mounted the steps*. ④ If you mount a horse, you climb on its back. ⑤ If you mount an object in a particular place, you fix it there to display it. ▶ NOUN ⑥ 'Mount' is also used as part of the name of a mountain • *Mount Everest*.

mountain, mountains NOUN ① a very high piece of land with steep sides. ② a large amount of something • *mountains of paperwork*.

mountaineer, mountaineers NOUN a person who climbs mountains.

mountainous ADJECTIVE A mountainous area has a lot of mountains.

mourn, mourns, mourning, mourned VERB ① If you mourn for someone who has died, you are very sad and think about them a lot. ② If you mourn something, you are sad because you no longer have it • *He mourned the loss of his favourite pet*.

mourner, mourners NOUN a person who attends a funeral.

mournful ADJECTIVE very sad.

mourning NOUN If someone is in mourning, they wear special black clothes or behave in a quiet and restrained way because a member of their family has died.

SPELLING TIP

Do not confuse the spellings of *mourning* and *morning*: *a week of national mourning; a sunny morning*.

---

mouse, mice NOUN ① a small rodent with a long tail. ② ICT a small device moved by hand to control the position of the cursor on a computer screen.

mousse, mousses *[Said moos]* NOUN Mousse is a light, fluffy food made from whipped eggs and cream.

moustache, moustaches *[Said mus-stahsh]* NOUN A man's moustache is hair growing on his upper lip.

WORD HISTORY: from Greek *mustax* meaning 'upper lip'

mouth, mouths, mouthing, mouthed NOUN ① your lips, or the space behind them where your tongue and teeth are. ② The mouth of a cave or a hole is the entrance to it. ③ GEOGRAPHY The mouth of a river is the place where it flows into the sea. ▶ VERB ④ If you mouth something, you form words with your lips without making any sound • *Dad mouthed 'Thank you' to me*.

mouthful NOUN

mouthpiece, mouthpieces NOUN ① the part you speak into on a telephone. ② the part of a musical instrument you put to your mouth. ③ The mouthpiece of an organisation is the person who publicly states its opinions and policies.

movable ADJECTIVE Something that is movable can be moved from one place to another.

move, moves, moving, moved VERB ① To move means to go to a different place or position. To move something means to change its place or position. ② If you move, or move house, you go to live in a different house. ③ If something moves you, it causes you to feel a deep emotion • *Her story moved us to tears*. ▶ NOUN ④ a change from one place or position to another • *We were watching his every move*. ⑤ an act of moving house. ⑥ the act of putting a piece or counter in a game in a different position • *It's your move next*.

SIMILAR WORDS: ① budge, go, shift, stir

movement, movements NOUN
① Movement involves changing position or going from one place to another. ② (*in plural, formal*) Your movements are everything you do during a period of time • *They asked him for an account of his movements during the previous morning.* ③ a group of people who share the same beliefs or aims • *the peace movement.* ④ one of the major sections of a piece of classical music.

movie, movies NOUN (*informal*) a film.

moving ADJECTIVE Something that is moving makes you feel deep sadness or emotion. **movingly** ADVERB

mow, mows, mowing, mowed, mown VERB To mow grass is to cut it with a lawnmower.

mower, mowers NOUN a machine for cutting grass.

MP, MPs NOUN CITIZENSHIP a person who has been elected to represent people in a country's parliament. MP is an abbreviation for 'Member of Parliament'.

MP3 player, MP3 players NOUN a device that plays audio or video files, often used for listening to music downloaded from the internet.

mpg an abbreviation for 'miles per gallon'.

mph an abbreviation for 'miles per hour'.

Mr [*Said* miss-ter] NOUN 'Mr' is used before a man's name when you are speaking or referring to him.

Mrs [*Said* miss-iz] NOUN 'Mrs' is used before the name of a married woman when you are speaking or referring to her.

Ms [*Said* miz] NOUN 'Ms' is used before a woman's name when you are speaking or referring to her. Ms does not specify whether a woman is married or not.

MSP, MSPs NOUN a person who has been elected to represent people in the Scottish Parliament. MSP is an abbreviation for 'Member of the Scottish Parliament'.

much ADVERB ① You use 'much' to emphasise that something is true to a great extent • *I feel much better now.* ② If something does not happen much, it does not happen very often. ▶ ADJECTIVE or PRONOUN ③ You use 'much' to ask questions or give information about the size or amount of something • *How much money do you need?* • *There isn't much left.*

muck, mucks, mucking, mucked NOUN ① (*informal*) Muck is dirt or some other unpleasant substance. ② Muck is also manure. **mucky** ADJECTIVE **muck about** VERB (*informal*) If you muck about, you behave stupidly and waste time.

mucus [*Said* myoo-kuss] NOUN Mucus is a liquid produced in parts of your body, for example in your nose.

mud NOUN Mud is wet, sticky earth.

muddle, muddles, muddling, muddled NOUN ① A muddle is a state of disorder or untidiness • *My room is in a muddle.* ▶ VERB ② If you muddle things, you mix them up. SIMILAR WORDS: ② jumble, mix up

muddy, muddier, muddiest ADJECTIVE ① covered in mud. ② A muddy colour is dull and not clear • *a mottled, muddy brown.*

muesli [*Said* myooz-lee] NOUN Muesli is a mixture of chopped nuts, cereal flakes and dried fruit that you can eat for breakfast with milk.

muffin, muffins NOUN ① a small, flat, sweet bread roll, which you eat hot. ② a small, domed cake, often containing fruit pieces or chocolate chips.

a
b
c
d
e
f
g
h
i
j
k
l
m
n
o
p
q
r
s
t
u
v
w
x
y
z

muffled ADJECTIVE A muffled sound is quiet or difficult to hear • *a muffled explosion*.

mug, mugs, mugging, mugged NOUN ① a large, deep cup. ② (*informal*) someone who is stupid and easily deceived. ▶ VERB ③ (*informal*) If someone mugs you, they attack you in order to steal your money. **mugging** NOUN **mugger** NOUN

muggy, muggier, muggiest ADJECTIVE Muggy weather is unpleasantly warm and damp.

mule, mules NOUN the offspring of a female horse and a male donkey.

mulga NOUN ① Mulga is an acacia shrub that is found in the desert regions of Australia. ② (*informal*) In Australian English, mulga is also the bush or outback.

mull, mulls, mulling, mulled VERB If you mull something over, you think about it for a long time before making a decision.

mullet, mullets NOUN a common edible fish.

mulloway, mulloways NOUN a large edible fish found in Australian waters.

multi- PREFIX 'Multi-' is used to form words that refer to something that has many parts or aspects • *a multistorey car park*.

multicellular ADJECTIVE SCIENCE An organism that is multicellular has many cells.

multicultural ADJECTIVE consisting of or relating to people of many different nationalities and cultures • *London is an extremely multicultural city*. **multiculturalism** NOUN

multimedia NOUN ① ICT in computing, you use 'multimedia' to refer to products which use sound, pictures, film and ordinary text to convey information. ② In the classroom, all the things like TV, computers and books which are used as teaching aids are called multimedia.

multinational, multinationals NOUN a very large company with branches in many countries.

multiple, multiples ADJECTIVE ① having or involving many different functions or things • *She displayed multiple talents at school*. ▶ NOUN ② The multiples of a number are other numbers that it will divide into exactly. For example, 6, 9 and 12 are multiples of 3.

multiple sclerosis [*Said skler-roe-siss*] NOUN Multiple sclerosis is a serious disease which attacks the nervous system, affecting your ability to move.

multiplication NOUN ① MATHS Multiplication is the process of multiplying one number by another. ② The multiplication of things is a large increase in their number • *the multiplication of universities*.

multiplicity NOUN If there is a multiplicity of things, there is a large number or variety of them.

multiply, multiplies, multiplying, multiplied VERB ① When something multiplies, it increases greatly in number • *The trip wore on and the hazards multiplied*. ② MATHS When you multiply one number by another, you calculate the total you would get if you added the first number to itself a particular number of times. For example, two multiplied by three is equal to two plus two plus two, which equals six.

multitude, multitudes NOUN (*formal*) a very large number of people or things.

mum, mums (*informal*) NOUN ① Your

mum is your mother. ▶ PHRASE ② If you **keep mum** about something, you keep it secret.

mumble, mumbles, mumbling, mumbled VERB If you mumble, you speak very quietly and indistinctly.

mummy, mummies NOUN ① (*informal*) Your mummy is your mother. ② a dead body which was preserved long ago by being rubbed with special oils and wrapped in cloth.

mumps NOUN Mumps is a disease that causes painful swelling in the neck glands.

munch, munches, munching, munched VERB If you munch something, you chew it steadily and thoroughly.

mundane ADJECTIVE very ordinary and not interesting or unusual • *a mundane job*.

municipal [*Said myoo-nis-si-pl*] ADJECTIVE belonging to a city or town which has its own local government • *a municipal golf course*.
WORD HISTORY: from Latin *municipium* meaning 'free town'

munitions PLURAL NOUN Munitions are bombs, guns and other military supplies.

mural, murals NOUN a picture painted on a wall.

murder, murders, murdering, murdered NOUN ① Murder is the deliberate killing of a person. ▶ VERB ② To murder someone is to kill them deliberately. **murderer** NOUN
SIMILAR WORDS: ① homicide, killing

murderous ADJECTIVE ① likely to murder someone • *murderous gangsters*. ② A murderous attack or other action results in the death of many people • *murderous acts of terrorism*.

murky, murkier, murkiest ADJECTIVE dark or dirty and unpleasant • *He rushed through the murky streets*.

murmur, murmurs, murmuring, murmured VERB ① If you murmur, you say something very softly. ▶ NOUN ② something that someone says which can hardly be heard.

muscle, muscles, muscling, muscled NOUN ① SCIENCE Your muscles are pieces of flesh which you can expand or contract in order to move parts of your body. An **agonistic muscle** is a muscle which is relaxed when another muscle is contracted; an **antagonistic muscle** is a muscle which is contracted when another muscle is relaxed, returning the limb to its original position; an **antagonistic pair of muscles** means two muscles which work together, for example one opening a joint and the other closing it. ▶ VERB ② (*informal*) If you muscle in on something, you force your way into a situation in which you are not welcome.
WORD HISTORY: from Latin *musculus* meaning 'little mouse', because muscles were thought to look like mice

muscular [*Said musk-yool-lar*] ADJECTIVE ① involving or affecting your muscles • *muscular strength*. ② Someone who is muscular has strong, firm muscles.

muse, muses, musing, mused VERB (*literary*) To muse is to think about something for a long time.

museum, museums NOUN a building where many interesting or valuable objects are kept and displayed.

mush NOUN A mush is a thick, soft paste.

a
b
c
d
e
f
g
h
i
j
k
l
m
n
o
p
q
r
s
t
u
v
w
x
y
z

mushroom, mushrooms, mushrooming, mushroomed NOUN ① a fungus with a short stem and a round top. Some types of mushroom are edible. ▸ VERB ② If something mushrooms, it appears and grows very quickly • *The mill towns mushroomed into cities.*

mushy, mushier, mushiest ADJECTIVE ① Mushy fruits or vegetables are too soft • *mushy tomatoes.* ② (*informal*) Mushy stories are too sentimental.

music NOUN ① Music is a pattern of sounds performed by people singing or playing instruments. ② Music is also the written symbols that represent musical sounds • *I taught myself to read music.*

musical, musicals ADJECTIVE ① relating to playing or studying music • *a musical instrument.* ▸ NOUN ② a play or film that uses songs and dance to tell the story. **musically** ADVERB

musician, musicians NOUN MUSIC a person who plays a musical instrument as their job or hobby.

musk NOUN Musk is a substance with a strong, sweet smell. It is used to make perfume. **musky** ADJECTIVE

musket, muskets NOUN an old-fashioned gun with a long barrel.

Muslim, Muslims NOUN RE ① a person who believes in Islam and lives according to its rules. ▸ ADJECTIVE ② relating to Islam.

muslin NOUN Muslin is a very thin cotton material.

mussel, mussels NOUN Mussels are a kind of shellfish with black shells.

must, musts VERB ① If something must happen, it is very important or necessary that it happens • *You must be over 18.* ② If you tell someone they must do something, you are suggesting that they do it • *You must try this pudding: it's delicious.* ▸ NOUN ③ something that is absolutely necessary • *The museum is a must for all visitors.*

mustard NOUN Mustard is a spicy-tasting yellow or brown paste made from seeds.

muster, musters, mustering, mustered VERB If you muster something such as energy or support, you gather it together • *as much calm as he could muster.*

musty, mustier, mustiest ADJECTIVE smelling stale and damp • *musty old books.*

mutate, mutates, mutating, mutated VERB SCIENCE If something mutates, its structure or appearance alters in some way • *Viruses react to change and can mutate fast.* **mutation** NOUN **mutant** NOUN or ADJECTIVE

mute, mutes, muting, muted (*formal*) ADJECTIVE ① not giving out sound or speech • *He stared in mute amazement.* ▸ VERB ② To mute a sound means to make it quieter. **WORD HISTORY:** from Latin *mutus* meaning 'silent'

muted ADJECTIVE ① Muted colours or sounds are soft and gentle. ② A muted reaction is not very strong.

muti [*Said moo-ti*] NOUN (*informal*) In South African English, muti is medicine.

mutilate, mutilates, mutilating, mutilated VERB ① If someone is mutilated, their body is badly injured. ② If you mutilate something, you deliberately damage or spoil it • *Almost every book had been mutilated.* **mutilation** NOUN

mutiny, mutinies NOUN A mutiny is a rebellion against someone in authority.

A B C D E F G H I J K L M N O P Q R S T U V W X Y Z

mutter, mutters, muttering, muttered VERB To mutter is to speak in a very low and perhaps cross voice • *Rory muttered something under his breath*.

mutton NOUN Mutton is the meat of an adult sheep.

muttonbird, muttonbirds NOUN a seabird in the Pacific Ocean that is often hunted for its flesh, which is said to taste like mutton.

mutual ADJECTIVE used to describe something that two or more people do to each other or share • *They had a mutual interest in rugby*.

USAGE NOTE
It used to be that *mutual* could only be used of something that was shared between two people or groups. Nowadays you can use it to mean 'shared between two or more people or groups'.

mutually ADVERB Mutually describes a situation in which two or more people feel the same way about each other • *a mutually supportive relationship*.

muzzle, muzzles, muzzling, muzzled NOUN ① the nose and mouth of an animal. ② a cover or a strap for a dog's nose and mouth to prevent it from biting. ③ the open end of a gun through which the bullets come out. ▶ VERB ④ To muzzle a dog is to put a muzzle on it.

my ADJECTIVE 'My' refers to something belonging or relating to the person speaking or writing • *I held my breath*.

mynah bird, mynah birds NOUN a tropical bird which can mimic speech and sounds.

myriad, myriads [Said mir-ree-ad] NOUN (literary) a very large number of people or things.

myrrh [Rhymes with purr] NOUN Myrrh is a fragrant substance used in perfume and incense.

myself PRONOUN ① 'Myself' is used when the person speaking or writing does an action and is affected by it • *I congratulated myself*. ② 'Myself' is also used to emphasise 'I' • *I find it a bit odd myself*.

mysterious ADJECTIVE ① strange and not well understood. ② secretive about something • *Stop being so mysterious*. **mysteriously** ADVERB
SIMILAR WORDS: ② enigmatic, secretive

mystery, mysteries NOUN something that is not understood or known about.

mystic, mystics NOUN ① a religious person who spends long hours meditating. ▶ ADJECTIVE ② Mystic means the same as mystical. **mysticism** NOUN

mystical ADJECTIVE involving spiritual powers and influences • *a mystical experience*.

mystify, mystifies, mystifying, mystified VERB If something mystifies you, you find it impossible to understand.

mystique [Said mis-steek] NOUN Mystique is an atmosphere of mystery and importance associated with a particular person or thing.

myth, myths NOUN ① an untrue belief or explanation. ② ENGLISH a story which was made up long ago to explain natural events and religious beliefs • *Viking myths*.

mythical ADJECTIVE imaginary, untrue or existing only in myths • *a mythical beast*.

mythology NOUN Mythology refers to stories that have been made up in the past to explain natural events or justify religious beliefs. **mythological** ADJECTIVE

a b c d e f g h i j k l m n o p q r s t u v w x y z

Nn

naartjie, naartjies [Said *nar-chi*] NOUN In South African English, a naartjie is a tangerine.

nab, nabs, nabbing, nabbed VERB (*informal*) To nab someone who has done something wrong means to catch them or arrest them.

nag, nags, nagging, nagged VERB ① If you nag someone, you keep complaining to them about something. ② If something nags at you, it keeps worrying you.

nail, nails, nailing, nailed NOUN ① a small piece of metal with a sharp point at one end, which you hammer into objects to hold them together. ② Your nails are the thin hard areas covering the ends of your fingers and toes. ▶ VERB ③ If you nail something somewhere, you fit it there using a nail. ④ (*informal*) If you nail someone who has done something wrong, you catch them and prove that they are guilty. ⑤ (*informal*) If you nail something, you do it extremely well or successfully.

naive [Said *ny-eev*]; also spelt **naïve** ADJECTIVE foolishly believing that things are easier or less complicated than they really are. **naively** ADVERB **naivety** NOUN

naked ADJECTIVE ① not wearing any clothes or not covered by anything. ② shown openly • *naked aggression*. **nakedness** NOUN

name, names, naming, named NOUN ① a word that you use to identify a person, place or thing. ② Someone's name is also their reputation • *My only wish now is to clear my name.* ▶ VERB ③ If you name someone or something, you give them a name or you say their name. ④ If you name a price or a date, you say what you want it to be.

nameless ADJECTIVE You describe someone or something as nameless when you do not know their name, or when a name has not yet been given to them.

namely ADVERB that is; used to introduce more detailed information about what you have just said • *The state stripped them of their rights, namely the right to own land.*

namesake, namesakes NOUN Your namesake is someone with the same name as you • *Audrey Hepburn and her namesake Katharine.*

nanny, nannies NOUN a person, usually a woman, whose job is looking after young children.

nanotechnology NOUN Nanotechnology is the science of making or working with things that are so small that they can only be seen using a powerful microscope.

nap, naps, napping, napped NOUN ① a short sleep. ▶ VERB ② When you nap, you have a short sleep.

nape, napes NOUN The nape of your neck is the back of it.

napkin, napkins NOUN a small piece of cloth or paper used to wipe your hands and mouth after eating.

nappy, **nappies** NOUN a piece of towelling or paper worn round a baby's bottom.

narcissism [Said nahr-siss-siz-um] NOUN Narcissism is the habit of always thinking about yourself and admiring yourself. **narcissist** NOUN **narcissistic** ADJECTIVE

WORD HISTORY: from *Narcissus*, a character in Greek mythology, who fell in love with his own reflection

narcotic, **narcotics** NOUN a drug which makes you sleepy and unable to feel pain.

WORD HISTORY: from Greek *narkoun* meaning 'to make numb'

narrate, **narrates**, **narrating**, **narrated** VERB If you narrate a story, you tell it. **narration** NOUN

narrative, **narratives** [Said nar-rat-tiv] NOUN ENGLISH a story or an account of events.

narrator, **narrators** NOUN ① a person who is reading or telling a story out loud. ② ENGLISH a character in a novel who tells the story.

narrow, **narrower**, **narrowest**; **narrows**, **narrowing**, **narrowed** ADJECTIVE ① having a small distance from one side to the other • *a narrow stream*. ② concerned only with a few aspects of something and ignoring the important points • *people with a narrow point of view*. ③ A narrow escape or victory is one that you only just achieve. ▶ VERB ④ To narrow means to become less wide • *The road narrowed*. **narrowly** ADVERB **narrowness** NOUN

narrow-minded ADJECTIVE unwilling to consider new ideas or opinions.

SIMILAR WORDS: bigoted, intolerant

nasal [Said nay-zal] ADJECTIVE ① relating to the nose • *the nasal passages*. ② Nasal sounds are made by breathing out through your nose as you speak.

nasty, **nastier**, **nastiest** ADJECTIVE very unpleasant • *a nasty shock*. **nastily** ADVERB **nastiness** NOUN

nation, **nations** NOUN GEOGRAPHY a large group of people sharing the same history and language and usually inhabiting a particular country.

national, **nationals** GEOGRAPHY ADJECTIVE ① relating to the whole of a country • *a national newspaper*. ② typical of a particular country • *women in Polish national dress*. ▶ NOUN ③ A national of a country is a citizen of that country • *Turkish nationals*. **nationally** ADVERB

national anthem, **national anthems** NOUN A country's national anthem is its official song.

nationalise, **nationalises**, **nationalising**, **nationalised**; also spelt **nationalize** VERB To nationalise an industry means to bring it under the control and ownership of the state. **nationalisation** NOUN

nationalism NOUN ① Nationalism is a desire for the independence of a country; also a political movement aiming to achieve such independence. ② Nationalism is also love of your own country. **nationalist** NOUN **nationalistic** ADJECTIVE

nationality, **nationalities** NOUN Nationality is the fact of belonging to a particular country.

national park, **national parks** NOUN an area of land protected by the government because of its natural beauty, which the public can visit.

National Party NOUN In Australia

a
b
c
d
e
f
g
h
i
j
k
l
m
n
o
p
q
r
s
t
u
v
w
x
y
z

and New Zealand, the National Party is a major political party.

national service NOUN National service is a compulsory period of service in the armed forces.

nationwide ADJECTIVE or ADVERB happening all over a country • *a nationwide search*.

native, natives ADJECTIVE ① Your native country is the country where you were born. ② Your native language is the language that you first learned to speak. ③ Animals or plants that are native to a place live or grow there naturally and have not been brought there by people. ▸ NOUN ④ A native of a place is someone who was born there.

Native American, Native Americans NOUN A Native American is someone descended from the people who lived in North America before Europeans arrived.

Nativity NOUN In Christianity, the Nativity is the birth of Christ or the festival celebrating this.

natter, natters, nattering, nattered VERB (*informal*) If you natter, you talk about unimportant things.

natural, naturals ADJECTIVE ① normal and to be expected • *It was only natural that he was tempted.* ② not trying to pretend or hide anything • *Caitlin's natural manner reassured her.* ③ DGT existing or happening in nature • *natural disasters* • *natural fabrics.* ④ A natural ability is one you were born with. ⑤ Your natural mother or father is your birth mother or father and not someone who has adopted you. ▸ NOUN ⑥ someone who is born with a particular ability • *She's a natural at tennis.* ⑦ In music, a natural is a note that is not a sharp or a flat. It is represented by the symbol (♮). **naturally** ADVERB

SIMILAR WORDS: ④ inborn, inherent, innate

natural resources PLURAL NOUN GEOGRAPHY materials such as minerals, trees and coal that exist naturally in a country and can be used by its people.

natural selection NOUN SCIENCE Natural selection is Darwin's theory that only the species of animals and plants that are best suited to their environment survive and reproduce, while those that are less well suited die.

nature, natures NOUN ① Nature is animals, plants and all the other things in the world not made by people. ② The nature of a person or thing is their basic character • *She liked his warm, generous nature.* WORD HISTORY: from Latin *natura* meaning 'birth'

naughty, naughtier, naughtiest ADJECTIVE ① behaving badly. ② rude or indecent. **naughtily** ADVERB **naughtiness** NOUN

nausea [*Said naw-zee-ah*] NOUN Nausea is a feeling in your stomach that you are going to be sick. **nauseous** ADJECTIVE

nautical [*Said naw-tik-kl*] ADJECTIVE relating to ships or navigation.

nautical mile, nautical miles NOUN A nautical mile is a unit of distance used at sea, equal to 1852 metres.

naval ADJECTIVE relating to or having a navy • *naval officers* • *naval bases*.

SPELLING TIP
Do not confuse the spellings of *naval* and *navel*: *a handsome man in a naval uniform; She had her navel pierced on her nineteenth birthday.*

---

navel, navels NOUN the small hollow on the front of your body just below your waist.

SPELLING TIP

Do not confuse the spellings of *navel* and *naval*: *She had her navel pierced on her nineteenth birthday; a handsome man in a naval uniform.*

navigable ADJECTIVE wide enough and deep enough to sail on.

navigate, **navigates**, **navigating**, **navigated** VERB ①When someone navigates, they work out the direction in which a ship, plane or car should go, using maps and sometimes instruments. ②To navigate a stretch of water means to travel safely across it • *It was the first time I had navigated the ocean.*
navigation NOUN **navigator** NOUN

navy, **navies** NOUN ①the part of a country's armed forces that fights at sea. ▸ADJECTIVE ②dark blue.

Nazi, **Nazis** [*Said* **naht**-*see*] NOUN
HISTORY The Nazis were members of the National Socialist German Workers' Party, which was led by Adolf Hitler.

NB You write NB to draw attention to what you are going to write next. NB is an abbreviation for the Latin 'nota bene', which means 'note well'.

Neanderthal [*Said* **nee**-*an*-*der*-*tahl*]
ADJECTIVE HISTORY Neanderthal man was a primitive species of man who lived in Europe before 12,000 BC. The name comes from Neandertal, a German valley where archaeological discoveries were made.

near, **nearer**, **nearest**; **nears**, **nearing**, **neared** PREPOSITION ①not far from. ▸ADJECTIVE ②not far away in distance. ③not far away in time. ④You can also use 'near' to mean almost • *a night of near disaster.*
▸VERB ⑤When you are nearing something, you are approaching it and will soon reach it • *The dog began to bark as he neared the porch.*
nearness NOUN

nearby ADJECTIVE ①only a short distance away • *a nearby town.*
▸ADVERB ②only a short distance away • *They built a house nearby.*

nearly ADVERB not completely but almost.

neat, **neater**, **neatest** ADJECTIVE ①tidy and smart. ②A neat alcoholic drink does not have anything added to it. **neatly** ADVERB **neatness** NOUN

necessarily ADVERB Something that is not necessarily the case is not always or inevitably the case.

necessary ADJECTIVE ①Something that is necessary is needed or must be done. ②(*formal*) Necessary also means certain or inevitable • *a necessary consequence of war.*
SIMILAR WORDS: ① essential, needed, requisite

necessitate, **necessitates**, **necessitating**, **necessitated** VERB (*formal*) To necessitate something means to make it necessary.

necessity, **necessities** NOUN ①Necessity is the need to do something • *There is no necessity for any of this.* ②Necessities are things needed in order to live.

neck, **necks** NOUN ①the part of your body which joins your head to the rest of your body. ②the long narrow part at the top of a bottle.

necklace, **necklaces** NOUN a piece of jewellery worn around the neck.

nectar NOUN Nectar is a sweet liquid produced by flowers that is attractive to insects.

nectarine, **nectarines** NOUN a kind of peach with a smooth skin.

née [*Rhymes with* **day**] ADJECTIVE 'Née' is used to indicate what a woman's surname was before she got married • *Sara Black, née Wells.*

need, needs, needing, needed VERB
① If you need something, you believe that you must have it or do it. ▶ NOUN ② Your needs are the things that you need to have. ③ a strong feeling that you must have or do something • *I just felt the need to write about it.*
SIMILAR WORDS: ② necessity, requirement

needle, needles, needling, needled NOUN ① a small thin piece of metal with a pointed end and a hole at the other, which is used for sewing. ② Needles are also long thin pieces of steel or plastic, used for knitting. ③ the small pointed part in a record player that touches the record and picks up the sound signals. ④ the part of a syringe which a doctor or nurse sticks into your body. ⑤ the thin piece of metal or plastic on a dial which moves to show a measurement. ⑥ The needles of a pine tree are its leaves. ▶ VERB ⑦ (*informal*) If someone needles you, they annoy or provoke you.

needless ADJECTIVE unnecessary.
needlessly ADVERB

needy, needier, neediest ADJECTIVE very poor.

negative, negatives ADJECTIVE ① A negative answer means 'no'. ② Someone who is negative sees only problems and disadvantages • *Why are you so negative about everything?* ③ If a medical or scientific test is negative, it shows that something has not happened or is not present • *The diabetes test came back negative.* ④ MATHS A negative number is less than zero. ▶ NOUN ⑤ the image on film that is first produced when you take a photograph. **negatively** ADVERB

neglect, neglects, neglecting, neglected VERB ① If you neglect something, you do not look after it

properly. ② (*formal*) If you neglect to do something, you fail to do it • *He had neglected to give her his address.* ▶ NOUN ③ Neglect is failure to look after something or someone properly • *Most of her plants died from neglect.*
neglectful ADJECTIVE

negligent ADJECTIVE not taking enough care • *her negligent driving.*
negligently ADVERB **negligence** NOUN

negligible ADJECTIVE very small and unimportant • *a negligible amount of fat.*

negotiable ADJECTIVE able to be changed or agreed by discussion • *All contributions are negotiable.*

negotiate, negotiates, negotiating, negotiated VERB ① When people negotiate, they have formal discussions in order to reach an agreement about something. ② If you negotiate an obstacle, you manage to get over it or round it.
negotiation NOUN **negotiator** NOUN

Negro, Negroes NOUN (*old-fashioned, offensive*) a person with black skin who comes from Africa or whose ancestors came from Africa.

neigh, neighs, neighing, neighed [Rhymes with **day**] VERB ① When a horse neighs, it makes a loud high-pitched sound. ▶ NOUN ② a loud high-pitched sound made by a horse.

neighbour, neighbours NOUN ① Your neighbour is someone who lives next door to you or near you. ② Your neighbour is also someone standing or sitting next to you • *I got chatting with my neighbour in the studio.*

neighbourhood, neighbourhoods NOUN a district where people live • *a safe neighbourhood.*

neighbouring ADJECTIVE situated nearby • *schools in neighbouring areas*.

neither ADJECTIVE or PRONOUN used to indicate that a negative statement refers to two or more things or people • *It's neither a play nor a musical* • *Neither of them spoke*.

GRAMMAR TIP
When *neither* is followed by a plural noun, the verb can be plural too: *Neither of these books are useful*. When you have two singular subjects the verb should be singular too: *Neither Jack nor John has done the work*.

nemesis NOUN The nemesis of a person or thing is a situation, event or person which causes them to be seriously harmed, especially as a punishment.

neo- PREFIX new or modern • *neo-fascism*.
WORD HISTORY: from Greek *neos* meaning 'new'

neolithic ADJECTIVE relating to the Stone Age period when people first started farming.

neon [*Said* nee-yon] NOUN SCIENCE Neon is a chemical element existing as a gas in very small amounts in the atmosphere. It is used in glass tubes to make bright electric lights and signs. Neon's atomic number is 10 and its symbol is Ne.

nephew, nephews NOUN Someone's nephew is the son of their sister or brother.

Neptune NOUN Neptune is the planet in the solar system which is eighth from the sun.
WORD HISTORY: from *Neptune*, the Roman god of the sea

nerve, nerves NOUN ① a long thin fibre that sends messages between your brain and other parts of your body. ② If you talk about someone's nerves, you are referring to how able they are to remain calm in a difficult situation • *It needs confidence and strong nerves*. ③ Nerve is courage • *O'Meara held his nerve to sink the putt*. ④ (informal) Nerve is boldness or rudeness • *He had the nerve to swear at me*. ▶ PHRASE ⑤ (informal) If someone **gets on your nerves**, they irritate you.

nerve cell, nerve cells NOUN SCIENCE A nerve cell is the same as a neuron.

nerve-racking ADJECTIVE making you feel very worried and tense • *a nerve-racking experience*.

nervous ADJECTIVE ① worried and frightened. ② relating to or affecting your nerves. **nervously** ADVERB **nervousness** NOUN
SIMILAR WORDS: ① apprehensive, edgy, jumpy

nervous breakdown, nervous breakdowns NOUN an illness in which someone suffers from severe depression or anxiety and needs psychiatric treatment.

nervous system, nervous systems NOUN SCIENCE Your nervous system is the nerves in your body together with your brain and spinal cord.

-ness SUFFIX '-ness' forms nouns from adjectives • *tenderness* • *happiness*.
WORD HISTORY: from an Old English suffix

nest, nests, nesting, nested NOUN ① a place that a bird makes to lay its eggs in; also a place that some insects and other animals make to rear their young in. ▶ VERB ② When birds nest, they build a nest and lay eggs in it.

nestle, nestles, nestling, nestled [*Said* ness-sl] VERB If you nestle somewhere, you settle there comfortably, often pressing up against someone else • *A new puppy nestled in her lap.*

nestling, nestlings NOUN a young bird that has not yet learned to fly and so has not left the nest.

net, nets NOUN ① a piece of material made of threads woven together with small spaces in between. ② The net is the same as the **internet**.
▸ ADJECTIVE ③ A net amount is final, after everything that should be subtracted from it has been subtracted • *a net profit of £171 million.* ④ The net weight of something is its weight without its wrapping.

netball NOUN Netball is a game played by two teams of seven players in which each team tries to score goals by throwing a ball through a net at the top of a pole.

netbook, netbooks NOUN ICT a type of small, lightweight laptop computer used especially for internet access and email.

netting NOUN Netting is material made of threads or metal wires woven together with small spaces in between.

nettle, nettles NOUN a wild plant covered with little hairs that sting.

network, networks NOUN ① a large number of lines or roads which cross each other at many points • *a small network of side roads.* ② A network of people or organisations is a large number of them that work together as a system • *the public telephone network.* ③ A television network is a group of broadcasting stations that all transmit the same programmes at the same time. ④ ICT a group of computers connected to each other.

neuron, neurons; also spelt **neurone**, neurones NOUN a cell that is part of the nervous system and conducts messages to and from the brain.

neurosis, neuroses [*Said* nyoor-roh-siss] NOUN a mental illness that causes people to have strong fears and worries.

neurotic [*Said* nyoor-rot-ik] ADJECTIVE having strong fears and worries • *He was almost neurotic about being followed.*

neuter, neuters, neutering, neutered [*Said* nyoo-ter] VERB ① When an animal is neutered, its reproductive organs are removed.
▸ ADJECTIVE ② In some languages, a neuter noun or pronoun is one which is not masculine or feminine.

neutral, neutrals ADJECTIVE ① People who are neutral do not support either side in a disagreement or war. ② DGT The neutral wire in an electric plug is the one that is not earth or live. ③ ART A neutral colour is not definite or striking, for example pale grey. ④ SCIENCE In chemistry, a neutral substance is neither acid nor alkaline. ▸ NOUN ⑤ a person or country that does not support either side in a disagreement or war. ⑥ DGT Neutral is the position between the gears of a vehicle in which the gears are not connected to the engine. **neutrality** NOUN

What is a Neuter Noun?

Neuter nouns refer to inanimate objects and abstract ideas:

The kettle will switch itself off. →

kettle is **neuter**

Also look at the grammar boxes at **gender**; **masculine**; **feminine**

neutralise, neutralises, neutralising, neutralised; also spelt **neutralize** VERB ①To neutralise something means to prevent it from working or taking effect, especially by doing or applying something that has the opposite effect. ② SCIENCE If you neutralise a substance, you make it neither acid nor alkaline.

neutron, neutrons NOUN SCIENCE an atomic particle that has no electrical charge.

neutron star, neutron stars NOUN SCIENCE a star that has collapsed under the weight of its own gravity.

never ADVERB at no time in the past, present or future.

USAGE NOTE
Do not use *never* to mean 'not' in writing. You should say *I didn't see her*, not *I never saw her*.

nevertheless ADVERB in spite of what has just been said • *They dress rather plainly but nevertheless look quite smart.*

new, newer, newest ADJECTIVE ① recently made, created or discovered • *a new house* • *a new plan* • *a new virus*. ② not used or owned before • *We've got a new car*. ③ different or unfamiliar • *a name which was new to me*. **newness** NOUN
SIMILAR WORDS: ① latest, modern, recent

newborn ADJECTIVE born recently.

newcomer, newcomers NOUN someone who has recently arrived in a place.

newly ADVERB recently • *the newly born baby*.

new moon, new moons NOUN The moon is a new moon when it is a thin crescent shape at the start of its four-week cycle.

news NOUN News is information about things that have happened.

newsagent, newsagents NOUN a person or shop that sells newspapers and magazines.

newspaper, newspapers NOUN a publication, on large sheets of paper, that is produced regularly and contains news and articles.

newt, newts NOUN a small amphibious creature with a moist skin, short legs, and a long tail.
WORD HISTORY: from a mistaken division of Middle English *an ewt*

New Testament NOUN RE The New Testament is the second part of the Bible, which deals with the life of Jesus Christ and with the early Church.

newton, newtons NOUN SCIENCE A newton is a unit of force. One newton causes one kilogram to have an acceleration of one metre per second. The newton is named after the English scientist Sir Isaac Newton (1643–1727).

New Year NOUN New Year is the time when people celebrate the start of a year.

New Zealander, New Zealanders NOUN someone who comes from New Zealand.

next ADJECTIVE ① coming immediately after something else • *Their next child was a girl*. ② in a position nearest to something • *in the next room*. ▶ ADVERB ③ coming immediately after something else • *Steve arrived next*. ▶ PHRASE ④ If one thing is **next to** another, it is at the side of it.
SIMILAR WORDS: ① following, subsequent

next door ADJECTIVE or ADVERB in the house next to yours.

NGO, NGOs NOUN an organisation which is not run by the government.

NGO is an abbreviation for 'non-governmental organisation'.

Nguni [Said un-**goo**-nee] NOUN Nguni is a group of languages of southern Africa, including Zulu, Xhosa and Swazi.

NHS In Britain, NHS is an abbreviation for 'National Health Service'.

nib, nibs NOUN the pointed end of a pen.

nibble, nibbles, nibbling, nibbled VERB ① When you nibble something, you take small bites of it. ▶ NOUN ② a small bite of something.

nice, nicer, nicest ADJECTIVE pleasant or attractive. **nicely** ADVERB **niceness** NOUN

nicety, niceties [Said **nigh**-se-tee] NOUN a small detail • the social niceties.

niche, niches [Said neesh] NOUN ① a hollow area in a wall. ② If you say that you have found your niche, you mean that you have found a job or way of life that is exactly right for you.

nick, nicks, nicking, nicked VERB ① If you nick something, you make a small cut in its surface • He nicked his chin. ② (informal) To nick something also means to steal it. ▶ NOUN ③ a small cut in the surface of something.

nickel, nickels NOUN ① SCIENCE Nickel is a silver-coloured metallic element that is used in alloys. Its atomic number is 28 and its symbol is Ni. ② A nickel is an American or Canadian coin worth five cents.

nickname, nicknames, nicknaming, nicknamed NOUN ① an informal name given to someone. ▶ VERB ② If you nickname someone, you give them a nickname.
WORD HISTORY: from Middle English

an ekename meaning 'an additional name'

nicotine NOUN SCIENCE Nicotine is an addictive substance found in tobacco. It is named after Jacques Nicot, who first brought tobacco to France.

niece, nieces NOUN Someone's niece is the daughter of their sister or brother.

nifty ADJECTIVE neat and pleasing or cleverly done.

Nigerian, Nigerians [Said nie-**jeer**-ee-an] ADJECTIVE ① belonging or relating to Nigeria. ▶ NOUN ② someone from Nigeria.

niggle, niggles, niggling, niggled VERB ① If something niggles you, it worries you slightly. ▶ NOUN ② a small worry that you keep thinking about.

night, nights NOUN Night is the time between sunset and sunrise when it is dark.

nightclub, nightclubs NOUN a place where people go late in the evening to drink and dance.

nightdress, nightdresses NOUN a loose dress that a woman or girl wears to sleep in.

nightfall NOUN Nightfall is the time of day when it starts to get dark.

nightie, nighties NOUN (informal) a nightdress.

nightingale, nightingales NOUN a small brown European bird, the male of which sings very beautifully, especially at night.

nightly ADJECTIVE OR ADVERB happening every night • the nightly news programme.

nightmare, nightmares NOUN a very frightening dream; also used of any very unpleasant or frightening situation • The meal itself was a

nightmare. **nightmarish** ADJECTIVE
WORD HISTORY: from *night* + Middle
English *mare* meaning 'evil spirit'

nil NOUN Nil means zero or nothing. It
is used especially in sports scores.

nimble, nimbler, nimblest ADJECTIVE
① able to move quickly and easily.
② able to think quickly and cleverly.
nimbly ADVERB

nimbus, nimbuses NOUN GEOGRAPHY
A nimbus is a dark cloud bringing rain
and snow.

nine the number 9. **ninth** ADJECTIVE

nineteen the number 19.
nineteenth ADJECTIVE

ninety, nineties the number 90.
ninetieth ADJECTIVE

nip, nips, nipping, nipped VERB
① (*informal*) If you nip somewhere,
you go there quickly. ② To nip
someone or something means to
pinch or squeeze them slightly.
▶ NOUN ③ a light pinch.

nipple, nipples NOUN Your nipples
are the two small pieces of projecting
flesh on your chest. Babies suck milk
through the nipples on their mothers'
breasts.

nirvana *[Said neer-vah-na]* NOUN RE
Nirvana is the ultimate state of
spiritual enlightenment which can
be achieved in the Buddhist religion.

nit, nits NOUN Nits are the eggs of a
kind of louse that sometimes lives in
people's hair.

nitrate, nitrates NOUN SCIENCE
A nitrate is a chemical compound
that includes nitrogen and oxygen.
Nitrates are used as fertilisers in
agriculture.

nitrogen NOUN SCIENCE Nitrogen is
a chemical element usually found as
a gas. It forms about 78 per cent of
the earth's atmosphere. Nitrogen's
atomic number is 7 and its symbol is N.

nitroglycerine NOUN Nitroglycerine
is a dense oily liquid used as an
explosive.

no INTERJECTION ① used to say that
something is not true or to refuse
something. ▶ ADJECTIVE ② none at
all or not at all • *She gave no reason*
• *You're no friend of mine.* ▶ ADVERB
③ used with a comparative to mean
'not' • *no later than July 24th.*

no. a written abbreviation for
number.

nobility NOUN ① Nobility is the
quality of being noble • *the
unmistakable nobility of her character.*
② The nobility of a society are all the
people who have titles and high
social rank.

noble, nobler, noblest; nobles
ADJECTIVE ① honest and brave, and
deserving admiration. ② very
impressive • *great parks with noble tall
trees.* ▶ NOUN ③ a member of the
nobility. **nobly** ADVERB

noble gas, noble gases NOUN
SCIENCE any of the gases which
belong to group 18 of the periodic
table and which do not react with
other elements. Examples include
helium, neon and argon.

nobleman, noblemen NOUN a man
who is a member of the nobility.

noblewoman, noblewomen NOUN
a woman who is a member of the
nobility.

nobody, nobodies PRONOUN ① not a
single person. ▶ NOUN ② Someone
who is a nobody is not at all
important.

USAGE NOTE
Nobody and *no-one* mean the same.

nocturnal ADJECTIVE ① happening
at night • *a nocturnal journey through
New York.* ② active at night • *a
nocturnal animal.*

a
b
c
d
e
f
g
h
i
j
k
l
m
n
o
p
q
r
s
t
u
v
w
x
y
z

nod, nods, nodding, nodded VERB ①When you nod, you move your head up and down, usually to show agreement. ▶ NOUN ②a movement of your head up and down. **nod off** VERB If you nod off, you fall asleep.

node, nodes NOUN SCIENCE In biology, a node is the place on the stem of a plant from which a branch or leaf grows.
WORD HISTORY: from Latin *nodus* meaning 'knot'

nodule, nodules [Said *nod-yool*] NOUN A nodule is a small, rounded lump, especially one on the root of a plant.

noise, noises NOUN a sound, especially one that is loud or unpleasant.
SIMILAR WORDS: din, racket, sound

noise pollution NOUN GEOGRAPHY noise that is annoying or harmful to people in the place where they live or work and that they have no control over.

noisy, noisier, noisiest ADJECTIVE making a lot of noise or full of noise • *a noisy crowd*. **noisily** ADVERB **noisiness** NOUN

nomad, nomads NOUN a person who belongs to a tribe which travels from place to place rather than living in just one place. **nomadic** ADJECTIVE

nominal ADJECTIVE ①Something that is nominal is supposed to have a particular identity or status, but in reality does not have it • *the nominal leader of his party*. ②A nominal amount of money is very small compared to the value of something • *I am prepared to do the work for a nominal fee*. **nominally** ADVERB

nominate, nominates, nominating, nominated VERB If you nominate someone for a job or position, you formally suggest that they have it. **nomination** NOUN

SIMILAR WORDS: name, propose, suggest

non- PREFIX not • *non-smoking*.
WORD HISTORY: from Latin

nonagon, nonagons NOUN MATHS a shape with nine straight sides.

nonchalant [Said *non-shal-nt*] ADJECTIVE seeming calm and not worried. **nonchalance** NOUN **nonchalantly** ADVERB

noncommissioned officer, noncommissioned officers NOUN an officer such as a sergeant or corporal who has been promoted from the lower ranks.

nondescript ADJECTIVE Someone or something nondescript has no special or interesting qualities or details • *a nondescript coat*.

none PRONOUN not a single thing or person, or not even a small amount of something.

nonetheless ADVERB in spite of what has just been said • *His face is serious but nonetheless very friendly*.

nonfiction NOUN LIBRARY Nonfiction is writing that gives facts and information rather than telling a story.

nonmetal, nonmetals NOUN SCIENCE a chemical element such as carbon, oxygen or sulphur. Nonmetals are poor conductors of heat and electricity and form negative ions.

nonplussed ADJECTIVE confused and unsure about how to react.

non-renewable resources PLURAL NOUN GEOGRAPHY substances such as coal and oil that occur naturally and cannot be replaced once they have been used up.

nonsense NOUN Nonsense is foolish and meaningless words or behaviour. **nonsensical** ADJECTIVE

non sequitur, non sequiturs [Said non **sek**-kwit-ter] NOUN ENGLISH A non sequitur is a remark that does not follow logically from what has just been said.

WORD HISTORY: from Latin *non sequitur* meaning 'It does not follow'

nonstop ADJECTIVE OR ADVERB continuing without any pauses or breaks • *nonstop excitement*.

noodle, noodles NOUN Noodles are a kind of pasta shaped into long, thin pieces.

nook, nooks NOUN (*literary*) a small sheltered place.

noon NOUN Noon is midday.

no-one; also spelt **no one** PRONOUN not a single person.

USAGE NOTE
No-one and *nobody* mean the same.

---

noose, nooses NOUN a loop at the end of a piece of rope, with a knot that tightens when the rope is pulled.

nor CONJUNCTION used after 'neither' or after a negative statement, to add something else that the negative statement applies to • *They had neither the time nor the money for the sport*.

norm NOUN If something is the norm, it is the usual and expected thing • *cultures where large families are the norm*.

WORD HISTORY: from Latin *norma* meaning 'carpenter's rule'

normal ADJECTIVE usual and ordinary • *I try to lead a normal life*. **normality** NOUN

SIMILAR WORDS: conventional, ordinary, usual

normally ADVERB ① usually • *I don't normally like dancing*. ② in a way that is normal • *The foetus is developing normally*.

north NOUN ① The north is the direction to your left when you are looking towards the place where the sun rises. ② The north of a place or country is the part which is towards the north when you are in the centre. ▶ ADVERB OR ADJECTIVE ③ North means towards the north • *The helicopter took off and headed north*. ▶ ADJECTIVE ④ A north wind blows from the north.

North America NOUN North America is the third largest continent, consisting of Canada, the United States and Mexico.
North American ADJECTIVE

north-east NOUN OR ADVERB OR ADJECTIVE North-east is halfway between north and east.

north-easterly ADJECTIVE ① North-easterly means to or towards the north-east. ② A north-easterly wind blows from the north-east.

north-eastern ADJECTIVE in or from the north-east.

northerly ADJECTIVE ① Northerly means to or towards the north. ② A northerly wind blows from the north.

northern ADJECTIVE in or from the north • *the mountains of northern Italy*.

North Pole NOUN GEOGRAPHY The North Pole is the most northerly place on the surface of the earth.

northward or **northwards** ADVERB ① Northward or northwards means towards the north • *We continued northwards*. ▶ ADJECTIVE ② The northward part of something is the north part.

north-west NOUN OR ADVERB OR ADJECTIVE North-west is halfway between north and west.

north-westerly ADJECTIVE ① North-westerly means to or towards the north-west. ② A north-westerly wind blows from the north-west.

a
b
c
d
e
f
g
h
i
j
k
l
m
n
o
p
q
r
s
t
u
v
w
x
y
z

What does Not do?

You can turn most sentences into negatives if you want to express the opposite meaning.

You can usually make a sentence into a negative by adding the word *not*:

*Robbie was **not** feeling tired.*

If a sentence already contains an auxiliary verb, such as *have*, *will*, *be* or *must*, the word *not* should go after this verb:

*She has **not** gone to the shops.*

If the sentence does not already contain an auxiliary verb, a form of the verb *do* is added, and the word *not* is placed after this:

*We **do not** expect to win.*

In spoken and informal English, the ending -*n't* may be added to an auxiliary verb in place of *not*:

*She **hasn't** gone to the shops.*

north-western ADJECTIVE in or from the north-west.

Norwegian, **Norwegians** [*Said nor-wee-jn*] ADJECTIVE ① belonging or relating to Norway. ▸ NOUN ② someone who comes from Norway. ③ Norwegian is the main language spoken in Norway.

nose, **noses** NOUN ① the part of your face above your mouth which you use for smelling and breathing. ② the front part of a car or plane.

nostalgia [*Said nos-tal-ja*] NOUN Nostalgia is a feeling of affection for the past, and sadness that things have changed. **nostalgic** ADJECTIVE

nostril, **nostrils** NOUN Your nostrils are the two openings in your nose which you breathe through.

nosy, **nosier**, **nosiest**; also spelt **nosey** ADJECTIVE trying to find out about things that do not concern you.

not ADVERB used to make a sentence negative, to refuse something, or to deny something.

notable ADJECTIVE important or interesting • *The production is notable for some outstanding performances.* **notably** ADVERB

notation, **notations** NOUN A notation is a set of written symbols, such as those used in music or mathematics.
WORD HISTORY: from Latin *notare* meaning 'to note'

notch, **notches** NOUN a small V-shaped cut in a surface.
WORD HISTORY: from a mistaken division of Middle English *an otch*

note, **notes**, **noting**, **noted** NOUN ① a short letter. ② a written piece of information that helps you to remember something • *You should make a note of that.* ③ In music, a note is a musical sound of a particular pitch, or a written symbol that represents it. ④ a banknote. ⑤ an atmosphere, feeling or quality • *There was a note of regret in his voice* • *I'm determined to close on an optimistic note.* ▸ VERB ⑥ If you note a fact, you become aware of it or you mention it • *I noted that the rain had stopped.* ▸ PHRASE ⑦ If you **take note** of something, you pay attention to it • *The world hardly took note of this crisis.*
note down VERB If you note something down, you write it down so that you will remember it.

notebook, **notebooks** NOUN a small book for writing notes in.

noted ADJECTIVE well-known and admired • *a noted opera singer.*

nothing PRONOUN not anything
• *There was nothing to do*.
SIMILAR WORDS: nil, nought, zero

GRAMMAR TIP
Nothing is followed by a singular verb:
Nothing was in the bag.

---

notice, notices, noticing, noticed
VERB ① If you notice something,
you become aware of it. ▶ NOUN
② Notice is attention or awareness
• *I'm glad he brought it to my notice*. ③ a
written announcement. ④ Notice is
also advance warning about
something • *We were lucky to get you at
such short notice*. ▶ PHRASE ⑤ If you
hand in your notice, you tell your
employer that you intend to leave
your job after a fixed period of time.
SIMILAR WORDS: ① detect, observe,
perceive

noticeable ADJECTIVE obvious and
easy to see • *a noticeable improvement*.
noticeably ADVERB

noticeboard, noticeboards NOUN a
board for notices.

notification, notifications NOUN
① a formal announcement. ② an
indication to the user of a computer
or smartphone that they have
received a message, alert or update.

notify, notifies, notifying, notified
VERB To notify someone of
something means to officially inform
them of it • *You must notify us of any
change of address*.

notion, notions NOUN an idea or belief.

notorious ADJECTIVE well-known for
something bad • *The river has become
notorious for pollution*. **notoriously**
ADVERB **notoriety** NOUN

notwithstanding PREPOSITION
(*formal*) in spite of • *He liked his
classmate, notwithstanding his different
views*.

nougat [*Said noo-gah*] NOUN Nougat
is a kind of chewy sweet containing
nuts and sometimes fruit.
WORD HISTORY: from Provençal *noga*
meaning 'nut'

nought the number 0.

noun, nouns NOUN ENGLISH MFL
a word which refers to a person,
thing or idea. Examples of nouns are
'president', 'table', 'sun' and 'beauty'.

What is a Noun?

A noun is a word that labels a person,
a thing or an idea. In any sentence,
the nouns will tell you which people
or things are involved. They are
sometimes called 'naming words'.

Common nouns are words which
indicate every example of a certain
type of thing. They begin with small
letters:

girl city picture

Proper nouns are words which give
the name of a particular person,
place or object. They begin with
capital letters:

Anna Jamieson

Los Angeles
The Mona Lisa

Some common nouns are **concrete
nouns**. These are words that
indicate things that you *can* touch:

cat pen apple

Other common nouns are **abstract
nouns**. These are words that
indicate things that you *cannot* touch:

beauty ambition popularity

Some common nouns are **collective
nouns**. These are words that indicate
a group or collection of things:

pack bunch flock

a
b
c
d
e
f
g
h
i
j
k
l
m
n
o
p
q
r
s
t
u
v
w
x
y
z

nourish, nourishes, nourishing, nourished [*Said* **nur**-rish] **VERB** To nourish people or animals means to provide them with food.

nourishing **ADJECTIVE** Food that is nourishing makes you strong and healthy.

nourishment **NOUN** Nourishment is food that your body needs in order to remain healthy • *poor nourishment*.

novel, novels **NOUN** ① LIBRARY a book that tells an invented story. ▶ **ADJECTIVE** ② new and interesting • *a very novel experience*.

novelist, novelists **NOUN** a person who writes novels.

novelty, novelties **NOUN** ① Novelty is the quality of being new and interesting • *The novelty had worn off*. ② something new and interesting • *Steam power was still a bit of a novelty then*. ③ a small, unusual object sold as a gift or souvenir.

November **NOUN** November is the eleventh month of the year. It has 30 days.

WORD HISTORY: from Latin *November* meaning 'the ninth month'

novice, novices **NOUN** ① someone who is not yet experienced at something. ② someone who is preparing to become a monk or nun.

now **ADVERB** ① at the present time or moment. ▶ **CONJUNCTION** ② as a result or consequence of a particular fact • *Things have got better now there is a new board*. ▶ **PHRASE** ③ **Just now** means very recently • *I drove Brenda back to the camp just now*. ④ If something happens **now and then**, it happens sometimes but not regularly.

SPELLING TIP
Do not confuse the spellings of *now* and *know*: *Lunch is ready now; I think I know that girl*.

nowadays **ADVERB** at the present time, in contrast with in the past • *I don't go swimming much nowadays*.

nowhere **ADVERB** not anywhere.

noxious [*Said* **nok**-shus] **ADJECTIVE** harmful or poisonous • *a noxious gas*.

nozzle, nozzles **NOUN** a spout fitted onto the end of a pipe or hose to control the flow of a liquid.

nuance, nuances [*Said* **nyoo**-ahnss] **NOUN** a small difference in sound, colour or meaning • *the nuances of his music*.

nuclear **ADJECTIVE** ① SCIENCE relating to the energy produced when the nuclei of atoms are split • *nuclear power* • *the nuclear industry*. ② relating to weapons that explode using the energy released by atoms • *nuclear war*. ③ SCIENCE relating to the structure and behaviour of the nuclei of atoms • *nuclear physics*.

nuclear reactor, nuclear reactors **NOUN** A nuclear reactor is a device which is used to obtain nuclear energy.

nucleus, nuclei [*Said* **nyoo**-klee-uss] **NOUN** ① SCIENCE The nucleus of an atom is the central part of it. It is positively charged and is made up of protons and neutrons. ② SCIENCE The nucleus of a cell is the part that contains the chromosomes and controls the growth and reproduction of the cell. ③ The nucleus of something is the basic central part of it to which other things are added • *They have retained the nucleus of the team that won the World Cup*.

WORD HISTORY: from Latin *nucleus* meaning 'kernel'

nude, nudes **ADJECTIVE** ① naked. ▶ **NOUN** ② a picture or statue of a naked person. **nudity** **NOUN**

nudge, nudges, nudging, nudged **VERB** ① If you nudge someone, you push them gently, usually with your elbow. ▸NOUN ② a gentle push.

nudist, nudists NOUN a person who believes in wearing no clothes.

nugget, nuggets NOUN a small rough lump of something, especially gold.

nuisance, nuisances NOUN someone or something that is annoying or inconvenient.
SIMILAR WORDS: bother, inconvenience, problem

null PHRASE Null and void means not legally valid • Other documents were declared to be null and void.

nulla-nulla, nulla-nullas NOUN a thick heavy stick used as a weapon by Aboriginal Australians.

numb, numbs, numbing, numbed ADJECTIVE ① unable to feel anything • My legs felt numb • numb with grief. ▸VERB ② If something numbs you, it makes you unable to feel anything • The cold numbed my fingers.

numbat, numbats NOUN a small Australian marsupial with a long snout and tongue and strong claws which it uses for hunting and eating insects.

number, numbers, numbering, numbered NOUN ① a word or a symbol used for counting or calculating. ② Someone's number is the series of numbers that you use to telephone them. ③ A number of things is a quantity of them • Adrian has introduced me to a large number of people. ④ a song or piece of music.

▸VERB ⑤ If things number a particular amount, there are that many of them • At that time London's population numbered about 460,000. ⑥ If you number something, you give it a number • The picture is signed and numbered by the artist. ⑦ To be numbered among a particular group means to belong to it • Only the best are numbered among their champions.
SIMILAR WORDS: ① digit, figure, numeral

numeral, numerals NOUN a symbol that represents a number • a clock with Roman numerals.

numerate [Said nyoo-mer-rit] ADJECTIVE MATHS able to do arithmetic. **numeracy** NOUN

numerator, numerators NOUN MATHS In maths, the numerator is the top part of a fraction.

numerical ADJECTIVE expressed in numbers or relating to numbers • a numerical value.

numerous ADJECTIVE existing or happening in large numbers.

nun, nuns NOUN a woman who has taken religious vows and lives in a convent.

nurse, nurses, nursing, nursed NOUN ① a person whose job is to look after people who are ill. ▸VERB ② If you nurse someone, you look after them when they are ill. ③ If you nurse a feeling, you feel it strongly for a long time • He nursed a grudge against his teacher.

What do Numbers do?

Numbers tell you how many of a thing there are.

Cardinal numbers tell you the total number of a thing:

Three figures huddled in the doorway.

Ordinal numbers tell you the order of something. They often end with the letters -th:

Her **sixth** novel was the most successful yet.

nursery, **nurseries** NOUN ① a place where young children are looked after while their parents are working. ② a room in which young children sleep and play. ③ a place where plants are grown and sold.

nursery rhyme, **nursery rhymes** NOUN ENGLISH A nursery rhyme is a short poem or song for young children.

nursery school, **nursery schools** NOUN a school for children from three to five years old.

nursing home, **nursing homes** NOUN a privately run hospital, especially for elderly people.

nurture, **nurtures**, **nurturing**, **nurtured** VERB (*formal*) If you nurture a young child or a plant, you look after it carefully.

nut, **nuts** NOUN ① a fruit with a hard shell and an edible centre that grows on certain trees. ② a piece of metal with a hole in the middle which a bolt screws into.

nutmeg NOUN Nutmeg is a spice used for flavouring in cooking.

nutrient, **nutrients** NOUN SCIENCE Nutrients are substances that help plants or animals to grow • *the nutrients in the soil.*

nutrition NOUN DGT Nutrition is the food that you eat, considered from the point of view of how it helps you to grow and remain healthy • *The effects of poor nutrition are evident.* **nutritional** ADJECTIVE **nutritionist** NOUN

nutritious ADJECTIVE containing substances that help you to grow and remain healthy.

nutty, **nuttier**, **nuttiest** ADJECTIVE ① (*informal*) mad or very foolish. ② tasting of nuts.

nylon, **nylons** NOUN ① Nylon is a type of strong artificial material. ② Nylons are stockings or tights.

nymph, **nymphs** [*Said nimf*] NOUN In Greek and Roman mythology, a nymph is a young goddess who lives in trees, rivers or mountains.

Oo

oaf, oafs NOUN a clumsy and stupid person.
WORD HISTORY: from Old Norse *alfr* meaning 'elf'

oak, oaks NOUN a large tree which produces acorns. It has a hard wood which is often used to make furniture.

OAP, OAPs NOUN In Britain, an OAP is a person who receives a pension. OAP is an abbreviation for 'old age pensioner'.

oar, oars NOUN a wooden pole with a wide, flat end, used for rowing a boat.

oasis, oases [Said oh-*ay*-siss] NOUN GEOGRAPHY a small area in a desert where water and plants are found.

oat, oats NOUN Oats are a type of grain.

oath, oaths NOUN a formal promise, especially a promise to tell the truth in a court of law.
SIMILAR WORDS: pledge, promise, vow

oatmeal NOUN Oatmeal is a rough flour made from oats.

OBE, OBEs NOUN a British honour awarded by the King or Queen. OBE is an abbreviation for 'Officer of the Order of the British Empire' • *Jane Smith, OBE.*

obedient ADJECTIVE If you are obedient, you do what you are told to do. **obediently** ADVERB **obedience** NOUN

obelisk, obelisks NOUN a stone pillar built in honour of a person or an event.

obese [Said oh-*bees*] ADJECTIVE extremely fat. **obesity** NOUN
WORD HISTORY: from Latin *ob-* meaning 'much' and *edere* meaning 'to eat'

obey, obeys, obeying, obeyed VERB If you obey a person or an order, you do what you are told to do.

obituary, obituaries NOUN a piece of writing about the life and achievements of someone who has just died.

object, objects, objecting, objected [Said *ob*-ject] NOUN ① anything solid that you can touch or see, and that is not alive. ② an aim or purpose. ③ The object of your feelings or actions is the person that they are directed towards. ④ MFL In grammar, the object of a verb or preposition is the word or phrase which follows it and describes the person or thing affected. ▶ VERB [Said ob-*ject*] ⑤ If you object to something, you dislike it or disapprove of it.
SIMILAR WORDS: ⑤ oppose, protest, take exception

objection, objections NOUN If you have an objection to something, you dislike it or disapprove of it.

objectionable ADJECTIVE unpleasant and offensive.

objective, objectives NOUN ① an aim • *The protection of the countryside is their main objective.* ▶ ADJECTIVE ② If you are objective, you are not

influenced by personal feelings or prejudices • *an objective approach*.
objectively ADVERB **objectivity** NOUN

obligation, obligations NOUN something that you must do because it is your duty.

obligatory [Said ob-**lig**-a-tree] ADJECTIVE required by a rule or law • *Religious education was made obligatory*.

oblige, obliges, obliging, obliged VERB ① If you are obliged to do something, you have to do it. ② If you oblige someone, you help them. **obliging** ADJECTIVE

oblique [Said o-**bleek**] ADJECTIVE ① An oblique remark is not direct, and is therefore difficult to understand. ② An oblique line slopes at an angle.

obliterate, obliterates, obliterating, obliterated VERB To obliterate something is to destroy it completely. **obliteration** NOUN

oblivion NOUN Oblivion is unconsciousness or complete lack of awareness of your surroundings. **oblivious** ADJECTIVE **obliviously** ADVERB

oblong, oblongs NOUN ① a four-sided shape with two parallel short sides, two parallel long sides, and four right angles. ▶ ADJECTIVE ② shaped like an oblong.

obnoxious [Said ob-**nok**-shuss] ADJECTIVE extremely unpleasant.

oboe, oboes NOUN a woodwind musical instrument with a double reed. **oboist** NOUN
WORD HISTORY: from French *haut bois* meaning literally 'high wood', a reference to the instrument's pitch

obscene ADJECTIVE indecent and likely to upset people • *obscene pictures*. **obscenely** ADVERB **obscenity** NOUN

SIMILAR WORDS: filthy, indecent, pornographic

obscure, obscures, obscuring, obscured ADJECTIVE ① Something that is obscure is known by only a few people • *an obscure Mongolian dialect*. ② Something obscure is difficult to see or to understand • *The news was shrouded in obscure language*. ▶ VERB ③ To obscure something is to make it difficult to see or understand • *His view was obscured by trees*. **obscurity** NOUN
SIMILAR WORDS: ② cryptic, unclear, vague

observance NOUN The observance of a law or custom is the practice of obeying or following it.

observant ADJECTIVE Someone who is observant notices things that are not easy to see.

observation, observations NOUN ① Observation is the act of watching something carefully • *Success hinges on close observation*. ② something that you have seen or noticed. ③ a remark. ④ Observation is the ability to notice things that are not easy to see.

observatory, observatories NOUN a room or building containing telescopes and other equipment for studying the sun, moon and stars.

observe, observes, observing, observed VERB ① To observe something is to watch it carefully. ② To observe something is to notice it. ③ If you observe that something is the case, you make a comment about it. ④ To observe a law or custom is to obey or follow it. **observer** NOUN **observable** ADJECTIVE

obsession, obsessions NOUN If someone has an obsession about something, they cannot stop thinking about that thing.

obsessional ADJECTIVE **obsessed** ADJECTIVE **obsessive** ADJECTIVE

obsolete ADJECTIVE out of date and no longer used.

SIMILAR WORDS: outmoded, passé

obstacle, obstacles NOUN something which is in your way and makes it difficult to do something.

SIMILAR WORDS: difficulty, stumbling block

obstetrician, obstetricians NOUN An obstetrician is a doctor who specialises in the care of women during pregnancy and childbirth.

obstetrics NOUN Obstetrics is the branch of medicine concerned with pregnancy and childbirth.

WORD HISTORY: from Latin *obstetrix* meaning 'midwife'

obstinate ADJECTIVE Someone who is obstinate is stubborn and unwilling to change their mind.

obstinately ADVERB **obstinacy** NOUN

obstruct, obstructs, obstructing, obstructed VERB If something obstructs a road or path, it blocks it.

obstruction NOUN **obstructive** ADJECTIVE

obtain, obtains, obtaining, obtained VERB If you obtain something, you get it. **obtainable** ADJECTIVE

obtrusive ADJECTIVE noticeable in an unpleasant way • *a remarkably obtrusive cigar.*

obtuse ADJECTIVE ① Someone who is obtuse is stupid or slow to understand things. ② MATHS An obtuse angle is between 90° and 180°.

obvious ADJECTIVE easy to see or understand. **obviously** ADVERB

SIMILAR WORDS: clear, evident, plain

occasion, occasions, occasioning, occasioned NOUN ① a time when something happens. ② an important event. ③ An occasion for doing something is an opportunity for doing it. ▶ VERB ④ (*formal*) To occasion something is to cause it • *damage occasioned by fire.*

occasional ADJECTIVE happening sometimes but not often • *an occasional outing.* **occasionally** ADVERB

occult NOUN The occult is the knowledge and study of supernatural and magical forces or powers.

occupancy NOUN The occupancy of a building is the act of living or working in it.

occupant, occupants NOUN The occupants of a building are the people who live or work in it.

occupation, occupations NOUN ① a job or profession. ② a hobby or something you do for pleasure. ③ The occupation of a country is the act of invading it and taking control of it. **occupational** ADJECTIVE

occupy, occupies, occupying, occupied VERB ① The people who occupy a building are the people who live or work there. ② When people occupy a place, they move into it and take control of it • *Demonstrators occupied the building.* ③ To occupy a position in a system or plan is to have that position • *His phone-in show occupies a daytime slot.* ④ If something occupies you, you spend your time doing it • *That problem occupies me night and day.* **occupier** NOUN

occur, occurs, occurring, occurred VERB ① If something occurs, it happens or exists • *The crash occurred yesterday evening.* ② If something occurs to you, you suddenly think of it.

a
b
c
d
e
f
g
h
i
j
k
l
m
n
o
p
q
r
s
t
u
v
w
x
y
z

A B C D E F G H I J K L M N O P Q R S T U V W X Y Z

USAGE NOTE
If an event has been planned, you should not say that it *occurred* or *happened: The wedding took place on Saturday.* Only something unexpected *occurs* or *happens: An accident has occurred; The burglary happened last night.*

occurrence, occurrences NOUN
① an event. ② The occurrence of something is the fact that it happens or exists • *the occurrence of diseases*.

OCD NOUN If someone has OCD, they cannot stop doing a particular thing, for example washing their hands. OCD is an abbreviation for 'obsessive-compulsive disorder'.

ocean, oceans NOUN ① the sea. ② The five oceans are the five very large areas of sea on the Earth's surface • *the Atlantic Ocean*. **oceanic** ADJECTIVE

o'clock ADVERB You use 'o'clock' after the number of the hour to say what the time is.

octagon, octagons NOUN MATHS a shape with eight straight sides. **octagonal** ADJECTIVE

octave, octaves NOUN ① MUSIC the difference in pitch between the first note and the eighth note of a musical scale. ② ENGLISH eight lines of poetry together.

octet, octets NOUN MUSIC a group of eight musicians who sing or play together; also a piece of music written for eight instruments or singers.

October NOUN October is the tenth month of the year. It has 31 days.
WORD HISTORY: from Latin *October* meaning 'the eighth month'

octopus, octopuses NOUN a sea creature with eight long tentacles which it uses to catch food.
WORD HISTORY: from Greek *okto* + *pous* meaning 'eight feet'

odd, odder, oddest ADJECTIVE
① Something odd is strange or unusual. ② Odd things do not match each other • *odd socks*. ③ Odd numbers are numbers that cannot be divided exactly by two. ▶ ADVERB
④ You use 'odd' after a number to say that it is approximate • *I've written twenty-odd plays.* **oddly** ADVERB **oddness** NOUN

oddity, oddities NOUN something very strange.

oddments PLURAL NOUN Oddments are things that are left over after other things have been used.

odds PLURAL NOUN The odds of something happening are how likely it is to happen • *The odds are against the record being beaten.*

odds and ends PLURAL NOUN You can refer to a collection of small unimportant things as odds and ends.

ode, odes NOUN ENGLISH a poem written in praise of someone or something.

odious ADJECTIVE extremely unpleasant.

odour, odours NOUN (*formal*) a strong smell. **odorous** ADJECTIVE

odyssey, odysseys [*Said od-i-see*] NOUN An odyssey is a long and eventful journey. The name comes from Odysseus, the Greek hero who wandered from adventure to adventure for ten years.

oesophagus, oesophaguses [*Said ee-sof-fag-uss*] NOUN the tube that carries food from your throat to your stomach.

oestrogen another spelling of **estrogen**.

of PREPOSITION ① consisting of or containing • *a collection of short stories* • *a cup of tea.* ② used when naming something or describing a characteristic of something • *the city of Canberra* • *a woman of great power and influence*. ③ belonging to or connected with • *a friend of Rachel* • *the cover of the book*.

GRAMMAR TIP

Where *of* means 'belonging to', it can be replaced by an apostrophe: *the cover of the book* is the same as *the book's cover*.

SPELLING TIP

Do not confuse the spellings of *of* and *off*: *a bunch of tulips; Do you want to take off your coat?*

---

off PREPOSITION or ADVERB
① indicating movement away from or out of a place • *They had just stepped off the plane* • *She got up and marched off*. ② indicating separation or distance from a place • *some islands off the coast of Australia* • *The whole crescent has been fenced off*. ③ not working • *It was Frank's night off*. ▶ ADVERB or ADJECTIVE ④ not switched on • *He turned the radio off* • *the off switch*. ▶ ADJECTIVE ⑤ cancelled or postponed • *The concert was off*. ⑥ Food that is off has gone sour or bad. ▶ PREPOSITION ⑦ not liking or not using something • *He went right off chocolate*.

GRAMMAR TIP

Do not use *of* after *off*. You should say *he stepped off the bus* not *he stepped off of the bus*. It is very informal to use *off* where you mean 'from': *They bought milk off a farmer* instead of *They bought milk from a farmer*. Always use *from* in written work.

---

offal NOUN Offal is liver, kidneys and internal organs of animals, which can be eaten.

offence, offences NOUN ① a crime • *a driving offence*. ▶ PHRASE ② If something **gives offence**, it upsets people. If you **take offence**, you are upset by someone or something.

offend, offends, offending, offended VERB ① If you offend someone, you upset them. ② *(formal)* To offend or to offend against a law is to commit a crime. **offender** NOUN

offensive, offensives ADJECTIVE ① Something offensive is rude and upsetting • *offensive behaviour*. ② Offensive actions or weapons are used in attacking someone. ▶ NOUN ③ an attack • *a full-scale offensive against the rebels*. **offensively** ADVERB

offer, offers, offering, offered VERB ① If you offer something to someone, you ask them if they would like it. ▶ NOUN ② something that someone says they will give you or do for you if you want them to • *Many refused the offer anyway*. ③ a specially low price for a product in a shop • *You will need a voucher to qualify for the special offer*.

offering, offerings NOUN something that is offered or given to someone.

offhand ADJECTIVE ① If someone is offhand, they are unfriendly and slightly rude. ▶ ADVERB ② If you know something offhand, you know it without having to think very hard • *I couldn't tell you offhand how long he's been here*.

office, offices NOUN ① a room where people work at desks. ② a government department • *the Office of Fair Trading*. ③ a place where people can go for information, tickets or other services. ④ Someone who holds office has an important job or position in government or in an organisation.

officer, officers NOUN a person with a position of authority in the armed forces, the police or a government organisation.

a
b
c
d
e
f
g
h
i
j
k
l
m
n
o
p
q
r
s
t
u
v
w
x
y
z

official, officials ADJECTIVE
① approved by the government or by someone in authority • *the official figures.* ② done or used by someone in authority as part of their job • *official notepaper.* ▶ NOUN ③ a person who holds a position of authority in an organisation.
officially ADVERB

officialdom NOUN You can refer to officials in government or other organisations as officialdom, especially when you find them difficult to deal with.

officiate, officiates, officiating, officiated VERB To officiate at a ceremony is to be in charge and perform the official part of the ceremony.

offing PHRASE If something is **in the offing**, it is likely to happen soon • *A change is in the offing.*

off-licence, off-licences NOUN a shop which sells alcoholic drinks.

offline ADJECTIVE ① If a computer is offline, it is switched off or not connected to the internet. ▶ ADVERB ② If you do something offline, you do it while not connected to the internet.

offset, offsets, offsetting, offset VERB If one thing is offset by another thing, its effect is reduced or cancelled out by that thing • *This tedium can be offset by watching the television.*

offshoot, offshoots NOUN something that has developed from another thing • *The technology we use is an offshoot of the motor industry.*

offshore ADJECTIVE or ADVERB in or from the part of the sea near the shore • *an offshore wind* • *a wreck fifteen kilometres offshore.*

offside ADJECTIVE If a soccer, rugby or hockey player is offside, they have broken the rules by moving too far forward.

offspring NOUN A person's or animal's offspring are their children.

often ADVERB happening many times or a lot of the time.

ogre, ogres [*Said oh-gur*] NOUN a cruel, frightening giant in a fairy story.

ohm, ohms [*Rhymes with home*] NOUN [SCIENCE] An ohm is a unit of electrical resistance. When the resistance is one ohm, each volt of electrical force produces one amp of current. The ohm is named after the German physicist G.S. Ohm (1787–1854).

oil, oils, oiling, oiled NOUN ① Oil is a thick, sticky liquid used as a fuel and for lubrication. ② Oil is also a thick, greasy liquid made from plants or animals • *cooking oil* • *bath oil.* ▶ VERB ③ If you oil something, you put oil in it or on it.

oil paint, oil paints NOUN Oil paint is a thick paint used by artists, made from a coloured powder and linseed oil.

oil painting, oil paintings NOUN An oil painting is a painting that has been painted with oil paints.

oilskin, oilskins NOUN a piece of clothing made from a thick, waterproof material, worn especially by fishermen.

oily ADJECTIVE Something that is oily is covered with or contains oil • *an oily rag* • *oily skin.*

ointment, ointments NOUN a smooth, thick substance that you put on sore skin to heal it.

okay; also spelt **OK** ADJECTIVE (*informal*) Okay means all right • *Tell me if this sounds okay.*
SIMILAR WORDS: acceptable, all right, satisfactory

old, older, oldest ADJECTIVE ① having lived or existed for a long time • *an old lady* • *old clothes*. ② 'Old' is used to give the age of someone or something • *This photo is five years old*. ③ 'Old' also means former • *my old art teacher*.

olden PHRASE In the olden days means long ago.

Old English NOUN Old English was the English language from the fifth century AD until about 1100. Old English is also known as Anglo-Saxon.

old-fashioned ADJECTIVE ① Something which is old-fashioned is no longer fashionable • *old-fashioned shoes*. ② Someone who is old-fashioned believes in the values and standards of the past.
SIMILAR WORDS: ① dated, outmoded, passé

Old Norse NOUN Old Norse was a language spoken in Scandinavia and Iceland from about 700 AD to about 1350 AD. Many English words are derived from Old Norse.

Old Testament NOUN RE The Old Testament is the first part of the Christian Bible. It is also the holy book of the Jewish religion and contains writings which relate to the history of the Jews.

oleander, oleanders NOUN an evergreen shrub with fragrant white, pink or purple flowers.

olive, olives NOUN ① a small green or black fruit containing a stone. Olives are usually pickled and eaten as a snack or crushed to produce oil.
▶ ADJECTIVE or NOUN ② dark yellowish-green.

-ology SUFFIX '-ology' is used to form words that refer to the study of something • *biology* • *geology*.
WORD HISTORY: from Greek *logos* meaning 'reason', 'speech' or 'discourse'

Olympic Games *[Said ol-lim-pik]* PLURAL NOUN (trademark) The Olympic Games are a set of sporting contests held in a different city every four years. It originated in Ancient Greece where a contest was regularly held in Olympia to honour the god Zeus.

ombudsman, ombudsmen NOUN The ombudsman is a person who investigates complaints against the government or a public organisation.

omelette, omelettes *[Said om-lit]* NOUN a dish made by beating eggs together and cooking them in a flat pan.

omen, omens NOUN something that is thought to be a sign of what will happen in the future • *John saw this success as a good omen for his trip*.
SIMILAR WORDS: portent, sign

ominous ADJECTIVE suggesting that something unpleasant is going to happen • *an ominous sign*. **ominously** ADVERB
SIMILAR WORDS: sinister, threatening

omission, omissions NOUN ① something that has not been included or done • *There are some striking omissions in the survey*. ② Omission is the act of not including or not doing something • *controversy over the omission of female novelists from the shortlist*.

SPELLING TIP
Do not confuse the spellings of *omission* and *emission*: *Her omission from the team is a big surprise; the plan to cut carbon emissions*.

---

omit, omits, omitting, omitted VERB ① If you omit something, you do not include it. ② (formal) If you omit to do something, you do not do it.

a b c d e f g h i j k l m n o p q r s t u v w x y z

omnibus, **omnibuses** NOUN ① a book containing a collection of stories or articles by the same author or about the same subject. ▶ ADJECTIVE ② An omnibus edition of a radio or television show contains two or more programmes that were originally broadcast separately.

omnipotent [Said om-**nip**-a-tent] ADJECTIVE having very great or unlimited power • omnipotent emperors. **omnipotence** NOUN

omniscient narrator, **omniscient narrators** NOUN ⎡ENGLISH⎤ A narrator who tells a story that he or she is not part of, and who knows everything about all the characters: their past, their future, and even what they think.

omnivore NOUN An omnivore is an animal that eats all kinds of food, including meat and plants. **omnivorous** ADJECTIVE

on PREPOSITION ① above and supported by, touching, or attached to something • The woman was sitting on the sofa. ② If you are on a bus, plane or train, you are inside it. ③ If something happens on a particular day, that is when it happens • It is his birthday on Monday. ④ If something is done on an instrument or machine, it is done using that instrument or machine • He preferred to play on his computer. ⑤ A book or talk on a particular subject is about that subject. ▶ ADVERB ⑥ If you have a piece of clothing on, you are wearing it. ▶ ADJECTIVE ⑦ A machine or switch that is on is working. ⑧ If an event is on, it is happening or taking place • The race is definitely on.

once ADVERB ① If something happens once, it happens one time only. ② If something was once true, it was true in the past, but is no longer true. ▶ CONJUNCTION ③ If something happens once another thing has happened, it happens immediately afterwards • Once we understood the problem, we tried to find a solution. ▶ PHRASE ④ If you do something **at once**, you do it immediately. If several things happen **at once**, they all happen at the same time.

one, **ones** ① the number 1. ▶ ADJECTIVE ② If you refer to the one person or thing of a particular kind, you mean the only person or thing of that kind • My one aim is to look after the horses well. ③ One also means 'a', used when emphasising something • They got one almighty shock. ▶ PRONOUN ④ One refers to a particular thing or person • Alf Brown's business was a good one. ⑤ One also means people in general • One likes to have the opportunity to chat.

one-off, **one-offs** NOUN something that happens or is made only once.

onerous [Said **ohn**-er-uss] ADJECTIVE (formal) difficult or unpleasant • an onerous task.

oneself PRONOUN 'Oneself' is used when you are talking about people in general • One could hardly hear oneself talk.

one-sided ADJECTIVE ① If an activity or relationship is one-sided, one of the people has a lot more success or involvement than the other • a one-sided contest. ② A one-sided argument or report considers the facts or a situation from only one point of view.

one-way ADJECTIVE ① One-way streets are streets along which vehicles can drive in only one direction. ② A one-way ticket is one that you can use to travel to a place, but not to travel back again.

ongoing ADJECTIVE continuing to

happen • *an ongoing process of learning*.

onion, onions NOUN a small, round vegetable with a brown skin like paper and a very strong taste.

online ADJECTIVE ① Online activity is carried out using the internet • *online shopping*. ② If a computer is online, it is switched on or connected to the internet. ▶ ADVERB ③ If you do something online, you do it while connected to the internet.

onlooker, onlookers NOUN someone who is watching an event.

only ADVERB ① You use 'only' to indicate the one thing or person involved • *Only Keith knows whether he will continue*. ② You use 'only' to emphasise that something is unimportant or small • *He's only a little boy*. ③ You can use 'only' to introduce something which happens immediately after something else • *She had thought of one plan, only to discard it for another*. ▶ ADJECTIVE ④ If you talk about the only thing or person, you mean that there are no others • *their only hit single*. ⑤ If you are an only child, you have no brothers or sisters. ▶ CONJUNCTION ⑥ 'Only' also means but or except • *He was like you, only blond*. ▶ PHRASE ⑦ Only too means extremely • *I would be only too happy to swap places*.

onomatopoeia [*Said on-o-mat-o-pee-a*] NOUN ENGLISH the use of words which sound like the thing that they represent. 'Hiss' and 'buzz' are examples of onomatopoeia.
onomatopoeic ADJECTIVE
WORD HISTORY: from Greek *onoma* meaning 'name' and *poiein* meaning 'to make'

onset NOUN The onset of something unpleasant is the beginning of it • *the onset of war*.

onslaught, onslaughts [*Said on-slawt*] NOUN a violent attack.

onto; also spelt **on to** PREPOSITION If you put something onto an object, you put it on it.

onus [*Rhymes with bonus*] NOUN (formal) If the onus is on you to do something, it is your duty or responsibility to do it.

onwards or **onward** ADVERB ① continuing to happen from a particular time • *He could not speak a word from that moment onwards*. ② travelling forwards • *Duncliffe escorted the pair onwards to his own room*.

onyx [*Said on-iks*] NOUN Onyx is a semiprecious stone used for making ornaments and jewellery.

ooze, oozes, oozing, oozed VERB When a thick liquid oozes, it flows slowly • *The cold mud oozed over her new footwear*.

opal, opals NOUN a pale or whitish semiprecious stone used for making jewellery.

opaque [*Said oh-pake*] ADJECTIVE If something is opaque, you cannot see through it • *opaque glass windows*.

open, opens, opening, opened VERB ① When you open something, or when it opens, you move it so that it is no longer closed • *She opened the door*. ② When a shop or office opens, people are able to go in. ③ To open something also means to start it • *He tried to open a bank account*.
▶ ADJECTIVE ④ Something that is open is not closed or fastened • *an open box of chocolates*. ⑤ If you have an open mind, you are willing to consider new ideas or suggestions. ⑥ Someone who is open is honest and frank. ⑦ When a shop or office is open, people are able to go in. ⑧ An open area of sea or land is a large,

a
b
c
d
e
f
g
h
i
j
k
l
m
n
o
p
q
r
s
t
u
v
w
x
y
z

empty area • *open country.* ⑨ If something is open to you, it is possible for you to do it • *There is no other course open to us but to fight it out.* ⑩ If a situation is still open, it is still being considered • *Even if the case remains open, the full facts may never be revealed.* ▸ **PHRASE** ⑪ **In the open** means outside. ⑫ **In the open** also means not secret. **openly ADVERB**

opening, openings ADJECTIVE ① Opening means coming first • *the opening day of the season.* ▸ **NOUN** ② The opening of a book or film is the first part of it. ③ a hole or gap. ④ an opportunity • *She waited for an opening to bring up the subject.*
SIMILAR WORDS: ③ aperture, gap, hole

open-minded ADJECTIVE willing to consider new ideas and suggestions.

open-plan ADJECTIVE An open-plan office or building has very few dividing walls inside.

opera, operas NOUN a play in which the words are sung rather than spoken. **operatic** ADJECTIVE
WORD HISTORY: from Latin *opera* meaning 'works'

operate, operates, operating, operated VERB ① To operate is to work • *We are shocked at the way that businesses operate.* ② When you operate a machine, you make it work. ③ When surgeons operate, they cut open a patient's body to remove or repair a damaged part.

operating system, operating systems NOUN ICT The operating system of a computer is its most basic program, which it needs in order to function and run other programs.

operation, operations NOUN ① a complex planned event • *a full-scale military operation.* ② a form of

medical treatment in which a surgeon cuts open a patient's body to remove or repair a damaged part. ③ MATHS any process in which a number or quantity is operated on according to a set of rules, for example addition, subtraction, multiplication and division.
▸ **PHRASE** ④ If something is **in operation**, it is working or being used • *The system is in operation from April to the end of September.*

operational ADJECTIVE working or able to be used • *an operational aircraft.*

operative ADJECTIVE Something that is operative is working or having an effect.

operator, operators NOUN ① someone who operates a machine • *a forklift operator.* ② someone who runs a business • *a tour operator.* ③ someone who connects telephone calls in places such as an office or hotel.

opinion, opinions NOUN a belief or view.
SIMILAR WORDS: belief, judgment, view

opinionated ADJECTIVE Someone who is opinionated has strong views and refuses to accept that they might be wrong.

opium NOUN Opium is a drug made from the seeds of a poppy. It is used in medicine to relieve pain.
WORD HISTORY: from Latin *opium* meaning 'poppy juice'

opossum, opossums NOUN An opossum is a small animal which carries its young in a pouch on its body and has a long tail. Opossums are found in North and South America. They are famous for pretending to be dead when in danger.

WORD HISTORY: an American Indian word

opponent, opponents NOUN someone who is against you in an argument or a contest.

opportune ADJECTIVE (*formal*) happening at a convenient time • *The king's death was opportune for the prince.*

opportunism NOUN Opportunism is taking advantage of any opportunity to gain money or power for yourself. **opportunist** NOUN

opportunity, opportunities NOUN a chance to do something.

oppose, opposes, opposing, opposed VERB If you oppose something, you disagree with it and try to prevent it.

opposed ADJECTIVE ① If you are opposed to something, you disagree with it • *He was totally opposed to bullying in schools.* ② Opposed also means opposite or very different • *two opposed schools of thought.* ▶ PHRASE ③ If you refer to one thing **as opposed to** another, you are emphasising that it is the first thing rather than the second which concerns you • *Real spectators, as opposed to invited guests, were hard to spot.*

opposite, opposites PREPOSITION or ADVERB ① If one thing is opposite another, it is facing it • *the shop opposite the station* • *the house opposite.* ▶ ADJECTIVE ② The opposite part of something is the part farthest away from you • *the opposite side of town.* ③ If things are opposite, they are completely different • *I take the opposite view to you.* ▶ NOUN ④ If two things are completely different, they are opposites.

SIMILAR WORDS: ④ antithesis, contrary, reverse

opposition NOUN ① If there is opposition to something, people disagree with it and try to prevent it. ② The political parties who are not in power are referred to as the opposition. ③ In a game or sports event, the opposition is the person or team that you are competing against.

oppressed ADJECTIVE People who are oppressed are treated cruelly or unfairly. **oppress** VERB **oppressor** NOUN

oppression NOUN cruel and unfair treatment of people.

oppressive ADJECTIVE ① If the weather is oppressive, it is hot and humid. ② An oppressive situation makes you feel dispirited or concerned • *The silence became oppressive.* ③ An oppressive system treats people cruelly or unfairly • *Some groups in the country were subject to oppressive laws.* **oppressively** ADVERB

opt, opts, opting, opted VERB If you opt for something, you choose it. If you opt out of something, you choose not to be involved in it.

optic ADJECTIVE relating to eyes • *the optic nerves.* **WORD HISTORY:** from Greek *optos* meaning 'seen' or 'visible'

optical ADJECTIVE ① SCIENCE concerned with vision, light or images. ② relating to the appearance of things.

optical fibre, optical fibres NOUN ICT a very thin thread of glass inside a protective coating. Optical fibres are used to carry information in the form of light.

optician, opticians NOUN someone who tests people's eyes, and makes and sells glasses and contact lenses.

optimism NOUN Optimism is a feeling of hopefulness about the future. **optimist** NOUN

a
b
c
d
e
f
g
h
i
j
k
l
m
n
o
p
q
r
s
t
u
v
w
x
y
z

optimistic ADJECTIVE hopeful about the future. **optimistically** ADVERB

optimum ADJECTIVE the best that is possible • *50 to 80 centimetres is the optimum size.*

option, options NOUN a choice between two or more things. **optional** ADJECTIVE

opulent [Said op-yool-nt] ADJECTIVE grand and expensive-looking • *an opulent seafront estate.* **opulence** NOUN

opus, opuses or opera NOUN ① MUSIC An opus is a musical composition. 'Opus' is often used with a number, indicating its position in a series of published works by the same composer. ② ART An opus is also a great artistic work, such as a piece of writing or a painting.

or CONJUNCTION ① used to link two different things • *I didn't know whether to laugh or cry.* ② used to introduce a warning • *Do what I say or else I will fire.*

-or SUFFIX '-or' is used to form nouns from verbs • *actor* • *conductor.*
WORD HISTORY: from Latin

oracle, oracles NOUN ① In ancient Greece, an oracle was a place where a priest or priestess made predictions about the future. ② a prophecy made by a priest or other person with great authority or wisdom.

oral, orals ADJECTIVE ① spoken rather than written • *oral history.* ② Oral describes things that are used in your mouth or done with your mouth • *an oral vaccine.* ▶ NOUN ③ an examination that is spoken rather than written. **orally** ADVERB
SIMILAR WORDS: ① spoken, verbal

SPELLING TIP
Do not confuse the spellings of *oral* and *aural*: *I failed the oral examination; sounds that test aural function.*

orange, oranges NOUN ① a round citrus fruit that is juicy and sweet and has a thick reddish-yellow skin. ▶ ADJECTIVE or NOUN ② reddish-yellow.
WORD HISTORY: from Sanskrit *naranga* meaning 'orange'

orang-utan, orang-utans; also spelt **orang-utang** NOUN An orang-utan is a large ape with reddish-brown hair. Orang-utans come from the forests of Borneo and Sumatra.
WORD HISTORY: from Malay *orang* meaning 'man' and *hutan* meaning 'forest'

orator, orators NOUN someone who is good at making speeches.

oratory NOUN Oratory is the art and skill of making formal public speeches.

orbit, orbits, orbiting, orbited NOUN ① SCIENCE the curved path followed by an object going round a planet or the sun. ▶ VERB ② If something orbits a planet or the sun, it goes round and round it.

orchard, orchards NOUN a piece of land where fruit trees are grown.

orchestra, orchestras [Said or-kess-tra] NOUN MUSIC a large group of musicians who play musical instruments together. **orchestral** ADJECTIVE
WORD HISTORY: from Greek *orkhēstra* meaning 'the area in a theatre reserved for musicians'

orchestrate, orchestrates, orchestrating, orchestrated VERB ① To orchestrate something is to organise it very carefully in order to produce a particular result. ② To orchestrate a piece of music is to rewrite it so that it can be played by an orchestra. **orchestration** NOUN

orchid, orchids [Said or-kid] NOUN Orchids are plants with beautiful and unusual flowers.

ordain, ordains, ordaining, ordained
VERB When someone is ordained,
they are made a member of the clergy.

ordeal, ordeals **NOUN** a difficult and
extremely unpleasant experience
• *the ordeal of being arrested and charged
with attempted murder*.
SIMILAR WORDS: hardship, torture,
tribulation

order, orders, ordering, ordered
NOUN ① a command given by
someone in authority. ② If things are
arranged or done in a particular
order, they are arranged or done in
that sequence • *in alphabetical order*.
③ Order is a situation in which
everything is in the correct place or
done at the correct time.
④ something that you ask to be
brought to you or sent to you. ⑤ An
order is a division of living organisms
that is smaller than a class and larger
than a family. ▶ **VERB** ⑥ To order
someone to do something is to tell
them firmly to do it. ⑦ When you
order something, you ask for it to be
brought or sent to you. ▶ **PHRASE** ⑧ If
you do something **in order to**
achieve a particular thing, you do it
because you want to achieve that
thing.

orderly **ADJECTIVE** Something that is
orderly is organised or arranged well.
SIMILAR WORDS: methodical,
well-organised

ordinal number, ordinal numbers
NOUN An ordinal number is a number
such as 'third' or 'fifth', which tells you
what position something has in a
group or series.

ordinarily **ADVERB** If something
ordinarily happens, it usually
happens.

ordinary **ADJECTIVE** Ordinary means
not special or different in any way.
SIMILAR WORDS: conventional,
normal, usual

ordination **NOUN** When someone's
ordination takes place, they are
made a member of the clergy.

ordnance **NOUN** Weapons and other
military supplies are referred to as
ordnance.

ore, ores **NOUN** GEOGRAPHY Ore is
rock or earth from which metal can
be obtained.

oregano [Said or-rig-**gah**-no] **NOUN**
Oregano is a herb used for flavouring
in cooking.

organ, organs **NOUN** ① SCIENCE
Your organs are parts of your body
that have a particular function, for
example your heart or lungs. ② a
large musical instrument with pipes
of different lengths through which
air is forced. It has various keyboards
which are played like a piano.

organic **ADJECTIVE** ① Something that
is organic is produced by or found in
plants or animals • *decaying organic
matter*. ② Organic food is produced
without the use of artificial fertilisers
or pesticides. **organically** **ADVERB**

organisation, organisations; also
spelt **organization** **NOUN** ① any
group or business. ② The
organisation of something is the act
of planning and arranging it.
organisational **ADJECTIVE**
SIMILAR WORDS: ① body, company,
group

organise, organises, organising,
organised; also spelt **organize** **VERB**
① If you organise an event, you plan
and arrange it. ② If you organise
things, you arrange them in a
sensible order. **organised** **ADJECTIVE**
organiser **NOUN**

organism, organisms **NOUN**
SCIENCE any living animal, plant,
fungus or bacterium.

organist, organists **NOUN** someone
who plays the organ.

a
b
c
d
e
f
g
h
i
j
k
l
m
n
o
p
q
r
s
t
u
v
w
x
y
z

orgy, orgies [Said or-jee] NOUN You can refer to a period of intense activity as an orgy of that activity • an orgy of violence.
WORD HISTORY: from Greek orgia meaning 'nocturnal festival'

Orient NOUN (literary) The Orient is eastern and south-eastern Asia.

oriental ADJECTIVE relating to eastern or south-eastern Asia.

orientated ADJECTIVE If someone is interested in a particular thing, you can say that they are orientated towards it • These people are very career-orientated.

orientation NOUN You can refer to an organisation's activities and aims as its orientation • Poland's political and military orientation.

oriented ADJECTIVE Oriented means the same as orientated.

orienteering NOUN Orienteering is a sport in which people run from one place to another in the countryside, using a map and compass to guide them.

origin, origins NOUN ① You can refer to the beginning or cause of something as its origin or origins. ② You can refer to someone's family background as their origin or origins • She was of Swedish origin. ③ In mathematics, the origin is the point where two or more axes meet.
SIMILAR WORDS: ① root, source

original, originals ADJECTIVE ① Original describes things that existed at the beginning, rather than being added later, or things that were the first of their kind to exist • the original owner of the cottage. ② Original means imaginative and clever • a stunningly original idea. ▶ NOUN ③ a work of art or a document that is the one that was first produced, and not a copy.

originally ADVERB **originality** NOUN

originate, originates, originating, originated VERB When something originates, or you originate it, it begins to happen or exist.
originator NOUN

ornament, ornaments NOUN a small, attractive object that you display in your home or that you wear in order to look attractive.

ornamental ADJECTIVE designed to be attractive rather than useful • an ornamental lake.

ornamentation NOUN Ornamentation is decoration on a building, a piece of furniture or a work of art.

ornate ADJECTIVE Something that is ornate has a lot of decoration on it.

ornithology NOUN Ornithology is the study of birds. **ornithologist** NOUN
WORD HISTORY: from Greek ornis meaning 'bird' and -logia meaning 'study of'

orphan, orphans, orphaning, orphaned NOUN ① a child whose parents are dead. ▶ VERB ② If a child is orphaned, its parents have died.

orphanage, orphanages NOUN a place where orphans are looked after.

orthodontics NOUN Orthodontics is the branch of dentistry concerned with straightening irregular teeth.
orthodontic ADJECTIVE
orthodontist NOUN

orthodox ADJECTIVE ① Orthodox beliefs or methods are the ones that most people have or use and that are considered standard. ② People who are orthodox believe in the older, more traditional ideas of their religion or political party. ③ RE The Orthodox Church is the part of the Christian Church which separated from the western European Church in the 11th century and is the main church in Greece and Russia. **orthodoxy** NOUN

oscillate, oscillates, oscillating, oscillated [Said *os-sil-late*] VERB ① SCIENCE If something oscillates, it moves repeatedly backwards and forwards. ② (*formal*) If you oscillate between two moods, you keep changing from one to the other. **oscillation** NOUN **oscillatory** ADJECTIVE

oscilloscope, oscilloscopes [Said *os-sil-los-scope*] NOUN SCIENCE a machine which shows the shape of a wave on a cathode-ray tube. WORD HISTORY: from Latin *oscillum* meaning 'swing' and Greek *skopein* meaning 'to look at'

osmosis [Said *oz-moh-siss*] NOUN SCIENCE Osmosis is the process by which a liquid moves through a semipermeable membrane from a weaker solution to a more concentrated one.

osprey, ospreys [Said *oss-pree*] NOUN a large bird of prey which catches fish with its feet.

ostensibly ADVERB If something is done ostensibly for a reason, that seems to be the reason for it • *Byrnes submitted his resignation, ostensibly on medical grounds.*

ostentatious ADJECTIVE ① Something that is ostentatious is intended to impress people, for example by looking expensive • *ostentatious sculptures.* ② People who are ostentatious try to impress other people with their wealth or importance. **ostentatiously** ADVERB **ostentation** NOUN

osteoporosis [Said *os-tee-oh-puh-roh-siss*] NOUN SCIENCE Osteoporosis is a condition in which the bones lose calcium and become more likely to break.

ostinato, ostinatos MUSIC NOUN ① a musical phrase that is continuously repeated throughout a piece. ▶ ADJECTIVE ② continuously repeated • *an ostinato passage.* WORD HISTORY: an Italian word meaning 'obstinate'

ostrich, ostriches NOUN The ostrich is the largest bird in the world. Ostriches cannot fly.

other, others ADJECTIVE OR PRONOUN ① Other people or things are different people or things • *All the other children had gone home* • *One of the cabinets came from the palace; the other is a copy.* ▶ PHRASE ② **The other day** or **the other week** means recently • *She had bought four pairs of shoes the other day.*

otherwise ADVERB ① You use 'otherwise' to say a different situation would exist if a particular fact or occurrence was not the case • *You had to learn to swim pretty quickly, otherwise you sank.* ② 'Otherwise' means apart from the thing mentioned • *She had written to her daughter, but otherwise refused to take sides.* ③ 'Otherwise' also means in a different way • *The majority voted otherwise.*

otter, otters NOUN a small, furry animal with a long tail. Otters swim well and eat fish.

ouch INTERJECTION You say ouch when you suddenly feel pain.

ought [Said *awt*] VERB If you say that someone ought to do something, you mean that they should do it • *He ought to see a doctor.*

GRAMMAR TIP
Do not use *did* and *had* with *ought*: *He ought not to come* is correct: *He didn't ought to come* is not correct.

ounce, ounces NOUN a unit of weight equal to one sixteenth of a pound or about 28.35 grams.

our ADJECTIVE 'Our' refers to something belonging or relating to the speaker or writer and one or more other people • *We recently sold our house.*

SPELLING TIP

Some people pronounce *our* and *are* in the same way, so do not confuse the spellings of these words.

---

ours PRONOUN 'Ours' refers to something belonging or relating to the speaker or writer and one or more other people • *a friend of ours from Korea.*

ourselves PRONOUN ① 'Ourselves' is used when the same speaker or writer and one or more other people do an action and are affected by it • *We haven't damaged ourselves too badly.* ② 'Ourselves' is used to emphasise 'we' • *We ourselves were delighted at the news.*

oust, ousts, ousting, ousted VERB If you oust someone, you force them out of a job or a place • *Cole was ousted from the board.*

out ADVERB ① towards the outside of a place • *Two dogs rushed out of the house.* ② not at home • *She was out when I rang last night.* ③ in the open air • *They are playing out in bright sunshine.* ④ no longer shining or burning • *The lights went out.* ▶ ADJECTIVE ⑤ on strike • *Over 800 construction workers are out in sympathy.* ⑥ unacceptable or unfashionable • *Miniskirts are out.* ⑦ incorrect • *Logan's timing was out in the first two rounds.*

out- PREFIX ① 'Out-' means 'exceeding' or 'going beyond' • *outdo* • *outclass.* ② 'Out-' also means on the outside or away from the centre • *outback* • *outpost.*

out-and-out ADJECTIVE entire or complete • *an out-and-out lie.*

outback NOUN In Australia, the outback is the remote parts where very few people live.

outboard motor, outboard motors NOUN a motor that can be fixed to the back of a small boat.

outbreak, outbreaks NOUN If there is an outbreak of something unpleasant, such as war, it suddenly occurs.

outburst, outbursts NOUN ① a sudden, strong expression of an emotion, especially anger • *John broke into an angry outburst about how unfairly the work was divided.* ② a sudden occurrence of violent activity • *an outburst of gunfire.*

outcast, outcasts NOUN someone who is rejected by other people.

outclassed ADJECTIVE If you are outclassed, you are much worse than your opponent at a particular activity.

outcome, outcomes NOUN a result • *the outcome of the election.*

outcrop, outcrops NOUN a large piece of rock that sticks out of the ground.

outcry, outcries NOUN If there is an outcry about something, a lot of people are angry about it • *a public outcry over alleged fraud.*

outdated ADJECTIVE no longer in fashion.

outdo, outdoes, outdoing, outdid, outdone VERB If you outdo someone, you do a particular thing better than they do.

outdoor ADJECTIVE happening or used outside • *outdoor activities.*

outdoors ADVERB outside • *It was too chilly to sit outdoors.*

outer ADJECTIVE The outer parts of

something are the parts furthest from the centre • *the outer door of the office*.

outer space NOUN Outer space is everything beyond the earth's atmosphere.

outfit, outfits NOUN ① a set of clothes. ② (*informal*) an organisation.

outgoing ADJECTIVE ① Outgoing describes someone who is leaving a job or place • *the outgoing President*. ② Someone who is outgoing is friendly and not shy.

outgoings PLURAL NOUN Your outgoings are the amount of money that you spend.

outgrow, outgrows, outgrowing, outgrew, outgrown VERB ① If you outgrow a piece of clothing, you grow too big for it. ② If you outgrow a way of behaving, you stop it because you have grown older and more mature.

outhouse, outhouses NOUN a small building in the grounds of a house to which it belongs.

outing, outings NOUN a trip made for pleasure.

outlandish ADJECTIVE very unusual or odd • *outlandish clothes*.

outlaw, outlaws, outlawing, outlawed VERB ① If something is outlawed, it is made illegal. ▶ NOUN ② In the past, an outlaw was a criminal.

outlay, outlays NOUN an amount of money spent on something • *a cash outlay of $300*.

outlet, outlets NOUN ① An outlet for your feelings or ideas is a way of expressing them. ② a hole or pipe through which water or air can flow away. ③ a shop which sells goods made by a particular manufacturer.

outlier, outliers NOUN MATHS SCIENCE a member of a group that is very different from normal members of the group.

outline, outlines, outlining, outlined VERB ① If you outline a plan or idea, you explain it in a general way. ② You say that something is outlined when you can see its shape because there is a light behind it. ▶ NOUN ③ a general explanation or description of something. ④ The outline of something is its shape.

outlive, outlives, outliving, outlived VERB To outlive someone is to live longer than they do.

outlook NOUN ① Your outlook is your general attitude towards life. ② The outlook of a situation is the way it is likely to develop • *The outlook for the business is uncertain*.

outlying ADJECTIVE Outlying places are far from cities.

outmoded ADJECTIVE old-fashioned and no longer useful • *an outmoded form of transport*.

outnumber, outnumbers, outnumbering, outnumbered VERB If there are more of one group than of another, the first group outnumbers the second.

out of PREPOSITION ① If you do something out of a particular feeling, you are motivated by that feeling • *Out of curiosity she went along*. ② 'Out of' also means from • *old instruments made out of wood*. ③ If you are out of something, you no longer have any of it • *I do hope we're not out of fuel again*. ④ If you are out of the rain, sun or wind, you are sheltered from it. ⑤ You also use 'out of' to indicate proportion. For example, one out of five means one in every five.

out of date ADJECTIVE old-fashioned and no longer useful.

out of doors ADVERB outside • *Sometimes we eat out of doors*.

a
b
c
d
e
f
g
h
i
j
k
l
m
n
o
p
q
r
s
t
u
v
w
x
y
z

outpatient, outpatients NOUN
Outpatients are people who receive treatment in hospital without staying overnight.

outpost, outposts NOUN a small collection of buildings a long way from a main centre • *a remote mountain outpost.*

output, outputs NOUN ① Output is the amount of something produced by a person or organisation.
② ICT The output of a computer is the information that it produces.

outrage, outrages, outraging, outraged VERB ① If something outrages you, it angers and shocks you • *I was outraged at what had happened to her.* ▶ NOUN ② Outrage is a feeling of anger and shock. ③ something very shocking or violent. **outrageous** ADJECTIVE **outrageously** ADVERB

outright ADJECTIVE [Said *owt-rite*] ① absolute • *an outright rejection.* ▶ ADVERB [Said *owt-rite*] ② in an open and direct way • *Have you asked him outright?* ③ completely and totally • *I own the company outright.*

outset NOUN The outset of something is the beginning of it • *the outset of his journey.*

outshine, outshines, outshining, outshone VERB If you outshine someone, you perform better than they do.

outside NOUN ① The outside of something is the part which surrounds or encloses the rest of it. ▶ PREPOSITION ② on or to the exterior of • *outside the house.* ③ Outside also means not included in something • *outside office hours.* ▶ ADJECTIVE ④ Outside means not inside • *an outside toilet.* ▶ ADVERB ⑤ out of doors.

GRAMMAR TIP
Do not use *of* after *outside*. You should write *she was waiting outside the school* and not *outside of the school.*

outsider, outsiders NOUN
① someone who does not belong to a particular group. ② a competitor considered unlikely to win in a race.

outsize or **outsized** ADJECTIVE
much larger than usual • *outsize feet.*

outskirts PLURAL NOUN The outskirts of a city or town are the parts around the edge of it.

outsource, outsources, outsourcing, outsourced NOUN
If a business organisation outsources work, it pays workers from outside the organisation to do the work.

outspan, outspans, outspanning, outspanned VERB In South Africa, if you outspan, you relax.

outspoken ADJECTIVE Outspoken people give their opinions openly, even if they shock other people.

outstanding ADJECTIVE ① extremely good • *The collection contains hundreds of outstanding works of art.* ② Money that is outstanding is still owed • *an outstanding mortgage of many thousands of pounds.*

outstretched ADJECTIVE If your arms are outstretched, they are stretched out as far as possible.

outstrip, outstrips, outstripping, outstripped VERB If one thing outstrips another thing, it becomes bigger or more successful or moves faster than the other thing.

outward ADJECTIVE or ADVERB
① Outward means away from a place or towards the outside • *the outward journey.* ▶ ADJECTIVE ② The outward features of someone are the ones they appear to have, rather than the ones they actually have • *She never*

showed any outward signs of emotion.
outwardly ADVERB

outwards ADVERB away from a place or towards the outside • *The door opened outwards.*

outweigh, **outweighs**, **outweighing**, **outweighed** VERB If you say that the advantages of something outweigh its disadvantages, you mean that the advantages are more important than the disadvantages.

outwit, **outwits**, **outwitting**, **outwitted** VERB If you outwit someone, you use your intelligence to defeat them.

ova the plural of **ovum**.

oval, **ovals** NOUN ① a round shape, similar to a circle but wider in one direction than the other. ▶ ADJECTIVE ② shaped like an oval • *an oval table.*

ovary, **ovaries** [Said oh-var-ree] NOUN
SCIENCE A woman's ovaries are the two organs in her body that produce eggs.

ovation, **ovations** NOUN a long burst of applause.

oven, **ovens** NOUN the part of a cooker that you use for baking or roasting food.

over, **overs** PREPOSITION ① Over something means directly above it or covering it • *the picture over the fireplace* • *He put his hands over his eyes.* ② A view over an area is a view across that area • *The pool and terrace look out over the sea.* ③ If something is over a road or river, it is on the opposite side of the road or river. ④ Something that is over a particular amount is more than that amount. ⑤ 'Over' indicates a topic of discussion • *A customer was arguing over the bill.* ⑥ If something happens over a period of time, it happens during that period • *I went to New Zealand over Christmas.*

▶ ADVERB or PREPOSITION ⑦ If you lean over, you bend your body in a particular direction • *He bent over and rummaged in a drawer* • *She was hunched over her keyboard.* ▶ ADVERB ⑧ 'Over' is used to indicate a position • *over by the window* • *Come over here.* ⑨ If something rolls or turns over, it is moved so that its other side is facing upwards • *He flipped over the envelope.* ▶ ADJECTIVE ⑩ Something that is over is completely finished. ▶ PHRASE ⑪ **All over** a place means everywhere in that place • *studios all over America.* ▶ NOUN ⑫ In cricket, an over is a set of six balls bowled by a bowler from the same end of the pitch.

over- PREFIX 'Over-' means to too great an extent or too much • *overprotective* • *overindulge* • *overact.*

overall, **overalls** ADJECTIVE ① Overall means taking into account all the parts or aspects of something • *The overall quality of pupils' work had shown a marked improvement.* ▶ ADVERB ② taking into account all the parts of something • *Overall, things are not really too bad.* ▶ NOUN ③ (in plural) Overalls are a piece of clothing that looks like trousers and a jacket combined. You wear overalls to protect your other clothes when you are working. ④ An overall is a piece of clothing like a coat that you wear to protect your other clothes when you are working.

overawed ADJECTIVE If you are overawed by something, you are very impressed by it and a little afraid of it.

overbearing ADJECTIVE trying to dominate other people • *Mozart had a difficult relationship with his overbearing father.*

overboard ADVERB If you fall overboard, you fall over the side of a ship into the water.

overcame the past tense of **overcome**.

overcast ADJECTIVE If it is overcast, the sky is covered by cloud.

overcoat, overcoats NOUN a thick, warm coat.

overcome, overcomes, overcoming, overcame, overcome VERB ① If you overcome a problem or a feeling, you manage to deal with it or control it. ▶ADJECTIVE ② If you are overcome by a feeling, you feel it very strongly.

overcrowded ADJECTIVE If a place is overcrowded, there are too many things or people in it.

overdo, overdoes, overdoing, overdid, overdone VERB If you overdo something, you do it too much or in an exaggerated way • It is important never to overdo new exercises.

overdose, overdoses NOUN a larger dose of a drug than is safe.

overdraft, overdrafts NOUN an agreement with a bank that allows someone to spend more money than they have in their account.

overdrawn ADJECTIVE If someone is overdrawn, they have taken more money from their bank account than the account has in it.

overdrive NOUN ① Overdrive is an extra, higher gear in a vehicle, which is used at high speeds to reduce engine wear and save fuel. ▶PHRASE ② If an activity goes into overdrive, people work at it in a very intense way.

overdue ADJECTIVE If someone or something is overdue, they are late • The payments are overdue.

overestimate, overestimates, overestimating, overestimated VERB If you overestimate something, you think that it is bigger, more important or better than it really is • We had overestimated his popularity.

overflow, overflows, overflowing, overflowed, overflown VERB If a liquid overflows, it spills over the edges of its container. If a river overflows, it flows over its banks.

overgrown ADJECTIVE A place that is overgrown is covered with weeds because it has not been looked after • an overgrown path.

overhang, overhangs, overhanging, overhung VERB If one thing overhangs another, it sticks out sideways above it • old trees whose branches overhang a footpath.

overhaul, overhauls, overhauling, overhauled VERB ① If you overhaul something, you examine it thoroughly and repair any faults. ▶NOUN ② If you give something an overhaul, you examine it and repair or improve it.

overhead ADJECTIVE ① Overhead means above you • overhead cables. ▶ADVERB ② Overhead means above you • seagulls flying overhead.

overheads PLURAL NOUN The overheads of a business are the costs of running it.

overhear, overhears, overhearing, overheard VERB If you overhear someone's conversation, you hear what they are saying to someone else.

overhung the past tense and past participle of **overhang**.

overjoyed ADJECTIVE extremely pleased • Colm was overjoyed to see me. SIMILAR WORDS: delighted, over the moon

overlaid ADJECTIVE If something is overlaid by something else, it is covered by it.

overland ADJECTIVE or ADVERB travelling across land rather than going by sea or air • an overland trek to India • Wray was returning to England overland.

overlander, overlanders NOUN
In Australian history, an overlander
was a man who drove cattle or
sheep long distances through the
outback.

overlap, overlaps, overlapping,
overlapped VERB If one thing
overlaps another, one part of it
covers part of the other thing.

overleaf ADVERB on the other side of
the page • *Write to us at the address
shown overleaf.*

overload, overloads, overloading,
overloaded VERB If you overload
someone or something, you give
them too much to do or to carry.

overlook, overlooks, overlooking,
overlooked VERB ① If a building or
window overlooks a place, it has a
view over that place. ② If you
overlook something, you ignore it or
do not notice it.

overly ADVERB excessively • *I'm not
overly fond of puddings.*

overnight ADVERB ① during the
night • *Further rain was forecast
overnight.* ② suddenly • *Good players
don't become bad ones overnight.*
▶ ADJECTIVE ③ during the night.
④ sudden • *an overnight success.* ⑤ for
use when you go away for one or two
nights • *an overnight bag.*

overpower, overpowers,
overpowering, overpowered VERB
① If you overpower someone, you
seize them despite their struggles,
because you are stronger than them.
② If a feeling overpowers you, it
affects you very strongly.
overpowering ADJECTIVE

overran the past tense of **overrun**.

overrate, overrates, overrating,
overrated VERB If you overrate
something, you think that it is better
or more important than it really is.
overrated ADJECTIVE

overreact, overreacts, overreacting,
overreacted VERB If you overreact,
you react in an extreme way.

overriding ADJECTIVE more
important than anything else • *an
overriding duty.*

overrule, overrules, overruling,
overruled VERB To overrule a person
or their decisions is to decide that
their decisions are incorrect.
SIMILAR WORDS: countermand,
override, reverse

overrun, overruns, overrunning,
overran, overrun VERB ① If an army
overruns a country, it occupies it very
quickly. ② If animals or plants
overrun a place, they spread quickly
over it. ③ If an event overruns, it
continues for longer than it was
meant to.

oversaw the past tense of **oversee**.

overseas ADVERB ① abroad
• *travelling overseas.* ▶ ADJECTIVE
② abroad • *an overseas tour.* ③ from
abroad • *overseas students.*

oversee, oversees, overseeing,
oversaw, overseen VERB To oversee
a job is to make sure it is done
properly. **overseer** NOUN

overshadow, overshadows,
overshadowing, overshadowed
VERB If something is overshadowed,
it is made unimportant by something
else that is better or more important.

oversight, oversights NOUN
something which you forget to do or
fail to notice.

overspill NOUN or ADJECTIVE
'Overspill' refers to the moving of
people from overcrowded cities to
houses in smaller towns • *an East End
overspill* • *overspill estates.*

overstate, overstates, overstating,
overstated VERB If you overstate
something, you exaggerate its
importance.

overstep, oversteps, overstepping, overstepped PHRASE If you **overstep the mark**, you behave in an unacceptable way.

overt ADJECTIVE open and obvious • *overt signs of stress.* **overtly** ADVERB

overtake, overtakes, overtaking, overtook, overtaken VERB If you overtake someone, you pass them because you are moving faster than them.

overthrow, overthrows, overthrowing, overthrew, overthrown VERB If a government is overthrown, it is removed from power by force.

overtime NOUN ① Overtime is time that someone works in addition to their normal working hours.
▶ ADVERB ② If someone works overtime, they do work in addition to their normal working hours.

overtones PLURAL NOUN If something has overtones of an emotion or attitude, it suggests it without showing it openly • *the political overtones of the trial.*

overtook the past tense of **overtake**.

overture, overtures NOUN ① a piece of music that is the introduction to an opera or play. ② If you make overtures to someone, you approach them because you want to start a friendly or business relationship with them.

overturn, overturns, overturning, overturned VERB ① To overturn something is to turn it upside down or onto its side. ② If someone overturns a legal decision, they change it by using their higher authority.

overview, overviews NOUN a general understanding or description of a situation.

overweight ADJECTIVE too fat, and therefore unhealthy.

overwhelm, overwhelms, overwhelming, overwhelmed VERB ① If you are overwhelmed by something, it affects you very strongly • *The priest appeared overwhelmed by the news.* ② If one group of people overwhelms another, they gain complete control or victory over them. **overwhelming** ADJECTIVE **overwhelmingly** ADVERB

overwork, overworks, overworking, overworked VERB If you overwork, you work too hard.

overwrought [*Said oh-ver-rawt*] ADJECTIVE extremely upset • *He didn't get angry or overwrought.*

ovulate, ovulates, ovulating, ovulated [*Said ov-yool-late*] VERB SCIENCE When a woman or female animal ovulates, she produces ova or eggs from her ovary.

ovule, ovules NOUN ① SCIENCE the part of a plant that develops into a seed. ② SCIENCE an immature ovum.

ovum, ova [*Said oh-vum*] NOUN SCIENCE a reproductive cell of a woman or female animal. The ovum is fertilised by a male sperm to produce young.
WORD HISTORY: a Latin word meaning 'egg'

owe, owes, owing, owed VERB ① If you owe someone money, they have lent it to you and you have not yet paid it back. ② If you owe a quality or skill to someone, they are responsible for giving it to you • *He owes his success to his mother.* ③ If you say that you owe someone gratitude or loyalty, you mean that they deserve it from you.

owl, owls NOUN Owls are birds of prey

that hunt at night. They have large eyes and short, hooked beaks.

own, owns, owning, owned ADJECTIVE ① If something is your own, it belongs to you or is associated with you • *She stayed in her own house.* ▶ VERB ② If you own something, it belongs to you. ▶ PHRASE ③ **On your own** means alone.

owner, owners NOUN The owner of something is the person it belongs to.

ownership NOUN If you have ownership of something, you own it • *He shared the ownership of a sailing dinghy.*

ox, oxen NOUN Oxen are cattle which are used for carrying or pulling things.

oxide, oxides NOUN a compound of oxygen and another chemical element.

oxidise, oxidises, oxidising, oxidised; also spelt **oxidize** VERB SCIENCE When a substance oxidises, it changes chemically by reacting with oxygen. **oxidation** NOUN

oxygen NOUN SCIENCE Oxygen is a chemical element in the form of a colourless gas. It makes up about 21 per cent of the earth's atmosphere. With an extremely small number of exceptions, living things need oxygen to live, and things cannot burn without it. Oxygen's atomic number is 8 and its symbol is O.

oxygen cycle NOUN The oxygen cycle is the continuous exchange of oxygen between the earth's atmosphere, soil and life forms.

oxymoron, oxymora or oxymorons NOUN ENGLISH two words that contradict each other placed beside each other, for example 'deafening silence'.

oyster, oysters NOUN Oysters are large, flat shellfish. Some oysters can be eaten, and others produce pearls. **WORD HISTORY:** from Greek *ostrakon* meaning 'shell'

oz an abbreviation for 'ounce' or 'ounces'.

ozone NOUN Ozone is a form of oxygen that is poisonous and has a strong smell. There is a layer of ozone high above the earth's surface.

ozone layer NOUN The ozone layer is that part of the earth's atmosphere that protects living things from the harmful radiation of the sun.

a
b
c
d
e
f
g
h
i
j
k
l
m
n
o
p
q
r
s
t
u
v
w
x
y
z

Pp

p ① an abbreviation for 'pence'. ② a written abbreviation for 'page'. The plural is pp.

pa, **pa** or **pas** NOUN In New Zealand, a pa is a Māori village or settlement.

pace, **paces**, **pacing**, **paced** NOUN ① The pace of something is the speed at which it moves or happens. ② a step; also used as a measurement of distance. ▶ VERB ③ If you pace up and down, you continually walk around because you are anxious or impatient.

pacemaker, **pacemakers** NOUN a small electronic device put into someone's heart to control their heartbeat.

Pacific [*Said pas-sif-ik*] NOUN The Pacific is the ocean separating North and South America from Asia and Australia.

pacifist, **pacifists** NOUN someone who is opposed to all violence and war. **pacifism** NOUN

pacify, **pacifies**, **pacifying**, **pacified** VERB If you pacify someone who is angry, you calm them.
SIMILAR WORDS: appease, calm, placate

pack, **packs**, **packing**, **packed** VERB ① If you pack, you put things neatly into a suitcase, bag or box. ② If people pack into a place, it becomes crowded with them. ▶ NOUN ③ a bag or rucksack carried on your back. ④ a packet or collection of something • *a pack of fish fingers.* ⑤ A pack of playing cards is a complete set. ⑥ A pack of

dogs or wolves is a group of them.

pack in VERB (*informal*) If you pack something in, you stop doing it.

pack up VERB If you pack up your belongings, you put them in a bag because you are leaving.

package, **packages** NOUN ① a small parcel. ② a set of proposals or offers presented as a whole • *a package of beauty treatments.* **packaged** ADJECTIVE

packaging NOUN DGT Packaging is the container or wrapping in which an item is sold or sent.

packed ADJECTIVE very full • *The church was packed with people.*

packet, **packets** NOUN a thin cardboard box or paper container in which something is sold.

pact, **pacts** NOUN a formal agreement or treaty.

pad, **pads**, **padding**, **padded** NOUN ① a thick, soft piece of material. ② a number of pieces of paper fixed together at one end. ③ The pads of an animal such as a cat or dog are the soft, fleshy parts on the bottom of its paws. ④ a flat surface from which helicopters take off or rockets are launched. ▶ VERB ⑤ If you pad something, you put a pad inside it or over it to protect it or change its shape. ⑥ If you pad around, you walk softly. **padding** NOUN

paddle, **paddles**, **paddling**, **paddled** NOUN ① a short pole with a broad blade at one or both ends, used to move a small boat or a canoe. ▶ VERB

②If someone paddles a boat, they move it using a paddle. ③If you paddle, you walk in shallow water.

paddock, paddocks NOUN a small field where horses are kept.

paddy, paddies NOUN A paddy or paddy field is an area in which rice is grown.

padlock, padlocks, padlocking, padlocked NOUN ①a lock made up of a metal case with a U-shaped bar attached to it, which can be put through a metal loop and then closed. It is unlocked by turning a key in the lock on the case. ▶VERB ②If you padlock something, you lock it with a padlock.

padre, padres [Said pah-dray] NOUN a priest, especially a chaplain to the armed forces.
WORD HISTORY: from Italian or Spanish *padre* meaning 'father'

paediatrician, paediatricians [Said pee-dee-ya-**trish**-n]; also spelt **pediatrician** NOUN a doctor who specialises in treating children.
WORD HISTORY: from Greek *pais* meaning 'child' and *iatros* meaning 'physician'

paediatrics [Said pee-dee-ya-triks]; also spelt **pediatrics** NOUN Paediatrics is the area of medicine which deals with children's diseases. **paediatric** ADJECTIVE

pagan, pagans [Said **pay**-gan] ADJECTIVE ①involving beliefs and worship outside the main religions of the world • *pagan myths and cults*. ▶NOUN ②someone who believes in a pagan religion. **paganism** NOUN

page, pages, paging, paged NOUN ①one side of one of the pieces of paper in a book or magazine; also the sheet of paper itself. ②In medieval times, a page was a young boy servant who was learning to be a knight. ▶VERB ③To page someone is to send a signal or message to a small electronic device which they are carrying.

pageant, pageants [Said paj-jent] NOUN a grand, colourful show or parade.

pagoda, pagodas NOUN a tall, elaborately decorated Buddhist or Hindu temple.

paid the past tense and past participle of **pay**.

pail, pails NOUN a bucket.

pain, pains, paining, pained NOUN ①Pain is an unpleasant feeling of physical hurt. ②Pain is also an unpleasant feeling of deep unhappiness. ▶VERB ③If something pains you, it makes you very unhappy. **painless** ADJECTIVE **painlessly** ADVERB
SIMILAR WORDS: ①ache, hurt, pang, twinge

painful ADJECTIVE ①causing emotional pain. ②causing physical pain. **painfully** ADVERB

painkiller, painkillers NOUN a drug that reduces or stops pain.

painstaking ADJECTIVE very careful and thorough • *years of painstaking research*.

paint, paints, painting, painted NOUN ① ART Paint is a coloured liquid used to decorate buildings, or to make a picture. ▶VERB ② ART If you paint something or paint a picture of it, you make a picture of it using paint. ③ DGT When you paint something such as a wall, you cover it with paint. **painter** NOUN **painting** NOUN

pair, pairs, pairing, paired NOUN ①two things of the same type or that do the same thing • *a pair of earrings*. ②You use 'pair' when referring to certain objects which have two main

a
b
c
d
e
f
g
h
i
j
k
l
m
n
o
p
q
r
s
t
u
v
w
x
y
z

matching parts • *a pair of scissors.*
▶ **VERB** ③ When people pair off, they become grouped in pairs. ④ If you pair up with someone, you agree to do something together.

GRAMMAR TIP
The verb following *pair* can be singular or plural. If *pair* refers to a unit, the verb is singular: *A pair of good shoes is essential.* If *pair* refers to two individual things, the verb is plural: *The pair are said to dislike each other.*

pakeha, pakeha or pakehas *[Said pa-ki-ha]* **NOUN** In New Zealand English, a pakeha is someone who is of European rather than Māori descent.

Pakistani, Pakistanis *[Said pah-kiss-**tah**-nee]* **ADJECTIVE**
① belonging or relating to Pakistan.
▶ **NOUN** ② someone who comes from Pakistan.

pal, pals **NOUN** (*informal*) a friend.

palace, palaces **NOUN** a large, grand house, especially the official home of a king or queen.

palaeolithic *[Said pal-lee-oh-**lith**-ik]* **ADJECTIVE** belonging or relating to the period about 2.5 to 3 million years ago when primitive man emerged and was making unpolished chipped stone tools.

palagi, palagi or palagis *[Said pa-**lang**-ee]* **NOUN** a Samoan name for a New Zealander of European descent.

palatable **ADJECTIVE** Palatable food tastes pleasant.

palate, palates *[Said **pall**-lat]* **NOUN**
① the top of the inside of your mouth.
② Someone's palate is their ability to judge good food and drink • *dishes to tempt every palate.*

pale, paler, palest **ADJECTIVE** rather white and without much colour or brightness.

Palestinian, Palestinians **ADJECTIVE**
① belonging or relating to the region of Palestine, between the River Jordan and the Mediterranean.
▶ **NOUN** ② an Arab who comes from Palestine.

palette, palettes **NOUN** ART a flat piece of wood on which an artist mixes colours.

palindrome, palindromes **NOUN** ENGLISH A palindrome is a word or phrase that is the same whether you read it forwards or backwards, for example the word 'refer'.

palisade cell, palisade cells **NOUN** SCIENCE In plants, palisade cells are cells lying below the surface of a leaf that contain many chloroplasts.

pall, palls, palling, palled *[Rhymes with **fall**]* **VERB** ① If something palls, it becomes less interesting or less enjoyable • *This record palls after ten minutes.* ▶ **NOUN** ② a thick cloud of smoke. ③ a cloth covering a coffin.

palm, palms **NOUN** ① A palm or palm tree is a tropical tree with no branches and a crown of long leaves. ② the flat surface of your hand which your fingers bend towards.

Palm Sunday **NOUN** RE Palm Sunday is the Sunday before Easter.

palpable **ADJECTIVE** obvious and easily sensed • *Happiness was palpable in the air.* **palpably** **ADVERB**
WORD HISTORY: from Latin *palpabilis* meaning 'able to be touched'

paltry *[Said **pawl**-tree]* **ADJECTIVE** A paltry sum of money is a very small amount.
SIMILAR WORDS: insignificant, trifling, trivial

pamper, pampers, pampering, pampered **VERB** If you pamper someone, you give them too much kindness and comfort.

pamphlet, pamphlets **NOUN** ENGLISH

a very thin book in paper covers giving information about something.

pan, pans, panning, panned NOUN ① a round metal container with a long handle, used for cooking things in on top of a cooker. ▶ VERB ② When a film camera pans, it moves in a wide sweep. ③ (informal) To pan something is to criticise it strongly.

panacea, panaceas [Said pan-nass-see-ah] NOUN something that is supposed to cure everything.

panache [Said pan-nash] NOUN Something that is done with panache is done confidently and stylishly.

pancake, pancakes NOUN a thin, flat piece of fried batter which can be served with savoury or sweet fillings.

pancreas, pancreases [Said pang-kree-ass] NOUN SCIENCE The pancreas is an organ in the body situated behind the stomach. It produces insulin and enzymes that help with digestion.

panda, pandas NOUN A panda or giant panda is a large animal rather like a bear that lives in China. It has black fur with large patches of white.

pandemonium [Said pan-dim-moan-ee-um] NOUN Pandemonium is a state of noisy confusion • scenes of pandemonium.
WORD HISTORY: from Pandemonium, the capital of Hell in Milton's 'Paradise Lost'

pander, panders, pandering, pandered VERB If you pander to someone, you do everything they want.

pane, panes NOUN a sheet of glass in a window or door.

panel, panels NOUN ① a small group of people who are chosen to do something • a panel of judges. ② a flat piece of wood that is part of a larger object • door panels. ③ A control panel is a surface containing switches and instruments to operate a machine.
panelled ADJECTIVE

panelling NOUN Panelling is rectangular pieces of wood covering an inside wall.

pang, pangs NOUN a sudden strong feeling of sadness or pain.

panic, panics, panicking, panicked NOUN ① Panic is a sudden overwhelming feeling of fear or anxiety. ▶ VERB ② If you panic, you become so afraid or anxious that you cannot act sensibly.

panorama, panoramas NOUN an extensive view over a wide area of land • a fine panorama over the hills.
panoramic ADJECTIVE

pansy, pansies NOUN a small garden flower with large round petals.

pant, pants, panting, panted VERB If you pant, you breathe quickly and loudly through your mouth.

panther, panthers NOUN a large wild animal belonging to the cat family, especially the black leopard.

pantomime, pantomimes NOUN a musical play, usually based on a fairy story and performed at Christmas.

pantry, pantries NOUN a small room where food is kept.
WORD HISTORY: from Old French paneterie meaning 'bread store'

pants PLURAL NOUN ① Pants are a piece of underwear with holes for your legs and elastic around the waist or hips. ② In American English, pants are trousers.

pantyhose; also spelt **pantihose** PLURAL NOUN in American English, pantyhose are the same as tights.

papaya, papayas NOUN a fruit with sweet yellow or reddish-orange flesh and small black seeds.

a
b
c
d
e
f
g
h
i
j
k
l
m
n
o
p
q
r
s
t
u
v
w
x
y
z

paper, papers, papering, papered
NOUN ① Paper is a material made from wood pulp and used for writing on or wrapping things. ② a newspaper. ③ (*in plural*) Papers are official documents, for example a passport for identification. ④ part of a written examination. ▶ VERB ⑤ If you paper a wall, you put wallpaper on it.
WORD HISTORY: from *papyrus*, the plant from which paper was made in ancient Egypt, Greece and Rome

paperback, paperbacks NOUN a book with a thin cardboard cover.

paperwork NOUN Paperwork is the part of a job that involves dealing with letters and records.

papier-mâché [*Said pap-yay mash-shay*] NOUN Papier-mâché is a hard substance made from mashed wet paper mixed with glue and moulded when moist to make things such as bowls and ornaments.
WORD HISTORY: from French *papier-mâché* meaning 'chewed paper'

paprika NOUN Paprika is a red powder made from a kind of pepper.
WORD HISTORY: a Hungarian word

papyrus [*Said pap-eye-russ*] NOUN HISTORY Papyrus was a type of paper made in ancient Egypt, Greece and Rome from the stems of a tall water plant which is also called papyrus.

par PHRASE ① Something that is **on a par** with something else is similar in quality or amount • *This match was on a par with the German Cup Final.* ② Something that is **below par** or **under par** is below its normal standard. ▶ NOUN ③ In golf, par is the number of strokes which it is thought a good player should take for a hole or all the holes on a particular golf course.

parable, parables NOUN RE a short story which makes a moral or religious point.

parabola, parabolas [*Said par-rab-bol-la*] NOUN MATHS A parabola is a regular curve like the path of something that is thrown up in the air and comes down in a different place. **parabolic** ADJECTIVE

parachute, parachutes [*Said par-rash-oot*] NOUN a circular piece of fabric attached by lines to a person or package so that they can fall safely to the ground from an aircraft.

parade, parades, parading, paraded NOUN ① a line of people or vehicles standing or moving together as a display. ▶ VERB ② When people parade, they walk together in a group as a display.

paradigm, paradigms [*Said pa-ra-dime*] NOUN ① a model for something which explains it or shows how it can be produced. ② a typical example of something.

Paradise NOUN According to some religions, Paradise is a wonderful place where good people go when they die.
WORD HISTORY: from Greek *paradeisos* meaning 'garden'

paradox, paradoxes NOUN something that contains two ideas that seem to contradict each other • *The paradox of exercise is that while you use a lot of energy, it seems to generate more.* **paradoxical** ADJECTIVE

paraffin NOUN Paraffin is a strong-smelling liquid which is used as a fuel.

paragon, paragons NOUN someone whose behaviour is perfect in some way • *a paragon of elegance.*

paragraph, paragraphs NOUN ENGLISH a section of a piece of writing. Paragraphs begin on a new line.

parallel, parallels NOUN
① Something that is a parallel to something else has similar qualities or features to it. ▶ADJECTIVE
② MATHS If two lines are parallel, they are the same distance apart along the whole of their length.
▶ PHRASE ③ SCIENCE If electrical circuits are arranged **in parallel**, the same voltage is applied to each of them.

parallelogram, parallelograms
NOUN MATHS a four-sided shape in which each side is parallel to the opposite side.

paralyse, paralyses, paralysing, paralysed VERB If something paralyses you, it causes loss of feeling and movement in your body.
SIMILAR WORDS: freeze, immobilise, numb

paralysis [Said par-ral-liss-iss] NOUN Paralysis is loss of the power to move.

paramedic, paramedics [Said par-ram-**med**-dik] NOUN a person who does some types of medical work, for example for the ambulance service.

parameter, parameters [Said par-**ram**-met-ter] NOUN a limit which affects the way something is done • the general parameters set by the president.

paramilitary ADJECTIVE A paramilitary organisation has a military structure but is not the official army of a country.

paramount ADJECTIVE more important than anything else • Safety is paramount.

paranoia [Said par-ran-**noy**-ah] NOUN Paranoia is a mental illness in which someone believes that other people are trying to harm them.

paranoid [Said par-ran-noyd] ADJECTIVE Someone who is paranoid believes wrongly that other people are trying to harm them.

parapet, parapets NOUN a low wall along the edge of a bridge or roof.
WORD HISTORY: from Italian parapetto meaning 'chest-high wall'

paraphernalia [Said par-raf-fan-**ale**-yah] NOUN Someone's paraphernalia is all their belongings or equipment.
WORD HISTORY: from Latin parapherna meaning 'personal property of a married woman'

paraphrase, paraphrases, paraphrasing, paraphrased NOUN
① A paraphrase of a piece of writing or speech is the same thing said in a different way • a paraphrase of the popular song. ▶ VERB ② If you paraphrase what someone has said, you express it in a different way.

parasite, parasites NOUN a small animal or plant that lives on or inside a larger animal or plant. **parasitic** ADJECTIVE
WORD HISTORY: from Greek parasitos meaning 'someone who eats at someone else's table'

parasol, parasols NOUN an object like an umbrella that provides shelter from the sun.

paratroops or **paratroopers**
PLURAL NOUN Paratroops are soldiers trained to be dropped by parachute.

parcel, parcels, parcelling, parcelled NOUN ① something wrapped up in paper. ▶ VERB ② If you parcel something up, you make it into a parcel.

parched ADJECTIVE ① If the ground is parched, it is very dry and in need of water. ② (informal) If you are parched, you are very thirsty.

parchment NOUN Parchment is thick yellowish paper of very good quality.

pardon, pardons, pardoning, pardoned INTERJECTION ① You say

a
b
c
d
e
f
g
h
i
j
k
l
m
n
o
p
q
r
s
t
u
v
w
x
y
z

pardon or **I beg your pardon** to express surprise or apology, or when you have not heard what someone has said. ▶**VERB** ② If you pardon someone, you forgive them for doing something wrong.

pare, pares, paring, pared **VERB** When you pare fruit or vegetables, you cut off the skin.

parent, parents **NOUN** Your parents are usually the people who caused you to be born and who look after you while you grow up. **parental ADJECTIVE**

parentage NOUN A person's parentage is their parents and ancestors.

parenthesis, parentheses [*Said par-renth-iss-iss*] **NOUN** ① ENGLISH A parenthesis is a phrase or remark inside brackets, dashes or commas that is inserted into a piece of writing or speech. ② ENGLISH Parentheses are a pair of brackets put round a word or phrase. **parenthetical ADJECTIVE**

parenthood NOUN Parenthood is the state of being a parent, or the time during which a person is a parent.

pariah, pariahs [*Said par-eye-ah*] **NOUN** A pariah is someone who is disliked and rejected by other people.

parish, parishes **NOUN** an area with its own church and member of the clergy, and often its own elected council.

parishioner, parishioners **NOUN** Parishioners are the people who live in a parish and attend its church.

parity NOUN (*formal*) If there is parity between things, they are equal • *By 1943 the USA had achieved a rough parity of power with the British.*

park, parks, parking, parked **NOUN** ① a public area with grass and trees.

② a private area of grass and trees around a large country house. ▶**VERB** ③ When someone parks a vehicle, they drive it into a position where it can be left. **parked ADJECTIVE parking NOUN**

parliament, parliaments **NOUN** CITIZENSHIP the group of elected representatives who make the laws of a country. **parliamentary ADJECTIVE**

parlour, parlours **NOUN** (*old-fashioned*) a sitting room.
WORD HISTORY: from Old French *parleur* meaning 'room for talking to visitors (in a convent)'

parochial [*Said par-roe-key-yal*] **ADJECTIVE** concerned only with local matters • *narrow parochial interests.*

parody, parodies, parodying, parodied **NOUN** ① an amusing imitation of the style of an author or of a familiar situation. ▶**VERB** ② If you parody something, you make a parody of it.
SIMILAR WORDS: ① send-up, spoof, takeoff

parole NOUN When prisoners are given parole, they are released early on condition that they behave well.
WORD HISTORY: from French *parole d'honneur* meaning 'word of honour'

parrot, parrots **NOUN** a brightly coloured tropical bird with a curved beak.

parry, parries, parrying, parried **VERB** ① If you parry a question, you cleverly avoid answering it • *My searching questions are simply parried with evasions.* ② If you parry a blow, you push aside your attacker's arm to defend yourself.

parsley NOUN Parsley is a herb with curly or flat leaves used for flavouring in cooking.

parsnip, parsnips **NOUN** a long,

pointed, cream-coloured root vegetable.

parson, parsons NOUN a vicar or other member of the clergy.

part, parts, parting, parted NOUN ① one of the pieces or aspects of something. ② one of the roles in a play or film, played by an actor or actress. ③ Someone's part in something is their involvement in it • *He was jailed for eleven years for his part in the plot.* ▶ PHRASE ④ If you **take part** in an activity, you do it together with other people. ▶ VERB ⑤ If things that are next to each other part, they move away from each other. ⑥ If two people part, they leave each other.

SIMILAR WORDS: ① bit, component, constituent, piece

partake, partakes, partaking, partook, partaken VERB (formal) If you partake of food, you eat it • *She partook of the refreshments offered.*

partial ADJECTIVE ① not complete or whole • *a partial explanation* • *partial success.* ② liking something very much • *I'm very partial to marigolds.* ③ supporting one side in a dispute, rather than being fair and without bias. **partially** ADVERB

participate, participates, participating, participated VERB CITIZENSHIP If you participate in an activity, you take part in it.
participant NOUN **participation** NOUN
SIMILAR WORDS: be involved in, join in, take part

participle, participles NOUN In grammar, a participle is a form of a verb used with an auxiliary verb in compound tenses and often as an adjective. English has two participles: the past participle, which describes a completed action, and the present participle, which

describes a continuing action. For example in 'He has gone', 'gone' is a past participle and in 'She was winning', 'winning' is a present participle.

particle, particles NOUN ① SCIENCE a basic unit of matter, such as an atom, molecule or electron. ② a very small piece of something.

particular ADJECTIVE ① relating or belonging to only one thing or person • *That particular place is dangerous.* ② especially great or intense • *Pay particular attention to the oral part of the exam.* ③ Someone who is particular has high standards and is not easily satisfied. **particularly** ADVERB

particulars PLURAL NOUN Particulars are facts or details.

parting, partings NOUN an occasion when one person leaves another.

partisan, partisans ADJECTIVE ① favouring or supporting one person or group • *a partisan crowd.* ▶ NOUN ② a member of an unofficial armed force fighting to free their country from enemy occupation • *Norwegian partisans in World War II.*

partition, partitions, partitioning, partitioned NOUN ① a screen separating one part of a room or vehicle from another. ② Partition is the division of a country into independent areas. ▶ VERB ③ To partition something is to divide it into separate parts.

partly ADVERB to some extent but not completely.

partner, partners, partnering, partnered NOUN ① Someone's partner is the person they are married to or are living with. ② Your partner is the person you are doing something with, for example in a dance or a game. ③ Business

partners are joint owners of their business. ▶ **VERB** ④ If you partner someone, you are their partner for a game or social occasion.
partnership NOUN

part of speech, parts of speech NOUN A part of speech is another name for a word class.

partook the past tense of **partake**.

partridge, partridges NOUN a brown game bird with a round body and a short tail.

part-time ADJECTIVE involving work for only a part of the working day or week.

party, parties NOUN ① a social event held for people to enjoy themselves. ② CITIZENSHIP an organisation whose members share the same political beliefs and campaign for election to government. ③ a group who are doing something together. ④ (formal) one of the people involved in a legal agreement or dispute.

pascal, pascals NOUN SCIENCE The pascal is the SI unit of pressure. It is named after the French physicist Blaise Pascal (1623–62).

pass, passes, passing, passed VERB ① To pass something is to move past it. ② To pass in a particular direction is to move in that direction • We passed through the gate. ③ If you pass something to someone, you hand it to them or transfer it to them. ④ If you pass a period of time doing something, you spend it that way • He hoped to pass the long night in meditation. ⑤ When a period of time passes, it happens and finishes. ⑥ If you pass a test, you are considered to be of an acceptable standard. ⑦ When a new law or proposal is passed, it is formally approved. ⑧ When a judge passes sentence on someone, the judge states what the punishment will be. ⑨ If you pass the ball in a ball game, you throw, kick or hit it to another player in your team. ▶ **NOUN** ⑩ the transfer of the ball in a ball game to another player in the same team. ⑪ an official document that allows you to go somewhere. ⑫ a narrow route between mountains. **pass away** or **pass on** VERB Someone who has passed away has died. **pass out** VERB If someone passes out, they faint. **pass up** VERB (informal) If you pass up an opportunity, you do not take advantage of it.
SIMILAR WORDS: ① go past, overtake ⑤ elapse, go by, lapse

SPELLING TIP
Do not confuse the spellings of passed and past: We passed an accident on the way here; Go past the garage and turn left.

passable ADJECTIVE of an acceptable standard • a passable imitation of his dad.

passage, passages NOUN ① a space that connects two places. ② a long, narrow corridor. ③ a section of a book or piece of music.

passcode, passcodes NOUN a series of numbers that you need to know to get into a computer, mobile phone, security system, etc.

passé [Said pas-say] ADJECTIVE no longer fashionable.

passenger, passengers NOUN a person travelling in a vehicle, aircraft or ship.

passer-by, passers-by NOUN someone who is walking past someone or something.

passing ADJECTIVE lasting only for a short time • a passing phase.
SIMILAR WORDS: brief, fleeting, momentary

The Passive Voice

The **passive** voice and the **active** voice are two different ways of presenting information in a sentence. The **passive** always uses a form of the auxiliary verb *to be* with the past participle of the verb. When a sentence is in the passive voice, the subject of the verb is affected by the action, rather than doing it:

*The cat **is being fed** by Anna.*
*The mouse **was chased** by a cat.*

It usually sounds more natural to use the active rather than the passive. However, it is sometimes better to use the passive if you want to avoid giving blame or if the name of the subject is not known:

The book has been mislaid.
We are being followed.

Also look at the grammar box at **active**

passion, passions NOUN ① Passion is a very strong feeling of attraction. ② Passion is also any strong emotion.
SIMILAR WORDS: ① emotion, fervour, intensity ② emotion, fervour, intensity

passionate ADJECTIVE involving very strong feelings about something.
passionately ADVERB
SIMILAR WORDS: emotional, fervent, intense

passive ADJECTIVE ① remaining calm and showing no feeling when provoked. ▶ NOUN ② ENGLISH In grammar, the passive or passive voice is the form of the verb in which the person or thing to which an action is being done is the grammatical subject of the sentence, and is given more emphasis as a result. For example, the passive of *The committee rejected your application* is *Your application was rejected by the committee.* **passively** ADVERB
passivity NOUN
SIMILAR WORDS: ① inactive, submissive

Passover NOUN RE The Passover is an eight-day Jewish festival held in spring.

passport, passports NOUN an official identification document which you need to show when you travel abroad.

password, passwords NOUN ① a secret word known to only a few people. It allows people on the same side to recognise a friend. ② ICT a word or series of numbers and letters that you need to know to get into a computer, mobile phone, security system, etc.

past NOUN ① The past is the period of time before the present. ▶ ADJECTIVE ② Past things are things that happened or existed before the present • *the past 30 years.* ③ ENGLISH MFL The past tense of a verb is the form used to express something that happened in the past. ▶ PREPOSITION OR ADVERB ④ You use 'past' when you are telling the time • *It was ten past eleven.* ⑤ If you go past something, you move towards it and continue until you are on the other side • *They drove rapidly past their cottage.*
▶ PREPOSITION ⑥ Something that is past a place is situated on the other side of it • *It's just past the church there.*

SPELLING TIP
Do not confuse the spellings of *past* and *passed* (from the verb pass): *Go past the garage and turn left; We passed an accident on the way here.*

pasta NOUN Pasta is a dried mixture of flour, eggs and water, formed into different shapes.

paste, pastes, pasting, pasted NOUN ① Paste is a soft, rather sticky mixture that can be easily spread • *tomato paste*. ▶ VERB ② If you paste something onto a surface, you stick it with glue.

pastel, pastels ADJECTIVE ① Pastel colours are pale and soft. ▶ NOUN ② ART Pastels are small sticks of coloured crayon, used for drawing pictures.

pasteurised [*Said* past-*yoor*-ized]; also spelt **pasteurized** ADJECTIVE Pasteurised milk has been treated in a special heating process to kill bacteria. It is named after the bacteriologist Louis Pasteur, who invented the process.

pastiche, pastiches [*Said* pass-*teesh*] NOUN ART A pastiche is a work of art that contains a mixture of styles or that copies the style of another artist.

pastime, pastimes NOUN a hobby or something you do just for pleasure. SIMILAR WORDS: activity, hobby, recreation

pastor, pastors NOUN a member of the clergy in charge of a congregation.

pastoral ADJECTIVE ① characteristic of peaceful country life and landscape • *pastoral scenes*. ② relating to the duties of the clergy in caring for the needs of their parishioners, or of a school in caring for the needs of its students • *a pastoral visit* • *Most schools have some system of pastoral care*.

past participle, past participles NOUN ENGLISH MFL In grammar, the past participle of an English verb is the form, usually ending in '-ed' or '-en', that is used to make some past tenses and the passive. For example 'killed' in 'She has killed the goldfish' and 'broken' in 'My leg was broken' are past participles.

pastry, pastries NOUN ① Pastry is a mixture of flour, fat and water, rolled flat and used for making pies. ② a small cake.

past tense NOUN ENGLISH MFL In grammar, the past tense is the tense of a verb that you use mainly to refer to things that happened or existed before the time of writing or speaking.

pasture, pastures NOUN Pasture is an area of grass on which farm animals graze.

pasty, pastier, pastiest; pasties ADJECTIVE ① [*Rhymes with* **hasty**] Someone who is pasty looks pale and unhealthy. ▶ NOUN ② [*Said* pass-*tee*] a small pie containing meat and vegetables.

pat, pats, patting, patted VERB ① If you pat something, you tap it lightly with your hand held flat. ▶ NOUN ② a small lump of butter.

patch, patches, patching, patched NOUN ① a piece of material used to cover a hole in something. ② an area of a surface that is different in appearance from the rest • *a bald patch*. ▶ VERB ③ If you patch something, you mend it by fixing a patch over the hole. **patch up** VERB If you patch something up, you mend it hurriedly or temporarily.

patchwork ADJECTIVE ① A patchwork quilt is made from many small pieces of material sewn together. ▶ NOUN ② Something that is a patchwork is made up of many parts.

patchy, patchier, patchiest ADJECTIVE Something that is patchy is unevenly spread or incomplete in parts • *patchy fog on the hills*.

Talking about the Past

You can talk about events that have already happened by using **simple past tenses** or **compound tenses**.

The **simple past tense** is formed without any auxiliary verbs. It is usually formed by taking the dictionary form of the verb and adding the ending -*ed*. (If the verb already ends in -*e*, then you only need to add -*d*.)

I **cook**_ed_ the dinner.
She **lik**_ed_ fish.

You can also use **compound tenses** to talk about actions that have happened.

One compound past tense is formed by using *was* or *were* in front of the main verb, and adding the ending -*ing*. This shows that an action happening in the past was continuous:

I **was cook**_ing_ the dinner.
We **were din**_ing_.

Notice that if the verb ends in *e*, the *e* is dropped.

Another compound past tense is formed by using a form of the verb *to have* in front of the main verb, and adding the ending -*ed*. This shows that an action has been completed:

I **have cook**_ed_ the dinner.
We **have din**_ed_.

Notice that if the verb already ends in *e* you don't need to add one.

Another compound past tense is formed by using *had* in front of the main verb, and adding the ending -*ed*. This form shows that an action in the past had been completed before something else took place:

I **had cook**_ed_ the dinner.
We **had din**_ed_.

Another compound past tense is formed by using *did* in front of the basic form of the verb. This can add emphasis:

We **did enjoy** that.

---

pâté [*Said pa-tay*] NOUN Pâté is a mixture of meat, fish or vegetables blended into a paste and spread on bread or toast.

patella, patellae NOUN SCIENCE Your patella is your kneecap.

patent, patents, patenting, patented NOUN ① an official right given to an inventor to be the only person or company allowed to make or sell a new product. ▶ VERB ② If you patent something, you obtain a patent for it. ▶ ADJECTIVE ③ obvious • *This was patent nonsense.* **patently** ADVERB

paternal ADJECTIVE relating to a father • *paternal pride*.

paternity NOUN Paternity is the state or fact of being a father.

path, paths NOUN ① a strip of ground for people to walk on. ② Your path is the area ahead of you and the direction in which you are moving.

pathetic ADJECTIVE ① If something is pathetic, it makes you feel pity. ② Pathetic also means very poor or unsuccessful • *a pathetic attempt*. **pathetically** ADVERB
SIMILAR WORDS: ① heart-rending, moving, sad

pathological ADJECTIVE extreme and uncontrollable • *a pathological fear of snakes*. **pathologically** ADVERB

pathology NOUN Pathology is the study of diseases and the way they develop. **pathologist** NOUN

pathos [Said **pay-thoss**] NOUN Pathos is a quality in literature or art that causes great sadness or pity.

pathway, pathways NOUN a path.

patience NOUN Patience is the ability to stay calm in a difficult or irritating situation.
SIMILAR WORDS: forbearance, tolerance

patient, patients ADJECTIVE ① If you are patient, you stay calm in a difficult or irritating situation.
▶ NOUN ② a person receiving medical treatment from a doctor or in a hospital. **patiently** ADVERB

patio, patios NOUN a paved area close to a house.

patois [Said **pat-twah**] NOUN A patois is an unwritten regional dialect, especially in France and the Caribbean.

patriarch, patriarchs [Said **pay-tree-ark**] NOUN a man who is the head of a family in a society in which power passes from father to son. **patriarchy** NOUN **patriarchal** ADJECTIVE

patrician ADJECTIVE (formal) belonging to a family of high rank.

patriot, patriots NOUN someone who loves their country and feels very loyal towards it. **patriotic** ADJECTIVE **patriotism** NOUN

patrol, patrols, patrolling, patrolled VERB ① When soldiers, police or guards patrol an area, they walk or drive around to make sure there is no trouble. ▶ NOUN ② a group of people patrolling an area.
WORD HISTORY: from French *patrouiller* meaning 'to flounder in mud'

patron, patrons NOUN ① a person who supports or gives money to artists, writers or musicians. ② The patrons of a hotel, pub or shop are the people who use it. **patronage** NOUN

patronise, patronises, patronising, patronised; also spelt **patronize** VERB ① If someone patronises you, they treat you kindly, but in a way that suggests that you are less intelligent than them or inferior to them. ② If you patronise a hotel, pub or shop, you are a customer there. **patronising** ADJECTIVE

patron saint, patron saints NOUN The patron saint of a group of people or place is a saint who is believed to look after them.

patter, patters, pattering, pattered VERB ① If something patters on a surface, it makes quick, light tapping sounds. ▶ NOUN ② a series of light tapping sounds • *a patter of light rain.*

pattern, patterns NOUN ① a decorative design of repeated shapes. ② The pattern of something is the way it is usually done or happens • *a perfectly normal pattern of behaviour.* ③ a diagram or shape used as a guide for making something, for example clothes. **patterned** ADJECTIVE

paunch, paunches NOUN If a person has a paunch, he or she has a fat stomach.

pauper, paupers NOUN (old-fashioned) a very poor person.

pause, pauses, pausing, paused VERB ① If you pause, you stop what you are doing for a short time. ▶ NOUN ② a short period when you stop what you are doing.

pave, paves, paving, paved VERB When an area of ground is paved, it is covered with flat blocks of stone or concrete.

pavement, pavements NOUN a path with a hard surface at the side of a road.

pavilion, pavilions NOUN a building at a sports ground where players can wash and change.

paw, paws, pawing, pawed NOUN ① The paws of an animal such as a cat or bear are its feet with claws and soft pads. ▶ VERB ② If an animal paws something, it hits it or scrapes at it with its paws.

pawn, pawns, pawning, pawned VERB ① If you pawn something, you leave it with a pawnbroker in exchange for money. ▶ NOUN ② the smallest and least valuable playing piece in chess.

pawnbroker, pawnbrokers NOUN a dealer who lends money in return for personal property left with him or her, which may be sold if the loan is not repaid on time.

pawpaw, pawpaws NOUN the same as a **papaya**.

pay, pays, paying, paid VERB ① When you pay money to someone, you give it to them because you are buying something or owe it to them. ② If it pays to do something, it is to your advantage to do it • They say it pays to advertise. ③ If you pay for something that you have done, you suffer as a result. ④ If you pay attention to something, you give it your attention. ⑤ If you pay a visit to someone, you visit them. ▶ NOUN ⑥ Someone's pay is their salary or wages.
SIMILAR WORDS: ① give, reimburse, settle

payable ADJECTIVE An amount of money that is payable has to be paid or can be paid • All fees are payable in advance.

payment, payments NOUN ① Payment is the act of paying money. ② a sum of money paid.

payroll, payrolls NOUN Someone who is on an organisation's payroll is employed and paid by them.

PC, PCs NOUN ① In Britain, PC is an abbreviation for 'police constable'. ② a personal computer. ▶ ADJECTIVE ③ short for **politically correct**.

PDF NOUN ICT a format for computer documents which makes a copy of the document look exactly like the original, regardless of which software or operating system was used to create it. PDF is an abbreviation for 'Portable Document Format'.

PE an abbreviation for 'physical education'.

pea, peas NOUN Peas are small, round, green seeds that grow in pods and are eaten as a vegetable.

peace NOUN ① Peace is a state of calm and quiet when there is no disturbance of any kind. ② When a country is at peace, it is not at war.
peaceable ADJECTIVE
SIMILAR WORDS: ① stillness, tranquillity

SPELLING TIP
Do not confuse the spellings of peace and piece: I love the peace and quiet here; a piece of cheese.

peaceful ADJECTIVE quiet and calm.
peacefully ADVERB
SIMILAR WORDS: serene, tranquil

peacekeeper, peacekeepers NOUN ① Someone who is a peacekeeper tries to prevent arguments between people. ② A peacekeeper is also a soldier whose job is to prevent further fighting between hostile forces in an area • United Nations peacekeepers.

peach, peaches NOUN ① a soft,

a
b
c
d
e
f
g
h
i
j
k
l
m
n
o
p
q
r
s
t
u
v
w
x
y
z

round fruit with yellow flesh and a yellow and red skin. ▸ **ADJECTIVE** ② pale orange with a hint of pink.

peacock, peacocks **NOUN** a large bird with green and blue feathers. The male has a long tail which it can spread out in a fan.

peak, peaks, peaking, peaked **NOUN** ① The peak of an activity or process is the point at which it is strongest or most successful. ② the pointed top of a mountain. ▸ **VERB** ③ When something peaks, it reaches its highest value or its greatest level of success. **peaked ADJECTIVE**
SIMILAR WORDS: ① climax, culmination, high point

peal, peals, pealing, pealed **NOUN** ① A peal of bells is the musical sound made by bells ringing one after another. ▸ **VERB** ② When bells peal, they ring one after the other.

SPELLING TIP
Do not confuse the spellings of *peal* and *peel*: *the peal of church bells; I slipped on a banana peel.*

---

peanut, peanuts **NOUN** Peanuts are small oval nuts that grow under the ground.

pear, pears **NOUN** a fruit which is narrow at the top and wide and rounded at the bottom.

pearl, pearls **NOUN** a hard, round, creamy-white object used to make jewellery. Pearls grow inside the shell of an oyster.

peasant, peasants **NOUN** In some countries, a peasant is a person who works on the land.

peat **NOUN** Peat is dark-brown decaying plant material found in cool, wet regions. Dried peat can be used as fuel.

pebble, pebbles **NOUN** a smooth, round stone.

peck, pecks, pecking, pecked **VERB** ① If a bird pecks something, it bites at it quickly with its beak. ② If you peck someone on the cheek, you give them a quick kiss. ▸ **NOUN** ③ a quick bite by a bird. ④ a quick kiss on the cheek.

peculiar **ADJECTIVE** ① strange and perhaps unpleasant. ② relating or belonging only to a particular person or thing • *a gesture peculiar to her.*
peculiarly ADVERB peculiarity NOUN

pedal, pedals, pedalling, pedalled **NOUN** ① a control lever on a machine or vehicle that you press with your foot. ▸ **VERB** ② When you pedal a bicycle, you push the pedals round with your feet to move along.

SPELLING TIP
Do not confuse the spellings of *pedal* and *peddle*: *You have to pedal hard when you go uphill; The market was full of people trying to peddle cheap jewellery and watches.*

---

pedantic **ADJECTIVE** If a person is pedantic, they are too concerned with unimportant details and traditional rules.

peddle, peddles, peddling, peddled **VERB** Someone who peddles something sells it.

SPELLING TIP
Do not confuse the spellings of *peddle* and *pedal*: *The market was full of people trying to peddle cheap jewellery and watches; You have to pedal hard when you go uphill.*

---

pedestal, pedestals **NOUN** a base on which a statue stands.

pedestrian, pedestrians **NOUN** ① someone who is walking. ▸ **ADJECTIVE** ② Pedestrian means ordinary and rather dull • *a pedestrian performance.*

pedestrian crossing, pedestrian crossings NOUN a specially marked place where you can cross the road safely.

pediatrician another spelling of **paediatrician**.

pediatrics another spelling of **paediatrics**.

pedigree, pedigrees ADJECTIVE ① A pedigree animal is descended from a single breed and its ancestors are known and recorded. ▶ NOUN ② Someone's pedigree is their background or ancestry.

peek, peeks, peeking, peeked VERB ① If you peek at something, you have a quick look at it • *I peeked round the corner.* ▶ NOUN ② a quick look at something.

peel, peels, peeling, peeled NOUN ① The peel of a fruit is the skin when it has been removed. ▶ VERB ② When you peel fruit or vegetables, you remove the skin. ③ If a surface is peeling, it is coming off in thin layers. **peelings** PLURAL NOUN

SPELLING TIP
Do not confuse the spellings of *peel* and *peal*: *I slipped on a banana peel; the peal of church bells.*

peep, peeps, peeping, peeped VERB ① If you peep at something, you have a quick look at it. ② If something peeps out from behind something else, a small part of it becomes visible • *a handkerchief peeping out of his breast pocket.* ▶ NOUN ③ a quick look at something.

peer, peers, peering, peered VERB ① If you peer at something, you look at it very hard. ▶ NOUN ② a member of the nobility. ③ Your peers are the people who are of the same age and social status as yourself.

peerage, peerages NOUN ① The peers in a country are called the peerage. ② A peerage is also the rank of being a peer.

peer group, peer groups NOUN Your peer group is the people who are of the same age and social status as yourself.

peerless ADJECTIVE so magnificent that nothing can equal it • *a peerless cast of actors.*

peer pressure NOUN PSHE Peer pressure is the influence that people of a person's own age have on him or her.

peewee, peewees NOUN a small black-and-white Australian bird with long, thin legs.

peg, pegs, pegging, pegged NOUN ① a plastic or wooden clip used for hanging wet clothes on a line. ② a hook on a wall where you can hang things. ▶ VERB ③ If you peg clothes on a line, you fix them there with pegs. ④ If a price is pegged at a certain level, it is fixed at that level.

peggy square, peggy squares NOUN In New Zealand, a peggy square is a small square of knitted wool which is sewn together with others to make a rug.

pejorative [*Said* pej-**jor**-ra-tiv] ADJECTIVE A pejorative word expresses criticism.

pelican, pelicans NOUN a large water bird with a pouch beneath its beak in which it stores fish.

pellet, pellets NOUN a small ball of paper, lead or other material.

pelt, pelts, pelting, pelted VERB ① If you pelt someone with things, you throw the things with force at them. ② (*informal*) If you pelt along, you run very fast. ▶ NOUN ③ the skin and fur of an animal.

pelvis, pelvises NOUN the wide, curved group of bones at hip level at

the base of your spine. **pelvic**
ADJECTIVE

pen, pens, penning, penned NOUN
① a long, thin instrument used for
writing with ink. ② a small fenced
area in which farm animals are kept
for a short time. ▸ VERB ③ (*literary*) If
someone pens a letter or article, they
write it. ④ If you are penned in or
penned up, you have to remain in an
uncomfortably small area.
WORD HISTORY: from Latin *penna*
meaning 'feather'; pens used to be
made from feathers

penal ADJECTIVE relating to the
punishment of criminals.

penalise, penalises, penalising,
penalised; also spelt **penalize** VERB
If you are penalised, you are made to
suffer some disadvantage as a
punishment for something.

penalty, penalties NOUN ① a
punishment or disadvantage that
someone is made to suffer. ② In
soccer, a penalty is a free kick at goal
that is given to the attacking team if
the defending team have committed
a foul near their goal.

penance NOUN If you do penance,
you do something unpleasant to
show that you are sorry for
something wrong that you have
done.

pence a plural form of **penny**.

penchant [*Said pon-shon*] NOUN
(*formal*) If you have a penchant for
something, you have a particular
liking for it • *a penchant for crime*.

pencil, pencils NOUN a long, thin
stick of wood with graphite in the
centre, used for drawing or writing.

pendant, pendants NOUN a piece of
jewellery attached to a chain and
worn round the neck.

pending (*formal*) ADJECTIVE
① Something that is pending is
waiting to be dealt with or will
happen soon. ▸ PREPOSITION
② Something that is done pending a
future event is done until the event
happens • *The army should stay in the
west pending a future war*.

pendulum, pendulums NOUN a rod
with a weight at one end in a clock
which swings regularly from side to
side to control the clock.

penetrate, penetrates,
penetrating, penetrated VERB To
penetrate an area that is difficult to
get into is to succeed in getting into
it. **penetration** NOUN

penetrating ADJECTIVE ① loud and
high-pitched • *a penetrating voice*.
② having or showing deep
understanding • *penetrating
questions*.

pen friend, pen friends NOUN
someone living in a different place or
country whom you write to regularly,
although you may never have met
each other.

penguin, penguins NOUN A penguin
is a black and white bird with webbed
feet and small wings like flippers.
Penguins are found mainly in the
Antarctic.

penicillin NOUN Penicillin is a
powerful antibiotic obtained from
fungus and used to treat infections.

peninsula, peninsulas NOUN
GEOGRAPHY an area of land almost
surrounded by water.

penis, penises NOUN SCIENCE A
man's penis is the part of his body
used for urination and reproduction.

penitent ADJECTIVE Someone who is
penitent is deeply sorry for having
done something wrong. **penitence**
NOUN

penknife, penknives NOUN a small
knife with a blade that folds back into
the handle.

pennant, pennants NOUN a triangular flag, especially one used by ships as a signal.

penniless ADJECTIVE Someone who is penniless has no money.

penny, pennies or **pence** NOUN a unit of currency in Britain and some other countries. In Britain a penny is worth one-hundredth of a pound.

pension, pensions [Said pen-shn] NOUN a regular sum of money paid to an old or retired person.

pensioner, pensioners NOUN an old or retired person who gets a pension paid by the state.

pensive ADJECTIVE deep in thought.
SIMILAR WORDS: dreamy, meditative, thoughtful

pentagon, pentagons NOUN MATHS a shape with five straight sides; a **regular pentagon** is a shape with five straight sides of the same length.
pentagonal ADJECTIVE

pentameter, pentameters [Said pen-tam-i-ter] NOUN ENGLISH a line of verse that has five metrical feet.

pentathlon, pentathlons [Said pen-tath-lon] NOUN a sports contest in which athletes compete in five different events.

penthouse, penthouses NOUN a luxurious flat at the top of a building.

pent-up ADJECTIVE Pent-up emotions have been held back for a long time without release.
SIMILAR WORDS: bottled up, suppressed

penultimate ADJECTIVE The penultimate thing in a series is the one before the last.

peony, peonies [Said pee-yon-ee] NOUN a garden plant with large pink, white or red flowers.

people, peoples, peopling, peopled PLURAL NOUN ① People are men,

women and children. ▶ NOUN ② all the men, women and children of a particular country or race. ▶ VERB ③ If an area is peopled by a particular group, that group of people live there.
SIMILAR WORDS: ① humanity, mankind, persons ② nation, population, race

people carrier, people carriers NOUN a large family car which has three rows of seats for passengers.

pepper, peppers NOUN ① a hot-tasting powdered spice used for flavouring in cooking. ② a hollow green, orange, red or yellow fruit eaten as a vegetable, with sweet-flavoured flesh.

peppermint, peppermints NOUN Peppermint is a plant with a strong taste. It is used for making sweets and in medicine.

pepperoni NOUN Pepperoni is a kind of spicy sausage which is often sliced and put on pizzas.

per PREPOSITION 'Per' is used to mean 'each' when expressing rates and ratios • The class meets two evenings per week.

perceive, perceives, perceiving, perceived VERB If you perceive something that is not obvious, you see it or realise it.
SIMILAR WORDS: notice, see, spot

per cent PHRASE You use **per cent** to talk about amounts as a proportion of a hundred. An amount that is 10 per cent (10%) of a larger amount is equal to 10 hundredths of the larger amount • 20 per cent of voters have still not decided who to vote for.
WORD HISTORY: from Latin per meaning 'each' and centum meaning 'hundred'

percentage, percentages NOUN MATHS a fraction expressed as a

a b c d e f g h i j k l m n o p q r s t u v w x y z

number of hundredths • *How do you show one fifth as a percentage?*

perceptible ADJECTIVE Something that is perceptible can be seen • *a barely perceptible nod.*

perception, perceptions NOUN ① Perception is the recognition of things using the senses, especially the sense of sight. ② Someone who has perception realises or notices things that are not obvious. ③ Your perception of something or someone is your understanding of them.

perceptive ADJECTIVE Someone who is perceptive realises or notices things that are not obvious.
perceptively ADVERB
SIMILAR WORDS: astute, observant, sharp

perch, perches, perching, perched VERB ① If you perch on something, you sit on the edge of it. ② When a bird perches on something, it stands on it. ▶ NOUN ③ a short rod for a bird to stand on. ④ an edible freshwater fish.

percolator, percolators NOUN a special pot for making and serving coffee.

percussion ADJECTIVE or NOUN MUSIC Percussion instruments or percussion are musical instruments that you hit to produce sounds.
percussionist NOUN

perennial ADJECTIVE continually occurring or never ending • *The damp cellar was a perennial problem.*

perfect, perfects, perfecting, perfected ADJECTIVE [Said **per**-fect] ① of the highest standard and without fault • *His English was perfect.* ② complete or absolute • *They have a perfect right to say so.* ③ ENGLISH MFL In grammar, the perfect tenses of a verb are used to talk about things that happened before a particular

time. The **present perfect** is formed in English with the present tense of 'have' and the past participle of the main verb, as in 'She has spoken'. The **past perfect** is formed with 'had' and the past participle of the main verb, as in 'She had spoken'. ▶ VERB [Said per-**fect**] ④ If you perfect something, you make it as good as it can possibly be. **perfectly** ADVERB **perfection** NOUN
SIMILAR WORDS: ① faultless, flawless ④ improve, refine

perfectionist, perfectionists NOUN someone who always tries to do everything perfectly.

perforated ADJECTIVE Something that is perforated has had small holes made in it. **perforation** NOUN

perform, performs, performing, performed VERB ① To perform a task or action is to do it. ② DRAMA To perform is to act, dance or play music in front of an audience.
performer NOUN

performance, performances NOUN ① DRAMA an entertainment provided for an audience. ② The performance of a task or action is the doing of it. ③ Someone's or something's performance is how successful they are • *the poor performance of the local economy.*

perfume, perfumes NOUN ① Perfume is a pleasant-smelling liquid for putting on the body. ② The perfume of something is its pleasant smell. **perfumed** ADJECTIVE

perfunctory ADJECTIVE done quickly without interest or care • *a perfunctory kiss.*

perhaps ADVERB You use 'perhaps' when you are not sure whether something is true or possible.

peril, perils NOUN (formal) Peril is

great danger. **perilous** ADJECTIVE
perilously ADVERB

perimeter, perimeters NOUN
MATHS The perimeter of a closed
figure or shape is the length of its
boundary.

period, periods NOUN ① a particular
length of time. ② one of the parts the
day is divided into at school. ③ A
woman's period is the monthly
bleeding from her womb. ④ In
American English, a period is a full
stop. ▶ ADJECTIVE ⑤ relating to a
historical period of time • *period
furniture*. **periodic** ADJECTIVE
periodically ADVERB

periodical, periodicals NOUN a
magazine.

periodic table NOUN SCIENCE The
periodic table is a table showing the
chemical elements arranged
according to their atomic numbers.

peripheral [*Said* per-rif-fer-ral]
ADJECTIVE ① of little importance in
comparison with other things • *a
peripheral activity*. ② on or relating to
the edge of an area.

periphery, peripheries NOUN The
periphery of an area is its outside
edge.

periscope, periscopes NOUN A
periscope is a tube with mirrors
which is used in a submarine to see
above the surface of the water.

perish, perishes, perishing, perished
VERB ① (*formal*) If someone or
something perishes, they are killed or
destroyed. ② If fruit or fabric perishes,
it rots. **perishable** ADJECTIVE

perjury NOUN (*Law*) If someone
commits perjury, they tell a lie in
court while under oath. **perjure**
VERB

perk, perks, perking, perked NOUN
① an extra, such as a company car,
offered by an employer in addition to

a salary. Perk is an abbreviation for
'perquisite'. ▶ VERB ② (*informal*)
When someone perks up, they
become more cheerful. **perky**
ADJECTIVE

perm, perms, perming, permed
NOUN ① If you have a perm, your hair
is curled and treated with chemicals
to keep the curls for several months.
▶ VERB ② To perm someone's hair
means to put a perm in it.

permanent ADJECTIVE lasting for
ever, or present all the time.
permanently ADVERB **permanence**
NOUN

permeable [*Said* per-mee-a-bl]
ADJECTIVE (*formal*) If something is
permeable, liquids are able to pass
through it • *permeable rock*.

permeate, permeates, permeating,
permeated VERB To permeate
something is to spread through it
and affect every part of it • *A sense of
optimism permeates everything that the
organisation does*.

permissible ADJECTIVE allowed by
the rules.
SIMILAR WORDS: allowable,
permitted

permission NOUN If you have
permission to do something, you are
allowed to do it.
SIMILAR WORDS: authorisation,
go-ahead

permissive ADJECTIVE A permissive
society allows things which some
people disapprove of.
permissiveness NOUN

permit, permits, permitting,
permitted VERB ① To permit
something is to allow it or make it
possible. ▶ NOUN ② an official
document which says that you are
allowed to do something.
SIMILAR WORDS: ① allow, give
permission, let

permutation, permutations NOUN one possible arrangement of a number of things.

pernicious ADJECTIVE (*formal*) very harmful • *the pernicious influence of television*.

peroxide NOUN Peroxide is a chemical used for bleaching hair or as an antiseptic.

perpendicular ADJECTIVE MATHS upright, or at right angles to a horizontal line.
WORD HISTORY: from Latin *perpendiculum* meaning 'plumb line'

perpetrate, perpetrates, perpetrating, perpetrated VERB (*formal*) To perpetrate a crime is to commit it. **perpetrator** NOUN

perpetual ADJECTIVE never ending • *a perpetual toothache*. **perpetually** ADVERB **perpetuity** NOUN

perpetuate, perpetuates, perpetuating, perpetuated VERB To perpetuate a situation or belief is to cause it to continue • *The television series will perpetuate the myths*.

perplexed ADJECTIVE If you are perplexed, you are puzzled and do not know what to do.

persecute, persecutes, persecuting, persecuted VERB To persecute someone is to treat them cruelly and unfairly over a long period of time. **persecution** NOUN **persecutor** NOUN
SIMILAR WORDS: pick on, victimise

persevere, perseveres, persevering, persevered VERB If you persevere, you keep trying to do something and do not give up. **perseverance** NOUN
SIMILAR WORDS: carry on, continue, keep going

Persian [*Said per-zhn*] ADJECTIVE or NOUN an old word for **Iranian**, used especially when referring to the older forms of the language.

persimmon, persimmons NOUN a sweet, red, tropical fruit.

persist, persists, persisting, persisted VERB ① If something undesirable persists, it continues to exist. ② If you persist in doing something, you continue in spite of opposition or difficulty. **persistence** NOUN **persistent** ADJECTIVE

person, people or persons NOUN ① a man, woman or child. ② MFL In grammar, the first person is the speaker (I), the second person is the person being spoken to (you), and the third person is anyone else being referred to (he, she, they).
SIMILAR WORDS: ① human being, individual

GRAMMAR TIP
The usual plural of *person* is *people*. *Persons* is much less common, and is used only in formal or official English.

---

persona, personas or personae [*Said per-soh-na*] NOUN (*formal*) Your persona is the image of yourself and your character that you choose to present to other people.

personal ADJECTIVE ① Personal means belonging or relating to a particular person rather than to people in general • *my personal feeling*. ② Personal matters relate to your feelings, relationships and health which you may not wish to discuss with other people. **personally** ADVERB
SIMILAR WORDS: ① individual, own, private

SPELLING TIP
Do not confuse the spellings of *personal* and *personnel*: *my personal belongings; a reduction in personnel*.

---

personality, personalities NOUN ① Your personality is your character and nature. ②a famous person in entertainment or sport.

personification NOUN ① ENGLISH Personification is a form of imagery in which something inanimate is described as if it has human qualities, for example 'The trees sighed and whispered as the impatient breeze stirred their branches'. ②Someone who is the personification of some quality is a living example of that quality • *He was the personification of evil.*

personify, personifies, personifying, personified VERB ①Someone who personifies a particular quality seems to be a living example of it. ②If you personify a thing or concept, you write or speak of it as if it has human abilities or qualities, for example 'The sun is trying to come out'.

personnel [Said per-son-**nell**] NOUN The personnel of an organisation are the people who work for it.

SPELLING TIP
Do not confuse the spellings of *personnel* and *personal*: *a reduction in personnel; my personal belongings*.

perspective, perspectives NOUN ①A particular perspective is one way of thinking about something. ② ART Perspective is a method artists use to make some people and things seem further away than others.

perspiration NOUN Perspiration is the moisture that appears on your skin when you are hot or frightened.

perspire, perspires, perspiring, perspired VERB If someone perspires, they sweat.

persuade, persuades, persuading, persuaded VERB If someone persuades you to do something or persuades you that something is true, they make you do it or believe it by giving you very good reasons.

persuasion NOUN **persuasive** ADJECTIVE
SIMILAR WORDS: convince, talk into

pertaining ADJECTIVE (*formal*) If information or questions are pertaining to a place or thing, they are about that place or thing • *issues pertaining to women.*

pertinent ADJECTIVE especially relevant to the subject being discussed • *He asks pertinent questions.*

perturbed ADJECTIVE Someone who is perturbed is worried.

Peruvian, Peruvians [Said per-**roo**-vee-an] ADJECTIVE ①belonging or relating to Peru. ▶NOUN ②someone who comes from Peru.

pervade, pervades, pervading, pervaded VERB Something that pervades a place is present and noticeable throughout it • *a fear that pervades the community.* **pervasive** ADJECTIVE

perverse ADJECTIVE Someone who is perverse deliberately does things that are unreasonable or harmful. **perversely** ADVERB **perversity** NOUN

pervert, perverts, perverting, perverted VERB (*formal*) To pervert something is to interfere with it so that it is no longer what it should be • *a conspiracy to pervert the course of justice.* **perversion** NOUN
WORD HISTORY: from Latin *pervertere* meaning 'to turn the wrong way'

perverted ADJECTIVE ①Someone who is perverted has disgusting or unacceptable behaviour or ideas. ②Something that is perverted is completely wrong • *a perverted sense of value.*

a b c d e f g h i j k l m n o p q r s t u v w x y z

peso, pesos [Said **pay**-soh] NOUN the main unit of currency in several South American countries.

pessimism NOUN Pessimism is the tendency to believe that bad things will happen. **pessimist** NOUN

pessimistic ADJECTIVE believing that bad things will happen.
pessimistically ADVERB

pest, pests NOUN ① an insect or small animal which damages plants or food supplies. ② (informal) someone who keeps bothering or annoying you.

pester, pesters, pestering, pestered VERB If you pester someone, you keep bothering them or asking them to do something.
SIMILAR WORDS: annoy, badger, hassle

pesticide, pesticides NOUN SCIENCE Pesticides are chemicals sprayed onto plants to kill insects and grubs.

pet, pets, petting, petted NOUN ① a tame animal kept at home.
▸ ADJECTIVE ② Someone's pet theory or pet project is something that they particularly support or feel strongly about. ▸ VERB ③ If you pet a person or animal, you stroke them affectionately.

petal, petals NOUN The petals of a flower are the coloured outer parts.

peter out, peters out, petering out, petered out VERB If something peters out, it gradually comes to an end.

petite [Said pet-**teet**] ADJECTIVE A woman who is petite is small and slim.

petition, petitions, petitioning, petitioned NOUN ① a document demanding official action which is signed by a lot of people. ② a formal request to a court for legal action to be taken. ▸ VERB ③ If you petition

someone in authority, you make a formal request to them • I petitioned the government for permission to visit its country.

petrified ADJECTIVE If you are petrified, you are very frightened.

petrol NOUN SCIENCE Petrol is a liquid obtained from petroleum and used as a fuel for motor vehicles.

petroleum NOUN Petroleum is thick, dark oil found under the earth or under the sea bed.
WORD HISTORY: from Latin petra meaning 'rock' and oleum meaning 'oil'

petticoat, petticoats NOUN a piece of women's underwear like a very thin skirt.

petty, pettier, pettiest ADJECTIVE ① Petty things are small and unimportant. ② Petty behaviour consists of doing small things which are selfish and unkind.

petulant ADJECTIVE showing unreasonable and childish impatience or anger. **petulantly** ADVERB **petulance** NOUN

petunia, petunias [Said pit-**yoon**-nee-ah] NOUN a garden plant with large trumpet-shaped flowers.

pew, pews NOUN a long wooden seat with a back, which people sit on in church.

pewter NOUN Pewter is a silvery-grey metal made from a mixture of tin and lead.

pH NOUN SCIENCE The pH of a solution or of the soil is a measurement of how acid or alkaline it is. Acid solutions have a pH of less than 7 and alkaline solutions have a pH greater than 7. pH is an abbreviation for 'potential of hydrogen'.

phalanger, phalangers [Said fal-**lan**-jer] NOUN an Australian marsupial with thick fur and a long tail. In Australia and New Zealand, it is also called a possum.

phantom, phantoms NOUN ① a ghost. ▶ADJECTIVE ② imagined or unreal • *a phantom illness*.

pharaoh, pharaohs [Said *fair-oh*] NOUN The pharaohs were kings of ancient Egypt.

pharmaceutical [Said *far-mass-yoo-tik-kl*] ADJECTIVE connected with the industrial production of medicines.

pharmacist, pharmacists NOUN a person who is qualified to prepare and sell medicines.

pharmacy, pharmacies NOUN a shop where medicines are sold.

phase, phases, phasing, phased NOUN ① a particular stage in the development of something. ▶VERB ② To phase something is to cause it to happen gradually in stages.

PhD, PhDs NOUN a degree awarded to someone who has done advanced research in a subject. PhD is an abbreviation for 'Doctor of Philosophy'.

pheasant, pheasants NOUN a large, long-tailed game bird.

phenomenal [Said *fin-nom-in-nal*] ADJECTIVE extraordinarily great or good. **phenomenally** ADVERB

phenomenon, phenomena NOUN something that happens or exists, especially something remarkable or something being considered in a scientific way • *a well-known geographical phenomenon*.

GRAMMAR TIP
The word *phenomenon* is singular. The plural form is *phenomena*.

---

philanthropist, philanthropists [Said *fil-lan-throp-pist*] NOUN someone who freely gives help or money to people in need.

philanthropic ADJECTIVE
philanthropy NOUN

philistine, philistines NOUN If you call someone a philistine, you mean that they do not like art, literature or music.

philosophical or **philosophic** ADJECTIVE Someone who is philosophical does not get upset when disappointing things happen.

philosophy, philosophies NOUN ① Philosophy is the study or creation of ideas about existence, knowledge or beliefs. ② a set of beliefs that a person has. **philosopher** NOUN WORD HISTORY: from Greek *philosophos* meaning 'lover of wisdom'

phishing NOUN Phishing is the practice of trying to trick people into giving secret personal information by sending fake emails to them.

phlegm [Said *flem*] NOUN Phlegm is a thick mucus which you get in your throat when you have a cold.

phlegmatic [Said *fleg-mat-tik*] ADJECTIVE Someone who is phlegmatic is calm and unemotional.

phobia, phobias NOUN a great fear or hatred of something • *The man had a phobia about flying*. **phobic** ADJECTIVE WORD HISTORY: from Greek *phobos* meaning 'fear'

-phobia SUFFIX '-phobia' means 'fear of' • *claustrophobia*.

phoenix, phoenixes [Said *fee-niks*] NOUN an imaginary bird which, according to myth, burns itself to ashes every five hundred years and rises from the fire again.

phone, phones, phoning, phoned NOUN ① a piece of electronic equipment which allows you to speak to someone in another place by keying in or dialling their number. ▶VERB ② If you phone someone, you

a b c d e f g h i j k l m n o **p** q r s t u v w x y z

key in or dial their number and speak to them using a phone.

-phone SUFFIX '-phone' means 'giving off sound' • *telephone* • *gramophone*.
WORD HISTORY: from Greek *phōnē* meaning 'voice' or 'sound'

phonetics NOUN ENGLISH
Phonetics is the study of speech sounds. **phonetic** ADJECTIVE

phoney, phonier, phoniest; phoneys; also spelt **phony** (*informal*) ADJECTIVE ① false and intended to deceive. ▸ NOUN ② Someone who is a phoney pretends to have qualities they do not possess.

phosphorus NOUN SCIENCE
Phosphorus is a whitish, nonmetallic element that burns easily and is used in making fertilisers and matches. Its atomic number is 15 and its symbol is P.

photo, photos NOUN (*informal*) a photograph.

photo- PREFIX 'Photo-' means 'light' or 'using light' • *photography*.

photocopier, photocopiers NOUN a machine which makes instant copies of documents by photographing them.

photocopy, photocopies, photocopying, photocopied LIBRARY NOUN ① a copy of a document produced by a photocopier. ▸ VERB ② If you photocopy a document, you make a copy of it using a photocopier.

photogenic ADJECTIVE Someone who is photogenic always looks nice in photographs.

photograph, photographs, photographing, photographed NOUN ① a picture made using a camera. ▸ VERB ② When you photograph someone, you take a picture of them by using a camera.
photographer NOUN **photography** NOUN

photographic ADJECTIVE connected with photography.

photosynthesis NOUN SCIENCE
Photosynthesis is the process by which the action of sunlight on the chlorophyll in plants produces the substances that keep the plants alive.

phrasal verb, phrasal verbs NOUN a verb such as 'take over' or 'break in', which is made up of a verb and an adverb or preposition.

phrase, phrases, phrasing, phrased NOUN ① a group of words considered as a unit. ▸ VERB ② If you phrase something in a particular way, you choose those words to express it • *I should have phrased that better*.

physical ADJECTIVE ① concerning the body rather than the mind. ② relating to things that can be touched or seen, especially with regard to their size or shape • *the physical characteristics of their machinery* • *the physical world*.
physically ADVERB

physical education NOUN Physical education consists of lessons in which gymnastics or sports are taught.

physician, physicians NOUN a doctor.

physics NOUN Physics is the scientific study of matter, energy, gravity, electricity, heat and sound.
physicist NOUN

physio- PREFIX 'Physio-' means to do with the body or natural functions • *physiotherapy*.
WORD HISTORY: from Greek *phusio-*, from *phuein* meaning 'to make grow'

physiology NOUN Physiology is the scientific study of the way the bodies of living things work.

physiotherapy NOUN
Physiotherapy is medical treatment

What is a Phrase?

A **phrase** is a group of words which combine together but which is not usually capable of standing on its own to describe an idea or situation. It requires additional words to form a meaningful sentence:

*She drank **a cup of tea**.*
*I **was reading** a book.*

Some phrases act as nouns:

***A stack of newspapers** lay on the floor.*
***My sister's friend** lives in Canada.*

Some phrases act as verbs. Verb phrases often contain an auxiliary verb. They may also contain adverbs:

*She **was always complaining** about the buses.*
*He **used to play** the piano.*

Some phrases act as adjectives. When words combine to act as an adjective, they are usually hyphenated if they occur before the noun:

*The food here is **of the highest quality**.*
*He asked for an **up-to-the-minute** report.*

Some phrases act as adverbs. Adverb phrases often begin with a preposition:

*She disappeared **in the blink of an eye**.*
*They played **with great gusto**.*

Some phrases are acceptable as substitutes for sentences. Although they do not contain a subject and a verb, they can be understood on their own:

Happy Birthday!
Good morning.
All right?

---

which involves exercise and massage. **physiotherapist** NOUN

physique, physiques *[Said fiz-zeek]* NOUN A person's physique is the shape and size of their body.

pi *[Rhymes with fly]* NOUN MATHS Pi is a number, approximately 3.142 and symbolised by the Greek letter π. Pi is the ratio of the circumference of a circle to its diameter.

pianissimo *[Said pee-an-iss-sim-moh]* ADVERB MUSIC In music, pianissimo is an instruction to play or sing something very quietly.

piano, pianos MUSIC NOUN ① a large musical instrument with a row of black and white keys. When the keys are pressed, little hammers hit wires to produce the different notes. ② In music, piano is an instruction to play or sing something quietly. **pianist** NOUN
WORD HISTORY: originally called

'pianoforte', from Italian *gravecembalo col piano e forte* meaning 'harpsichord with soft and loud (sounds)'

piccolo, piccolos NOUN a high-pitched wind instrument like a small flute.
WORD HISTORY: from Italian *piccolo* meaning 'small'

pick, picks, picking, picked VERB ① To pick something is to choose it. ② If you pick a flower or fruit, or pick something from a place, you remove it with your fingers. ③ If someone picks a lock, they open it with a piece of wire instead of a key. ▶ NOUN ④ The pick of a group of people or things are the best ones in it. ⑤ a pickaxe. **pick on** VERB If you pick on someone, you criticise them unfairly or treat them unkindly. **pick out** VERB If you pick out someone or something, you recognise them when they are difficult to see, or you choose them from among other things. **pick up** VERB If you pick someone or something up, you collect them from the place where they are waiting.

pickaxe, pickaxes NOUN a tool consisting of a curved pointed iron bar attached in the middle to a long handle.

picket, pickets, picketing, picketed VERB ① When a group of people picket a place of work, they stand outside to persuade other workers to join a strike. ▶ NOUN ② someone who is picketing a place.

pickings PLURAL NOUN Pickings are goods or money that can be obtained very easily • *rich pickings*.

pickle, pickles, pickling, pickled NOUN ① Pickle or pickles consists of vegetables or fruit preserved in vinegar or salt water. ▶ VERB ② To pickle food is to preserve it in vinegar or salt water.

pickpocket, pickpockets NOUN a thief who steals from people's pockets or handbags.

picnic, picnics, picnicking, picnicked NOUN ① a meal eaten out of doors. ▶ VERB ② People who are picnicking are having a picnic.

pictorial ADJECTIVE relating to or using pictures • *a pictorial record of the railway*.

picture, pictures, picturing, pictured NOUN ① a drawing, painting or photograph of someone or something. ② If you have a picture of something in your mind, you have an idea or impression of it. ▶ VERB ③ If someone is pictured in a newspaper or magazine, a photograph of them is printed in it. ④ If you picture something, you think of it and imagine it clearly • *That is how I always picture him*.

picturesque [*Said pik-chur-esk*] ADJECTIVE A place that is picturesque is very attractive and unspoiled.

pie, pies NOUN a dish of meat, vegetables or fruit covered with pastry.

piece, pieces, piecing, pieced NOUN ① a portion or part of something. ② something that has been written or created, such as a work of art or a musical composition. ③ a coin • *a 50 pence piece*. ▶ VERB ④ If you piece together a number of things, you gradually put them together to make something complete.

SPELLING TIP
Do not confuse the spellings of *piece* and *peace*: *a piece of cheese; I love the peace and quiet here*.

SPELLING TIP
Remember this mnemonic: *have a plEce of plE*.

piecemeal ADVERB or ADJECTIVE done gradually and at irregular intervals • *He built up a piecemeal knowledge of the subject, but it was not complete*.

pie chart, pie charts NOUN MATHS a circular graph divided into sections to show the relative sizes of things.

pier, piers NOUN a large structure which sticks out into the sea at a seaside town, and which people can walk along.

pierce, pierces, piercing, pierced VERB If a sharp object pierces something, it goes through it, making a hole.
SIMILAR WORDS: penetrate, puncture

piercing ADJECTIVE ① A piercing sound is high-pitched and unpleasant. ② Someone with piercing eyes seems to look at you very intensely.

SIMILAR WORDS: ① penetrating, shrill

piety [Said pie-it-tee] NOUN Piety is strong and devout religious belief or behaviour.

pig, pigs NOUN a farm animal kept for its meat. It has pinkish skin, short legs, and a snout.

pigeon, pigeons NOUN a largish bird with grey feathers, often seen in towns.

pigeonhole, pigeonholes NOUN one of the sections in a frame on a wall where letters can be left.

piggyback, piggybacks NOUN If you give someone a piggyback, you carry them on your back, supporting them under their knees.

piglet, piglets NOUN a young pig.

pigment, pigments NOUN a substance that gives something a particular colour. **pigmentation** NOUN

pigsty, pigsties NOUN a hut with a small enclosed area where pigs are kept.

pigtail, pigtails NOUN a length of plaited hair.

pike, pikes NOUN ① a large freshwater fish of northern countries with strong teeth. ② a medieval weapon consisting of a pointed metal blade attached to a long pole.

Pilates [Said pil-lah-teez] NOUN Pilates is a system of gentle exercises designed to make the body stronger and more flexible.

pilchard, pilchards NOUN a small sea fish.

pile, piles, piling, piled NOUN ① a quantity of things lying one on top of another. ② the soft surface of a carpet consisting of many threads standing on end. ③ (in plural) Piles are painful swellings that appear in the veins inside or just outside a person's anus. ▶ VERB ④ If you pile things somewhere, you put them one on top of the other.

pile-up, pile-ups NOUN (informal) a road accident involving several vehicles.

pilfer, pilfers, pilfering, pilfered VERB Someone who pilfers steals small things over a period of time.

pilgrim, pilgrims NOUN ⟦RE⟧ a person who travels to a holy place for religious reasons. **pilgrimage** NOUN

pill, pills NOUN ① a small, hard tablet of medicine that you swallow. ② The pill is a type of drug that women can take regularly to prevent pregnancy. WORD HISTORY: from Latin pilula meaning 'little ball'

pillage, pillages, pillaging, pillaged VERB If a group of people pillage a place, they steal from it using violence.

pillar, pillars NOUN ① a tall, narrow, solid structure, usually supporting part of a building. ② Someone who is described as a pillar of a particular group is an active and important member of it • a pillar of the Church.

pillar box, pillar boxes NOUN a red cylinder or box in which you post letters.

pillory, pillories, pillorying, pilloried VERB If someone is pilloried, they are criticised severely by a lot of people.

pillow, pillows NOUN a rectangular cushion which you rest your head on when you are in bed.

pillowcase, pillowcases NOUN a cover for a pillow which can be removed and washed.

pilot, pilots, piloting, piloted NOUN ① a person who is trained to fly an aircraft. ② a person who goes on board ships to guide them through local waters to a port. ▶ VERB ③ To pilot something is to control its

a
b
c
d
e
f
g
h
i
j
k
l
m
n
o
p
q
r
s
t
u
v
w
x
y
z

movement or to guide it. ④ To pilot a scheme or product is to test it to see if it would be successful.

pimple, pimples NOUN a small spot on the skin. **pimply** ADJECTIVE

pin, pins, pinning, pinned NOUN ① a thin, pointed piece of metal used to fasten together things such as pieces of fabric or paper. ▶ VERB ② If you pin something somewhere, you fasten it there with a pin or a drawing pin. ③ If someone pins you in a particular position, they hold you there so that you cannot move. ④ If you try to pin something down, you try to get or give a clear and exact description of it or statement about it.

PIN, PINs NOUN a security number used by the holder of a cash card or credit card. PIN is an abbreviation for 'personal identification number'.

pinafore, pinafores NOUN a dress with no sleeves, worn over a blouse.

pincers PLURAL NOUN ① Pincers are a tool used for gripping and pulling things. They consist of two pieces of metal hinged in the middle. ② The pincers of a crab or lobster are its front claws.

pinch, pinches, pinching, pinched VERB ① If you pinch something, you squeeze it between your thumb and first finger. ② (informal) If someone pinches something, they steal it. ▶ NOUN ③ A pinch of something is the amount that you can hold between your thumb and first finger • a pinch of salt.

pinched ADJECTIVE If someone's face is pinched, it looks thin and pale.

pine, pines, pining, pined NOUN ① A pine or pine tree is an evergreen tree with very thin leaves. ▶ VERB ② If you pine for something, you are sad because you cannot have it.

pineapple, pineapples NOUN a large, oval fruit with sweet, yellow flesh and a thick, lumpy brown skin.

ping-pong NOUN the same as **table tennis**.

pink, pinker, pinkest ADJECTIVE pale reddish-white.

pinnacle, pinnacles NOUN ① a tall pointed piece of stone or rock. ② The pinnacle of something is its best or highest level • the pinnacle of his career.

pinpoint, pinpoints, pinpointing, pinpointed VERB If you pinpoint something, you explain or discover exactly what or where it is.

pinstripe ADJECTIVE Pinstripe cloth has very narrow vertical stripes.

pint, pints NOUN a unit of liquid volume equal to one eighth of a gallon or about 0.568 litres.

pioneer, pioneers, pioneering, pioneered [Said pie-on-ear] NOUN ① Someone who is a pioneer in a particular activity is one of the first people to develop it. ▶ VERB ② Someone who pioneers a new process or invention is the first person to develop it.

pious [Said pie-uss] ADJECTIVE very religious and moral.

pip, pips NOUN Pips are the hard seeds in a fruit.

pipe, pipes, piping, piped NOUN ① a long, hollow tube through which liquid or gas can flow. ② an object used for smoking tobacco. It consists of a small hollow bowl attached to a tube. ▶ VERB ③ To pipe a liquid or gas somewhere is to transfer it through a pipe.

pipeline, pipelines NOUN a large underground pipe that carries oil or gas over a long distance.

piper, pipers NOUN a person who plays the bagpipes.

piping NOUN Piping consists of pipes and tubes.

piranha, piranhas [Said pir-rah-nah] NOUN a small, fierce fish with sharp teeth.

pirate, pirates NOUN Pirates were sailors who attacked and robbed other ships.

pirouette, pirouettes [Said pir-roo-et] NOUN In ballet, a pirouette is a fast spinning step done on the toes.

Pisces [Said pie-seez] NOUN Pisces is the twelfth sign of the zodiac, represented by two fish. People born between February 19th and March 20th are born under this sign.
WORD HISTORY: the plural of Latin *piscis* meaning 'a fish'

pistol, pistols NOUN a small gun held in the hand.

piston, pistons NOUN a cylinder or disc that slides up and down inside a tube. Pistons make parts of engines move.

pit, pits NOUN ① a large hole in the ground. ② a small hollow in the surface of something. ③ a coal mine.

pitch, pitches, pitching, pitched NOUN ① PE an area of ground marked out for playing a game such as football. ② MUSIC The pitch of a sound is how high or low it is. ③ a black substance used in road tar and also for making boats and roofs waterproof. ▶ VERB ④ If you pitch something somewhere, you throw it with a lot of force. ⑤ If you pitch something at a particular level of difficulty, you set it at that level • *Any film must be pitched at a level to suit its intended audience.* ⑥ When you pitch a tent, you fix it in an upright position.

pitcher, pitchers NOUN a large jug.

pitfall, pitfalls NOUN The pitfalls of a situation are its difficulties or dangers.

pith NOUN the white substance between the outer skin and the flesh of an orange or lemon.

pitiful ADJECTIVE Someone or something that is pitiful is in such a sad or weak situation that you feel pity for them.

pittance NOUN a very small amount of money.

pitted ADJECTIVE covered in small hollows • *Nails often become pitted.*

pity, pities, pitying, pitied VERB ① If you pity someone, you feel very sorry for them. ▶ NOUN ② Pity is a feeling of being sorry for someone. ③ If you say that it is a pity about something, you are expressing your disappointment about it.

pivot, pivots, pivoting, pivoted VERB ① If something pivots, it balances or turns on a central point • *The keel pivots on a large stainless steel pin.* ▶ NOUN ② the central point on which something balances or turns.

pivotal ADJECTIVE A pivotal role, point or figure is very important to the success of something • *This was a pivotal moment in Stevenson's career.*

pixel, pixels NOUN ICT the smallest area on a computer screen which can be given a separate colour by the computer.

pixie, pixies NOUN an imaginary little creature in fairy stories.

pizza, pizzas [Said peet-sah] NOUN a flat piece of dough covered with cheese, tomato and other savoury food.

pizzicato [Said pit-sik-kat-oh] ADVERB MUSIC If a stringed instrument such as a violin is played pizzicato, it is played by plucking the strings.

placard, placards NOUN a large notice carried at a demonstration or displayed in a public place.

placate, placates, placating, placated VERB If you placate

a
b
c
d
e
f
g
h
i
j
k
l
m
n
o
p
q
r
s
t
u
v
w
x
y
z

someone, you stop them feeling angry by doing something to please them.

place, places, placing, placed NOUN ① any point, building or area. ② the position where something belongs • *She set the holder in its place on the table.* ③ a space at a table set with cutlery where one person can eat. ④ If you have a place in a group or at a college, you are a member or are accepted as a student. ⑤ a particular point or stage in a sequence of things • *second place in the race.* ▶ PHRASE ⑥ When something **takes place**, it happens. ▶ VERB ⑦ If you place something somewhere, you put it there. ⑧ If you place an order, you order something.
SIMILAR WORDS: ① location, site, spot

placebo, placebos [Said plas-**see**-boh] NOUN a substance given to a patient in place of a drug and from which, though it has no active ingredients, the patient may imagine they get some benefit.

placenta, placentas [Said plas-**sen**-tah] NOUN SCIENCE The placenta is the mass of veins and tissues in the womb of a pregnant woman or animal. It gives the foetus food and oxygen.

placid ADJECTIVE calm and not easily excited or upset. **placidly** ADVERB
SIMILAR WORDS: even-tempered, unexcitable

plagiarism [Said play-jer-rizm] NOUN Plagiarism is copying someone else's work or ideas and pretending that it is your own. **plagiarist** NOUN **plagiarise** VERB
WORD HISTORY: from Latin *plagiarus* meaning 'plunderer'

plague, plagues, plaguing, plagued [Said playg] NOUN ① Plague is a very infectious disease that kills large numbers of people. ② A plague of unpleasant things is a large number of them occurring at the same time • *a plague of rats.* ▶ VERB ③ If problems plague you, they keep causing you trouble.

plaice, plaice NOUN an edible European flat fish.

SPELLING TIP
Remember this mnemonic: *plaice the fish has a glittering eye (i).*

plaid, plaids [Said plad] NOUN Plaid is woven material with a tartan design.

plain, plainer, plainest; plains ADJECTIVE ① very simple in style with no pattern or decoration • *plain walls.* ② obvious and easy to recognise or understand • *plain language.* ③ A person who is plain is not at all beautiful or attractive. ▶ ADVERB ④ You can use 'plain' before a noun or adjective to emphasise it • *You were just plain stupid.* ▶ NOUN ⑤ a large, flat area of land with very few trees.
plainly ADVERB
SIMILAR WORDS: ① bare, simple, unadorned

SPELLING TIP
Do not confuse the spellings of *plain* and *plane*: *lions who live on the African plains; If you don't hurry up you will miss your plane.*

plaintiff, plaintiffs NOUN a person who has brought a court case against another person.

plait, plaits, plaiting, plaited VERB ① If you plait three lengths of hair or rope together, you twist them over each other in turn to make one thick length. ▶ NOUN ② a length of hair that has been plaited.

plan, plans, planning, planned NOUN ① a method of achieving something that has been worked out

beforehand. ②a detailed diagram or drawing of something that is to be made. ▸ **VERB** ③If you plan something, you decide in detail what it is to be and how to do it. ④If you are planning to do something, you intend to do it • *They plan to marry in the summer.*
SIMILAR WORDS: ①scheme, strategy ③devise, scheme, think out ④intend, mean, propose

plane, planes, planing, planed **NOUN** ①a vehicle with wings and engines that enable it to fly. ②a flat surface. ③You can refer to the standard at which something is done as a particular plane • *I want to take gymnastics to a higher plane.* ④a tool with a flat bottom with a sharp blade in it. You move it over a piece of wood to remove thin pieces from the surface. ▸ **VERB** ⑤If you plane a piece of wood, you smooth its surface with a plane.

SPELLING TIP
Do not confuse the spellings of *plane* and *plain*: *If you don't hurry up you will miss your plane; lions who live on the African plains.*

planet, planets **NOUN** a round object in space which moves around the sun or a star and is lit by light from it. **planetary ADJECTIVE**

plank, planks **NOUN** a long rectangular piece of wood.

plankton NOUN Plankton is a layer of tiny plants and animals that live just below the surface of a sea or lake.

plant, plants, planting, planted **NOUN** ①a living thing that grows in the earth and has stems, leaves and roots. ②a factory or power station • *a giant bottling plant.* ▸ **VERB** ③When you plant a seed or plant, you put it into the ground. ④If you plant something somewhere, you

put it there firmly or secretly.

plantation, plantations **NOUN** ①a large area of land where crops such as tea, cotton or sugar are grown. ②a large number of trees planted together.

plaque, plaques [*Rhymes with* **black**] **NOUN** ①a flat piece of metal which is fixed to a wall and has an inscription in memory of a famous person or event. ②Plaque is a substance which forms around your teeth and consists of bacteria, saliva and food.

plasma [*Said* plaz-*mah*] **NOUN** Plasma is the clear fluid part of blood.

plasma screen, plasma screens **NOUN** a thin screen on a television or computer that produces high-quality images.

plaster, plasters, plastering, plastered **NOUN** ①Plaster is a paste made of sand, lime and water, which is used to form a smooth surface for inside walls and ceilings. ②a strip of sticky material with a small pad, used for covering cuts on your body. ▸ **VERB** ③To plaster a wall is to cover it with a layer of plaster. ▸ **PHRASE** ④If your arm or leg is **in plaster**, it has a plaster cast on it to protect a broken bone. **plasterer NOUN**

plastered ADJECTIVE ①If something is plastered to a surface, it is stuck there. ②If something is plastered with things, they are all over its surface.

plastic, plastics **NOUN** ①Plastic is a substance made by a chemical process that can be moulded when soft to make a wide range of objects. ▸ **ADJECTIVE** ②made of plastic.

plastic surgery NOUN Plastic surgery is surgery to replace or repair damaged skin or to improve a person's appearance by changing the shape of their features.

a
b
c
d
e
f
g
h
i
j
k
l
m
n
o
p
q
r
s
t
u
v
w
x
y
z

plate | 590

plate, **plates** NOUN ① a flat dish used to hold food. ② a flat piece of metal or other hard material used for various purposes in machinery or building • *heavy steel plates used in shipbuilding.* ③ GEOGRAPHY a large part of the earth's surface.

plateau, **plateaus** or **plateaux** [*Rhymes with* **snow**] NOUN GEOGRAPHY a large area of high and fairly flat land.

plated ADJECTIVE Metal that is plated is covered with a thin layer of silver or gold.

platform, **platforms** NOUN ① a raised structure on which someone or something can stand. ② the raised area in a railway station where passengers get on and off trains.

platinum NOUN Platinum is a valuable silver-coloured metal. Its atomic number is 78 and its symbol is Pt.

platitude, **platitudes** NOUN a statement made as if it were significant but which has become meaningless or boring because it has been used so many times before.

platonic ADJECTIVE A platonic relationship is simply one of friendship and does not involve romantic attraction.
WORD HISTORY: from the name of the Greek philosopher Plato

platoon, **platoons** NOUN a small group of soldiers, commanded by a lieutenant.

platteland [*Said* plat-uh-lant] NOUN In South Africa, the platteland is the country districts or rural areas.

platter, **platters** NOUN a large serving plate.

platypus, **platypuses** NOUN A platypus or duck-billed platypus is an Australian mammal which lives in rivers. It has brown fur, webbed feet, and a bill like a duck.

WORD HISTORY: from Greek *platus* meaning 'flat' and *pous* meaning 'foot'

plaudits PLURAL NOUN (*formal*) Plaudits are expressions of admiration.

plausible ADJECTIVE An explanation that is plausible seems likely to be true. **plausibility** NOUN

play, **plays**, **playing**, **played** VERB ① When children play, they take part in games or use toys. ② When you play a sport or match, you take part in it. ③ If an actor plays a character in a play or film, he or she performs that role. ④ If you play a musical instrument, you produce music from it. ⑤ If you play recorded music, you operate a machine in order to produce that music. ▶ NOUN ⑥ a piece of drama performed in the theatre or on television. **player** NOUN

playboy, **playboys** NOUN a rich man who spends his time enjoying himself.

playful ADJECTIVE ① friendly and light-hearted • *a playful kiss on the tip of his nose.* ② lively • *a playful puppy.* **playfully** ADVERB

playground, **playgrounds** NOUN a special area for children to play in.

playgroup, **playgroups** NOUN an informal kind of school for very young children where they learn by playing.

playing card, **playing cards** NOUN Playing cards are cards printed with numbers or pictures which are used to play various games.

playing field, **playing fields** NOUN an area of grass where people play sports.

playwright, **playwrights** NOUN ENGLISH DRAMA a person who writes plays.

plaza, **plazas** [Said *plah-za*] NOUN an open square in a city.

plea, **pleas** NOUN ① an emotional request • *a plea for help*. ② In a court of law, someone's plea is their statement that they are guilty or not guilty.

plead, **pleads**, **pleading**, **pleaded** VERB ① If you plead with someone, you ask them in an intense emotional way to do something. ② When a person pleads guilty or not guilty, they state in court that they are guilty or not guilty of a crime.

pleasant ADJECTIVE ① enjoyable or attractive. ② friendly or charming. **pleasantly** ADVERB
SIMILAR WORDS: ① agreeable, nice, pleasing ② agreeable, nice, pleasing

please, **pleases**, **pleasing**, **pleased** ADVERB ① You say please when you are asking someone politely to do something. ▸ VERB ② If something pleases you, it makes you feel happy and satisfied.
SIMILAR WORDS: ② delight, gladden, satisfy

pleased ADJECTIVE happy or satisfied.

pleasing ADJECTIVE attractive, satisfying or enjoyable • *a pleasing appearance*.

pleasure, **pleasures** NOUN ① Pleasure is a feeling of happiness, satisfaction or enjoyment. ② an activity that you enjoy. **pleasurable** ADJECTIVE

pleat, **pleats** NOUN a permanent fold in fabric made by folding one part over another.

plebiscite, **plebiscites** [Said *pleb-iss-ite*] NOUN (*formal*) a vote on a matter of national importance in which all the voters in a country can take part.
WORD HISTORY: from Latin *plebiscitum* meaning 'decree of the people'

pledge, **pledges**, **pledging**, **pledged** NOUN ① a solemn promise. ▸ VERB ② If you pledge something, you promise that you will do it or give it.

plentiful ADJECTIVE existing in large numbers or amounts and readily available • *Fruit and vegetables were plentiful*. **plentifully** ADVERB

plenty NOUN If there is plenty of something, there is a lot of it.

plethora [Said *pleth-thor-ah*] NOUN A plethora of something is an amount that is greater than you need.

pleurisy [Said *ploor-ris-see*] NOUN Pleurisy is a serious illness in which a person's lungs become inflamed and breathing is difficult.

pliable ADJECTIVE ① If something is pliable, you can bend it without breaking it. ② Someone who is pliable can be easily influenced or controlled.
SIMILAR WORDS: ① bendy, flexible, supple

pliers PLURAL NOUN Pliers are a small tool with metal jaws for holding small objects and bending wire.

plight NOUN Someone's plight is the very difficult or dangerous situation that they are in • *the plight of the refugees*.

plinth, **plinths** NOUN a block of stone on which a statue or pillar stands.

plod, **plods**, **plodding**, **plodded** VERB If you plod somewhere, you walk there slowly and heavily.

plonk, **plonks**, **plonking**, **plonked** VERB (*informal*) If you plonk something down, you put it down heavily and carelessly.

plop, **plops**, **plopping**, **plopped** (*informal*) NOUN ① a gentle sound made by something light dropping into a liquid. ▸ VERB ② If something plops into a liquid, it drops into it with a gentle sound.

a
b
c
d
e
f
g
h
i
j
k
l
m
n
o
p
q
r
s
t
u
v
w
x
y
z

plot, plots, plotting, plotted NOUN
① a secret plan made by a group of
people. ② ENGLISH The plot of a
novel or play is the story. ③ a small
piece of land. ▶ VERB ④ If people plot
to do something, they plan it secretly
• *His family is plotting to disinherit him.*
⑤ If someone plots the course of a
plane or ship on a map, or plots a
graph, they mark the points in the
correct places.
SIMILAR WORDS: ① conspiracy,
scheme ④ conspire, plan, scheme

plough, ploughs, ploughing,
ploughed [*Rhymes with cow*] NOUN
① a large farming tool that is pulled
across a field to turn the soil over
before planting seeds. ▶ VERB
② When someone ploughs land, they
use a plough to turn over the soil.

ploy, ploys NOUN a clever plan or way
of behaving in order to get
something that you want.

pluck, plucks, plucking, plucked
VERB ① To pluck a fruit or flower is to
remove it with a sharp pull. ② To
pluck a chicken or other dead bird
means to pull its feathers out before
cooking it. ③ When you pluck a
stringed instrument, you pull the
strings and let them go. ▶ NOUN
④ Pluck is courage. **plucky**
ADJECTIVE

plug, plugs, plugging, plugged
NOUN ① a plastic object with metal
prongs that can be pushed into a
socket to connect an appliance to the
electricity supply. ② a disc of rubber
or metal with which you block up the
hole in a sink or bath. ▶ VERB ③ If you
plug a hole, you block it with
something.

plum, plums NOUN a small fruit with
a smooth red or yellow skin and a
large stone in the middle.

plumage [*Said ploom-mage*] NOUN A
bird's plumage is its feathers.

plumber, plumbers NOUN a person
who connects and repairs water
pipes.
WORD HISTORY: from Old French
plommier meaning 'worker in lead'

plumbing NOUN The plumbing in a
building is the system of water pipes,
sinks and toilets.

plume, plumes NOUN a large,
brightly coloured feather.

plummet, plummets, plummeting,
plummeted VERB If something
plummets, it falls very quickly • *Sales
have plummeted.*

plump, plumper, plumpest
ADJECTIVE rather fat • *a small plump
baby.*
SIMILAR WORDS: chubby, podgy,
tubby

plunder, plunders, plundering,
plundered VERB If someone
plunders a place, they steal things
from it.

plunge, plunges, plunging, plunged
VERB ① If something plunges, it falls
suddenly. ② If you plunge an object
into something, you push it in
quickly. ③ If you plunge into an
activity or state, you suddenly
become involved in it or affected by it
• *The United States had just plunged into
the war.* ▶ NOUN ④ a sudden fall.
SIMILAR WORDS: ① dive, drop, fall,
plummet

Plunket Society NOUN In New
Zealand, the Plunket Society was an
organisation for the care of mothers
and babies. It is now called the Royal
New Zealand Society for the Health
of Women and Children.

plural, plurals NOUN ENGLISH MFL
the form of a word that is used to
refer to two or more people or things,
for example the plural of 'chair' is
'chairs', and the plural of 'mouse' is
'mice'.

What is a Plural?

Most nouns can exist in either the singular or plural.

The **singular** form of the noun is used to mean only one instance of a thing. This is the main form given in the dictionary:

one book
a raven

The **plural** form of the noun is used to mean more than one instance of a thing. The plural form is given in the dictionary in smaller type after the main form:

two books
some ravens

The plural form of the noun is usually formed by adding the letter -s to the singular:

book → books
raven → ravens

Words that end in -s, -z, -x, -ch or -sh in the singular are made plural by adding the letters -es:

cross → crosses
box → boxes

Words that end in a consonant + -y in the singular are made plural by removing the -y and adding -ies:

pony → ponies
party → parties

Words that end in -ife in the singular are made plural by removing the -fe and adding -ves:

knife → knives
life → lives

Some words that end in -f in the singular are made plural by removing the -f and adding -ves. Other words that end in -f in the singular are made plural by simply adding -s:

hoof → hooves

roof → roofs

BE CAREFUL not to use an apostrophe (') when you add an -s to make a plural.

Irregular Plurals
Some words that have come to English from a foreign language have plurals that do not end in -s.

Some words that came into English from French have plurals ending in -x:

bureau → bureaux
gateau → gateaux

Some words that came into English from Italian have plurals ending in -i:

paparazzo → paparazzi
graffito → graffiti

Some words that came into English from Hebrew have plurals ending in -im:

cherub → cherubim
kibbutz → kibbutzim

Some words that came into English from Latin have plurals ending in -i, -a or -ae:

cactus → cacti
medium → media
formula → formulae

Some words that came into English from Ancient Greek have plurals ending in -a:

phenomenon → phenomena
criterion → criteria

The plural forms of a few words are not formed according to any regular rule. However, there are very few words like this. Here are some of the most common ones: *child, children; deer, deer; fish, fish or fishes; foot, feet; man, men; mouse, mice; ox, oxen; sheep, sheep; woman, women.*

a b c d e f g h i j k l m n o **p** q r s t u v w x y z

pluralism NOUN Pluralism is the belief that it is possible for different social and religious groups to live together peacefully while keeping their own beliefs and traditions. **pluralist** ADJECTIVE or NOUN

plural noun, plural nouns NOUN In this dictionary, 'plural noun' is the name given to a noun that is normally used only in the plural, for example 'scissors' or 'police'.

plus ① You use 'plus' to show that one number is being added to another • *Two plus two equals four.* ② You can use 'plus' when you mention an additional item • *He wrote a history of Scotland plus a history of British literature.* ▸ ADJECTIVE ③ slightly more than the number mentioned • *a career of 25 years plus.*

USAGE NOTE
Although you can use *plus* to mean 'additionally' in spoken language, you should avoid it in written work: *Plus, you could win a holiday in Florida.*

plush ADJECTIVE (*informal*) very expensive and smart • *a plush hotel.*

Pluto NOUN Pluto is a dwarf planet in the solar system.

ply, plies, plying, plied VERB ① If you ply someone with things or questions, you keep giving them things or asking them questions. ② To ply a trade is to do a particular job as your work. ▸ NOUN ③ Ply is the thickness of wool or thread, measured by the number of strands it is made from.

plywood NOUN Plywood is wooden board made from several thin sheets of wood glued together under pressure.

PM, PMs NOUN an abbreviation for 'prime minister' or 'private message'.

p.m. used to specify times between 12 noon and 12 midnight, eg *He went to bed at 9 p.m.* It is an abbreviation for the Latin phrase 'post meridiem', which means 'after noon'.

pneumatic [Said new-*mat*-ik] ADJECTIVE DGT operated by or filled with compressed air • *a pneumatic drill.* WORD HISTORY: from Latin *pneumaticus* meaning 'of air or wind'

pneumonia [Said new-*moan*-ee-ah] NOUN Pneumonia is a serious disease which affects a person's lungs and makes breathing difficult.

poach, poaches, poaching, poached VERB ① If someone poaches animals from someone else's land, they illegally catch the animals for food. ② When you poach food, you cook it gently in hot liquid. **poacher** NOUN

pocket, pockets NOUN ① a small pouch that forms part of a piece of clothing. ② A pocket of something is a small area of it • *There are still pockets of resistance.*

pocket money NOUN Pocket money is an amount of money given regularly to children by their parents.

pod, pods NOUN a long, narrow seed container that grows on plants such as peas or beans.

podcast, podcasts NOUN an audio file that can be downloaded and listened to on a computer or electronic device.

poddy, poddies NOUN In Australian English, a poddy is a calf or lamb that is being fed by hand.

podium, podiums NOUN a small platform, often one on which someone stands to make a speech.

poem, poems NOUN a piece of writing in which the words are arranged in short rhythmic lines, often with a rhyme.

poet, poets NOUN a person who writes poems.

poetic ADJECTIVE ①very beautiful and expressive • *a pure and poetic love.* ②relating to poetry. **poetically** ADVERB

poetic licence NOUN ENGLISH If a writer or poet uses poetic licence, they change the facts or the usual rules to make what they are writing more powerful or interesting.

poetry NOUN Poetry is poems, considered as a form of literature.

poignant [*Said poyn-yant*] ADJECTIVE Something that is poignant has a strong emotional effect on you, often making you feel sad • *a moving and poignant moment.* **poignancy** NOUN

point, points, pointing, pointed NOUN ①an opinion or fact expressed by someone • *You've made a good point.* ②a quality • *Tact was never her strong point.* ③the purpose or meaning something has • *He completely missed the point in most of his argument.* ④a position or time • *At some point during the party, a fight erupted.* ⑤a single mark in a competition. ⑥the thin, sharp end of something such as a needle or knife. ⑦The points of a compass are the 32 directions indicated on it. ⑧The decimal point in a number is the dot separating the whole number from the fraction. ⑨On a railway track, the points are the levers and rails which enable a train to move from one track to another. ▶VERB ⑩If you point at something, you stick out your finger to show where it is. ⑪If something points in a particular direction, it faces that way.

point-blank ADJECTIVE ①Something that is shot at point-blank range is shot with a gun held very close to it. ▶ADVERB ②If you say something point-blank, you say it directly without explanation or apology.

pointed ADJECTIVE ①A pointed object has a thin, sharp end. ②Pointed comments express criticism. **pointedly** ADVERB

pointer, pointers NOUN a piece of information which helps you to understand something • *Here are a few pointers to help you make a choice.*

pointless ADJECTIVE Something that is pointless has no purpose. **pointlessly** ADVERB

point of view, points of view NOUN ①Your point of view is your opinion about something or your attitude towards it. ②ENGLISH The point of view is also the mental position from which a story is observed or narrated.

poise NOUN Someone who has poise is calm and dignified.

poised ADJECTIVE If you are poised to do something, you are ready to do it at any moment.

poison, poisons, poisoning, poisoned NOUN ①Poison is a substance that can kill people or animals if they swallow it or absorb it. ▶VERB ②To poison someone is to try to kill them with poison.

poisonous ADJECTIVE containing something that causes death or illness.

poke, pokes, poking, poked VERB ①If you poke someone or something, you push at them quickly with your finger or a sharp object. ②Something that pokes out of another thing appears from underneath or behind it • *roots poking out of the earth.* ▶NOUN ③a sharp jab or prod.

SIMILAR WORDS: ①dig, jab, prod

poker, pokers NOUN ①Poker is a card game in which the players make bets on the cards dealt to them. ②a long metal rod used for moving coals or logs in a fire.

a
b
c
d
e
f
g
h
i
j
k
l
m
n
o
p
q
r
s
t
u
v
w
x
y
z

polar ADJECTIVE relating to the area around the North and South Poles.

polar bear, polar bears NOUN a large white bear which lives in the area around the North Pole.

polarise, polarises, polarising, polarised; also spelt **polarize** VERB If groups polarise, they form opposite opinions from each other. **polarisation** NOUN

pole, poles NOUN ① a long rounded piece of wood or metal. ② The earth's poles are the two opposite ends of its axis • *the North Pole*.

Pole, Poles NOUN someone who comes from Poland.

pole vault NOUN The pole vault is an athletics event in which contestants jump over a high bar using a long flexible pole to lift themselves into the air.

police, polices, policing, policed PLURAL NOUN ① CITIZENSHIP The police are the people who are officially responsible for making sure that people obey the law. ▶ VERB ② To police an area is to keep law and order there by means of the police or an armed force.

policeman, policemen NOUN a man who is an officer in a police force.

policewoman, policewomen NOUN a woman who is an officer in a police force.

policy, policies NOUN ① a set of plans, especially in politics or business • *the new economic policy*. ② An insurance policy is a document which shows an agreement made with an insurance company.

polio NOUN Polio is an infectious disease that is caused by a virus and often results in paralysis. Polio is short for 'poliomyelitis'.

polish, polishes, polishing, polished VERB ① If you polish something, you put polish on it or rub it with a cloth to make it shine. ② If you polish a skill or technique you have, you work on it in order to improve it. ▶ NOUN ③ Polish is a substance that you put on an object to clean it and make it shine • *shoe polish*. ④ Something that has polish is elegant and of good quality. **polished** ADJECTIVE

Polish [Said pole-ish] ADJECTIVE ① belonging or relating to Poland. ▶ NOUN ② Polish is the main language spoken in Poland.

polite ADJECTIVE ① Someone who is polite has good manners and behaves considerately towards other people. ② Polite society is cultivated and refined. **politely** ADVERB SIMILAR WORDS: ① civil, courteous, well-mannered ② refined, sophisticated

politeness NOUN the quality of having good manners and behaving considerately.

political ADJECTIVE ① GEOGRAPHY relating to the state, government or public administration. ② relating to or interested in politics. **politically** ADVERB

politically correct ADJECTIVE careful not to offend or designed not to offend minority or disadvantaged groups.

politician, politicians NOUN a person involved in the government of a country.

politics NOUN HISTORY Politics is the activity and planning concerned with achieving power and control in a country or organisation.

polka, polkas NOUN a fast dance in which couples dance together in circles around the room.

poll, polls, polling, polled NOUN ① a survey in which people are asked their opinions about something.

② (in plural) A political election can be referred to as the polls. ▶ VERB ③ If you are polled on something, you are asked your opinion about it as part of a survey.

pollen NOUN SCIENCE Pollen is a fine yellow powder produced by flowers in order to fertilise other flowers of the same species.

pollen tube, pollen tubes NOUN SCIENCE a hollow tube that grows out of a pollinated grain and carries pollen to the reproductive part of a plant.

pollinate, pollinates, pollinating, pollinated VERB SCIENCE To pollinate a plant is to fertilise it with pollen. **pollination** NOUN

pollutant, pollutants NOUN a substance that causes pollution.

pollute, pollutes, polluting, polluted VERB To pollute water or air is to make it dirty and dangerous to use or live in. **polluted** ADJECTIVE
SIMILAR WORDS: contaminate, foul, poison

pollution NOUN GEOGRAPHY Pollution of the environment happens when dirty, dangerous or unwanted substances get into the air, water or soil.

polo NOUN Polo is a game played between two teams of players on horseback. The players use wooden hammers with long handles to hit a ball.

polo-neck ADJECTIVE A polo-neck jumper has a deep fold of material at the neck.

poly- PREFIX 'Poly-' means many or much • polygon.
WORD HISTORY: from Greek polus meaning 'many' or 'much'

polyester NOUN DGT a synthetic fibre, used especially to make clothes.

polygamy [Said pol-**lig**-gam-ee] NOUN Polygamy is having more than one wife at the same time. **polygamous** ADJECTIVE

polygon, polygons NOUN MATHS any two-dimensional shape whose sides are all straight; a **regular polygon** has straight sides of the same length.

polyhedron, polyhedrons or **polyhedra** NOUN MATHS A polyhedron is any three-dimensional shape whose edges are all straight and whose sides are all flat.

polymer, polymers NOUN SCIENCE A polymer is a chemical compound with large molecules made up of many simple repeated units.

polystyrene NOUN Polystyrene is a very light plastic, used especially as insulating material or to make containers.

polythene NOUN SCIENCE Polythene is a type of plastic that is used to make thin sheets or bags.

polyunsaturated ADJECTIVE Polyunsaturated oils and margarines are made mainly from vegetable fats and are considered to be healthier than most other oils.
polyunsaturate NOUN

pomegranate, pomegranates NOUN a round fruit with a thick reddish skin. It contains a lot of small seeds.
WORD HISTORY: from Latin pomum granatum meaning 'apple full of seeds'

pomp NOUN Pomp is the use of ceremony, fine clothes and decorations on special occasions • Sir Patrick was buried with much pomp.

pompous ADJECTIVE behaving in a way that is too serious and self-important. **pomposity** NOUN

pond, ponds NOUN a small, usually man-made area of water.

a b c d e f g h i j k l m n o **p** q r s t u v w x y z

ponder, ponders, pondering, pondered VERB If you ponder, you think about something deeply • *He was pondering the problem when Phillipson drove up.*
SIMILAR WORDS: consider, mull over, think about

ponderous ADJECTIVE dull, slow and serious • *the ponderous commentary.* **ponderously** ADVERB

pong, pongs NOUN (*informal*) an unpleasant smell.

pontiff, pontiffs NOUN (*formal*) The pontiff is the Pope.

pony, ponies NOUN a small horse.

ponytail, ponytails NOUN a hairstyle in which long hair is tied at the back of the head and hangs down like a tail.

pony trekking NOUN Pony trekking is a leisure activity in which people ride across country on ponies.

poodle, poodles NOUN a type of dog with curly hair.

pool, pools, pooling, pooled NOUN ① a small area of still water. ② Pool is a game in which players try to hit coloured balls into pockets around the table using long sticks called cues. ③ A pool of people, money or things is a group or collection used or shared by several people. ④ (*in plural*) The pools are a competition in which people try to guess the results of football matches. ▶ VERB ⑤ If people pool their resources, they gather together the things they have so that they can be shared or used by all of them.

poor, poorer, poorest ADJECTIVE ① Poor people have very little money and few possessions. ② Poor places are inhabited by people with little money and show signs of neglect. ③ You use 'poor' to show sympathy • *Poor you!* ④ 'Poor' also means of a low quality or standard • *a poor performance.*
SIMILAR WORDS: ① impoverished, penniless, poverty-stricken

poorly ADJECTIVE ① feeling unwell or ill. ▶ ADVERB ② badly • *a poorly planned operation.*

pop, pops, popping, popped NOUN ① Pop is modern music played and enjoyed especially by young people. ② (*informal*) You can refer to fizzy, nonalcoholic drinks as pop. ③ a short, sharp sound. ▶ VERB ④ If something pops, it makes a sudden sharp sound. ⑤ (*informal*) If you pop something somewhere, you put it there quickly • *I'd just popped the pie in the oven.* ⑥ (*informal*) If you pop somewhere, you go there quickly • *His mother popped out to buy him an ice cream.*

popcorn NOUN Popcorn is a snack consisting of grains of maize heated until they puff up and burst.

Pope, Popes NOUN RE The Pope is the head of the Roman Catholic Church.
WORD HISTORY: from Latin *Papa* meaning 'bishop' or 'father'

poplar, poplars NOUN a type of tall, thin tree.

poppy, poppies NOUN a plant with a large, red flower on a hairy stem.

populace NOUN (*formal*) The populace of a country is its people.

popular ADJECTIVE ① liked or approved of by a lot of people. ② involving or intended for ordinary people • *the popular press.* **popularly** ADVERB **popularity** NOUN **popularise** VERB
SIMILAR WORDS: ① fashionable, well-liked

populate, populates, populating, populated VERB The people or animals that populate an area live there.

population, populations NOUN The population of a place is the people who live there, or the number of people living there.

population density NOUN
GEOGRAPHY a measure of the number of people living in a given area of land, usually expressed as the number of people per square kilometre.

population pyramid NOUN
GEOGRAPHY a pyramid-shaped diagram that uses horizontal bars to show the number of males and females within different age categories for a particular country.

porcelain NOUN Porcelain is a delicate, hard material used to make crockery and ornaments.

porch, porches NOUN a covered area at the entrance to a building.

porcupine, porcupines NOUN a large rodent with long spines covering its body.
WORD HISTORY: from Old French *porc d'espins* meaning 'pig with spines'

pore, pores, poring, pored NOUN ① The pores in your skin or on the surface of a plant are very small holes which allow moisture to pass through. ▸ VERB ② If you pore over a piece of writing or a diagram, you study it carefully.

SPELLING TIP
Do not confuse the spellings of *pore* and *pour*: *Aila was poring over a book; The rain was pouring down the window.*

pork NOUN Pork is meat from a pig which has not been salted or smoked.

porous ADJECTIVE containing many holes through which water and air can pass.

porpoise, porpoises [Said por-pus] NOUN a sea mammal related to the dolphin.

WORD HISTORY: from Latin *porcus* meaning 'pig' and *piscis* meaning 'fish'

porridge NOUN Porridge is a thick, sticky food made from oats cooked in water or milk.

port, ports NOUN ① a town or area which has a harbour or docks. ② Port is a kind of strong, sweet red wine. ▸ ADJECTIVE ③ The port side of a ship is the left side when you are facing the front.

-port SUFFIX '-port' comes at the end of words that have something to do with 'carrying' in their meaning • *transport*.
WORD HISTORY: from Latin *portāre* meaning 'to carry'

portable ADJECTIVE designed to be easily carried • *a portable speaker*.

porter, porters NOUN ① a person whose job is to be in charge of the entrance of a building, greeting and directing visitors. ② A porter in a railway station or hospital is a person whose job is to carry or move things.

portfolio, portfolios NOUN ① a thin, flat case for carrying papers. ② A portfolio is also a group of selected duties, investments or items of artwork • *the education portfolio* • *Choose your share portfolio wisely*.
WORD HISTORY: from Italian *portafoglio* meaning 'carrier for papers'

porthole, portholes NOUN a small window in the side of a ship or aircraft.

portion, portions NOUN a part or amount of something • *a portion of fresh fruit*.
SIMILAR WORDS: bit, part, piece

portrait, portraits NOUN ART a picture or photograph of someone.

portray, portrays, portraying, portrayed VERB When an actor, artist or writer portrays someone or something, they represent or describe them. **portrayal** NOUN

Portuguese [Said por-tyoo-**geez**] ADJECTIVE ① belonging or relating to Portugal. ▶ NOUN ② someone who comes from Portugal. ③ Portuguese is the main language spoken in Portugal and Brazil.

pose, poses, posing, posed VERB ① If something poses a problem, it is the cause of the problem. ② If you pose a question, you ask it. ③ If you pose as someone else, you pretend to be that person in order to deceive people. ▶ NOUN ④ a way of standing, sitting or lying • *Mr Clark assumes a pose for the photographer.*
SIMILAR WORDS: ④ attitude, posture

poser, posers NOUN ① someone who behaves or dresses in an exaggerated way in order to impress people. ② a difficult problem.

posh, posher, poshest ADJECTIVE (informal) ① smart, fashionable and expensive • *a posh restaurant.* ② upper-class • *the man with the posh voice.*

position, positions, positioning, positioned NOUN ① DRAMA The position of someone or something is the place where they are or ought to be • *Would the cast take their positions, please.* ② When someone or something is in a particular position, they are sitting or lying in that way • *I raised myself to a sitting position.* ③ a job or post in an organisation. ④ The position that you are in at a particular time is the situation that you are in • *This puts the president in a difficult position.* ▶ VERB ⑤ To position something somewhere is to put it there • *Llewelyn positioned a cushion behind Joanna's back.*

positive ADJECTIVE ① completely sure about something • *I was positive he'd known about that money.* ② confident and hopeful • *I felt very positive about everything.* ③ showing approval or encouragement • *I anticipate a positive response.* ④ providing definite proof of something • *positive evidence.* ⑤ MATHS A positive number is greater than zero. **positively** ADVERB
SIMILAR WORDS: ④ absolute, certain, definite

possess, possesses, possessing, possessed VERB ① If you possess a particular quality, you have it. ② If you possess something, you own it. ③ If a feeling or belief possesses you, it strongly influences you • *Absolute terror possessed her.* **possessor** NOUN

possession, possessions NOUN ① If something is in your possession or if you are in possession of it, you have it. ② Your possessions are the things that you own or that you have with you.
SIMILAR WORDS: ② belongings, property

possessive ADJECTIVE ① A person who is possessive about someone or something wants to keep them to themselves. ▶ NOUN ② In grammar, the possessive is the form of a noun or pronoun used to show possession • *my car* • *That's hers.*

possibility, possibilities NOUN something that might be true or might happen • *the possibility of a ban.*
SIMILAR WORDS: chance, likelihood, probability

possible ADJECTIVE ① likely to happen or able to be done • *the best possible result.* ② likely or capable of being true or correct • *I can think of no possible explanation.* **possibly** ADVERB
SIMILAR WORDS: ① feasible, practicable

possum, possums NOUN In Australian

What is the Possessive?

The possessive case is formed by adding an apostrophe (') and the letter s to the dictionary form of the word.

The **possessive** is used when a noun indicates a person or thing that owns another person or thing:

*The **cat's** fur was wet.*
*The **doctor's** cat was called Joey.*

If the noun is plural and already ends in -s, the possessive is formed by simply adding an apostrophe:

*The vet often trims **cats'** claws.*

Doctors' surgeries make me nervous.

The possessive can also be shown by using the word of in front of the noun. This is usually used when you are talking about something that is not alive or cannot be touched:

*We climbed to the top **of the hill**.*
*She read the first chapter **of the book**.*

When a possessive is not followed by another noun, it refers to the place where that person lives or works:

*I am going to stay at my **aunt's**.*
*I bought a loaf at the **baker's**.*

---

and New Zealand English, a possum is a phalanger, a marsupial with thick fur and a long tail.

post, posts, posting, posted NOUN ① The post is the system by which letters and parcels are collected and delivered. ② a job or official position in an organisation. ③ a strong, upright pole fixed into the ground • *They are tied to a post.* ④ a message or article published on a website. ▶ VERB ⑤ If you post a letter, you send it to someone by putting it into a postbox. ⑥ If you are posted somewhere, you are sent by your employers to work there. ⑦ If you post a message or article, you publish it on a website. **postal** ADJECTIVE

post- PREFIX after a particular time or event • *his postwar career.*
WORD HISTORY: from Latin *post* meaning 'after'

postage NOUN Postage is the money that you pay to send letters and parcels by post.

postal order, postal orders NOUN a piece of paper representing a sum of money which you can buy at a post office.

postbox, postboxes NOUN a metal box with a hole in it which you put letters into for collection by the postman.

postcard, postcards NOUN a card, often with a picture on one side, which you write on and send without an envelope.

postcode, postcodes NOUN a short sequence of letters and numbers at the end of an address which helps the post office to sort the mail.

poster, posters NOUN a large notice or picture that is stuck on a wall as an advertisement or for decoration.

posterior, posteriors NOUN (*humorous*) A person's posterior is their bottom.

posterity NOUN (*formal*) You can refer to the future and the people who will be alive then as posterity • *to record the voyage for posterity.*
WORD HISTORY: from Latin *posteritas* meaning 'future generations'

posthumous [*Said poss-tyum-uss*] ADJECTIVE happening or awarded after a person's death • *a posthumous medal.* **posthumously** ADVERB

a
b
c
d
e
f
g
h
i
j
k
l
m
n
o
p
q
r
s
t
u
v
w
x
y
z

postman, postmen NOUN someone who collects and delivers letters and parcels sent by post.

postmortem, postmortems NOUN a medical examination of a dead body to find out how the person died.

post office, post offices NOUN ① The Post Office is the national organisation responsible for postal services. ② a building where you can buy stamps and post letters.

postpone, postpones, postponing, postponed VERB If you postpone an event, you arrange for it to take place at a later time than was originally planned. **postponement** NOUN
SIMILAR WORDS: put off, shelve

posture, postures NOUN Your posture is the position or manner in which you hold your body.

posy, posies NOUN a small bunch of flowers.

pot, pots NOUN a deep round container; also used to refer to its contents.

potassium NOUN SCIENCE
Potassium is a soft silver-coloured element used in making soap, detergents, fertilisers and glass. Its atomic number is 19 and its symbol is K.

potassium nitrate NOUN a white chemical compound used to make gunpowder, fireworks and fertilisers. Potassium nitrate is also called saltpetre.

potato, potatoes NOUN a white vegetable that has a brown or red skin and grows underground.

potent ADJECTIVE effective or powerful • *a potent cocktail*. **potency** NOUN

potential ADJECTIVE ① capable of becoming the thing mentioned • *potential customers* • *potential sources of finance*. ▶ NOUN ② Your potential is your ability to achieve success in the future. **potentially** ADVERB

potential difference NOUN
SCIENCE Potential difference is the work done in moving a unit of positive electric charge from one point to another.

potential energy NOUN (*technical*) Potential energy is the energy stored in something.

pothole, potholes NOUN ① a hole in the surface of a road caused by bad weather or traffic. ② an underground cavern.

potion, potions NOUN a drink containing medicine, poison or supposed magical powers.

potted ADJECTIVE Potted meat or fish is cooked and put into a small sealed container to preserve it.

potter, potters, pottering, pottered NOUN ① a person who makes pottery. ▶ VERB ② If you potter about, you pass the time doing pleasant, unimportant things.

pottery NOUN ① Pottery is pots, dishes and other items made from clay and fired in a kiln. ② Pottery is also the craft of making pottery.

potty, potties; pottier, pottiest NOUN ① a bowl which a small child can sit on and use instead of a toilet. ▶ ADJECTIVE ② (*informal*) crazy or foolish.

pouch, pouches NOUN ① a small, soft container with a fold-over top. ② Animals like kangaroos have a pouch, which is a pocket of skin in which they carry their young.

poultry NOUN Chickens, turkeys and other birds kept for their meat or eggs are referred to as poultry.

pounce, pounces, pouncing, pounced VERB If an animal or person pounces on something, they leap and grab it.

pound, **pounds**, **pounding**, **pounded**
NOUN ①The pound is the main unit of currency in Britain and in some other countries. ②a unit of weight equal to 16 ounces or about 0.454 kilograms. ▸VERB ③If you pound something, you hit it repeatedly with your fist • *Someone was pounding on the door*. ④If you pound a substance, you crush it into a powder or paste • *Wooden mallets were used to pound the meat*. ⑤If your heart is pounding, it is beating very strongly and quickly. ⑥If you pound somewhere, you run there with heavy noisy steps.

pour, **pours**, **pouring**, **poured** VERB ①If you pour a liquid out of a container, you make it flow out by tipping the container. ②If something pours somewhere, it flows there quickly and in large quantities • *Sweat poured down his face*. ③When it is raining heavily, you can say that it is pouring.

SPELLING TIP
Do not confuse the spellings of *pour* and *pore*: *The rain was pouring down the window; Aila was poring over a book*.

pout, **pouts**, **pouting**, **pouted** VERB If you pout, you stick out your lips or bottom lip.

poverty NOUN GEOGRAPHY the state of being very poor.
SIMILAR WORDS: destitution, pennilessness, want

powder, **powders**, **powdering**, **powdered** NOUN ①Powder consists of many tiny particles of a solid substance. ▸VERB ②If you powder a surface, you cover it with powder.
powdery ADJECTIVE

power, **powers**, **powering**, **powered** NOUN ①Someone who has power has a lot of control over people and activities. ②Someone who has the power to do something has the ability to do it • *the power of speech*. ③Power is also the authority to do something • *the power of arrest*. ④The power of something is the physical strength that it has to move things. ⑤Power is energy obtained, for example, by burning fuel or using the wind or waves. ⑥ MATHS In maths, a power is the product of a number multiplied by itself a certain number of times. For example, the third power of 10 is 1000. ⑦ SCIENCE In physics, power is the energy transferred from one thing to another in one second. It is measured in watts. ▸VERB ⑧Something that powers a machine provides the energy for it to work.
SIMILAR WORDS: ③force, strength

powerful ADJECTIVE ①able to control people and events. ②having great physical strength. ③having a strong effect. **powerfully** ADVERB

powerhouse, **powerhouses** NOUN (*informal*) a person or organisation that has a lot of energy, power and influence.

powerless ADJECTIVE unable to control or influence events • *I was powerless to save her*.
SIMILAR WORDS: helpless, impotent, incapable

power station, **power stations** NOUN a place where electricity is generated.

practicable ADJECTIVE If a task or plan is practicable, it can be carried out successfully • *a practicable option*.

practical, **practicals** ADJECTIVE ①The practical aspects of something are those that involve experience and real situations rather than ideas or theories • *the practical difficulties of teaching science*. ②sensible and likely to be effective • *practical low-heeled shoes*. ③Someone who is practical is able to deal effectively and sensibly with problems. ▸ NOUN ④ an examination in which you make or perform something rather than simply write. **practicality** NOUN

SIMILAR WORDS: ② functional, utilitarian

practically ADVERB ① almost but not completely or exactly • *The house was practically a wreck.* ② in a practical way • *practically minded.*

practice, practices NOUN ① You can refer to something that people do regularly as a practice • *the practice of shaking hands.* ② Practice is regular training or exercise • *I need more practice to improve my football skills.* ③ A doctor's or lawyer's practice is his or her business.

SPELLING TIP

Do not confuse the spellings of the noun *practice* and the verb *practise*: *You won't get better without practice; I practise the piano every day.*

SPELLING TIP

Remember this mnemonic: *I went to see (C) the doctor's new practiCe.*

---

practise, practises, practising, practised VERB ① If you practise something, you do it regularly in order to improve. ② People who practise a religion, custom or craft regularly take part in the activities associated with it • *a practising Buddhist.* ③ Someone who practises medicine or law works as a doctor or lawyer.

SPELLING TIP

Do not confuse the spellings of the verb *practise* and the noun *practice*: *I practise the piano every day; You won't get better without practice.*

SPELLING TIP

Remember this mnemonic: *you must practiSe your Spelling.*

---

practised ADJECTIVE Someone who is practised at doing something is very skilful at it • *a practised performer.*

practitioner, practitioners NOUN You can refer to someone who works in a particular profession as a practitioner • *a medical practitioner.*

pragmatic ADJECTIVE A pragmatic way of considering or doing something is a practical rather than theoretical way • *He is pragmatic about the risks involved.*
pragmatically ADVERB
pragmatism NOUN

prairie, prairies NOUN a large area of flat, grassy land in North America.

praise, praises, praising, praised VERB ① If you praise someone or something, you express strong approval of their qualities or achievements. ▸ NOUN ② Praise is what is said or written in approval of someone's qualities or achievements.

SIMILAR WORDS: ① acclaim, approve, compliment ② acclaim, approval, commendation

pram, prams NOUN a baby's cot on wheels.

prance, prances, prancing, pranced VERB Someone who is prancing around is walking with exaggerated movements.

prank, pranks NOUN a childish trick.

prattle, prattles, prattling, prattled VERB If someone prattles on, they talk a lot without saying anything important.

prawn, prawns NOUN a small, pink, edible shellfish with a long tail.

pray, prays, praying, prayed VERB
RE When someone prays, they speak to God to give thanks or to ask for help.

SPELLING TIP
Do not confuse the spellings of *pray* and *prey*: *Muslims pray five times a day; Owls prey on mice and small birds.*

prayer, prayers NOUN ① RE Prayer is the activity of praying. ② RE the words said when someone prays.

pre- PREFIX 'Pre-' means before a particular time or event • *pre-war*.
WORD HISTORY: from Latin *prae* meaning 'before'

preach, preaches, preaching, preached VERB When someone preaches, they give a short talk on a religious or moral subject as part of a church service. **preacher** NOUN

precarious ADJECTIVE ① If your situation is precarious, you may fail in what you are doing at any time. ② Something that is precarious is likely to fall because it is not well balanced or secured. **precariously** ADVERB
SIMILAR WORDS: ② insecure, shaky, unsafe

precaution, precautions NOUN an action that is intended to prevent something from happening • *It's still worth taking precautions against accidents.* **precautionary** ADJECTIVE

precede, precedes, preceding, preceded VERB ① Something that precedes another thing happens or occurs before it. ② If you precede someone somewhere, you go in front of them. **preceding** ADJECTIVE

SPELLING TIP
Do not confuse the spellings of *precede* and *proceed*: *Summer precedes autumn; I think we should proceed with the meeting.*

precedence [Said *press-id-ens*] NOUN If something takes precedence over other things, it is the most important thing and should be dealt with first.

precedent, precedents NOUN An action or decision that is regarded as a precedent is used as a guide in taking similar action or decisions later.

precinct, precincts NOUN ① A shopping precinct is a pedestrian shopping area. ② (*in plural, formal*) The precincts of a place are its buildings and land.

precious ADJECTIVE Something that is precious is valuable or very important and should be looked after or used carefully.

precipice, precipices [Said *press-sip-piss*] NOUN a very steep rock face.

precipitate, precipitates, precipitating, precipitated VERB (*formal*) If something precipitates an event or situation, it causes it to happen suddenly.

precipitation NOUN GEOGRAPHY Precipitation is any kind of moisture that falls from the sky; used especially when stating the amount that falls during a particular period.

precise ADJECTIVE exact and accurate in every detail • *precise measurements*. **precisely** ADVERB **precision** NOUN

preclude, precludes, precluding, precluded VERB (*formal*) If something precludes an event or situation, it prevents it from happening • *The meal precluded serious conversation*.

precocious ADJECTIVE Precocious children behave in a way that seems too advanced for their age.

preconceived ADJECTIVE Preconceived ideas about something have been formed without any real experience or information. **preconception** NOUN

precondition, preconditions NOUN If something is a precondition for another thing, it must happen before the second thing can take place.

precursor, precursors NOUN A precursor of something that exists now is a similar thing that existed at an earlier time • *real tennis, an ancient precursor of the modern game.*

predator, predators [*Said pred-dat-tor*] NOUN SCIENCE an animal that kills and eats other animals. **predatory** ADJECTIVE

predecessor, predecessors NOUN Someone's predecessor is a person who used to do their job before.

predetermined ADJECTIVE decided in advance or controlled by previous events rather than left to chance.

predicament, predicaments NOUN a difficult situation.
SIMILAR WORDS: dilemma, fix, jam

predicate, predicates NOUN In grammar, the predicate of a sentence is the part that is not the subject. In the sentence 'I decided what to do', 'decided what to do' is the predicate.

predict, predicts, predicting, predicted VERB If someone predicts an event, they say that it will happen in the future.
SIMILAR WORDS: forecast, foretell, prophesy

prediction, predictions NOUN something that is forecast.

predominant ADJECTIVE more important or more noticeable than anything else in a particular set of people or things • *Yellow is the predominant colour in the house.*
predominantly ADVERB
SIMILAR WORDS: chief, main, prevailing

predominate, predominates, predominating, predominated VERB If one type of person or thing predominates, it is the most common, frequent or noticeable

• *Fresh flowers predominate in the bouquet.* **predominance** NOUN

pre-eminent ADJECTIVE recognised as being the most important in a particular group • *the pre-eminent experts in the area.* **pre-eminence** NOUN

pre-empt, pre-empts, pre-empting, pre-empted VERB (*formal*) If you pre-empt something, you prevent it by doing something else which makes it pointless or impossible • *By resigning, he pre-empted the decision to sack him.*

preen, preens, preening, preened VERB When a bird preens its feathers, it cleans them using its beak.

preface, prefaces [*Said pref-fiss*] NOUN an introduction at the beginning of a book explaining what the book is about or why it was written.

prefect, prefects NOUN a pupil who has special duties at a school.
WORD HISTORY: from Latin *praefectus* meaning 'someone put in charge'

prefer, prefers, preferring, preferred VERB If you prefer one thing to another, you like it better than the other thing. **preferable** ADJECTIVE **preferably** ADVERB

preference, preferences [*Said pref-fer-enss*] NOUN ① If you have a preference for something, you like it more than other things • *a preference for tea over coffee.* ② When making a choice, if you give preference to one type of person or thing, you try to choose that type.

preferential ADJECTIVE A person who gets preferential treatment is treated better than others.

prefix, prefixes NOUN ENGLISH a letter or group of letters added to the beginning of a word to make a new word, for example 'semi-', 'pre-' and 'un-'.

What is a Prefix?

A prefix is a letter or group of letters that is added to the beginning of a word to make a new word with a different meaning.

When you add a prefix to another word, you usually drop the hyphen. Sometimes, however, you do keep the hyphen, especially if the word could be misunderstood without it, for example *co-worker* or *re-elect*.

Here are some common examples of prefixes and their meanings:

anti- (opposed to), *co-* (together), *inter-* (between), *post-* (after), *pre-* (before), *re-* (again), *semi-* (half) and *un-* (not).

anti- + *racism* = *antiracism*
co- + *worker* = *co-worker*
inter- + *continental* = *intercontinental*
post- + *war* = *postwar*
pre- + *order* = *pre-order*
re- + *elect* = *re-elect*
semi- + *circle* = *semicircle*
un- + *wrap* = *unwrap*

pregnant ADJECTIVE A woman who is pregnant has a baby developing in her womb. **pregnancy** NOUN

prehistoric ADJECTIVE HISTORY existing at a time in the past before anything was written down.

prejudice, prejudices NOUN ① Prejudice is an unreasonable and unfair dislike or preference formed without carefully examining the facts. ② Prejudice is also an intolerance towards certain people or groups • *racial prejudice*.
prejudiced ADJECTIVE **prejudicial** ADJECTIVE

preliminary ADJECTIVE Preliminary activities take place before something starts, in preparation for it • *the preliminary rounds of the competition*.
SIMILAR WORDS: first, initial, preparatory

prelude, preludes NOUN Something that is an introduction to a more important event can be described as a prelude to that event.

premature ADJECTIVE happening too early, or earlier than expected • *premature baldness*. **prematurely** ADVERB

premeditated ADJECTIVE planned in advance • *a premeditated attack*.

premier, premiers NOUN ① The leader of a government is sometimes referred to as the premier. ② In Australia, a premier is the leader of a State government. ▶ ADJECTIVE ③ considered to be the best or most important • *Wellington's premier jewellers*.

premiere, premieres [Said *prem-mee-er*] NOUN the first public performance of a new play or film.

premise, premises [Said *prem-iss*] NOUN ① (*in plural*) The premises of an organisation are all the buildings it occupies on one site. ② a statement which you suppose is true and use as the basis for an idea or argument.

premium, premiums NOUN ① A sum of money paid regularly to an insurance company for an insurance policy. ② an extra sum of money that has to be paid • *Paying a premium for space is worthwhile*.

premolar, premolars NOUN SCIENCE Your premolars are the teeth between the canines and the molars.

premonition, premonitions [Said *prem-on-ish-on*] NOUN a feeling that something unpleasant is going to happen.

a b c d e f g h i j k l m n o **p** q r s t u v w x y z

A
B
C
D
E
F
G
H
I
J
K
L
M
N
O
P
Q
R
S
T
U
V
W
X
Y
Z

What is a Preposition?

A preposition is a word that is used before a noun or pronoun to relate it to other words.

Prepositions may tell you the **place** of something in relation to another thing:

*She saw the cat **in** the garden.*
*The cat was sheltering **under** a bench.*

Prepositions may also indicate **movement**:

*The train came **into** the station.*
*We pushed **through** the crowd.*

Prepositions may indicate **time**:

*They will arrive **on** Friday.*
*They will stay **for** two days.*

SIMILAR WORDS: feeling, foreboding, presentiment

preoccupation, preoccupations NOUN If you have a preoccupation with something, it is very important to you and you keep thinking about it.

preoccupied ADJECTIVE Someone who is preoccupied is deep in thought or totally involved with something.

preparatory ADJECTIVE Preparatory activities are done before doing something else in order to prepare for it.

prepare, prepares, preparing, prepared VERB If you prepare something, you make it ready for a particular purpose or event • *He was preparing the meal.* **preparation** NOUN

prepared ADJECTIVE If you are prepared to do something, you are willing to do it.

preposition, prepositions NOUN ENGLISH MFL a word such as 'by', 'for', 'into' or 'with', which usually has a noun as its object.

preposterous ADJECTIVE extremely unreasonable and ridiculous • *a preposterous statement.*

prerequisite, prerequisites [Said pree-rek-wiz-zit] NOUN (formal) Something that is a prerequisite for

another thing must happen or exist before the other thing is possible • *Self-esteem is a prerequisite for a happy life.*

prerogative, prerogatives [Said prir-rog-at-tiv] NOUN (formal) Something that is the prerogative of a person is their special privilege or right.

prescribe, prescribes, prescribing, prescribed VERB When a doctor prescribes treatment, he or she states what treatment a patient should have.

prescription, prescriptions NOUN a piece of paper on which the doctor has written the name of a medicine needed by a patient.

presence NOUN ① Someone's presence in a place is the fact of their being there • *His presence made me happy.* ② If you are in someone's presence, you are in the same place as they are. ③ Someone who has presence has an impressive appearance or manner.

present, presents, presenting, presented ADJECTIVE [Said prez-ent] ① If someone is present somewhere, they are there • *He had been present at the birth of his son.* ② A present situation is one that exists now rather than in the past or the future. ③ ENGLISH MFL The present tense of a verb is the form used to express something that is happening in the present. ▶ NOUN [Said prez-ent] ④ The present is the period of time that is taking place now. ⑤ something that you give to someone for them to keep. ▶ VERB [Said pri-zent] ⑥ If you present someone with something, you give it to them • *She presented a bravery award to the girl*. ⑦ Something that presents a difficulty or a challenge causes it or provides it. ⑧ The person who presents a radio or television show introduces each part or each guest. **presenter** NOUN

SIMILAR WORDS: ② contemporary, current, existing

presentable ADJECTIVE neat or attractive and suitable for people to see.

presentation, presentations NOUN ① the act of presenting or a way of presenting something. ② The presentation of a piece of work is the way it looks or the impression it gives. ③ To give a presentation is to give a talk or demonstration to an audience of something you have been studying or working on.

present-day ADJECTIVE existing or happening now • *present-day farming practices*.

presently ADVERB ① If something will happen presently, it will happen soon • *I'll finish the job presently*. ② Something that is presently happening is happening now • *Some progress is presently being made*.

present participle, present participles NOUN ENGLISH MFL In grammar, the present participle of an English verb is the form that ends in '-ing'. It is used to form some tenses, and can be used to form adjectives and nouns from a verb.

present tense NOUN ENGLISH MFL In grammar, the present tense is the tense of a verb that you use mainly to talk about things that happen or exist at the time of writing or speaking.

Talking about the Present

You can talk about events that are happening now by using **simple tenses** or **compound tenses**.

The **simple present tense** is formed by using the verb on its own, without any auxiliary verbs. For the first and second person, and for all plural forms, the simple present tense of the verb is the same as the main form given in the dictionary:

I **cook** the dinner.

For the third person singular, however, you need to add an -s to the dictionary form to make the simple present tense:

He **cook**s the dinner.

You can also talk about an event that is happening in the present by using **compound tenses**. Compound tenses are formed by adding an auxiliary verb to a form of the main verb.

The most common compound present tense is formed by putting a form of the verb *to be* in front of the main verb, and adding the ending *-ing*. This shows that the action is going on at the present time and is continuous:

I **am listening** to the radio.

You can also talk about the present using a form of the verb *to do* in front of the basic form of the verb. This can add emphasis:

I **do like** fish.

a
b
c
d
e
f
g
h
i
j
k
l
m
n
o
p
q
r
s
t
u
v
w
x
y
z

preservative, preservatives NOUN a substance or chemical that stops things decaying.

preserve, preserves, preserving, preserved VERB ① If you preserve something, you take action so that it remains as it is. ② If you preserve food, you treat it to prevent it from decaying. ▶ NOUN ③ Preserves are foods such as jam or chutney that have been made with a lot of sugar or vinegar. **preservation** NOUN

preside, presides, presiding, presided VERB A person who presides over a formal event is in charge of it.

president, presidents NOUN ① In a country which has no king or queen, the president is the elected leader • *the President of the United States of America*. ② The president of an organisation is the person who has the highest position. **presidency** NOUN **presidential** ADJECTIVE

press, presses, pressing, pressed VERB ① If you press something, you push it or hold it firmly against something else • *Lisa pressed his hand* • *Press the blue button*. ② If you press clothes, you iron them. ③ If you press for something, you try hard to persuade someone to agree to it • *She was pressing for improvements to the education system*. ④ If you press charges, you make an accusation against someone which has to be decided in a court of law. ▶ NOUN ⑤ Newspapers and the journalists who work for them are called the press.

press conference, press conferences NOUN When someone gives a press conference, they have a meeting to answer questions put by reporters.

pressing ADJECTIVE Something that is pressing needs to be dealt with immediately • *pressing needs*.

pressure, pressures, pressuring, pressured NOUN ① SCIENCE Pressure is the force that is produced by pushing on something. ② PSHE If you are under pressure, you have too much to do and not enough time, or someone is trying hard to persuade you to do something. ▶ VERB ③ If you pressure someone, you try hard to persuade them to do something.

pressurise, pressurises, pressurising, pressurised; also spelt **pressurize** VERB If you pressurise someone, you try hard to persuade them to do something.

prestige [*Said press-teezh*] NOUN If you have prestige, people admire you because of your position. **prestigious** ADJECTIVE SIMILAR WORDS: honour, standing, status

presumably ADVERB If you say that something is presumably the case, you mean you assume that it is • *Your audience, presumably, are younger*.

presume, presumes, presuming, presumed [*Said priz-yoom*] VERB If you presume something, you think that it is the case although you have no proof. **presumption** NOUN SIMILAR WORDS: assume, believe, suppose

presumptuous ADJECTIVE Someone who behaves in a presumptuous way does things that they have no right to do.

pretence, pretences NOUN a way of behaving that is false and intended to deceive people.

pretend, pretends, pretending, pretended VERB If you pretend that something is the case, you try to make people believe that it is, although in fact it is not • *Latimer pretended not to notice*.

SIMILAR WORDS: affect, feign, sham

pretender, pretenders NOUN A pretender to a throne or title is someone who claims it but whose claim is being questioned.

pretension, pretensions NOUN Someone with pretensions claims that they are more important than they really are.

pretentious ADJECTIVE Someone or something that is pretentious is trying to seem important when in fact they are not.

pretext, pretexts NOUN a false reason given to hide the real reason for doing something.

pretty, prettier, prettiest ADJECTIVE ① attractive in a delicate way. ▶ADVERB ② (informal) quite or rather • He spoke pretty good English. **prettily** ADVERB **prettiness** NOUN

prevail, prevails, prevailing, prevailed VERB ① If a custom or belief prevails in a particular place, it is normal or most common there • This attitude has prevailed in Britain for many years. ② If someone or something prevails, they succeed in their aims • In recent years better sense has prevailed. **prevailing** ADJECTIVE

prevalent ADJECTIVE very common or widespread • the hooliganism so prevalent today. **prevalence** NOUN

prevent, prevents, preventing, prevented VERB If you prevent something, you stop it from happening or being done. **preventable** ADJECTIVE **prevention** NOUN
SIMILAR WORDS: avert, forestall, stop

preventive or **preventative** ADJECTIVE intended to help prevent things such as disease or crime • preventive health care.

preview, previews NOUN ① an opportunity to see something, such as a film or exhibition, before it is shown to the public. ② ICT a part of a computer program which allows you to look at what you have keyed or added to a document or spreadsheet as it will appear when it is printed.

previous ADJECTIVE happening or existing before something else in time or position • previous reports • the previous year. **previously** ADVERB
SIMILAR WORDS: earlier, former, preceding

prey, preys, preying, preyed [Rhymes with *say*] NOUN ① The creatures that an animal hunts and eats are called its prey. ▶ VERB ② An animal that preys on a particular kind of animal lives by hunting and eating it.

SPELLING TIP
Do not confuse the spellings of *prey* and *pray*: *Owls prey on mice and small birds; Muslims pray five times a day.*

price, prices, pricing, priced NOUN ① The price of something is the amount of money you have to pay to buy it. ▶ VERB ② To price something at a particular amount is to fix its price at that amount.
SIMILAR WORDS: ① charge, cost, expense

priceless ADJECTIVE Something that is priceless is so valuable that it is difficult to work out how much it is worth.

pricey, pricier, priciest ADJECTIVE (informal) expensive.

prick, pricks, pricking, pricked VERB ① If you prick something, you stick a sharp pointed object into it. ▶ NOUN ② a small, sharp pain caused when something pricks you.

prickle, prickles, prickling, prickled NOUN ① Prickles are small sharp points or thorns on plants. ▶ VERB

② If your skin prickles, it feels as if a lot of sharp points are being stuck into it. **prickly** ADJECTIVE

pride, prides, priding, prided NOUN ① Pride is a feeling of satisfaction you have when you have done something well. ② Pride is also a feeling of being better than other people. ③ A pride of lions is a group of them. ▶ VERB ④ If you pride yourself on a quality or skill, you are proud of it • *She prides herself on punctuality.*
SIMILAR WORDS: ① gratification, pleasure, satisfaction

priest, priests NOUN ① RE a member of the clergy in some Christian Churches. ② RE In many non-Christian religions, a priest is a man who has special duties in the place where people worship.
priestly ADJECTIVE

priestess, priestesses NOUN a female priest in a non-Christian religion.

priesthood NOUN The priesthood is the position of being a priest.

prim, primmer, primmest ADJECTIVE Someone who is prim always behaves very correctly and is easily shocked by anything rude.
SIMILAR WORDS: priggish, prudish, strait-laced

primaeval another spelling of **primeval**.

primarily ADVERB You use 'primarily' to indicate the main or most important feature of something • *I still rated people primarily on their looks*.

primary ADJECTIVE 'Primary' is used to describe something that is extremely important for someone or something • *the primary aim of his research*.

primary colour, primary colours NOUN In art, the primary colours are red, yellow and blue, from which other colours can be obtained by mixing.

primary school, primary schools NOUN a school for children aged up to 11.

primate, primates NOUN ① an archbishop. ② a member of the group of animals which includes humans, monkeys and apes.

prime, primes, priming, primed ADJECTIVE ① main or most important • *a prime cause of brain damage*. ② of the best quality • *in prime condition*.
▶ NOUN ③ Someone's prime is the stage when they are at their strongest, most active or most successful.
▶ VERB ④ If you prime someone, you give them information about something in advance to prepare them • *We are primed for every lesson*.
SIMILAR WORDS: ③ height, heyday, peak

prime minister, prime ministers NOUN The prime minister is the leader of the government.

prime number, prime numbers NOUN MATHS A prime number is a whole number greater than 1 that cannot be divided exactly by any whole number except itself and 1. The numbers 2, 3, 7 and 11 are prime numbers.

primeval [Said pry-**mee**-vl]; also spelt **primaeval** ADJECTIVE belonging to a very early period in the history of the world.

primitive ADJECTIVE ① connected with a society that lives very simply without industries or a writing system • *the primitive peoples of the world*. ② very simple, basic or old-fashioned • *a very small primitive cottage*.

primordial [Said pry-**mor**-dee-al] ADJECTIVE (formal) existing at the beginning of time.

primrose, primroses NOUN a small plant that has pale yellow flowers in spring.

WORD HISTORY: from Latin *prima rosa* meaning 'first rose'

prince, princes NOUN a male member of a royal family, especially the son of a king or queen. **princely** ADJECTIVE

princess, princesses NOUN a female member of a royal family, usually the daughter of a king or queen, or the wife of a prince.

principal, principals ADJECTIVE ① main or most important • *the principal source of food.* ▸ NOUN ② the person in charge of a school or college. **principally** ADVERB

SPELLING TIP
Do not confuse the spellings of *principal* and *principle*: *the principal reason; the school principal; Eating meat is against my principles.*

SPELLING TIP
Remember this mnemonic: *pAL up with the principAL and principAL teachers.*

principality, principalities NOUN a country ruled by a prince.

principle, principles NOUN ① a belief you have about the way you should behave • *a woman of principle.* ② a general rule or scientific law which explains how something happens or works • *the principle of evolution in nature.*

SIMILAR WORDS: ① precept, standard, rule

SPELLING TIP
Do not confuse the spellings of *principle* and *principal*: *Eating meat is against my principles; the principal reason; the school principal.*

SPELLING TIP
Remember this mnemonic: *LEarn the principLEs.*

print, prints, printing, printed VERB ① To print a newspaper or book is to reproduce it in large quantities using a mechanical or electronic copying process. ② If you print when you are writing, you do not join the letters together. ▸ NOUN ③ The letters and numbers on the pages of a book or newspaper are referred to as the print. ④ a photograph, or a printed copy of a painting. ⑤ Footprints and fingerprints can be referred to as prints.

printer, printers NOUN ① a machine that can be connected to a computer to reproduce copies of documents or pictures on paper. ② a person or company that prints newspapers or books.

printing NOUN the process of producing printed material such as books and newspapers.

print-out, print-outs NOUN a printed copy of information from a computer.

prior, priors ADJECTIVE ① planned or done at an earlier time • *I have a prior engagement.* ▸ PHRASE ② Something that happens **prior to** a particular time or event happens before it. ▸ NOUN ③ a monk in charge of a small group of monks in a priory. **prioress** NOUN

prioritise, prioritises, prioritising, prioritised; also spelt **prioritize** VERB To prioritise things is to decide which is the most important and deal with it first.

priority, priorities NOUN something that needs to be dealt with first • *The priority is building homes.*

priory, priories NOUN a place where a small group of monks live under the charge of a prior.

a b c d e f g h i j k l m n o p q r s t u v w x y z

prise, prises, prising, prised VERB If you prise something open or away from a surface, you force it open or away • *She prised his fingers loose.*

SPELLING TIP
Do not confuse the spellings of *prise* and *prize*: *A prisoner had prised the wire fence apart; Analytical skills are highly prized in business.*

prism, prisms NOUN ① an object made of clear glass with many flat sides. It separates light passing through it into the colours of the rainbow. ② MATHS A prism is any polyhedron with two identical parallel ends and sides which are parallelograms.

prison, prisons NOUN a building where criminals are kept in captivity.

prisoner, prisoners NOUN someone who is kept in prison or held in captivity against their will.

pristine [*Said* priss-teen] ADJECTIVE (*formal*) very clean or new and in perfect condition.

private, privates ADJECTIVE ① for the use of one person rather than people in general • *a private bathroom.* ② taking place between a small number of people and kept secret from others • *a private conversation.* ③ owned or run by individuals or companies rather than by the state • *a private company.* ▶ NOUN ④ a soldier of the lowest rank. **privacy** NOUN **privately** ADVERB

private message, private messages NOUN On a computer network, a private message is a message that can be read only by the person you send it to.

private school, private schools NOUN a school that does not receive money from the government, and which parents pay for their children to attend.

privatise, privatises, privatising, privatised; also spelt **privatize** VERB If the government privatises a state-owned industry or organisation, it allows it to be bought and owned by a private individual or group.

privilege, privileges NOUN a special right or advantage given to a person or group • *the privileges of monarchy.* **privileged** ADJECTIVE

privy ADJECTIVE (*formal*) If you are privy to something secret, you have been told about it.

prize, prizes, prizing, prized NOUN ① a reward given to the winner of a competition or game. ▶ ADJECTIVE ② of the highest quality or standard • *his prize dahlia.* ▶ VERB ③ Something that is prized is wanted and admired for its value or quality.
SIMILAR WORDS: ① award, reward, trophy

SPELLING TIP
Do not confuse the spellings of *prize* and *prise*: *Analytical skills are highly prized in business; A prisoner had prised the wire fence apart.*

pro, pros NOUN ① (*informal*) a professional. ▶ PHRASE ② The **pros and cons** of a situation are its advantages and disadvantages.

pro- PREFIX 'Pro-' means supporting or in favour of • *pro-democracy protests.*

probability, probabilities NOUN ① The probability of something happening is how likely it is to happen • *the probability of success.* ② If something is a probability, it is likely to happen • *The probability is that you will be feeling better.*
SIMILAR WORDS: ① chances, likelihood, odds

probable ADJECTIVE Something that is probable is likely to be true or correct, or likely to happen • *the most probable outcome*.

probably ADVERB Something that is probably the case is likely but not certain.

probation NOUN Probation is a period of time during which a person convicted of a crime is supervised by a probation officer instead of being sent to prison. **probationary** ADJECTIVE

probe, probes, probing, probed VERB ① If you probe, you ask a lot of questions to discover the facts about something. ▶ NOUN ② a long thin instrument used by doctors and dentists when examining a patient.

problem, problems NOUN ① an unsatisfactory situation that causes difficulties. ② a puzzle or question that you solve using logical thought or mathematics. **problematic** ADJECTIVE
SIMILAR WORDS: ① difficulty, predicament

procedure, procedures NOUN a way of doing something, especially the correct or usual way • *It's standard procedure*. **procedural** ADJECTIVE

proceed, proceeds, proceeding, proceeded VERB ① If you proceed to do something, you start doing it, or continue doing it • *She proceeded to tell them*. ② (*formal*) If you proceed in a particular direction, you move in that direction • *The taxi proceeded along a lonely road*.

SPELLING TIP
Do not confuse the spellings of *proceed* and *precede*: *I think we should proceed with the meeting; Summer precedes autumn*.

---

proceedings PLURAL NOUN ① You can refer to an organised and related series of events as the proceedings • *She was determined to see the proceedings from start to finish*. ② Legal proceedings are legal action taken against someone.

proceeds PLURAL NOUN The proceeds from a fund-raising event are the money obtained from it.

process, processes, processing, processed NOUN ① a series of actions intended to achieve a particular result or change. ▶ PHRASE ② If you are **in the process** of doing something, you have started doing it but have not yet finished. ▶ VERB ③ When food is processed, it is prepared in factories before it is sold. ④ When information is processed, it is put through a system or into a computer to organise it.

procession, processions NOUN a group of people or vehicles moving in a line, often as part of a ceremony.

processor, processors NOUN ICT In computing, a processor is the central chip in a computer which controls its operations.

proclaim, proclaims, proclaiming, proclaimed VERB If someone proclaims something, they announce it or make it known • *You have proclaimed your innocence*. **proclamation** NOUN

procrastinate, procrastinates, procrastinating, procrastinated VERB (*formal*) If you procrastinate, you put off doing something.

procure, procures, procuring, procured VERB (*formal*) If you procure something, you obtain it.

prod, prods, prodding, prodded VERB If you prod something, you give it a push with your finger or with something pointed.

prodigal ADJECTIVE (*literary*) Someone who is prodigal spends money freely and wastefully.

prodigy, prodigies [Said **prod**-dij-ee] NOUN someone who shows an extraordinary natural ability at an early age.

produce, produces, producing, produced VERB [Said pro-**dyoos**] ①To produce something is to make it or cause it • a factory producing circuits for computers. ② If you produce something from somewhere, you bring it out so it can be seen. ▶ NOUN [Said **prod**-yoos] ③ Produce is food that is grown to be sold • fresh produce.

producer, producers NOUN ① a person or business that generates goods for sale. ② The producer of a record, film or show is the person in charge of making it or putting it on.

product, products NOUN ① something that is made to be sold • high-quality products. ② MATHS The product of two or more numbers or quantities is the result of multiplying them together. ③ SCIENCE a substance formed in a chemical reaction.

production, productions NOUN ① DGT Production is the process of manufacturing or growing something in large quantities • modern methods of production. ② Production is also the amount of goods manufactured or food grown by a country or company • Production has fallen by 13.2%. ③ A production of a play, opera or other show is a series of performances of it.

productive ADJECTIVE ①To be productive means to produce a large number of things • Farms were more productive in these areas. ② If something such as a meeting is productive, good or useful things happen as a result of it.
SIMILAR WORDS: ② beneficial, useful, worthwhile

productivity NOUN Productivity is the rate at which things are produced or dealt with.

profane ADJECTIVE (formal) showing disrespect for a religion or religious things • profane language.

profess, professes, professing, professed VERB ① (formal) If you profess to do or have something, you claim to do or have it. ② If you profess a feeling or opinion, you express it • He professes a lasting affection for Trinidad.

profession, professions NOUN ① a type of job that requires advanced education or training. ② You can use 'profession' to refer to all the people who have a particular profession • the medical profession.

professional, professionals ADJECTIVE ① Professional means relating to the work of someone who is qualified in a particular profession • I think you need professional advice. ② Professional also describes activities when they are done to earn money rather than as a hobby • professional football. ③ A professional piece of work is of a very high standard. ▶ NOUN ④ a person who has been trained in a profession. ⑤ someone who plays a sport to earn money rather than as a hobby.

professor, professors NOUN the senior teacher in a department of a British university. **professorial** ADJECTIVE

proficient ADJECTIVE If you are proficient at something, you can do it well. **proficiency** NOUN

profile, profiles NOUN ① Your profile is the outline of your face seen from the side. ② A profile of someone is a short description of their life and character. ③ Your profile on a social networking site is the basic information about you that appears on the site.

WORD HISTORY: from Italian *profilare* meaning 'to sketch lightly'

profit, profits, profiting, profited
NOUN ①When someone sells something, the profit is the amount they gain by selling it for more than it cost them to buy or make. ▶VERB ②If you profit from something, you gain or benefit from it. **profitable** ADJECTIVE

SIMILAR WORDS: ①gain, proceeds, return

profound ADJECTIVE ①great in degree or intensity • *a profound need to please.* ②showing great and deep intellectual understanding • *a profound question.* **profoundly** ADVERB **profundity** NOUN

profuse [Said prof-*yooss*] ADJECTIVE very large in quantity or number • *There were profuse apologies for his absence.* **profusely** ADVERB **profusion** NOUN

program, programs, programming, programmed ICT NOUN ①a set of instructions that a computer follows to perform a particular task. ▶VERB ②When someone programs a computer, they write a program and put it into the computer. **programmer** NOUN

programme, programmes NOUN ①a planned series of events • *a programme of official engagements.* ②a particular piece presented as a unit on television or radio, such as a play, show or discussion. ③a booklet giving information about a play, concert or show that you are attending.

SIMILAR WORDS: ①agenda, plan, schedule

progress, progresses, progressing, progressed NOUN ①Progress is the process of gradually improving or getting near to achieving something • *Gerry is now making some real progress towards fitness.* ②The progress of something is the way in which it develops or continues • *news on the progress of the war.* ▶PHRASE ③Something that is **in progress** is happening • *A cricket match was in progress.* ▶VERB ④If you progress, you become more advanced or skilful. ⑤To progress is to continue • *As the evening progressed, sadness turned to rage.* **progression** NOUN

SIMILAR WORDS: ①advance, headway②course, movement

progressive ADJECTIVE ①having modern ideas about how things should be done. ②happening gradually • *a progressive illness.*

prohibit, prohibits, prohibiting, prohibited VERB If someone prohibits something, they forbid it or make it illegal. **prohibition** NOUN

GRAMMAR TIP
You *prohibit* a person *from* doing something.

prohibitive ADJECTIVE If the cost of something is prohibitive, it is so high that people cannot afford it.

project, projects, projecting, projected NOUN [Said pro-*ject*]①a carefully planned attempt to achieve something or to study something over a period of time. ▶VERB [Said pro-*ject*]②Something that is projected is planned or expected to happen in the future • *The population aged 65 or over is projected to increase.* ③To project an image onto a screen is to make it appear there using equipment such as a projector. ④Something that projects sticks out beyond a surface or edge. **projection** NOUN

projector, projectors NOUN a piece of equipment which produces a large image on a screen by shining light through a photographic slide or film strip.

prokaryote, prokaryotes NOUN SCIENCE a living organism whose genetic material is not enclosed in a nucleus. Bacteria are prokaryotes.

proletariat [Said proh-la-**tair**-ree-at] NOUN (formal) Working-class people are sometimes referred to as the proletariat. **proletarian** ADJECTIVE

proliferate, proliferates, proliferating, proliferated VERB If things proliferate, they quickly increase in number. **proliferation** NOUN
WORD HISTORY: from Latin prolifer meaning 'having children'

prolific ADJECTIVE producing a lot of something • this prolific artist.

prologue, prologues NOUN a speech or section that introduces a play or book.

prolong, prolongs, prolonging, prolonged VERB If you prolong something, you make it last longer. **prolonged** ADJECTIVE

prom, proms NOUN (informal) a concert at which some of the audience stand.

promenade, promenades [Said prom-min-**ahd**] NOUN a road or path next to the sea at a seaside resort.
WORD HISTORY: a French word, from se promener meaning 'to go for a walk'

prominent ADJECTIVE ① Prominent people are well-known and important. ② Something that is prominent is very noticeable • a prominent nose. **prominence** NOUN **prominently** ADVERB

promise, promises, promising, promised VERB ① If you promise to do something, you say that you will definitely do it. ② Something that

promises to have a particular quality shows signs that it will have that quality • This promised to be a very long night. ▶ NOUN ③ a statement made by someone that they will definitely do something • He made a promise to me. ④ Someone or something that shows promise seems likely to be very successful. **promising** ADJECTIVE
SIMILAR WORDS: ① guarantee, pledge, vow ③ guarantee, oath, vow

promontory, promontories [Said prom-mon-tree] NOUN an area of high land sticking out into the sea.

promote, promotes, promoting, promoted VERB ① If someone promotes something, they try to make it happen. ② If someone promotes a product such as a film or a book, they try to make it popular by advertising. ③ If someone is promoted, they are given a more important job at work. **promoter** NOUN **promotion** NOUN

prompt, prompts, prompting, prompted VERB ① If something prompts someone to do something, it makes them decide to do it • Curiosity prompted him to push at the door. ② If you prompt someone when they stop speaking, you tell them what to say next or encourage them to continue. ▶ ADVERB ③ exactly at the time mentioned • Wednesday morning at 10.40 prompt. ▶ ADJECTIVE ④ A prompt action is done without any delay • a prompt reply. **promptly** ADVERB

prone ADJECTIVE ① If you are prone to something, you have a tendency to be affected by it or to do it • She is prone to headaches. ② If you are prone, you are lying flat and face downwards • lying prone on the grass.

What is a Pronoun?

A **pronoun** is a word that is used in place of a noun. Pronouns may be used instead of naming a person or thing.

Personal pronouns replace the subject or object of a sentence:

She caught a fish.
*The nurse reassured **him**.*

Reflexive pronouns replace the object when it is the same person or thing as the subject:

*Adil saw **himself** in the mirror.*

Demonstrative pronouns replace the subject or object when you want to show where something is:

That is a nice jacket.
*Have you seen **this**?*

Possessive pronouns replace the subject or object when you want to show who owns it:

*The blue car is **mine**.*

Hers is a strange story.

Relative pronouns replace a noun to link two different parts of the sentence:

*Do you know the man **who** lives next door?*
*I watched a programme **that** I had recorded yesterday.*

Interrogative pronouns ask questions:

What are you doing?

Indefinite pronouns replace a subject or object to talk about a broad or vague range of people or things:

Everybody knew the exercise was a waste of time.
Some say he cheats at cards.

Also look at the grammar box at **relative pronoun**

SIMILAR WORDS: ① inclined, liable, subject

prong, prongs NOUN The prongs of a fork are the long, narrow, pointed parts.

pronoun, pronouns NOUN
[ENGLISH] [MFL] In grammar, a pronoun is a word that is used to replace a noun. 'He', 'she' and 'them' are all pronouns.

pronounce, pronounces, pronouncing, pronounced VERB
[ENGLISH] [MFL] When you pronounce a word, you say it.

SPELLING TIP
There is an *o* before the *u* in *pronounce*. Compare this spelling with *pronunciation*.

pronounced ADJECTIVE very noticeable • *He talks with a pronounced lowland accent.*

pronunciation, pronunciations
[Said pron-nun-see-**ay**-shn] NOUN
the way a word is usually said.

SPELLING TIP
There is no *o* before the *u* in *pronunciation*. Compare this spelling with *pronounce*.

proof NOUN If you have proof of something, you have evidence which shows that it is true or exists.
SIMILAR WORDS: confirmation, evidence, verification

prop, props, propping, propped
VERB ① If you prop an object somewhere, you support it or rest it against something • *The barman propped himself against the counter.*
▶ NOUN ② a stick or other object used to support something. ③ The props in a play are all the objects and

furniture used by the actors.

propaganda NOUN HISTORY
Propaganda is exaggerated or false information that is published or broadcast in order to influence people.

propagate, propagates, propagating, propagated VERB
① If people propagate an idea, they spread it to try to influence many other people. ② If you propagate plants, you grow more of them from an original one. **propagation** NOUN

propane NOUN Propane is a gas found in petroleum and used as a fuel for cooking and heating.

propel, propels, propelling, propelled VERB To propel something is to cause it to move in a particular direction.

propeller, propellers NOUN a device on a boat or aircraft with rotating blades which make the boat or aircraft move.

propensity, propensities NOUN (formal) a tendency to behave in a particular way.

proper ADJECTIVE ① real and satisfactory • He was no nearer having a proper job. ② correct or suitable • Put things in their proper place. ③ accepted or conventional • a proper wedding. **properly** ADVERB

proper fraction, proper fractions NOUN MATHS a fraction in which the numerator has a lower value than the denominator, for example, $3/5$.

proper noun, proper nouns NOUN the name of a person, place or institution.

property, properties NOUN
① A person's property is the things that belong to them. ② a building and the land belonging to it. ③ a characteristic or quality • Mint has powerful healing properties.

prophecy, prophecies [Said prof-iss-see] NOUN a statement about what someone believes will happen in the future.

SPELLING TIP
The noun prophecy ends in cy.

prophesy, prophesies, prophesying, prophesied [Said prof-iss-sigh] VERB If someone prophesies something, they say it will happen.

SPELLING TIP
The verb prophesy ends in sy.

prophet, prophets NOUN RE a person who predicts what will happen in the future.

prophetic ADJECTIVE correctly predicting what will happen • It was a prophetic warning.

proportion, proportions NOUN ① A proportion of an amount or group is a part of it • a tiny proportion of the population. ② The proportion of one amount to another is its size in comparison with the other amount • the highest proportion of women to men. ③ (in plural) You can refer to the size of something as its proportions • a red umbrella of vast proportions.

proportional or **proportionate** ADJECTIVE If one thing is proportional to another, it remains the same size in comparison with the other • proportional increases in profit. **proportionally** or **proportionately** ADVERB

proportional representation NOUN Proportional representation is a system of voting in elections in which the number of representatives of each party is in proportion to the number of people who voted for it.

proposal, proposals NOUN a plan that has been suggested • business proposals.

propose, proposes, proposing, proposed VERB ① If you propose a plan or idea, you suggest it. ② If you propose to do something, you intend to do it • *And how do you propose to do that?* ③ When someone proposes a toast to a particular person, they ask people to drink a toast to that person. ④ If someone proposes to another person, they ask that person to marry them.

proposition, propositions NOUN ① a statement expressing a theory or opinion. ② an offer or suggestion • *I made her a proposition.*

proprietor, proprietors NOUN The proprietor of a business is the owner.

propriety NOUN (*formal*) Propriety is what is socially or morally acceptable • *a model of propriety.*

propulsion NOUN Propulsion is the power that moves something.

prose NOUN Prose is ordinary written language in contrast to poetry. **WORD HISTORY:** from Latin *prosa oratio* meaning 'straightforward speech'

prosecute, prosecutes, prosecuting, prosecuted VERB If someone is prosecuted, they are charged with a crime and have to stand trial. **prosecutor** NOUN

prosecution NOUN The lawyers who try to prove that a person on trial is guilty are called the prosecution.

prospect, prospects, prospecting, prospected NOUN ① If there is a prospect of something happening, there is a possibility that it will happen • *There was little prospect of going home.* ② Someone's prospects are their chances of being successful in the future. ▶ VERB ③ If someone prospects for gold or oil, they look for it. **prospector** NOUN

prospective ADJECTIVE 'Prospective' is used to say that someone wants to be or is likely to be something. For example, the prospective owner of something is the person who wants to own it.

prospectus, prospectuses NOUN a booklet giving details about a college or a company.

prosper, prospers, prospering, prospered VERB When people or businesses prosper, they are successful and make a lot of money. **prosperous** ADJECTIVE **prosperity** NOUN

prostate, prostates NOUN an organ in the body of male mammals which is situated at the neck of the bladder.

prostrate ADJECTIVE lying face downwards on the ground.

protagonist, protagonists NOUN (*formal*) ① a main character in a play or story. ② Someone who is a protagonist of an idea or movement is a leading supporter of it. **WORD HISTORY:** from Greek *prōtagōnistēs* meaning 'main actor in a play'

protea, proteas NOUN an evergreen African shrub with colourful flowers.

protect, protects, protecting, protected VERB To protect someone or something is to prevent them from being harmed or damaged. **protection** NOUN **protective** ADJECTIVE **protector** NOUN

protection, protections NOUN ① the act of preventing harm or damage. ② something that keeps a person or thing safe.

protégé, protégés [*Said* **proh-tij-ay**] NOUN Someone who is the protégé of an older, more experienced person is helped and guided by that person.

protein, proteins NOUN SCIENCE Protein is a complex compound consisting of amino acid chains, found in many foods and essential for all living things.

WORD HISTORY: from Greek *prōteios* meaning 'primary'

protest, protests, protesting, protested VERB [Said pro-**test**] ① If you protest about something, you say or demonstrate publicly that you disagree with it • *They protested against the new law.* ▸ NOUN [Said pro-test] ② a demonstration or statement showing that you disagree with something. **protester** NOUN

Protestant, Protestants NOUN or ADJECTIVE RE (a member) of one of the Christian Churches which separated from the Catholic Church in the 16th century.

protestation, protestations NOUN a strong declaration that something is true or not true • *his protestations of love.*

protocol NOUN Protocol is the system of rules about the correct way to behave in formal situations.

proton, protons NOUN SCIENCE a particle which forms part of the nucleus of an atom and has a positive electrical charge.

prototype, prototypes NOUN D&T a first model of something that is made so that the design can be tested and improved.

protracted ADJECTIVE lasting longer than usual • *a protracted dispute.*

protrude, protrudes, protruding, protruded VERB (formal) If something is protruding from a surface or edge, it is sticking out. **protrusion** NOUN

proud, prouder, proudest ADJECTIVE ① feeling pleasure and satisfaction at something you own or have achieved • *I was proud of our players today.*
② having great dignity and self-respect • *too proud to ask for money.* **proudly** ADVERB

prove, proves, proving, proved or **proven** VERB ① To prove that something is true is to provide evidence that it is definitely true • *A letter from Kathleen proved that he lived there.* ② If something proves to be the case, it becomes clear that it is so • *His first impressions of her proved wrong.*
SIMILAR WORDS: ① confirm, show, verify

proverb, proverbs NOUN a short sentence which gives advice or makes a comment about life. **proverbial** ADJECTIVE

provide, provides, providing, provided VERB ① If you provide something for someone, you give it to them or make it available for them. ② If you provide for someone, you give them the things they need.
SIMILAR WORDS: ① furnish, supply

provided or **providing** CONJUNCTION If you say that something will happen provided something else happens, you mean that the first thing will happen only if the second thing does.

GRAMMAR TIP
Provided can be followed by *that*, but *providing* cannot: *I'll come, providing he doesn't; You can go, provided that you phone as soon as you get there.*

providence NOUN Providence is God or a force which is believed to arrange the things that happen to us.

province, provinces NOUN ① one of the areas into which some large countries are divided, each province having its own administration. ② (in plural) You can refer to the parts of a country which are not near the capital as the provinces.

WORD HISTORY: from Latin *provincia* meaning 'a conquered territory'

provincial ADJECTIVE ① connected with the parts of a country outside the capital • *a provincial theatre.* ② narrow-minded and lacking sophistication.

provision, provisions NOUN ① The provision of something is the act of making it available to people • *the provision of health care.* ② (*in plural*) Provisions are supplies of food.

provisional ADJECTIVE A provisional arrangement has not yet been made definite and so might be changed.

proviso, provisos [*Said* prov-**eye**-zoh] NOUN a condition in an agreement.

provocation, provocations NOUN an act done deliberately to annoy someone.

provocative ADJECTIVE intended to annoy people or make them react • *a provocative speech.*

provoke, provokes, provoking, provoked VERB ① If you provoke someone, you deliberately try to make them angry. ② If something provokes an unpleasant reaction, it causes it • *illness provoked by tension or worry.*

prow, prows NOUN the front part of a boat.

prowess NOUN Prowess is outstanding ability • *his prowess at tennis.*

prowl, prowls, prowling, prowled VERB If a person or animal prowls around, they move around quietly and secretly, as if hunting.

proximity NOUN (*formal*) Proximity is nearness to someone or something.

proxy PHRASE If you do something by proxy, someone else does it on your behalf • *voting by proxy.*

prude, prudes NOUN someone who is very easily shocked by things.

prudish ADJECTIVE

WORD HISTORY: from Old French *prode femme* meaning 'respectable woman'

prudent ADJECTIVE behaving in a sensible and cautious way • *It is prudent to plan ahead.* **prudence** NOUN **prudently** ADVERB

prune, prunes, pruning, pruned NOUN ① a dried plum. ▶ VERB ② When someone prunes a tree or shrub, they cut back some of the branches.

pry, pries, prying, pried VERB If someone is prying, they are trying to find out about something secret or private.

PS PS is written before an additional message at the end of a letter. PS is an abbreviation for 'postscript'.

psalm, psalms [*Said* sahm] NOUN one of the 150 songs, poems and prayers which together form the Book of Psalms in the Bible.

pseudo- [*Said* syoo-doh] PREFIX 'Pseudo-' is used to form adjectives and nouns indicating that something is not what it is claimed to be • *pseudo-scientific theories.*

WORD HISTORY: from Greek *pseudēs* meaning 'false'

pseudonym, pseudonyms [*Said* syoo-doe-nim] NOUN a name an author uses rather than their real name.

PSHE NOUN a part of the school curriculum concerned with social and personal issues. PSHE is an abbreviation for 'Personal, Social and Health Education'.

psyche, psyches [*Said* sigh-kee] NOUN your mind and your deepest feelings.

psychiatry NOUN Psychiatry is the branch of medicine concerned with mental health. **psychiatrist** NOUN

a
b
c
d
e
f
g
h
i
j
k
l
m
n
o
p
q
r
s
t
u
v
w
x
y
z

psychiatric ADJECTIVE

psychic ADJECTIVE having unusual mental powers such as the ability to read people's minds or predict the future.

psychoanalysis NOUN Psychoanalysis is the examination and treatment of someone who has mental health problems by encouraging them to talk about their feelings and past events in order to discover the cause of the illness.
psychoanalyst NOUN
psychoanalyse VERB

psychology NOUN Psychology is the scientific study of the mind and of the reasons for people's behaviour.
psychological ADJECTIVE
psychologist NOUN

psychopath, psychopaths NOUN a person with a psychiatric disorder who can commit antisocial or violent acts without feeling guilt.
psychopathic ADJECTIVE

psychosis, psychoses [Said sigh-koe-siss] NOUN a severe mental illness that causes people to interpret reality in a different way from the people around them.
psychotic ADJECTIVE

pterodactyl, pterodactyls [Said ter-rod-dak-til] NOUN Pterodactyls were flying reptiles in prehistoric times.
WORD HISTORY: from Greek *pteron* meaning 'wing' and *daktulos* meaning 'finger'

PTO PTO is an abbreviation for 'please turn over'. It is written at the bottom of a page to indicate that the writing continues on the other side.

pub, pubs NOUN a building where people go to buy and drink alcoholic or soft drinks.

puberty [Said pyoo-ber-tee] NOUN Puberty is the stage when a person's body changes from that of a child into that of an adult.

pubic [Said pyoo-bik] ADJECTIVE relating to the area around and above a person's genitals.

public NOUN ① You can refer to people in general as the public.
▶ ADJECTIVE ② relating to people in general • *There was some public support for the idea.* ③ provided for everyone to use, or open to anyone • *public transport.* **publicly** ADVERB

publican, publicans NOUN a person who owns or manages a pub.

publication, publications NOUN ① The publication of a book is the act of printing it and making it available. ② a book or magazine • *medical publications*.

public domain NOUN If a piece of music or writing is in the public domain, no one has the copyright and it is available for people to use freely.

publicise, publicises, publicising, publicised; also spelt **publicize** VERB When someone publicises a fact or event, they advertise it and make it widely known.

publicist, publicists NOUN a person whose job involves getting publicity for people, events or things.

publicity NOUN Publicity is information or advertisements about an item or event.

public school, public schools NOUN In Britain, a public school is a school that is privately run and that charges fees for the pupils to attend.

public servant, public servants NOUN In Australia and New Zealand, a public servant is someone who works in the public service.

public service NOUN In Australia and New Zealand, the public service is the government departments responsible for the administration of the country.

public transport NOUN Public transport is a system of buses, trains, etc., running on fixed routes at fixed times, on which the public may travel.

publish, publishes, publishing, published VERB LIBRARY When a company publishes a book, newspaper or magazine, they print copies of it and distribute it. **publishing** NOUN

publisher, publishers NOUN LIBRARY The publisher of a book, newspaper or magazine is the person or company that prints copies of it and distributes it.

pudding, puddings NOUN ① a sweet cake mixture cooked with fruit or other flavouring and served hot. ② You can refer to the sweet course of a meal as the pudding.

puddle, puddles NOUN a small shallow pool of liquid.

puerile [Said pyoo-rile] ADJECTIVE Puerile behaviour is silly and childish. WORD HISTORY: from Latin puerilis, from puer meaning 'boy'

puff, puffs, puffing, puffed VERB ① To puff on a cigarette or pipe is to smoke it. ② If you are puffing, you are breathing loudly and quickly with your mouth open. ③ If something puffs out or puffs up, it swells and becomes larger and rounder. ▶ NOUN ④ a small amount of air or smoke that is released.

puffin, puffins NOUN a black and white sea bird with a large, brightly coloured beak.

pug, pugs NOUN a small, short-haired dog with a flat nose.

puja [Said poo-jah] NOUN Puja is a variety of practices which make up Hindu worship.

puke, pukes, puking, puked VERB (informal) If someone pukes, they vomit.

pull, pulls, pulling, pulled VERB ① When you pull something, you hold it and move it towards you. ② When something is pulled by a vehicle or animal, it is attached to it and moves along behind it • Four oxen can pull a single plough. ③ When you pull a curtain or blind, you move it so that it covers or uncovers the window. ④ If you pull a muscle, you injure it by stretching it too far or too quickly. ⑤ When a vehicle pulls away, pulls out or pulls in, it moves in that direction. ▶ NOUN ⑥ The pull of something is its attraction or influence • the pull of the past.

pull down VERB When a building is pulled down, it is deliberately destroyed. **pull out** VERB If you pull out of something, you leave it or decide not to continue with it • The German government has pulled out of the project. **pull through** VERB When someone pulls through, they recover from a serious illness.

pulley, pulleys NOUN DGT a device for lifting heavy weights. The weight is attached to a rope which passes over a wheel or series of wheels.

pullover, pullovers NOUN a woollen piece of clothing that covers the top part of your body.

pulmonary ADJECTIVE relating to the lungs or to the veins and arteries carrying blood between the lungs and the heart.

pulp NOUN If something is turned into a pulp, it is crushed until it is soft and moist.

What does Punctuation do?

Punctuation marks are essential parts of written language. By linking sequences of written words, or by dividing them into sentences and clauses, they help the reader to understand what is being read.

Look at the punctuation boxes at **apostrophe**; **bracket**; **colon**; **comma**; **dash**; **exclamation mark**; **full stop**; **hyphen**; **inverted comma**; **question mark**; **semicolon**

pulpit, pulpits *[Said pool-pit]* NOUN the small raised platform in a church where a member of the clergy stands to preach.

pulse, pulses, pulsing, pulsed NOUN ① Your pulse is the regular beating of blood through your body, the rate of which you can feel at your wrists and elsewhere. ② The seeds of beans, peas and lentils are called pulses when they are used for food. ▶ VERB ③ If something is pulsing, it is moving or vibrating with rhythmic, regular movements • *She could feel the blood pulsing in her eardrums.*

puma, pumas *[Said pyoo-mah]* NOUN a wild animal belonging to the cat family.

pumice *[Said pum-miss]* NOUN Pumice stone is very lightweight grey stone that can be used to soften areas of hard skin.

pummel, pummels, pummelling, pummelled VERB If you pummel something, you beat it with your fists.

pump, pumps, pumping, pumped NOUN ① a machine that is used to force a liquid or gas to move in a particular direction. ② Pumps are light shoes with flat soles which people wear for sport or leisure. ▶ VERB ③ To pump a liquid or gas somewhere is to force it to flow in that direction, using a pump. ④ If you pump money into something, you put a lot of money into it.

pumpkin, pumpkins NOUN a very large, round, orange fruit eaten as a vegetable.

pun, puns NOUN a clever and amusing use of words so that what you say has two different meanings, such as *my dog's a champion boxer*.

punch, punches, punching, punched VERB ① If you punch someone, you hit them hard with your fist. ▶ NOUN ② a hard blow with the fist. ③ a tool used for making holes. ④ Punch is a drink made from a mixture of wine, spirits and fruit.

punctual ADJECTIVE arriving at the correct time. **punctually** ADVERB **punctuality** NOUN
SIMILAR WORDS: on time, prompt

punctuate, punctuates, punctuating, punctuated VERB ① Something that is punctuated by a particular thing is interrupted by it at intervals • *a grey day punctuated by bouts of rain.* ② ENGLISH When you punctuate a piece of writing, you put punctuation into it.

punctuation NOUN ENGLISH The marks in writing such as full stops, question marks and commas are called punctuation or punctuation marks.

puncture, punctures, puncturing, punctured NOUN ① If a tyre has a puncture, a small hole has been made in it and it has become flat. ▶ VERB ② To puncture something is to make a small hole in it.

pungent ADJECTIVE having a strong, often unpleasant, smell or taste. **pungency** NOUN

punish, punishes, punishing, punished VERB To punish someone who has done something wrong is to make them suffer because of it. SIMILAR WORDS: chastise, discipline, penalise

punishment, punishments NOUN something unpleasant done to someone because they have done something wrong.

punitive [Said pyoo-nit-tiv] ADJECTIVE harsh and intended to punish people • punitive military action.

Punjabi, Punjabis [Said pun-jah-bee] ADJECTIVE ① belonging or relating to the Punjab, a state in north-western India. ▸ NOUN ② someone who comes from the Punjab. ③ Punjabi is a language spoken in the Punjab.

punk NOUN Punk or punk rock is an aggressive style of rock music.

punt, punts NOUN a long, flat-bottomed boat. You move it along by pushing a pole against the river bottom.

puny, punier, puniest ADJECTIVE very small and weak.

pup, pups NOUN a young dog. Some other young animals such as seals are also called pups.

pupil, pupils NOUN ① The pupils at a school are the children who go there. ② Your pupils are the small, round, black areas in the centre of your eyes.

puppet, puppets NOUN a doll or toy animal that is moved by pulling strings or by putting your hand inside its body.

puppy, puppies NOUN a young dog.

purchase, purchases, purchasing, purchased VERB ① When you purchase something, you buy it.

▸ NOUN ② something you have bought. **purchaser** NOUN

pure, purer, purest ADJECTIVE ① Something that is pure is not mixed with anything else • pure wool • pure white. ② Pure also means clean and free from harmful substances • The water is pure enough to drink. ③ People who are pure have not done anything considered to be sinful. ④ Pure also means complete and total • a matter of pure luck. **purity** NOUN SIMILAR WORDS: ② clean, uncontaminated ③ chaste, innocent, virtuous

purée, purées [Said pyoo-ray] NOUN a food which has been mashed or blended to a thick, smooth consistency.

purely ADVERB involving only one feature and not including anything else • purely professional.

Purgatory NOUN RE Roman Catholics believe that Purgatory is where souls are purified before going to Heaven.

purge, purges, purging, purged VERB To purge something is to remove undesirable things from it • to purge the country of criminals.

purify, purifies, purifying, purified VERB To purify something is to remove all dirty or harmful substances from it. **purification** NOUN

purist, purists NOUN someone who believes that something should be done in a particular, correct way • a football purist.

puritan, puritans NOUN someone who believes in strict moral principles and avoids physical pleasures. **puritanical** ADJECTIVE

purple NOUN or ADJECTIVE reddish-blue.

a b c d e f g h i j k l m n o **p** q r s t u v w x y z

purport, purports, purporting, purported [Said pur-**port**] VERB (formal) Something that purports to be or have a particular thing claims to be or have it • a country which purports to disapprove of smokers.

purpose, purposes NOUN ① The purpose of something is the reason for it • the purpose of the meeting. ② If you have a particular purpose, this is what you want to achieve • To make music is my purpose in life. ▶ PHRASE ③ If you do something **on purpose**, you do it deliberately. **purposely** ADVERB **purposeful** ADJECTIVE

purr, purrs, purring, purred VERB When a cat purrs, it makes a low vibrating sound because it is contented.

purse, purses, pursing, pursed NOUN ① a small leather or fabric container for carrying money. ② In American English, a purse is a handbag. ▶ VERB ③ If you purse your lips, you move them into a tight, rounded shape.

purser, pursers NOUN the officer responsible for the paperwork and the welfare of passengers on a ship.

pursue, pursues, pursuing, pursued VERB ① If you pursue an activity or plan, you do it or make efforts to achieve it • I decided to pursue a career in photography. ② If you pursue someone, you follow them to try to catch them. **pursuer** NOUN **pursuit** NOUN

purveyor, purveyors NOUN (formal) A purveyor of goods or services is a person who sells them or provides them.

pus NOUN Pus is a thick yellowish liquid that forms in an infected wound.

push, pushes, pushing, pushed VERB ① When you push something, you press it using force in order to move it. ② If you push someone into doing something, you force or persuade them to do it • His agent pushed him into auditioning for a part. ③ (informal) Someone who pushes drugs sells them illegally. **push off** VERB (informal) If you tell someone to push off, you are telling them rudely to go away.

SIMILAR WORDS: ① shove, thrust

pushchair, pushchairs NOUN a small folding chair on wheels in which a baby or toddler can be wheeled around.

pusher, pushers NOUN (informal) someone who sells illegal drugs.

pushing PREPOSITION Someone who is pushing a particular age is nearly that age • pushing sixty.

pushover NOUN (informal) ① something that is easy. ② someone who is easily persuaded or defeated.

pushy, pushier, pushiest ADJECTIVE (informal) behaving in a forceful and determined way.

pussy, pussies NOUN (informal) a cat.

put, puts, putting, put VERB ① When you put something somewhere, you move it into that place or position. ② If you put an idea or remark in a particular way, you express it that way • I think you've put that very well. ③ To put someone or something in a particular state or situation means to cause them to be in it • It puts us both in an awkward position. ④ You can use 'put' to express an estimate of the size or importance of something • Her wealth is now put at £290 million. **put down** VERB ① To put someone down is to criticise them and make them appear foolish. ② If an animal is put down, it is killed because it is very ill or dangerous. **put off** VERB

①If you put something off, you delay doing it. ②To put someone off is to discourage them. **put out** VERB ①If you put a fire out or put the light out, you make it stop burning or shining. ②If you are put out, you are annoyed or upset. **put up** VERB If you put up resistance to something, you argue or fight against it • *She put up a tremendous struggle.* **put up with** VERB If you put up with something, you tolerate it even though you disagree with it or dislike it.
SIMILAR WORDS: ① place, position, set

putt, putts NOUN In golf, a putt is a gentle stroke made when the ball is near the hole.

putting NOUN Putting is a game played on a small grass course with no obstacles. You hit a ball gently with a club so that it rolls towards one of a series of holes around the course.

putty NOUN Putty is a paste used to fix panes of glass into frames.

puzzle, puzzles, puzzling, puzzled VERB ①If something puzzles you, it confuses you and you do not understand it • *There was something about her that puzzled me.* ▶ NOUN ②A puzzle is a game or question that requires a lot of thought to complete or solve. **puzzled** ADJECTIVE **puzzlement** NOUN

SIMILAR WORDS: ① baffle, mystify, perplex

PVC NOUN PVC is a plastic used for making clothing, pipes and many other things. PVC is an abbreviation for 'polyvinyl chloride'.

pygmy, pygmies [*Said* **pig**-mee]; also spelt **pigmy** NOUN a very small person, especially one who belongs to a racial group in which all the people are small.
WORD HISTORY: from Greek *pugmaios* meaning 'undersized'

pyjamas PLURAL NOUN Pyjamas are loose trousers and a jacket or top that you wear in bed.
WORD HISTORY: from Persian *pay jama* meaning 'leg clothing'

pylon, pylons NOUN a very tall metal structure which carries overhead electricity cables.

pyramid, pyramids NOUN ①a three-dimensional shape with a flat base and flat triangular sides sloping upwards to a point. ② HISTORY The Pyramids are ancient stone structures built over the tombs of Egyptian kings and queens.

pyre, pyres NOUN a high pile of wood on which a dead body or religious offering is burned.

python, pythons NOUN a large snake that kills animals by squeezing them with its body.

Qq

quack, quacks, quacking, quacked
VERB When a duck quacks, it makes a
loud, harsh sound.

quad, quads *[Said kwod]* **NOUN**
① *(informal)* Quad is the same as
quadruplet. ②A quad is a courtyard
with buildings all round it.

quadrangle, quadrangles *[Said
kwod-rang-gl]* **NOUN** a courtyard with
buildings all round it.

quadratic *[Said kwod-rat-ik]*
ADJECTIVE MATHS A quadratic
equation involves a variable raised to
the power of two, but no higher.

quadri- **PREFIX** 'Quadri-' means 'four'.

quadriceps **NOUN** PE a large
muscle in four parts at the front of
your thigh.

quadrilateral, quadrilaterals *[Said
kwod-ril-lat-ral]* **NOUN** MATHS a
shape with four straight sides.

quadruped, quadrupeds *[Said
kwod-roo-ped]* **NOUN** any animal with
four legs.

quadruple, quadruples,
quadrupling, quadrupled *[Said
kwod-roo-pl]* **VERB** When an amount
or number quadruples, it becomes
four times as large as it was.

quadruplet, quadruplets *[Said
kwod-roo-plet]* **NOUN** Quadruplets
are four children born at the same
time to the same mother.

quagga, quaggas *[Said kwog-ga]*
NOUN A quagga was a type of zebra
with stripes only on the head and
shoulders. They are now extinct.

quagmire, quagmires *[Said
kwag-mire]* **NOUN** a soft, wet area of
land which you sink into if you walk
on it.

quail, quails, quailing, quailed **NOUN**
① a type of small game bird with a
round body and short tail. ▶**VERB**
②If you quail, you feel or look afraid.

quaint, quainter, quaintest
ADJECTIVE attractively old-fashioned
or unusual • *quaint customs*. **quaintly**
ADVERB

quake, quakes, quaking, quaked
VERB If you quake, you shake and
tremble because you are very
frightened.

Quaker, Quakers **NOUN** RE a
member of a Christian group, the
Society of Friends.

qualification, qualifications **NOUN**
①Your qualifications are your skills
and achievements, especially as
officially recognised at the end of a
course of training or study.
②something you add to a statement
to make it less strong • *It is a good
novel and yet cannot be recommended
without qualification*.

qualify, qualifies, qualifying,
qualified **VERB** ① PE When you
qualify, you pass the examinations or
tests that you need to pass to do a
particular job or to take part in a
sporting event. ②If you qualify a
statement, you add a detail or
explanation to make it less strong • *I
would qualify that by putting it into
context*. ③If you qualify for

something, you become entitled to have it • *You qualify for a discount*.
qualified ADJECTIVE

qualitative ADJECTIVE relating to the quality of something.

quality, qualities NOUN ① The quality of something is how good it is • *The quality of food is very poor*. ② a characteristic • *These qualities are essential for success*.

qualm, qualms *[Said kwahm]* NOUN If you have qualms about what you are doing, you worry that it might not be right.

quandary, quandaries *[Said kwon-dree]* NOUN If you are in a quandary, you cannot decide what to do.

quango, quangos NOUN a body responsible for a particular area of public administration, which is financed by the government but is outside direct government control. Quango is short for 'quasi-autonomous non-governmental organisation'.

quantitative ADJECTIVE relating to the size or amount of something.

quantity, quantities NOUN ① an amount you can measure or count • *a small quantity of the mixture*. ② Quantity is the amount of something that there is • *emphasis on quantity rather than quality*.

quantum, quanta *[Said kwon-tum]* NOUN ① (formal) A quantum of something is an amount of it. ▶ADJECTIVE ② Quantum is used to describe various theories in physics and mathematics which are concerned with the properties and behaviour of atomic particles. ③ A quantum leap is a very great advance.

quarantine *[Said kwor-an-teen]* NOUN If an animal is in quarantine, it is kept away from other animals for

a time because it might have an infectious disease.
WORD HISTORY: from Italian *quarantina* meaning 'forty days'

quarrel, quarrels, quarrelling, quarrelled NOUN ① an angry argument. ▶VERB ② If people quarrel, they have an angry argument.
SIMILAR WORDS: ① argument, disagreement, fight ② argue, disagree, fall out

quarrelsome ADJECTIVE often quarrelling • *His brothers were greedy and quarrelsome*.

quarry, quarries, quarrying, quarried *[Said kwor-ree]* NOUN ① a place where stone is removed from the ground by digging or blasting. ② A person's or animal's quarry is the animal that they are hunting. ▶VERB ③ To quarry stone means to remove it from a quarry by digging or blasting.
WORD HISTORY: sense 2 is from Middle English *quirre* meaning 'entrails given to the hounds to eat'

quart, quarts *[Said kwort]* NOUN a unit of liquid volume equal to two pints or about 1.136 litres.

quarter, quarters NOUN ① one of four equal parts. ② an American coin worth 25 cents. ③ You can refer to a particular area in a city as a quarter • *the French quarter*. ④ You can use 'quarter' to refer vaguely to a particular person or group of people • *You are very popular in certain quarters*. ⑤ (in plural) A soldier's or a servant's quarters are the rooms that they live in.

quarterly, quarterlies ADJECTIVE or ADVERB ① Quarterly means happening regularly every three months • *my quarterly report*. ▶NOUN ② a magazine or journal published every three months.

quartet, quartets [Said kwor-**tet**]
NOUN a group of four musicians who
sing or play together; also a piece of
music written for four instruments or
singers.

quartile, quartiles NOUN MATHS
When you divide data into quartiles,
you divide it into four equal groups.

quartz NOUN Quartz is a kind of hard,
shiny crystal used in making very
accurate watches and clocks.

quash, quashes, quashing, quashed
[Said kwosh] VERB To quash a decision
or judgment means to reject it
officially • The judges quashed their
convictions.

quasi- [Said kway-sie] PREFIX 'Quasi-'
means resembling something but
not actually being that thing • a
quasi-religious order.
WORD HISTORY: a Latin word
meaning 'as if'

quatrain, quatrains [Said kwot-rain]
NOUN ENGLISH A quatrain is a verse
of poetry with four lines.

quaver, quavers, quavering,
quavered [Said kway-ver] VERB ① If
your voice quavers, it sounds
unsteady, usually because you are
nervous. ▶ NOUN ② MUSIC a
musical note (♪) that has the time
value of an eighth of a semibreve. In
the United States and Canada, a
quaver is known as an eighth note.

quay, quays [Said kee] NOUN a place
where boats are tied up and loaded
or unloaded.

SPELLING TIP
Remember this mnemonic: the
QUeen stood on the QUay.

queasy, queasier, queasiest [Said
kwee-zee] ADJECTIVE feeling slightly
sick. **queasiness** NOUN

queen, queens NOUN ① a female
monarch or a woman married to a
king. ② a female bee or ant which
can lay eggs. ③ In chess, the queen is
the most powerful piece and can
move in any direction. ④ In a pack of
cards, a queen is a card with a picture
of a queen on it.

queen mother, queen mothers
NOUN the widow of a king and the
mother of the reigning monarch.

queer, queerer, queerest ADJECTIVE
Queer means very strange.

quell, quells, quelling, quelled VERB
① To quell a rebellion or riot means to
put an end to it by using force. ② If
you quell a feeling such as fear or
grief, you stop yourself from feeling it
• trying to quell the loneliness.

quench, quenches, quenching,
quenched VERB If you quench your
thirst, you have a drink so that you
are no longer thirsty.

query, queries, querying, queried
[Said qweer-ree] NOUN ① a question.
▶ VERB ② If you query something,
you ask about it because you think it
might not be right • No-one queried my
decision.

quest, quests NOUN a long search for
something.

question, questions, questioning,
questioned NOUN ① a sentence
which asks for information. ② If
there is some question about
something, there is doubt about it.
③ a problem that needs to be
discussed • Can we get back to the
question of the car? ▶ VERB ④ If you
question someone, you ask them
questions. ⑤ If you question
something, you express doubts
about it • He never stopped questioning
his own beliefs. ▶ PHRASE ⑥ If
something is **out of the question**, it
is impossible.

SIMILAR WORDS: ① inquiry, query
⑤ challenge, dispute

What is a Question?

Questions are used to ask for information.

A question has a question mark at the end of the sentence:

What is your name?

Questions are often introduced by a questioning word such as *what*, *who*, *where*, *when*, *why* or *how*:

Where do you live?

If a sentence does not already contain an auxiliary verb, a form of the auxiliary verb *do* may be placed at the start to turn it into a question:

Does Anna have a sister?

If there is already an auxiliary verb in the sentence, you can turn it into a question by reversing the word order so the auxiliary verb comes before the subject instead of after it:

Are you going to the swimming baths?
Must they keep doing that?

A question can also be made by adding a phrase, such as *isn't it?* or *don't you?*, onto the end of a statement:

It is hot today, isn't it?
You like chocolate, don't you?

questionable ADJECTIVE possibly not true or not honest.

question mark, question marks NOUN the punctuation mark (?) which is used at the end of a question.

PUNCTUATION TIP
If a piece of direct speech ends in a question, you put the question mark inside the quotation marks: *Bob said, 'Did you get my message?'*.

questionnaire, questionnaires NOUN a list of questions which asks for information.

queue, queues, queuing or queueing, queued [*Said kyoo*] NOUN ① a line of people or vehicles waiting for something.

▸ VERB ② When people queue, they stand in a line waiting for something.

SPELLING TIP
Do not confuse the spellings of *queue* and *cue*: *a long queue at the bank*; *That's the lead singer's cue.*

quibble, quibbles, quibbling, quibbled VERB ① If you quibble, you argue about something unimportant. ▸ NOUN ② a minor objection.

quiche, quiches [*Said keesh*] NOUN a tart with a savoury filling.
WORD HISTORY: a French word, originally from German *Kuchen* meaning 'cake'

What does the Question Mark do?

The **question mark** (?) marks the end of a question:

When is the train leaving?

After an indirect question or a polite request, a full stop is used rather

than a question mark:

Anna asked when the train was leaving.
Will you please send me an application form.

a b c d e f g h i j k l m n o p q r s t u v w x y z

quick, quicker, quickest ADJECTIVE
① moving with great speed.
② lasting only a short time • *a quick chat*. ③ happening without any delay • *a quick response*. ④ intelligent and able to understand things easily.

quickly ADVERB with great speed.

quicksand, quicksands NOUN an area of deep wet sand that you sink into if you walk on it.

quid, quid NOUN (*informal*) In British English, a pound in money.

quiet, quieter, quietest ADJECTIVE
① Someone or something that is quiet makes very little noise or no noise at all. ② Quiet also means peaceful • *a quiet evening at home*. ③ A quiet event happens with very little fuss or publicity • *a quiet wedding*.
▶ NOUN ④ Quiet is silence. **quietly** ADVERB **quietness** NOUN

SPELLING TIP
Do not confuse the spellings of *quiet* and the adverb *quite*.

quieten, quietens, quietening, quietened VERB To quieten someone means to make them become quiet.

quill, quills NOUN ① a pen made from a feather. ② A bird's quills are the large feathers on its wings and tail. ③ A porcupine's quills are its spines.

quilt, quilts NOUN A quilt for a bed is a cover, especially a cover that is padded.

quilted ADJECTIVE Quilted clothes or coverings are made of thick layers of material sewn together.

quin, quins NOUN (*informal*) Quin is the same as **quintuplet**.

quince, quinces NOUN a sour-tasting fruit used for making jam and marmalade.

quinoa [*Said* keen-wah] NOUN Quinoa is a South American grain that contains a lot of nutrients.

quintessential ADJECTIVE
(*formal*) A person or thing that is quintessential seems to represent the basic nature of something in a pure, concentrated form • *It was the quintessential Hollywood party*.

quintet, quintets [*Said* kwin-**tet**] NOUN a group of five musicians who sing or play together; also a piece of music written for five instruments or singers.

quintuplet, quintuplets [*Said* kwin-**tyoo**-plit] NOUN Quintuplets are five children born at the same time to the same mother.

quip, quips, quipping, quipped NOUN ① an amusing or clever remark. ▶ VERB ② To quip means to make an amusing or clever remark.

quirk, quirks NOUN ① an odd habit or characteristic • *an interesting quirk of human nature*. ② an unexpected event or development • *a quirk of fate*. **quirky** ADJECTIVE

quit, quits, quitting, quit VERB If you quit something, you leave it or stop doing it • *Leigh quit his job as a salesman*.

quite ADVERB ① fairly but not very • *quite old*. ② completely • *Jane lay quite still*. ▶ PHRASE ③ You use **quite a** to emphasise that something is large or impressive • *It was quite a party*.

USAGE NOTE
You should be careful about using *quite*. It can mean 'completely': *quite amazing*. It can also mean 'fairly but not very': *quite friendly*.

SPELLING TIP
Do not confuse the spellings of *quite* and the adjective *quiet*.

quiver, quivers, quivering, quivered
VERB ① If something quivers, it
trembles. ▶ NOUN ② a trembling
movement • *a quiver of panic*.

quixotic *[Said kwik-sot-ik]* ADJECTIVE
unrealistic and romantic.

quiz, quizzes, quizzing, quizzed
NOUN ① a game in which the
competitors are asked questions to
test their knowledge. ▶ VERB ② If
you quiz someone, you question
them closely about something.

quizzical *[Said kwiz-ik-kl]* ADJECTIVE
amused and questioning • *a quizzical
smile*.

quota, quotas NOUN a number or
quantity of something which is
officially allowed • *a quota of three
foreign players allowed in each team*.

quotation, quotations NOUN an
extract from a book or speech which
is quoted.

quotation mark, quotation marks
NOUN Quotation marks are the
punctuation marks ('...' or "...") that
show where a speech or quotation
begins and ends.

PUNCTUATION TIP

When you use quotation marks to
show exactly what someone has
said, you put the comma,
exclamation mark or question
mark inside the quotation marks:
*'You're late!' cried Hashem. 'I'm really
sorry,' said Louis. 'What happened?'
asked Scott.*

quote, quotes, quoting, quoted
VERB ① If you quote something that
someone has written or said, you
repeat their exact words. ② If you
quote a fact, you state it because it
supports what you are saying. ③ To
quote for a piece of work means to

What is a Quotation?

There are two ways of writing what
people say. You can write down the
exact words that are spoken. This is
called **direct speech**. The second way
is to write down the meaning of
what they say without using the
exact words. This is called **indirect
speech** or **reported speech**.

When you use direct speech, the
exact words spoken go into
quotation marks:

*Robbie said, 'Thank you very much for
the prize.'*

The sentence will contain a main
verb which indicates speaking, such
as *say*, *tell*, *ask* or *answer*. The words
contained in quotation marks begin
with a capital letter. If there is no
other punctuation, they are
separated from the rest of the

sentence by a comma:

'This is the best picture,' said the judge.

When you use indirect or reported
speech, there is a subordinate
clause which reports the meaning
of what was said.

*The judge said **that Robbie's picture
was the best**.*

When the reported words are a
statement, the clause that reports
them is usually introduced by *that*.
The main clause usually contains a
verb such as *say*, *tell*, *explain* or *reply*:

*The judge said **that** Robbie should win
first prize.*

Sometimes the word *that* can be
left out.

*The judge said Robbie should win first
prize.*

a b c d e f g h i j k l m n o p **q** r s t u v w x y z

state what it would cost to do it.

▶ NOUN ④ an extract from a book or speech. ⑤ an estimate of how much a piece of work will cost.

quoth [*Said kwohth*] VERB (old-fashioned) Quoth means the same as 'said' • *Not I, quoth he.*

quotient, quotients [*Said kwoh-shent*] NOUN MATHS A quotient is the number that you get when you divide one number into another.

WORD HISTORY: from Latin *quotiens* meaning 'how often'

Qur'an another spelling of **Koran**.

Rr

RAAF In Australia, RAAF is an abbreviation for 'Royal Australian Air Force'.

rabbi, rabbis [Said *rab-by*] NOUN a Jewish religious leader.
WORD HISTORY: from Hebrew *rabh* + *-i* meaning 'my master'

rabbit, rabbits NOUN a small mammal with long ears.

rabble NOUN a noisy, disorderly crowd.

rabid ADJECTIVE ① used to describe someone with very strong views that you do not approve of • *a rabid Nazi*. ② A rabid dog or other animal has rabies.

rabies [Said *ray-beez*] NOUN an infectious disease which causes people and animals, especially dogs, to go mad and die.

raccoon, raccoons; also spelt **racoon** NOUN a small North American mammal with a long striped tail.

race, races, racing, raced NOUN ① a competition to see who is fastest, for example in running or driving. ② one of the major groups that human beings can be divided into according to their physical features. ▶ VERB ③ If you race someone, you compete with them in a race. ④ If you race something or if it races, it goes at its greatest rate • *Her heart raced uncontrollably*. ⑤ If you race somewhere, you go there as quickly as possible • *The hares raced away out of sight*. **racing** NOUN

racecourse, racecourses NOUN a grass track, sometimes with jumps, along which horses race.

racehorse, racehorses NOUN a horse trained to run in races.

racial ADJECTIVE relating to the different races that people belong to • *racial harmony*. **racially** ADVERB

racism or **racialism** NOUN Racism or racialism is the treatment of some people as inferior because of their race or skin colour. **racist** NOUN or ADJECTIVE

rack, racks, racking, racked NOUN ① a piece of equipment for holding things or hanging things on. ▶ VERB ② If you are racked by something, you suffer because of it • *She was racked by guilt*. ▶ PHRASE ③ (*informal*) If you **rack your brains**, you try hard to think of or remember something.

racket, rackets NOUN ① If someone is making a racket, they are making a lot of noise. ② an illegal way of making money • *a racket selling fake designer bags*. ③ Racket is another spelling of **racquet**.

racquet, racquets; also spelt **racket** NOUN a bat with strings across it used in tennis and similar games.
WORD HISTORY: from Arabic *rahat* meaning 'palm of the hand'

radar NOUN Radar is equipment used to track ships or aircraft that are out of sight by using radio signals that are reflected back from the object and shown on a screen.

WORD HISTORY: from RA(dio) D(etecting) A(nd) R(anging)

radiant ADJECTIVE ① Someone who is radiant is so happy that it shows in their face. ② glowing brightly. **radiance** NOUN

radiate, radiates, radiating, radiated VERB ① If things radiate from a place, they form a pattern like lines spreading out from the centre of a circle. ② If you radiate a quality or emotion, it shows clearly in your face and behaviour • He radiated health.

radiation NOUN SCIENCE the stream of particles given out by a radioactive substance.

radiator, radiators NOUN ① a hollow metal device for heating a room, usually connected to a central heating system. ② the part of a car that is filled with water to cool the engine.

radical, radicals NOUN ① Radicals are people who think there should be great changes in society, and try to make them happen. ▶ ADJECTIVE ② very significant, important or basic • a radical change in the law. **radically** ADVERB **radicalism** NOUN

radii the plural of radius.

radio, radios, radioing, radioed NOUN ① Radio is a system of sending sound over a distance by transmitting electrical signals. ② Radio is also the broadcasting of programmes to the public by radio. ③ a piece of equipment for listening to radio programmes. ▶ VERB ④ To radio someone means to send them a message by radio • The pilot radioed that a fire had started.

radioactive ADJECTIVE giving off powerful and harmful rays. **radioactivity** NOUN

radiotherapy NOUN the treatment of diseases such as cancer using radiation. **radiotherapist** NOUN

radish, radishes NOUN a small salad vegetable with a red skin and white flesh and a hot taste.

radium NOUN SCIENCE Radium is a radioactive element used in the treatment of cancer and other diseases. Its atomic number is 88 and its symbol is Ra. Radium was discovered in 1898 by Marie Curie.

radius, radii or radiuses NOUN MATHS The radius of a circle is the length of a straight line drawn from its centre to its circumference.

RAF In Britain, RAF is an abbreviation for 'Royal Air Force'.

raffia NOUN a material made from palm leaves and used for making mats and baskets.

raffle, raffles NOUN a competition in which people buy numbered tickets and win a prize if they have the ticket that is chosen.

raft, rafts NOUN a floating platform made from long pieces of wood tied together.

rafter, rafters NOUN Rafters are the sloping pieces of wood that support a roof.

rag, rags NOUN ① a piece of old cloth used to clean or wipe things. ② If someone is dressed in rags, they are wearing old torn clothes.

rage, rages, raging, raged NOUN ① Rage is great anger. ▶ VERB ② To rage about something means to speak angrily about it. ③ If something such as a storm or battle is raging, it is continuing with great force or violence • The fire still raged out of control.

SIMILAR WORDS: ① anger, fury, wrath

ragged ADJECTIVE ① Ragged clothes are old and torn.

raid, raids, raiding, raided VERB ① To raid a place means to enter it by force

to attack it or steal something.
▶ **NOUN** ② the raiding of a building or a place • *an armed raid on a bank.*

rail, rails **NOUN** ① a fixed horizontal bar used as a support or for hanging things on. ② Rails are the steel bars which trains run along. ③ Rail is the railway considered as a means of transport • *I plan to go by rail.*

railing, railings **NOUN** Railings are a fence made from metal bars.

railroad, railroads **NOUN** in American English, a railroad is a railway.

railway, railways **NOUN** a route along which trains travel on steel rails.

rain, rains, raining, rained **NOUN** ① water falling from the clouds in small drops. ▶ **VERB** ② When it is raining, rain is falling. **rainy** **ADJECTIVE**

SPELLING TIP
Do not confuse the spellings of *rain*, *rein* and *reign*: *The rain has finally stopped; Pull the reins sharply if you want to turn; the reign of King John.*

rainbird, rainbirds **NOUN** Especially in South African English, a rainbird is a bird whose call is believed to be a sign that it will rain.

rainbow, rainbows **NOUN** an arch of different colours that sometimes appears in the sky when it is raining.

raincoat, raincoats **NOUN** a waterproof coat.

rainfall **NOUN** the amount of rain that falls in a place during a particular period.

rainforest, rainforests **NOUN** GEOGRAPHY a dense forest of tall trees where there is a lot of rain.

rainwater **NOUN** rain that has been stored.

raise, raises, raising, raised **VERB** ① If you raise something, you make it higher • *She went to the window and raised the blinds* • *a drive to raise standards of literacy.* ② If you raise your voice, you speak more loudly. ③ To raise money for a cause means to get people to donate money towards it. ④ To raise a child means to look after it until it is grown up. ⑤ If you raise a subject, you mention it.

raisin, raisins **NOUN** Raisins are dried grapes.

rake, rakes, raking, raked **NOUN** a garden tool with a row of metal teeth and a long handle. **rake up** **VERB** If you rake up something embarrassing from the past, you remind someone about it.

rally, rallies, rallying, rallied **NOUN** ① a large public meeting held to show support for something. ② a competition in which vehicles are raced over public roads. ③ In tennis or squash, a rally is a continuous series of shots exchanged by the players. ▶ **VERB** ④ When people rally to something, they gather together to continue a struggle or to support something.

ram, rams, ramming, rammed **VERB** ① If one vehicle rams another, it crashes into it. ② To ram something somewhere means to push it there firmly • *He rammed his key into the lock.* ▶ **NOUN** ③ an adult male sheep.

RAM **NOUN** ICT a storage space which can be filled with data but which loses its contents when the machine is switched off. RAM stands for 'random access memory'.

Ramadan **NOUN** RE the ninth month of the Muslim year, during which Muslims eat and drink nothing during daylight.
WORD HISTORY: from Arabic *Ramadan* meaning literally 'the hot month'

a
b
c
d
e
f
g
h
i
j
k
l
m
n
o
p
q
r
s
t
u
v
w
x
y
z

ramble, rambles, rambling, rambled
NOUN ①a long walk in the
countryside. ▶VERB ②To ramble
means to go for a ramble. ③To
ramble also means to talk in a
confused way • *He then started
rambling and repeating himself.*
rambler NOUN

ramification, ramifications NOUN
The ramifications of a decision or
plan are all its consequences and
effects.

ramp, ramps NOUN a sloping surface
connecting two different levels.

rampage, rampages, rampaging,
rampaged VERB ①To rampage
means to rush about wildly causing
damage. ▶PHRASE ②To go **on the
rampage** means to rush about in a
wild or violent way.
SIMILAR WORDS: ① go berserk, run
amok

rampant ADJECTIVE If something
such as crime or disease is rampant,
it is growing or spreading
uncontrollably.

rampart, ramparts NOUN Ramparts
are earth banks, often with a wall on
top, built to protect a castle or city.

ramshackle ADJECTIVE A ramshackle
building is in very poor condition.

ran the past tense of **run**.

ranch, ranches NOUN a large farm
where cattle or horses are reared,
especially in the USA.
WORD HISTORY: from Mexican
Spanish *rancho* meaning 'small farm'

rancid [*Said ran-sid*] ADJECTIVE Rancid
food has gone bad.
WORD HISTORY: from Latin *rancere*
meaning 'to stink'

rancour [*Said rang-kur*] NOUN (*formal*)
Rancour is bitter hatred. **rancorous**
ADJECTIVE

rand NOUN The rand is the main unit
of currency in South Africa.

random ADJECTIVE ①A random
choice or arrangement is not based
on any definite plan. ▶PHRASE ②If
you do something **at random**, you do
it without any definite plan • *He chose
his victims at random.* **randomly**
ADVERB
SIMILAR WORDS: ① chance,
haphazard, incidental

rang the past tense of **ring**.

range, ranges, ranging, ranged
NOUN ①The range of something is
the maximum distance over which it
can reach things or detect things
• *This mortar has a range of 15,000
metres.* ②a number of different
things of the same kind • *A wide range
of colours are available.* ③a set of
values on a scale • *The average age
range is between 35 and 55.* ④A range of
mountains is a line of them. ⑤A rifle
range or firing range is a place where
people practise shooting at targets.
▶VERB ⑥When a set of things ranges
between two points, they vary
within these points on a scale • *prices
ranging between £370 and £1200.*
SIMILAR WORDS: ② series, variety

ranger, rangers NOUN someone
whose job is to look after a forest or
park.

rank, ranks, ranking, ranked NOUN
①Someone's rank is their official
level in a job or profession. ②The
ranks are the ordinary members of
the armed forces, rather than the
officers. ③The ranks of a group are
its members • *We welcomed five new
members to our ranks.* ④a row of
people or things. ▶VERB ⑤To rank as
something means to have that
status or position on a scale • *His
dismissal ranks as the worst humiliation
he has ever known.* ▶ADJECTIVE
⑥complete and absolute • *rank
stupidity.* ⑦having a strong,
unpleasant smell • *the rank smell of
unwashed clothes.*

ransack, ransacks, ransacking, ransacked VERB To ransack a place means to disturb everything and leave it in a mess, in order to search for or steal something.
WORD HISTORY: from Old Norse *rann* meaning 'house' and *saka* meaning 'to search'

ransom, ransoms NOUN money that is demanded to free someone who has been kidnapped.

rant, rants, ranting, ranted VERB To rant means to talk loudly in an excited or angry way.

rap, raps, rapping, rapped VERB ① If you rap something, you hit it with a series of quick blows. ▶ NOUN ② a quick knock or blow on something • *A rap on the door signalled his arrival.* ③ Rap is a style of poetry spoken to music with a strong rhythmic beat.

SPELLING TIP

Do not confuse the spellings of *rap* and *wrap*: *The teacher rapped the table with a ruler; I have wrapped all my Christmas presents.*

---

rape, rapes, raping, raped VERB ① If someone is raped, they are forced to have sex against their will. ▶ NOUN ② Rape is the act or crime of raping someone. ③ Rape is a plant with yellow flowers that is grown as a crop for oil and fodder. **rapist** NOUN

rapid ADJECTIVE happening or moving very quickly • *rapid industrial expansion* • *He took a few rapid steps.* **rapidly** ADVERB **rapidity** NOUN

rapids PLURAL NOUN An area of a river where the water moves extremely fast over rocks is referred to as rapids.

rapier, rapiers NOUN a long, thin sword with a sharp point.

rapport [Said rap-por] NOUN (formal) If there is a rapport between two people, they find it easy to understand each other's feelings and attitudes.

rapt ADJECTIVE If you are rapt, you are so interested in something that you are not aware of other things • *sitting with rapt attention in front of the screen.*

rapture NOUN Rapture is a feeling of extreme delight. **rapturous** ADJECTIVE **rapturously** ADVERB

rare, rarer, rarest ADJECTIVE ① Something that is rare is not common or does not happen often • *a rare flower* • *Such major disruptions are rare.* ② Rare meat has been lightly cooked. **rarely** ADVERB

rarefied [Said rare-if-eyed] ADJECTIVE seeming to have little connection with ordinary life • *He grew up in a rarefied literary atmosphere.*

raring ADJECTIVE If you are raring to do something, you are very eager to do it.

rarity, rarities NOUN ① something that is interesting or valuable because it is unusual. ② The rarity of something is the fact that it is not common.

rascal, rascals NOUN If you refer to someone as a rascal, you mean that they do bad or mischievous things.

rash, rashes ADJECTIVE ① If you are rash, you do something hasty and foolish. ▶ NOUN ② an area of red spots that appear on your skin when you are ill or have an allergy. ③ A rash of events is a lot of them happening in a short time • *a rash of strikes.*
rashly ADVERB
SIMILAR WORDS: ① foolhardy, reckless

rasher, rashers NOUN a thin slice of bacon.

rasp, rasps, rasping, rasped VERB ① To rasp means to make a harsh unpleasant sound. ▶ NOUN ② a coarse file with rows of raised teeth, used for smoothing wood or metal.

raspberry, **raspberries** NOUN a small, red soft fruit that grows on a bush.

Rasta, **Rastas** NOUN or ADJECTIVE short for Rastafarian.

Rastafarian, **Rastafarians** NOUN ① a member of a religious group of Jamaican origin that regards Ras Tafari, the former emperor of Ethiopia, as God. ▶ ADJECTIVE ② of or relating to Rastafarians.

rat, **rats** NOUN a long-tailed animal which looks like a large mouse.

rate, **rates**, **rating**, **rated** NOUN ① The rate of something is the speed or frequency with which it happens • New diet books appear at the rate of nearly one a week. ② The rate of interest is its level • a further cut in interest rates. ③ the cost or charge for something. ④ In some countries, rates are a local tax paid by people who own buildings. ▶ PHRASE ⑤ If you say **at this rate** something will happen, you mean it will happen if things continue in the same way • At this rate we'll be lucky to get home before six. ⑥ You say **at any rate** when you want to add to or amend what you have just said • He is the least appealing character, to me at any rate. ▶ VERB ⑦ The way you rate someone or something is your opinion of them • He was rated as one of England's top young players.

rather ADVERB ① Rather means to a certain extent • We got along rather well • The reality is rather more complex. ▶ PHRASE ② If you **would rather** do a particular thing, you would prefer to do it. ③ If you do one thing **rather than** another, you choose to do the first thing instead of the second.

SIMILAR WORDS: ① quite, relatively, somewhat ② preferably, sooner

ratify, **ratifies**, **ratifying**, **ratified** VERB (formal) To ratify a written agreement means to approve it formally, usually by signing it.
ratification NOUN

rating, **ratings** NOUN ① a score based on the quality or status of something. ② The ratings are statistics showing how popular each television programme is.

ratio, **ratios** NOUN ① a relationship which shows how many times one thing is bigger than another • The adult to child ratio is 1 to 6. ② MATHS a relationship between two numbers, which shows how many times one number goes into another • The ratio of 1 to 6 is shown as 1:6.

ration, **rations**, **rationing**, **rationed** NOUN ① Your ration of something is the amount you are allowed to have. ② Rations are the food given each day to a soldier or member of an expedition. ▶ VERB ③ When something is rationed, you are only allowed a limited amount of it, because there is a shortage.

rational ADJECTIVE When people are rational, their judgments are based on reason rather than emotion.
rationally ADVERB **rationality** NOUN

rationale [Said rash-on-nahl] NOUN The rationale for a course of action or for a belief is the set of reasons on which it is based.

rattle, **rattles**, **rattling**, **rattled** VERB ① When something rattles, it makes short, regular knocking sounds. ② If something rattles you, it upsets you • He was obviously rattled by events. ▶ NOUN ③ the noise something makes when it rattles. ④ a baby's toy which makes a noise when it is shaken.

rattlesnake, **rattlesnakes** NOUN a poisonous American snake.

raucous [Said *raw-kuss*] ADJECTIVE A raucous voice is loud and rough.

ravage, ravages, ravaging, ravaged (*formal*) VERB ① To ravage something means to seriously harm or damage it • *a country ravaged by floods.* ▶ NOUN ② The ravages of something are its damaging effects • *the ravages of two world wars.*

rave, raves, raving, raved VERB ① If someone raves, they talk in an angry, uncontrolled way • *He started raving about being treated badly.* ② (*informal*) If you rave about something, you talk about it very enthusiastically. ▶ ADJECTIVE ③ (*informal*) If something gets a rave review, it is praised enthusiastically. ▶ NOUN ④ (*informal*) a large party with electronic dance music.

raven, ravens NOUN ① a large black bird with a deep, harsh call. ▶ ADJECTIVE ② Raven hair is black and shiny.

ravenous ADJECTIVE very hungry.

ravine, ravines NOUN a deep, narrow valley with steep sides.

raving, ravings ADJECTIVE ① If someone is raving, they are speaking in a strange, wild way. ▶ NOUN ② Someone's ravings are strange things they write or say.

ravioli [Said *rav-ee-oh-lee*] NOUN Ravioli consists of small squares of pasta filled with meat or other ingredients and served with a sauce.

ravishing ADJECTIVE Someone or something that is ravishing is very beautiful • *a ravishing landscape.*

raw ADJECTIVE ① Raw food has not been cooked. ② A raw substance is in its natural state • *raw sugar.* ③ If part of your body is raw, the skin has come off or been rubbed away. ④ Someone who is raw is too young or too new in a situation to know how to behave.

raw material, raw materials NOUN Raw materials are the natural substances used to make something.

ray, rays NOUN ① a beam of light or radiation. ② A ray of hope is a small amount that makes an unpleasant situation seem slightly better. ③ a large sea fish with eyes on the top of its body, and a long tail.

raze, razes, razing, razed VERB To raze a building, town or forest means to completely destroy it • *The town was razed to the ground during the occupation.*

razor, razors NOUN a tool that people use for shaving.

razor blade, razor blades NOUN a small, sharp, flat piece of metal fitted into a razor for shaving.

re- PREFIX ① 'Re-' is used to form nouns and verbs that refer to the repetition of an action or process • *reread* • *remarry.* ② 'Re-' is also used to form verbs that refer to going back to a previous condition • *refresh* • *renew.*

WORD HISTORY: from a Latin prefix

reach, reaches, reaching, reached VERB ① When you reach a place, you arrive there. ② When you reach for something, you stretch out your arm to it. ③ If something reaches a place or point, it extends as far as that place or point • *She has a cloak that reaches to the ground.* ④ If something or someone reaches a stage or level, they get to it • *Unemployment has reached record levels.* ⑤ To reach an agreement or decision means to succeed in achieving it. ▶ PHRASE ⑥ If a place is **within reach**, you can get there • *a cycle route well within reach of most people.* ⑦ If something is **out of reach**, you cannot get it to it by stretching out your arm • *Store out of reach of children.*

react, reacts, reacting, reacted VERB
When you react to something, you behave in a particular way because of it • *He reacted badly to the news.*

reactant, reactants NOUN SCIENCE
In a chemical reaction, a reactant is a substance that reacts with another one.

reaction, reactions NOUN ① Your reaction to something is what you feel, say or do because of it • *Reaction to the visit is mixed.* ② Your reactions are your ability to move quickly in response to something that happens • *Squash requires fast reactions.* ③ If there is a reaction against something, it becomes unpopular • *a reaction against the government.* ④ SCIENCE In a chemical reaction, a chemical change takes place when two substances are put together.

reactionary, reactionaries ADJECTIVE ① Someone who is reactionary tries to prevent political or social change. ▸ NOUN ② Reactionaries are reactionary people.

reactive ADJECTIVE SCIENCE a chemical substance that is reactive will react readily with another. **reactivity** NOUN

reactor, reactors NOUN a device which is used to produce nuclear energy.

read, reads, reading, read VERB ① When you read, you look at something written and follow it or say it aloud. ② If you can read someone's moods or mind, you can judge what they are feeling or thinking. ③ When you read a meter or gauge, you look at it and record the figure on it. ④ If you read a subject at university, you study it.

reader, readers NOUN ① The readers of a newspaper or magazine are the people who read it regularly. ② At a university, a reader is a senior lecturer just below the rank of professor.

readership NOUN The readership of a newspaper or magazine consists of the people who read it regularly.

readily ADVERB ① willingly and eagerly • *She readily agreed to see Alex.* ② easily done or quickly obtainable • *Help is readily available.*

reading, readings NOUN ① Reading is the activity of reading books. ② The reading on a meter or gauge is the figure or measurement it shows.

readjust, readjusts, readjusting, readjusted [Said ree-aj-*just*] VERB ① If you readjust, you adapt to a new situation. ② If you readjust something, you alter it to a different position.

ready ADJECTIVE ① having reached the required stage, or prepared for action or use • *In a few days' time the plums will be ready to eat.* ② willing or eager to do something • *She says she's not ready for university.* ③ easily produced or obtained • *ready cash.* **readiness** NOUN

ready-made ADJECTIVE already made and therefore able to be used immediately.

reaffirm, reaffirms, reaffirming, reaffirmed VERB To reaffirm something means to state it again • *He reaffirmed his support for the campaign.*

real ADJECTIVE ① actually existing and not imagined or invented. ② genuine and not imitation • *Who's to know if they're real diamonds?* ③ true or actual and not mistaken • *This was the real reason for her call.*
SIMILAR WORDS: ① authentic, genuine, true

real estate NOUN Real estate is

property in the form of land and buildings rather than personal possessions.

realise, realises, realising, realised; also spelt **realize** VERB ① If you realise something, you become aware of it. ② (*formal*) If your hopes or fears are realised, what you hoped for or feared actually happens • *Our worst fears were realised.* ③ To realise a sum of money means to receive it as a result of selling goods or shares. **realisation** NOUN

realism NOUN Realism is the recognition of the true nature of a situation • *a triumph of muddled thought over realism and common sense.* **realist** NOUN

realistic ADJECTIVE ① recognising and accepting the true nature of a situation. ② representing things in a way that is true to real life • *His novels are more realistic than his short stories.* **realistically** ADVERB

reality NOUN ① Reality is the real nature of things, rather than the way someone imagines it • *Fiction and reality were increasingly blurred.* ② If something has become reality, it actually exists or is actually happening.
SIMILAR WORDS: ① fact, truth

really ADVERB ① used to add emphasis to what is being said • *I'm not really surprised.* ② used to indicate that you are talking about the true facts about something • *What was really going on?*

GRAMMAR TIP
If you want to emphasise an adjective, you should always use *really* rather than *real*: *really interesting*.

---

realm, realms [*Said* realm] NOUN (*formal*) ① You can refer to any area of thought or activity as a realm • *the*

realm of politics. ② a country with a king or queen • *defence of the realm.*

reap, reaps, reaping, reaped VERB ① To reap a crop such as corn means to cut and gather it. ② When people reap benefits or rewards, they get them as a result of hard work or careful planning. **reaper** NOUN

reappear, reappears, reappearing, reappeared VERB When people or things reappear, you can see them again, because they have come back • *The stolen ring reappeared three years later in a pawn shop.* **reappearance** NOUN

reappraisal, reappraisals NOUN (*formal*) If there is a reappraisal, people think about something and decide whether they want to change it • *a reappraisal of the government's economic policies.*

rear, rears, rearing, reared NOUN ① The rear of something is the part at the back. ▶ VERB ② To rear children or young animals means to bring them up until they are able to look after themselves. ③ When a horse rears, it raises the front part of its body, so that its front legs are in the air.

rear admiral, rear admirals NOUN a senior officer in the navy.

rearrange, rearranges, rearranging, rearranged VERB To rearrange something means to organise or arrange it in a different way.

reason, reasons, reasoning, reasoned NOUN ① The reason for something is the fact or situation which explains why it happens or which causes it to happen. ② If you have reason to believe or feel something, there are definite reasons why you believe it or feel it • *He had every reason to be upset.*

a
b
c
d
e
f
g
h
i
j
k
l
m
n
o
p
q
r
s
t
u
v
w
x
y
z

③ Reason is the ability to think and make judgments. ▶ **VERB** ④ If you reason that something is true, you decide it is true after considering all the facts. ⑤ If you reason with someone, you persuade them to accept sensible arguments.

SIMILAR WORDS: ① cause, motive ③ rationality, sense, senses, understanding

reasonable **ADJECTIVE**
① Reasonable behaviour is fair and sensible. ② If an explanation is reasonable, there are good reasons for thinking it is correct. ③ A reasonable amount is a fairly large amount. ④ A reasonable price is fair and not too high. **reasonably** **ADVERB**

reasoning **NOUN** Reasoning is the process by which you reach a conclusion after considering all the facts.

reassess, reassesses, reassessing, reassessed **VERB** If you reassess something, you consider whether it still has the same value or importance. **reassessment** **NOUN**

reassure, reassures, reassuring, reassured **VERB** If you reassure someone, you say or do things that make them less worried.
reassurance **NOUN**

rebate, rebates **NOUN** money paid back to someone who has paid too much tax or rent.

rebel, rebels, rebelling, rebelled **NOUN** [Said reb-l] ① HISTORY Rebels are people who are fighting their own country's army to change the political system. ② Someone who is a rebel rejects society's values and behaves differently from other people. ▶ **VERB** [Said ri-bel] ③ To rebel means to fight against authority or reject accepted values.

rebellion, rebellions **NOUN** HISTORY A rebellion is organised and often violent opposition to authority.
SIMILAR WORDS: mutiny, revolution, uprising

rebellious **ADJECTIVE** unwilling to obey and likely to rebel against authority.

rebound, rebounds, rebounding, rebounded **VERB** When something rebounds, it bounces or springs back after hitting a solid surface.

rebuff, rebuffs, rebuffing, rebuffed **VERB** ① If you rebuff someone, you reject what they offer • She rebuffed their offers of help. ▶ **NOUN** ② a rejection of an offer.

rebuild, rebuilds, rebuilding, rebuilt **VERB** When a town or building is rebuilt, it is built again after being damaged or destroyed.

rebuke, rebukes, rebuking, rebuked [Said rib-yook] **VERB** To rebuke someone means to speak severely to them about something they have done.

recall, recalls, recalling, recalled **VERB** ① To recall something means to remember it. ② If you are recalled to a place, you are ordered to return there. ③ If a company recalls products, it asks people to return them because they are faulty.

recap, recaps, recapping, recapped **VERB** ① To recap means to repeat and summarise the main points of an explanation or discussion. ▶ **NOUN** ② a summary of the main points of an explanation or discussion.

recapture, recaptures, recapturing, recaptured **VERB** ① When you recapture a pleasant feeling, you experience it again • She may never recapture that past assurance. ② When soldiers recapture a place, they capture it from the people who took it from them. ③When animals or prisoners are recaptured, they are caught after they have escaped.

recede, recedes, receding, receded VERB ①When something recedes, it moves away into the distance. ②If a man's hair is receding, he is starting to go bald at the front.

receipt, receipts [Said ris-*seet*] NOUN ①a piece of paper confirming that money or goods have been received. ②In a shop or theatre, the money received is often called the receipts • *Box-office receipts were down last month.* ③(formal) The receipt of something is the receiving of it • *You have to sign here and acknowledge receipt.*

receive, receives, receiving, received VERB ①When you receive something, someone gives it to you, or you get it after it has been sent to you. ②To receive something also means to have it happen to you • *injuries she received in a car crash.* ③When you receive visitors or guests, you welcome them. ④If something is received in a particular way, that is how people react to it • *The decision has been received with great disappointment.*

receiver, receivers NOUN the part of a telephone you hold near to your ear and mouth.

recent ADJECTIVE Something recent happened a short time ago. **recently** ADVERB

reception, receptions NOUN ①In a hotel or office, reception is the place near the entrance where appointments or enquiries are dealt with. ②a formal party. ③The reception someone or something gets is the way people react to them • *Her tour met with a rapturous reception.* ④If your radio or television gets good reception, the sound or picture is clear.

receptionist, receptionists NOUN The receptionist in a hotel or office deals with people when they arrive, answers the telephone, and arranges appointments.

receptive ADJECTIVE Someone who is receptive to ideas or suggestions is willing to consider them.

recess, recesses NOUN ①a period when no work is done by a committee or parliament • *the Christmas recess.* ②a place where part of a wall has been built further back than the rest.

recession, recessions NOUN a period when a country's economy is less successful and more people become unemployed.

recessive ADJECTIVE [SCIENCE] A recessive gene produces a particular characteristic only if a person has two of these genes, one from each parent.

recharge, recharges, recharging, recharged VERB To recharge a battery means to charge it with electricity again after it has been used.

recipe, recipes [Said *res*-sip-ee] NOUN ①[DGT] a list of ingredients and instructions for cooking something. ②If something is a recipe for disaster or for success, it is likely to result in disaster or success.

recipient, recipients NOUN The recipient of something is the person receiving it.

reciprocal ADJECTIVE ①A reciprocal agreement involves two people, groups or countries helping each other in a similar way • *a reciprocal agreement on trade.* ▶ NOUN ②[MATHS] If one number is the reciprocal of another number, the two numbers give a product of 1 when they are multiplied together • *The reciprocal of 2 is 0.5.*

A
B
C
D
E
F
G
H
I
J
K
L
M
N
O
P
Q
R
S
T
U
V
W
X
Y
Z

reciprocate, reciprocates, reciprocating, **reciprocated** VERB If you reciprocate someone's feelings or behaviour, you feel or behave in the same way towards them.

recital, recitals NOUN a performance of music or poetry, usually by one person.

recite, recites, reciting, recited VERB If you recite a poem or something you have learnt, you say it aloud. **recitation** NOUN

reckless ADJECTIVE showing a complete lack of care about danger or damage • a reckless tackle. **recklessly** ADVERB **recklessness** NOUN

reckon, reckons, reckoning, reckoned VERB ① (informal) If you reckon that something is true, you think it is true • I reckoned he was still fond of her. ② (informal) If someone reckons to do something, they claim or expect to do it • Officers on the case are reckoning to charge someone shortly. ③ To reckon an amount means to calculate it. ④ If you reckon on something, you rely on it happening when making your plans • He reckons on being world champion. ⑤ If you had not reckoned with something, you had not expected it and therefore were unprepared when it happened • Giles had not reckoned with the strength of Sally's feelings.

reckoning, reckonings NOUN a calculation • There were a thousand or so, by my reckoning.

reclaim, reclaims, reclaiming, reclaimed VERB ① When you reclaim something, you collect it after leaving it somewhere or losing it. ② To reclaim land means to make it suitable for use, for example by draining it. **reclamation** NOUN

recline, reclines, reclining, reclined VERB To recline means to lie or lean back at an angle • a photo of him reclining on his bed.

recluse, recluses NOUN Someone who is a recluse lives alone and avoids other people. **reclusive** ADJECTIVE

recognise, recognises, recognising, recognised; also spelt **recognize** VERB ① If you recognise someone or something, you realise that you know who or what they are • The receptionist recognised me at once. ② To recognise something also means to accept and acknowledge it • The RAF recognised him as an outstanding pilot. **recognition** NOUN **recognisable** ADJECTIVE **recognisably** ADVERB SIMILAR WORDS: ① identify, know, place

recoil, recoils, recoiling, recoiled VERB To recoil from something means to draw back in shock or horror.

recommend, recommends, recommending, recommended VERB If you recommend something to someone, you praise it and suggest they try it. **recommendation** NOUN

reconcile, reconciles, reconciling, reconciled VERB ① To reconcile two things that seem to oppose one another, means to make them work or exist together successfully • The designs reconciled style with comfort. ② When people are reconciled, they become friendly again after a quarrel. ③ If you reconcile yourself to an unpleasant situation, you accept it. **reconciliation** NOUN

reconnaissance [Said rik-kon-iss-sanss] NOUN Reconnaissance is the gathering of military information by soldiers, planes or satellites.

reconsider, reconsiders, reconsidering, reconsidered VERB To reconsider something means to think about it again to decide whether to change it.

reconsideration NOUN

reconstruct, reconstructs, reconstructing, reconstructed VERB ① To reconstruct something that has been damaged means to build it again. ② To reconstruct a past event means to get a complete description of it from small pieces of information. **reconstruction** NOUN

record, records, recording, recorded NOUN [Said **rek**-ord] ① If you keep a record of something, you keep a written account or store information in a computer • *medical records*. ② a round, flat piece of plastic on which music has been recorded. ③ an achievement which is the best of its type. ④ Your record is what is known about your achievements or past activities • *He had a distinguished war record.* ▶ VERB [Said ri-**kord**] ⑤ If you record information, you write it down or put it into a computer. ⑥ To record sound means to preserve it on tape or disc, or digitally. ▶ ADJECTIVE [Said **rek**-ord] ⑦ higher, lower, better or worse than ever before • *Profits were at a record level.*

SIMILAR WORDS: ① document, file, register ⑤ note, register, write down

recorder, recorders NOUN a small woodwind instrument.

recording, recordings NOUN A recording of something is a tape, disc etc of it.

recount, recounts, recounting, recounted VERB [Said ri-**kownt**] ① If you recount a story, you tell it. ▶ NOUN [Said **ree**-kownt] ② a second count of votes in an election when the result is very close.

recoup, recoups, recouping, recouped [Said rik-**koop**] VERB If you recoup money that you have spent or lost, you get it back.

recourse NOUN (*formal*) If you have recourse to something, you use it to help you • *The members settled their differences without recourse to war.*

recover, recovers, recovering, recovered VERB ① To recover from an illness or unhappy experience means to get well again or get over it. ② If you recover a lost object or your ability to do something, you get it back.

SIMILAR WORDS: ① convalesce, get better, recuperate ② regain, retrieve

recovery NOUN ① the act of getting better again. ② the act of getting something back.

recreate, recreates, recreating, recreated VERB To recreate something means to succeed in making it happen or exist again • *a museum that faithfully recreates an old farmhouse.*

recreation, recreations [Said rek-kree-**ay**-shn] NOUN Recreation is all the things that you do for enjoyment in your spare time. **recreational** ADJECTIVE

recrimination, recriminations NOUN Recriminations are accusations made by people about each other.

recruit, recruits, recruiting, recruited VERB ① To recruit people means to get them to join a group or help with something. ▶ NOUN ② someone who has joined the army or some other organisation. **recruitment** NOUN

rectangle, rectangles NOUN MATHS a four-sided shape with four right angles. **rectangular** ADJECTIVE

rectify, rectifies, rectifying, rectified VERB (*formal*) If you rectify something that is wrong, you put it right.

rector, rectors NOUN a Church of England priest in charge of a parish.

a b c d e f g h i j k l m n o p q r s t u v w x y z

rectory, rectories NOUN a house where a rector lives.

rectum, rectums NOUN (*technical*) the bottom end of the tube down which waste food passes out of your body. **rectal** ADJECTIVE

recuperate, recuperates, recuperating, recuperated VERB When you recuperate, you gradually recover after being ill or injured. **recuperation** NOUN

recur, recurs, recurring, recurred VERB If something recurs, it happens or occurs again • *His hamstring injury recurred after the first game.* **recurrence** NOUN **recurrent** ADJECTIVE

recurring ADJECTIVE ① happening or occurring many times • *a recurring dream.* ② MATHS A recurring digit is one that is repeated over and over again after the decimal point.

recycle, recycles, recycling, recycled VERB GEOGRAPHY To recycle used products means to process them so that they can be used again • *recycled glass.*

red, redder, reddest; reds NOUN or ADJECTIVE ① Red is the colour of blood or of a ripe tomato.
▶ ADJECTIVE ② Red hair is between red and brown in colour.

redback, redbacks NOUN a small Australian spider with a poisonous bite.

red blood cell, red blood cells NOUN SCIENCE Your red blood cells are the cells in your blood that carry oxygen, carbon dioxide and haemoglobin to and from your tissues.

redcurrant, redcurrants NOUN Redcurrants are very small, bright red fruits that grow in bunches on a bush.

redeem, redeems, redeeming, redeemed VERB ① If a feature redeems an unpleasant thing or situation, it makes it seem less bad. ② If you redeem yourself, you do something that gives people a good opinion of you again. ③ If you redeem something, you get it back by paying for it. ④ RE In Christianity, Jesus Christ is said to have redeemed the human race by paying the price of his life to save them from sin and death.

redemption NOUN Redemption is the state of being redeemed.

red giant, red giants NOUN SCIENCE In astronomy, a red giant is a large star that is coming towards the end of its life and emits red light.

red-handed PHRASE To catch someone red-handed means to catch them doing something wrong.

red-hot ADJECTIVE Red-hot metal has been heated to such a high temperature that it has turned red.

redress, redresses, redressing, redressed (*formal*) VERB ① To redress a wrong means to put it right.
▶ NOUN ② If you get redress for harm done to you, you are compensated for it.

red tape NOUN Red tape is official rules and procedures that seem unnecessary and cause delay. In the 18th century, red tape was used to bind official government documents.

reduce, reduces, reducing, reduced VERB ① To reduce something means to make it smaller in size or amount. ② You can use 'reduce' to say that someone or something is changed to a weaker or inferior state • *She reduced them to tears* • *The village was reduced to rubble.*
SIMILAR WORDS: ① cut, decrease, lessen

reduction, reductions NOUN When there is a reduction in something, it is made smaller.

redundancy, redundancies NOUN
① Redundancy is the state of being redundant. ② The number of redundancies is the number of people made redundant.

redundant ADJECTIVE ① When people are made redundant, they lose their jobs because there is no more work for them or no money to pay them. ② When something becomes redundant, it is no longer needed.

reed, reeds NOUN ① Reeds are hollow stemmed plants that grow in shallow water or wet ground. ② a thin piece of cane or metal inside some wind instruments which vibrates when air is blown over it.

reef, reefs NOUN GEOGRAPHY a long line of rocks or coral close to the surface of the sea.

reek, reeks, reeking, reeked VERB ① To reek of something means to smell strongly and unpleasantly of it. ▸ NOUN ② If there is a reek of something, there is a strong unpleasant smell of it.

reel, reels, reeling, reeled NOUN ① a cylindrical object around which you wrap something; often part of a device which you turn as a control. ② a fast Scottish dance. ▸ VERB ③ When someone reels, they move unsteadily as if they are going to fall. ④ If your mind is reeling, you are confused because you have too much to think about. **reel off** VERB If you reel off information, you repeat it from memory quickly and easily.

re-elect, re-elects, re-electing, re-elected VERB When someone is re-elected, they win an election again and are able to stay in power.

refer, refers, referring, referred VERB ① If you refer to something, you mention it. ② If you refer to a book or record, you look at it to find something out. ③ When a problem or issue is referred to someone, they are formally asked to deal with it
• *The case was referred to the European Court*.

WORD HISTORY: from Latin *referre* meaning 'to carry back'

GRAMMAR TIP
The word *refer* contains the sense 'back' in its meaning. Therefore, you should not use *back* after *refer*: *This refers to what has already been said*, not *refers back*.

referee, referees NOUN ① the official who controls a football game or a boxing or wrestling match. ② someone who gives a reference to a person who is applying for a job.

reference, references NOUN ① A reference to something or someone is a mention of them. ② Reference is the act of referring to something or someone for information or advice
• *He makes that decision without reference to her*. ③ a number or name that tells you where to find information or identifies a document. ④ If someone gives you a reference when you apply for a job, they write a letter about your abilities.

referendum, referendums or referenda NOUN a vote in which all the people in a country are officially asked whether they agree with a policy or proposal.

refine, refines, refining, refined VERB To refine a raw material such as oil or sugar means to process it to remove impurities.

refined ADJECTIVE ① very polite and well-mannered. ② processed to remove impurities.

refinement, refinements NOUN ① Refinements are minor

improvements. ②Refinement is politeness and good manners.

refinery, refineries NOUN a factory where substances such as oil or sugar are refined.

reflect, reflects, reflecting, reflected VERB ① If something reflects an attitude or situation, it shows what it is like • *His off-duty hobbies reflected his maritime interests*. ② If something reflects light or heat, the light or heat bounces off it. ③When something is reflected in a mirror or water, you can see its image in it. ④ MATHS If something reflects, its direction is reversed. ⑤When you reflect, you think about something. **reflective** ADJECTIVE **reflectively** ADVERB

reflection, reflections NOUN ① If something is a reflection of something else, it shows what it is like • *This is a terrible reflection of the times*. ② an image in a mirror or water. ③ SCIENCE Reflection is the process by which light and heat are bounced off a surface. ④ MATHS In maths, reflection is also the turning back of something on itself • *reflection of an axis*. ⑤ Reflection is also thought • *After days of reflection she decided to leave*.

reflex, reflexes NOUN ① A reflex or reflex action is a sudden uncontrollable movement that you make as a result of pressure or a blow. ② If you have good reflexes, you respond very quickly when something unexpected happens. ▶ ADJECTIVE ③ MATHS A reflex angle is between 180° and 360°.

reflexive ADJECTIVE ENGLISH MFL In grammar, a reflexive verb or pronoun is one that refers back to the subject of the sentence. For example, *She washed herself*.

reform, reforms, reforming, reformed NOUN ① Reforms are major changes to laws or institutions • *a programme of economic reform*. ▶ VERB ②When laws or institutions are reformed, major changes are made to them. ③When people reform, they stop committing crimes or doing other unacceptable things. **reformer** NOUN

Reformation NOUN HISTORY The Reformation was a religious and political movement in Europe in the 16th century that began as an attempt to reform the Roman Catholic Church, but ended in the establishment of the Protestant Churches.

refraction NOUN SCIENCE Refraction is the bending of a ray of light, for example when it enters water or glass.

refrain, refrains, refraining, refrained VERB ① (*formal*) If you refrain from doing something, you do not do it • *Please refrain from running in the corridors*. ▶ NOUN ② MUSIC The refrain of a song is a short, simple part, repeated after each verse.

refresh, refreshes, refreshing, refreshed VERB ① If something refreshes you when you are hot or tired, it makes you feel cooler or more energetic • *A glass of fruit juice will refresh you*. ▶ PHRASE ②To **refresh someone's memory** means to remind them of something they had forgotten.

refreshing ADJECTIVE You say that something is refreshing when it is pleasantly different from what you are used to • *She is a refreshing contrast to her father*.

refreshment, refreshments NOUN Refreshments are drinks and small amounts of food provided at an event.

refrigerator, refrigerators NOUN an electrically cooled container in which you store food to keep it fresh.

refuel, refuels, refuelling, refuelled VERB When an aircraft or vehicle is refuelled, it is filled with more fuel.

refuge, refuges NOUN ① a place where you go for safety. ② If you take refuge, you go somewhere for safety or behave in a way that will protect you • *They took refuge in a bomb shelter* • *Father Rowan took refuge in silence.*
SIMILAR WORDS: ① haven, sanctuary, shelter

refugee, refugees NOUN Refugees are people who have been forced to leave their country and live elsewhere.

refund, refunds, refunding, refunded NOUN [Said re-fund] ① money returned to you because you have paid too much for something or because you have returned goods. ▶VERB [Said re-fund] ② To refund someone's money means to return it to them after they have paid for something with it.

refurbish, refurbishes, refurbishing, refurbished VERB (formal) To refurbish a building means to decorate it and repair damage.
refurbishment NOUN

refusal, refusals NOUN A refusal is when someone says firmly that they will not do, allow or accept something.

refuse¹, refuses, refusing, refused [Said rif-*yooz*] VERB ① If you refuse to do something, you say or decide firmly that you will not do it. ② If someone refuses something, they do not allow it or do not accept it • *The United States has refused him a visa* • *He offered me a second drink which I refused.*

refuse² [Said *ref-yoos*] NOUN Refuse is rubbish or waste.

refute, refutes, refuting, refuted VERB (formal) To refute a theory or argument means to prove that it is wrong.

USAGE NOTE
Refute does not mean the same as *deny*. If you *refute* something, you provide evidence to show that it is not true. If you *deny* something, you say that it is not true.

regain, regains, regaining, regained VERB To regain something means to get it back.

regal ADJECTIVE very grand and suitable for a king or queen • *regal splendour.* **regally** ADVERB

regard, regards, regarding, regarded VERB ① To regard someone or something in a particular way means to think of them in that way or have that opinion of them • *We all regard him as a friend* • *Many disapprove of the tax, regarding it as unfair.* ② (literary) To regard someone in a particular way also means to look at them in that way • *She regarded him curiously for a moment.* ▶NOUN ③ If you have a high regard for someone, you have a very good opinion of them. ▶PHRASE ④ **Regarding**, **as regards**, **with regard to** and **in regard to** are all used to indicate what you are talking or writing about • *There was always some question regarding education* • *As regards the war, he believed in victory at any price.* ⑤ 'Regards' is used in various expressions to express friendly feelings • *Give my regards to your husband.*

regardless PREPOSITION or ADVERB done or happening in spite of something else • *He led from the front, regardless of the danger.*

regatta, regattas NOUN a race meeting for sailing or rowing boats.

a
b
c
d
e
f
g
h
i
j
k
l
m
n
o
p
q
r
s
t
u
v
w
x
y
z

regency, regencies NOUN a period when a country is ruled by a regent.

regenerate, regenerates, regenerating, regenerated VERB (formal) To regenerate something means to develop and improve it after it has been declining • *a scheme to regenerate the docks area of the city.* **regeneration** NOUN

regent, regents NOUN someone who rules in place of a king or queen who is ill or too young to rule.

reggae NOUN Reggae is a type of music, originally from Jamaica, with a strong beat.

regime, regimes [Said ray-*jeem*] NOUN a system of government, and the people who are ruling a country • *a communist regime.*

regiment, regiments NOUN a large group of soldiers commanded by a colonel. **regimental** ADJECTIVE

regimented ADJECTIVE very strictly controlled • *the regimented life of the orphanage.* **regimentation** NOUN

region, regions NOUN ① GEOGRAPHY a large area of land. ② You can refer to any area or part as a region • *the pelvic region of the body.* ▶ PHRASE ③ **In the region of** means approximately • *The scheme will cost in the region of six million.* **regional** ADJECTIVE **regionally** ADVERB
SIMILAR WORDS: ① area, district, territory

register, registers, registering, registered NOUN ① an official list or record of things • *the electoral register.* ② (technical) a style of speaking or writing used in particular circumstances or social occasions. ▶ VERB ③ When something is registered, it is recorded on an official list • *The car was registered in my name.* ④ If an instrument registers a measurement, it shows it. ⑤ If your

face registers a feeling, it expresses it. **registration** NOUN

registrar, registrars NOUN ① a person who keeps official records of births, marriages and deaths. ② At a college or university, the registrar is a senior administrative official. ③ a senior hospital doctor.

registration number, registration numbers NOUN the sequence of letters and numbers on the front and back of a motor vehicle that identify it.

registry, registries NOUN a place where official records are kept.

registry office, registry offices NOUN a place where births, marriages and deaths are recorded, and where people can marry without a religious ceremony.

regret, regrets, regretting, regretted VERB ① If you regret something, you are sorry that it happened. ② You can say that you regret something as a way of apologising • *We regret any inconvenience to passengers.* ▶ NOUN ③ If you have regrets you are sad or sorry about something. **regretful** ADJECTIVE **regretfully** ADVERB
SIMILAR WORDS: ① repent, rue

regrettable ADJECTIVE unfortunate and undesirable • *a regrettable accident.* **regrettably** ADVERB

regular, regulars ADJECTIVE ① even and equally spaced • *soft music with a regular beat.* ② MATHS A regular shape has equal angles and equal sides • *a regular polygon.* ③ Regular events or activities happen often and according to a pattern, for example each day or each week • *The trains to London are fairly regular.* ④ If you are a regular customer or visitor somewhere, you go there often. ⑤ usual or normal • *I was filling in for the regular receptionist.* ⑥ having a well balanced appearance • *a regular geometrical shape*. ▸ NOUN ⑦ People who go to a place often are known as its regulars. **regularly** ADVERB **regularity** NOUN

SIMILAR WORDS: ① even, steady, uniform

regulate, regulates, regulating, regulated VERB To regulate something means to control the way it operates • *Sweating helps to regulate the body's temperature.* **regulator** NOUN

regulation, regulations NOUN ① Regulations are official rules. ② Regulation is the control of something • *regulation of the betting industry.*

regurgitate, regurgitates, regurgitating, regurgitated [*Said* rig-**gur**-jit-tate] VERB To regurgitate food means to bring it back from the stomach before it is digested.

rehabilitate, rehabilitates, rehabilitating, rehabilitated VERB To rehabilitate someone who has been ill or in prison means to help them lead a normal life. **rehabilitation** NOUN

rehearsal, rehearsals NOUN DRAMA a practice of a performance in preparation for the actual event.

rehearse, rehearses, rehearsing, rehearsed VERB DRAMA To rehearse a performance means to practise it in preparation for the actual event.

reign, reigns, reigning, reigned [*Said* rain] VERB ① When a king or queen reigns, he or she rules a country. ② You can say that something reigns when it is a noticeable feature of a situation or period of time • *Panic reigned after his assassination.* ▸ NOUN ③ HISTORY The reign of a king or queen is the period during which he or she reigns.

SPELLING TIP
Do not confuse the spellings of *reign, rein* and *rain: the reign of King John; Pull the reins sharply if you want to turn; The rain has finally stopped.*

rein, reins NOUN ① Reins are the thin leather straps which you hold when you are riding a horse. ▸ PHRASE ② To **keep a tight rein on** someone or something means to control them firmly.

SPELLING TIP
Do not confuse the spellings of *rein, rain* and *reign: Pull the reins sharply if you want to turn; The rain has finally stopped; the reign of King John.*

reincarnation NOUN RE People who believe in reincarnation believe that when you die, you are born again as another creature.

reindeer, reindeer NOUN Reindeer are deer with large antlers that live in northern regions.

reinforce, reinforces, reinforcing, reinforced VERB ① To reinforce something means to strengthen it • *a reinforced steel barrier.* ② If something reinforces an idea or claim, it provides evidence to support it.

reinforcement, reinforcements NOUN ① Reinforcements are additional soldiers sent to join an army in battle. ② Reinforcement is the reinforcing of something.

reinstate, reinstates, reinstating, reinstated VERB ① To reinstate someone means to give them back a position they have lost. ② To reinstate something means to bring it back • *Parliament voted against reinstating capital punishment.* **reinstatement** NOUN

reiterate, reiterates, reiterating, reiterated [*Said* ree-**it**-er-ate] VERB (*formal*) If you reiterate something, you say it again. **reiteration** NOUN

reject, rejects, rejecting, rejected
VERB [Said re-**ject**] ① If you reject a
proposal or request, you do not
accept it or agree to it. ② If you reject
a belief, political system or way of
life, you decide that it is not for you.
▶ NOUN [Said **re**-ject] ③ a product that
cannot be used, because there is
something wrong with it. **rejection**
NOUN
SIMILAR WORDS: ① decline, refuse,
turn down

rejoice, rejoices, rejoicing, rejoiced
VERB To rejoice means to be very
pleased about something • The whole
country rejoiced after his downfall.

rejoin, rejoins, rejoining, rejoined
VERB If you rejoin someone, you go
back to them soon after leaving them
• She rejoined her friends in the pool.

rejuvenate, rejuvenates,
rejuvenating, rejuvenated [Said
ree-**joo**-vin-ate] VERB To rejuvenate
someone means to make them feel
young again. **rejuvenation** NOUN

relapse, relapses NOUN If a sick
person has a relapse, their health
suddenly gets worse after improving.

relate, relates, relating, related
VERB ① If something relates to
something else, it is connected or
concerned with it • The statistics relate
only to western Germany. ② If you can
relate to someone, you can
understand their thoughts and
feelings. ③ To relate a story means to
tell it.

relation, relations NOUN ① If there is
a relation between two things, they
are similar or connected in some way
• This theory bears no relation to reality.
② Your relations are the members of
your family. ③ Relations between
people are their feelings and
behaviour towards each other

• Relations between brother and sister
had not improved.

relationship, relationships NOUN
① The relationship between two
people or groups is the way they feel
and behave towards each other.
② PSHE a close friendship, especially
one involving romantic feelings.
③ The relationship between two
things is the way in which they are
connected • the relationship between
slavery and the sugar trade.

relative, relatives ADJECTIVE
① compared to other things or
people of the same kind • The fighting
resumed after a period of relative calm
• He is a relative novice. ② You use
'relative' when comparing the size or
quality of two things • the relative
strengths of the British and German
forces. ▶ NOUN ③ Your relatives are
the members of your family.

relative pronoun, relative
pronouns NOUN a pronoun that
replaces a noun that links two parts
of a sentence.

relax, relaxes, relaxing, relaxed
VERB ① If you relax, you become
calm and your muscles lose their
tension. ② If you relax your hold, you
hold something less tightly. ③ To
relax something also means to make
it less strict or controlled • The rules
governing student conduct were relaxed.
relaxation NOUN
SIMILAR WORDS: ① rest, take it easy,
unwind ② lessen, loosen, slacken

relaxed ADJECTIVE ① calm and not
worried or tense. ② If a place or
situation is relaxed, it is calm and
peaceful.

relay, relays, relaying, relayed NOUN
[Said **re**-lay] ① PE A relay race or relay
is a race between teams, with each
team member running one part of
the race. ▶ VERB [Said re-**lay**] ② To
relay a television or radio signal

What is a Relative Pronoun?

Relative pronouns are used to replace a noun which links two different parts of a sentence. The relative pronouns are *who*, *whom*, *whose*, *which* and *that*.

Relative pronouns always refer to a word in the earlier part of the sentence. The word they refer to is called the **antecedent**. (In the examples that follow, the antecedents are underlined.)

*I have <u>a friend</u> **who** lives in Rome.*
*We could go to <u>a place</u> **that** I know.*

The forms *who*, *whom* and *whose* are used when the antecedent is a person. *Who* indicates the subject of the verb, while *whom* indicates the object of the verb:

*It was <u>the same person</u> **who** saw me yesterday.*
*It was <u>the person</u> **whom** I saw yesterday.*

The distinction between *who* and *whom* is often ignored in everyday English, and *who* is often used as the object:

*It was <u>the person</u> **who** I saw yesterday.*

Whom is used immediately after a preposition. However, if the preposition is separated from the relative pronoun, *who* is usually used:

*He is <u>a man</u> **in whom** I have great confidence.*
*He is <u>a man</u> **who** I have great confidence **in**.*

Whose is the possessive form of the relative pronoun. It can refer to things as well as people:

*Anna has <u>a sister</u> **whose** name is Rosa.*
*I found <u>a book</u> **whose** pages were torn.*

Which is only used when the antecedent is not a person:

*We took <u>the road</u> **which** leads to the sea.*

That refers to things or people. It is never used immediately after a preposition, but it can be used if the preposition is separated from the relative pronoun:

*It was <u>a film</u> **that** I had little interest **in**.*

means to send it on. ③ If you relay information, you tell it to someone else.

release, releases, releasing, released VERB ①To release someone or something means to set them free or remove restraints from them. ②To release something also means to issue it or make it available • *He is releasing an album of love songs.* ▶ NOUN ③When the release of someone or something takes place, they are set free. ④A press release or publicity release is an official written statement given to reporters. ⑤A new release is a new film or record that has just become available.

relegate, relegates, relegating,

relegated VERB To relegate something or someone means to give them a less important position or status. **relegation** NOUN

relent, relents, relenting, relented VERB If someone relents, they agree to something they had previously not allowed.

relentless ADJECTIVE never stopping and never becoming less intense • *the relentless rise of business closures.* **relentlessly** ADVERB

relevant ADJECTIVE If something is relevant, it is connected with and is appropriate to what is being discussed • *We have passed all relevant information on to the police.* **relevance** NOUN

SIMILAR WORDS: appropriate, pertinent, significant

reliable ADJECTIVE ① Reliable people and things can be trusted to do what you want. ② If information is reliable, you can assume that it is correct. **reliably** ADVERB **reliability** NOUN

reliant ADJECTIVE If you are reliant on someone or something, you depend on them • *They are not wholly reliant on charity.* **reliance** NOUN

relic, relics NOUN ① Relics are objects or customs that have survived from an earlier time. ② an object regarded as holy because it is thought to be connected with a saint.

relief NOUN ① If you feel relief, you are glad and thankful because a bad situation is over or has been avoided. ② Relief is also money, food or clothing provided for people in need.

relief map, relief maps NOUN GEOGRAPHY a map showing the shape of mountains and hills by shading.

relieve, relieves, relieving, relieved VERB ① If something relieves an unpleasant feeling, it makes it less unpleasant • *Meditation can help relieve stress.* ② (formal) If you relieve someone, you do their job or duty for a period. ③ If someone is relieved of their duties, they are dismissed from their job. ④ If you relieve yourself, you urinate.

religion, religions NOUN ① RE Religion is the belief in a god or gods and all the activities connected with such beliefs. ② RE a system of religious belief.

religious ADJECTIVE ① connected with religion • *religious worship.* ② RE Someone who is religious has a strong belief in a god or gods.

SIMILAR WORDS: ② devout, pious

religiously ADVERB If you do something religiously, you do it regularly as a duty • *He stuck religiously to the rules.*

relinquish, relinquishes, relinquishing, relinquished [Said ril-**ling**-kwish] VERB (formal) If you relinquish something, you give it up.

relish, relishes, relishing, relished VERB ① If you relish something, you enjoy it • *He relished the idea of getting some cash.* ▶ NOUN ② Relish is enjoyment • *He told me with relish of the wonderful times he had.* ③ Relish is also a savoury sauce or pickle.

relive, relives, reliving, relived VERB If you relive a past experience, you remember it and imagine it happening again.

relocate, relocates, relocating, relocated VERB If people or businesses are relocated, they are moved to a different place. **relocation** NOUN

reluctant ADJECTIVE If you are reluctant to do something, you are unwilling to do it. **reluctance** NOUN

reluctantly ADVERB If you do something reluctantly, you do it although you do not want to.

rely, relies, relying, relied VERB ① If you rely on someone or something, you need them and depend on them • *She has to rely on payments from her parents.* ② If you can rely on someone to do something, you can trust them to do it • *They can always be relied on to turn up.*

remain, remains, remaining, remained VERB ① If you remain in a particular place, you stay there. ② If you remain in a particular state, you stay the same and do not change • *The two men remained silent.* ③ Something that remains still exists or is left over • *Huge amounts of weapons remain to be collected.*

remainder NOUN ① The remainder of something is the part that is left • *He gulped down the remainder of his coffee.* ② the amount left over when one number cannot be exactly divided by another • *For 10 ÷ 3, the remainder is 1.*

remains PLURAL NOUN ① The remains of something are the parts that are left after most of it has been destroyed • *the remains of an ancient mosque.* ② You can refer to a dead body as remains.
SIMILAR WORDS: ① debris, remnants

remand, remands, remanding, remanded VERB ① If a judge remands someone who is accused of a crime, the trial is postponed and the person is ordered to come back at a later date. ▸ PHRASE ② If someone is **on remand**, they are in prison waiting for their trial to begin.

remark, remarks, remarking, remarked VERB ① If you remark on something, you mention it or comment on it • *She had remarked on the boy's improvement.* ▸ NOUN ② something you say, often in a casual way.

remarkable ADJECTIVE impressive and unexpected • *It was a remarkable achievement.* **remarkably** ADVERB
SIMILAR WORDS: extraordinary, outstanding, wonderful

remarry, remarries, remarrying, remarried VERB If someone remarries, they get married again.

remedial ADJECTIVE ① Remedial activities are to help someone improve their health after they have been ill. ② Remedial exercises are designed to improve someone's ability in something • *the remedial reading class.*

remedy, remedies, remedying, remedied NOUN ① a way of dealing with a problem • *a remedy for colic.* ▸ VERB ② If you remedy something that is wrong, you correct it • *We have to remedy the situation immediately.*

remember, remembers, remembering, remembered VERB ① If you can remember someone or something from the past, you can bring them into your mind or think about them. ② If you remember to do something, you do it when you intended to • *Ben had remembered to book reservations.*
SIMILAR WORDS: ① recall, recollect

remembrance NOUN If you do something in remembrance of a dead person, you are showing that they are remembered with respect and affection.

remind, reminds, reminding, reminded VERB ① If someone reminds you of a fact, they say something to make you think about it • *Remind me to buy a bottle of water, will you?* ② If someone reminds you of another person, they look similar and make you think of them.

reminder, reminders NOUN ① If one thing is a reminder of another, the first thing makes you think of the second • *a reminder of better times.* ② a note sent to tell someone they have forgotten to do something.

reminiscent ADJECTIVE Something that is reminiscent of something else reminds you of it.

remission NOUN When prisoners get remission for good behaviour, their sentences are reduced.

remit, remits, remitting, remitted (*formal*) VERB [*Said ri-mit*] ① To remit money to someone means to send it to them in payment for something. ▸ NOUN [*Said ree-mit*] ② The remit of a person or committee is the subject or task they are responsible for • *Their remit is to research into a wide range of health problems.*

remittance, remittances NOUN (*formal*) payment for something sent through the post.

remnant, remnants NOUN a small part of something left after the rest has been used or destroyed.

remorse NOUN (*formal*) Remorse is a strong feeling of guilt. **remorseful** ADJECTIVE
SIMILAR WORDS: contrition, regret, repentance

remote, remoter, remotest ADJECTIVE ① Remote areas are far away from places where most people live. ② far away in time • *the remote past.* ③ If you say a person is remote, you mean they do not want to be friendly • *She is severe, solemn and remote.* ④ If there is only a remote possibility of something happening, it is unlikely to happen. **remoteness** NOUN

remote control NOUN Remote control is a system of controlling a machine or vehicle from a distance using radio or electronic signals.

remotely ADVERB used to emphasise a negative statement • *He isn't remotely keen.*

removal NOUN ① The removal of something is the act of taking it away. ② A removal company transports furniture from one building to another.

remove, removes, removing, removed VERB ① If you remove something from a place, you take it off or away. ② If you are removed from a position of authority, you are not allowed to continue your job. ③ If you remove an undesirable feeling or attitude, you get rid of it

• *Most of her fears had been removed.*
removable ADJECTIVE
SIMILAR WORDS: ① extract, take away, withdraw

Renaissance [*Said ren-nay-sonss*] NOUN HISTORY The Renaissance was a period from the 14th to 16th centuries in Europe when there was a great revival in the arts and learning.
WORD HISTORY: a French word, meaning 'rebirth'

renal ADJECTIVE concerning the kidneys • *renal failure.*

rename, renames, renaming, renamed VERB If you rename something, you give it a new name.

render, renders, rendering, rendered VERB You can use 'render' to say that something is changed into a different state • *The bomb was quickly rendered harmless.*

rendezvous [*Said ron-day-voo*] NOUN ① a meeting • *Baxter arranged a six o'clock rendezvous.* ② a place where you have arranged to meet someone • *The pub became a popular rendezvous.*

rendition, renditions NOUN (*formal*) a performance of a play, poem or piece of music.

renew, renews, renewing, renewed VERB ① To renew an activity or relationship means to begin it again. ② To renew a licence or contract means to extend the period of time for which it is valid. **renewal** NOUN

renewable, renewables ADJECTIVE ① able to be renewed. ▶ NOUN ② GEOGRAPHY a renewable form of energy, such as wind power or solar power.

renewable resources PLURAL NOUN GEOGRAPHY sources of energy, such as wind, sun and water, which are constantly replaced so do not become used up.

renounce, renounces, renouncing,

renounced VERB (*formal*) If you renounce something, you reject it or give it up. **renunciation** NOUN

renovate, renovates, renovating, renovated VERB If you renovate an old building or machine, you repair it and restore it to good condition. **renovation** NOUN

renowned [*Rhymes with* **sound**] ADJECTIVE well-known for something good • *He is not renowned for his patience.* **renown** NOUN

rent, rents, renting, rented VERB ① If you rent something, you pay the owner a regular sum of money in return for being able to use it. ▶ NOUN ② Rent is the amount of money you pay regularly to rent land or accommodation.

rental ADJECTIVE ① concerned with the renting out of goods and services • *Scotland's largest car rental company.* ▶ NOUN ② the amount of money you pay when you rent something.

reorganise, reorganises, reorganising, reorganised; also spelt **reorganize** VERB To reorganise something means to organise it in a new way in order to make it more efficient or acceptable. **reorganisation** NOUN

rep, reps (*informal*) NOUN ① A rep is a travelling salesperson. Rep is an abbreviation for **representative**. ▶ PHRASE ② When actors work **in rep**, they are working with a repertory company.

repair, repairs, repairing, repaired NOUN ① something you do to mend something that is damaged or broken. ▶ VERB ② If you repair something, you mend it.

repay, repays, repaying, repaid VERB ① To repay money means to give it back to the person who lent it. ② If you repay a favour, you do something to help the person who helped you. **repayment** NOUN

repeal, repeals, repealing, repealed VERB If the government repeals a law, it cancels it so that it is no longer valid.

repeat, repeats, repeating, repeated VERB ① If you repeat something, you say, write or do it again. ② If you repeat what someone has said, you tell someone else about it • *I trust you not to repeat that to anyone.* ▶ NOUN ③ something which is done or happens again • *the number of repeats shown on TV.* **repeatable** ADJECTIVE **repeated** ADJECTIVE **repeatedly** ADVERB

repel, repels, repelling, repelled VERB ① If something repels you, you find it horrible and disgusting. ② When soldiers repel an attacking force, they successfully defend themselves against it. ③ SCIENCE When a magnetic pole repels an opposite pole, it forces the opposite pole away.

SIMILAR WORDS: ① disgust, revolt, sicken

repellent, repellents ADJECTIVE ① (*formal*) horrible and disgusting • *I found him repellent.* ▶ NOUN ② Repellents are chemicals used to keep insects or other creatures away.

repent, repents, repenting, repented VERB (*formal*) If you repent, you are sorry for something bad you have done. **repentance** NOUN **repentant** ADJECTIVE

repercussion, repercussions NOUN The repercussions of an event are the effects it has at a later time.

repertoire, repertoires [*Said* rep-et-twar] NOUN A performer's repertoire is all the pieces of music or dramatic parts he or she has learned and can perform.

a
b
c
d
e
f
g
h
i
j
k
l
m
n
o
p
q
r
s
t
u
v
w
x
y
z

repertory, repertories NOUN
① Repertory is the practice of performing a small number of plays in a theatre for a short time, using the same actors in each play. ② In Australian, New Zealand and South African English, repertory is the same as **repertoire**.

repetition, repetitions NOUN ① If there is a repetition of something, it happens again • *We don't want a repetition of last week's fiasco.*
② ENGLISH Repetition is when a word, phrase or sound is repeated, for example to emphasise a point or to make sure it is understood, or for poetic effect.

repetitious ADJECTIVE Repetitious means the same as repetitive.

repetitive ADJECTIVE A repetitive activity involves a lot of repetition and is boring • *dull and repetitive work.*

replace, replaces, replacing, replaced VERB ① When one thing replaces another, the first thing takes the place of the second. ② If you replace something that is damaged or lost, you get a new one. ③ If you replace something, you put it back where it was before • *She replaced the receiver.*
SIMILAR WORDS: ① supersede, supplant

replacement, replacements NOUN
① The replacement for someone or something is the person or thing that takes their place. ② The replacement of a person or thing happens when they are replaced by another person or thing.

replay, replays, replaying, replayed VERB [Said re-play] ① If a match is replayed, the teams play it again. ② If you replay a recording, you play it again • *Replay the first few seconds of the DVD please.* ▶ NOUN [Said re-play] ③ a match that is played for a second time.

replenish, replenishes, replenishing, replenished VERB (formal) If you replenish something, you make it full or complete again.

replica, replicas NOUN an accurate copy of something • *a replica of Columbus's ship.* **replicate** VERB

reply, replies, replying, replied VERB
① If you reply to something, you say or write an answer. ▶ NOUN ② what you say or write when you answer someone.

report, reports, reporting, reported VERB ① If you report that something has happened, you tell someone about it or give an official account of it • *He reported the theft to the police.*
② To report someone to an authority means to make an official complaint about them. ③ If you report to a person or place, you go there and say you have arrived. ▶ NOUN ④ an account of an event or situation.
SIMILAR WORDS: ④ account, description

reported speech NOUN ENGLISH a report of what someone said that gives the content of the speech without repeating the exact words.

reporter, reporters NOUN someone who writes news articles or broadcasts news reports.

repossess, repossesses, repossessing, repossessed VERB If a shop or company repossesses goods that have not been paid for, they take them back.

represent, represents, representing, represented VERB
① If you represent someone, you act on their behalf • *lawyers representing relatives of the victims.* ② If a sign or symbol represents something, it stands for it. ③ To represent something in a particular way means to describe it in that way • *The popular press tends to represent him as a hero.*

representation, representations
NOUN ① Representation is the state
of being represented by someone
• *Was there any student representation?*
② You can describe a picture or statue
of someone as a representation of
them.

representative, representatives
NOUN ① a person chosen to act on
behalf of another person or a group.
▶ ADJECTIVE ② A representative
selection is typical of the group it
belongs to • *The photos chosen are not
representative of his work.*

repress, represses, repressing,
repressed VERB ① If you repress a
feeling, you succeed in not showing
or feeling it • *I couldn't repress my anger
any longer.* ② To repress people
means to restrict their freedom and
control them by force. **repression**
NOUN

repressive ADJECTIVE Repressive
governments use force and unjust
laws to restrict and control people.

reprieve, reprieves, reprieving,
reprieved [*Said* rip-**preev**] VERB ① If
someone who has been sentenced to
death is reprieved, their sentence is
changed and they are not killed.
▶ NOUN ② a delay before something
unpleasant happens • *The zoo won a
reprieve from closure.*

reprimand, reprimands,
reprimanding, reprimanded VERB
① If you reprimand someone, you
officially tell them that they should
not have done something. ▶ NOUN
② something said or written by a
person in authority when they are
reprimanding someone.

reprisal, reprisals NOUN Reprisals
are violent actions taken by one
group of people against another
group that has harmed them.

reproach, reproaches, reproaching,

reproached (*formal*) NOUN ① If you
express reproach, you show that you
feel sad and angry about what
someone has done • *a long letter of
reproach.* ▶ VERB ② If you reproach
someone, you tell them, rather sadly,
that they have done something
wrong. **reproachful** ADJECTIVE
reproachfully ADVERB

reproduce, reproduces,
reproducing, reproduced VERB
① To reproduce something means to
make a copy of it. ② SCIENCE When
living things reproduce, they produce
more of their own kind • *Bacteria
reproduce by splitting into two.*

reproduction, reproductions NOUN
① a modern copy of a painting or
piece of furniture. ② SCIENCE
Reproduction is the process by which
a living thing produces more of its
kind • *the study of animal reproduction.*

reproductive ADJECTIVE relating to
the reproduction of living things • *the
female reproductive system.*

reptile, reptiles NOUN a cold-blooded
animal, such as a snake or a lizard,
which has scaly skin and lays eggs.
reptilian ADJECTIVE
WORD HISTORY: from Latin *reptilis*
meaning 'creeping'

republic, republics NOUN a country
which has a president rather than a
king or queen. **republican** NOUN or
ADJECTIVE **republicanism** NOUN
WORD HISTORY: from Latin *res publica*
meaning literally 'public thing'

repulse, repulses, repulsing,
repulsed VERB ① If you repulse
someone who is being friendly, you
put them off by behaving coldly
towards them • *He repulses friendly
advances.* ② To repulse an attacking
force means to fight it and cause it to
retreat. ③ If something repulses you,
you find it horrible and disgusting
and you want to avoid it.

repulsion NOUN ① Repulsion is a strong feeling of disgust. ② Repulsion is a force separating two objects, such as the force between two like electric charges.

repulsive ADJECTIVE horrible and disgusting.

reputable ADJECTIVE known to be good and reliable • *a well-established and reputable firm*.

reputation, reputations NOUN The reputation of something or someone is the opinion that people have of them • *The college had a good reputation*.

SIMILAR WORDS: name, renown, standing

reputed ADJECTIVE If something is reputed to be true, some people say that it is true • *He is the reputed writer of a number of the plays*. **reputedly** ADVERB

request, requests, requesting, requested VERB ① If you request something, you ask for it politely or formally. ▶ NOUN ② If you make a request for something, you request it.

requiem, requiems [Said rek-wee-em] NOUN ① A requiem or requiem mass is a mass celebrated for someone who has recently died. ② a piece of music for singers and an orchestra, originally written for a requiem mass • *Mozart's Requiem*.

WORD HISTORY: from Latin *requies* meaning 'rest'

require, requires, requiring, required VERB ① If you require something, you need it. ② If you are required to do something, you have to do it because someone says you must • *The rules require employers to provide safety training*.

requirement, requirements NOUN something that you must have or must do • *A good degree is a requirement for entry*.

requisite, requisites (formal) ADJECTIVE ① necessary for a particular purpose • *She filled in the requisite paperwork*. ▶ NOUN ② something that is necessary for a particular purpose.

rescue, rescues, rescuing, rescued VERB ① If you rescue someone, you save them from a dangerous or unpleasant situation. ▶ NOUN ② Rescue is help which saves someone from a dangerous or unpleasant situation. **rescuer** NOUN

research, researches, researching, researched NOUN ① Research is work that involves studying something and trying to find out facts about it. ▶ VERB ② If you research something, you try to discover facts about it. **researcher** NOUN

resemblance NOUN If there is a resemblance between two things, they are similar to each other • *There was a remarkable resemblance between them*.

SIMILAR WORDS: likeness, similarity

resemble, resembles, resembling, resembled VERB To resemble something means to be similar to it.

resent, resents, resenting, resented VERB If you resent something, you feel bitter and angry about it.

resentful ADJECTIVE bitter and angry • *He felt very resentful about losing his job*. **resentfully** ADVERB

resentment, resentments NOUN a feeling of anger or bitterness.

reservation, reservations NOUN ① If you have reservations about something, you are not sure that it is right. ② If you make a reservation, you book a place in advance. ③ an area of land set aside for American Indian peoples • *a Cherokee reservation*.

reserve, reserves, reserving, reserved VERB ① If something is reserved for a particular person or purpose, it is kept specially for them. ▸ NOUN ② a supply of something for future use. ③ In sport, a reserve is someone who is available to play in case one of the team is unable to play. ④ A nature reserve is an area of land where animals, birds or plants are officially protected. ⑤ If someone shows reserve, they keep their feelings hidden. **reserved** ADJECTIVE
SIMILAR WORDS: ① put by, save, set aside

reservoir, reservoirs [Said rez-ev-wahr] NOUN a lake used for storing water before it is supplied to people.

reshuffle, reshuffles NOUN a reorganisation of people or things.

reside, resides, residing, resided [Said riz-**zide**] VERB (formal) ① If someone resides somewhere, they live there or are staying there. ② If a quality resides in something, the quality is in that thing.

residence, residences (formal) NOUN ① A residence is a house. ▸ PHRASE ② If you **take up residence** somewhere, you go and live there.

resident, residents NOUN ① A resident of a house or area is someone who lives there. ▸ ADJECTIVE ② If someone is resident in a house or area, they live there.

residential ADJECTIVE ① A residential area contains mainly houses rather than offices or factories. ② providing accommodation • residential care for elderly people.

residue, residues NOUN a small amount of something that remains after most of it has gone • an increase in toxic residues found in drinking water. **residual** ADJECTIVE

resign, resigns, resigning, resigned VERB ① If you resign from a job, you formally announce that you are leaving it. ② If you resign yourself to an unpleasant situation, you realise that you have to accept it. **resigned** ADJECTIVE

resignation, resignations NOUN ① Someone's resignation is a formal statement of their intention to leave a job. ② Resignation is the reluctant acceptance of an unpleasant situation or fact.

resilient ADJECTIVE PSHE able to recover quickly from unpleasant or damaging events. **resilience** NOUN

resin, resins NOUN ① Resin is a sticky substance produced by some trees. ② Resin is also a substance produced chemically and used to make plastics.

resist, resists, resisting, resisted VERB ① If you resist something, you refuse to accept it and try to prevent it • The pay squeeze will be fiercely resisted by the unions. ② If you resist someone, you fight back against them.
SIMILAR WORDS: ① fight, oppose

resistance, resistances NOUN ① Resistance to something such as change is a refusal to accept it. ② Resistance to an attack consists of fighting back • The demonstrators offered no resistance. ③ Your body's resistance to germs or disease is its power to not be harmed by them. ④ SCIENCE Resistance is also the power of a substance to resist the flow of an electrical current through it.

resistant ADJECTIVE ① opposed to something and wanting to prevent it • People were very resistant to change. ② If something is resistant to a particular thing, it is not harmed or affected by it • *Certain insects are resistant to this spray.*

resistor, resistors NOUN A resistor is a device which is designed to increase the resistance in an electrical circuit.

resolute [*Said* rez-ol-loot] ADJECTIVE (*formal*) Someone who is resolute is determined not to change their mind. **resolutely** ADVERB

resolution, resolutions NOUN ① Resolution is determination. ② If you make a resolution, you promise yourself to do something. ③ a formal decision taken at a meeting. ④ ENGLISH The resolution of a problem is the solving of it.

resolve, resolves, resolving, resolved VERB ① If you resolve to do something, you firmly decide to do it. ② If you resolve a problem, you find a solution to it. ▶ NOUN ③ Resolve is absolute determination.

resonance, resonances NOUN ① Resonance is sound produced by an object vibrating as a result of another sound nearby. ② Resonance is also a deep, clear and echoing quality of sound.

resonate, resonates, resonating, resonated VERB If something resonates, it vibrates and produces a deep, strong sound.

resort, resorts, resorting, resorted VERB ① If you resort to a course of action, you do it because you have no alternative. ▶ NOUN ② a place where people spend their holidays. ▶ PHRASE ③ If you do something **as a last resort**, you do it because you can find no other way of solving a problem.

resounding ADJECTIVE ① loud and echoing • *a resounding round of applause.* ② A resounding success is a great success.

resource, resources NOUN The resources of a country, organisation or person are the materials, money or skills they have.

resourceful ADJECTIVE A resourceful person is good at finding ways of dealing with problems. **resourcefulness** NOUN

respect, respects, respecting, respected VERB ① If you respect someone, you have a good opinion of their character or ideas. ② If you respect someone's rights or wishes, you do not do things that they would not like, or would consider wrong • *It is about time they started respecting the law.* ▶ NOUN ③ If you have respect for someone, you have a good opinion of them. ▶ PHRASE ④ You can say **in this respect** to refer to a particular feature • *At least in this respect we are equals.*

respectable ADJECTIVE ① considered to be acceptable and morally correct • *respectable families.* ② adequate or reasonable • *a respectable rate of economic growth.* **respectability** NOUN **respectably** ADVERB

respectful ADJECTIVE showing respect for someone • *Our children are always respectful to their elders.* **respectfully** ADVERB

respective ADJECTIVE belonging or relating individually to the people or things just mentioned • *They went into their respective rooms to pack.*

respectively ADVERB in the same order as the items just mentioned • *Amanda and Emily finished first and second respectively.*

respiration NOUN SCIENCE Your respiration is your breathing.

respiratory ADJECTIVE SCIENCE relating to breathing • *respiratory diseases.*

respite NOUN (*formal*) a short rest

from something unpleasant.

respond, responds, responding, responded VERB When you respond to something, you react to it by doing or saying something.

respondent, respondents NOUN ① a person who answers a questionnaire or a request for information. ② In a court case, the respondent is the defendant.

response, responses NOUN Your response to an event is your reaction or reply to it • *There has been no response to his remarks yet.*

responsibility, responsibilities NOUN ① PSHE CITIZENSHIP If you have responsibility for something, it is your duty to deal with it or look after it • *The garden was to have been his responsibility.* ② If you accept responsibility for something that has happened, you agree that you caused it or were to blame • *We must all accept responsibility for our own mistakes.*

responsible ADJECTIVE ① If you are responsible for something, it is your job to deal with it. ② If you are responsible for something bad that has happened, you are to blame for it. ③ If you are responsible to someone, that person is your boss and tells you what you have to do. ④ A responsible person behaves properly and sensibly without needing to be supervised. ⑤ A responsible job involves making careful judgments about important matters. **responsibly** ADVERB
SIMILAR WORDS: ① accountable, answerable, liable

responsive ADJECTIVE ① quick to show interest and pleasure. ② taking notice of events and reacting in an appropriate way • *The course is responsive to students' needs.*

rest, rests, resting, rested NOUN ① The rest of something is all the remaining parts of it. ② If you have a rest, you sit or lie quietly and relax.
▸ VERB ③ If you rest, you relax and do not do anything active for a while.

restaurant, restaurants [*Said rest-er-ront*] NOUN a place where you can buy and eat a meal.
WORD HISTORY: a French word; from *restaurer* meaning 'to restore'

restaurateur, restaurateurs [*Said rest-er-a-tur*] NOUN someone who owns or manages a restaurant.

SPELLING TIP
There is no *n* in *restaurateur*.

restful ADJECTIVE Something that is restful helps you feel calm and relaxed.

restless ADJECTIVE finding it hard to remain still or relaxed because of boredom or impatience. **restlessly** ADVERB **restlessness** NOUN

restore, restores, restoring, restored VERB ① To restore something means to cause it to exist again or to return to its previous state • *He was anxious to restore his reputation.* ② To restore an old building or work of art means to clean and repair it. **restoration** NOUN
SIMILAR WORDS: ② refurbish, renovate

restrain, restrains, restraining, restrained VERB To restrain someone or something means to hold them back or prevent them from doing what they want to.

restrained ADJECTIVE behaving in a controlled way.

restraint, restraints NOUN ① Restraints are rules or conditions that limit something • *wage restraints.* ② Restraint is calm, controlled behaviour.

a b c d e f g h i j k l m n o p q r s t u v w x y z

restrict, restricts, restricting, restricted VERB ① If you restrict something, you prevent it becoming too large or varied. ② To restrict people or animals means to limit their movement or actions. **restrictive** ADJECTIVE

restriction, restrictions NOUN a rule or situation that limits what you can do • *financial restrictions*.

result, results, resulting, resulted NOUN ① The result of an action or situation is the situation that is caused by it • *As a result of the incident he got a two-year suspension*. ② The result is also the final marks, figures or situation at the end of an exam, calculation or contest • *election results* • *The result was calculated to three decimal places*. ▸ VERB ③ If something results in a particular event, it causes that event to happen. ④ If something results from a particular event, it is caused by that event • *The fire had resulted from carelessness*. **resultant** ADJECTIVE SIMILAR WORDS: ① consequence, outcome, upshot

resume, resumes, resuming, resumed *[Said riz-yoom]* VERB If you resume an activity or position, you return to it after a break. **resumption** NOUN

resurgence NOUN If there is a resurgence of an attitude or activity, it reappears and grows stronger. **resurgent** ADJECTIVE

resurrect, resurrects, resurrecting, resurrected VERB If you resurrect something, you make it exist again after it has disappeared or ended. **resurrection** NOUN

Resurrection NOUN RE In Christian belief, the Resurrection is the coming back to life of Jesus Christ three days after he had been killed.

resuscitate, resuscitates, resuscitating, resuscitated *[Said ris-suss-it-tate]* VERB If you resuscitate someone, you make them conscious again after an accident. **resuscitation** NOUN

retail NOUN The retail price is the price at which something is sold in the shops. **retailer** NOUN

retain, retains, retaining, retained VERB To retain something means to keep it. **retention** NOUN

retaliate, retaliates, retaliating, retaliated VERB If you retaliate, you do something to harm or upset someone because they have already acted in a similar way against you. **retaliation** NOUN

retch, retches, retching, retched VERB If you retch, your stomach moves as if you are vomiting.

SPELLING TIP
Do not confuse the spellings of *retch* and *wretch*: *The smell inside the fridge made me retch; He is an ungrateful wretch*.

retention NOUN The retention of something is the keeping of it.

rethink, rethinks, rethinking, rethought VERB If you rethink something, you think about how it should be changed • *We have to rethink our strategy*.

reticent ADJECTIVE Someone who is reticent is unwilling to tell people about things. **reticence** NOUN

retina, retinas NOUN SCIENCE the light-sensitive part at the back of your eyeball, which receives an image and sends it to your brain.

retinue, retinues NOUN a group of helpers or friends travelling with an important person.

retire, retires, retiring, retired VERB ① When older people retire, they give up work. ② (*formal*) If you retire, you leave to go into another room, or to bed • *She retired early with a good book.* **retired** ADJECTIVE **retirement** NOUN

retort, retorts, retorting, retorted VERB ① To retort means to reply angrily. ▶ NOUN ② a short, angry reply.

retract, retracts, retracting, retracted VERB ① If you retract something you have said, you say that you did not mean it. ② When something is retracted, it moves inwards or backwards • *The undercarriage was retracted shortly after takeoff.* **retraction** NOUN **retractable** ADJECTIVE

retreat, retreats, retreating, retreated VERB ① To retreat means to move backwards away from something or someone. ② If you retreat from something difficult or unpleasant, you avoid doing it. ▶ NOUN ③ If an army moves away from the enemy, this is referred to as a retreat. ④ a quiet place that you can go to rest or do things in private.

retribution NOUN (*formal*) Retribution is punishment • *the threat of retribution.*

retrieve, retrieves, retrieving, retrieved VERB If you retrieve something, you get it back. **retrieval** NOUN

retriever, retrievers NOUN a large dog often used by hunters to bring back birds and animals which have been shot.

retro ADJECTIVE Retro clothes, music and objects are based on the styles of the past.

retro- PREFIX 'Retro-' means 'back' or 'backwards' • *retrospective.* WORD HISTORY: from Latin *retrō* meaning 'behind' or 'backwards'

retrospect PHRASE When you consider something **in retrospect**, you think about it afterwards and often have a different opinion from the one you had at the time • *In retrospect, I probably shouldn't have resigned.*

retrospective ADJECTIVE ① concerning things that happened in the past. ② taking effect from a date in the past. **retrospectively** ADVERB

return, returns, returning, returned VERB ① When you return to a place, you go back after you have been away. ② If you return something to someone, you give it back to them. ③ When you return a ball during a game, you hit it back to your opponent. ④ When a judge or jury returns a verdict, they announce it. ▶ NOUN ⑤ Your return is your arrival back at a place. ⑥ The return on an investment is the profit or interest you get from it. ⑦ a ticket for the journey to a place and back again. ▶ PHRASE ⑧ If you do something **in return** for a favour, you do it to repay the favour.

reunion, reunions NOUN a party or meeting for people who have not seen each other for a long time.

reunite, reunites, reuniting, reunited VERB If people are reunited, they meet again after they have been separated for some time.

rev, revs, revving, revved (*informal*) VERB ① When you rev the engine of a vehicle, you press the accelerator to increase the engine speed. ▶ NOUN ② The speed of an engine is measured in revolutions per minute, referred to as revs • *I noticed that the engine revs had dropped.*

Rev or **Revd** abbreviations for **Reverend**.

a
b
c
d
e
f
g
h
i
j
k
l
m
n
o
p
q
r
s
t
u
v
w
x
y
z

revamp, revamps, revamping, revamped VERB To revamp something means to improve or repair it.

reveal, reveals, revealing, revealed VERB ① To reveal something means to tell people about it • *They were not ready to reveal any of the details.* ② If you reveal something that has been hidden, you uncover it. ▶ NOUN ③ an occasion when something that has been kept secret is shown or explained • *The series is building up to the big reveal.*

revel, revels, revelling, revelled VERB If you revel in a situation, you enjoy it very much. **revelry** NOUN

revelation, revelations NOUN ① a surprising or interesting fact made known to people. ② If an experience is a revelation, it makes you realise or learn something.

revenge, revenges, revenging, revenged NOUN ① Revenge involves hurting someone who has hurt you. ▶ VERB ② If you revenge yourself on someone who has hurt you, you hurt them in return.
SIMILAR WORDS: ① retaliation, vengeance ② avenge, retaliate

revenue, revenues NOUN Revenue is money that a government, company or organisation receives • *government tax revenues.*

revered ADJECTIVE If someone is revered, he or she is respected and admired • *He is still revered as the father of the nation.*

reverence NOUN Reverence is a feeling of great respect.

Reverend ADJECTIVE Reverend is a title used before the name of a member of the clergy • *the Reverend George Young.*

reversal, reversals NOUN If there is a reversal of a process or policy, it is changed to the opposite process or policy.

reverse, reverses, reversing, reversed VERB ① When someone reverses a process, they change it to the opposite process • *They won't reverse the decision to increase prices.* ② If you reverse the order of things, you arrange them in the opposite order. ③ When you reverse a car, you drive it backwards. ▶ NOUN ④ The reverse is the opposite of what has just been said or done. ▶ ADJECTIVE ⑤ Reverse means opposite to what is usual or to what has just been described.

reversible ADJECTIVE Reversible clothing can be worn with either side on the outside.

revert, reverts, reverting, reverted VERB (*formal*) To revert to a former state or type of behaviour means to go back to it.

review, reviews, reviewing, reviewed NOUN ① an article or an item on television or radio, giving an opinion of a new book, play or film. ② When there is a review of a situation or system, it is examined to decide whether changes are needed. ▶ VERB ③ To review a book, play or film means to write an account expressing an opinion of it. ④ To review something means to examine it to decide whether changes are needed. **reviewer** NOUN
SIMILAR WORDS: ② examination, survey ④ reassess, reconsider, revise

revise, revises, revising, revised VERB ① If you revise something, you alter or correct it. ② When you revise for an examination, you go over your work to learn things thoroughly. **revision** NOUN

revive, revives, reviving, revived VERB ① When a feeling or practice is revived, it becomes active or popular again. ② If someone who has fainted revives, they become conscious again. **revival** NOUN

revolt, revolts, revolting, revolted NOUN ① HISTORY a violent attempt by a group of people to change their country's political system. ▶ VERB ② HISTORY When people revolt, they fight against the authority that governs them. ③ If something revolts you, it is so horrible that you feel disgust.

revolting ADJECTIVE horrible and disgusting • *The smell in the cell was revolting*.

revolution, revolutions NOUN ① HISTORY a violent attempt by a large group of people to change the political system of their country. ② an important change in an area of human activity • *the Industrial Revolution*. ③ one complete turn in a circle.

revolutionary, revolutionaries ADJECTIVE ① involving great changes • *a revolutionary new cooling system*. ▶ NOUN ② a person who takes part in a revolution.

revolve, revolves, revolving, revolved VERB ① If something revolves round something else, it centres on that as the most important thing • *My job revolves around the telephone*. ② When something revolves, it turns in a circle around a central point • *The moon revolves round the earth*.

revolver, revolvers NOUN a small gun held in the hand.

revulsion NOUN Revulsion is a strong feeling of disgust or disapproval.

reward, rewards, rewarding, rewarded PSHE NOUN ① something you are given because you have done something good. ▶ VERB ② If you reward someone,

you give them a reward.

rewarding ADJECTIVE Something that is rewarding gives you a lot of satisfaction.

rewind, rewinds, rewinding, rewound VERB If you rewind a tape on a tape recorder or video, you make the tape go backwards.

rhapsody, rhapsodies [Said *rap-sod-ee*] NOUN a short piece of music which is very passionate and flowing.

rhetoric NOUN [Said *ret-or-ik*] Rhetoric is speech or writing that is intended to impress people.

rhetorical ADJECTIVE ① A rhetorical question is one which is asked in order to make a statement rather than to get an answer. ② Rhetorical language is intended to be grand and impressive.

rheumatism [Said *room-at-izm*] NOUN Rheumatism is an illness that makes your joints and muscles stiff and painful. **rheumatic** ADJECTIVE

rhino, rhinos NOUN (informal) a rhinoceros.

rhinoceros, rhinoceroses NOUN a large African or Asian animal with one or two horns on its nose. WORD HISTORY: from Greek *rhin* meaning 'of the nose' and *keras* meaning 'horn'

rhododendron, rhododendrons NOUN an evergreen bush with large coloured flowers.

rhombus, rhombuses or rhombi NOUN MATHS a shape with four equal sides and no right angles.

rhubarb NOUN Rhubarb is a plant with long red stems which can be cooked with sugar and eaten.

rhyme, rhymes, rhyming, rhymed ENGLISH VERB ① If two words rhyme, they have a similar sound • *Sally rhymes with valley*. ▶ NOUN

a
b
c
d
e
f
g
h
i
j
k
l
m
n
o
p
q
r
s
t
u
v
w
x
y
z

②a word that rhymes with another.
③a short poem with rhyming lines.

rhythm, rhythms NOUN ① MUSIC
Rhythm is a regular movement or
beat. ②a regular pattern of changes,
for example, in the seasons.
rhythmic ADJECTIVE **rhythmically**
ADVERB

SPELLING TIP
Remember this mnemonic:
Rhythmical Hounds Yap To Heavy Music.

rib, ribs NOUN Your ribs are the curved
bones that go from your backbone to
your chest. **ribbed** ADJECTIVE

ribbon, ribbons NOUN a long, narrow
piece of cloth used for decoration.

ribcage, ribcages NOUN Your ribcage
is the framework of bones made up
of your ribs which protects your
internal organs like your heart and
lungs.

rice NOUN Rice is a tall grass that
produces edible grains. Rice is grown
in warm countries on wet ground.

rich, richer, richest; riches
ADJECTIVE ① Someone who is rich
has a lot of money and possessions.
②Something that is rich in
something contains a large amount
of it • *Liver is particularly rich in vitamin
A*. ③ Rich food contains a large
amount of fat, oil or sugar. ④ Rich
colours, smells and sounds are
strong and pleasant. **richness**
NOUN

riches PLURAL NOUN Riches are
valuable possessions or large
amounts of money • *the oil riches of
the Middle East*.

richly ADVERB ① If someone is richly
rewarded, they are rewarded well
with something valuable. ② If you
feel strongly that someone deserves
something, you can say it is richly
deserved.

Richter scale [*Said rik-ter*] NOUN
GEOGRAPHY a scale which is used for
describing how strong an
earthquake is.

rick, ricks NOUN a large pile of hay or
straw.

rickets NOUN Rickets is a disease that
causes soft bones in children if they
do not get enough vitamin D.

rickety ADJECTIVE likely to collapse or
break • *a rickety wooden jetty*.

rickshaw, rickshaws NOUN a
hand-pulled cart used in Asia for
carrying passengers.

ricochet, ricochets, ricocheting or
ricochetting, ricocheted or
ricochetted [*Said rik-osh-ay*] VERB
When a bullet ricochets, it hits a
surface and bounces away from it.

rid, rids, ridding, rid PHRASE ①When
you **get rid of** something you do not
want, you remove or destroy it.
▶VERB ②(*formal*) To rid a place of
something unpleasant means to
succeed in removing it.

ridden the past participle of **ride**.

riddle, riddles NOUN ①a puzzle
which seems to be nonsense, but
which has an entertaining solution.
②Something that is a riddle puzzles
and confuses you.
SIMILAR WORDS: ② enigma, mystery

riddled ADJECTIVE full of something
undesirable • *The report was riddled
with errors*.
WORD HISTORY: from Old English
hriddel meaning 'sieve'

ride, rides, riding, rode, ridden VERB
①When you ride a horse or a bike,
you sit on it and control it as it moves
along. ②When you ride in a car, you
travel in it. ▶NOUN ③a journey on a
horse or bike or in a vehicle.

rider, riders NOUN ①a person riding
on a horse or bicycle. ②an additional
statement which changes or puts a

condition on what has already been said.

ridge, ridges NOUN ① a long, narrow piece of high land. ② a raised line on a flat surface.

ridicule, ridicules, ridiculing, ridiculed VERB ① To ridicule someone means to make fun of them in an unkind way. ▶ NOUN ② Ridicule is unkind laughter and mockery.

ridiculous ADJECTIVE very foolish.
ridiculously ADVERB

rife ADJECTIVE (*formal*) very common • *Unemployment was rife.*

riff, riffs NOUN MUSIC in jazz or rock music, a riff is a short repeated tune.

rifle, rifles, rifling, rifled NOUN ① a gun with a long barrel. ▶ VERB ② When someone rifles something, they make a quick search through it to steal things.

rift, rifts NOUN ① a serious quarrel between friends that damages their friendship. ② a split in something solid, especially in the ground.

rig, rigs, rigging, rigged VERB ① If someone rigs an election or contest, they dishonestly arrange for a particular person to succeed.
▶ NOUN ② a large structure used for extracting oil or gas from the ground or sea bed. **rig up** VERB If you rig up a device or structure, you make it quickly and fix it in place • *They had even rigged up a makeshift aerial.*

right, rights, righting, righted ADJECTIVE or ADVERB ① correct and in accordance with the facts • *That clock never tells the right time* • *That's absolutely right.* ② 'Right' means on or towards the right side of something.
▶ ADJECTIVE ③ The right choice or decision is the best or most suitable one. ④ The right people or places are those that have influence or are socially admired • *He was always to be seen in the right places.* ⑤ The right

side of something is the side intended to be seen and to face outwards. ▶ NOUN ⑥ 'Right' is used to refer to principles of morally correct behaviour • *At least he knew right from wrong.* ⑦ PSHE CITIZENSHIP If you have a right to do something, you are morally or legally entitled to do it. ⑧ The right is one of the two sides of something. For example, when you look at the word 'to', the 'o' is to the right of the 't'. ⑨ The Right refers to people who support the political ideas of capitalism and conservatism rather than socialism.
▶ ADVERB ⑩ 'Right' is used to emphasise a precise place • *I'm right here.* ⑪ 'Right' means immediately • *I had to decide right then.* ▶ VERB ⑫ If you right something, you correct it or put it back in an upright position.
rightly ADVERB
SIMILAR WORDS: ③ appropriate, proper, suitable ⑦ prerogative, privilege

---

SPELLING TIP
Do not confuse the spellings of *right*, *write* and *rite*: *Is that the right answer?*; *Write your name on the jotter*; *the marriage rites of the Christian Church*.

---

right angle, right angles NOUN MATHS an angle of 90°.

righteous ADJECTIVE Righteous people behave in a way that is morally good and religious.

rightful ADJECTIVE Someone's rightful possession is one which they have a moral or legal right to.
rightfully ADVERB

right-handed ADJECTIVE or ADVERB Someone who is right-handed does things such as writing and painting with their right hand.

right-wing ADJECTIVE believing more strongly in capitalism or conservatism, or less strongly in socialism, than other members of the same party or group. **right-winger** NOUN

rigid ADJECTIVE ① Rigid laws or systems cannot be changed and are considered severe. ② A rigid object is stiff and does not bend easily. **rigidly** ADVERB **rigidity** NOUN
SIMILAR WORDS: ① inflexible, strict

rigorous ADJECTIVE very careful and thorough. **rigorously** ADVERB

rigour, rigours NOUN (formal) The rigours of a situation are the things which make it hard or unpleasant • the rigours of his world tour.

rim, rims NOUN the outside or top edge of an object such as a wheel or a cup. **rimmed** ADJECTIVE

rimu, rimu or rimus [Said ree-moo] NOUN a New Zealand tree with narrow, pointed leaves, which produces wood used for furniture.

rind, rinds NOUN Rind is the thick outer skin of fruit, cheese or bacon.

ring, rings, ringing, ringed, rang, rung VERB ① If you ring someone, you phone them. ② When a bell rings, it makes a clear, loud sound. ③ To ring something means to draw a circle around it. ④ If something is ringed with something else, it has that thing all the way around it • The courthouse was ringed with police. ▶ NOUN ⑤ the sound made by a bell. ⑥ a small circle of metal worn on your finger. ⑦ an object or group of things in the shape of a circle. ⑧ At a boxing match or circus, the ring is the place where the fight or performance takes place. ⑨ an organised group of people who are involved in an illegal activity • an international spy ring.

GRAMMAR TIP
The past tense of ring is rang, and the past participle is rung. Do not confuse these words: She rang the bell; I had rung the police.

ringbark, ringbarks, ringbarking, ringbarked VERB If you ringbark a tree, you kill it by cutting away a strip of bark from around its trunk.

ringer, ringers NOUN ① a person or thing that is almost identical to another. ② In Australian English, a ringer is someone who works on a sheep farm. ③ In Australian and New Zealand English, a ringer is also the fastest shearer in a woolshed.

ring-in, ring-ins NOUN (informal) ① In Australian English, a ring-in is a person or thing that is not normally a member of a particular group. ② In Australian and New Zealand English, a ring-in is also someone who is brought in at the last minute as a replacement for someone else.

ringleader, ringleaders NOUN the leader of a group of people who get involved in mischief or crime.

ring road, ring roads NOUN A ring road is a road that goes round the edge of a town, avoiding the centre.

ringworm NOUN Ringworm is a fungal infection of the skin that causes itching circular patches.

rink, rinks NOUN a large indoor area for ice-skating or roller-skating.

rinse, rinses, rinsing, rinsed VERB ① When you rinse something, you wash it in clean water. ▶ NOUN ② a liquid you can put on your hair to give it a different colour.

riot, riots, rioting, rioted NOUN ① When there is a riot, a crowd of people behave noisily and violently. ▶ VERB ② To riot means to behave noisily and violently. ▶ PHRASE ③ To **run riot** means to behave in a wild and uncontrolled way.

rip, rips, ripping, ripped VERB ① When you rip something, you tear it violently. ② If you rip something away, you remove it quickly and violently. ▶ NOUN ③ a long split in cloth or paper. **rip off** VERB (*informal*) If someone rips you off, they cheat you by charging you too much money.

RIP an abbreviation often written on gravestones, meaning 'rest in peace'.

ripe, riper, ripest ADJECTIVE ① When fruit or grain is ripe, it is fully developed and ready to be eaten. ② If a situation is ripe for something to happen, it is ready for it. **ripeness** NOUN

ripen, ripens, ripening, ripened VERB When crops ripen, they become ripe.

ripper, rippers NOUN (*informal*) In Australian and New Zealand English, a ripper is an excellent person or thing.

ripple, ripples, rippling, rippled NOUN ① Ripples are little waves on the surface of calm water. ② If there is a ripple of laughter or applause, people laugh or applaud gently for a short time. ▶ VERB ③ When the surface of water ripples, little waves appear on it.

rise, rises, rising, rose, risen VERB ① If something rises, it moves upwards. ② (*formal*) When you rise, you stand up. ③ To rise also means to get out of bed. ④ When the sun rises, it first appears. ⑤ The place where a river rises is where it begins. ⑥ If land rises, it slopes upwards. ⑦ If a sound or wind rises, it becomes higher or stronger. ⑧ If an amount rises, it increases. ⑨ If you rise to a challenge or a remark, you respond to it rather than ignoring it • *He rose to the challenge with enthusiasm.* ⑩ When people rise up, they start fighting against people in authority. ▶ NOUN ⑪ an increase. ⑫ Someone's rise is the process by which they become more powerful or successful • *his rise to fame.*

SIMILAR WORDS: ① ascend, climb, go up

riser, risers NOUN An early riser is someone who likes to get up early in the morning.

risk, risks, risking, risked NOUN ① PSHE a chance that something unpleasant or dangerous might happen. ▶ VERB ② If you risk something unpleasant, you do something knowing that the unpleasant thing might happen as a result • *If he doesn't play, he risks losing his place in the team.* ③ If you risk someone's life, you put them in a dangerous situation in which they might be killed. **risky** ADJECTIVE WORD HISTORY: from Italian *rischiare* meaning 'to be in danger'

rite, rites NOUN a religious ceremony.

SPELLING TIP
Do not confuse the spellings of *rite*, *right* and *write*: *the marriage rites of the Christian Church*; *Is that the right answer?*; *Write your name on the jotter.*

ritual, rituals NOUN ① a series of actions carried out according to the custom of a particular society or group • *This is the most ancient of the Buddhist rituals.* ▶ ADJECTIVE ② Ritual activities happen as part of a tradition or ritual • *fasting and ritual dancing.* **ritualistic** ADJECTIVE

rival, rivals, rivalling, rivalled NOUN ① Your rival is the person you are competing with. ▶ VERB ② If something rivals something else, it is of the same high standard or quality • *As a holiday destination, South Africa rivals Kenya for weather.* SIMILAR WORDS: ① adversary, opponent

rivalry, rivalries NOUN Rivalry is active competition between people.

river, rivers NOUN a natural feature consisting of water flowing for a long

a b c d e f g h i j k l m n o p q **r** s t u v w x y z

distance between two banks.

rivet, rivets NOUN a short, round pin with a flat head which is used to fasten sheets of metal together.

riveting ADJECTIVE If you find something riveting, you find it fascinating and it holds your attention • *I find tennis riveting.*

road, roads NOUN a long piece of hard ground specially surfaced so that people and vehicles can travel along it easily.

road map, road maps NOUN ① a map intended for drivers. ② a plan or guide for future actions • *a road map for peace.*

road rage NOUN Road rage is aggressive behaviour by a driver as a reaction to the behaviour of another driver.

road train, road trains NOUN in Australia, a road train is a line of linked trailers pulled by a truck, used for transporting cattle or sheep.

roadworks PLURAL NOUN Roadworks are repairs being done on a road.

roam, roams, roaming, roamed VERB If you roam around, you wander around without any particular purpose • *Hens were roaming around the yard.*

roar, roars, roaring, roared VERB ① If something roars, it makes a very loud noise. ② To roar with laughter or anger means to laugh or shout very noisily. ③ When a lion roars, it makes a loud, angry sound. ▶ NOUN ④ a very loud noise.

roast, roasts, roasting, roasted VERB ① When you roast meat or other food, you cook it using dry heat in an oven or over a fire. ▶ ADJECTIVE ② Roast meat has been roasted. ▶ NOUN ③ a piece of meat that has been roasted.

rob, robs, robbing, robbed VERB ① If someone robs you, they steal your possessions. ② If you rob someone of something they need or deserve, you deprive them of it • *He robbed me of my childhood.*

robber, robbers NOUN Robbers are people who steal money or property using force or threats • *bank robbers.*

robbery, robberies NOUN Robbery is the act of stealing money or property using force or threats.

robe, robes NOUN a long, loose piece of clothing which covers the body • *He knelt in his white robes before the altar.*

robin, robins NOUN a small bird with a red breast.

robot, robots NOUN ① a machine which is programmed to move and perform tasks automatically. ② in South African English, a robot is a set of traffic lights.

WORD HISTORY: from Czech *robota* meaning 'work'

robust ADJECTIVE very strong and healthy. **robustly** ADVERB

rock, rocks, rocking, rocked NOUN ① Rock is the hard mineral substance that forms the surface of the earth. ② a large piece of rock • *She picked up a rock and threw it into the lake.* ③ Rock or rock music is music with simple tunes and a very strong beat. ④ Rock is also a sweet shaped into long, hard sticks, sold in holiday resorts. ▶ VERB ⑤ When something rocks or when you rock it, it moves regularly backwards and forwards or from side to side • *She rocked the baby.* ⑥ If something rocks people, it shocks and upsets them • *Palermo was rocked by a crime wave.* ▶ PHRASE ⑦ If someone's marriage or relationship is **on the rocks**, it is unsuccessful and about to end.

rock and roll NOUN Rock and roll is a style of music with a strong beat that was especially popular in the 1950s.

rock cycle NOUN GEOGRAPHY the series of events in which a rock of one type is changed to one or more other types, and then back to the original type.

rocket, rockets, rocketing, rocketed NOUN ① a space vehicle, usually shaped like a long pointed tube. ② an explosive missile • *They fired rockets into a number of government buildings*. ③ a firework that explodes when it is high in the air. ▶ VERB ④ If prices rocket, they increase very quickly.

rocking chair, rocking chairs NOUN a chair on two curved pieces of wood that rocks backwards and forwards when you sit in it.

rock melon, rock melons NOUN In Australian, New Zealand and American English, a rock melon is a cantaloupe, a melon with orange flesh and a hard, lumpy skin.

rocky, rockier, rockiest ADJECTIVE covered with rocks.

rod, rods NOUN a long, thin pole or bar, usually made of wood or metal • *a fishing rod*.

rode the past tense of **ride**.

rodent, rodents NOUN a small mammal with sharp front teeth which it uses for gnawing.
WORD HISTORY: from Latin *rodere* meaning 'to gnaw'

rodeo, rodeos NOUN a public entertainment in which cowboys show different skills.

roe NOUN Roe is the eggs of a fish.

rogue, rogues NOUN ① You can refer to a man who behaves dishonestly as a rogue. ▶ ADJECTIVE ② a vicious animal that lives apart from its herd or pack.

role, roles; also spelt **rôle** NOUN ① Someone's role is their position and function in a situation or society. ② DRAMA An actor's role is the character that he or she plays • *her first leading role*.

SPELLING TIP
Do not confuse the spellings of *role* and *roll*: *He has won a leading role in a musical*; *We need another roll of wallpaper*.

---

role play NOUN Role play is an activity in which a person acts out a scenario without previously preparing for it.

roll, rolls, rolling, rolled VERB ① When something rolls or when you roll it, it moves along a surface, turning over and over. ② When vehicles roll along, they move • *Tanks rolled into the village*. ③ If you roll your eyes, you make them turn up or go from side to side. ④ If you roll something flexible into a cylinder or ball, you wrap it several times around itself • *He rolled up the bag with the money in it*. ▶ NOUN ⑤ A roll of paper or cloth is a long piece of it that has been rolled into a tube • *a roll of wrapping paper*. ⑥ a small, rounded, individually baked piece of bread. ⑦ an official list of people's names • *the electoral roll*. ⑧ A roll on a drum is a long, rumbling sound made on it.
roll up VERB ① If you roll up something flexible, you wrap it several times around itself. ② If you roll up your sleeves or trousers, you fold them over from the bottom to make them shorter. ③ (*informal*) If you roll up, you arrive.

SPELLING TIP
Do not confuse the spellings of *roll* and *role*: *We need another roll of wallpaper*; *He has won a leading role in a musical*.

---

roll-call, roll-calls NOUN If you take a roll-call, you call a register of names to see who is present.

roller, rollers NOUN ① a cylinder that turns round in a machine or piece of equipment. ② Rollers are tubes which you can wind your hair around to make it curly.

Rollerblade, Rollerblades NOUN (*trademark*) Rollerblades are a brand of roller-skates which have the wheels set in one straight line on the bottom of the boot.

roller-coaster, roller-coasters NOUN a pleasure ride at a fair, consisting of a small railway that goes up and down very steep slopes.

roller-skate, roller-skates, roller-skating, roller-skated NOUN ① Roller-skates are shoes with four small wheels underneath. ▶ VERB ② If you roller-skate, you move along wearing roller-skates.

rolling pin, rolling pins NOUN a cylinder used for rolling pastry dough to make it flat.

ROM NOUN ICT ROM is a storage device that holds data permanently and cannot be altered by the programmer. ROM stands for 'read only memory'.

Roman Catholic, Roman Catholics RE ADJECTIVE ① relating or belonging to the branch of the Christian Church that accepts the Pope in Rome as its leader. ▶ NOUN ② someone who belongs to the Roman Catholic Church. **Roman Catholicism** NOUN

romance, romances NOUN ① a relationship between two people who are in love with each other. ② Romance is the pleasure and excitement of doing something new and unusual • *the romance of foreign travel*. ③ LIBRARY a novel about a love affair.

Romanian, Romanians [*Said roe-may-nee-an*]; also spelt **Rumanian** ADJECTIVE ① belonging or relating to Romania. ▶ NOUN ② someone who comes from Romania. ③ Romanian is the main language spoken in Romania.

Roman numeral, Roman numerals NOUN HISTORY Roman numerals are the letters used by the Romans in ancient times to write numbers. For example, V means five, VI means six, X means ten, and IX means nine.

romantic ADJECTIVE ① A romantic person has ideas that are not realistic, for example about love or about ways of changing society • *a romantic idealist*. ② connected with love • *a romantic relationship*. ③ Something that is romantic is beautiful in a way that strongly affects your feelings • *It is one of the most romantic ruins in Scotland*. ④ Romantic describes a style of music, literature and art popular in Europe in the late 18th and early 19th centuries, which emphasised feeling and imagination rather than order and form. **romantically** ADVERB **romanticism** NOUN

rondavel, rondavels NOUN In South Africa, a rondavel is a small circular building with a conical roof.

roo, roos NOUN (*informal*) In Australian English, a roo is a kangaroo.

roof, roofs NOUN ① The roof of a building or car is the covering on top of it. ② The roof of your mouth or of a cave is the highest part.

roofing NOUN Roofing is material used for covering roofs.

rooftop, rooftops NOUN the outside part of the roof of a building.

rook, rooks NOUN ① a large black bird. ② a chess piece which can move any number of squares in a straight but not diagonal line.

rookie, rookies NOUN (*informal*) someone who has just started doing a job and does not have much experience.

room, rooms NOUN ① a separate section in a building, divided from other rooms by walls. ② If there is room somewhere, there is enough space for things to be fitted in or for people to do what they want to do • *There wasn't enough room for his gear*.

roost, roosts, roosting, roosted NOUN ① a place where birds rest or build their nests. ▶ VERB ② When birds roost, they settle somewhere for the night.

rooster, roosters NOUN A rooster is an adult male chicken.

root, roots, rooting, rooted NOUN ① The roots of a plant are the parts that grow under the ground. ② The root of a hair is the part beneath the skin. ③ You can refer to the place or culture that you grew up in as your roots. ④ The root of something is its original cause or basis • *We got to the root of the problem*. ▶ VERB ⑤ To root through things means to search through them, pushing them aside • *She rooted through his bag*. **root out** VERB If you root something or someone out, you find them and force them out • *a major drive to root out corruption*.

rooted ADJECTIVE developed from or strongly influenced by something • *songs rooted in traditional African music*.

root word, root words NOUN ENGLISH A root word is a word from which other words can be made by adding a suffix or a prefix. For example, *clearly* and *unclear* can be made from the root word *clear*.

rope, ropes, roping, roped NOUN ① a thick, strong length of twisted cord. ▶ VERB ② If you rope one thing to another, you tie them together with rope.

rosary, rosaries NOUN a string of beads that Roman Catholics use for counting prayers.

rose, roses ① Rose is the past tense of **rise**. ▶ NOUN ② a large garden flower which has a pleasant smell and grows on a bush with thorns. ▶ NOUN or ADJECTIVE ③ reddish-pink.

rosella, rosellas NOUN a brightly coloured Australian parrot.

rosemary NOUN Rosemary is a herb with fragrant spiky leaves, used for flavouring in cooking.

rosette, rosettes NOUN a large badge of coloured ribbons gathered into a circle, which is worn as a prize in a competition or to support a political party.

Rosh Hashanah; also spelt **Rosh Hashana** NOUN RE the festival celebrating the Jewish New Year. WORD HISTORY: a Hebrew phrase meaning 'head of the year'

roster, rosters NOUN a list of people who take it in turn to do a particular job • *He put himself first on the new roster for domestic chores*.

rostrum, rostrums or rostra NOUN a raised platform on which someone stands to speak to an audience or conduct an orchestra. WORD HISTORY: from Latin *rostrum* meaning 'ship's prow'; Roman orators' platforms were decorated with the prows of captured ships

rosy, rosier, rosiest ADJECTIVE ① reddish-pink. ② If a situation seems rosy, it is likely to be good or successful. ③ If a person looks rosy, they have pink cheeks and look healthy.

rot, rots, rotting, rotted VERB ① When food or wood rots, it decays and can no longer be used. ② When something rots another substance, it causes it to decay • *Sugary drinks rot your teeth.* ▸ NOUN ③ Rot is the condition that affects things when they rot • *The timber frame was not protected against rot.*

SIMILAR WORDS: ① decay, decompose

rota, rotas NOUN a list of people who take turns to do a particular job.

rotate, rotates, rotating, rotated VERB MATHS When something rotates, it turns with a circular movement • *He rotated the camera 180°.* **rotation** NOUN

rotor, rotors NOUN ① The rotor is the part of a machine that turns. ② The rotors or rotor blades of a helicopter are the four long, flat pieces of metal on top of it which rotate and lift it off the ground.

rotten ADJECTIVE ① decayed and no longer of use • *The front bay window is rotten.* ② (*informal*) of very poor quality • *I think it's a rotten idea.* ③ (*informal*) very unfair, unkind or unpleasant • *That's a rotten thing to say!*

rouble, roubles [*Said* roo-bl] NOUN the main unit of currency in Russia.
WORD HISTORY: In Russian *rubl* means 'silver bar'

rough, rougher, roughest; roughs [*Said* **ruff**] ADJECTIVE ① uneven and not smooth. ② not using enough care or gentleness • *Don't be so rough or you'll break it.* ③ difficult or unpleasant • *Teenagers have been given a rough time.* ④ approximately correct • *At a rough guess it is five times more profitable.* ⑤ If the sea is rough, there are large waves because of bad weather. ⑥ A rough town or area has

a lot of crime or violence. ▸ NOUN or ADJECTIVE ⑦ A rough or a rough sketch is a drawing or description that shows the main features but does not show the details. ▸ NOUN ⑧ On a golf course, the rough is the part of the course next to a fairway where the grass has not been cut.

roughly ADVERB **roughness** NOUN

roulette [*Said* roo-**let**] NOUN Roulette is a gambling game in which a ball is dropped onto a revolving wheel with numbered holes in it.

round, rounder, roundest; rounds, rounding, rounded ADJECTIVE ① Something round is shaped like a ball or a circle. ② complete or whole • *round numbers.* ▸ PREPOSITION or ADVERB ③ If something is round something else, it surrounds it. ④ The distance round something is the length of its circumference or boundary • *I'm about two inches larger round the waist.* ⑤ You can refer to an area near a place as the area round it • *There's nothing to do round here.* ▸ PREPOSITION ⑥ If something moves round you, it keeps moving in a circle with you in the centre. ⑦ When someone goes to the other side of something, they have gone round it. ▸ ADVERB or PREPOSITION ⑧ If you go round a place, you go to different parts of it to look at it • *We went round the museum.* ▸ ADVERB ⑨ If you turn or look round, you turn so you are facing in a different direction. ⑩ When someone comes round, they visit you • *He came round with a bunch of flowers.* ▸ NOUN ⑪ one of a series of events • *After round three, two Americans shared the lead.* ⑫ If you buy a round of drinks, you buy a drink for each member of the group you are with. **round up** VERB If you round up people or animals, you gather them together.

SIMILAR WORDS: ① globular, spherical

roundabout, roundabouts NOUN ① a meeting point of several roads with a circle in the centre which vehicles have to travel around. ② a circular platform which rotates and which children can ride on in a playground. ③ the same as a merry-go-round.

round character, round characters NOUN ENGLISH a character in a story or play that is complicated and fully developed, like a real person, and often undergoes a significant change.

rounded ADJECTIVE curved in shape, without any points or sharp edges.

rounders NOUN a game played by two teams, in which a player scores points by hitting a ball and running around four sides of a square pitch.

round-the-clock ADJECTIVE happening continuously.

roundworm, roundworms NOUN A roundworm is a type of parasitic worm that lives in the intestines of dogs and cats.

rouse, rouses, rousing, roused VERB ① If someone rouses you, they wake you up. ② If you rouse yourself to do something, you make yourself get up and do it. ③ If something rouses you, it makes you feel very emotional and excited.

rouseabout, rouseabouts NOUN In Australian and New Zealand English, a rouseabout is an unskilled worker who does odd jobs, especially on a farm.

rout, routs, routing, routed [Rhymes with out] VERB To rout your opponents means to defeat them completely and easily.

route, routes [Said root] NOUN a way from one place to another.

router, routers [Said roo-ta] NOUN a piece of equipment which allows computers to access the internet.

routine, routines ADJECTIVE ① Routine activities are done regularly. ▸ NOUN ② the usual way or order in which you do things. ③ a boring repetition of tasks. **routinely** ADVERB

roving ADJECTIVE ① wandering or roaming • roving gangs of youths. ② not restricted to any particular location or area • a roving reporter.

row¹, rows, rowing, rowed [Rhymes with snow] NOUN ① A row of people or things is several of them arranged in a line. ▸ VERB ② When you row a boat, you use oars to make it move through the water.

row², rows, rowing, rowed [Rhymes with now] NOUN ① a serious argument. ② If someone is making a row, they are making too much noise. ▸ VERB ③ If people are rowing, they are quarrelling noisily.

rowdy, rowdier, rowdiest ADJECTIVE rough and noisy.

royal, royals ADJECTIVE ① belonging to or involving a queen, a king or a member of their family. ② 'Royal' is used in the names of organisations appointed or supported by a member of a royal family. ▸ NOUN ③ (informal) Members of the royal family are sometimes referred to as the royals. SIMILAR WORDS: ① imperial, regal

royalist, royalists NOUN someone who supports their country's royal family.

royalty, royalties NOUN ① The members of a royal family are sometimes referred to as royalty. ② Royalties are payments made to authors and musicians from the sales of their books or records.

RSS NOUN a way of allowing internet

users to receive the most recent news from particular websites as soon as it is published.

rub, rubs, rubbing, rubbed VERB If you rub something, you move your hand or a cloth backwards and forwards over it. **rub out** VERB To rub out something written means to remove it by rubbing it with a rubber or a cloth.

rubber, rubbers NOUN ① Rubber is a strong elastic substance used for making tyres, boots and other products. ② a small piece of rubber used to rub out pencil mistakes.

rubbish NOUN ① Rubbish is unwanted things or waste material. ② (*informal*) You can refer to nonsense or something of very poor quality as rubbish.
SIMILAR WORDS: ① garbage, refuse, trash, waste ② garbage, nonsense, twaddle

rubble NOUN Bits of old brick and stone are referred to as rubble.

rubric, rubrics [*Said roo-brik*] NOUN (*formal*) a set of instructions at the beginning of an official document.

ruby, rubies NOUN a type of red jewel.

rucksack, rucksacks NOUN a bag with shoulder straps for carrying things on your back.

rudder, rudders NOUN a piece of wood or metal at the back of a boat or plane which is moved to make the boat or plane turn.

rude, ruder, rudest ADJECTIVE ① not polite. ② embarrassing or offensive • *rude jokes*. ③ unexpected and unpleasant • *a rude awakening*.
rudely ADVERB **rudeness** NOUN
SIMILAR WORDS: ① discourteous, ill-mannered, impolite, uncivil

rudimentary ADJECTIVE (*formal*) very basic or not developed • *He had only a rudimentary knowledge of French*.

rudiments PLURAL NOUN When you learn the rudiments of something, you learn only the simplest and most basic things about it.
WORD HISTORY: from Latin *rudimentum* meaning 'beginning'

rueful ADJECTIVE expressing sorrow or regret in a quiet and gentle way.

ruff, ruffs NOUN ① a stiff circular collar with many pleats in it, worn especially in the 16th century. ② a thick band of fur or feathers around the neck of a bird or animal.

ruffle, ruffles, ruffling, ruffled VERB ① If you ruffle someone's hair, you move your hand quickly backwards and forwards over their head. ② If something ruffles you, it makes you annoyed or upset. ▸ NOUN ③ Ruffles are small folds made in a piece of material for decoration.

rug, rugs NOUN ① a small, thick carpet. ② a blanket which you can use to cover your knees or for sitting on outdoors.

rugby NOUN Rugby is a game played by two teams, who try to kick and throw an oval ball to their opponents' end of the pitch. Rugby League is played with 13 players in each side; Rugby Union is played with 15 players in each side.

rugged ADJECTIVE ① rocky and wild • *the rugged west coast of Ireland*. ② having strong features • *his rugged good looks*.

rugger NOUN (*informal*) Rugger is the same as rugby.

ruin, ruins, ruining, ruined VERB ① If you ruin something, you destroy or spoil it completely. ② If someone is ruined, they have lost all their money. ▸ NOUN ③ Ruin is the state of being destroyed or completely spoilt. ④ A ruin or the ruins of something refers to the parts that are left after it has been severely damaged • *the ruins of a thirteenth-century monastery.*

rule, **rules**, **ruling**, **ruled** NOUN
① Rules are statements which tell you what you are allowed to do.
▸ VERB ② To rule a country or group of people means to have power over it and be in charge of its affairs.
③ (*formal*) When someone in authority rules on a particular matter, they give an official decision about it. ▸ PHRASE ④ **As a rule** means usually or generally • *As a rule, I eat my meals in front of the TV.*

rule out VERB ① If you rule out an idea or course of action, you reject it.
② If one thing rules out another, it prevents it from happening or being possible • *The accident ruled out a future for him in football.*
SIMILAR WORDS: ① law, regulation

ruler, **rulers** NOUN ① a person who rules a country. ② a long, flat piece of wood or plastic with straight edges marked in centimetres or inches, used for measuring or drawing straight lines.

rum NOUN Rum is a strong alcoholic drink made from sugar cane juice.

Rumanian [*Said* roo-*may*-nee-*an*] another spelling of **Romanian**.

rumble, **rumbles**, **rumbling**, **rumbled** VERB ① If something rumbles, it makes a continuous low noise • *Another train rumbled past the house.* ▸ NOUN ② a continuous low noise • *the distant rumble of traffic.*

rummage, **rummages**, **rummaging**, **rummaged** VERB If you rummage somewhere, you search for something, moving things about carelessly.

rumour, **rumours**, **rumoured** NOUN
① a story that people are talking about, which may or may not be true.
▸ VERB ② If something is rumoured,

people are suggesting that it has happened.
SIMILAR WORDS: ① gossip, hearsay, story
WORD HISTORY: from Latin *rumor* meaning 'common talk'

rump, **rumps** NOUN ① An animal's rump is its rear end. ② Rump or rump steak is meat cut from the rear end of a cow.

rumpus NOUN A rumpus is a lot of noise or argument.

run, **runs**, **running**, **ran**, **run** VERB
① When you run, you move quickly, leaving the ground during each stride. ② If you say that a road or river runs in a particular direction, you are describing its course. ③ If you run your hand or an object over something, you move it over it. ④ If someone runs in an election, they stand as a candidate • *He announced he would run for President.* ⑤ If you run a business or an activity, you are in charge of it. ⑥ If you run an experiment, a computer program, or a tape, you start it and let it continue • *He ran a series of computer checks.*
⑦ To run a car means to have it and use it. ⑧ If you run someone somewhere in a car, you drive them there • *Could you run me up to town?*
⑨ If you run water, you turn on a tap to make it flow • *We heard him running the kitchen tap.* ⑩ If your nose is running, it is producing a lot of mucus. ⑪ If the dye in something runs, the colour comes out when it is washed. ⑫ If a feeling runs through your body, it affects you quickly and strongly. ⑬ If an amount is running at a particular level, it is at that level • *Inflation is currently running at 2.6 per cent.* ⑭ If someone or something is running late, they have taken more time than was planned. ⑮ If an event or contract runs for a particular time,

it lasts for that time. ▶NOUN ⑯ If you go for a run, you run for pleasure or exercise. ⑰ a journey somewhere • *It was quite a run to the village.* ⑱ If a play or show has a run of a particular length of time, it is on for that time. ⑲ A run of success or failure is a series of successes or failures. ⑳ In cricket or baseball, a player scores one run by running between marked places on the pitch after hitting the ball.

run away VERB If you run away from a place, you leave it suddenly and secretly. **run down** VERB ① To run someone down means to criticise them strongly. ② To run down an organisation means to reduce its size and activity. **run out** VERB If you run out of something, you have no more left. **run over** VERB If someone is run over, they are hit by a moving vehicle. SIMILAR WORDS: ① dash, race, sprint bolt, flee

runaway, runaways NOUN a person who has escaped from a place or left it secretly and hurriedly.

rundown ADJECTIVE ① tired and not well. ② neglected and in poor condition. ▶NOUN ③ (*informal*) If you give someone the rundown on a situation, you tell them the basic, important facts about it.

rung, rungs ① Rung is the past participle of **ring**. ▶NOUN ② The rungs on a ladder are the bars that form the steps.

runner, runners NOUN ① a person who runs, especially as a sport. ② a person who takes messages or runs errands. ③ A runner on a plant such as a strawberry is a long shoot from which a new plant develops. ④ The runners on drawers and ice-skates are the thin strips on which they move.

runner bean, runner beans NOUN Runner beans are long green pods

eaten as a vegetable, which grow on a climbing plant.

runner-up, runners-up NOUN a person or team that comes second in a race or competition.

running ADJECTIVE ① continuing without stopping over a period of time • *a running commentary.* ② Running water is flowing rather than standing still.

runny, runnier, runniest ADJECTIVE ① more liquid than usual • *Warm the honey until it becomes runny.* ② If someone's nose or eyes are runny, liquid is coming out of them.

runt, runts NOUN The runt of a litter of animals is the smallest and weakest.

runway, runways NOUN a long strip of ground used by aeroplanes for taking off or landing.

rupee, rupees [*Said* roo-pee] NOUN the main unit of currency in India, Pakistan and some other countries.

rupture, ruptures, rupturing, ruptured NOUN ① a severe injury in which part of your body tears or bursts open. ▶VERB ② To rupture part of the body means to cause it to tear or burst • *a ruptured spleen.*

rural ADJECTIVE GEOGRAPHY relating to or involving the countryside.

ruse, ruses NOUN (*formal*) an action which is intended to trick someone.

rush, rushes, rushing, rushed VERB ① To rush means to move fast or do something quickly. ② If you rush someone into doing something, you make them do it without allowing them enough time to think. ▶NOUN ③ If you are in a rush, you are busy and do not have enough time to do things. ④ If there is a rush for something, there is a sudden increase in demand for it • *There was a rush for tickets.* ⑤ Rushes are plants with long, thin stems that grow near water.

rush hour, rush hours NOUN The rush hour is one of the busy parts of the day when most people are travelling to or from work.

rusk, rusks NOUN a hard, dry biscuit given to babies.

Russian, Russians ADJECTIVE ① belonging or relating to Russia. ▶ NOUN ② someone who comes from Russia. ③ Russian is the main language spoken in Russia.

rust, rusts, rusting, rusted NOUN ① Rust is a reddish-brown substance that forms on iron or steel which has been in contact with water and which is decaying gradually. ▶ NOUN or ADJECTIVE ② reddish-brown. ▶ VERB ③ When a metal object rusts, it becomes covered in rust.

rustic ADJECTIVE simple in a way considered to be typical of the countryside • *a rustic old log cabin*.

rustle, rustles, rustling, rustled VERB When something rustles, it makes soft sounds as it moves.
rustling ADJECTIVE or NOUN

rusty, rustier, rustiest ADJECTIVE ① affected by rust • *a rusty iron gate*. ② If someone's knowledge is rusty, it is not as good as it used to be because they have not used it for a long time • *My German is a bit rusty these days*.

rut, ruts NOUN ① a deep, narrow groove in the ground made by the wheels of a vehicle. ▶ PHRASE ② If someone is **in a rut**, they have become fixed in their way of doing things.

ruthless ADJECTIVE very harsh or cruel • *a ruthless dictator*.
ruthlessness NOUN **ruthlessly** ADVERB

rye NOUN a type of grass that produces light brown grain.

Ss

Sabbath NOUN RE The Sabbath is the day of the week when members of some religious groups, especially Jews and Christians, do not work.
WORD HISTORY: from Hebrew *shabbath* meaning 'to rest'

sabotage, sabotages, sabotaging, sabotaged [Said *sab-ot-ahj*] NOUN ① the deliberate damaging of things such as machinery and railway lines. ▶ VERB ② If something is sabotaged, it is deliberately damaged. **saboteur** NOUN
WORD HISTORY: from French *saboter* meaning 'to spoil through clumsiness'

sabre, sabres NOUN ① a heavy curved sword. ② a light sword used in fencing.

sachet, sachets [Said *sash-ay*] NOUN a small closed packet, containing a small amount of something such as sugar or shampoo.

sack, sacks, sacking, sacked NOUN ① a large bag made of rough material used for carrying or storing goods. ▶ VERB ② (*informal*) If someone is sacked, they are dismissed from their job by their employer. ▶ PHRASE ③ (*informal*) If someone gets **the sack**, they are dismissed from their job by their employer.

sacrament, sacraments NOUN RE an important Christian ceremony such as communion, baptism or marriage.

sacred [Said *say-krid*] ADJECTIVE holy, or connected with religion or religious ceremonies • *sacred ground*.

sacrifice, sacrifices, sacrificing, sacrificed [Said *sak-riff-ice*] VERB ① If you sacrifice something valuable or important, you give it up. ② To sacrifice an animal means to kill it as an offering to a god. ▶ NOUN ③ the killing of an animal as an offering to a god or gods. ④ the action of giving something up. **sacrificial** ADJECTIVE
SIMILAR WORDS: ① forfeit, give up

sacrilege [Said *sak-ril-ij*] NOUN Sacrilege is behaviour that shows great disrespect for something holy. **sacrilegious** ADJECTIVE

sacrosanct [Said *sak-roe-sangkt*] ADJECTIVE regarded as too important to be criticised or changed • *Freedom of the press is sacrosanct.*

sad, sadder, saddest ADJECTIVE ① If you are sad, you feel unhappy. ② Something sad makes you feel unhappy • *a sad story.* **sadly** ADVERB
SIMILAR WORDS: ① low, melancholy, unhappy

sadden, saddens, saddening, saddened VERB If something saddens you, it makes you feel sad.

saddle, saddles, saddling, saddled NOUN ① a leather seat that you sit on when you are riding a horse. ② The saddle on a bicycle is the seat. ▶ VERB ③ If you saddle a horse, you put a saddle on it.

sadism [Said *say-diz-m*] NOUN Sadism is the obtaining of pleasure from making people suffer pain or humiliation. **sadist** NOUN **sadistic** ADJECTIVE **sadistically** ADVERB

WORD HISTORY: from the Marquis de *Sade* (1740–1814), who got his pleasure in this way

sadness NOUN the feeling of being unhappy.

safari, safaris NOUN an expedition for hunting or observing wild animals, especially in Africa.
WORD HISTORY: from Swahili *safari* meaning 'journey'

safari park, safari parks NOUN a large park where wild animals such as lions and elephants roam freely.

safe, safer, safest; safes ADJECTIVE ① PSHE Something that is safe does not cause harm or danger. ② If you are safe, you are not in any danger. ③ If it is safe to say something, you can say it with little risk of being wrong. ▶ NOUN ④ a strong metal box with special locks, in which you can keep valuable things. **safely** ADVERB
SIMILAR WORDS: ② out of danger, secure

safeguard, safeguards, safeguarding, safeguarded VERB ① To safeguard something means to protect it. ▶ NOUN ② something designed to protect people or things.

safekeeping NOUN If something is given to you for safekeeping, it is given to you to look after.

safety NOUN the state of being safe from harm or danger.

sag, sags, sagging, sagged VERB When something sags, it hangs down loosely or sinks downwards in the middle. **sagging** ADJECTIVE

saga, sagas [*Said sah-ga*] NOUN a very long story, usually with many different adventures • *a saga of rivalry, honour and love*.
WORD HISTORY: from Old Norse *saga* meaning 'story'

sage, sages NOUN ① (literary) a very wise person. ② Sage is also a herb used for flavouring in cooking.

WORD HISTORY: sense 1 is from Latin *sapere* meaning 'to be wise'; sense 2 is from Latin *salvus* meaning 'healthy', because of the supposed medicinal properties of the plant

Sagittarius [*Said saj-it-tair-ee-uss*] NOUN Sagittarius is the ninth sign of the zodiac, represented by a creature who is half horse, half man, holding a bow and arrow. People born between November 22nd and December 21st are born under this sign.
WORD HISTORY: from Latin *sagittarius* meaning 'archer'

said the past tense and past participle of **say**.

sail, sails, sailing, sailed NOUN ① Sails are large pieces of material attached to a ship's mast. The wind blows against the sail and moves the ship. ▶ VERB ② When a ship sails, it moves across water. ③ If you sail somewhere, you go there by ship.

sailor, sailors NOUN a member of a ship's crew.

saint, saints NOUN a person who after death is formally recognised by a Christian Church as deserving special honour because of having lived a very holy life.
WORD HISTORY: from Latin *sanctus* meaning 'holy'

saintly ADJECTIVE behaving in a very good or holy way.

sake, sakes PHRASE ① If you do something **for someone's sake**, you do it to help or please them. ② You use **for the sake of** to say why you are doing something • *a one-off expedition for interest's sake*.

salad, salads NOUN a mixture of raw vegetables.
WORD HISTORY: from Old Provençal *salar* meaning 'to season with salt'

salamander, salamanders NOUN A salamander is an amphibian that looks rather like a lizard.

salami [Said sal-**lah**-mee] NOUN
Salami is a kind of spicy sausage.

salary, salaries NOUN a regular
monthly payment to an employee.
salaried ADJECTIVE
WORD HISTORY: from Latin *salarium*
meaning 'money given to soldiers to
buy salt'

salat, salats NOUN RE a prayer that
Muslims say five times a day.

sale, sales NOUN ① The sale of goods
is the selling of them. ② an occasion
when a shop sells things at reduced
prices. ③ (*in plural*) The sales of a
product are the numbers that are sold.

saleable ADJECTIVE easy to sell or
suitable for being sold.

salesman, salesmen NOUN a man
who sells products for a company.

saleswoman, saleswomen NOUN a
woman who sells products for a
company.

salient [Said **say**-lee-ent] ADJECTIVE
(*formal*) The salient points or facts are
the important ones.

saliva [Said sal-**live**-a] NOUN Saliva is
the watery liquid in your mouth that
helps you chew and digest food.

sallow ADJECTIVE Sallow skin is pale
and unhealthy.

salmon, salmons or salmon [Said
sam-on] NOUN a large edible
silver-coloured fish with pink flesh.

salmonella [Said sal-mon-**nell**-a]
NOUN Salmonella is a kind of bacteria
which can cause severe food
poisoning.

salon, salons NOUN a place where
hairdressers work.

saloon, saloons NOUN ① a car with a
fixed roof and a separate boot. ② in
the Wild West of America, a place
where alcoholic drinks were sold
and drunk.

salt, salts NOUN ① Salt is a white
substance found naturally in sea
water. It is used to flavour and
preserve food. ② SCIENCE a
chemical compound formed from an
acid base.

salty, saltier, saltiest ADJECTIVE
containing salt or tasting of salt.

salute, salutes, saluting, saluted
NOUN ① a formal sign of respect.
Soldiers give a salute by raising their
right hand to their forehead. ▶ VERB
② If you salute someone, you give
them a salute.

salvage, salvages, salvaging,
salvaged VERB ① If you salvage
things, you save them, for example
from a wrecked ship or a destroyed
building. ▶ NOUN ② You refer to
things saved from a wrecked ship or
destroyed building as salvage.

salvation NOUN ① When someone's
salvation takes place, they are saved
from harm or evil. ② To be someone's
salvation means to save them from
harm or evil.

salvo, salvos or salvoes NOUN the
firing of several guns or missiles at
the same time.

same ADJECTIVE (*usually preceded by
the*) ① If two things are the same,
they are like one another. ② Same
means just one thing and not two
different ones • *They were born in the
same town.*

Samoan, Samoans ADJECTIVE
① belonging or relating to Samoa.
▶ NOUN ② someone who comes from
Samoa.

sample, samples, sampling,
sampled NOUN ① A sample of
something is a small amount of it
that you can try or test • *a free sample
of a new product.* ▶ VERB ② If you
sample something, you try it • *I
sampled his cooking.*

samsara NOUN ① RE in Hinduism, the endless cycle of birth, death and rebirth. ② RE in Buddhism, someone's rebirth.

samurai [Said *sam-oor-eye*] NOUN A samurai was a member of an ancient Japanese warrior class.

sanctimonious [Said *sank-tim-moan-ee-uss*] ADJECTIVE pretending to be very religious and virtuous.

sanction, sanctions, sanctioning, sanctioned VERB ① To sanction something means to officially approve of it or allow it. ▶ NOUN ② Sanction is official approval of something. ③ a severe punishment or penalty intended to make people obey the law. ④ Sanctions are sometimes taken by countries against a country that has broken international law.

sanctity NOUN If you talk about the sanctity of something, you are saying that it should be respected because it is very important • *the sanctity of marriage*.

sanctuary, sanctuaries NOUN ① a place where you are safe from harm or danger. ② a place where wildlife is protected • *a bird sanctuary*.

sand, sands, sanding, sanded NOUN ① Sand consists of tiny pieces of stone. Beaches are made of sand. ▶ VERB ② If you sand something, you rub sandpaper over it to make it smooth.

sandal, sandals NOUN Sandals are light open shoes with straps, worn in warm weather.

sandpaper NOUN DGT Sandpaper is strong paper with a coating of sand on it, used for rubbing surfaces to make them smooth.

sandstone NOUN Sandstone is a type of rock formed from sand, often used for building.

sandwich, sandwiches, sandwiching, sandwiched NOUN ① two slices of bread with a filling between them. ▶ VERB ② If one thing is sandwiched between two others, it is in a narrow space between them • *a small shop sandwiched between a bar and an office*.

WORD HISTORY: sense 1 is named after the 4th Earl of *Sandwich* (1718–1792), for whom they were invented so that he could eat and gamble at the same time

SPELLING TIP
Remember this mnemonic: *there's SAND in my SANDwich.*

sandy, sandier, sandiest ADJECTIVE ① A sandy area is covered with sand. ② Sandy hair is light orange-brown.

sane, saner, sanest ADJECTIVE ① If someone is sane, they have a normal and healthy mind. ② A sane action is sensible and reasonable.

sang the past tense of **sing**.

sangoma, sangomas [Said *san-goh-ma*] NOUN In traditional South African societies, a man who appears to have magic powers.

sanguine [Said *sang-gwin*] ADJECTIVE (*formal*) cheerful and confident.

sanitary ADJECTIVE Sanitary means concerned with keeping things clean and hygienic • *improving sanitary conditions*.

sanitary towel, sanitary towels NOUN Sanitary towels are pads of thick, soft material which women wear during their periods.

sanitation NOUN Sanitation is the process of keeping places clean and hygienic, especially by providing a sewage system and clean water supply.

sanity NOUN Your sanity is your ability to think and act normally and reasonably.

a b c d e f g h i j k l m n o p q r **s** t u v w x y z

sank the past tense of **sink**.

sap, saps, sapping, sapped VERB ① If something saps your strength or confidence, it gradually weakens and destroys it. ▶ NOUN ② Sap is the watery liquid in plants.

sapling, saplings NOUN a young tree.

sapphire, sapphires NOUN a blue precious stone.

sarcastic ADJECTIVE saying or doing the opposite of what you really mean in order to mock or insult someone • *a sarcastic remark.* **sarcasm** NOUN **sarcastically** ADVERB

WORD HISTORY: from Greek *sarkazein* meaning 'to tear the flesh'

sarcophagus, sarcophagi or sarcophaguses [*Said sar-kof-fag-uss*] NOUN HISTORY a stone coffin used in ancient times.

sardine, sardines NOUN a small edible sea fish.

sardonic ADJECTIVE mocking or scornful • *a sardonic grin.* **sardonically** ADVERB

sari, saris [*Said sah-ree*] NOUN a piece of clothing worn especially by Indian women, consisting of a long piece of material folded around the body.

sarmie, sarmies NOUN In South African English, a sarmie is a slang word for a sandwich.

sartorial ADJECTIVE (formal) relating to clothes • *sartorial elegance.*

sash, sashes NOUN a long piece of cloth worn round the waist or over one shoulder.

WORD HISTORY: from Arabic *shash* meaning 'muslin'

sat the past tense and past participle of **sit**.

Satan NOUN Satan is the Devil.

satanic [*Said sa-tan-ik*] ADJECTIVE caused by or influenced by Satan • *satanic forces.*

satchel, satchels NOUN a leather or cloth bag with a long strap.

satellite, satellites NOUN ① a spacecraft sent into orbit round the earth to collect information or as part of a communications system. ② a natural object in space that moves round a planet or star.

satin, satins NOUN Satin is a kind of smooth, shiny silk.

satire, satires NOUN Satire is the use of mocking or ironical humour, especially in literature, to show how foolish or wicked some people are. **satirical** ADJECTIVE

satisfaction NOUN Satisfaction is the feeling of pleasure you get when you do something you wanted or needed to do.

satisfactory ADJECTIVE acceptable or adequate • *a satisfactory explanation.* **satisfactorily** ADVERB

satisfied ADJECTIVE happy because you have got what you want.

satisfy, satisfies, satisfying, satisfied VERB ① To satisfy someone means to give them enough of something to make them pleased or contented. ② To satisfy someone that something is the case means to convince them of it. ③ To satisfy the requirements for something means to fulfil them.

SIMILAR WORDS: ① content, indulge, please

satisfying ADJECTIVE Something that is satisfying gives you a feeling of pleasure and fulfilment.

sat nav NOUN a computer in a car that gives directions to the driver's destination by using satellites.

satsuma, satsumas [*Said sat-soo-ma*] NOUN a fruit like a small orange.

saturated ADJECTIVE ① very wet. ② If a place is saturated with things, it is completely full of them • *If you*

thought the area was already saturated with supermarkets, think again.
saturation NOUN

Saturday, Saturdays NOUN the day between Friday and Sunday.
WORD HISTORY: from Latin *Saturni dies* meaning 'day of Saturn'

Saturn NOUN Saturn is the planet in the solar system which is sixth from the sun.

sauce, sauces NOUN a liquid eaten with food to give it more flavour.

SPELLING TIP
Do not confuse the spellings of *sauce* and *source*, which can sound very similar in some accents.

---

saucepan, saucepans NOUN a deep metal cooking pot with a handle and a lid.

saucer, saucers NOUN a small curved plate for a cup.

saucy, saucier, sauciest ADJECTIVE cheeky in an amusing way.

Saudi, Saudis [Rhymes with **cloudy**] ADJECTIVE ① belonging or relating to Saudi Arabia. ▸ NOUN ② someone who comes from Saudi Arabia.

sauna, saunas [Said **saw-na**] NOUN If you have a sauna, you go into a very hot room in order to sweat, then have a cold bath or shower.
WORD HISTORY: a Finnish word

saunter, saunters, sauntering, sauntered VERB To saunter somewhere means to walk there slowly and casually.

sausage, sausages NOUN a mixture of minced meat and herbs formed into a tubular shape and served cooked.

sauté, sautés, sautéing or sautéeing, sautéed [Said **soh-tay**] VERB To sauté food means to fry it quickly in a small amount of oil or butter.

savage, savages, savaging, savaged ADJECTIVE ① cruel and violent
• *savage fighting.* ▸ NOUN ② If you call someone a savage, you mean that they are violent and uncivilised.
▸ VERB ③ If an animal savages you, it attacks you and bites you. **savagely** ADVERB
SIMILAR WORDS: ① brutal, cruel, vicious

savagery NOUN Savagery is cruel and violent behaviour.

save, saves, saving, saved VERB ① If you save someone, you rescue them
• *He saved my life.* ② If you save someone or something, you keep them safe. ③ If you save something, you keep it so that you can use it later
• *He'd saved up enough money for the deposit.* ④ To save time, money or effort means to prevent it from being wasted • *You could have saved us the trouble.* ▸ PREPOSITION ⑤ (formal) Save means except • *I was alone in the house save for a very old woman.*

saving, savings NOUN ① a reduction in the amount of time or money used. ② (in plural) Your savings are the money you have saved.

saviour, saviours NOUN ① If someone saves you from danger, you can refer to them as your saviour.
▸ PROPER NOUN ② RE In Christianity, the Saviour is Jesus Christ.

savour, savours, savouring, savoured VERB If you savour something, you take your time with it and enjoy it fully • *I settled down and savoured a cup of strong coffee.*

savoury ADJECTIVE ① Savoury is salty or spicy. ② Something that is not very savoury is not very pleasant or respectable • *the less savoury places.*

saw, saws, sawing, sawed, sawn ① Saw is the past tense of **see**.
▸ VERB ② If you saw something, you

a
b
c
d
e
f
g
h
i
j
k
l
m
n
o
p
q
r
s
t
u
v
w
x
y
z

cut it with a saw. ▶ **NOUN** ③ a tool, with a blade with sharp teeth along one edge, for cutting wood.

sawdust **NOUN** Sawdust is the fine powder produced when you saw wood.

saxophone, saxophones **NOUN** a curved metal wind instrument often played in jazz bands.

WORD HISTORY: named after Adolphe *Sax* (1814–1894), who invented the instrument

say, says, saying, said **VERB** ① When you say something, you speak words. ② 'Say' is used to give an example • *a maximum fee of, say, a million.* ▶ **NOUN** ③ If you have a say in something, you can give your opinion and influence decisions.

SIMILAR WORDS: ① remark, speak, utter

saying, sayings **NOUN** a well-known sentence or phrase that tells you something about human life.

SIMILAR WORDS: adage, proverb

scab, scabs **NOUN** a hard, dry covering that forms over a wound.

scabby **ADJECTIVE**

scaffolding **NOUN** Scaffolding is a framework of poles and boards that is used by workmen to stand on while they are working on the outside structure of a building.

scald, scalds, scalding, scalded [*Said skawld*] **VERB** ① If you scald yourself, you burn yourself with very hot liquid or steam. ▶ **NOUN** ② a burn caused by scalding.

SPELLING TIP

Do not confuse *scald* and *scold*: *She was scalded by hot sauce; I was scolded for wearing the wrong shoes.*

---

scale, scales, scaling, scaled **NOUN** ① The scale of something is its size or extent • *the sheer scale of the disaster.*

② a set of levels or numbers used for measuring things. ③ GEOGRAPHY The scale of a map, plan or model is the relationship between the size of something in the map, plan or model and its size in the real world • *a scale of* 1:30,000. ④ MUSIC an upward or downward sequence of musical notes. ⑤ The scales of a fish or reptile are the small pieces of hard skin covering its body. ⑥ (*in plural*) Scales are a piece of equipment used for weighing things. ▶ **VERB** ⑦ If you scale something high, you climb it.

scale drawing, scale drawings **NOUN** a drawing whose proportions are exactly the same as those of the object represented.

scalene **ADJECTIVE** MATHS A scalene triangle has sides which are all of different lengths.

scallop, scallops **NOUN** Scallops are edible shellfish with two flat fan-shaped shells.

scalp, scalps, scalping, scalped **NOUN** ① Your scalp is the skin under the hair on your head. ② the piece of skin and hair removed when someone is scalped. ▶ **VERB** ③ To scalp someone means to remove the skin and hair from their head in one piece.

scalpel, scalpels **NOUN** a knife with a thin, sharp blade, used by surgeons.

scaly, scalier, scaliest **ADJECTIVE** covered with scales.

scam, scams **NOUN** (*informal*) an illegal trick, usually done to get money from a person.

scamper, scampers, scampering, scampered **VERB** To scamper means to move quickly and lightly.

scampi **PLURAL NOUN** Scampi are large prawns often eaten fried in breadcrumbs.

scan, scans, scanning, scanned
VERB ① If you scan something, you look at all of it carefully • *I scanned the horizon to the north-east.* ② If you scan a piece of writing, you read it very quickly to find the important or interesting parts. ③ If a machine scans something, it examines it by means of a beam of light or X-rays. ④ ENGLISH If the words of a poem scan, they fit into a regular, rhythmical pattern. ⑤ ENGLISH If you scan a line of poetry you count the number of beats or metrical feet it has. ▸ NOUN ⑥ an examination or search by a scanner • *a brain scan.*

scandal, scandals NOUN a situation or event that people think is shocking and immoral. **scandalous** ADJECTIVE

Scandinavia [Said skan-din-*nay*-vee-a] NOUN Scandinavia is the name given to a group of countries in Northern Europe, including Norway, Sweden, Denmark and sometimes Finland and Iceland. **Scandinavian** NOUN or ADJECTIVE

scanner, scanners NOUN ① a machine which is used to examine, identify or record things by means of a beam of light or X-rays. ② ICT a machine which converts text or images into a form that can be stored on a computer.

scansion NOUN ENGLISH Scansion is the analysis of the rhythmic arrangement of syllables in lines of poetry.

scant, scanter, scantest ADJECTIVE You use 'scant' to show that there is not as much of something as there should be • *Some drivers pay scant attention to the laws of the road.*

scapegoat, scapegoats NOUN If someone is made a scapegoat, they are blamed for something, although it may not be their fault.

scar, scars, scarring, scarred NOUN ① a mark left on your skin after a wound has healed. ② a permanent effect on someone's mind that results from a very unpleasant experience • *the scars of war.* ▸ VERB ③ If an injury scars you, it leaves a permanent mark on your skin. ④ If an unpleasant experience scars you, it has a permanent effect on you.

scarce, scarcer, scarcest ADJECTIVE If something is scarce, there is not very much of it. **scarcity** NOUN

scarcely ADVERB Scarcely means hardly • *I can scarcely hear her.*

GRAMMAR TIP
As *scarcely* already has a negative sense, it is followed by *ever* or *any*, and not by *never* or *no*.

scare, scares, scaring, scared VERB ① If something scares you, it frightens you. ▸ NOUN ② If something gives you a scare, it scares you. ③ If there is a scare about something, a lot of people are worried about it • *a health scare.* **scared** ADJECTIVE
SIMILAR WORDS: ① alarm, frighten, startle

scarecrow, scarecrows NOUN an object shaped like a person, put in a field to scare birds away.

scarf, scarfs or scarves NOUN a piece of cloth worn round your neck or head to keep you warm.

scarlet NOUN or ADJECTIVE bright red.

scary, scarier, scariest ADJECTIVE (*informal*) frightening.

scathing [Said *skayth*-ing] ADJECTIVE harsh and scornful • *They were scathing about his job.*

scatter, scatters, scattering, scattered VERB ① To scatter things means to throw or drop them all over an area. ② If people scatter, they suddenly move away in different directions.

SIMILAR WORDS: ① sprinkle, strew, throw about

scattering NOUN A scattering of things is a small number of them spread over a large area • *the scattering of islands*.

scavenge, scavenges, scavenging, scavenged VERB If you scavenge for things, you search for them among waste and rubbish. **scavenger** NOUN

scenario, scenarios *[Said sin-nar-ee-oh]* NOUN ① DRAMA The scenario of a film or play is a summary of its plot. ② the way a situation could possibly develop in the future • *the worst possible scenario*.

scene, scenes NOUN ① ENGLISH DRAMA part of a play or film in which a series of events happen in one place. ② Pictures and views are sometimes called scenes • *a village scene*. ③ The scene of an event is the place where it happened. ④ an area of activity • *the music scene*.

scenery NOUN ① In the countryside, you can refer to everything you see as the scenery. ② In a theatre, the scenery is the painted cloth on the stage which represents the place where the action is happening.

scenic ADJECTIVE A scenic place or route has nice views.

scent, scents, scenting, scented NOUN ① a smell, especially a pleasant one. ② Scent is perfume. ▶ VERB ③ When an animal scents something, it becomes aware of it by smelling it.

SPELLING TIP
Do not confuse the spellings of *scent* and *sent*, the past tense of *send*: *the scent of lilies; I sent Anna a birthday card.*

sceptic, sceptics *[Said skep-tik]* NOUN someone who has doubts about things that other people believe. **scepticism** NOUN

SPELLING TIP
Do not confuse the spellings of *sceptic* and *septic*: *Eve is a sceptic when it comes to ghosts; The doctor said the wound had gone septic.*

sceptical *[Said skep-tik-kl]* ADJECTIVE If you are sceptical about something, you have doubts about it.

sceptically ADVERB **scepticism** NOUN

sceptre, sceptres *[Said sep-ter]* NOUN an ornamental rod carried by a king or queen as a symbol of power.

schedule, schedules, scheduling, scheduled *[Said shed-yool]* NOUN ① a plan that gives a list of events or tasks, together with the times at which each thing should be done. ▶ VERB ② If something is scheduled to happen, it has been planned and arranged • *Their journey was scheduled for the beginning of May.*

schema, schemata *[Said skee-ma]* NOUN ① (*technical*) an outline of a plan or theory. ② a mental model which the mind uses to understand new experiences or to view the world.

scheme, schemes, scheming, schemed NOUN ① a plan or arrangement • *a five-year development scheme*. ▶ VERB ② When people scheme, they make secret plans.

schism, schisms *[Said skizm]* NOUN a split or division within a group or organisation.

schizophrenia *[Said skit-soe-free-nee-a]* NOUN Schizophrenia is a serious mental illness which prevents someone relating their thoughts and feelings to what is happening around

them. **schizophrenic** ADJECTIVE
WORD HISTORY: from Greek *skhizein*
meaning 'to split' and *phrēn* meaning
'mind'

scholar, scholars NOUN ① a person
who studies an academic subject and
knows a lot about it. ② In South
African English, a scholar is a school
pupil.

scholarly ADJECTIVE having or
showing a lot of knowledge.

scholarship, scholarships NOUN
① If you get a scholarship to a school
or university, your studies are paid for
by the school or university or by some
other organisation. ② Scholarship is
academic study and knowledge.

school, schools, schooling, schooled
NOUN ① a place where children are
educated. ② University departments
and colleges are sometimes called
schools • *My oldest son is in medical
school.* ③ You can refer to a large
group of dolphins or fish as a school.
▶ VERB ④ When someone is schooled
in something, they are taught it
• *They were schooled in the modern
techniques.*

schoolchild, schoolchildren NOUN
Schoolchildren are children who go
to school. **schoolboy** NOUN
schoolgirl NOUN

schooling NOUN Your schooling is
the education you get at school.

schooner, schooners NOUN a sailing
ship.

science, sciences NOUN ① Science is
the study of the nature and
behaviour of natural things and the
knowledge obtained about them.
② a branch of science, for example
physics or biology.

science fiction NOUN Stories about
events happening in the future or in
other parts of the universe are called
science fiction.

scientific ADJECTIVE ① relating to
science or to a particular science
• *scientific knowledge.* ② done in a
systematic way, using experiments
or tests • *this scientific method.*
scientifically ADVERB

scientist, scientists NOUN an expert
in one of the sciences who does work
connected with it.

scimitar, scimitars [Said sim-mit-ar]
NOUN HISTORY A scimitar is a
curved sword used in the past in
some Eastern countries.

scintillating [Said sin-til-late-ing]
ADJECTIVE lively and witty
• *scintillating conversation.*

scissors PLURAL NOUN Scissors are a
cutting tool with two sharp blades.

scoff, scoffs, scoffing, scoffed VERB
① If you scoff, you speak in a scornful,
mocking way about something.
② (informal) If you scoff food, you eat
it quickly and greedily.

scold, scolds, scolding, scolded VERB
If you scold someone, you tell them
off.
SIMILAR WORDS: rebuke, reprimand,
tell off

SPELLING TIP
Do not confuse *scold* and *scald*: *I was
scolded for wearing the wrong shoes; She
was scalded by hot sauce.*

scone, scones [Said skon or skoan]
NOUN Scones are small cakes made
from flour and fat and usually eaten
with butter.

scoop, scoops, scooping, scooped
VERB ① If you scoop something up,
you pick it up using a spoon or the
palm of your hand. ▶ NOUN ② an
object like a large spoon which is
used for picking up food such as ice
cream.

scooter, scooters NOUN ① a small,
light motorcycle. ② a simple cycle

which a child rides by standing on it and pushing the ground with one foot.

scope NOUN ① If there is scope for doing something, the opportunity to do it exists. ② The scope of something is the whole subject area which it deals with or includes.

-scope SUFFIX '-scope' is used to form nouns meaning an instrument used for observing or detecting • *microscope* • *telescope*.
WORD HISTORY: from Greek *skopein* meaning 'to look at'

scorch, scorches, scorching, scorched VERB To scorch something means to burn it slightly.

scorching ADJECTIVE extremely hot • *another scorching summer*.

score, scores, scoring, scored VERB ① If you score in a game, you get a goal, run or point. ② To score in a game also means to record the score obtained by the players. ③ If you score a success or victory, you achieve it. ④ To score a surface means to cut a line into it. ▶ NOUN ⑤ The score in a game is the number of goals, runs or points obtained by the two teams. ⑥ Scores of things means very many of them • *Ros entertained scores of celebrities.* ⑦ (*old-fashioned*) A score is twenty. ⑧ MUSIC The score of a piece of music is the written version of it.
scorer NOUN

scorn, scorns, scorning, scorned NOUN ① Scorn is great contempt • *a look of scorn.* ▶ VERB ② If you scorn someone, you treat them with great contempt. ③ (*formal*) If you scorn something, you refuse to accept it.

scornful ADJECTIVE showing contempt • *his scornful comment.*
scornfully ADVERB
SIMILAR WORDS: contemptuous, disdainful, sneering

Scorpio NOUN Scorpio is the eighth sign of the zodiac, represented by a scorpion. People born between October 23rd and November 21st are born under this sign.

scorpion, scorpions NOUN an animal that looks like a small lobster, with a long tail with a poisonous sting on the end.

Scot, Scots NOUN ① a person who comes from Scotland. ▶ ADJECTIVE ② Scots means the same as **Scottish**.

scotch, scotches NOUN Scotch is whisky made in Scotland.

scot-free ADVERB If you get away scot-free, you get away without being punished.
WORD HISTORY: from Old English *scot* meaning 'payment'; hence 'payment-free'

Scotsman, Scotsmen NOUN a man who comes from Scotland.

Scotswoman, Scotswomen NOUN a woman who comes from Scotland.

Scottish ADJECTIVE belonging or relating to Scotland.

scoundrel, scoundrels NOUN (*old-fashioned*) a man who cheats and deceives people.

scour, scours, scouring, scoured VERB ① If you scour a place, you look all over it in order to find something • *The police scoured the area.* ② If you scour something such as a pan, you clean it by rubbing it with something rough.

scourge, scourges [*Rhymes with urge*] NOUN something that causes a lot of suffering • *hay fever, that scourge of summer.*

scout, scouts, scouting, scouted NOUN ① a boy who is a member of the Scout Association, an organisation for boys which aims to develop character and responsibility. ② someone who is sent to an area to find out the position of an enemy army. ▸ **VERB** ③ If you scout around for something, you look around for it.

scowl, scowls, scowling, scowled **VERB** ① If you scowl, you frown because you are angry • *They were scowling at me.* ▸ **NOUN** ② an angry expression.

scrabble, scrabbles, scrabbling, scrabbled **VERB** If you scrabble at something, you scrape at it with your hands or feet.

WORD HISTORY: from Old Dutch *schrabbelen* meaning 'to scrape repeatedly'

scramble, scrambles, scrambling, scrambled **VERB** ① If you scramble over something, you climb over it using your hands to help you. ▸ **NOUN** ② a motorcycle race over rough ground.

scrap, scraps, scrapping, scrapped **NOUN** ① A scrap of something is a very small piece of it • *a scrap of cloth.* ② (*in plural*) Scraps are pieces of leftover food. ▸ **ADJECTIVE** or **NOUN** ③ Scrap metal or scrap is metal from old machinery or cars that can be re-used. ▸ **VERB** ④ If you scrap something, you get rid of it • *They considered scrapping passport controls.*

scrapbook, scrapbooks **NOUN** a book in which you stick things such as pictures or newspaper articles.

scrape, scrapes, scraping, scraped **VERB** ① If you scrape a surface, you rub a rough or sharp object against it. ② If something scrapes, it makes a harsh noise by rubbing against something • *his shoes scraping across the stone ground.*

scratch, scratches, scratching, scratched **VERB** ① To scratch something means to make a small cut on it accidentally • *They were always getting scratched by cats.* ② If

you scratch, you rub your skin with your nails because it is itching. ▸ **NOUN** ③ a small cut.

scratchcard, scratchcards **NOUN** a ticket in a competition with a surface that you scratch off to show whether or not you have won a prize.

scrawl, scrawls, scrawling, scrawled **VERB** ① If you scrawl something, you write it in a careless and untidy way. ▸ **NOUN** ② You can refer to careless and untidy writing as a scrawl.

scrawny, scrawnier, scrawniest **ADJECTIVE** thin and bony • *a small scrawny man.*

scream, screams, screaming, screamed **VERB** ① If you scream, you shout or cry in a loud, high-pitched voice. ▸ **NOUN** ② a loud, high-pitched cry.

SIMILAR WORDS: ② cry, shriek, yell

screech, screeches, screeching, screeched **VERB** ① To screech means to make an unpleasant high-pitched noise • *The car wheels screeched.* ▸ **NOUN** ② an unpleasant high-pitched noise.

screen, screens, screening, screened **NOUN** ① a flat vertical surface on which a picture is shown • *a television screen.* ② a vertical panel used to separate different parts of a room or to protect something. ▸ **VERB** ③ To screen a film or television programme means to show it. ④ If you screen someone, you put something in front of them to protect them.

screenplay, screenplays **NOUN** The screenplay of a film is the script.

screen saver, screen savers **NOUN** a piece of computer software that produces changing images on a monitor when the computer is idle.

screenshot, screenshots **NOUN** A screenshot is an image copied from a computer screen at a particular moment.

screw, screws, screwing, screwed
NOUN ① a small, sharp piece of metal used for fixing things together or for fixing something to a wall. ▶VERB ② If you screw things together, you fix them together using screws. ③ If you screw something onto something else, you fix it there by twisting it round and round • *He screwed the top on the ink bottle.*

screw up VERB If you screw something up, you twist it or squeeze it so that it no longer has its proper shape • *Amy screwed up her face.*

screwdriver, screwdrivers NOUN a tool for turning screws.

scribble, scribbles, scribbling, scribbled VERB ① If you scribble something, you write it quickly and roughly. ② To scribble also means to make meaningless marks • *When Caroline was five she scribbled on a wall.* ▶NOUN ③ You can refer to something written or drawn quickly and roughly as a scribble.

scrimp, scrimps, scrimping, scrimped VERB If you scrimp, you live cheaply and spend as little money as you can.

script, scripts NOUN DRAMA the written version of a play or film.

scripture, scriptures NOUN RE Scripture refers to sacred writings, especially the Bible. **scriptural** ADJECTIVE

scroll, scrolls NOUN a long roll of paper or parchment with writing on it.

scrounge, scrounges, scrounging, scrounged VERB (*informal*) If you scrounge something, you get it by asking for it rather than by earning or buying it. **scrounger** NOUN

SIMILAR WORDS: cadge, sponge

scrub, scrubs, scrubbing, scrubbed
VERB ① If you scrub something, you clean it with a stiff brush and water. ▶NOUN ② If you give something a scrub, you scrub it. ③ GEOGRAPHY Scrub consists of low trees and bushes.

scruff NOUN The scruff of your neck is the back of your neck or collar.

scruffy, scruffier, scruffiest
ADJECTIVE dirty and untidy • *four scruffy youths.*
SIMILAR WORDS: tatty, unkempt

scrum, scrums NOUN When rugby players form a scrum, they form a group and push against each other with their heads down in an attempt to get the ball.

scrunchie, scrunchies NOUN a loop of elastic loosely covered with material which is used to hold hair in a ponytail.

scruple, scruples [*Said skroo-pl*]
NOUN Scruples are moral principles that make you unwilling to do something that seems wrong • *The West must drop its scruples and fight back.*

scrupulous ADJECTIVE ① always doing what is honest or morally right. ② paying very careful attention to detail • *a long and scrupulous search.* **scrupulously** ADVERB

scrutinise, scrutinises, scrutinising, scrutinised; also spelt **scrutinize** VERB If you scrutinise something, you examine it very carefully.

scrutiny NOUN If something is under scrutiny, it is being observed very carefully.

scuba diving NOUN Scuba diving is the sport of swimming underwater while breathing from tanks of compressed air on your back.

scuff, scuffs, scuffing, scuffed VERB ① If you scuff your feet, you drag them along the ground when you are walking. ② If you scuff your shoes, you mark them by scraping or rubbing them.

scuffle, scuffles, scuffling, scuffled NOUN ① a short, rough fight. ▸ VERB ② When people scuffle, they fight roughly.

scullery, sculleries NOUN a small room next to a kitchen where washing and cleaning are done.

sculpt, sculpts, sculpting, sculpted VERB When something is sculpted, it is carved or shaped in stone, wood or clay.

sculptor, sculptors NOUN someone who makes sculptures.

sculpture, sculptures NOUN ① a work of art produced by carving or shaping stone or clay. ② Sculpture is the art of making sculptures.

scum NOUN Scum is a layer of a dirty substance on the surface of a liquid.

scungy, scungier, scungiest [Said skun-jee] ADJECTIVE In Australia and New Zealand, 'scungy' is a slang word for 'dirty or messy'.

scurrilous [Said skur-ril-luss] ADJECTIVE abusive and damaging to someone's good name • scurrilous stories.

scurry, scurries, scurrying, scurried VERB To scurry means to run quickly with short steps.

scurvy NOUN Scurvy is a disease caused by a lack of vitamin C.

scuttle, scuttles, scuttling, scuttled VERB ① To scuttle means to run quickly. ② To scuttle a ship means to sink it deliberately by making holes in the bottom. ▸ NOUN ③ a container for coal.

scythe, scythes [Said sythe] NOUN a tool with a long handle and a curved blade used for cutting grass or grain.

sea, seas NOUN ① The sea is the salty water that covers much of the earth's surface. ② A sea of people or things is a very large number of them • a sea of red flags.

seagull, seagulls NOUN Seagulls are common white, grey and black birds that live near the sea.

seahorse, seahorses NOUN a small fish which swims upright, with a head that resembles a horse's head.

seal, seals, sealing, sealed NOUN ① an official mark on a document which shows that it is genuine. ② a piece of wax fixed over the opening of a container. ③ a large mammal with flippers that lives partly on land and partly in the sea. ▸ VERB ④ If you seal an envelope, you stick down the flap. ⑤ If you seal an opening, you cover it securely so that air, gas or liquid cannot get through.

sea lion, sea lions NOUN a type of large seal.

seam, seams NOUN ① a line of stitches joining two pieces of cloth. ② A seam of coal is a long, narrow layer of it beneath the ground.

seaman, seamen NOUN a sailor.

seance, seances [Said say-ahnss]; also spelt **séance** NOUN a meeting in which people try to communicate with the spirits of dead people.

search, searches, searching, searched VERB ① If you search for something, you look for it in several places. ② If a person is searched their body and clothing are examined to see if they are hiding anything. ▸ NOUN ③ an attempt to find something.

SIMILAR WORDS: ① hunt, look, scour ③ look, hunt, quest

a
b
c
d
e
f
g
h
i
j
k
l
m
n
o
p
q
r
s
t
u
v
w
x
y
z

search engine, search engines
NOUN a service on the internet which
enables users to search for items of
interest.

searching ADJECTIVE intended to
discover the truth about something
• *searching questions*.

searchlight, searchlights NOUN a
powerful light whose beam can be
turned in different directions.

searing ADJECTIVE A searing pain is
very sharp.

seashore NOUN The seashore is the
land along the edge of the sea.

seasick ADJECTIVE feeling sick
because of the movement of a boat.
seasickness NOUN

seaside NOUN The seaside is an area
next to the sea.

season, seasons, seasoning,
seasoned NOUN ① The seasons are
the periods into which a year is
divided and which have their own
typical weather conditions. The
seasons are spring, summer, autumn
and winter. ② a period of the year
when something usually happens
• *the football season* • *the hunting
season*. ▶ VERB ③ If you season
food, you add salt, pepper or spices
to it.

seasonal ADJECTIVE happening
during one season or one time of the
year • *seasonal work*.

seasoned ADJECTIVE very
experienced • *a seasoned professional*.

seasoning NOUN Seasoning is
flavouring such as salt and pepper.

season ticket, season tickets
NOUN a train or bus ticket that you
can use as many times as you like
within a certain period.

seat, seats, seating, seated NOUN
① something you can sit on. ② The
seat of a piece of clothing is the part
that covers your bottom. ③ If
someone wins a seat in parliament,
they are elected. ▶ VERB ④ If you seat
yourself somewhere, you sit down.
⑤ If a place seats a particular number
of people, it has enough seats for
that number • *The theatre seats
570 people*.

seat belt, seat belts NOUN a strap
that you fasten across your body for
safety when travelling in a car or an
aircraft.

seating NOUN The seating in a place
is the number or arrangement of
seats there.

seaweed NOUN Plants that grow in
the sea are called seaweed.

secateurs [Said sek-at-**turz**] PLURAL
NOUN Secateurs are small shears for
pruning garden plants.

secluded ADJECTIVE quiet and hidden
from view • *a secluded beach*.
seclusion NOUN

second, seconds, seconding,
seconded ADJECTIVE [Said sek-ond]
① The second item in a series is the
one counted as number two. ▶ NOUN
[Said sek-ond] ② one of the sixty parts
that a minute is divided into.
③ Seconds are goods that are sold
cheaply because they are slightly
faulty. ▶ VERB ④ [Said sek-ond] If you
second a proposal, you formally
agree with it so that it can be
discussed or voted on. ⑤ [Said
si-kond] If you are seconded
somewhere, you are sent there
temporarily to work. **secondly**
ADVERB
WORD HISTORY: from Latin *secundus*

secondary ADJECTIVE ① Something
that is secondary is less important
than something else. ② Secondary
education is education for pupils
between the ages of eleven and
eighteen.

secondary school, secondary schools NOUN a school for pupils between the ages of eleven and eighteen.

second-class ADJECTIVE ① Second-class things are regarded as less important than other things of the same kind • *He has been treated as a second-class citizen*. ② Second-class services are cheaper and therefore slower or less comfortable than first-class ones.

second cousin, second cousins NOUN Your second cousins are the children of your parents' cousins.

second-hand ADJECTIVE or ADVERB ① Something that is second-hand has already been owned by someone else • *a second-hand car*. ② If you hear a story second-hand, you hear it indirectly, rather than from the people involved.

second person NOUN ENGLISH MFL In grammar, the second person is the person being spoken to (*you*).

second-person narrator NOUN ENGLISH A second-person narrator addresses the reader directly using the pronoun *you* and tells a story as if the reader is the character whose thoughts and actions are being described. For example, a **second-person narrative** might begin 'You are standing in a dusty street, pretending to be doing nothing.'

second-rate ADJECTIVE of poor quality • *a second-rate movie*.

secret, secrets ADJECTIVE ① Something that is secret is told to only a small number of people and hidden from everyone else • *a secret meeting*. ▶ NOUN ② a fact told to only a small number of people and hidden from everyone else. **secretly** ADVERB **secrecy** NOUN SIMILAR WORDS: ① confidential, concealed, hidden

secret agent, secret agents NOUN a spy.

secretary, secretaries NOUN ① a person employed by an organisation to keep records, write letters, and do office work. ② Ministers in charge of some government departments are also called secretaries • *the Health Secretary*. **secretarial** ADJECTIVE

secrete, secretes, secreting, secreted [Said sik-*kreet*] VERB ① When part of a plant or animal secretes a liquid, it produces it. ② (formal) If you secrete something somewhere, you hide it. **secretion** NOUN

secretive ADJECTIVE Secretive people tend to hide their feelings and intentions.
SIMILAR WORDS: reticent, tight-lipped

secret service NOUN A country's secret service is the government department in charge of espionage.

sect, sects NOUN a religious or political group which has broken away from a larger group.

sectarian [Said sek-*tair*-ee-an] ADJECTIVE strongly supporting a particular sect • *sectarian violence*.

section, sections NOUN A section of something is one of the parts it is divided into • *this section of the motorway*.
SIMILAR WORDS: part, portion, segment

sector, sectors NOUN ① A sector of something, especially a country's economy, is one part of it • *the private sector*. ② MATHS A sector of a circle is one of the two parts formed when you draw two straight lines from the centre to the circumference.

secular ADJECTIVE having no connection with religion • *secular education*.

a b c d e f g h i j k l m n o p q r s t u v w x y z

secure, secures, securing, secured
VERB ① (formal) If you secure
something, you manage to get it
• *They secured the rights to her story*.
② If you secure a place, you make it
safe from harm or attack. ③ To
secure something also means to
fasten it firmly • *One end was secured
to the pier*. ▶ ADJECTIVE ④ If a place is
secure, it is tightly locked or well
protected. ⑤ If an object is secure, it
is firmly fixed in place. ⑥ If you feel
secure, you feel safe and confident.
securely ADVERB

security NOUN ① Security means all
the precautions taken to protect a
place • *The airports have increased the
level of security*. ② A feeling of security
is a feeling of being safe.

sedate, sedates, sedating, sedated
[Said sid-**date**] ADJECTIVE ① quiet and
dignified. ▶ VERB ② To sedate
someone means to give them a drug
to calm them down or make them
sleep. **sedately** ADVERB

sedative, sedatives [Said sed-at-tiv]
NOUN ① a drug that calms you down
or makes you sleep. ▶ ADJECTIVE
② having a calming or soothing effect
• *antihistamines which have a sedative
effect*. **sedation** NOUN

sedentary [Said sed-en-tree]
ADJECTIVE A sedentary occupation is
one in which you spend most of your
time sitting down.

sediment NOUN ① Sediment is solid
material that settles at the bottom of
a liquid • *A bottle of beer with sediment
in it is usually a guarantee of quality*.
② GEOGRAPHY Sediment is also
small particles of rock that have been
worn down and deposited together
by water, ice and wind.

sedimentary ADJECTIVE
GEOGRAPHY Sedimentary rocks are
formed from fragments of shells or
rocks that have become compressed.

Sandstone and limestone are
sedimentary rocks.

seduce, seduces, seducing, seduced
VERB If you are seduced into doing
something, you are persuaded to do
it because it seems very attractive.

seductive ADJECTIVE Something
seductive is very attractive and
tempting. **seductively** ADVERB

see, sees, seeing, saw, seen VERB
① If you see something, you are
looking at it or you notice it. ② If you
see someone, you visit them or meet
them • *I went to see my dentist*. ③ If
you see someone to a place, you
accompany them there. ④ To see
something also means to realise or
understand it • *I see what you mean*.
⑤ If you say you will see what is
happening, you mean you will find
out. ⑥ If you say you will see if you
can do something, you mean you will
try to do it. ⑦ If you see that
something is done, you make sure
that it is done. ⑧ If you see to
something, you deal with it. ⑨ 'See' is
used to say that an event takes place
during a particular period of time
• *The next couple of years saw two
momentous developments*. ▶ PHRASE
⑩ (informal) **Seeing that** or **seeing as**
means because • *I took John for lunch,
seeing as it was his birthday*. ▶ NOUN
⑪ A bishop's see is his diocese.
SIMILAR WORDS: ① notice, perceive,
spot

seed, seeds NOUN ① SCIENCE The
seeds of a plant are the small, hard
parts from which new plants can
grow. ② The seeds of a feeling or
process are its beginning or origins
• *the seeds of mistrust*.

seedling, seedlings NOUN a young
plant grown from a seed.

seedy, seedier, seediest ADJECTIVE
untidy and shabby • *a seedy hotel*.

seek, seeks, seeking, sought VERB
(formal) ① To seek something means
to try to find it, obtain it or achieve it
• *The police were still seeking
information.* ② If you seek to do
something, you try to do it • *De Gaulle
sought to reunite the country.*

seem, seems, seeming, seemed
VERB If something seems to be the
case, it appears to be the case or you
think it is the case • *He seemed such a
quiet chap.*

seeming ADJECTIVE appearing to be
real or genuine • *this seeming disregard
for human life.* **seemingly** ADVERB

seep, seeps, seeping, seeped VERB If
a liquid or gas seeps through
something, it flows through very
slowly.

seesaw, seesaws NOUN a long plank,
supported in the middle, on which
two children sit, one on each end,
and move up and down in turn.

seething ADJECTIVE If you are
seething about something, you are
very angry but it does not show.

segment, segments NOUN ① A
segment of something is one part of
it. ② The segments of an orange or
grapefruit are the sections which you
can divide it into. ③ MATHS A
segment of a circle is one of the two
parts formed when you draw a
straight line across it.

segmentation NOUN Segmentation
is the dividing of something into
segments.

segregate, segregates,
segregating, segregated VERB To
segregate two groups of people
means to keep them apart from each
other. **segregated** ADJECTIVE
segregation NOUN

seismograph, seismographs [Said
size-moh-grahf] NOUN GEOGRAPHY
A seismograph is an instrument for

measuring the strength of
earthquakes.

seismology [Said size-mol-loj-ee]
NOUN GEOGRAPHY Seismology is
the scientific study of earthquakes.
seismic ADJECTIVE

seize, seizes, seizing, seized VERB
① If you seize something, you grab it
firmly • *He seized the phone.* ② To seize
a place or to seize control of it means
to take control of it quickly and
suddenly. ③ If you seize an
opportunity, you take advantage of
it. ④ If you seize on something, you
immediately show great interest in it
• *MPs have seized on a new report.*

seize up VERB ① If a part of your
body seizes up, it becomes stiff and
painful. ② If an engine seizes up, it
becomes jammed and stops
working.

seizure, seizures [Said seez-yer] NOUN
① a sudden violent attack of an
illness, especially a heart attack or a
fit. ② If there is a seizure of power, a
group of people suddenly take
control using force.

seldom ADVERB not very often • *They
seldom speak to each other.*

select, selects, selecting, selected
VERB ① If you select something, you
choose it. ▶ ADJECTIVE ② of good
quality • *a select social club.* **selector**
NOUN

selection, selections NOUN
① Selection is the choosing of people
or things • *the selection of
parliamentary candidates.* ② A
selection of people or things is a set
of them chosen from a larger group.
③ The selection of goods in a shop is
the range of goods available • *a good
selection of shoes.*

selective ADJECTIVE choosing things
carefully • *I am selective about what I
eat.* **selectively** ADVERB

a b c d e f g h i j k l m n o p q r s t u v w x y z

selective breeding NOUN SCIENCE taking control of breeding in order to produce animals or plants with or without particular characteristics • *Selective breeding can be used to develop plants that are resistant to disease.*

self, selves NOUN Your self is your basic personality or nature • *Hershey is her normal dependable self.*

self- PREFIX ① done to yourself or by yourself • *self-help* • *self-control*. ② doing something automatically • *a self-loading rifle.*

self-assured ADJECTIVE behaving in a way that shows confidence in yourself.

self-centred ADJECTIVE thinking only about yourself and not about other people.

self-confessed ADJECTIVE admitting to having bad habits or unpopular opinions • *a self-confessed liar.*

self-confident ADJECTIVE confident of your own abilities or worth. **self-confidence** NOUN

self-conscious ADJECTIVE nervous and easily embarrassed, and worried about what other people think of you. **self-consciously** ADVERB

self-control NOUN PSHE Self-control is the ability to restrain yourself and not show your feelings.

self-defence NOUN Self-defence is the use of special physical techniques to protect yourself when someone attacks you.

self-discipline NOUN the power to control one's own feelings and actions, especially in order to improve oneself.

self-employed ADJECTIVE working for yourself and organising your own finances, rather than working for an employer.

self-esteem NOUN PSHE Your self-esteem is your good opinion of yourself.

self-evident ADJECTIVE Self-evident facts are completely obvious and need no proof or explanation.

self-harm, self-harms, self-harming, self-harmed VERB If you self-harm, you deliberately hurt yourself, for example by cutting yourself, because of a psychological problem.

selfie, selfies NOUN (*informal*) a photograph taken by pointing a camera at yourself.

self-indulgent ADJECTIVE allowing yourself to do or have things you enjoy, especially as a treat.

self-interest NOUN If you do something out of self-interest, you do it for your own benefit rather than to help other people.

selfish ADJECTIVE caring only about yourself, and not about other people. **selfishly** ADVERB **selfishness** NOUN

selfless ADJECTIVE putting other people's interests before your own.

self-raising ADJECTIVE Self-raising flour contains baking powder to make cakes and bread rise when they are baked.

self-respect NOUN Self-respect is a belief in your own worth and opinions.

self-righteous ADJECTIVE convinced that you are better or more virtuous than other people. **self-righteousness** NOUN
SIMILAR WORDS: holier-than-thou, sanctimonious

self-service ADJECTIVE A self-service shop or restaurant is one where you serve yourself.

self-sufficient ADJECTIVE ① producing or making everything you need, and so not needing to buy things. ② able to live in a way in which you do not need other people.

sell, sells, selling, sold VERB
① If you sell something, you let someone have it in return for money.
② If a shop sells something, it has it available for people to buy • *a tobacconist that sells stamps.*
③ If something sells, people buy it • *This book will sell.* **seller** NOUN
sell out VERB If a shop has sold out of something, it has sold it all.
SIMILAR WORDS: ② deal in, retail, stock

Sellotape NOUN (*trademark*)
Sellotape is a transparent sticky tape.

semblance NOUN If there is a semblance of something, it seems to exist, although it might not really exist • *an effort to restore a semblance of normality.*

semen [*Said see-men*] NOUN SCIENCE
Semen is the liquid containing sperm produced by a man's or male animal's sex organs.

semi- PREFIX 'Semi-' means half or partly • *semiskilled workers.*
WORD HISTORY: from Latin *semi-* meaning 'half' or 'partly'

semibreve, semibreves NOUN MUSIC
a musical note (○) which can be divided by any power of 2 to give all other notes. In the United States and Canada, a semibreve is known as a whole note.

semicircle, semicircles NOUN a half of a circle, or something with this shape. **semicircular** ADJECTIVE

semicolon, semicolons NOUN
ENGLISH the punctuation mark (;), used to separate different parts of a sentence or to indicate a pause.

PUNCTUATION TIP
If two main clauses could be written as separate sentences, you can join them with a semicolon: *The plane's engine started; the propellers began to turn.*

---

semidetached ADJECTIVE A semidetached house is joined to another house on one side.

semifinal, semifinals NOUN The semifinals are the two matches in a competition played to decide who plays in the final. **semifinalist** NOUN

seminar, seminars NOUN a meeting of a small number of university students or teachers to discuss a particular topic.

semipermeable ADJECTIVE A semipermeable material is one that certain substances with small

What does the Semicolon do?

The **semicolon** (;) and the **colon** (:) are often confused and used incorrectly.

The **semicolon** is stronger than a comma, but weaker than a full stop. It can be used to mark the break between two main clauses, especially where there is balance or contrast between them:

I'm not that interested in jazz; I prefer classical music.

The semicolon can also be used instead of a comma to separate clauses or items in a long list:

They did not enjoy the meal: the food was cold; the service was poor; and the music was too loud.

Also look at the punctuation box at **colon**

a
b
c
d
e
f
g
h
i
j
k
l
m
n
o
p
q
r
s
t
u
v
w
x
y
z

enough molecules can pass through but which others with larger molecules can not.

semiprecious ADJECTIVE
Semiprecious stones are stones such as opals or turquoises that are used in jewellery. They are less valuable than precious stones.

semitone, semitones NOUN [MUSIC]
an interval representing the difference in pitch between a note and its sharpened or flattened equivalent. Two semitones are equal to one tone.

Senate, Senates NOUN The Senate is the smaller, more important of the two councils in the government of some countries, for example Australia, Canada and the USA.

senator, senators NOUN a member of a Senate.

send, sends, sending, sent VERB ① If you send something to someone, you arrange for it to be delivered to them. ② To send a radio signal or message means to transmit it. ③ If you send someone somewhere, you tell them to go there or arrange for them to go. ④ If you send for someone, you send a message asking them to come and see you. ⑤ If you send off for something, you write and ask for it to be sent to you. ⑥ To send people or things in a particular direction means to make them move in that direction • *It should have sent him tumbling from the saddle.* **send up** VERB If you send someone or something up, you imitate them and make fun of them.

SIMILAR WORDS: ① direct, dispatch, forward

SPELLING TIP
Do not confuse the spellings of *sent*, the past tense of *send*, and *scent*: *I sent Anna a birthday card; the scent of lilies.*

senile ADJECTIVE If elderly people become senile, they become confused and cannot look after themselves. **senility** NOUN

senior, seniors ADJECTIVE ① The senior people in an organisation or profession have the highest and most important jobs. ▸ NOUN ② Someone who is your senior is older than you. **seniority** NOUN

senior citizen, senior citizens NOUN an elderly person, especially one receiving a retirement pension.

sensation, sensations NOUN ① a feeling, especially a physical feeling. ② If something is a sensation, it causes great excitement and interest.

sensational ADJECTIVE ① causing great excitement and interest. ② (*informal*) extremely good • *a sensational party.* **sensationally** ADVERB

sense, senses, sensing, sensed NOUN ① Your senses are the physical abilities of sight, hearing, smell, touch and taste. ② a feeling • *a sense of guilt.* ③ A sense of a word is one of its meanings. ④ Sense is the ability to think and behave sensibly. ▸ VERB ⑤ If you sense something, you become aware of it. ▸ PHRASE ⑥ If something **makes sense**, you can understand it or it seems sensible • *It makes sense to find out as much as you can.*

senseless ADJECTIVE ① A senseless action has no meaning or purpose • *senseless destruction.* ② If someone is senseless, they are unconscious.

sensibility, sensibilities NOUN Your sensibility is your ability to experience deep feelings • *a man of sensibility rather than reason.*

sensible ADJECTIVE showing good sense and judgment. **sensibly** ADVERB
SIMILAR WORDS: prudent, rational, wise

sensitive ADJECTIVE ① If you are sensitive to other people's feelings, you understand them. ② If you are sensitive about something, you are worried or easily upset about it • *He was sensitive about his height.* ③ A sensitive subject or issue needs to be dealt with carefully because it can make people angry or upset. ④ Something that is sensitive to a particular thing is easily affected or harmed by it. **sensitively** ADVERB

sensitivity NOUN ① the quality of being sensitive. ② the ability of a plant or animal to respond to external stimuli such as light, sound, movement or temperature.

sensor, sensors NOUN an instrument which reacts to physical conditions such as light or heat.

sensual [*Said senss-yool*] ADJECTIVE giving pleasure to your physical senses rather than to your mind • *the sensual rhythm of his voice.* **sensuality** NOUN

sensuous ADJECTIVE giving pleasure through the senses. **sensuously** ADVERB

sentence, sentences, sentencing, sentenced NOUN ① a group of words which make a statement, question or command. When written down a sentence begins with a capital letter and ends with a full stop. ② In a law court, a sentence is a punishment given to someone who has been found guilty. ▶ VERB ③ When a guilty person is sentenced, they are told officially what their punishment will be.
▶ SEE GRAMMAR BOX ON NEXT PAGE

sentiment, sentiments NOUN ① a feeling, attitude or opinion • *I doubt my parents share my sentiments.* ② Sentiment consists of feelings such as tenderness or sadness • *There's no room for sentiment in business.*

sentimental ADJECTIVE ① feeling or expressing tenderness or sadness to an exaggerated extent • *sentimental love stories.* ② relating to a person's emotions • *things of sentimental value.* ③ ENGLISH Sentimental literature is intended to provoke an emotional response to the story, rather than relying on the reader's own natural response. **sentimentality** NOUN
SIMILAR WORDS: ① emotional, romantic, slushy

sentinel, sentinels NOUN (*old-fashioned*) a sentry.

sentry, sentries NOUN a soldier who keeps watch and guards a camp or building.

separate, separates, separating, separated ADJECTIVE [*Said sep-ir-it*] ① If something is separate from something else, the two things are not connected. ▶ VERB [*Said sep-ir-ate*] ② To separate people or things means to cause them to be apart from each other. ③ If people or things separate, they move away from each other. ④ If a married couple separate, they decide to live apart. **separately** ADVERB **separation** NOUN
SIMILAR WORDS: ② divide, split, part ③ diverge, part, part company

sepia [*Said see-pee-a*] ADJECTIVE or NOUN deep brown, like the colour of old photographs.
WORD HISTORY: from Latin *sepia* meaning 'cuttlefish', because the brown dye is obtained from the ink of this fish

September NOUN September is the ninth month of the year. It has 30 days.
WORD HISTORY: from Latin *September* meaning 'the seventh month'

septic ADJECTIVE If a wound becomes septic, it becomes infected with poison.

a b c d e f g h i j k l m n o p q r s t u v w x y z

A
B
C
D
E
F
G
H
I
J
K
L
M
N
O
P
Q
R
S
T
U
V
W
X
Y
Z

What is a Sentence?

The different types of word can go together to make sentences. A sentence is a group of words which expresses an idea or describes a situation.

Sentences begin with a **capital letter**:

The child was sleeping.

Sentences usually end with a **full stop**:

Anna lives in Lisbon.

If a sentence is a question, it ends with a **question mark** instead of a full stop:

Where is my purse?

If a sentence is an exclamation of surprise, anger or excitement, it ends with an **exclamation mark** instead of a full stop:

You must be joking!

Sentences have a **subject**, which indicates a person or thing. The rest of the sentence usually says something about the subject. The subject is usually the first word or group of words in a sentence:

Anna laughed.
Robbie likes bananas.

Most sentences have a **verb**. The verb says what the subject of the sentence is doing or what is happening to the subject. The verb usually follows immediately after the subject:

Matthew smiled.

Simple Sentences, Compound Sentences and Complex Sentences

Simple sentences consist of only one main clause, and no subordinate clause:

Anna fed the cat.

The **subject** of a simple sentence is the person or thing that the sentence is about. It usually comes at the start of the sentence. The subject may be a noun, a pronoun or a noun phrase:

We often go to the cinema.

The remaining part of the sentence contains a verb phrase and says something about the subject:

Katia likes to go swimming.
She is a strong swimmer.
A ginger cat was sitting on the stair.

Compound sentences consist of two or more main clauses joined together by a conjunction. Both clauses are equally important:

Katia likes to go swimming, but Matthew likes to go fishing.

Complex sentences consist of a main clause with one or more subordinate clauses joined to it.

Numerous subordinate clauses can be added to a main clause:

After looking at all the pictures, the judges gave the first prize, which was a silver trophy, to Robbie, because his work was the best.

SPELLING TIP

Do not confuse the spellings of *septic* and *sceptic*: *The doctor said the wound had gone septic; Eve is a sceptic when it comes to ghosts.*

---

sepulchre, sepulchres [*Said* sep-pul-ka]

NOUN (*literary*) a large tomb.

sequel, sequels NOUN ① A sequel to a book or film is another book or film which continues the story. ② The sequel to an event is a result or consequence of it • *There's a sequel to my egg story.*

sequence, sequences NOUN ①A sequence of events is a number of them coming one after the other • *the whole sequence of events that had brought me to this place*. ②The sequence in which things are arranged is the order in which they are arranged • *Do things in the right sequence*.

sequin, sequins NOUN Sequins are small, shiny, coloured discs sewn on clothes to decorate them.

Serbian, Serbians ADJECTIVE ①belonging or relating to Serbia. ▶ NOUN ②someone who comes from Serbia. ③Serbian is the form of Serbo-Croat spoken in Serbia.

Serbo-Croat [Said ser-boh-**kroh**-at] NOUN Serbo-Croat is the main language spoken in Serbia and Croatia.

serenade, serenades, serenading, serenaded VERB ①If you serenade someone you love, you sing or play music to them outside their window. ▶ NOUN ②a song sung outside a person's window by someone who loves them.

serene ADJECTIVE peaceful and calm • *She had a serene air.* **serenely** ADVERB **serenity** NOUN

serf, serfs NOUN HISTORY Serfs were servants in medieval Europe who had to work on their master's land and could not leave without his permission.

sergeant, sergeants NOUN ①a noncommissioned officer of middle rank in the army or air force. ②a police officer just above a constable in rank.

sergeant major, sergeant majors NOUN a noncommissioned army officer of the highest rank.

serial, serials NOUN a story which is broadcast or published in a number of parts over a period of time • *a television serial.*

SPELLING TIP
Do not confuse the spellings of *serial* and *cereal: a new drama serial; my favourite breakfast cereal.*

serial number, serial numbers NOUN An object's serial number is a number you can see on it which identifies it and distinguishes it from other objects of the same kind.

series, series NOUN ①A series of things is a number of them coming one after the other • *a series of loud explosions*. ②A radio or television series is a set of programmes with the same title. ▶ PHRASE ③ SCIENCE If electrical circuits are arranged **in series**, the same current flows through each of them in turn.
SIMILAR WORDS: ① sequence, set, succession

serious ADJECTIVE ①A serious problem or situation is very bad and worrying. ②Serious matters are important and should be thought about carefully. ③If you are serious about something, you are sincere about it • *You are really serious about having a baby.* ④People who are serious are thoughtful, quiet and do not laugh much. **seriousness** NOUN
SIMILAR WORDS: ① grave, severe ④ grave, solemn

seriously ADVERB ①You say seriously to emphasise that you mean what you say • *Seriously, though, something must be done.* ▶ PHRASE ②If you **take something seriously**, you regard it as important.

sermon, sermons NOUN a talk on a religious or moral subject given as part of a church service.

serpent, serpents NOUN (*literary*) a snake.

a b c d e f g h i j k l m n o p q r s t u v w x y z

A
B
C
D
E
F
G
H
I
J
K
L
M
N
O
P
Q
R
S
T
U
V
W
X
Y
Z

serrated ADJECTIVE having a row of V-shaped points along the edge, like a saw • *green serrated leaves*.

servant, servants NOUN someone who is employed to work in another person's house.

serve, serves, serving, served VERB ①If you serve a country, an organisation or a person, you do useful work for them. ②To serve as something means to act or be used as that thing • *the room that served as their office*. ③If something serves people in a particular place, it provides them with something they need • *a recycling plant which serves the whole of the county*. ④If you serve food or drink to people, you give it to them. ⑤To serve customers in a shop means to help them and provide them with what they want. ⑥To serve a prison sentence or an apprenticeship means to spend time doing it. ⑦When you serve in tennis or badminton, you throw the ball or shuttlecock into the air and hit it over the net to start playing. ▶ NOUN ⑧the act of serving in tennis or badminton.

server, servers NOUN ① ICT a computer or computer program which supplies information or resources to a number of computers on a network. ②a spoon or fork used for serving food • *salad servers*.

service, services, servicing, serviced NOUN ①a system organised to provide something for the public • *the bus service*. ②Some government organisations are called services • *the diplomatic service*. ③The services are the army, the navy and the air force. ④If you give your services to a person or organisation, you work for them or help them in some way • *services to the community*. ⑤In a shop or restaurant, service is the process of

being served. ⑥a religious ceremony. ⑦When it is your service in a game of tennis or badminton, it is your turn to serve. ⑧(*in plural*) Motorway services consist of a petrol station, restaurant, shop and toilets. ▶ VERB ⑨When a machine or vehicle is serviced, it is examined and adjusted so that it will continue working efficiently.

serviceman, servicemen NOUN a man in the army, navy or air force.

service station, service stations NOUN a garage that sells petrol, oil, spare parts and snacks.

servicewoman, servicewomen NOUN a woman in the army, navy or air force.

servile ADJECTIVE too eager to obey people. **servility** NOUN
SIMILAR WORDS: obsequious, subservient

serving, servings NOUN ①a helping of food. ▶ ADJECTIVE ②A serving spoon or dish is used for serving food.

session, sessions NOUN ①a meeting of an official group • *the emergency session of the Indiana Supreme Court*. ②a period during which meetings are held regularly • *the end of the parliamentary session*. ③The period during which an activity takes place can also be called a session • *a yoga session*.

set, sets, setting, set NOUN ①Several things make a set when they belong together or form a group • *a set of weights*. ② MATHS In maths, a set is a collection of numbers or other things which are treated as a group. ③A television set is a television. ④The set for a play or film is the scenery or furniture on the stage or in the studio. ⑤In tennis, a set is a group of six or more games. There are usually several sets in a match.

▶ VERB ⑥ If something is set somewhere, that is where it is • *The house was set back from the beach*. ⑦ When the sun sets, it goes below the horizon. ⑧ When you set the table, you prepare it for a meal by putting plates and cutlery on it. ⑨ When you set a clock or a control, you adjust it to a particular point or position. ⑩ If you set someone a piece of work or a target, you give it to them to do or to achieve. ⑪ When something such as jelly or cement sets, it becomes firm or hard.

▶ ADJECTIVE ⑫ Something that is set is fixed and not varying • *a set charge*. ⑬ If you are set to do something, you are ready or likely to do it. ⑭ If you are set on doing something, you are determined to do it. ⑮ If a play or story is set at a particular time or in a particular place, the events in it take place at that time or in that place.

set about VERB If you set about doing something, you start doing it.

set back VERB If something sets back a project or scheme, it delays it.

set off VERB ① When you set off, you start a journey. ② To set something off means to cause it to start.

set out VERB ① When you set out, you start a journey. ② If you set out to do something, you start trying to do it. **set up** VERB If you set something up, you make all the necessary preparations for it • *We have done all we can about setting up a system of communication*.

SIMILAR WORDS: ⑫ fixed, hard and fast, inflexible

setback, setbacks NOUN PSHE something that stops you from making progress.

settee, settees NOUN a long comfortable seat for two or three people to sit on.

setter, setters NOUN a long-haired breed of dog originally used in hunting.

setting, settings NOUN ① The setting of something is its surroundings or circumstances • *The Irish setting made the story realistic*. ② The settings on a machine are the different positions to which the controls can be adjusted.

settle, settles, settling, settled VERB ① To settle an argument means to put an end to it • *The dispute was settled*. ② If something is settled, it has all been decided and arranged. ③ If you settle on something or settle for it, you choose it • *We settled for orange juice and coffee*. ④ When you settle a bill, you pay it. ⑤ If you settle in a place, you make it your permanent home. ⑥ If you settle yourself somewhere, you sit down and make yourself comfortable. ⑦ If something settles, it sinks slowly down and comes to rest • *A black dust settled on the walls*. **settle down** VERB ① When someone settles down, they start living a quiet life in one place, especially when they get married. ② To settle down means to become quiet or calm.

settlement, settlements NOUN ① an official agreement between people who have been involved in a conflict • *the last chance for a peaceful settlement*. ② GEOGRAPHY a place where people have settled and built homes.

settler, settlers NOUN someone who settles in a new country • *the first settlers in Cuba*.

seven the number 7.

seventeen the number 17. **seventeenth** ADJECTIVE

seventh, sevenths ADJECTIVE ① The seventh item in a series is the one counted as number seven. ▶ NOUN ② one of seven equal parts.

a b c d e f g h i j k l m n o p q r **s** t u v w x y z

seventy, **seventies** the number 70. **seventieth** ADJECTIVE

sever, **severs**, **severing**, **severed** VERB ① To sever something means to cut it off or cut right through it. ② If you sever a connection with someone or something, you end it completely • *She severed her ties with England.*

SPELLING TIP
Do not confuse the spellings of *sever* and *severe*: *If we move him, there is a chance we will sever an artery; The explosion caused severe injuries.*

several ADJECTIVE Several people or things means a small number of them.

severe ADJECTIVE ① extremely bad or unpleasant • *severe stomach pains.* ② stern and harsh • *Perhaps I was too severe with that young man.* **severely** ADVERB **severity** NOUN

SPELLING TIP
Do not confuse the spellings of *severe* and *sever*: *The explosion caused severe injuries; If we move him, there is a chance we will sever an artery.*

sew, **sews**, **sewing**, **sewed**, **sewn** [Said so] VERB DGT When you sew things together, you join them using a needle and thread. **sewing** NOUN

sewage [Said soo-ij] NOUN Sewage is dirty water and waste which is carried away in sewers.

sewer, **sewers** NOUN an underground channel that carries sewage to a place where it is treated to make it harmless.

sewerage NOUN Sewerage is the system by which sewage is carried away and treated.

sex, **sexes** NOUN ① The sexes are the two groups, male and female, into which people and animals are divided. ② The sex of a person or animal is their characteristic of being either male or female. ③ Sex is the physical activity by which people and animals produce young.

sex cell, **sex cells** NOUN SCIENCE a male or female cell with half the usual number of chromosomes that unites with a cell of the opposite sex during sexual reproduction. Ova and sperms are sex cells.

sexism NOUN Sexism is discrimination against the members of one gender, usually women. **sexist** ADJECTIVE or NOUN

sextet, **sextets** NOUN ① MUSIC a group of six musicians who sing or play together; also a piece of music written for six instruments or singers. ② ENGLISH six lines of poetry together, especially linked by a pattern of rhyme.

sextuplet, **sextuplets** NOUN Sextuplets are six children born at the same time to the same mother.

sexual ADJECTIVE ① connected with the act of sex or with people's desire for sex • *sexual attraction.* ② relating to the difference between males and females • *sexual equality.* ③ relating to the biological process by which people and animals produce young • *sexual reproduction.* **sexually** ADVERB

sexual intercourse NOUN Sexual intercourse is the physical act of sex between two people.

sexuality [Said seks-yoo-al-it-ee] NOUN ① A person's sexuality is their ability to experience sexual feelings. ② You can refer to a person's sexuality when you are talking about whether they are sexually attracted to people of the same sex or a different sex.

sexy, **sexier**, **sexiest** ADJECTIVE attractive or exciting.

sforzando, sforzandos [Said sfort-**san**-doh] ADVERB MUSIC ① In music, sforzando is an instruction to sing or play something with sudden, strong emphasis. ▶ NOUN ② a symbol, such as >, written above a note to indicate that it should be played or sung in this way.
WORD HISTORY: an Italian word

shabby, shabbier, shabbiest ADJECTIVE ① old and worn in appearance • *a shabby overcoat.* ② dressed in old, worn-out clothes • *a shabby figure crouching in a doorway.* ③ behaving in a mean or unfair way • *shabby treatment.* **shabbily** ADVERB
SIMILAR WORDS: ① tatty, threadbare, worn

shack, shacks NOUN a small hut.

shackle, shackles, shackling, shackled NOUN ① In the past, shackles were two metal rings joined by a chain fastened around a prisoner's wrists or ankles. ▶ VERB ② To shackle someone means to put shackles on them. ③ (*literary*) If you are shackled by something, it restricts or hampers you.

shade, shades, shading, shaded NOUN ① Shade is an area of darkness and coolness which the sun does not reach • *The table was in the shade.* ② a lampshade. ③ The shades of a colour are its different forms. For example, olive green is a shade of green. ▶ VERB ④ If a place is shaded by trees or buildings, they prevent the sun from shining on it. ⑤ If you shade your eyes, you put your hand in front of them to protect them from a bright light.

shadow, shadows, shadowing, shadowed NOUN ① the dark shape made when an object prevents light from reaching a surface. ② Shadow is darkness caused by light not reaching a place. ▶ VERB ③ To shadow someone means to follow them and watch them closely.

shadow cabinet NOUN The shadow cabinet consists of the leaders of the main opposition party, each of whom is concerned with a particular policy.

shadowy ADJECTIVE ① A shadowy place is dark and full of shadows. ② A shadowy figure or shape is difficult to see because it is dark or misty.

shady, shadier, shadiest ADJECTIVE A shady place is sheltered from sunlight by trees or buildings.

shaft, shafts NOUN ① a vertical passage, for example one for a lift or one in a mine. ② A shaft of light is a beam of light. ③ DGT A shaft in a machine is a rod which revolves and transfers movement in the machine • *the drive shaft.*

shaggy, shaggier, shaggiest ADJECTIVE Shaggy hair or fur is long and untidy.

shahada NOUN RE the Islamic declaration of faith, repeated every day by Muslims. It begins 'There is no God but Allah and Mohammed is the prophet of Allah'.

shake, shakes, shaking, shook, shaken VERB ① To shake something means to move it quickly from side to side or up and down. ② If something shakes, it moves from side to side or up and down with small, quick movements. ③ If your voice shakes, it trembles because you are nervous or angry. ④ If something shakes you, it shocks and upsets you. ⑤ When you shake your head, you move it from side to side in order to say 'no'. ▶ NOUN ⑥ If you give something a shake, you shake it. ▶ PHRASE ⑦ When you **shake hands** with someone, you grasp their hand as a way of greeting them.

a
b
c
d
e
f
g
h
i
j
k
l
m
n
o
p
q
r
s
t
u
v
w
x
y
z

A
B
C
D
E
F
G
H
I
J
K
L
M
N
O
P
Q
R
S
T
U
V
W
X
Y
Z

The Verbs Shall and Will

The verbs *shall* and *will* have only one form. They do not have a present form ending in -*s*, and they do not have a present participle, a past tense or a past participle.

These verbs are used as auxiliary verbs to form the future tense:

We **shall** *arrive on Thursday.*
She **will** *give a talk about Chinese history.*

People used to use *shall* to indicate the first person, and *will* to indicate the second person and the third person. However, this distinction is often ignored now:

I **shall** *see you on Sunday.*
I **will** *see you on Sunday.*

Shall is always used in questions involving *I* and *we*. *Will* is avoided in these cases:

Shall *I put the cat out?*
Shall *we dance?*

Will is always used when making polite requests, giving orders, and indicating persistence. *Shall* is avoided in these cases:

Will *you please help me?*
Will *you be quiet!*
She **will** *keep going on about Al Pacino.*

SIMILAR WORDS: ② quiver, tremble, vibrate

shaky, **shakier**, **shakiest** ADJECTIVE rather weak and unsteady
• *Confidence in the economy is still shaky.* **shakily** ADVERB

shall VERB ① If I say I shall do something, I mean that I intend to do it. ② If I say something shall happen, I am emphasising that it will definitely happen, or I am ordering it to happen • *You shall go to the ball!* ③ 'Shall' is also used in questions when you are asking what to do, or making a suggestion • *Shall we sit down? • Shall I go and check for you?*

shallow, **shallower**, **shallowest**; ADJECTIVE ① Shallow means not deep. ② Shallow also means not involving serious thought or sincere feelings • *a well-meaning but shallow man.*

shallows PLURAL NOUN The shallows are the shallow part of a river or lake.

sham, **shams** NOUN ① Something that is a sham is not real or genuine.
▶ ADJECTIVE ② not real or genuine • *a sham display of affection.*

shambles NOUN (*informal*) If an event is a shambles, it is confused and badly organised.

shame, **shames**, **shaming**, **shamed** NOUN ① Shame is the feeling of guilt or embarrassment you get when you know you have done something wrong or foolish. ② Shame is also something that makes people lose respect for you • *the scenes that brought shame to English soccer.* ③ If you say something is a shame, you mean you are sorry about it • *It's a shame you can't come round.*
▶ INTERJECTION ④ (*informal*) In South African English, you say 'Shame!' to show sympathy. ▶ VERB ⑤ If something shames you, it makes you feel ashamed. ⑥ If you shame someone into doing something, you force them to do it by making them feel ashamed not to • *Two children shamed their parents into giving up cigarettes.*

shameful ADJECTIVE If someone's behaviour is shameful, they ought to be ashamed of it. **shamefully** ADVERB

shameless ADJECTIVE behaving in an indecent or unacceptable way, but showing no shame • *shameless dishonesty.* **shamelessly** ADVERB SIMILAR WORDS: barefaced, brazen, flagrant

shampoo, shampoos, shampooing, shampooed NOUN ① Shampoo is a soapy liquid used for washing your hair. ▸VERB ② When you shampoo your hair, you wash it with shampoo. WORD HISTORY: from Hindi *champna* meaning 'to knead'

shamrock, shamrocks NOUN a plant with three round leaves on each stem which is the national emblem of Ireland. WORD HISTORY: from Irish Gaelic *seamrog* meaning 'little clover'

shanghai, shanghais, shanghaiing, shanghaied (*informal*) VERB ① If someone is shanghaied, they are kidnapped and forced to work on a ship. ② If you shanghai someone, you trick or force them into doing something. ▸NOUN ③ In Australian and New Zealand English, a shanghai is a catapult.

shanty, shanties NOUN ① a small, rough hut. ② A sea shanty is a song sailors used to sing.

shanty town, shanty towns NOUN GEOGRAPHY A shanty town is a collection of small rough huts in which poor people live.

shape, shapes, shaping, shaped NOUN ① The shape of something is the form or pattern of its outline, for example whether it is round or square. ② MATHS something with a definite shape, for example a circle or triangle. ③ The shape of something such as an organisation is its structure and size. ▸VERB ④ If you shape an object, you form it into a particular shape • *Shape the dough into an oblong.* ⑤ To shape something means to cause it to develop in a particular way • *events that shaped the lives of some of the leading characters.* SIMILAR WORDS: ① figure, form, outline

shapeless ADJECTIVE not having a definite shape.

shapely, shapelier, shapeliest ADJECTIVE having an attractive figure.

shard, shards NOUN a small fragment of pottery, glass or metal.

share, shares, sharing, shared VERB ① If two people share something, they both use it, do it or have it • *We shared a bottle of orange juice.* ② If you share an idea or a piece of news with someone, you tell it to them. ▸NOUN ③ A share of something is a portion of it. ④ The shares of a company are the equal parts into which its ownership is divided. People can buy shares as an investment. **share out** VERB If you share something out, you give it out equally among a group of people. SIMILAR WORDS: ③ lot, part, portion

shareholder, shareholders NOUN a person who owns shares in a company.

share-milker, share-milkers NOUN In New Zealand, a share-milker is someone who works on a dairy farm and shares the profit from the sale of its produce.

Sharia [*Said* shuh-ree-uh] NOUN RE In Islam, Sharia is a set of laws providing guidance on all aspects of life.

shark, sharks NOUN ① Sharks are large, powerful fish with sharp teeth. ② (*informal*) a person who cheats people out of money.

sharp, sharper, sharpest; sharps ADJECTIVE ① A sharp object has a fine edge or point that is good for cutting or piercing things. ② A sharp outline or distinction is easy to see.

a b c d e f g h i j k l m n o p q r **s** t u v w x y z

③A sharp person is quick to notice or understand things. ④A sharp change is sudden and significant • *a sharp rise in prices.* ⑤If you say something in a sharp way, you say it firmly and rather angrily. ⑥A sharp sound is short, sudden and quite loud. ⑦A sharp pain is a sudden pain. ⑧A sharp taste is slightly sour. ⑨A musical instrument or note that is sharp is slightly too high in pitch. ▸ ADVERB ⑩If something happens at a certain time sharp, it happens at that time precisely • *You'll begin at eight o'clock sharp.* ▸ NOUN ⑪In music, a sharp is a note or key a semitone higher than that described by the same letter. It is represented by the symbol (♯). **sharply** ADVERB **sharpness** NOUN

SIMILAR WORDS: ③ astute, perceptive, quick-witted

sharpen, sharpens, sharpening, sharpened VERB ①To sharpen an object means to make its edge or point sharper. ②If your senses or abilities sharpen, you become quicker at noticing or understanding things. ③If you voice sharpens, you begin to speak more angrily or harshly. ④If something sharpens the disagreements between people, it makes them greater.

sharpener, sharpeners NOUN A sharpener is a device for sharpening things.

shatter, shatters, shattering, shattered VERB ①If something shatters, it breaks into a lot of small pieces. ②If something shatters your hopes or beliefs, it destroys them completely. ③If you are shattered by an event or piece of news, you are shocked and upset by it.

shattered ADJECTIVE (*informal*) completely exhausted • *He must be absolutely shattered after all his efforts.*

shattering ADJECTIVE making you feel shocked and upset • *a shattering event.*

shave, shaves, shaving, shaved VERB ①When a person shaves, they remove hair from a part of their body with a razor. ②If you shave off part of a piece of wood, you cut thin pieces from it. ▸ NOUN ③When a man has a shave, he shaves.

shaven ADJECTIVE If part of someone's body is shaven, it has been shaved • *a shaven head.*

shaver, shavers NOUN an electric razor.

shavings PLURAL NOUN Shavings are small, very thin pieces of wood which have been cut from a larger piece.

shawl, shawls NOUN a large piece of woollen cloth worn round a person's head or shoulders or used to wrap a baby in.

she PRONOUN 'She' is used to refer to a woman or girl whose identity is clear. 'She' is also used to refer to a country, a ship or a car.

sheaf, sheaves NOUN ①A sheaf of papers is a bundle of them. ②A sheaf of corn is a bundle of ripe corn tied together.

shear, shears, shearing, sheared, shorn VERB To shear a sheep means to cut off its wool.

shearer, shearers NOUN someone whose job is to shear sheep.

shears PLURAL NOUN Shears are a tool like a large pair of scissors, used especially for cutting hedges.

sheath, sheaths NOUN a covering for the blade of a knife.

shed, sheds, shedding, shed NOUN ①a small building used for storing things. ▸ VERB ②When an animal sheds hair or skin, some of its hair or skin drops off. When a tree sheds its leaves, its leaves fall off. ③ (*formal*) To shed something also means to get rid of it • *The firm is to shed 700 jobs*. ④ If a lorry sheds its load, the load falls off the lorry onto the road. ⑤ If you shed tears, you cry.

sheen NOUN a gentle brightness on the surface of something.

sheep, sheep NOUN A sheep is a farm animal with a thick woolly coat. Sheep are kept for meat and wool.

GRAMMAR TIP
The plural of *sheep* is *sheep*.

---

sheep dip, sheep dips NOUN a liquid disinfectant used to keep sheep clean and free of pests.

sheepdog, sheepdogs NOUN a breed of dog often used for controlling sheep.

sheepish ADJECTIVE If you look sheepish, you look embarrassed because you feel shy or foolish. **sheepishly** ADVERB

sheepskin NOUN Sheepskin is the skin and wool of a sheep, used for making rugs and coats.

sheer, sheerer, sheerest ADJECTIVE ① Sheer means complete and total • *sheer exhaustion*. ② A sheer cliff or drop is vertical. ③ Sheer fabrics are very light and delicate.

sheet, sheets NOUN ① a large rectangular piece of cloth used to cover a bed. ② A sheet of paper is a rectangular piece of it. ③ A sheet of glass or metal is a large, flat piece of it.

sheik, sheiks [*Said shake*]; also spelt **sheikh** NOUN an Arab chief or ruler. **WORD HISTORY**: from Arabic *shaykh* meaning 'old man'

shelf, shelves NOUN a flat piece of wood, metal or glass fixed to a wall and used for putting things on.

shell, shells, shelling, shelled NOUN ① The shell of an egg or nut is its hard covering. ② The shell of a tortoise, snail or crab is the hard protective covering on its back. ③ The shell of a building or other structure is its frame • *The room was just an empty shell*. ④ a container filled with explosives that can be fired from a gun. ▶ VERB ⑤ If you shell peas or nuts, you remove their natural covering. ⑥ To shell a place means to fire large explosive shells at it.

shellfish, shellfish or shellfishes NOUN a small sea creature with a shell.

shelter, shelters, sheltering, sheltered NOUN ① a small building made to protect people from bad weather or danger. ② If a place provides shelter, it provides protection from bad weather or danger. ▶ VERB ③ If you shelter in a place, you stay there and are safe. ④ If you shelter someone, you provide them with a place to stay when they are in danger.

sheltered ADJECTIVE ① A sheltered place is protected from wind and rain. ② If you lead a sheltered life, you do not experience unpleasant or upsetting things. ③ Sheltered accommodation is accommodation designed for old or disabled people.

shelve, shelves, shelving, shelved VERB If you shelve a plan, you decide to postpone it for a while.

shepherd, shepherds, shepherding, shepherded NOUN ① a person who looks after sheep. ▶ VERB ② If you shepherd someone somewhere, you accompany them there.

sheriff, sheriffs NOUN ① In America, a sheriff is a person elected to enforce the law in a county. ② In Australia, a sheriff is an administrative officer of the Supreme Court who carries out writs and judgments.

a b c d e f g h i j k l m n o p q r **s** t u v w x y z

WORD HISTORY: from Old English *scir* meaning 'shire' and *gerefa* meaning 'reeve', an official

sherry, **sherries** NOUN Sherry is a kind of strong wine.

WORD HISTORY: from the Spanish town *Jerez* where it was first made

shield, **shields**, **shielding**, **shielded** NOUN ① a large piece of a strong material like metal or plastic which soldiers or police officers carry to protect themselves. ② If something is a shield against something, it gives protection from it. ▶ VERB ③ To shield someone means to protect them from something.

shift, **shifts**, **shifting**, **shifted** VERB ① If you shift something, you move it. If something shifts, it moves • *to shift the rubble*. ② If an opinion or situation shifts, it changes slightly. ▶ NOUN ③ A shift in an opinion or situation is a slight change. ④ a set period during which people work • *the night shift*.

Shiite, **Shiites** [*Said* shee-ite] NOUN RE a member of a minority branch of the Islamic religion.

shilling, **shillings** NOUN a former British, Australian and New Zealand coin worth one-twentieth of a pound.

shimmer, **shimmers**, **shimmering**, **shimmered** VERB ① If something shimmers, it shines with a faint, flickering light. ▶ NOUN ② a faint, flickering light.

shin, **shins**, **shinning**, **shinned** NOUN ① Your shin is the front part of your leg between your knee and your ankle. ▶ VERB ② If you shin up a tree or pole, you climb it quickly by gripping it with your hands and legs.

shine, **shines**, **shining**, **shone** VERB ① When something shines, it gives out or reflects a bright light • *The stars shone brilliantly.* ② If you shine a torch or lamp somewhere, you point it there.

shingle, **shingles** NOUN ① GEOGRAPHY Shingle consists of small pebbles on the seashore. ② Shingles are small wooden roof tiles. ③ Shingles is a disease that causes a painful red rash, especially around the waist.

shining ADJECTIVE ① Shining things are very bright, usually because they are reflecting light • *shining stainless steel tables.* ② A shining example of something is a very good or typical example of that thing • *a shining example of courage.*

SIMILAR WORDS: ① bright, gleaming

shiny, **shinier**, **shiniest** ADJECTIVE Shiny things are bright and look as if they have been polished • *a shiny brass plate.*

ship, **ships**, **shipping**, **shipped** NOUN ① a large boat which carries passengers or cargo. ▶ VERB ② If people or things are shipped somewhere, they are transported there.

-ship SUFFIX '-ship' is used to form nouns that refer to a condition or position • *fellowship.*

shipment, **shipments** NOUN ① a quantity of goods that are transported somewhere • *a shipment of olive oil.* ② The shipment of goods is the transporting of them.

shipping NOUN ① Shipping is the transport of cargo on ships. ② You can also refer to ships generally as shipping • *Attention all shipping!*

shipwreck, **shipwrecks** NOUN When there is a shipwreck, a ship is destroyed in an accident at sea • *He was drowned in a shipwreck.*

shipyard, **shipyards** NOUN a place where ships are built and repaired.

shiralee, shiralees NOUN (*old-fashioned*) In Australian English, a shiralee is the bundle of possessions carried by a swagman.

shire, shires NOUN ① In Britain, 'shire' is an old word for a county. ② In Australia, a shire is a rural district with its own local council.

shirk, shirks, shirking, shirked VERB To shirk a task means to avoid doing it.

shirt, shirts NOUN a piece of clothing worn on the upper part of the body, with a collar, sleeves, and buttons down the front.

Shiva [*Said sheev-a*] PROPER NOUN RE Shiva is a Hindu god and one of the Trimurti.

shiver, shivers, shivering, shivered VERB ① When you shiver, you tremble slightly because you are cold or scared. ▶ NOUN ② a slight trembling caused by cold or fear.

shoal, shoals NOUN A shoal of fish is a large group of them swimming together.

shock, shocks, shocking, shocked NOUN ① If you have a shock, you have a sudden upsetting experience. ② Shock is a person's emotional and physical condition when something very unpleasant or upsetting has happened to them. ③ In medicine, shock is a serious physical condition in which the blood cannot circulate properly because of an injury. ④ a slight movement in something when it is hit by something else • *The straps help to absorb shocks*. ⑤ A shock of hair is a thick mass of it. ▶ VERB ⑥ If something shocks you, it upsets you because it is unpleasant and unexpected • *I was shocked by his appearance*. ⑦ You can say that something shocks you when it offends you because it is rude or

immoral. **shocked** ADJECTIVE
SIMILAR WORDS: ⑥ appal, horrify ⑦ disgust, scandalise

shock absorber, shock absorbers NOUN Shock absorbers are devices fitted near the wheels of a vehicle. They help to prevent the vehicle from bouncing up and down.

shocking ADJECTIVE ① (*informal*) very bad • *a shocking set of exam results*. ② disgusting or horrifying • *shocking images*.

shod the past tense and past participle of **shoe**.

shoddy, shoddier, shoddiest ADJECTIVE badly made or done • *a shoddy piece of work*.

shoe, shoes, shoeing, shod NOUN ① Shoes are strong coverings for your feet. They cover most of your foot, but not your ankle. ▶ VERB ② To shoe a horse means to fix horseshoes onto its hooves.

shoestring NOUN (*informal*) If you do something on a shoestring, you do it using very little money.

shone the past tense and past participle of **shine**.

shook the past tense of **shake**.

shoot, shoots, shooting, shot VERB ① To shoot a person or animal means to kill or injure them by firing a gun at them. ② To shoot an arrow means to fire it from a bow. ③ If something shoots in a particular direction, it moves there quickly and suddenly • *They shot back into Green Street*. ④ When a film is shot, it is filmed • *The whole film was shot in California*. ⑤ In games such as football or hockey, to shoot means to kick or hit the ball towards the goal. ▶ NOUN ⑥ an occasion when people hunt animals or birds with guns. ⑦ a plant that is beginning to grow, or a new part growing from a plant.

a
b
c
d
e
f
g
h
i
j
k
l
m
n
o
p
q
r
s
t
u
v
w
x
y
z

shooting, shootings NOUN an incident in which someone is shot.

shooting star, shooting stars NOUN a meteor.

shop, shops, shopping, shopped NOUN ① a place where things are sold. ② a place where a particular type of work is done • *a bicycle repair shop.* ▶ VERB ③ When you shop, you go to the shops to buy things. **shopper** NOUN

shopkeeper, shopkeepers NOUN someone who owns or manages a small shop.

shoplifting NOUN Shoplifting is stealing goods from shops. **shoplifter** NOUN

shopping NOUN Your shopping is the goods you have bought from the shops.

shop steward, shop stewards NOUN a trade union member elected to represent the workers in a factory or office.

shore, shores, shoring, shored NOUN ① The shore of a sea, lake or wide river is the land along the edge of it. ▶ VERB ② If you shore something up, you reinforce it or strengthen it • *a short-term solution to shore up the worst defence in the League.*

shoreline, shorelines NOUN the edge of a sea, lake or wide river.

shorn ① Shorn is the past participle of **shear**. ▶ ADJECTIVE ② Grass or hair that is shorn is cut very short.

short, shorter, shortest; shorts ADJECTIVE ① not lasting very long. ② small in length, distance or height • *a short climb* • *the short road.* ③ not using many words • *a short speech.* ④ If you are short with someone, you speak to them crossly. ⑤ If you have a short temper, you get angry very quickly. ⑥ If you are short of something, you do not have enough

of it. ⑦ If a name is short for another name, it is a short version of it. ▶ NOUN ⑧ (*in plural*) Shorts are trousers with short legs. ▶ ADVERB ⑨ If you stop short of a place, you do not quite reach it. ▶ PHRASE ⑩ **Short of** is used to say that a level or amount has not quite been reached • *a hundred votes short of a majority.* SIMILAR WORDS: ④ abrupt, curt, sharp

shortage, shortages NOUN If there is a shortage of something, there is not enough of it.

shortbread NOUN Shortbread is a crumbly biscuit made from flour and butter. WORD HISTORY: from an old-fashioned use of *short* meaning 'crumbly'

short circuit, short circuits NOUN a fault in an electrical system when two points accidentally become connected and the electricity travels directly between them rather than through the complete circuit.

shortcoming, shortcomings NOUN Shortcomings are faults or weaknesses.

shortcut, shortcuts NOUN ① a quicker way of getting somewhere than the usual route. ② a quicker way of doing something • *Stencils have been used as a shortcut to hand painting.*

shorten, shortens, shortening, shortened VERB If you shorten something or if it shortens, it becomes shorter • *This might help to shorten the conversation.*

shortfall, shortfalls NOUN If there is a shortfall in something, there is less than you need.

shorthand NOUN Shorthand is a way of writing in which signs represent words or syllables. It is used to write down quickly what someone is saying.

short-list, short-lists, short-listing, short-listed NOUN ① a list of people selected from a larger group, from which one person is finally selected for a job or prize. ▶ VERB ② If someone is short-listed for a job or prize, they are put on a short-list.

shortly ADVERB ① Shortly means soon • *I'll be back shortly.* ② If you speak to someone shortly, you speak to them in a cross and impatient way.

short-sighted ADJECTIVE ① If you are short-sighted, you cannot see things clearly when they are far away. ② A short-sighted decision does not take account of the way things may develop in the future.

short-term ADJECTIVE happening or having an effect within a short time or for a short time.

shot, shots ① Shot is the past tense and past participle of **shoot**. ▶ NOUN ② the act of firing a gun. ③ Someone who is a good shot can shoot accurately. ④ In football, golf and tennis, a shot is the act of kicking or hitting the ball. ⑤ a photograph or short film sequence • *I'd like to get some shots of the river.* ⑥ (informal) If you have a shot at something, you try to do it.

shotgun, shotguns NOUN a gun that fires a lot of small pellets all at once.

shot put NOUN In athletics, the shot put is an event in which the contestants throw a heavy metal ball called a shot as far as possible.

shot putter NOUN

should VERB ① You use 'should' to say that something ought to happen • *Ward should have done better.* ② You also use 'should' to say that you expect something to happen • *He should have heard by now.* ③ (formal) You can use 'should' to announce

that you are about to do or say something • *I should like to express my thanks to the Professor.* ④ 'Should' is used in conditional sentences • *If you should see Kerr, tell him I have his umbrella.* ⑤ 'Should' is sometimes used in 'that' clauses • *It is inevitable that you should go.* ⑥ If you say that you should think something, you mean that it is probably true • *I should think that's unlikely.*

shoulder, shoulders, shouldering, shouldered NOUN ① Your shoulders are the parts of your body between your neck and the tops of your arms. ▶ VERB ② If you shoulder something heavy, you put it across one of your shoulders to carry it. ③ If you shoulder the responsibility or blame for something, you accept it.

shoulder blade, shoulder blades NOUN Your shoulder blades are the two large, flat bones in the upper part of your back, below your shoulders.

shout, shouts, shouting, shouted NOUN ① a loud call or cry. ▶ VERB ② If you shout something, you say it very loudly • *He shouted something to his brother.* **shout down** VERB If you shout someone down, you prevent them from being heard by shouting at them.

SIMILAR WORDS: ② call, cry, yell

shove, shoves, shoving, shoved VERB ① If you shove someone or something, you push them roughly • *He shoved his wallet into a back pocket.* ▶ NOUN ② a rough push. **shove off** VERB (informal) If you tell someone to shove off, you are telling them angrily and rudely to go away.

shovel, shovels, shovelling, shovelled NOUN ① a tool like a spade, used for moving earth or snow. ▶ VERB ② If you shovel earth or snow, you move it with a shovel.

a b c d e f g h i j k l m n o p q r s t u v w x y z

show, shows, showing, showed, shown VERB ① To show that something exists or is true means to prove it • *The survey showed that 29 per cent would now approve the treaty.* ② If a picture shows something, it represents it • *The painting shows supporters and crowd scenes.* ③ If you show someone something, you let them see it • *Show me your passport.* ④ If you show someone to a room or seat, you lead them there. ⑤ If you show someone how to do something, you demonstrate it to them. ⑥ If something shows, it is visible. ⑦ If something shows a quality or characteristic, you can see that it has it • *Her sketches and watercolours showed promise.* ⑧ If you show your feelings, you let people see them • *She was flustered, but too proud to show it.* ⑨ If you show affection or mercy, you behave in an affectionate or merciful way • *the first person who showed me some affection.* ⑩ To show a film or television programme means to let the public see it. ▶ NOUN ⑪ a form of light entertainment at the theatre or on television. ⑫ an exhibition • *the Napier Antiques Show.* ⑬ A show of a feeling or attitude is behaviour in which you show it • *a show of optimism.* ▶ PHRASE ⑭ If something is **on show**, it is being exhibited for the public to see. **show off** VERB (*informal*) If someone is showing off, they are trying to impress people. **show up** VERB ① (*informal*) If you show up, you arrive at a place. ② If something shows up, it can be seen clearly • *Her bones were too soft to show up on an X-ray.*
SIMILAR WORDS: ① demonstrate, prove ⑦ display, indicate, reveal ⑫ display, exhibition

show business NOUN Show business is entertainment in the theatre, films and television.

showcase, showcases, showcasing, showcased NOUN A showcase for something is a situation or setting in which it is shown to its best advantage.

showdown, showdowns NOUN (*informal*) a major argument or conflict intended to end a dispute.

shower, showers, showering, showered NOUN ① a device which sprays you with water so that you can wash yourself. ② If you have a shower, you wash yourself by standing under a shower. ③ a short period of rain. ④ You can refer to a lot of things falling at once as a shower • *a shower of confetti.* ▶ VERB ⑤ If you shower, you have a shower. ⑥ If you are showered with a lot of things, they fall on you.

showing, showings NOUN A showing of a film or television programme is a presentation of it so that the public can see it.

showjumping NOUN Showjumping is a horse-riding competition in which the horses jump over a series of high fences.

show-off, show-offs NOUN (*informal*) someone who tries to impress people with their knowledge or skills.

showroom, showrooms NOUN a shop where goods such as cars or electrical appliances are displayed.

showy, showier, showiest ADJECTIVE large or bright and intended to impress people • *a showy house.*
SIMILAR WORDS: flamboyant, flashy, ostentatious

shrank the past tense of **shrink**.

shrapnel NOUN Shrapnel consists of small pieces of metal scattered from an exploding shell.
WORD HISTORY: named after General

Henry *Shrapnel* (1761–1842), who invented it

shred, shreds, shredding, shredded
VERB ① If you shred something, you cut or tear it into very small pieces. ▸ **NOUN** ② A shred of paper or material is a small, narrow piece of it. ③ If there is not a shred of something, there is absolutely none of it • *He was left without a shred of self-esteem*.

shrew, shrews [*Said shroo*] **NOUN** a small mouse-like animal with a long pointed nose.

shrewd, shrewder, shrewdest **ADJECTIVE** Someone who is shrewd is intelligent and makes good judgments. **shrewdly ADVERB** **shrewdness NOUN**
SIMILAR WORDS: astute, clever, sharp

shriek, shrieks, shrieking, shrieked
NOUN ① a high-pitched scream. ▸ **VERB** ② If you shriek, you make a high-pitched scream.

shrift **PHRASE** If you give someone or something **short shrift**, you pay very little attention to them.

shrill, shriller, shrillest **ADJECTIVE** A shrill sound is unpleasantly high-pitched and piercing. **shrilly ADVERB**

shrimp, shrimps **NOUN** a small edible shellfish with a long tail and many legs.

shrine, shrines **NOUN** RE a place of worship associated with a sacred person or object.

shrink, shrinks, shrinking, shrank, shrunk **VERB** ① If something shrinks, it becomes smaller. ② If you shrink from something, you move away from it because you are afraid of it. **shrinkage NOUN**

shrivel, shrivels, shrivelling, shrivelled **VERB** When something shrivels, it becomes dry and withered.

shroud, shrouds, shrouding, shrouded **NOUN** ① a cloth in which a dead body is wrapped before it is buried. ▸ **VERB** ② If something is shrouded in darkness or fog, it is hidden by it.

shrub, shrubs **NOUN** a low, bushy plant.

shrug, shrugs, shrugging, shrugged **VERB** ① If you shrug your shoulders, you raise them slightly as a sign of indifference of if you don't know something. ▸ **NOUN** ② If you give a shrug of your shoulders, you shrug them.

shrunk the past participle of **shrink**.

shrunken ADJECTIVE (*formal*) Someone or something that is shrunken has become smaller than it used to be • *a shrunken old man*.

shudder, shudders, shuddering, shuddered **VERB** ① If you shudder, you tremble with fear or horror. ② If a machine or vehicle shudders, it shakes violently. ▸ **NOUN** ③ a shiver of fear or horror.

shuffle, shuffles, shuffling, shuffled **VERB** ① If you shuffle, you walk without lifting your feet properly off the ground. ② If you shuffle about, you move about and fidget because you feel uncomfortable or embarrassed. ③ If you shuffle a pack of cards, you mix them up before you begin a game. ▸ **NOUN** ④ the way someone walks when they shuffle.

shun, shuns, shunning, shunned **VERB** If you shun someone or something, you deliberately avoid them.

shunt, shunts, shunting, shunted **VERB** (*informal*) If you shunt people or things to a place, you move them there • *You are shunted from room to room*.

shut, shuts, shutting, shut VERB ①If you shut something, you close it. ②When a shop or pub shuts, it is closed and you can no longer go into it. ▶ADJECTIVE ③If something is shut, it is closed. **shut down** VERB When a factory or business is shut down, it is closed permanently. **shut up** VERB (*informal*) If you shut up, you stop talking.

shutter, shutters NOUN Shutters are hinged wooden or metal covers fitted on the outside or inside of a window.

shuttle, shuttles ADJECTIVE ①A shuttle service is an air, bus or train service which makes frequent journeys between two places. ▶NOUN ②a plane used in a shuttle service.

shuttlecock, shuttlecocks NOUN the feathered object used like a ball in the game of badminton.

shy, shyer, shyest; shies, shying, shied ADJECTIVE ①A shy person is nervous and uncomfortable in the company of other people. ▶VERB ②When a horse shies, it moves away suddenly because something has frightened it. ③If you shy away from doing something, you avoid doing it because you are afraid or nervous. **shyly** ADVERB **shyness** NOUN SIMILAR WORDS: ① bashful, self-conscious, timid

sibling, siblings NOUN (*formal*) Your siblings are your brothers and sisters.

sick, sicker, sickest ADJECTIVE ①If you are sick, you are ill. ②If you feel sick, you feel as if you are going to vomit. If you are sick, you vomit. ③ (*informal*) If you are sick of doing something, you feel you have been doing it too long. ④ (*informal*) A sick joke or story deals with death or suffering in an unpleasantly frivolous way. ▶PHRASE ⑤If something

makes you sick, it makes you angry. **sickness** NOUN SIMILAR WORDS: ② nauseous, queasy

sicken, sickens, sickening, sickened VERB If something sickens you, it makes you feel disgusted. **sickening** ADJECTIVE

sickle, sickles NOUN a tool with a short handle and a curved blade used for cutting grass or grain.

sickly, sicklier, sickliest ADJECTIVE ①A sickly person or animal is weak and unhealthy. ② Sickly also means very unpleasant to smell or taste.

side, sides, siding, sided NOUN ① Side refers to a position to the left or right of something • *the two armchairs on either side of the fireplace*. ②The sides of a boundary or barrier are the two areas it separates • *this side of the border*. ③Your sides are the parts of your body from your armpits down to your hips. ④The sides of something are its outside surfaces, especially the surfaces which are not its front or back. ⑤The sides of a hill or valley are the parts that slope. ⑥The two sides in a war, argument or relationship are the two people or groups involved. ⑦A particular side of something is one aspect of it • *the sensitive, caring side of human nature*. ▶ADJECTIVE ⑧ situated on a side of a building or vehicle • *the side door*. ⑨A side road is a small road leading off a larger one. ⑩A side issue is an issue that is less important than the main one. ▶VERB ⑪If you side with someone in an argument, you support them.

sidebar, sidebars NOUN a short article placed alongside a longer one on a website.

sideboard, sideboards NOUN ①a long, low cupboard for plates and glasses. ② (*in plural*) A man's sideboards are his sideburns.

sideburns PLURAL NOUN A man's sideburns are areas of hair growing on his cheeks in front of his ears.
WORD HISTORY: from a 19th-century US army general called *Burnside* who wore his whiskers like this

side effect, side effects NOUN The side effects of a drug are the effects it has in addition to its main effects.

sidekick, sidekicks NOUN (*informal*) Someone's sidekick is their close friend who spends a lot of time with them.

sideline, sidelines NOUN an extra job in addition to your main job.

sideshow, sideshows NOUN Sideshows are stalls at a fairground.

sidestep, sidesteps, sidestepping, sidestepped VERB If you sidestep a difficult problem or question, you avoid dealing with it.

sidewalk, sidewalks NOUN In American English, a sidewalk is a pavement.

sideways ADVERB ① from or towards the side of something or someone.
▸ ADJECTIVE ② to or from one side • *a sideways step*.

siding, sidings NOUN a short railway track beside the main tracks, where engines and carriages are left when not in use.

sidle, sidles, sidling, sidled VERB If you sidle somewhere, you walk there cautiously and slowly, as if you do not want to be noticed.

siege, sieges [*Said seej*] NOUN HISTORY a military operation in which an army surrounds a place and prevents food or help from reaching the people inside.

sieve, sieves, sieving, sieved [*Said siv*] NOUN ① a kitchen tool made of mesh, used for sifting or straining things.
▸ VERB ② If you sieve a powder or liquid, you pass it through a sieve.

sift, sifts, sifting, sifted VERB ① If you sift a powdery substance, you pass it through a sieve to remove lumps. ② If you sift through something such as evidence, you examine it all thoroughly.

sigh, sighs, sighing, sighed VERB ① When you sigh, you let out a deep breath. ▸ NOUN ② the breath you let out when you sigh.

sight, sights, sighting, sighted NOUN ① Sight is the ability to see • *His sight was so poor that he could not follow the cricket.* ② something you see • *It was a ghastly sight.* ③ (*in plural*) Sights are interesting places which tourists visit. ▸ VERB ④ If you sight someone or something, you see them briefly or suddenly • *He had been sighted in Cairo.* ▸ PHRASE ⑤ If something is **in sight**, you can see it. If it is **out of sight**, you cannot see it.

SPELLING TIP
Do not confuse the spellings of *sight* and *site*: *The bombed city was a terrible sight; the site of a battle in World War One.*

sighted ADJECTIVE Someone who is sighted can see.

sighting, sightings NOUN A sighting of something rare or unexpected is an occasion when it is seen.

sightseeing NOUN Sightseeing is visiting the interesting places that tourists usually visit. **sightseer** NOUN

sign, signs, signing, signed NOUN ① a mark or symbol that always has a particular meaning, for example in mathematics or music. ② a gesture with a particular meaning. ③ A sign can also consist of words, a picture or a symbol giving information or a warning. ④ A sign is an event or happening that some people believe God has sent as a warning or instruction to an individual or to people in general. ⑤ If there are signs of something, there is evidence that it exists or is happening • *We are now seeing the first signs of recovery.* ▶ VERB ⑥ If you sign a document, you write your name on it • *He hurriedly signed the death certificate.* ⑦ If you sign, you communicate by using sign language. **sign on** VERB ① If you sign on for a job or course, you officially agree to do it by signing a contract. ② When people sign on, they officially state that they are unemployed and claim benefit from the state. **sign up** VERB If you sign up for a job or course, you officially agree to do it.

SIMILAR WORDS: ② gesture, signal

signage NOUN signs collectively, especially street signs or signs that give directions.

signal, signals, signalling, signalled NOUN ① a gesture, sound or action intended to give a message to someone. ② A railway signal is a piece of equipment beside the track which tells train drivers whether to stop or not. ▶ VERB ③ If you signal to someone, you make a gesture or sound to give them a message.

signature, signatures NOUN If you write your signature, you write your name the way you usually write it.

significant ADJECTIVE large or important • *a significant amount* • *a significant victory.* **significance** NOUN **significantly** ADVERB

significant figure, significant figures NOUN MATHS each of the figures of a number that express its size to a particular degree of accuracy; for example, 4.271 expressed to three significant figures is 4.27.

signify, signifies, signifying, signified VERB A gesture that signifies something has a particular meaning • *She screwed up her face to signify her disgust.*

sign language NOUN Sign language is a way of communicating using your hands, used especially by deaf people.

signpost, signposts NOUN a road sign with information on it such as the name of a town and how far away it is.

Sikh, Sikhs [Said *seek*] NOUN RE a person who believes in Sikhism, an Indian religion which separated from Hinduism in the 16th century and which teaches that there is only one God. **Sikhism** NOUN
WORD HISTORY: from Hindi *sikh* meaning 'disciple'

silence, silences, silencing, silenced NOUN ① Silence is quietness. ② Someone's silence about something is their failure or refusal to talk about it. ▶ VERB ③ To silence someone or something means to stop them talking or making a noise.

silent ADJECTIVE ① If you are silent, you are not saying anything. ② If you are silent about something, you do not tell people about it. ③ When something is silent, it makes no noise. ④ A silent film has only pictures and no sound. **silently** ADVERB

SIMILAR WORDS: ① dumb, mute, speechless

silhouette, silhouettes [Said *sil-loo-ett*] NOUN the outline of a dark shape against a light background. **silhouetted** ADJECTIVE

silicon NOUN SCIENCE Silicon is an element found in sand, clay and stone. It is used to make glass and also to make parts of computers. Its atomic number is 14 and its symbol is Si.

silk, silks NOUN Silk is a fine, soft cloth made from a substance produced by silkworms.

silken ADJECTIVE (*literary*) smooth and soft • *silken hair*.

silkworm, silkworms NOUN Silkworms are the larvae of a particular kind of moth.

silky, silkier, silkiest ADJECTIVE smooth and soft.

sill, sills NOUN a ledge at the bottom of a window.

silly, sillier, silliest ADJECTIVE foolish or childish.
SIMILAR WORDS: daft, foolish, stupid

silt NOUN GEOGRAPHY Silt is fine sand or soil which is carried along by a river.

silver NOUN ① SCIENCE Silver is a valuable greyish-white metallic element used for making jewellery and ornaments. Its atomic number is 47 and its symbol is Ag. ② Silver is also coins made from silver or from silver-coloured metal • *He's won a handful of silver on the fruit machine.* ③ In a house, the silver is all the things made from silver, especially the cutlery. ▶ ADJECTIVE or NOUN ④ greyish-white.

silver beet, silver beets NOUN a type of beet grown in Australia and New Zealand.

silver fern NOUN a tall fern that is found in New Zealand. It is the symbol of New Zealand national sports teams.

silverfish, silverfishes or silverfish NOUN a small silver insect with no wings that eats paper and clothing.

silver jubilee, silver jubilees NOUN the 25th anniversary of an important event.

silver medal, silver medals NOUN a medal made from silver awarded to the competitor who comes second in a competition.

silver wedding, silver weddings NOUN A couple's silver wedding is the 25th anniversary of their wedding.

silvery ADJECTIVE having the appearance or colour of silver • *the silvery moon*.

similar ADJECTIVE ① If one thing is similar to another, or if two things are similar, they are like each other. ② In maths, two triangles are similar if the angles in one correspond exactly to the angles in the other.
similarly ADVERB

USAGE NOTE
Be careful when deciding whether to use *similar* or *same*. *Similar* means 'alike but not identical', and *same* means 'identical'. Do not put *as* after *similar*: *Her dress was similar to mine.*

similarity, similarities NOUN If there is a similarity between things, they are alike in some way.
SIMILAR WORDS: likeness, resemblance

simile, similes [*Said sim-ill-ee*] NOUN ENGLISH an expression in which a person or thing is described as being similar to someone or something else. Examples of similes are *She runs like a deer* and *He's as white as a sheet*.

simmer, simmers, simmering, simmered VERB When food simmers, it cooks gently at just below boiling point.

simple, simpler, simplest ADJECTIVE ① Something that is simple is uncomplicated and easy to understand or do. ② Simple also means plain and not elaborate in style • *a simple coat*. ③ A simple way of life is uncomplicated. ④ You use 'simple' to emphasise that what you are talking about is the only important thing • *simple stubbornness*. ⑤ In grammar, a simple sentence consists of one main clause and no subordinate clause. **simplicity** NOUN

simple-minded ADJECTIVE not very intelligent or sophisticated • *simple-minded pleasures*.

simplify, simplifies, simplifying, simplified VERB To simplify something means to make it easier to do or understand. **simplification** NOUN

simplistic ADJECTIVE too simple or naive • *a rather simplistic approach to the subject*.

simply ADVERB ① Simply means merely • *It was simply a question of making the decision*. ② You use 'simply' to emphasise what you are saying • *It is simply not true*. ③ If you say or write something simply, you do it in a way that makes it easy to understand.

simulate, simulates, simulating, simulated VERB To simulate something means to imitate it • *The wood has been painted to simulate stone* • *He simulated shock*.
WORD HISTORY: from Latin *simulare* meaning 'to copy'

simulation, simulations NOUN ① Simulation is the process of simulating something or the result of simulating it. ② (*technical*) A simulation is an attempt to solve a problem by representing it mathematically, often on a computer.

simulator, simulators NOUN A simulator is a device designed to reproduce actual conditions, for example in order to train pilots or astronauts.

simultaneous ADJECTIVE Things that are simultaneous happen at the same time. **simultaneously** ADVERB

simultaneous equations PLURAL NOUN MATHS Simultaneous equations are all satisfied by the same values of the variables.

sin, sins, sinning, sinned NOUN ① RE Sin is wicked and immoral behaviour. ▶ VERB ② To sin means to do something wicked and immoral.
SIMILAR WORDS: ① evil, iniquity, wrongdoing ② lapse, transgress

since PREPOSITION or CONJUNCTION or ADVERB ① Since means from a particular time until now • *I've been waiting patiently since half past three*. ▶ ADVERB ② Since also means at some time after a particular time in the past • *The band split up and he has since gone solo*. ▶ CONJUNCTION ③ Since also means because • *I'm forever on a diet, since I put on weight easily*.

GRAMMAR TIP
Do not put *ago* before *since*, as it is not needed: *It is ten years since she wrote her book*, not *ten years ago since*.

sincere ADJECTIVE If you are sincere, you say things that you really mean • *a sincere expression of friendliness*. **sincerity** NOUN
SIMILAR WORDS: genuine, honest

sincerely ADVERB ① If you say or feel something sincerely, you mean it or feel it genuinely. ▶ PHRASE ② You write **Yours sincerely** before your signature at the end of a letter in which you have named the person you are writing to in the greeting at the beginning of the letter. For example, if you began your letter 'Dear Mr Brown' you would use 'Yours sincerely'.

sine, sines NOUN MATHS In mathematics, a sine is a function of an angle. If B is the right angle in a right-angled triangle ABC, the sine of the angle at A is BC divided by AC.

sinew, sinews [Said *sin-yoo*] NOUN a tough cord in your body that connects a muscle to a bone.

sinful ADJECTIVE RE wicked and immoral.

sing, sings, singing, sang, sung VERB ①When you sing, you make musical sounds with your voice, usually producing words that fit a tune. ②When birds or insects sing, they make pleasant sounds. **singer** NOUN

GRAMMAR TIP

The past tense of *sing* is *sang*, and the past participle is *sung*. Do not confuse these words: *The team sang the national anthem; We have sung together many times.*

---

singe, singes, singeing, singed VERB ①To singe something means to burn it slightly so that it goes brown but does not catch fire. ▶ NOUN ②a slight burn.

single, singles, singling, singled ADJECTIVE ①Single means only one and not more • *A single shot was fired.* ②People who are single are not married. ③A single bed or bedroom is for one person. ④A single ticket is a one-way ticket. ▶ NOUN ⑤a recording of one or two short pieces of music on a small record, CD or download. ⑥Singles is a game of tennis, badminton or squash between just two players. **single out** VERB If you single someone out from a group, you give them special treatment • *He'd been singled out for some special award.*

single-handed ADVERB If you do something single-handed, you do it on your own, without any help.

single-minded ADJECTIVE A single-minded person has only one aim and is determined to achieve it.

singly ADVERB If people do something singly, they do it on their own or one by one.

singular NOUN ① MFL In grammar, the singular is the form of a word that refers to just one person or thing. ▶ ADJECTIVE ②(formal) unusual and remarkable • *her singular beauty.* **singularity** NOUN **singularly** ADVERB

sinister ADJECTIVE seeming harmful or evil • *something cold and sinister about him.*

WORD HISTORY: from Latin *sinister* meaning 'left-hand side', because the left side was considered unlucky

sink, sinks, sinking, sank, sunk NOUN ①a basin with taps supplying water, usually in a kitchen or bathroom. ▶ VERB ②If something sinks, it moves downwards, especially through water • *An Indian cargo ship sank in icy seas.* ③To sink a ship means to cause it to sink by attacking it. ④If an amount or value sinks, it decreases. ⑤If you sink into an unpleasant state, you gradually pass into it • *He sank into black despair.* ⑥To sink something sharp into an object means to make it go deeply into it • *The tiger sank its teeth into his leg.* **sink in** VERB When a fact sinks in, you fully understand it or realise it • *The truth was at last sinking in.*

sinner, sinners NOUN someone who has committed a sin.

sinus, sinuses NOUN Your sinuses are the air passages in the bones of your skull, just behind your nose.

sip, sips, sipping, sipped VERB ①If you sip a drink, you drink it by taking a small amount at a time. ▶ NOUN ②a small amount of drink that you take into your mouth.

siphon, siphons, siphoning, siphoned [Said *sigh-fn*]; also spelt

syphon VERB If you siphon off a liquid, you draw it out of a container through a tube and transfer it to another place.

sir NOUN ① Sir is a polite, formal way of addressing a man. ② Sir is also the title used in front of the name of a knight or baronet.

siren, sirens NOUN a warning device, for example on a police car, which makes a loud wailing noise.
WORD HISTORY: the Sirens in Greek mythology were sea nymphs who had beautiful voices and sang in order to lure sailors to their deaths on the rocks where the nymphs lived

sirloin NOUN Sirloin is a prime cut of beef from the lower part of a cow's back.
WORD HISTORY: from Old French *sur* meaning 'above' and *longe* meaning 'loin'

sis [Said *siss*]; also spelt **sies**
INTERJECTION (*informal*) In South African English, you say 'Sis!' to show disgust.

sister, sisters NOUN ① Your sister is a girl or woman who has the same parents as you. ② a member of a female religious order. ③ In a hospital, a sister is a senior nurse who supervises a ward. ▶ ADJECTIVE ④ Sister means closely related to something or very similar to it
• *Voyager 2 and its sister ship, Voyager 1.*

sisterhood NOUN Sisterhood is a strong feeling of companionship between women.

sister-in-law, sisters-in-law NOUN Someone's sister-in-law is the sister of their husband or wife, or their sibling's wife.

sit, sits, sitting, sat VERB ① If you are sitting, your weight is supported by your buttocks rather than your feet. ② When you sit or sit down

somewhere, you lower your body until you are sitting. ③ If you sit an examination, you take it. ④ (*formal*) When a parliament, law court or other official body sits, it meets and officially carries out its work.

sitcom, sitcoms NOUN (*informal*) a television comedy series which shows characters in amusing situations that are similar to everyday life.
WORD HISTORY: shortened from *situation comedy*

site, sites, siting, sited NOUN ① a piece of ground where a particular thing happens or is situated • *a building site.* ② A site is the same as a website. ▶ VERB ③ If something is sited in a place, it is built or positioned there.

SPELLING TIP
Do not confuse the spellings of *site* and *sight*: *the site of a battle in World War One; The bombed city was a terrible sight.*

sitting, sittings NOUN ① one of the times when a meal is served. ② one of the occasions when a parliament or law court meets and carries out its work.

sitting room, sitting rooms NOUN a room in a house where people sit and relax.

situated ADJECTIVE If something is situated somewhere, that is where it is • *a town situated 45 minutes from Geneva.*

situation, situations NOUN ① what is happening in a particular place at a particular time • *the political situation.* ② The situation of a building or town is its surroundings • *a beautiful situation.*
SIMILAR WORDS: ① circumstances, condition, state of affairs

Siva [Said *seev-a*] PROPER NOUN Siva is another name for Shiva.

six the number 6.

sixteen the number 16. **sixteenth** ADJECTIVE

sixth, sixths ADJECTIVE ①The sixth item in a series is the one counted as number six. ▶ NOUN ②one of six equal parts.

sixth sense NOUN You say that someone has a sixth sense when they know something instinctively, without having any evidence of it.

sixty, sixties the number 60. **sixtieth** ADJECTIVE

sizable; also spelt **sizeable** ADJECTIVE fairly large • *a sizable amount of money*.

size, sizes NOUN ①The size of something is how big or small it is • *the size of the audience*. ②The size of something is also the fact that it is very large • *the sheer size of Australia*. ③one of the standard graded measurements of clothes and shoes.
size up VERB If you size up people or situations, you look at them carefully and make a judgment about them.
SIMILAR WORDS: ① dimensions, magnitude, proportions

sizzle, sizzles, sizzling, sizzled VERB If something sizzles, it makes a hissing sound like the sound of frying food.

sjambok, sjamboks [Said *sham-bok*] NOUN In South African English, a sjambok is a long whip made from animal hide.

skate, skates, skating, skated NOUN ① Skates are ice skates or roller skates. ②a flat edible sea fish. ▶ VERB ③If you skate, you move about on ice wearing ice skates. ④If you skate round a difficult subject, you avoid discussing it.

skateboard, skateboards NOUN a narrow board on wheels, which you stand on and ride for fun.

skeleton, skeletons NOUN Your skeleton is the framework of bones in your body.

sketch, sketches, sketching, sketched NOUN ① ART a quick, rough drawing. ②A sketch of a situation or incident is a brief description of it. ③a short, humorous piece of acting, usually forming part of a comedy show. ▶ VERB ④If you sketch something, you draw it quickly and roughly.

sketchy, sketchier, sketchiest ADJECTIVE giving only a rough description or account • *Details surrounding his death are sketchy*.

skew [Said *skyoo*] or **skewed** ADJECTIVE in a slanting position, rather than straight or upright.

skewer, skewers, skewering, skewered NOUN ① a long metal pin used to hold pieces of food together during cooking. ▶ VERB ②If you skewer something, you push a skewer through it.

ski, skis, skiing, skied NOUN ① Skis are long pieces of wood, metal or plastic that you fasten to special boots so you can move easily on snow. ▶ VERB ②When you ski, you move on snow wearing skis, especially as a sport.

skid, skids, skidding, skidded VERB If a vehicle skids, it slides in an uncontrolled way, for example because the road is wet or icy.

skilful ADJECTIVE If you are skilful at something, you can do it very well. **skilfully** ADVERB
SIMILAR WORDS: able, expert, proficient

skill, skills NOUN ① Skill is the knowledge and ability that enables you to do something well. ②a type of work or technique which requires special training and knowledge.

a
b
c
d
e
f
g
h
i
j
k
l
m
n
o
p
q
r
s
t
u
v
w
x
y
z

SIMILAR WORDS: ① ability, expertise, proficiency

skilled ADJECTIVE ① A skilled person has the knowledge and ability to do something well. ② Skilled work is work which can only be done by people who have had special training.

skim, skims, skimming, skimmed VERB ① If you skim something from the surface of a liquid, you remove it. ② If something skims a surface, it moves along just above it • *seagulls skimming the waves*. ③ If you skim a piece of writing, you read through it quickly and without taking in the details.

skimmed milk NOUN Skimmed milk has had the cream removed.

skin, skins, skinning, skinned NOUN ① Your skin is the natural covering of your body. An animal skin is the skin and fur of a dead animal. ② The skin of a fruit or vegetable is its outer covering. ③ a solid layer which forms on the surface of a liquid. ▶ VERB ④ If you skin a dead animal, you remove its skin. ⑤ If you skin a part of your body, you accidentally graze it.

skinny, skinnier, skinniest ADJECTIVE extremely thin.

skip, skips, skipping, skipped VERB ① If you skip along, you move along jumping from one foot to the other. ② (*informal*) If you skip something, you miss it out or avoid doing it • *It is all too easy to skip meals*. ▶ NOUN ③ Skips are the movements you make when you skip. ④ a large metal container for holding rubbish and rubble.

skipper, skippers NOUN (*informal*) The skipper of a ship or boat is its captain.
WORD HISTORY: from Old Dutch *schipper* meaning 'shipper'

skirmish, skirmishes NOUN a short, rough fight.

skirt, skirts, skirting, skirted NOUN ① A skirt is a piece of clothing which fastens at the waist and hangs down over the legs. ▶ VERB ② Something that skirts an area is situated around the edge of it. ③ If you skirt something, you go around the edge of it • *We skirted the town*. ④ If you skirt a problem, you avoid dealing with it • *He was skirting the real question*.
WORD HISTORY: from Old Norse *skyrta* meaning 'shirt'

skirting, skirtings NOUN A skirting or skirting board is a narrow strip of wood running along the bottom of a wall in a room.

skite, skites, skiting, skited (*informal*) VERB ① In Australian and New Zealand English, to skite is to talk in a boastful way about something that you own or that you have done. ▶ NOUN ② In Australian and New Zealand English, a skite is someone who boasts.

skittle, skittles NOUN Skittles is a game in which players roll a ball and try to knock down wooden objects called skittles.

skull, skulls NOUN Your skull is the bony part of your head which surrounds your brain.

skunk, skunks NOUN a small black and white mammal from North America which gives off an unpleasant smell when it is frightened.

sky, skies NOUN The sky is the space around the earth which you can see when you look upwards.
WORD HISTORY: from Old Norse *sky* meaning 'cloud'

skylight, skylights NOUN a window in a roof or ceiling.

skyline, skylines NOUN The skyline is the line where the sky meets buildings or the ground • *the New York City skyline*.

Skype, Skypes, Skyping, Skyped NOUN (*trademark*) ① a computer program for making phone calls and video calls on the internet. ▶ VERB ② If you Skype someone, you use a computer program to speak to them on the internet.

skyscraper, skyscrapers NOUN a very tall building.

slab, slabs NOUN a thick, flat piece of something.

slack, slacker, slackest; slacks ADJECTIVE ① Something that is slack is loose and not firmly stretched or positioned. ② A slack period is one in which there is not much work to do. ▶ NOUN ③ The slack in a rope is the part that hangs loose. ④ (*in plural*, *old-fashioned*) Slacks are casual trousers. **slackness** NOUN

slacken, slackens, slackening, slackened VERB ① If something slackens, it becomes slower or less intense • *The rain had slackened to a drizzle*. ② To slacken also means to become looser • *Her grip slackened on Arnold's arm*.

slag, slags, slagging, slagged NOUN ① Slag is the waste material left when ore has been melted down to remove the metal • *a slag heap*. ▶ VERB ② (*informal*) To slag someone off means to criticise them in an unpleasant way, usually behind their back.

slain the past participle of **slay**.

slalom, slaloms [*Said slah-lom*] NOUN a skiing competition in which the competitors have to twist and turn quickly to avoid obstacles. **WORD HISTORY:** from Norwegian *slad* + *lom* meaning 'sloping path'

slam, slams, slamming, slammed VERB ① If you slam a door or if it slams, it shuts noisily and with great force. ② If you slam something down, you put it down violently • *She slammed the phone down*.

slander, slanders, slandering, slandered NOUN ① Slander is something untrue and malicious said about someone. ▶ VERB ② To slander someone means to say untrue and malicious things about them.
slanderous ADJECTIVE
SIMILAR WORDS: ① defamation, smear

slang NOUN Slang consists of very informal words and expressions.

slant, slants, slanting, slanted VERB ① If something slants, it slopes • *The back can be adjusted to slant into the most comfortable position*. ② If news or information is slanted, it is presented in a biased way. ▶ NOUN ③ a slope. ④ A slant on a subject is one way of looking at it, especially a biased one.

slap, slaps, slapping, slapped VERB ① If you slap someone, you hit them with the palm of your hand. ② If you slap something onto a surface, you put it there quickly and noisily. ▶ NOUN ③ If you give someone a slap, you slap them.
WORD HISTORY: from German *Schlappe*, an imitation of the sound

slash, slashes, slashing, slashed VERB ① If you slash something, you make a long, deep cut in it. ② (*informal*) To slash money means to reduce it greatly • *Car makers could be forced to slash prices*. ▶ NOUN ③ a diagonal line that separates letters, words or numbers, for example in the number 340/21/K.

PUNCTUATION TIP
The slash that rises from left to right (/) is called a forward slash, and this is the one used in web addresses: *www.bbc.co.uk/news/world*.

slat, slats NOUN Slats are the narrow pieces of wood, metal or plastic in things such as Venetian blinds. **slatted** ADJECTIVE

slate, slates, slating, slated NOUN ① Slate is a dark grey rock that splits easily into thin layers. ② Slates are small, flat pieces of slate used for covering roofs. ▶ VERB ③ (*informal*) If critics slate a play, film or book, they criticise it severely.

slaughter, slaughters, slaughtering, slaughtered VERB ① To slaughter a large number of people means to kill them unjustly or cruelly. ② To slaughter farm animals means to kill them for meat. ▶ NOUN ③ Slaughter is the killing of many people.
SIMILAR WORDS: ③ carnage, massacre, murder

slave, slaves, slaving, slaved NOUN ① someone who is forced to work for another person. ▶ VERB ② If you slave for someone, you work very hard for them. **slavery** NOUN
WORD HISTORY: from Latin *Sclavus* meaning 'a Slav', because the Slavonic races were frequently conquered and made into slaves

slay, slays, slaying, slew, slain VERB (*literary*) To slay someone means to kill them.

sleazy, sleazier, sleaziest ADJECTIVE A sleazy place looks dirty, run-down and not respectable.

sled or **sledge**, sleds or sledges NOUN a vehicle on runners used for travelling over snow.

sledgehammer, sledgehammers NOUN a large, heavy hammer.

sleek, sleeker, sleekest ADJECTIVE ① Sleek hair is smooth and shiny. ② Someone who is sleek looks rich and dresses elegantly.

sleep, sleeps, sleeping, slept NOUN ① Sleep is the natural state of rest in which your eyes are closed and you are unconscious. ② If you have a sleep, you sleep for a while • *He'll be ready for a sleep soon.* ▶ VERB ③ When you sleep, you rest in a state of sleep. ▶ PHRASE ④ If a sick or injured animal **is put to sleep**, it is painlessly killed.
SIMILAR WORDS: ② doze, nap, slumber

sleeper, sleepers NOUN ① You use 'sleeper' to say how deeply someone sleeps • *I'm a very heavy sleeper.* ② a bed on a train, or a train which has beds on it. ③ Railway sleepers are the large beams that support the rails of a railway track.

sleeping bag, sleeping bags NOUN a large, warm bag for sleeping in, especially when you are camping.

sleeping pill, sleeping pills or **sleeping tablet** NOUN A sleeping pill or a sleeping tablet is a pill which you take to help you sleep.

sleepout, sleepouts NOUN ① In Australia, a sleepout is an area of veranda or porch which has been closed off to be used as a bedroom. ② In New Zealand, a sleepout is a small building outside a house, used for sleeping.

sleepover, sleepovers NOUN a gathering or party at which friends spend the night at another friend's house.

sleepwalk, sleepwalks, sleepwalking, sleepwalked VERB If you sleepwalk, you walk around while you are asleep.

sleepy, sleepier, sleepiest ADJECTIVE ① tired and ready to go to sleep. ② A sleepy town or village is very quiet. **sleepily** ADVERB **sleepiness** NOUN

sleet NOUN Sleet is a mixture of rain and snow.

sleeve, sleeves NOUN The sleeves of a piece of clothing are the parts that cover your arms. **sleeveless** ADJECTIVE

sleigh, sleighs [Said *slay*] NOUN a sledge.

slender ADJECTIVE ① attractively thin and graceful. ② small in amount or degree • *the first slender hopes of peace.* SIMILAR WORDS: ① slim, willowy

slept the past tense and past participle of **sleep**.

sleuth, sleuths [Said *slooth*] NOUN (old-fashioned) a detective. WORD HISTORY: a shortened form of *sleuthhound*, a tracker dog, from Old Norse *sloth* meaning 'track'

slew, slews, slewing, slewed VERB ▶ ① Slew is the past tense of **slay**. ② If a vehicle slews, it slides or skids • *The bike slewed into the crowd.*

slice, slices, slicing, sliced NOUN ① A slice of cake, bread or other food is a piece of it cut from a larger piece. ② a kitchen tool with a broad, flat blade • *a fish slice.* ③ In sport, a slice is a stroke in which the player makes the ball go to one side, rather than straight ahead. ▶ VERB ④ If you slice food, you cut it into thin pieces. ⑤ To slice through something means to cut or move through it quickly, like a knife • *The ship sliced through the water.*

slick, slicker, slickest; slicks ADJECTIVE ① A slick action is done quickly and smoothly • *slick passing and strong running.* ② A slick person speaks easily and persuasively but is not sincere • *a slick TV presenter.* ▶ NOUN ③ An oil slick is a layer of oil floating on the surface of the sea or a lake.

slide, slides, sliding, slid VERB ① When something slides, it moves smoothly over or against something else. ▶ NOUN ② a small piece of photographic film which can be projected onto a screen so that you can see the picture. ③ a small piece of glass on which you put something that you want to examine through a microscope. ④ In a playground, a slide is a structure with a steep, slippery slope for children to slide down.

slight, slighter, slightest; slights, slighting, slighted ADJECTIVE ① Slight means small in amount or degree • *a slight dent.* ② A slight person has a slim body. ▶ PHRASE ③ **Not in the slightest** means not at all • *This doesn't surprise me in the slightest.* ▶ VERB ④ If you slight someone, you insult them by behaving rudely towards them. ▶ NOUN ⑤ A slight is an example of rude or insulting behaviour. **slightly** ADVERB

slim, slimmer, slimmest; slims, slimming, slimmed ADJECTIVE ① A slim person is attractively thin. ② A slim object is thinner than usual • *a slim book.* ③ If there is only a slim chance that something will happen, it is unlikely to happen. ▶ VERB ④ If you are slimming, you are trying to lose weight. **slimmer** NOUN

slime NOUN Slime is an unpleasant, thick, slippery substance.

slimy, slimier, slimiest ADJECTIVE ① covered in slime. ② Slimy people are friendly and pleasant in an insincere way.

sling, slings, slinging, slung VERB ① (informal) If you sling something somewhere, you throw it there. ② If you sling a rope between two points, you attach it so that it hangs loosely between them. ▶ NOUN ③ a piece of cloth tied round a person's neck to support a broken or injured arm. ④ a device made of ropes or cloth used for carrying things.

slip, slips, slipping, slipped VERB ① If you slip, you accidentally slide and lose your balance. ② If something slips, it slides out of place accidentally • *One of the knives slipped from her grasp.* ③ If you slip somewhere, you go there quickly and quietly • *She slipped out of the house.* ④ If you slip something somewhere, you put it there quickly and quietly. ⑤ If something slips to a lower level or standard, it falls to that level or standard • *The shares slipped to an all-time low.* ▶ NOUN ⑥ a small mistake. ⑦ A slip of paper is a small piece of paper. ⑧ a piece of clothing worn under a dress or skirt. **slip up** VERB (*informal*) If you slip up, you make a mistake.

slipped disc, slipped discs NOUN a painful condition in which one of the discs in your spine has moved out of its proper position.

slipper, slippers NOUN Slippers are loose, soft shoes that you wear indoors.

slippery ADJECTIVE ① smooth, wet or greasy, and difficult to hold or walk on. ② (*informal*) You describe a person as slippery when they cannot be trusted.

slippery dip, slippery dips NOUN (*informal*) In Australian English, a slippery dip is a children's slide at a playground or funfair.

slip rail, slip rails NOUN In Australian and New Zealand English, a slip rail is a rail in a fence that can be slipped out of place to make an opening.

slipstream, slipstreams NOUN The slipstream of a car or plane is the flow of air directly behind it.

slit, slits, slitting, slit VERB ① If you slit something, you make a long, narrow cut in it. ▶ NOUN ② a long, narrow cut or opening.

slither, slithers, slithering, slithered VERB To slither somewhere means to move there by sliding along the ground in an uneven way • *The snake slithered into the water.*

sliver, slivers NOUN a small, thin piece of something.

slob, slobs NOUN (*informal*) a lazy, untidy person.

slog, slogs, slogging, slogged VERB (*informal*) ① If you slog at something, you work hard and steadily at it • *They are still slogging away at algebra.* ② If you slog somewhere, you move along with difficulty • *people willing to slog round the streets delivering catalogues.*

slogan, slogans NOUN a short, easily remembered phrase used in advertising or by a political party.
SIMILAR WORDS: catch phrase, motto
WORD HISTORY: from Gaelic *sluagh-ghairm* meaning 'war cry'

slop, slops, slopping, slopped VERB ① If a liquid slops, it spills over the edge of a container in a messy way. ② (*in plural*) You can refer to dirty water or liquid waste as slops.

slope, slopes, sloping, sloped NOUN ① a flat surface that is at an angle, so that one end is higher than the other. ② The slope of something is the angle at which it slopes. ▶ VERB ③ If a surface slopes, it is at an angle. ④ If something slopes, it leans to one side rather than being upright • *sloping handwriting.*
SIMILAR WORDS: ① incline, slant, tilt ② gradient, inclination

sloppy, sloppier, sloppiest ADJECTIVE (*informal*) ① very messy or careless • *two sloppy performances.* ② foolishly sentimental • *some sloppy love story.* **sloppily** ADVERB **sloppiness** NOUN

slot, slots, slotting, slotted NOUN

① a narrow opening in a machine or container, for example for putting coins in. ▶ **VERB** ② When you slot something into something else, you put it into a space where it fits.

sloth, **sloths** [*Rhymes with* **growth**] **NOUN** ① (*formal*) Sloth is laziness. ② a South and Central American animal that moves very slowly and hangs upside down from the branches of trees.

slouch, **slouches**, **slouching**, **slouched VERB** If you slouch, you stand or sit with your shoulders and head drooping forwards.

slouch hat, **slouch hats NOUN** a hat with a wide, flexible brim, especially an Australian army hat with the left side of the brim turned up.

Slovak, **Slovaks ADJECTIVE** ① belonging or relating to Slovakia. ▶ **NOUN** ② someone who comes from Slovakia. ③ Slovak is the language spoken in Slovakia.

Slovene, **Slovenes ADJECTIVE** ① belonging or relating to Slovenia. ▶ **NOUN** ② someone who comes from Slovenia. ③ Slovene is the language spoken in Slovenia.

slow, **slower**, **slowest**; **slows**, **slowing**, **slowed ADJECTIVE** ① moving, happening or doing something with very little speed • *His progress was slow.* ② Someone who is slow is not very clever. ③ If a clock or watch is slow, it shows a time earlier than the correct one. ▶ **VERB** ④ If something slows, slows down or slows up, it moves or happens more slowly. **slowness NOUN**

slowly ADVERB not quickly or hurriedly.

slow motion NOUN Slow motion is movement which is much slower than normal, especially in a film • *It all seemed to happen in slow motion.*

sludge NOUN Sludge is thick mud or sewage.

slug, **slugs NOUN** ① a small, slow-moving creature with a slimy body, like a snail without a shell. ② (*informal*) A slug of a strong alcoholic drink is a mouthful of it.

sluggish ADJECTIVE moving slowly and without energy • *the sluggish waters.* **sluggishly ADVERB**

sluice, **sluices**, **sluicing**, **sluiced** [*Said* **sloose**] **NOUN** ① a channel which carries water, with an opening called a sluicegate which can be opened or closed to control the flow of water. ▶ **VERB** ② If you sluice something, you wash it by pouring water over it • *He had sluiced his hands under a tap.* **WORD HISTORY:** from Latin *exclusa aqua* meaning 'water shut out'

slum, **slums NOUN** a poor, run-down area of a city.

slumber, **slumbers**, **slumbering**, **slumbered** (*literary*) **NOUN** ① Slumber is sleep. ▶ **VERB** ② When you slumber, you sleep.

slump, **slumps**, **slumping**, **slumped VERB** ① If an amount or a value slumps, it falls suddenly by a large amount. ② If you slump somewhere, you fall or sit down heavily • *He slumped against the side of the car.* ▶ **NOUN** ③ a sudden, severe drop in an amount or value • *the slump in house prices.* ④ a time when there is economic decline and high unemployment.

slung the past tense and past participle of **sling**.

slur, **slurs**, **slurring**, **slurred NOUN** ① an insulting remark. ▶ **VERB** ② When people slur their speech, they do not say their words clearly, often because they are drunk or ill.

slurp, **slurps**, **slurping**, **slurped VERB** If you slurp a drink, you drink it noisily.

WORD HISTORY: from Old Dutch *slorpen* meaning 'to sip'

slurry NOUN Slurry is a watery mixture of something such as mud, cement or clay.

slush NOUN ① Slush is wet melting snow. ② (*informal*) You can refer to sentimental love stories as slush. **slushy** ADJECTIVE

sly, slyer or slier, slyest or sliest ADJECTIVE ① A sly expression or remark shows that you know something other people do not know • *a sly smile*. ② A sly person is cunning and good at deceiving people. **slyly** ADVERB
SIMILAR WORDS: ② crafty, cunning, devious

smack, smacks, smacking, smacked VERB ① If you smack someone, you hit them with your open hand. ② If something smacks of something else, it reminds you of it • *His tale smacks of fantasy.* ▶ NOUN ③ If you give someone a smack, you smack them. ④ a loud, sharp noise • *He landed with a smack on the tank.*

small, smaller, smallest; smalls ADJECTIVE ① Small means not large in size, number or amount. ② Small means not important or significant • *small changes*. ▶ NOUN ③ The small of your back is the narrow part where your back curves slightly inwards. **smallness** NOUN
SIMILAR WORDS: ① little, tiny ② insignificant, minor, trivial

smallpox NOUN Smallpox is a serious contagious disease that causes a fever and a rash.

small talk NOUN Small talk is conversation about unimportant things.

smart, smarter, smartest; smarts, smarting, smarted ADJECTIVE ① A smart person is clean and neatly dressed. ② Smart means clever • *a smart idea*. ③ A smart movement is quick and sharp. ④ A smart machine or system is one that uses computer technology. ▶ VERB ⑤ If a wound smarts, it stings. ⑥ If you are smarting from criticism or unkindness, you are feeling upset by it. **smartly** ADVERB **smartness** NOUN

smart card, smart cards NOUN a plastic card which can store and process computer data.

smarten, smartens, smartening, smartened VERB If you smarten something up, you make it look neater and tidier.

smartphone, smartphones NOUN a mobile phone allowing access to the internet.

smash, smashes, smashing, smashed VERB ① If you smash something, you break it into a lot of pieces by hitting it or dropping it. ② To smash through something such as a wall means to go through it by breaking it. ③ To smash against something means to hit it with great force • *An immense wave smashed against the hull*. ▶ NOUN ④ (*informal*) If a play or film is a smash or a smash hit, it is very successful. ⑤ a car crash. ⑥ In tennis, a smash is a stroke in which the player hits the ball downwards very hard.

smashing ADJECTIVE (*informal*) If you describe something as smashing, you mean you like it very much.

smattering NOUN A smattering of knowledge or information is a very small amount of it • *a smattering of Russian*.

smear, smears, smearing, smeared NOUN ① a dirty, greasy mark on a surface • *a smear of pink lipstick*. ② an untrue and malicious rumour. ▶ VERB ③ If something smears a surface, it makes dirty, greasy marks on it • *The blade was chipped and smeared.* ④ If you smear a surface with a thick substance, you spread a layer of the substance over the surface.

smell, smells, smelling, smelled or smelt NOUN ① The smell of something is a quality it has which you perceive through your nose • *a smell of damp wood.* ② Your sense of smell is your ability to smell things. ▶ VERB ③ If something smells, it has a quality you can perceive through your nose, especially an unpleasant quality. ④ If you smell something, you become aware of it through your nose. ⑤ If you can smell something such as danger or trouble, you feel it is present or likely to happen.

SIMILAR WORDS: ① odour, scent

smelly, smellier, smelliest ADJECTIVE having a strong, unpleasant smell.

smelt, smelts, smelting, smelted VERB To smelt a metal ore means to heat it until it melts, so that the metal can be extracted.

smile, smiles, smiling, smiled VERB ① When you smile, the corners of your mouth move outwards and slightly upwards because you are pleased or amused. ▶ NOUN ② the expression you have when you smile.

smirk, smirks, smirking, smirked VERB ① When you smirk, you smile in a sneering or sarcastic way • *The boy smirked and turned the volume up.* ▶ NOUN ② a sneering or sarcastic smile.

smith, smiths NOUN someone who makes things out of iron, gold or another metal.

smitten ADJECTIVE If you are smitten with someone or something, you are very impressed with or enthusiastic about them • *They were totally smitten with each other.*

smock, smocks NOUN a loose garment like a long blouse.

smog NOUN Smog is a mixture of smoke and fog which occurs in some industrial cities.

smoke, smokes, smoking, smoked NOUN ① Smoke is a mixture of gas and small particles sent into the air when something burns. ▶ VERB ② If something is smoking, smoke is coming from it. ③ When someone smokes a cigarette or pipe, they suck smoke from it into their mouth and blow it out again. ④ To smoke fish or meat means to hang it over burning wood so that the smoke preserves it and gives it a pleasant flavour • *smoked bacon.* **smoker** NOUN **smoking** NOUN or ADJECTIVE

smoky, smokier, smokiest ADJECTIVE A smoky place is full of smoke.

smooth, smoother, smoothest; smooths, smoothing, smoothed ADJECTIVE ① A smooth surface has no roughness and no holes in it. ② A smooth liquid or mixture has no lumps in it. ③ A smooth movement or process happens evenly and steadily • *smooth acceleration.* ④ Smooth also means successful and without problems • *staff responsible for the smooth running of the hall.* ▶ VERB ⑤ If you smooth something, you move your hands over it to make it smooth and flat. **smoothly** ADVERB **smoothness** NOUN

smoothie, smoothies NOUN a thick type of drink made in an electric blender from milk, fruit and crushed ice.

smother, smothers, smothering, smothered VERB ① If you smother a fire, you cover it with something to put it out. ② To smother a person means to cover their face with something so that they cannot breathe. ③ To smother someone also means to give them too much love and protection. ④ If you smother an emotion, you control it so that people do not notice it • *They tried to smother their glee.*

smothered ADJECTIVE completely covered with something • *a spectacular trellis smothered in climbing roses.*

smoulder, smoulders, smouldering, smouldered VERB ① When something smoulders, it burns slowly, producing smoke but no flames. ② If a feeling is smouldering inside you, you feel it very strongly but do not show it • *smouldering with resentment.*

smudge, smudges, smudging, smudged NOUN ① a dirty or blurred mark or a smear on something. ▸ VERB ② If you smudge something, you make it dirty or messy by touching it or marking it.

smug, smugger, smuggest ADJECTIVE Someone who is smug is very pleased with how good or clever they are. **smugly** ADVERB **smugness** NOUN

smuggle, smuggles, smuggling, smuggled VERB To smuggle things or people into or out of a place means to take them there illegally or secretly.

smuggler, smugglers NOUN someone who smuggles goods illegally into a country.

snack, snacks NOUN a light, quick meal.

snag, snags, snagging, snagged NOUN ① a small problem or disadvantage • *There is one snag: it is not true.* ② (*informal*) In Australian and New Zealand English, a snag is a sausage. ▸ VERB ③ If you snag your clothing, you damage it by catching it on something sharp.

snail, snails NOUN a small, slow-moving creature with a long, shiny body and a shell on its back.

snail mail NOUN (*informal*) the conventional postal system, as opposed to email or text messaging.

snake, snakes, snaking, snaked NOUN ① a long, thin, scaly reptile with no legs. ▸ VERB ② Something that snakes moves in long winding curves • *The queue snaked out of the shop.*

snap, snaps, snapping, snapped VERB ① If something snaps or if you snap it, it breaks with a sharp cracking noise. ② If you snap something into a particular position, you move it there quickly with a sharp sound. ③ If an animal snaps at you, it shuts its jaws together quickly as if to bite you. ④ If someone snaps at you, they speak in a sharp, unfriendly way. ⑤ If you snap someone, you take a quick photograph of them. ▸ NOUN ⑥ the sound of something snapping. ⑦ (*informal*) a photograph taken quickly and casually. ▸ ADJECTIVE ⑧ A snap decision or action is taken suddenly without careful thought.

snapper, snappers NOUN a fish with edible pink flesh, found in waters around Australia, New Zealand and the US.

snapshot, snapshots NOUN a photograph taken quickly and casually.

snare, snares, snaring, snared NOUN ① a trap for catching birds or small animals. ▸ VERB ② To snare an animal or bird means to catch it using a snare.

snarl, snarls, snarling, snarled VERB ① When an animal snarls, it bares its teeth and makes a fierce growling noise. ② If you snarl, you say something in a fierce, angry way.

▸ NOUN ③ the noise an animal makes when it snarls.

snatch, snatches, snatching, snatched VERB ① If you snatch something, you reach out for it quickly and take it. ② If you snatch an amount of time or an opportunity, you quickly make use of it. ▸ NOUN ③ If you make a snatch at something, you reach out for it quickly to try to take it. ④ A snatch of conversation or song is a very small piece of it.

sneak, sneaks, sneaking, sneaked VERB ① If you sneak somewhere, you go there quickly trying not to be seen or heard. ② If you sneak something somewhere, you take it there secretly. ▸ NOUN ③ (informal) someone who tells people in authority that someone else has done something wrong.

sneaker, sneakers NOUN Sneakers are casual shoes with rubber soles.

sneaking ADJECTIVE If you have a sneaking feeling about something or someone, you have this feeling rather reluctantly • I had a sneaking suspicion that she was enjoying herself.

sneaky, sneakier, sneakiest ADJECTIVE (informal) Someone who is sneaky does things secretly rather than openly.

sneer, sneers, sneering, sneered VERB ① If you sneer at someone or something, you show by your expression and your comments that you think they are stupid or inferior. ▸ NOUN ② the expression on someone's face when they sneer.

sneeze, sneezes, sneezing, sneezed VERB ① When you sneeze, you suddenly take in breath and blow it down your nose noisily, because something has irritated the inside of your nose. ▸ NOUN ② an act of sneezing.

snide ADJECTIVE A snide comment or remark criticises someone in a nasty but indirect way.

sniff, sniffs, sniffing, sniffed VERB ① When you sniff, you breathe in air through your nose hard enough to make a sound. ② If you sniff something, you smell it by sniffing. ③ You can say that a person sniffs at something when they do not think very much of it • Bessie sniffed at his household arrangements. ▸ NOUN ④ the noise you make when you sniff. ⑤ A sniff of something is a smell of it • a sniff at the flowers.

snigger, sniggers, sniggering, sniggered VERB ① If you snigger, you laugh in a quiet, disrespectful way • They were sniggering at her accent. ▸ NOUN ② a quiet, disrespectful laugh.

snip, snips, snipping, snipped VERB ① If you snip something, you cut it with scissors or shears in a single quick action. ▸ NOUN ② a small cut made by scissors or shears.

snippet, snippets NOUN A snippet of something such as information or news is a small piece of it.

snob, snobs NOUN ① someone who admires upper-class people and looks down on lower-class people. ② someone who believes that they are better than other people. **snobbery** NOUN **snobbish** ADJECTIVE

snooker NOUN Snooker is a game played on a large table covered with smooth green cloth. Players score points by hitting different coloured balls into side pockets using a long stick called a cue.

snoop, snoops, snooping, snooped VERB (informal) Someone who is snooping is secretly looking round a place to find out things.

a b c d e f g h i j k l m n o p q r s t u v w x y z

WORD HISTORY: from Dutch *snoepen* meaning 'to eat furtively'

snooper NOUN (*informal*) a person who interferes in other people's business.

snooze, snoozes, snoozing, snoozed (*informal*) VERB ① If you snooze, you sleep lightly for a short time, especially during the day. ▸ NOUN ② a short, light sleep.

snore, snores, snoring, snored VERB ① When a sleeping person snores, they make a loud noise each time they breathe. ▸ NOUN ② the noise someone makes when they snore.

snorkel, snorkels NOUN a tube you can breathe through when you are swimming just under the surface of the sea. **snorkelling** NOUN
WORD HISTORY: from German *Schnorchel*, originally an air pipe for a submarine

snort, snorts, snorting, snorted VERB ① When people or animals snort, they force breath out through their nose in a noisy way • *Sarah snorted with laughter.* ▸ NOUN ② the noise you make when you snort.

snout, snouts NOUN An animal's snout is its nose.

snow, snows, snowing, snowed NOUN ① Snow consists of flakes of ice crystals which fall from the sky in cold weather. ▸ VERB ② When it snows, snow falls from the sky.

snowball, snowballs, snowballing, snowballed NOUN ① a ball of snow for throwing. ▸ VERB ② When something such as a project snowballs, it grows rapidly.

snowdrift, snowdrifts NOUN a deep pile of snow formed by the wind.

snowdrop, snowdrops NOUN a small white flower which appears in early spring.

snowman, snowmen NOUN a large mound of snow moulded into the shape of a person.

snub, snubs, snubbing, snubbed VERB ① To snub someone means to behave rudely towards them, especially by making an insulting remark or ignoring them. ▸ NOUN ② an insulting remark or a piece of rude behaviour. ▸ ADJECTIVE ③ A snub nose is short and turned-up.
SIMILAR WORDS: ② affront, insult, slap in the face

snuff NOUN Snuff is powdered tobacco which people take by sniffing it up their noses.

snug, snugger, snuggest ADJECTIVE A snug place is warm and comfortable. If you are snug, you are warm and comfortable. **snugly** ADVERB

snuggle, snuggles, snuggling, snuggled VERB If you snuggle somewhere, you cuddle up more closely to something or someone.

SO ADVERB ① 'So' is used to refer to what has just been mentioned • *Had he locked the car? If so, where were the keys?* ② 'So' is used to mean also • *He laughed, and so did Jarvis.* ③ 'So' can be used to mean 'therefore' • *It's a bit expensive, so I don't think I will get one.* ④ 'So' is used when you are talking about the degree or extent of something • *Why are you so cruel?* ⑤ 'So' is used before words like 'much' and 'many' to say that there is a definite limit to something • *There are only so many questions that can be asked about the record.* ▸ PHRASE ⑥ **So that** and **so as** are used to introduce the reason for doing something • *to die so that you might live.*

soak, soaks, soaking, soaked VERB ① To soak something or leave it to soak means to put it in a liquid and leave it there. ② When a liquid soaks

something, it makes it very wet.
③When something soaks up a liquid, the liquid is drawn up into it.

SIMILAR WORDS: ②saturate, wet

soaked ADJECTIVE extremely wet.

soaking ADJECTIVE If something is soaking, it is very wet.

soap, soaps NOUN Soap is a substance made of natural oils and fats and used for washing yourself. **soapy** ADJECTIVE

soap opera, soap operas NOUN a popular television drama serial about people's daily lives.

soar, soars, soaring, soared VERB ①If an amount soars, it quickly increases by a great deal • *Property prices soared*. ②If something soars into the air, it quickly goes up into the air. **soaring** ADJECTIVE

sob, sobs, sobbing, sobbed VERB ①When someone sobs, they cry in a noisy way, breathing in short breaths. ▶ NOUN ②the noise made when you cry.

sober, soberer, soberest; sobers, sobering, sobered ADJECTIVE ①If someone is sober, they are not drunk. ②Sober also means serious and thoughtful. ③Sober colours are plain and rather dull. **soberly** ADVERB
sober up VERB To sober up means to become sober after being drunk.

sobering ADJECTIVE Something which is sobering makes you serious and thoughtful • *the sobering lesson of the last year*.

so-called ADJECTIVE You use 'so-called' to say that the name by which something is called is incorrect or misleading • *so-called environmentally-friendly products*.

soccer NOUN Soccer is a game played by two teams of eleven players who try to kick or head a ball into the opposing team's net.

WORD HISTORY: formed from *Association* Football

sociable ADJECTIVE Sociable people are friendly and enjoy talking to other people. **sociability** NOUN
SIMILAR WORDS: friendly, gregarious, outgoing

social ADJECTIVE ①to do with society or life within a society • *people from similar social backgrounds*. ②to do with leisure activities that involve meeting other people. **socially** ADVERB

socialise, socialises, socialising, socialised; also spelt **socialize** VERB When people socialise, they meet other people socially, for example at parties.

socialism NOUN Socialism is the political belief that the state should own industries on behalf of the people and that everyone should be equal. **socialist** ADJECTIVE or NOUN

social media PLURAL NOUN ICT websites and applications used by large groups of people to share information and to develop social and professional contacts.

GRAMMAR TIP
Although *social media* is a plural noun, it is becoming more common for it to be used as a singular: *Social media is very powerful*.

social networking site, social networking sites NOUN ICT a website where users can connect with other people to chat and share photographs and videos.

social security NOUN Social security is a system by which the government pays money regularly to people who have no other income or only a very small income.

social work NOUN Social work involves giving help and advice to

a b c d e f g h i j k l m n o p q r s t u v w x y z

people with serious financial or family problems. **social worker** NOUN

society, societies NOUN
① CITIZENSHIP Society is the people in a particular country or region • *a major problem in society*. ② an organisation for people who have the same interest or aim • *the school debating society*. ③ Society is also rich, upper-class, fashionable people.
SIMILAR WORDS: ① civilisation, culture

sociology NOUN Sociology is the study of human societies and the relationships between groups in these societies. **sociological** ADJECTIVE **sociologist** NOUN

sock, socks NOUN Socks are pieces of clothing covering your foot and ankle.

socket, sockets NOUN ① a place on a wall or on a piece of electrical equipment into which you can put a plug or bulb. ② Any hollow part or opening into which another part fits can be called a socket • *eye sockets*.

sod NOUN (*literary*) The sod is the surface of the ground, together with the grass and roots growing in it.

soda, sodas NOUN ① Soda is the same as **soda water**. ② in American English, a sweet fizzy drink. ③ Soda is also sodium in the form of crystals or a powder, and is used for baking or cleaning.

soda water, soda waters NOUN Soda water is fizzy water used for mixing with alcoholic drinks or fruit juice.

sodden ADJECTIVE soaking wet.

sodium NOUN SCIENCE Sodium is a silvery-white chemical element which combines with other chemicals. Salt is a sodium compound. Sodium's atomic number is 11 and its symbol is Na.

sofa, sofas NOUN a long comfortable seat with a back and arms for two or three people.
WORD HISTORY: from Arabic *suffah* meaning 'an upholstered raised platform'

soft, softer, softest ADJECTIVE
① Something soft is not hard, stiff or firm. ② Soft also means very gentle • *a soft breeze*. ③ A soft sound or voice is quiet and not harsh. ④ A soft colour or light is not bright. **softly** ADVERB

soft drink, soft drinks NOUN any cold, nonalcoholic drink.

soften, softens, softening, softened VERB ① If something is softened or softens, it becomes less hard, stiff or firm. ② If you soften, you become more sympathetic and less critical • *Phillida softened as she spoke*.

software NOUN ICT Computer programs are known as software.

soggy, soggier, soggiest ADJECTIVE unpleasantly wet or full of water.

soil, soils, soiling, soiled NOUN ① Soil is the top layer on the surface of the earth in which plants grow. ▶ VERB ② If you soil something, you make it dirty. **soiled** ADJECTIVE
SIMILAR WORDS: ① earth, ground

solace [*Said* sol-iss] NOUN (*literary*) Solace is something that makes you feel less sad • *I found solace in writing*.

solar ADJECTIVE ① SCIENCE relating or belonging to the sun. ② using the sun's light and heat as a source of energy • *a solar-powered calculator*.

solar system NOUN The solar system is the sun and all the planets, comets and asteroids that orbit round it.

sold the past tense and past participle of **sell**.

solder, solders, soldering, soldered VERB ① To solder two pieces of metal together means to join them with molten metal. ▸ NOUN ②Solder is the soft metal used for soldering.

SPELLING TIP
Do not confuse the spellings of *solder* and *soldier*: *Never use lead solder to repair plumbing; a soldier in the Japanese army.*

soldier, soldiers NOUN a person in an army.

sole, soles, soling, soled ADJECTIVE ①The sole thing or person of a particular type is the only one of that type. ▸ NOUN ②The sole of your foot or shoe is the underneath part. ③a flat seawater fish which you can eat. ▸ VERB ④When a shoe is soled, a sole is fitted to it.

solely ADVERB If something involves solely one thing, it involves that thing and nothing else.

solemn ADJECTIVE Solemn means serious rather than cheerful or humorous. **solemnly** ADVERB **solemnity** NOUN

solenoid, solenoids NOUN SCIENCE a cylindrical coil of wire which acts as a magnet when an electric current is passed through it.

solicitor, solicitors NOUN a lawyer who gives legal advice and prepares legal documents and cases.

solid, solids ADJECTIVE ①A solid substance or object is hard or firm, and not in the form of a liquid or gas. ②You say that something is solid when it is not hollow • *solid steel.* ③You say that a structure is solid when it is strong and not likely to fall down • *solid fences.* ④You use 'solid' to say that something happens for a period of time without interruption • *I cried for two solid days.* ▸ NOUN ⑤a solid substance or object.
solidly ADVERB

solidarity NOUN If a group of people show solidarity, they show unity and support for each other.

soliloquy, soliloquies [Said *sol-lill-ok-wee*] NOUN ENGLISH a speech in a play made by a character who is alone on the stage.
WORD HISTORY: from Latin *solus* meaning 'alone' and *loqui* meaning 'to speak'

solitary ADJECTIVE ①A solitary activity is one that you do on your own. ②A solitary person or animal spends a lot of time alone. ③If there is a solitary person or object somewhere, there is only one.

solitary confinement NOUN A prisoner in solitary confinement is being kept alone in a prison cell.

solitude NOUN Solitude is the state of being alone.
SIMILAR WORDS: isolation, seclusion

solo, solos NOUN ①a piece of music played or sung by one person alone. ▸ ADJECTIVE ②A solo performance or activity is done by one person alone • *my first solo flight.* ▸ ADVERB ③Solo means alone • *to sail solo around the world.*

soloist, soloists NOUN a person who performs a solo.

solstice, solstices NOUN one of the two times in the year when the sun is at its furthest point south or north of the equator.
WORD HISTORY: from Latin *sol* meaning 'sun' and *sistere* meaning 'to stand still'

soluble ADJECTIVE SCIENCE A soluble substance is able to dissolve in liquid.

solute, solutes NOUN SCIENCE In chemistry, the solute is the substance which dissolves in a liquid to form a solution.

solution, solutions NOUN ①a way of dealing with a problem or difficult situation • *a quick solution to our problem*. ② The solution to a riddle or a puzzle is the answer. ③ SCIENCE a liquid in which a solid substance has been dissolved.

solve, solves, solving, solved VERB If you solve a problem or a question, you find a solution or answer to it.
SIMILAR WORDS: answer, resolve, work out

solvent, solvents ADJECTIVE ① If a person or company is solvent, they have enough money to pay all their debts. ▶ NOUN ② SCIENCE a liquid that can dissolve other substances.
solvency NOUN

Somali, Somalis ADJECTIVE ① belonging or relating to Somalia. ▶ NOUN ② The Somalis are a group of people who live in Somalia. ③ Somali is the language spoken by Somalis.

sombre ADJECTIVE ① Sombre colours are dark and dull. ② A sombre person is serious, sad or gloomy.

some ① You use 'some' to refer to a quantity or number when you are not stating the quantity or number exactly • *There's some money on the table*. ② You use 'some' to emphasise that a quantity or number is fairly large • *She had been there for some days*. ▶ ADVERB ③ You use 'some' in front of a number to show that it is not exact • *a fishing village some seven miles north*.

somebody PRONOUN You use 'somebody' to refer to a person without saying exactly who you mean.

USAGE NOTE
Somebody and *someone* mean the same.

some day ADVERB Some day means at a date in the future that is unknown or that has not yet been decided.

somehow ADVERB ① You use 'somehow' to say that you do not know how something was done or will be done • *You'll find a way of doing it somehow*. ② You use 'somehow' to say that you do not know the reason for something • *Somehow it didn't feel quite right*.

someone PRONOUN You use 'someone' to refer to a person without saying exactly who you mean.

USAGE NOTE
Someone and *somebody* mean the same.

somersault, somersaults NOUN a forwards or backwards roll in which the head is placed on the ground and the body is brought over it.
WORD HISTORY: from Old Provençal *sobre* meaning 'over' and *saut* meaning 'jump'

something PRONOUN You use 'something' to refer to anything that is not a person without saying exactly what you mean.

sometime ADVERB ① at a time in the future or the past that is unknown or that has not yet been fixed • *He has to find out sometime*. ▶ ADJECTIVE ② (*formal*) 'Sometime' is used to say that a person had a particular job or role in the past • *a sometime actor, dancer and singer*.

sometimes ADVERB occasionally, rather than always or never.

somewhat ADVERB to some extent or degree • *The future seemed somewhat bleak*.

somewhere ADVERB ① 'Somewhere' is used to refer to a place without stating exactly where it is • *There has to be a file somewhere*. ② 'Somewhere' is used when giving an approximate amount, number or time • *somewhere* *between the winter of 2009 and the summer of 2011.*

son, **sons** NOUN Someone's son is their male child.

sonar NOUN Sonar is equipment on a ship which calculates the depth of the sea or the position of an underwater object using sound waves.
WORD HISTORY: from *So(und) Na(vigation) R(anging)*

sonata, **sonatas** NOUN MUSIC a piece of classical music, usually in three or more movements, for piano or for another instrument with or without piano.

song, **songs** NOUN a piece of music with words that are sung to the music.

songbird, **songbirds** NOUN a bird that produces musical sounds like singing.

sonic ADJECTIVE involving or producing sound.
WORD HISTORY: from Latin *sonus* meaning 'sound'

son-in-law, **sons-in-law** NOUN Someone's son-in-law is the husband of their grown-up child.

sonnet, **sonnets** NOUN ENGLISH a poem with 14 lines, in which lines rhyme according to fixed patterns.
WORD HISTORY: from Old Provençal *sonet* meaning 'little poem'

soon, **sooner**, **soonest** ADVERB If something is going to happen soon, it will happen in a very short time.

soot NOUN Soot is black powder which rises in the smoke from a fire.
sooty ADJECTIVE

soothe, **soothes**, **soothing**, **soothed** VERB ① If you soothe someone who is angry or upset, you make them calmer. ② Something that soothes pain makes the pain less severe.
soothing ADJECTIVE

sophisticated ADJECTIVE ① Sophisticated people have refined or cultured tastes or habits. ② A sophisticated machine or device is made using advanced and complicated methods.
sophistication NOUN
SIMILAR WORDS: ① cultured, urbane

soppy, **soppier**, **soppiest** ADJECTIVE (*informal*) silly or foolishly sentimental.

soprano, **sopranos** NOUN MUSIC a woman, girl or boy with a singing voice in the highest range of musical notes.

sorcerer, **sorcerers** [*Said sor-ser-er*] NOUN a person who performs magic by using the power of evil spirits.

sorceress, **sorceresses** NOUN a female sorcerer.

sorcery NOUN Sorcery is magic that uses the power of evil spirits.

sordid ADJECTIVE ① dishonest or immoral • *a rather sordid business*. ② dirty, unpleasant or miserable • *the sordid guest house*.
SIMILAR WORDS: ② seedy, sleazy, squalid

sore, **sorer**, **sorest**; **sores** ADJECTIVE ① If part of your body is sore, it causes you pain and discomfort. ② (*literary*) 'Sore' is used to emphasise something • *The President is in sore need of friends.* ▶ NOUN ③ a painful place where your skin has become infected. **sorely** ADVERB **soreness** NOUN
SIMILAR WORDS: ① painful, sensitive, tender

sorghum [*Said saw-gum*] NOUN a type of tropical grass that is grown for hay, grain and syrup.

sorrow, **sorrows** NOUN ① Sorrow is deep sadness or regret. ② Sorrows are things that cause sorrow • *the sorrows of this world.*

a
b
c
d
e
f
g
h
i
j
k
l
m
n
o
p
q
r
s
t
u
v
w
x
y
z

sorry, sorrier, **sorriest** ADJECTIVE
① If you are sorry about something, you feel sadness or regret about it.
② feeling sympathy for someone.
③ 'Sorry' is used to describe people and things that are in a bad physical or mental state • *She was in a pretty sorry state when we found her.*
SIMILAR WORDS: ① apologetic, contrite, regretful

sort, sorts, sorting, **sorted** NOUN
① The different sorts of something are the different types of it. ▸ VERB
② To sort things means to arrange them into different groups or sorts.
sort out VERB If you sort out a problem or misunderstanding, you deal with it and find a solution to it.
SIMILAR WORDS: ① kind, type, variety

GRAMMAR TIP
When you use *sort* in its singular form, the adjective before it should also be singular: *that sort of car.* When you use the plural form *sorts*, the adjective before it should be plural: *those sorts of shop.*

SOS NOUN An SOS is a signal that you are in danger and need help.

SO-SO ADJECTIVE (*informal*) neither good nor bad • *The food is so-so.*

Sotho [*Said soo-too or soh-toh*] NOUN
① The Sotho are a group of Black people who live in southern Africa.
② Sotho is the language spoken by the Sotho.

soufflé, soufflés [*Said soo-flay*]; also spelt **souffle** NOUN a light, fluffy food made from beaten egg whites and other ingredients that is baked in the oven.

sought the past tense and past participle of **seek**.

soul, souls NOUN ① RE A person's soul is the spiritual part of them that is supposed to continue after their body is dead. ② People also use 'soul' to refer to a person's mind, character, thoughts and feelings. ③ 'Soul' can be used to mean person • *There was not a soul there.* ④ Soul is a type of pop music.

sound, sounds, sounding, **sounded**; sounder, **soundest** NOUN
① SCIENCE Sound is everything that can be heard. It is caused by vibrations travelling through air or water to your ear. ② A particular sound is something that you hear.
③ The sound of someone or something is the impression you have of them through what other people have told you • *I like the sound of your father's grandfather.* ▸ VERB ④ If something sounds or if you sound it, it makes a noise. ⑤ To sound something deep, such as a well or the sea, means to measure how deep it is using a weighted line or sonar.
▸ ADJECTIVE ⑥ in good condition • *a guarantee that a house is sound.*
⑦ reliable and sensible • *The logic behind the argument seems sound.*
soundly ADVERB

sound bite, sound bites NOUN a short and memorable sentence or phrase extracted from a longer speech for use on radio or television.

sound effect, sound effects NOUN Sound effects are sounds created artificially to make a play, television programme or film more realistic.

soundproof ADJECTIVE If a room is soundproof, sound cannot get into it or out of it.

soundtrack, soundtracks NOUN The soundtrack of a film is the part you hear, especially the music.

soup, soups NOUN Soup is liquid food made by cooking meat, fish or vegetables in water.

sour, sours, souring, soured
  ADJECTIVE ① If something is sour, it has a sharp, acid taste. ② Sour milk has an unpleasant taste because it is no longer fresh. ③ A sour person is bad-tempered and unfriendly.
  ▶ VERB ④ If a friendship, situation or attitude sours or if something sours it, it becomes less friendly, enjoyable or hopeful.

source, sources NOUN ① The source of something is the person, place or thing that it comes from • *the source of his confidence*. ② A source is a person or book that provides information for a news story or for research. ③ GEOGRAPHY The source of a river or stream is the place where it begins.

SPELLING TIP
Do not confuse the spellings of *source* and *sauce*, which can sound very similar in some accents.

sour grapes PLURAL NOUN You describe someone's behaviour as sour grapes when they say something is worthless but secretly want it and cannot have it.

south NOUN ① The south is the direction to your right when you are looking towards the place where the sun rises. ② The south of a place or country is the part which is towards the south when you are in the centre.
  ▶ ADVERB OR ADJECTIVE ③ South means towards the south • *The taxi headed south* • *the south end of the site*.
  ▶ ADJECTIVE ④ A south wind blows from the south.

South America NOUN South America is the fourth largest continent. It has the Pacific Ocean on its west side, the Atlantic on the east, and the Antarctic to the south. South America is joined to Central America by the Isthmus of Panama.
South American ADJECTIVE

south-east NOUN OR ADVERB OR ADJECTIVE South-east is halfway between south and east.

south-easterly ADJECTIVE ① South-easterly means to or towards the south-east. ② A south-easterly wind blows from the south-east.

south-eastern ADJECTIVE in or from the south-east.

southerly ADJECTIVE ① Southerly means to or towards the south. ② A southerly wind blows from the south.

southern ADJECTIVE in or from the south.

Southern Cross NOUN The Southern Cross is a small group of stars which can be seen from the southern part of the earth, and which is represented on the national flags of Australia and New Zealand.

South Pole NOUN GEOGRAPHY The South Pole is the most southerly place on the surface of the earth.

southward or **southwards**
  ADVERB ① Southward or southwards means towards the south • *the dusty road which led southwards*. ▶ ADJECTIVE ② The southward part of something is the south part.

south-west NOUN OR ADVERB OR ADJECTIVE South-west is halfway between south and west.

south-westerly ADJECTIVE ① South-westerly means to or towards the south-west. ② A south-westerly wind blows from the south-west.

south-western ADJECTIVE in or from the south-west.

souvenir, souvenirs NOUN something you keep to remind you of a holiday, place or event.
  WORD HISTORY: from French *se souvenir* meaning 'to remember'

a
b
c
d
e
f
g
h
i
j
k
l
m
n
o
p
q
r
s
t
u
v
w
x
y
z

sovereign, sovereigns [Said **sov**-rin] NOUN ① a king, queen or royal ruler of a country. ② In the past, a sovereign was a British gold coin worth one pound. ▶ ADJECTIVE ③ A sovereign state or country is independent and not under the authority of any other country.

sovereignty [Said **sov**-rin-tee] NOUN Sovereignty is the political power that a country has to govern itself.

Soviet, Soviets [Said **soh**-vee-et] HISTORY ADJECTIVE ① belonging or relating to the Soviet Union, a former country consisting of Russia and neighbouring states. ▶ NOUN ② The people and the government of the Soviet Union were sometimes referred to as the Soviets.

sow¹, sows, sowing, sowed, sown [Said **soh**] VERB ① To sow seeds or sow an area of land with seeds means to plant them in the ground. ② To sow undesirable feelings or attitudes means to cause them • *You have sown discontent*.

sow², sows [Rhymes with **now**] NOUN an adult female pig.

soya NOUN Soya flour, margarine, oil and milk are made from soya beans.
WORD HISTORY: from Chinese *chiang yu* meaning 'paste sauce'

soya bean, soya beans NOUN Soya beans are a type of edible Asian bean.

spa, spas NOUN a place where water containing minerals bubbles out of the ground, at which people drink or bathe in the water to improve their health.
WORD HISTORY: from the Belgian town *Spa* where there are mineral springs

space, spaces, spacing, spaced NOUN ① Space is the area that is empty or available in a place, building or container. ② Space is the area beyond the earth's atmosphere surrounding the stars and planets. ③ a gap between two things • *the space between the tables*. ④ Space can also refer to a period of time • *two incidents in the space of a week*. ▶ VERB ⑤ If you space a series of things, you arrange them with gaps between them.

spacecraft NOUN a rocket or other vehicle that can travel in space.

spaceman, spacemen NOUN a man who travels in space.

spaceship, spaceships NOUN a spacecraft that carries people through space.

space shuttle, space shuttles NOUN a spacecraft designed to be used many times for travelling out into space and back again.

spacewoman, spacewomen NOUN a woman who travels in space.

spacious ADJECTIVE having or providing a lot of space • *the spacious living room*.
SIMILAR WORDS: capacious, commodious, roomy

spade, spades NOUN ① a tool with a flat metal blade and a long handle used for digging. ② Spades is one of the four suits in a pack of playing cards. It is marked by a black symbol like a heart-shaped leaf with a stem.

spaghetti [Said spag-**get**-ee] NOUN Spaghetti consists of long, thin pieces of pasta.

spam NOUN unwanted emails, usually containing advertising.

span, spans, spanning, spanned NOUN ① the period of time during which something exists or functions • *looking back today over a span of 40 years*. ② The span of something is the total length of it from one end to the other. ▶ VERB ③ If something spans a particular length of time, it lasts throughout that time • *a career that spanned 50 years*. ④A bridge that spans something stretches right across it.

spangle, spangles, spangling, spangled VERB ① If something is spangled, it is covered with small, sparkling objects. ▶ NOUN ② Spangles are small sparkling pieces of metal or plastic used to decorate clothing or hair.

Spaniard, Spaniards [*Said* span-yard] NOUN someone who comes from Spain.

spaniel, spaniels NOUN a dog with long drooping ears and a silky coat. WORD HISTORY: from Old French *espaigneul* meaning 'Spanish dog'

Spanish ADJECTIVE ① belonging or relating to Spain. ▶ NOUN ② Spanish is the main language spoken in Spain, and is also spoken by many people in Central and South America.

spank, spanks, spanking, spanked VERB If a child is spanked, it is punished by being slapped, usually on its leg or bottom.

spanner, spanners NOUN a tool with a specially shaped end that fits round a nut to turn it.

spar, spars, sparring, sparred VERB ① When boxers spar, they hit each other with light punches for practice. ② To spar with someone also means to argue with them, but not in an unpleasant or serious way. ▶ NOUN ③ a strong pole that a sail is attached to on a yacht or ship.

spare, spares, sparing, spared ADJECTIVE ① extra to what is needed • *What does she do in her spare time?* ▶ NOUN ② a thing that is extra to what is needed. ▶ VERB ③ If you spare something for a particular purpose, you make it available • *Few troops could be spared to go*

abroad. ④ If someone is spared an unpleasant experience, they are prevented from suffering it • *The class was spared the misery of detention.*

sparing ADJECTIVE If you are sparing with something, you use it in very small quantities. **sparingly** ADVERB

spark, sparks, sparking, sparked NOUN ① a tiny, bright piece of burning material thrown up by a fire. ② a small flash of light caused by electricity. ③ A spark of feeling is a small amount of it • *that tiny spark of excitement*. ▶ VERB ④ If something sparks, it throws out sparks. ⑤ If one thing sparks another thing off, it causes the second thing to start happening • *The tragedy sparked off a wave of sympathy among staff.*

sparkle, sparkles, sparkling, sparkled VERB ① If something sparkles, it shines with a lot of small, bright points of light. ▶ NOUN ② Sparkles are small, bright points of light. **sparkling** ADJECTIVE SIMILAR WORDS: ① gleam, glitter, twinkle

sparrow, sparrows NOUN a common small bird with brown and grey feathers.

sparse, sparser, sparsest ADJECTIVE small in number or amount and spread out over an area • *the sparse audience*. **sparsely** ADVERB

spartan ADJECTIVE A spartan way of life is very simple with no luxuries • *spartan accommodation*. WORD HISTORY: from *Sparta*, a city in Ancient Greece, whose inhabitants were famous for their discipline, military skill, and stern and plain way of life

spasm, spasms NOUN ① a sudden tightening of the muscles. ② a sudden, short burst of something • *a spasm of fear.*

a
b
c
d
e
f
g
h
i
j
k
l
m
n
o
p
q
r
s
t
u
v
w
x
y
z

A
B
C
D
E
F
G
H
I
J
K
L
M
N
O
P
Q
R
S
T
U
V
W
X
Y
Z

spasmodic ADJECTIVE happening suddenly for short periods of time at irregular intervals • *spasmodic movements*. **spasmodically** ADVERB

spat the past tense and past participle of **spit**.

spate NOUN A spate of things is a large number of them that happen or appear in a rush • *a recent spate of first novels from older writers*.

spatial [*Said* spay-shl] ADJECTIVE to do with size, area or position.

spatter, spatters, spattering, spattered VERB ① If something spatters a surface, it covers the surface with drops of liquid. ▶ NOUN ② A spatter of something is a small amount of it in drops or tiny pieces.

spawn, spawns, spawning, spawned NOUN ① Spawn is a jelly-like substance containing the eggs of fish or amphibians. ▶ VERB ② When fish or amphibians spawn, they lay their eggs. ③ If something spawns something else, it causes it • *The depressed economy spawned the riots*.

spaza shop, spaza shops [*Said* spah-za] NOUN (*slang*) a small informal shop in a South African township.

speak, speaks, speaking, spoke, spoken VERB ① When you speak, you use your voice to say words. ② If you speak a foreign language, you know it and can use it. **speak out** VERB To speak out about something means to publicly state an opinion about it.
SIMILAR WORDS: ① say, talk, utter

speaker, speakers NOUN ① a person who is speaking, especially someone making a speech. ② A speaker on a device that reproduces sound is a loudspeaker.

spear, spears, spearing, speared NOUN ① a weapon consisting of a long pole with a sharp point. ▶ VERB ② To spear something means to push or throw a spear or other pointed object into it.

spearhead, spearheads, spearheading, spearheaded VERB If someone spearheads a campaign, they lead it.

spec PHRASE If you do something **on spec**, you do it hoping for a result but without any certainty • *He turned up at the same event on spec*.

special ADJECTIVE ① Something special is more important or better than other things of its kind. ② Special describes someone who is officially appointed, or something that is needed for a particular purpose • *Karen actually had to get special permission to go there*. ③ Special also describes something that belongs or relates to only one particular person, group or place • *the special needs of the chronically sick*.

specialise, specialises, specialising, specialised; also spelt **specialize** VERB If you specialise in something, you make it your speciality • *a shop specialising in ceramics*. **specialisation** NOUN

specialised; also spelt **specialized** ADJECTIVE developed for a particular purpose or trained in a particular area of knowledge • *a specialised sales team*.

specialist, specialists NOUN ① someone who has a particular skill or who knows a lot about a particular subject • *a skin specialist*. ▶ ADJECTIVE ② having a skill or knowing a lot about a particular subject • *a specialist teacher*. **specialism** NOUN

speciality, specialities NOUN A person's speciality is something they are especially good at or know a lot about • *Roses are her speciality*.

specially ADVERB If something has been done specially for a particular person or purpose, it has been done only for that person or purpose.

species [Said *spee-sheez*] NOUN ⌊SCIENCE⌋ a division of plants or animals whose members have the same characteristics and are able to breed with each other.

specific ADJECTIVE ① particular • *specific areas of difficulty*. ② precise and exact • *She will ask for specific answers*. **specifically** ADVERB

specification, specifications NOUN ⌊DGT⌋ a detailed description of what is needed for something, such as the necessary features in the design of something • *I like to build it to my own specifications*.

specify, specifies, specifying, specified VERB To specify something means to state or describe it precisely • *In his will he specified that these documents were never to be removed*.

specimen, specimens NOUN A specimen of something is an example or small amount of it which gives an idea of what the whole is like • *a specimen of your writing*.

speck, specks NOUN a very small stain or amount of something.

speckled ADJECTIVE Something that is speckled is covered in very small marks or spots.

specs PLURAL NOUN (*informal*) short for **spectacles**.

spectacle, spectacles NOUN ① a strange or interesting sight or scene • *an astonishing spectacle*. ② a grand and impressive event or performance.

spectacles PLURAL NOUN Someone's spectacles are their glasses.

spectacular, spectaculars ADJECTIVE ① Something spectacular is very impressive or dramatic.

▶ NOUN ② a grand and impressive show or performance.
SIMILAR WORDS: ① impressive, sensational, stunning

spectator, spectators NOUN a person who is watching something.
SIMILAR WORDS: observer, onlooker, watcher

spectre, spectres NOUN ① a frightening idea or image • *the spectre of war*. ② a ghost.

spectrum, spectra or spectrums NOUN ① ⌊ART⌋ The spectrum is the range of different colours produced when light passes through a prism or a drop of water. A rainbow shows the colours in a spectrum. ② A spectrum of opinions or emotions is a range of them.

speculate, speculates, speculating, speculated VERB If you speculate about something, you think about it and form opinions about it.
speculation NOUN

speculative ADJECTIVE ① A speculative piece of information is based on guesses and opinions rather than known facts. ② Someone with a speculative expression seems to be trying to guess something • *His mother regarded him with a speculative eye*.

speech, speeches NOUN ① Speech is the ability to speak or the act of speaking. ② a formal talk given to an audience. ③ In a play, a speech is a group of lines spoken by one of the characters.
SIMILAR WORDS: ② address, talk

speechless ADJECTIVE Someone who is speechless is unable to speak for a short time because something has shocked them.

speed, speeds, speeding, sped or speeded NOUN ① The speed of something is the rate at which it

a b c d e f g h i j k l m n o p q r s t u v w x y z

moves or happens. ② Speed is very fast movement or travel. ▸ VERB ③ If you speed somewhere, you move or travel there quickly. ④ Someone who is speeding is driving a vehicle faster than the legal speed limit.
SIMILAR WORDS: ② rapidity, swiftness, velocity

speedboat, speedboats NOUN a small, fast motorboat.

speed limit, speed limits NOUN The speed limit is the maximum speed at which vehicles are legally allowed to drive on a particular road.

speedway NOUN Speedway is the sport of racing lightweight motorcycles on special tracks.

speedy, speedier, speediest ADJECTIVE done very quickly. **speedily** ADVERB

spell, spells, spelling, spelt or spelled VERB ① When you spell a word, you name or write its letters in order. ② When letters spell a word, they form that word when put together in a particular order. ③ If something spells a particular result, it suggests that this will be the result • *This haphazard method could spell disaster for you.* ▸ NOUN ④ A spell of something is a short period of it • *a spell of rough weather.* ⑤ a word or sequence of words used to perform magic. **spell out** VERB If you spell something out, you explain it in detail • *I don't have to spell it out, do I?*

spellbound ADJECTIVE so fascinated by something that you cannot think about anything else • *She had sat spellbound through the film.*

spelling, spellings NOUN The spelling of a word is the correct order of letters in it.

spend, spends, spending, spent VERB ① When you spend money, you buy things with it. ② To spend time or energy means to use it.

spent ADJECTIVE ① Spent describes things which have been used and therefore cannot be used again • *spent matches.* ② If you are spent, you are exhausted and have no energy left.

sperm, sperms NOUN a cell produced in the reproductive organ of a male animal which can enter a female animal's egg and fertilise it.

spew, spews, spewing, spewed VERB ① When things spew from something or when it spews them out, they come out of it in large quantities. ② (informal) To spew means to vomit.

sphere, spheres NOUN ① a perfectly round object, such as a ball. ② An area of activity or interest can be referred to as a sphere of activity or interest. **spherical** ADJECTIVE

sphinx, sphinxes [Said sfingks] NOUN In mythology, the sphinx was a monster with a person's head and a lion's body.

spice, spices, spicing, spiced NOUN ① Spice is powder or seeds from a plant added to food to give it flavour. ② Spice is something which makes life more exciting • *Variety is the spice of life.* ▸ VERB ③ To spice food means to add spice to it. ④ If you spice something up, you make it more exciting or lively.

spicy, spicier, spiciest ADJECTIVE strongly flavoured with spices.

spider, spiders NOUN a small insect-like creature with eight legs that spins webs to catch insects for food.
WORD HISTORY: from Old English *spinnan* meaning 'to spin'

spike, spikes NOUN ① a long pointed piece of metal. ② The spikes on a sports shoe are the pointed pieces of metal attached to the sole. ③ Some other long pointed objects are called spikes • *beautiful pink flower spikes*.

spiky, spikier, spikiest ADJECTIVE Something spiky has sharp points.

spill, spills, spilling, spilled or **spilt** VERB ① If you spill something or if it spills, it accidentally falls or runs out of a container. ② If people or things spill out of a place, they come out of it in large numbers.

spillage, spillages NOUN the spilling of something, or something that has been spilt • *the oil spillage in the Shetlands*.

spin, spins, spinning, spun VERB ① If something spins, it turns quickly around a central point. ② When spiders spin a web, they give out a sticky substance and make it into a web. ③ When people spin, they make thread by twisting together pieces of fibre using a machine. ④ If your head is spinning, you feel dizzy or confused. ▶ NOUN ⑤ a rapid turn around a central point • *a golf club which puts more spin on the ball*.

spin out VERB If you spin something out, you make it last longer than it otherwise would.

spinach *[Said spin-itch]* NOUN Spinach is a vegetable with large green leaves.

spinal ADJECTIVE to do with the spine.

spine, spines NOUN ① Your spine is your backbone. ② Spines are long, sharp points on an animal's body or on a plant.

spinifex NOUN Spinifex is a coarse, spiny Australian grass.

spinning wheel, spinning wheels NOUN a wooden machine for spinning flax or wool.

spin-off, spin-offs NOUN something useful that unexpectedly results from an activity.

spinster, spinsters NOUN (*old-fashioned*) a woman who has never married.

WORD HISTORY: originally a person whose occupation was spinning; later, the official label of an unmarried woman

spiny, spinier, spiniest ADJECTIVE covered with spines.

spiral, spirals, spiralling, spiralled NOUN ① a continuous curve which winds round and round, with each curve above or outside the previous one. ▶ ADJECTIVE ② in the shape of a spiral • *a spiral staircase*. ▶ VERB ③ If something spirals, it moves up or down in a spiral curve • *The aircraft spiralled down*. ④ If an amount or level spirals, it rises or falls quickly at an increasing rate • *Prices have spiralled recently*.

spire, spires NOUN The spire of a church is the tall cone-shaped structure on top.

spirit, spirits, spiriting, spirited NOUN ① Your spirit is the part of you that is not physical and that is connected with your deepest thoughts and feelings. ② RE The spirit of a dead person is a nonphysical part that is believed to remain alive after death. ③ a supernatural being, such as a ghost. ④ Spirit is liveliness, energy and self-confidence • *a band full of spirit*. ⑤ Spirit can refer to an attitude • *his old fighting spirit*. ⑥ (*in plural*) Spirits can describe how happy or unhappy someone is • *in good spirits*. ⑦ Spirits are strong alcoholic drinks such as whisky and gin. ▶ VERB ⑧ If you spirit someone or something into or out of a place, you get them in or out quickly and secretly.

spirited ADJECTIVE showing energy and courage.

spirit level, spirit levels NOUN a device for finding out if a surface is level, consisting of a bubble of air sealed in a tube of liquid in a wooden or metal frame.

spiritual, spirituals ADJECTIVE ① to do with people's thoughts and beliefs, rather than their bodies and physical surroundings. ② RE to do with people's religious beliefs • *spiritual guidance*. ▶ NOUN ③ a religious song originally sung by enslaved Black people in America. **spiritually** ADVERB **spirituality** NOUN

spit, spits, spitting, spat NOUN ① Spit is saliva. ② a long stick made of metal or wood which is pushed through a piece of meat so that it can be hung over a fire and cooked. ③ GEOGRAPHY a long, flat, narrow piece of land sticking out into the sea. ▶ VERB ④ If you spit, you force saliva or some other substance out of your mouth. ⑤ (*informal*) When it is spitting, it is raining very lightly.

spite, spites, spiting, spited PHRASE ① If you do something **in spite of** something else, you do the first thing even though the second thing makes it unpleasant or difficult • *In spite of all the gossip, Virginia stayed behind.* ▶ VERB ② If you do something to spite someone, you do it deliberately to hurt or annoy them. ▶ NOUN ③ If you do something out of spite, you do it to hurt or annoy someone.

spiteful ADJECTIVE A spiteful person does or says nasty things to people deliberately to hurt them.
SIMILAR WORDS: malicious, nasty, vindictive

spitting image NOUN If someone is the spitting image of someone else, they look just like them.

splash, splashes, splashing, splashed VERB ① If you splash around in water, your movements disturb the water in a noisy way. ② If liquid splashes something, it scatters over it in a lot of small drops. ▶ NOUN ③ A splash is the sound made when something hits or falls into water. ④ A splash of liquid is a small quantity of it that has been spilt on something. **splash out** VERB To splash out on something means to spend a lot of money on it.

splatter, splatters, splattering, splattered VERB When something is splattered with a substance, the substance is splashed all over it • *fur coats splattered with paint.*

spleen, spleens NOUN Your spleen is an organ near your stomach which controls the quality of your blood.

splendid ADJECTIVE ① very good indeed • *a splendid career.* ② beautiful and impressive • *a splendid old mansion.* **splendidly** ADVERB
SIMILAR WORDS: ② grand, magnificent

splendour, splendours NOUN ① If something has splendour, it is beautiful and impressive. ② (*in plural*) The splendours of something are its beautiful and impressive features.

splint, splints NOUN a long piece of wood or metal fastened to a broken limb to hold it in place.

splinter, splinters, splintering, splintered NOUN ① a thin, sharp piece of wood or glass which has broken off a larger piece. ▶ VERB ② If something splinters, it breaks into thin, sharp pieces.

split, splits, splitting, split VERB ① If something splits or if you split it, it divides into two or more parts. ② If something such as wood or fabric splits, a long crack or tear appears in it. ③ If people split something, they share it between them. ▶ NOUN ④ A split in a piece of wood or fabric is a crack or tear. ⑤ A split between two things is a division or difference between them • *the split between rugby league and rugby union.* **split up** VERB If two people split up, they end their relationship or marriage.

SIMILAR WORDS: ① break, divide, separate ⑤ division, schism

split infinitive, split infinitives NOUN ENGLISH A split infinitive is an infinitive with a word between the 'to' and the verb, as in 'to boldly go'. This is often thought to be incorrect.

split second NOUN an extremely short period of time.

splitting ADJECTIVE A splitting headache is a very painful headache.

splutter, splutters, spluttering, spluttered VERB ① If someone splutters, they speak in a confused way because they are embarrassed. ② If something splutters, it makes a series of short, sharp sounds.

spoil, spoils, spoiling, spoiled or spoilt VERB ① If you spoil something, you prevent it from being successful or satisfactory. ② To spoil children means to give them everything they want, with harmful effects on their character. ③ To spoil someone also means to give them something nice as a treat.

SIMILAR WORDS: ① mess up, ruin, wreck ② overindulge, pamper

spoils PLURAL NOUN Spoils are valuable things obtained during war or as a result of violence • *the spoils of war.*

spoilsport, spoilsports NOUN (*informal*) someone who spoils people's fun.

spoke, spokes ① Spoke is the past tense of **speak**. ▸ NOUN ② The spokes of a wheel are the bars which connect the hub to the rim.

spoken the past participle of **speak**.

spokesperson, spokespersons NOUN someone who speaks on behalf of another person or a group.

spokesman NOUN **spokeswoman** NOUN

sponge, sponges, sponging, sponged NOUN ① a sea creature with a body made up of many cells. ② part of the very light skeleton of a sponge, used for bathing and cleaning. ③ A sponge or sponge cake is a very light cake. ▸ VERB ④ If you sponge something, you clean it by wiping it with a wet sponge.

sponsor, sponsors, sponsoring, sponsored VERB ① To sponsor something, such as an event or someone's training, means to support it financially • *The visit was sponsored by the London Natural History Society.* ② If you sponsor someone who is doing something for charity, you agree to give them a sum of money for the charity if they manage to do it. ③ If you sponsor a proposal or suggestion, you officially put it forward and support it • *the MP who sponsored the Bill.* ▸ NOUN ④ a person or organisation sponsoring something or someone.

sponsorship NOUN

spontaneous ADJECTIVE ① Spontaneous acts are not planned or arranged in advance. ② A spontaneous event happens because of processes within something rather than being caused by things outside it • *spontaneous bleeding.*

spontaneously ADVERB **spontaneity** NOUN

spoof, spoofs NOUN something such as an article or television programme that seems to be about a serious matter but is actually a joke.

spooky, spookier, spookiest ADJECTIVE eerie and frightening.

spool, spools NOUN a cylindrical object onto which thread, tape or film can be wound.

spoon, **spoons** NOUN an object shaped like a small shallow bowl with a long handle, used for eating, stirring and serving food.

spoonful, **spoonfuls** or **spoonsful** NOUN the amount held by a spoon.

sporadic ADJECTIVE happening at irregular intervals • *a few sporadic attempts at keeping a diary.*
sporadically ADVERB

spore, **spores** NOUN SCIENCE Spores are cells produced by bacteria and nonflowering plants such as fungi which develop into new bacteria or plants.

sporran, **sporrans** NOUN a large purse made of leather or fur, worn by a Scotsman over his kilt.
WORD HISTORY: from Scottish Gaelic *sporan* meaning 'purse'

sport, **sports**, **sporting**, **sported** NOUN ① Sports are games and other enjoyable activities which need physical effort and skill. ② (*informal*) You say that someone is a sport when they accept defeat or teasing cheerfully • *Be a sport, Minister!* ▶ VERB ③ If you sport something noticeable or unusual, you wear it • *One girl sported a bowler hat.*

sporting ADJECTIVE ① relating to sport. ② behaving in a fair and decent way.

sports car, **sports cars** NOUN a low, fast car, usually with room for only two people.

sportsman, **sportsmen** NOUN a man who takes part in sports and is good at them.

sportsmanship NOUN the behaviour and attitudes of a good sportsman or sportswoman, for example fairness, generosity and cheerfulness when losing.

sportswoman, **sportswomen** NOUN a woman who takes part in sports and is good at them.

sporty, **sportier**, **sportiest** ADJECTIVE ① A sporty car is fast and flashy. ② A sporty person is good at sports.

spot, **spots**, **spotting**, **spotted** NOUN ① Spots are small, round, coloured areas on a surface. ② Spots on a person's skin are small lumps, usually caused by an infection or allergy. ③ A spot of something is a small amount of it • *spots of rain.* ④ A place can be called a spot • *the most beautiful spot in the garden.* ▶ VERB ⑤ If you spot something, you notice it. ▶ PHRASE ⑥ If you do something **on the spot**, you do it immediately.

spot check, **spot checks** NOUN a random examination made without warning on one of a group of things or people • *spot checks by road safety officers.*

spotless ADJECTIVE perfectly clean.
spotlessly ADVERB
SIMILAR WORDS: clean, immaculate, impeccable

spotlight, **spotlights**, **spotlighting**, **spotlit** or **spotlighted** NOUN ① DRAMA a powerful light which can be directed to light up a small area. ▶ VERB ② If something spotlights a situation or problem, it draws the public's attention to it • *a national campaign to spotlight the problem.*

spot-on ADJECTIVE (*informal*) exactly correct or accurate.

spotted ADJECTIVE Something spotted has a pattern of spots on it.

spotter, **spotters** NOUN a person whose hobby is looking out for things of a particular kind • *a train spotter.*

spotty, **spottier**, **spottiest** ADJECTIVE Someone who is spotty has spots or pimples on their skin, especially on their face.

spouse, spouses NOUN Someone's spouse is the person they are married to.

spout, spouts, spouting, spouted VERB ① When liquid or flame spouts out of something, it shoots out in a long stream. ② When someone spouts what they have learned, they say it in a boring way. ▶ NOUN ③ a tube with a lip-like end for pouring liquid • *a teapot with a long spout*.

sprain, sprains, spraining, sprained VERB ① If you sprain a joint, you accidentally damage it by twisting it violently. ▶ NOUN ② the injury caused by spraining a joint.

sprang the past tense of **spring**.

sprawl, sprawls, sprawling, sprawled VERB ① If you sprawl somewhere, you sit or lie there with your legs and arms spread out. ② A place that sprawls is spread out over a large area • *a Monday market which sprawls all over town*. ▶ NOUN ③ anything that spreads in an untidy and uncontrolled way • *a sprawl of skyscrapers*. **sprawling** ADJECTIVE

spray, sprays, spraying, sprayed NOUN ① Spray consists of many drops of liquid splashed or forced into the air • *A spray of water shot upwards from the fountain*. ② Spray is also a liquid kept under pressure in a can or other container • *hair spray*. ③ a piece of equipment for spraying liquid • *a garden spray*. ④ A spray of flowers or leaves consists of several of them on one stem. ▶ VERB ⑤ To spray a liquid over something means to cover it with drops of the liquid.

spread, spreads, spreading, spread VERB ① If you spread something out, you open it out or arrange it so that it can be seen or used easily • *He spread the map out on his knees*. ② If you spread a substance on a surface, you put a thin layer on the surface. ③ If

something spreads, it gradually reaches or affects more people • *The news spread quickly*. ④ If something spreads over a period of time, it happens regularly or continuously over that time • *His four international appearances were spread over eight years*. ⑤ If something such as work is spread, it is distributed evenly. ▶ NOUN ⑥ The spread of something is the extent to which it gradually reaches or affects more people • *the spread of technology*. ⑦ A spread of ideas, interests or other things is a wide variety of them. ⑧ soft food put on bread • *cheese spread*.

spread-eagled ADJECTIVE Someone who is spread-eagled is lying with their arms and legs spread out.

spreadsheet, spreadsheets NOUN ICT a computer program that is used for entering and arranging figures, used mainly for financial planning.

spree, sprees NOUN a period of time spent doing something enjoyable • *a shopping spree*.

sprig, sprigs NOUN ① a small twig with leaves on it. ② In Australian and New Zealand English, sprigs are studs on the sole of a football boot.

sprightly, sprightlier, sprightliest ADJECTIVE lively and active.

spring, springs, springing, sprang, sprung NOUN ① Spring is the season between winter and summer. ② a coil of wire which returns to its natural shape after being pressed or pulled. ③ a place where water comes up through the ground. ④ an act of springing • *With a spring he had opened the door*. ▶ VERB ⑤ To spring means to jump upwards or forwards • *Martha sprang to her feet*. ⑥ If something springs in a particular direction, it moves suddenly and quickly • *The door sprang open*. ⑦ If one thing

a
b
c
d
e
f
g
h
i
j
k
l
m
n
o
p
q
r
s
t
u
v
w
x
y
z

springs from another, it is the result of it • *The failures sprang from three facts*.

springboard, springboards NOUN ① a flexible board on which a diver or gymnast jumps to gain height. ② If something is a springboard for an activity or enterprise, it makes it possible for it to begin.

springbok, springboks NOUN ① a small South African antelope which moves in leaps. ② A Springbok is a person who has represented South Africa in a sports team.

spring-clean, spring-cleans, spring-cleaning, spring-cleaned VERB To spring-clean a house means to clean it thoroughly throughout.

spring onion, spring onions NOUN a small onion with long green shoots, often eaten raw in salads.

sprinkle, sprinkles, sprinkling, sprinkled VERB If you sprinkle a liquid or powder over something, you scatter it over it.

sprinkling, sprinklings NOUN A sprinkling of something is a small quantity of it • *a light sprinkling of snow*.

sprint, sprints, sprinting, sprinted NOUN ① a short, fast race. ▸ VERB ② To sprint means to run fast over a short distance.

sprinter, sprinters NOUN an athlete who runs fast over short distances.

sprite, sprites NOUN a type of fairy.

sprout, sprouts, sprouting, sprouted VERB ① When something sprouts, it grows. ② If things sprout up, they appear rapidly • *Their houses sprouted up in that region*. ▸ NOUN ③ A sprout is the same as a **brussels sprout**.

spruce, spruces; sprucer, sprucest; spruces, sprucing, spruced NOUN ① an evergreen tree with needle-like leaves. ▸ ADJECTIVE ② Someone who is spruce is very neat and smart. ▸ VERB ③ To spruce something up means to make it neat and smart.

spruit, spruits [*Rhymes with* **gate**] NOUN In South African English, a spruit is a small stream that flows into a larger body of water.

sprung the past participle of **spring**.

spun the past tense and past participle of **spin**.

spur, spurs, spurring, spurred VERB ① If something spurs you to do something or spurs you on, it encourages you to do it. ▸ NOUN ② Something that acts as a spur encourages a person to do something. ③ Spurs are sharp metal points attached to the heels of a rider's boots and used to urge a horse on. ▸ PHRASE ④ If you do something **on the spur of the moment**, you do it suddenly, without planning it.

spurious [*Said* **spyoor-ee-uss**] ADJECTIVE not genuine or real.

spurn, spurns, spurning, spurned VERB If you spurn something, you refuse to accept it • *You spurned his last offer*.

spurt, spurts, spurting, spurted VERB ① When a liquid or flame spurts out of something, it comes out quickly in a thick, powerful stream. ▸ NOUN ② A spurt of liquid or flame is a thick powerful stream of it • *a small spurt of blood*. ③ A spurt of activity or effort is a sudden, brief period of it.

spy, spies, spying, spied NOUN ① a person sent to find out secret information about a country or organisation. ▸ VERB ② Someone who spies tries to find out secret information about another country or organisation. ③ If you spy on someone, you watch them secretly. ④ If you spy something, you notice it.

spyware NOUN Computer programs that secretly record information which websites you visit are known as spyware.

squabble, **squabbles**, **squabbling**, **squabbled** VERB ① When people squabble, they quarrel about something trivial. ▶ NOUN ② a quarrel.

squad, **squads** NOUN a small group chosen to do a particular activity • the fraud squad • the England football squad.
WORD HISTORY: from Old Spanish escuadra meaning 'square', because of the square formation used by soldiers

squadron, **squadrons** NOUN a section of one of the armed forces, especially the air force.
WORD HISTORY: from Italian squadrone meaning 'soldiers drawn up in a square formation'

squalid ADJECTIVE ① dirty, untidy and in bad condition. ② Squalid activities are unpleasant and often dishonest.

squall, **squalls** NOUN a brief, violent storm.

squalor NOUN Squalor consists of bad or dirty conditions or surroundings.

squander, **squanders**, **squandering**, **squandered** VERB To squander money or resources means to waste them • They have squandered huge amounts of money.

square, **squares**, **squaring**, **squared** NOUN ① MATHS a shape with four equal sides and four right angles. ② In a town or city, a square is a flat, open place, bordered by buildings or streets. ③ MATHS The square of a number is the number multiplied by itself. For example, the square of 3, written 3^2, is 3×3. ▶ ADJECTIVE ④ shaped like a square • her delicate square face. ⑤ 'Square' is used before units of length when talking about the area of something • 24 square metres. ⑥ 'Square' is used after units of length when you are giving the length of each side of something square • a towel measuring a foot square. ▶ VERB ⑦ MATHS If you square a number, you multiply it by itself.

squarely ADVERB ① Squarely means directly rather than indirectly or at an angle • I looked squarely in the mirror. ② If you approach a subject squarely, you consider it fully, without trying to avoid unpleasant aspects of it.

square root, **square roots** NOUN MATHS A square root of a number is a number that makes the first number when it is multiplied by itself. For example, the square roots of 25 are 5 and –5.

squash, **squashes**, **squashing**, **squashed** VERB ① If you squash something, you press it, so that it becomes flat or loses its shape. ▶ NOUN ② If there is a squash in a place, there are a lot of people squashed in it. ③ Squash is a game in which two players hit a small rubber ball against the walls of a court using rackets. ④ Squash is a drink made from fruit juice, sugar and water.

squat, **squats**, **squatting**, **squatted**; **squatter**, **squattest** VERB ① If you squat down, you crouch, balancing on your feet with your legs bent. ② A person who squats in an unused building lives there as a squatter. ▶ NOUN ③ a building used by squatters. ▶ ADJECTIVE ④ short and thick.

squatter, **squatters** NOUN ① a person who lives in an unused building without permission and without paying rent. ② In Australian English, a squatter is someone who owns a large amount of land for sheep or cattle farming. ③ In Australia and New Zealand in the past, a squatter was someone who rented land from the King or Queen.

squawk, squawks, squawking, squawked VERB ① When a bird squawks, it makes a loud, harsh noise. ▶ NOUN ② a loud, harsh noise made by a bird.

squeak, squeaks, squeaking, squeaked VERB ① If something squeaks, it makes a short, high-pitched sound. ▶ NOUN ② a short, high-pitched sound. **squeaky** ADJECTIVE

squeal, squeals, squealing, squealed VERB ① When things or people squeal, they make long, high-pitched sounds. ▶ NOUN ② a long, high-pitched sound.

squeamish ADJECTIVE easily upset by unpleasant sights or situations.

squeeze, squeezes, squeezing, squeezed VERB ① When you squeeze something, you press it firmly from two sides. ② If you squeeze something into a small amount of time or space, you manage to fit it in. ▶ NOUN ③ If you give something a squeeze, you squeeze it • *She gave my hand a quick squeeze.* ④ If getting into something is a squeeze, it is just possible to fit into it • *It would take four comfortably, but six would be a squeeze.*

squelch, squelches, squelching, squelched VERB ① To squelch means to make a wet, sucking sound. ▶ NOUN ② a wet, sucking sound.

squid, squids NOUN a sea creature with a long soft body and many tentacles.

squiggle, squiggles NOUN a wriggly line.

squint, squints, squinting, squinted VERB ① If you squint at something,

you look at it with your eyes screwed up. ▶ NOUN ② If someone has a squint, their eyes look in different directions from each other.

squire, squires NOUN HISTORY In a village, the squire was a gentleman who owned a large house with a lot of land.

squirm, squirms, squirming, squirmed VERB If you squirm, you wriggle and twist your body about, usually because you are nervous or embarrassed.

squirrel, squirrels NOUN a small furry mammal with a long bushy tail. WORD HISTORY: from Greek *skia* meaning 'shadow' and *oura* meaning 'tail'

squirt, squirts, squirting, squirted VERB ① If a liquid squirts, it comes out of a narrow opening in a thin, fast stream. ▶ NOUN ② a thin, fast stream of liquid.

Sri Lankan, Sri Lankans [Said *shree-lang-kan*] ADJECTIVE ① belonging or relating to Sri Lanka. ▶ NOUN ② someone who comes from Sri Lanka.

stab, stabs, stabbing, stabbed VERB ① To stab someone means to wound them by pushing a knife into their body. ② To stab at something means to push at it sharply with your finger or with something long and narrow. ▶ PHRASE ③ (*informal*) If you **have a stab** at something, you try to do it. ▶ NOUN ④ You can refer to a sudden unpleasant feeling as a stab of something • *He felt a stab of guilt.*

stable, stables ADJECTIVE ① not likely to change or come to an end suddenly • *I am in a stable relationship.* ② firmly fixed or balanced and not likely to move, wobble or fall. ▶ NOUN ③ a building in which horses are kept. **stability** NOUN **stabilise** VERB

staccato [Said stak-*kah-toe*] ADJECTIVE consisting of a series of short, sharp, separate sounds.

stack, stacks, stacking, stacked NOUN ① A stack of things is a pile of them, one on top of the other. ▶ VERB ② If you stack things, you arrange them one on top of the other in a pile.

stacks PLURAL NOUN (*informal*) If someone has stacks of something, they have a lot of it.

stadium, stadiums NOUN a sports ground with rows of seats around it. WORD HISTORY: from Greek *stadion* meaning 'racecourse'

staff, staffs, staffing, staffed NOUN ① The staff of an organisation are the people who work for it. ▶ VERB ② To staff an organisation means to find and employ people to work in it. ③ If an organisation is staffed by particular people, they are the people who work for it.

stag, stags NOUN an adult male deer.

stage, stages, staging, staged NOUN ① a part of a process that lasts for a period of time. ② DRAMA In a theatre, the stage is a raised platform where the actors or entertainers perform. ③ DRAMA You can refer to the profession of acting as the stage. ▶ VERB ④ If someone stages a play or event, they organise it and present it or take part in it. SIMILAR WORDS: ① period, phase, point

stagecoach, stagecoaches NOUN a large carriage pulled by horses which used to carry passengers and mail.

stagger, staggers, staggering, staggered VERB ① If you stagger, you walk unsteadily, for example because you are ill. ② If something staggers you, it amazes you. ③ If events are staggered, they are arranged so that they do not all happen at the same time.

staggering ADJECTIVE **staggered** ADJECTIVE SIMILAR WORDS: ① lurch, reel, totter

stagnant ADJECTIVE Stagnant water is not flowing and is unhealthy and dirty.

stag night, stag nights NOUN a party for a man who is about to get married, which only men go to.

staid ADJECTIVE serious and dull.

stain, stains, staining, stained NOUN ① a mark on something that is difficult to remove. ▶ VERB ② If a substance stains something, the thing becomes marked or coloured by it.

stained glass NOUN Stained glass is coloured pieces of glass held together with strips of lead.

stainless steel NOUN Stainless steel is a metal made from steel and chromium which does not rust.

stair, stairs NOUN Stairs are a set of steps inside a building going from one floor to another.

staircase, staircases NOUN a set of stairs.

stairway, stairways NOUN a set of stairs.

stake, stakes, staking, staked PHRASE ① If something is **at stake**, it might be lost or damaged if something else is not successful • *The whole future of the company was at stake.* ▶ VERB ② If you say you would stake your money, life or reputation on the success or truth of something, you mean you would risk it • *He is prepared to stake his own career on this.* ▶ NOUN ③ If you have a stake in something such as a business, you own part of it and its success is important to you. ④ a pointed wooden post that can be hammered into the ground and used as a support. ⑤ (*in plural*) The stakes involved in something are the things that can be lost or gained.

stakeholder, stakeholders NOUN someone who gains or loses from the success or failure of an organisation.

stalactite, stalactites NOUN GEOGRAPHY A stalactite is a piece of rock like a huge icicle hanging from the roof of a cave.

stalagmite, stalagmites NOUN GEOGRAPHY A stalagmite is a large pointed piece of rock sticking up from the floor of a cave.

stale, staler, stalest ADJECTIVE
① Stale food or air is no longer fresh.
② If you feel stale, you have no new ideas and are bored.
SIMILAR WORDS: ① fusty, musty, old

stalemate NOUN ① Stalemate is a situation in which neither side in an argument or contest can win. ② In chess, stalemate is a situation in which a player cannot make any move permitted by the rules, so that the game ends and no-one wins.

stalk, stalks, stalking, stalked [Said stawk] NOUN ① The stalk of a flower or leaf is its stem. ▶ VERB ② To stalk a person or animal means to follow them quietly in order to catch, kill or observe them. ③ If someone stalks into a room, they walk in a stiff, proud or angry way.

stall, stalls, stalling, stalled NOUN ① a large table containing goods for sale or information. ② (in plural) In a theatre, the stalls are the seats at the lowest level, in front of the stage. ▶ VERB ③ When a vehicle stalls, the engine suddenly stops. ④ If you stall when someone asks you to do something, you try to avoid doing it until a later time.

stallion, stallions NOUN an adult male horse that can be used for breeding.

stamen, stamens NOUN SCIENCE The stamens of a flower are the small delicate stalks which grow inside the blossom and produce pollen.

stamina NOUN Stamina is the physical or mental energy needed to do something for a very long time.

stammer, stammers, stammering, stammered VERB ① When someone stammers, they speak with difficulty, repeating words and sounds and hesitating awkwardly. ▶ NOUN ② Someone who has a stammer tends to stammer when they speak.

stamp, stamps, stamping, stamped NOUN ① a small piece of gummed paper which you stick on a letter or parcel before posting it. ② a small block with a pattern cut into it, which you press onto an inky pad and make a mark with it on paper; also the mark made by the stamp. ③ If something bears the stamp of a particular quality or person, it shows clear signs of that quality or of the person's style or characteristics. ▶ VERB ④ If you stamp a piece of paper, you make a mark on it using a stamp. ⑤ If you stamp, you lift your foot and put it down hard on the ground. **stamp out** VERB To stamp something out means to put an end to it • We must stamp out bullying in schools.

stampede, stampedes, stampeding, stampeded VERB ① When a group of animals stampede, they run in a wild, uncontrolled way. ▶ NOUN ② a group of animals stampeding.
WORD HISTORY: from Spanish estampida meaning 'crash' or 'din'

stance, stances NOUN Your stance on a particular matter is your attitude and way of dealing with it • He takes no particular stance on animal rights.

stand, stands, standing, stood VERB
① If you are standing, you are upright, your legs are straight, and your weight is supported by your feet. When you stand up, you get into a standing position. ② If something stands somewhere, that is where it is • *The house stands alone on the top of a small hill.* ③ If you stand something somewhere, you put it there in an upright position • *Stand the containers on bricks.* ④ If a decision or offer stands, it is still valid • *My offer still stands.* ⑤ You can use 'stand' when describing the state or condition of something • *Youth unemployment stands at 35 per cent.* ⑥ If a letter stands for a particular word, it is an abbreviation for that word. ⑦ If you say you will not stand for something, you mean you will not tolerate it. ⑧ If something can stand a situation or test, it is good enough or strong enough not to be damaged by it. ⑨ If you cannot stand something, you cannot bear it • *I can't stand that woman.* ⑩ If you stand in an election, you are one of the candidates.
▶ PHRASE ⑪ When someone **stands trial**, they are tried in a court of law.
▶ NOUN ⑫ a stall or very small shop outdoors or in a large public building. ⑬ a large structure at a sports ground, where the spectators sit. ⑭ a piece of furniture designed to hold something • *an umbrella stand.*
stand by VERB ① If you stand by to provide help or take action, you are ready to do it if necessary. ② If you stand by while something happens, you do nothing to stop it.
stand down VERB If someone stands down, they resign from their job or position. **stand in** VERB If you stand in for someone, you take their place while they are ill or away.
stand out VERB If something stands out, it can be easily noticed or is more important than other similar things.
stand up VERB ① If something stands up to rough treatment, it is not damaged or harmed. ② If you stand up to someone who is criticising or attacking you, you defend yourself.

standard, standards NOUN ① a level of quality or achievement that is considered acceptable • *The work is not up to standard.* ② (*in plural*) Standards are moral principles of behaviour. ▶ ADJECTIVE ③ usual, normal and correct • *The practice became standard procedure for most motor companies.*

standard English NOUN Standard English is the form of English taught in schools, used in text books and broadsheet newspapers, and spoken and written by most educated people.

standardise, standardises, standardising, standardised; also spelt **standardize** VERB To standardise things means to change them so that they all have a similar set of features • *We have decided to standardise our equipment.*

stand-by, stand-bys NOUN ① something available for use when you need it • *a useful stand-by.* ▶ ADJECTIVE ② A stand-by ticket is a cheap ticket that you buy just before a theatre performance or a flight if there are any seats left.

stand-in, stand-ins NOUN someone who takes a person's place while the person is ill or away • *The school had to employ a stand-in while the teacher was ill.*

standing ADJECTIVE ① permanently in existence or used regularly • *a standing joke.* ▶ NOUN ② A person's standing is their status and reputation. ③ 'Standing' is used to say how long something has existed • *a friend of 20 years' standing.*

a b c d e f g h i j k l m n o p q r **s** t u v w x y z

standpoint, standpoints NOUN
If you consider something from a particular standpoint, you consider it from that point of view • *from a military standpoint*.

standstill NOUN If something comes to a standstill, it stops completely.

stank the past tense of **stink**.

stanza, stanzas NOUN ENGLISH
a verse of a poem.

staple, staples, stapling, stapled NOUN ① Staples are small pieces of wire that hold sheets of paper firmly together. You insert them with a stapler. ▸ VERB ② If you staple sheets of paper, you fasten them together with staples. ▸ ADJECTIVE ③ A staple food forms a regular and basic part of someone's everyday diet.
WORD HISTORY: senses 1 and 2 are from Old English *stapol* meaning 'prop'; sense 3 is from Old Dutch *stapel* meaning 'warehouse'

star, stars, starring, starred NOUN ① a large ball of burning gas in space that appears as a point of light in the sky at night. ② a shape with four or more points sticking out in a regular pattern. ③ Famous actors, sports players and musicians are referred to as stars. ④ (*in plural*) The horoscope in a newspaper or magazine can be referred to as the stars • *I'm a Virgo, but don't read my stars every day.* ▸ VERB ⑤ If an actor or actress stars in a film or if the film stars that person, he or she has one of the most important parts in it.

starboard ADJECTIVE The starboard side of a ship is the right-hand side when you are facing the front.
WORD HISTORY: from Old English *steorbord* meaning 'steering side', because boats were formerly steered with a paddle over the right-hand side

starch, starches, starching, starched NOUN ① Starch is a substance used for stiffening fabric such as cotton and linen. ② SCIENCE Starch is a carbohydrate found in foods such as bread and potatoes. ▸ VERB ③ To starch fabric means to stiffen it with starch.

stare, stares, staring, stared VERB ① If you stare at something, you look at it for a long time. ▸ NOUN ② a long fixed look at something.
SIMILAR WORDS: ① gawp, gaze, goggle

starfish, starfishes or starfish NOUN a flat, star-shaped sea creature with five limbs.

stark, starker, starkest ADJECTIVE ① harsh, unpleasant and plain • *the stark choice.* ▸ PHRASE ② If someone is **stark naked**, they have no clothes on at all.

starling, starlings NOUN a common European bird with shiny dark feathers.

start, starts, starting, started VERB ① If something starts, it begins to take place or comes into existence • *When does the party start?* ② If you start to do something, you begin to do it • *Susie started to cry.* ③ If you start something, you cause it to begin or to come into existence • *as good a time as any to start a business.* ④ If you start a machine or car, you operate the controls to make it work. ⑤ If you start, your body suddenly jerks because of surprise or fear. ▸ NOUN ⑥ The start of something is the point or time at which it begins. ⑦ If you do something with a start, you do it with a sudden jerky movement because of surprise or fear • *I awoke with a start.*

starter, starters NOUN a small quantity of food served as the first part of a meal.

startle, startles, startling, startled
VERB If something sudden and
unexpected startles you, it surprises
you and makes you slightly
frightened. **startled** ADJECTIVE
startling ADJECTIVE

starve, starves, starving, starved
VERB ① If people are starving, they
are suffering from a serious lack of
food and are likely to die. ② To starve
a person or animal means to prevent
them from having any food.
③ (informal) If you say you are
starving, you mean you are very
hungry. ④ If someone or something
is starved of something they need,
they are suffering because they are
not getting enough of it • The hospital
was starved of cash. **starvation** NOUN

stash, stashes, stashing, stashed
VERB (informal) If you stash
something away in a secret place,
you store it there to keep it safe.

state, states, stating, stated NOUN
① The state of something is its
condition, what it is like, or its
circumstances. ② Countries are
sometimes referred to as states • the
state of Denmark. ③ Some countries
are divided into regions called states
which make some of their own laws
• the State of Vermont. ④ You can refer
to the government or administration
of a country as the state. ▶ PHRASE
⑤ If you are **in a state**, you are
nervous or upset and unable to
control your emotions. ▶ ADJECTIVE
⑥ A state ceremony involves the ruler
or leader of a country. ▶ VERB ⑦ If
you state something, you say it or
write it, especially in a formal way.

state house, state houses NOUN
In New Zealand, a state house is a
house built and owned by the
government and rented out.

stately home, stately homes NOUN
In Britain, a stately home is a very

large old house which belongs to an
upper-class family.

statement, statements NOUN
① something you say or write when
you give facts or information in a
formal way. ② a document provided
by a bank showing all the money paid
into and out of an account during a
period of time.

state school, state schools NOUN a
school maintained and financed by
the government in which education
is free.

statesman, statesmen NOUN an
important and experienced politician.

static ADJECTIVE ① never moving or
changing • The temperature remains
fairly static. ▶ NOUN ② SCIENCE
Static or static electricity is an
electrical charge caused by friction. It
builds up in metal objects.

station, stations, stationing,
stationed NOUN ① a building and
platforms where trains stop for
passengers. ② A bus or coach station
is a place where some buses start
their journeys. ③ A radio station is
the frequency on which a particular
company broadcasts. ④ In Australian
and New Zealand English, a station is
a large sheep or cattle farm.
⑤ (old-fashioned) A person's station is
their position or rank in society.
▶ VERB ⑥ Someone who is stationed
somewhere is sent there to work or
do a particular job • Her husband was
stationed in Vienna.

stationary ADJECTIVE not moving
• a stationary car.
SIMILAR WORDS: fixed, motionless

SPELLING TIP
Do not confuse the spellings of
stationary the adjective and stationery
the noun: He drove into a stationary
bus; paper, pens and other office
stationery.

a
b
c
d
e
f
g
h
i
j
k
l
m
n
o
p
q
r
s
t
u
v
w
x
y
z

stationery NOUN Stationery is paper, pens and other writing equipment.

SPELLING TIP
Do not confuse the spellings of *stationery* the noun and *stationary* the adjective: *paper, pens and other office stationery; He drove into a stationary bus.*

statistic, statistics NOUN
① Statistics are facts obtained by analysing numerical information.
② Statistics is the branch of mathematics that deals with the analysis of numerical information. **statistical** ADJECTIVE **statistically** ADVERB

statistician, statisticians [Said *stat-iss-tish-an*] NOUN a person who studies or works with statistics.

statue, statues NOUN a sculpture of a person.

SPELLING TIP
Do not confuse the spellings of *statue* and *statute*: *a marble statue of the Roman goddess Venus; an anti-terrorism statute passed by the Russian parliament.*

stature NOUN ① Someone's stature is their height and size. ② Someone's stature is also their importance and reputation • *the desire to gain international stature.*

status, statuses [Said *stay-tuss*] NOUN ① A person's status is their position and importance in society. ② Status is also the official classification given to someone or something • *I am not sure what your legal status is.*
SIMILAR WORDS: ① position, prestige, standing

status quo [Said *stay-tuss kwoh*] NOUN The status quo is the situation that exists at a particular time • *They want to keep the status quo.*

WORD HISTORY: a Latin expression, meaning literally 'the state in which'

statute, statutes NOUN a law. **statutory** ADJECTIVE

SPELLING TIP
Do not confuse the spellings of *statute* and *statue*: *an anti-terrorism statute passed by the Russian parliament; a marble statue of the Roman goddess Venus.*

staunch, stauncher, staunchest; staunches, staunching, staunched ADJECTIVE ① A staunch supporter is a strong and loyal supporter • *a staunch supporter of the Royal family.* ▶ VERB ② If you staunch blood, you stop it from flowing out of a wound.
WORD HISTORY: from Old French *estanche* meaning 'watertight'

stave, staves, staving, staved NOUN ① MUSIC A stave is the five lines that music is written on. ▶ VERB ② If you stave something off, you try to delay or prevent it.

stay, stays, staying, stayed VERB ① If you stay in a place, you do not move away from it • *She stayed in bed until noon.* ② If you stay at a hotel or a friend's house, you spend some time there as a guest or visitor. ③ If you stay in a particular state, you continue to be in it • *I stayed awake the first night.* ④ In Scottish and South African English, to stay in a place can also mean to live there. ▶ NOUN ⑤ a short time spent somewhere • *a very pleasant stay in Cornwall.*
SIMILAR WORDS: ① linger, remain

stead PHRASE (*formal*) Something that will stand someone **in good stead** will be useful to them in the future.

steadfast ADJECTIVE refusing to change or give up. **steadfastly** ADVERB

steady, steadier, steadiest; steadies, steadying, steadied
ADJECTIVE ① continuing or developing gradually without major interruptions or changes • *a steady rise in profits*. ② firm and not shaking or wobbling • *O'Brien held out a steady hand*. ③ A steady look or voice is calm and controlled. ④ Someone who is steady is sensible and reliable. ▶ VERB ⑤ When you steady something, you hold on to prevent it from shaking or wobbling. ⑥ When you steady yourself, you control and calm yourself. **steadily** ADVERB
SIMILAR WORDS: ② firm, secure, stable

steak, steaks NOUN ① Steak is good-quality beef without much fat. ② A fish steak is a large piece of fish.
WORD HISTORY: from Old Norse *steik* meaning 'roast'

steal, steals, stealing, stole, stolen VERB ① To steal something means to take it without permission and without intending to return it. ② To steal somewhere means to move there quietly and secretively.
SIMILAR WORDS: ① nick, purloin, take

SPELLING TIP
Do not confuse the spellings of *steal* and *steel*: *He is accused of stealing a car; The government is steeling itself to take action*.

stealth [Rhymes with **health**] NOUN If you do something with stealth, you do it quietly and secretively.
stealthy ADJECTIVE **stealthily** ADVERB

steam, steams, steaming, steamed NOUN ① Steam is the hot vapour formed when water boils.
▶ ADJECTIVE ② Steam engines are operated using steam as a means of power. ▶ VERB ③ If something steams, it gives off steam. ④ To

steam food means to cook it in steam. **steamy** ADJECTIVE

steam engine, steam engines NOUN any engine that uses the energy of steam to produce mechanical work.

steamer, steamers NOUN ① a ship powered by steam. ② a container with small holes in the bottom in which you steam food.

steed, steeds NOUN (*literary*) a horse.

steel, steels, steeling, steeled NOUN ① Steel is a very strong metal containing mainly iron with a small amount of carbon. ▶ VERB ② To steel yourself means to prepare to deal with something unpleasant.

SPELLING TIP
Do not confuse the spellings of *steel* and *steal*: *The government is steeling itself to take action; He is accused of stealing a car*.

steel band, steel bands NOUN a group of people who play music on special metal drums.

steel drum, steel drums NOUN a drum made from the head of an oil drum, hammered or embossed to create a certain note, played in a steel band.

steep, steeper, steepest; steeps, steeping, steeped ADJECTIVE ① A steep slope rises sharply and is difficult to go up. ② larger than is reasonable • *a steep price increase*.
▶ VERB ③ To steep something in a liquid means to soak it thoroughly.
steeply ADVERB
SIMILAR WORDS: ① precipitous, sheer

steeped ADJECTIVE If a person or place is steeped in a particular quality, they are surrounded by it or have been deeply influenced by it • *an industry steeped in tradition*.

a b c d e f g h i j k l m n o p q r s t u v w x y z

steeple, **steeples** NOUN a tall pointed structure on top of a church tower.

steeplechase, **steeplechases** NOUN a long horse race in which the horses jump over obstacles such as hedges and water jumps.

WORD HISTORY: originally a race with a church steeple in sight as the goal

steer, **steers**, **steering**, **steered** VERB ①To steer a vehicle or boat means to control it so that it goes in the right direction. ②To steer someone towards a particular course of action means to influence and direct their behaviour or thoughts. ▶ NOUN ③a castrated bull.

SIMILAR WORDS: ① direct, guide, pilot

stellar ADJECTIVE relating to the stars.

WORD HISTORY: from Latin *stella* meaning 'star'

stem, **stems**, **stemming**, **stemmed** NOUN ①The stem of a plant is the long, thin central part above the ground that carries the leaves and flowers. ②The stem of a glass is the long, narrow part connecting the bowl to the base. ▶ VERB ③If a problem stems from a particular situation, that situation is the original starting point or cause of the problem. ④If you stem the flow of something, you restrict it or stop it from spreading • *to stem the flow of blood*.

STEM an abbreviation for 'science, technology, engineering and mathematics'.

stench, **stenches** NOUN a very strong, unpleasant smell.

stencil, **stencils**, **stencilling**, **stencilled** NOUN ①a thin sheet with a cut-out pattern through which ink or paint passes to form the pattern on the surface below. ▶ VERB ②To stencil a design on a surface means to create it using a stencil.

WORD HISTORY: from Middle English *stanselen* meaning 'to decorate with bright colours'

step, **steps**, **stepping**, **stepped** NOUN ①If you take a step, you lift your foot and put it down somewhere else. ②one of a series of actions that you take in order to achieve something. ③a raised flat surface, usually one of a series that you can walk up or down. ▶ VERB ④If you step in a particular direction, you move your foot in that direction. ⑤If someone steps down or steps aside from an important position, they resign.

step in VERB If you step in, you become involved in a difficult situation in order to help to resolve it.

step up VERB If you step up the rate of something, you increase it.

step- PREFIX If a word like 'father' or 'sister' has 'step-' in front of it, it shows that the family relationship has come about as a result of a parent marrying again • *stepfather* • *stepsister*.

steppe, **steppes** [*Said step*] NOUN GEOGRAPHY a large area of open grassland with no trees.

WORD HISTORY: from Old Russian *step* meaning 'lowland'

stepping stone, **stepping stones** NOUN ① Stepping stones are a line of large stones that you walk on to cross a shallow river. ②a job or event that is regarded as a stage in your progress, especially in your career.

stereo, **stereos** ADJECTIVE ①A stereo recording or music system is one in which the sound is directed through two speakers. ▶ NOUN ②a piece of equipment that reproduces sound from records, tapes or CDs directing the sound through two speakers.

stereotype, **stereotypes**, **stereotyping**, **stereotyped** PSHE NOUN ①a fixed image or set of characteristics that people consider to represent a particular type of person or thing • *the stereotype of the polite, industrious Japanese.* ▶ VERB ② If you stereotype someone, you assume they are a particular type of person and will behave in a particular way.

sterile ADJECTIVE ① Sterile means completely clean and free from germs. ② A sterile person or animal is unable to produce offspring. **sterility** NOUN
SIMILAR WORDS: ① germ-free, sterilised

sterilise, sterilises, sterilising, sterilised; also spelt **sterilize** VERB ① To sterilise something means to make it completely clean and free from germs, usually by boiling it or treating it with an antiseptic. ② If a person or animal is sterilised, they have an operation that makes it impossible for them to produce offspring.

sterling NOUN ① Sterling is the money system of the United Kingdom. ▶ ADJECTIVE ② excellent in quality • *Volunteers are doing sterling work.*

stern, sterner, sternest; sterns ADJECTIVE ① very serious and strict • *a stern father* • *a stern warning.* ▶ NOUN ② The stern of a boat is the back part.

sternum, sternums or sterna NOUN
SCIENCE Your sternum is the flat bone in the centre of your chest that is joined to your ribs.

steroid, steroids NOUN Steroids are chemicals that occur naturally in your body. Sometimes sportsmen and sportswomen illegally take them as drugs to improve their performance.

stethoscope, stethoscopes NOUN a device used by doctors to listen to a patient's heart and breathing, consisting of earpieces connected to a hollow tube and a small disc.
WORD HISTORY: from Greek *stēthos* meaning 'chest' and *skopein* meaning 'to look at'

stew, stews, stewing, stewed NOUN ① a dish of small pieces of savoury food cooked together slowly in a liquid. ▶ VERB ② To stew meat, vegetables or fruit means to cook them slowly in a liquid.
WORD HISTORY: from Middle English *stuen* meaning 'to take a very hot bath'

steward, stewards NOUN ① a man who works on a ship or plane looking after passengers and serving meals. ② a person who helps to direct the public at a race, march or other event.
WORD HISTORY: from Old English *stigweard* meaning 'hall protector'

stewardess, stewardesses NOUN a woman who works on a ship or plane looking after passengers and serving meals.

stewardship NOUN Stewardship is the responsibility of looking after something, such as land or property.

stick, sticks, sticking, stuck NOUN ① a long, thin piece of wood. ② A stick of something is a long, thin piece of it • *a stick of celery.* ▶ VERB ③ If you stick a long or pointed object into something, you push it in. ④ If you stick one thing to another, you attach it with glue or sticky tape. ⑤ If one thing sticks to another, it becomes attached and is difficult to remove. ⑥ If a movable part of something sticks, it becomes fixed and will no longer move or work properly • *My gears keep sticking.* ⑦ (*informal*) If you stick something somewhere, you put it there. ⑧ If you stick by someone, you continue to help and support them. ⑨ If you

a b c d e f g h i j k l m n o p q r **s** t u v w x y z

stick to something, you keep to it and do not change to something else • *He should have stuck to the old ways of doing things.* ⑩ When people stick together, they stay together and support each other. **stick out** VERB ① If something sticks out, it projects from something else. ② To stick out also means to be very noticeable.

stick up VERB ① If something sticks up, it points upwards from a surface. ② (*informal*) If you stick up for a person or principle, you support or defend them.

sticker, stickers NOUN a small piece of paper or plastic with writing or a picture on it, that you stick onto a surface.

sticking plaster, sticking plasters NOUN a small piece of fabric that you stick over a cut or sore to protect it.

stick insect, stick insects NOUN an insect with a long cylindrical body and long legs, which looks like a twig.

sticky, stickier, stickiest ADJECTIVE ① A sticky object is covered with a substance that can stick to other things • *sticky hands.* ② Sticky paper or tape has glue on one side so that you can stick it to a surface. ③ (*informal*) A sticky situation is difficult or embarrassing to deal with. ④ Sticky weather is unpleasantly hot and humid.

stiff, stiffer, stiffest ADJECTIVE ① DGT Something that is stiff is firm and not easily bent. ② If you feel stiff, your muscles or joints ache when you move. ③ Stiff behaviour is formal and not friendly or relaxed. ④ Stiff also means difficult or severe • *stiff competition for places.* ⑤ A stiff breeze is blowing strongly. ► ADVERB ⑥ (*informal*) If you are bored stiff or scared stiff, you are very bored or very scared. **stiffly** ADVERB **stiffness** NOUN

stiffen, stiffens, stiffening, stiffened VERB ① If you stiffen, you suddenly stop moving and your muscles become tense • *I stiffened with tension.* ② If your joints or muscles stiffen, they become sore and difficult to bend or move. ③ If fabric or material is stiffened, it is made firmer so that it does not bend easily.

stifle, stifles, stifling, stifled [*Said sty-fl*] VERB ① If the atmosphere stifles you, you feel you cannot breathe properly. ② To stifle something means to stop it from happening or continuing • *Martin stifled a yawn.* **stifling** ADJECTIVE

stigma, stigmas NOUN ① If something has a stigma attached to it, people consider it unacceptable or a disgrace • *the stigma of poverty.* ② SCIENCE The stigma of a flower is the part which receives the pollen.

stile, stiles NOUN a step on either side of a wall or fence to enable you to climb over.

stiletto, stilettos NOUN Stilettos are women's shoes with very high, narrow heels.
WORD HISTORY: from Italian *stilo* meaning 'dagger', because of the shape of the heels

still, stiller, stillest; stills ADVERB ① If a situation still exists, it has continued to exist and it exists now. ② If something could still happen, it might happen although it has not happened yet. ③ 'Still' emphasises that something is the case in spite of other things • *Whatever you think of him, he's still your father.* ► ADVERB or ADJECTIVE ④ Still means staying in the same position without moving • *Sit still* • *The air was still.* ► ADJECTIVE ⑤ A still place is quiet and peaceful with no signs of activity. ► NOUN ⑥ a photograph taken from a film or video. **stillness** NOUN

stillborn ADJECTIVE A stillborn baby is dead when it is born.

stilt, **stilts** NOUN ① Stilts are long upright poles on which a building is built, for example on wet land. ② Stilts are also two long pieces of wood or metal on which people balance and walk.

stilted ADJECTIVE formal, unnatural and rather awkward • *a stilted conversation*.

stimulant, **stimulants** NOUN a drug or other substance that makes your body work faster, increasing your heart rate and making it difficult to sleep.

stimulate, **stimulates**, **stimulating**, **stimulated** VERB ① To stimulate something means to encourage it to begin or develop • *to stimulate discussion*. ② If something stimulates you, it gives you new ideas and enthusiasm. **stimulating** ADJECTIVE **stimulation** NOUN
SIMILAR WORDS: ① arouse, encourage, inspire

stimulus, **stimuli** NOUN something that causes a process or event to begin or develop.

sting, **stings**, **stinging**, **stung** VERB ① If a creature or plant stings you, it pricks your skin and injects a substance which causes pain. ② If a part of your body stings, you feel a sharp tingling pain there. ③ If someone's remarks sting you, they make you feel upset and hurt. ▶ NOUN ④ A creature's sting is the part it stings you with.
SIMILAR WORDS: ② hurt, smart

stink, **stinks**, **stinking**, **stank**, **stunk** VERB ① Something that stinks smells very unpleasant. ▶ NOUN ② a very unpleasant smell.
SIMILAR WORDS: ② pong, stench

stint, **stints** NOUN a period of time spent doing a particular job • *a three-year stint in the army*.

stipulate, **stipulates**, **stipulating**, **stipulated** VERB (*formal*) If you stipulate that something must be done, you state clearly that it must be done. **stipulation** NOUN

stir, **stirs**, **stirring**, **stirred** VERB ① When you stir a liquid, you move it around using a spoon or a stick. ② To stir means to move slightly. ③ If something stirs you, it makes you feel strong emotions • *The power of the singing stirred me.* ▶ NOUN ④ If an event causes a stir, it causes general excitement or shock • *two books which have caused a stir*.

stirring, **stirrings** ADJECTIVE ① causing excitement, emotion and enthusiasm • *a stirring account of the action.* ▶ NOUN ② If there is a stirring of emotion, people begin to feel it.

stirrup, **stirrups** NOUN Stirrups are two metal loops hanging by leather straps from a horse's saddle, which you put your feet in when riding.

stitch, **stitches**, **stitching**, **stitched** VERB ① When you stitch pieces of material together, you use a needle and thread to sew them together. ② To stitch a wound means to use a special needle and thread to hold the edges of skin together. ▶ NOUN ③ one of the pieces of thread that can be seen where material has been sewn. ④ one of the pieces of thread that can be seen where a wound has been stitched • *He had eleven stitches in his lip.* ⑤ If you have a stitch, you feel a sharp pain at the side of your abdomen, usually because you have been running or laughing.

stoat, **stoats** NOUN a small wild animal with a long body and brown fur.

stock, **stocks**, **stocking**, **stocked** NOUN ① Stocks are shares bought as an investment in a company; also the amount of money raised by the company through the issue of shares. ②A shop's stock is the total amount of goods it has for sale. ③If you have a stock of things, you have a supply ready for use. ④The stock an animal or person comes from is the type of animal or person they are descended from • *She was descended from Scots Highland stock.* ⑤ Stock is farm animals. ⑥ Stock is a liquid made from boiling meat, bones or vegetables together in water. Stock is used as a base for soups, stews and sauces. ▶**VERB** ⑦A shop that stocks particular goods keeps a supply of them to sell. ⑧If you stock a shelf or cupboard, you fill it with food or other things. ▶**ADJECTIVE** ⑨A stock expression or way of doing something is one that is commonly used. **stock up VERB** If you stock up on something, you buy a supply of it.

stockbroker, stockbrokers **NOUN** A stockbroker is a person whose job is to buy and sell shares for people who want to invest money.

stock exchange, stock exchanges **NOUN** a place where there is trading in stocks and shares • *the New York Stock Exchange.*

stocking, stockings **NOUN** Stockings are long pieces of thin clothing that cover the leg.

stockman, stockmen **NOUN** a man who looks after sheep or cattle on a farm.

stock market, stock markets **NOUN** The stock market is the organisation and activity involved in buying and selling stocks and shares.

stockpile, stockpiles, stockpiling, stockpiled **VERB** ①If someone stockpiles something, they store large quantities of it for future use. ▶**NOUN** ②a large store of something.

stocktaking **NOUN** Stocktaking is the counting and checking of all a shop's or business's goods.

stocky, stockier, stockiest **ADJECTIVE** A stocky person is rather short, but broad and solid-looking.

stoep, stoeps [*Rhymes with* **hoop**] **NOUN** In South African English, a stoep is a veranda.

stoke, stokes, stoking, stoked **VERB** To stoke a fire means to keep it burning by moving or adding fuel.

stole the past tense of **steal**.

stolen the past participle of **steal**.

stoma, stomata **NOUN** SCIENCE In botany, stomata are pores in the outer layer of cells in a plant which control the passage of gases into and out of the plant.

stomach, stomachs, stomaching, stomached **NOUN** ①Your stomach is the organ inside your body where food is digested. ②You can refer to the front part of your body above your waist as your stomach. ▶**VERB** ③If you cannot stomach something, you strongly dislike it and cannot accept it.

stone, stones, stoning, stoned **NOUN** ①Stone is the hard solid substance found in the ground and used for building. ②a small piece of rock. ③The stone in a fruit such as a plum or cherry is the large seed in the centre. ④a unit of weight equal to 14 pounds or about 6.35 kilograms. ⑤You can refer to a jewel as a stone • *a diamond ring with three stones.* ▶**VERB** ⑥To stone something or someone means to throw stones at them.

Stone Age **NOUN** HISTORY The Stone Age is the earliest known period of human history when people used stone to make weapons and tools. The Stone Age is often divided into three periods: the Palaeolithic, the Mesolithic and the Neolithic.

stony, stonier, stoniest ADJECTIVE ① Stony ground is rough and contains a lot of stones or rocks. ② If someone's expression is stony, it shows no friendliness or sympathy.

stood the past tense and past participle of **stand**.

stool, stools NOUN ① a seat with legs but no back or arms. ② a lump of faeces.

stoop, stoops, stooping, stooped VERB ① If you stoop, you stand or walk with your shoulders bent forwards. ② If you would not stoop to something, you would not disgrace yourself by doing it.

stop, stops, stopping, stopped VERB ① If you stop doing something, you no longer do it. ② If an activity or process stops, it comes to an end or no longer happens. ③ If a machine stops, it no longer functions or it is switched off. ④ To stop something means to prevent it. ⑤ If people or things that are moving stop, they no longer move. ⑥ If you stop somewhere, you stay there for a short while. ▶ PHRASE ⑦ To **put a stop to** something means to prevent it from happening or continuing. ▶ NOUN ⑧ a place where a bus, train or other vehicle stops during a journey. ⑨ If something that is moving comes to a stop, it no longer moves.

SIMILAR WORDS: ① cease, desist, halt

stoppage, stoppages NOUN If there is a stoppage, people stop work because of a disagreement with their employer.

stopper, stoppers NOUN a piece of glass or cork that fits into the neck of a jar or bottle.

stopwatch, stopwatches NOUN a watch that can be started and stopped by pressing buttons, which is used to time events.

storage NOUN ① The storage of something is the keeping of it somewhere until it is needed. ② Storage is the place where something is stored. ③ ICT Storage is the process of storing information in a computer.

store, stores, storing, stored NOUN ① a shop. ② A store of something is a supply kept for future use. ③ a place where things are kept while they are not used. ▶ VERB ④ When you store something somewhere, you keep it there until it is needed. ▶ PHRASE ⑤ Something that is **in store for** you is going to happen to you in the future.

SIMILAR WORDS: ① hoard, stockpile, supply

storeroom, storerooms NOUN a room where things are kept until they are needed.

storey, storeys NOUN A storey of a building is one of its floors or levels.

SPELLING TIP
Do not confuse the spellings of *storey* and *story: Jack's office is on the third storey of the building; The children want a bedtime story.*

stork, storks NOUN A stork is a very large white and black bird with long red legs and a long bill. Storks live mainly near water in Eastern Europe and Africa.

storm, storms, storming, stormed NOUN ① When there is a storm, there is heavy rain, a strong wind, and often thunder and lightning. ② If something causes a storm, it causes an angry or excited reaction • *His words caused a storm of protest.* ▶ VERB

③If someone storms out, they leave quickly, noisily and angrily. ④To storm means to say something in a loud, angry voice • *'It's a fiasco!' he stormed.* ⑤If people storm a place, they attack it. **stormy** ADJECTIVE

story, stories NOUN ① ENGLISH a description of imaginary people and events written or told to entertain people. ②The story of something or someone is an account of the important events that have happened to them • *his life story.*
SIMILAR WORDS: ①tale, yarn

SPELLING TIP
Do not confuse the spellings of *story* and *storey*: *The children want a bedtime story; Jack's office is on the third storey of the building.*

stout, stouter, stoutest ADJECTIVE ①rather fat. ②thick, strong and sturdy • *stout walking shoes.* ③determined, firm and strong • *He can outrun the stoutest opposition.* **stoutly** ADVERB

stove, stoves NOUN a piece of equipment for heating a room or for cooking.

stow, stows, stowing, stowed VERB ①If you stow something somewhere or stow it away, you store it until it is needed. ②If someone stows away in a ship or plane, they hide in it to go somewhere secretly without paying.

straddle, straddles, straddling, straddled VERB ①If you straddle something, you stand or sit with one leg on either side of it. ②If something straddles a place, it crosses it, linking different parts together • *The town straddles a river.*

straight, straighter, straightest ADJECTIVE or ADVERB ①continuing in the same direction without curving or bending • *the straight path* • *Amy stared straight ahead of her.* ②upright or level rather than sloping or bent • *Keep your arms straight.* ▶ADVERB ③immediately and directly • *We will go straight to the hotel.* ▶ADJECTIVE ④neat and tidy • *Get this room straight.* ⑤honest, frank and direct • *They wouldn't give me a straight answer.* ⑥A straight choice involves only two options.

SPELLING TIP
Do not confuse the spellings of *straight* and *strait*: *a straight line; the Strait of Messina.*

straightaway ADVERB If you do something straightaway, you do it immediately.

straighten, straightens, straightening, straightened VERB ①To straighten something means to remove any bends or curves from it. ②To straighten something also means to make it neat and tidy. ③To straighten out a confused situation means to organise and deal with it.

straightforward ADJECTIVE ①easy and involving no problems. ②honest, open and frank.

strain, strains, straining, strained NOUN ①Strain is worry and nervous tension. ②If a strain is put on something, it is affected by a strong force which may damage it. ③You can refer to an aspect of someone's character, remarks or work as a strain • *There was a strain of bitterness in his voice.* ④You can refer to distant sounds of music as strains of music. ⑤A particular strain of plant is a variety of it • *strains of rose.* ▶VERB ⑥To strain something means to force it or use it more than is reasonable or normal. ⑦If you strain a muscle, you injure it by moving awkwardly. ⑧To strain food means to pour away the liquid from it.

SIMILAR WORDS: ①anxiety, stress ⑥overexert, tax

strained ADJECTIVE ①worried and anxious. ②If a relationship is strained, people feel unfriendly and do not trust each other.

strait, straits NOUN ①You can refer to a narrow strip of sea as a strait or the straits • *the Straits of Hormuz*. ②(*in plural*) If someone is in a bad situation, you can say they are in difficult straits.

SPELLING TIP
Do not confuse the spellings of *strait* and *straight*: *the Strait of Messina; a straight line*.

straitjacket, straitjackets NOUN a special jacket used to tie the arms of a violent person tightly around their body.

strait-laced ADJECTIVE having a very strict and serious attitude to moral behaviour.

strand, strands NOUN ①A strand of thread or hair is a single long piece of it. ②You can refer to a part of a situation or idea as a strand of it • *the different strands of the problem*.

stranded ADJECTIVE If someone or something is stranded somewhere, they are stuck and cannot leave.

strange, stranger, strangest ADJECTIVE ①unusual or unexpected. ②not known, seen or experienced before • *alone in a strange country*. **strangely** ADVERB **strangeness** NOUN

SIMILAR WORDS: ①curious, odd, peculiar ②alien, new, unfamiliar

stranger, strangers NOUN ①someone you have never met before. ②If you are a stranger to a place or situation, you have not been there or experienced it before.

strangle, strangles, strangling, strangled VERB To strangle someone

means to kill them by squeezing their throat. **strangulation** NOUN

strangled ADJECTIVE A strangled sound is unclear and muffled.

stranglehold, strangleholds NOUN To have a stranglehold on something means to have control over it and prevent it from developing.

strap, straps, strapping, strapped NOUN ①a narrow piece of leather or cloth, used to fasten or hold things together. ▶ VERB ②To strap something means to fasten it with a strap.

strapping ADJECTIVE tall, strong and healthy-looking.

strata the plural of **stratum**.

stratagem, stratagems NOUN A stratagem is a plan or tactic.

strategic [*Said strat-tee-jik*] ADJECTIVE planned or intended to achieve something or to gain an advantage • *a strategic plan*. **strategically** ADVERB

strategy, strategies NOUN ① PSHE a plan for achieving something. ②Strategy is the skill of planning the best way to achieve something, especially in war. **strategist** NOUN

stratosphere NOUN GEOGRAPHY The stratosphere is the layer of the earth's atmosphere which lies between 10 and 50 kilometres above the earth.

stratum, strata NOUN SCIENCE The strata in the earth's surface are the different layers of rock.

straw, straws NOUN ①Straw is the dry, yellowish stalks from cereal crops. ②a hollow tube of paper or plastic which you use to suck a drink into your mouth. ▶ PHRASE ③If something is **the last straw**, it is the latest in a series of bad events and makes you feel you cannot stand any more.

a
b
c
d
e
f
g
h
i
j
k
l
m
n
o
p
q
r
s
t
u
v
w
x
y
z

strawberry, strawberries NOUN a small red fruit with tiny seeds in its skin.

stray, strays, straying, strayed VERB ①When people or animals stray, they wander away from where they should be. ②If your thoughts stray, you stop concentrating. ▶ADJECTIVE ③A stray dog or cat is one that has wandered away from home. ④Stray things are separated from the main group of things of their kind • *a stray piece of lettuce.* ▶ NOUN ⑤a stray dog or cat.

streak, streaks, streaking, streaked NOUN ①a long mark or stain. ②If someone has a particular streak, they have that quality in their character. ③A lucky or unlucky streak is a series of successes or failures. ▶VERB ④If something is streaked with a colour, it has lines of the colour in it. ⑤To streak somewhere means to move there very quickly. **streaky** ADJECTIVE

stream, streams, streaming, streamed NOUN ①a small river. ②You can refer to a steady flow of something as a stream • *a constant stream of people.* ③In a school, a stream is a group of children of the same age and ability. ▶VERB ④To stream somewhere means to move in a continuous flow in large quantities • *Rain streamed down the windscreen.* ⑤To stream video or audio material is to send it over the internet so that the receiving system can play it almost simultaneously.

streamer, streamers NOUN a long, narrow strip of coloured paper used for decoration.

streamline, streamlines, streamlining, streamlined VERB ①To streamline a vehicle, aircraft or boat means to improve its shape so that it moves more quickly and efficiently. ②To streamline an organisation means to make it more efficient by removing parts of it.

street, streets NOUN a road in a town or village, usually with buildings along it.

streetcar, streetcars NOUN In American English, a streetcar is a tram.

street child, street children NOUN a homeless child who lives on the streets.

strength, strengths NOUN ①Your strength is your physical energy and the power of your muscles. ②Strength can refer to the degree of someone's confidence or courage. ③You can refer to power or influence as strength • *The campaign against factory closures gathered strength.* ④Someone's strengths are their good qualities and abilities. ⑤The strength of an object is the degree to which it can stand rough treatment. ⑥The strength of a substance is the amount of other substances that it contains • *coffee with sugar and milk in it at the correct strength.* ⑦The strength of a feeling or opinion is the degree to which it is felt or supported. ⑧The strength of a relationship is its degree of closeness or success. ⑨The strength of a group is the total number of people in it. ▶ PHRASE ⑩If people do something **in strength**, a lot of them do it together • *The press were here in strength.*

SIMILAR WORDS: ① might, muscle ③ force, intensity, power

strengthen, strengthens, strengthening, strengthened VERB ①To strengthen something means to give it more power, influence or support and make it more likely to succeed. ②To strengthen an object means to improve it or add to its structure so that it can withstand rough treatment.

SIMILAR WORDS: ② fortify, reinforce

strenuous [Said **stren-yoo-uss**]
ADJECTIVE involving a lot of effort or energy. **strenuously** ADVERB

stress, stresses, stressing, stressed
NOUN ① Stress is worry and nervous tension. ② Stresses are strong physical forces applied to an object. ③ [ENGLISH] Stress is emphasis put on a word or part of a word when it is pronounced, making it slightly louder. ▶ VERB ④ If you stress a point, you emphasise it and draw attention to its importance. **stressful** ADJECTIVE

SIMILAR WORDS: ① anxiety, pressure, strain ③ accent, emphasis ④ accentuate, emphasise

stretch, stretches, stretching, stretched VERB ① Something that stretches over an area extends that far. ② When you stretch, you hold out part of your body as far as you can. ③ To stretch something soft or elastic means to pull it to make it longer or bigger. ▶ NOUN ④ A stretch of land or water is an area of it. ⑤ A stretch of time is a period of time.

stretcher, stretchers NOUN a long piece of material with a pole along each side, used to carry an injured person.

strewn ADJECTIVE If things are strewn about, they are scattered about untidily • The costumes were strewn all over the floor.

stricken ADJECTIVE severely affected by something unpleasant.

strict, stricter, strictest ADJECTIVE ① Someone who is strict controls other people very firmly. ② A strict rule must always be obeyed absolutely. ③ The strict meaning of something is its precise and accurate

meaning. ④ You can use 'strict' to describe someone who never breaks the rules or principles of a particular belief • a strict Muslim.

SIMILAR WORDS: ① severe, stern ② stringent

strictly ADVERB ① Strictly means only for a particular purpose • I was in it strictly for the money. ▶ PHRASE ② You say **strictly speaking** to correct a statement or add more precise information • Somebody pointed out that, strictly speaking, electricity was a discovery, not an invention.

stride, strides, striding, strode, stridden VERB ① To stride along means to walk quickly with long steps. ▶ NOUN ② a long step; also the length of a step.

strident [Said **stry-dent**] ADJECTIVE loud, harsh and unpleasant.

strife NOUN (formal) Strife is trouble, conflict and disagreement.

strike, strikes, striking, struck NOUN ① If there is a strike, people stop working as a protest. ② A hunger strike is a refusal to eat anything as a protest. A rent strike is a refusal to pay rent. ③ a military attack • the threat of air strikes. ▶ VERB ④ To strike someone or something means to hit them. ⑤ If an illness, disaster or enemy strikes, it suddenly affects or attacks someone. ⑥ If a thought strikes you, it comes into your mind. ⑦ If you are struck by something, you are impressed by it. ⑧ When a clock strikes, it makes a sound to indicate the time. ⑨ To strike a deal with someone means to come to an agreement with them. ⑩ If someone strikes oil or gold, they discover it in the ground. ⑪ If you strike a match, you rub it against something to make it burst into flame. **strike off** VERB If a professional person is struck

a
b
c
d
e
f
g
h
i
j
k
l
m
n
o
p
q
r
s
t
u
v
w
x
y
z

off for bad behaviour, their name is removed from an official register and they are not allowed to practise their profession. **strike out** VERB If someone strikes out, they go off to do something different on their own. **strike up** VERB To strike up a conversation or friendship means to begin it.

striker, strikers NOUN ① Strikers are people who are refusing to work as a protest. ② in soccer, a player whose function is to attack and score goals.

striking ADJECTIVE very noticeable because of being unusual or very attractive. **strikingly** ADVERB

string, strings, stringing, strung NOUN ① String is thin cord made of twisted threads. ② You can refer to a row or series of similar things as a string of them • *a string of islands* • *a string of injuries*. ③ The strings of a musical instrument are tightly stretched lengths of wire or nylon which vibrate to produce the notes. ④ (*in plural*) The section of an orchestra consisting of stringed instruments is called the strings. **string along** VERB (*informal*) To string someone along means to deceive them by letting them believe you have the same desires, hopes or plans as them. **string out** VERB ① If things are strung out, they are spread out in a long line. ② To string something out means to make it last longer than necessary.

stringed ADJECTIVE A stringed instrument is one with strings, such as a guitar or violin.

stringent ADJECTIVE Stringent laws or conditions are very severe or are strictly controlled • *stringent security checks*.

stringy-bark, stringy-barks NOUN any Australian eucalypt that has bark that peels off in long, tough strands.

strip, strips, stripping, stripped NOUN ① A strip of something is a long, narrow piece of it. ② A comic strip is a series of drawings which tell a story. ③ A sports team's strip is the clothes worn by the team when playing a match. ▶ VERB ④ If you strip, you take off all your clothes. ⑤ To strip something means to remove whatever is covering its surface. ⑥ To strip someone of their property or rights means to take their property or rights away from them officially.

stripe, stripes NOUN Stripes are long, thin lines, usually of different colours. **striped** ADJECTIVE

strive, strives, striving, strove, striven VERB If you strive to do something, you make a great effort to achieve it.

strode the past tense of **stride**.

stroke, strokes, stroking, stroked VERB ① If you stroke something, you move your hand smoothly and gently over it. ▶ NOUN ② If someone has a stroke, they suddenly lose consciousness as a result of a blockage or rupture in a blood vessel in the brain. A stroke can result in damage to speech and paralysis. ③ The strokes of a brush or pen are the movements that you make with it. ④ The strokes of a clock are the sounds that indicate the hour. ⑤ A swimming stroke is a particular style of swimming. ▶ PHRASE ⑥ If you have **a stroke of luck**, then you are lucky and something good happens to you.

stroll, strolls, strolling, strolled VERB ① To stroll along means to walk slowly in a relaxed way. ▶ NOUN ② a slow, pleasurable walk.
SIMILAR WORDS: ② amble, saunter, walk

stroller, strollers NOUN In Australian

and American English, a stroller is a pushchair.

strong, stronger, strongest
ADJECTIVE ① Someone who is strong has powerful muscles. ② You also say that someone is strong when they are confident and have courage. ③ Strong objects are able to withstand rough treatment. ④ Strong also means great in degree or intensity • *a strong wind*. ⑤ A strong argument or theory is supported by a lot of evidence. ⑥ If a group or organisation is strong, it has a lot of members or influence. ⑦ You can use 'strong' to say how many people there are in a group • *The audience was about two dozen strong*. ⑧ Your strong points are the things you are good at. ⑨ A strong economy or currency is stable and successful. ⑩ A strong liquid or drug contains a lot of a particular substance.
▶ ADVERB ⑪ If someone or something is still going strong, they are still healthy or working well after a long time. **strongly** ADVERB
SIMILAR WORDS: ① muscular, powerful ④ acute, intense

stronghold, strongholds NOUN ① a place that is held and defended by an army. ② A stronghold of an attitude or belief is a place in which the attitude or belief is strongly held • *a Conservative stronghold*.

strove the past tense of **strive**.

struck the past tense and past participle of **strike**.

structure, structures, structuring, structured NOUN ① DGT The structure of something is the way it is made, built or organised. ② something that has been built or constructed. ▶ VERB ③ DGT To structure something means to arrange it into an organised pattern or system. **structural** ADJECTIVE **structurally** ADVERB

SIMILAR WORDS: ① arrangement, construction, make-up

struggle, struggles, struggling, struggled VERB ① If you struggle to do something, you try hard to do it in difficult circumstances. ② When people struggle, they twist and move violently during a fight. ▶ NOUN ③ Something that is a struggle is difficult to achieve and takes a lot of effort. ④ a fight.

strum, strums, strumming, strummed VERB To strum a guitar means to play it by moving your fingers backwards and forwards across all the strings.

strung the past tense and past participle of **string**.

strut, struts, strutting, strutted VERB ① To strut means to walk in a stiff, proud way with your chest out and your head high. ▶ NOUN ② a piece of wood or metal which strengthens or supports part of a building or structure.

Stuart, Stuarts HISTORY NOUN Stuart was the family name of the monarchs who ruled Scotland from 1371 to 1714 and England from 1603 to 1714.

stub, stubs, stubbing, stubbed NOUN ① The stub of a pencil or cigarette is the short piece that remains when the rest has been used. ② The stub of a ticket is the small part that you keep. ▶ VERB ③ If you stub your toe, you hurt it by accidentally kicking something.
stub out VERB To stub out a cigarette means to put it out by pressing the end against something.

stubble NOUN ① The short stalks remaining in the ground after a crop is harvested are called stubble. ② If a man has stubble on his face, he has very short hair growing there because he has not shaved recently.

a b c d e f g h i j k l m n o p q r **s** t u v w x y z

stubborn ADJECTIVE ① Someone who is stubborn is determined not to change their opinion or course of action. ② A stubborn stain is difficult to remove. **stubbornly** ADVERB **stubbornness** NOUN
SIMILAR WORDS: ① inflexible, obstinate, pig-headed

stuck ① Stuck is the past tense and past participle of **stick**. ▶ ADJECTIVE ② If something is stuck in a particular position, it is fixed or jammed and cannot be moved • *His car's stuck in a snowdrift.* ③ If you are stuck, you are unable to continue what you were doing because it is too difficult. ④ If you are stuck somewhere, you are unable to get away.

stuck-up ADJECTIVE (*informal*) proud and conceited.

stud, studs NOUN ① a small piece of metal fixed into something. ② A male horse or other animal that is kept for stud is kept for breeding purposes.

studded ADJECTIVE decorated with small pieces of metal or precious stones.

student, students NOUN a person studying at university or college.

studied ADJECTIVE A studied action or response has been carefully planned and is not natural • *She sipped her glass of white wine with studied boredom.*

studio, studios NOUN ① a room where a photographer or painter works. ② a room containing special equipment where records, films or radio or television programmes are made.

studious [*Said* **styoo-dee-uss**] ADJECTIVE spending a lot of time studying.

studiously ADVERB carefully and deliberately • *She was studiously ignoring me.*

study, studies, studying, studied VERB ① If you study a particular subject, you spend time learning about it. ② If you study something, you look at it carefully • *He studied the map in silence.* ▶ NOUN ③ Study is the activity of studying a subject • *the serious study of medieval archaeology.* ④ Studies are subjects which are studied • *media studies.* ⑤ a piece of research on a particular subject • *a detailed study of the world's most remote places.* ⑥ a room used for writing and studying.

stuff, stuffs, stuffing, stuffed NOUN ① You can refer to a substance or group of things as stuff. ▶ VERB ② (*informal*) If you stuff something somewhere, you push it there quickly and roughly. ③ If you stuff something with a substance or objects, you fill it with the substance or objects.

stuffing NOUN Stuffing is a mixture of small pieces of food put inside poultry or a vegetable before it is cooked.

stuffy, stuffier, stuffiest ADJECTIVE ① very formal and old-fashioned. ② If it is stuffy in a room, there is not enough fresh air.
SIMILAR WORDS: ② airless, close, fusty

stumble, stumbles, stumbling, stumbled VERB ① If you stumble while you are walking or running, you trip and almost fall. ② If you stumble when speaking, you make mistakes when pronouncing the words. ③ If you stumble across something or stumble on it, you find it unexpectedly.

stump, stumps, stumping, stumped NOUN ① a small part of something that is left when the rest has been removed • *the stump of a dead tree.* ② In cricket, the stumps are the three upright wooden sticks that support the bails, forming the wicket. ▸**VERB** ③ (*informal*) If a question or problem stumps you, you cannot think of an answer or solution.

stun, stuns, stunning, stunned **VERB** ① If you are stunned by something, you are very shocked by it. ② To stun a person or animal means to knock them unconscious with a blow to the head.

stung the past tense and past participle of **sting**.

stunk the past participle of **stink**.

stunning ADJECTIVE very beautiful or impressive • *a stunning first novel*.

stunt, stunts, stunting, stunted **NOUN** ① an unusual or dangerous and exciting action that someone does to get publicity or as part of a film. ▸**VERB** ② To stunt the growth or development of something means to prevent it from developing as it should.

stupendous ADJECTIVE very large or impressive • *a stupendous amount of money*. **stupendously ADVERB**

stupid, stupider, stupidest **ADJECTIVE** showing lack of good judgment or intelligence and not at all sensible. **stupidly ADVERB** **SIMILAR WORDS:** foolish, obtuse, unintelligent

stupidity NOUN a lack of intelligence or good judgment.

sturdy, sturdier, sturdiest **ADJECTIVE** strong and firm and unlikely to be damaged or injured • *a sturdy chest of drawers*.

sturgeon [*Said* stur-jon] **NOUN** a large edible fish, the eggs of which are also eaten and are known as caviar.

stutter, stutters, stuttering, stuttered **NOUN** ① Someone who has a stutter finds it difficult to speak smoothly and often repeats sounds through being unable to complete a

word. ▸**VERB** ② When someone stutters, they hesitate or repeat sounds when speaking.

sty, sties **NOUN** a pigsty.

style, styles, styling, styled **NOUN** ① The style of something is the general way in which it is done or presented, often showing the attitudes of the people involved. ② A person or place that has style is smart, elegant and fashionable. ③ The style of something is its design • *new windows that fit in with the style of the house*. ④ SCIENCE In botany, the style is the slender part of a flower which comes out of the ovary and is tipped by the stigma. ▸**VERB** ⑤ To style a piece of clothing or a person's hair means to design and create its shape.
SIMILAR WORDS: ② elegance, flair, panache

stylised; also spelt **stylized** **ADJECTIVE** using a particular artistic or literary form as a basis rather than being natural or spontaneous • *a stylised picture of a Japanese garden*.

stylish ADJECTIVE smart, elegant and fashionable. **stylishly ADVERB** **SIMILAR WORDS:** chic, smart

suave [*Said* swahv] **ADJECTIVE** charming, polite and confident • *a suave Italian*.

sub- **PREFIX** ① 'Sub-' is used at the beginning of words that have 'under' as part of their meaning • *submarine*. ② 'Sub-' is also used to form nouns that refer to the parts into which something is divided • *Subsection 2 of section 49* • *a particular subgroup of citizens*.

subconscious NOUN ① Your subconscious is the part of your mind that can influence you without your being aware of it. ▸**ADJECTIVE** ② happening or existing in someone's subconscious and therefore not directly realised or understood by them • *a subconscious fear of rejection*.

subconsciously ADVERB

subcontinent, subcontinents NOUN a large mass of land, often consisting of several countries, and forming part of a continent • *the Indian subcontinent*.

subdue, subdues, subduing, subdued VERB ① To subdue a person or group of people is to bring them under control by using force. ② To subdue a colour, light or emotion means to make it less bright or strong.

SIMILAR WORDS: ① control, overcome, quell

subdued ADJECTIVE ① rather quiet and sad. ② not very noticeable or bright.

subject, subjects, subjecting, subjected NOUN ① The subject of writing or a conversation is the thing or person being discussed. ② MFL In grammar, the subject is the word or words representing the person or thing doing the action expressed by the verb. For example, in the sentence 'My cat keeps catching birds', 'my cat' is the subject. ③ an area of study. ④ The subjects of a king or queen are the people who are ruled by them. ▶ VERB ⑤ To subject someone to something means to make them experience it • *He was subjected to constant interruption*. ▶ ADJECTIVE ⑥ Someone or something that is subject to something is affected by it • *He was subject to attacks at various times*.

subjective ADJECTIVE influenced by personal feelings and opinion rather than based on fact or rational thought.

subjunctive NOUN ENGLISH In grammar, the subjunctive or

subjunctive mood is one of the forms a verb can take. It is used to express attitudes such as wishing and doubting.

sublime ADJECTIVE Something that is sublime is wonderful and affects people emotionally • *sublime music*.

submarine, submarines NOUN a ship that can travel beneath the surface of the sea.

submerge, submerges, submerging, submerged VERB ① To submerge means to go beneath the surface of a liquid. ② If you submerge yourself in an activity, you become totally involved in it.

submission, submissions NOUN ① Submission is a state in which someone accepts the control of another person • *Now he must beat us into submission*. ② The submission of a proposal or application is the act of sending it for consideration.

submissive ADJECTIVE behaving in a quiet, obedient way.

submit, submits, submitting, submitted VERB ① If you submit to something, you accept it because you are not powerful enough to resist it. ② If you submit an application or proposal, you send it to someone for consideration.

subordinate, subordinates, subordinating, subordinated NOUN [Said sub-**ord**-in-it] ① A person's subordinate is someone who is in a less important position than them. ▶ ADJECTIVE [Said sub-**ord**-in-it] ② If one thing is subordinate to another, it is less important • *The House of Lords would always remain subordinate to the Commons*. ▶ VERB [Said sub-**ord**-in-ate] ③ To subordinate one thing to another means to treat it as being less important.

subordinate clause, subordinate clauses NOUN ENGLISH In grammar, a subordinate clause is a clause which adds details to the main clause of a sentence.

subscribe, subscribes, subscribing, subscribed VERB ① If you subscribe to a particular belief or opinion, you support it or agree with it. ② If you subscribe to a magazine, you pay to receive regular copies. **subscriber** NOUN

subscription, subscriptions NOUN a sum of money that you pay regularly to belong to an organisation or to receive regular copies of a magazine.

subsequent ADJECTIVE happening or coming into existence at a later time than something else • *the December uprising and the subsequent political violence.* **subsequently** ADVERB

subservient ADJECTIVE Someone who is subservient does whatever other people want them to do.

subset, subsets NOUN [MATHS] A subset of a larger set or group is a smaller set or group contained within it.

subside, subsides, subsiding, subsided VERB ① To subside means to become less intense or quieter • *Her excitement suddenly subsided.* ② If water or the ground subsides, it sinks to a lower level.

subsidence [Said sub-*side-ins*] NOUN If a place is suffering from subsidence, parts of the ground have sunk to a lower level.

subsidiary, subsidiaries [Said sub-*sid-yer-ee*] NOUN ① a company which is part of a larger company. ▶ ADJECTIVE ② treated as being of less importance and additional to another thing • *Drama is offered as a subsidiary subject.*

subsidise, subsidises, subsidising, subsidised; also spelt **subsidize** VERB To subsidise something means

to provide part of the cost of it • *He feels the government should do much more to subsidise films.* **subsidised** ADJECTIVE

subsidy, subsidies NOUN a sum of money paid to help support a company or provide a public service.

substance, substances NOUN ① Anything which is a solid, a powder, a liquid or a paste can be referred to as a substance. ② If a speech or piece of writing has substance, it is meaningful or important • *a good speech, but there was no substance.* SIMILAR WORDS: ① material, stuff

substantial ADJECTIVE ① very large in degree or amount • *a substantial pay rise.* ② large and strongly built • *a substantial stone building.*

substantially ADVERB Something that is substantially true is generally or mostly true.

substitute, substitutes, substituting, substituted VERB ① To substitute one thing for another means to use it instead of the other thing or to put it in the other thing's place. ② [MATHS] to replace one mathematical element with another. ▶ NOUN ③ If one thing is a substitute for another, it is used instead of it or put in its place. **substitution** NOUN SIMILAR WORDS: ① exchange, replace ③ alternative, replacement, surrogate

subtend, subtends, subtending, subtended VERB [MATHS] to be opposite to and mark the limit of an angle or the side of a geometric shape. For example, a right angle is subtended by a hypotenuse.

subterfuge, subterfuges [Said sub-*ter-fyooj*] NOUN Subterfuge is the use of deceitful or dishonest methods.

a
b
c
d
e
f
g
h
i
j
k
l
m
n
o
p
q
r
s
t
u
v
w
x
y
z

subtitle, subtitles NOUN A film with subtitles has a printed translation of the dialogue at the bottom of the screen.

subtle, subtler, subtlest [Said **sut-tl**] ADJECTIVE ① very fine, delicate or small in degree • *a subtle change*. ② using indirect methods to achieve something. **subtly** ADVERB **subtlety** NOUN

subtract, subtracts, subtracting, subtracted VERB If you subtract you remove one number from another.

subtraction, subtractions NOUN ⟨MATHS⟩ Subtraction is the process of subtracting one number from another.

suburb, suburbs NOUN an area of a town or city that is away from its centre.

suburban ADJECTIVE ① relating to a suburb or suburbs. ② dull and conventional.

suburbia NOUN You can refer to the suburbs of a city as suburbia.

subversive, subversives ADJECTIVE ① intended to destroy or weaken a political system • *subversive activities*. ▶ NOUN ② Subversives are people who try to destroy or weaken a political system. **subversion** NOUN

subvert, subverts, subverting, subverted VERB (*formal*) To subvert something means to cause it to weaken or fail • *a cunning campaign to subvert the music industry*.

subway, subways NOUN ① a footpath that goes underneath a road. ② an underground railway.

succeed, succeeds, succeeding, succeeded VERB ① To succeed means to achieve the result you intend. ② To succeed someone means to be the next person to have their job. ③ If one thing succeeds another, it comes after it in time

• *The explosion was succeeded by a crash.* **succeeding** ADJECTIVE SIMILAR WORDS: ① be successful, do well, make it

success, successes NOUN ① Success is the achievement of something you have been trying to do. ② Someone who is a success has achieved an important position or made a lot of money.

successful ADJECTIVE having achieved what you intended to do. **successfully** ADVERB

succession, successions NOUN ① A succession of things is a number of them occurring one after the other. ② When someone becomes the next person to have an important position, you can refer to this event as their succession to this position • *his succession to the throne*. ▶ PHRASE ③ If something happens a number of weeks, months or years **in succession**, it happens that number of times without a break • *Borg won Wimbledon five years in succession.*

successive ADJECTIVE occurring one after the other without a break • *three successive victories*.

successor, successors NOUN Someone's successor is the person who takes their job when they leave.

succinct [Said **suk-singkt**] ADJECTIVE expressing something clearly and in very few words. **succinctly** ADVERB

succulent ADJECTIVE Succulent food is juicy and delicious.

succumb, succumbs, succumbing, succumbed VERB If you succumb to something, you are unable to resist it any longer • *She never succumbed to temptation.*

such ADJECTIVE or PRONOUN ① You use 'such' to refer to the person or thing you have just mentioned, or to someone or something similar

• *Naples or Palermo or some such place.*
▶ **PHRASE** ②You can use **such as** to introduce an example of something • *herbal teas such as camomile.* ③You can use **such as it is** to indicate that something is not great in quality or quantity • *The action, such as it is, is set in Egypt.* ④You can use **such and such** when you want to refer to something that is not specific • *A good trick is to ask whether they have seen such and such a film.* ▶ **ADJECTIVE** ⑤'Such' can be used for emphasising • *I have such a terrible sense of guilt.*

suchlike **ADJECTIVE** or **PRONOUN** used to refer to things similar to those already mentioned • *shampoos, talcs, toothbrushes and suchlike.*

suck, sucks, sucking, sucked **VERB**
①If you suck something, you hold it in your mouth and pull at it with your cheeks and tongue, usually to get liquid out of it. ②To suck something in a particular direction means to draw it there with a powerful force.
suck up **VERB** (*informal*) To suck up to someone means to do things to please them in order to obtain praise or approval.

sucker, suckers **NOUN** ①(*informal*) If you call someone a sucker, you mean that they are easily fooled or cheated. ②Suckers are pads on the bodies of some animals and insects which they use to cling to a surface. ③A sucker is also a cup-shaped piece of plastic or rubber on an object that sticks to a surface when pressed flat.

suckle, suckles, suckling, suckled **VERB** When a mother suckles a baby, she feeds it with milk from her breast.

sucrose [*Said* soo-kroze] **NOUN**
SCIENCE Sucrose is sugar in crystalline form found in sugar cane and sugar beet.

suction **NOUN** ①Suction is the force involved when a substance is drawn or sucked from one place to another. ②Suction is the process by which two surfaces stick together when the air between them is removed • *They stay there by suction.*

Sudanese [*Said* soo-dan-**neez**]
ADJECTIVE ①belonging or relating to the Sudan. ▶ **NOUN** ②someone who comes from the Sudan.

sudden **ADJECTIVE** happening quickly and unexpectedly • *a sudden cry.*
suddenly **ADVERB** **suddenness** **NOUN**

sudoku [*Said* soo-**doh**-koo] **NOUN** a puzzle in which you have to enter numbers in a square made up of nine three-by-three grids, so that every column, row and grid contains the numbers one to nine.
WORD HISTORY: Japanese for 'numbers singly'

sue, sues, suing, sued **VERB** To sue someone means to start a legal case against them, usually to claim money from them.

suede [*Said* swayd] **NOUN** Suede is a thin, soft leather with a rough surface.
WORD HISTORY: from French *gants de Suède* meaning 'gloves from Sweden'

suffer, suffers, suffering, suffered **VERB** ①If someone is suffering pain, or suffering as a result of an unpleasant situation, they are badly affected by it. ②If something suffers as a result of neglect or a difficult situation, its condition or quality becomes worse • *The bus service is suffering.* **sufferer** **NOUN** **suffering** **NOUN**

suffice, suffices, sufficing, sufficed **VERB** (*formal*) If something suffices, it is enough or adequate for a purpose.

A
B
C
D
E
F
G
H

What is a Suffix?

A suffix is a letter or group of letters that is added to the end of a word to make a new word with a different meaning.

When you add a suffix to another word, you drop the hyphen.

Here are some common examples of suffixes and their meanings:
-able (capable of doing or being), *-er* (a person who does an activity), *-ful* (full of), *-ism* (a system of beliefs),

-less (without), *-like* (similar to), *-ly* (in a particular way) and *-ment* (a particular state or feeling).

say + -able = sayable
golf + -er = golfer
pain + -ful = painful
Sikh + -ism = Sikhism
friend + -less = friendless
dog + -like = doglike
silent + -ly = silently
disappoint + -ment = disappointment

I
J
K
L
M
N
O
P
Q
R
S
T
U
V
W
X
Y
Z

sufficient ADJECTIVE If a supply or quantity is sufficient for a purpose, there is enough of it available.
sufficiently ADVERB

suffix, suffixes NOUN ENGLISH a group of letters which is added to the end of a word to form a new word, for example '-ology' or '-itis'.

suffocate, suffocates, suffocating, suffocated VERB To suffocate means to die as a result of having too little air or oxygen to breathe.
suffocation NOUN

suffrage NOUN Suffrage is the right to vote in political elections.

suffragette, suffragettes NOUN a woman who, at the beginning of the 20th century, campaigned for women to be given the right to vote.

suffused ADJECTIVE (*literary*) If something is suffused with light or colour, light or colour has gradually spread over it.

sugar NOUN Sugar is a sweet substance used to sweeten food or drinks. Sugar is obtained from sugar cane or sugar beet.
WORD HISTORY: from Arabic *sukkar*

sugar beet, sugar beets NOUN a plant with white roots from which sugar is obtained.

sugar cane, sugar canes NOUN a tropical plant with thick stems from which sugar is obtained.

suggest, suggests, suggesting, suggested VERB ① If you suggest a plan or idea to someone, you mention it as a possibility for them to consider. ② If something suggests a particular thought or impression, it makes you think in that way or gives you that impression • *Nothing you say suggests he is worried*.
SIMILAR WORDS: ① advocate, propose, recommend ② hint, imply

suggestion, suggestions NOUN ① a plan or idea that is mentioned as a possibility for someone to consider. ② A suggestion of something is a very slight indication or faint sign of it • *a suggestion of dishonesty*.
SIMILAR WORDS: ① proposal, recommendation

suggestive ADJECTIVE Something that is suggestive of a particular thing gives a slight hint or sign of it.
suggestively ADVERB

suicidal ADJECTIVE ① People who are suicidal want to kill themselves. ② Suicidal behaviour is so dangerous that it is likely to result in death • *a suicidal leap*. **suicidally** ADVERB

suicide NOUN People who die by suicide deliberately kill themselves.
WORD HISTORY: from Latin *sui* meaning 'of oneself' and *caedere* meaning 'to kill'

suicide bomber, suicide bombers NOUN a terrorist who carries out a bomb attack, knowing that he or she will be killed in the explosion.
suicide bombing NOUN

suit, suits, suiting, suited NOUN ① a matching jacket and trousers or skirt. ② In a court of law, a suit is a legal action taken by one person against another. ③ one of four different types of card in a pack of playing cards. The four suits are hearts, clubs, diamonds and spades. ▶ VERB ④ If a situation or course of action suits you, it is appropriate or acceptable for your purpose. ⑤ If a piece of clothing or a colour suits you, you look good when you are wearing it. ⑥ If you do something to suit yourself, you do it because you want to and without considering other people.

suitable ADJECTIVE right or acceptable for a particular purpose or occasion. **suitability** NOUN **suitably** ADVERB
SIMILAR WORDS: appropriate, apt, fitting

suitcase, suitcases NOUN a case in which you carry your clothes when you are travelling.

suite, suites [*Said* sweet] NOUN ① In a hotel, a suite is a set of rooms. ② a set of matching furniture or bathroom fittings.

suited ADJECTIVE right or appropriate for a particular purpose or person • *He is well suited to be minister for the arts.*

suitor, suitors NOUN (old-fashioned) A person's suitor is someone who wants to marry them.

sulk, sulks, sulking, sulked VERB Someone who is sulking is showing their annoyance by being silent and moody.

sulky, sulkier, sulkiest ADJECTIVE showing annoyance by being silent and moody.

sullen ADJECTIVE behaving in a bad-tempered and disagreeably silent way. **sullenly** ADVERB

sully, sullies, sullying, sullied VERB To sully something means to spoil it or make it dirty.

sulphate, sulphates NOUN [SCIENCE] A sulphate is a salt or compound containing sulphuric acid.

sulphur NOUN [SCIENCE] Sulphur is a pale yellow nonmetallic element which burns with a very unpleasant smell. Its atomic number is 16 and its symbol is S.

sultan, sultans NOUN In some Muslim countries, the ruler of the country is called the sultan.

sultana, sultanas NOUN ① a dried grape. ② the wife of a sultan.

sum, sums, summing, summed NOUN ① an amount of money. ② In arithmetic, a sum is a calculation. ③ The sum of something is the total amount of it. **sum up** VERB If you sum something up, you briefly describe its main points.

summarise, summarises, summarising, summarised; also spelt **summarize** VERB [EXAM TERM] To summarise something means to give a short account of its main points.

summary, summaries NOUN ① A summary of something is a short account of its main points. ▶ ADJECTIVE ② A summary action is done without delay or careful thought • *Summary punishments are common.* **summarily** ADVERB

a
b
c
d
e
f
g
h
i
j
k
l
m
n
o
p
q
r
s
t
u
v
w
x
y
z

SIMILAR WORDS: ① précis, résumé, synopsis

summer, summers NOUN
Summer is the season between spring and autumn.

summit, summits NOUN ① The summit of a mountain is its top. ② a meeting between leaders of different countries to discuss particular issues.

summon, summons, summoning, summoned VERB ① If someone summons you, they order you to go to them. ② If you summon up strength or energy, you make a great effort to be strong or energetic.

summons, summonses NOUN ① an official order to appear in court. ② an order to go to someone • *The result was a summons to headquarters.*

sumptuous ADJECTIVE Something that is sumptuous is magnificent and obviously very expensive.

sum total NOUN The sum total of a number of things is all of them added or considered together.

sun, suns, sunning, sunned NOUN ① The sun is the star providing heat and light for the planets revolving around it in our solar system. ② You refer to heat and light from the sun as sun • *We need a bit of sun.* ▶ VERB ③ If you sun yourself, you sit in the sunshine.

sunbathe, sunbathes, sunbathing, sunbathed VERB If you sunbathe, you sit in the sunshine to get a suntan.

sunburn NOUN Sunburn is sore red skin on someone's body due to too much exposure to the rays of the sun. **sunburnt** ADJECTIVE

sundae, sundaes [Said *sun-day*] NOUN a dish of ice cream with cream and fruit or nuts.

Sunday, Sundays NOUN Sunday is the day between Saturday and Monday.
WORD HISTORY: from Old English *sunnandæg* meaning 'day of the sun'

Sunday school, Sunday schools NOUN Sunday school is a special class held on Sundays to teach children about Christianity.

sundial, sundials NOUN an object used for telling the time, consisting of a pointer which casts a shadow on a flat base marked with the hours.

sundown NOUN In American English, sundown is sunset.

sundry ADJECTIVE ① 'Sundry' is used to refer to several things or people of various sorts • *sundry journalists and lawyers.* ▶ PHRASE ② All and sundry means everyone.

sunflower, sunflowers NOUN a tall plant with very large yellow flowers.

sung the past participle of **sing**.

sunglasses PLURAL NOUN Sunglasses are spectacles with dark lenses that you wear to protect your eyes from the sun.

sunk the past participle of **sink**.

sunken ADJECTIVE ① having sunk to the bottom of the sea, a river, or a lake • *sunken ships.* ② A sunken object or area has been constructed below the level of the surrounding area • *a sunken garden.* ③ curving inwards • *Her cheeks were sunken.*

sunlight NOUN Sunlight is the bright light produced when the sun is shining. **sunlit** ADJECTIVE

Sunni, Sunnis NOUN RE a member of the main branch of the Islamic religion.

sunny, sunnier, sunniest ADJECTIVE When it is sunny, the sun is shining.

sunrise, sunrises NOUN Sunrise is the time in the morning when the sun first appears, and the colours produced in the sky at that time.

sunset, sunsets NOUN Sunset is the time in the evening when the sun disappears below the horizon, and the colours produced in the sky at that time.

sunshine NOUN Sunshine is the bright light produced when the sun is shining.

sunspot, sunspots NOUN SCIENCE Sunspots are dark cool patches that appear on the surface of the sun. Sunspots have a strong magnetic field.

sunstroke NOUN Sunstroke is an illness caused by spending too much time in hot sunshine.

suntan, suntans NOUN If you have a suntan, the sun has turned your skin brown. **suntanned** ADJECTIVE

super ADJECTIVE very nice or very good • *a super party*.

super- PREFIX 'Super-' is used to describe something that is larger or better than similar things • *a European superstate*.

superb ADJECTIVE very good indeed. **superbly** ADVERB

supercilious [Said soo-per-**sill**-ee-uss] ADJECTIVE If you are supercilious, you behave in a scornful way towards other people because you think they are inferior to you.

superego NOUN (technical) Your superego is the part of your mind that controls your ideas of right and wrong and produces feelings of guilt.

superficial ADJECTIVE ① involving only the most obvious or most general aspects of something • *a superficial knowledge of music*. ② not having a deep, serious or genuine interest in anything • *a superficial and rather silly character*. ③ Superficial wounds are not very deep or severe. **superficially** ADVERB

superfluous [Said soo-per-**floo**-uss] ADJECTIVE (formal) unnecessary or no longer needed.

superhuman ADJECTIVE having much greater power or ability than is normally expected of humans • *superhuman strength*.

superimpose, superimposes, superimposing, superimposed VERB To superimpose one image on another means to put the first image on top of the other so that they are seen as one image.

superintendent, superintendents NOUN ① a police officer above the rank of inspector. ② a person whose job is to be responsible for a particular thing • *the superintendent of prisons*.

superior, superiors ADJECTIVE ① better or of higher quality than other similar things. ② in a position of higher authority than another person. ③ showing too much pride and self-importance • *Jerry smiled in a superior way.* ▶ NOUN ④ Your superiors are people who are in a higher position than you in society or an organisation. **superiority** NOUN

superlative, superlatives [Said soo-per-**lat**-tiv] NOUN ① ENGLISH In grammar, the superlative is the form of an adjective which indicates that the person or thing described has more of a particular quality than anyone or anything else. For example, 'quickest', 'best' and 'easiest' are all superlatives. ▶ ADJECTIVE ② (formal) very good indeed • *a superlative performance*.

▶ SEE GRAMMAR BOX ON NEXT PAGE

a
b
c
d
e
f
g
h
i
j
k
l
m
n
o
p
q
r
s
t
u
v
w
x
y
z

A
B
C
D
E
F
G
H
I
J
K
L
M
N
O
P
Q
R
S
T
U
V
W
X
Y
Z

What is a Superlative?

Many adjectives have three different forms. These are known as the **positive**, the **comparative** and the **superlative**. The comparative and superlative are used when you make comparisons.

The **positive** form of an adjective is given as the entry in the dictionary. It is used when there is no comparison between different objects:

Matthew is tall.

The **superlative** form is usually made by adding the ending *-est* to the positive form of the adjective. It shows that something possesses a quality to a greater extent than all the others in its class or group:

Matthew is the tallest boy in his class.

You can also express superlatives by using the words *most* or *least* with the positive (not the superlative) form of the adjective:

Matthew is the most energetic member of the family.

Also look at the grammar box at **comparative**

supermarket, supermarkets NOUN a shop selling food and household goods arranged so that you can help yourself and pay for everything at a till by the exit.

supernatural ADJECTIVE
① Something that is supernatural, for example ghosts or witchcraft, cannot be explained by normal scientific laws. ▶ NOUN ② You can refer to supernatural things as the supernatural.

supernova, supernovae or **supernovas** NOUN SCIENCE A supernova is a star that explodes and for a few days becomes very much brighter than the sun.

superpower, superpowers NOUN a very powerful and influential country such as the USA.

supersede, supersedes, superseding, superseded [*Said soo-per-seed*] VERB If something supersedes another thing, it replaces it because it is more modern • *New York superseded Paris as the centre for modern art.*

supersonic ADJECTIVE A supersonic aircraft can travel faster than the speed of sound.

superstar, superstars NOUN You can refer to a very famous entertainer or sports player as a superstar.

superstition, superstitions NOUN Superstition is a belief in things like magic and powers that bring good or bad luck. **superstitious** ADJECTIVE
WORD HISTORY: from Latin *superstitio* meaning 'dread of the supernatural'

supervise, supervises, supervising, supervised VERB To supervise someone means to check and direct what they are doing to make sure that they do it correctly. **supervision** NOUN **supervisor** NOUN
SIMILAR WORDS: oversee, superintend

supper, suppers NOUN Supper is a meal eaten in the evening or a snack eaten before you go to bed.

supplant, supplants, supplanting, supplanted VERB (*formal*) To supplant someone or something means to take their place • *By the 1930s the wristwatch had supplanted the pocket watch.*

supple ADJECTIVE able to bend and move easily.

supplement, supplements, supplementing, supplemented **VERB** ① To supplement something means to add something to it to improve it • *Many village men supplemented their wages by fishing for salmon.* ▶ **NOUN** ② something that is added to something else to improve it. ③ a separate part of a newspaper or magazine, often dealing with a particular subject.

supplementary **ADJECTIVE** added to something else to improve it • *supplementary doses of vitamin E.*

supplementary angle, supplementary angles **NOUN** MATHS A supplementary angle is either of two angles that together make up 180°.

supplier, suppliers **NOUN** a firm which provides particular goods.

supply, supplies, supplying, supplied **VERB** ① To supply someone with something means to provide it or send it to them. ▶ **NOUN** ② A supply of something is an amount available for use • *the world's supply of precious metals.* ③ (*in plural*) Supplies are food and equipment for a particular purpose.

support, supports, supporting, supported **VERB** ① If you support someone, you agree with their aims and want them to succeed. ② If you support someone who is in difficulties, you are kind, encouraging and helpful to them. ③ If something supports an object, it is underneath it and holding it up. ④ To support someone or something means to prevent them from falling by holding them. ⑤ To support someone financially means to provide them with money. ▶ **NOUN** ⑥ an object that is holding something up. ⑦ PSHE Moral support is encouragement given to

someone to help them do something difficult. ⑧ Financial support is money that is provided for someone or something. **supportable** **ADJECTIVE**

supporter, supporters **NOUN** a person who agrees with or helps someone.

supportive **ADJECTIVE** A supportive person is encouraging and helpful to someone who is in difficulties.

suppose, supposes, supposing, supposed **VERB** ① If you suppose that something is the case, you think that it is likely • *I supposed that would be too obvious.* ▶ **PHRASE** ② You can say **I suppose** when you are not entirely certain or enthusiastic about something • *Yes, I suppose he could come.* ▶ **CONJUNCTION** ③ You can use 'suppose' or 'supposing' when you are considering or suggesting a possible situation or action • *Supposing he were to break down under interrogation?*

supposed **ADJECTIVE** ① 'Supposed' is used to express doubt about something that is generally believed • *the supposed culprit.* ② If something is supposed to be done or to happen, it is planned, expected or required to be done or to happen • *You are supposed to report it to the police* • *It was supposed to be this afternoon.* ③ Something that is supposed to be the case is generally believed or thought to be so • *Wimbledon is supposed to be the best tournament of them all.* **supposedly** **ADVERB**

supposition, suppositions **NOUN** something that is believed or assumed to be true • *the supposition that science requires an ordered universe.*

suppress, suppresses, suppressing, suppressed **VERB** ① If an army or government suppresses an activity, it prevents people from doing it. ② If someone suppresses a piece of

information, they prevent it from becoming generally known. ③ If you suppress your feelings, you stop yourself expressing them.
suppression NOUN
SIMILAR WORDS: ① crush, quell, stop

supremacy [*Said soo-prem-mass-ee*] NOUN If a group of people has supremacy over others, it is more powerful than the others.

supreme ADJECTIVE ① 'Supreme' is used as part of a title to indicate the highest level of an organisation or system • *the Supreme Court*. ② 'Supreme' is used to emphasise the greatness of something • *the supreme achievement of the human race*.
supremely ADVERB
SIMILAR WORDS: ② greatest, highest, paramount

surcharge, surcharges NOUN an additional charge.

sure, surer, surest ADJECTIVE ① If you are sure about something, you have no doubts about it. ② If you are sure of yourself, you are very confident. ③ If something is sure to happen, it will definitely happen. ④ Sure means reliable or accurate • *a sure sign that something is wrong*. ▸ PHRASE ⑤ If you **make sure** about something, you check it or take action to see that it is done. ▸ INTERJECTION ⑥ Sure is an informal way of saying 'yes' • *'Can I come too?' – 'Sure'*.

surely ADVERB 'Surely' is used to emphasise the belief that something is the case • *Surely these people here knew that?*

surf, surfs, surfing, surfed VERB ① When you surf, you take part in the sport of surfing. ② When you surf the internet, you go from website to website reading the information. ▸ NOUN ③ Surf is the white foam that forms on the top of waves when they break near the shore.

surface, surfaces, surfacing, surfaced NOUN ① The surface of something is the top or outside area of it. ② The surface of a situation is what can be seen easily rather than what is hidden or not immediately obvious. ▸ VERB ③ If someone surfaces, they come up from under water to the surface.

surfboard, surfboards NOUN a long narrow lightweight board used for surfing.

surf club, surf clubs NOUN In Australia, a surf club is an organisation of lifesavers in charge of safety on a particular beach, and which often provides leisure facilities.

surfeit [*Said sur-fit*] NOUN If there is a surfeit of something, there is too much of it.

surfing NOUN Surfing is a sport which involves riding towards the shore on the top of a large wave while standing on a surfboard.

surge, surges, surging, surged NOUN ① a sudden great increase in the amount of something • *a surge of panic*. ▸ VERB ② If something surges, it moves suddenly and powerfully • *The soldiers surged forwards*.

surgeon, surgeons NOUN a doctor who performs operations.

surgery, surgeries NOUN ① Surgery is medical treatment involving cutting open part of the patient's body to treat the damaged part. ② The room or building where a doctor or dentist works is called a surgery. ③ A period of time during which a doctor is available to see patients is called surgery • *evening surgery*.

surgical ADJECTIVE used in or involving a medical operation • *surgical gloves*. **surgically** ADVERB

surly, surlier, surliest ADJECTIVE rude and bad-tempered. **surliness** NOUN

surmise, surmises, surmising, surmised VERB (*formal*) To surmise something means to guess it • *I surmised it was of French manufacture.*

surmount, surmounts, surmounting, surmounted VERB ①To surmount a difficulty means to manage to solve it. ②(*formal*) If something is surmounted by a particular thing, that thing is on top of it • *The island is surmounted by a huge black castle.*

surname, surnames NOUN Your surname is your last name, which you share with other members of your family.

surpass, surpasses, surpassing, surpassed VERB (*formal*) To surpass someone or something means to be better than them.

surplus, surpluses NOUN If there is a surplus of something there is more of it than is needed.
SIMILAR WORDS: excess, surfeit

surprise, surprises, surprising, surprised NOUN ①an unexpected event. ②Surprise is the feeling caused when something unexpected happens. ▸ VERB ③If something surprises you, it gives you a feeling of surprise. ④If you surprise someone, you do something they were not expecting. **surprising** ADJECTIVE

surreal ADJECTIVE very strange and dreamlike.

surrealism NOUN ART Surrealism began in the 1920s. It involves the putting together of strange images and things that are not normally seen together.

surrender, surrenders, surrendering, surrendered VERB ①To surrender means to stop fighting and agree that the other side has won. ②If you surrender to a temptation or feeling, you let it take control of you. ③To surrender something means to give it up to someone else • *The gallery director surrendered his keys.* ▸ NOUN ④Surrender is a situation in which one side in a fight agrees that the other side has won and gives in.
SIMILAR WORDS: ① give in, submit, yield ④ capitulation, submission

surreptitious [*Said sur-rep-**tish**-uss*] ADJECTIVE A surreptitious action is done secretly or so that no-one will notice • *a surreptitious glance.* **surreptitiously** ADVERB

surrogate, surrogates ADJECTIVE ① acting as a substitute for someone or something. ▸ NOUN ②a person or thing that acts as a substitute.

surrogate mother, surrogate mothers NOUN a woman who agrees to conceive and give birth to a baby for people who are not able to have children of their own.

surround, surrounds, surrounding, surrounded VERB ①To surround someone or something means to be situated all around them. ▸ NOUN ②The surround of something is its outside edge or border.
SIMILAR WORDS: ① encircle, enclose

surrounding ADJECTIVE The surrounding area of a particular place is the area around it • *the surrounding countryside.*

surroundings PLURAL NOUN You can refer to the area and environment around a place or person as their surroundings • *very comfortable surroundings.*

surveillance [*Said sur-**vay**-lanss*] NOUN Surveillance is the close watching of a person's activities by the police or army.
WORD HISTORY: from French *surveiller* meaning 'to watch over'

a b c d e f g h i j k l m n o p q r s t u v w x y z

survey, surveys, surveying, surveyed VERB [Said *sur-vay*] ① To survey something means to look carefully at the whole of it. ② To survey a building or piece of land means to examine it carefully in order to make a report or plan of its structure and features. ▸ NOUN [Said *sir-vay*] ③ A survey of something is a detailed examination of it, often in the form of a report.
SIMILAR WORDS: ① look over, scan, view

surveyor, surveyors NOUN a person whose job is to survey buildings or land.

survival, survivals NOUN Survival is being able to continue living or existing in spite of great danger or difficulties • *There was no hope of survival.*

survive, survives, surviving, survived VERB To survive means to continue to live or exist in spite of great danger or difficulties • *a German monk who survived the shipwreck.*
survivor NOUN

susceptible ADJECTIVE If you are susceptible to something, you are likely to be influenced or affected by it • *Elderly people are more susceptible to infection.* **susceptibility** NOUN

sushi NOUN Sushi is a Japanese dish of rice with sweet vinegar, often served with raw fish.

suspect, suspects, suspecting, suspected VERB [Said *sus-pekt*] ① If you suspect something, you think that it is likely or is probably true • *I suspected that the report would be sent.* ② If you suspect something, you have doubts about its reliability or genuineness • *Given his previous behaviour, I suspected his remorse.* ③ If you suspect someone of doing something wrong, you think that they have done it. ▸ NOUN [Said

sus-pekt] ④ someone who is thought to be guilty of a crime. ▸ ADJECTIVE [Said **sus**-pekt] ⑤ If something is suspect, it cannot be trusted or relied upon • *a rather suspect holy man.*

suspend, suspends, suspending, suspended VERB ① If something is suspended, it is hanging from somewhere • *the television set suspended above the bar.* ② To suspend an activity or event means to delay it or stop it for a while. ③ If someone is suspended from their job, they are told not to do it for a period of time, usually as a punishment.

suspender, suspenders NOUN Suspenders are fastenings which hold up stockings.

suspense NOUN Suspense is a state of excitement or anxiety caused by having to wait for something.

suspension NOUN ① The suspension of something is the delaying or stopping of it. ② A person's suspension is their removal from a job for a period of time, usually as a punishment. ③ The suspension of a vehicle consists of springs and shock absorbers which provide a smooth ride. ④ a liquid mixture in which very small bits of a solid material are contained and are not dissolved.

suspicion, suspicions NOUN ① Suspicion is the feeling of not trusting someone or the feeling that something is wrong. ② a feeling that something is likely to happen or is probably true • *the suspicion that more could have been achieved.*
SIMILAR WORDS: ① distrust, misgiving, scepticism

suspicious ADJECTIVE ① If you are suspicious of someone, you do not trust them. ② 'Suspicious' is used to describe things that make you think that there is something wrong with a situation • *suspicious circumstances.*

suspiciously ADVERB
SIMILAR WORDS: ② dubious, questionable, suspect

sustain, sustains, sustaining, sustained VERB ① To sustain something means to continue it for a period of time • *Their team-mates were unable to sustain the challenge.* ② If something sustains you, it gives you energy and strength. ③ (*formal*) To sustain an injury or loss means to suffer it.

sustainable ADJECTIVE ① capable of being sustained. ② If economic development or energy resources are sustainable they are capable of being maintained at a steady level without exhausting natural resources or causing ecological damage • *sustainable forestry*.

sustenance NOUN (*formal*) Sustenance is food and drink.

swab, swabs, swabbing, swabbed NOUN ① a small piece of cotton wool used for cleaning a wound. ▶ VERB ② To swab something means to clean it using a large mop and a lot of water. ③ To swab a wound means to clean it or take specimens from it using a swab.

swag, swags NOUN (*informal*) ① goods or valuables, especially ones which have been gained dishonestly. ② in Australian and New Zealand English, a swag is the bundle of possessions belonging to a tramp. ③ In Australian and New Zealand English, swags of something is lots of it.

swagger, swaggers, swaggering, swaggered VERB ① To swagger means to walk in a proud, exaggerated way. ▶ NOUN ② an exaggerated walk.

swagman, swagmen NOUN (*informal*) In Australia and New Zealand in the past, a swagman was a tramp who carried his possessions on his back.

swallow, swallows, swallowing, swallowed VERB ① If you swallow something, you make it go down your throat and into your stomach. ② When you swallow, you move your throat muscles as if you were swallowing something, especially when you are nervous. ▶ NOUN ③ a bird with pointed wings and a long forked tail.

swam the past tense of **swim**.

swamp, swamps, swamping, swamped NOUN ① an area of permanently wet land. ▶ VERB ② If something is swamped, it is covered or filled with water. ③ If you are swamped by things, you have more than you are able to deal with • *She was swamped with calls.* **swampy** ADJECTIVE

swan, swans NOUN a large, usually white, bird with a long neck that lives on rivers or lakes.

swap, swaps, swapping, swapped [Rhymes with *stop*] VERB To swap one thing for another means to replace the first thing with the second, often by making an exchange with another person • *Webb swapped shirts with a Leeds player.*
SIMILAR WORDS: exchange, switch, trade

swarm, swarms, swarming, swarmed NOUN ① A swarm of insects is a large group of them flying together. ▶ VERB ② When bees or other insects swarm, they fly together in a large group. ③ If people swarm somewhere, a lot of people go there quickly and at the same time • *the crowds of office workers who swarm across the bridge.* ④ If a place is swarming with people, there are a lot of people there.

a
b
c
d
e
f
g
h
i
j
k
l
m
n
o
p
q
r
s
t
u
v
w
x
y
z

swarthy, swarthier, swarthiest
ADJECTIVE A swarthy person has a dark complexion.

swashbuckling ADJECTIVE 'Swashbuckling' is used to describe people who have the exciting behaviour or appearance of pirates.
WORD HISTORY: from Middle English *swashbuckling* meaning 'making a noise by striking your sword against a shield'

swastika, swastikas [Said *swoss-tik-ka*] NOUN a symbol in the shape of a cross with each arm bent over at right angles. It was the official symbol of the Nazis in Germany, but in India it is a good luck sign.
WORD HISTORY: from Sanskrit *svasti* meaning 'prosperity'

swat, swats, swatting, swatted VERB To swat an insect means to hit it sharply in order to kill it.

swathe, swathes [Rhymes with *bathe*] NOUN ① a long strip of cloth that is wrapped around something • *swathes of white silk*. ② A swathe of land is a long strip of it.

swathed ADJECTIVE If someone is swathed in something, they are wrapped in it • *She was swathed in towels.*

sway, sways, swaying, swayed VERB ① To sway means to lean or swing slowly from side to side. ② If something sways you, it influences your judgment. ▶ NOUN ③ (literary) Sway is the power to influence people • *under the sway of more powerful neighbours.*

swear, swears, swearing, swore, sworn VERB ① To swear means to say words that are considered to be very rude or blasphemous. ② If you swear to something, you state solemnly that you will do it or that it is true. ③ If you swear by something,

you firmly believe that it is a reliable cure or solution • *Some people swear by extra vitamins.* **swear in** VERB When someone is sworn in to a new position, they solemnly promise to fulfil the duties and are officially appointed.

swearword, swearwords NOUN a word which is considered to be rude or blasphemous, which people use when they are angry.

sweat, sweats, sweating, sweated NOUN ① Sweat is the salty liquid produced by your body when you are hot or afraid. ▶ VERB ② When you sweat, sweat comes through the pores in your skin in order to lower the temperature of your body.

sweater, sweaters NOUN a knitted piece of clothing covering your upper body and arms.

sweatshirt, sweatshirts NOUN a piece of clothing made of thick cotton, covering your upper body and arms.

sweaty, sweatier, sweatiest ADJECTIVE covered or soaked with sweat.

swede, swedes NOUN a large round root vegetable with yellow flesh and a brownish-purple skin.
WORD HISTORY: from *Swedish turnip* because it was introduced from Sweden in the 18th century

Swede, Swedes NOUN someone who comes from Sweden.

Swedish ADJECTIVE ① belonging or relating to Sweden. ▶ NOUN ② Swedish is the main language spoken in Sweden.

sweep, sweeps, sweeping, swept VERB ① If you sweep the floor, you use a brush to gather up dust or rubbish from it. ② To sweep things off a surface means to push them all off with a quick, smooth movement.

③ If something sweeps from one place to another, it moves there very quickly • *A gust of wind swept over the terrace.* ④ If an attitude or new fashion sweeps a place, it spreads rapidly through it • *a phenomenon that is sweeping America.* ▶ NOUN ⑤ If you do something with a sweep of your arm, you do it with a wide curving movement of your arm.

sweeping ADJECTIVE ① A sweeping curve or movement is long and wide. ② A sweeping statement is based on a general assumption rather than on careful thought. ③ affecting a lot of people to a great extent • *sweeping changes.*

sweet, sweeter, sweetest; sweets ADJECTIVE ① containing a lot of sugar • *a mug of sweet tea.* ② pleasant and satisfying • *sweet success.* ③ A sweet smell is soft and fragrant. ④ A sweet sound is gentle and tuneful. ⑤ attractive and pleasant • *a sweet little baby.* ▶ NOUN ⑥ Things such as toffees, chocolates and mints are sweets. ⑦ a dessert. **sweetly** ADVERB **sweetness** NOUN SIMILAR WORDS: ⑤ charming, cute, delightful

sweet corn NOUN Sweet corn is a long stalk covered with juicy yellow seeds that can be eaten as a vegetable.

sweeten, sweetens, sweetening, sweetened VERB To sweeten food means to add sugar or another sweet substance to it.

sweetener, sweeteners NOUN a very sweet, artificial substance that can be used instead of sugar.

sweetheart, sweethearts NOUN ① You can call someone who you are very fond of 'sweetheart'. ② (*old-fashioned*) A young person's sweetheart is their boyfriend or girlfriend.

sweet pea, sweet peas NOUN Sweet peas are delicate, very fragrant climbing flowers.

sweet tooth NOUN If you have a sweet tooth, you like sweet food very much.

swell, swells, swelling, swelled, swollen VERB ① If something swells, it becomes larger and rounder • *It causes the abdomen to swell.* ② If an amount swells, it increases in number. ▶ NOUN ③ The regular up and down movement of the waves at sea can be called a swell.

swelling, swellings NOUN ① an enlarged area on your body as a result of injury or illness. ② The swelling of something is an increase in its size.

sweltering ADJECTIVE If the weather is sweltering, it is very hot.

swept the past tense and past participle of **sweep**.

swerve, swerves, swerving, swerved VERB To swerve means to suddenly change direction to avoid colliding with something.

swift, swifter, swiftest; swifts ADJECTIVE ① happening or moving very quickly • *a swift glance.* ▶ NOUN ② a bird with narrow crescent-shaped wings. **swiftly** ADVERB **swiftness** NOUN

swig, swigs, swigging, swigged (*informal*) VERB ① To swig a drink means to drink it in large mouthfuls, usually from a bottle. ▶ NOUN ② If you have a swig of a drink, you take a large mouthful of it.

swill, swills, swilling, swilled VERB ① To swill something means to pour water over it to clean it • *Swill the can out thoroughly.* ▶ NOUN ② Swill is a liquid mixture containing waste food that is fed to pigs.

a
b
c
d
e
f
g
h
i
j
k
l
m
n
o
p
q
r
s
t
u
v
w
x
y
z

swim, swims, swimming, swam, swum VERB ①To swim means to move through water using various movements with parts of the body. ②If things are swimming, it seems as if everything you see is moving and you feel dizzy. ▶ NOUN ③If you go for a swim, you go into water to swim for pleasure. **swimmer** NOUN

swimming NOUN Swimming is the activity of moving through water using your arms and legs.

swimming bath, swimming baths NOUN a public swimming pool.

swimming costume, swimming costumes NOUN a piece of clothing worn for swimming, especially by women and girls.

swimming pool, swimming pools NOUN a large hole that has been tiled and filled with water for swimming.

swimming trunks PLURAL NOUN Swimming trunks are shorts worn by a man when he goes swimming.

swimsuit, swimsuits NOUN a swimming costume.

swindle, swindles, swindling, swindled VERB ①To swindle someone means to deceive them to obtain money or property. ▶ NOUN ②a trick in which someone is cheated out of money or property. **swindler** NOUN

swine, swine or swines NOUN ①(old-fashioned) A swine is another name for a pig. ②(informal) If you call someone a swine, you mean they are nasty and spiteful.

GRAMMAR TIP
The plural of the animal is *swine*. The plural of the spiteful person is *swines*.

swing, swings, swinging, swung VERB ①If something swings, it moves repeatedly from side to side from a fixed point. ②If someone or something swings in a particular direction, they turn quickly or move in a sweeping curve in that direction. ▶ NOUN ③a seat hanging from a frame or a branch, which you sit on and move backwards and forwards. ④A swing in opinion is a significant change in people's opinion.

swipe, swipes, swiping, swiped VERB ①To swipe at something means to try to hit it making a curving movement with the arm. ②(informal) To swipe something means to steal it. ③To swipe a credit card means to pass it through a machine that electronically reads the information stored in the card. ④To swipe a touchscreen on an electronic device is to move your finger across it in order to activate a function on the device. ▶ NOUN ⑤To take a swipe at something means to swipe at it.

swirl, swirls, swirling, swirled VERB To swirl means to move quickly in circles • *The black water swirled around his legs*.

swish, swishes, swishing, swished VERB ①To swish means to move quickly through the air making a soft sound • *The curtains swished back.* ▶ NOUN ②the sound made when something swishes.

Swiss, Swiss ADJECTIVE ①belonging or relating to Switzerland. ▶ NOUN ②someone who comes from Switzerland.

switch, switches, switching, switched NOUN ①a small control for an electrical device or machine. ②a change • *a switch in routine.* ▶ VERB ③To switch to a different task or topic means to change to it. ④If you switch things, you exchange one for the other. **switch off** VERB To switch off a light or machine means to stop it working by pressing a switch. **switch on** VERB To switch on a light or machine means to start it working by pressing a switch.

switchboard, switchboards NOUN The switchboard in an organisation is the part where all telephone calls are received.

swivel, swivels, swivelling, swivelled VERB ①To swivel means to turn round on a central point. ▸ ADJECTIVE ②A swivel chair or lamp is made so that you can move the main part of it while the base remains in a fixed position.

swollen a past participle of **swell**. SIMILAR WORDS: distended, enlarged, puffed up

swoon, swoons, swooning, swooned VERB (literary) To swoon means to faint as a result of strong emotion.

swoop, swoops, swooping, swooped VERB To swoop means to move downwards through the air in a fast curving movement • A flock of pigeons swooped low over the square.

swop another spelling of **swap**.

sword, swords [Said sord] NOUN a weapon consisting of a very long blade with a short handle.

swordfish, swordfishes or swordfish NOUN a large sea fish with an upper jaw which sticks out like a sword.

swore the past tense of **swear**.

sworn the past participle of **swear**.

swot, swots, swotting, swotted (informal) VERB ①To swot means to study or revise very hard. ②If you swot up on a subject you find out as much about it as possible in a short time. ▸ NOUN ③someone who spends too much time studying.

swum the past participle of **swim**.

swung the past tense and past participle of **swing**.

sycamore, sycamores [Said sik-am-mor] NOUN a tree that has large leaves with five points.

syllable, syllables NOUN ENGLISH a part of a word that contains a single vowel sound and is pronounced as a unit. For example, 'book' has one syllable and 'reading' has two.

syllabus, syllabuses or syllabi NOUN The subjects that are studied for a particular course or examination are called the syllabus.

GRAMMAR TIP
The plural *syllabuses* is much more common than *syllabi*.

symbiosis [Said sim-bee-oh-siss] NOUN SCIENCE Symbiosis is a relationship between two organisms which benefits both. **symbiotic** ADJECTIVE

symbol, symbols NOUN a shape, design or idea that is used to represent something • The fish has long been a symbol of Christianity. SIMILAR WORDS: emblem, representation, sign

SPELLING TIP
Do not confuse the spellings of *symbol* and *cymbal*: The dove is the symbol of peace; a sudden crash of cymbals.

symbolic ADJECTIVE Something that is symbolic has a special meaning that is considered to represent something else • Six tons of ivory were burned in a symbolic ceremony.

symbolise, symbolises, symbolising, symbolised; also spelt **symbolize** VERB If a shape, design or idea symbolises something, it is regarded as being a symbol of it • In China and Japan the carp symbolises courage. **symbolism** NOUN

symmetrical ADJECTIVE MATHS If

a b c d e f g h i j k l m n o p q r **s** t u v w x y z

something is symmetrical, it could be split into two halves, one being the exact reflection of the other.
symmetrically ADVERB

symmetry NOUN MATHS
Something that has symmetry is symmetrical.

sympathetic ADJECTIVE ①A sympathetic person shows kindness and understanding to other people. ②If you are sympathetic to a proposal or an idea, you approve of it.

sympathise, sympathises, sympathising, sympathised; also spelt **sympathize** VERB To sympathise with someone who is in difficulties means to show them understanding and care.

sympathiser, sympathisers; also spelt **sympathizer** NOUN People who support a particular cause can be referred to as sympathisers.

sympathy, sympathies NOUN ① Sympathy is kindness and understanding towards someone who is in difficulties. ② If you have sympathy with someone's ideas or actions, you agree with them. ▶ PHRASE ③ If you do something **in sympathy** with someone, you do it to show your support for them.
SIMILAR WORDS: ① compassion, pity

symphony, symphonies NOUN a piece of music for an orchestra, usually in four movements.
WORD HISTORY: from Greek *sumphōnos* meaning 'harmonious'

symptom, symptoms NOUN ① something wrong with your body that is a sign of an illness. ② Something that is considered to be a sign of a bad situation can be referred to as a symptom of it • *another symptom of the unrest sweeping across the country.*
symptomatic ADJECTIVE

synagogue, synagogues [Said *sin-a-gog*] NOUN RE a building where Jewish people meet for worship and religious instruction.
WORD HISTORY: from Greek *sunagōgē* meaning 'meeting'

synchronise, synchronises, synchronising, synchronised [Said *sing-kron-nize*]; also spelt **synchronize** VERB ① To synchronise two actions means to do them at the same time and speed. ② To synchronise watches means to set them to show exactly the same time as each other. **synchronisation** NOUN

syncopation NOUN MUSIC Syncopation in rhythm is the stressing of weak beats instead of the usual strong ones.
WORD HISTORY: from Greek *suncopē* meaning 'cutting off'

syndicate, syndicates NOUN an association of business people formed to carry out a particular project.

syndrome, syndromes NOUN ① a medical condition characterised by a particular set of symptoms • *Down's syndrome.* ② You can refer to a typical set of characteristics as a syndrome • *the syndrome of skipping from one wonder diet to the next.*

synecdoche [Said sin-**ek**-dok-kee] NOUN ENGLISH a figure of speech in which part of something is used to mean the whole. For example, in *Give us this day our daily bread*, *bread* means 'food'.

synod, synods [Said **sin**-od] NOUN a council of church leaders which meets regularly to discuss religious and moral issues.

synonym, synonyms NOUN ENGLISH If two words have the same or a very similar meaning, they are synonyms.

synonymous ADJECTIVE ①Two words that are synonymous have the same or very similar meanings. ②If two things are closely associated, you can say that one is synonymous with the other • *New York is synonymous with the Statue of Liberty*.

synopsis, synopses NOUN a summary of a book, play or film.

syntax NOUN ENGLISH The syntax of a language is its grammatical rules and the way its words are arranged.

synthesis, syntheses NOUN A synthesis of different ideas or styles is a blended combination of them. **synthesise** VERB

synthetic ADJECTIVE made from artificial substances rather than natural ones.

syphon another spelling of **siphon**.

Syrian, Syrians [Said *sirr-ee-an*] ADJECTIVE ①belonging or relating to Syria. ▶ NOUN ②someone who comes from Syria.

syringe, syringes [Said *si-rinj*] NOUN a hollow tube with a part which is pushed down inside and a fine hollow needle at one end, used for injecting or extracting liquids.

syrup, syrups NOUN a thick sweet liquid made by boiling sugar with water. **syrupy** ADJECTIVE
WORD HISTORY: from Arabic *sharab* meaning 'drink'

system, systems NOUN ① LIBRARY an organised way of doing or arranging something according to a fixed plan or set of rules. ②People sometimes refer to the government and administration of the country as the system. ③You can also refer to a set of equipment as a system • *an old stereo system*. ④In biology, a system of a particular kind is the set of organs that perform that function • *the immune system*.
SIMILAR WORDS: ① method, procedure, routine

systematic ADJECTIVE following a fixed plan and done in an efficient way • *a systematic study*.
systematically ADVERB

Tt

tab, tabs NOUN a small extra piece that is attached to something, for example on a curtain so it can be hung on a pole.

tabby, tabbies NOUN a cat whose fur has grey, brown or black stripes.
WORD HISTORY: from Old French *tabis* meaning 'striped silk cloth'

tabernacle, tabernacles [Said *tab-er-nak-kl*] NOUN ① a place of worship for certain Christian groups. ② a sanctuary in which the ancient Hebrews carried the Ark of the Covenant as they wandered from place to place. ③ a Jewish temple.
WORD HISTORY: from Latin *tabernaculum* meaning 'tent'

table, tables, tabling, tabled NOUN ① a piece of furniture with a flat horizontal top supported by one or more legs. ② a set of facts or figures arranged in rows or columns. ▶ VERB ③ If you table something such as a proposal, you say formally that you want it to be discussed.

tablecloth, tablecloths NOUN a cloth used to cover a table and keep it clean.

tablespoon, tablespoons NOUN a large spoon used for serving food; also the amount that a tablespoon contains.

tablet, tablets NOUN ① any small, round pill made of powdered medicine. ② a slab of stone with words cut into it. ③ ICT a small mobile personal computer with a screen that is manipulated by swiping or tapping with the hand.

table tennis NOUN Table tennis is a game for two or four people in which you use bats to hit a small hollow ball over a low net across a table.

tabloid, tabloids NOUN ENGLISH a newspaper with small pages, short news stories, and lots of photographs.

taboo, taboos NOUN ① a social custom that some words, subjects or actions must be avoided because they are considered embarrassing or offensive • *We have a powerful taboo against boasting.* ② a religious custom that forbids people to do something. ▶ ADJECTIVE ③ forbidden or disapproved of • *a taboo subject*.

tacit [Said *tass-it*] ADJECTIVE understood or implied without actually being said or written.
tacitly ADVERB

taciturn [Said *tass-it-urn*] ADJECTIVE Someone who is taciturn does not talk very much and so seems unfriendly.

tack, tacks, tacking, tacked NOUN ① a short nail with a broad, flat head. ② If you change tack, you start to use a different method for dealing with something. ▶ VERB ③ If you tack something to a surface, you nail it there with tacks. ④ If you tack a piece of fabric, you sew it with long loose stitches.

tackies; also spelt **takkies** PLURAL NOUN (*informal*) In South African English, tackies are tennis shoes or plimsolls.

tackle, tackles, tackling, tackled **VERB** ① If you tackle a difficult task, you start dealing with it in a determined way. ② If you tackle someone in a game such as soccer, you try to get the ball away from them. ③ If you tackle someone about something, you talk to them about it in order to get something changed or dealt with. ▶ **NOUN** ④ A tackle in sport is an attempt to get the ball away from your opponent. ⑤ Tackle is the equipment used for fishing. **SIMILAR WORDS:** ① deal with, undertake

tacky, tackier, tackiest **ADJECTIVE** ① slightly sticky to touch • *The cream feels tacky to the touch.* ② (*informal*) badly made and in poor taste • *tacky furniture.*

tact **NOUN** Tact is the ability to see when a situation is difficult or delicate and to handle it without upsetting people. **tactless ADJECTIVE** **tactlessly ADVERB** **SIMILAR WORDS:** delicacy, diplomacy, discretion

tactful ADJECTIVE behaving with or showing tact. **tactfully ADVERB**

tactic, tactics **NOUN** ① Tactics are the methods you use to achieve what you want, especially to win a game. ② Tactics are also the ways in which troops and equipment are used in order to win a battle.

tactical ADJECTIVE relating to or using tactics • *England made some tactical errors in the game.* **tactically ADVERB**

tactile ADJECTIVE involving the sense of touch.

tadpole, tadpoles **NOUN** Tadpoles are the larvae of frogs and toads. They are black with round heads and long tails and live in water. **WORD HISTORY:** from Middle English *tadde* meaning 'toad' and *pol* meaning 'head'

taffeta [*Said* **taf-fit-a**] **NOUN** Taffeta is a stiff, shiny fabric that is used mainly for making women's clothes.

tag, tags, tagging, tagged **NOUN** a small label made of cloth, paper or plastic.

tail, tails, tailing, tailed **NOUN** ① The tail of an animal, bird or fish is the part extending beyond the end of its body. ② Tail can be used to mean the end part of something • *the tail of the plane.* ③ (*in plural*) If a man is wearing tails, he is wearing a formal jacket which has two long pieces hanging down at the back. ▶ **VERB** ④ (*informal*) If you tail someone, you follow them in order to find out where they go and what they do. ▶ **ADJECTIVE** *or* **ADVERB** ⑤ The 'tails' side of a coin is the side which does not have a person's head. **tail off VERB** If something tails off, it becomes gradually less.

tailback, tailbacks **NOUN** a long queue of traffic stretching back from whatever is blocking the road.

tailor, tailors, tailoring, tailored **NOUN** ① a person who makes, alters and repairs clothes, especially for men. ▶ **VERB** ② If something is tailored for a particular purpose, it is specially designed for it.

tailor-made ADJECTIVE suitable for a particular person or purpose, or specifically designed for them.

taint, taints, tainting, tainted **VERB** ① To taint something is to spoil it by adding something undesirable to it. ▶ **NOUN** ② an undesirable quality in something which spoils it.

taipan, taipans **NOUN** a large and very poisonous Australian snake.

take, takes, taking, took, taken **VERB** ① 'Take' is used to show what action or activity is being done • *Amy took a bath* • *She took her driving test.* ② If something takes a certain amount of time, or a particular quality or ability, it requires it • *He takes three hours to get ready.* ③ If you take something, you put your hand round it and hold it or carry it • *Here, let me take your coat.* ④ If you take someone somewhere, you drive them there by car or lead them there. ⑤ If you take something that is offered to you, you accept it • *He had to take the job.* ⑥ If you take the responsibility or blame for something, you accept responsibility or blame. ⑦ If you take something that does not belong to you, you steal it. ⑧ If you take pills or medicine, you swallow them. ⑨ If you can take something painful, you can bear it • *We can't take much more of this.* ⑩ If you take someone's advice, you do what they say you should do. ⑪ If you take a person's temperature or pulse, you measure it. ⑫ If you take a car or train, or a road or route, you use it to go from one place to another. ▶ PHRASE ⑬ If you **take care of** someone or something, you look after them. ⑭ If you **take care of** a problem or situation, you deal with it and get it sorted. **take after** VERB If you take after someone in your family, you look or behave like them. **take down** VERB If you take down what someone is saying, you write it down. **take in** VERB ① If someone is taken in, they are deceived. ② If you take something in, you understand it. **take off** VERB When an aeroplane takes off, it leaves the ground and begins to fly. **takeoff** NOUN **take over** VERB To take something over means to start controlling it. **takeover** NOUN **take to** VERB If you take to someone or something, you like them immediately.

takeaway, takeaways NOUN ① a shop or restaurant that sells hot cooked food to be eaten elsewhere. ② a hot cooked meal bought from a takeaway.

takings PLURAL NOUN Takings are the money that a shop or cinema gets from selling its goods or tickets.

talc NOUN ① Talc is a white, grey or pale green mineral used to make talcum powder. ② Talc is also talcum powder.
WORD HISTORY: a Persian word

talcum powder NOUN Talcum powder is a soft perfumed powder made of purified talc and used for absorbing moisture on the body.

tale, tales NOUN a story.

talent, talents NOUN Talent is the natural ability to do something well. **talented** ADJECTIVE
SIMILAR WORDS: ability, flair, gift

talisman, talismans [*Said* tal-iz-man] NOUN an object which you believe has magic powers to protect you or bring luck.
WORD HISTORY: from Greek *telesma* meaning 'holy object'

talk, talks, talking, talked VERB ① When you talk, you say things to someone. ② If people talk, especially about other people's private affairs, they gossip about them • *The neighbours might talk.* ③ If you talk on or about something, you make an informal speech about it. ▶ NOUN ④ Talk is discussion or gossip. ⑤ an informal speech about something. **talk down** VERB If you talk down to someone, you talk to them in a way that shows that you think you are more important or clever than them.

talkative ADJECTIVE talking a lot.
SIMILAR WORDS: chatty, garrulous, loquacious

tall, taller, tallest ADJECTIVE ① of

more than average or normal height.
② having a particular height • *a wall ten metres tall*. ▸ **PHRASE** ③ If you describe something as **a tall story**, you mean that it is difficult to believe because it is so unlikely.

tally, tallies, tallying, tallied NOUN
① an informal record of amounts which you keep adding to as you go along • *He ended with a reasonable goal tally last season*. ▸ **VERB** ② If numbers or statements tally, they are exactly the same or they give the same results or conclusions.

Talmud [Said *tal-mood*] NOUN RE
The Talmud consists of the books containing the ancient Jewish ceremonies and civil laws.
WORD HISTORY: a Hebrew word meaning 'instruction'

talon, talons NOUN Talons are sharp, hooked claws, especially of a bird of prey.

tambourine, tambourines NOUN a percussion instrument made of a skin stretched tightly over a circular frame, with small round pieces of metal around the edge that jingle when the tambourine is beaten or shaken.

tame, tamer, tamest; tames, taming, tamed ADJECTIVE ① A tame animal or bird is not afraid of people and is not violent towards them.
② Something that is tame is uninteresting and lacks excitement or risk • *The report was pretty tame*.
▸ **VERB** ③ If you tame people or things, you bring them under control. ④ To tame a wild animal or bird is to train it to be obedient and live with humans.

tamper, tampers, tampering, tampered VERB If you tamper with something, you interfere or meddle with it.

tampon, tampons NOUN a firm, specially shaped piece of cotton wool that a woman places inside her vagina to absorb the blood during her period.

tan, tans, tanning, tanned NOUN
① If you have a tan, your skin is darker than usual because you have been in the sun. ▸ **VERB** ② To tan an animal's hide is to turn it into leather by treating it with chemicals.
▸ **ADJECTIVE** ③ Something that is tan is of a light yellowish-brown colour
• *a tan dress*.

tandem, tandems NOUN a bicycle designed for two riders sitting one behind the other.

tang, tangs NOUN a strong, sharp smell or flavour • *the tang of lemon*.
tangy ADJECTIVE

tangata whenua [Said *tang-ah-tah feh-noo-ah*] NOUN Tangata whenua is a Māori term for the original Polynesian settlers in New Zealand, and their descendants.

tangent, tangents NOUN ① MATHS
A tangent of a curve is any straight line that touches the curve at one point only. ② MATHS A tangent is also a function of an angle. If B is the right angle in a right-angled triangle ABC, the tangent of the angle at A is BC divided by AB. ▸ **PHRASE** ③ If you **go off at a tangent**, you start talking or thinking about something that is not completely relevant to what has gone before.

tangerine, tangerines NOUN ① a type of small sweet orange with a loose rind. ▸ **NOUN** or **ADJECTIVE**
② reddish-orange.

tangible [Said *tan-jib-bl*] ADJECTIVE
clear or definite enough to be easily seen or felt • *tangible proof*.

tangle, tangles, tangling, tangled
NOUN ① a mass of things such as

hairs or fibres knotted or coiled together and difficult to separate. ▸ **VERB** ② If you are tangled in wires or ropes, you are caught or trapped in them so that it is difficult to get free.

tango, **tangos** NOUN A tango is a Latin American dance using long gliding steps and sudden pauses; also a piece of music composed for this dance.

taniwha, **taniwha** or **taniwhas** [Said tun-ee-fah] NOUN In New Zealand, a taniwha is a monster of Māori legends that lives in water.

tank, **tanks** NOUN ① a large container for storing liquid or gas. ② an armoured military vehicle which moves on tracks and is equipped with guns or rockets.

tankard, **tankards** NOUN a large metal mug used for drinking beer.

tanker, **tankers** NOUN a ship or lorry designed to carry large quantities of gas or liquid • a petrol tanker.

tannin NOUN a brown or yellow substance found in plants and used in making leather.

tantalising; also spelt **tantalizing** ADJECTIVE Something that is tantalising makes you feel hopeful and excited, although you know that you probably will not be able to have what you want • a tantalising glimpse of riches to come.

tantamount ADJECTIVE If you say that something is tantamount to something else, you mean that it is almost the same as it • That would be tantamount to treason.

tantrum, **tantrums** NOUN a noisy and sometimes violent outburst of temper, especially by a child.

Tanzanian, **Tanzanians** [Said tan-zan-nee-an] ADJECTIVE ① belonging or relating to Tanzania.

▸ NOUN ② someone who comes from Tanzania.

tap, **taps**, **tapping**, **tapped** NOUN ① a device that you turn to control the flow of liquid or gas from a pipe or container. ② the action of hitting something lightly; also the sound that this action makes. ▸ **VERB** ③ If you tap something or tap on it, you hit it lightly. ④ If a telephone is tapped, a device is fitted to it so that someone can listen secretly to the calls.

tap-dancing NOUN Tap-dancing is a type of dancing in which the dancers wear special shoes with pieces of metal on the toes and heels which click against the floor.

tape, **tapes**, **taping**, **taped** NOUN ① Tape is plastic ribbon covered with a magnetic substance and used to record sounds, pictures and computer data. ② A tape is a recording of sounds, pictures or computer data. ③ Tape is a long, thin strip of fabric that is used for binding or fastening. ④ Tape is also a strip of sticky plastic which you use for sticking things together. ▸ **VERB** ⑤ If you tape sounds or television pictures, you record them. ⑥ If you tape one thing to another, you attach them using sticky tape.

tape measure, **tape measures** NOUN a strip of plastic or metal that is marked off in inches or centimetres and used for measuring things.

taper, **tapers**, **tapering**, **tapered** VERB ① Something that tapers becomes thinner towards one end. ▸ NOUN ② a thin candle.

tape recorder, **tape recorders** NOUN a machine used for recording sounds onto magnetic tape, and for playing these sounds back.

tapestry, tapestries NOUN a piece of heavy cloth with designs embroidered on it.

tar NOUN Tar is a thick, black, sticky substance which is used in making roads.

tarantula, tarantulas [Said tar-**rant**-yoo-la] NOUN a large, hairy, poisonous spider.

tardy, tardier, tardiest; tardies ADJECTIVE (literary) happening later or more slowly than expected.
▸ NOUN

target, targets NOUN ① something which you aim at when firing weapons. ② The target of an action or remark is the person or thing at which it is directed • You become a target for our hatred. ③ Your target is the result that you are trying to achieve.

tariff, tariffs NOUN ① a tax that a government collects on imported goods. ② any list of prices or charges.

tarmac NOUN Tarmac is a material used for making road surfaces. It consists of crushed stones mixed with tar.
WORD HISTORY: short for tarmacadam, from the name of John McAdam, the Scottish engineer who invented it

tarnish, tarnishes, tarnishing, tarnished VERB ① If metal tarnishes, it becomes stained and loses its shine. ② If something tarnishes your reputation, it spoils it and causes people to lose their respect for you.

tarot [Said tar-roh] NOUN A tarot card is one of a special pack of cards used for fortune-telling.

tarpaulin, tarpaulins NOUN a sheet of heavy waterproof material used as a protective covering.

tarragon NOUN Tarragon is a herb with narrow green leaves used in cooking.

tarry, tarries, tarrying, tarried VERB (old-fashioned) To tarry is to wait, or to stay somewhere for a little longer.

tarseal NOUN In New Zealand English, tarseal is the tarmac surface of a road.

tart, tarts; tarter, tartest NOUN ① a pastry case with a sweet filling.
▸ ADJECTIVE ② Something that is tart is sour or sharp to taste. ③ A tart remark is unpleasant and cruel.

tartan, tartans NOUN Tartan is a woollen fabric from Scotland with checks of various colours and sizes, depending on which clan it belongs to.

tartar NOUN Tartar is a hard, crusty substance that forms on teeth.

tarwhine, tarwhines NOUN an edible Australian marine fish.

task, tasks NOUN any piece of work which has to be done.
SIMILAR WORDS: chore, duty, job

Tasmanian devil, Tasmanian devils NOUN a black-and-white marsupial of Tasmania, which eats flesh.

tassel, tassels NOUN a tuft of loose threads tied by a knot and used for decoration.

taste, tastes, tasting, tasted NOUN ① Your sense of taste is your ability to recognise the flavour of things in your mouth. ② The taste of something is its flavour. ③ If you have a taste of food or drink, you have a small amount of it to see what it is like. ④ If you have a taste for something, you enjoy it • a taste for publicity. ⑤ If you have a taste of something, you experience it • my first taste of defeat. ⑥ A person's taste is their choice in the things they like to buy or have around them • His *taste in music is great.* ▶ VERB ⑦When you can taste something in your mouth, you are aware of its flavour. ⑧If you taste food or drink, you have a small amount of it to see what it is like. ⑨If food or drink tastes of something, it has that flavour.

taste bud, taste buds NOUN Your taste buds are the little points on the surface of your tongue which enable you to taste things.

tasteful ADJECTIVE attractive and elegant. **tastefully** ADVERB

tasteless ADJECTIVE ①vulgar and unattractive. ②A tasteless remark or joke is offensive. ③Tasteless food has very little flavour.

tasty, tastier, tastiest ADJECTIVE having a pleasant flavour.

tatters PHRASE Clothes that are in tatters are badly torn. **tattered** ADJECTIVE

tattoo, tattoos, tattooing, tattooed VERB ①If someone tattoos you or tattoos a design on you, they draw it on your skin by pricking little holes and filling them with coloured dye. ▶ NOUN ②a picture or design tattooed on someone's body. ③a public military display of exercises and music.

tatty, tattier, tattiest ADJECTIVE worn out or untidy and rather dirty.

taught the past tense and past participle of **teach**.

taunt, taunts, taunting, taunted VERB ①To taunt someone is to speak to them about their weaknesses or failures in order to make them angry or upset. ▶ NOUN ②an offensive remark intended to make a person angry or upset.

Taurus NOUN Taurus is the second sign of the zodiac, represented by a bull. People born between April 20th and May 20th are born under this sign.

WORD HISTORY: from Latin *taurus* meaning 'bull'

taut ADJECTIVE stretched very tight • *taut wires.*

tautology, tautologies NOUN ENGLISH Tautology is using different words to say the same thing twice in the same sentence. For example, *She repeated the task again* is a tautology.

tavern, taverns NOUN (*old-fashioned*) a pub.

tawdry, tawdrier, tawdriest [*Said taw-dree*] ADJECTIVE cheap, gaudy and of poor quality.

tawny NOUN or ADJECTIVE brownish-yellow.

tax, taxes, taxing, taxed NOUN ①Tax is an amount of money that the people in a country have to pay to the government so that it can provide public services such as health care and education. ▶ VERB ②If a sum of money is taxed, a certain amount of it has to be paid to the government. ③If goods are taxed, a certain amount of their price has to be paid to the government. ④If a person or company is taxed, they have to pay a certain amount of their income to the government. ⑤If something taxes you, it makes heavy demands on you • *They must be told not to tax your patience.* **taxation** NOUN

taxi, taxis, taxiing, taxied NOUN ①a car with a driver which you hire to take you to where you want to go. ▶ VERB ②When an aeroplane taxis, it moves slowly along the runway before taking off or after landing.

taxonomy NOUN SCIENCE the process of naming and classifying animals and plants.

tea, teas NOUN ①Tea is the dried leaves of an evergreen shrub found in Asia. ②Tea is a drink made by brewing the leaves of the tea plant in hot water; also a cup of this. ③Tea is also any drink made with hot water and leaves or flowers • *peppermint tea*. ④Tea is a meal taken in the late afternoon or early evening.

tea bag, tea bags NOUN a small paper bag with tea leaves in it which is placed in boiling water to make tea.

teach, teaches, teaching, taught VERB ① If you teach someone something, you give them instructions so that they know about it or know how to do it. ② If you teach a subject, you help students learn about a subject at school, college or university. **teaching** NOUN
SIMILAR WORDS: ① educate, instruct, train, tutor

teacher, teachers NOUN a person who teaches other people, especially children.

teak NOUN Teak is a hard wood which comes from a large Asian tree.

team, teams, teaming, teamed NOUN ① a group of people who work together or play together against another group in a sport or game. ▶ VERB ② If you team up with someone, you join them and work together with them.

team-mate, team-mates NOUN In a game or sport, your team-mates are the other members of your team.

teamwork NOUN Teamwork is the ability of a group of people to work well together.

teapot, teapots NOUN a round pot with a handle, a lid and a spout, used for brewing and pouring tea.

tear¹, tears [*Rhymes with fear*] NOUN Tears are the drops of salty liquid that come out of your eyes when you cry.

tear², tears, tearing, tore, torn

[*Rhymes with hair*] NOUN ① a hole that has been made in something. ▶ VERB ② If you tear something, it is damaged by being pulled so that a hole appears in it. ③ If you tear somewhere, you rush there • *He tore through busy streets in a high-speed chase*.
SIMILAR WORDS: ① hole, rip, rupture

tearaway, tearaways NOUN someone who is wild and uncontrollable.

tearful ADJECTIVE about to cry or crying gently. **tearfully** ADVERB

tease, teases, teasing, teased VERB ① If you tease someone, you deliberately make fun of them or embarrass them because it amuses you. ▶ NOUN ② someone who enjoys teasing people.

teaspoon, teaspoons NOUN a small spoon used for stirring drinks; also the amount that a teaspoon holds.

teat, teats NOUN ① a nipple on a female animal. ② a piece of rubber or plastic that is shaped like a nipple and fitted to a baby's feeding bottle.

tea tree, tea trees NOUN a tree found in Australia and New Zealand with leaves that yield an oil used as an antiseptic • *Tea tree oil has many uses*.

tech, techs NOUN (*informal*) a technical college.

technical ADJECTIVE ① involving machines, processes and materials used in industry, transport and communications. ② skilled in practical and mechanical things rather than theories and ideas. ③ involving a specialised field of activity • *I never understood the technical jargon*.

technical college, technical colleges NOUN a college where you can study subjects like technology and secretarial skills.

technicality, technicalities NOUN ① The technicalities of a process or activity are the detailed methods used to do it. ② an exact detail of a law or a set of rules, especially one some people might not notice • *The verdict may have been based on a technicality.*

technically ADVERB If something is technically true or correct, it is true or correct when you consider only the facts, rules or laws, but may not be important or relevant in a particular situation • *Technically, they were not supposed to drink on duty.*

technician, technicians NOUN someone whose job involves skilled practical work with scientific equipment.

technique, techniques NOUN ① a particular method of doing something • *these techniques of manufacture.* ② Technique is skill and ability in an activity which is developed through training and practice • *Jim's unique vocal technique.*

techno- PREFIX 'Techno-' means a craft or art • *technology.*
WORD HISTORY: from Greek *tekhnē* meaning 'a skill'

technology, technologies NOUN ① DGT Technology is the study of the application of science and scientific knowledge for practical purposes in industry, farming, medicine or business. ② a particular area of activity that requires scientific methods and knowledge • *computer technology.* **technological** ADJECTIVE **technologically** ADVERB

tectonic ADJECTIVE ① SCIENCE relating to or involving the geological forces that shape the earth's crust. ② SCIENCE tectonic plates are large, slow-moving pieces of the earth's crust. The movement of tectonic plates against or away from

one another is one of the main causes of earthquakes.

teddy, teddies NOUN A teddy or teddy bear is a stuffed toy that looks like a friendly bear.
WORD HISTORY: named after the American President Theodore (*Teddy*) Roosevelt, who hunted bears

tedious [*Said tee-dee-uss*] ADJECTIVE boring and lasting for a long time • *the tedious task of clearing up.*

tedium [*Said tee-dee-um*] NOUN the quality of being boring and lasting for a long time • *the tedium of unemployment.*

tee, tees, teeing, teed NOUN the small wooden or plastic peg on which a golf ball is placed before the golfer first hits it. **tee off** VERB To tee off is to hit the golf ball from the tee, or to start a round of golf.

teem, teems, teeming, teemed VERB ① If a place is teeming with people or things, there are a lot of them moving about. ② If it teems, it rains very heavily • *The rain was teeming down.*

teenage ADJECTIVE ① aged between thirteen and nineteen. ② typical of people aged between thirteen and nineteen • *teenage fashion.* **teenager** NOUN

teens PLURAL NOUN Your teens are the period of your life when you are between thirteen and nineteen years old.

tee shirt another spelling of **T-shirt**.

teeter, teeters, teetering, teetered VERB To teeter is to shake or sway slightly in an unsteady way and seem about to fall over.

teeth the plural of **tooth**.

teethe, teethes, teething, teethed [*Rhymes with breathe*] VERB When babies are teething, their teeth are starting to come through, usually causing them pain.

teetotal [Said tee-toe-tl] ADJECTIVE Someone who is teetotal never drinks alcohol. **teetotaller** NOUN

tele- PREFIX 'Tele-' means at or over a distance • *telegraph*.
WORD HISTORY: from Greek *telē* meaning 'far'

telecommunications NOUN Telecommunications is the science and activity of sending signals and messages over long distances using electronic equipment.

telegram, telegrams NOUN a message sent by telegraph.

telegraph NOUN The telegraph is a system of sending messages over long distances using electrical or radio signals.

telepathy [Said til-lep-ath-ee] NOUN Telepathy is direct communication between people's minds. **telepathic** ADJECTIVE

telephone, telephones, telephoning, telephoned NOUN ① a piece of electrical equipment for talking directly to someone who is in a different place. ▶ VERB ② If you telephone someone, you speak to them using a telephone.

telescope, telescopes NOUN a long instrument shaped like a tube which has lenses which make distant objects appear larger and nearer.

teletext NOUN Teletext is an electronic system that broadcasts pages of information onto a television set.

televise, televises, televising, televised VERB If an event is televised, it is filmed and shown on television.

television, televisions NOUN a piece of electronic equipment which receives pictures and sounds by

electrical signals over a distance.

tell, tells, telling, told VERB ① If you tell someone something, you let them know about it. ② If you tell someone to do something, you order or advise them to do it. ③ If you can tell something, you are able to judge correctly what is happening or what the situation is • *I could tell he was scared*. ④ If an unpleasant or tiring experience begins to tell, it begins to have a serious effect • *The pressure began to tell*.
SIMILAR WORDS: ① inform, notify

teller, tellers NOUN a person who receives or gives out money in a bank.

telling ADJECTIVE Something that is telling has an important effect, often because it shows the true nature of a situation • *a telling account of the war*.

telltale ADJECTIVE A telltale sign reveals information • *the sad telltale signs of a recent accident*.

telly, tellies NOUN (informal) a television.

temerity [Said tim-mer-it-ee] NOUN If someone has the temerity to do something, they do it even though it upsets or annoys other people • *She had the temerity to call him Bob*.

temp, temps NOUN (informal) an employee who works for short periods of time in different places.

temper, tempers, tempering, tempered NOUN ① Your temper is the frame of mind or mood you are in. ② a sudden outburst of anger.
▶ PHRASE ③ If you **lose your temper**, you become very angry. ▶ VERB ④ To temper something is to make it more acceptable or suitable • *curiosity tempered with some caution*.

temperament, temperaments [Said tem-pra-ment] NOUN Your temperament is your nature or

a
b
c
d
e
f
g
h
i
j
k
l
m
n
o
p
q
r
s
t
u
v
w
x
y
z

personality, shown in the way you react towards people and situations • *an artistic temperament*.

temperamental ADJECTIVE
Someone who is temperamental has moods that change often and suddenly.

temperate ADJECTIVE GEOGRAPHY
A temperate place has weather that is neither extremely hot nor extremely cold.

temperature, temperatures NOUN
① SCIENCE The temperature of something is how hot or cold it is. ② Your temperature is the temperature of your body. ▶ PHRASE ③ If you **have a temperature**, the temperature of your body is higher than it should be, because you are ill.

tempest, tempests NOUN (*literary*) a violent storm.

tempestuous [*Said tem-pest-yoo-uss*] ADJECTIVE violent or strongly emotional • *a tempestuous relationship*.

template, templates NOUN a shape or pattern cut out in wood, metal, plastic or card which you draw or cut around to reproduce that shape or pattern.

temple, temples NOUN ① RE a building used for the worship of a god in various religions • *a Buddhist temple*. ② Your temples are the flat parts on each side of your forehead.

tempo, tempos or tempi NOUN
① The tempo of something is the speed at which it happens • *the slow tempo of change*. ② MUSIC The tempo of a piece of music is its speed.

temporary ADJECTIVE lasting for only a short time. **temporarily** ADVERB

tempt, tempts, tempting, tempted VERB ① If you tempt someone, you

try to persuade them to do something by offering them something they want. ② If you are tempted to do something, you want to do it but you think it might be wrong or harmful • *He was tempted to reply with sarcasm*.
SIMILAR WORDS: ① entice, lure

temptation, temptations NOUN
① Temptation is the state you are in when you want to do or have something, even though you know it might be wrong or harmful.
② something that you want to do or have, even though you know it might be wrong or harmful.

ten the number 10. **tenth** ADJECTIVE

tenacious [*Said tin-nay-shuss*]
ADJECTIVE determined and not giving up easily. **tenaciously** ADVERB
tenacity NOUN

tenant, tenants NOUN someone who pays rent for the place they live in, or for land or buildings that they use. **tenancy** NOUN

tend, tends, tending, tended VERB
① If something tends to happen, it happens usually or often. ② If you tend someone or something, you look after them • *the way we tend our cattle*.
SIMILAR WORDS: ① be apt to, be inclined to, be liable to

tendency, tendencies NOUN a trend or type of behaviour that happens very often • *a tendency to be critical*.

tender, tenderest; tenders, tendering, tendered ADJECTIVE
① Someone who is tender has gentle and caring feelings. ② If someone is at a tender age, they are young and do not know very much about life.
③ Tender meat is easy to cut or chew. ④ If a part of your body is tender, it is painful and sore. ▶ VERB ⑤ If someone tenders an apology or their

What is a Tense?

The tense of the verb tells us whether the action is in the past, the present or the future.

Some forms of the verb indicate that the action has already happened. These forms are **past tenses**:

*The captain **asked** Omar for advice.*
*The captain **has asked** Omar for advice.*
*The captain **was asking** Omar for advice this morning.*
*The captain **had asked** Omar for advice that morning.*

Some forms of the verb indicate that the action is happening at the present time. These forms are **present tenses**:

*I **see** some cause for optimism.*
*I **do see** some cause for optimism.*

Some forms of the verb indicate that the action will happen in the future. These forms are **future tenses**:

*They **will go** to Fiji in September.*
*They **will have gone** to Fiji by the end of September.*

Also look at the grammar boxes at **future**; **past tense**; **present tense**

---

resignation, they offer it. ▶ NOUN ⑥ a formal offer to supply goods or to do a job for a particular price.
SIMILAR WORDS: ① affectionate, gentle, loving

tendon, tendons NOUN SCIENCE a strong cord of tissue which joins a muscle to a bone.

tendril, tendrils NOUN Tendrils are short, thin stems which grow on climbing plants and attach them to walls.

tenement, tenements [Said *ten-em-ent*] NOUN a large house or building divided into many flats.

tenet, tenets NOUN The tenets of a theory or belief are the main ideas it is based upon.

tenner, tenners NOUN (*informal*) a ten-pound or ten-dollar note.

tennis NOUN Tennis is a game played by two or four players on a rectangular court in which a ball is hit by players over a central net.

tenor, tenors NOUN ① a man who sings in a fairly high voice. ② The tenor of something is the general meaning or mood that it expresses • *the whole tenor of his poetry had*

changed. ▶ ADJECTIVE ③ A tenor recorder, saxophone or other musical instrument has a range of notes of a fairly low pitch.

tense, tenser, tensest; tenses, tensing, tensed ADJECTIVE ① If you are tense, you are nervous and cannot relax. ② A tense situation or period of time is one that makes people nervous and worried. ③ If your body is tense, your muscles are tight. ▶ VERB ④ If you tense, or if your muscles tense, your muscles become tight and stiff. ▶ NOUN ⑤ The tense of a verb is the form which shows whether you are talking about the past, present or future.
SIMILAR WORDS: ① anxious, nervous, uptight

tension, tensions NOUN ① Tension is the feeling of nervousness or worry that you have when something dangerous or important is happening. ② DGT The tension in a rope or wire is how tightly it is stretched.

tent, tents NOUN a shelter made of canvas or nylon held up by poles and pinned down with pegs and ropes.

a b c d e f g h i j k l m n o p q r s **t** u v w x y z

tentacle, **tentacles** NOUN The tentacles of an animal such as an octopus are the long, thin parts that it uses to feel and hold things.

tentative ADJECTIVE acting or speaking cautiously because of being uncertain or afraid. **tentatively** ADVERB

tenterhooks PLURAL NOUN If you are on tenterhooks, you are nervous and excited about something that is going to happen.

WORD HISTORY: from the hooks called *tenterhooks* which were used to stretch cloth tight while it was drying

tenuous [Said *ten-yoo-uss*] ADJECTIVE If an idea or connection is tenuous, it is so slight and weak that it may not really exist or may easily cease to exist • *a very tenuous friendship*.

tenure, **tenures** [Said *ten-yoor*] NOUN ①Tenure is the legal right to live in a place or to use land or buildings for a period of time. ②Tenure is the period of time during which someone holds an important job • *His tenure ended in 2014*.

tepee, **tepees** [Said *tee-pee*] NOUN a cone-shaped tent of animal skins used by North American Indians.

tepid ADJECTIVE Tepid liquid is only slightly warm.

term, **terms**, **terming**, **termed** NOUN ①a fixed period of time • *her second term as manager*. ②one of the periods of time that each year is divided into at a school or college. ③a name or word used for a particular thing. ④(*in plural*) The terms of an agreement are the conditions that have been accepted by the people involved in it. ⑤If you express something in particular terms, you express it using a particular type of language or in a way that clearly shows your attitude • *The young priest spoke of her in glowing terms*. ▶ PHRASE ⑥If you **come to terms with** something difficult or unpleasant, you learn to accept it. ▶ VERB ⑦To term something is to give it a name or to describe it • *He termed my performance memorable*.

terminal, **terminals** ADJECTIVE ①A terminal illness or disease cannot be cured and causes death gradually. ▶ NOUN ②a place where vehicles, passengers or goods begin or end a journey. ③A computer terminal is a keyboard and a visual display unit that is used to put information into or get information out of a computer. ④one of the parts of an electrical device through which electricity enters or leaves. **terminally** ADVERB

terminate, **terminates**, **terminating**, **terminated** VERB When you terminate something or when it terminates, it stops or ends. **termination** NOUN

terminology, **terminologies** NOUN The terminology of a subject is the set of special words and expressions used in it.

terminus, **terminuses** [Said *ter-min-uss*] NOUN a place where a bus or train route ends.

termite, **termites** NOUN Termites are small white insects that feed on wood.

tern, **terns** NOUN a small black and white sea bird with long wings and a forked tail.

ternary ADJECTIVE MUSIC Ternary form is a musical structure of three sections, the first and the second contrasting with each other and the third being a repetition of the first.

terrace, **terraces** NOUN ①a row of houses joined together. ②a flat area of stone next to a building where people can sit.

terracotta NOUN a type of brown pottery with no glaze.
WORD HISTORY: from Italian *terra cotta* meaning 'baked earth'

terrain NOUN The terrain of an area is the type of land there • *the region's hilly terrain*.

terrapin, terrapins NOUN a small North American freshwater turtle.

terrestrial ADJECTIVE involving the earth or land.

terrible ADJECTIVE ① serious and unpleasant • *a terrible illness*. ② (*informal*) very bad or of poor quality • *Paddy's terrible haircut*.

terribly ADVERB very or very much • *I was terribly upset*.

terrier, terriers NOUN a small, short-bodied dog.

terrific ADJECTIVE ① (*informal*) very pleasing or impressive • *a terrific film*. ② great in amount, degree or intensity • *a terrific blow on the head*.
terrifically ADVERB

terrify, terrifies, terrifying, terrified VERB If something terrifies you, it makes you feel extremely frightened.

territorial ADJECTIVE involving or relating to the ownership of a particular area of land or water • *a territorial dispute*.

territory, territories NOUN ① The territory of a country is the land that it controls. ② An animal's territory is an area which it regards as its own and defends when other animals try to enter it.

terror, terrors NOUN ① Terror is great fear or panic. ② something that makes you feel very frightened.

terrorise, terrorises, terrorising, terrorised; also spelt **terrorize** VERB If someone terrorises you, they frighten you by threatening you or being violent to you.

terrorism NOUN Terrorism is the use of violence for political reasons.
terrorist NOUN or ADJECTIVE

terse, terser, tersest ADJECTIVE A terse statement is short and rather unfriendly.

tertiary [*Said* ter-shar-ee] ADJECTIVE ① third in order or importance. ② Tertiary education is education at university or college level.

test, tests, testing, tested VERB ① When you test something, you try it to find out what it is, what condition it is in, or how well it works. ② If you test someone, you ask them questions to find out how much they know. ▸ NOUN ③ a deliberate action or experiment to find out whether something works or how well it works. ④ a set of questions or tasks given to someone to find out what they know or can do.

testament, testaments NOUN ① (*Law*) a will. ② a copy of either the Old or the New Testament of the Bible.

test case, test cases NOUN a legal case that becomes an example for deciding other similar cases.

testicle, testicles NOUN [SCIENCE] A man's testicles are the two sex glands beneath the penis that produce sperm.

testify, testifies, testifying, testified VERB ① When someone testifies, they make a formal statement, especially in a court of law • *He later testified at the inquiry*. ② To testify to something is to show that it is likely to be true • *a consultant's certificate testifying to her good health*.

testimonial, testimonials [*Said* tess-tim-**moh**-nee-al] NOUN a statement saying how good someone or something is.

testimony, testimonies NOUN
A person's testimony is a formal statement they make, especially in a court of law.

testing ADJECTIVE Testing situations or problems are very difficult to deal with • *It is a testing time for his team*.

testis, testes NOUN A man's testes are his testicles.

test match, test matches NOUN one of a series of international cricket or rugby matches.

testosterone [*Said tess-toss-ter-rone*] NOUN Testosterone is a hormone that produces male characteristics.

test tube, test tubes NOUN a small cylindrical glass container that is used in chemical experiments.

tetanus [*Said tet-ah-nuss*] NOUN Tetanus is a painful infectious disease caused by germs getting into wounds.

tether, tethers, tethering, tethered VERB ① If you tether an animal, you tie it to a post. ▶ PHRASE ② If you are **at the end of your tether**, you are extremely tired and have no more patience or energy left to deal with your problems.

tetrahedron, tetrahedrons or tetrahedra [*Said tet-ra-hee-dron*] NOUN MATHS A tetrahedron is a three-dimensional shape with six straight edges and four triangular sides.

Teutonic [*Said tyoo-tonn-ik*] ADJECTIVE (*formal*) involving or related to German people.

text, texts, texting, texted NOUN ① The text of a book is the main written part of it, rather than the pictures or index. ② Text is any written material. ③ a book or other piece of writing used for study or an exam at school or college. ④ Text is

short for 'text message'. ▶ VERB ⑤ If you text someone, you send them a text message. **textual** ADJECTIVE

textbook, textbooks NOUN a book about a particular subject for students to use.

textile, textiles NOUN DGT a woven cloth or fabric.

text message, text messages NOUN a written message sent using a mobile phone.

texture, textures NOUN The texture of something is the way it feels when you touch it.
SIMILAR WORDS: consistency, feel

Thai, Thais ADJECTIVE ① belonging or relating to Thailand. ▶ NOUN ② someone who comes from Thailand. ③ Thai is the main language spoken in Thailand.

than PREPOSITION or CONJUNCTION ① You use 'than' to link two parts of a comparison • *She was older than me*. ② You use 'than' to link two parts of a contrast • *Players would rather play than train*.

thank, thanks, thanking, thanked VERB When you thank someone, you show that you are grateful for something, usually by saying 'thank you'.

thankful ADJECTIVE happy and relieved about something.
thankfully ADVERB

thankless ADJECTIVE A thankless job or task involves doing a lot of hard work that other people do not notice or are not grateful for • *Referees have a thankless task*.

thanks PLURAL NOUN ① When you express your thanks to someone, you tell or show them how grateful you are for something. ▶ PHRASE ② If something happened **thanks to** someone or something, it happened

What does That do?

That is a relative pronoun. A relative pronoun replaces a noun which links two different parts of a sentence.

Relative pronouns always refer to a word in the earlier part of the sentence. The word they refer to is called the **antecedent**. (In the examples that follow, the antecedents are underlined.)

I have <u>a friend</u> **who** lives in Rome.
We could go to <u>a place</u> **that** I know.

That refers to things or people. It is never used immediately after a preposition, but it can be used if the preposition is separated from the relative pronoun:

It was <u>a film</u> **that** I had little interest **in**.

Also look at the grammar box at **relative pronoun**

---

because of them • *I'm as prepared as I can be, thanks to you*. ▶ **INTERJECTION** ③ You say 'thanks' to show that you are grateful for something.

thanksgiving NOUN
① Thanksgiving is an act of thanking God, especially in prayer or in a religious ceremony. ② In the United States, Thanksgiving is a public holiday in the autumn.

thank you INTERJECTION You say 'thank you' to show that you are grateful to someone for something.

that, those ADJECTIVE or PRONOUN
① 'That' or 'those' is used to refer to things or people already mentioned or known about • *That man was waving*. ▶ **CONJUNCTION** ② 'That' is used to introduce a clause • *I said that I was coming home*. ▶ **PRONOUN** ③ 'That' is also used to introduce a relative clause • *I followed Alex to a door that led inside*.

GRAMMAR TIP
You can use either *that* or *which* in clauses known as defining clauses. These are clauses that identify the object you are talking about. In the sentence *The book that is on the table is mine*, 'that is on the table' is a defining clause which distinguishes the book

from other books that are not on the table. Some people think these types of clause should only be introduced by *that*, and *which* should be kept for nondefining clauses. These nondefining clauses add extra information about the object, but do not identify it. In the sentence *The book, which is on the table, is mine*, 'which is on the table' is a nondefining clause which gives the reader extra detail about the book.

thatch, thatches, thatching, thatched NOUN ① Thatch is straw and reeds used to make roofs. ▶ **VERB** ② To thatch a roof is to cover it with thatch.

thaw, thaws, thawing, thawed VERB
① When snow or ice thaws, it melts.
② When you thaw frozen food, or when it thaws, it returns to its normal state in a warmer atmosphere. ③ When people who are unfriendly thaw, they begin to be more friendly and relaxed. ▶ **NOUN** ④ a period of warmer weather in winter when snow or ice melts.

the ADJECTIVE The definite article 'the' is used when you are talking about something that is known about, that has just been mentioned, or that you are going to give details about.

a b c d e f g h i j k l m n o p q r s t u v w x y z

A
B
C
D
E
F

The Definite Article

The word *the* is known as the **definite article**. You use it before a noun to refer to a specific example of that noun:

the kitchen table
the school I attend

The definite article *the* may be used before singular and plural nouns. However, you cannot use the

indefinite article *a* or *an* before a plural noun. You need to use the word *some* in this case:

the tables
some tables
the schools
some schools

Also look at the grammar box at **a**

G
H
I
J
K
L
M
N
O
P
Q
R
S
T
U
V
W
X
Y
Z

theatre, theatres *[Said thee-uh-tuh]* NOUN ① DRAMA a building where plays and other entertainments are performed on a stage. ② In American, Australian and New Zealand English, a theatre is also a cinema. ③ Theatre is work such as writing, producing and acting in plays. ④ An operating theatre is a room in a hospital designed and equipped for surgical operations. **WORD HISTORY:** from Greek *theatron* meaning 'viewing place'

theatrical *[Said thee-at-rik-kl]* ADJECTIVE ① DRAMA involving the theatre or performed in a theatre • *his theatrical career.* ② Theatrical behaviour is exaggerated, unnatural and done for effect. **theatrically** ADVERB

thee PRONOUN *(old-fashioned)* Thee means you.

theft, thefts NOUN Theft is the crime of stealing. **SIMILAR WORDS:** robbery, stealing

their ADJECTIVE 'Their' refers to something belonging or relating to people or things, other than yourself or the person you are talking to, which have already been mentioned • *It was their fault.*

SPELLING TIP
Do not confuse the spellings of *their*, *there* and *they're*: *Their house is the blue*

one; *That's my car over there*; *They're always late.*

theirs PRONOUN 'Theirs' refers to something belonging or relating to people or things, other than yourself or the person you are talking to, which have already been mentioned • *Amy had been Helen's friend, not theirs.*

them PRONOUN 'Them' refers to things or people, other than yourself or the people you are talking to, which have already been mentioned • *He picked up the pillows and threw them to the floor.*

theme, themes NOUN ① ENGLISH a main idea or topic in a piece of writing, painting, film or music • *the main theme of the book.* ② a tune, especially one played at the beginning and end of a television or radio programme.

themselves PRONOUN ① 'Themselves' is used when people, other than yourself or the person you are talking to, do an action and are affected by it • *They think they've made a fool of themselves.* ② 'Themselves' is used to emphasise 'they' • *He was as excited as they themselves were.*

then ADVERB at a particular time in the past or future • *I'd left home by then.*

theologian, theologians *[Said thee-ol-loe-jee-an]* NOUN someone who studies religion and the nature of God.

theology NOUN RE Theology is the study of religion and God.

theological ADJECTIVE

theorem, theorems [Said *theer-um*] NOUN MATHS A theorem is a statement in mathematics that can be proved to be true by reasoning.

theoretical ADJECTIVE ① based on or to do with ideas of a subject rather than the practical aspects. ② not proved to exist or be true.

theoretically ADVERB

theory, theories NOUN ① an idea or set of ideas that is meant to explain something • *Darwin's theory of evolution*. ② Theory is the set of rules and ideas that a particular subject or skill is based upon. ▶ PHRASE ③ You use **in theory** to say that although something is supposed to happen, it may not in fact happen • *In theory, prices should rise by 2 per cent*.

SIMILAR WORDS: ① conjecture, hypothesis

therapeutic [Said *ther-ap-yoo-tik*] ADJECTIVE ① If something is therapeutic, it helps you to feel happier and more relaxed • *Laughing is therapeutic*. ② In medicine, therapeutic treatment is designed to treat a disease or to improve a person's health.

therapy NOUN Therapy is the treatment of mental or physical health problems, often without the use of drugs or operations.

therapist NOUN

there ADVERB ① in, at or to that place, point or case • *He's sitting over there*. ▶ PRONOUN ② 'There' is used to say that something exists or does not exist, or to draw attention to something • *There are flowers on the table*.

SPELLING TIP
Do not confuse the spellings of *there*, *their* and *they're*. A good way to remember that *there* is connected to the idea of place is by remembering the spelling of two other place words, *here* and *where*.

thereby ADVERB (formal) as a result of the event or action mentioned • *They had recruited 200 new members, thereby making the day worthwhile*.

therefore ADVERB as a result.

thermal ADJECTIVE ① to do with or caused by heat • *thermal energy*. ② Thermal clothes are specially designed to keep you warm in cold weather.

thermometer, thermometers NOUN SCIENCE an instrument for measuring the temperature of a room or a person's body.

thermostat, thermostats NOUN a device used to control temperature, for example on a central heating system.

thesaurus, thesauruses [Said *this-saw-russ*] NOUN LIBRARY a reference book in which words with similar meanings are grouped together.

WORD HISTORY: from Greek *thēsauros* meaning 'treasure'

these the plural of **this**.

thesis, theses [Said *thee-siss*] NOUN a long piece of writing, based on research, that is done as part of a university degree.

they PRONOUN ① 'They' refers to people or things, other than you or the people you are talking to, that have already been mentioned • *They married two years later*. ② 'They' is sometimes used instead of 'he' or 'she' where the gender of the person is unknown or unspecified. Some people consider this to be incorrect

• *Someone could have a nasty accident if they tripped over that.*

GRAMMAR TIP
Do not use *they are* to say that a number of things are in a particular place. You should say *there are two bottles in the fridge* not *they are two bottles in the fridge*.

thick, thicker, thickest ADJECTIVE
① Something thick has a large distance between its two opposite surfaces. ② If something is a particular amount thick, it measures that amount between its two sides. ③ Thick means growing or grouped closely together and in large quantities • *thick dark hair.* ④ Thick liquids contain little water and do not flow easily • *thick soup.* ⑤ (*informal*) A thick person is stupid or slow to understand things.

thicken, thickens, thickening, thickened VERB If something thickens, it becomes thicker • *The clouds thickened.*

thicket, thickets NOUN a small group of trees growing closely together.

thief, thieves NOUN a person who steals.

thieving NOUN Thieving is the act of stealing.

thigh, thighs NOUN Your thighs are the top parts of your legs, between your knees and your hips.

thimble, thimbles NOUN a small metal or plastic cap that you put on the end of your finger to protect it when you are sewing.

thin, thinner, thinnest; thins, thinning, thinned ADJECTIVE
① Something that is thin is much narrower than it is long. ② A thin person or animal has very little fat on their body. ③ Thin liquids contain a lot of water • *thin soup.* ▶ VERB ④ If

you thin something such as paint or soup, you add water or other liquid to it.
SIMILAR WORDS: ② lean, skinny, slim

thing, things NOUN ① an object, rather than a plant, an animal or a human being. ② (*in plural*) Your things are your clothes or possessions.
SIMILAR WORDS: ① article, object

think, thinks, thinking, thought VERB ① When you think about ideas or problems, you use your mind to consider them. ② If you think something, you have the opinion that it is true or the case • *I think she has a secret boyfriend.* ③ If you think of something, you remember it or it comes into your mind. ④ If you think a lot of someone or something, you admire them or think they are good.

third, thirds ADJECTIVE ① The third item in a series is the one counted as number three. ▶ NOUN ② one of three equal parts.

third person NOUN ENGLISH MFL In grammar, the third person is anyone or anything being referred to which isn't a first or second person (*he*, *she*, *they* or *it*).

third-person narrator NOUN ENGLISH A third-person narrator is either a minor character in the story or not a character at all and uses the pronouns *he*, *she*, *it* and *they*.

Third World NOUN The poorer countries of Africa, Asia and South America are sometimes referred to as the Third World.

thirst, thirsts NOUN ① If you have a thirst, you feel a need to drink something. ② A thirst for something is a very strong desire for it • *a thirst for money.* **thirsty** ADJECTIVE **thirstily** ADVERB

thirteen the number 13. **thirteenth** ADJECTIVE

thirty, thirties the number 30.
thirtieth ADJECTIVE

this, these ADJECTIVE or PRONOUN
① 'This' is used to refer to something or someone that is nearby or has just been mentioned • *This is Robert.*
② 'This' is used to refer to the present time or place • *this week.*

thistle, thistles NOUN a wild plant with prickly-edged leaves and purple flowers.

thong, thongs NOUN a long narrow strip of leather.

thorn, thorns NOUN one of many sharp points growing on some plants and trees.

thorny, thornier, thorniest
ADJECTIVE ① covered with thorns.
② A thorny subject or question is difficult to discuss or answer.

thorough [*Said thur-ruh*] ADJECTIVE
① done very carefully and completely
• *a thorough examination.* ② A thorough person is very careful in what they do and makes sure nothing has been missed out.
thoroughly ADVERB

thoroughbred, thoroughbreds
NOUN an animal that has parents that are of the same high quality breed.

thoroughfare, thoroughfares
NOUN a main road in a town.

those the plural of **that**.

thou PRONOUN (*old-fashioned*) Thou means you.

though [*Rhymes with show*]
CONJUNCTION ① despite the fact that
• *Meg felt cold, even though the sun was out.* ② if • *It looks as though you were right.*

thought, thoughts ① Thought is the past tense and past participle of **think**. ▸ NOUN ② an idea that you have in your mind. ③ Thought is the activity of thinking • *She was lost in thought.* ④ Thought is a particular way of thinking or a particular set of ideas • *this school of thought.*
SIMILAR WORDS: ③ consideration, reflection, thinking

thoughtful ADJECTIVE ① When someone is thoughtful, they are quiet and serious because they are thinking about something. ② A thoughtful person remembers what other people want or need, and tries to be kind to them. **thoughtfully** ADVERB
SIMILAR WORDS: ① meditative, pensive, reflective ② caring, considerate, kind

thoughtless ADJECTIVE A thoughtless person forgets or ignores what other people want, need or feel. **thoughtlessly** ADVERB

thousand, thousands the number 1000. **thousandth** ADJECTIVE

thrash, thrashes, thrashing, thrashed VERB ① To thrash someone is to beat them by hitting them with something. ② To thrash someone in a contest or fight is to defeat them completely. ③ To thrash out a problem or an idea is to discuss it in detail until a solution is reached.

thread, threads, threading, threaded NOUN ① a long, fine piece of cotton, silk, nylon or wool. ② The thread on something such as a screw or the top of a container is the raised spiral line of metal or plastic round it. ③ The thread of an argument or story is an idea or theme that connects the different parts of it. ④ On the internet, a thread is a series of messages from different people about a particular subject. ▸ VERB ⑤ When you thread something, you pass thread, tape or cord through it. ⑥ If you thread your way through people or things, you carefully make your way through them.

a
b
c
d
e
f
g
h
i
j
k
l
m
n
o
p
q
r
s
t
u
v
w
x
y
z

threadbare ADJECTIVE Threadbare cloth or clothing is old and thin.

threat, **threats** NOUN ① a statement that someone will harm you, especially if you do not do what they want. ② anything or anyone that seems likely to harm you. ③ If there is a threat of something unpleasant happening, it is very possible that it will happen.

threaten, **threatens**, **threatening**, **threatened** VERB ① If you threaten to harm someone or threaten to do something that will upset them, you say that you will do it. ② If someone or something threatens a person or thing, they are likely to harm them.
SIMILAR WORDS: ② endanger, jeopardise

three the number 3.

three-dimensional ADJECTIVE
MATHS A three-dimensional object or shape is not flat, but has height or depth as well as length and width.

threesome, **threesomes** NOUN a group of three.

threshold, **thresholds** [Said thresh-hold] NOUN ① the doorway or the floor in the doorway of a building or room. ② The threshold of something is the lowest amount, level or limit at which something happens or changes • the tax threshold • His boredom threshold was exceptionally low.

threw the past tense of **throw**.

SPELLING TIP
Do not confuse the spellings of threw and through: Aidan threw the ball over the fence; The river runs through the centre of town.

---

thrice ADVERB (old-fashioned) If you do something thrice, you do it three times.

thrift NOUN Thrift is the practice of saving money and not wasting things.

thrifty, **thriftier**, **thriftiest** ADJECTIVE A thrifty person saves money and does not waste things.

thrill, **thrills**, **thrilling**, **thrilled** NOUN ① a sudden feeling of great excitement, pleasure or fear; also any event or experience that gives you such a feeling. ▶ VERB ② If something thrills you, or you thrill to it, it gives you a feeling of great pleasure and excitement. **thrilled** ADJECTIVE **thrilling** ADJECTIVE
SIMILAR WORDS: ① buzz, kick

thriller, **thrillers** NOUN a book, film or play that tells an exciting story about dangerous or mysterious events.

thrive, **thrives**, **thriving**, **thrived** or **throve** VERB When people or things thrive, they are healthy, happy or successful. **thriving** ADJECTIVE

throat, **throats** NOUN ① the back of your mouth and the top part of the passages inside your neck. ② the front part of your neck.

throb, **throbs**, **throbbing**, **throbbed** VERB ① If a part of your body throbs, you feel a series of strong beats or dull pains. ② If something throbs, it vibrates and makes a loud, rhythmic noise • The engines throbbed.

throes PLURAL NOUN ① Throes are a series of violent pangs or movements • death throes. ▶ PHRASE ② If you are in the throes of something, you are deeply involved in it.

thrombosis, **thromboses** [Said throm-boe-siss] NOUN a blood clot which blocks the flow of blood in the body. Thromboses are dangerous and often fatal.

throne, **thrones** NOUN ① a ceremonial chair used by a king or queen on important official occasions. ② The throne is a way of referring to the position of being king or queen • *The Queen is celebrating 60 years on the throne.*

throng, throngs, thronging, thronged NOUN ① a large crowd of people. ▶ VERB ② If people throng somewhere or throng a place, they go there in great numbers • *Hundreds of city workers thronged the scene.*

throttle, throttles, throttling, throttled VERB To throttle someone is to kill or injure them by squeezing their throat.

through [*Said* threw] PREPOSITION ① moving all the way from one side of something to the other • *a path through the woods.* ② because of • *He had been exhausted through lack of sleep.* ③ during • *He has to work through the summer.* ④ If you go through an experience, it happens to you • *I don't want to go through that again.* ▶ ADJECTIVE ⑤ If you are through with something, you have finished doing it or using it.

SPELLING TIP

Do not confuse the spellings of *through* and *threw*, the past tense of *throw*: *The river runs through the centre of town; Aidan threw the ball over the fence.*

---

throughout PREPOSITION ① during • *I stayed awake throughout the night.* ▶ ADVERB ② happening or existing through the whole of a place • *The house was painted brown throughout.*

throve the past tense of **thrive**.

throw, throws, throwing, threw, thrown VERB ① When you throw something you are holding, you move your hand quickly and let it go, so that it moves through the air. ② If you throw yourself somewhere, you move there suddenly and with force • *We threw ourselves on the ground.*

③ To throw someone into an unpleasant situation is to put them there • *It threw them into a panic.* ④ If something throws light or shadow on something else, it makes that thing have light or shadow on it. ⑤ If you throw yourself into an activity, you become actively and enthusiastically involved in it. ⑥ If you throw a fit or tantrum, you suddenly begin behaving in an uncontrolled way.
SIMILAR WORDS: ① chuck, fling, hurl

throwback, throwbacks NOUN something which has the characteristics of something that existed a long time ago • *Everything about her was a throwback to the fifties.*

thrush, thrushes NOUN ① a small brown songbird. ② Thrush is a disease of the mouth or of the vagina, caused by a fungus.

thrust, thrusts, thrusting, thrust VERB ① If you thrust something somewhere, you push or move it there quickly with a lot of force. ② If you thrust your way somewhere, you move along, pushing between people or things. ▶ NOUN ③ a sudden forceful movement. ④ The main thrust of an activity or idea is the most important part of it • *the general thrust of his argument.*

thud, thuds, thudding, thudded NOUN ① a dull sound, usually made by a solid, heavy object hitting something soft. ▶ VERB ② If something thuds somewhere, it makes a dull sound, usually by hitting something else.

thug, thugs NOUN a very rough and violent person.
WORD HISTORY: from Hindi *thag* meaning 'thief'

thumb, thumbs, thumbing, thumbed NOUN ① the short, thick finger on the side of your hand.

a
b
c
d
e
f
g
h
i
j
k
l
m
n
o
p
q
r
s
t
u
v
w
x
y
z

▸**VERB** ②If someone thumbs a lift, they stand at the side of the road and stick out their thumb until a driver stops and gives them a lift.

thump, thumps, thumping, thumped **VERB** ①If you thump someone or something, you hit them hard with your fist. ②If something thumps somewhere, it makes a fairly loud, dull sound, usually when it hits something else. ③When your heart thumps, it beats strongly and quickly. ▸**NOUN** ④a hard hit • *a great thump on the back.* ⑤a fairly loud, dull sound.

thunder, thunders, thundering, thundered **NOUN** ①Thunder is a loud cracking or rumbling noise caused by expanding air which is suddenly heated by lightning. ②Thunder is any loud rumbling noise • *the distant thunder of bombs.* ▸**VERB** ③When it thunders, a loud cracking or rumbling noise occurs in the sky after a flash of lightning. ④If something thunders, it makes a loud continuous noise • *The helicopter thundered low over the trees.*

thunderbolt, thunderbolts **NOUN** a flash of lightning, accompanied by thunder.

thunderous **ADJECTIVE** A thunderous noise is very loud • *thunderous applause.*

Thursday, Thursdays **NOUN** Thursday is the day between Wednesday and Friday.
WORD HISTORY: from Old English *Thursdæg* meaning 'Thor's day'; Thor was the Norse god of thunder

thus **ADVERB** (*formal*) ①in this way • *I sat thus for nearly half an hour.* ②therefore • *She is more experienced than him, thus better paid.*

thwart, thwarts, thwarting, thwarted **VERB** To thwart someone or their plans is to prevent them from doing or getting what they want.

thy **ADJECTIVE** (*old-fashioned*) Thy means your.

thyme [*Said time*] **NOUN** Thyme is a bushy herb with very small leaves.

thyroid gland, thyroid glands **NOUN** Your thyroid gland is situated at the base of your neck. It releases hormones which control your growth and your metabolism.

tiara, tiaras [*Said tee-ah-ra*] **NOUN** a semicircular crown of jewels worn by a woman on formal occasions.

Tibetan, Tibetans **ADJECTIVE** ①belonging or relating to Tibet. ▸**NOUN** ②someone who comes from Tibet.

tic, tics **NOUN** a twitching of a group of muscles, especially the muscles in the face.

tick, ticks, ticking, ticked **NOUN** ①a written mark to show that something is correct or has been dealt with. ②The tick of a clock is the series of short sounds it makes when it is working. ③a tiny, blood-sucking, insect-like creature that usually lives on the bodies of people or animals. ▸**VERB** ④To tick something written on a piece of paper is to put a tick next to it. ⑤When a clock ticks, it makes a regular series of short sounds as it works. **ticking NOUN**
tick off **VERB** (*informal*) If you tick someone off, you speak angrily to them because they have done something wrong.

ticket, tickets **NOUN** a piece of paper or card which shows that you have paid for a journey or have paid to enter a place of entertainment.

tickle, tickles, tickling, tickled **VERB** ①When you tickle someone, you move your fingers lightly over their body in order to make them laugh.

② If something tickles you, it amuses you or gives you pleasure • *Simon is tickled by the idea*.

tidal ADJECTIVE to do with or produced by tides • *a tidal estuary*.

tidal wave, tidal waves NOUN
GEOGRAPHY a very large wave, often caused by an earthquake, that comes over land and destroys things.

tide, tides, tiding, tided NOUN ①The tide is the regular change in the level of the sea on the shore, caused by the gravitational pull of the sun and the moon. ②The tide of opinion or fashion is what the majority of people think or do at a particular time. ③A tide of something is a large amount of it • *the tide of anger and bitterness*. **tide over** VERB If something will tide someone over, it will help them through a difficult period of time.

tidings PLURAL NOUN (*formal*) Tidings are news.

tidy, tidier, tidiest; tidies, tidying, tidied ADJECTIVE ① Something that is tidy is neat and arranged in an orderly way. ② Someone who is tidy always keeps their things neat and arranged in an orderly way. ③ (*informal*) A tidy amount of money is a fairly large amount of it. ▶ VERB ④To tidy a place is to make it neat by putting things in their proper place.

tie, ties, tying, tied VERB ① If you tie one thing to another or tie it in a particular position, you fasten it using cord of some kind. ② If you tie a knot or a bow in a piece of cord or cloth, you fasten the ends together to make a knot or bow. ③ Something or someone that is tied to something else is closely linked with it • *40,000 jobs are tied to the project*. ④ If you tie with someone in a competition or game, you have the same number of points. ▶ NOUN ⑤ a long, narrow

piece of cloth worn around the neck under a shirt collar and tied in a knot at the front. ⑥ a connection or feeling that links you with a person, place or organisation • *I had very close ties with the family*.
SIMILAR WORDS: ① bind, fasten

tied up ADJECTIVE If you are tied up, you are busy.

tier, tiers NOUN one of a number of rows or layers of something • *Take the stairs to the upper tier*.

tiff, tiffs NOUN (*informal*) a small unimportant quarrel.

tiger, tigers NOUN a large meat-eating animal of the cat family. It comes from Asia and has an orange coloured coat with black stripes.

tiger snake, tiger snakes NOUN a fierce, very poisonous Australian snake with dark stripes across its back.

tight, tighter, tightest ADJECTIVE ① fitting closely • *The shoes are too tight*. ② firmly fastened and difficult to move • *a tight knot*. ③ stretched or pulled so as not to be slack • *a tight cord*. ④ A tight plan or arrangement allows only the minimum time or money needed to do something • *Our schedule tonight is very tight*. ▶ ADVERB ⑤ held firmly and securely • *He held me tight*. **tightly** ADVERB **tightness** NOUN
SIMILAR WORDS: ③ stretched, taut

tighten, tightens, tightening, tightened VERB ① If you tighten your hold on something, you hold it more firmly. ② If you tighten a rope or chain, or if it tightens, it is stretched or pulled until it is straight. ③ If someone tightens a rule or system, they make it stricter or more efficient.

tightrope, tightropes NOUN a tightly stretched rope on which an

a
b
c
d
e
f
g
h
i
j
k
l
m
n
o
p
q
r
s
t
u
v
w
x
y
z

acrobat balances and performs tricks.

tights PLURAL NOUN Tights are a piece of clothing made of thin stretchy material that fit closely round a person's hips, legs and feet.

tiki, tiki or tikis NOUN In New Zealand, a tiki is a small carving of an ancestor worn as a pendant in some Māori cultures.

tile, tiles, tiling, tiled NOUN ① a small flat square piece of something, for example slate or carpet, that is used to cover surfaces. ▶ VERB ② To tile a surface is to fix tiles to it. **tiled** ADJECTIVE

till, tills, tilling, tilled PREPOSITION or CONJUNCTION ① Till means the same as until. ▶ NOUN ② a drawer or box in a shop where money is kept, usually in a cash register. ▶ VERB ③ To till the ground is to plough it for raising crops.

tiller, tillers NOUN the handle fixed to the top of the rudder for steering a boat.

tilt, tilts, tilting, tilted VERB ① If you tilt an object or it tilts, it changes position so that one end or side is higher than the other. ▶ NOUN ② a position in which one end or side of something is higher than the other. SIMILAR WORDS: ① incline, lean, tip

timber, timbers NOUN ① Timber is wood that has been cut and prepared ready for building and making furniture. ② The timbers of a ship or house are the large pieces of wood that have been used to build it.

timbre [Said tam-ber] NOUN MUSIC The timbre of a musical instrument, voice or sound is the particular quality or characteristic it has. WORD HISTORY: from Old French timbre meaning 'bell'

time, times, timing, timed NOUN ① Time is what is measured in hours, days and years • We still have plenty of time. ② 'Time' is used to mean a particular period or point • I enjoyed my time in Durban. ③ If you say it is time for something or it is time to do it, you mean that it ought to happen or be done now • It is time for a change. ④ 'Times' is used after numbers to indicate how often something happens • I saw my father four times a year. ⑤ 'Times' is used after numbers when you are saying how much bigger, smaller, better or worse one thing is compared to another • The Belgians drink three times as much beer as the French. ⑥ 'Times' is used in arithmetic to link numbers that are multiplied together • Two times three is six. ▶ VERB ⑦ If you time something for a particular time, you plan that it should happen then • We could not have timed our arrival better. ⑧ If you time an activity or action, you measure how long it lasts. SIMILAR WORDS: ② interval, period, spell

timeless ADJECTIVE Something timeless is so good or beautiful that it cannot be affected by the passing of time or by changes in fashion.

timely ADJECTIVE happening at just the right time • a timely appearance. SIMILAR WORDS: opportune, well-timed

timer, timers NOUN a device that measures time, especially one that is part of a machine.

timescale, timescales NOUN The timescale of an event is the length of time during which it happens.

time signature, time signatures NOUN MUSIC A time signature is a sign at the beginning of a line of music showing the number of beats in a bar.

timetable, timetables NOUN ① a plan of the times when particular activities or jobs should be done. ② a list of the times when particular trains, boats, buses or aeroplanes arrive and depart.

timid ADJECTIVE shy and having no courage or self-confidence. **timidity** NOUN **timidly** ADVERB
SIMILAR WORDS: fearful, shy, timorous

timing NOUN ① Someone's timing is their skill in judging the right moment at which to do something. ② The timing of an event is when it actually happens.

timpani [Said tim-pan-ee] PLURAL NOUN Timpani are large drums with curved bottoms that are played in an orchestra.

tin, tins NOUN ① SCIENCE Tin is a soft, silvery-white metallic element used in alloys. Its atomic number is 50, and its symbol is Sn. ② A tin is a metal container which is filled with food and then sealed in order to preserve the food. ③ A tin is a small metal container which may have a lid • a baking tin • the biscuit tin.

tinder NOUN Tinder is small pieces of dry wood or grass that burn easily and can be used for lighting a fire.

tinge, tinges NOUN a small amount of something • a tinge of envy. **tinged** ADJECTIVE

tingle, tingles, tingling, tingled VERB ① When a part of your body tingles, you feel a slight prickling feeling in it. ▸ NOUN ② a slight prickling feeling. **tingling** NOUN or ADJECTIVE

tinker, tinkers, tinkering, tinkered NOUN ① a person who travels from place to place mending metal pots and pans or doing other small repair jobs. ▸ VERB ② If you tinker with something, you make a lot of small changes to it in order to repair or improve it • All he wanted was to tinker with engines.

tinkle, tinkles, tinkling, tinkled VERB ① If something tinkles, it makes a sound like a small bell ringing. ▸ NOUN ② a sound like that of a small bell ringing.

tinned ADJECTIVE Tinned food has been preserved by being sealed in a tin.

tinsel NOUN Tinsel is long threads with strips of shiny paper attached, used as a decoration at Christmas.

tint, tints, tinting, tinted NOUN ① a small amount of a particular colour • a distinct tint of green. ▸ VERB ② If a person tints their hair, they change its colour by adding a weak dye to it. **tinted** ADJECTIVE

tiny, tinier, tiniest ADJECTIVE extremely small.
SIMILAR WORDS: diminutive, minute

tip, tips, tipping, tipped NOUN ① the end of something long and thin • a fingertip. ② a place where rubbish is dumped. ③ If you give someone such as a waiter a tip, you give them some money to thank them for their services. ④ a useful piece of advice or information. ▸ VERB ⑤ If you tip an object, you move it so that it is no longer horizontal or upright. ⑥ If you tip something somewhere, you pour it there quickly or carelessly. **tipped** ADJECTIVE

tipple, tipples NOUN A person's tipple is the alcoholic drink that they normally drink.

tipsy, tipsier, tipsiest ADJECTIVE slightly drunk.

tiptoe, tiptoes, tiptoeing, tiptoed VERB If you tiptoe somewhere, you walk there very quietly on your toes.

tirade, tirades [Said tie-rade] NOUN a long, angry speech in which you criticise someone or something.

a
b
c
d
e
f
g
h
i
j
k
l
m
n
o
p
q
r
s
t
u
v
w
x
y
z

WORD HISTORY: from Italian *tirata* meaning 'volley of shots'

tire, tires, tiring, tired VERB ① If something tires you, it makes you use a lot of energy so that you want to rest or sleep. ② If you tire of something, you become bored with it. SIMILAR WORDS: ① exhaust, fatigue, weary

SPELLING TIP
Do not confuse the spellings of *tire* and *tyre*: *Since my illness I tire easily; Jonny's car needs a new front tyre.*

tired ADJECTIVE having little energy. **tiredness** NOUN

tireless ADJECTIVE Someone who is tireless has a lot of energy and never seems to need a rest.

tiresome ADJECTIVE A person or thing that is tiresome makes you feel irritated or bored.

tiring ADJECTIVE Something that is tiring makes you tired.

tissue, tissues [Said tiss-yoo] NOUN ① SCIENCE The tissue in plants and animals consists of cells that are similar in appearance and function • *scar tissue* • *dead tissue*. ② Tissue is thin paper that is used for wrapping breakable objects. ③ a small piece of soft paper that you use as a handkerchief.

tit, tits NOUN a small European bird • *a blue tit*.

titanic ADJECTIVE very big or important.
WORD HISTORY: in Greek legend, the *Titans* were a family of giants

tithe, tithes, tithing, tithed NOUN A tithe was a fixed amount of money or goods that people used to give regularly to support churches and charities.
WORD HISTORY: from Old English *teogoth* meaning 'tenth part'

titillate, titillates, titillating, titillated VERB If something titillates someone, it pleases and excites them. **titillation** NOUN

title, titles NOUN ① the name of a book, film or piece of music. ② a word that describes someone's rank or job • *My official title is Design Manager.* ③ the position of champion in a sports competition • *the European featherweight title*.

titled ADJECTIVE Someone who is titled has a high social rank and has a title such as 'Princess', 'Lord', 'Lady' or 'Sir'.

titration NOUN SCIENCE a way of calculating the concentration of a solution by adding to it amounts of another substance which reacts with it, until the reaction between them is complete.

titter, titters, tittering, tittered VERB If you titter, you laugh in a way that shows you are nervous or embarrassed.

TNT NOUN TNT is a type of powerful explosive. It is an abbreviation for 'trinitrotoluene'.

to PREPOSITION ① 'To' is used to indicate the place that someone or something is moving towards or pointing at • *They are going to China.* ② 'To' is used to indicate the limit of something • *Goods to the value of 500 pounds.* ③ 'To' is used in ratios and rates when saying how many units of one type there are for each unit of another • *I only get about 30 kilometres to the gallon from it.* ▶ ADVERB ④ If you push or shut a door to, you close it but do not shut it completely.

SPELLING TIP
The preposition *to* is spelt with one *o*, the adverb *too* has two *os*, and the number *two* is spelt with *wo*.

toad, toads NOUN an amphibian that looks like a frog but has a drier skin and lives less in the water.

toadstool, toadstools NOUN a type of poisonous fungus.

toast, toasts, toasting, toasted NOUN ①Toast is slices of bread made brown and crisp by cooking at a high temperature. ②To drink a toast to someone is to drink an alcoholic drink in honour of them. ▸ VERB ③If you toast bread, you cook it at a high temperature so that it becomes brown and crisp. ④If you toast yourself, you sit in front of a fire so that you feel pleasantly warm. ⑤To toast someone is to drink an alcoholic drink in honour of them.
WORD HISTORY: from Latin *tostus* meaning 'parched'

toaster, toasters NOUN a piece of electrical equipment used for toasting bread.

tobacco NOUN Tobacco is the dried leaves of the tobacco plant which people smoke in pipes, cigarettes and cigars.

tobacconist, tobacconists NOUN a shop where tobacco, cigarettes and cigars are sold.

toboggan, toboggans NOUN a flat seat with two wooden or metal runners, used for sliding over the snow.

today ADVERB or NOUN ①Today means the day on which you are speaking or writing. ②Today also means the present period of history • *the challenges of growing up in today's society*.

toddle, toddles, toddling, toddled VERB To toddle is to walk in short, quick steps, as a very young child does.

toddler, toddlers NOUN a small child who has just learned to walk.

to-do, to-dos NOUN A to-do is a situation in which people are very agitated or confused • *It's just like him to make such a to-do about nothing*.

toe, toes NOUN ①Your toes are the five movable parts at the end of your foot. ②The toe of a shoe or sock is the part that covers the end of your foot.

toff, toffs NOUN (*informal, old-fashioned*) a rich person or one from an aristocratic family.

toffee, toffees NOUN Toffee is a sticky, chewy sweet made by boiling sugar and butter together with water.

toga, togas NOUN a long loose robe worn in ancient Rome.

together ADVERB ①If people do something together, they do it with each other. ②If two things happen together, they happen at the same time. ③If things are joined or fixed together, they are joined or fixed to each other. ④If things or people are together, they are very near to each other.
SIMILAR WORDS: ① collectively, jointly ② concurrently, simultaneously

GRAMMAR TIP
Two nouns joined by *together with* do not make a plural subject, so the following verb is not plural: *Jones, together with his partner, has had great success*.

togetherness NOUN Togetherness is a feeling of closeness and friendship.

toil, toils, toiling, toiled VERB ①When people toil, they work hard doing unpleasant, difficult or tiring tasks or jobs. ▸ NOUN ②Toil is unpleasant, difficult or tiring work.

toilet, toilets NOUN ①a large bowl, connected by a pipe to the drains,

a
b
c
d
e
f
g
h
i
j
k
l
m
n
o
p
q
r
s
t
u
v
w
x
y
z

A
B
C
D
E
F
G
H
I
J
K
L
M
N
O
P
Q
R
S
T
U
V
W
X
Y
Z

which you use when you want to get rid of urine or faeces. ② a small room containing a toilet.

toiletries PLURAL NOUN Toiletries are the things you use when cleaning and taking care of your body, such as soap and talc.

token, tokens NOUN ① a piece of paper or card that is worth a particular amount of money and can be exchanged for goods • *book tokens*. ② a flat round piece of metal or plastic that can sometimes be used instead of money. ③ If you give something to someone as a token of your feelings for them, you give it to them as a way of showing those feelings. ▶ ADJECTIVE ④ If something is described as token, it shows that it is not being treated as important • *a token contribution to your fees*.

told Told is the past tense and past participle of **tell**.

tolerable ADJECTIVE ① able to be put up with. ② fairly satisfactory or reasonable • *a tolerable salary*.

tolerance NOUN ① A person's tolerance is their ability to accept or put up with something which may not be enjoyable or pleasant for them. ② Tolerance is the quality of allowing other people to have their own attitudes or beliefs, or to behave in a particular way, even if you do not agree or approve • *religious tolerance*.

tolerant ADJECTIVE accepting of different views and behaviour.

tolerate, tolerates, tolerating, tolerated VERB ① If you tolerate things that you do not approve of or agree with, you allow them. ② If you can tolerate something, you accept it, even though it is unsatisfactory or unpleasant. **toleration** NOUN
SIMILAR WORDS: ② bear, endure, stand

toll, tolls, tolling, tolled NOUN ① The death toll in an accident is the number of people who have died in it. ② a sum of money that you have to pay in order to use a particular bridge or road. ▶ VERB ③ When someone tolls a bell, it is rung slowly, often as a sign that someone has died.

tom, toms NOUN a male cat.

tomahawk, tomahawks NOUN a small axe used by North American Indians.

tomato, tomatoes NOUN a small round red fruit, used as a vegetable and often eaten raw in salads.

tomb, tombs NOUN a large grave for one or more corpses.

tomboy, tomboys NOUN a girl who likes playing rough or noisy games.

tome, tomes NOUN (*formal*) a very large heavy book.

tomorrow ADVERB or NOUN ① Tomorrow means the day after today. ② You can refer to the future, especially the near future, as tomorrow.

ton, tons NOUN ① a unit of weight equal to 2240 pounds or about 1016 kilograms. ② (*in plural, informal*) If you have tons of something, you have a lot of it.

tonal ADJECTIVE involving the quality or pitch of a sound or of music.

tone, tones, toning, toned NOUN ① Someone's tone is a quality in their voice which shows what they are thinking or feeling. ② MUSIC The tone of a musical instrument or a singer's voice is the kind of sound it has. ③ ENGLISH The tone of a piece of writing is its style and the ideas or opinions expressed in it • *I was shocked at the tone of your leading article*. ④ ART a lighter, darker or brighter shade of the same colour

• *The whole room is painted in two tones of orange.* **tone down** VERB If you tone down something, you make it less forceful or severe.

tone-deaf ADJECTIVE unable to sing in tune or to recognise different tunes.

tongs PLURAL NOUN Tongs consist of two long narrow pieces of metal joined together at one end. You press the pieces together to pick an object up.

tongue, tongues NOUN ① Your tongue is the soft part in your mouth that you can move and use for tasting, licking and speaking. ② a language. ③ Tongue is the cooked tongue of an ox. ④ The tongue of a shoe or boot is the piece of leather underneath the laces.

tonic, tonics NOUN ① Tonic or tonic water is a colourless, fizzy drink that has a slightly bitter flavour and is often mixed with alcoholic drinks. ② a medicine that makes you feel stronger, healthier and less tired. ③ anything that makes you feel stronger or more cheerful • *It was a tonic just being with her.*

tonight ADVERB or NOUN Tonight is the evening or night that will come at the end of today.

tonne, tonnes [*Said* tun] NOUN a unit of weight equal to 1000 kilograms.

tonsil, tonsils NOUN Your tonsils are the two small, soft lumps in your throat at the back of your mouth.

tonsillitis [*Said* ton-sil-*lie*-tiss] NOUN Tonsillitis is a painful swelling of your tonsils caused by an infection.

too ADVERB ① also or as well • *You were there too.* ② more than a desirable, necessary or acceptable amount • *We had spent too long in the sun.*

SPELLING TIP
The adverb *too* has two *o*s, the preposition *to* is spelt with one *o*, and the number *two* is spelt with *wo*.

took the past tense of **take**.

tool, tools NOUN ① any hand-held instrument or piece of equipment that you use to help you do a particular kind of work. ② an object, skill or idea that is needed or used for a particular purpose • *You can use the survey as a bargaining tool in the negotiations.*
SIMILAR WORDS: ① implement, instrument, utensil

toot, toots, tooting, tooted VERB If a car horn toots, it produces a short sound.

tooth, teeth NOUN ① Your teeth are the hard, enamel-covered objects in your mouth that you use for biting and chewing food. ② The teeth of a comb, saw or zip are the parts that stick out in a row on its edge.

toothbrush, toothbrushes NOUN a small brush that you use for cleaning your teeth.

toothpaste NOUN Toothpaste is a substance which you use to clean your teeth.

top, tops, topping, topped NOUN ① The top of something is its highest point, part or surface. ② The top of a bottle, jar or tube is its cap or lid. ③ a piece of clothing worn on the upper half of your body. ④ a toy with a pointed end on which it spins.
▶ ADJECTIVE ⑤ The top thing of a series of things is the highest one • *the top floor of the building.* ▶ VERB ⑥ If someone tops a poll or popularity chart, they do better than anyone else in it • *It has topped the bestseller lists in almost every country.* ⑦ If something tops a particular amount, it is greater than that amount • *The*

temperature topped 90°. **top up** VERB To top something up is to add something to it in order to keep it at an acceptable or usable level.

top hat, top hats NOUN a tall hat with a narrow brim that men wear on special occasions.

topic, topics NOUN a particular subject that you write about or discuss.

topical ADJECTIVE involving or related to events that are happening at the time you are speaking or writing.

topography, topographies NOUN ① GEOGRAPHY Topography is the study and description of the physical features of an area, for example the hills, valleys or rivers. ② The topography of a particular area is its physical shape.

topping, toppings NOUN food that is put on top of other food in order to decorate it or add to its flavour.

topple, topples, toppling, toppled VERB If something topples, it becomes unsteady and falls over.

top-secret ADJECTIVE meant to be kept completely secret.

topsy-turvy ADJECTIVE in a confused state • *My life was truly topsy-turvy.*

Torah NOUN RE The Torah is Jewish law and teaching.

torch, torches NOUN ① a small electric light carried in the hand and powered by batteries. ② a long stick with burning material wrapped around one end.

tore the past tense of **tear²**.

torment, torments, tormenting, tormented NOUN [Said tor-ment] ① Torment is extreme pain or unhappiness. ② something that causes extreme pain and unhappiness • *It's a torment to see them staring at me.* ▶ VERB [Said tor-ment] ③ If something torments

you, it causes you extreme unhappiness.

torn ① Torn is the past participle of **tear²**. ▶ ADJECTIVE ② If you are torn between two or more things, you cannot decide which one to choose and this makes you unhappy • *torn between duty and pleasure.*

tornado, tornadoes or **tornados** [Said tor-nay-doh] NOUN a violent storm with strong circular winds around a funnel-shaped cloud.

torpedo, torpedoes, torpedoing, torpedoed [Said tor-pee-doh] NOUN ① a tube-shaped bomb that travels underwater and explodes when it hits a target. ▶ VERB ② If a ship is torpedoed, it is hit, and usually sunk, by a torpedo.

torque [Rhymes with fork] NOUN Torque is a force that causes something to spin around a central point such as an axle.

torrent, torrents NOUN ① When a lot of water is falling very rapidly, it can be said to be falling in torrents. ② A torrent of speech is a lot of it directed continuously at someone • *torrents of abuse.*

torrential ADJECTIVE Torrential rain pours down very rapidly and in great quantities.

torrid ADJECTIVE ① Torrid weather is very hot and dry. ② If something is described as torrid, it involves very strong emotions.

torso, torsos NOUN the main part of your body, excluding your head, arms and legs.

tortoise, tortoises NOUN a slow-moving reptile with a large hard shell over its body into which it can pull its head and legs for protection.

tortuous ADJECTIVE ① A tortuous road is full of bends and twists.

②A tortuous piece of writing is long and complicated.

torture, tortures, torturing, tortured NOUN ①Torture is great pain that is deliberately caused to someone to punish them or get information from them. ▶VERB ②If someone tortures another person, they deliberately cause that person great pain to punish them or get information. ③To torture someone is also to cause them to suffer mentally • *Memory tortured her.*

torturer NOUN

Tory, Tories NOUN In Britain, a Tory is a member or supporter of the Conservative Party.
WORD HISTORY: from Irish *toraidhe* meaning 'outlaw'

toss, tosses, tossing, tossed VERB ①If you toss something somewhere, you throw it there lightly and carelessly. ②If you toss a coin, you decide something by throwing a coin into the air and guessing which side will face upwards when it lands. ③If you toss your head, you move it suddenly backwards, especially when you are angry or annoyed or want your own way. ④To toss is to move repeatedly from side to side • *We tossed and turned and tried to sleep.*
SIMILAR WORDS: ①fling, sling, throw

tot, tots, totting, totted NOUN ①a very young child. ②a small amount of strong alcohol such as whisky. ▶VERB ③To tot up numbers is to add them together.

total, totals, totalling, totalled NOUN ①the number you get when you add several numbers together. ▶ADJECTIVE ②Total means complete • *a total failure.* ▶VERB ③When you total a set of numbers or objects, you add them all together. ④If several numbers total a certain figure, that is the figure you get when all the

numbers are added together • *Their debts totalled over 300,000 dollars.*
totally ADVERB
SIMILAR WORDS: ①aggregate, sum, whole

totalitarian [*Said toe-tal-it-tair-ee-an*] ADJECTIVE A totalitarian political system is one in which one political party controls everything and does not allow any other parties to exist.
totalitarianism NOUN

tote, totes, toting, toted (*informal*) NOUN ①The tote is a system of betting money on horses at a racetrack, in which all the money is divided among the people who have bet on the winning horses. Tote is an abbreviation for 'totalisator'. ▶VERB ②To tote a gun means to carry it.

totem pole, totem poles NOUN a long wooden pole with symbols and pictures carved and painted on it. Totem poles are made by some North American Indians.

totter, totters, tottering, tottered VERB When someone totters, they walk in an unsteady way.

toucan, toucans [*Said too-kan*] NOUN a large tropical bird with a very large beak.

touch, touches, touching, touched VERB ①If you touch something, you put your fingers or hand on it. ②When two things touch, their surfaces come into contact • *Their knees were touching.* ③If you are touched by something, you are emotionally affected by it • *I was touched by his thoughtfulness.* ▶NOUN ④Your sense of touch is your ability to tell what something is like by touching it. ⑤a detail which is added to improve something • *finishing touches.* ⑥a small amount of something • *a touch of mustard.* ▶PHRASE ⑦If you are **in touch** with someone, you are in contact with them.

touchdown, touchdowns NOUN
Touchdown is the landing of an
aircraft.

touching ADJECTIVE causing feelings
of sadness and sympathy.
SIMILAR WORDS: moving, poignant,
sad

touchscreen, touchscreens NOUN a
computer screen that allows the user
to give commands by touching parts
of the screen instead of using a
keyboard or mouse.

touchy, touchier, touchiest
ADJECTIVE ① If someone is touchy,
they are easily upset or irritated. ② A
touchy subject is one that needs to
be dealt with carefully, because it
might upset or offend people.

tough, tougher, toughest [Said tuff]
ADJECTIVE ① A tough person is strong
and independent and able to put up
with hardship. ② A tough substance
is difficult to break. ③ A tough task,
problem or way of life is difficult or
full of hardship. ④ Tough policies or
actions are strict and firm • tough
measures against organised crime.
toughly ADVERB **toughness** NOUN
toughen VERB
SIMILAR WORDS: ② durable, resilient,
strong

toupee, toupees [Said too-pay] NOUN
a small wig worn by a man to cover a
bald patch on his head.

tour, tours, touring, toured NOUN
① a long journey during which you
visit several places. ② a short trip
round a place such as a city or famous
building. ▶ VERB ③ If you tour a
place, you go on a journey or a trip
round it.

tourism NOUN Tourism is the
business of providing services for
people on holiday, for example hotels
and sightseeing trips.

tourist, tourists GEOGRAPHY NOUN

a person who visits places for
pleasure or interest.

tournament, tournaments NOUN
PE a sports competition in which
players who win a match play further
matches, until just one person or
team is left.

tourniquet, tourniquets [Said
toor-nik-kay] NOUN a strip of cloth
tied tightly round a wound to stop it
bleeding.

tousled ADJECTIVE Tousled hair is
untidy.

tout, touts, touting, touted VERB
① If someone touts something, they
try to sell it. ② If someone touts for
business or custom, they try to
obtain it in a very direct way
• volunteers who spend days touting for
donations. ▶ NOUN ③ someone who
sells tickets outside a sports ground
or theatre, charging more than the
original price.

tow, tows, towing, towed VERB ① If
a vehicle tows another vehicle, it
pulls it along behind it. ▶ NOUN ② To
give a vehicle a tow is to tow it.
▶ PHRASE ③ If you have someone in
tow, they are with you because you
are looking after them.

towards PREPOSITION ① in the
direction of • He turned towards the
door. ② about or involving • My
feelings towards Susan have changed.
③ as a contribution for • a huge
donation towards the new opera house.
④ near to • We sat towards the back.

towel, towels NOUN a piece of thick,
soft cloth that you use to dry yourself
with.

towelling NOUN Towelling is thick,
soft cloth that is used for making
towels.

tower, towers, towering, towered
NOUN ① a tall, narrow building,
sometimes attached to a larger

building such as a castle or church.
▶ **VERB** ② Someone or something that towers over other people or things is much taller than them.
towering ADJECTIVE

town, towns NOUN ① a place with many streets and buildings where people live and work. ② Town is the central shopping and business part of a town rather than the suburbs • *She has gone into town*.

town hall, town halls NOUN a large building in a town containing the council offices and a hall for public meetings.

township, townships NOUN Especially in the United States, Canada and South Africa, a township is a small area containing a town and the land surrounding it.

towpath, towpaths NOUN a path along the side of a canal or river.

toxic ADJECTIVE poisonous • *toxic waste*.
WORD HISTORY: from Greek *toxikon* meaning 'poison used on arrows' from *toxon* meaning 'arrow'

toxin, toxins NOUN SCIENCE a poison, especially one produced by bacteria and very harmful to living creatures.

toy, toys, toying, toyed NOUN ① any object made to play with. ▶ **VERB** ② If you toy with an idea, you consider it without being very serious about it • *She toyed with the idea of telephoning him*. ③ If you toy with an object, you fiddle with it • *Jessica was toying with her glass*.

toyi-toyi or **toy-toy** NOUN In South Africa, a toyi-toyi is a dance performed to protest about something.

trace, traces, tracing, traced VERB ① If you trace something, you find it after looking for it • *Police are trying to*

trace the owner of the car.
② EXAM TERM To trace the development of something is to find out or describe how it developed. ③ If you trace a drawing or a map, you copy it by covering it with a piece of transparent paper and drawing over the lines underneath. ▶ NOUN ④ a sign which shows you that someone or something has been in a place • *No trace of his father had been found*. ⑤ a very small amount of something. **tracing** NOUN

trachea, tracheas [Said trak-**kee**-a] NOUN SCIENCE Your trachea is your windpipe.
WORD HISTORY: from Greek *arteria trakheia* meaning 'rough artery'

track, tracks, tracking, tracked NOUN ① a narrow road or path. ② a strip of ground with rails on it that a train travels along. ③ a piece of ground, shaped like a ring, which horses, cars or athletes race around. ④ (*in plural*) Tracks are marks left on the ground by a person or animal • *the deer tracks by the side of the path*.
▶ ADJECTIVE ⑤ In an athletics competition, the track events are the races on a running track. ▶ VERB ⑥ If you track animals or people, you find them by following their footprints or other signs that they have left behind. **track down** VERB If you track down someone or something, you find them by searching for them.

track and field NOUN track events and field events in an athletics competition.

track record, track records NOUN The track record of a person or a company is their past achievements or failures • *the track record of the film's star*.

tracksuit, tracksuits NOUN a loose, warm suit of trousers and a top, worn for outdoor sports.

tract, tracts NOUN ①A tract of land or forest is a large area of it. ②a pamphlet which expresses a strong opinion on a religious, moral or political subject. ③a system of organs and tubes in an animal's or person's body that has a particular function • *the digestive tract*.

traction NOUN Traction is a form of medical treatment given to an injured limb which involves pulling it gently for long periods of time using a system of weights and pulleys.

tractor, tractors NOUN a vehicle with large rear wheels that is used on a farm for pulling machinery and other heavy loads.

trade, trades, trading, traded NOUN ①Trade is the activity of buying, selling or exchanging goods or services between people, firms or countries. ②Someone's trade is the kind of work they do, especially when it requires special training in practical skills • *a joiner by trade*. ▶VERB ③When people, firms or countries trade, they buy, sell or exchange goods or services. ④If you trade things, you exchange them • *Their mother had traded her rings for a few potatoes*.
SIMILAR WORDS: ①business, commerce ③deal, do business, traffic

trademark, trademarks NOUN a name or symbol that a manufacturer always uses on its products. Trademarks are usually protected by law so that no-one else can use them.

trader, traders NOUN a person whose job is to buy and sell goods • *a timber trader*.

tradesman, tradesmen NOUN a person, for example a shopkeeper, whose job is to sell goods.

trade union, trade unions NOUN an organisation of workers that tries to improve the pay and conditions in a particular industry.

tradition, traditions NOUN a custom or belief that has existed for a long time without changing.
SIMILAR WORDS: convention, custom

traditional ADJECTIVE ①Traditional customs or beliefs have existed for a long time without changing • *her traditional Indian dress*. ②A traditional organisation or institution is one in which older methods are used rather than modern ones • *a traditional school*. **traditionally** ADVERB

traditionalist, traditionalists NOUN someone who supports the established customs and beliefs of their society, and does not want to change them.

traffic, traffics, trafficking, trafficked NOUN ①Traffic is the movement of vehicles or people along a route at a particular time. ②Traffic in something such as drugs is an illegal trade in them. ▶VERB ③Someone who traffics in drugs or other goods buys and sells them illegally. **trafficker** NOUN **trafficking** NOUN

traffic light, traffic lights NOUN Traffic lights are the set of red, amber and green lights at a road junction which control the flow of traffic.

traffic warden, traffic wardens NOUN a person whose job is to make sure that cars are not parked in the wrong place or for longer than is allowed.

tragedy, tragedies [*Said* traj-id-ee] NOUN ①an event or situation that is disastrous or very sad. ②a serious story or play, that usually ends with the death of the main character.

tragic ADJECTIVE ①Something tragic

is very sad because it involves death, suffering or disaster • *a tragic accident*. ②Tragic films, plays and books are sad and serious • *a tragic love story*. **tragically** ADVERB

trail, trails, trailing, trailed NOUN ①a rough path across open country or through forests. ②a series of marks or other signs left by someone or something as they move along. ▶ VERB ③If you trail something or it trails, it drags along behind you as you move, or it hangs down loosely • *a small plane trailing a banner*. ④If someone trails along, they move slowly, without any energy or enthusiasm. ⑤If a voice trails away or trails off, it gradually becomes more hesitant until it stops completely.

trailer, trailers NOUN ①a small vehicle which can be loaded with things and pulled behind a car. ②In American English, a trailer is a caravan.

train, trains, training, trained NOUN ①a number of carriages or trucks which are pulled by a railway engine. ②A train of thought is a connected series of thoughts. ③A train of vehicles or people is a line or group following behind something or someone • *a train of oil tankers*. ▶ VERB ④If you train someone, you teach them how to do something. ⑤If you train, you learn how to do a particular job • *She trained as a serious actor*. ⑥If you train for a sports match or a race, you prepare for it by doing exercises. **training** NOUN

trainee, trainees NOUN someone who is being taught how to do a job.

trainers PLURAL NOUN Trainers are shoes with thick rubber soles, originally designed for running.

trait, traits NOUN a particular characteristic or tendency. In literature, a trait is an aspect of a character in a story, for example, kind, greedy, funny or stupid • *a very English trait*.

traitor, traitors NOUN HISTORY someone who betrays their country or the group which they belong to.

trajectory, trajectories [Said *traj-jek-tor-ee*] NOUN The trajectory of an object moving through the air is the curving path that it follows.

tram, trams NOUN a vehicle which runs on rails along the street and is powered by electricity from an overhead wire.

tramp, tramps, tramping, tramped NOUN ①a person who has no home, no job, and very little money. ②a long country walk • *I took a long, wet tramp through the fine woodlands*. ▶ VERB ③If you tramp from one place to another, you walk with slow, heavy footsteps.

trample, tramples, trampling, trampled VERB ①If you trample on something, you tread heavily on it so that it is damaged. ②If you trample on someone or on their rights or feelings, you behave in a way that shows you don't care about them.

trampoline, trampolines NOUN a piece of gymnastic equipment consisting of a large piece of strong cloth held taut by springs in a frame, on which a person jumps for exercise or fun.

trance, trances NOUN a mental state in which someone seems to be asleep but is conscious enough to be aware of their surroundings and to respond to questions and commands.

tranquil [Said *trang-kwil*] ADJECTIVE calm and peaceful • *tranquil lakes* • *I have a tranquil mind*. **tranquillity** NOUN

a
b
c
d
e
f
g
h
i
j
k
l
m
n
o
p
q
r
s
t
u
v
w
x
y
z

A
B
C
D
E
F
G
H
I
J
K
L
M
N
O
P
Q
R
S
T
U
V
W
X
Y
Z

tranquillise, tranquillises, tranquillising, **tranquillised**; also spelt **tranquillize** VERB If people or animals are tranquillised, they are given a drug to make them become calm, sleepy or unconscious.

tranquilliser, tranquillisers; also spelt **tranquillizer** NOUN a drug that makes people feel less anxious or nervous.

trans- PREFIX Trans- means across, through or beyond • *transatlantic*.

transaction, transactions NOUN a business deal which involves buying and selling something.

transcend, transcends, transcending, **transcended** VERB If one thing transcends another, it goes beyond it or is superior to it • *The story transcends belief.*

transcribe, transcribes, transcribing, **transcribed** VERB If you transcribe something that is spoken or written, you write it down, copy it, or change it into a different form of writing • *These letters were often transcribed by his wife Patti.*

transcript, transcripts NOUN a written copy of something that is spoken.

transfer, transfers, transferring, **transferred** VERB ① If you transfer something from one place to another, you move it • *They transferred the money to the Swiss account.* ② If you transfer to a different place or job, or are transferred to it, you move to a different place or job within the same organisation. ▶ NOUN ③ the movement of something from one place to another. ④ a piece of paper with a design on one side which can be ironed or pressed onto cloth, paper or china. **transferable** ADJECTIVE

transfixed ADJECTIVE If a person is transfixed by something, they are so impressed or frightened by it that they cannot move • *Price stood transfixed at the sight of that tiny figure.*

transform, transforms, transforming, **transformed** VERB ① If something is transformed, it is changed completely • *The frown is transformed into a smile.* ② MATHS To transform a shape is to change how it looks, for example by translation, reflection, rotation or enlargement. **transformation** NOUN

transfusion, transfusions NOUN A transfusion or blood transfusion is a process in which blood from a healthy person is injected into the body of another person who is badly injured or ill.

transgender ADJECTIVE Someone who is transgender has a gender identity which does not fully correspond to the sex assigned to them at birth.

transient [Said tran-zee-ent] ADJECTIVE Something transient does not stay or exist for very long • *transient emotions.* **transience** NOUN

transistor, transistors NOUN ① a small electrical device in something such as a television or radio which is used to control electric currents. ② A transistor or a transistor radio is a small portable radio.

transit NOUN ① Transit is the carrying of goods or people by vehicle from one place to another. ▶ PHRASE ② People or things that are **in transit** are travelling or being taken from one place to another • *damage that had occurred in transit.*

transition, transitions NOUN PSHE a change from one form, state or stage of life to another • *the transition from war to peace.*

transitional ADJECTIVE A transitional period or stage is one during which something changes from one form or state to another.

transition metal, transition metals NOUN SCIENCE one of a group of metals which includes chromium, copper and gold. Transition metals have an incomplete penultimate electron shell, can have more than one valency, and tend to form compounds.

transitive ADJECTIVE In grammar, a transitive verb is a verb which has an object.

transitory ADJECTIVE lasting for only a short time.

translate, translates, translating, translated VERB ① To translate something that someone has said or written is to say it or write it in a different language. ② MATHS To translate a shape is to move it up or down, or from side to side, but not change it in any other way.
translation NOUN **translator** NOUN

translucent ADJECTIVE If something is translucent, light passes through it so that it seems to glow • *translucent petals.*

transmission, transmissions NOUN ① The transmission of something involves passing or sending it to a different place or person • *the transmission of infectious diseases.* ② The transmission of television or radio programmes is the broadcasting of them. ③ a broadcast.

transmit, transmits, transmitting, transmitted VERB ① When a message or an electronic signal is transmitted, it is sent by radio waves. ② To transmit something to a different place or person is to pass it or send it to the place or person • *the teacher's role in transmitting knowledge.*
transmitter NOUN

transparency, transparencies NOUN ① a small piece of photographic film which can be projected onto a screen. ② Transparency is the quality that an object or substance has if you can see through it.

transparent ADJECTIVE If an object or substance is transparent, you can see through it. **transparently** ADVERB
SIMILAR WORDS: clear, limpid, see-through

transpire, transpires, transpiring, transpired VERB ① (*formal*) When it transpires that something is the case, people discover that it is the case • *It transpired that he had flown off on holiday.* ② When something transpires, it happens • *You start to wonder what transpired between them.*

USAGE NOTE
Some people think that it is wrong to use *transpire* to mean 'happen'. However, it is very widely used in this sense, especially in spoken English.

transplant, transplants, transplanting, transplanted NOUN ① a process of removing something from one place and putting it in another • *a man who needs a heart transplant.* ▸ VERB ② When something is transplanted, it is moved to a different place.

transport, transports, transporting, transported NOUN ① Vehicles that you travel in are referred to as transport • *public transport.* ② Transport is the moving of goods or people from one place to another • *The prices quoted include* transport costs. ▶ **VERB** ③ When goods or people are transported from one place to another, they are moved there.

SIMILAR WORDS: ③ carry, convey, transfer

transportation NOUN
Transportation is the transporting of people and things from one place to another.

transpose, transposes, transposing, transposed VERB
① (formal) If you transpose something to a different place or position, you move it there. ② To transpose something also means to alter it to a different form, while keeping its essential features.
transposition NOUN

transverse ADJECTIVE SCIENCE
Transverse is used to describe something that is at right angles to something else • the transverse muscles run from side to side.

transvestite, transvestites NOUN a person who enjoys wearing clothes normally worn by people of the opposite gender.

trap, traps, trapping, trapped NOUN
① a piece of equipment or a hole that is carefully positioned in order to catch animals or birds. ② a trick that is intended to catch or deceive someone. ▶ **VERB** ③ Someone who traps animals catches them using traps. ④ If you trap someone, you trick them so that they do or say something which they did not want to. ⑤ If you are trapped somewhere, you cannot move or escape because something is blocking your way or holding you down. ⑥ If you are trapped, you are in an unpleasant situation that you cannot easily change. **trapper** NOUN
SIMILAR WORDS: ③ catch, snare ④ dupe, trick

trap door, trap doors NOUN a small horizontal door in a floor, ceiling or stage.

trapeze, trapezes NOUN a bar of wood or metal hanging from two ropes on which acrobats and gymnasts swing and perform skilful movements.

trapezium, trapeziums or trapezia [Said trap-**pee**-zee-um] NOUN MATHS a four-sided shape with two sides parallel to each other.

trappings PLURAL NOUN The trappings of a particular rank, position or state are the clothes or equipment that go with it.

trash NOUN ① Trash is rubbish • He picks up your trash on Mondays. ② (informal) If you say that something such as a book, painting or film is trash, you mean that it is not very good.

trauma, traumas [Said **traw**-ma] NOUN a very upsetting experience which causes great stress.

traumatic ADJECTIVE A traumatic experience is very upsetting.

travel, travels, travelling, travelled VERB ① To travel is to go from one place to another. ② When something reaches one place from another, you say that it travels there • Gossip travels fast. ▶ NOUN ③ Travel is the act of travelling • air travel. ④ (in plural) Someone's travels are the journeys that they make to places a long way from their home • my travels in the Himalayas. **traveller** NOUN
travelling ADJECTIVE
SIMILAR WORDS: ① go, journey

traveller's cheque, traveller's cheques NOUN Traveller's cheques are cheques for use abroad. You buy them at home and then exchange them when you are abroad for foreign currency.

traverse, traverses, traversing, traversed VERB (formal) If you traverse an area of land or water, you go across it or over it • *They have traversed the island from the west coast.*

travesty, travesties NOUN a very bad or ridiculous representation or imitation of something • *The case is a travesty of justice.*

trawl, trawls, trawling, trawled VERB When fishermen trawl, they drag a wide net behind a boat in order to catch fish.

trawler, trawlers NOUN a fishing boat that is used for trawling.

tray, trays NOUN a flat object with raised edges which is used for carrying food or drinks.

treacherous ADJECTIVE ① A treacherous person is likely to betray you and cannot be trusted. ② The ground or the sea can be described as treacherous when it is dangerous or unreliable • *treacherous mountain roads.* **treacherously** ADVERB SIMILAR WORDS: ① disloyal, untrustworthy

treachery NOUN Treachery is behaviour in which someone betrays their country or a person who trusts them.

treacle NOUN Treacle is a thick, sweet syrup used to make cakes and toffee • *treacle tart.*

tread, treads, treading, trod, trodden VERB ① If you tread on something, you walk on it or step on it. ② If you tread something into the ground or into a carpet, you crush it in by stepping on it • *bubblegum that has been trodden into the pavement.*
▸ NOUN ③ A person's tread is the sound they make with their feet as they walk • *his heavy tread.* ④ The tread of a tyre or shoe is the pattern of ridges on it that stops it slipping.

treadmill, treadmills NOUN ① an exercise machine with a continuous moving belt for walking or running on. ② Any task or job that you must keep doing even though it is unpleasant or tiring can be referred to as a treadmill • *My life is one constant treadmill of making music.*

treason NOUN Treason is the crime of betraying your country, for example by helping its enemies.

treasure, treasures, treasuring, treasured NOUN ① Treasure is a collection of gold, silver, jewels or other precious objects, especially one that has been hidden • *buried treasure.* ② Treasures are valuable works of art • *the finest art treasures in the world.*
▸ VERB ③ If you treasure something, you are very pleased that you have it and regard it as very precious • *He treasures his friendship with her.*
treasured ADJECTIVE

treasurer, treasurers NOUN a person who is in charge of the finance and accounts of an organisation.

Treasury NOUN The Treasury is the government department that deals with the country's finances.

treat, treats, treating, treated VERB ① If you treat someone in a particular way, you behave that way towards them. ② If you treat something in a particular way, you deal with it that way or see it that way • *We are now treating this case as murder.* ③ When a doctor treats a patient or an illness, he or she gives them medical care and attention. ④ If something such as wood or cloth is treated, a special substance is put on it in order to protect it or give it special properties • *The carpet's been treated with a stain protector.* ⑤ If you treat someone, you buy or arrange something special for them which they will enjoy. ▶ NOUN ⑥ If you give someone a treat, you buy or arrange something special for them which they will enjoy • *my birthday treat*.

treatment NOUN

treatise, treatises [*Said* **tree**-*tiz*] NOUN a long formal piece of writing about a particular subject.

treaty, treaties NOUN a written agreement between countries in which they agree to do something or to help each other.

treble, trebles, trebling, trebled VERB ① If something trebles or is trebled, it becomes three times greater in number or amount • *Next year we can treble that amount*. ▶ ADJECTIVE ② Treble means three times as large or three times as strong as previously • *a treble dose*.

tree, trees NOUN a large plant with a hard woody trunk, branches and leaves.

trek, treks, trekking, trekked VERB ① If you trek somewhere, you go on a long and difficult journey. ▶ NOUN ② a long and difficult journey, especially one made by walking.

WORD HISTORY: an Afrikaans word

trellis, trellises NOUN a frame made of horizontal and vertical strips of wood or metal and used to support plants.

tremble, trembles, trembling, trembled VERB ① If you tremble, you shake slightly, usually because you are frightened or cold. ② If something trembles, it shakes slightly. ③ If your voice trembles, it sounds unsteady, usually because you are frightened or upset.

trembling ADJECTIVE

tremendous ADJECTIVE ① large or impressive • *a tremendous size*. ② (*informal*) very good or pleasing

• *tremendous fun*. **tremendously** ADVERB

tremor, tremors NOUN ① a shaking movement of your body which you cannot control. ② an unsteady quality in your voice, for example when you are upset. ③ a small earthquake.

trench, trenches NOUN a long narrow channel dug into the ground.

trenchant [*Said* **trent**-*shent*] ADJECTIVE Trenchant writings or comments are bold and firmly expressed.

trench warfare NOUN HISTORY Trench warfare is a type of fighting between two armies who both take up positions in trenches to defend themselves.

trend, trends, trending, trended NOUN ① a change towards doing or being something different. ▶ VERB ② If a topic is trending on a social media site, it is being discussed by a large number of users.

trendy, trendier, trendiest ADJECTIVE (*informal*) Trendy things or people are fashionable.

trepidation NOUN (*formal*) Trepidation is fear or anxiety • *He saw the look of trepidation on my face*.

trespass, trespasses, trespassing, trespassed VERB If you trespass on someone's land or property, you go onto it without their permission.

trespasser NOUN

tresses PLURAL NOUN (*old-fashioned*) A woman's tresses are her long flowing hair.

trestle, trestles NOUN a wooden or metal structure that is used as one of the supports for a table.

trevally, trevallies NOUN an Australian and New Zealand fish that is caught for both food and sport.

tri- PREFIX three • *tricycle*.

triad, triads [Said **try-ad**] NOUN
① (formal) a group of three similar
things. ② MUSIC In music, a triad is
a chord of three notes consisting of
the tonic and the third and fifth
above it.

trial, trials NOUN ① the legal process
in which a judge and jury decide
whether a person is guilty of a
particular crime after listening to all
the evidence about it. ② an
experiment in which something is
tested • Trials of the drug start next
month.

triangle, triangles NOUN ① MATHS
a shape with three straight sides. ② a
percussion instrument consisting of
a thin steel bar bent in the shape of a
triangle. **triangular** ADJECTIVE

triangulation NOUN GEOGRAPHY
Triangulation is a method of
surveying land, in which the land is
divided into triangles and the areas
of the triangles are calculated.
triangulate VERB

triathlon, triathlons [Said tri-**ath**-lon]
NOUN a sports contest in which
athletes compete in three different
events.

tribe, tribes NOUN a group of people
of the same race, who have the same
customs, religion, language or land,
especially when they are thought to
be primitive. **tribal** ADJECTIVE

tribulation, tribulations NOUN
(formal) Tribulation is trouble or
suffering • the tribulations of everyday
life.

tribunal, tribunals [Said try-**byoo**-nl]
NOUN a special court or committee
appointed to deal with particular
problems • an industrial tribunal.

tributary, tributaries NOUN
GEOGRAPHY a stream or river that
flows into a larger river.

tribute, tributes NOUN ① A tribute is
something said or done to show
admiration and respect for someone
• Police paid tribute to her courage. ② If
one thing is a tribute to another, it is
the result of the other thing and
shows how good it is • His success has
been a tribute to hard work.

trice NOUN If someone does
something in a trice, they do it very
quickly.

triceps [Said try-**seps**] NOUN Your
triceps is the large muscle at the back
of your upper arm that straightens
your arm.

trick, tricks, tricking, tricked NOUN
① an action done to deceive
someone. ② Tricks are clever or
skilful actions done in order to
entertain people • magic tricks.
▶ VERB ③ If someone tricks you, they
deceive you.

trickery NOUN Trickery is deception
• He obtained the money by trickery.

trickle, trickles, trickling, trickled
VERB ① When a liquid trickles
somewhere, it flows slowly in a thin
stream. ② When people or things
trickle somewhere, they move there
slowly in small numbers or
quantities. ▶ NOUN ③ a thin stream
of liquid. ④ A trickle of people or
things is a small number or quantity
of them.

tricky, trickier, trickiest ADJECTIVE
difficult to do or deal with.

tricycle, tricycles NOUN a vehicle
similar to a bicycle but with two
wheels at the back and one at the
front.

trifle, trifles, trifling, trifled NOUN
① A trifle means a little • He seemed a
trifle annoyed. ② Trifles are things that
are not very important or valuable.
③ a cold pudding made of layers of
sponge cake, fruit, jelly and custard.
▶ VERB ④ If you trifle with someone

or something, you treat them in a disrespectful way • *He was not to be trifled with.*

trifling ADJECTIVE small and unimportant.

trigger, triggers, triggering, triggered NOUN ① the small lever on a gun which is pulled in order to fire it. ▶VERB ② If something triggers an event or triggers it off, it causes it to happen.

WORD HISTORY: from Dutch *trekken* meaning 'to pull'

trigonometry [*Said* trig-gon-**nom**-it-ree] NOUN [MATHS] Trigonometry is the branch of mathematics that is concerned with calculating the angles of triangles or the lengths of their sides.

trill, trills, trilling, trilled VERB If a bird trills, it sings with short high-pitched repeated notes.

trillion, trillions NOUN ① A trillion is a million million. This is shown as one followed by twelve zeros. ② (*informal*) Trillions of things means an extremely large number of them.

trilogy, trilogies NOUN a series of three books or plays that have the same characters or are on the same subject.

trim, trimmer, trimmest; trims, trimming, trimmed ADJECTIVE ① neat, tidy and attractive. ▶VERB ② To trim something is to clip small amounts off it. ③ If you trim off parts of something, you cut them off because they are not needed • *Trim off the excess marzipan.* ▶NOUN ④ If something is given a trim, it is cut a little • *All styles need a trim every six to eight weeks.* ⑤ a decoration on something, especially along its edges • *a velvet trim.* **trimmed** ADJECTIVE

trimming, trimmings NOUN Trimmings are extra parts added to

something for decoration or as a luxury • *a turkey dinner with all the trimmings.*

Trimurti NOUN [RE] In the Hindu religion, the Trimurti are the three deities Brahma, Vishnu and Shiva.

trinity NOUN ① [RE] In the Christian religion, the Trinity is the joining of God the Father, God the Son, and God the Holy Spirit. ② (*literary*) A trinity is a group of three things or people.

trinket, trinkets NOUN a cheap ornament or piece of jewellery.

trio, trios NOUN ① a group of three musicians who sing or play together; also a piece of music written for three instruments or singers. ② any group of three things or people together • *a trio of children's tales.*

trip, trips, tripping, tripped NOUN ① a journey made to a place. ▶VERB ② If you trip, you catch your foot on something and fall over. ③ If you trip someone or trip them up, you make them fall over by making them catch their foot on something.

SIMILAR WORDS: ① excursion, journey, outing

tripe NOUN Tripe is the stomach lining of a pig, cow or ox, which is cooked and eaten.

triple, triples, tripling, tripled ADJECTIVE ① consisting of three things or three parts • *the Triple Alliance.* ▶VERB ② If you triple something or if it triples, it becomes three times greater in number or size.

triplet, triplets NOUN Triplets are three children born at the same time to the same mother.

tripod, tripods [*Said* **try**-pod] NOUN a stand with three legs used to support something like a camera or telescope.

tripper, trippers NOUN a tourist or someone on an excursion.

trite ADJECTIVE dull and not original • *his trite novels*.

triumph, triumphs, triumphing, triumphed NOUN ① a great success or achievement. ② Triumph is a feeling of great satisfaction when you win or achieve something. ▸ VERB ③ If you triumph, you win a victory or succeed in overcoming something.

triumphal ADJECTIVE done or made to celebrate a victory or great success • *a triumphal return to Rome*.

triumphant ADJECTIVE Someone who is triumphant feels very happy because they have won a victory or have achieved something • *a triumphant shout*.

trivia PLURAL NOUN Trivia are unimportant things.

trivial ADJECTIVE Something trivial is unimportant.
WORD HISTORY: from Latin *trivialis* meaning 'found everywhere'

trod the past tense of **tread**.

trodden the past participle of **tread**.

troll, trolls, trolling, trolled NOUN ① an imaginary creature in Scandinavian mythology that lives in caves or mountains and is believed to turn to stone at daylight. ② (*slang*) a person who makes offensive or provocative posts on a website. ▸ VERB ③ (*slang*) If you troll, you deliberately make offensive or provocative posts on a website.

trolley, trolleys NOUN ① a small table on wheels. ② a small cart on wheels used for carrying heavy objects • *a supermarket trolley*.

trombone, trombones NOUN a brass wind instrument with a U-shaped slide which you move to produce different notes.

troop, troops, trooping, trooped NOUN ① Troops are soldiers. ② A troop of people or animals is a group of them. ▸ VERB ③ If people troop somewhere, they go there in a group.

trooper, troopers NOUN a low-ranking soldier in the cavalry.

trophic level, trophic levels NOUN SCIENCE A living organism's trophic level is a measure of how many organisms are below it on a food chain.

trophy, trophies NOUN ① a cup or shield given as a prize to the winner of a competition. ② something you keep to remember a success or victory.
WORD HISTORY: from Greek *trope* meaning 'defeat of the enemy'

tropical ADJECTIVE belonging to or typical of the tropics • *a tropical island*.

tropics PLURAL NOUN GEOGRAPHY The tropics are the hottest parts of the world, between two lines of latitude, the Tropic of Cancer, 23½° north of the equator, and the Tropic of Capricorn, 23½° south of the equator.

trot, trots, trotting, trotted VERB ① When a horse trots, it moves at a speed between a walk and a canter, lifting its feet quite high off the ground. ② If you trot, you run or jog using small quick steps. ▸ NOUN ③ When a horse breaks into a trot, it starts trotting.

trotter, trotters NOUN A pig's trotters are its feet.

trouble, troubles, troubling, troubled NOUN ① Troubles are difficulties or problems. ② If there is trouble, people are quarrelling or fighting • *There was more trouble after the match*. ▸ PHRASE ③ If you are **in trouble**, you are in a situation where you may be punished because you have done something wrong. ▸ VERB ④ If something troubles you, it

makes you feel worried or anxious.
⑤ If you trouble someone for
something, you disturb them in order
to ask them for it • *Can I trouble you for
some milk?* **troubling** ADJECTIVE
troubled ADJECTIVE
SIMILAR WORDS: ① difficulty,
problem, worry ⑤ bother,
inconvenience

troublesome ADJECTIVE causing
problems or difficulties • *a
troublesome cough.*

trough, troughs [*Said* **troff**] NOUN
① a long, narrow container from
which animals drink or feed.
② SCIENCE In weather forecasting,
a trough of low pressure is a long,
narrow area of low air pressure.

trounce, trounces, trouncing,
trounced VERB If you trounce
someone, you defeat them
completely.

troupe, troupes [*Said* **troop**] NOUN a
group of actors, singers or dancers
who work together and often travel
around together.

trousers PLURAL NOUN Trousers are a
piece of clothing covering the body
from the waist down, enclosing each
leg separately.
WORD HISTORY: from Gaelic *triubhas*

trout NOUN a type of freshwater fish.

trowel, trowels NOUN ① a small
garden tool with a curved, pointed
blade used for planting or weeding.
② a small tool with a flat blade used
for spreading cement or plaster.

truant, truants NOUN ① a child who
stays away from school without
permission. ▸ PHRASE ② If children
play truant, they stay away from
school without permission. **truancy**
NOUN

truce, truces NOUN an agreement
between two people or groups to
stop fighting for a short time.

truck, trucks NOUN ① a large motor
vehicle used for carrying heavy loads.
② an open vehicle used for carrying
goods on a railway.

truculent [*Said* **truk-yoo-lent**]
ADJECTIVE bad-tempered and
aggressive. **truculence** NOUN

trudge, trudges, trudging, trudged
VERB ① If you trudge, you walk with
slow, heavy steps. ▸ NOUN ② a slow
tiring walk • *the long trudge home.*

true, truer, truest ADJECTIVE ① A true
story or statement is based on facts
and is not made up. ② 'True' is used
to describe things or people that are
genuine • *She was a true friend.* ③ True
feelings are sincere and genuine.
▸ PHRASE ④ If something **comes
true**, it actually happens. **truly**
ADVERB
SIMILAR WORDS: ① accurate, correct,
factual

truffle, truffles NOUN ① a soft, round
sweet made from chocolate. ② a
round mushroom-like fungus which
grows underground and is
considered very good to eat.

trump, trumps NOUN In a game of
cards, trumps is the suit with the
highest value.

trumpet, trumpets, trumpeting,
trumpeted NOUN ① a brass wind
instrument with a narrow tube
ending in a bell-like shape. ▸ VERB
② When an elephant trumpets, it
makes a sound like a very loud
trumpet.

truncated ADJECTIVE Something
that is truncated is made shorter.

truncheon, truncheons [*Said
trunt-shn*] NOUN a stick carried by
police officers as a weapon,
especially the short, thick kind
formerly used by British police.
WORD HISTORY: from Old French
tronchon meaning 'stump'

trundle, trundles, trundling, trundled VERB If you trundle something or it trundles somewhere, it moves or rolls along slowly.

trunk, trunks NOUN ① the main stem of a tree from which the branches and roots grow. ② the main part of your body, excluding your head, neck, arms and legs. ③ the long flexible nose of an elephant. ④ a large, strong case or box with a hinged lid used for storing things. ⑤ (in plural) A man's trunks are his bathing pants or shorts. ⑥ in American English, the covered space in a car, usually at the back, for carrying things in.

truss, trusses, trussing, trussed VERB To truss someone or truss them up is to tie them up so that they cannot move.

trust, trusts, trusting, trusted VERB ① If you trust someone, you believe that they are honest and will not harm you. ② If you trust someone to do something, you believe they will do it successfully or properly. ③ If you trust someone with something, you give it to them or tell it to them • One member of the group cannot be trusted with the secret. ④ If you do not trust something, you feel that it is not safe or reliable • I didn't trust my arms and legs to work. ▶ NOUN ⑤ Trust is the responsibility you are given to deal with or look after important or secret things • He had built up a position of trust. ⑥ a financial arrangement in which an organisation looks after and invests money for someone.
trusting ADJECTIVE

trustee, trustees NOUN someone who is allowed by law to control money or property they are keeping or investing for another person.

trustworthy ADJECTIVE A trustworthy person is reliable and responsible and can be trusted.

trusty, trustier, trustiest ADJECTIVE Trusty things and animals are considered to be reliable because they have always worked well in the past • a trusty black labrador.

truth, truths NOUN ① The truth is the facts about something, rather than things that are imagined or made up • I know she was telling the truth. ② an idea or principle that is generally accepted to be true • the basic truths in life.
SIMILAR WORDS: ① fact, reality

truthful ADJECTIVE A truthful person is honest and tells the truth.
truthfully ADVERB

truth table, truth tables NOUN ICT a diagram that shows what the output of a computer circuit will be for every possible combination of inputs.

try, tries, trying, tried VERB ① To try to do something is to make an effort to do it. ② If you try something, you use it or do it to test how useful or enjoyable it is • Howard wanted me to try the cake. ③ When a person is tried, they appear in court and a judge and jury decide if they are guilty after hearing the evidence. ▶ NOUN ④ an attempt to do something. ⑤ a test of something • You gave it a try. ⑥ In rugby, a try is scored when someone carries the ball over the goal line of the opposing team and touches the ground with it.
SIMILAR WORDS: ① attempt, endeavour, strive ④ attempt, go, shot

GRAMMAR TIP
You can use try to in speech and writing: Try to get here on time for once. Try and is very common in speech, but you should avoid it in written work: Just try and stop me!

a b c d e f g h i j k l m n o p q r s **t** u v w x y z

trying ADJECTIVE A trying person or thing is difficult to deal with and makes you feel impatient or annoyed.

tryst, trysts [Said *trist*] NOUN an appointment or meeting, especially between lovers in a quiet, secret place.

tsar, tsars [Said *zar*]; also spelt **czar** NOUN a Russian emperor or king between 1547 and 1917.

tsarina, tsarinas [Said *zah-ree-na*]; also spelt **czarina** NOUN a female tsar or the wife of a tsar.

tsetse fly, tsetse flies [Said *tset-tsee*] NOUN an African fly that feeds on blood and causes serious diseases in people and animals.

T-shirt, T-shirts; also spelt **tee shirt** NOUN a simple short-sleeved cotton shirt with no collar.

tsunami, tsunamis NOUN GEOGRAPHY a large, often destructive sea wave, caused by an earthquake or volcanic eruption under the sea.
WORD HISTORY: from Japanese *tsunami* meaning 'harbour wave'

tuatara, tuatara or tuataras [Said *too-ah-tah-rah*] NOUN a large, lizard-like reptile found on certain islands off the coast of New Zealand.

tub, tubs NOUN ① a wide circular container. ② a bath.

tuba, tubas NOUN a large brass musical instrument that can produce very low notes.

tubby, tubbier, tubbiest ADJECTIVE rather fat.

tube, tubes NOUN ① a round, hollow pipe. ② a soft metal or plastic cylindrical container with a screw cap at one end • *a tube of toothpaste*.
tubing NOUN

tuberculosis [Said *tyoo-ber-kyoo-loe-siss*] NOUN Tuberculosis is a serious infectious disease affecting the lungs.

tubular ADJECTIVE in the shape of a tube.

TUC In Britain, the TUC is an association of trade unions. TUC is an abbreviation for 'Trades Union Congress'.

tuck, tucks, tucking, tucked VERB ① If you tuck something somewhere, you put it there so that it is safe or comfortable • *She tucked the letter into her handbag*. ② If you tuck a piece of fabric into or under something, you push the loose ends inside or under it to make it tidy. ③ If something is tucked away, it is in a quiet place where few people go • *a little house tucked away in a valley*.

tucker, tuckers, tuckering, tuckered (*informal*) NOUN ① In Australian and New Zealand English, tucker is food. ▶ VERB ② In Australian, New Zealand and American English, if you are tuckered out you are tired out.

Tudor, Tudors HISTORY NOUN Tudor was the family name of the English monarchs who reigned from 1485 to 1603.

Tuesday, Tuesdays NOUN Tuesday is the day between Monday and Wednesday.
WORD HISTORY: from Old English *tiwesdæg* meaning 'Tiw's day'; Tiw was the Scandinavian god of war and the sky

tuft, tufts NOUN A tuft of something such as hair is a bunch of it growing closely together.

tug, tugs, tugging, tugged VERB ① To tug something is to give it a quick, hard pull. ▶ NOUN ② a quick, hard pull • *He felt a tug at his arm*. ③ a small, powerful boat which tows large ships.

tug of war NOUN A tug of war is a sport in which two teams test their strength by pulling against each other on opposite ends of a rope.

tuition NOUN Tuition is the teaching of a subject, especially to one person or to a small group.

tulip, tulips NOUN a brightly coloured spring flower.

WORD HISTORY: from Turkish *tulbend* meaning 'turban', because of its shape

tumble, tumbles, tumbling, tumbled VERB ① To tumble is to fall with a rolling or bouncing movement. ▸ NOUN ② a fall.

tumbler, tumblers NOUN a drinking glass with straight sides.

tummy, tummies NOUN (informal) Your tummy is your stomach.

tumour, tumours [*Said tyoo-mur*] NOUN a mass of diseased or abnormal cells that has grown in a person's or animal's body.

tumultuous ADJECTIVE A tumultuous event or welcome is very noisy because people are happy or excited.

tuna, tuna [*Said tyoo-na*] NOUN Tuna are large fish that live in warm seas and are caught for food.

tundra NOUN GEOGRAPHY The tundra is a vast treeless Arctic region.

WORD HISTORY: a Russian word

tune, tunes, tuning, tuned NOUN ① a series of musical notes arranged in a particular way. ▸ VERB ② To tune a musical instrument is to adjust it so that it produces the right notes. ③ To tune an engine or machine is to adjust it so that it works well. ④ If you tune to a particular radio or television station you turn or press the controls to select the station you want to listen to or watch. ▸ PHRASE ⑤ If your voice or an instrument is **in tune**, it produces the right notes.

tuneful ADJECTIVE having a pleasant and easily remembered tune.

tuner, tuners NOUN A piano tuner is a person whose job it is to tune pianos.

tungsten NOUN SCIENCE Tungsten is a greyish-white metallic element used for electric light filaments and cutting tools. Its atomic number is 74 and its symbol is W.

tunic, tunics NOUN a sleeveless garment covering the top part of the body and reaching to the hips, thighs or knees.

Tunisian, Tunisians [*Said tyoo-niz-ee-an*] ADJECTIVE ① belonging or relating to Tunisia. ▸ NOUN ② someone who comes from Tunisia.

tunnel, tunnels, tunnelling, tunnelled NOUN ① a long underground passage. ▸ VERB ② To tunnel is to make a tunnel.

turban, turbans NOUN a head-covering worn by a Hindu, Muslim or Sikh man, consisting of a long piece of cloth wound round his head.

turbine, turbines NOUN a machine or engine in which power is produced when a stream of air, gas, water or steam pushes the blades of a wheel and makes it turn round.

WORD HISTORY: from Latin *turbo* meaning 'whirlwind'

turbot, turbot, turbots NOUN a large European flat fish that is caught for food.

turbulent ADJECTIVE ① A turbulent period of history is one where there is much uncertainty, and possibly violent change. ② Turbulent air or water currents make sudden changes of direction. **turbulence** NOUN

tureen, tureens [*Said tur-reen*] NOUN a large dish with a lid for serving soup.

turf, turves; turfs, turfing, turfed NOUN Turf is short, thick, even grass and the layer of soil beneath it.

a
b
c
d
e
f
g
h
i
j
k
l
m
n
o
p
q
r
s
t
u
v
w
x
y
z

turf out VERB (*informal*) To turf someone out is to force them to leave a place.

turgid [*Said* tur-jid] ADJECTIVE (*literary*) A turgid play, film or piece of writing is difficult to understand and rather boring.

Turk, Turks NOUN someone who comes from Turkey.

turkey, turkeys NOUN a large bird kept for food; also the meat of this bird.

Turkish ADJECTIVE ① belonging or relating to Turkey. ▶ NOUN ② Turkish is the main language spoken in Turkey.

turmoil NOUN Turmoil is a state of confusion, disorder or great anxiety • *Europe is in a state of turmoil*.

turn, turns, turning, turned VERB ① When you turn, you move so that you are facing or going in a different direction. ② When you turn something or when it turns, it moves or rotates so that it faces in a different direction or is in a different position. ③ If you turn your attention or thoughts to someone or something, you start thinking about them or discussing them. ④ When something turns or is turned into something else, it becomes something different • *A hobby can be turned into a career*. ▶ NOUN ⑤ an act of turning something so that it faces in a different direction or is in a different position. ⑥ a change in the way something is happening or being done • *Her career took a turn for the worse*. ⑦ If it is your turn to do something, you have the right, chance or duty to do it. ▶ PHRASE ⑧ **In turn** is used to refer to people, things or actions that are in sequence one after the other. **turn down** VERB If you turn down someone's request or offer, you refuse or reject it.

turn up VERB ① If someone or something turns up, they arrive or appear somewhere. ② If something turns up, it is found or discovered. SIMILAR WORDS: ⑦ chance, go, opportunity

turncoat, turncoats NOUN a person who leaves one political party or group for an opposing one.

turning, turnings NOUN a road which leads away from the side of another road.

turning effect, turning effects NOUN SCIENCE the effect of a force to make something rotate around a point. For example, effort applied to a lever produces a turning effect to work on a load at the other end.

turning point, turning points NOUN the moment when decisions are taken and events start to move in a different direction.

turnip, turnips NOUN a round root vegetable with a white or yellow skin.

turnout, turnouts NOUN The turnout at an event is the number of people who go to it.

turnover, turnovers NOUN ① The turnover of people in a particular organisation or group is the rate at which people leave it and are replaced by others. ② The turnover of a company is the value of the goods or services sold during a particular period.

turnstile, turnstiles NOUN a revolving mechanical barrier at the entrance to places like football grounds or zoos.

turpentine NOUN Turpentine is a strong-smelling colourless liquid used for cleaning and for thinning paint.

turps NOUN (*informal*) Turps is turpentine.

turquoise [Said *tur-kwoyz*] NOUN or ADJECTIVE ① light bluish-green. ▸ NOUN ② Turquoise is a bluish-green stone used in jewellery.

turret, turrets NOUN a small narrow tower on top of a larger tower or other buildings.

turtle, turtles NOUN a large reptile with a thick shell covering its body and flippers for swimming. It lays its eggs on land but lives the rest of its life in the sea.

tusk, tusks NOUN The tusks of an elephant, wild boar or walrus are the pair of long curving pointed teeth it has.

tussle, tussles NOUN an energetic fight or argument between two people, especially about something they both want.

tutor, tutors, tutoring, tutored NOUN ① a teacher at a college or university. ② a private teacher. ▸ VERB ③ If someone tutors a person or subject, they teach that person or subject.

tutorial, tutorials NOUN a teaching session involving a tutor and a small group of students.

tutu, tutus [Said *too-too*] NOUN a short, stiff skirt worn by female ballet dancers.

TV, TVs NOUN ① TV is television. ② a television set.

twang, twangs, twanging, twanged NOUN ① a sound like the one made by pulling and then releasing a tight wire. ② A twang is a nasal quality in a person's voice. ▸ VERB ③ If a tight wire or string twangs or you twang it, it makes a sound as it is pulled and then released.

tweak, tweaks, tweaking, tweaked VERB ① If you tweak something, you twist it or pull it. ▸ NOUN ② a short twist or pull of something.

twee ADJECTIVE sweet and pretty but in bad taste or sentimental.

tweed, tweeds NOUN Tweed is a thick woollen cloth.

tweet, tweets, tweeting, tweeted VERB ① When a small bird tweets, it makes a short, high-pitched sound. ② If you tweet, you send a message on the social networking site Twitter. ▸ NOUN ③ a short high-pitched sound made by a small bird. ④ a message sent on the social networking site Twitter.

tweezers PLURAL NOUN Tweezers are a small tool with two arms which can be closed together and are used for pulling out hairs or picking up small objects.

twelve the number 12. **twelfth** ADJECTIVE

twenty, twenties the number 20. **twentieth** ADJECTIVE

twice ADVERB Twice means two times.

twiddle, twiddles, twiddling, twiddled VERB To twiddle something is to twist it or turn it quickly.

twig, twigs NOUN a very small thin branch growing from a main branch of a tree or bush.

twilight [Said *twy-lite*] NOUN ① Twilight is the time after sunset when it is just getting dark. ② The twilight of something is the final stages of it • *the twilight of his career*.

twin, twins NOUN ① If two people are twins, they have the same mother and were born on the same day. ② 'Twin' is used to describe two similar things that are close together or happen together • *the little twin islands*.

twine, twines, twining, twined NOUN ① Twine is strong smooth string. ▸ VERB ② If you twine one

a b c d e f g h i j k l m n o p q r s **t** u v w x y z

thing round another, you twist or wind it round.

twinge, twinges NOUN ① a sudden, unpleasant feeling • *a twinge of jealousy*. ② a sudden sharp pain • *a twinge in my lower back*.

twinkle, twinkles, twinkling, twinkled VERB ① If something twinkles, it sparkles or seems to sparkle with an unsteady light • *Her green eyes twinkled.* ▸ NOUN ② a sparkle or brightness that something has.

twirl, twirls, twirling, twirled VERB If something twirls, or if you twirl it, it spins or twists round and round.

twist, twists, twisting, twisted VERB ① When you twist something you turn one end of it in one direction while holding the other end or turning it in the opposite direction. ② When something twists or is twisted, it moves or bends into a strange shape. ③ If you twist a part of your body, you injure it by turning it too sharply or in an unusual direction • *I've twisted my ankle.* ④ If you twist something that someone has said, you change the meaning slightly. ▸ NOUN ⑤ a twisting action or motion. ⑥ an unexpected development or event in a story or film, especially at the end • *Each day now seemed to bring a new twist to the story.*
SIMILAR WORDS: ① coil, wind ② contort, distort

twisted ADJECTIVE ① Something twisted has been bent or moved into a strange shape • *a tangle of twisted metal*. ② If someone's mind or behaviour is twisted, it is unpleasantly abnormal • *He's bitter and twisted.*

twit, twits NOUN (*informal*) a silly person.

twitch, twitches, twitching, twitched VERB ① If you twitch, you make little jerky movements which you cannot control. ② If you twitch something, you give it a little jerk in order to move it. ▸ NOUN ③ a little jerky movement.

twitter, twitters, twittering, twittered VERB When birds twitter, they make short high-pitched sounds.

two the number 2.

SPELLING TIP
Do not confuse the spelling of the preposition *to*, the adverb *too*, and the number *two*.

two-dimensional ADJECTIVE MATHS A two-dimensional shape has height and width but not depth.

two-faced ADJECTIVE A two-faced person is not honest in the way they behave towards other people.

twofold ADJECTIVE Something twofold has two equally important parts or reasons • *Their concern was twofold: personal and political*.

twosome, twosomes [*Said too-sum*] NOUN two people or things that are usually seen together.

two-time, two-times, two-timing, two-timed VERB (*informal*) If you two-time your boyfriend or girlfriend, you deceive them, by having a romantic relationship with someone else without telling them.

two-up NOUN In Australia and New Zealand, two-up is a popular gambling game in which two coins are tossed and bets are placed on whether they land heads or tails.

tycoon, tycoons NOUN a person who is successful in business and has become rich and powerful.
WORD HISTORY: from Chinese *ta* + *chun* meaning 'great ruler'

type, types, typing, typed NOUN ①A type of something is a class of it that has common features and belongs to a larger group of related things • *What type of dog should we get?* ②A particular type of person has a particular appearance or quality • *Andrea is the type who likes to play safe.* ▶VERB ③If you type something, you use a typewriter or computer keyboard to write it.

typewriter, typewriters NOUN a machine with a keyboard with individual keys which are pressed to produce letters and numbers on a page.

typhoid [Said **tie**-foyd] NOUN Typhoid, or typhoid fever, is an infectious disease caused by dirty water or food. It produces fever and can kill.

typhoon, typhoons NOUN GEOGRAPHY a very violent tropical storm.
WORD HISTORY: from Chinese *tai fung* meaning 'great wind'

typhus NOUN Typhus is an infectious disease transmitted by lice or mites. It results in fever, severe headaches and a skin rash.

typical ADJECTIVE showing the most usual characteristics or behaviour.
typically ADVERB
SIMILAR WORDS: characteristic, standard, usual

typify, typifies, typifying, typified VERB If something typifies a situation or thing, it is characteristic of it or a typical example of it • *This story is one that typifies our times.*

typing NOUN Typing is the work or activity of producing something on a typewriter or computer keyboard.

typist, typists NOUN ①a person whose job is typing. ②a person who types in a particular way • *a painfully slow typist.*

tyrannosaurus, tyrannosauruses [Said tir-ran-oh-**saw**-russ] NOUN a very large meat-eating dinosaur which walked upright on its hind legs.
WORD HISTORY: from Greek *turannos* meaning 'tyrant' and *sauros* meaning 'lizard'

tyranny, tyrannies NOUN ①A tyranny is cruel and unjust rule of people by a person or group • *the evils of Nazi tyranny.* ②You can refer to something which is not human but is harsh as tyranny • *the tyranny of fate.*
tyrannical ADJECTIVE

tyrant, tyrants NOUN a person who treats the people he or she has authority over cruelly and unjustly.

tyre, tyres NOUN a thick ring of rubber fitted round each wheel of a vehicle and filled with air.

SPELLING TIP
Do not confuse the spellings of *tyre* and *tire*: *Jonny's car needs a new front tyre; Since my illness I tire easily.*

a
b
c
d
e
f
g
h
i
j
k
l
m
n
o
p
q
r
s
t
u
v
w
x
y
z

Uu

ubiquitous [Said yoo-**bik**-wit-tuss] **ADJECTIVE** Something that is ubiquitous seems to be everywhere at the same time • *the ubiquitous jeans*.
WORD HISTORY: from Latin *ubique* meaning 'everywhere'

ubuntu [Said oo-**boon**-too] **NOUN** In South Africa, ubuntu is the principle of behaving humanely and kindly towards other people.

udder, udders **NOUN** the baglike organ that hangs below a cow's body and produces milk.

UFO, UFOs **NOUN** a strange object seen in the sky, which some people believe to be a spaceship from another planet. UFO is an abbreviation for 'unidentified flying object'.

Ugandan, Ugandans [Said yoo-**gan**-dan] **ADJECTIVE** ① belonging or relating to Uganda. ▶ **NOUN** ② someone who comes from Uganda.

ugly, uglier, ugliest **ADJECTIVE** very unattractive in appearance.
SIMILAR WORDS: unattractive, unsightly
WORD HISTORY: from Old Norse *uggligr* meaning 'terrifying'

UK an abbreviation for **United Kingdom**.

ulcer, ulcers **NOUN** a sore area on the skin or inside the body, which takes a long time to heal • *stomach ulcers*.
ulcerous ADJECTIVE

ulterior [Said ul-**teer**-ee-or] **ADJECTIVE** If you have an ulterior motive for doing something, you have a hidden reason for it.

ultimate ADJECTIVE ① final or eventual • *a gold medal is the ultimate goal*. ② most important or powerful • *the ultimate ambition of any player*. ▶ **NOUN** ③ You can refer to the best or most advanced example of something as the ultimate • *This hotel is the ultimate in luxury*. **ultimately ADVERB**

ultimatum, ultimatums [Said ul-tim-**may**-tum] **NOUN** a warning stating that unless someone meets your conditions, you will take action against them.

ultra- **PREFIX** Ultra- is used to form adjectives describing something as having a quality to an extreme degree • *the ultra-competitive world of sport today*.

ultramarine NOUN or **ADJECTIVE** bright blue.
WORD HISTORY: from Latin *ultramarinus* meaning 'beyond the sea', because the pigment was imported from abroad

ultrasonic ADJECTIVE An ultrasonic sound has a very high frequency that cannot be heard by the human ear.

ultrasound NOUN SCIENCE Ultrasound is sound which cannot be heard by the human ear because its frequency is too high.

ultraviolet ADJECTIVE SCIENCE Ultraviolet light is not visible to the human eye. It is a form of radiation that causes your skin to darken after being exposed to the sun.

umbilical cord, umbilical cords [Said um-**bil**-lik-kl] NOUN SCIENCE the tube of blood vessels which connects an unborn baby to its mother and through which the baby receives nutrients and oxygen.

umbrella, umbrellas NOUN a device that you use to protect yourself from the rain. It consists of a folding frame covered in cloth attached to a long stick.

umpire, umpires, umpiring, umpired NOUN ① The umpire in cricket or tennis is the person who makes sure that the game is played according to the rules and who makes a decision if there is a dispute. ▶ VERB ② If you umpire a game, you are the umpire.

umpteen ADJECTIVE (informal) very many • *tomatoes and umpteen other plants.* **umpteenth** ADJECTIVE

un- PREFIX Un- is added to the beginning of many words to form a word with the opposite meaning • *an uncomfortable chair* • *He unlocked the door.*

unabashed ADJECTIVE not embarrassed or discouraged by something • *Samuel was unabashed.*

unabated ADJECTIVE OR ADVERB continuing without any reduction in intensity or amount • *The noise continued unabated.*

unable ADJECTIVE If you are unable to do something, you cannot do it.

unacceptable ADJECTIVE If you find something unacceptable, you disapprove of it because you think it is of a very low standard.

unaccompanied ADJECTIVE alone.

unaccustomed ADJECTIVE If you are unaccustomed to something, you are not used to it.

unaffected ADJECTIVE ① not changed in any way by a particular thing • *unaffected by the recession.* ② behaving in a natural and genuine way • *the most down-to-earth, unaffected person I've ever met.*

unaided ADVERB OR ADJECTIVE without help • *He was incapable of walking unaided.*

unambiguous ADJECTIVE An unambiguous statement has only one meaning.

unanimous [Said yoon-**nan**-nim-mus] ADJECTIVE When people are unanimous, they all agree about something. **unanimously** ADVERB **unanimity** NOUN WORD HISTORY: from Latin *unanimus* meaning 'of one mind'

unannounced ADJECTIVE happening unexpectedly and without warning.

unarmed ADJECTIVE not carrying any weapons.

unassuming ADJECTIVE modest and quiet.

unattached ADJECTIVE An unattached person is not married and is not having a steady relationship with someone.

unattended ADJECTIVE not being watched or looked after • *an unattended handbag.*

unauthorised; also spelt **unauthorized** ADJECTIVE done without official permission • *unauthorised parking.*

unavoidable ADJECTIVE unable to be prevented or avoided.

unaware ADJECTIVE If you are unaware of something, you do not know about it.

GRAMMAR TIP
Unaware is usually followed by *of* or *that*.

a
b
c
d
e
f
g
h
i
j
k
l
m
n
o
p
q
r
s
t
u
v
w
x
y
z

unawares ADVERB If something catches you unawares, it happens when you are not expecting it.

SPELLING TIP

Do not confuse *unawares* with the adjective *unaware*.

---

unbalanced ADJECTIVE ① with more weight or emphasis on one side than the other • *an unbalanced load* • *an unbalanced relationship*. ② slightly mad. ③ made up of parts that do not work well together • *an unbalanced lifestyle*. ④ An unbalanced account of something is an unfair one because it emphasises some things and ignores others.

unbearable ADJECTIVE Something unbearable is so unpleasant or upsetting that you feel you cannot stand it • *The pain was unbearable*. **unbearably** ADVERB
SIMILAR WORDS: insufferable, intolerable

unbeatable ADJECTIVE Something that is unbeatable is the best thing of its kind.

unbelievable ADJECTIVE
① extremely great or surprising • *unbelievable courage*. ② so unlikely that you cannot believe it.
unbelievably ADVERB
SIMILAR WORDS: ① astonishing, incredible ② far-fetched, implausible

unborn ADJECTIVE not yet born.

unbroken ADJECTIVE continuous or complete • *ten days of almost unbroken sunshine*.

uncanny ADJECTIVE strange and difficult to explain • *an uncanny resemblance*.
WORD HISTORY: from Scottish *uncanny* meaning 'unreliable' or 'not safe to deal with'

uncertain ADJECTIVE ① not knowing what to do • *For a minute he looked*

uncertain. ② doubtful or not known • *The outcome of the war was uncertain*.
uncertainty NOUN

unchallenged ADJECTIVE accepted without any questions being asked • *an unchallenged decision*.

uncharacteristic ADJECTIVE not typical or usual • *My father reacted with uncharacteristic speed*.

uncivilised; also spelt **uncivilized** ADJECTIVE unacceptable, for example by being very cruel or rude • *the uncivilised behaviour of football hooligans*.

uncle, **uncles** NOUN Your uncle is the brother of your mother or father, or the husband of one of your parents' siblings.

unclean ADJECTIVE dirty • *unclean water*.

unclear ADJECTIVE confusing and not obvious.

uncomfortable ADJECTIVE ① If you are uncomfortable, you are not physically relaxed and feel slight pain or discomfort. ② Uncomfortable also means slightly worried or embarrassed. **uncomfortably** ADVERB

uncommon ADJECTIVE ① not happening often or not seen often. ② unusually great • *She had read Cecilia's last letter with uncommon interest*. **uncommonly** ADVERB

uncompromising ADJECTIVE determined not to change an opinion or aim in any way • *an uncompromising approach to life*. **uncompromisingly** ADVERB

unconcerned ADJECTIVE not interested in something or not worried about it.

unconditional ADJECTIVE with no conditions or limitations • *a full three-year unconditional guarantee*.
unconditionally ADVERB

A B C D E F G H I J K L M N O P Q R S T U V W X Y Z

unconscious ADJECTIVE ① Someone who is unconscious is asleep or in a state similar to sleep as a result of a shock, accident or injury. ② If you are unconscious of something, you are not aware of it. **unconsciously** ADVERB **unconsciousness** NOUN

uncontrollable ADJECTIVE If someone or something is uncontrollable, they or it cannot be controlled or stopped • *uncontrollable anger*. **uncontrollably** ADVERB

unconventional ADJECTIVE not behaving in the same way as most other people.

unconvinced ADJECTIVE not at all certain that something is true or right • *Some critics remain unconvinced by the plan*.

uncouth [*Said un-kooth*] ADJECTIVE bad-mannered and unpleasant. SIMILAR WORDS: boorish, coarse, vulgar

uncover, uncovers, uncovering, uncovered VERB ① If you uncover a secret, you find it out. ② To uncover something is to remove the cover or lid from it.

undaunted ADJECTIVE If you are undaunted by something disappointing, you are not discouraged by it.

undecided ADJECTIVE If you are undecided, you have not yet made a decision about something.

undemanding ADJECTIVE not difficult to do or deal with • *undemanding work*.

undeniable ADJECTIVE certainly true • *undeniable evidence*. **undeniably** ADVERB

under PREPOSITION ① below or beneath. ② You can use 'under' to say that a person or thing is affected by a particular situation or condition • *The country was under threat* • *It is wrong to keep animals under unnatural conditions*. ③ If someone studies or works under a particular person, that person is their teacher or their boss. ④ less than • *under five kilometres* • *children under the age of 14*. ▶ PHRASE ⑤ **Under way** means already started • *A murder investigation is already under way*.

under- PREFIX Under- is used in words that describe something as being below, not being provided to a sufficient extent, or not having happened to a sufficient extent.

underarm ADJECTIVE ① under your arm • *underarm hair*. ▶ ADVERB ② If you throw a ball underarm, you throw it without raising your arm over your shoulder.

undercarriage, undercarriages NOUN the part of an aircraft, including the wheels, that supports the aircraft when it is on the ground.

underclass NOUN The underclass is the people in society who are the most poor and whose situation is unlikely to improve.

underclothes PLURAL NOUN Your underclothes are the clothes that you wear under your other clothes and next to your skin.

undercover ADJECTIVE involving secret work to obtain information • *a police undercover operation*.

undercurrent, undercurrents NOUN a weak, partly hidden feeling that may become stronger later.

undercut, undercuts, undercutting, undercut VERB ① To undercut someone's prices is to sell a product more cheaply than they do. ② If something undercuts your attempts to achieve something, it prevents them from being effective.

underdeveloped ADJECTIVE An underdeveloped country does not

a
b
c
d
e
f
g
h
i
j
k
l
m
n
o
p
q
r
s
t
u
v
w
x
y
z

have modern industries, and usually has a low standard of living.

underdog, underdogs NOUN The underdog in a competition is the person who seems likely to lose.

underestimate, underestimates, underestimating, underestimated VERB If you underestimate something or someone, you do not realise how large, great or capable they are.

underfoot ADJECTIVE or ADVERB under your feet • *the icy ground underfoot.*

undergo, undergoes, undergoing, underwent, undergone VERB If you undergo something unpleasant, it happens to you.

underground ADJECTIVE or ADVERB ① below the surface of the ground. ② secret, unofficial and usually illegal. ▶ NOUN ③ The underground is a railway system in which trains travel in tunnels below ground.

undergrowth NOUN Small bushes and plants growing under trees are called the undergrowth.

underhand ADJECTIVE secret and dishonest • *underhand behaviour.*

underlie, underlies, underlying, underlay, underlain VERB The thing that underlies a situation is the cause or basis of it. **underlying** ADJECTIVE

underline, underlines, underlining, underlined VERB ① If something underlines a feeling or a problem, it emphasises it. ② If you underline a word or sentence, you draw a line under it.

underling, underlings NOUN someone who is less important than someone else in rank or status.

undermine, undermines, undermining, undermined VERB To undermine an idea, feeling or system is to make it less strong or secure

• *You're trying to undermine my confidence again.*

SIMILAR WORDS: subvert, weaken
WORD HISTORY: from the practice in warfare of digging tunnels under enemy fortifications in order to make them collapse

underneath PREPOSITION ① below or beneath. ▶ ADVERB or PREPOSITION ② Underneath describes feelings and qualities that do not show in your behaviour • *Alex knew that underneath she was shattered.* ▶ ADJECTIVE ③ The underneath part of something is the part that touches or faces the ground.

underpants PLURAL NOUN Underpants are a piece of clothing worn by men and boys under their trousers.

underpass, underpasses NOUN a road or footpath that goes under a road or railway.

underpin, underpins, underpinning, underpinned VERB If something underpins something else, it helps it to continue by supporting and strengthening it • *Australian skill is usually underpinned by an immense team spirit.*

underprivileged ADJECTIVE Underprivileged people have less money and fewer opportunities than other people.

underrate, underrates, underrating, underrated VERB If you underrate someone, you do not realise how clever or valuable they are.

understand, understands, understanding, understood VERB ① If you understand what someone says, you know what they mean. ② If you understand a situation, you know what is happening and why.

③ If you say that you understand that something is the case, you mean that you have heard that it is the case • *I understand that she's a lot better now.*
SIMILAR WORDS: ① comprehend, follow, grasp, see

understandable ADJECTIVE If something is understandable, people can easily understand it.
understandably ADVERB

understanding, understandings NOUN ① If you have an understanding of something, you have some knowledge about it. ② an informal agreement between people. ▶ ADJECTIVE ③ kind and sympathetic.
SIMILAR WORDS: ① comprehension, grasp, perception

understatement, understatements NOUN a statement that does not say fully how true something is • *To say I was pleased was an understatement.*

understood the past tense and past participle of **understand**.

understudy, understudies NOUN someone who has learnt a part in a play so that they can act it if the main actor or actress is ill.

undertake, undertakes, undertaking, undertook, undertaken VERB When you undertake a task or job, you agree to do it.

undertaker, undertakers NOUN someone whose job is to prepare bodies for burial and arrange funerals.

undertaking, undertakings NOUN a task which you have agreed to do.

undertone, undertones NOUN ① If you say something in an undertone, you say it very quietly. ② If something has undertones of a particular kind, it indirectly suggests ideas of this kind • *unsettling undertones of anger.*

undertook the past tense of **undertake**.

undervalue, undervalues, undervaluing, undervalued VERB If you undervalue something, you think it is less important than it really is.

underwater ADVERB OR ADJECTIVE ① beneath the surface of the sea, a river or a lake. ▶ ADJECTIVE ② designed to work in water • *an underwater camera.*

underwear NOUN Your underwear is the clothing that you wear under your other clothes, next to your skin.

underwent the past tense of **undergo**.

underworld NOUN You can refer to organised crime and the people who are involved in it as the underworld.

undesirable ADJECTIVE unwelcome and likely to cause harm • *undesirable behaviour.*

undid the past tense of **undo**.

undisputed ADJECTIVE definite and without any doubt • *the undisputed champion.*

undivided ADJECTIVE If you give something your undivided attention, you concentrate on it totally.

undo, undoes, undoing, undid, undone VERB ① If you undo something that is tied up, you untie it. ② If you undo something that has been done, you reverse the effect of it.

undoing NOUN If something is someone's undoing, it is the cause of their failure.

undoubted ADJECTIVE You use 'undoubted' to emphasise something • *The event was an undoubted success.*
undoubtedly ADVERB

a
b
c
d
e
f
g
h
i
j
k
l
m
n
o
p
q
r
s
t
u
v
w
x
y
z

undress, undresses, undressing, undressed VERB When you undress, you take off your clothes.

undue ADJECTIVE greater than is reasonable • *undue pressure*. **unduly** ADVERB

undulating ADJECTIVE (*formal*) moving gently up and down • *undulating hills*.

undying ADJECTIVE lasting forever • *his undying love for his wife*.

unearth, unearths, unearthing, unearthed VERB If you unearth something that is hidden, you discover it.

unearthly ADJECTIVE strange and unnatural.

uneasy ADJECTIVE If you are uneasy, you feel worried that something may be wrong. **unease** NOUN **uneasily** ADVERB **uneasiness** NOUN

unemployed ADJECTIVE ① without a job • *an unemployed mechanic*. ▶ PLURAL NOUN ② The unemployed are all the people who are without a job.

unemployment NOUN Unemployment is the state of being without a job.

unending ADJECTIVE Something unending has continued for a long time and seems as if it will never stop • *unending joy*.

unenviable ADJECTIVE An unenviable situation is one that you would not like to be in.

unequal ADJECTIVE ① An unequal society does not offer the same opportunities and privileges to all people. ② Unequal things are different in size, strength or ability.

uneven ADJECTIVE ① An uneven surface is not level or smooth. ② not the same or consistent • *six lines of uneven length*. **unevenly** ADVERB

uneventful ADJECTIVE An uneventful period of time is one when nothing interesting happens.

unexpected ADJECTIVE Something unexpected is surprising because it was not thought likely to happen. **unexpectedly** ADVERB

unfailing ADJECTIVE continuous and not weakening as time passes • *his unfailing cheerfulness*.

unfair ADJECTIVE not right or just. **unfairly** ADVERB

unfaithful ADJECTIVE If someone is unfaithful, they are not loyal.

unfamiliar ADJECTIVE If something is unfamiliar to you, or if you are unfamiliar with it, you have not seen or heard it before.

unfashionable ADJECTIVE Something that is unfashionable is not popular or is no longer used by many people.

unfavourable ADJECTIVE not encouraging or promising, or not providing any advantage.

unfit ADJECTIVE ① If you are unfit, your body is not in good condition because you have not been taking enough exercise. ② Something that is unfit for a particular purpose is not suitable for that purpose.

unfold, unfolds, unfolding, unfolded VERB ① When a situation unfolds, it develops and becomes known. ② If you unfold something that has been folded, you open it out so that it is flat.

unfollow, unfollows, unfollowing, unfollowed VERB If you unfollow a person on a social networking site, you stop reading his or her messages.

unforeseen ADJECTIVE happening unexpectedly.

unforgettable ADJECTIVE Something unforgettable is so good or so bad that you are unlikely to forget it. **unforgettably** ADVERB

unforgivable ADJECTIVE Something unforgivable is so bad or cruel that it can never be forgiven or justified. **unforgivably** ADVERB

unfortunate ADJECTIVE ① Someone who is unfortunate is unlucky. ② If you describe an event as unfortunate, you mean that it is a pity that it happened • *an unfortunate accident.* **unfortunately** ADVERB

unfounded ADJECTIVE Something that is unfounded has no evidence to support it • *unfounded allegations.*

unfriend, unfriends, unfriending, **unfriended** VERB If you unfriend a person on a social networking site, you remove them from your list of friends so that you no longer have contact.

unfriendly ADJECTIVE ① A person who is unfriendly is not pleasant to you. ② A place that is unfriendly makes you feel uncomfortable or is not welcoming.

ungainly ADJECTIVE moving in an awkward or clumsy way.
WORD HISTORY: from Old Norse *ungegn* meaning 'not straight'

ungrateful ADJECTIVE not grateful or thankful.

unhappy, unhappier, unhappiest ADJECTIVE ① sad and depressed. ② not pleased or satisfied • *I am unhappy at being left out.* ③ If you describe a situation as an unhappy one, you are sorry that it exists • *an unhappy state of affairs.* **unhappily** ADVERB **unhappiness** NOUN

unhealthy ADJECTIVE ① likely to cause illness • *an unhealthy lifestyle.* ② An unhealthy person is often ill.

unheard-of ADJECTIVE never having happened before and therefore surprising or shocking.

unhinged ADJECTIVE Someone who is unhinged is mentally unbalanced.

unhurried ADJECTIVE Unhurried is used to describe actions or movements that are slow and relaxed.

unicellular ADJECTIVE SCIENCE consisting of only one cell.

unicorn, unicorns NOUN an imaginary animal that looks like a white horse with a straight horn growing from its forehead.
WORD HISTORY: from Latin *unicornis* meaning 'having one horn'

unidentified ADJECTIVE You say that someone or something is unidentified when nobody knows who or what they are.

uniform, uniforms NOUN ① a special set of clothes worn by people at work or school. ▶ ADJECTIVE ② Something that is uniform does not vary but is even and regular throughout. **uniformity** NOUN

unify, unifies, unifying, unified VERB If you unify a number of things, you bring them together. **unification** NOUN

unilateral ADJECTIVE A unilateral decision or action is one taken by only one of several groups involved in a particular situation. **unilaterally** ADVERB

unimaginable ADJECTIVE impossible to imagine or understand properly • *a fairyland of unimaginable beauty.*

unimportant ADJECTIVE having very little significance or importance.
SIMILAR WORDS: insignificant, minor, trivial

uninhabited ADJECTIVE An uninhabited place is a place where nobody lives.

uninhibited ADJECTIVE If you are uninhibited, you behave freely and naturally and show your true feelings.

a b c d e f g h i j k l m n o p q r s t **u** v w x y z

unintelligible ADJECTIVE (formal) impossible to understand.

uninterested ADJECTIVE If you are uninterested in something, you are not interested in it.

uninterrupted ADJECTIVE continuing without breaks or interruptions • uninterrupted views.

union, unions NOUN ① an organisation of people or groups with mutual interests, especially workers aiming to improve their pay and conditions. ② When the union of two things takes place, they are joined together to become one thing.

unique [Said yoo-neek] ADJECTIVE ① being the only one of its kind. ② If something is unique to one person or thing, it concerns or belongs to that person or thing only • trees and vegetation unique to the Canary islands. **uniquely** ADVERB **uniqueness** NOUN

USAGE NOTE
Something is either unique or not unique, so you should avoid saying things like rather unique or very unique.

unisex ADJECTIVE designed to be used by both men and women • unisex clothing.

unison NOUN If a group of people do something in unison, they all do it together at the same time.
WORD HISTORY: from Latin unisonus meaning 'making the same musical sound'

unit, units NOUN ① If you consider something as a unit, you consider it as a single complete thing. ② a group of people who work together at a particular job • the Police Support Unit. ③ a machine or piece of equipment which has a particular function • a remote control unit. ④ A unit of measurement is a fixed standard that is used for measuring things.

unite, unites, uniting, united VERB If a number of people unite, they join together and act as a group.

United Kingdom NOUN The United Kingdom consists of Great Britain and Northern Ireland.

United Nations NOUN The United Nations is an international organisation which tries to encourage peace, cooperation and friendship between countries.

unity NOUN Where there is unity, people are in agreement and act together for a particular purpose.

universal ADJECTIVE concerning or relating to everyone in the world or every part of the universe • Music and sports programmes have a universal appeal • universal destruction. **universally** ADVERB

universe, universes NOUN The universe is the whole of space, including all the stars and planets.

university, universities NOUN a place where students study for degrees.

unjust ADJECTIVE not fair or reasonable. **unjustly** ADVERB

unjustified ADJECTIVE If a belief or action is unjustified, there is no good reason for it.

unkempt ADJECTIVE untidy and not looked after properly • unkempt hair.

unkind ADJECTIVE unpleasant and rather cruel. **unkindly** ADVERB **unkindness** NOUN
SIMILAR WORDS: cruel, nasty, uncharitable

unknown ADJECTIVE ① If someone or something is unknown, people do not know about them or have not heard of them. ▶ NOUN ② You can refer to the things that people in general do not know about as the unknown.

unlawful ADJECTIVE not legal • *the unlawful possession of a gun.*

unleaded ADJECTIVE Unleaded petrol has a reduced amount of lead in it in order to reduce the pollution from cars.

unleash, **unleashes**, **unleashing**, **unleashed** VERB When a powerful or violent force is unleashed, it is released.

unless CONJUNCTION You use 'unless' to introduce the only circumstances in which something will not take place or is not true • *Unless it was raining, they played in the little garden.*

unlike PREPOSITION ① You can use 'unlike' to show how two people, things or situations are different from each other • *Unlike me, she enjoys ballet.* ▸ ADJECTIVE ② If one thing is unlike another, the two things are different.

unlikely ADJECTIVE ① If something is unlikely, it is probably not true or probably will not happen. ② strange and unexpected • *There are riches in unlikely places.*

unlimited ADJECTIVE If a supply of something is unlimited, you can have as much as you want or need.

unload, **unloads**, **unloading**, **unloaded** VERB If you unload things from a container or vehicle, you remove them.

unlock, **unlocks**, **unlocking**, **unlocked** VERB If you unlock a door or container, you open it by turning a key in the lock.

unlucky ADJECTIVE Someone who is unlucky has bad luck. **unluckily** ADVERB
SIMILAR WORDS: hapless, unfortunate

unmarked ADJECTIVE ① with no marks of damage or injury. ② with no signs or marks of identification • *unmarked police cars.*

unmistakable; also spelt **unmistakeable** ADJECTIVE Something unmistakable is so obvious that it cannot be mistaken for something else. **unmistakably** ADVERB

unmitigated ADJECTIVE (*formal*) You use unmitigated to describe a situation or quality that is completely bad • *an unmitigated disaster.*

unmoved ADJECTIVE not emotionally affected • *He is unmoved by criticism.*

unnatural ADJECTIVE ① strange and rather frightening because it is not usual • *There was an unnatural stillness.* ② artificial and not typical • *My voice sounded high-pitched and unnatural.* **unnaturally** ADVERB

unnecessary ADJECTIVE If something is unnecessary, there is no need for it to happen or be done. **unnecessarily** ADVERB

unnerve, **unnerves**, **unnerving**, **unnerved** VERB If something unnerves you, it frightens or startles you. **unnerving** ADJECTIVE

unobtrusive ADJECTIVE Something that is unobtrusive does not draw attention to itself.

unoccupied ADJECTIVE not occupied. For example, if a house is unoccupied, there is nobody living in it.

unofficial ADJECTIVE without the approval or permission of a person in authority • *unofficial strikes.* **unofficially** ADVERB

unorthodox ADJECTIVE unusual and not generally accepted • *an unorthodox theory.*

unpack, **unpacks**, **unpacking**, **unpacked** VERB When you unpack, you take everything out of a suitcase or bag.

a
b
c
d
e
f
g
h
i
j
k
l
m
n
o
p
q
r
s
t
u
v
w
x
y
z

unpaid ADJECTIVE ① If you do unpaid work, you do not receive any money for doing it. ② An unpaid bill has not yet been paid.

unpalatable ADJECTIVE ① Unpalatable food is unpleasant to eat. ② An unpalatable idea is so unpleasant that it is difficult to accept.

unparalleled ADJECTIVE greater than anything else of its kind • *an unparalleled success*.

unpleasant ADJECTIVE ① Something unpleasant causes you to have bad feelings, for example by making you uncomfortable or upset. ② An unpleasant person is unfriendly or rude. **unpleasantly** ADVERB **unpleasantness** NOUN

unpopular ADJECTIVE disliked by most people • *an unpopular idea*.

unprecedented [Said un-*press*-id-en-tid] ADJECTIVE (formal) Something that is unprecedented has never happened before or is the best of its kind so far.

unpredictable ADJECTIVE If someone or something is unpredictable, you never know how they will behave or react.

unprepared ADJECTIVE If you are unprepared for something, you are not ready for it and are therefore surprised or at a disadvantage when it happens.

unproductive ADJECTIVE not producing anything useful.
SIMILAR WORDS: fruitless, useless

unqualified ADJECTIVE ① having no qualifications or not having the right qualifications for a particular job • *supervision of unqualified doctors*. ② total • *an unqualified success*.

unquestionable ADJECTIVE so obviously true or real that nobody can doubt it • *His devotion is unquestionable*. **unquestionably** ADVERB

unravel, unravels, unravelling, unravelled VERB ① If you unravel something such as a twisted and knotted piece of string, you unwind it so that it is straight. ② If you unravel a mystery, you work out the answer to it.

unreal ADJECTIVE so strange that you find it difficult to believe.

unrealistic ADJECTIVE ① An unrealistic person does not face the truth about something or deal with it in a practical way. ② Something unrealistic is not true to life • *an unrealistic picture*.

unreasonable ADJECTIVE unfair and difficult to deal with or justify • *an unreasonable request*. **unreasonably** ADVERB

unrelated ADJECTIVE Things that are unrelated have no connection with each other.

unrelenting ADJECTIVE continuing in a determined way • *unrelenting criticism*.

unreliable ADJECTIVE If people, machines or methods are unreliable, you cannot rely on them.

unremitting ADJECTIVE never stopping.

unrest NOUN If there is unrest, people are angry and dissatisfied.

unrivalled ADJECTIVE better than anything else of its kind • *an unrivalled range of health and beauty treatments*.

unroll, unrolls, unrolling, unrolled VERB If you unroll a roll of cloth or paper, you open it up and make it flat.

unruly ADJECTIVE difficult to control or organise • *unruly children* • *unruly hair*.

unsafe ADJECTIVE If a building, machine, activity or area is unsafe, it is dangerous.

unsatisfactory ADJECTIVE not good enough.

unscathed ADJECTIVE not injured or harmed as a result of a dangerous experience.

unscrew, unscrews, unscrewing, unscrewed VERB If you unscrew something, you remove it by turning it or by removing the screws that are holding it.

unscrupulous ADJECTIVE willing to behave dishonestly in order to get what you want.

unseemly ADJECTIVE Unseemly behaviour is not suitable for a particular situation and shows a lack of control and good manners • *an unseemly squabble*.

unseen ADJECTIVE You use 'unseen' to describe things that you cannot see or have not seen.

unsettle, unsettles, unsettling, unsettled VERB If something unsettles you, it makes you restless or worried.

unshakable; also spelt **unshakeable** ADJECTIVE An unshakable belief is so strong that it cannot be destroyed.

unsightly ADJECTIVE very ugly • *an unsightly scar*.

unskilled ADJECTIVE Unskilled work does not require any special training or ability.

unsolicited ADJECTIVE given or happening without being asked for.

unsound ADJECTIVE ① If a conclusion or method is unsound, it is based on ideas that are likely to be wrong. ② An unsound building is likely to collapse.

unspeakable ADJECTIVE very unpleasant.

unspecified ADJECTIVE You say that something is unspecified when you are not told exactly what it is • *It was being stored in some unspecified place*.

unspoilt or **unspoiled** ADJECTIVE If you describe a place as unspoilt or unspoiled, you mean it has not been changed and it is still in its natural or original state.

unspoken ADJECTIVE An unspoken wish or feeling is one that is not mentioned to other people.

unstable ADJECTIVE ① likely to change suddenly and create difficulty or danger • *The political situation in Moscow is unstable*. ② not firm or fixed properly and likely to wobble or fall.

unsteady ADJECTIVE ① having difficulty in controlling the movement of your legs or hands • *unsteady on her feet*. ② not held or fixed securely and likely to fall over.
unsteadily ADVERB

unstuck ADJECTIVE separated from the thing that it was stuck to.

unsuccessful ADJECTIVE If you are unsuccessful, you do not succeed in what you are trying to do.
unsuccessfully ADVERB

unsuitable ADJECTIVE not right or appropriate for a particular purpose.
unsuitably ADVERB

unsuited ADJECTIVE not appropriate for a particular task or situation • *He's totally unsuited to the job*.

unsung ADJECTIVE You use 'unsung' to describe someone who is not appreciated or praised for their good work • *George is the unsung hero of the club*.
WORD HISTORY: from the custom of celebrating in song the exploits of heroes

unsure ADJECTIVE uncertain or doubtful.

unsuspecting ADJECTIVE having no idea of what is happening or going to

a
b
c
d
e
f
g
h
i
j
k
l
m
n
o
p
q
r
s
t
u
v
w
x
y
z

happen • *His horse escaped and collided with an unsuspecting cyclist.*

untangle, untangles, untangling, untangled VERB If you untangle something that is twisted together, you undo the twists.

untenable ADJECTIVE (*formal*) A theory, argument or position that is untenable cannot be successfully defended.

unthinkable ADJECTIVE so shocking or awful that you cannot imagine it to be true.

untidy, untidier, untidiest ADJECTIVE not neat or well arranged. **untidily** ADVERB

untie, unties, untying, untied VERB If you untie something, you undo the knots in the string or rope around it.

until PREPOSITION or CONJUNCTION ① If something happens until a particular time, it happens before that time and stops at that time • *The shop stayed open until midnight* • *She waited until her sister was asleep and crept out.* ② If something does not happen until a particular time, it does not happen before that time and only starts happening at that time • *It didn't rain until the middle of the afternoon* • *It was not until they arrived that they found out who he was.*

untimely ADJECTIVE happening too soon or sooner than expected • *his untimely death.*

unto PREPOSITION (*old-fashioned*) Unto means the same as to • *Nation shall speak peace unto nation.*

untold ADJECTIVE You use untold to emphasise how great or extreme something is • *The island possessed untold wealth.*

untouched ADJECTIVE ① not changed, moved or damaged • *a small village untouched by tourism.*

② If a meal is untouched, none of it has been eaten.

untoward ADJECTIVE unexpected and causing difficulties • *no untoward problems.*

untrue ADJECTIVE not true.

unused ADJECTIVE ① [*Said un-**yoozd**]* not yet used. ② [*Said un-**yoost**]* If you are unused to something, you have not often done or experienced it.

unusual ADJECTIVE Something that is unusual does not occur very often. **unusually** ADVERB

SIMILAR WORDS: exceptional, extraordinary, rare

unveil, unveils, unveiling, unveiled VERB When someone unveils a new statue or plaque, they draw back a curtain that is covering it.

unwanted ADJECTIVE Unwanted things are not desired or wanted, either by a particular person or by people in general • *He felt lonely and unwanted.*

unwarranted ADJECTIVE (*formal*) not justified or not deserved • *unwarranted fears.*

unwelcome ADJECTIVE not wanted • *an unwelcome visitor* • *unwelcome news.*

unwell ADJECTIVE If you are unwell, you are ill.

unwieldy ADJECTIVE difficult to move or carry because of being large or an awkward shape.

unwilling ADJECTIVE If you are unwilling to do something, you do not want to do it. **unwillingly** ADVERB

SIMILAR WORDS: averse, loath, reluctant

unwind, unwinds, unwinding, unwound VERB ① When you unwind after working hard, you relax. ② If you unwind something that is wrapped round something else, you undo it.

unwise ADJECTIVE foolish or not sensible.

unwitting ADJECTIVE Unwitting describes someone who becomes involved in something without realising what is really happening • *her unwitting victims*. **unwittingly** ADVERB

unworthy ADJECTIVE (*formal*) Someone who is unworthy of something does not deserve it.

unwound the past tense and past participle of **unwind**.

unwrap, unwraps, unwrapping, unwrapped VERB When you unwrap something, you take off the paper or covering around it.

unwritten ADJECTIVE An unwritten law is one which is generally understood and accepted without being officially laid down.

up ADVERB or PREPOSITION ① towards or in a higher place • *He ran up the stairs* • *high up in the mountains*. ② towards or in the north • *I'm flying up to Darwin*. ▶ PREPOSITION ③ If you go up a road or river, you go along it. ④ You use 'up to' to say how large something can be or what level it has reached • *traffic jams up to 15 kilometres long*. ⑤ (*informal*) If someone is up to something, they are secretly doing something they should not be doing. ⑥ If it is up to someone to do something, it is their responsibility. ▶ ADJECTIVE ⑦ If you are up, you are not in bed. ⑧ If a period of time is up, it has come to an end. ▶ ADVERB ⑨ If an amount of something goes up, it increases.

up-and-coming ADJECTIVE Up-and-coming people are likely to be successful.

upbeat ADJECTIVE If you are upbeat, you are cheerful and hopeful about a situation.

upbringing NOUN Your upbringing is the way that your parents have taught you to behave.

update, updates, updating, updated VERB If you update something, you make it more modern or add new information to it • *He updated his timetable for the new term*.

upgrade, upgrades, upgrading, upgraded VERB If a person or their job is upgraded, they are given more responsibility or status and usually more money.

upheaval, upheavals NOUN a big change which causes a lot of trouble.

upheld the past tense and past participle of **uphold**.

uphill ADVERB ① If you go uphill, you go up a slope. ▶ ADJECTIVE ② An uphill task requires a lot of effort and determination.

uphold, upholds, upholding, upheld VERB If someone upholds a law or a decision, they support and maintain it.

upholstery NOUN Upholstery is the soft covering on chairs and sofas that makes them comfortable.

upkeep NOUN The upkeep of something is the continual process and cost of keeping it in good condition.

upland, uplands ADJECTIVE ① An upland area is an area of high land. ▶ NOUN ② (*in plural*) Uplands are areas of high land.

uplifting ADJECTIVE something that is uplifting makes you feel happy.

upload, uploads, uploading, uploaded ICT VERB ① If you upload data you transfer it from the memory of a computer to a larger computer system. ▶ NOUN ② a piece of data transferred in this way.

a
b
c
d
e
f
g
h
i
j
k
l
m
n
o
p
q
r
s
t
u
v
w
x
y
z

upmarket ADJECTIVE Upmarket products or services are expensive and of good quality • *an upmarket restaurant*.

upon PREPOSITION ① (*formal*) Upon means on • *I stood upon the stair*. ② You use upon when mentioning an event that is immediately followed by another • *Upon entering the hall he took a quick glance round*. ③ If an event is upon you, it is about to happen • *The football season is upon us once more*.

upper, uppers ADJECTIVE ① referring to something that is above something else, or the higher part of something • *the upper arm*. ▶ NOUN ② the top part of a shoe.

upper case ADJECTIVE ENGLISH Upper case letters are the capital letters used in printing.

upper class, upper classes NOUN The upper classes are people who belong to a very wealthy or aristocratic group in a society.

uppermost ADJECTIVE or ADVERB ① on top or in the highest position • *the uppermost leaves* • *Lay your arms beside your body with the palms turned uppermost*. ▶ ADJECTIVE ② most important • *His family is now uppermost in his mind*.

upright ADJECTIVE or ADVERB ① standing or sitting up straight, rather than bending or lying down. ② behaving in a very respectable and moral way.

uprising, uprisings NOUN If there is an uprising, a large group of people begin fighting against the existing government to bring about political changes.

uproar NOUN If there is uproar or an uproar, there is a lot of shouting and noise, often because people are angry.

SIMILAR WORDS: commotion, furore, pandemonium
WORD HISTORY: from Dutch *oproer* meaning 'revolt'

uproot, uproots, uprooting, uprooted VERB ① If someone is uprooted, they have to leave the place where they have lived for a long time. ② If a tree is uprooted, it is pulled out of the ground.

upset, upsets, upsetting, upset ADJECTIVE [*Said* up-**set**] ① worried or unhappy. ▶ VERB [*Said* up-**set**] ② If something upsets you, it makes you feel worried or unhappy. ③ If you upset something, you turn it over or spill it accidentally. ▶ NOUN [*Said* up-*set*] ④ A stomach upset is a slight stomach illness caused by an infection or by something you have eaten.

upshot NOUN The upshot of a series of events is the final result.

upside down ADJECTIVE or ADVERB the wrong way up.

upstage, upstages, upstaging, upstaged VERB If someone upstages you, they draw people's attention away from you by being more attractive or interesting.

upstairs ADVERB ① If you go upstairs in a building, you go up to a higher floor. ▶ ADJECTIVE or ADVERB ② on a higher floor or on the top floor. ▶ NOUN ③ The upstairs of a building is its upper floor or floors.

upstart, upstarts NOUN someone who has risen too quickly to an important position and is too arrogant.

upstream ADVERB towards the source of a river • *They made their way upstream*.

upsurge NOUN An upsurge of something is a sudden large increase in it.

uptake NOUN You can say that someone is quick on the uptake if they understand things quickly.

upthrust, upthrusts NOUN
① SCIENCE a block of rock that has moved upwards during a violent raising of part of the earth's crust.
② SCIENCE a violent raising of part of the earth's crust.

uptight ADJECTIVE (informal) tense or annoyed.

up-to-date ADJECTIVE ① being the newest thing of its kind. ② having the latest information.

up-to-the-minute ADJECTIVE Up-to-the-minute information is the latest available information.

upturn, upturns NOUN an improvement in a situation.

upturned ADJECTIVE ① pointing upwards • *rain splashing down on her upturned face.* ② upside down • *an upturned bowl.*

upwards ADVERB ① If you move or look upwards, you move or look towards the sky or towards a higher level • *People stared upwards and pointed.* ② If an amount or rate moves upwards, it increases.
upward ADJECTIVE

uranium [Said yoo-ray-nee-um] NOUN SCIENCE Uranium is a radioactive metallic element used in the production of nuclear power and weapons. Its atomic number is 92 and its symbol is U.

Uranus NOUN Uranus is the planet in the solar system which is seventh from the sun.

urban ADJECTIVE GEOGRAPHY relating to a town or city • *She found urban life very different from country life.*

urbane ADJECTIVE well-mannered, and comfortable in social situations.

Urdu [Said oor-doo] NOUN Urdu is the official language of Pakistan. It is also spoken by many people in India.

urethra, urethras NOUN SCIENCE The urethra is the tube in the body that carries urine from the bladder out of the body.

urge, urges, urging, urged NOUN ① If you have an urge to do something, you have a strong wish to do it.
▸ VERB ② If you urge someone to do something, you try hard to persuade them to do it.
SIMILAR WORDS: ① compulsion, desire, impulse ② beg, implore

urgent ADJECTIVE needing to be dealt with as soon as possible. **urgently** ADVERB **urgency** NOUN
SIMILAR WORDS: crucial, pressing

urinal, urinals [Said yoor-**rye**-nl] NOUN a bowl or trough fixed to the wall in a public toilet for men to urinate in.

urinate, urinates, urinating, urinated [Said **yoor**-rin-ate] VERB When you urinate, you go to the toilet and get rid of urine from your body.

urine [Said yoor-rin] NOUN the waste liquid that you get rid of from your body when you go to the toilet.

URL, URLs NOUN ICT A URL is a technical name for an internet address. URL is an abbreviation for 'uniform resource locator'.

urn, urns NOUN a decorated container, especially one that is used to hold the ashes of a person who has been cremated.

us PRONOUN A speaker or writer uses us to refer to himself or herself and one or more other people • *Why don't you tell us?*

US or **USA** an abbreviation for 'United States (of America)'.

usage NOUN ① the degree to which something is used, or the way in which it is used. ② the way in which

a b c d e f g h i j k l m n o p q r s t **u** v w x y z

words are actually used • *The terms soon entered common usage.*

USB, USBs NOUN ICT a socket on a computer or other electronic device where you can connect another piece of equipment, such as a keyboard, camera or flash drive. USB is an abbreviation for 'universal serial bus'.

use, uses, using, used VERB [*Said yooz*] ① If you use something, you do something with it in order to do a job or achieve something • *May I use your phone?* ② If you use someone, you take advantage of them by making them do things for you. ▶ NOUN [*Said yoos*] ③ The use of something is the act of using it • *the use of force.* ④ If you have the use of something, you have the ability or permission to use it. ⑤ If you find a use for something, you find a purpose for it. **usable**; also spelt **useable** ADJECTIVE **user** NOUN
SIMILAR WORDS: ① apply, employ, utilise ③ application, employment, usage

used [*Said yoost*] VERB ① Something that used to be done or used to be true was done or was true in the past. ▶ PHRASE ② If you are **used to** something, you are familiar with it and have often experienced it. ▶ ADJECTIVE [*Said yoozd*] ③ A used object has had a previous owner.

useful ADJECTIVE If something is useful, you can use it in order to do something or to help you in some way. **usefully** ADVERB **usefulness** NOUN

useless ADJECTIVE ① If something is useless, you cannot use it because it is not suitable or helpful. ② If a course of action is useless, it will not achieve what is wanted.

username, usernames NOUN a name that someone uses when logging into a computer or website.

usher, ushers, ushering, ushered VERB ① If you usher someone somewhere, you show them where to go by going with them. ▶ NOUN ② a person who shows people where to sit at a wedding or a concert.

USSR HISTORY an abbreviation for 'Union of Soviet Socialist Republics', a country which was made up of a lot of smaller countries including Russia, but which is now broken up.

usual ADJECTIVE ① happening, done or used most often • *his usual seat.* ▶ PHRASE ② If you do something **as usual**, you do it in the way that you normally do it, or you do something that you do regularly. **usually** ADVERB
SIMILAR WORDS: ① customary, normal, regular

usurp, usurps, usurping, usurped [*Said yoo-zerp*] VERB (*formal*) If someone usurps another person's job or title they take it when they have no right to do so.

ute, utes [*Said yoot*] NOUN (*informal*) in Australian and New Zealand English, a ute is a utility truck.

utensil, utensils [*Said yoo-ten-sil*] NOUN Utensils are tools • *cooking utensils.*
WORD HISTORY: from Latin *utensilis* meaning 'available for use'

uterus, uteruses [*Said yoo-ter-russ*] NOUN SCIENCE A woman's uterus is her womb.

utilise, utilises, utilising, utilised; also spelt **utilize** VERB (*formal*) To utilise something is to use it. **utilisation** NOUN

utilitarian ADJECTIVE ① intended to produce the greatest benefit for the greatest number of people. ② designed to be useful rather than beautiful.

utility, utilities NOUN ① The utility of

something is its usefulness. ② a service, such as water or gas, that is provided for everyone.

utility truck, utility trucks NOUN In Australian and New Zealand English, a utility truck is a small motor vehicle with an open body and low sides.

utmost ADJECTIVE used to emphasise a particular quality • *I have the utmost respect for Richard.*

utter, utters, uttering, uttered VERB ① When you utter sounds or words, you make or say them. ▶ ADJECTIVE ② Utter means complete or total • *scenes of utter chaos.* **utterly** ADVERB

utterance, utterances NOUN something that is said • *his first utterance.*

uvula, uvulas or uvulae [*Said yoo-vyoo-la*] NOUN (technical) Your uvula is the small piece of flesh that hangs down above the back of your tongue.

a
b
c
d
e
f
g
h
i
j
k
l
m
n
o
p
q
r
s
t
u
v
w
x
y
z

Vv

v an abbreviation for **versus**.

vacant ADJECTIVE ① If something is vacant, it is not occupied or being used. ② If a job or position is vacant, no-one holds it at present. ③ A vacant look suggests that someone does not understand something or is not very intelligent. **vacancy** NOUN **vacantly** ADVERB

vacate, vacates, vacating, vacated VERB (formal) If you vacate a room or job, you leave it and it becomes available for someone else.

vacation, vacations NOUN ① the period between academic terms at a university or college • the summer vacation. ② a holiday.

vaccinate, vaccinates, vaccinating, vaccinated [Said vak-sin-ate] VERB To vaccinate someone means to give them a vaccine, usually by injection, to protect them against a disease. **vaccination** NOUN

vaccine, vaccines [Said vak-seen] NOUN a substance made from the germs that cause a disease, given to people to make them immune to that disease.
WORD HISTORY: from Latin vacca meaning 'cow', because smallpox vaccine is based on cowpox, a disease of cows

vacuole, vacuoles [Said vak-yoo-ole] NOUN SCIENCE the area in a cell containing air, fluid or partially digested food.
WORD HISTORY: from French vacuole meaning 'little vacuum'

vacuum, vacuums, vacuuming, vacuumed [Said vak-yoom] NOUN ① SCIENCE a space containing no air, gases or other matter. ▶ VERB ② If you vacuum something, you clean it using a vacuum cleaner.

vacuum cleaner, vacuum cleaners NOUN an electric machine which cleans by sucking up dirt.

vagina, vaginas [Said vaj-jie-na] NOUN SCIENCE A woman's vagina is the passage that connects her outer sex organs to her womb.
WORD HISTORY: from Latin vagina meaning 'sheath'

vagrant, vagrants NOUN a person who moves from place to place, and has no home or regular job. **vagrancy** NOUN

vague, vaguer, vaguest [Said vayg] ADJECTIVE ① If something is vague, it is not expressed or explained clearly, or you cannot see or remember it clearly • vague statements. ② Someone looks or sounds vague if they are not concentrating or thinking clearly. **vaguely** ADVERB **vagueness** NOUN
SIMILAR WORDS: ① imprecise, indefinite, unclear

vain, vainer, vainest ADJECTIVE ① A vain action or attempt is one which is not successful • He made a vain effort to cheer her up. ② A vain person is very proud of their looks, intelligence or other qualities. ▶ PHRASE ③ If you do something **in vain**, you do not succeed in achieving what you intend. **vainly** ADVERB

a
b
c
d
e
f
g
h
i
j
k
l
m
n
o
p
q
r
s
t
u
v
w
x
y
z

SPELLING TIP
Do not confuse the spellings of *vain*, *vein* and *vane*: *a vain attempt to conquer Everest; Veins carry blood back to the heart; the vanes of a windmill.*

vale, vales NOUN (*literary*) a valley.

valentine, valentines NOUN ①Your valentine is someone you love and send a card to on Saint Valentine's Day, February 14th. ②A valentine or a valentine card is the card you send to the person you love on Saint Valentine's Day.

valet, valets [*Said* **val**-lit *or* **val**-lay] NOUN a male servant who is employed to look after another man, particularly caring for his clothes.

valiant ADJECTIVE very brave. **valiantly** ADVERB

valid ADJECTIVE ①Something that is valid is based on sound reasoning. ②A valid ticket or document is one which is officially accepted. **validity** NOUN

validate, validates, validating, validated VERB If something validates a statement or claim, it proves that it is true or correct.

valley, valleys NOUN GEOGRAPHY a long stretch of land between hills, often with a river flowing through it.

valour NOUN Valour is great bravery.

valuable, valuables ADJECTIVE ①having great importance or usefulness. ②worth a lot of money.
SIMILAR WORDS: ②costly, expensive, precious

valuables PLURAL NOUN Valuables are things that you own that cost a lot of money.

valuation, valuations NOUN a judgment about how much money something is worth or how good it is.

value, values, valuing, valued NOUN ①The value of something is its importance or usefulness • *information of great value.* ②The value of something you own is the amount of money that it is worth. ③The values of a group or a person are the moral principles and beliefs that they think are important • *the values of liberty and equality.* ▶ VERB ④If you value something, you think it is important and you appreciate it. ⑤When experts value something, they decide how much money it is worth. **valued** ADJECTIVE **valuer** NOUN

valve, valves NOUN ①a part attached to a pipe or tube which controls the flow of gas or liquid. ②a small flap in your heart or in a vein which controls the flow and direction of blood.

vampire, vampires NOUN In horror stories, vampires are corpses that come out of their graves at night and suck the blood of living people.

van, vans NOUN a covered vehicle larger than a car but smaller than a lorry, used for carrying goods.

vandal, vandals NOUN someone who deliberately damages or destroys things, particularly public property. **vandalise** VERB **vandalism** NOUN

vane, vanes NOUN a flat blade that is part of a mechanism for using the energy of the wind or water to drive a machine.

SPELLING TIP
Do not confuse the spellings of *vane*, *vain* and *vein*: *the vanes of a windmill; a vain attempt to conquer Everest; Veins carry blood back to the heart.*

vanguard [*Said* van-**gard**] NOUN If someone is in the vanguard of something, they are in the most advanced part of it.

vanilla NOUN Vanilla is a flavouring for food such as ice cream, which comes from the pods of a tropical plant.

vanish, **vanishes**, **vanishing**, **vanished** VERB ① If something vanishes, it disappears • *The moon vanished behind a cloud.* ② If something vanishes, it ceases to exist • *a vanishing civilisation.*

vanity NOUN Vanity is a feeling of excessive pride about your looks or abilities.

vanquish, **vanquishes**, **vanquishing**, **vanquished** [*Said vang-kwish*] VERB (*literary*) To vanquish someone means to defeat them completely.

vapour NOUN SCIENCE Vapour is a mass of tiny drops of water or other liquids in the air which looks like mist.

variable, **variables** ADJECTIVE ① Something that is variable is likely to change at any time. ▶ NOUN ② In any situation, a variable is something in it that can change. ③ MATHS a symbol such as x which can represent any value or any one of a set of values. **variability** NOUN

variance NOUN If one thing is at variance with another, the two seem to contradict each other.

variant, **variants** NOUN ① A variant of something has a different form from the usual one, for example *gaol* is a variant of *jail*. ▶ ADJECTIVE ② alternative or different.

variation, **variations** NOUN ① a change from the normal or usual pattern • *a variation of the same route.* ② a change in level, amount or quantity • *a large variation in demand.*

varicose veins PLURAL NOUN Varicose veins are swollen painful veins in the legs.

varied ADJECTIVE of different types, quantities or sizes.

variety, **varieties** NOUN ① If something has variety, it consists of things which are not all the same. ② A variety of things is a number of different kinds of them • *a wide variety of readers.* ③ A variety of something is a particular type of it • *a new variety of celery.* ④ Variety is a form of entertainment consisting of short unrelated acts, such as singing, dancing and comedy.
SIMILAR WORDS: ② assortment, mixture, range

various ADJECTIVE Various means of several different types • *trees of various sorts.* **variously** ADVERB
SIMILAR WORDS: different, miscellaneous, sundry

GRAMMAR TIP
You should avoid putting *different* after *various*: *The disease exists in various forms* not *various different forms.*

---

varnish, **varnishes**, **varnishing**, **varnished** NOUN ① a liquid which when painted onto a surface gives it a hard, clear, shiny finish. ▶ VERB ② If you varnish something, you paint it with varnish.

vary, **varies**, **varying**, **varied** VERB ① If things vary, they change • *Weather patterns vary greatly.* ② If you vary something, you introduce changes in it • *Vary your routes as much as possible.* **varied** ADJECTIVE

vascular ADJECTIVE relating to tubes or ducts that carry fluids within animals or plants.

vase, **vases** NOUN a glass or china jar for flowers.

vasectomy, **vasectomies** [*Said vas-sek-tom-ee*] NOUN an operation to sterilise a man by cutting the tube in his body that carries the sperm.

A B C D E F G H I J K L M N O P Q R S T U V W X Y Z

Vaseline NOUN (*trademark*) Vaseline is a soft, clear jelly made from petroleum and used as an ointment or as grease.

vast ADJECTIVE extremely large. **vastly** ADVERB **vastness** NOUN

vat, vats NOUN a large container for liquids.

VAT [*Said* **vee-ay-tee** *or* **vat**] NOUN In Britain, VAT is a tax which is added to the costs of making or providing goods and services. VAT is an abbreviation for 'value-added tax'.

vault, vaults, vaulting, vaulted [*Rhymes with* **salt**] NOUN ① a strong secure room, often underneath a building, where valuables are stored, or underneath a church where people are buried. ② an arched roof, often found in churches. ▶ VERB ③ If you vault over something, you jump over it using your hands or a pole to help.

VDU, VDUs NOUN a monitor screen attached to a computer or word processor. VDU is an abbreviation for 'visual display unit'.

veal NOUN Veal is the meat from a calf.

vector, vectors NOUN MATHS In maths, a vector is a quantity, such as a force, which has magnitude and direction.

Veda, Vedas [*Said* **vay-da**] NOUN an ancient sacred text of the Hindu religion; also these texts as a collection. **Vedic** ADJECTIVE

veer, veers, veering, veered VERB If something which is moving veers in a particular direction, it suddenly changes course • *The aircraft veered sharply to one side*.

vegan, vegans [*Said* **vee-gn**] NOUN someone who does not eat any food made from animal products, such as meat, eggs, cheese or milk.

vegetable, vegetables NOUN ① Vegetables are edible roots or leaves such as carrots or cabbage. ▶ ADJECTIVE ② Vegetable is used to refer to any plants in contrast to animals or minerals • *vegetable life*. WORD HISTORY: from Latin *vegetabilis* meaning 'enlivening'

vegetarian, vegetarians NOUN a person who does not eat meat, poultry or fish. **vegetarianism** NOUN

vegetation NOUN GEOGRAPHY Vegetation is the plants in a particular area.

vegetation cover NOUN GEOGRAPHY The vegetation cover of a particular area of land is the type and number of plants growing there.

vehement [*Said* **vee-im-ent**] ADJECTIVE Someone who is vehement has strong feelings or opinions and expresses them forcefully • *He wrote a letter of vehement protest*. **vehemence** NOUN **vehemently** ADVERB

vehicle, vehicles [*Said* **vee-ik-kl**] NOUN ① a machine, often with an engine, used for transporting people or goods. ② something used to achieve a particular purpose or as a means of expression • *The play seemed an ideal vehicle for his music*. **vehicular** ADJECTIVE

veil, veils [*Rhymes with* **male**] NOUN a piece of thin, soft cloth that women sometimes wear over their heads. **veiled** ADJECTIVE

vein, veins [*Rhymes with* **rain**] NOUN ① Your veins are the tubes in your body through which your blood flows to your heart. ② Veins are the thin lines on leaves or on insects' wings. ③ A vein of a metal or a mineral is a layer of it in rock. ④ Something that is in a particular vein is in that style or mood • *in a more serious vein*.

SPELLING TIP

Do not confuse the spellings of *vein*, *vain* and *vane*: *Veins carry blood back to the heart; a vain attempt to conquer Everest; the vanes of a windmill.*

veld [*Said felt*] NOUN The veld is flat high grassland in Southern Africa.

veldskoen, veldskoens [*Said felt-skoon*] NOUN In South Africa, a veldskoen is a tough ankle-length boot.

velocity NOUN (*technical*) Velocity is the speed at which something is moving in a particular direction.

velvet NOUN Velvet is a very soft material which has a thick layer of fine short threads on one side. **velvety** ADJECTIVE

WORD HISTORY: from Latin *villus* meaning 'shaggy hair'

vendetta, vendettas NOUN a long-lasting bitter quarrel in which people try to harm each other.

vending machine, vending machines NOUN a machine which provides things such as drinks or sweets when you put money in it.

vendor, vendors NOUN a person who sells something.

veneer NOUN ①You can refer to a superficial quality that someone has as a veneer of that quality • *a veneer of calm.* ②Veneer is a thin layer of wood or plastic used to cover a surface.

venerable ADJECTIVE ①A venerable person is someone you treat with respect because they are old and wise. ②Something that is venerable is impressive because it is old or important historically.

venerate, venerates, venerating, venerated VERB (*formal*) If you venerate someone, you feel great respect for them. **veneration** NOUN

vengeance NOUN ①Vengeance is the act of harming someone because they have harmed you. ▶ PHRASE ②If something happens **with a vengeance**, it happens to a much greater extent than was expected • *It began to rain again with a vengeance.*

venison NOUN Venison is the meat from a deer.

WORD HISTORY: from Latin *venatio* meaning 'hunting'

Venn diagram, Venn diagrams NOUN MATHS In mathematics, a Venn diagram is a drawing which uses circles to show the relationships between different sets.

WORD HISTORY: named after the English logician John *Venn* (1834–1923), who invented them

venom NOUN ①The venom of a snake, scorpion or spider is its poison. ②Venom is a feeling of great bitterness or spitefulness towards someone • *He was glaring at me with venom.* **venomous** ADJECTIVE

vent, vents, venting, vented NOUN ①a hole in something through which gases and smoke can escape and fresh air can enter • *air vents.* ▶ VERB ②If you vent strong feelings, you express them • *She wanted to vent her anger upon me.* ▶ PHRASE ③If you **give vent** to strong feelings, you express them • *Pamela gave vent to a lot of bitterness.*

ventilate, ventilates, ventilating, ventilated VERB To ventilate a room means to allow fresh air into it. **ventilated** ADJECTIVE

ventilation NOUN ①Ventilation is the process of breathing air in and out of the lungs. ②A ventilation system supplies fresh air into a building.

ventilator, ventilators NOUN a machine that helps people breathe when they cannot breathe naturally, for example if they are very ill.

ventricle, ventricles NOUN
① SCIENCE A ventricle is a chamber of the heart that pumps blood to the arteries. ② SCIENCE A ventricle is also one of the four main cavities of the brain.

ventriloquist, ventriloquists [Said ven-**trill**-o-kwist] NOUN an entertainer who can speak without moving their lips so that the words seem to come from a dummy.
ventriloquism NOUN
WORD HISTORY: from Latin venter meaning 'belly' and loqui meaning 'to speak'

venture, ventures, venturing, ventured NOUN ① something new which involves the risk of failure or of losing money • a successful venture in television films. ▶ VERB ② If you venture something such as an opinion, you say it cautiously or hesitantly because you are afraid it might be foolish or wrong • I would not venture to agree. ③ If you venture somewhere that might be dangerous, you go there.
SIMILAR WORDS: ① enterprise, undertaking

venue, venues [Said **ven**-yoo] NOUN The venue for an event is the place where it will happen.

Venus NOUN Venus is the planet in the solar system which is second from the sun.

veranda, verandas [Said ver-**ran**-da]; also spelt **verandah** NOUN a platform with a roof that is attached to an outside wall of a house at ground level.

verb, verbs NOUN ENGLISH MFL In grammar, a verb is a word that expresses actions and states, for example 'be', 'become', 'take' and 'run'.
▶ SEE GRAMMAR BOX ON NEXT PAGE

verbal ADJECTIVE ① ENGLISH You use 'verbal' to describe things connected with words and their use • verbal attacks on referees. ② 'Verbal' describes things which are spoken rather than written • a verbal agreement. **verbally** ADVERB

verdict, verdicts NOUN ① In a law court, a verdict is the decision which states whether a prisoner is guilty or not guilty. ② If you give a verdict on something, you give your opinion after thinking about it.

verge, verges, verging, verged NOUN ① The verge of a road is the narrow strip of grassy ground at the side. ▶ PHRASE ② If you are **on the verge** of something, you are going to do it soon or it is likely to happen soon • on the verge of crying. ▶ VERB ③ Something that verges on something else is almost the same as it • dark blue that verged on purple.

verify, verifies, verifying, verified VERB If you verify something, you check that it is true • None of his statements could be verified. **verifiable** ADJECTIVE **verification** NOUN

veritable ADJECTIVE You use veritable to emphasise something • a veritable jungle of shops.

vermin PLURAL NOUN Vermin are small animals or insects, such as rats and cockroaches, which carry disease and damage crops.

vernacular, vernaculars [Said ver-**nak**-yoo-lar] NOUN The vernacular of a particular country or district is the language widely spoken there.

verruca, verrucas [Said ver-**roo**-ka] NOUN a small, hard infectious growth rather like a wart, occurring on the sole of the foot.

versatile ADJECTIVE ① If someone is versatile, they have many different skills. ② If a tool or material is versatile, it can be used for many different purposes. **versatility** NOUN

a b c d e f g h i j k l m n o p q r s t u v w x y z

A
B
C
D
E
F
G
H
I
J
K
L
M
N
O
P
Q
R
S
T
U
V
W
X
Y
Z

What is a Verb?

A verb is a word that describes an action or a state of being. Verbs are sometimes called 'doing words'.

Verbs of state indicate the way things are:

Robert is a Taurus.
Anna has one sister.

Verbs of action indicate specific events that happen, have happened or will happen:

Anna visits the dentist.
The man faxed his order.

Auxiliary verbs are used in combination with other verbs to allow the user to distinguish between different times, different degrees of completion and different amounts of certainty:

Anna will visit the dentist.
The man is faxing his order.
They may talk for up to three hours.

A **phrasal verb** consists of a verb followed by either an adverb or a preposition. The two words taken together have a special meaning which could not be deduced from their literal meanings:

The car broke down again.
When did you take up croquet?

An **impersonal verb** is a verb that does not have a subject and is only used after *it* or *there*:

It rains here every day.

Modal Verbs

Can, could, may, might, must, should, would and *ought* are called 'modal verbs'. They are usually used as auxiliary verbs to change the tone of the meaning of another verb:

I wonder if you can come.

Even when they are used on their own, they *suggest* another verb:

I certainly can. (i.e. I certainly *can come*)

There is no difference between the third person present and the other forms of the present tense. No form of the verb ends in -s:

I can speak German.
She can speak German.

These verbs do not have a present participle or a past participle.

The verb *could* may be used as the past tense of *can*:

I could speak German when I was younger.

You can talk about past time by using *could have, may have, might have, must have, should have, would have* and *ought to have*:

We may have taken a wrong turning.
She must have thought I was stupid.

---

verse, verses NOUN ① Verse is another word for poetry. ② one part of a poem or song, or a chapter of the Bible.

versed ADJECTIVE If you are versed in something, you know a lot about it.

version, versions NOUN ① A version of something is a form of it in which some details are different from earlier or later forms • *a cheaper version of the aircraft*. ② Someone's version of an event is their personal description of what happened.

versus PREPOSITION Versus is used to indicate that two people or teams are competing against each other.

vertebra, vertebrae [Said *ver-tib-bra*] NOUN SCIENCE Vertebrae are the small bones which form a person's or animal's backbone.

vertebrate, vertebrates NOUN SCIENCE Vertebrates are any creatures which have a backbone.

vertex, vertices NOUN MATHS a point at which two or more lines intersect.

vertical ADJECTIVE MATHS Something that is vertical points straight up and forms a ninety-degree angle with the surface on which it stands. **vertically** ADVERB

vertigo NOUN Vertigo is a feeling of dizziness caused by looking down from a high place.

verve NOUN Verve is lively and forceful enthusiasm.

very ADVERB ① to a great degree • *very bad dreams*. ▶ADJECTIVE ② 'Very' is used before words to emphasise them • *the very end of the book*. ▶PHRASE ③ You use 'not very' to mean that something is the case only to a small degree • *You're not very like your sister.*
SIMILAR WORDS: ① extremely, greatly, really

vessel, vessels NOUN ① a ship or large boat. ② (*literary*) any bowl or container in which a liquid can be kept. ③ a thin tube along which liquids such as blood or sap move in animals and plants.

vest, vests NOUN ① a piece of underwear worn for warmth on the top half of the body. ② In American English, a vest is a waistcoat.

vestige, vestiges [Said *vest-ij*] NOUN (*formal*) A vestige is a tiny part of something that is left over when the rest has been used up • *They have a vestige of strength left.*

vestry, vestries NOUN The vestry is the part of the church building where a priest or minister changes into their official clothes.

vet, vets, vetting, vetted NOUN ① a doctor for animals. ▶VERB ② If you vet someone or something, you check them carefully to see if they are acceptable • *He refused to let them vet his speeches.*

veteran, veterans NOUN ① someone who has served in the armed forces, particularly during a war. ② someone who has been involved in a particular activity for a long time • *a veteran of 25 political campaigns.*

veterinary [Said *vet-er-in-ar-ee*] ADJECTIVE Veterinary is used to describe the work of a vet and the medical treatment of animals.
WORD HISTORY: from Latin *veterinae* meaning 'animals used for pulling carts and ploughs'

veterinary surgeon, veterinary surgeons NOUN the same as a **vet**.

veto, vetoes, vetoing, vetoed [Said *vee-toh*] VERB ① If someone in authority vetoes something, they say no to it. ▶NOUN ② Veto is the right that someone in authority has to say no to something • *Dr Baker has the power of veto.*

vexed ADJECTIVE If you are vexed, you are annoyed, worried or puzzled.

VHF NOUN VHF is a range of high radio frequencies. VHF is an abbreviation for 'very high frequency'.

via PREPOSITION ① If you go to one place via another, you travel through that place to get to your destination • *He drove directly from Bonn via Paris.* ② Via also means done or achieved by making use of a particular thing or person • *to follow proceedings via newspapers or television.*

a
b
c
d
e
f
g
h
i
j
k
l
m
n
o
p
q
r
s
t
u
v
w
x
y
z

viable [Said vy-a-bl] ADJECTIVE Something that is viable is capable of doing what it is intended to do without extra help or financial support • *a viable business*. **viability** NOUN

viaduct, viaducts [Said vy-a-dukt] NOUN a long, high bridge that carries a road or railway across a valley.

WORD HISTORY: from Latin *via* meaning 'road' and *ducere* meaning 'to bring'

vibrant ADJECTIVE Something or someone that is vibrant is full of life, energy and enthusiasm. **vibrantly** ADVERB **vibrancy** NOUN

vibrate, vibrates, vibrating, vibrated VERB SCIENCE If something vibrates, it moves a tiny amount backwards and forwards very quickly. **vibration** NOUN

vicar, vicars NOUN a priest in the Church of England.

vicarage, vicarages NOUN a house where a vicar lives.

vice, vices NOUN ① a serious moral fault in someone's character, such as greed, or a weakness, such as smoking. ② a tool with a pair of jaws that hold an object tightly while it is being worked on.

vice- PREFIX 'Vice-' is used before a title or position to show that the holder is the deputy of the person with that title or position • *vice-president*.

viceregal ADJECTIVE ① of or concerning a viceroy. ② In Australia and New Zealand, viceregal means of or concerning a governor or governor-general.

viceroy, viceroys NOUN A viceroy is someone who has been appointed to govern a place as a representative of a monarch.

vice versa ADVERB 'Vice versa' is used to indicate that the reverse of what you have said is also true • *Brothers sometimes annoy their sisters, and vice versa*.

vicinity [Said vis-sin-it-ee] NOUN If something is in the vicinity of a place, it is in the surrounding or nearby area.

vicious ADJECTIVE cruel and violent. **viciously** ADVERB **viciousness** NOUN

victim, victims NOUN someone who has been harmed or injured by someone or something.

victor, victors NOUN The victor in a fight or contest is the person who wins.

Victorian ADJECTIVE ① HISTORY Victorian describes things that happened or were made during the reign of Queen Victoria (1837–1901). ② Victorian also describes people or things connected with the state of Victoria in Australia.

victory, victories NOUN a success in a battle or competition. **victorious** ADJECTIVE

SIMILAR WORDS: conquest, triumph, win

video, videos, videoing, videoed NOUN ① Video is the recording and showing of films and events using a video recorder, video tape and a television set. ② a sound and picture recording which can be played back on a television set. ③ a video recorder. ▶ VERB ④ If you video something, you record it on magnetic tape for later viewing.

vie, vies, vying, vied VERB (*formal*) If you vie with someone, you compete to do something sooner than or better than they do.

Vietnamese [Said vyet-nam-meez] ADJECTIVE ① belonging or relating to

Vietnam. ▸ **NOUN** ② someone who comes from Vietnam. ③ Vietnamese is the main language spoken in Vietnam.

view, views, viewing, viewed **NOUN** ① Your views are your personal opinions • *his political views.* ② everything you can see from a particular place. ▸ **VERB** ③ If you view something in a particular way, you think of it in that way • *They viewed me with contempt.* ▸ **PHRASE** ④ You use **in view of** to specify the main fact or event influencing your actions or opinions • *He wore a lighter suit in view of the heat.* ⑤ If something is **on view**, it is being shown or exhibited to the public.
SIMILAR WORDS: ② prospect, scene, vista

viewer, viewers **NOUN** Viewers are the people who watch television.

viewpoint, viewpoints **NOUN** ① Your viewpoint is your attitude towards something. ② a place from which you get a good view of an area or event.

vigil, vigils [Said **vij-jil**] **NOUN** a period of time, especially at night, when you stay quietly in one place, for example because you are making a political protest or praying.

vigilant **ADJECTIVE** careful and alert to danger or trouble. **vigilance NOUN** **vigilantly ADVERB**

vigilante, vigilantes [Said **vij-il-ant-ee**] **NOUN** Vigilantes are unofficially organised groups of people who try to protect their community and catch and punish criminals.

vignette, vignettes [Said **vin-yet**] **NOUN** ENGLISH A vignette is a short description or piece of writing about a particular subject or thing.

vigorous **ADJECTIVE** energetic or enthusiastic. **vigorously ADVERB** **vigour NOUN**

Viking, Vikings **NOUN** HISTORY The Vikings were seamen from Scandinavia who raided parts of north-western Europe from the 8th to the 11th centuries.

vile, viler, vilest **ADJECTIVE** unpleasant or disgusting • *a vile accusation* • *a vile smell.*

villa, villas **NOUN** a house, especially a pleasant holiday home in a country with a warm climate.

village, villages **NOUN** a collection of houses and other buildings in the countryside. **villager NOUN**

villain, villains **NOUN** ① someone who harms others or breaks the law. ② the main evil character in a story. **villainous** **ADJECTIVE** **villainy NOUN** **SIMILAR WORDS:** ① criminal, evildoer, rogue

vindicate, vindicates, vindicating, vindicated **VERB** (formal) If someone is vindicated, their views or ideas are proved to be right • *My friend's instincts have been vindicated.* **vindication NOUN**

vindictive **ADJECTIVE** Someone who is vindictive is deliberately hurtful towards someone, often as an act of revenge. **vindictiveness NOUN**

vine, vines **NOUN** a trailing or climbing plant which winds itself around and over a support, especially one which produces grapes.

vinegar **NOUN** Vinegar is a sharp-tasting liquid made from sour wine, beer or cider, which is used for salad dressing. **vinegary ADJECTIVE** **WORD HISTORY:** from French *vin* meaning 'wine' and *aigre* meaning 'sour'

vineyard, vineyards [Said **vin-yard**] **NOUN** an area of land where grapes are grown.

vintage, vintages **ADJECTIVE** ① A vintage wine is a good quality wine

a
b
c
d
e
f
g
h
i
j
k
l
m
n
o
p
q
r
s
t
u
v
w
x
y
z

A
B
C
D
E
F
G
H
I
J
K
L
M
N
O
P
Q
R
S
T
U
V
W
X
Y
Z

which has been stored for a number of years to improve its quality. ②Vintage describes something which is the best or most typical of its kind • *a vintage guitar*. ③A vintage car is one made between 1918 and 1930. ▶ NOUN ④a grape harvest of one particular year and the wine produced from it.

vinyl NOUN Vinyl is a strong plastic used to make things such as furniture and floor coverings.

viola, violas [*Said vee-oh-la*] NOUN a musical instrument like a violin, but larger and with a lower pitch.

violate, violates, violating, violated VERB ①If you violate an agreement, law or promise, you break it. ②If you violate someone's peace or privacy, you disturb it. ③If you violate a place, especially a holy place, you treat it with disrespect or violence. **violation** NOUN

violence NOUN ①Violence is behaviour which is intended to hurt or kill people. ②If you do or say something with violence, you use a lot of energy in doing or saying it, often because you are angry.

violent ADJECTIVE ①If someone is violent, they try to hurt or kill people. ②A violent event happens unexpectedly and with great force. ③Something that is violent is said, felt or done with great force. **violently** ADVERB

violet, violets NOUN ①a plant with dark purple flowers. ▶ NOUN or ADJECTIVE ②bluish purple.

violin, violins NOUN a musical instrument with four strings that is held under the chin and played with a bow. **violinist** NOUN

VIP, VIPs NOUN VIPs are famous or important people. VIP is an abbreviation for 'very important person'.

viper, vipers NOUN Vipers are types of poisonous snakes.

viral [*Said vie-rul*] ADJECTIVE ①relating to or caused by a virus. ▶ ADVERB ②If a story or a video goes viral, it spreads quickly and widely among users of the internet.

virgin, virgins NOUN ①someone who has never had sexual intercourse. ▶ PROPER NOUN ② RE The Virgin, or the Blessed Virgin, is a name given to Mary, the mother of Jesus Christ. ▶ ADJECTIVE ③Something that is virgin is fresh and unused • *virgin land*. **virginity** NOUN

virginal ADJECTIVE ①Someone who is virginal looks young and innocent. ②Something that is virginal is fresh and clean.

Virgo NOUN Virgo is the sixth sign of the zodiac, represented by a girl. People born between August 23rd and September 22nd are born under this sign.

virile ADJECTIVE A virile man has all the qualities that a man is traditionally expected to have, such as strength. **virility** NOUN

virtual [*Said vur-tyool*] ADJECTIVE ①Virtual means that something has all the characteristics of a particular thing, but it is not formally recognised as being that thing • *The country is in a virtual state of war*. ② ICT Virtual objects and activities are generated by a computer to simulate real objects and activities. ③Virtual activities are also any activities conducted using computers or the internet. **virtually** ADVERB

virtual reality NOUN ICT Virtual reality is a situation or setting that has been created by a computer and that looks real to the person using it.

virtue, virtues NOUN ① Virtue is thinking and doing what is morally right and avoiding what is wrong. ② a good quality in someone's character. ③ A virtue of something is an advantage • *The virtue of neatness is that you can always find things*.
▶ PHRASE ④ (*formal*) **By virtue of** means because of • *The article stuck in my mind by virtue of one detail*.
SIMILAR WORDS: ① goodness, integrity, morality

virtuoso, virtuosos or virtuosi [*Said vur-tyoo-**oh**-soh*] NOUN someone who is exceptionally good at something, particularly playing a musical instrument.
WORD HISTORY: from Italian *virtuoso* meaning 'skilled'

virtuous ADJECTIVE behaving with or showing moral virtue. **virtuously** ADVERB
SIMILAR WORDS: good, moral, upright

virus, viruses [*Said vie-russ*] NOUN ① SCIENCE a kind of germ that can cause disease. ② ICT a program that alters or damages the information stored in a computer system.

visa, visas NOUN an official stamp that allows you to visit a particular country.

viscount, viscounts [*Said vie-kount*] NOUN a British nobleman.
viscountess NOUN

viscous [*Said viss-kuss*] ADJECTIVE SCIENCE Something which is viscous is thick and sticky and does not flow easily.

Vishnu NOUN RE Vishnu is a Hindu god and is one of the Trimurti.

visibility NOUN You use visibility to say how far or how clearly you can see in particular weather conditions.

visible ADJECTIVE ① able to be seen. ② noticeable or evident • *There was little visible excitement*. **visibly** ADVERB

vision, visions NOUN ① Vision is the ability to see clearly. ② a mental picture, in which you imagine how things might be different • *the vision of a possible future*. ③ Vision is also imaginative insight • *a total lack of vision and imagination*. ④ an unusual experience that some people claim to have, in which they see things that other people cannot see. **visionary** NOUN or ADJECTIVE

visit, visits, visiting, visited VERB ① If you visit someone, you go to see them and spend time with them. ② If you visit a place, you go to see it.
▶ NOUN ③ a trip to see a person or place. **visitor** NOUN

visor, visors [*Said vie-zor*] NOUN a transparent movable shield attached to a helmet, which can be pulled down to protect the eyes or face.

visual ADJECTIVE relating to sight • *a visual inspection*.

visual arts PLURAL NOUN the arts of painting, sculpting, photography, etc.

visualise, visualises, visualising, visualised [*Said viz-yool-eyes*]; also spelt **visualize** VERB If you visualise something, you form a mental picture of it.

vital ADJECTIVE ① necessary or very important • *vital evidence*. ② energetic, exciting and full of life • *an active and vital life outside school*. **vitally** ADVERB
SIMILAR WORDS: ① essential, necessary

vitality NOUN People who have vitality are energetic and lively.

vitamin, vitamins NOUN SCIENCE Vitamins are organic compounds which you need in order to remain healthy. They occur naturally in food.

vitriolic ADJECTIVE (*formal*) Vitriolic

a
b
c
d
e
f
g
h
i
j
k
l
m
n
o
p
q
r
s
t
u
v
w
x
y
z

A
B
C
D
E
F
G
H
I
J
K
L
M
N
O
P
Q
R
S
T
U
V
W
X
Y
Z

language or behaviour is full of bitterness and hate.

vivacious [Said viv-**vay**-shuss] ADJECTIVE A vivacious person is attractively lively and high-spirited. **vivacity** NOUN

vivid ADJECTIVE very bright in colour or clear in detail • vivid red paint • vivid memories. **vividly** ADVERB **vividness** NOUN

SIMILAR WORDS: intense, powerful

vivisection NOUN Vivisection is the act of cutting open living animals for medical research. **vivisectionist** NOUN

vixen, vixens NOUN a female fox.

vlog, vlogs NOUN a video diary that a person puts on the internet so that other people can read it.

vocabulary, vocabularies NOUN ① ENGLISH Someone's vocabulary is the total number of words they know in a particular language. ② ENGLISH The vocabulary of a language is all the words in it.

vocal ADJECTIVE ① You say that someone is vocal if they express their opinions strongly and openly. ② MUSIC Vocal means involving the use of the human voice, especially in singing. **vocalist** NOUN **vocally** ADVERB

vocal cords PLURAL NOUN Your vocal cords are the part of your throat which can be made to vibrate when you breathe out, making the sounds you use for speaking.

vocation, vocations NOUN ① a strong wish to do a particular job, especially one which involves serving other people. ② a profession or career.

vocational ADJECTIVE 'Vocational' is used to describe the skills needed for a particular job or profession • vocational training.

vociferous [Said voe-**sif**-fer-uss] ADJECTIVE (formal) Someone who is vociferous speaks a lot, or loudly, because they want to make a point strongly • vociferous critics. **vociferously** ADVERB

vodka, vodkas NOUN a strong clear alcoholic drink which originally came from Russia.

vogue [Said vohg] PHRASE If something is **the vogue** or **in vogue**, it is fashionable and popular • Colour photographs became the vogue.

voice, voices, voicing, voiced NOUN ① Your voice is the sounds produced by your vocal cords, or the ability to make such sounds. ▶ VERB ② If you voice an opinion or an emotion, you say what you think or feel • A range of opinions were voiced.

voicemail NOUN Voicemail is a system that stores telephone messages so that the person being called can listen to them later.

void, voids NOUN ① a situation which seems empty because it has no interest or excitement • Cats fill a very large void in your life. ② a large empty hole or space • His feet dangled in the void.

volatile ADJECTIVE liable to change often and unexpectedly • The situation at work is volatile.

volcanic ADJECTIVE A volcanic region has many volcanoes or was created by volcanoes.

volcano, volcanoes NOUN GEOGRAPHY a hill with an opening through which lava, gas and ash burst out from inside the earth onto the surface. **WORD HISTORY:** named after Vulcan, the Roman god of fire

vole, voles NOUN a small mammal like a mouse with a short tail, which lives in fields and near rivers.

volition NOUN (formal) If you do

something of your own volition, you do it because you have decided for yourself, without being persuaded by others • *He attended of his own volition*.

volley, volleys NOUN ①A volley of shots or gunfire is a lot of shots fired at the same time. ②In tennis, a volley is a stroke in which the player hits the ball before it bounces.

volleyball NOUN Volleyball is a game in which two teams hit a large ball back and forth over a high net with their hands. The ball is not allowed to bounce on the ground.

volt, volts NOUN SCIENCE A volt is a unit of electrical force. One volt produces one amp of electricity when the resistance is one ohm. **WORD HISTORY:** named after the Italian physicist Count Alessandro *Volta* (1745–1827)

voltage, voltages NOUN The voltage of an electric current is its force measured in volts.

voltmeter, voltmeters NOUN SCIENCE an instrument for measuring potential difference in volts.

volume, volumes NOUN ① MATHS The volume of something is the amount of space it contains or occupies. ②The volume of something is also the amount of it that there is • *a large volume of letters*. ③The volume of a radio, TV or MP3 player is the strength of the sound that it produces. ④a book, or one of a series of books.

voluminous *[Said vol-loo-min-uss]* ADJECTIVE very large or full in size or quantity • *voluminous skirts*.

voluntary ADJECTIVE ①Voluntary actions are ones that you do because you choose to do them and not because you have been forced to do them. ②Voluntary work is done by

people who are not paid for what they do. **voluntarily** ADVERB

volunteer, volunteers, volunteering, volunteered NOUN ① CITIZENSHIP someone who does work for which they are not paid • *a volunteer for Greenpeace*. ②someone who chooses to join the armed forces, especially during wartime. ▶ VERB ③ CITIZENSHIP If you volunteer to do something, you offer to do it rather than being forced into it. ④If you volunteer information, you give it without being asked.

voluptuous *[Said vol-lupt-yoo-uss]* ADJECTIVE having a figure which is considered to be full and attractive. **voluptuously** ADVERB **voluptuousness** NOUN

vomit, vomits, vomiting, vomited VERB ①If you vomit, food and drink comes back up from your stomach and out through your mouth. ▶ NOUN ②Vomit is partly digested food and drink that has come back up from someone's stomach and out through their mouth.

voodoo NOUN Voodoo is a form of magic practised in the Caribbean, especially in Haiti.

Voortrekker, Voortrekkers *[Said foor-trek-er]* NOUN an Afrikaner settler who migrated from the Cape Colony to the Transvaal and the Orange Free State in the 1830s.

vortex, vortexes or vortices NOUN A vortex is a mass of wind or water which spins round so fast that it pulls objects into its empty centre.

vote, votes, voting, voted NOUN ① CITIZENSHIP Someone's vote is their choice in an election, or at a meeting where decisions are taken. ②When a group of people have a vote, they make a decision by allowing each person in the group to

a
b
c
d
e
f
g
h
i
j
k
l
m
n
o
p
q
r
s
t
u
v
w
x
y
z

say what they would prefer. ③ In an election, the vote is the total number of people who have made their choice • *the average Liberal vote.* ④ If people have the vote, they have the legal right to vote in an election.
▶ **VERB** ⑤ CITIZENSHIP When people vote, they indicate their choice or opinion, usually by writing on a piece of paper or by raising their hand. ⑥ If you vote that a particular thing should happen, you are suggesting it should happen • *I vote that we all go to the Netherlands.* **voter NOUN**

vouch, vouches, vouching, vouched **VERB** ① If you say that you can vouch for something, you mean that you have evidence from your own experience that it is true or correct. ② If you say that you can vouch for someone, you mean that you are sure that you can guarantee their good behaviour or support • *Her employer will vouch for her.*

voucher, vouchers **NOUN** a piece of paper that can be used instead of money to pay for something.

vow, vows, vowing, vowed **VERB** ① If you vow to do something, you make a solemn promise to do it • *He vowed to do better in future.*

▶ **NOUN** ② a solemn promise.

vowel, vowels **NOUN** ENGLISH a sound made without your tongue touching the roof of your mouth or your teeth, or one of the letters a, e, i, o, u, which represent such sounds.

voyage, voyages **NOUN** a long journey on a ship or in a spacecraft. **voyager NOUN**

vulgar **ADJECTIVE** ① socially unacceptable or offensive • *vulgar language.* ② showing a lack of taste or quality • *IShe thought it was a very vulgar house.* **vulgarity NOUN** **vulgarly ADVERB**

vulnerable **ADJECTIVE** weak and without protection. **vulnerably ADVERB** **vulnerability NOUN** SIMILAR WORDS: defenceless, susceptible, weak

vulture, vultures **NOUN** a large bird which lives in hot countries and eats the flesh of dead animals.

vuvuzela, vuvuzelas [*Said voo-voo-***zel**-*a*] **NOUN** in South Africa, a vuvuzela is a plastic instrument that is blown to make a trumpeting sound.

vying the present participle of **vie**.

Ww

wacky, wackier, wackiest
ADJECTIVE (*informal*) odd or crazy
• *wacky clothes*.

wad, wads NOUN ①A wad of papers
or banknotes is a thick bundle of
them. ②A wad of something is a
lump of it • *a wad of cotton wool*.

waddle, waddles, waddling,
waddled VERB When a duck or a fat
person waddles, they walk with
short, quick steps, swaying slightly
from side to side.

waddy, waddies NOUN a heavy
wooden club used by Aboriginal
Australians as a weapon in war.

wade, wades, wading, waded VERB
① If you wade through water or mud,
you walk slowly through it. ② If you
wade through a book or document,
you spend a lot of time and effort
reading it because you find it dull or
difficult.

wader, waders NOUN Waders are
long waterproof rubber boots worn
by fishermen.

wafer, wafers NOUN ① a thin, crisp,
sweet biscuit often eaten with ice
cream. ② a thin disc of special bread
used in the Christian service of Holy
Communion.

waffle, waffles, waffling, waffled
[*Said wof-fl*] VERB ① When someone
waffles, they talk or write a lot
without being clear or without
saying anything of importance.
▶ NOUN ② Waffle is vague and
lengthy speech or writing. ③ a thick,
crisp pancake with squares marked

on it often eaten with syrup poured
over it.

waft, wafts, wafting, wafted [*Said
wahft*] VERB If a sound or scent wafts
or is wafted through the air, it moves
gently through it.

wag, wags, wagging, wagged VERB
① When a dog wags its tail, it shakes
it repeatedly from side to side. ② If
you wag your finger, you move it
repeatedly up and down.

wage, wages, waging, waged
NOUN ①A wage or wages is the
regular payment made to someone
each week for the work they do,
especially for manual or unskilled
work. ▶ VERB ② If a person or
country wages a campaign or war,
they start it and carry it on over a
period of time.

wager, wagers NOUN a bet.

wagon, wagons; also spelt **waggon**
NOUN ① a strong four-wheeled
vehicle for carrying heavy loads,
usually pulled by a horse or tractor.
② Wagons are also the containers for
freight pulled by a railway engine.

waif, waifs NOUN a young, thin
person who looks hungry and
homeless.

wail, wails, wailing, wailed VERB
① To wail is to cry loudly with sorrow
or pain. ▶ NOUN ② a long, unhappy
cry.

waist, waists NOUN the middle part
of your body where it narrows
slightly above your hips.

waistcoat, waistcoats NOUN a sleeveless piece of clothing, often worn under a suit or jacket, which buttons up the front.

wait, waits, waiting, waited VERB ① If you wait, you spend time, usually doing little or nothing, before something happens. ② If something can wait, it is not urgent and can be dealt with later. ③ If you wait on people in a restaurant, it is your job to serve them food. ▶ NOUN ④ a period of time before something happens. ▶ PHRASE ⑤ If you **can't wait** to do something, you are very excited and eager to do it.

waiter, waiters NOUN a person who works in a restaurant, serving people with food and drink.

waiting list, waiting lists NOUN a list of people who have asked for something which cannot be given to them immediately, for example medical treatment.

waitress, waitresses NOUN a woman who works in a restaurant, serving people with food and drink.

waive, waives, waiving, waived [Said wave] VERB If someone waives something such as a rule or a right, they decide not to insist on it being applied.

SPELLING TIP

Do not confuse the spellings of waive and wave: All the bands in the concert have waived their fees; Aileen looked over and waved to me.

---

wake, wakes, waking, woke, woken VERB ① When you wake or when something wakes you, you become conscious again after being asleep. ▶ NOUN ② The wake of a boat or other object moving in water is the track of waves it leaves behind it. ③ a gathering of people who have got together to mourn someone's death. ▶ PHRASE ④ If one thing follows **in the wake of** another, it follows it as a result of it, or in imitation of it • a project set up in the wake of last year's riots. **wake up** VERB ① When you wake up or something wakes you up, you become conscious again after being asleep. ② If you wake up to a dangerous situation, you become aware of it.

SIMILAR WORDS: ① awaken, rouse

waken, wakens, wakening, wakened VERB (literary) When you waken someone, you wake them up.

walk, walks, walking, walked VERB ① When you walk, you move along by putting one foot in front of the other on the ground. ② If you walk away with or walk off with something such as a prize, you win it or achieve it easily. ▶ NOUN ③ a journey made by walking • We'll have a quick walk. ④ Your walk is the way you walk • his rolling walk. **walk out** VERB ① If you walk out on someone, you leave them suddenly. ② If workers walk out, they go on strike.

walkabout, walkabouts NOUN ① an informal walk amongst crowds in a public place by royalty or by some other well-known person. ② Walkabout is a period when an Aboriginal Australian wanders in the bush to return to a traditional way of life.

walker, walkers NOUN a person who walks, especially for pleasure or to keep fit.

walking stick, walking sticks NOUN a wooden stick which people can lean on while walking.

walk of life, walks of life NOUN The walk of life that you come from is the position you have in society and the kind of job you have.

walkover, walkovers NOUN
(*informal*) a very easy victory in a
competition or contest.

walkway, walkways NOUN a
passage between two buildings for
people to walk along.

wall, walls NOUN ① one of the
vertical sides of a building or a room.
② a long, narrow vertical structure
made of stone or brick that
surrounds or divides an area of land.
③ a lining or membrane enclosing a
bodily cavity or structure • *the wall of
the womb*.

wallaby, wallabies NOUN an
Australian animal like a small
kangaroo.
WORD HISTORY: from *wolaba*, from
an Aboriginal language

wallaroo, wallaroos NOUN a large,
stocky kangaroo that lives in rocky
or mountainous regions of
Australia.

wallet, wallets NOUN a small, flat
case made of leather or plastic, used
for keeping paper money and
sometimes credit cards.

wallop, wallops, walloping,
walloped VERB (*informal*) If you
wallop someone, you hit them very
hard.

wallow, wallows, wallowing,
wallowed VERB ① If you wallow in
an unpleasant feeling or situation,
you allow it to continue longer than
is reasonable or necessary because
you are getting a kind of enjoyment
from it • *We're wallowing in misery*.
② When an animal wallows in mud or
water, it lies or rolls about in it slowly
for pleasure.

wallpaper, wallpapers NOUN
Wallpaper is thick coloured or
patterned paper for pasting onto the
walls of rooms in order to decorate
them.

walnut, walnuts NOUN ① an edible
nut with a wrinkled shape and a
hard, round, light-brown shell.
② Walnut is wood from the walnut
tree which is often used for making
expensive furniture.
WORD HISTORY: from Old English
walh-hnutu meaning 'foreign nut'

walrus, walruses NOUN an animal
which lives in the sea and which
looks like a large seal with a tough
skin, coarse whiskers, and two tusks.

waltz, waltzes, waltzing, waltzed
NOUN ① a dance which has a rhythm
of three beats to the bar. ▶ VERB ② If
you waltz with someone, you dance
a waltz with them. ③ (*informal*) If you
waltz somewhere, you walk there in
a relaxed and confident way.
WORD HISTORY: from Old German
walzen meaning 'to revolve'

wan [*Rhymes with* **on**] ADJECTIVE pale
and tired-looking.

WAN, WANs NOUN ICT a large group
of computers that are linked by
telephone lines or wireless
technology. WAN is an abbreviation
for 'wide area network'.

wand, wands NOUN a long, thin rod
that magicians wave when they are
performing tricks and magic.

wander, wanders, wandering,
wandered VERB ① If you wander in a
place, you walk around in a casual
way. ② If your mind wanders or your
thoughts wander, you lose
concentration and start thinking
about other things. **wanderer**
NOUN
SIMILAR WORDS: ① ramble, roam,
stroll

SPELLING TIP
Do not confuse the spellings of
wander and *wonder*: *We wandered
through the gardens; I wondered why she
had been trying to contact me.*

a
b
c
d
e
f
g
h
i
j
k
l
m
n
o
p
q
r
s
t
u
v
w
x
y
z

wane, wanes, waning, waned VERB
If a condition, attitude or emotion wanes, it becomes gradually weaker.

wangle, wangles, wangling, wangled VERB (*informal*) If you wangle something that you want, you manage to get it by being crafty or persuasive.

want, wants, wanting, wanted VERB ① If you want something, you feel a desire to have it. ② If something is wanted, it is needed or needs to be done. ③ If someone is wanted, the police are searching for them • *John was wanted for fraud*. ▶ NOUN ④ (*formal*) A want of something is a lack of it.

wanting ADJECTIVE If you find something wanting or if it proves wanting, it is not as good in some way as you think it should be.

wanton ADJECTIVE A wanton action deliberately causes unnecessary harm or waste • *wanton destruction*.

war, wars, warring, warred NOUN ① a period of fighting between countries or states when weapons are used and many people may be killed. ② a competition between groups of people, or a campaign against something • *a trade war* • *the war against crime*. ▶ VERB ③ When two countries war with each other, they are fighting a war against each other. **warring** ADJECTIVE
SIMILAR WORDS: ① battle, fighting, hostilities ③ battle, fight

waratah, waratahs [*Said* wor-ra-**tah**] NOUN an Australian shrub with dark green leaves and large clusters of crimson flowers.

warble, warbles, warbling, warbled VERB When a bird warbles, it sings pleasantly with high notes.

ward, wards, warding, warded NOUN ① a room in a hospital which has beds for several people who need similar treatment. ② an area or district which forms a separate part of a political constituency or local council. ③ A ward or a ward of court is a child who is officially put in the care of an adult or a court of law, because their parents are dead or because they need protection.

ward off VERB If you ward off a danger or an illness, you do something to prevent it from affecting or harming you.

-ward or **-wards** SUFFIX '-ward' and '-wards' form adverbs or adjectives that show the way something is moving or facing • *homeward* • *westwards*.

warden, wardens NOUN ① a person in charge of a building or institution such as a youth hostel or prison. ② an official who makes sure that certain laws or rules are obeyed in a particular place or activity • *a traffic warden*.

warder, warders NOUN a person who is in charge of prisoners in a jail.

wardrobe, wardrobes NOUN ① a tall cupboard in which you can hang your clothes. ② Someone's wardrobe is their collection of clothes.

ware, wares NOUN ① Ware is manufactured goods of a particular kind • *kitchenware*. ② Someone's wares are the things they sell, usually in the street or in a market.

warehouse, warehouses NOUN a large building where raw materials or manufactured goods are stored.

warfare NOUN Warfare is the activity of fighting a war.

warhead, warheads NOUN the front end of a bomb or missile, where the explosives are carried.

warlock, warlocks NOUN a male witch.

warm, warmer, warmest; warms, warming, warmed ADJECTIVE
① Something that is warm has some heat, but not enough to be hot • *a warm day*. ② Warm clothes or blankets are made of a material which protects you from the cold. ③ Warm colours or sounds are pleasant and make you feel comfortable and relaxed. ④ A warm person is friendly and affectionate. ▶ VERB ⑤ If you warm something, you heat it up gently so that it stops being cold. **warmly** ADVERB
warm up VERB If you warm up for an event or an activity, you practise or exercise gently to prepare for it.

warm-blooded ADJECTIVE An animal that is warm-blooded has a relatively high body temperature which remains constant and does not change with the surrounding temperature.

warmth NOUN ① Warmth is a moderate amount of heat. ② Someone who has warmth is friendly and affectionate.

warn, warns, warning, warned VERB ① If you warn someone about a possible problem or danger, you tell them about it in advance so that they are aware of it • *I warned him what it would be like*. ② If you warn someone not to do something, you advise them not to do it, in order to avoid possible danger or punishment • *I have warned her not to train for 10 days*. **warn off** VERB If you warn someone off, you tell them to go away or to stop doing something.
SIMILAR WORDS: ① alert, caution, notify

warning, warnings NOUN something said or written to tell people of a possible problem or danger.

warp, warps, warping, warped VERB ① If something warps or is warped, it becomes bent, often because of the effect of heat or water. ② If something warps someone's mind or character, it makes them abnormal or corrupt.

warrant, warrants, warranting, warranted VERB ① (*formal*) If something warrants a particular action, it makes the action seem necessary • *no evidence to warrant a murder investigation*. ▶ NOUN ② an official document which gives permission to the police to do something • *a warrant for his arrest*.

warranty, warranties NOUN a guarantee • *a three-year warranty*.

warren, warrens NOUN a group of holes under the ground connected by tunnels, which rabbits live in.

warrigal, warrigals [*Said* **wor**-rih-gl] NOUN ① In Australian English, a warrigal is a dingo. ② In Australian English, a wild horse or other wild creature. ▶ ADJECTIVE ③ In Australian English, wild.

warrior, warriors NOUN a fighting man or soldier, especially in former times.

warship, warships NOUN a ship built with guns and used for fighting in wars.

wart, warts NOUN a small, hard piece of skin which can grow on someone's face or hands.

wartime NOUN Wartime is a period of time during which a country is at war.

wary, warier, wariest ADJECTIVE cautious and on one's guard • *Michelle is wary of strangers*. **warily** ADVERB **wariness** NOUN

was a past tense of **be**.

wash, washes, washing, washed VERB ① If you wash something, you

a
b
c
d
e
f
g
h
i
j
k
l
m
n
o
p
q
r
s
t
u
v
w
x
y
z

clean it with water and soap. ② If you wash, you clean yourself using soap and water. ③ If something is washed somewhere, it is carried there gently by water • *The infant Arthur was washed ashore.* ▸ NOUN ④ The wash is all the clothes and bedding that are washed together at one time • *a typical family's weekly wash.* ⑤ The wash in water is the disturbance and waves produced at the back of a moving boat. ▸ PHRASE ⑥ If you **wash your hands of** something or someone, you refuse to have anything more to do with it or them.

wash up VERB ① If you wash up, you wash the dishes, pans and cutlery used in preparing and eating a meal. ② If something is washed up on land, it is carried by a river or sea and left there • *Some wreckage had been washed up on the beach.*

washable ADJECTIVE able to be washed without being damaged.

washbasin, washbasins NOUN a deep bowl, usually fixed to a wall, with taps for hot and cold water.

washer, washers NOUN ① a thin, flat ring of metal or plastic which is placed over a bolt before the nut is screwed on, so that it is fixed more tightly. ② In Australian English, a washer is a small piece of towelling for washing yourself.

washing NOUN Washing consists of clothes and bedding which need to be washed or are in the process of being washed and dried.

washing machine, washing machines NOUN a machine for washing clothes in.

washing-up NOUN If you do the washing-up, you wash the dishes, pans and cutlery which have been used in the cooking and eating of a meal.

wasp, wasps NOUN an insect with yellow and black stripes across its body, which can sting like a bee.

wastage NOUN Wastage is loss and misuse of something • *wastage of resources.*

waste, wastes, wasting, wasted VERB ① If you waste time, money or energy, you use too much of it on something that is not important or necessary. ② If you waste an opportunity, you do not take advantage of it when it is available. ③ If you say that something is wasted on someone, you mean that it is too good, too clever, or too sophisticated for them • *This book is wasted on us.* ▸ NOUN ④ If an activity is a waste of time, money or energy, it is not important or necessary. ⑤ Waste is the use of more money or some other resource than is necessary. ⑥ Waste is also material that is no longer wanted, or material left over from a useful process • *nuclear waste.* ▸ ADJECTIVE ⑦ unwanted in its present form • *waste paper.* ⑧ Waste land is land which is not used or looked after by anyone. **waste away** VERB If someone is wasting away, they are becoming very thin and weak because they are ill or not eating properly.
SIMILAR WORDS: ① fritter away, misuse, squander ⑤ misuse, squandering

wasted ADJECTIVE not necessary or useful • *a wasted journey.*

wasteful ADJECTIVE extravagant or causing waste by using something in a careless and inefficient way.
SIMILAR WORDS: extravagant, prodigal, spendthrift

wasteland, wastelands NOUN A wasteland is land which is of no use because it is infertile or has been misused.

wasting ADJECTIVE A wasting disease is one that gradually reduces the strength and health of the body.

watch, watches, watching, watched NOUN ① a small clock usually worn on a strap on the wrist. ② a period of time during which a guard is kept over something. ▸ VERB ③ If you watch something, you look at it for some time and pay close attention to what is happening. ④ If you watch someone or something, you take care of them. ⑤ If you watch a situation, you pay attention to it or are aware of it • *I had watched Jimmy's progress with interest.*

watch out VERB ① If you watch out for something, you keep alert to see if it is near you • *Watch out for more fog and ice.* ② If you tell someone to watch out, you are warning them to be very careful.

watchdog, watchdogs NOUN ① a dog used to guard property. ② a person or group whose job is to make sure that companies do not act illegally or irresponsibly.

watchful ADJECTIVE careful to notice everything that is happening • *the watchful eye of her father.*

watchman, watchmen NOUN a person whose job is to guard property.

water, waters, watering, watered NOUN ① Water is a clear, colourless, tasteless and odourless liquid that is necessary for all plant and animal life. ② You use 'water' or 'waters' to refer to a large area of water, such as a lake or sea • *the black waters of the lake.* ▸ VERB ③ If you water a plant or an animal, you give it water to drink. ④ If your eyes water, you have tears in them because they are hurting. ⑤ If your mouth waters, it produces extra saliva, usually because you think of or can smell something

appetising. **water down** VERB If you water something down, you make it weaker.

watercolour, watercolours NOUN ① Watercolours are paints for painting pictures, which are diluted with water or put on the paper using a wet brush. ② a picture which has been painted using watercolours.

watercress NOUN Watercress is a small plant which grows in streams and pools. Its leaves taste hot and are eaten in salads.

water cycle NOUN GEOGRAPHY The water cycle is the continuous process in which water evaporates from the sea, forming clouds. The clouds break as rain, which makes its way back to the sea, where the process starts again.

waterfall, waterfalls NOUN GEOGRAPHY A waterfall is water from a river or stream as it flows over the edge of a steep cliff in hills or mountains and falls to the ground below.

waterfront, waterfronts NOUN a street or piece of land next to an area of water such as a river or harbour.

watering can, watering cans NOUN a container with a handle and a long spout, which you use to water plants.

waterlogged ADJECTIVE Land that is waterlogged is so wet that the soil cannot contain any more water, so that some water remains on the surface of the ground.

watermelon, watermelons NOUN a large, round fruit which has a hard green skin and red juicy flesh.

waterproof, waterproofs ADJECTIVE ① not letting water pass through • *waterproof clothing.* ▸ NOUN ② a coat which keeps water out.

a
b
c
d
e
f
g
h
i
j
k
l
m
n
o
p
q
r
s
t
u
v
w
x
y
z

water quality NOUN GEOGRAPHY a measurement of how pure a body of water is.

watershed, watersheds NOUN ① an event or period which marks a turning point or the beginning of a new way of life • *a watershed in European history.* ② GEOGRAPHY A watershed is an area of high ground, such as a ridge, which divides two river systems, so that they flow in different directions.

watersider, watersiders NOUN In Australian and New Zealand English, a watersider is a person who loads and unloads the cargo from ships.

water-skiing NOUN Water-skiing is the sport of skimming over the water on skis while being pulled by a boat.

water table, water tables NOUN GEOGRAPHY The water table is the level below the surface of the ground at which water can be found.

watertight ADJECTIVE ① Something that is watertight does not allow water to pass through. ② An agreement or an argument that is watertight has been so carefully put together that nobody should be able to find a fault in it.

waterway, waterways NOUN a canal, river or narrow channel of sea which ships or boats can sail along.

waterworks NOUN A waterworks is the system of pipes, filters and tanks where the public supply of water is stored and cleaned, and from where it is distributed.

watery ADJECTIVE ① pale or weak • *a watery smile.* ② Watery food or drink contains a lot of water or is thin like water.

watt, watts [Said *wot*] NOUN SCIENCE a unit of power equal to one joule per second. It is named after James Watt (1736–1819), the inventor of the modern steam engine.

wattle, wattles [Said *wot-tl*] NOUN an Australian acacia tree with spikes of brightly coloured flowers.

wave, waves, waving, waved VERB ① If you wave your hand, you move it from side to side, usually to say hello or goodbye. ② If you wave someone somewhere or wave them on, you make a movement with your hand to tell them which way to go. ③ If you wave something, you hold it up and move it from side to side • *The doctor waved a piece of paper at him.* ▶ NOUN ④ a ridge of water on the surface of the sea caused by wind or by tides. ⑤ A wave is the form in which some types of energy such as heat, light or sound travel through a substance. ⑥ A wave of sympathy, alarm or panic is a steady increase in it which spreads through you or through a group of people. ⑦ an increase in a type of activity or behaviour • *the crime wave.*
SIMILAR WORDS: ③ brandish, flourish

SPELLING TIP
Do not confuse the spellings of *wave* and *waive: Aileen looked over and waved to me; All the bands in the concert have waived their fees.*

wave-cut notch, wave-cut notches NOUN GEOGRAPHY a place where a cliff is eroded by the sea at the high-water mark.

wave-cut platform, wave-cut platforms NOUN GEOGRAPHY a flat surface at the base of a cliff formed after erosion by the sea has created a wave-cut notch which eventually causes the cliff above it to fall away.

wavelength, wavelengths NOUN ① SCIENCE the distance between the same point on two adjacent waves of energy. ② the size of radio wave which a particular radio station uses to broadcast its programmes.

waver, wavers, wavering, wavered
VERB ① If you waver or if your confidence or beliefs waver, you are no longer as firm, confident or sure in your beliefs • *Ben has never wavered from his belief.* ② If something wavers, it moves slightly • *The shadows wavered on the wall.*

wavy, wavier, waviest **ADJECTIVE** having waves or regular curves • *wavy hair.*

wax, waxes, waxing, waxed **NOUN** ① Wax is a solid, slightly shiny substance made of fat or oil and used to make candles and polish. ② Wax is also the sticky yellow substance in your ears. ▸ **VERB** ③ If you wax a surface, you treat it or cover it with a thin layer of wax, especially to polish it. ④ (*formal*) If you wax eloquent, you talk in an eloquent way.

way, ways **NOUN** ① A way of doing something is the manner of doing it • *an excellent way of cooking meat.* ② The ways of a person or group are their customs or their normal behaviour • *Their ways are certainly different.* ③ The way you feel about something is your attitude to it or your opinion about it. ④ If you have a way with people or things, you are very skilful at dealing with them. ⑤ The way to a particular place is the route that you take to get there. ⑥ If you go or look a particular way, you go or look in that direction • *She glanced the other way.* ⑦ If you divide something a number of ways, you divide it into that number of parts. ⑧ Way is used with words such as 'little' or 'long' to say how far off in distance or time something is • *They lived a long way away.* ▸ **PHRASE** ⑨ If something or someone is **in the way**, they prevent you from moving freely or seeing clearly. ⑩ You say **by the way** when adding something to

what you are saying • *By the way, I asked Brad to drop in.* ⑪ If you **go out of your way** to do something, you make a special effort to do it.
SIMILAR WORDS: ⑤ course, path, route

SPELLING TIP
Do not confuse the spellings of *way* and *weigh*: *What is the quickest way to the station from here?*; *Weigh your ingredients carefully.*

---

wayside **PHRASE** If someone or something **falls by the wayside**, they fail in what they are trying to do, or become forgotten and ignored.

wayward **ADJECTIVE** difficult to control and likely to change suddenly • *a wayward teenager.*

WC, WCs **NOUN** a toilet. WC is an abbreviation for 'water closet'.

we **PRONOUN** A speaker or writer uses 'we' to refer to himself or herself and one or more other people • *We are going to see Eddie.*

weak, weaker, weakest **ADJECTIVE** ① not having much strength • *weak from lack of sleep.* ② If something is weak, it is likely to break or fail • *Russia's weak economy.* ③ If you describe someone as weak, you mean they are easily influenced by other people. **weakly** **ADVERB**
SIMILAR WORDS: ① feeble, frail, puny

weaken, weakens, weakening, weakened **VERB** ① If someone weakens something, they make it less strong or certain. ② If someone weakens, they become less certain about something.

weakling, weaklings **NOUN** a person who lacks physical strength or who is weak in character or health.

weakness, weaknesses **NOUN** ① Weakness is lack of moral or physical strength. ② If you have a weakness for something, you have a great liking for it • *a weakness for whisky*.

wealth NOUN ① GEOGRAPHY Wealth is the large amount of money or property which someone owns. ②A wealth of something is a lot of it • *a wealth of information*.

SIMILAR WORDS: ①fortune, prosperity, riches

wealthy, **wealthier**, **wealthiest** ADJECTIVE having a large amount of money, property or other valuable things.

SIMILAR WORDS: affluent, rich, well-off

wean, **weans**, **weaning**, **weaned** VERB To wean a baby or animal is to start feeding it food other than its mother's milk.

weapon, **weapons** NOUN ①an object used to kill or hurt people in a fight or war. ② anything which can be used to get the better of an opponent • *Surprise was his only weapon*. **weaponry** NOUN

wear, **wears**, **wearing**, **wore**, **worn** VERB ①When you wear something such as clothes, make-up or jewellery, you have them on your body or face. ② If you wear a particular expression, it shows on your face. ③ If something wears, it becomes thinner or worse in condition. ▶ NOUN ④You can refer to clothes that are suitable for a particular time or occasion as a kind of wear • *beach wear*. ⑤Wear is the amount or type of use that something has and which causes damage or change to it • *signs of wear*.

wear down VERB If you wear people down, you weaken them by repeatedly doing something or asking them to do something.

wear off VERB If a feeling such as pain wears off, it gradually

disappears. **wear on** VERB If time wears on, it seems to pass very slowly or boringly. **wear out** VERB ①When something wears out or when you wear it out, it is used so much that it becomes thin, weak and no longer usable. ② (*informal*) If you wear someone out, you make them feel extremely tired.

wear and tear NOUN Wear and tear is the damage caused to something by normal use.

wearing ADJECTIVE Someone or something that is wearing makes you feel extremely tired.

weary, **wearier**, **weariest**; **wearies**, **wearying**, **wearied** ADJECTIVE ①very tired. ▶ VERB ②If you weary of something, you become tired of it. **wearily** ADVERB **weariness** NOUN

weasel, **weasels** NOUN a small wild mammal with a long, thin body and short legs.

weather, **weathers**, **weathering**, **weathered** NOUN ①The weather is the condition of the atmosphere at any particular time and the amount of rain, wind or sunshine occurring. ▶ VERB ②If something such as rock or wood weathers, it changes colour or shape as a result of being exposed to the wind, rain or sun. ③If you weather a problem or difficulty, you come through it safely. ▶ PHRASE ④If you are **under the weather**, you feel slightly ill.

weather forecast, **weather forecasts** NOUN a statement saying what the weather will be like the next day or for the next few days.

weather vane, **weather vanes** NOUN a metal object on the roof of a building which turns round in the wind and shows which way the wind is blowing.

weave, weaves, weaving, wove, woven VERB ① To weave cloth is to make it by crossing threads over and under each other, especially by using a machine called a loom. ② If you weave your way somewhere, you go there by moving from side to side through and round the obstacles. ▶ NOUN ③ The weave of cloth is the way in which the threads are arranged and the pattern that they form • *a tight weave*.

weaver, weavers NOUN a person who weaves cloth.

web, webs NOUN ① a fine net of threads that a spider makes from a sticky substance which it produces in its body. ② something that has a complicated structure or pattern • *a web of lies*. ③ The Web is the same as the **World Wide Web**.

webbed ADJECTIVE Webbed feet have the toes connected by a piece of skin.

webcam, webcams NOUN a video camera that takes pictures which can be viewed on a website.

weblog, weblogs NOUN the full name for a **blog**.

webmail NOUN ICT Webmail is electronic mail that you access on a website rather than downloading to your computer.

website, websites NOUN a publication on the World Wide Web which contains information about a particular subject.

wed, weds, wedding, wedded or wed VERB (old-fashioned) If you wed someone or if you wed, you get married.

wedding, weddings NOUN a marriage ceremony.

wedge, wedges, wedging, wedged VERB ① If you wedge something, you force it to remain there by holding it there tightly, or by fixing something next to it to prevent it from moving • *I shut the shed door and wedged it with a log of wood*. ▶ NOUN ② a piece of something such as wood, metal or rubber with one pointed edge and one thick edge which is used to wedge something. ③ a piece of something that has a thick triangular shape • *a wedge of cheese*.

wedlock NOUN (old-fashioned) Wedlock is the state of being married.

Wednesday, Wednesdays NOUN Wednesday is the day between Tuesday and Thursday.

WORD HISTORY: from Old English *Wodnes dæg* meaning 'Woden's day'

SPELLING TIP
Remember this mnemonic: *JoeWED NESsa on WEDNESday*.

wee, weer, weest ADJECTIVE In Scotland, a term for small.

weed, weeds, weeding, weeded NOUN ① a wild plant that prevents cultivated plants from growing properly. ▶ VERB ② If you weed a place, you remove the weeds from it.

weed out VERB If you weed out unwanted things, you get rid of them.

weedkiller, weedkillers NOUN a chemical used for killing weeds.

week, weeks NOUN ① a period of seven days, especially one beginning on a Sunday and ending on a Saturday. ② A week is also the number of hours you spend at work during a week • *a 35-hour week*. ③ The week can refer to the part of a week that does not include Saturday and Sunday • *They are working during the week*.

weekday, weekdays NOUN any day except Saturday and Sunday.

a b c d e f g h i j k l m n o p q r s t u v w x y z

weekend, weekends NOUN Saturday and Sunday.

weekly, weeklies ADJECTIVE ① happening or appearing once a week. ▶ ADVERB ② once a week • *I see my mother weekly.* ▶ NOUN ③ A weekly is a newspaper or magazine that is published once a week.

weep, weeps, weeping, wept VERB ① If someone weeps, they cry. ② If something such as a wound weeps, it oozes blood or other liquid.

weevil, weevils NOUN a type of beetle which eats grain, seeds or plants.

weft NOUN The weft of a piece of woven material is the threads which are passed sideways in and out of the threads held in a loom.

weigh, weighs, weighing, weighed VERB ① If something weighs a particular amount, that is how heavy it is. ② If you weigh something, you measure how heavy it is using scales. ③ If you weigh facts or words, you think about them carefully before coming to a decision or before speaking. ④ If a problem weighs on you or weighs upon you, it makes you very worried. **weigh down** VERB ① If a load weighs you down, it stops you moving easily. ② If you are weighed down by a difficulty, it is making you very worried. **weigh up** VERB If you weigh up a person or a situation, you make an assessment of them.

SPELLING TIP
Do not confuse the spellings of *weigh* and *way*: *Weigh your ingredients carefully; What is the quickest way to the station from here?*

weight, weights, weighting, weighted NOUN ① The weight of something is its heaviness. ② a metal object which has a certain known heaviness. Weights are used with sets of scales in order to weigh things. ③ any heavy object. ④ The weight of something is its large amount or importance which makes it hard to fight against or contradict • *the weight of the law.* ▶ VERB ⑤ If you weight something or weight it down, you make it heavier, often so that it cannot move. ▶ PHRASE ⑥ If you **pull your weight**, you work just as hard as other people involved in the same activity.

weighted ADJECTIVE A system that is weighted in favour of a particular person or group is organised in such a way that this person or group will have an advantage.

weightless ADJECTIVE SCIENCE Something that is weightless has no weight or very little weight, for example because it is in space and not affected by the Earth's gravity. **weightlessness** NOUN

weightlifting NOUN Weightlifting is the sport of lifting heavy weights in competition or for exercise. **weightlifter** NOUN

weighty, weightier, weightiest ADJECTIVE serious or important • *a weighty problem.*

weir, weirs [*Rhymes with near*] NOUN a low dam which is built across a river to raise the water level, control the flow of water, or change its direction.

weird, weirder, weirdest [*Said weerd*] ADJECTIVE strange or odd. **weirdly** ADVERB
SIMILAR WORDS: bizarre, odd, strange

weirdo, weirdos [*Said weer-doe*] NOUN (*informal*) If you call someone a weirdo, you mean they behave in a strange way.

welcome, welcomes, welcoming, welcomed VERB ① If you welcome a visitor, you greet them in a friendly way when they arrive. ② 'Welcome' can be said as a greeting to a visitor who has just arrived. ③ If you welcome something, you approve of it and support it • *He welcomed the decision.* ▶ NOUN ④ a greeting to a visitor • *a warm welcome.* ▶ ADJECTIVE ⑤ If someone is welcome at a place, they will be warmly received there. ⑥ If something is welcome, it brings pleasure or is accepted gratefully • *a welcome rest.* ⑦ If you tell someone they are welcome to something or welcome to do something, you mean you are willing for them to have or to do it. **welcoming** ADJECTIVE

weld, welds, welding, welded VERB To weld two pieces of metal together is to join them by heating their edges and fixing them together so that when they cool they harden into one piece. **welder** NOUN

welfare NOUN ① The welfare of a person or group is their general state of health and comfort. ② Welfare services are provided to help with people's living conditions and financial problems • *welfare workers.*

welfare state NOUN The welfare state is a system in which the government uses money from taxes to provide health care and education services, and to give benefits to people who are old, unemployed or sick.

well, better, best; wells, welling, welled ADVERB ① If something goes well, it happens in a satisfactory way • *The interview went well.* ② in a good, skilful or pleasing way • *He draws well.* ③ thoroughly and completely • *well established.* ④ kindly • *We treat our*

employees well. ⑤ If something may well or could well happen, it is likely to happen. ⑥ You use 'well' to emphasise an adjective, adverb or phrase • *He was well aware of that.* ▶ ADJECTIVE ⑦ If you are well, you are healthy. ▶ PHRASE ⑧ As well means also • *He was a bus driver as well.* ⑨ As well as means in addition to • *a meal which includes meat or fish, as well as rice.* ⑩ If you say you **may as well** or **might as well** do something, you mean you will do it, not because you are keen to, but because there is nothing better to do. ▶ NOUN ⑪ a hole drilled in the ground from which water, oil or gas is obtained. ▶ VERB ⑫ If tears well or well up, they appear in someone's eyes.

well-advised ADJECTIVE sensible or wise • *Bill would be well-advised to retire.*

well-balanced ADJECTIVE sensible and without serious emotional problems • *a well-balanced happy teenager.*

wellbeing NOUN PSHE Someone's wellbeing is their health and happiness.

well-earned ADJECTIVE thoroughly deserved.

well-heeled ADJECTIVE (*informal*) wealthy.

well-informed ADJECTIVE having a great deal of knowledge about a subject or subjects.

wellington, wellingtons NOUN Wellingtons or wellington boots are long waterproof rubber boots. Long boots were popularised by the 1st Duke of Wellington.

well-meaning ADJECTIVE A well-meaning person tries to be helpful but is often unsuccessful.

well-off ADJECTIVE (*informal*) quite wealthy.

well-to-do ADJECTIVE quite wealthy.

well-worn ADJECTIVE ①A well-worn expression or saying has been used too often and has become boring. ②A well-worn object or piece of clothing has been used and worn so much that it looks old and shabby.

welly, **wellies** NOUN (*informal*) Wellies are wellingtons.

Welsh ADJECTIVE ①belonging or relating to Wales. ▶NOUN ②Welsh is a language spoken in parts of Wales.

Welshman, **Welshmen** NOUN a man who comes from Wales.

Welshwoman, **Welshwomen** NOUN a woman who comes from Wales.

welt, **welts** NOUN a raised mark on someone's skin made by a blow from something like a whip or a stick.

welter NOUN (*formal*) A welter of things is a large number of them that happen or appear together in a state of confusion • *a welter of rumours*.

wench, **wenches** NOUN (*old-fashioned*) a woman or young girl.

wend, **wends**, **wending**, **wended** VERB (*literary*) If you wend your way in a particular direction, you walk slowly in that direction.

went the past tense of **go**.

wept the past tense and past participle of **weep**.

were a past tense of **be**.

werewolf, **werewolves** NOUN In horror stories, a werewolf is a person who changes into a wolf.
WORD HISTORY: from Old English *wer* + *wulf* meaning 'man wolf'

Wesak [*Said* **wess-suck**] NOUN Wesak is the Buddhist festival celebrating the Buddha, held in May.

west NOUN ①The west is the direction in which you look to see the sun set. ②The west of a place or country is the part which is towards the west when you are in the centre • *the west of America*. ③The West refers to the countries of North America and western and southern Europe. ▶ADVERB or ADJECTIVE ④West means towards the west. ▶ADJECTIVE ⑤A west wind blows from the west.

westerly ADJECTIVE ①Westerly means to or towards the west. ②A westerly wind blows from the west.

western, **westerns** ADJECTIVE ①in or from the west. ②coming from or associated with the countries of North America and western and southern Europe • *western dress*. ▶NOUN ③a book or film about life in the west of America in the 19th century.

westward or **westwards** ADVERB ①Westward or westwards means towards the west • *He stared westwards towards the clouds*. ▶ADJECTIVE ②The westward part of something is the west part.

wet, **wetter**, **wettest**; **wets**, **wetting**, **wet** or **wetted** ADJECTIVE ①If something is wet, it is covered in water or another liquid. ②If the weather is wet, it is raining. ③If something such as paint, ink or cement is wet, it is not yet dry or solid. ④(*informal*) If you say someone is wet, you mean they are weak and lacking confidence • *Don't be so wet!* ▶NOUN ⑤In Australia, the wet is the rainy season. ▶VERB ⑥To wet something is to put water or some other liquid over it. ⑦If people wet themselves or wet their beds, they urinate in their clothes or bed because they cannot control their bladder. **wetness** NOUN

wet suit, wet suits NOUN a close-fitting rubber suit which a diver wears to keep his or her body warm.

whack, whacks, whacking, whacked VERB If you whack someone or something, you hit them hard.

whale, whales NOUN a very large sea mammal which breathes through a hole on the top of its head.

whaling NOUN Whaling is the work of hunting and killing whales for oil or food.

wharf, wharves [Said worf] NOUN a platform beside a river or the sea, where ships load or unload.

what PRONOUN ① 'What' is used in questions • What time is it? ② 'What' is used in indirect questions and statements • I don't know what you mean. ③ 'What' can be used at the beginning of a clause to refer to something with a particular quality • It is impossible to decide what is real and what is invented. ▸ ADJECTIVE ④ 'What' can be used at the beginning of a clause to show that you are talking about the whole amount that is available to you • Their spouses try to earn what money they can. ⑤ You say 'what' to emphasise an opinion or reaction • What nonsense! ▸ PHRASE ⑥ You say **what about** at the beginning of a question when you are making a suggestion or offer • What about a drink?

whatever PRONOUN ① You use 'whatever' to refer to anything or everything of a particular type • He said he would do whatever he could. ② You use 'whatever' when you do not know the precise nature of something • Whatever it is, I don't like it. ▸ CONJUNCTION ③ You use 'whatever' to mean no matter what • Whatever happens, you have to behave decently. ▸ ADVERB ④ You use 'whatever' to emphasise a negative statement or a question • You have no proof whatever • Whatever is wrong with you?

whatsoever ADVERB You use 'whatsoever' to emphasise a negative statement • I have no memory of it whatsoever.

wheat NOUN Wheat is a cereal plant grown for its grain, which is used to make flour.

wheel, wheels, wheeling, wheeled NOUN ① DGT a circular object which turns on a rod attached to its centre. Wheels are fixed underneath vehicles so that they can move along. ② DGT The wheel of a car is its steering wheel. ▸ VERB ③ If you wheel something such as a bicycle, you push it. ④ If someone or something wheels, they move round in the shape of a circle • Cameron wheeled around and hit him.

wheelbarrow, wheelbarrows NOUN a small cart with a single wheel at the front, used for carrying things in the garden.

wheelchair, wheelchairs NOUN a chair with wheels in which sick or injured people, or people with certain disabilities, can move around.

wheeze, wheezes, wheezing, wheezed VERB If someone wheezes, they breathe with difficulty, making a whistling sound, usually because they have a chest complaint such as asthma. **wheezy** ADJECTIVE

whelk, whelks NOUN a snail-like shellfish with a strong shell and a soft edible body.

when ADVERB ① You use 'when' to ask what time something happened or will happen • When are you leaving?

▶ **CONJUNCTION** ②You use 'when' to refer to a time in the past • *I met him when I was sixteen.* ③You use 'when' to introduce the reason for an opinion, comment or question • *How did you pass the exam when you hadn't studied for it?* ④'When' is used to mean although • *He drives when he could walk.*

whence ADVERB or CONJUNCTION (*old-fashioned*) 'Whence' means from where.

GRAMMAR TIP
You should not write *from whence* because *whence* already means 'from where'.

---

whenever CONJUNCTION 'Whenever' means at any time, or every time that something happens • *I still go on courses whenever I can.*

where ADVERB ①You use 'where' to ask which place something is in, is coming from, or is going to • *Where is Philip?* ▶ **CONJUNCTION** or **PRONOUN** or **ADVERB** ②You use 'where' when asking about or referring to something • *I hardly know where to begin.* ▶ **CONJUNCTION** ③You use 'where' to refer to the place in which something is situated or happening • *I don't know where we are.* ④'Where' can introduce a clause that contrasts with the other part of the sentence • *Some people took music lessons, where others learned dance.*

whereabouts NOUN ①The whereabouts of a person or thing is the place where they are. ▶ **ADVERB** ②You use 'whereabouts' when you are asking more precisely where something is • *Whereabouts in Canada are you from?*

whereas CONJUNCTION 'Whereas' introduces a comment that contrasts with the other part of the sentence • *Her eyes were blue, whereas*

mine were brown.

whereby PRONOUN (*formal*) 'Whereby' means by which • *a new system whereby you pay the bill quarterly.*

whereupon CONJUNCTION (*formal*) 'Whereupon' means at which point • *His enemies rejected his message, whereupon he tried again.*

wherever CONJUNCTION ①'Wherever' means in every place or situation • *Alex heard the same thing wherever he went.* ②You use 'wherever' to show that you do not know where a place or person is • *the nearest police station, wherever that is.*

wherewithal NOUN If you have the wherewithal to do something, you have enough money to do it.

whet, whets, whetting, whetted PHRASE To **whet someone's appetite** for something means to increase their desire for it.

whether CONJUNCTION You use 'whether' when you are talking about two or more alternatives • *I don't know whether that's true or false.*

whey [*Rhymes with* **day**] NOUN Whey is the watery liquid that is separated from the curds in sour milk when cheese is made.

which ADJECTIVE or PRONOUN ①You use 'which' to ask about alternatives or to refer to a choice between alternatives • *Which room are you in?* ▶ **PRONOUN** ②'Which' at the beginning of a clause identifies the thing you are talking about or gives more information about it • *certain wrongs which exist in our society.*

GRAMMAR TIP
See the grammar tip at *that.*

What does Which do?

Which is a relative pronoun. A relative pronoun replaces a noun which links two different parts of a sentence.

Relative pronouns always refer to a word in the earlier part of the sentence. The word they refer to is called the **antecedent**. (In the examples that follow, the antecedents are underlined.)

*I have <u>a friend</u> **who** lives in Rome.*
*We could go to <u>a place</u> **that** I know.*

Which is only used when the antecedent is not a person:

*We took <u>the road</u> **which** leads to the sea.*

Also look at the grammar box at **relative pronoun**

whichever ADJECTIVE or PRONOUN You use 'whichever' when you are talking about different alternatives or possibilities • *Make your pizzas round or square, whichever you prefer.*

whiff, whiffs NOUN ① a slight smell of something. ② a slight sign or trace of something • *a whiff of criticism.*

Whig, Whigs NOUN HISTORY In the 18th and 19th centuries, a Whig was a member of a British political party that was in favour of social change.

while, whiles, whiling, whiled CONJUNCTION ① If something happens while something else is happening, the two things happen at the same time. ② While also means but • *The first issue is free, while the second costs £5.* ▶ NOUN ③ a period of time • *a little while earlier.* ▶ PHRASE ④ If an action or activity is **worth your while**, it will be helpful or useful to you if you do it. **while away** VERB If you while away the time in a particular way, you pass the time that way because you have nothing else to do.

whilst CONJUNCTION Whilst means the same as while.

whim, whims NOUN a sudden desire or fancy.

SIMILAR WORDS: fancy, impulse

whimper, whimpers, whimpering, whimpered VERB ① When children or animals whimper, they make soft, low, unhappy sounds. ② If you whimper something, you say it in an unhappy or frightened way, as if you are about to cry.

whimsical ADJECTIVE unusual and slightly playful • *an endearing, whimsical charm.*

whine, whines, whining, whined VERB ① To whine is to make a long, high-pitched noise, especially one which sounds sad or unpleasant. ② If someone whines about something, they complain about it in an annoying way. ▶ NOUN ③ A whine is the noise made by something or someone whining.

whinge, whinges, whingeing, whinged VERB If someone whinges about something, they complain about it in an annoying way.

whinny, whinnies, whinnying, whinnied VERB When a horse whinnies, it neighs softly.

whip, whips, whipping, whipped NOUN ① a thin piece of leather or rope attached to a handle, which is used for hitting people or animals. ▶ VERB ② If you whip a person or animal, you hit them with a whip. ③ When the wind whips something, it strikes it. ④ If you whip something out or off, you take it out or off very quickly • *She had whipped off her* *glasses.* ⑤If you whip cream, you beat it until it is thick and frothy or stiff. **whip up** VERB If you whip up a strong emotion, you make people feel it • *The thought whipped up his temper.*

whip bird, whip birds NOUN an Australian bird whose cry ends with a sound like the crack of a whip.

whiplash injury, whiplash injuries NOUN a neck injury caused by your head suddenly jerking forwards and then back again, for example in a car accident.

whippet, whippets NOUN a small, thin dog used for racing.

whirl, whirls, whirling, whirled VERB ①When something whirls, or when you whirl it round, it turns round very fast. ▸NOUN ②You can refer to a lot of intense activity as a whirl of activity.

whirlpool, whirlpools NOUN a small circular area in a river or the sea where the water is moving quickly round and round so that objects floating near it are pulled into its centre.

whirlwind, whirlwinds NOUN ①a tall column of air which spins round and round very fast. ▸ADJECTIVE ②more rapid than usual • *a whirlwind tour.*

whirr, whirrs, whirring, whirred; also spelt **whir** VERB ①When something such as a machine whirrs, it makes a series of low sounds so fast that it sounds like one continuous sound. ▸NOUN ②the noise made by something whirring.

whisk, whisks, whisking, whisked VERB ①If you whisk someone or something somewhere, you take them there quickly • *We were whisked away into a private room.* ②If you whisk eggs or cream, you stir air into them quickly. ▸NOUN ③a kitchen

tool used for quickly stirring air into eggs or cream.

whisker, whiskers NOUN The whiskers of an animal such as a cat or mouse are the long, stiff hairs near its mouth.

whisky, whiskies NOUN Whisky is a strong alcoholic drink made from grain such as barley.
WORD HISTORY: from Scottish Gaelic *uisge beatha* meaning 'water of life'

whisper, whispers, whispering, whispered VERB ①When you whisper, you talk to someone very quietly, using your breath and not your throat. ▸NOUN ②If you talk in a whisper, you whisper.

whist NOUN Whist is a card game for four players in which one pair of players tries to win more tricks than the other pair.

whistle, whistles, whistling, whistled VERB ①When you whistle a tune or whistle, you produce a clear musical sound by forcing your breath out between your lips. ②If something whistles, it makes a loud, high sound • *The kettle whistled.* ▸NOUN ③A whistle is the sound something or someone makes when they whistle. ④a small metal tube that you blow into to produce a whistling sound.

whit NOUN (*formal*) You say 'not a whit' or 'no whit' to emphasise that something is not the case at all • *It does not matter a whit to the customer.*

white, whiter, whitest; whites NOUN or ADJECTIVE ①White is the lightest possible colour. ②Someone who is white has a pale skin and is of European origin. ▸ADJECTIVE ③If someone goes white, their face becomes very pale because they are afraid, shocked or ill. ④White coffee contains milk or cream. ▸NOUN

⑤ The white of an egg is the transparent liquid surrounding the yolk which turns white when it is cooked. **whiteness** NOUN

white blood cell, white blood cells NOUN SCIENCE Your white blood cells are the cells in your blood that cannot carry oxygen.

whiteboard, whiteboards NOUN a white board on which people can write or draw using special coloured pens.

white-collar ADJECTIVE White-collar workers work in offices rather than doing manual work • *a white-collar union*.

white lie, white lies NOUN a harmless lie, especially one told to prevent someone's feelings from being hurt.

white paper, white papers NOUN A white paper is an official report published by the British Government, which gives the policy of the Government on a particular subject.

whitewash NOUN ① Whitewash is a mixture of lime and water used for painting walls white. ② an attempt to hide unpleasant facts • *the refusal to accept official whitewash in the enquiry*.

whither ADVERB or CONJUNCTION (*old-fashioned*) Whither means to what place • *Whither shall I wander?*

whiting NOUN a sea fish related to the cod.

whittle, whittles, whittling, whittled VERB If you whittle a piece of wood, you shape it by shaving or cutting small pieces off it.

whittle away or **whittle down** VERB To whittle away at something or to whittle it down means to make it smaller or less effective • *The 250 entrants had been whittled down to 34.*

whizz, whizzes, whizzing, whizzed; also spelt **whiz** (*informal*) VERB ① If you whizz somewhere, you move there quickly • *Could you whizz down to the shop and get me some milk?* ▶ NOUN ② If you are a whizz at something, you are very good at it.

who PRONOUN ① You use 'who' when you are asking about someone's identity • *Who gave you that black eye?* ② 'Who' at the beginning of a clause refers to the person or people you are talking about • *a shipyard worker who wants to be a postman.*

a b c d e f g h i j k l m n o p q r s t u v **w** x y z

What does Who do?

Who is a relative pronoun. A relative pronoun replaces a noun which links two different parts of a sentence.

Relative pronouns always refer to a word in the earlier part of the sentence. The word they refer to is called the **antecedent**. (In the examples that follow, the antecedents are underlined.)

*I have a friend **who** lives in Rome.*
*We could go to a place **that** I know.*

The forms *who, whom* and *whose* are used when the antecedent is a person. *Who* indicates the subject of the verb:

*It was the same person **who** saw me yesterday.*
*It was the person **whom** I saw yesterday.*

The distinction between *who* and *whom* is often ignored in everyday English, and *who* is often used as the object:

*It was the person **who** I saw yesterday.*

Also look at the grammar box at **relative pronoun**

whoa [Said **woh**] INTERJECTION Whoa
is a command used to slow down or
stop a horse.

whoever PRONOUN ① 'Whoever'
means the person who • *Whoever
bought it for you has to make the claim.*
② 'Whoever' also means no matter
who • *I pity him, whoever he is.*
③ 'Whoever' is used in questions to
give emphasis to 'who' • *Whoever
thought of such a thing?*

whole, wholes ADJECTIVE
① indicating all of something • *Have
the whole cake.* ▸ NOUN ② the full
amount of something • *the whole
of Africa.* ▸ ADVERB ③ in one piece
• *He swallowed it whole.* ▸ PHRASE
④ You use **as a whole** to emphasise
that you are talking about all of
something • *The country as a whole is
in a very odd mood.* ⑤ You say **on the
whole** to mean that something is
generally true • *On the whole, we
should be glad they are gone.*
wholeness NOUN

wholehearted ADJECTIVE
enthusiastic and totally sincere
• *wholehearted approval.*
wholeheartedly ADVERB

wholemeal ADJECTIVE Wholemeal
flour is made from the complete
grain of the wheat plant, including
the husk.

wholesale ADJECTIVE OR ADVERB
① Wholesale refers to the activity
of buying goods cheaply in large
quantities and selling them again,
especially to shopkeepers • *We buy
fruit and vegetables wholesale.*
▸ ADJECTIVE ② Wholesale also means
done to an excessive extent • *the
wholesale destruction of wild plant
species.* **wholesaler** NOUN

wholesome ADJECTIVE ① Something
that is wholesome is good and likely

What does Whom do?

Whom is a relative pronoun. A
relative pronoun replaces a noun
which links two different parts of a
sentence.

Relative pronouns always refer to a
word in the earlier part of the
sentence. The word they refer to is
called the **antecedent**. (In the
examples that follow, the
antecedents are underlined.)

*I have a friend **who** lives in Rome.
We could go to a place **that** I know.*

The forms *who*, *whom* and *whose* are
used when the antecedent is a person.
Whom indicates the object of the verb:

*It was the same person **who** saw me
yesterday.*

*It was the person **whom** I saw yesterday.*

The distinction between *who* and
whom is often ignored in everyday
English, and *who* is often used as
the object:

*It was the person **who** I saw yesterday.*

Whom is used immediately after
a preposition. However, if the
preposition is separated from the
relative pronoun, *who* is usually
used:

*He is a man **in whom** I have great
confidence.*
*He is a man **who** I have great
confidence **in**.*

Also look at the grammar box at
relative pronoun

to improve your life, behaviour or health • *good wholesome entertainment*. ② If you describe a person as wholesome, you mean that their appearance suggests health and wellbeing • *wholesome individuals who will make a positive contribution to society*.

wholly [Said *hoe-lee*] ADVERB completely.

whom PRONOUN 'Whom' is the object form of 'who' • *the girl whom Albert would marry*.

whoop, whoops, whooping, whooped VERB ① If you whoop, you shout loudly in a happy or excited way. ▶ NOUN ② a loud cry of happiness or excitement • *whoops of delight*.

whooping cough [Said *hoop-ing*] NOUN Whooping cough is an acute infectious disease which makes people cough violently and produce a loud sound when they breathe.

whorl, whorls [Said *wurl*] NOUN A whorl is a spiral shape, such as the coiled lines that make up a fingerprint.

whose PRONOUN ① You use 'whose' to ask who something belongs to • *Whose gun is this?* ② You use 'whose' at the beginning of a clause which gives information about something relating or belonging to the thing or person you have just mentioned • *a wealthy gentleman whose mansion is for sale*.

GRAMMAR TIP
Many people are confused about the difference between *whose* and *who's*. *Whose* is used to show possession in a question or when something is being described: *Whose bag is this?*; *the person whose car is blocking the exit*. *Who's*, with the apostrophe, is a short form of *who is* or *who has*: *Who's that girl?*; *Who's got my ruler?*

---

why ADVERB or PRONOUN You use 'why' when you are asking about the reason for something, or talking about it • *Why did you do it?* • *He wondered why she suddenly looked happier*.

wick, wicks NOUN the cord in the middle of a candle, which you set alight.

wicked ADJECTIVE ① very bad • *a wicked thing to do*. ② mischievous in an amusing or attractive way • *a wicked sense of humour*. **wickedly** ADVERB **wickedness** NOUN
SIMILAR WORDS: ① bad, evil, sinful
WORD HISTORY: from Old English *wicce* meaning 'witch'

What does Whose do?

Whose is a relative pronoun. A relative pronoun replaces a noun which links two different parts of a sentence.

Relative pronouns always refer to a word in the earlier part of the sentence. The word they refer to is called the **antecedent**. (In the examples that follow, the antecedents are underlined.)

I have a friend who lives in Rome.

We could go to a place that I know.

The forms *who*, *whom* and *whose* are used when the antecedent is a person.

Whose is the possessive form of the relative pronoun. It can refer to things as well as people:

Anna has a sister whose name is Rosa. I found a book whose pages were torn.

Also look at the grammar box at **relative pronoun**

a
b
c
d
e
f
g
h
i
j
k
l
m
n
o
p
q
r
s
t
u
v
w
x
y
z

A B C D E F G H I J K L M N O P Q R S T U V W X Y Z

wicker ADJECTIVE A wicker basket or chair is made from twigs, canes or reeds that have been woven together.
WORD HISTORY: from Swedish *vika* meaning 'bend'

wicket, wickets NOUN ① In cricket, the wicket is one of the two sets of stumps and bails at which the bowler aims the ball. ② The grass between the wickets on a cricket pitch is also called the wicket.

wide, wider, widest ADJECTIVE ① measuring a large distance from one side to the other. ② If there is a wide variety, range or selection of something, there are many different kinds of it • *a wide range of colours*.
▶ ADVERB ③ If you open or spread something wide, you open it to its fullest extent. **widely** ADVERB
SIMILAR WORDS: ② broad, extensive, large

wide-awake ADJECTIVE completely awake.

widen, widens, widening, widened VERB ① If something widens or if you widen it, it becomes bigger from one side to the other. ② You can say that something widens when it becomes greater in size or scope • *the opportunity to widen your outlook*.

wide-ranging ADJECTIVE extending over a variety of different things or over a large area • *a wide-ranging survey*.

widespread ADJECTIVE existing or happening over a large area or to a great extent • *the widespread use of chemicals*.
SIMILAR WORDS: common, general, universal

widow, widows NOUN a woman whose spouse has died.

widowed ADJECTIVE If someone is widowed, their husband or wife has died.

widower, widowers NOUN a man whose spouse has died.

width, widths NOUN The width of something is the distance from one side or edge to the other.

wield, wields, wielding, wielded [Said *weeld*] VERB ① If you wield a weapon or tool, you carry it and use it. ② If someone wields power, they have it and are able to use it.

wife, wives NOUN A person's wife is the woman they are married to.

Wi-Fi NOUN ICT a system of accessing the internet from machines such as laptop computers that aren't physically connected to a network.

wig, wigs NOUN a false head of hair worn to cover someone's own hair or to hide their baldness.

wiggle, wiggles, wiggling, wiggled VERB ① If you wiggle something, you move it up and down or from side to side with small jerky movements.
▶ NOUN ② a small jerky movement.

wigwam, wigwams NOUN a kind of tent used by North American Indians.
WORD HISTORY: from American Indian *wikwam* meaning 'their house'

wiki, wikis NOUN ICT a website (or page within one) that can be edited by anyone who looks it up on the internet.

wild, wilder, wildest; wilds ADJECTIVE ① Wild animals, birds and plants live and grow in natural surroundings and are not looked after by people. ② Wild land is natural and has not been cultivated • *wild areas of countryside*. ③ Wild weather or sea is stormy and rough. ④ Wild behaviour is excited and uncontrolled. ⑤ A wild idea or scheme is original and crazy.
▶ NOUN ⑥ The wild is a free and

The Verbs Will and Shall

The verbs *will* and *shall* have only one form. They do not have a present form ending in -*s*, and they do not have a present participle, a past tense or a past participle.

These verbs are used as auxiliary verbs to form the future tense:

*She **will** give a talk about Chinese history.*
*We **shall** arrive on Thursday.*

People used to use *shall* to indicate the first person, and *will* to indicate the second person and the third person. However, this distinction is often ignored now:

*I **will** see you on Sunday.*
*I **shall** see you on Sunday.*

Shall is always used in questions involving *I* and *we*. *Will* is avoided in these cases:

***Shall** I put the cat out?*
***Shall** we dance?*

Will is always used when making polite requests, giving orders, and indicating persistence. *Shall* is avoided in these cases:

***Will** you please help me?*
***Will** you be quiet!*
*She **will** keep going on about Al Pacino.*

---

a b c d e f g h i j k l m n o p q r s t u v **w** x y z

natural state of living • *There are about 200 left in the wild.* ⑦ The wilds are remote areas where few people live, far away from towns. **wildly** ADVERB

wilderness, **wildernesses** NOUN an area of natural land which is not cultivated.

wildfire NOUN If something spreads like wildfire, it spreads very quickly.

wild-goose chase, **wild-goose chases** NOUN (*informal*) a hopeless or useless search.

wildlife NOUN Wildlife means wild animals and plants.

Wild West NOUN The Wild West was the western part of the United States when it was first being settled by Europeans.

wiles PLURAL NOUN Wiles are clever or crafty tricks used to persuade people to do something • *You are going to need all your wiles to get a pay rise from the new boss.*

wilful ADJECTIVE ① Wilful actions or attitudes are deliberate and often intended to hurt someone • *wilful damage.* ② Someone who is wilful is obstinate and determined to get

their own way • *a wilful little boy.*
wilfully ADVERB
SIMILAR WORDS: ② headstrong, stubborn

will¹ VERB ① You use 'will' to form the future tense • *Robin will be quite annoyed.* ② You use 'will' to say that you intend to do something • *I will not deceive you.* ③ You use 'will' when inviting someone to do or have something • *Will you have another coffee?* ④ You use 'will' when asking or telling someone to do something • *Will you do me a favour?* • *You will do as I say.* ⑤ You use 'will' to say that you are assuming something to be the case • *As you will have gathered, I was surprised.*

will², **wills**, **willing**, **willed** VERB ① If you will something to happen, you try to make it happen by mental effort • *I willed my eyes to open.* ② If you will something to someone, you leave it to them when you die • *Penbrook Farm is willed to her.* ▶ NOUN ③ Will is the determination to do something • *the will to win.* ④ If something is the will of a person or group, they want it to happen • *the will of the people.* ⑤ a legal document in which you say what you want to happen to your money and property when you die. ▶ **PHRASE** ⑥ If you can do something **at will**, you can do it whenever you want.

willing ADJECTIVE ready and eager to do something • *a willing helper.*
willingly ADVERB **willingness** NOUN
SIMILAR WORDS: game, prepared, ready

willow, willows NOUN A willow or willow tree is a tree with long, thin branches and narrow leaves that often grows near water.

wilt, wilts, wilting, wilted VERB ① If a plant wilts, it droops because it needs more water or is dying. ② If someone wilts, they gradually lose strength or confidence • *James visibly wilted under pressure.*

wily, wilier, wiliest [Said *wie-lee*] ADJECTIVE clever and cunning.

wimp, wimps NOUN (*informal*) someone who is feeble and timid.

win, wins, winning, won VERB ① If you win a fight, game or argument, you defeat your opponent. ② If you win something, you succeed in obtaining it. ▶ NOUN ③ a victory in a game or contest. **win over** VERB If you win someone over, you persuade them to support you.

wince, winces, wincing, winced VERB When you wince, the muscles of your face tighten suddenly because of pain, fear or distress.

winch, winches, winching, winched NOUN ① a machine used to lift heavy objects. It consists of a cylinder around which a rope or chain is wound. ▶ VERB ② If you winch an object or person somewhere, you lift, lower or pull them using a winch.

wind¹, winds [*Rhymes with* **tinned**] NOUN ① a current of air moving across the earth's surface. ② Your wind is the ability to breathe easily • *Brown had recovered her wind.* ③ Wind is air swallowed with food or drink, or gas produced in your stomach, which causes discomfort. ④ MUSIC The wind section of an orchestra is the group of musicians who play wind instruments.

wind², winds, winding, wound [*Rhymes with* **mind**] VERB ① If a road or river winds in a particular direction, it twists and turns in that direction. ② When you wind something round something else, you wrap it round it several times. ③ When you wind a clock or machine or wind it up, you turn a key or handle several times to make it work.
wind up VERB ① When you wind up something such as an activity or a business, you finish it or close it. ② If you wind up in a particular place, you end up there.

windfall, windfalls NOUN a sum of money that you receive unexpectedly.

wind farm, wind farms NOUN GEOGRAPHY a collection of wind-powered turbines for generating electricity.

wind instrument, wind instruments NOUN an instrument you play by using your breath, for example a flute, an oboe or a trumpet.

windmill, windmills NOUN a machine for grinding grain or pumping water. It is driven by vanes or sails turned by the wind.

window, windows NOUN a space in a wall or roof or in the side of a vehicle, usually with glass in it so that light can pass through and people can see in or out.

window box, window boxes NOUN a long, narrow container on a windowsill in which plants are grown.

windowsill, windowsills NOUN a ledge along the bottom of a window, either on the inside or outside of a building.

windpipe, windpipes NOUN Your windpipe is the tube which carries air into your lungs when you breathe. The technical name for windpipe is **trachea**.

windscreen, windscreens NOUN the glass at the front of a vehicle through which the driver looks.

windshield, windshields NOUN In American English, a windshield is the same as a windscreen.

windsurfing NOUN Windsurfing is the sport of moving along the surface of the sea or a lake standing on a board with a sail on it.

windswept ADJECTIVE A windswept place is exposed to strong winds • *a windswept beach*.

windward ADJECTIVE or ADVERB ①facing the direction from which the wind is blowing, or moving in that direction. ▸ NOUN ②(*Nautical*) the direction from which the wind is blowing.

windy, windier, windiest ADJECTIVE If it is windy, there is a lot of wind.

wine, wines NOUN Wine is the red or white alcoholic drink which is normally made from grapes.
WORD HISTORY: from Latin *vinum* meaning 'wine'

wing, wings NOUN ①A bird's or insect's wings are the parts of its body that it uses for flying. ②An aeroplane's wings are the long, flat parts on each side that support it while it is in the air. ③A wing of a building is a part which sticks out

from the main part or which has been added later. ④A wing of an organisation, especially a political party, is a group within it with a particular role or particular beliefs • *the left wing of the party*. ⑤(*in plural*) The wings in a theatre are the sides of the stage which are hidden from the audience. **winged** ADJECTIVE

wink, winks, winking, winked VERB ①When you wink, you close one eye briefly, often as a signal that something is a joke or a secret. ▸ NOUN ②the closing of your eye when you wink.

winkle, winkles NOUN a small sea-snail with a hard shell and a soft edible body.

winner, winners NOUN The winner of a prize, race or competition is the person or thing that wins it.
SIMILAR WORDS: champion, victor

winning ADJECTIVE ①The winning team or entry in a competition is the one that has won. ②attractive and charming • *a winning smile*.

winter, winters NOUN Winter is the season between autumn and spring.

wintry ADJECTIVE Something wintry has features that are typical of winter • *the wintry dawn*.

wipe, wipes, wiping, wiped VERB ①If you wipe something, you rub its surface lightly to remove dirt or liquid. ②If you wipe dirt or liquid off something, you remove it using a cloth or your hands • *Anne wiped the tears from her eyes*. ③If you wipe a video or audio recording, you remove the sounds or pictures recorded on it.
wipe out VERB To wipe out people or places is to destroy them completely.

wire, wires, wiring, wired NOUN ①Wire is metal in the form of a long, thin, flexible thread which can be used to make or fasten things or to

a
b
c
d
e
f
g
h
i
j
k
l
m
n
o
p
q
r
s
t
u
v
w
x
y
z

conduct an electric current. ▶ **VERB**
② If you wire one thing to another,
you fasten them together using wire.
③ DG-T If you wire something or wire
it up, you connect it so that
electricity can pass through it.
wired ADJECTIVE

wireless, wirelesses NOUN
① (*old-fashioned*) a radio. ▶ ADJECTIVE
② communicating without
connecting wires • *wireless internet
connection*.

wiring NOUN The wiring in a building
is the system of wires that supply
electricity to the rooms.

wiry, wirier, wiriest ADJECTIVE
① Wiry people are thin but with
strong muscles. ② Wiry things are
stiff and rough to the touch • *wiry
hair*.

wisdom NOUN ① Wisdom is the
ability to use experience and
knowledge in order to make sensible
decisions or judgments. ② If you talk
about the wisdom of an action or a
decision, you are talking about how
sensible it is.

wisdom tooth, wisdom teeth
NOUN Your wisdom teeth are the four
molar teeth at the back of your
mouth which grow much later than
other teeth.

wise, wiser, wisest ADJECTIVE
① Someone who is wise can use their
experience and knowledge to make
sensible decisions and judgments.
▶ PHRASE ② If you say that someone
is **none the wiser** or **no wiser**, you
mean that they know no more about
something than they did before • *I left
the lesson none the wiser*.
SIMILAR WORDS: ① judicious,
prudent, sensible

-wise SUFFIX ① -wise means
behaving like someone or something
• *I edged crabwise to my seat*. ② -wise

also means relating to • *I'm a bit of a
novice, cooking-wise*.

wisecrack, wisecracks NOUN a
clever remark, intended to be
amusing but often unkind.

wish, wishes, wishing, wished NOUN
① a longing or desire for something,
often something difficult to achieve
or obtain. ② something desired or
wanted • *That wish came true two years
later*. ③ (*in plural*) Good wishes are
expressions of hope that someone
will be happy or successful • *best
wishes on your birthday*. ▶ VERB ④ If
you wish to do something, you want
to do it • *We wished to return*. ⑤ If you
wish something were the case, you
would like it to be the case, but know
it is not very likely • *I wish I were tall*.

wishbone, wishbones NOUN a
V-shaped bone in the breast of most
birds.

wishful thinking NOUN If
someone's hope or wish is wishful
thinking, it is unlikely to come true.

wishy-washy ADJECTIVE (*informal*) If
a person or their ideas are wishy-
washy, then their ideas are not firm
or clear • *wishy-washy reasons*.

wisp, wisps NOUN ① A wisp of grass
or hair is a small, thin, untidy bunch
of it. ② A wisp of smoke is a long, thin
streak of it. **wispy** ADJECTIVE

wistful ADJECTIVE sadly thinking
about something, especially
something you want but cannot
have • *A wistful look came into her eyes*.
wistfully ADVERB

wit, wits NOUN ① Wit is the ability to
use words or ideas in an amusing and
clever way. ② Wit means sense • *They
haven't got the wit to realise what they're
doing*. ③ (*in plural*) Your wits are the
ability to think and act quickly in a
difficult situation • *the man who lived
by his wits*. ▶ PHRASE ④ If someone is

at their wits' end, they are so worried and exhausted by problems or difficulties that they do not know what to do.

witch, witches NOUN a woman claimed to have magic powers and to be able to use them for good or evil.

witchcraft NOUN Witchcraft is the skill or art of using magic powers, especially evil ones.
SIMILAR WORDS: black magic, sorcery, wizardry

witch doctor, witch doctors NOUN a man in some societies, especially in Africa, who appears to have magic powers.

witchetty grub, witchetty grubs NOUN a large, wood-eating Australian caterpillar.

with PREPOSITION ① If you are with someone, you are in their company • *He was at home with me.* ② 'With' is used to show who your opponent is in a fight or competition • *next week's game with Brazil.* ③ 'With' can mean using or having • *Apply the colour with a brush* • *a bloke with a moustache.* ④ 'With' is used to show how someone does something or how they feel • *She looked at him with hatred.* ⑤ 'With' can mean concerning • *a problem with her telephone bill.* ⑥ 'With' is used to show support • *Are you with us or against us?*

withdraw, withdraws, withdrawing, withdrew, withdrawn VERB ① If you withdraw something, you remove it or take it out • *He withdrew the money from his bank account.* ② If you withdraw to another place, you leave where you are and go there • *He withdrew to his study.* ③ If you withdraw from an activity, you back out of it • *They withdrew from the conference.*

withdrawal, withdrawals NOUN ① The withdrawal of something is the act of taking it away • *the withdrawal of Russian troops.* ② The withdrawal of a statement is the act of saying formally that you wish to change or deny it. ③ an amount of money you take from your bank or building society account.

withdrawal symptoms PLURAL NOUN Withdrawal symptoms are the unpleasant effects suffered by someone who has suddenly stopped taking a drug to which they are addicted.

withdrawn ① Withdrawn is the past participle of **withdraw**.
▶ ADJECTIVE ② unusually shy or quiet.

withdrew the past tense of **withdraw**.

wither, withers, withering, withered VERB ① When something withers or withers away, it becomes weaker until it no longer exists. ② If a plant withers, it wilts or shrivels up and dies.

withering ADJECTIVE A withering look or remark makes you feel ashamed, stupid or inferior.

withhold, withholds, withholding, withheld VERB (*formal*) If you withhold something that someone wants, you do not let them have it.

within PREPOSITION or ADVERB ① Within means in or inside.
▶ PREPOSITION ② Within can mean not going beyond certain limits • *Stay within the budget.* ③ Within can mean before a period of time has passed • *You must write back within fourteen days.*

without PREPOSITION ① Without means not having, feeling or showing • *Didier looked on without emotion.* ② Without can mean not using • *You can't get in without a key.* ③ Without can mean not in someone's company • *He went*

a
b
c
d
e
f
g
h
i
j
k
l
m
n
o
p
q
r
s
t
u
v
w
x
y
z

without me. ④Without can indicate that something does not happen when something else happens • *Stone signalled the ship, again without response.*

withstand, withstands, withstanding, withstood VERB When something or someone withstands a force or action, they survive it or do not give in to it • *ships designed to withstand the North Atlantic winter.*

witness, witnesses, witnessing, witnessed NOUN ① someone who has seen an event such as an accident and can describe what happened. ② someone who appears in a court of law to say what they know about a crime or other event. ③ someone who writes their name on a document that someone else has signed, to confirm that it is really that person's signature. ▶ VERB ④ (formal) If you witness an event, you see it.

SIMILAR WORDS: ① bystander, observer, onlooker

witticism, witticisms [Said wit-tiss-izm] NOUN a clever and amusing remark or joke.

witty, wittier, wittiest ADJECTIVE amusing in a clever way • *this witty novel.* **wittily** ADVERB

wives the plural of **wife**.

wizard, wizards NOUN a man in a fairy story who has magic powers.

wizardry NOUN Wizardry is something that is very cleverly done • *technological wizardry.*

wizened [Said wiz-nd] ADJECTIVE having a wrinkled skin, especially with age.

WMD NOUN an abbreviation for 'weapon(s) of mass destruction'.

wobbegong, wobbegongs [Said wob-bi-gong] NOUN an Australian shark with a richly patterned brown-and-white skin.

wobble, wobbles, wobbling, wobbled VERB If something wobbles, it shakes or moves from side to side because it is loose or unsteady • *a cyclist who wobbled into my path.*

wobbly, wobblier, wobbliest ADJECTIVE unsteady • *a wobbly table.*

woe, woes (literary) NOUN ①Woe is great unhappiness or sorrow. ② (in plural) Someone's woes are their problems or misfortunes.

wok, woks NOUN a large bowl-shaped metal pan used for Chinese-style cooking.

woke the past tense of **wake**.

woken the past participle of **wake**.

wolf, wolves; wolfs, wolfing, wolfed NOUN ① a wild animal related to the dog. Wolves hunt in packs and kill other animals for food. ▶ VERB ② (informal) If you wolf food or wolf it down, you eat it up quickly and greedily.

woman, women NOUN ① an adult female human being. ②Woman can refer to women in general • *a problem affecting both man and woman.*

womanhood NOUN Womanhood is the state of being a woman rather than a girl • *on the verge of womanhood.*

womb, wombs [Said woom] NOUN A woman's womb is the part inside her body where her unborn baby grows.

wombat, wombats [Said wom-bat] NOUN a short-legged furry Australian mammal which eats plants.

women the plural of **woman**.

won the past tense and past participle of **win**.

wonder, wonders, wondering, wondered VERB ① If you wonder

about something, you think about it with curiosity or doubt. ② If you wonder at something, you are surprised and amazed at it • *He wondered at her anger.* ▶ **NOUN** ③ Wonder is a feeling of surprise and amazement. ④ something or someone that surprises and amazes people • *the wonders of science.*
SIMILAR WORDS: ④ marvel, miracle, phenomenon

SPELLING TIP
Do not confuse the spellings of *wonder* and *wander*: *I wondered why she had been trying to contact me; We wandered through the gardens.*

wonderful ADJECTIVE ① making you feel very happy and pleased • *It was wonderful to be together.* ② very impressive • *Nature is a wonderful thing.* **wonderfully** ADVERB
SIMILAR WORDS: ② amazing, magnificent, remarkable

wondrous ADJECTIVE (*literary*) amazing and impressive.

wont [*Rhymes with don't*] ADJECTIVE (*old-fashioned*) If someone is wont to do something, they do it often • *a gesture he was wont to use when preaching.*

woo, woos, wooing, wooed VERB ① If you woo people, you try to get them to help or support you • *attempts to woo the women's vote.* ② (*old-fashioned*) If you woo someone you are attracted to, you try to get them to marry you.

wood, woods NOUN ① Wood is the substance which forms the trunks and branches of trees. ② a large area of trees growing near each other.

wooded ADJECTIVE covered in trees • *a wooded area nearby.*

wooden ADJECTIVE made of wood • *a wooden box.*

woodland, woodlands NOUN Woodland is land that is mostly covered with trees.

woodpecker, woodpeckers NOUN a climbing bird with a long, sharp beak that it uses to drill holes into trees to find insects.

woodwind ADJECTIVE Woodwind instruments are musical instruments such as flutes, oboes, clarinets and bassoons, that are played by being blown into.

woodwork NOUN ① Woodwork refers to the parts of a house, such as stairs, doors or window-frames, that are made of wood. ② Woodwork is the craft or skill of making things out of wood.

woodworm, woodworm or woodworms NOUN ① Woodworm are the larvae of a kind of beetle. They make holes in wood by feeding on it. ② Woodworm is damage caused to wood by woodworm making holes in it.

woody, woodier, woodiest ADJECTIVE ① Woody plants have hard tough stems. ② A woody area has a lot of trees in it.

woof, woofs NOUN the sound that a dog makes when it barks.

wool, wools NOUN ① Wool is the hair that grows on sheep and some other animals. ② Wool is also yarn spun from the wool of animals which is used to knit, weave and make such things as clothes, blankets and carpets.

woollen, woollens ADJECTIVE ① made from wool. ▶ NOUN ② Woollens are clothes made of wool.

woolly, woollier, woolliest ADJECTIVE ① made of wool or looking like wool • *a woolly hat.* ② If you describe people or their thoughts as

a b c d e f g h i j k l m n o p q r s t u v **w** x y z

woolly, you mean that they seem confused and unclear.

woolshed, woolsheds NOUN In Australian and New Zealand English, a woolshed is a large building in which sheep are sheared.

woomera, woomeras NOUN a stick with a notch at one end used by Aboriginal Australians to help fire a dart or spear.

word, words, wording, worded NOUN ① a single unit of language in speech or writing which has a meaning. ② a remark • *a word of praise.* ③ a brief conversation • *Could I have a word?* ④ A word can also be a message • *The word is that Sharon is exhausted.* ⑤ Your word is a promise • *He gave me his word.* ⑥ The word can be a command • *I gave the word to start.* ⑦ (in plural) The words of a play or song are the spoken or sung text. ▶ VERB ⑧ When you word something, you choose your words in order to express your ideas accurately or acceptably • *the best way to word our invitations.*

word class, word classes NOUN a group of words that behave in the same way in terms of grammar, for example nouns, adjectives or verbs.

wording NOUN The wording of a piece of writing or a speech is the words used in it, especially when these words have been carefully chosen to have a certain effect.

wordplay NOUN ENGLISH Wordplay is the making of jokes by clever use of words.

word processor, word processors NOUN ICT a computer program or a computer which is used to produce printed documents.

wore the past tense of **wear**.

work, works, working, worked VERB ① People who work have a job which they are paid to do • *My husband works for a national newspaper.* ② When you work, you do the tasks that your job involves. ③ To work the land is to cultivate it. ④ If someone works a machine, they control or operate it. ⑤ If a machine works, it operates properly and effectively • *The radio doesn't work.* ⑥ If something such as an idea or a system works, it is successful • *The housing benefit system is not working.* ⑦ If something works its way into a particular position, it gradually moves there • *The cable had worked loose.* ▶ NOUN ⑧ People who have work or who are in work have a job which they are paid to do • *She's trying to find work.* ⑨ Work is the tasks that have to be done. ⑩ something done or made • *a work of art.* ⑪ SCIENCE In physics, work is transfer of energy. It is calculated by

What is a Word Class?

Every word in the dictionary can be classified into a group. These groups are known as **word classes**. If we know which group a word belongs to, we can understand what sort of idea the word represents, and how it can be combined with other words to produce meaningful statements.

You can check the word class of any word by looking it up in the dictionary. The word class is given after the main entry word. The most common word classes in this dictionary are noun, verb, adjective, adverb, pronoun, preposition, interjection and conjunction. There are separate grammar boxes for all of these.

multiplying a force by the distance moved by the point to which the force has been applied. Work is measured in joules. ⑫(*in plural*) A works is a place where something is made by an industrial process • *the old steel works*. ⑬Works are large-scale building, digging or general construction activities • *building works*. **work out** VERB ①If you work out a solution to a problem, you find the solution. ②If a situation works out in a particular way, it happens in that way. **work up** VERB ①If you work up to something, you gradually progress towards it. ②If you work yourself up or work someone else up, you make yourself or the other person very upset or angry about something. **worked up** ADJECTIVE

SIMILAR WORDS: ④control, handle, operate ⑤function, go, run

workable ADJECTIVE Something workable can operate successfully or can be used for a particular purpose • *a workable solution* • *This plan simply isn't workable.*

workaholic, workaholics NOUN a person who finds it difficult to stop working and do other things.

worker, workers NOUN a person employed in a particular industry or business • *a defence worker.*

workforce, workforces NOUN The workforce is all the people who work in a particular place.

workhouse, workhouses NOUN
HISTORY In the past a workhouse was a building to which very poor people were sent and made to work in return for food and shelter.

working, workings ADJECTIVE ①Working people have jobs which they are paid to do. ②Working can mean related to, used for, or suitable for work • *the working week* • *working*

conditions. ③Working can mean sufficient to be useful or to achieve what is required • *a working knowledge of Hebrew.* ④(*in plural*) The workings of a piece of equipment, an organisation or a system are the ways in which it operates • *the workings of the European Union.*

working class, working classes NOUN The working class or working classes are the group of people in society who do not own much property and who do jobs which involve physical rather than intellectual skills.

workload, workloads NOUN the amount of work that a person or a machine has to do.

workman, workmen NOUN a man whose job involves using physical rather than intellectual skills.

workmanship NOUN Workmanship is the skill with which something is made or a job is completed.

workmate, workmates NOUN Someone's workmate is the fellow worker with whom they do their job.

workout, workouts NOUN a session of physical exercise or training.

workplace NOUN Your workplace is the building or company where you work.

workshop, workshops NOUN ①a room or building that contains tools or machinery used for making or repairing things • *an engineering workshop.* ②a period of discussion or practical work in which a group of people learn about a particular subject • *a theatre workshop.*

world, worlds NOUN ①The world is the earth, the planet we live on. ②You can use 'world' to refer to people generally • *The eyes of the world are upon me.* ③Someone's world is the life they lead and the things they

a b c d e f g h i j k l m n o p q r s t u v w x y z

experience • *We come from different worlds*. ④A world is a division or section of the earth, its history, or its people, such as the Arab World or the Ancient World. ⑤A particular world is a field of activity and the people involved in it • *the world of football*. ▶ **ADJECTIVE** ⑥'World' is used to describe someone or something that is one of the best or most important of its kind • *a world leader*. ▶ **PHRASE** ⑦If you **think the world** of someone, you like or admire them very much.
WORD HISTORY: from Old English *weorold* from *wer* meaning 'man' and *ald* meaning 'age'

worldly, **worldlier**, **worldliest**
ADJECTIVE ①relating to the ordinary activities of life rather than spiritual things • *opportunities for worldly pleasures*. ②experienced and knowledgeable about life.

world war, **world wars** **NOUN** a war that involves countries all over the world.

worldwide **ADJECTIVE** throughout the world • *a worldwide flu epidemic*.

World Wide Web **NOUN** The World Wide Web is a system of linked documents accessed via the internet.

worm, **worms**, **worming**, **wormed**
NOUN ①a small thin animal without bones or legs, which lives in the soil or off other creatures. ②an insect such as a beetle or moth at a very early stage in its life. ③a computer program that makes many copies of itself within a network, usually harming the system. ▶ **VERB** ④If you worm an animal, you give it medicine in order to kill the worms that are living as parasites in its intestines.

worm out **VERB** If you worm information out of someone, you gradually persuade them to give you it.

worn ①Worn is the past participle of **wear**. ▶ **ADJECTIVE** ②damaged or thin because of long use. ③looking old or exhausted • *He appeared frail and worn*.

worn-out **ADJECTIVE** ①used until it is too thin or too damaged to be of further use • *a worn-out cardigan*. ②extremely tired • *You must be worn-out after the drive*.

worried **ADJECTIVE** unhappy and anxious about a problem or about something unpleasant that might happen.
SIMILAR WORDS: anxious, concerned, troubled

worry, **worries**, **worrying**, **worried**
VERB ①If you worry, you feel anxious and fearful about a problem or about something unpleasant that might happen. ②If something worries you, it causes you to feel uneasy or fearful • *a puzzle which had worried her all her life*. ③If you worry someone with a problem, you disturb or bother them by telling them about it • *I didn't want to worry the boys with this*. ④If a dog worries sheep or other animals, it frightens or harms them by chasing them or biting them. ▶ **NOUN** ⑤Worry is a feeling of unhappiness and unease caused by a problem or by thinking of something unpleasant that might happen • *the major source of worry*. ⑥a person or thing that causes you to feel anxious or uneasy • *Inflation is the least of our worries*.
worrying **ADJECTIVE**
SIMILAR WORDS: ①be anxious, fret ②bother, perturb, trouble ⑤anxiety, concern
WORD HISTORY: from Old English *wyrgan* meaning 'strangle'

worse **ADJECTIVE** OR **ADVERB** ①Worse is the comparative form of **bad** and **badly**. ②If someone who is ill gets worse, they become more ill than before. ▶ **PHRASE** ③If someone or something is **none the worse** for something, they have not been harmed by it • *He appeared none the worse for the accident.*

worsen, worsens, worsening, worsened **VERB** If a situation worsens, it becomes more difficult or unpleasant • *The weather conditions worsened.*
SIMILAR WORDS: decline, deteriorate, get worse

worse off **ADJECTIVE** If you are worse off, you have less money or are in a more unpleasant situation than before • *There are people much worse off than me.*

worship, worships, worshipping, worshipped **VERB** ① RE If you worship a god, you show your love and respect by praying or singing hymns. ② If you worship someone or something, you love them or admire them very much. ▶ **NOUN** ③ Worship is the feeling of respect, love or admiration you feel for something or someone. **worshipper** **NOUN**
SIMILAR WORDS: ② adore, idolise, love ③ adoration, devotion

worst **ADJECTIVE** OR **ADVERB** Worst is the superlative of **bad** and **badly**.

worth **PREPOSITION** ① If something is worth a sum of money, it has that value • *a house worth $850,000.* ② If something is worth doing, it deserves to be done. ▶ **NOUN** ③ A particular amount of money's worth of something is the quantity of it that you can buy for that money • *five pounds' worth of petrol.* ④ Someone's worth is the value or usefulness they are considered to have.

worthless **ADJECTIVE** having no real value or use • *a worthless piece of junk.*

worthwhile **ADJECTIVE** important enough to justify the time, money or effort spent on it • *a worthwhile career.*

worthy, worthier, worthiest **ADJECTIVE** If someone or something is worthy of something, they deserve it • *a worthy champion.*

would **VERB** ① You use 'would' to say what someone thought was going to happen • *We were sure it would be a success.* ② You use 'would' when you are referring to the result or effect of a possible situation • *If readers can help I would be most grateful.* ③ You use 'would' when referring to someone's willingness to do something • *I wouldn't change places with him if you paid me.* ④ You use 'would' in polite questions • *Would you like some lunch?*

would-be **ADJECTIVE** wanting to be or claiming to be • *a would-be pop singer.*

wound¹, wounds, wounding, wounded [Rhymes with **spooned**] **NOUN** ① an injury to part of your body, especially a cut in your skin and flesh. ▶ **VERB** ② If someone wounds you, they damage your body using a gun, knife or other weapon. ③ If you are wounded by what someone says or does, your feelings are hurt.
wounded **ADJECTIVE**

wound² [Rhymes with **sound**] the past tense and past participle of **wind²**.

wove the past tense of **weave**.

woven the past participle of **weave**.

wow **INTERJECTION** Wow is an expression of admiration or surprise.

wraith, wraiths [Said *rayth*] **NOUN** (literary) A wraith is a ghost or apparition.
WORD HISTORY: a Scottish word

wrangle, wrangles, wrangling, wrangled **VERB** ① If you wrangle with someone, you argue noisily or angrily, often about something unimportant. ▶ **NOUN** ② an argument that is difficult to settle.
wrangling **NOUN**

a
b
c
d
e
f
g
h
i
j
k
l
m
n
o
p
q
r
s
t
u
v
w
x
y
z

wrap, **wraps**, **wrapping**, **wrapped**
VERB ① If you wrap something or wrap something up, you fold a piece of paper or cloth tightly around it to cover or enclose it. ② If you wrap paper or cloth round something, you put or fold the paper round it. ③ If you wrap your arms, fingers or legs round something, you coil them round it. **wrap up** VERB If you wrap up, you put warm clothes on.

SPELLING TIP
Do not confuse the spellings of *wrap* and *rap*: *I have wrapped all my Christmas presents; The teacher rapped the table with a ruler.*

wrapped up ADJECTIVE (*informal*) If you are wrapped up in a person or thing, you give that person or thing all your attention.

wrapper, **wrappers** NOUN a piece of paper, plastic or foil which covers and protects something that you buy • *sweet wrappers*.

wrapping, **wrappings** NOUN Wrapping is the material used to cover and protect something.

wrath [*Said* roth] NOUN (*literary*) Wrath is great anger • *The manager faced the wrath of the fans.*

wreak, **wreaks**, **wreaking**, **wreaked** [*Said* reek] VERB To wreak havoc or damage is to cause it.

wreath, **wreaths** [*Said* reeth] NOUN an arrangement of flowers and leaves, often in the shape of a circle, which is put on a grave as a sign of remembrance for the dead person.

wreck, **wrecks**, **wrecking**, **wrecked** VERB ① If someone wrecks something, they break it, destroy it, or spoil it completely. ② If a ship is wrecked, it has been so badly damaged that it can no longer sail.
▶ NOUN ③ a vehicle which has been badly damaged in an accident. ④ If you say someone is a wreck, you mean that they are in very poor physical or mental health or completely exhausted. **wrecked** ADJECTIVE

wreckage NOUN Wreckage is what remains after something has been badly damaged or destroyed.

wren, **wrens** NOUN a very small brown songbird.

wrench, **wrenches**, **wrenching**, **wrenched** VERB ① If you wrench something, you give it a sudden and violent twist or pull • *Nick wrenched open the door.* ② If you wrench a limb or a joint, you twist and injure it.
▶ NOUN ③ a metal tool with parts which can be adjusted to fit around nuts or bolts to loosen or tighten them. ④ a painful parting from someone or something.

wrest, **wrests**, **wresting**, **wrested** [*Said* **rest**] VERB (*formal*) If you wrest something from someone else you take it from them violently or with effort • *to try and wrest control of the island from the Mafia.*

wrestle, **wrestles**, **wrestling**, **wrestled** VERB ① If you wrestle someone or wrestle with them, you fight them by holding or throwing them, but not hitting them. ② When you wrestle with a problem, you try to deal with it. **wrestler** NOUN

wrestling NOUN Wrestling is a sport in which two people fight and try to win by throwing or holding their opponent on the ground.

wretch, **wretches** NOUN (*old-fashioned*) someone who is thought to be wicked or very unfortunate.
WORD HISTORY: from Old English *wrecca* meaning 'exile' or 'despised person'

SPELLING TIP
Do not confuse the spellings of *wretch* and *retch*: *He is an ungrateful wretch*; *The smell inside the fridge made me retch.*

wretched [Said *ret-shid*] ADJECTIVE ① very unhappy or unfortunate • *a wretched childhood.* ② (*informal*) You use wretched to describe something or someone you feel angry about or dislike • *a wretched bully.*

wriggle, wriggles, wriggling, wriggled VERB ① If someone wriggles, they twist and turn their body or a part of their body using quick movements • *He wriggled his arms and legs.* ② If you wriggle somewhere, you move there by twisting and turning • *I wriggled out of the van.* **wriggly** ADJECTIVE

-wright, -wrights [Said *rite*] SUFFIX '-wright' is used to form nouns that refer to a person who creates, builds or repairs something • *a playwright.* WORD HISTORY: from Old English *wryhta* meaning 'craftsman'

wring, wrings, wringing, wrung VERB ① When you wring a wet cloth or wring it out, you squeeze the water out of it by twisting it. ② If you wring your hands, you hold them together and twist and turn them, usually because you are worried or upset. ③ If someone wrings a bird's neck, they kill the bird by twisting and breaking its neck.

wrinkle, wrinkles, wrinkling, wrinkled NOUN ① Wrinkles are lines in someone's skin, especially on the face, which form as they grow old. ▶ VERB ② If something wrinkles, folds or lines develop on it • *Fold the paper carefully so that it doesn't wrinkle.* ③ When you wrinkle your nose, forehead or eyes, you tighten the muscles in your face so that the skin folds into lines. **wrinkled** ADJECTIVE **wrinkly** ADJECTIVE

SIMILAR WORDS: ① crease, fold
WORD HISTORY: from Old English *wrinclian* meaning 'to wind around'

wrist, wrists NOUN the part of your body between your hand and your arm which bends when you move your hand.

writ, writs NOUN a legal document that orders a person to do or not to do a particular thing.

write, writes, writing, wrote, written VERB ① When you write something, you use a pen or pencil to form letters, words or numbers on a surface. ② If you write something such as a poem, a book or a piece of music, you create it. ③ When you write to someone or write them a letter, you express your feelings in a letter. ④ When someone writes something such as a cheque, they put the necessary information on it and sign it. ⑤ When you write data you transfer it to a computer's memory. **write down** VERB If you write something down, you record it on a piece of paper. **write up** VERB If you write up something, you write a full account of it, often using notes that you have made.

SPELLING TIP
Do not confuse the spellings of *write*, *right* and *rite*: *Write your name on the jotter; Is that the right answer?; the marriage rites of the Christian church.*

writer, writers NOUN ① a person who writes books, stories or articles as a job. ② The writer of something is the person who wrote it.

writhe, writhes, writhing, writhed VERB If you writhe, you twist and turn your body, often because you are in pain.

writing, writings NOUN ① Writing is something that has been written or printed • *Apply in writing for the* *information*. ②Your writing is the way you write with a pen or pencil. ③Writing is also a piece of written work, especially the style of language used • *witty writing*. ④An author's writings are his or her written works.

written ①Written is the past participle of **write**. ▶ ADJECTIVE ②taken down in writing • *a written agreement*.

wrong, wrongs, wronging, wronged ADJECTIVE ①not working properly or unsatisfactory • *There was something wrong with the car*. ②not correct or truthful • *the wrong answer*. ③bad or immoral • *It is wrong to kill people*. ▶ NOUN ④an unjust action or situation • *the wrongs of our society*. ▶ VERB ⑤If someone wrongs you, they treat you in an unfair or unjust way. **wrongly** ADVERB

SIMILAR WORDS: ②erroneous, inaccurate, incorrect

wrongful ADJECTIVE A wrongful act is regarded as illegal, unfair or immoral • *wrongful imprisonment*. **wrongfully** ADVERB

wrote the past tense of **write**.

wrought iron NOUN Wrought iron is a pure type of iron that is formed into decorative shapes.

wrung the past tense and past participle of **wring**.

wry ADJECTIVE A wry expression shows that you find a situation slightly amusing because you know more about it than other people. **wryly** ADVERB **wryness** NOUN

Xx

a
b
c
d
e
f
g
h
i
j
k
l
m
n
o
p
q
r
s
t
u
v
w
x
y
z

X or **x** ① 'X' is used to represent the name of an unknown or secret person or place • *The witness was referred to as Mr X throughout the trial.* ② In algebra, 'x' is used as a symbol to represent a number whose value is not known. ③ People sometimes write 'X' on a map to mark a precise position. ④ 'X' is used to represent a kiss at the bottom of a letter, a vote on a ballot paper, or the signature of someone who cannot write.

X chromosome, X chromosomes NOUN SCIENCE In biology, an X chromosome is one of an identical pair of chromosomes found in a woman's cells, or one of a nonidentical pair found in a man's cells. X chromosomes are associated with female characteristics.

xenon [*Said* zen-non] NOUN SCIENCE Xenon is a chemical element in the form of a colourless, odourless gas found in very small quantities in the atmosphere. It is used in radio valves and in some lamps. Its atomic number is 54 and its symbol is Xe.

xenophobia [*Said* zen-nof-foe-bee-a] NOUN a fear or strong dislike of people from other countries.
xenophobic ADJECTIVE
WORD HISTORY: from Greek *xenos* meaning 'stranger' and *phobos* meaning 'fear'

Xerox, Xeroxes [*Said* zeer-roks] NOUN (trademark) ① a machine that makes photographic copies of sheets of paper with writing or printing on them. ② a copy made by a Xerox machine.

Xmas NOUN (*informal*) Xmas means the same as Christmas.

X-ray, X-rays, X-raying, X-rayed NOUN ① a stream of radiation of very short wavelength that can pass through some solid materials. X-rays are used by doctors to examine the bones or organs inside a person's body. ② a picture made by sending X-rays through someone's body in order to examine the inside of it.
▶ VERB ③ If you are X-rayed, a picture is made of the inside of your body by passing X-rays through it.

xylem [*Said* zy-lem] NOUN SCIENCE Xylem is a plant tissue that conducts water and mineral salts from the roots and carries them through the plant. It forms the wood in trees and shrubs.

xylophone, xylophones [*Said* zy-lo-fone] NOUN a musical instrument made of a row of wooden bars of different lengths. It is played by hitting the bars with special hammers.

Yy

-y SUFFIX -y forms nouns • *anarchy*.
WORD HISTORY: from Old French *-ie*

yabby, yabbies NOUN a small edible Australian crayfish.

yacht, yachts [*Said yot*] NOUN a boat with sails or an engine, used for racing or for pleasure trips.

yachting NOUN Yachting is the sport or activity of sailing a yacht.

yachtsman, yachtsmen NOUN a man who sails a yacht.

yachtswoman, yachtswomen NOUN a woman who sails a yacht.

yak, yaks NOUN a type of long-haired ox with long horns, found mainly in Tibet.

yakka or **yacker** NOUN (*informal*) In Australian and New Zealand English, yakka or yacker is work.

yam, yams NOUN a root vegetable which grows in tropical regions.

yank, yanks, yanking, yanked (*informal*) VERB ① If you yank something, you pull or jerk it suddenly with a lot of force. ▶ NOUN ② A Yank is an American.

SPELLING TIP
When *Yank* means 'an American' it starts with a capital letter.

Yankee, Yankees NOUN (*informal*) the same as a Yank.

yap, yaps, yapping, yapped VERB If a dog yaps, it barks with a high-pitched sound.

yard, yards NOUN ① a unit of length equal to 36 inches or about 91.4 centimetres. ② an enclosed area that is usually next to a building and is often used for a particular purpose • *a ship repair yard*. ③ In the United States, Canada and Australia, a yard is the garden of a house.

yardstick, yardsticks NOUN someone or something you use as a standard against which to judge other people or things • *He had no yardstick by which to judge university*.

yarn, yarns NOUN ① [DGT] Yarn is thread used for knitting or making cloth. ② (*informal*) a story that someone tells, often with invented details to make it more interesting or exciting • *fishermen's yarns*.

yawn, yawns, yawning, yawned VERB ① When you yawn, you open your mouth wide and take in more air than usual. You often yawn when you are tired or bored. ② A gap or opening that yawns is large and wide. ▶ NOUN ③ an act of yawning.

yawning ADJECTIVE A yawning gap or opening is very wide.

Y chromosome, Y chromosomes NOUN [SCIENCE] In biology, a Y chromosome is the single chromosome in a man's cells which will produce a male baby if it joins with an X chromosome during reproduction.

ye (*old-fashioned*) PRONOUN ① Ye is used to mean 'you'. ▶ ADJECTIVE ② Ye is also used to mean 'the'.

yeah INTERJECTION (*informal*) Yeah means 'yes'.

year, years NOUN ① a period of twelve months or 365 days (366 days in a leap year), which is the time taken for the earth to travel once around the sun. ② a period of twelve consecutive months, not always January to December, on which administration or organisation is based • *the current financial year*. ▶ PHRASE ③ If something happens **year in, year out**, it happens every year • *a tradition kept up year in, year out*.

yearling, yearlings NOUN an animal between one and two years old.

yearly ADJECTIVE ① happening or appearing once a year. ▶ ADVERB ② once a year • *He goes to New York yearly, in the spring*.

yearn, yearns, yearning, yearned [*Rhymes with* ***learn***] VERB If you yearn for something, you want it very much indeed • *He yearned to sleep*. **yearning** NOUN

yeast NOUN SCIENCE Yeast is a kind of fungus which is used to make bread rise, and to make liquids ferment in order to produce alcohol.

yell, yells, yelling, yelled VERB ① If you yell, you shout loudly, usually because you are angry, excited or in pain. ▶ NOUN ② a loud shout.

yellow, yellower, yellowest; yellows, yellowing, yellowed NOUN or ADJECTIVE ① Yellow is the colour of buttercups, egg yolks and lemons. ▶ VERB ② When something yellows or is yellowed, it becomes yellow, often because it is old. ▶ ADJECTIVE ③ (*informal*) If you say someone is yellow, you mean they are cowardly. **yellowish** ADJECTIVE

yellow box, yellow boxes NOUN a large spreading Australian tree from which honey is collected.

yellow fever NOUN Yellow fever is a serious infectious disease that is found in tropical countries. It causes fever and jaundice.

yelp, yelps, yelping, yelped VERB ① When people or animals yelp, they give a sudden, short cry. ▶ NOUN ② a sudden, short cry.

yen NOUN ① The yen is the main unit of currency in Japan. ② (*informal*) If you have a yen to do something, you have a strong desire to do it • *Mike had a yen to try cycling*.

yeoman, yeomen [*Said* ***yoe-man***] NOUN HISTORY In the past, a yeoman was a man who owned and farmed his own land.

yes INTERJECTION You use 'yes' to agree with someone, to say that something is true, or to accept something.

yesterday NOUN or ADVERB ① Yesterday is the day before today. ② You also use 'yesterday' to refer to the past • *Leave yesterday's sadness behind you*.

yet ADVERB ① If something has not happened yet, it has not happened up to the present time • *It isn't quite dark yet*. ② If something should not be done yet, it should not be done now, but later • *Don't switch off yet*. ③ 'Yet' can mean there is still a possibility that something can happen • *We'll make a soldier of you yet*. ④ You can use 'yet' when you want to say how much longer a situation will continue • *The service doesn't start for an hour yet*. ⑤ 'Yet' can be used for emphasis • *She'd changed her mind yet again*. ▶ CONJUNCTION ⑥ You can use 'yet' to introduce a fact which is rather surprising • *He isn't a smoker yet he always carries a lighter*.

yeti, yetis [*Said* ***yet-tee***] NOUN A yeti, or abominable snowman, is a large hairy apelike animal which some people believe exists in the Himalayas.

yew, yews NOUN an evergreen tree with bright red berries.

Yiddish NOUN Yiddish is a language derived mainly from German, which many Jewish people of European origin speak.

WORD HISTORY: from German *jüdisch* meaning 'Jewish'

yield, yields, yielding, yielded VERB ① If you yield to someone or something, you stop resisting and give in to them • *Russia recently yielded to US pressure.* ② If you yield something that you have control of or responsibility for, you surrender it • *They refused to yield control of their weapons.* ③ If something yields, it breaks or gives way • *The handle would yield to her grasp.* ④ To yield something is to produce it • *One season's produce yields food for the following year.* ▸ NOUN ⑤ A yield is an amount of food, money or profit produced from a given area of land or from an investment.

yippee INTERJECTION (*informal*) 'Yippee!' is an exclamation of happiness or excitement.

yob, yobs NOUN (*informal*) a noisy, badly behaved boy or young man.

yodel, yodels, yodelling, yodelled [*Said* **yoe-dl**] VERB When someone yodels, they sing normal notes with high quick notes in between. This style of singing is associated with the Swiss and Austrian Alps.

yoga [*Said* **yoe-ga**] NOUN Yoga is a Hindu method of mental and physical exercise or discipline.

WORD HISTORY: from Sanskrit *yoga* meaning 'union'

yogurt, yogurts [*Said* **yog-gurt** *or* **yoe-gurt**]; also spelt **yoghurt** NOUN Yogurt is a slightly sour thick liquid made from milk that has had bacteria added to it.

yoke, yokes NOUN ① a wooden bar attached to two collars which is laid across the necks of animals such as oxen to hold them together, and to which a plough or other tool may be attached. ② (*literary*) If people are under a yoke of some kind, they are being oppressed • *People are still suffering under the yoke of slavery.*

SPELLING TIP

Do not confuse the spellings of *yoke* and *yolk*: *People are still suffering under the yoke of slavery; Beat the yolks of three large eggs.*

yokel, yokels [*Said* **yoe-kl**] NOUN someone who lives in the country and is regarded as being rather stupid and old-fashioned.

yolk, yolks [*Rhymes with* **joke**] NOUN the yellow part in the middle of an egg.

WORD HISTORY: from Old English *geoloca*, from *geolu* meaning 'yellow'

SPELLING TIP

Do not confuse the spellings of *yolk* and *yoke*: *Beat the yolks of three large eggs; People are still suffering under the yoke of slavery.*

Yom Kippur [*Said* **yom kip-poor**] NOUN RE Yom Kippur is an annual Jewish religious holiday, which is a day of fasting and prayers. It is also called the Day of Atonement.

yonder ADVERB *or* ADJECTIVE (*old-fashioned*) over there • *There's an island yonder.*

yore PHRASE (*old-fashioned*) **Of yore** means existing a long time ago • *nostalgia for the days of yore.*

Yorkshire pudding, Yorkshire puddings NOUN In Britain, Yorkshire pudding is a kind of baked batter made of flour, milk and eggs, and usually eaten with roast beef.

you PRONOUN ① 'You' refers to the person or group of people that a person is speaking or writing to. ② 'You' also refers to people in general • *You can get a two-bedroom villa quite cheaply here.*

young, younger, youngest ADJECTIVE ① A young person, animal or plant has not lived very long and is not yet mature. ▶ PLURAL NOUN ② The young are young people in general. ③ The young of an animal are its babies.
SIMILAR WORDS: ① immature, undeveloped ③ babies, offspring, progeny

youngster, youngsters NOUN a child or young person.

your ADJECTIVE ① 'Your' means belonging or relating to the person or group of people that someone is speaking to • *I do like your name.* ② 'Your' is used to show that something belongs or relates to people in general • *Some of these chemicals can cause serious damage to your health.*

SPELLING TIP
Do not confuse the spellings of *your* and *you're*. *Your* is an adjective showing possession and *you're* is short for 'you are': *Don't forget your phone; You're joking, aren't you?*

---

yours PRONOUN 'Yours' refers to something belonging or relating to the person or group of people that someone is speaking to • *His hair is longer than yours.*

yourself, yourselves PRONOUN ① 'Yourself' is used when the person being spoken to does the action and is affected by it • *Why can't you do it yourself?* ② 'Yourself' is used to emphasise 'you' • *Do you yourself want to go?*

youth, youths NOUN ① Someone's youth is the period of their life before they are a fully mature adult. ② Youth is the quality or condition of being young and often inexperienced. ③ a boy or young man. ④ The youth are young people thought of as a group • *the youth of today.* **youthful** ADJECTIVE

youth hostel, youth hostels NOUN a place where young people can stay cheaply when they are on holiday.

yo-yo, yo-yos NOUN a round wooden or plastic toy attached to a piece of string. You play by making the yo-yo rise and fall on the string.

Yule NOUN (*old-fashioned*) Yule means Christmas.
WORD HISTORY: from Old English *geola* meaning a pagan winter feast

yuppie, yuppies NOUN A yuppie is a young, middle-class person who earns a lot of money which he or she spends on himself or herself.
WORD HISTORY: from *y*(oung) *u*(rban) or *u*(pwardly-mobile) *p*(rofessional) + *-ie*

Zz

zakat NOUN RE a tax that all Muslims must pay which is used to help the poor in their community.

Zambian, Zambians [Said *zam-bee-an*] ADJECTIVE ① belonging or relating to Zambia. ▶ NOUN ② someone who comes from Zambia.

zany, zanier, zaniest ADJECTIVE (*informal*) odd and ridiculous • *zany humour*.

WORD HISTORY: from Italian *zanni* meaning 'clown'

zap, zaps, zapping, zapped VERB (*informal*) ① To zap someone is to kill them, usually by shooting. ② To zap also is to move somewhere quickly • *I zapped over to Paris*.

zeal NOUN Zeal is very great enthusiasm. **zealous** ADJECTIVE **zealously** ADVERB

zealot, zealots [Said *zel-lot*] NOUN a person who acts with very great enthusiasm, especially in following a political or religious cause.

zebra, zebras NOUN a type of African wild horse with black and white stripes over its body.

zebra crossing, zebra crossings NOUN a place where people can cross the road safely. The road is marked with black and white stripes.

Zen or **Zen Buddhism** NOUN RE Zen is a form of Buddhism that concentrates on learning through meditation and intuition.

zenith NOUN (*literary*) The zenith of something is the time when it is at its most successful or powerful • *the zenith of his military career*.

zero, zeros or zeroes, zeroing, zeroed ① nothing or the number 0. ② Zero is freezing point, 0° Centigrade. ▶ ADJECTIVE ③ Zero means there is none at all of a particular thing • *His chances are zero*. **zero in** VERB To zero in on a target is to aim at or to move towards it • *The headlines zeroed in on the major news stories*.

WORD HISTORY: from Arabic *sifr* meaning 'cipher' or 'empty'

zest NOUN ① Zest is a feeling of pleasure and enthusiasm • *zest for life*. ② Zest is a quality which adds extra flavour or interest to something • *brilliant ideas to add zest to your wedding list*. ③ The zest of an orange or lemon is the outside of the peel which is used to flavour food or drinks.

zigzag, zigzags, zigzagging, zigzagged NOUN ① a line which has a series of sharp, angular turns to the right and left in it, like a continuous series of 'W's. ▶ VERB ② To zigzag is to move forward by going at an angle first right and then left • *He zigzagged his way across the racecourse*.

Zimbabwean, Zimbabweans [Said *zim-bahb-wee-an*] ADJECTIVE ① belonging or relating to Zimbabwe. ▶ NOUN ② someone who comes from Zimbabwe.

zinc NOUN SCIENCE Zinc is a bluish-white metallic element used in alloys and to coat other metals to stop them rusting. Its atomic number is 30 and its symbol is Zn.

zing NOUN (*informal*) Zing is a quality in something that makes it lively or interesting • *There's a real zing around the studio.*

Zionism [*Said* **zie**-on-izm] NOUN RE Zionism is a political movement which was originally concerned with the establishment of a state in Palestine for Jewish people. It is now concerned with the development of the modern state of Israel. **Zionist** NOUN

zip, zips, zipping, zipped NOUN ① a long narrow fastener with two rows of teeth that are closed or opened by a small clip pulled between them. ▶ VERB ② When you zip something or zip it up, you fasten it using a zip.

zipper, zippers NOUN the same as a **zip**.

zodiac [*Said* **zoe**-dee-ak] NOUN The zodiac is an imaginary strip in the sky which contains the planets and stars which astrologers think are important influences on people. It is divided into 12 sections, each with a special name and symbol.

WORD HISTORY: from Greek *zōidiakos kuklos* meaning 'circle of signs'

zombie, zombies NOUN ① (*informal*) If you refer to someone as a zombie, you mean that they seem to be unaware of what is going on around them and to act without thinking

about what they are doing. ② In voodoo, a zombie is a dead person who has been brought back to life by witchcraft.

WORD HISTORY: from an African word *zumbi* meaning 'good-luck charm'

zone, zones NOUN an area that has particular features or properties • *a war zone.*

zoo, zoos NOUN a place where live animals are kept so that people can look at them.

zoology [*Said* zoo-**ol**-loj-jee] NOUN Zoology is the scientific study of animals. **zoological** ADJECTIVE **zoologist** NOUN

zoom, zooms, zooming, zoomed VERB ① To zoom is to move very quickly • *They zoomed to safety.* ② If a camera zooms in on something, it gives a close-up picture of it.

zucchini [*Said* zoo-**keen**-nee] PLURAL NOUN Zucchini are small vegetable marrows with dark green skin. They are also called **courgettes**.

Zulu, Zulus [*Said* **zoo**-loo] NOUN ① The Zulus are a group of Black people who live in southern Africa. ② Zulu is the language spoken by the Zulus.

Zumba [*Said* **zoom**-bah] NOUN (*trademark*) a form of exercise involving dance moves performed to Latin American music.

zygote, zygotes [*Said* **zye**-goat] NOUN SCIENCE an egg that has been fertilised by sperm and which could develop into an embryo.

a
b
c
d
e
f
g
h
i
j
k
l
m
n
o
p
q
r
s
t
u
v
w
x
y
z